DISCOVERING COMPUTERS 2000

Concepts for a Connected World

Web and  Enhanced

Gary B. Shelly
Thomas J. Cashman
Misty E. Vermaat
Tim J. Walker

COURSE TECHNOLOGY
ONE MAIN STREET
CAMBRIDGE MA 02142

an International Thomson Publishing company I(T)P

SHELLY
CASHMAN
SERIES®

CAMBRIDGE • ALBANY • BONN • CINCINNATI • LONDON • MADRID • MELBOURNE

MEXICO CITY • NEW YORK • PARIS • SAN FRANCISCO • TOKYO • TORONTO • WASHINGTON

COURSE
TECHNOLOGY

© 1999 by Course Technology — I(T)P

Printed in the United States of America

For more information, contact:

Course Technology One Main Street Cambridge, Massachusetts 02142, USA	International Thomson Editores Saneca, 53 Colonia Polanco 11560 Mexico D.F. Mexico
ITP Europe Berkshire House 168-173 High Holborn London, WC1V 7AA, United Kingdom	ITP GmbH Konigswinterer Strasse 418 53227 Bonn, Germany
ITP Australia 102 Dodds Street South Melbourne Victoria 3205 Australia	ITP Asia 60 Albert Street, #15-01 Albert Complex Singapore 189969
ITP Nelson Canada 1120 Birchmount Road Scarborough, Ontario Canada M1K 5G4	ITP Japan Hirakawa-cho Kyowa Building, 3F 2-2-1 Hirakawa-cho, Chiyoda-ku Tokyo 102, Japan

TRADEMARKS

DISCLAIMER

ISBN 0-7895-4618-3 (Perfect bound)
ISBN 0-7895-4703-1 (Case bound)

3 4 5 6 7 8 9 10   BC   03 02 01 00 99

CONTENTS

DISCOVERING COMPUTERS 2000
Concepts for a Connected World, Web and CNN Enhanced

CHAPTER 3

THE COMPONENTS IN THE SYSTEM UNIT

CHAPTER 4

INPUT

CHAPTER 5

OUTPUT

CHAPTER 6

STORAGE

CHAPTER 7

THE INTERNET

CHAPTER 8

OPERATING SYSTEMS AND UTILITY PROGRAMS

CHAPTER 11
INFORMATION SYSTEMS DEVELOPMENT

CHAPTER 12
PROGRAM DEVELOPMENT AND PROGRAMMING LANGUAGES

SPECIAL FEATURE **12.47**

CAREERS 2000
Planning, Prerequisites, Potential

CHAPTER 13

MULTIMEDIA

CHAPTER 14

SECURITY, PRIVACY, AND ETHICS

SPECIAL FEATURE **14.39**

TRENDS 2000
A Look to the Future

APPENDIX

CODING SCHEMES AND NUMBER SYSTEMS

PREFACE

The previous four editions of this textbook have been runaway best-sellers. Each of the these editions included new learning innovations such as integration of the World Wide Web, CyberClass, Interactive Labs, and Teaching Tools that set it apart from its competitors. *Discovering Computers 2000: Concepts for a Connected World, Web and CNN Enhanced* continues with the innovation, quality, and reliability that you have come to expect from the Shelly Cashman Series®. The newest edition of *Discovering Computers* includes these enhancements:

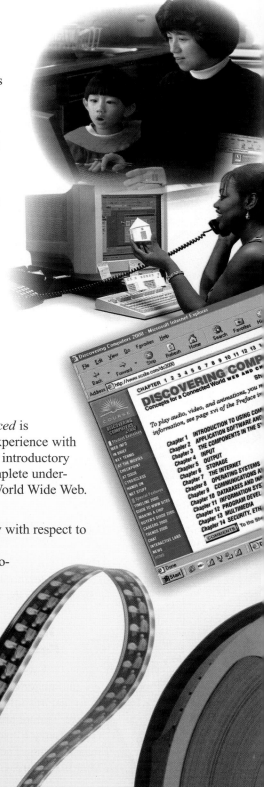

- Updates of the latest hardware, software, and trends in the computer field with particular emphasis placed on the personal computer and its practical use
- An exercise section at the end of each chapter titled AT THE MOVIES that includes streaming up-to-date, computer-related CNN videos on the Web; these videos offer a unique way for students to solidify, reinforce, and extend the concepts presented in the chapter
- Step-by-step illustrations that significantly simplify the complexity of the computer concepts presented
- Chapter-ending sections titled Technology Trailblazer and Company on the Cutting Edge; these one-page briefs introduce students to the people and companies they should know as they move into the job market
- Web pages with dramatically improved functionality

OBJECTIVES OF THIS TEXTBOOK

Discovering Computers 2000: Concepts for a Connected World, Web and CNN Enhanced is intended for use in a one-quarter or one-semester introductory computer course. No experience with computers is assumed. The material presented provides the most in-depth treatment of introductory computer subjects ever found in a textbook. Students will finish the course with a complete understanding of computers, how to use computers, and how to access information on the World Wide Web. The objectives of this book are as follows:

- Teach the fundamentals of computers and computer nomenclature, particularly with respect to personal computer hardware and software, and the World Wide Web
- Give students an in-depth understanding of why computers are essential components in business and society in general
- Make use of the World Wide Web as a repository of the latest information and as an integrated learning tool
- Present the material in a visually appealing and exciting manner that invites students to learn
- Offer alternative learning techniques with streaming audio and video on the Web
- Recognize the personal computer's position as the backbone of the computer industry and emphasize its use as a stand-alone and networked device
- Provide exercises and lab assignments that allow students to interact with a computer and actually learn by using the computer and the World Wide Web
- Present strategies for purchasing, installing, and maintaining a personal computer
- Assist students in planning a career in the computer field

DISTINGUISHING FEATURES

Discovering Computers 2000: Concepts for a Connected World, Web and CNN Enhanced includes the following distinguishing features.

A Proven Book

More than three million students have learned about computers using Shelly and Cashman computer fundamentals textbooks. With the additional World Wide Web integration and interactivity, streaming up-to-date, computer-related CNN videos, extraordinary visual drawings and photographs, unprecedented currency, and the Shelly and Cashman touch, this book will make your computer concepts course exciting and dynamic, an experience your students will remember as a highlight of their educational careers.

World Wide Web and CNN Enhanced

Each of the Shelly Cashman Series computer fundamentals books has included significant educational innovations that have set them apart from all other textbooks in the field. *Discovering Computers 2000* sustains this tradition of innovation with its continued integration of the World Wide Web and the agreement with CNN to make available its up-to-date, computer-related videos on the Web.

The purpose of integrating the World Wide Web into the book is to (1) offer students additional information and currency topics of importance; (2) make available alternative learning techniques with Web-based streaming audio and up-to-date, computer-related CNN videos; (3) underscore the relevance of the World Wide Web as a basic information tool that can be used in all facets of society; and (4) offer instructors the opportunity to organize and administer their campus-based or distance-education-based courses on the Web using CyberClass. The World Wide Web is integrated into the book in four central ways:

▲ End-of-chapter pages and most of the special features in the book have been stored as Web pages on the World Wide Web. While working on an end-of-chapter page, students can display the corresponding Web page to obtain additional information on a term or exercise, and get an alternative point of view. See page xv for more information.

▲ Streaming audio on the Web in the end-of-chapter IN BRIEF sections, streaming up-to-date, computer-related CNN videos on the Web in the end-of-chapter AT THE MOVIES sections, and the Interactive Labs in the end-of-chapter NET STUFF sections on the Web.

▲ Throughout the text, marginal annotations titled WEB INFO provide suggestions on how to obtain additional information via the Web on an important topic covered on the page.

▲ CyberClass Web-based teaching and learning system as described on page xiv.

This textbook, however, does not depend on Web access in order to be used successfully. The Web access adds to the already complete treatment of topics within the book.

Technology Trailblazer and Company on the Cutting Edge Features

Every student graduating from an institution of higher education should be aware of the leaders and major companies in the field of computers. Thus, each chapter ends with two full pages devoted to features titled Technology Trailblazer and Company on the Cutting Edge. The Technology Trailblazer feature presents people who have made a difference in the computer revolution, such as Bill Gates, Larry Ellison, Steve Wozniak, Steve Jobs, Marc Andreessen, Tim Berners-Lee, Michael Dell, and Linus Torvalds. The Company on the Cutting Edge feature presents the major computer companies, such as Microsoft, Sun Microsystems, AOL, SAP, Compaq, and IBM.

A Visually Appealing Book that Maintains Student Interest

Using the latest technology, pictures, drawings, and text have been artfully combined to produce a visually appealing and easy-to-understand book. Many of the figures show a step-by-step pedagogy, which simplifies the more complex computer concepts. Pictures and drawings reflect the latest trends in computer technology. Finally, the text was set in two columns, which research shows is easier for students to read. This combination of pictures, step-by-step drawings, and text sets a new standard for computer textbook design.

Latest Computer Trends

The terms and technologies your students see in this book are those they will encounter when they start using computers. Only the latest application software packages are shown throughout the book. New topics and terms include Pentium® III and Pentium® Xeon™ chips; Microsoft Windows 2000; Microsoft Office 2000; IrDA ports; the latest on the World Wide Web, networks, intranets, and extranets; USB; video digitizers; video decoders; video capture cards; HDTV; LCD monitors; large-format printers; DLP projectors; SuperDisk™ and HiFD drives; Zip® and Jaz® drives; flash cards; DVD-ROMs; streaming audio and video; Webcasting; electronic credit; Web publishing; portals; chat rooms; Linux; e-money; e-commerce; telephony; digital subscriber lines; ATM; T-3 lines; cable modems; object-oriented databases; JavaScript; dynamic HTML; XML; distance learning; Web-based training; e-books; secure servers; digital signatures; and much more.

Shelly Cashman Series Interactive Labs

Eighteen unique, hands-on exercises, developed specifically for this book, allow students to use the computer to learn about computers. Students can step through each Lab exercise in about 15 minutes. Assessment is available. The Interactive Labs are described in detail on page xvi. These Labs are available free on the Web (see page 1.46) or on CD-ROM for an additional cost (ISBN 0-7895-5679-0).

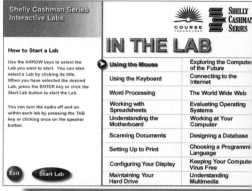

End-of-Chapter Exercises

Unlike other books on the subject of computer fundamentals, a major effort was undertaken in *Discovering Computers 2000* to offer exciting, rich, and thorough end-of-chapter material to reinforce the chapter objectives and assist you in making your course the finest ever offered. As indicated earlier, each and every one of the end-of-chapter pages is stored as a Web page on the World Wide Web to provide your students in-depth information and alternative methods of preparing for examinations. Each chapter ends with the following:

- ▲ **IN BRIEF**   This section summarizes the chapter material in the form of questions and answers. Each question addresses a chapter objective, making this section invaluable in reviewing and preparing for examinations. Links on the Web page provide additional current information. With a single-click on the Web page, the review section is read to the student using streaming audio.

- ▲ **KEY TERMS**   This list of the key terms found in the chapter together with the page number on which the terms are defined will aid students in mastering the chapter material. A complete summary of all key terms in the book, together with their definitions, appears in the Index at the end of the book. On the Web page, students can click terms to view a definition and a picture, and then click a link to visit a page that offers an alternative explanation.

- ▲ **AT THE MOVIES**   In this section, students complete exercises that requires them to click photographs on the Web page to view streaming up-to-date CNN videos. These videos, which present computer-related topics, reinforce the chapter or provide extended knowledge of important concepts.

- ▲ **CHECKPOINT**   Matching and short-answer questions, together with a figure from the chapter that must be labeled, reinforce the material presented within the chapter. Students accessing the Web page answer the questions in an interactive forum.

- ▲ **AT ISSUE**   The computer industry is not without its controversial issues. At the end of each chapter, several scenarios are presented that challenge students to critically examine their perspective of technology in society. The Web pages provide links to challenge students further.

- ▲ **CYBERCLASS**   These exercises have students connect to the CyberClass Web page where they complete tasks that include online flash cards; practice tests; e-mail; bulletin board activities; visiting and evaluating Web sites; and CyberChallenge.

- ▲ **HANDS ON**   To complete their introduction to computers, students must interact with and use a computer. A series of Windows Lab exercises begins with the simplest exercises within Windows. Students then are led through additional activities that, by the end of the book, will enable them to be proficient in using Windows.

♠ **NET STUFF**   In this section, students gain an appreciation for the World Wide Web by visiting interesting and exciting Web pages and completing suggested tasks. Also included in this section are exercises that have students complete the Shelly Cashman Series Interactive Labs. These Interactive Labs can be done directly from the World Wide Web. The last NET STUFF exercise sends students into a Chat room where they can discuss engaging issues and topics presented in the book with other students throughout the world.

Timeline 2000: Milestones in Computer History

A colorful, highly informative ten-page timeline following Chapter 1 steps students through the major computer technology developments over the past 50 years, including the most recent advances.

Guide to World Wide Web Sites

More than 100 popular Web sites are listed and described in a new guide to Web sites that follows Chapter 2.

How Computer Chips Are Made

This special feature following Chapter 3 steps through the intricate details of making a computer chip.

Buyer's Guide 2000: How to Purchase, Install, and Maintain a Personal Computer

A ten-page guide following Chapter 8 introduces students to purchasing, installing, and maintaining a desktop or laptop computer.

Careers 2000: Planning, Prerequisites, Potential

This special feature following Chapter 12 provides students with practical information on careers in the computer field and covers preparing for a career in computers, obtaining the necessary foundation, and recognizing the opportunities presented.

Trends 2000: A Look to the Future

Following Chapter 14, a fourteen-page special feature examines several trends that will influence the direction of the computer field. The feature then looks at computers in the future in both the workplace and at home.

INSTRUCTOR'S SUPPORT PACKAGE

A comprehensive instructor's support package accompanies this textbook in the form of two CD-ROM packages. The two packages titled Teaching Tools (ISBN 0-7895-4620-5) and Course Presenter (ISBN 0-7895-5645-6) are described in the following sections. Both packages are available free to adopters through your Course Technology representative or by calling one of the following telephone numbers: Colleges and Universities, 1-800-648-7450; High Schools, 1-800-824-5179; and Career Colleges, 1-800-477-3692.

Teaching Tools

The Teaching Tools for this textbook include both teaching and testing aids. The contents of the Teaching Tools CD-ROM are listed below.

♠ **Instructor's Manual**   The Instructor's Manual is made up of Microsoft Word files. The files include the following for each chapter: chapter objectives; chapter overview; detailed lesson plans with page number references; teacher notes and activities; answers to the exercises; test bank (100 true/false, 50 multiple-choice, and 70 fill-in-the-blank questions per chapter); and figure references. The figures are available in the Figures in the Book ancillary. The test bank questions are numbered the same as in Course Test Manager. You can print a copy of the chapter test bank and use the printout to select your questions in Course Test Manager. You also can use your word processing software to generate quizzes and exams from the test bank.

▲ **Figures in the Book**   Illustrations for every picture, table, and screen in the textbook are available in electronic form. Use this ancillary to present a slide show in lecture or to print transparencies for use in lecture with an overhead projector. If you have a personal computer and LCD device, this ancillary can be an effective tool for presenting lectures.

▲ **Course Test Manager**   Course Test Manager is a powerful testing and assessment package that enables instructors to create and print tests quickly from the large test bank. Instructors with access to a networked computer lab (LAN) can administer, grade, and track tests online. Students also can take online practice tests, which generate customized study guides that indicate where in the textbook students can find more information for each question.

▲ **Student Files**   A few of the exercises in the end-of-chapter HANDS ON section ask students to use these files. You can distribute the files on the Teaching Tools CD-ROM to your students over a network or you can have them follow the instructions on the inside back cover of this book to obtain a copy of the Discover 2000 Data Disk.

▲ **Interactive Labs**   These are the non-audio versions of the eighteen hands-on Interactive Labs exercises. Students can step through each lab in about fifteen minutes to solidify and reinforce computer concepts. Assessment requires students to answer questions about the contents of the Interactive Labs.

▲ **Interactive Lab Solutions**   This ancillary includes the solutions for the Interactive Labs assessment quizzes.

Course Presenter with Figures, Animations, and CNN Video Clips

Course Presenter is a multimedia lecture presentation system that provides Power-Point slides for every subject in each chapter. Use this presentation system to present well-organized lectures that are both interesting and knowledge-based. Fourteen presentation files are provided for the book, one for each chapter. Each file contains PowerPoint slides for every subject in each chapter together with optional choices to show any figure in the chapter as you introduce the material in class. More than 40 current, two- to three-minute up-to-date, computer-related CNN video clips and more than 35 animations that reinforce chapter material also are available for optional presentation. Course Presenter provides consistent coverage for multiple lecturers.

SUPPLEMENTS

Three supplements can be used in combination with *Discovering Computers 2000: Concepts for a Connected World, Web and CNN Enhanced*. These supplements reinforce the computer concepts presented in the book.

Audio Chapter Review on CD-ROM

The Audio Chapter Review on CD-ROM (ISBN 0-7895-5680-4) vocalizes the end-of-chapter IN BRIEF pages (see page 1.38). Students can use this supplement with a CD player or PC to solidify their understanding of the concepts presented. It is a great tool for preparing for examinations. This same Audio Chapter Review also is available at no cost on the Web by clicking the Audio button on the IN BRIEF page at the end of any chapter.

Shelly Cashman Series Interactive Labs with Audio on CD-ROM

The Shelly Cashman Series Interactive Labs with Audio on CD-ROM (ISBN 0-7895-5679-0) may be used in combination with this textbook to augment your students' learning process. See page xvi for a description of each lab. These Interactive Labs also are available at no cost on the Web by clicking the appropriate button on the NET STUFF exercise pages (see page 1.46).

Study Guide

This highly popular supplement (ISBN 0-7895-4633-7) includes a variety of activities that help students recall, review, and master introductory computer concepts. The *Study Guide* complements the end-of-chapter material with a guided chapter outline; a self-test consisting of true/false, multiple-choice, short answer, fill-in, and matching questions, an entertaining puzzle, and other challenging exercises.

ACKNOWLEDGMENTS

The Shelly Cashman Series would not be the most successful computer textbook series ever published without the contributions of outstanding publishing professionals. First, and foremost, among them is Becky Herrington, director of production and designer. She is the heart and soul of the Shelly Cashman Series, and it is only through her leadership, dedication, and tireless efforts that superior products are produced.

Under Becky's direction, the following individuals made significant contributions to this book: Doug Cowley, production manager; Ginny Harvey, series specialist, developmental editor, and copy editor; Ken Russo, senior graphic designer/Web developer; Mike Bodnar, Stephanie Nance, Mark Norton, and Ellana Russo, graphic artists; Greg Herrington, Web developer; Marlo Mitchem, associate production editor; Jeanne Black, Quark expert; Nancy Lamm and Marilyn Martin, proofreaders; Sarah Evertson of Image Quest, photo researcher; Jeanne Busemeyer, CNN video editor; and Cristina Haley, indexer. Special thanks go to Jim Quasney, series editor, for the tremendous effort he put forth during the development of this book; Lisa Strite, senior editor and developmental editor; Lora Wade, associate product manager; Tonia Grafakos, associate Web product manager; Meagan Walsh, editorial assistant; Scott Wiseman, online developer; Francis Schurgot, Web product manager; and Kathryn Cronin, product marketing manager.

Our sincere thanks go to Dennis Tani, who together with Becky Herrington, designed this book. In addition, Dennis designed the cover, performed all the initial layout, typography, and executed the magnificent drawings contained in this book. Thanks go to Stephanie Nance and Mark Norton for the extraordinary design of the Special Feature sections in this book.

Thanks go to Charles Aitkenhead, Virgil Brewer, Kay Delk, and Harry Rosenblatt (Chapters 1 through 5) for reviewing the manuscript; William Vermaat for researching, reviewing the manuscript, and taking photographs; and to Darrell Ward of *Hyper*Graphics Corporation for the development of CyberClass. We hope you find using this book an exciting and rewarding experience.

Gary B. Shelly
Thomas J. Cashman
Misty E. Vermaat
Tim J. Walker

CYBERCLASS — A WEB-BASED TEACHING AND LEARNING SYSTEM

CyberClass is a Web-based teaching and learning system that adopters of *Discovering Computers 2000: Concepts for a Connected World, Web and CNN Enhanced* can use in a traditional campus setting or distance learning setting. CyberClass is available in three levels so you can choose the one that best fits your course needs.

CyberClass Level I is free to adopters of this book and includes (1) 25 interactive flash cards per chapter that serve as a self-study aid to help students master chapter content; (2) practice tests that enable students to test their mastery of a chapter; includes study guide feedback; (3) case scenarios that show how corporations use computers; and (4) a link to this book's award-winning Web site.

CyberClass Level II is available for an additional cost and includes (1) a customizable and secure Web site that the instructor can use to organize and administer a campus-based or distance learning-based course; (2) access to all CyberClass Level I capabilities; (3) posting class syllabi for students to read; (4) posting class assignments for students to read; (5) the capability of sending messages to and receiving messages from class members and instructors; (6) an option to submit assignments electronically to instructors; (7) access to a student bulletin board; (8) posting of hot links for class members; (9) electronic flash cards for every bold term in the book, organized by chapter; (10) Cyber-Challenge, a self-study game; and (11) a class administrative system that includes Web-based testing and class rosters.

CyberClass Level III is available for an additional cost and includes (1) all the capabilities of Level I and Level II; (2) audio-conferencing, which allows instructor and students to meet for Web-based lectures; and (3) live assessment, which allows instructors to send questions real-time to students who then respond back immediately.

NOTES TO THE STUDENT

If you have access to the World Wide Web, you can obtain current and additional information on topics covered in this book in the three ways listed below.

1. Throughout the book, marginal annotations called WEB INFO (Figure 1) specify subjects about which you can obtain additional current information. Enter the designated URL and then click the appropriate term on the Web page.
2. Each chapter ends with seven sections titled IN BRIEF, KEY TERMS, AT THE MOVIES, CHECKPOINT, AT ISSUE, CYBERCLASS, HANDS ON, and NET STUFF. These sections in your book are stored as Web pages on the Web. You can visit them by starting your browser and entering the URL in the instructions at the top of the end-of-chapter pages. When the Web page displays, you can click links or buttons on the page to broaden your understanding of the topics and obtain current information about the topic.
3. Use CyberClass as described on the previous page.

Each time you reference a Web page from *Discovering Computers 2000*, a sidebar displays on the left. To display one of the Student Exercises (Figure 2), click the chapter number and then click the Student Exercise title in the sidebar. To display one of the Special Features, click the desired Special Feature title in the sidebar.

WEB INFO provides additional current information on a topic

WEB INFO

For more information on personal computers, visit the Discovering Computers 2000 Chapter 1 WEB INFO page (**www.scsite.com/dc2000/ch1/webinfo.htm**) and click Personal Computers.

Figure 1

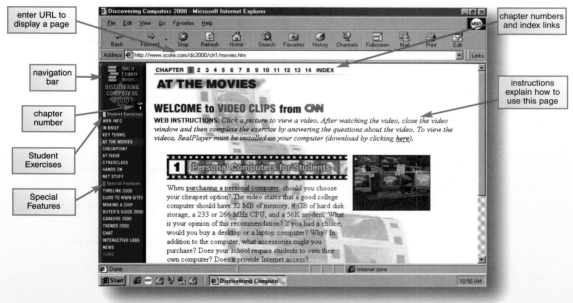

- enter URL to display a page
- navigation bar
- chapter number
- Student Exercises
- Special Features
- chapter numbers and index links
- instructions explain how to use this page

Figure 2

TO DOWNLOAD PLAYERS

For best viewing results of the Web pages referenced in this book, download the Shockwave and Flash Player. To play the audio in the IN BRIEF section and view the video in the AT THE MOVIES section at the end of each chapter, you must download RealPlayer. Follow the steps below:

Shockwave and Flash Player — (1) Launch your browser; (2) enter the URL, `www.macromedia.com`; (3) click shockwave; (4) click the download shockwave and flash button; (5) follow the instructions in the STEP boxes on the Macromedia Web Player Download Center Web page.

RealPlayer — (1) Launch your browser; (2) enter the URL, `www.real.com`; (3) click the FREE RealPlayer G2 button; (4) click RealPlayer G2; (5) click Free RealPlayer with basic features; (6) step through and respond to the forms, requests, and dialog boxes; (7) when the File Download dialog box displays, click Save this program to disk; (8) save the file to a folder and remember the folder name; and (9) launch Explorer and then double-click the downloaded file in step 8.

SHELLY CASHMAN SERIES INTERACTIVE LABS WITH AUDIO

Each of the fourteen chapters in this book includes the NET STUFF exercises, which utilize the World Wide Web. The eighteen Shelly Cashman Series Interactive Labs described below are included as exercises in the NET STUFF section. These Interactive Labs are available on the Web (see page 1.46) or on CD-ROM. The CD-ROM version (ISBN 0-7895-5679-0) is available at an additional cost. A non-audio version is also available at no extra cost on the Shelly Cashman Series Teaching Tools CD-ROM that is available free to adopters. Each lab takes the students approximately 15 minutes to complete using a personal computer and helps them gain a better understanding of a specific subject covered in the chapter.

Shelly Cashman Series Interactive Labs with Audio

Lab	Function	Page
Using the Mouse	Master how to use a mouse. The Lab includes exercises on pointing, clicking, double-clicking, and dragging.	1.46
Using the Keyboard	Learn how to use the keyboard. The Lab discusses different categories of keys, including the edit keys, function keys, ESC, CTRL, and ALT keys and how to press keys simultaneously.	1.47
Word Processing	Gain a basic understanding of word processing concepts, from creating a document to printing and saving the final result.	2.55
Working with Spreadsheets	Learn how to create and utilize spreadsheets, including entering formulas, creating graphs, and performing what-if analysis.	2.55
Understanding the Motherboard	Step through the components of a motherboard. The Lab shows how different motherboard configurations affect the overall speed of a computer.	3.40
Scanning Documents	Understand how document scanners work.	4.38
Setting Up to Print	See how information flows from the system unit to the printer and how drivers, fonts, and physical connections play a role in generating a printout.	5.36
Configuring Your Display	Recognize the different monitor configurations available, including screen size, display cards, and number of colors.	5.36
Maintaining Your Hard Drive	Understand how files are stored on disk, what causes fragmentation, and how to maintain an efficient hard drive.	6.38
Connecting to the Internet	Learn how a computer is connected to the Internet. The Lab presents using the Internet to access information.	7.44
The World Wide Web	Understand the significance of the World Wide Web and how to use Web browser software and search tools.	7.44
Evaluating Operating Systems	Evaluate the advantages and disadvantages of different categories of operating systems.	8.36
Working at Your Computer	Learn the basic ergonomic principles that prevent back and neck pain, eye strain, and other computer-related physical ailments.	8.36
Exploring the Computers of the Future	Learn about computers of the future and how they will work.	9.44
Designing a Database	Create a database structure and optimize a database to support searching.	10.44
Choosing a Programming Language	Differentiate between traditional languages and the newer object-oriented languages.	12.46
Understanding Multimedia	Gain an understanding of the types of media used in multimedia applications, the components of a multimedia PC, and the newest applications of multimedia.	13.40
Keeping Your Computer Virus Free	Learn what a virus is and about the different kinds of viruses. The Lab discusses how to prevent your computer from being infected with a virus.	14.38

CHAPTER 1

INTRODUCTION TO USING COMPUTERS

OBJECTIVES

After completing this chapter, you will be able to:

Explain why it is important to be computer literate

Define the term computer

Identify the components of a computer

Explain why a computer is a powerful tool

Differentiate among the various categories of software

Explain the purpose of a network

Discuss the uses of the Internet and the World Wide Web

Describe the categories of computers and their uses

Whether you are attending classes, working in an office, or participating in recreational activities, you use computers every day. Even activities in your daily routine – typing a report, driving your car, paying for goods and services with a credit card, or using an ATM – can involve the use of computers. Computers have become the tools people use to access information and communicate with others around the world. Today, computers are everywhere.

The purpose of this book is to present the knowledge you need to understand how computers work and how computers are used. Chapter 1 introduces you to basic computer concepts such as what a computer is, how it works, and what makes it a powerful tool. You will begin to learn about the many different categories of computers and their applications. In the process, you will gain an understanding of the vocabulary used to describe computers. While you are reading, remember that this chapter is an overview and that many of the terms and concepts that are introduced will be discussed further in later chapters.

COMPUTER LITERACY

The vocabulary of computing is all around you. Before the advent of computers, memory was the mental ability to recall previous experiences; storage was an area where you kept out-of-season clothing; and communication was the act of exchanging opinions and information through writing, speaking, or signs. In today's world, these words and countless others have taken on new meanings as part of the common terminology used to describe computers and their use.

When you hear the word computer, initially you may think of those found in the workplace – the computers used to create business letters, memos, and other correspondence; calculate payroll; track inventory; or generate invoices. In the course of a day or week, however, you encounter many other computers. Your home, for instance, may contain a myriad of electronic devices, such as cordless telephones, VCRs, handheld video games, cameras, and stereo systems, that include small computers.

Computers help you with your banking in the form of automatic teller machines (ATMs) used to deposit or withdraw funds. When you buy groceries, a computer tracks your purchases and calculates the amount of money you owe; and sometimes generates coupons customized to your buying patterns.

Even your car is equipped with computers that operate the electrical system, control the temperature, and run sophisticated antitheft devices. Figure 1-1 shows a variety of computers being used in everyday life.

Computers are valuable tools. As technology advances and computers extend into every facet of daily living, it is essential you gain some level of **computer literacy**. To be successful in today's world, you must have a knowledge and understanding of computers and their uses.

WHAT IS A COMPUTER AND WHAT DOES IT DO?

A **computer** is an electronic machine, operating under the control of instructions stored in its own memory, that can accept data (input), manipulate the data according to specified rules (process), produce results (output), and store the results for future use.

Data is a collection of unorganized facts, which can include words, numbers, images, and sounds. Computers manipulate and process data to create information.

WEB INFO
WEB INFO

For more information on computer literacy, visit the Discovering Computers 2000 Chapter 1 WEB INFO page (**www.scsite.com/dc2000/ch1/webinfo.htm**) and click Computer Literacy.

Figure 1-1 Computers are present in every aspect of daily living – in the workplace, at home, and in the classroom.

Information is data that is organized, has meaning, and is useful. Examples are reports, newsletters, a receipt, a picture, an invoice, or a check. In Figure 1-2, data is processed and manipulated to create a check.

Data entered into a computer is called **input**. The processed results are called **output**. Thus, a computer processes input to create output. A computer also can hold data and information for future use in an area called **storage**. This cycle of input, process, output, and storage is called the **information processing cycle**.

A person that communicates with a computer or uses the information it generates is called a **user**.

The electric, electronic, and mechanical equipment that makes up a computer is called **hardware**. **Software** is the series of instruction that tells the hardware how to perform tasks. Without software, hardware is useless; hardware needs the instructions provided by software to process data into information.

The next section discusses various hardware components. Later in the chapter, categories of software are discussed.

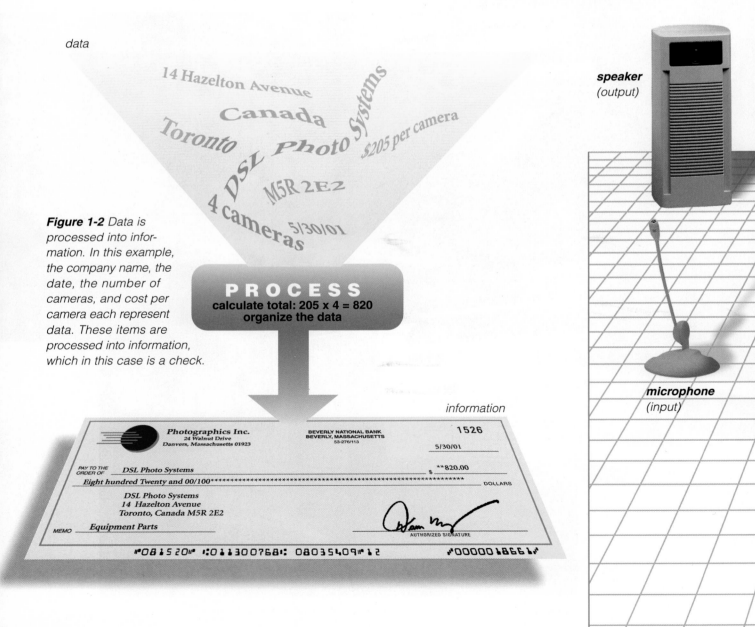

data

14 Hazelton Avenue
Canada
Toronto
DSL Photo Systems
$205 per camera
M5R 2E2
4 cameras   5/30/01

Figure 1-2 Data is processed into information. In this example, the company name, the date, the number of cameras, and cost per camera each represent data. These items are processed into information, which in this case is a check.

P R O C E S S
calculate total: 205 x 4 = 820
organize the data

information

Photographics Inc.
24 Walnut Drive
Danvers, Massachusetts 01923

BEVERLY NATIONAL BANK
BEVERLY, MASSACHUSETTS
53-276/113

1526

5/30/01

PAY TO THE
ORDER OF   DSL Photo Systems $ **820.00

Eight hundred Twenty and 00/100** DOLLARS

DSL Photo Systems
14 Hazelton Avenue
Toronto, Canada M5R 2E2

MEMO   Equipment Parts   AUTHORIZED SIGNATURE

⑈081520⑈ ⑆011300768⑆ 08035409⑈12   ⑈000001866⑈

speaker
(output)

microphone
(input)

THE COMPONENTS OF A COMPUTER

A computer consists of a variety of hardware components that work together with software to perform calculations, organize data, and communicate with other computers.

These hardware components include input devices, output devices, a system unit, storage devices, and communications devices. Figure 1-3 shows some common computer hardware components.

Input Devices

An **input device** allows a user to enter data and commands into the memory of a computer. Three commonly used input devices are the keyboard, the mouse, and a microphone.

A computer keyboard contains keys that allow you to type letters of the alphabet, numbers, spaces, punctuation marks, and other symbols. A computer keyboard also contains special keys that allow you to perform specific functions on the computer.

WEB INFO

For more information on input devices, visit the Discovering Computers 2000 Chapter 1 WEB INFO page (**www.scsite.com/dc2000/ch1/webinfo.htm**) and click Input Devices.

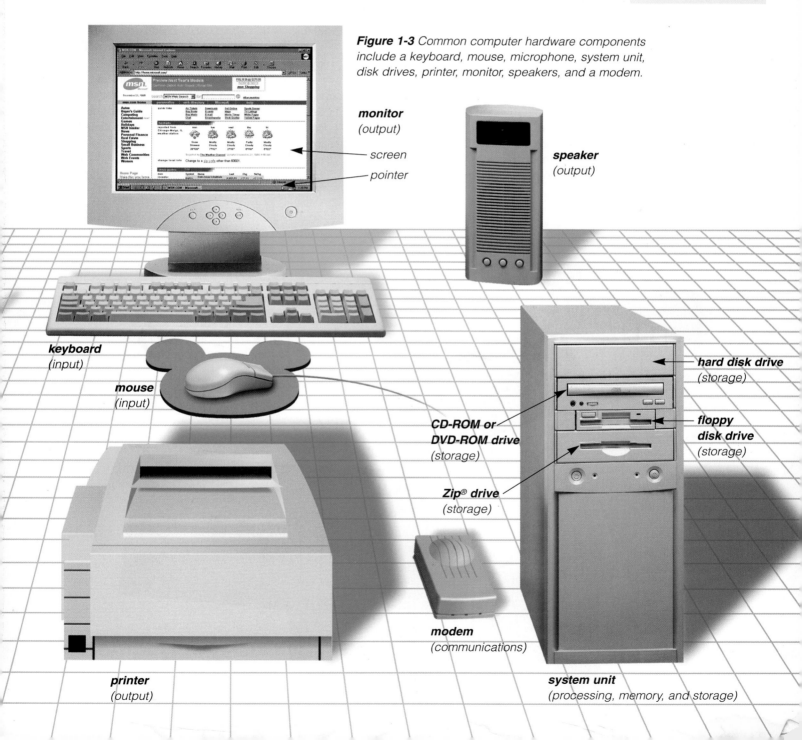

Figure 1-3 *Common computer hardware components include a keyboard, mouse, microphone, system unit, disk drives, printer, monitor, speakers, and a modem.*

monitor
(output)

screen

pointer

speaker
(output)

keyboard
(input)

mouse
(input)

hard disk drive
(storage)

CD-ROM or DVD-ROM drive
(storage)

floppy disk drive
(storage)

Zip® drive
(storage)

modem
(communications)

printer
(output)

system unit
(processing, memory, and storage)

A mouse is a small handheld device that contains at least one button. The mouse controls the movement of a symbol on the screen called a pointer. For example, moving the mouse across a flat surface allows you to move the pointer on the screen. You also can make choices and initiate processing on the computer by using a mouse.

A microphone allows you to speak to the computer in order to enter data and control the actions of the computer.

Output Devices

An **output device** is used to convey the information generated by a computer to a user. Three commonly used output devices are a printer, a monitor, and speakers.

A printer produces text and graphics, such as photographs, on paper or other hard-copy medium. A monitor, which looks like a television screen, is used to display text and graphics. Speakers allow you to hear music, voice, and other sounds generated by the computer.

System Unit

The **system unit** is a box-like case made from metal or plastic that houses the computer electronic circuitry. The circuitry in the system unit usually is part of or is connected to a circuit board called the motherboard.

Two main components on the motherboard are the central processing unit (CPU) and memory. The **central processing unit (CPU)**, also called a **processor**, is the electronic device that interprets and carries out the instructions that operate the computer.

Memory is a series of electronic elements that temporarily holds data and instructions while they are being processed by the CPU.

Both the processor and memory are chips. A chip is an electronic device that contains many microscopic pathways designed to carry electrical current. Chips, which usually are no bigger than one-half inch square, are packaged so they can be connected to a motherboard or other circuit boards (Figure 1-4).

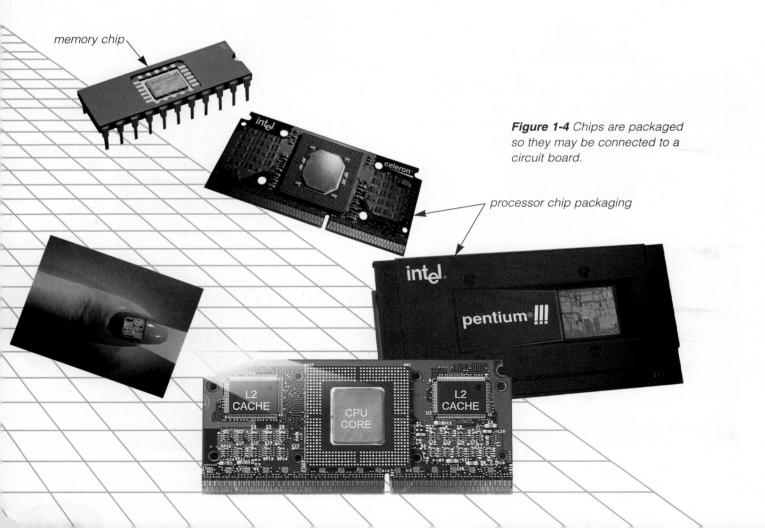

memory chip

Figure 1-4 Chips are packaged so they may be connected to a circuit board.

processor chip packaging

Some computer components, such as the processor and memory, reside inside the system unit; that is, they are internal. Other components, such as the keyboard, mouse, microphone, monitor, and printer, often are located outside the system unit. These devices are considered external. Any external device that attaches to the system unit is called a **peripheral** device.

Storage Devices

Storage holds data, instructions, and information for future use. Storage differs from memory, in that it can hold these items permanently, whereas memory holds these items only temporarily while they are being processed. A **storage medium** (media is the plural) is the physical material on which data, instructions, and information are stored. One commonly used storage medium is a disk, which is a round, flat piece of plastic or metal on which items can be encoded, or written.

A **storage device** is used to record and retrieve data, instructions, and information to and from a storage medium. Storage devices often function as a source of input because they transfer items from storage into memory. Four common storage devices are a floppy disk drive, a hard disk drive, a CD-ROM drive, and a DVD-ROM drive. A disk drive is a device that reads from and may write onto a disk.

A floppy disk consists of a thin, circular, flexible disk enclosed in a plastic shell. A floppy disk stores data, instructions, and information using magnetic patterns and can be inserted into and removed from a floppy disk drive (Figure 1-5). A Zip® disk is a higher capacity floppy disk that can store the equivalent of about 70 standard floppy disks.

A hard disk provides much greater storage capacity than a floppy disk. A hard disk usually consists of several circular disks on which data, instructions, and information are stored magnetically. These disks are enclosed in an airtight, sealed case, which often is housed inside the system unit (Figure 1-6). Some hard disks are removable, which means they can be inserted and removed from a hard disk drive, much like a floppy disk. Removable disks are enclosed in plastic or metal cartridges so that they can be removed from the drive. The advantage of removable

Figure 1-5 *A floppy disk is inserted and removed from a floppy disk drive.*

WEB INFO
WEB INFO

For more information on storage devices, visit the Discovering Computers 2000 Chapter 1 WEB INFO page (**www.scsite.com/ dc2000/ch1/webinfo.htm**) and click Storage Devices.

self-contained hard disk

removable hard disks

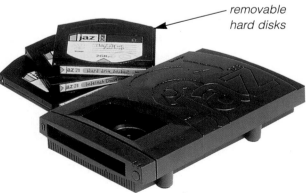

Figure 1-6 *Some hard disks are self-contained devices housed inside the system unit (picture above). Removable hard disks, in contrast, are inserted and removed from a drive (picture below).*

media such as a floppy disk and removable hard disk is it can be taken out of the computer and transported or secured.

Another type of disk used to store data is the compact disc (Figure 1-7). A compact disc stores data using microscopic pits, which are created by a laser light. One type of compact disc is a *CD-ROM,* which is accessed or played using a CD-ROM drive. A newer type of compact disc is a *DVD-ROM,* which has tremendous storage capacities – enough for a full-length movie. To use a DVD-ROM, you need a DVD-ROM drive.

Figure 1-7 *A compact disc (CD) is a round, flat piece of metal with a protective plastic coating. Two types of compact discs are CD-ROMs and DVD-ROMs.*

Communications Devices

Communications devices enable computer users to communicate and to exchange items such as data, instructions, and information with another computer. Communications devices transmit these items over transmission media, such as cables, telephone lines, or other means, used to establish a connection between two computers. A modem is a communications device that enables computers to communicate via telephone lines or other means. Although modems are available as both external and internal devices, most are internal; that is, contained within the system unit.

WEB INFO
WEB INFO

For more information on communications devices, visit the Discovering Computers 2000 Chapter 1 WEB INFO page (**www.scsite.com/dc2000/ ch1/webinfo.htm**) and click Communications Devices.

WHY IS A COMPUTER SO POWERFUL?

A computer's power is derived from its capability of performing the information processing cycle operations (input, process, output, and storage) with amazing speed, reliability, and accuracy; its capacity to store huge amounts of data and information; and its ability to communicate with other computers.

Speed

Inside the system unit, operations occur through electronic circuits. When data, instructions, and information flow along these circuits, they travel at close to the speed of light. This allows billions of operations to be carried out in a single second.

Reliability

The electronic components in modern computers are dependable because they have a low failure rate. The high reliability of the components enables the computer to produce consistent results.

Accuracy

Computers can process large amounts of data and generate error-free results, provided the data is entered correctly. If inaccurate data is entered, the resulting output will be incorrect. This computing principle – known as garbage in, garbage out (GIGO) – points out that the accuracy of a computer's output depends on the accuracy of the input.

Storage

Many computers can store enormous amounts of data and make this data available for processing any time it is needed. Using current storage devices, the data can be transferred quickly from storage to memory, processed, and then stored again for future use.

Communications

Most computers today have the capability of communicating with other computers. Computers with this capability can share any of the four information processing cycle operations – input, process, output, and storage – with another computer. For example, two computers connected by a communications device such as a modem can share stored data, instructions, and information. When two or more computers are connected together via communications media and devices, they comprise a network. The most widely known network is the Internet, a worldwide collection of networks that links together millions of businesses, government installations, educational institutions, and individuals (Figure 1-8).

COMPUTER SOFTWARE

Software, also called a **computer program** or simply a **program**, is a series of instructions that tells the hardware of a computer what to do. For example, some instructions direct the computer to allow you to input data from the keyboard and store it in memory. Other instructions cause data stored in memory to be used in calculations such as adding a series of numbers to obtain a total. Some instructions compare two values stored in memory and direct the computer to perform alternative operations based on the results of the comparison; and some instructions direct

the computer to print a report, display information on the monitor, draw a color graph on the monitor, or store information on a disk.

Before a computer can perform, or **execute**, a program, the instructions in the program must be placed, or loaded, into the memory of the computer. Usually, they are loaded into memory from storage. For example, a program might be loaded from the hard disk of a computer into memory for execution.

When you purchase a program, such as one that contains legal documents, you will receive one or more floppy disks, one or more CD-ROMs, or a single DVD-ROM on which the software is stored (Figure 1-9). To use this software, you often must **install** the software on the computer's hard disk.

Figure 1-9 *When you buy software, you receive media such as floppy disks, CD-ROMs, or a DVD-ROM that contains the software program.*

Figure 1-8 *The Internet is a worldwide collection of networks that links together millions of businesses, the government, educational institutions, and individuals.*

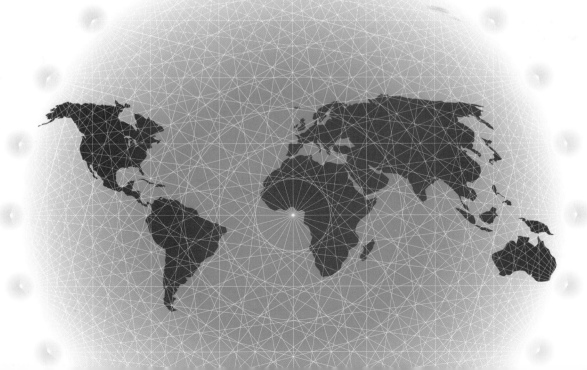

WEB INFO
WEB INFO

For more information on operating systems, visit the Discovering Computers 2000 Chapter 1 WEB INFO page (**www.scsite.com/dc2000/ch1/webinfo.htm**) and click Operating Systems.

Sometimes, a program can be loaded in memory directly from a floppy disk, CD-ROM, or DVD-ROM so you do not have to install it on a hard disk first.

When you buy a computer, it usually has some software already installed on its hard disk. Thus, you can use the computer as soon as you receive it.

Figure 1-10 illustrates the steps for running a computer program that simulates flying an airplane.

Software is the key to productive use of computers. With the correct software, a computer can become a valuable tool.

Software can be categorized into two types: system software and application software. The following sections describe these categories of software.

System Software

System software, which consists of programs that control the operations of the computer and its devices, serves as the interface between a user and the computer's hardware. Two types of system software are the operating system and utility programs.

OPERATING SYSTEM The **operating system** contains instructions that coordinate all of the activities of hardware devices. The operating system also contains instructions that allow you to run application software. Microsoft Windows is the name of a popular operating system that is used on many of today's computers.

When you start a computer, the operating system is loaded, or copied, into memory from the computer's hard disk. It remains in memory while the computer is running and allows you to communicate with the computer and other software.

Figure 1-10 Running a program.

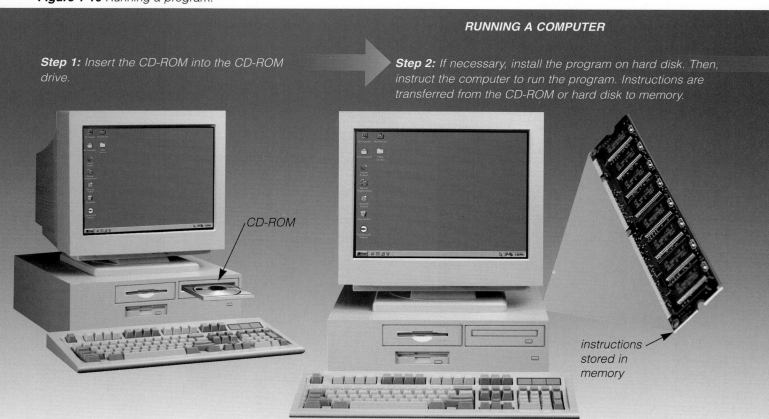

RUNNING A COMPUTER

Step 1: Insert the CD-ROM into the CD-ROM drive.

Step 2: If necessary, install the program on hard disk. Then, instruct the computer to run the program. Instructions are transferred from the CD-ROM or hard disk to memory.

CD-ROM

instructions stored in memory

UTILITY PROGRAMS A utility program is a type of system software that performs a specific task, usually related to managing a computer, its devices, or its programs. An example of a utility program is an uninstaller, which removes a program that has been installed on a computer. Most operating systems include several utility programs for managing disk drives, printers, and other devices. You also can buy stand-alone utility programs to perform additional computer management functions.

USER INTERFACE All software has a **user interface** that is the part of the software with which you interact. The user interface controls how data and instructions are entered and how information is presented on the screen. Many of today's software programs have a **graphical user interface**, or **GUI** (pronounced gooey), which allows you to interact with the software using visual images such as icons. An **icon** is a small image that

represents a program, an instruction, or some other object. Figure 1-11 shows a widely used operating system, Microsoft Windows 98, which has a graphical user interface.

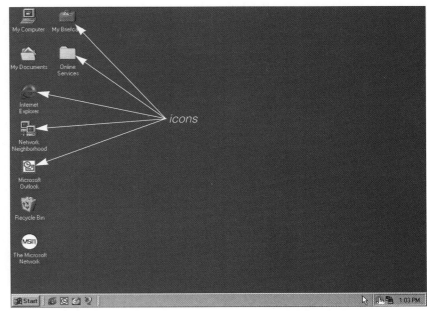

Figure 1-11 *Microsoft Windows 98 is an operating system with a graphical user interface.*

Step 3: *The program executes and the screen displays graphics that simulate flying an aircraft.*

Application Software

Application software consists of programs designed to perform specific tasks for users. Popular application software includes word processing software, spreadsheet software, database software, and presentation graphics software. Word processing software allows you to create documents such as letters and memos. Spreadsheet software allows you to calculate numbers arranged in rows and columns and often is used for budgeting, forecasting, and other financial tasks. Database software is used to store data in an organized fashion, as well as to retrieve, manipulate, and display that data in a meaningful form. Presentation graphics software allows you to create documents called slides that are used in making presentations. These four applications often are sold together as a single unit, called a suite, in which individual applications are packaged in the same box and sold for a price that is significantly less than buying the applications individually.

Many other types of application software exist, thus enabling users to perform a variety of tasks. Some widely used software applications include: reference, education, and entertainment; desktop publishing; photo and video editing; multimedia authoring; network, communications, electronic mail, and Web browsers; accounting; project management; and personal information management. Each of these applications is discussed in depth in Chapter 2.

WEB INFO

For more information on application software, visit the Discovering Computers 2000 Chapter 1 WEB INFO page (**www.scsite.com/dc2000/ch1/webinfo.htm**) and click Application Software.

Figure 1-12a

Application software is available as packaged software, custom software, shareware, freeware, and public-domain software.

PACKAGED SOFTWARE **Packaged software** is designed to meet the needs of a wide variety of users, not just a single user or company. Packaged software sometimes is called commercial off-the-shelf software because you can purchase these programs off the shelf from software vendors or stores that sell computer products (Figure 1-12a). You also can purchase packaged software on the Internet (Figure 1-12b).

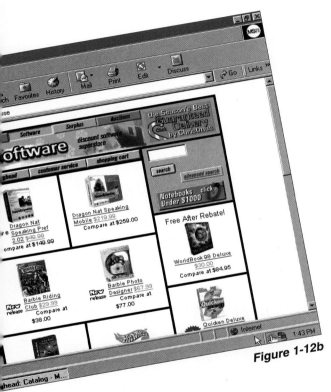

Figure 1-12b

Figure 1-12 Packaged software programs can be purchased from computer stores, office equipment suppliers, retailers, and software vendors.

CUSTOM SOFTWARE Sometimes a user or organization with unique software requirements cannot find packaged software that meets all of its needs. In this case, the user or organization can use **custom software**, which is a program or programs developed at a user's request to perform specific functions.

SHAREWARE **Shareware** is software that is distributed free for a trial period. If you want to use a shareware program beyond that period of time, you are expected to send a payment to the person or company that developed the program. Upon sending this small fee, the developer registers you to receive service assistance and updates.

FREEWARE AND PUBLIC-DOMAIN SOFTWARE **Freeware** is software that is provided at no cost to a user by an individual or company. Although free, freeware is copyrighted, meaning you cannot resell it as your own. **Public-domain software** is free software that has been donated for public use and has no copyright restrictions.

Examples of shareware, freeware, and public-domain software include utility programs, graphics programs, and games. Thousands of these programs are available on the Internet; you also can obtain copies of the program from the developer, a coworker, or a friend.

Software Development

People who write software programs are called **computer programmers** or **programmers**. Programmers write the instructions necessary to direct the computer to process data into information. The instructions must be placed in the correct sequence so the desired results occur. Complex programs can require hundreds of thousands of program instructions.

When writing complex programs for large businesses, programmers often follow a plan developed by a systems analyst. A **systems analyst** manages the development of a program, working with both the user and the programmer to determine and design the desired output of the program.

Programmers use a programming language to write computer programs. Some programming languages, such as Microsoft Visual Basic, have a graphical user interface that makes it easier to include the correct instructions in a program. Figure 1-13 illustrates the steps involved to create a program using the Microsoft Visual Basic programming language.

NETWORKS AND THE INTERNET

A **network** is a collection of computers and devices connected together via communications media and devices such as cables, telephone lines, modems, or other means. When your computer is connected to a network, you are said to be online.

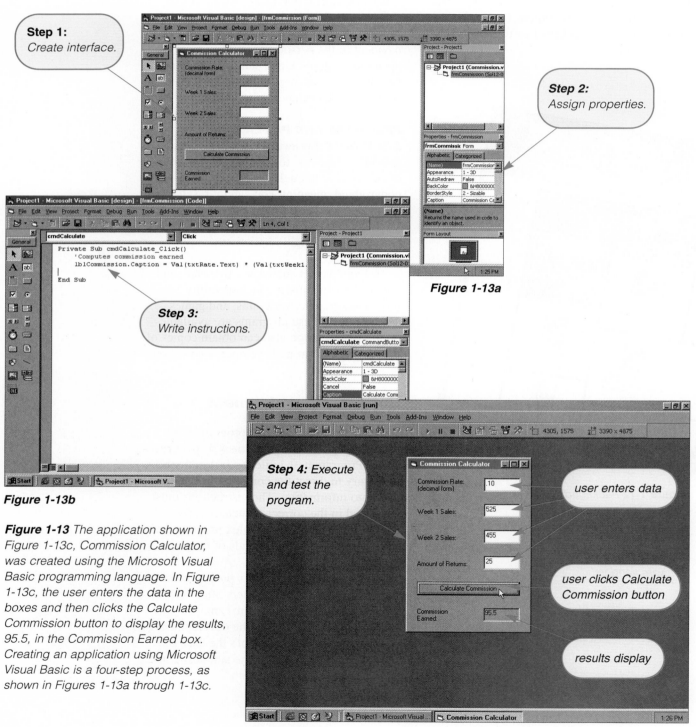

Figure 1-13a

Figure 1-13b

Figure 1-13 The application shown in Figure 1-13c, Commission Calculator, was created using the Microsoft Visual Basic programming language. In Figure 1-13c, the user enters the data in the boxes and then clicks the Calculate Commission button to display the results, 95.5, in the Commission Earned box. Creating an application using Microsoft Visual Basic is a four-step process, as shown in Figures 1-13a through 1-13c.

Figure 1-13c

Computers are networked together so users can share **resources**, such as hardware devices, software programs, data, and information. Sharing resources saves time and money. For example, instead of purchasing one printer for every computer in a company, the firm can connect a single printer and all computers via a network (Figure 1-14); the network enables all of the computers to access the same printer.

Most business computers are networked together. These networks can be relatively small or quite extensive. A network that connects computers in a limited geographic area, such as a school computer laboratory, office, or group of buildings, is called a local area network (LAN). A network that covers a large geographical area, such as one that connects the district offices of a national corporation, is called a wide area network (WAN) (Figure 1-15).

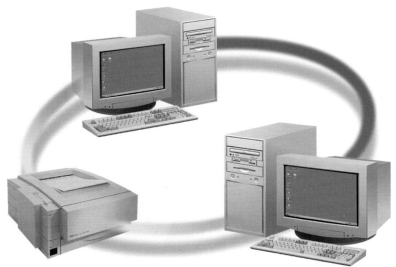

Figure 1-14 *This local area network (LAN) enables two separate computers to share the same printer.*

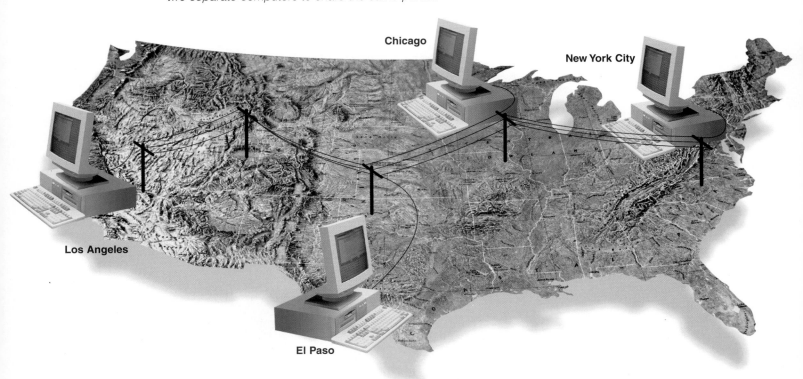

Figure 1-15 *A network can be quite large and complex, connecting users in district offices around the country (WAN).*

The world's largest network is the **Internet**, which is a worldwide collection of networks that links together millions of computers by means of modems, telephone lines, and other communications devices and media. With an abundance of resources and data accessible via the Internet, more than 125 million users around the world are making use of the Internet for a variety of reasons, some of which include the following (Figure 1-16):

- Sending messages to other connected users (e-mail)
- Accessing a wealth of information, such as news, maps, airline schedules, and stock market data
- Shopping for goods and services
- Meeting or conversing with people around the world
- Accessing sources of entertainment and leisure, such as online games, magazines, and vacation planning guides

Figure 1-16b (stock market data)

Figure 1-16a (e-mail)

Figure 1-16 *Users access the Internet for a variety of reasons: to send messages to other connected users, to access a wealth of information, to shop for goods and services, to meet or converse with people around the world, and for entertainment.*

Most users connect to the Internet in one of two ways: through an Internet service provider or through an online service. An Internet service provider (ISP) is an organization that supplies connections to the Internet for a monthly fee. Like an ISP, an online service provides access to the Internet, but it also provides a variety of other specialized content and services such as financial data, hardware and software guides, news, weather, legal information, and other similar commodities. For this reason, the fees for using an online service usually are slightly higher than fees for using an ISP. Two popular online services are America Online and The Microsoft Network.

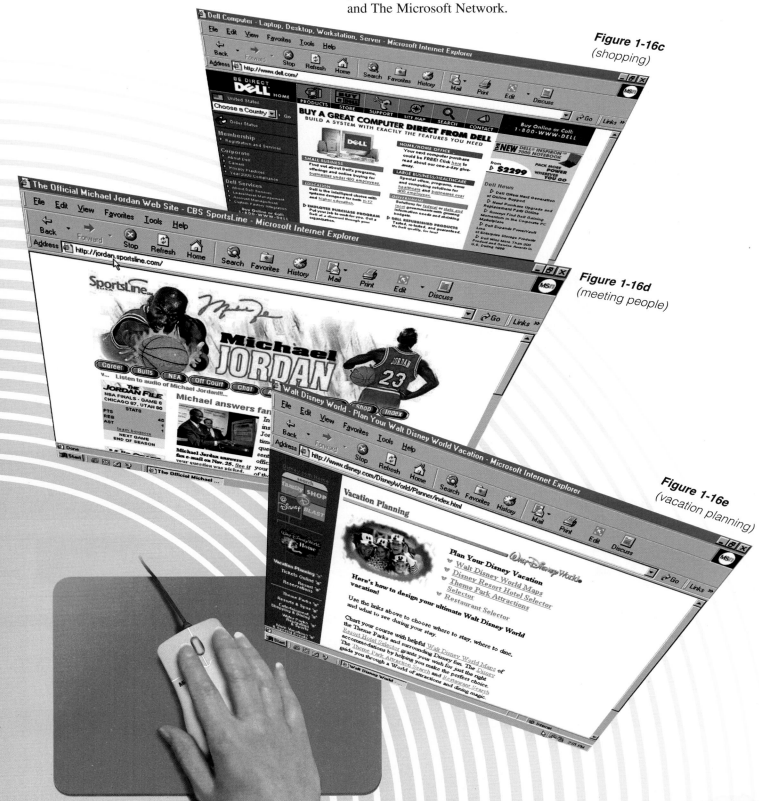

Figure 1-16c
(shopping)

Figure 1-16d
(meeting people)

Figure 1-16e
(vacation planning)

One of the more popular segments of the Internet is the World Wide Web, also called the Web, which contains billions of documents called Web pages. A Web page is a document that contains text, graphics, sound, or video, and has built-in connections, or hyperlinks, to other Web documents. Web pages are stored on computers throughout the world. A Web site is a related collection of Web pages. You access and view Web pages using a software program called a Web browser. The two most popular Web browsers are Microsoft Internet Explorer and Netscape Navigator. Figure 1-17 illustrates one method of connecting to the Web and displaying a Web page.

CATEGORIES OF COMPUTERS

The four major categories of computers are personal computers, minicomputers, mainframe computers, and supercomputers. These categories are based on the differences in the size, speed, processing capabilities, and price of computers. Due to rapidly changing

Figure 1-17 *One method of connecting to the Web and displaying a Web page.*

Step 1: *Use your computer and modem to make a local telephone call to an online service, such as The Microsoft Network.*

CONNECTING TO THE WEB AND DISPLAYING A WEB PAGE

ONLINE SERVICE

Step 2: *A Web browser such as Internet Explorer displays on your screen.*

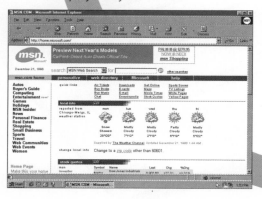

Web address

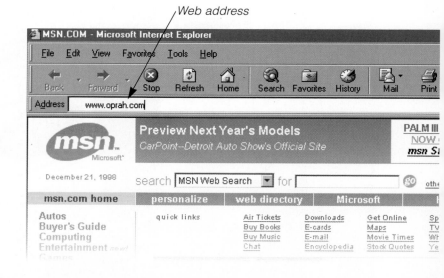

Step 3: *Enter the address of the Web site you wish to visit.*

technology, the categories cannot be defined precisely. For example, the speed used to define a mainframe today may be used to define a minicomputer next year. Some characteristics may overlap categories. Still, they frequently are used and should be understood. Figure 1-18 summarizes the four categories of computers, which are discussed in the following pages.

PERSONAL COMPUTERS

A **personal computer (PC)** is a computer that can perform all of its input, processing, output, and storage activities by itself; that is, it contains at least one input device, one output device, one storage device, memory, and a processor. The processor, sometimes called a microprocessor, is a central processing unit (CPU) on a single chip and is the basic building block of a PC.

CATEGORIES OF COMPUTERS

Category	Physical size	Number of instructions executed per second	Number of simultaneously connected users	General price range
Personal computer	Fits in your hand or on a desk	Up to 400 million	One stand-alone or many networked	Several thousand dollars or less
Minicomputer	Small cabinet	Thousands to millions	Two to 4,000	$5,000 to $150,000
Mainframe	Partial room to a full room of equipment	Millions	Hundreds to thousands	$300,00 to several million dollars
Supercomputer	Full room of equipment	Millions to billions	Hundreds to thousands	Several million dollars and up

Figure 1-18 *This table summarizes some of the differences among the categories of computers. Because of rapid changes in technology, these should be considered general guidelines only.*

Step 4: *The Web browser locates the Web site for the entered address and displays a Web page on your screen.*

Two popular series of personal computers are the PC (Figure 1-19) and the Apple Macintosh (Figure 1-20). These two types of computers have different processors and use different operating systems. The PC and compatibles use the Windows operating system, whereas the Apple Macintosh uses the Macintosh operating system. Today, the terms PC and compatible are used to refer to any personal computer that is based on specifications of the original IBM PC computer. Companies such as Gateway 2000, Compaq, Dell, and Toshiba all sell PC-compatible computers.

Two major categories of personal computers are desktop computers and portable computers. These types of personal computers are discussed in the next two sections.

Desktop Computers

A **desktop computer** is designed so the system unit, input devices, output devices, and any other devices fit entirely on or under a desk or table (Figure 1-21). In some desktop models, the system unit is placed horizontally on top of a desk along with the other devices. A **tower model**, in contrast, has a tall and narrow system unit that is designed to be placed on the floor vertically. Tower model desktop computers are available in a variety of heights: a full tower is at least 21 inches tall, a mid-tower is about 16 inches tall, and a mini-tower is usually 13 inches tall. The model of desktop computer you use often is determined by the design of your workspace.

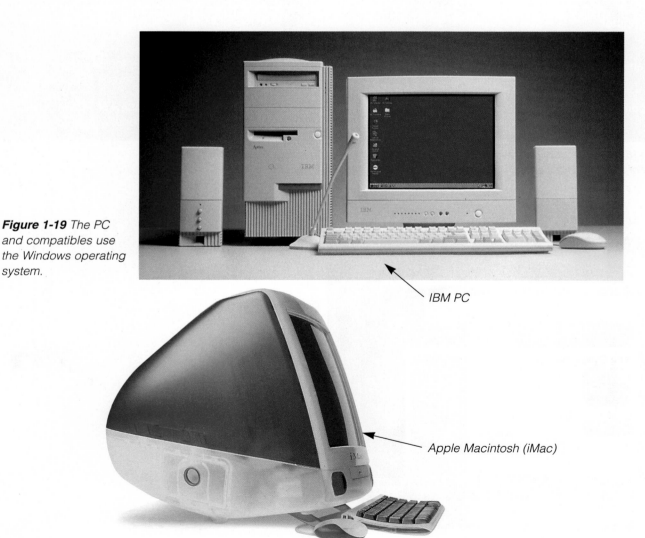

Figure 1-19 *The PC and compatibles use the Windows operating system.*

IBM PC

Apple Macintosh (iMac)

Figure 1-20 *The Apple Macintosh uses the Macintosh operating system.*

A more expensive and powerful desktop computer, called a **workstation**, is designed for work that requires intense calculations and graphics capabilities (Figure 1-22). Users in fields such as engineering, desktop publishing, and graphic art use workstations. For example, a workstation would be used to view and create maps or create computer-animated special effects for Hollywood movies.

A computer that is not connected to a network and has the capability of performing the information processing cycle operations (input, process, output, and storage) by itself is called a **stand-alone** computer. Most desktop computers today, however, have networking capabilities. Another use of the term workstation refers to any computer connected to a network, regardless of its category.

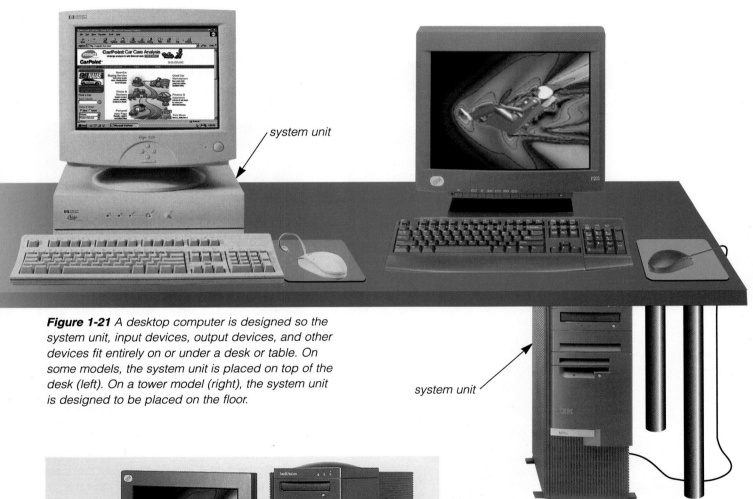

system unit

system unit

Figure 1-21 *A desktop computer is designed so the system unit, input devices, output devices, and other devices fit entirely on or under a desk or table. On some models, the system unit is placed on top of the desk (left). On a tower model (right), the system unit is designed to be placed on the floor.*

Figure 1-22 *An expensive, powerful, desktop computer designed for intense graphics and calculating is called a workstation.*

A desktop computer also can function as a server on a network. A **server** is a computer that manages the resources on a network. Servers control access to the software, printers, and other devices on the network as well as provide a centralized storage area for software programs and data. The other computers on the network, called clients, can access the contents of the storage area on the servers (Figure 1-23). In a network, one or more computers usually are designated as the server(s). The major difference between the server and client computers is that the server ordinarily is faster and has more storage space.

NETWORK COMPUTERS Another type of personal computer is called a **network computer (NC)**. It is designed specifically to connect to a network, especially the Internet. Most network computers cannot operate as stand-alone computers; that is, they have to be connected to a network to be functional. Because a network computer relies on the network for storage, it typically does not have a hard disk or CD-ROM drive. When used in the home, a network computer often does not have a monitor; instead it uses a television set as the display device. This type of computer, called a set-top box, sits on top of your television set and allows you to access the Internet and navigate Web pages using a device that looks like a remote control (Figure 1-24).

Figure 1-24 A network computer that uses a television set as the display device is called a set-top box.

SERVER

CLIENT

CLIENT

Figure 1-23 A server is a computer that manages resources on a network. Other computers on the network are called clients.

Portable Computers

A **portable computer** is a personal computer that is small enough to carry. Two types of portable computers are laptop and handheld. Each of these types of portable computers is discussed next.

LAPTOP COMPUTERS Designed for mobility, a **laptop computer**, also called a **notebook computer**, is a personal computer small enough to fit on your lap. Today's laptop computers are thin, lightweight, and can be just as powerful as the average desktop computer. Laptop computers generally are more expensive than their desktop counterparts.

On a typical laptop computer, the keyboard is located on top of the system unit, the monitor attaches to the system unit with a hinge, and the drives are built into the system unit (Figure 1-25). Weighing on average between four and ten pounds, these computers can be transported easily from place to place. Most laptop computers can run either on batteries or using a standard power supply. Users with mobile computing needs, such as business travelers, often use a laptop.

HANDHELD COMPUTERS A **handheld computer** or **palmtop computer** is a small personal computer designed to fit in your hand (Figure 1-26). Because of their reduced size, the keyboards and screens on handheld computers are quite small. Computers in the handheld category usually do not have disk drives; instead, programs and data are stored on chips inside the system unit. Many handheld computers can be connected to a larger computer for the purpose of exchanging information. A business traveler or other mobile user might use a handheld computer if a laptop computer is too large.

A popular type of handheld computer is the **Personal Digital Assistant (PDA)**. A PDA often supports personal information management (PIM) applications such as a calendar, appointment book, calculator, memo pad, and even telephone services and Internet access. Today, a wide variety of people use PDAs instead of writing in a pocket-sized appointment book.

Because handheld computers have such small keyboards, many of these computers use pen input, which allows you to write on the screen instead of typing on a keyboard (Figure 1-27). These computers, called **pen computers**, contain special software that permits the computer to recognize handwritten characters and other symbols. Many PDAs use pen input and can be considered pen computers. Pen computers also are used by parcel delivery individuals, meter readers, and other people whose jobs require them to move from place to place.

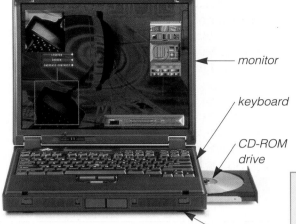
monitor

keyboard

CD-ROM drive

system unit

Figure 1-25 *On a typical laptop computer, the keyboard is located on top of the system unit, the monitor attaches to the system unit with a hinge, and the drives are built into the system unit.*

Figure 1-26 *A handheld computer is a small personal computer designed to fit in your hand.*

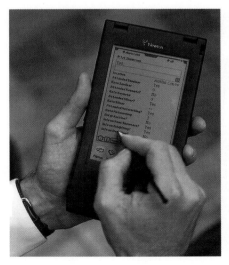

Figure 1-27 *Pen computers, such as this PDA, allow you to write directly on the screen of the handheld computer.*

WEB INFO
WEB INFO

For more information on laptop computers, visit the Discovering Computers 2000 Chapter 1 WEB INFO page (**www.scsite.com/dc2000/ch1/webinfo.htm**) and click Laptop Computers.

WEB INFO
WEB INFO

For more information on PDAs, visit the Discovering Computers 2000 Chapter 1 WEB INFO page (**www.scsite.com/dc2000/ch1/webinfo.htm**) and click PDAs.

Figure 1-28
Minicomputers are more powerful than a workstation but less powerful than a mainframe.

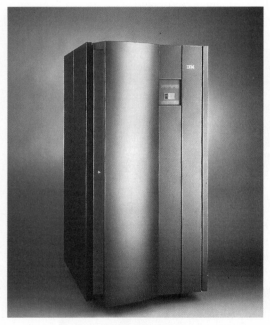

Figure 1-29 *Mainframe computers are large, expensive, powerful machines that can handle thousands of connected users simultaneously and process up to millions of instructions per second.*

MINICOMPUTERS

A **minicomputer**, such as the one shown in Figure 1-28, is more powerful and larger than a workstation computer. Minicomputers often can support up to 4,000 connected users at the same time. Users often access a minicomputer via a **terminal**, which is a device with a monitor and keyboard. Such terminals – sometimes called **dumb terminals** because they have no processing power – cannot act as stand-alone computers and must be connected to the minicomputer to operate.

A minicomputer also can act as a server in a network environment. In this case, personal computers access the minicomputer.

MAINFRAME COMPUTERS

A **mainframe** is a large, expensive, very powerful computer that can handle hundreds or thousands of connected users simultaneously (Figure 1-29). Like minicomputers, mainframes also can act as a server in a network environment. Mainframes can store tremendous amounts of data, instructions, and information, which users can access with terminals or personal computers.

SUPERCOMPUTERS

A **supercomputer**, shown in Figure 1-30, is the fastest, most powerful computer – and the most expensive. Capable of processing more than 64 billion instructions in a single second, supercomputers are used for applications requiring complex, sophisticated mathematical calculations. For example, a supercomputer would be used for weather forecasting, nuclear energy research, and petroleum exploration.

Figure 1-30 *This Intel supercomputer at Sandia National Laboratories in New Mexico contains 86 cabinets that house over 9,000 processor chips.*

EXAMPLES OF COMPUTER USAGE

Every day, numerous users rely on different types of computers for a variety of applications. Whether used to run complex application software, connect to a network, or perform countless other functions, computers are powerful tools at home, at work, and at play. To illustrate the variety of uses for computers, this section takes you on a visual and narrative tour of five categories of users: a home user, a small business user, a mobile user, a large business user, and a power user (Figure 1-31). Examples of hardware and software listed in the table below are presented on the following pages.

USER	HARDWARE/NETWORK	SOFTWARE
Home User	• Desktop computer; set-top box; handheld computer • Internet	• Reference (e.g., encyclopedias, medical dictionaries, road atlas) • Entertainment (e.g., games, music composition, greeting card publishing) • Educational (e.g., foreign language tutorials, children's math and reading software) • Productivity (e.g., word processor, spreadsheet) • Personal finance, online banking • Communications and Web browser • E-mail
SMALL BUSINESS USER	• Desktop computer; handheld computer (PDA); shared network printer • Local area network • Internet	• Productivity (e.g., word processor, spreadsheet, database) • Company specific (e.g., accounting, legal reference) • Communications and Web browser • May use network versions of some software packages • E-mail
 MOBILE USER	• Laptop computer equipped with a modem; laptop carrying case; video projector • Internet • Local area network	• Productivity (e.g., word processor, spreadsheet, presentation graphics) • Personal information management • Communications and Web browser • E-mail
LARGE BUSINESS USER	• Minicomputer or mainframe computer • Desktop or laptop computer; handheld computer (PDA); kiosk • Local area network or wide area network, depending on the size of the company • Internet	• Productivity (e.g., word processor, spreadsheet, database, presentation graphics) • Personal information management • Desktop publishing • Accounting • Network management • Communications and Web browser • May use network versions of some software packages • E-mail
POWER USER	• Workstation or other powerful computer with multimedia capabilities • Local area network • Internet	• Desktop publishing • Multimedia authoring • Photo, sound, and video editing • Communications and Web browser • Computer-aided design

Figure 1-31 *Today, computers are used in millions of businesses and homes to support work tasks and leisure activities. Depending on their intended usage, different computer users require different kinds of hardware and software to meet their needs effectively. The types of users are listed here together with the hardware, software, and network types used most commonly by each.*

Home User

An increasingly common item in the home is a desktop computer, which can be used for different purposes by various family members, including entertainment; research and education; budgeting and personal financial management; home business management; personal and business communications; Web access; and shopping.

More than likely, the home user has purchased a variety of software applications (Figure 1-32). Reference software, such as encyclopedias, medical dictionaries, or a road atlas, provides valuable and thorough information for everyone in the family. Software also provides hours of entertainment. For example, you can play games such as solitaire, chess, and Monopoly™; compose music; make a family tree; or create a greeting card. Educational software helps adults learn to speak a foreign language and youngsters to read, write, count, and spell. To make computers easier for children to use, many companies design special hardware just for kids (Figure 1-33).

Figure 1-32a (encyclopedia)

Figure 1-32 Among the variety of software products used in a typical household are an interactive encyclopedia, a children's learning tool, and a flight simulator.

Figure 1-32b (educational software)

Figure 1-32c (flight simulator)

Figure 1-33 To assist young children at the computer, special keyboards are designed for their small hands.

For other users in the house, a variety of productivity software exists. Most computers today are sold with word processing and spreadsheet software already installed. Personal finance software helps to prepare taxes, balance a checkbook, and manage investments and family budgets, as well as allowing you to connect to your bank via the Internet to pay bills online. Other software assists in organizing names and addresses, setting up maintenance schedules, preparing legal documents, and purchasing stocks online.

Today, more than 50 million home users also access the Web (Figure 1-34). Once online, users can retrieve a tremendous amount of information, shop for products and services, communicate with others around the world using e-mail or chat rooms, or even take college classes. Some home users access the Web through the desktop computer, while others use a set-top box.

Handheld computers also find a place in the home. For example, a handheld computer commonly is used to maintain daily schedules and address lists or is used for a more specialized purpose such as managing and monitoring the health condition of a family member.

Already, half of today's homes have one or more computers. As computers continue to drop in price, they will become a more common component of the family household.

Figure 1-34 *Some family members use the computer to access the Web. Shown are Web sites where individuals can take college classes on the Web and grocery shop online.*

Figure 1-34a *(college class)*

Figure 1-34b *(grocery store)*

Figure 1-35 *Small businesses often provide a desktop personal computer for some or all of their employees.*

Small Business User

Computers also play an important role in helping **small business users** manage their resources effectively. A small business, sometimes called a **small office/home office (SOHO)**, such as a local law practice, accounting firm, travel agency, or florist, usually has fewer than fifty employees. Small businesses often provide a desktop personal computer for some or all of their employees (Figure 1-35). Many individuals also will have handheld computers, specifically PDAs, to manage appointments and contact information.

Small businesses often have a local area network to connect the computers in the company. Networking the computers saves money on both hardware and software. For example, a company can avoid the expense of buying multiple printers by connecting a single shared printer to the network. The company also can purchase a network version of a software package, which usually costs less than purchasing a separate software license for each individual desktop computer. Employees can access the software on a server as needed.

For business document preparation, finances, and tracking, a small business owner usually purchases basic productivity software such as word processing and spreadsheet software (Figure 1-36).

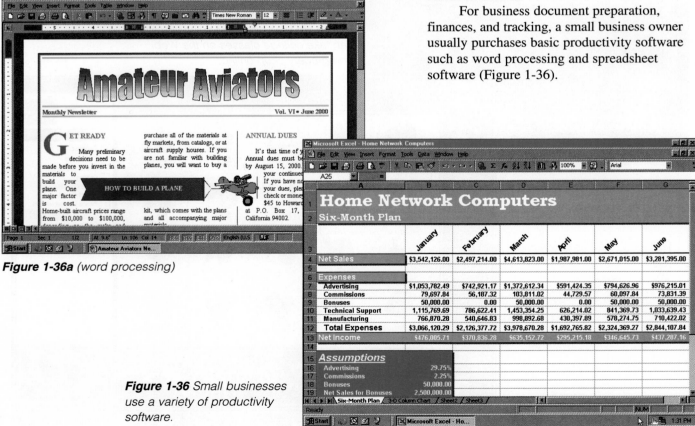

Figure 1-36a *(word processing)*

Figure 1-36 *Small businesses use a variety of productivity software.*

Figure 1-36b *(spreadsheet)*

Businesses may use other types of software, specific to the industry or company. An accounting firm, for example, will have accounting software to prepare journals, ledgers, income statements, balance sheets, and other documents (Figure 1-37).

The employees in a small business usually have access to the Web, so they can connect to online references such as the Yellow Pages, package shipping information (Figure 1-38), and postal rates, as well as legal information relevant to small businesses. Today, many small businesses are building their own Web sites to advertise their products and services and take orders and requests from customers (Figure 1-39).

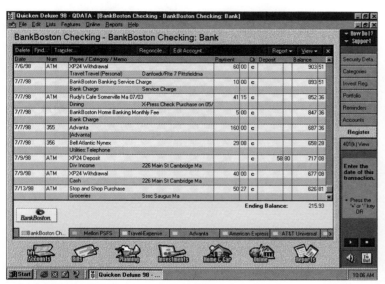

Figure 1-37 *Small businesses often use specialized software such as the accounting software shown here.*

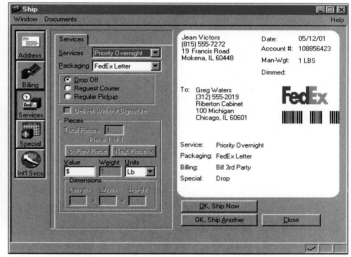

Figure 1-38 *With access to the Web, small businesses can send or track packages.*

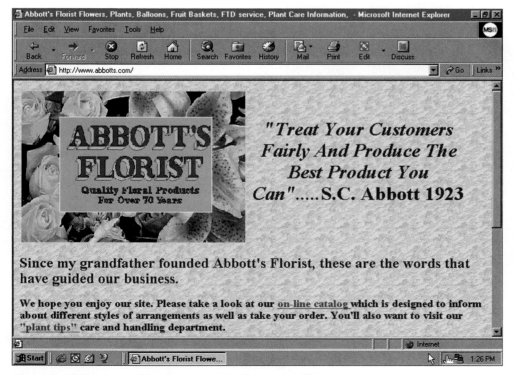

Figure 1-39 *Some small businesses advertise on the Web.*

Mobile User

As businesses expand to serve customers across the country and around the world, more and more people find themselves traveling to and from a main office to conduct business. Such users – who need to use a computer while on the road – are examples of those with mobile computing needs (Figure 1-40). **Mobile users** include a range of people, such as outside sales representatives,

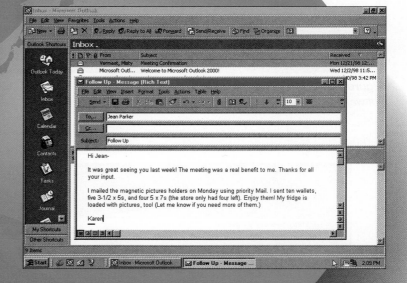

Figure 1-40 Mobile users have laptop computers so they can work while on the road.

marketing managers, real estate and insurance agents, and consultants.

Mobile users often have a laptop computer equipped with a modem, which enables them to transfer information between their computer and another computer, such as one at the main office.

The software utilized by mobile users includes basic productivity software such as word processing and spreadsheet software, as well as presentation graphics software that allows the creation and delivery of presentations.

Figure 1-41 *Mobile users often connect their laptops to multimedia video projectors for presentations.*

To deliver such presentations to a large audience, the user connects the laptop to a video projector that displays the presentation on a full screen (Figure 1-41). Other types of software, such as communications software and a Web browser, allow a mobile user to access the company network and the Internet.

While transporting the laptop computer, a mobile user needs a durable, well-insulated carrying case to protect the computer if it is dropped or bumped. Back in their main office or residence, many laptop owners have a **docking station**, which is a platform into which you place a laptop. The docking station contains connections to peripherals such as a keyboard, monitor, printer, and other devices (Figure 1-42). When a laptop is in the docking station, it essentially functions as a desktop computer. With a docking station, a mobile user can enjoy the features of a desktop computer, such as a full-sized keyboard and monitor, while accessing the software and data stored on the laptop computer.

Figure 1-42 *When you insert a laptop into a docking station, you can use peripherals such as a full-sized keyboard, a full-sized monitor, and a printer with your laptop.*

laptop computer

docking station

Large Business User

A large business can have hundreds or thousands of employees in offices across a region, the country, or the world. The company may have an equally large number of computers, all of which are connected in a network. This network – a local area network or a wide area network depending on the size of the company – enables communications between employees at all locations.

Throughout a large business, computers help employees perform a variety of tasks related to their job. For example, **large business users** in a typical large company use an automated telephone system to route calls to the appropriate department or person. The inside sales representatives enter orders into desktop computers while on the telephone with a customer (Figure 1-43). Outside sales representatives – the mobile users in the firm – use laptop computers as described in the previous section. The marketing department uses desktop publishing software to prepare marketing literature such as newsletters, product brochures, and advertising material. The accounting department uses software to pay invoices, bill customers, and process payroll. The employees in the information systems department have a huge responsibility: to keep the computers and the network running and determine when and if new hardware or software is required.

Figure 1-43 *Computers are used throughout a large business for tasks such as entering orders.*

Figure 1-44a *(PDA being used at a meeting)*

Figure 1-44 *Employees in a large business often use PDAs. Many models allow you to transfer data from a desktop computer to the PDA so you have important information at your fingertips while you attend meetings.*

In addition to word processing, spreadsheet, database, and presentation graphics software, employees in a large firm also may use calendar programs to post their schedules on the network and PDAs to maintain personal or company information (Figure 1-44). Electronic mail and Web browsers also enable communication between employees and others around the world.

Most large organizations have their own Web site to showcase products, services, and selected company information (Figure 1-45). Customers, vendors, and any other interested parties can access the information on the Web without having to speak to a company employee.

Some large businesses also use a kiosk to provide information to the public. A **kiosk** is a freestanding computer, usually with a touch screen that serves as an input device (Figure 1-46). More advanced kiosks allow customers to place orders, make payments, or even access the Web.

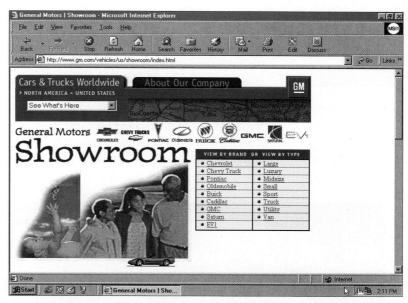

Figure 1-45 *Large businesses often have their own Web site to showcase products, services, and company information.*

Figure 1-44b *(PDA connected to a desktop computer)*

Figure 1-46 *A kiosk is a freestanding computer, usually with multimedia capabilities and a touch screen. This kiosk allows customers to place orders.*

Power User

Another category of user, called a **power user**, requires the capabilities of a workstation or other powerful computer. Examples of power users include engineers, architects, desktop publishers, and graphic artists (Figure 1-47). Workstations also are used by developers working with **multimedia**, in which they combine text, graphics, sound, video and other media elements into one application. Because of the nature of their work, all of these users need computers with extremely fast processors that have multi-media capabilities.

In addition to powerful hardware, a workstation contains software specific to the needs of the power user (Figure 1-48). For example, engineers and architects use software to draft and design items such as floor plans, mechanical assemblies, and computer chips. The desktop publisher uses specialized software to prepare marketing literature such as newsletters, brochures, and annual reports. A multimedia developer uses multimedia authoring software to create presentations containing text, graphics, video, sound, and animation. Animation is the appearance of motion. Many of these users also have software that enables them to create and edit drawings, photographs, audio, and video. Because of its specialized design, this software usually is quite expensive.

Power users are found in all types of businesses, both large and small; some also work at home. Depending on where he or she works, a power user might fit into one of the previously discussed categories, as well. Thus, in addition to their specific needs, these users often have additional hardware and software requirements such as network capabilities and Internet access.

Figure 1-47 *Examples of power users are engineers, architects, desktop publishers, graphic artists, and multimedia authors.*

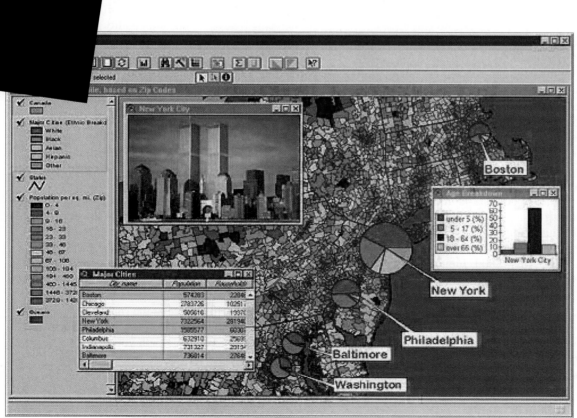

Figure 1-48 *One application for a power user is to create maps.*

TECHNOLOGY TRAILBLAZER

BILL GATES

Bill Gates is the wealthiest person in America, and one of the richest people in the world. Admirers call him insightful, innovative, and dedicated, while critics claim he is haughty, opportunistic, and lucky. Admirers and critics agree, however, that William Henry Gates III is the most powerful man in the computer industry.

Despite his larger-than-life presence today, Gates's early years were inauspicious. Even with parental encouragement (25 cents for each A), he was an underachiever in school. His reputation as "class clown" changed when his parents transferred him to Lakeside, a distinguished private school. At Lakeside, Gates says, "there was no position called the clown. I applied for it, but either they didn't like my brand of humor or humor wasn't in that season." For the first time Gates studied – and he earned straight A's. At Lakeside, Gates was introduced to computers and lifelong friend, Paul Allen. Gates and Allen spent hours writing programs on a teletype machine connected to a large computer and soon were writing programs for local companies. After graduation, Gates enrolled at Harvard, but he spent more time playing games and in the computer laboratory than in class. The best classes, Gates feels, dealt in fundamentals. "The goal [of school] should be to learn how the world works, the underlying principles. You must study specifics in order to do that, but the specifics aren't what you're learning."

In 1975, an excited call from Paul Allen interrupted Gates's studies. A company called MITS planned to release the first microcomputer, the Altair 8800. Jumping the gun slightly, they called MITS and declared that they had developed a form of the programming language BASIC for the new computer. MITS was interested. After a marathon eight-week programming session, Allen flew to MITS headquarters to test the language. It worked! MITS agreed to pay a royalty for licensing rights; Gates dropped out of Harvard; and he and Allen formed Microsoft.

Certain that computing power would increase steadily, Gates convinced Allen they should concentrate on software. "What is it that limits being able to get value out of infinite computing power? Software." Microsoft's big break came in 1980, when IBM sought an operating system for its first personal computer. IBM's conservative, middle-aged, business-suited executives met with Microsoft's twenty-five year old, tousle-haired headman in his smudged glasses and wrinkled chinos. Gates agreed to supply an operating system, provided he kept the rights to market it to other manufacturers. The IBM PC was an immediate success, and Gates's foresight was evident when IBM-compatible computers also adopted the operating system.

Throughout his administration, Gates has shown an uncanny ability to anticipate technological developments and customer needs. With these factors in mind, Gates has focused not on originating new products, but on modifying existing products. The once casually garbed micromanager today acts as chief strategist, monitoring and promoting Microsoft's many ventures – often clothed in a suit and tie. Gates's vision, however, remains unchanged: to do "better software than anyone else."

It is a profitable vision, to be sure. Yet, even with personal assets estimated at more than $50 billion (much of it in Microsoft stock), Gates is wary of the trappings of wealth. "It's easy to get spoiled," he says, "by things that alienate you from what's important." Gates has given more than $270 million to various charities, and proceeds from his book, *The Road Ahead*, are donated to nonprofit organizations. Gates admits some of his success was luck – being born in the right place at the right time. But in the end, his achievements seem grounded in his own advice: "To succeed, put yourself on a path you enjoy that leads somewhere important."

COMPANY ON THE CUTTING EDGE

COMPANY ON THE CUTTING EDGE

MICROSOFT

In 1975, Microsoft had three programmers, one product, and revenues of $16,000. Less than twenty-five years later, the software giant employs 25,000 people, offers scores of software titles, and has earnings of more than $11 billion. Microsoft's rapid ascent is an achievement almost unparalleled in the history of American business.

Bill Gates and Paul Allen, former high-school classmates, founded Microsoft in 1975. The company's name is a contraction of "microcomputer software;" an advantage of being the first in a field, Gates points out, is the ability to choose an obvious name. The founders had no business plan, no capital, and no financial backing, but they did have a product – a form of the BASIC programming language tailored for the first microcomputer – that they licensed for about $30 a copy. Within five years, Microsoft employed a staff of forty and had developed and licensed versions of other programming languages, opened an international office, and marketed some computer games.

In 1980 IBM, a $30 billion behemoth, asked Microsoft to provide an operating system for its new IBM personal computer. The deadline? Three months. Luckily, Gates was able to find and purchase the core of a suitable operating system, dubbed Q-DOS ("Quick and Dirty Operating System"), from another company. Microsoft's version, called MS-DOS, would become the international standard for IBM and IBM-compatible personal computers. With 80 percent of the PC market, Microsoft's sales rocketed to $97 million in 1984.

Microsoft did not rest. While the company continued to update MS-DOS, it also worked on the operating system's successor, Windows. Like Apple's Macintosh operating system, Windows had a graphical user interface. (Apple Corporation later sued unsuccessfully for copyright infringement.) Acceptance was slow when Windows was released in 1985. Critics wondered if graphical user interfaces were as inevitable as Microsoft believed. Yet, while Windows struggled,

Microsoft's application software packages enjoyed great success. In 1988, Microsoft surpassed Lotus Development Corporation to become the world's top software vendor.

Microsoft had not given up on Windows. A new version, Windows 3.0, was released in 1990. Aided by more powerful processors, a greater variety of compatible software, and a $10 million promotion, four million copies were shipped in just one year. With the introduction of a networking version, called Windows NT, Windows became the most popular graphical operating system in the world with more than 25 million users. "We bet the company on Windows," Gates later said, "and we deserve the benefit."

In 1995, Microsoft reinvented itself in response to the growing Internet. The new Windows 95 operating system incorporated Internet Explorer, a Web browser, and elements that made it easy to access Microsoft's new online service. Windows 95 sold one million copies in its first four days. The next year Microsoft debuted a cable television news network and a corresponding Web site. In less than two years, Microsoft had moved from the periphery to the vanguard of the information revolution.

Almost ninety percent of personal computers sold use a Microsoft operating system. Ironically, this dominance resulted in what may be Microsoft's greatest challenge to date – an antitrust suit. Sparked by manufacturers of rival Web browsers, the United States Department of Justice claimed that, with actions such as including Internet Explorer in Windows 98, Microsoft stifled competition. Microsoft denied the charge, countering that restrictions on these innovations punish creativity, harming consumers.

Despite the lawsuit, Microsoft's huge customer acceptance, sound financial base, state-of-the-art facilities, and talented staff point to a bright future. In the ever-changing arena of computer software, however, even a colossus may be vulnerable. "Microsoft won't be immortal," Gates warns. "All companies fail...My goal is to keep my company vital as long as possible."

Microsoft
WHERE DO YOU WANT TO GO TODAY?™

CHAPTER 1 **2 3 4 5 6 7 8 9 10 11 12 13 14 INDEX**

IN BRIEF www.scsite.com/dc2000/ch1/brief.htm

WEB INSTRUCTIONS: *To display this page from the Web, launch your browser and enter the URL,* *www.scsite.com/dc2000/ch1/brief.htm. Click the links for current and additional information. To listen to* *an audio version of this IN BRIEF, click the Audio button to the right of the title, IN BRIEF, at the top of the* *page. To play the audio, RealPlayer must be installed on your computer (download by clicking* <u>*here*</u>*).*

 ## 1. Why Is Computer Literacy Important?

To be successful in today's world, it is crucial to have knowledge and understanding of computers and their uses. This knowledge, called **<u>computer literacy</u>**, is essential as technology advances and computers extend into every facet of daily living.

 ## 2. What Is a Computer?

A **<u>computer</u>** is an electronic machine, operating under the control of instructions stored in its own memory, that can accept data (input), manipulate the data according to specified rules (process), produce results (output), and store the results for future use (**storage**). **Data** is a collection of unorganized facts, which can include words, numbers, images, and sounds. Computers manipulate data to create information. **Information** is data that is organized, has meaning, and is useful. Examples are reports, newsletters, a receipt, or a check. Data entered into a computer is called **input**. The processed results are called **output**. The cycle of input, process, output, and storage is called the **information processing cycle**.

 ## 3. What Are the Components of a Computer?

Hardware is the electric, electronic, and mechanical equipment that makes up a computer. An **input device** allows a user to enter data and commands into the memory of a computer. Three commonly used input devices are the keyboard, the mouse, and a microphone. An **output device** is used to convey information generated by a computer to the user. Three commonly used output devices are a printer, a monitor, and speakers. The **system unit** is a box-like case made from metal or plastic that houses the computer circuitry. The system unit contains the **<u>central processing unit (CPU)</u>**, which interprets and carries out the instructions that operate a computer, including computations; and **memory**, which is a series of electronic elements that temporarily holds the data and instructions while the CPU is processing them. **Storage devices** are mechanisms used to record and retrieve data, information, and instructions to and from a storage medium. Common storage devices are a floppy disk drive, hard disk drive, CD-ROM drive, and DVD-ROM drive. **Communications devices** enable a computer to exchange items such as data, instructions, and information with another computer.

 ## 4. Why Is a Computer a Powerful Tool?

A computer's power is derived from its capability of performing the <u>information processing cycle</u> operations with speed, reliability, and accuracy; its capacity to store huge amounts of data, instructions, and information; and its ability to communicate with other computers.

 ## 5. What Is Computer Software?

Software is the series of instructions that tells the hardware of a computer what to do. <u>Software</u> can be categorized into two types: system software and application software. **System software** controls the operation of the computer and its devices and serves as the interface between a user and the

 **www.scsite.com/dc2000/ch1/brief.htm**

computer's hardware. Two types of system software are the **operating system**, which contains instructions that coordinate the activities of hardware devices; and utility programs, which perform specific tasks usually related to managing a computer. **Application software** performs specific tasks for users, such as creating documents, spreadsheets, databases, or presentation graphics. **Computer programmers** write software programs, often following a plan developed by a **systems analyst**.

6. What Is the Purpose of a Network?

A network is a collection of computers and devices connected together via communications media. Computers are networked so users can share resources such as hardware devices, software programs, data, and information.

7. How Is the Internet Used?

The world's largest network is the **Internet**, which is a worldwide collection of networks that links together millions of computers. The Internet is used to send messages to other users, obtain information, shop for goods and services, meet or converse with people around the world, and access sources of entertainment and leisure. The World Wide Web, which contains billions of Web pages with text, graphics, sound, and built-in connections to other Web pages, is one of the more popular segments of the Internet.

8. What Are the Categories of Computers?

The four major categories of computers are personal computers, minicomputers, mainframe computers, and supercomputers. These categories are based on differences in size, speed, processing capabilities, and price. A **personal computer** (**PC**) can perform all of its input, processing, output, and storage by itself. Two types of personal computers are **desktop computers**, which are designed to fit entirely on or under a desk or table, and **portable computers**, which are small enough to carry. **Minicomputers** are larger and more powerful than personal computers and often can support up to 4,000 connected users. A **mainframe** is a large, expensive, very powerful computer that can handle hundreds or thousands of connected users simultaneously. **Supercomputers** – the fastest, most powerful, and most expensive computers – are capable of processing more than 64 billion instructions in a single second.

9. How Are Computers Used?

Every day, people depend on different types of computers for a variety of applications. **Home users** rely on their computers for entertainment; communications; research and education; Web access; shopping; personal finance; and productivity applications such as word processing and spreadsheets. Small business users utilize productivity software as well as communications software, Web browsers, e-mail, and specialized software. **Mobile users** have laptop computers so they can work on the road. They often use presentation software. **Large business users** use computers to run their businesses by using productivity software, communications software, automated systems for most departments in the company, and large networks. **Power users** require the capabilities of workstations or other powerful computers to design plans, produce publications, create graphic art, and work with multimedia that includes text, graphics, sound, video, and other media elements.

KEY TERMS www.scsite.com/dc2000/ch1/terms.htm

WEB INSTRUCTIONS: *To display this page from the Web, launch your browser and enter the URL, www.scsite.com/dc2000/ch1/terms.htm. Scroll through the list of terms. Click a term to display its definition and a picture. Click KEY TERMS on the left to redisplay the KEY TERMS page. Click the TO WEB button for current and additional information about the term from the Web. To see animations, Shockwave and the Flash Player must be installed on your computer (download by clicking here).*

application software (1.12)
central processing unit (CPU) (1.6)
communications devices (1.8)
computer (1.3)
computer literacy (1.3)
computer program (1.9)
computer programmers (1.13)
custom software (1.13)
data (1.3)
desktop computer (1.20)
docking station (1.31)
dumb terminals (1.24)
execute (1.10)
freeware (1.13)
graphical user interface (GUI) (1.11)
handheld computer (1.23)
hardware (1.4)
home users (1.26)
icon (1.11)
information (1.4)
information processing cycle (1.4)
input (1.4)
input device (1.5)
install (1.10)
Internet (1.16)
kiosk (1.33)
laptop computer (1.23)
large business users (1.32)
mainframe (1.24)

APPLICATION SOFTWARE: Programs designed to perform specific tasks for users; include word processing software, spreadsheet software, database software, presentation graphics software, and many other types of software for a variety of tasks. (1.12)

memory (1.6)
minicomputer (1.24)
mobile users (1.30)
multimedia (1.34)
network (1.14)
network computer (NC) (1.22)
notebook computer (1.23)
operating system (1.10)
output (1.4)
output device (1.6)
packaged software (1.13)
palmtop computer (1.23)

pen computers (1.23)
personal computer (PC) (1.19)
Personal Digital Assistant (PDA) (1.23)
portable computer (1.22)
power user (1.34)
processing (1.4)
processor (1.6)
program (1.9)
programmers (1.13)
public-domain software (1.13)
resources (1.15)
server (1.22)
shareware (1.13)
small business users (1.28)
small office/home office (SOHO) (1.28)
software (1.4)
stand-alone (1.21)
storage (1.4)
storage device (1.7)
storage medium (1.7)
supercomputer (1.24)
system software (1.10)
system unit (1.6)
systems analyst (1.13)
terminal (1.24)
tower model (1.20)
user (1.4)
user interface (1.11)
workstation (1.21)

Student Exercises
WEB INFO
IN BRIEF
KEY TERMS
AT THE MOVIES
CHECKPOINT
AT ISSUE
CYBERCLASS
HANDS ON
NET STUFF
Special Features
TIMELINE 2000
GUIDE TO WWW SITES
MAKING A CHIP
BUYER'S GUIDE 2000
CAREERS 2000
TRENDS 2000
CHAT
INTERACTIVE LABS
NEWS
HOME

CHAPTER **1** 2 3 4 5 6 7 8 9 10 11 12 13 14 **INDEX**

AT THE MOVIES
www.scsite.com/dc2000/ch1/movies.htm

WELCOME to VIDEO CLIPS from CNN

WEB INSTRUCTIONS: *To display this page from the Web, launch your browser and enter the URL,*
www.scsite.com/dc2000/ch1/movies.htm. Click a picture to view a video. After watching the video, close
the video window and then complete the exercise by answering the questions about the video. To view the
videos, RealPlayer must be installed on your computer (download by clicking here).

1 Personal Computers for Students

When purchasing a personal computer, should you choose
your cheapest option? The video states that a good college
computer should have 32 MB of memory, 4 GB of hard disk
storage, a 233 or 266 MHz CPU, and a 56K modem. What is
your opinion of this recommendation? If you had a choice,
would you buy a desktop or a laptop computer? Why? In addition to the computer, what accessories might you purchase?
Does your school require students to own their own computer?
Does it provide Internet access?

2 Handheld Computers

A handheld computer is a small personal computer designed to
fit in your hand. What are some other terms used to describe
handheld computers? Many of these small computers run basic
operating systems such as Windows CE. What does CE stand
for? What other productivity or Internet software can you run
on a handheld computer? Who might use one of these computers and why? Would you purchase a handheld computer
instead of desktop or laptop? Why?

3 Microsoft Inner Workings

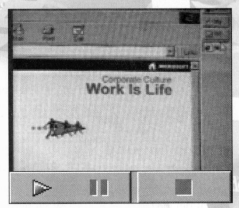

Have you ever wondered what it would be like to work for the
world's largest software company? At Microsoft Corporation, a
$200 billion company that holds a 90 percent market share in
key PC markets, the only rule is to win. How would you
describe the corporate culture at Microsoft? How do you think
Microsoft's culture differs from the culture at other large corporations? What do you think the advantages and disadvantages would be of working for a company whose motto is,
work is life?

Student Exercises
WEB INFO
IN BRIEF
KEY TERMS
AT THE MOVIES
CHECKPOINT
AT ISSUE
CYBERCLASS
HANDS ON
NET STUFF
Special Features
TIMELINE 2000
GUIDE TO WWW SITES
MAKING A CHIP
BUYER'S GUIDE 2000
CAREERS 2000
TRENDS 2000
CHAT
INTERACTIVE LABS
NEWS
HOME

CHAPTER 1 2 3 4 5 6 7 8 9 10 11 12 13 14 **INDEX**

CHECKPOINT   www.scsite.com/dc2000/ch1/check.htm

WEB INSTRUCTIONS: *To display this page from the Web, launch your browser and enter the URL, www.scsite.com/dc2000/ch1/check.htm. Click the links for current and additional information. To experience the animation and interactivity, Shockwave and the Flash Player must be installed on your computer (download by clicking here).*

Label the Figure

Instructions: *Categorize these common computer hardware components. Write the letter next to each component on the right in an appropriate blue box. Then write the words from the list on the left in the appropriate yellow boxes to identify the hardware components.*

monitor
speakers
keyboard
mouse
printer
system unit
hard disk drive
CD-ROM drive
floppy disk drive
Zip drive
modem
microphone

INPUT   OUTPUT   STORAGE   COMMUNICATIONS

PROCESSING

a b c d e f g h i j k l

Matching

Instructions: *Match each term from the column on the left with the best description from the column on the right.*

_____ 1. network computer (NC)

_____ 2. workstation

_____ 3. Personal Digital Assistant (PDA)

_____ 4. laptop computer

_____ 5. server

a. PC with a tall and narrow system unit designed to be placed vertically on the floor.
b. Powerful desktop computer designed for work that requires intense calculation and graphics capabilities.
c. A type of personal computer designed specifically to connect to a network.
d. Portable computer designed for mobility, small enough to fit on a lap.
e. Desktop computer that manages the resources on a network.
f. Popular handheld computer that often supports personal information management applications.
g. Large, expensive, powerful computers that can handle thousands of connected users simultaneously.

Short Answer

Instructions: *Write a brief answer to each of the following questions.*

1. How is hardware different from software? _____ Why is hardware useless without software? _____
2. What is a peripheral device? _____ What hardware components are considered peripheral devices? _____
3. What are four common storage devices? _____ How are they different? _____
4. How is packaged software different from custom software? _____ How is shareware different from freeware and public-domain software? _____
5. Why do people use the Internet? _____ How do most users connect to the Internet? _____

AT ISSUE www.scsite.com/dc2000/ch1/issue.htm

SHELLY
CASHMAN
SERIES®
DISCOVERING
COMPUTERS
2000

WEB INSTRUCTIONS: *To display this page from the Web, launch your browser and enter the URL, www.scsite.com/dc2000/ch1/issue.htm. Click the links for current and additional information.*

ONE *A survey of senior executives found 75 percent could not* explain the purpose of a modem, 65 percent believed the Internet was privately controlled, and 50 percent thought an Arch Deluxe was a PC part. Almost 100 percent of sixth graders questioned knew that modems let computers communicate over telephone lines, the Internet is not owned by anyone, and an Arch Deluxe is a McDonald's sandwich. In the race for computer literacy, many fear that some people have an unfair head start because of their youth, education, or economic status. Is this fear justified? Why or why not? What, if anything, can be done to level the playing field?

TWO *In one county, the number of computers purchased by local* school districts increased by 85 percent, while the supply of library books declined by almost ten percent. School officials claim computers extend learning opportunities and develop the computer literacy needed in today's technological world. Yet, some parents complain that computer purchases represent frivolous, status-seeking spending. How should a school district's money be spent? If you were an administrator, what percentage of your budget would you spend on computers? On library books and textbooks? Why? What factors would influence your decision?

THREE *Popular theory says that if an auditorium full of monkeys* each was given a typewriter, eventually they would produce a known classic. Monkeys may or may not be able to emulate Shakespeare, but today, computers can perform assignments once thought exclusively human. Computers have been programmed to read written work and answer questions demonstrating comprehension. One computer has been programmed to paint, producing pictures that have sold for more than $20,000. Computer-controlled robots have been programmed to play soccer. What types of activities or problems, if any, still do not embrace computer involvement? Why? Will computers someday be capable of handling these activities or problems? Why or why not?

FOUR *In 1997, the Graduate Management Admissions Test (GMAT) became the first* computerized standardized test. Other tests – including the GRE and even the SAT – intend to follow suit. Computer Adaptive Tests show one question at a time, and a student's response dictates the difficulty of the next question. Grades are based on the difficulty of questions and the number of correct answers. Advocates claim the tests are multidimensional and better reflect individual abilities. Critics argue the tests favor those with computer experience, demand unfamiliar test-taking skills, and evaluate computer literacy as much as knowledge of the subject matter. Are computerized standardized tests a good idea? Why or why not? Would you be comfortable taking one? How would you prepare differently for a computerized standardized test?

FIVE *The chess world was stunned when Gary Kasparov, reigning* world champion, was defeated in a six-game match by Deep Blue, an IBM supercomputer. Computer experts point out that the machine can consider 200 million moves per second; and its victory humbles mankind no more than would a race between a world-class sprinter and a cheetah. Some, however, feel the win symbolizes a new presence on the top rung of the intelligence ladder. Kasparov would like a rematch: "Man versus machine, the match is not over. I believe I have a noble cause to defend." How important is Deep Blue's victory, both realistically and symbolically? Might emerging computer technology change people's lives in unanticipated and unasked-for ways? Is there cause for concern? Why or why not?

Student Exercises
WEB INFO
IN BRIEF
KEY TERMS
AT THE MOVIES
CHECKPOINT
AT ISSUE
CYBERCLASS
HANDS ON
NET STUFF
Special Features
TIMELINE 2000
GUIDE TO WWW SITES
MAKING A CHIP
BUYER'S GUIDE 2000
CAREERS 2000
TRENDS 2000
CHAT
INTERACTIVE LABS
NEWS
HOME

CHAPTER **1** 2 3 4 5 6 7 8 9 10 11 12 13 14 **INDEX**

CYBERCLASS www.scsite.com/dc2000/ch1/class.htm

WEB INSTRUCTIONS: *To display this page from the Web, launch your browser and enter the URL, www.scsite.com/dc2000/ch1/class.htm. To start Level I CyberClass, click a Level I link on this page or enter the URL, www.cyber-class.com. Click the Student button, click* Discovering Computers 2000 *in the list of titles, and then click the Enter a site button. To start Level II or III CyberClass (available only to those purchasers of a CyberClass floppy disk), place your CyberClass floppy disk in drive A, click Start on the taskbar, click Run on the Start menu, type* a:connect *in the Open text box, click the OK button, click the Enter CyberClass button, and then follow the instructions.*

(I) (II) (III) LEVEL **1. Flash Cards** Click Flash Cards on the Main Menu of the CyberClass web page. Click the plus sign before the Chapter 1 title. Click The Components of a Computer and answer all the cards in that section. Then, click Computer Software and answer the cards in that section. If you have less than 85% correct, continue to answer cards in other sections until you have more than 85% correct. All users: Answer as many more Flash Cards as you desire. Close the Electronic Flash Card window and the Flash Cards window by clicking the Close button in the upper-right corner of each window.

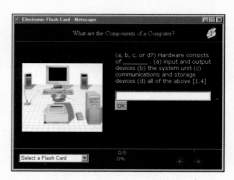

(I) (II) (III) LEVEL **2. Practice Test** Click Testing on the Main Menu of the CyberClass web page. Click the Select a book box arrow and then click Discovering Computers 2000. Click the Select a test to take box arrow and then click the Chapter 1 title in the list. Click the Take Test button. If necessary, maximize the window. Take the practice test and then click the Submit Test button. Click the Display Study Guide button. Review the Study Guide. Scroll down and click the Return To CyberClass button. Click the Yes button to close the Study Guide window. If your score was less than 80%, click the Take another Test button to take another practice test. Continue taking tests until your score is greater than 80%. Then, click the Done button.

(I) (II) (III) LEVEL **3. Web Guide** Click Web Guide on the Main Menu of the CyberClass web page. When the Guide to World Wide Web Sites page displays, click Computers and Computing. Take a tour of the Computer Museum. In particular, review the history of computers. When you are finished, close the window and then prepare a brief report on your tour.

(I) (II) (III) LEVEL **4. Company Briefs** Click Company Briefs on the Main Menu of the CyberClass web page. Click a corporation name to display a case study. Read the case study. Write a brief report on what contribution to computing this company has made.

(II) (III) LEVEL **5. Assignments and Syllabus** Click Assignments on the Main Menu of the CyberClass web page. Ensure you are aware of all assignments and when they are due. Click Syllabus on the Main Menu of the CyberClass web page. Verify you are up to date on all activities for the class.

(II) (III) LEVEL **6. CyberChallenge** Click CyberChallenge on the Main Menu of the CyberClass web page. Click the Select a book box arrow and then click Discovering Computers 2000. Click the Select a board to play box arrow and then click Chapter 1 in the list. Click the Play CyberChallenge button. Maximize the CyberChallenge window. Play CyberChallenge until your score for a complete game is 500 points or more. Close the CyberChallenge window.

(II) (III) LEVEL **7. Hot Links** Click Hot Links on the Main Menu of the CyberClass web page. Review the sites in the Hot Links section and then write a brief report indicating which site you like best and why you like it.

HANDS ON

www.scsite.com/dc2000/ch1/hands.htm

Student Exercises
WEB INFO
IN BRIEF
KEY TERMS
AT THE MOVIES
CHECKPOINT
AT ISSUE
CYBERCLASS
HANDS ON
NET STUFF
Special Features
TIMELINE 2000
GUIDE TO WWW SITES
MAKING A CHIP
BUYER'S GUIDE 2000
CAREERS 2000
TRENDS 2000
CHAT
INTERACTIVE LABS
NEWS
HOME

WEB INSTRUCTIONS: *To display this page from the Web, launch your browser and enter the URL,* www.scsite.com/dc2000/ch1/hands.htm. *Click the links for current and additional information.*

One — Using Windows Help

This exercise uses Windows 98 procedures. In the past, when you purchased computer software, you also received large printed manuals that attempted to answer any questions you might have. Today, Help usually is offered directly on the computer. To make it easy to find exactly the Help you need, Windows Help is arranged on three sheets: Contents, Index, and Search. Click the Start button on the taskbar and then click Help on the Start menu. Click the Contents tab. What do you see? When would you use the Contents sheet to find Help? Click the Index tab. What do you see? When would you use the Index sheet to find Help? Click the Search tab. What do you see? When would you use the Search sheet to find Help?

Two — What's New in Microsoft Windows?

This exercise uses Windows 98 procedures. Click the Start button on the taskbar and then click Help on the Start menu. Click the Contents tab in the Windows Help window. Click the Introducing Windows 98 book, and then click the What's New in Windows 98 book. Click a topic in which you are interested. Click each topic in the right pane. How is this version of Windows better than previous versions of Windows? Will the improvement make your work more efficient? Why or why not? What improvement, if any, would you still like to see? Close the Windows Help window.

Three — Improving Mouse Skills

This exercise uses Windows 98 procedures. Click the Start button on the taskbar. Point to Programs, then point to Accessories on the Programs submenu. Point to Games on the Accessories submenu, and then click Solitaire on the Games submenu. When the Solitaire window displays, click the Maximize button. Click Help on the Solitaire menu bar, and then click Help Topics. Click the Contents tab. Click the object of Solitaire topic and read the information. Click the Playing Solitaire topic. Read and print the information by clicking the Solitaire Help window's Option button, clicking Print, and then clicking the OK button. Click the Close button in the Solitaire Help window. Play the game of Solitaire. Close the Solitare window.

Four — Learning About Your System

You can learn some important information about your computer system by studying the System Properties. Click the Start button. Point to Settings and then click Control Panel on the Settings submenu. Double-click System in the Control Panel window. Click the General tab in the System dialog box. Use the General sheet to find out the answers to these questions:

- ▲ What operating system does your computer use?
- ▲ To whom is your system registered?
- ▲ What type of processor does your computer have?
- ▲ How much memory (RAM) does your computer have?

Close the System Properties dialog box.

SHELLY CASHMAN SERIES®
DISCOVERING COMPUTERS 2000

■ **Student Exercises**
WEB INFO
IN BRIEF
KEY TERMS
AT THE MOVIES
CHECKPOINT
AT ISSUE
CYBERCLASS
HANDS ON
NET STUFF
■ Special Features
TIMELINE 2000
GUIDE TO WWW SITES
MAKING A CHIP
BUYER'S GUIDE 2000
CAREERS 2000
TRENDS 2000
CHAT
INTERACTIVE LABS
NEWS
HOME

CHAPTER **1** **2** **3** **4** **5** **6** **7** **8** **9** **10** **11** **12** **13** **14** **INDEX**

NET STUFF   www.scsite.com/dc2000/ch1/net.htm

WEB INSTRUCTIONS: *To display this page from the Web, launch your browser and enter the URL, www.scsite.com/dc2000/ch1/net.htm. To use the Mouse lab or the Keyboard lab from the Web, Shockwave and the Flash Player must be installed on your computer (download by clicking here).*

MOUSE LAB

1. Shelly Cashman Series Mouse Lab

a) To start the Shelly Cashman Series Mouse Lab, complete the step that applies to you.

   (1) **Running from the World Wide Web:** Enter the URL, www.scsite.com/sclabs/menu.htm; or display the NET STUFF page (see instructions at the top of this page) and then click the MOUSE LAB button.

   (2) **Running from a CD:** Insert the Shelly Cashman Series Labs with Audio CD in your CD-ROM drive.

   (3) **Running the No-Audio Version from a Hard Disk or Network:** Click the Start button on the taskbar, point to Shelly Cashman Series Labs on the Programs submenu, and click Interactive Labs.

b) When the Shelly Cashman Series IN THE LAB screen displays (Figure 1-49), if necessary maximize the window, and then follow the instructions on the screen to start the Using the Mouse lab.

c) When the Using the Mouse screen displays, if necessary maximize the window, and then read the objectives.

d) If assigned, follow the instructions on the screen to print the questions associated with the lab.

e) Follow the instructions on the screen to continue in the lab.

f) When completed, follow the instructions on the screen to terminate the lab.

g) If assigned, hand in your answers for the printed questions to your instructor.

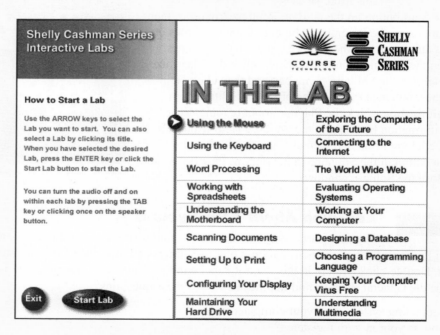

Figure 1-49

NET STUFF   www.scsite.com/dc2000/ch1/net.htm

2. Shelly Cashman Series Keyboard Lab

Follow the appropriate instructions in NET STUFF Exercise 1 on the previous page to start and use the Using the Keyboard lab. If you are running from the Web, enter the URL, www.scsite.com/sclabs/menu.htm; or display the NET STUFF page (see instructions at the top of the previous page) and then click the KEYBOARD LAB button.

KEYBOARD LAB

3. Learn the Net

LEARN THE NET

No matter how much computer experience you have, navigating the Net for the first time can be intimidating. How do you get started? Click the LEARN THE NET button and complete this exercise to discover how you can find out everything you wanted to know about the Internet.

4. In the News

IN THE NEWS

Companies can have problems with their products, or problems with perceptions of their products. In the computer industry, a flaw in a software program or a failure in a hardware device would be a product problem. An accusation of unfair business practices or a rumor of a program malfunction would be a perception problem. Click the IN THE NEWS button and read a news article about a problem experienced by a company in the computer industry. What is the problem? Is the problem affecting the company's profits? If so, why? How is the company addressing the problem? Do you think the company's efforts will be successful? Why or why not?

5. Web Chat

WEB CHAT

Everyone who works with computers has experienced moments of enormous frustration – incomprehensible error messages, software glitches that produce unanticipated results, or even the entire system freezing up. Many people feel reactions to computer problems tend to be more extreme than reactions to problems with other tools they use. If you are viewing this page on the Web, start the video on the right to see how one individual handled a problem with his computer. Do computer problems make people angrier than problems with other tools? Why? How can individuals reduce their frustration when dealing with computer failures? Click the WEB CHAT button to enter a Web Chat discussion related to this topic.

WEB INSTRUCTIONS: *To gain World Wide Web access to additional and up-to-date information regarding this special feature, launch your browser and enter the URL shown at the top of the page you want to view.*

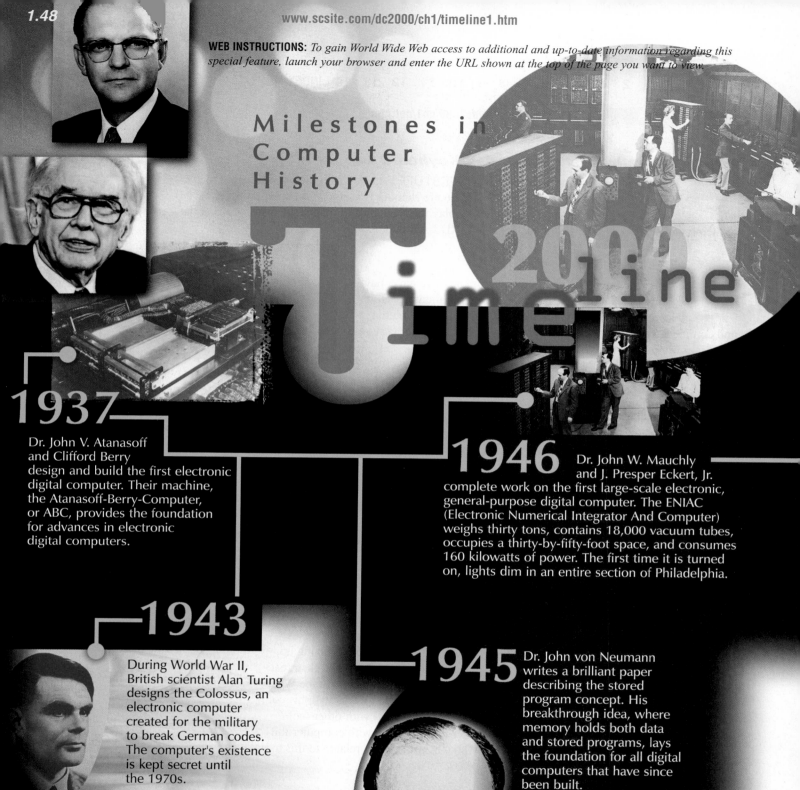

Milestones in Computer History

Timeline 2000

1937

Dr. John V. Atanasoff and Clifford Berry design and build the first electronic digital computer. Their machine, the Atanasoff-Berry-Computer, or ABC, provides the foundation for advances in electronic digital computers.

1946

Dr. John W. Mauchly and J. Presper Eckert, Jr. complete work on the first large-scale electronic, general-purpose digital computer. The ENIAC (Electronic Numerical Integrator And Computer) weighs thirty tons, contains 18,000 vacuum tubes, occupies a thirty-by-fifty-foot space, and consumes 160 kilowatts of power. The first time it is turned on, lights dim in an entire section of Philadelphia.

1943

During World War II, British scientist Alan Turing designs the Colossus, an electronic computer created for the military to break German codes. The computer's existence is kept secret until the 1970s.

1945

Dr. John von Neumann writes a brilliant paper describing the stored program concept. His breakthrough idea, where memory holds both data and stored programs, lays the foundation for all digital computers that have since been built.

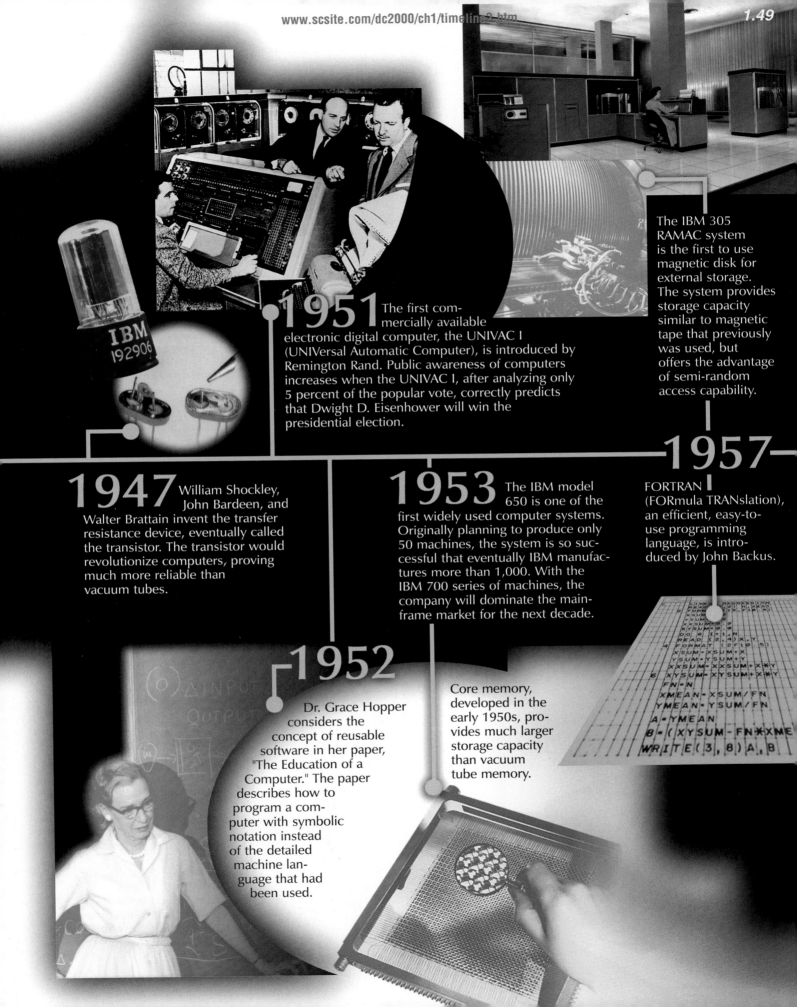

1951 The first commercially available electronic digital computer, the UNIVAC I (UNIVersal Automatic Computer), is introduced by Remington Rand. Public awareness of computers increases when the UNIVAC I, after analyzing only 5 percent of the popular vote, correctly predicts that Dwight D. Eisenhower will win the presidential election.

The IBM 305 RAMAC system is the first to use magnetic disk for external storage. The system provides storage capacity similar to magnetic tape that previously was used, but offers the advantage of semi-random access capability.

1957 FORTRAN (FORmula TRANslation), an efficient, easy-to-use programming language, is introduced by John Backus.

1947 William Shockley, John Bardeen, and Walter Brattain invent the transfer resistance device, eventually called the transistor. The transistor would revolutionize computers, proving much more reliable than vacuum tubes.

1953 The IBM model 650 is one of the first widely used computer systems. Originally planning to produce only 50 machines, the system is so successful that eventually IBM manufactures more than 1,000. With the IBM 700 series of machines, the company will dominate the mainframe market for the next decade.

1952 Dr. Grace Hopper considers the concept of reusable software in her paper, "The Education of a Computer." The paper describes how to program a computer with symbolic notation instead of the detailed machine language that had been used.

Core memory, developed in the early 1950s, provides much larger storage capacity than vacuum tube memory.

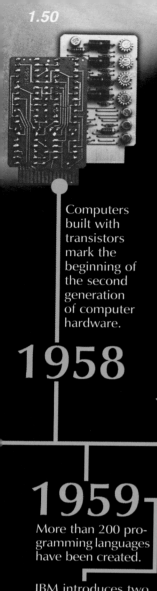

Dr. John Kemeny of Dartmouth leads the development of the BASIC programming language. BASIC will be widely used on personal computers.

Computers built with transistors mark the beginning of the second generation of computer hardware.

1958

COBOL, a high-level business application language, is developed by a committee headed by Dr. Grace Hopper. COBOL uses English-like phrases and runs on most business computers, making it one of the more widely used programming languages.

1960

Digital Equipment Corporation (DEC) introduces the first mini-computer, the PDP-8. The machine is used extensively as an interface for time-sharing systems.

1965

1964

1959

More than 200 programming languages have been created.

IBM introduces two smaller, desk-sized computers: the IBM 1401 for business and the IBM 1602 for scientists. The IBM 1602 initially is called the CADET, but IBM drops the name when campus wags claim it is an acronym for, Can't Add, Doesn't Even Try.

The number of computers has grown to 18,000.

Third-generation computers, with their controlling circuitry stored on chips, are introduced. The IBM System/360 computer is the first family of compatible machines, merging science and business lines.

1968

Alan Shugart at IBM demonstrates the first regular use of an 8-inch floppy (magnetic storage) disk.

In a letter to the editor titled, "GO TO Statements Considered Harmful," Dr. Edsger Dijsktra introduces the concept of structured programming, developing standards for constructing computer programs.

Computer Science Corporation becomes the first software company listed on the New York Stock Exchange.

CSC STOCK PRICE NYSE/COMPOSITE Corrected Data for Dividends		
DATE	PRICE	HIGH	LO
1/02/68	2.83	2.97	
1/03/68	2.60	2.81	
1/04/68	2.61	2.62	
1/05/68			
1/08/68	2.54	2.60	
1/09/68	2.55	2.60	
1/10/68	2.46		
		2.51	30,100
		13,500	
		2.48	23,400
		2.49	7,800
		2.50	18,800

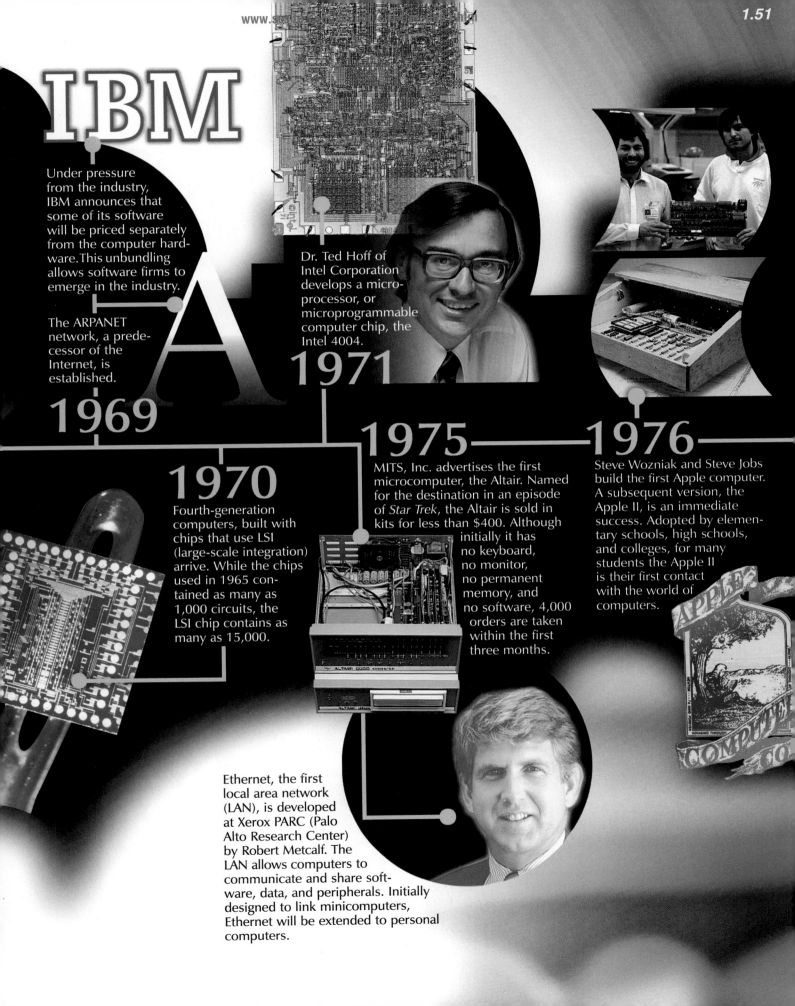

IBM

Under pressure from the industry, IBM announces that some of its software will be priced separately from the computer hardware. This unbundling allows software firms to emerge in the industry.

The ARPANET network, a predecessor of the Internet, is established.

1969

Dr. Ted Hoff of Intel Corporation develops a microprocessor, or microprogrammable computer chip, the Intel 4004.

1971

1970

Fourth-generation computers, built with chips that use LSI (large-scale integration) arrive. While the chips used in 1965 contained as many as 1,000 circuits, the LSI chip contains as many as 15,000.

1975

MITS, Inc. advertises the first microcomputer, the Altair. Named for the destination in an episode of *Star Trek*, the Altair is sold in kits for less than $400. Although initially it has no keyboard, no monitor, no permanent memory, and no software, 4,000 orders are taken within the first three months.

1976

Steve Wozniak and Steve Jobs build the first Apple computer. A subsequent version, the Apple II, is an immediate success. Adopted by elementary schools, high schools, and colleges, for many students the Apple II is their first contact with the world of computers.

Ethernet, the first local area network (LAN), is developed at Xerox PARC (Palo Alto Research Center) by Robert Metcalf. The LAN allows computers to communicate and share software, data, and peripherals. Initially designed to link minicomputers, Ethernet will be extended to personal computers.

Creators of VisiCalc®

...ARE ARTS, INC.

VisiCalc, a spreadsheet program written by Bob Frankston and Dan Bricklin, is introduced. Originally written to run on Apple II computers, VisiCalc will be seen as the most important reason for the acceptance of personal computers in the business world.

The first public online information services, CompuServe and the Source, are founded.

1979

The IBM PC is introduced, signaling IBM's entrance into the personal computer marketplace. The IBM PC quickly garners the largest share of the personal computer market and becomes the personal computer of choice in business.

1981

Lotus Development Corpora... is founded. Its spreadsheet software, Lotus 1-2-3, which combines spreadsheet, graph... and database programs in or... package, becomes the best-s... program for IBM personal computers.

1983

1980

Alan Shugart presents the Winchester hard drive, revolutionizing storage for personal computers.

IBM offers Microsoft Corporation co-founder, Bill Gates, the opportunity to develop the operating system for the soon-to-be announced IBM personal computer. With the development of MS-DOS, Microsoft achieves tremendous growth and success.

1982

3,275,000 personal computers are sold, almost 3,000,000 more than in 1981.

3,275,000

Hayes introduces the 300 bps smart modem. The modem is an immediate success.

COMPAQ

Compaq, Inc. is founded to develop and market IBM-compatible PCs.

Instead of choosing a person for its annual award, *TIME* magazine names the computer Machine of the Year for 1982, acknowledgin... the impact of computers on society.

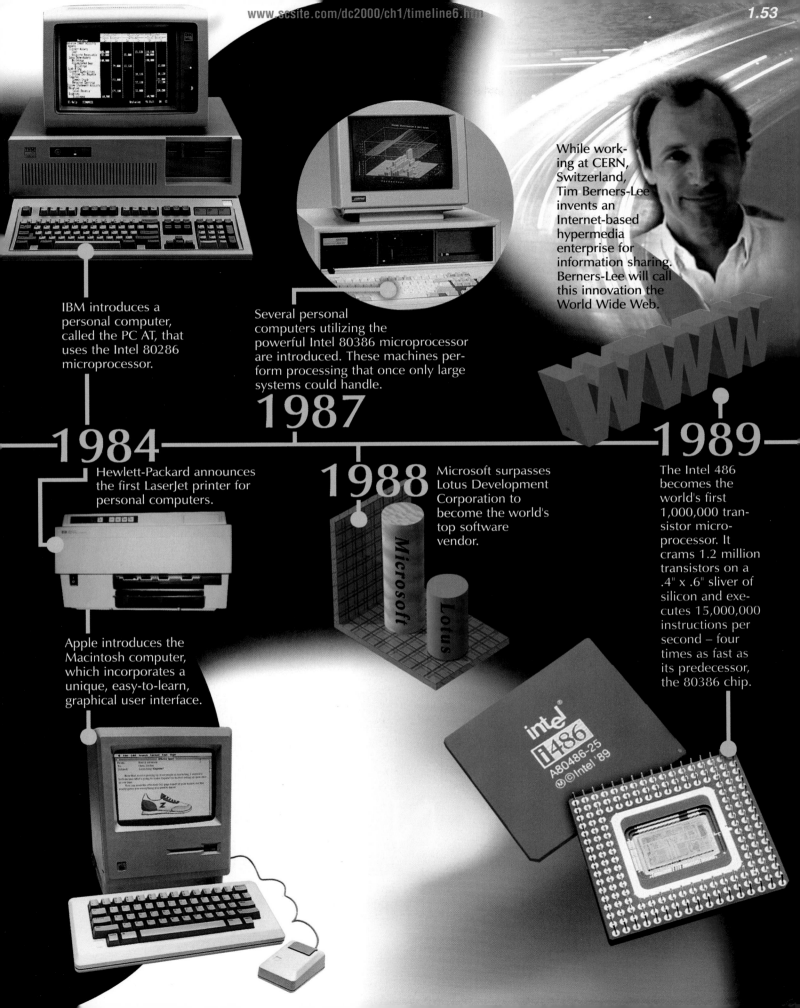

While working at CERN, Switzerland, Tim Berners-Lee invents an Internet-based hypermedia enterprise for information sharing. Berners-Lee will call this innovation the World Wide Web.

IBM introduces a personal computer, called the PC AT, that uses the Intel 80286 microprocessor.

Several personal computers utilizing the powerful Intel 80386 microprocessor are introduced. These machines perform processing that once only large systems could handle.

1987

1984

1989

Hewlett-Packard announces the first LaserJet printer for personal computers.

1988

Microsoft surpasses Lotus Development Corporation to become the world's top software vendor.

The Intel 486 becomes the world's first 1,000,000 transistor microprocessor. It crams 1.2 million transistors on a .4" x .6" sliver of silicon and executes 15,000,000 instructions per second – four times as fast as its predecessor, the 80386 chip.

Apple introduces the Macintosh computer, which incorporates a unique, easy-to-learn, graphical user interface.

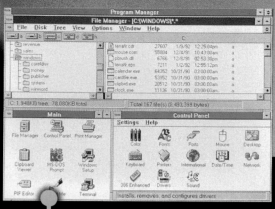

Microsoft releases Windows 3.1, the latest version of its Windows operating system. Windows 3.1 offers improvements such as TrueType fonts, multimedia capability, and object linking and embedding (OLE). In two months, 3,000,000 copies of Windows 3.1 are sold.

Several companies introduce computer systems using the Pentium® microprocessor from Intel. The Pentium® chip is the successor to the Intel 486 processor. It contains 3.1 million transistors and is capable of performing 112,000,000 instructions per second

Jim Clark and Marc Andreessen found Netscape and launch Netscape Navigator 1.0, a browser for the World Wide Web.

1992

1991

1993

1994

World Wide Web Consortium releases standards that describe a framework for linking documents on different computers.

The White House launches its Web page. The site includes an interactive citizens' handbook and White House history and tours.

Linus Torvalds creates the Linux kernal, a UNIX-like operating system that he releases free across the Internet for further enhancement by other programmers.

Marc Andreessen creates a graphical Web browser called Mosaic. This success leads to the organization of Netscape Communications Corporation.

NCSA
MOSAIC
X Window System • Microsoft Windows • Macintosh

N

Linux

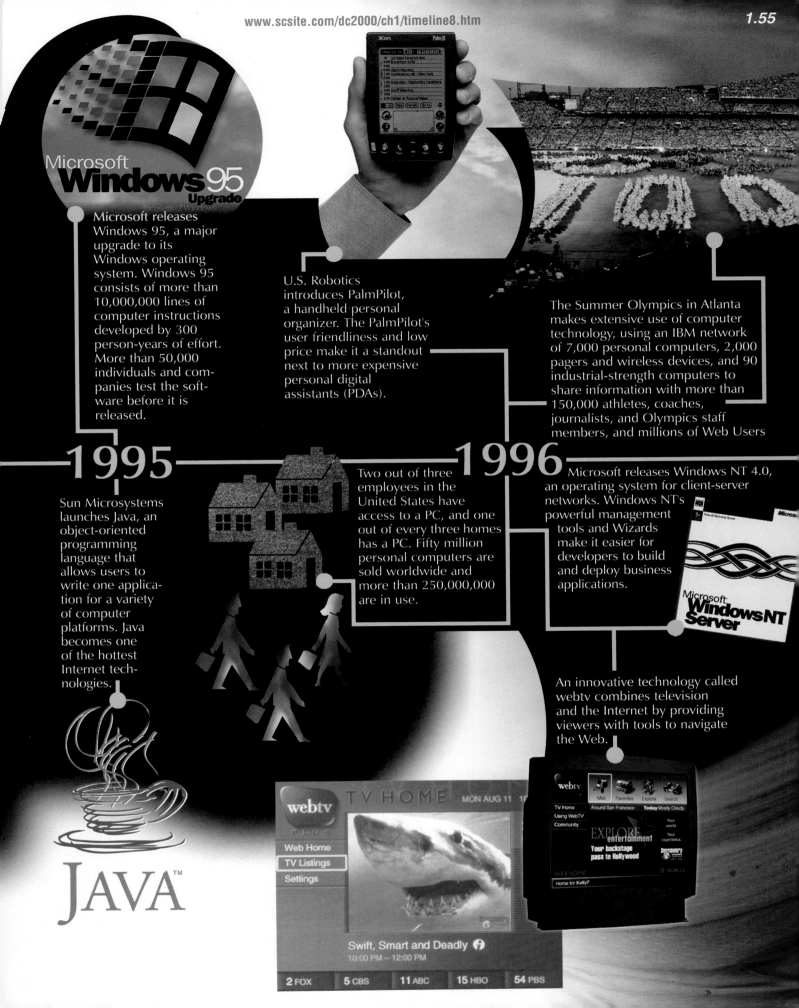

Microsoft releases Windows 95, a major upgrade to its Windows operating system. Windows 95 consists of more than 10,000,000 lines of computer instructions developed by 300 person-years of effort. More than 50,000 individuals and companies test the software before it is released.

U.S. Robotics introduces PalmPilot, a handheld personal organizer. The PalmPilot's user friendliness and low price make it a standout next to more expensive personal digital assistants (PDAs).

The Summer Olympics in Atlanta makes extensive use of computer technology, using an IBM network of 7,000 personal computers, 2,000 pagers and wireless devices, and 90 industrial-strength computers to share information with more than 150,000 athletes, coaches, journalists, and Olympics staff members, and millions of Web Users

1995

1996

Sun Microsystems launches Java, an object-oriented programming language that allows users to write one application for a variety of computer platforms. Java becomes one of the hottest Internet technologies.

Two out of three employees in the United States have access to a PC, and one out of every three homes has a PC. Fifty million personal computers are sold worldwide and more than 250,000,000 are in use.

Microsoft releases Windows NT 4.0, an operating system for client-server networks. Windows NT's powerful management tools and Wizards make it easier for developers to build and deploy business applications.

An innovative technology called webtv combines television and the Internet by providing viewers with tools to navigate the Web.

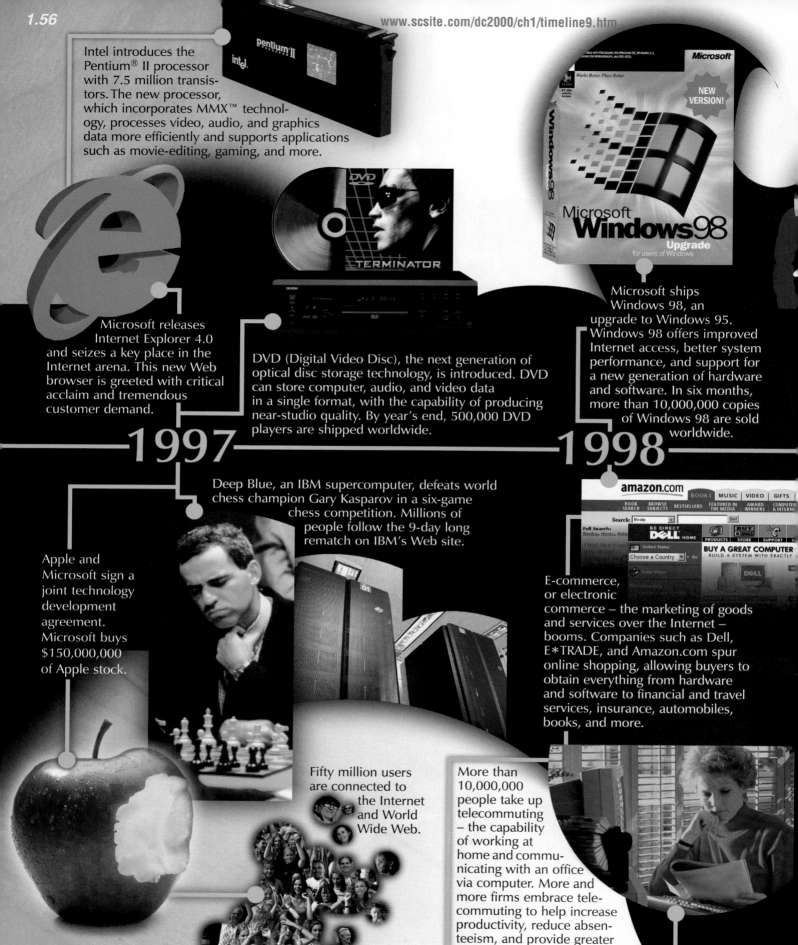

Intel introduces the Pentium® II processor with 7.5 million transistors. The new processor, which incorporates MMX™ technology, processes video, audio, and graphics data more efficiently and supports applications such as movie-editing, gaming, and more.

Microsoft releases Internet Explorer 4.0 and seizes a key place in the Internet arena. This new Web browser is greeted with critical acclaim and tremendous customer demand.

DVD (Digital Video Disc), the next generation of optical disc storage technology, is introduced. DVD can store computer, audio, and video data in a single format, with the capability of producing near-studio quality. By year's end, 500,000 DVD players are shipped worldwide.

Microsoft ships Windows 98, an upgrade to Windows 95. Windows 98 offers improved Internet access, better system performance, and support for a new generation of hardware and software. In six months, more than 10,000,000 copies of Windows 98 are sold worldwide.

1997

1998

Deep Blue, an IBM supercomputer, defeats world chess champion Gary Kasparov in a six-game chess competition. Millions of people follow the 9-day long rematch on IBM's Web site.

Apple and Microsoft sign a joint technology development agreement. Microsoft buys $150,000,000 of Apple stock.

E-commerce, or electronic commerce – the marketing of goods and services over the Internet – booms. Companies such as Dell, E*TRADE, and Amazon.com spur online shopping, allowing buyers to obtain everything from hardware and software to financial and travel services, insurance, automobiles, books, and more.

Fifty million users are connected to the Internet and World Wide Web.

More than 10,000,000 people take up telecommuting – the capability of working at home and communicating with an office via computer. More and more firms embrace telecommuting to help increase productivity, reduce absenteeism, and provide greater job satisfaction.

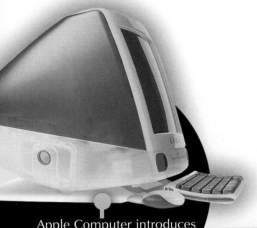

Apple Computer introduces the iMac, the latest version of its popular Macintosh computer. The iMac abandons such conventional features as a floppy disk drive but wins customers with its futuristic design, see-through case, and easy setup. Consumer demand outstrips Apple's production capabilities, and some vendors are forced to begin waiting lists.

Intel releases its Pentium III processor, which provides enhanced multimedia capabilities.

Microsoft introduces Office 2000, its premier productivity suite, offering new tools for users to create content and save it directly to a Web site without any file conversion or special steps.

1999

1998

Compaq Computer, the United States' leading personal computer manufacturer, buys Digital Equipment Corporation in the biggest take-over in the history of the computer industry. Compaq becomes the world's second largest computer firm, behind IBM.

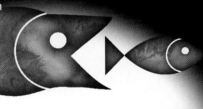

2000

The Millennium Bug, Year 2000 Bug, or Y2K Bug has the potential to cause serious financial losses. On 1 January 2000, dates are read by non-compliant computers as 01/01/00, a year that is indistinguishable from 1900 or 3000, and some computer hardware and software will operate according to the wrong date. Y2K affects computer chips embedded in switchboards, automatic teller machines, video recorders, lifts, and security systems in the new millennium.

The Department of Justice's broad antitrust lawsuit asks that Microsoft offer Windows 98 without the Internet Explorer browser or that it bundle the competing Netscape Navigator browser with the operating system.

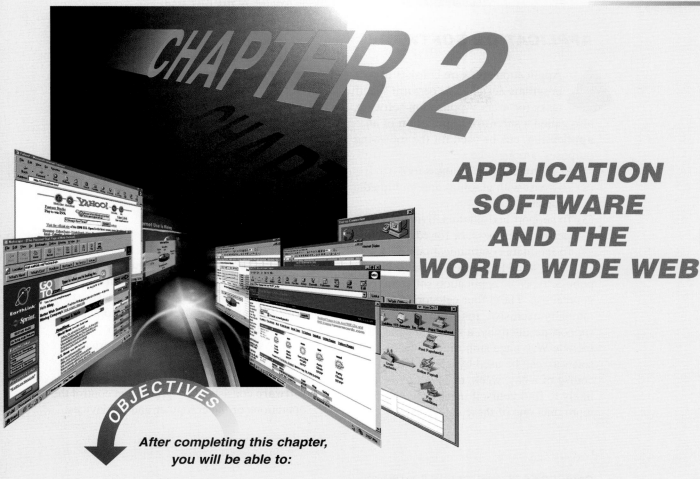

CHAPTER 2

APPLICATION SOFTWARE AND THE WORLD WIDE WEB

OBJECTIVES

After completing this chapter, you will be able to:

Define application software

Explain how to start a software application

Explain the key features of widely used software applications

Provide examples illustrating the importance of the World Wide Web

Describe how to use a Web browser

Explain how to search for information on the Web

Describe the learning aids available with many software applications

A key aspect of building computer literacy is learning about software, which is the series of instructions that tells computer hardware how to perform tasks. Having a solid understanding of software — especially application software — will help you use your computer to be more productive, organized, and well informed.

Application software, such as word processing, spreadsheets, and e-mail, can help you perform tasks such as creating documents, analyzing finances, and sending messages. One type of application software, called a Web browser, allows you to view pages on the World Wide Web, thus giving you access to a vast resource of information.

Understanding application software also can help advance your personal and professional goals. In fact, many employers today consider an understanding of software to be a hiring requirement. Because application software concepts are so important, this book discusses them early so you can refer back to them as you learn more about computers, how they are used today, and how they can help you in your future.

APPLICATION SOFTWARE

Application software consists of programs designed to perform specific tasks for users. Application software, also called a **software application** or an **application**, can be used for the following purposes, among others:

(1) As a productivity/business tool
(2) To assist with graphics and multimedia projects
(3) To support household activities, for personal business, or for education
(4) To facilitate communications

The table in Figure 2-1 categorizes popular types of application software by their general use. These four categories are not mutually exclusive; for example, e-mail can support productivity, a software suite can include Web page authoring tools, and legal software can be used by a business. In the course of a day, week, or month, you are likely to find yourself using software from more than one of these categories.

A variety of application software is available as packaged software that you can purchase from software vendors in retail stores or on the Web. A specific software product, such as Microsoft Word, often is called a **software package**. Many application software packages also are available as shareware, freeware, and public-domain software; these packages, however, usually have fewer capabilities than retail software packages.

The Role of the Operating System

Like most computer users, you probably are somewhat familiar with application software. To run any application software, however, your computer must be running another type of software — an operating system.

As described in Chapter 1, software can be categorized into two types: system software and application software. **System software** consists of programs that control the operations of the computer and its devices.

CATEGORIES OF APPLICATION SOFTWARE

Productivity/ Business	Graphic Design/ Multimedia	Home/Personal/ Educational	Communications
• Word Processing	• Computer-Aided Design	• Integrated Software	• Groupware
• Spreadsheet		• Personal Finance	• E-mail
• Database	• Desktop Publishing (Professional)	• Legal	• Web Browser
• Presentation Graphics	• Paint/Image Editing (Professional)	• Tax Preparation	
• Personal Information Management	• Video and Audio Editing	• Desktop Publishing (Personal)	
• Software Suite		• Paint/Image Editing (Personal)	
• Accounting	• Multimedia Authoring	• Home Design/ Landscaping	
• Project Management	• Web Page Authoring	• Educational	
		• Reference	
		• Entertainment	

Figure 2-1 *The four major categories of popular application software. You likely will use software from more than one of these categories.*

As shown in Figure 2-2, system software serves as the interface between you (the user), your application software, and your computer's hardware. One type of system software, the **operating system**, contains instructions that coordinate all of the activities of the hardware devices in a computer. The operating system also contains instructions that allow you to run application software. The other type of system software is a utility program, or utility, which is discussed in Chapter 8.

Before a computer can run any application software, the operating system must be loaded from the hard disk into the computer's memory. Each time you start your computer, the operating system is loaded, or copied, into memory from the computer's hard disk. Once the operating system is loaded, it tells the computer how to perform functions such as processing program instructions and transferring data among input and output devices and memory. The operating system, which remains in memory while the computer is running, allows you to communicate with the computer and other software, such as application software. The operating system continues to run until the computer is turned off.

The Role of the User Interface

All software, including the operating system, communicates with the user in a certain way, through a portion of the program called a user interface. A **user interface** controls how you enter data or instructions and how information and processing options are presented to you.

One of the more common user interfaces is a graphical user interface (GUI). A **graphical user interface**, or **GUI**, combines text, graphics, and other visual cues to make software easier to use.

In 1984, Apple Computer introduced the Macintosh operating system, which used a graphical user interface. Recognizing the value of this easy-to-use interface, many software companies followed suit, developing their own GUI software. Since then, Apple has developed several new versions (modifications) of their original GUI operating system for their Macintosh computers. Today's most widely used personal computer operating system and graphical user interface, however, is Microsoft Windows, which often is referred to simply as **Windows**.

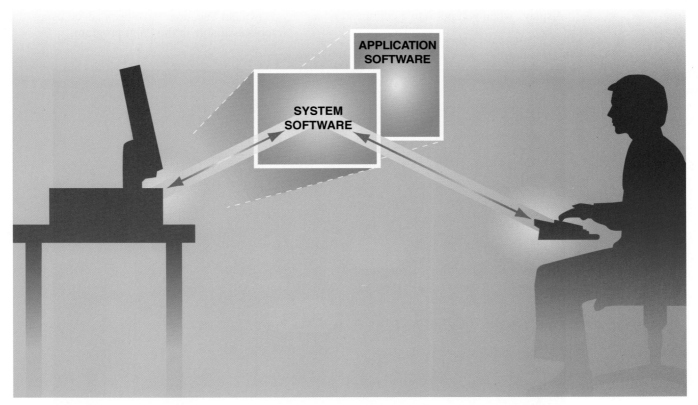

Figure 2-2 *A user does not communicate directly with the computer hardware; instead, the user communicates with the system software or with the application software to control the hardware.*

Starting a Software Application

Both the Apple Macintosh and Microsoft Windows operating systems use the concept of a desktop to make the computer easier to use. The **desktop** is an onscreen work area that uses common graphical elements such as icons, buttons, windows, menus, links, and dialog boxes, all of which can display on the desktop. The Windows desktop shown in Figure 2-3 contains many icons and buttons.

An **icon** is a small image that displays on the screen to represent a program, a document, or some other object. A **button** is a graphical element (usually a rectangular or circular shape) that you can click to cause a specific action to take place. To click a button, you typically point to it with a mouse and then press and release a mouse button.

The Windows desktop contains a Start button in its lower-left corner, which can be used to start an application. When you click the Start button, the Start menu displays on the desktop. A **menu** contains commands you can select. **Commands** are instructions that cause a computer program to perform a specific action.

Some menus have a **submenu**, which displays when you point to a command on a previous menu. For example, as shown in Figure 2-4, when you click the Start button and point to the Programs command on the Start menu, the Programs submenu displays. Pointing to the Accessories command on the Programs submenu displays the Accessories submenu. As shown on the Accessories submenu, Windows includes several applications such as Calculator, Paint, and WordPad.

You can start an application by clicking its program name on a menu or submenu. Doing so instructs the operating system to start the application by transferring the program's instructions from a storage medium into memory. For example, if you click Paint on the Accessories submenu, Windows transfers the Paint program instructions from the computer's hard disk into memory.

Once started, an application displays in a window on the desktop. A **window** is a rectangular area of the screen that is used to display a program, data, and/or information. The top of a window has a **title bar**, which is a horizontal space that contains the window's name. Figure 2-5 shows the Paint window. This window contains a photographic image that has been converted from a paper document to an electronic document using special hardware and software. The words, Our Hawaiian Vacation, have been added using tools available in the Paint program.

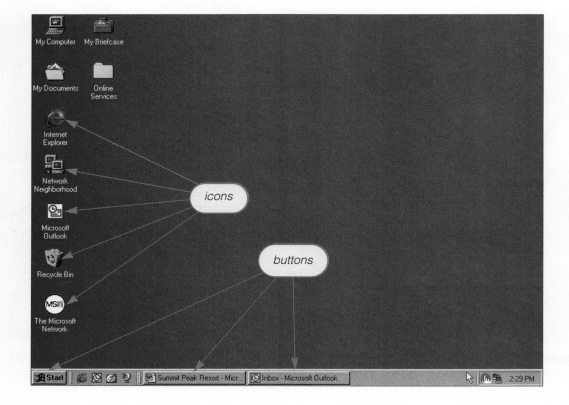

Figure 2-3 This Windows desktop shows a variety of icons and buttons.

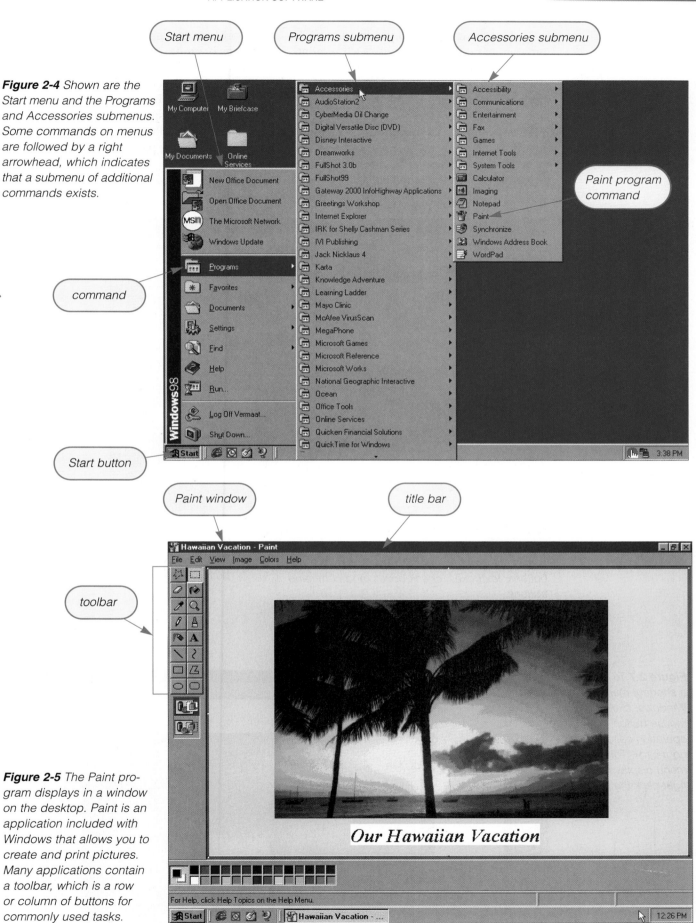

Figure 2-4 Shown are the Start menu and the Programs and Accessories submenus. Some commands on menus are followed by a right arrowhead, which indicates that a submenu of additional commands exists.

Figure 2-5 The Paint program displays in a window on the desktop. Paint is an application included with Windows that allows you to create and print pictures. Many applications contain a toolbar, which is a row or column of buttons for commonly used tasks.

In some cases, when you instruct a program to perform an activity such as printing, a dialog box displays. A **dialog box** is a special window displayed by a program to provide information, present available options, or request a response (Figure 2-6). A Print dialog box, for example, gives you many printing options, such as printing multiple copies, using different printers, or printing all or part of a document.

Many applications also use **shortcut menus** or **context-sensitive menus** that display a list of commands commonly used to complete a task related to the current activity or selected item. For example, one shortcut menu for Paint displays an abbreviated list of commands that allows you to change the appearance of the picture (Figure 2-7).

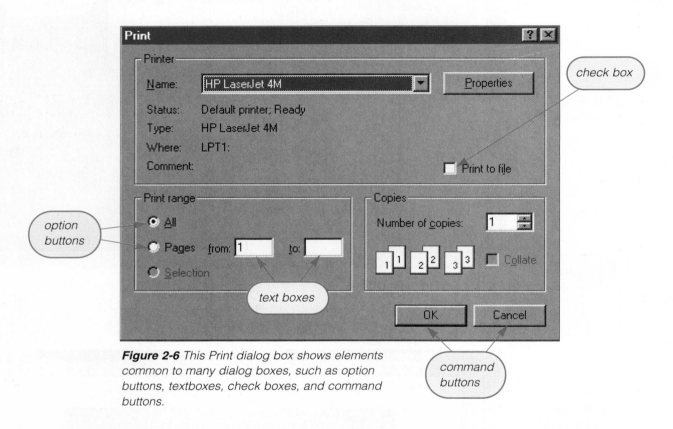

Figure 2-6 *This Print dialog box shows elements common to many dialog boxes, such as option buttons, textboxes, check boxes, and command buttons.*

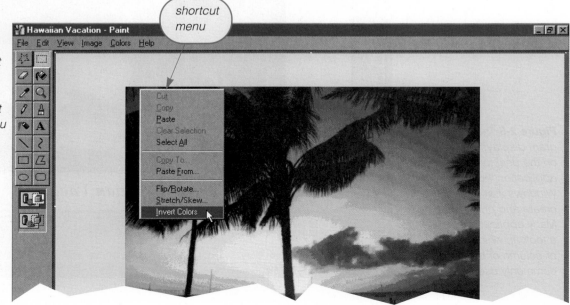

Figure 2-7 *To display a shortcut menu in Windows, click the right mouse button, a mouse operation called a right-click. This shortcut menu displays when you right-click the picture.*

Many elements shown on the previous pages, such as icons, buttons, and menus are part of the graphical user interface that allows you to communicate with software. One of the major advantages of a graphical user interface is that these elements usually are common across most applications. Once you learn the purpose and functionality of these elements, you can apply that knowledge to other software applications.

PRODUCTIVITY SOFTWARE

Productivity software is designed to make people more effective and efficient while performing daily activities. Productivity software includes applications such as word processing, spreadsheet, database, presentation graphics, personal information management, accounting, project management, and other related types of software. Figure 2-8 lists popular software packages for each of these applications. The features and functions of each of these applications are discussed in the following sections.

POPULAR PRODUCTIVITY SOFTWARE PACKAGES

Software Application	Popular Packages
Word Processing	• Corel WordPerfect • Lotus Word Pro • Microsoft Word 2000
Spreadsheet	• Corel Quattro Pro • Lotus 1-2-3 • Microsoft Excel 2000
Database	• Corel Paradox • Lotus Approach • Microsoft Access 2000 • Microsoft Visual FoxPro
Presentation Graphics	• Corel Presentations • Lotus Freelance Graphics • Microsoft PowerPoint 2000
Personal Information Manager	• 3Com Palm Desktop • Lotus Organizer • Microsoft Outlook 2000
Software Suite	• Corel WordPerfect Suite • Lotus SmartSuite • Microsoft Office 2000
Accounting	• Intuit QuickBooks • Peachtree Complete Accounting
Project Management	• Microsoft Project • Primavera SureTrak Project Manager

Figure 2-8 Popular productivity software products.

Word Processing Software

A widely used application software package is **word processing software**, which is used to create, edit, and format textual documents (Figure 2-9). Millions of people use word processing software every day to create documents such as letters, memos, reports, fax cover sheets, mailing labels, and newsletters.

DEVELOPING A DOCUMENT While using many software applications, you have the ability to create, edit, format, print, and save documents. During the process of developing a document, you likely will switch back and forth among all of these activities.

Creating involves developing the document by entering text or numbers, inserting graphical images, and performing other tasks using an input device such as a keyboard or mouse. If you design an announcement in Microsoft Word, for example, you are creating a document.

Editing is the process of making changes to the document's existing content. Common editing features include inserting, deleting, cutting, copying, and pasting items into a document. For example, using Microsoft Word, you can insert, or add, text to an announcement, such as the cost of various vacation packages. When you delete, you remove text or other content. To cut involves removing a portion of the document and electronically storing it in a temporary storage location called the **Clipboard**. When you copy, a portion of the document is duplicated and stored on the Clipboard. To place whatever is stored on the Clipboard into the document, you paste it into the document.

document displays in word processing window

printed document

Figure 2-9 With word processing software, you can create documents that are professional and visually appealing.

Formatting involves changing the appearance of a document. Formatting is important because the overall look of a document can significantly affect its ability to communicate effectively.

Examples of formatting tasks are changing the font, font size, or font style of text (Figure 2-10). A **font** is a name assigned to a specific design of characters. Times New Roman and Arial are examples of fonts. The **font size** specifies the size of the characters in a particular font. Font size is gauged by a measurement system called points. A single **point** is about 1/72 of an inch in height. The text you are reading in this book is 10 point.

Thus, each character is about 10/72 of an inch in height. A **font style** adds emphasis to a font. Examples of font styles are **bold**, *italic*, and underline.

While you are creating, editing, and formatting a document, it is held temporarily in memory. Once you have completed these steps, you may want to save your document for future use. **Saving** is the process of copying a document from memory to a storage medium such as a floppy disk or hard disk. You also should save the document frequently while working with it, to ensure your work is not lost. Many applications have an optional **AutoSave** feature that automatically saves open documents at specified time periods.

Figure 2-10 *The Times New Roman and Arial fonts are shown in three font sizes and a variety of font styles.*

Any document that you are working with or have saved exists as a file. A **file** is a named collection of data, instructions, or information, such as a document that you create. To distinguish among various files, each file has a **file name**, which is a unique set of letters of the alphabet, numbers, and other characters that identifies the file.

Once you have created a document, you can print it many times, with each copy looking just like the first. **Printing** is the process of sending a file to a printer to generate output on a medium such as paper. You also can send the document to others electronically, if your computer is connected in a network.

BASIC WORD PROCESSING FEATURES

Word processing software has many formatting features to make documents look professional and visually appealing. For example, you can change the font and font size of headlines and headings, change the color of characters, or organize text into newspaper-style columns. Any colors used for characters or other formatting will print as black or gray unless you have a color printer.

Most word processing software allows you to incorporate graphical images of many types into your document. For example, you can enhance a document by adding a **border**, which is a decorative line or pattern along one or more edges of a page or around a graphical image. One type of graphical image commonly included with word processing software is **clip art**, which is a collection of drawings, diagrams, and photographs that can be inserted in other documents. Figure 2-9 on page 2.8 includes a clip art image of a skier. Clip art collections, which can contain several hundred to several thousand images, usually are grouped by type, such as buildings, nature, or people.

While some clip art is included in your word processing package, you can create clip art and other graphics using Paint or another application and **import** (bring in) the clip art into the word processing document. Once you insert or import a clip art image or other graphical image into a document, you can move it, resize it, rotate it, crop it, and adjust its color.

All word processing software provides at least some basic capabilities to help you create, edit, and format documents. For example, you can define the size of the paper on which to print, as well as the **margins** — that is, the portion of the page outside the main body of text, on the top, bottom, and sides of the paper. The word processing software automatically readjusts any text so it fits within the new definitions.

With **wordwrap**, if you type text that extends beyond the right page margin, the word processing software automatically positions text at the beginning of the next line. Wordwrap allows you to type words in a paragraph continually without pressing the ENTER key at the end of each line.

As you type more lines of text than can display on the screen, the top portion of the document moves upward, or scrolls, off the screen. Because of the size of the screen, you can view only a portion of a document on the screen at a time. **Scrolling** is the process of moving different portions of the document on the screen into view.

A major advantage of using word processing software is that you easily can change what you have written. You can insert, delete, or rearrange words, sentences, paragraphs, or entire sections. You can use the **find** or **search** feature to locate all occurrences of a particular character, word, or phrase. This feature can be used in combination with the **replace** feature to substitute existing characters or words with new ones. For example, you can instruct the word processing software to locate the word, vacation, and replace it with the word, holiday.

Current word processing packages even have a feature that automatically corrects errors and makes word substitutions as you type text. For instance, you can type an abbreviation such as asap and the word processing software will replace this abbreviation with the phrase, as soon as possible.

To review the spelling of individual words, sections of a document, or the entire document, you can use a **spelling checker** (sometimes called a spell checker). The spelling checker compares the words in the document to an electronic dictionary that is part of the word processing software. You can customize the electronic dictionary by adding words such as companies, streets, cities, and personal names, so the software can check the spelling of those words as well. Many word processing software packages allow you to check the spelling of a whole document at one time, or to check the spelling of individual words as you type them.

You also can insert headers and footers into a word processing document. A **header** is text you want at the top of each page; a **footer** is text you want at the bottom of each page. Page numbers, as well as company names, report titles, or dates are examples of items frequently included in headers and footers.

In addition to these basic features, most current word processing packages provide numerous additional features. The table in Figure 2-11 lists these additional features.

POPULAR WORD PROCESSING FEATURES

Feature	Description
AutoCorrect	As you type words, the AutoCorrect feature corrects common spelling errors. For example, if you type the word, adn, the word processing software automatically changes it to the correct word, and. AutoCorrect also corrects errors in capitalization. For example, it capitalizes names of days and the first letter in a sentence.
AutoFormat	As you type, the AutoFormat feature automatically applies formatting to your text. For example, it automatically can number a list or convert a Web address to a hyperlink. AutoFormat also automatically creates symbols, fractions, and ordinal numbers. For example, when you type :), it changes to a smiling face symbol ☺; the fraction $1/2$ is created when you type 1/2; and the ordinal 2nd is created when you type 2nd.
Columns	Most word processing software can arrange text in two or more columns like a newspaper or magazine. The text from the bottom of one column automatically flows to the top of the next column.
Grammar Checker	You can use the grammar checker to proofread documents for grammar, writing style, and sentence structure errors in your document. You can check the grammar of a document all at one time, or instruct the word processing software to check grammar as you enter text.
Tables	Tables are a way of organizing information into rows and columns. With tables, you easily can rearrange rows and columns, change column widths, sort rows and columns, sum the contents of rows and columns, or format the contents of a table. Instead of evenly spaced rows and columns, some word processing packages allow you to draw the tables of any size or shape directly into the document.
Templates	A template is a document that contains the formatting necessary for a specific document type. For example, a letter template would contain the proper spacing and indicate the position of elements common to a business letter such as a date, inside address, salutation, body, closing, and signature block. Templates usually exist for documents such as memos, fax cover sheets, and letters.
Thesaurus	With a thesaurus, you can look up synonyms (words with the same meaning) for words in a document while you are using your word processing software.
Tracking Changes/ Comments	If multiple users work with a document, you can instruct the word processing software to highlight or color-code the changes made by various users. This way, you can see easily what changes have been made to the document. You also can add comments to a document, without changing the text itself. These comments allow you to communicate with the other users working on the document.
Voice Recognition	With some of the newer word processing packages, you can speak into your computer's microphone and watch the spoken words display on your screen as you talk. With these packages, you also can edit and format the document by speaking or spelling an instruction.
Web Page Development	Most word processing software supports Internet connectivity, allowing you to create, edit, and format documents for the World Wide Web. You automatically can convert an existing word processing document into the standard document format for the World Wide Web. You also can view and browse Web pages directly from your word processing software.

Figure 2-11 *Additional features included with many word processing software packages.*

Spreadsheet Software

WEB INFO
WEB INFO

For more information
on spreadsheet software,
visit the Discovering
Computers 2000
Chapter 2 WEB INFO page
(**www.scsite.com/
dc2000/ch2/webinfo.htm**)
and click Spreadsheet
Software.

Another widely used software application is **spreadsheet software**, which allows you to organize data in rows and columns. These rows and columns collectively are called a **worksheet**. For years, people used manual methods, such as those performed with pencil and paper, to organize data in rows and columns. The data in an electronic worksheet is organized in the same manner as it is in a manual worksheet (Figure 2-12).

As with word processing software, most spreadsheet software has basic features to help you create, edit, and format worksheets. These features, as included in several popular spreadsheet software packages, are described in the following sections.

SPREADSHEET ORGANIZATION A spreadsheet file is like a notebook with up to 255 individual worksheets. On each worksheet, data is organized vertically in columns and horizontally in rows. Each worksheet typically has 256 columns and 65,536 rows. A letter identifies each column, and a number identifies each row. The column letters begin with A and end with IV; row numbers begin with 1 and end with 65,536. Only a small fraction of these columns and rows displays on the screen at one time. To view a different part of a worksheet, you can scroll to display it on your screen.

The intersection of a column and row is called a **cell**. Each worksheet has more than 16 million (256 x 65,536) cells into which you can enter data. Cells are identified by the column and row in which they are located. For example, the intersection of column B and row 10 is referred to as cell B10. In Figure 2-12, cell B10 contains the number, 5,000.00, which represents the Software expense for January through April.

Cells may contain three types of data: labels (text), values (numbers), and formulas. The text, or **label**, entered in a cell identifies the data and helps organize the worksheet. Using descriptive labels, such as Community College Revenue, Total Income, and Classroom Rental, helps make a worksheet more meaningful.

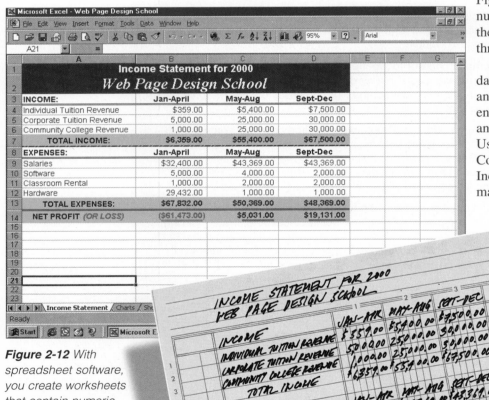

Figure 2-12 With
spreadsheet software,
you create worksheets
that contain numeric
data arranged in rows
and columns.

CALCULATIONS Many of the worksheet cells shown in Figure 2-12 contain a number, or a **value**. Other cells, however, contain formulas that generate values. A **formula** performs calculations on the data in the worksheet and displays the resulting value in a cell, usually the cell containing the formula. In Figure 2-12, for example, cell B7 could contain the formula =B4+B5+B6 to calculate the total income for January through April.

When creating a worksheet, you can enter your own formulas or, in some cases, you can use a function that is included with the spreadsheet software. A **function** is a predefined formula that performs common calculations such as adding the values in a group of cells or generating a value such as the time or date. For example, instead of using the formula =B4+B5+B6 to calculate the total income for January through April, you could use the function =SUM(B4:B6), which adds, or sums, the contents of cells B4, B5, and B6. Figure 2-13 is a list of functions commonly included in spreadsheet software packages.

MACROS Spreadsheet software and other programs often include a timesaving feature called a macro. A **macro** is a sequence of keystrokes and instructions that are recorded and saved. When you run the macro, the macro performs the sequence of keystrokes and instructions. Creating a macro can help you save time by allowing you to enter a single character or word to perform frequently used tasks. For example, you can create a macro to format cells automatically or print a portion of a worksheet.

SPREADSHEET FUNCTIONS

FINANCIAL	
FV (rate, number of periods, payment)	Calculates the future value of an investment
NPV (rate, range)	Calculates the net present value of an investment
PMT (rate, number of periods, present value)	Calculates the periodic payment for an annuity
PV (rate, number of periods, payment)	Calculates the present value of an investment
RATE (number of periods, payment, present value)	Calculates the periodic interest rate of an annuity
DAY & TIME	
DATE	Returns the current date
NOW	Returns the current date and time
TIME	Returns the current time
MATHEMATICAL	
ABS (number)	Returns the absolute value of a number
INT (number)	Rounds a number down to the nearest integer
LN (number)	Calculates the natural logarithm of a number
LOG (number, base)	Calculates the logarithm of a number to a specified base
ROUND (number, number of digits)	Rounds a number to a specified number of digits
SQRT (number)	Calculates the square root of a number
SUM (range)	Calculates the total of a range of numbers
STATISTICAL	
AVERAGE (range)	Calculates the average value of a range of numbers
COUNT (range)	Counts how many cells in the range have entries
MAX (range)	Returns the maximum value in a range
MIN (range)	Returns the minimum value in a range
STDEV (range)	Calculates the standard deviation of a range of numbers
LOGICAL	
IF (logical test, value if true, value if false)	Performs a test and returns one value if the result of the test is true and another value if the result is false

Figure 2-13 *Functions included with many spreadsheet software packages.*

RECALCULATION One of the more powerful features of spreadsheet software is its capability of recalculating the rest of the worksheet when data in a worksheet changes. To appreciate this capability, consider that each time you change a value in a manual worksheet, you must erase the old value, write in a new value, erase any totals that contain calculations referring to the changed value, and then recalculate these totals and enter the new results. When working with a manual worksheet, accurately making changes and updating the affected values can be time consuming and result in new errors.

Making changes in an electronic worksheet is much easier and faster. When you enter a new value to change data in a cell, any value that is affected by the change is updated automatically and instantaneously. In Figure 2-12 on page 2.12 for example, if you change the Software Expenses for May through August from 4,000.00 to 5,000.00, the total in cell C13 automatically changes to $51,369.00 and the net profit in cell C14 changes to $4,031.00.

Spreadsheet software's capability of recalculating data also makes it a valuable tool for decision making using what-if analysis. **What-if analysis** is a process in which certain values in a spreadsheet are changed in order to reveal the effects of those changes.

CHARTING Charting, which is another standard feature of spreadsheet software, allows you to display data in a chart that shows the relationship of data in graphical, rather than numerical, form. A visual representation of data through charts often makes it easier to analyze and interpret information. Three popular chart types are line charts, column charts, and pie charts (Figure 2-14).

Line charts are effective for showing a trend over a period of time, as indicated by a rising or falling line. A line chart for an Income Statement, for example, could show total expenses and total income over a period of time. **Column charts**, also called **bar charts**, display bars of various lengths to show the relationship of data. The bars can be horizontal, vertical, or stacked on top of one another. A column chart for an Income Statement might show the income breakdown by

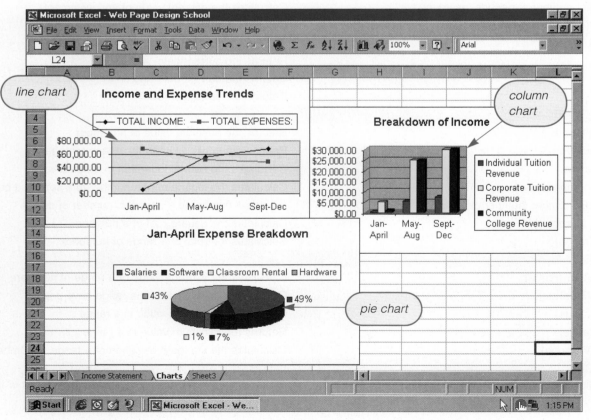

Figure 2-14 *Three basic types of charts provided with spreadsheet software are line charts, column charts, and pie charts. The line chart, column chart, and pie chart shown were created from the data in the worksheet in Figure 2-12 on page 2.12.*

category, with each bar representing a different category. **Pie charts**, which have the shape of round pies cut into pieces or slices, are used to show the relationship of parts to a whole. You might use a pie chart to show what percentage (part) each expense category contributed to the total expense (whole) for a time period.

Spreadsheet software also incorporates many of the features found in word processing software such as a spelling checker, changing fonts and font sizes, adding colors, tracking changes, and the capability of converting an existing spreadsheet document into the standard document format for the World Wide Web.

Database Software

A **database** is a collection of data organized in a manner that allows access, retrieval, and use of that data. In a manual database, data might be recorded on paper and stored in a filing cabinet. In a computerized database, such as the one shown in Figure 2-15, data is stored in an electronic format on a storage

medium. **Database software**, also called a **database management system (DBMS)**, allows you to create a computerized database; add, change, and delete data; sort and retrieve data from the database; and create forms and reports using the data in the database.

With most popular personal computer database software packages, a database consists of a collection of tables, organized in rows and columns. A row in a table is called a **record**, and contains information about a given person, product, or event. A column in a table is called a **field**, and contains a specific piece of information within a record.

The Museum Gift Shop database shown in Figure 2-15 consists of two tables: a Product table and a Vendor table. The Product table contains ten records (rows), each of which contains data about one product. The product data is listed in the table's six fields (columns): product identification number, description, quantity on hand, cost of product, selling price, and vendor code. The description field, for instance, contains a name of a particular product.

Figure 2-15 This database contains two tables: one for products and one for vendors. The product table has ten records and six fields; the vendor table has three records and seven fields.

DATABASE ORGANIZATION Before you begin creating a database, you should perform some preliminary tasks. Make a list of the data items you want to organize; each of these will become a field in the database. To identify the different fields, assign each field a unique name that is short, yet descriptive. For example, the field name for a product identification number could be Product Id, and the field name for the quantity on hand could be On Hand.

Once you have determined the fields and field names, you also must decide the field lengths and data types. The **field length** is the maximum number of characters to be stored for data in a particular field. The Description field, for instance, may be defined as 25 characters in length. The **data type** specifies the type of data that the field can contain. Common data types include:

- **Text**: letters, numbers, or special characters
- **Numeric**: numbers only
- **Currency**: dollar and cents amounts
- **Date**: month, day, and year information
- **Memo**: freeform text of any type or length
- **Hyperlink**, or **link**: Web address that links to Web page

Completing these steps provides a general description of the records and fields in a table, including the number of fields, field names, field lengths, and data types. These items collectively are referred to as the table **structure** (Figure 2-16).

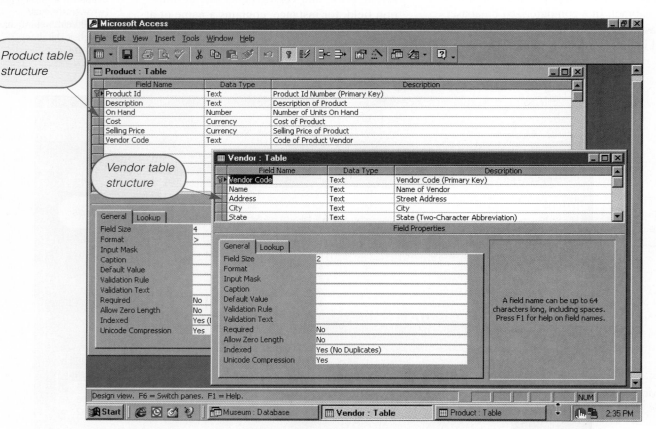

Figure 2-16 *The structure of a table includes the field names, field lengths, and data types. This Microsoft Access 2000 screen illustrates the structures for the Product and the Vendor tables.*

ENTERING DATA After a table structure is created, you can enter individual records into a table. Records usually are entered one at a time using the keyboard, often through a data entry form (Figure 2-17). As you are entering the data, the database software checks, or validates, the data. **Validation** is the process of comparing the data to a set of defined rules or values to determine if the data is acceptable. For example, designating a field as a numeric data type allows a user to enter only numbers into the field. Validation is important because it helps to ensure that data entered into the database is error free.

Another way to enter data into a database is to import data from an existing file. For example, you can import data saved in a spreadsheet file into a database.

MANIPULATING DATA Once the records are entered, you can use the database software to manipulate the data to generate information. For example, you can **sort**, or organize, a set of records in a particular order, such as alphabetical or by entry date. You also can retrieve information from the database by running a query. A **query** is a specific set of instructions for retrieving data from the database. You can specify which data the query retrieves by specifying **criteria**, or restrictions that the data must meet. For example, suppose you wanted to generate a list of all products that cost less than $15.00. You could set up a query to list the Product Id, Description, On Hand, and Cost for all records that meet this criteria. The list could be sorted to display the most expensive products first (Figure 2-18).

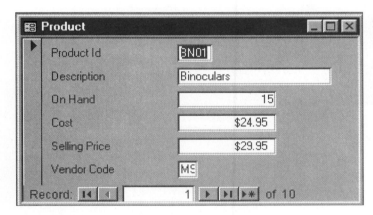

Figure 2-17 *After you define the table structure, you can enter data into the database using a data entry form. Most database software will create a data entry form automatically, based on the way fields are defined. In this data entry form, you enter data into the Product table.*

Product Id	Description	On Hand	Cost
PC03	Pick Up Sticks	5	$8.50
WI10	Wizard Cards	10	$7.50
JG01	Jigsaw Puzzle	3	$5.40
ST23	Stationery	8	$3.95
DI24	Dinosaurs	14	$3.75
WL34	Wildlife Posters	15	$2.50
YO12	Wooden YoYo	9	$1.60

Record: 7 of 7 (Filtered)

Figure 2-18 *Database software can produce reports based on criteria specified by a user. For example, this screen shows the result of a request, called a query, to list the Product Id, Description, On Hand, and Cost fields for all records that have a cost less than $15.00. The results of the query can be displayed or printed.*

Presentation Graphics Software

Presentation graphics software allows you to create documents called presentations, which are used to communicate ideas, messages, and other information to a group. The presentations can be viewed as slides that display on a large monitor or on a projection screen (Figure 2-19).

Presentation graphics software typically provides an array of predefined presentation formats that define complementary colors for backgrounds, text, and other items on the slides. Presentation graphics software also provides a variety of layouts for each individual slide such as a title slide, a two-column slide, and a slide with clip art. Any text, charts, and graphical images used in a slide can be enhanced with 3-D and other special effects such as shading, shadows, and textures.

WEB INFO
WEB INFO

For more information on presentation graphics software, visit the Discovering Computers 2000 Chapter 2 WEB INFO page (**www.scsite.com/ dc2000/ch2/webinfo.htm**) and click Presentation Graphics Software.

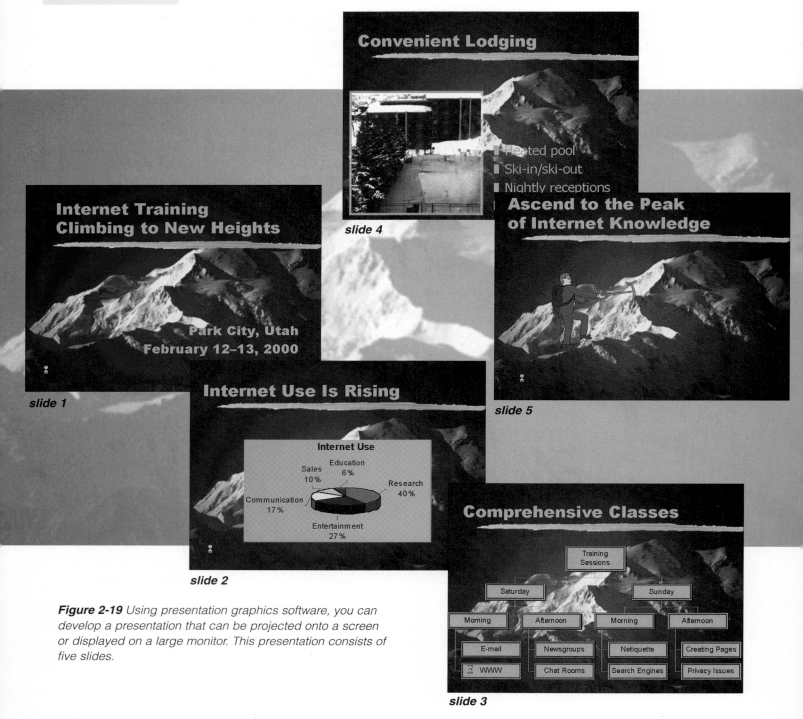

Figure 2-19 *Using presentation graphics software, you can develop a presentation that can be projected onto a screen or displayed on a large monitor. This presentation consists of five slides.*

With presentation graphics software, you can incorporate objects from the clip gallery into your slides to create multimedia presentations. A **clip gallery** includes clip art images, pictures, video clips, and audio clips. A clip gallery can be stored on your hard disk, a CD-ROM, or a DVD-ROM; in other cases, you access the clip gallery on the Web. As with clip art collections, a clip gallery typically is organized by categories that can include academic, business, entertainment, transportation, and so on. For example, the transportation category may contain a clip art image of a bicycle, a photograph of a locomotive, a video clip of an airplane in flight, and an audio clip of a Model T car horn.

When building a presentation, you also can set the slide timing, so that the presentation automatically displays the next slide after a predetermined delay. Special effects can be applied to the transition between each slide. One slide, for example, might slowly dissolve as the next slide comes into view.

To help organize the presentation, you can view small versions of all the slides in slide sorter view (Figure 2-20). Slide sorter view presents a screen view similar to how 35mm slides would look on a photographer's light table. The slide sorter allows you to arrange the slides in any order.

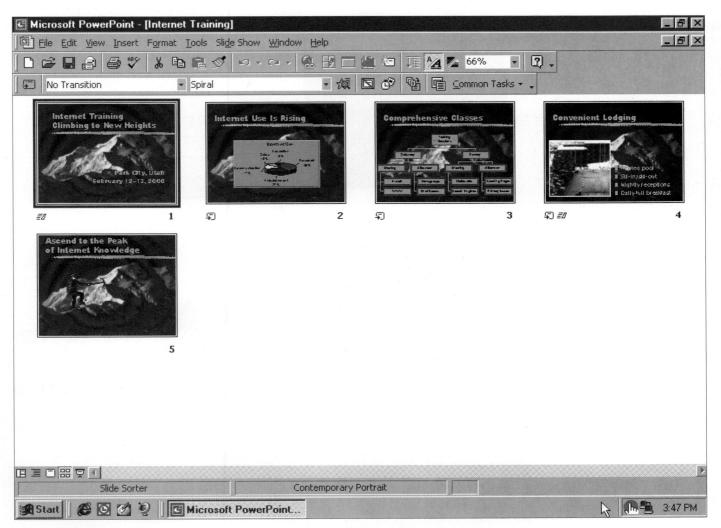

Figure 2-20 *Slide sorter view shows a small version of each slide. Using a pointing device or the keyboard, you can rearrange the slides to change the order of the presentation.*

Once you have created a presentation, you can view or print the presentation as slides or in several other formats. An outline includes only the text from each slide, such as the slide title and the key points (Figure 2-21a). Audience handouts include images of two or more slides on a page that you can distribute to presentation attendees (Figure 2-21b). You also may wish to print a notes page to help you deliver the presentation; a notes page shows a picture of the slide along with any notes you want to see while discussing a topic or slide (Figure 2-21c).

Presentation graphics software also incorporates some of the features found in word processing software such as a spelling checker, font formatting capabilities, and the capability of converting an existing slide show into the standard document format for the World Wide Web.

Figure 2-21 *In addition to viewing the presentation as slides, presentation graphics packages allow you to view or print the presentation as an outline, as audience handouts, or as notes pages for the speaker.*

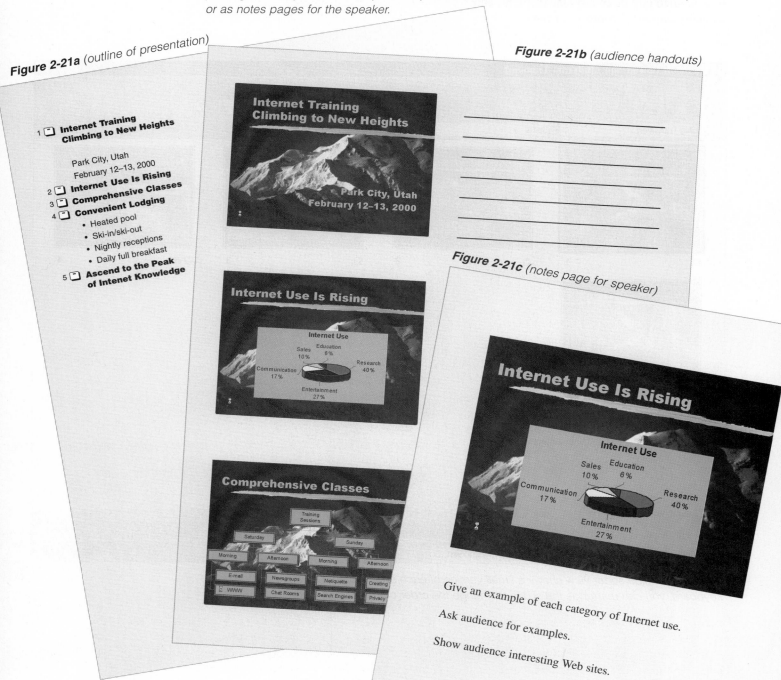

Figure 2-21a (outline of presentation)

Figure 2-21b (audience handouts)

Figure 2-21c (notes page for speaker)

Personal Information Managers

A **personal information manager** (**PIM**) is a software application that includes an appointment calendar, address book, and notepad to help you organize personal information such as appointments and task lists (Figure 2-22). A PIM allows you to take information that you previously tracked in a weekly or daily calendar, and organize and store it on your computer. PIMs can manage many different types of information such as telephone messages, project notes, reminders, task and address lists, and important dates and appointments.

Figure 2-22 *Some handheld computers such as the Palm III™ Connected Organizer run PIM software. With these computers, you can transfer information from the handheld computer to your desktop computer so appointments, address lists, and other important information always are available.*

Precisely defining a PIM is difficult because personal information managers offer a range of capabilities. As noted, however, most include at least an appointment calendar, address book, and notepad. An **appointment calendar** allows you to schedule activities for a particular day and time. With an **address book**, you can enter and maintain names,

addresses, and telephone numbers of customers, co-workers, family members, and friends. Instead of writing notes on a piece of paper, you can use a **notepad** to record ideas, reminders, and other important information. Many PIMs also include a calculator or a simple spreadsheet application; some also include e-mail capabilities.

Software Suite

A software **suite** is a collection of individual application software packages sold as a single package (Figure 2-23). When you install the suite, you install the entire collection of applications at once instead of installing each application individually. At a minimum, suites typically include the following software applications: word processing, spreadsheet, database, and presentation graphics.

Software suites offer two major advantages: lower cost and ease of use. Typically, buying a collection of software packages in a suite costs significantly less than purchasing each of the application packages separately. Software suites provide ease of use because the applications within a suite normally use a similar interface and have some common features. Thus, once you learn how to use one application in the suite, you are familiar with the interface in the other applications in the suite. For example, once you learn how to print using the suite's word processing package, you can apply the same skill to the spreadsheet, database, and presentation graphics software in the suite.

Figure 2-23 *Two popular software suites are Lotus SmartSuite and Microsoft Office 2000. Lotus SmartSuite includes WordPro, 1-2-3, Approach, FastSite, Freelance, Organizer, and ScreenCam. Microsoft Office 2000 Premium contains Word, Excel, PowerPoint, Access, Outlook, Publisher, FrontPage, and PhotoDraw.*

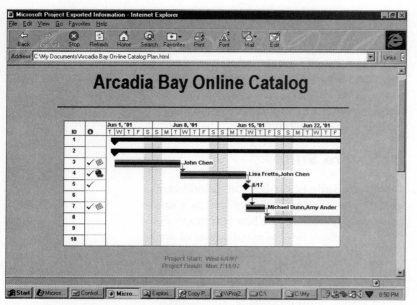

Figure 2-24 *Project management software allows you to plan, schedule, track, and analyze the events, resources, and costs of a project.*

Project Management Software

Project management software allows you to plan, schedule, track, and analyze the events, resources, and costs of a project (Figure 2-24). A general contractor, for example, might use project management software to manage a home-remodeling schedule, or a publisher might use it to coordinate the process of producing a textbook. The value of project management software is that it helps managers track, control, and manage project variables, thereby allowing them to complete a project on time and within budget. Project management is discussed in more detail in Chapter 11.

Accounting Software

Accounting software helps companies record and report their financial transactions (Figure 2-25). Accounting software allows you to perform accounting activities involved with the general ledger, accounts receivable, accounts payable, purchasing, invoicing, job costing, and payroll. With accounting software, you also can write and print checks, track checking account activity, and update and reconcile balances on demand. Newer accounting software packages support online direct deposit and payroll services, which makes it possible for a company to deposit paychecks directly into employee's checking accounts and pay employee taxes electronically.

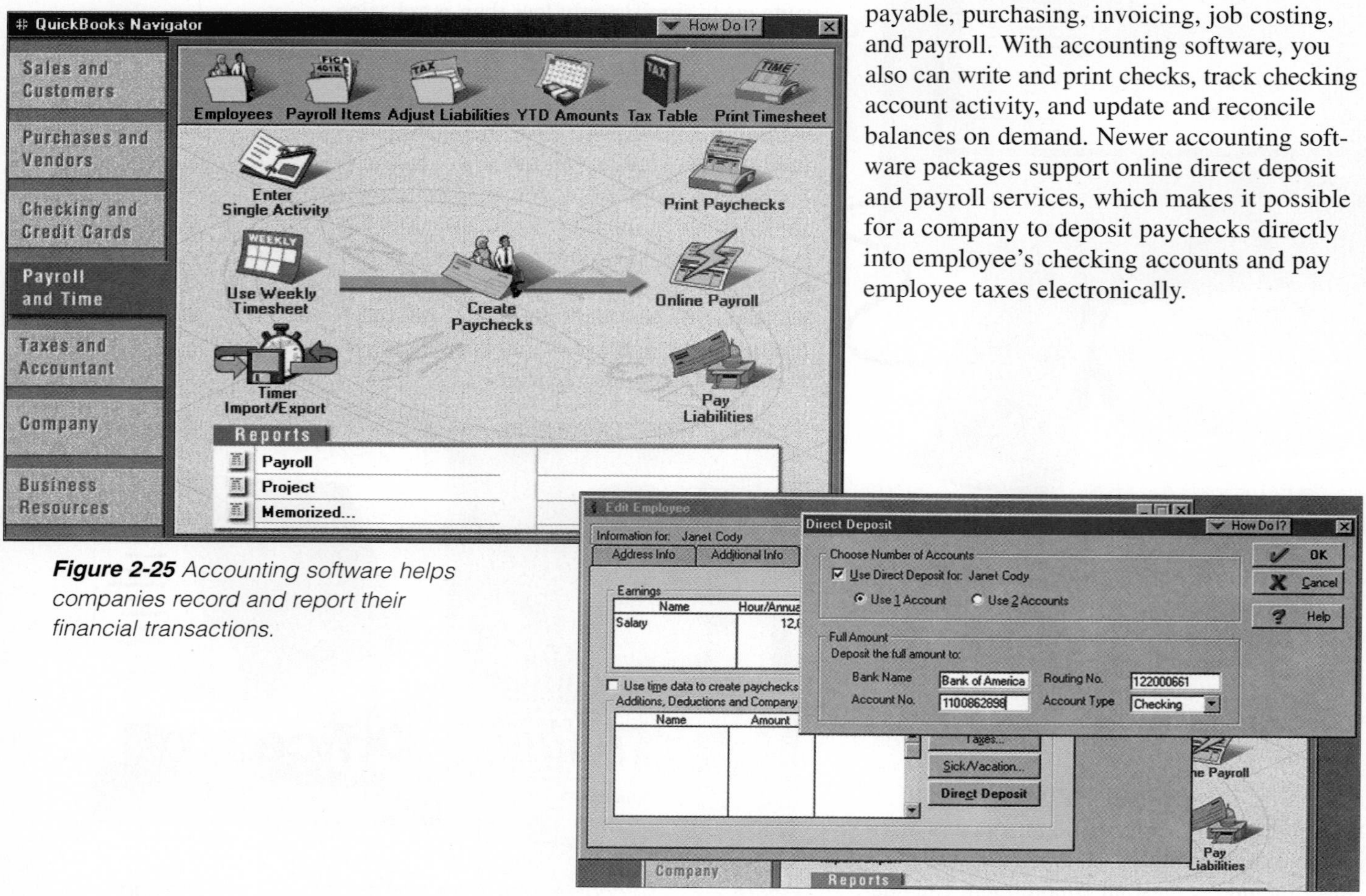

Figure 2-25 *Accounting software helps companies record and report their financial transactions.*

Some accounting software offers more sophisticated features such as multiple company reporting, foreign currency reporting, and forecasting the amount of raw materials needed for products. The cost of accounting software for small businesses ranges from less than one hundred to several thousand dollars. Accounting software for large businesses can cost several hundred thousand dollars.

GRAPHICS AND MULTIMEDIA SOFTWARE

In addition to productivity software, many individuals also work with software designed specifically for their fields of work. Power users such as engineers, architects, desktop publishers, and graphic artists, for example, often use powerful software that allows them to work with graphics and multimedia. Types of graphics and multimedia software include computer-aided design, desktop publishing, paint/image editing, video and audio editing, multimedia authoring, and Web page authoring. Figure 2-26 lists the more popular products for each of these applications. The features and functions of each of these applications are discussed in the following sections.

POPULAR GRAPHICS AND MULTIMEDIA SOFTWARE PACKAGES

Software Application	Popular Packages
Computer-Aided Design (CAD)	• Autodesk AutoCAD • Visio Technical
Desktop Publishing (Professional)	• Adobe PageMaker • QuarkXPress
Paint/Image Editing (Professional)	• Adobe Illustrator • Adobe Photoshop • MetaCreations Painter 3D
Video and Audio Editing	• Adobe Premiere
Multimedia Authoring	• Asymetrix ToolBook • Macromedia Authorware • Macromedia Director
Web Page Authoring	• Adobe PageMill • Microsoft FrontPage 2000

Figure 2-26 Popular graphics and multimedia software products.

Computer-Aided Design

Computer-aided design (CAD) software is a sophisticated type of application software that assists a user in creating engineering, architectural, and scientific designs (Figure 2-27). For example, using CAD, engineers can create design plans for airplanes and security systems; architects can design building structures and floor plans; and scientists can design drawings of molecular structures.

CAD software eliminates the laborious manual drafting that design processes can require. With CAD, designers can make changes to a drawing or design and view the results. Three-dimensional CAD programs allow designers to rotate designs of 3-D objects to view them from any angle. Some CAD software even can generate material lists for building designs.

Desktop Publishing Software (Professional)

Desktop publishing (DTP) software allows you to design and produce sophisticated documents that contain text, graphics, and brilliant colors (Figure 2-28). Although many word processing packages have some of the capabilities of DTP software, professional designers and graphic artists use DTP software because it is designed specifically to support **page layout**, which is the process of arranging text and graphics in a document. DTP software thus is ideal for the production of high-quality color documents such as newsletters, marketing literature, catalogs, and annual reports. In the past, documents of this type were created by slower, more expensive traditional publishing methods such as typesetting. Today's DTP software also allows you to convert a color document into a format for use on the World Wide Web.

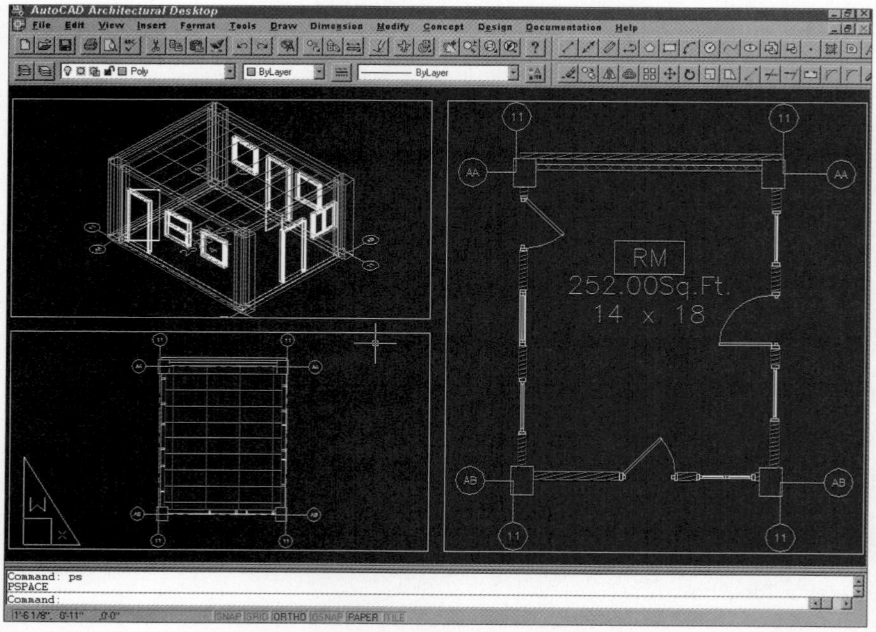

WEB INFO

For more information on desktop publishing software, visit the Discovering Computers 2000 Chapter 2 WEB INFO page (www.scsite.com/dc2000/ch2/webinfo.htm) and click Desktop Publishing Software.

Figure 2-27 CAD software is sophisticated software that assists engineers, architects, and scientists in creating designs.

Figure 2-28 Professional designers and graphic artists use DTP software to produce sophisticated publications such as marketing literature, catalogs, and annual reports.

When creating a document using DTP software, you can add text and graphical images directly into the document, or you can import existing text and graphics from other files. For example, you can import text from a word processing file into a desktop publishing document. Graphics files such as illustrations and photographs also can be imported into a DTP document. One type of input device, called a scanner, can be used to convert printed graphics such as photographs and drawings into files that DTP software can use.

Once you have created or inserted a graphical image into a document, the DTP software can crop, sharpen, and change the colors in the image by adding tints or percentages of colors. To help you select a color for a graphical image or text, DTP software packages include color libraries. A **color library** is a standard set of colors used by designers and printers to ensure that colors will print exactly as specified. Using a color library, you can choose standard colors or specialty colors such as metallic or fluorescent colors.

Paint/Image Editing Software (Professional)

Graphic artists, multimedia professionals, technical illustrators, and desktop publishers use paint software and image editing software to create and modify graphical images such as those used in DTP documents and Web pages (Figure 2-29). **Paint software**, also called **illustration software**, allows you to draw pictures, shapes, and other graphical images using various tools on the screen such as a pen, brush, eyedropper, and paint bucket. **Image editing software** provides the capabilities of paint software as well as the capability of modifying existing images. For example, you can retouch photographs; adjust or enhance image colors; and add special effects such as shadows and glows.

WEB INFO
WEB INFO

For more information on paint/image editing software, visit the Discovering Computers 2000 Chapter 2 WEB INFO page (**www.scsite.com/ dc2000/ch2/webinfo.htm**) and click Paint/Image Editing Software.

Figure 2-29 With image editing software, artists can create and modify a variety of graphical images.

Video and Audio Editing Software

Video consists of images that are played back at speeds that provide the appearance of full motion. With **video editing software** (Figure 2-30), you can modify a segment of a video, called a clip. For example, you can reduce the length of a video clip, reorder a series of clips, or add special effects such as words that move horizontally across the screen. Video editing software typically includes audio editing capabilities.

Audio is any music, speech, or other sound that is stored and produced by the computer. With **audio editing software**, you can modify audio clips. Audio editing software usually includes filters, which are designed to enhance audio quality. A filter, for example, might remove a distracting background noise from the audio clip.

Multimedia Authoring Software

Multimedia authoring software is used to create electronic interactive presentations that can include text, images, video, audio, and animation (Figure 2-31). The software helps you create presentations by allowing you to control the placement of text and images and the duration of sounds, video, and animation. Once created, such multimedia presentations often take the form of interactive computer-based presentations designed to facilitate learning and elicit direct student participation. Multimedia presentations usually are stored and delivered via a CD-ROM or DVD-ROM, over a local area network, or via the Internet.

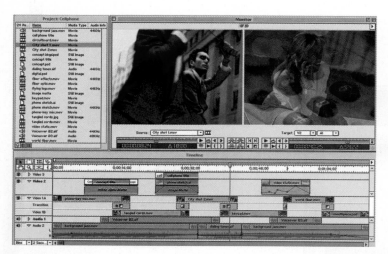

Figure 2-30 Video professionals can modify video images using video-editing software.

Figure 2-31 Multimedia authoring software allows you to create dynamic presentations that include text, graphics, video, sound, and animation.

Web Page Authoring Software

Web page authoring software is software specifically designed to help you create Web pages, in addition to organizing, managing, and maintaining Web sites. As noted in previous sections, many application software packages include Web page authoring features you can use to create basic Web pages that contain text and graphical images. Web page authoring software, however, includes features that also allow you to create sophisticated multimedia Web pages that include graphical images, video, audio, animation, and other special effects. With Web page authoring software, both new and experienced users can create fascinating Web sites. Web page authoring software is presented in more detail in Chapter 7.

SOFTWARE FOR HOME, PERSONAL, AND EDUCATIONAL USE

Many software applications are designed specifically for use at home or for personal or educational use. Examples of such software packages are integrated software that includes word processing, spreadsheet, database, and other software in a single package; personal finance; legal; tax preparation; desktop publishing; paint image/editing; clip art/image gallery; home design/landscaping; educational; reference; and entertainment. Most of the products in this category are relatively inexpensive, often priced at less than $100. Figure 2-32 lists popular software packages for many of these applications. The features and functions of each of these applications are discussed in the following sections.

WEB INFO
WEB INFO

For more information on Web page authoring software, visit the Discovering Computers 2000 Chapter 2 WEB INFO page (**www.scsite.com/dc2000/ch2/webinfo.htm**) and click Web Page Authoring Software.

POPULAR SOFTWARE PACKAGES FOR HOME/PERSONAL/EDUCATIONAL USE

Software Application	Popular Packages
Integrated Software	• Microsoft Works
Personal Finance	• Intuit Quicken • Microsoft Money
Legal	• E-Z Legal Advisor • Kiplinger's Home Legal Advisor • WillMaker
Tax Preparation	• Intuit TurboTax • Kiplinger TaxCut
Desktop Publishing (Personal)	• Broderbund Print Shop Premier • Microsoft Publisher 2000
Paint/Image Editing (Personal)	• Adobe PhotoDeluxe • Corel Photo-Paint • Microsoft PhotoDraw 2000 • Paint Shop Pro
Clip Art/Image Gallery	• Corel Gallery • Nova Art Explosion
Home Design/Landscaping	• Autodesk Planix Complete Home Suite • Broderbund 3D Home Design Suite
Reference	• Microsoft Encarta • Microsoft Streets/TripPlanner • Mosby's Medical Encyclopedia • The American Heritage Talking Dictionary

Figure 2-32 Popular software products for home, personal, and educational use.

WEB INFO
WEB INFO

For more information on
personal finance software,
visit the Discovering
Computers 2000
Chapter 2 WEB INFO page
(www.scsite.com/
dc2000/ch2/webinfo.htm)
and click Personal
Finance Software.

Integrated Software

Integrated software is software that combines applications such as word processing, spreadsheet, and database into a single, easy-to-use package. Like a software suite, the applications within the integrated software package use a similar interface and share some common features. Once you learn how to use one application in the integrated software package, you are familiar with the interface in the other applications.

Unlike a software suite, however, you cannot purchase the applications in the integrated software package individually. Each application in an integrated software package is designed specifically to work as part of a larger set of applications (thus the name integrated).

The applications within the integrated software package typically do not have all the capabilities of stand-alone productivity software applications such as word processing and spreadsheets. Integrated software thus is less expensive than a more powerful software suite. For many home and personal users, however, the capabilities of an integrated software package more than meet their needs.

Personal Finance Software

Personal finance software is a simplified accounting program that helps you pay bills; balance your checkbook; track your personal income and expenses, such as credit-card bills; track investments; and evaluate financial plans (Figure 2-33).

Using personal finance software can help you determine where, and for what purpose, you are spending money so that you can manage your finances. Reports can summarize transactions by category (such as dining), by payee (such as the electric company), or by time period (such as the last two months). Bill-paying features include the capability of printing checks on your printer or having an outside service print your checks.

Personal finance software packages usually offer a variety of online services which require access to the Web. For example, you can track your investments online; compare insurance rates from leading insurance companies; and even do your banking transactions online. With online banking, you can transfer money electronically from your checking or credit card accounts to payees' accounts. To obtain current credit card statements, bank statements, and account balances, you can download monthly transaction information

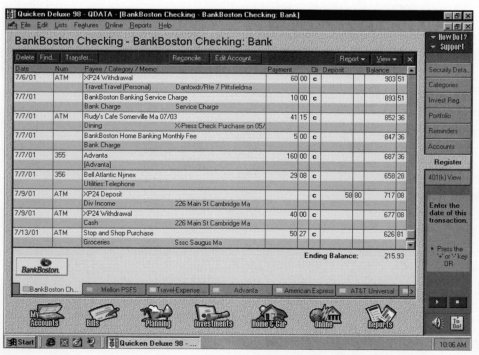

Figure 2-33 *Personal finance software assists you with paying bills; balancing your checkbook; tracking credit card activity, personal income and expenses, and investments; and evaluating financial plans.*

from the Web or copy it from a monthly transaction disk.

Financial planning features include analyzing home and personal loans, preparing income taxes, and managing retirement savings. Other features found in many personal finance packages include home inventory, budgeting, and tax-related transactions.

Legal Software

Legal software assists in the preparation of legal documents and provides legal advice to individuals, families, and small businesses (Figure 2-34). Legal software provides standard contracts and documents associated with buying, selling, and renting property; estate planning; and preparing a will. By answering a series of questions or completing a form, the legal software tailors the legal document to your needs.

Once the legal document is created, you can file the paperwork with the appropriate agency, court, or office; or you can take the document to your attorney for his or her review and signature.

Tax Preparation Software

Tax preparation software guides individuals, families, or small businesses through the process of filing federal taxes (Figure 2-35). These software packages also offer money saving tax tips, designed to lower your tax bill. After you answer a series of questions and complete basic forms, the tax preparation software creates and analyzes your tax forms to search for missed potential errors and deduction opportunities.

Once the forms are complete, you can print any necessary paperwork, completed and ready for you to file. Some tax preparation software packages even allow you to file your tax forms electronically.

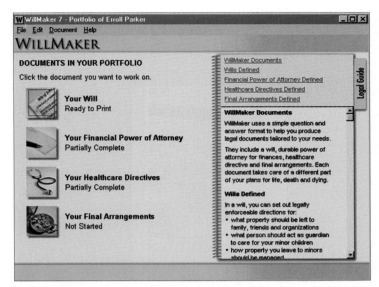

Figure 2-34 Legal software provides legal advice to individuals, families, and small businesses and assists in the preparation of legal documents.

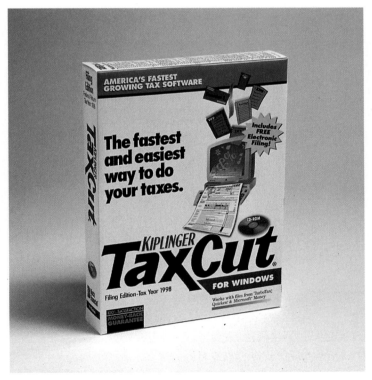

Figure 2-35 Tax preparation software guides individuals, families, or small businesses through the process of filing federal taxes.

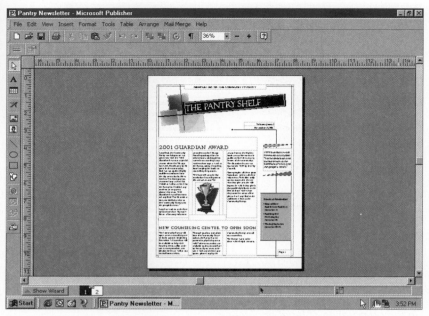

Figure 2-36 *With Microsoft Publisher 2000, home and small business users can create professional looking publications, such as this newsletter.*

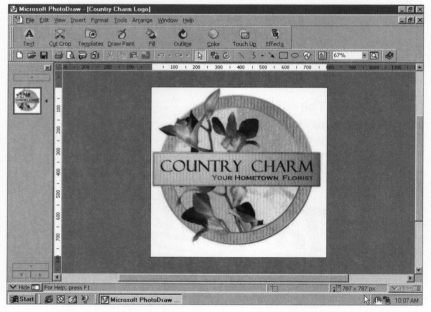

Figure 2-37 *Microsoft PhotoDraw 2000 is an easy-to-use illustration and photo-editing package designed for users without formal graphics or design training.*

Desktop Publishing (Personal)

Instead of using professional DTP software (as discussed earlier in this chapter), many home and small business users utilize much simpler, easy-to-understand DTP software designed for smaller-scale desktop publishing projects (Figure 2-36). Using **personal DTP software**, you can create newsletters, brochures, and advertisements; postcards and greeting cards; letterhead and business cards; banners, calendars, and logos. Personal DTP software guides you through the development of these documents by asking a series of questions, offering numerous predefined layouts, and providing standard text you can add to documents. In some packages, as you enter text, the personal DTP software checks your spelling. You can print your finished publications on a color printer or place them on the Web.

Paint/Image Editing Software (Personal)

Personal paint/image editing software provides an easy-to-use interface, usually with more simplified capabilities than its professional counterpart, including functions tailored to meet the needs of the home and small business user (Figure 2-37).

Like the professional versions, personal paint software includes various simplified tools that allow you to draw pictures, shapes, and other images.

Personal image editing software provides the capabilities of paint software and the capability of modifying existing graphics. One popular type of image editing software, called **photo-editing software**, allows you to edit digital photographs by removing red-eye, adding special effects, or creating electronic photo albums. When the photograph is complete, you can print it on labels, calendars, business cards, and banners; or place it on a Web page.

Clip Art/Image Gallery

Many applications include a **clip art/image gallery**, which is a collection of clip art and photographs (Figure 2-38). You also can purchase clip art/image galleries if you need a wider selection of images. In addition to clip art, many clip art/image galleries provide fonts, animations, sounds, video clips, and audio clips. You can use the images, fonts, and other items from the clip art/image gallery in all types of documents, including word processing, desktop publishing, spreadsheets, and presentation graphics.

Home Design/Landscaping Software

Homeowners or potential homeowners can use **home design/landscaping software** to assist with the design or remodeling of a home, deck, or landscape (Figure 2-39). Home design/landscaping software includes hundreds of predrawn plans which you can customize to meet your needs. Once designed, many home design/landscaping packages will print a material list outlining costs and quantities for the entire project.

WEB INFO
WEB INFO

For more information on clip art/image galleries, visit the Discovering Computers 2000 Chapter 2 WEB INFO page (**www.scsite.com/dc2000/ch2/webinfo.htm**) and click Clip Art/Image Gallery.

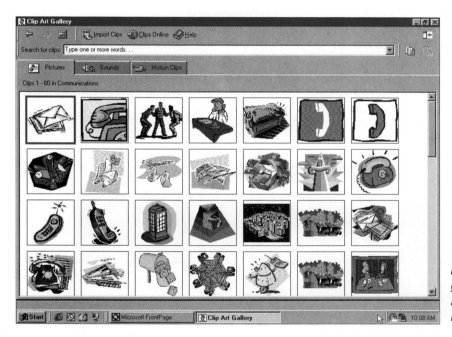

Figure 2-38 Clip art/image galleries are included with many applications, such as Microsoft FrontPage 2000 shown here.

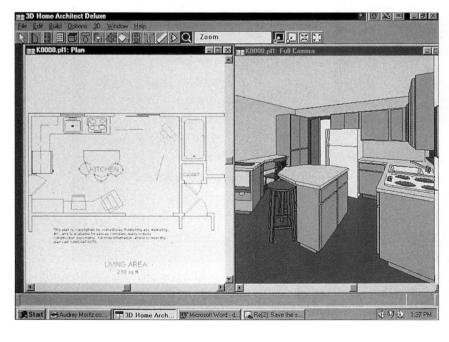

Figure 2-39 Home design/landscaping software can help you design or remodel a home, deck, or landscape.

Educational/Reference/ Personal Computer Entertainment Software

Educational software is software designed to teach a particular skill. Educational software exists for just about any subject, from learning a foreign language to learning how to cook. Pre-school to high school learners can use educational software to assist them with subjects such as reading and math, or to prepare them for class or college entry exams.

Reference software provides valuable and thorough information for all individuals (Figure 2-40). Popular reference software includes encyclopedias, dictionaries, health/medical guides, and travel directories.

Personal computer entertainment software includes interactive games, videos, and other programs designed to support a hobby or provide amusement and enjoyment. For example, you can use personal computer entertainment software to play games, make a family tree, compose music, or fly an aircraft.

WEB INFO
WEB INFO

For more information on reference software, visit the Discovering Computers 2000 Chapter 2 WEB INFO page (**www.scsite.com/ dc2000/ch2/webinfo.htm**) and click Reference Software.

SOFTWARE FOR COMMUNICATIONS

One of the more valuable aspects of software is its capability of supporting communications. Certain applications specifically are designed to facilitate communications, thus allowing you to share information with others. Communications software, which is a utility program that allows you to dial a modem, is discussed in a later chapter. Software for communications discussed in the following sections includes groupware, e-mail, and Web browsers.

Groupware

Groupware identifies any type of software that helps groups of people on a network collaborate on projects and share information, in addition to providing PIM functions, such

Figure 2-40 *Reference software provides valuable and thorough information for all types of users. This reference package includes text you can read about earthquakes, pictures you can view of earthquake fault lines and damages, and a video you can watch about earthquakes.*

as an address book (Figure 2-41) and appointment calendar. A major feature of groupware is group scheduling, in which a group calendar tracks the schedules of multiple users and helps coordinate appointments and meeting times.

Electronic Mail Software

E-mail (**electronic mail**) is the transmission of messages via a computer network such as a local area network or the Internet. The message can be simple text or can include an attachment such as a word processing document, a graphical image, or an audio or video clip. Using **electronic mail software**, you can create, send, receive, forward, store, print, and delete e-mail messages (Figure 2-42). Most e-mail software has a mail notification alert that informs you via a message or sound that you have received new mail, even if you are working in another application.

When you receive an e-mail message, the message is placed in your **mailbox**, which is a storage location usually residing on the computer that connects you to the local area network or the Internet, such as the server operated by your Internet service provider (ISP). The server that contains the mailboxes often is called a **mail server**. Most ISPs and online services provide an Internet e-mail program and a mailbox on a mail server as a standard part of their Internet access services.

To make the sending of messages more efficient, e-mail software allows you to send a single message to a distribution list consisting of two or more individuals. The e-mail software copies the message and sends it to each person on the distribution list. For example, a message addressed to the Accounting Department distribution list would be sent to each of the employees in the accounting department.

Just as you address a letter when using the postal system, you must address an e-mail message with the e-mail address of your intended recipient. Likewise, when someone sends you a message, they must have your e-mail address. An Internet **e-mail address**, which is a combination of a user name and a domain name, identifies a user so he or she can receive Internet e-mail (Figure 2-43).

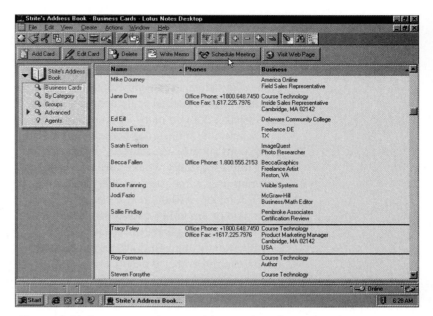

Figure 2-41 *Groupware often provides services for personal information management, such as the business cards shown in this example.*

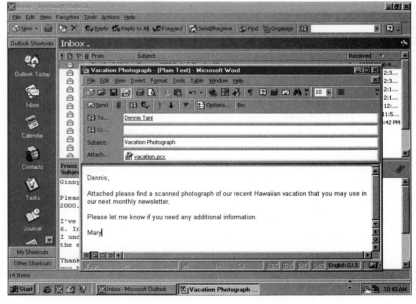

Figure 2-42 *Using e-mail software, you can create, send, receive, forward, store, print, and delete e-mail messages.*

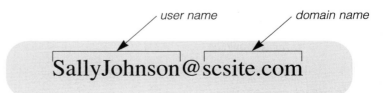

Figure 2-43 *An Internet e-mail address is a combination of a user name and a domain name.*

A **user name**, or **user-ID**, is a unique combination of characters, such as letters of the alphabet or numbers, that identifies you. Your user name must be different from the other user names in the same domain. For example, a user named Sally Johnson whose server has a domain name of scsite.com might select S_Johnson as her user name. If scsite.com already has a user S_Johnson (for Sam Johnson), Sally would have to select a different user name, such as SallyJohnson or Sally_Johnson. Although you can select a nickname or any other combination of characters for your user name, many users select a combination of their first and last names so others can remember it easily.

In an Internet e-mail address, an at symbol (@) separates the user name from the domain name. Using the example in Figure 2-43 on the previous page, a possible e-mail address would be SallyJohnson@scsite.com, which would be read as follows: Sally Johnson at s c site dot com. Most e-mail programs allow you to create an **address book**, which contains a list of names and e-mail addresses.

Although no complete listing of Internet e-mail addresses exists, several Internet sites list addresses collected from public sources. These sites also allow you to list your e-mail address voluntarily so others can find it. The site also might ask for other information, such as your high school or college, so others can determine if you are the person they want to reach.

When sending messages, you can append additional information to the message. Called a **signature**, this information usually is located at the bottom of the message and is attached automatically to each outgoing message. Your signature, for example, could include your name, company affiliation, and a favorite quotation.

Today, e-mail quickly is becoming a primary communication method for both personal and business use. Mobile users can send and receive e-mail messages at any time of the day. As e-mail has gained in popularity, several informal rules for using e-mail have developed; some of these are outlined in Figure 2-44.

Web Browsers

A software application called a **Web browser**, or **browser**, allows you to access and view Web pages. Today's browsers have graphical user interfaces and are quite easy to learn and use. The two more popular browsers are Netscape Navigator and Microsoft Internet Explorer (Figure 2-45). Browsers have many special features including buttons and navigation to help guide you through Web sites. In addition to displaying Web pages, most browsers allow you to use other Internet services such as electronic mail (e-mail). Using a Web browser to navigate the World Wide Web is discussed in depth in the next section.

E-MAIL RULES

1. Keep messages brief using proper grammar and spelling.

2. Be careful when using sarcasm and humor as it might be misinterpreted.

3. Be polite, be diplomatic, and avoid offensive language.

4. Do not use all capital letters, which is the equivalent of SHOUTING!

5. Use **emoticons** to express emotion. Popular emoticons include

   :)   Smile

   :(Frown

   :l   Indifference

   :\   Undecided

   :o   Surprised

6. Use abbreviations and acronyms for phrases such as

   BTW   by the way

   FYI   for your information

   FWIW   for what it's worth

   IMHO   in my humble opinion

   TTFN   ta ta for now

   TYVM   thank you very much

Figure 2-44 E-mail rules.

BROWSING THE WORLD WIDE WEB

Today's computer users of all types must have a Web browser to access the vast resources available on the World Wide Web. In fact, one of the major reasons that business, home, and other users purchase computers is for Internet access. It is apparent in advertising that many companies and organizations assume you are familiar with the Internet. Web addresses appear on television, in radio broadcasts, and in printed newspapers and magazines. Companies encourage you to browse their Web-based catalogs and buy their products online. Many colleges give tours of their campuses on the Web, accept applications online, and offer classes on the Internet. To be successful today, you must have an understanding of the Internet — particularly the World Wide Web. Without it, you are missing a tremendous resource for products, services, and information. This chapter discusses the World Wide Web; other services on the Internet are discussed in Chapter 7.

Although many people use the terms World Wide Web and Internet interchangeably, the World Wide Web is just one of the many services available on the Internet. The **World Wide Web** (**WWW**), or **Web**, consists of a worldwide collection of electronic documents. Each of these electronic documents on the Web is called a Web page. A **Web page** can contain text, graphical images, sound, and video, as well as connections to other documents. A collection of related Web pages that you can access electronically is called a **Web site**. The following sections explain how to navigate Web pages on the World Wide Web.

WEB INFO

WEB INFO

For more information on Web browsers, visit the Discovering Computers 2000 Chapter 2 WEB INFO page (**www.scsite.com/ dc2000/ch2/webinfo.htm**) and click Web Browsers.

Figure 2-45a *(Netscape Navigator)*

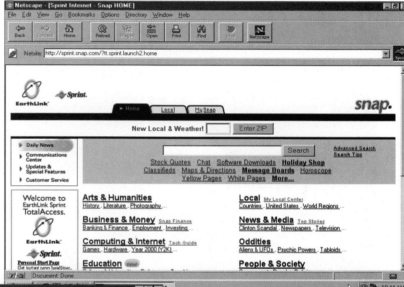

Figure 2-45 *The two more popular Web browsers are Netscape Navigator and Microsoft Internet Explorer.*

Figure 2-45b *(Microsoft Internet Explorer)*

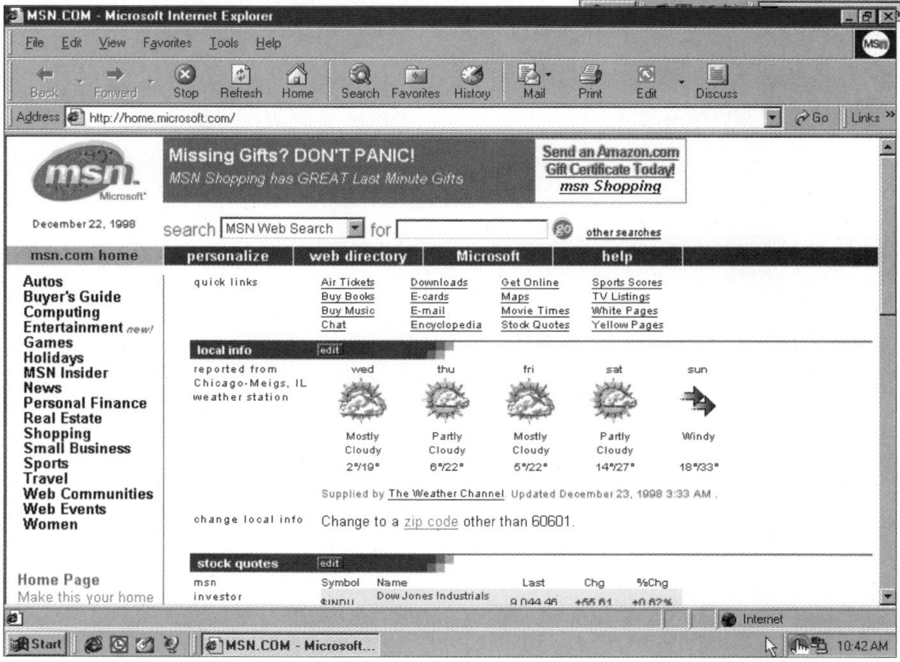

Connecting to the Web and Starting a Browser

As noted, to access and view Web pages you need browser software and a computer that is connected to the Internet. You can connect to the Internet in one of several ways. Some users connect through an Internet service provider or through an online service, using a modem to establish a connection by dialing a specific telephone number. Organizations such as schools and businesses often provide Internet access for students and employees. These users connect to the Internet through the business or school network, which is connected to an Internet service provider.

An **Internet service provider** (**ISP**) is an organization that has a permanent connection to the Internet and provides temporary connections to individuals and companies for a fee, usually about $20 per month. Like an ISP, an **online service** provides access to the Internet, but online services also have members-only features that offer a variety of special content and services such as news, weather, legal information, financial data, hardware and software guides, games, and travel guides. Two popular online services are The Microsoft Network (MSN) and America Online (AOL). The specifics of connecting to the Internet and using ISPs and online services are discussed in more depth in Chapter 7.

To establish the connection, you typically click an icon on your desktop to start the Web browser (Figure 2-46). Your modem will dial the telephone number to the ISP or online service. Once a telephone connection to the

Figure 2-46
ONE METHOD OF CONNECTING TO THE INTERNET

Step 1: Click an icon on the desktop to start your browser.

icons to start a browser

Step 4: Connection to the Internet occurs as shown in Figure 2-47.

Step 3: The modem begins dialing to establish a connection with your Internet service provider or online service.

Step 2: If you are not connected to the Internet already, you may be asked if you want to connect.

Internet is established, the browser retrieves and displays a home page (Figure 2-47). A starting page for a Web site, called a **home page** or sometimes a portal, is similar to a book cover or a table of contents for the site and provides information about the site's purpose and content. Most browsers use the manufacturer's Web page as their initial home page, but you can change your browser's home page at any time.

The process of receiving information, such as a Web page, onto your computer from a server on the Internet is called **downloading**. While your browser is downloading a page, it typically displays an animated logo or icon in the top-right corner of the browser window; when the download is complete, the animation stops. Downloading a Web page to your screen can take from a few seconds to several minutes, depending on the speed of your connection and the amount of graphics on the Web page. To speed up the display of pages, most Web browsers let you turn off the graphics and display only text.

Navigating Web Pages Using Links

Most Web pages contain hyperlinks. A **hyperlink**, also called a **link**, is a built-in connection to another related Web page.

Links allow you to obtain information in a nonlinear way; that is, to make associations between topics instead of moving sequentially through the topics. Reading a book from cover to cover is a linear way of learning. Branching off and investigating related topics as you encounter them is a nonlinear way of learning. For example, while reading an article on nutrition, you might want to learn more about counting calories. Having linked to and read information on counting calories, you might want to find several low-fat, low-calorie recipes. Reading these might inspire you to learn about a chef that specializes in healthy but tasty food preparation. The capability of branching from one related topic to another in

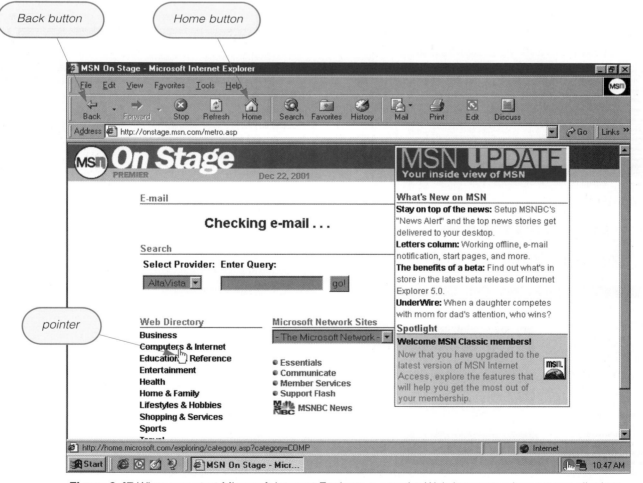

Figure 2-47 *When you start Microsoft Internet Explorer, a popular Web browser, a home page displays. You can change the home page that displays when you start a browser.*

a nonlinear fashion is what makes links so powerful and the World Wide Web such an interesting place to explore.

On the Web, links can be a word, phrase, or image; you can identify them because they are underlined, are a different color from the rest of the document, or are highlighted graphical images. In many cases, when you point to a link, the pointer shape changes to a small hand with a pointing index finger. For example, in Figure 2-47 on the previous page, the pointer is on the Computers & Internet link.

To activate a link, you click it, which then causes the Web page or the location within a Web page associated with the link to display on the screen. The link can point to the same Web page, a different Web page at the same Web site, or a separate Web page at a different Web site in another city or country. In essence, when you navigate using links, you are jumping from Web page to Web page. Displaying pages from one Web site after another is called **surfing the Web**. The steps in Figure 2-48 illustrate navigating using a variety of types of links.

To remind you visually that you have visited a location or document, some browsers change the color of a text link after you click it.

Figure 2-48
NAVIGATING USING A VARIETY OF LINKS

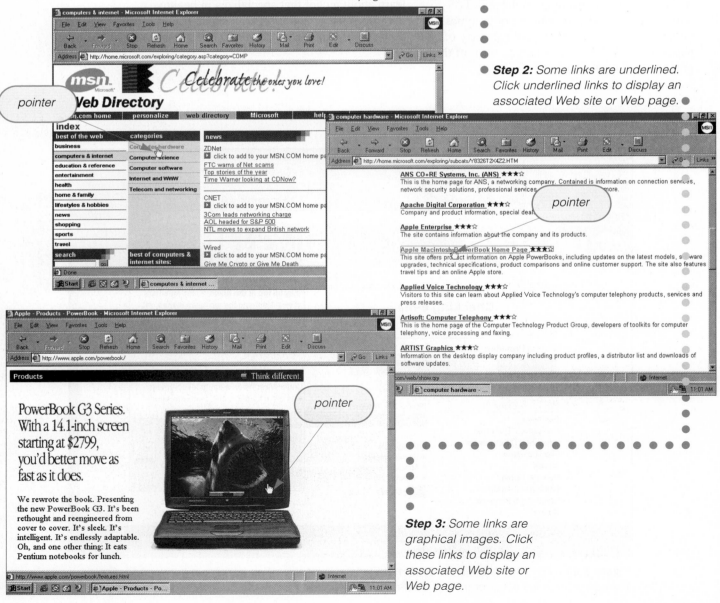

Step 1: Some links are a different color. Click these links to display an associated Web site or Web page.

Step 2: Some links are underlined. Click underlined links to display an associated Web site or Web page.

Step 3: Some links are graphical images. Click these links to display an associated Web site or Web page.

Using the Browser Toolbars

In addition to navigating using links, browsers have buttons, text boxes, and other features to help you navigate and work with Web sites. The Back button, for example, displays the previously displayed Web page. The Home button redisplays the home page (see Figure 2-47 on page 2.37). The table in Figure 2-49 identifies the functions of buttons on the Microsoft Internet Explorer toolbar.

Entering a URL

A Web page has a unique address, called a **Uniform Resource Locator** (**URL**). A browser retrieves a Web page by using its URL, which tells the browser where the document is located. URLs make it possible for you to navigate using links because a link is associated with a URL. When you click a link, you are issuing a request to display the Web site or the document specified by the URL.

MICROSOFT INTERNET EXPLORER TOOLBAR BUTTONS

Button Name	Function
⇐ Back	Goes back to the previous Web page
⇒ Forward	Goes forward to the next Web page
⊗ Stop	Stops loading a Web page
⟳ Refresh	Redisplays the current Web page
🏠 Home	Displays the Internet Explorer starting Web page
🔍 Search	Displays a Search window
📁 Favorites	Displays the Favorites window
🕐 History	Displays the History window
✉ Mail	Displays the Mail menu
🖨 Print	Prints the current Web page
Edit	Edits page with an Office application
📄 Discuss	Accesses discussion server(s)

Figure 2-49 *Functions of the buttons on the Microsoft Internet Explorer toolbar.*

If you know the URL of a Web page, you can type it into a text box at the top of the browser window. For example, if you type the URL of http://www.suntimes.com/index/business.html in the Address text box and then press the ENTER key, the browser will download and display the Business Section of the Chicago Sun-Times Online Newspaper (Figure 2-50).

As shown in Figure 2-50, a URL consists of a protocol, domain name, and sometimes the path to a specific Web page or location in a Web page. Most Web page URLs begin with **http**://, which stands for **hypertext transfer protocol**, the communications standard used to transfer pages on the Web. The domain name identifies the Web site, which is stored on a Web server. A **Web server** is a computer that delivers (serves) requested Web pages.

If you do not enter a URL exactly, your browser will not be able to locate the site or Web page you want to visit (view). To help minimize errors, most current browsers allow you to type URLs without the http:// portion. For example, you can type the text www.suntimes.com/index/business.html instead of http:// www.suntimes.com/index/business.html. If you enter an incorrect address, some browsers search for similar addresses and provide a list from which you can select.

Searching for Information on the Web

No single organization controls additions, deletions, and changes to Web sites, which means no central menu or catalog of Web site content and addresses exists. Several companies, however, maintain organized directories of Web sites to help you find information on specific topics.

A **search engine** is a software program you can use to find Web sites, Web pages, and Internet files. Search engines are particularly helpful in locating Web pages on certain topics or in locating specific pages for which you do not know the exact URL. To find a page or pages, you enter a word or phrase, called **search text** or **keywords**, in the search engine's text box; the search engine then displays a list of all Web pages that contain the word or phrase you entered. Any Web page listed as the result of a search is called a **hit**. For example, if you did not know the URL of the Chicago Sun-Times Online newspaper, you could enter Chicago Sun-Times as your search text. The search engine would return a list of hits, or Web pages, that contain the phrase Chicago Sun-Times (Figure 2-51). You then click an appropriate link in the list to display the associated Web site or Web page.

Figure 2-50 The URL for the Chicago Sun-Times Online Business section is http://www.suntimes.com/index/business.html. When you enter this URL in the Address text box, the associated Web page displays.

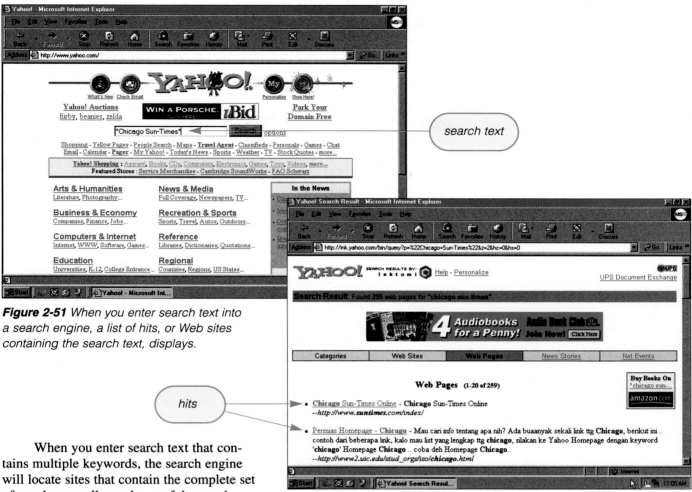

search text

Figure 2-51 When you enter search text into a search engine, a list of hits, or Web sites containing the search text, displays.

hits

When you enter search text that contains multiple keywords, the search engine will locate sites that contain the complete set of words, as well as subsets of the words. For example, a search with the keywords, Chicago Sun-Times, results in 645,573 hits, or Web pages, that contain the word Chicago or the word Sun-Times. To reduce the number of hits, you should search for Web pages that contain both words. In one search engine, for example, surrounding your keywords with quotation marks instructs the search engine to look for Web pages containing that exact phrase. The search text, "Chicago Sun-Times", for example, reduces the number of hits to 259.

Search engines actually do not search the entire Internet; such a search would take an extremely long time. Instead, they search an index of Internet sites and Web pages that constantly is updated by the company that provides the search engine.

The table in Figure 2-52 lists the Web site addresses of several Internet search engines. Most of these sites also provide directories of Web sites organized in categories such as sports, entertainment, or business.

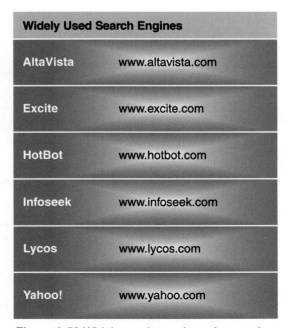

Widely Used Search Engines	
AltaVista	www.altavista.com
Excite	www.excite.com
HotBot	www.hotbot.com
Infoseek	www.infoseek.com
Lycos	www.lycos.com
Yahoo!	www.yahoo.com

Figure 2-52 Widely used search engines and their URLs.

LEARNING AIDS AND SUPPORT TOOLS

Learning how to use an application software package or the Web effectively involves time and practice. To aid you in that learning process, many software applications and Web sites provide online Help, FAQs, tutorials, and wizards (Figure 2-53).

Online Help is the electronic equivalent of a user manual; it usually is integrated into an application software package. Online Help provides assistance that can increase your productivity and reduce your frustrations by minimizing the time you spend learning how to use an application software package.

In most packages, a function key or a button on the screen starts the Help feature. When you are using an application and have a question, you can use the Help feature to ask a question or access the Help topics in subject or alphabetical order. Often the Help is **context-sensitive**, meaning that the Help information is related to the current task being attempted. Most online Help also points you to Web sites that provide updates and more comprehensive resources to answer your software questions.

Figure 2-53a *(online Help)*

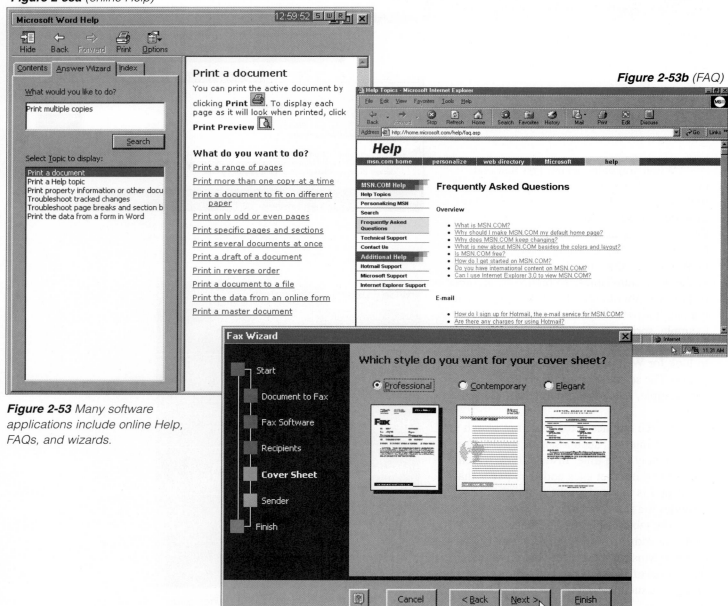

Figure 2-53b *(FAQ)*

Figure 2-53 *Many software applications include online Help, FAQs, and wizards.*

Figure 2-53c *(wizard)*

In many cases, online Help has replaced the user manual altogether, and software developers no longer include user's manuals with the software. If you want to learn more about the software package from a printed manual, however, many books are available to help you learn to use the features of personal computer application packages (Figure 2-54). These books typically are available in bookstores and software stores.

You also can find Web pages with an application software **FAQ** (Frequently Asked Questions) to help you find answers to common questions.

Tutorials are step-by-step instructions using real examples that show you how to use an application. Some tutorials are available in printed manuals; others are software-based or Internet-based, thus allowing you to use your computer to learn about a package.

A **wizard** is an automated assistant that helps you complete a task by asking you questions and then automatically performing actions based on your answers. Many software applications include wizards. For example, word processing software uses wizards to help you create memorandums, meeting agendas, fax cover sheets, and letters; spreadsheet software includes chart and function wizards; and database software has form and report wizards.

Many colleges and schools provide training on several of the applications discussed in this chapter. If you would like more direction than is provided in online Help, FAQs, tutorials, wizards, and trade books, contact your local school for a list of classes they offer.

Figure 2-54 Many bookstores sell trade books to help you learn to use the features of personal computer application packages.

TECHNOLOGY TRAILBLAZER

MARC ANDREESSEN

In 1982, Jim Clark founded Silicon Graphics, a billion-dollar manufacturer of visual computing systems. A dozen years later, Clark was eager for a fresh venture. Seeking a horse on which to hitch his new wagon, Clark asked an engineer for promising names in the computer industry. He wanted more than a technician. "I believe in athletes," he insists, "not first basemen." With Clark's requirements in mind, the engineer offered only one name — Marc Andreessen.

Andreessen grew up in Wisconsin but earned his reputation at the University of Illinois. Working part-time, for about $7.00 an hour, at the school's National Center for Supercomputing Applications (NCSA), he developed UNIX programs for supercomputers. Here, Andreessen became familiar with the Internet, a primarily text-based resource used almost exclusively by scientists and academics. Andreessen envisioned a program that would make the Internet and its subset, the World Wide Web, accessible to the general population. The program itself, Andreessen admits, "wasn't a breakthrough. It was just that nobody had developed a tool that would allow the next wave to come along and be able to take advantage of the Internet."

Andreessen convinced a friend, Eric Bina, to help with the project. The pair worked eighteen hours a day, writing code and debating other issues – from current events ("I'm a news junkie," Andreessen says) to the best snack food (Andreessen liked Pepperidge Farm pastries, while Bina preferred Skittles candy). In three months, they completed the program, which they called Mosaic.

On the face of it, Mosaic did not look like much. Only 9,000 lines long – the Windows operating system is almost a thousand times longer – the program was fairly slow and unstable. Mosaic's impact, however, was phenomenal. Mosaic translated the hypertext markup language (HTML) formatting code in which Web documents are written into colorful, graphical pages connected by hyperlinks. For the first time people had a user-friendly, graphical tool they could use to *browse* the Web, jumping from hyperlinks to other Web pages with a click of the mouse. NCSA engineers developed versions of the program for Windows and Macintosh computers. People could download Mosaic free on the Internet, and its popularity exploded. "We introduced Mosaic to twelve people at the beginning of 1993," Andreessen recalls, "and by the end, there were one million people using it. It grew like a virus."

After graduating from the University of Illinois, Andreessen accepted a job as a programmer at a small company in California's Silicon Valley. Here, Jim Clark contacted him, and the two met to consider ideas for a new company. Eventually, the talk came around to Mosaic. Several people who helped develop the browser were about to leave NCSA, and this gave Andreessen an idea. "We can always create a Mosaic killer — do the program right," he suggested. Andreessen recruited his NCSA friends, who were happy to rejoin him. Later, in a *Newsweek* article, an NCSA coworker would claim he and the other programmers were plumbers, but Andreessen was the architect who "showed us where all the bathrooms went." Clark invested four million dollars in the new company, which was called Netscape Communications Corporation. *Mozilla* (Mosaic killer) became the company's virtual mascot. The Netscape browser was its product.

The company was an immediate success, and stock options made the Andreessen, Clark, and the former NCSA programmers wealthy. As VP of technology Andreessen no longer writes code, but he still tests programs and, perhaps more importantly, keeps abreast of the present so he can anticipate the future. "What always amazes me is that people…find all sorts of creative uses for [our] product that I would never have thought of, and finding out what they're doing is really interesting to me. I try to figure out what we should do next."

COMPANY ON THE CUTTING EDGE

COMPANY ON THE CUTTING EDGE

AMERICA ONLINE, INC.

Each day, nearly 15 million people in the world hear the trademark voice intoning the familiar, "you've got mail." Millions more are likely to be introduced to it if recent events play out for America Online, Inc.

America Online, Inc. (AOL) is the world leader in online services, including electronic mail, software, computer support services, and Internet access. Headquartered in Dulles, Virginia, AOL employs nearly 9,000 people in 45 locations worldwide. It was founded in 1985 as Quantum Computer Services Corporation, but the idea really started earlier than that. In 1982, Stephen M. Case, a marketer for PepsiCo, Inc., became interested in electronic communications. Then, the Internet still was a place where only scholars and specialists felt comfortable. Case believed that online communications could be used and enjoyed by more people if using the Internet could be simplified.

In 1985, he founded Quantum and partnered with Commodore International, Ltd., a personal computer manufacturer. Case created an online service strictly for use by owners of Commodore computers. Dubbed Q-link, it was an archaic precursor to today's online offerings. The idea came at the right time.

Having sown the seeds of his idea, Case began a series of partnerships with strategic businesses. Early alliances included Tandy Corporation, a maker of IBM-clones, and Apple Computer. By 1989, Quantum introduced its America Online network, and by 1991 had changed the company name to America Online. AOL then began focusing on growth, concentrating mainly on services for IBM compatibles and Apple computers.

AOL has been called a niche-based product, and its early alliances with specific groups explains why. One of AOL's first joint ventures was with The Tribune Company, owner of the *Chicago Tribune* newspaper. Another was with SeniorNet, a senior citizens organization formed primarily to get senior citizens to use computers. Explained Case in 1992, "We see ourselves as a series of specialized magazines catering to specific interests."

This narrower view did not last long. Between 1991 and 1992, AOL's subscriber base grew by 50 percent. Between 1992 and 1993, its annual revenues had increased by 50 percent, and its subscriber base by nearly 80 percent. As AOL continued to expand, it began offering Internet access. Although the Internet still was considered the private playground of techies, AOL hoped to market software to make using it easier. The company aggressively

began to make its presence known through mailing campaigns, membership kits, and magazine inserts, easing the way for new subscribers to get online. Additionally, IBM, Apple, Tandy, and Compaq, among others, began incorporating AOL software into their products. It worked; revenues and users alike doubled that year and growth continued.

In 1998, AOL acquired Netscape Communications Corporation, forming a particularly vital alliance. AOL's Internet service has been criticized for being too simplistic and lacking in sophistication. As one media pundit put it, "AOL is the gateway through which the unwashed masses have flooded the Internet." AOL's marketing skills and popularity, coupled with Netscape's cutting-edge technology, make a formidable competitor for Microsoft, with ideas for information appliances (i.e., Internet set-top boxes) that will compete with Microsoft's WebTV.

AOL's growth continues today. A 1998 estimate claimed that 40 percent of the Internet traffic from U.S. homes came through AOL. Today, AOL's partnerships with news media, manufacturers (now including Dell Computer Corporation and U.S. Robotics), television networks, and many others ensure that it is poised to remain on top of the online services heap.

With all its success and growth, perhaps AOL's ultimate nod of recognition as a household catchword comes from Hollywood. In December 1998, a movie starring Tom Hanks and Meg Ryan was released. The title? *You've Got Mail*, what else?

SHELLY CASHMAN SERIES®

DISCOVERING COMPUTERS 2000

CHAPTER 1 **2** 3 4 5 6 7 8 9 10 11 12 13 14 **INDEX**

IN BRIEF www.scsite.com/dc2000/ch2/brief.htm

WEB INSTRUCTIONS: *To display this page from the Web, launch your browser and enter the URL, www.scsite.com/dc2000/ch2/brief.htm. Click the links for current and additional information. To listen to an audio version of this IN BRIEF, click the Audio button to the right of the title, IN BRIEF, at the top of the page. To play the audio, RealPlayer must be installed on your computer (download by clicking here).*

1. What Is Application Software?

Application software consists of programs designed to perform specific tasks for users. Application software can be grouped into four major categories: productivity software; graphics and multimedia software; home, personal, and educational software; and communications software.

2. What Is the Role of System Software?

System software consists of programs that control the operations of the computer and its devices. The operating system, one type of system software, coordinates the activities of hardware devices and allows application software to be run. The **user interface** is the portion of the operating system that controls how data or instructions are entered and how information and processing options are presented.

3. What Are the Elements of a Graphical User Interface?

A graphical user interface (GUI) combines text, graphics, and other visual clues to make software easier to use. The **desktop** is an onscreen work area with common graphical elements such as icons, buttons, menus, links, windows, and dialog boxes. An **icon** is a small image that represents a program, a document, or some other object. A **button** is a graphical element that causes a specific action to take place. A **menu** is a list of **commands** that make a computer program perform a specific action. A **window** is a rectangular area used to display a program, data, and/or information. A special window called a **dialog box** provides information, presents options, or requests a response.

4. How Is a Software Application Started?

An application can be started by clicking its program name in a menu or **submenu**. Clicking the program name instructs the operating system to start the application by transferring the program's instructions from a storage medium into memory.

5. What Are Key Features of Productivity Software?

Productivity software is designed to make people more effective and efficient while performing daily activities. **Word processing software** is used to **create**, **edit**, and **format** documents that consist primarily of text. **Spreadsheet software** organizes numeric data in a **worksheet** made up of rows and columns. **Database software** is used to create a **database**, an organized collection of data that can be accessed, retrieved, and used. **Presentation graphics software** creates documents called **presentations** that communicate ideas, messages, and other information to a group. A **personal information manager (PIM)** is software that includes an **appointment calendar**, **address book**, and **notepad** to help organize personal information. Project management software is used to plan, schedule, track, and analyze the progress of a project. **Accounting software** helps companies record and report their financial transactions.

IN BRIEF   www.scsite.com/dc2000/ch2/brief.htm

 6. What Are Key Features of Graphics and Multimedia Software?

Power users often use software that allows them to work with graphics and multimedia. **Computer-aided design (CAD) software** assists in creating engineering, architectural, and scientific designs. **Desktop publishing (DTP)** software is used in designing and producing sophisticated documents. **Paint software** is used to draw graphical images with various tools, while **image editing software** provides the capability of modifying existing images. **Video editing software** and **audio editing software** modify **video** and **audio** segments called clips. **Multimedia authoring software** creates electronic interactive presentations that can include text, images, video, audio, and animation. Web page authoring software is designed to create Web pages and to organize, manage, and maintain Web sites.

 7. What Are Key Features of Software for Home, Personal, and Educational Use?

Integrated software combines several productivity software applications into a single, easy-to-use package. **Personal finance software** is an accounting program that helps pay bills, balance a checkbook, track income and expenses, follow investments, and evaluate financial plans. **Legal software** assists in the creation of legal documents and provides legal advice. **Tax preparation software** guides users through the process of filing federal taxes. **Personal DTP software** helps develop conventional documents by asking questions, offering predefined layouts, and providing standard text. **Photo-editing software** is used to edit digital photographs. Clip art/image galleries are collections of clip art and photographs. **Home design/landscaping software** assists with design or remodeling. **Educational software** teaches a particular skill. **Reference software** provides information. **Personal computer entertainment software** includes programs designed to support a hobby or provide amusement.

 8. What Are Key Features of Software for Communications?

Groupware identifies any type of software that helps groups of people on a network collaborate on projects and share information, in addition to providing PIM functions. Electronic mail software is used to create, send, receive, forward, store, print, and delete **e-mail (electronic mail)**. A **Web browser** is a software application used to access and view Web pages.

 9. Why Is the World Wide Web Important?

The **World Wide Web (WWW)**, one of the services available on the Internet, consists of a worldwide collection of electronic documents called Web pages. The **Web** is a tremendous resource for products, services, and information.

 10. How Are Web Pages Connected?

A Web page can contain text, graphical images, sound, video, and connections to other Web pages. A **hyperlink**, or **link**, is a built-in connection to another related Web page. Links can be used to obtain information in a nonlinear way; that is, to make associations between topics instead of moving sequentially through topics. When a link is clicked, the Web page or the location within a Web page associated with it displays on the screen. Navigating using links is called **surfing the Web**.

CHAPTER **1** **2** **3** **4** **5** **6** **7** **8** **9** **10** **11** **12** **13** **14** **INDEX**

IN BRIEF www.scsite.com/dc2000/ch2/brief.htm

11. How Is a Web Browser Used?

When a Web browser is started, a connection to the Internet typically is established through an **Internet service provider (ISP)** or an **online service**. The browser retrieves and displays a **home page**, or starting page. Other Web pages can be viewed by clicking a link on the home page, typing the <u>Uniform Resource Locator (URL)</u> for a Web page, or using buttons on the browser toolbar.

12. How Do You Search for Information on the Web?

A **search engine** is a software program that finds Web sites, Web pages, and Internet files. To find a Web page(s), a word or phrase called **search text** or **keywords** is entered in the search engine text box. The <u>search engine</u> then displays a list of Web pages that contain the word or phrase entered.

KEY TERMS
www.scsite.com/dc2000/ch2/terms.htm

WEB INSTRUCTIONS: *To display this page from the Web, launch your browser and enter the URL,* www.scsite.com/dc2000/ch2/terms.htm. *Scroll through the list of terms. Click a term to display its definition and a picture. Click KEY TERMS on the left to redisplay the KEY TERMS page. Click the TO WEB button for current and additional information about the term from the Web. To see animations, Shockwave and the Flash Player must be installed on your computer (download by clicking* here).

accounting software (2.22)
address book (2.21, 2.34)
application (2.2)
appointment calendar (2.21)
audio (2.26)
audio editing software (2.26)
AutoSave (2.9)
bar charts (2.14)
border (2.10)
browser (2.34)
button (2.4)
cell (2.12)
charting (2.14)
clip art (2.10)
clip art/image gallery (2.31)
Clipboard (2.8)
clip gallery (2.19)
color library (2.25)
column charts (2.14)
commands (2.4)
computer-aided design (CAD) software (2.24)
context-sensitive (2.42)
context-sensitive menus (2.6)
creating (2.8)
criteria (2.17)
currency (2.16)
data type (2.16)
database (2.15)
database management system (DBMS) (2.15)
database software (2.15)
date (2.16)
desktop (2.4)
desktop publishing (DTP) software (2.24)
dialog box (2.6)
downloading (2.37)
editing (2.8)
educational software (2.32)
electronic mail software (2.33)
e-mail (electronic mail) (2.33)
e-mail address (2.33)
FAQ (2.43)
field (2.15)
field length (2.16)
file (2.10)
file name (2.10)
find (2.10)
font (2.9)
font size (2.9)
font style (2.9)
footer (2.11)
formatting (2.9)
formula (2.13)
function (2.13)
graphical user interface (GUI) (2.3)
groupware (2.32)

TO WEB

SUITE: Collection of individual application software packages sold as a single package. Two popular software suites are Microsoft Office 2000 and Lotus SmartSuite. (2.21)

header (2.11)
hit (2.40)
home design/landscaping software (2.31)
home page (2.37)
http:// (2.40)
hyperlink (2.16, 2.37)
hypertext transfer protocol (2.40)
icon (2.4)
illustration software (2.25)
image editing software (2.25)
import (2.10)
integrated software (2.28)
Internet service provider (ISP) (2.36)
keywords (2.40)
label (2.12)
legal software (2.29)
line charts (2.14)
link (2.16, 2.37)
macro (2.13)
mailbox (2.33)
mail server (2.33)
margins (2.10)
memo (2.16)
menu (2.4)
multimedia authoring software (2.26)
notepad (2.21)
numeric (2.16)
online Help (2.42)
online service (2.36)
operating system (2.3)
page layout (2.24)
paint software (2.25)
personal computer entertainment software (2.32)
personal DTP software (2.30)

personal finance software (2.28)
personal information manager (PIM) (2.21)
photo-editing software (2.30)
pie charts (2.15)
point (2.9)
presentation graphics software (2.18)
printing (2.10)
productivity software (2.7)
project management software (2.22)
query (2.17)
record (2.15)
reference software (2.32)
replace (2.10)
saving (2.9)
scrolling (2.10)
search (2.10)
search engine (2.40)
search text (2.40)
shortcut menus (2.6)
signature (2.34)
software application (2.2)
software package (2.2)
sort (2.17)
spelling checker (2.10)
spreadsheet software (2.12)
structure (2.16)
submenu (2.4)
suite (2.21)
surfing the Web (2.38)
system software (2.2)
tax preparation software (2.29)
text (2.16)
title bar (2.4)
tutorials (2.43)
Uniform Resource Locator (URL) (2.39)
user-ID (2.34)
user interface (2.3)
user name (2.34)
validation (2.17)
value (2.13)
video (2.26)
video editing software (2.26)
Web (2.35)
Web browser (2.34)
Web page (2.35)
Web page authoring software (2.27)
Web server (2.40)
Web site (2.35)
what-if analysis (2.14)
window (2.4)
Windows (2.3)
wizard (2.43)
word processing software (2.8)
wordwrap (2.10)
worksheet (2.12)
World Wide Web (WWW) (2.35)

Student Exercises
WEB INFO
IN BRIEF
KEY TERMS
AT THE MOVIES
CHECKPOINT
AT ISSUE
CYBERCLASS
HANDS ON
NET STUFF
Special Features
TIMELINE 2000
GUIDE TO WWW SITES
MAKING A CHIP
BUYER'S GUIDE 2000
CAREERS 2000
TRENDS 2000
CHAT
INTERACTIVE LABS
NEWS
HOME

SHELLY CASHMAN SERIES
DISCOVERING COMPUTERS 2000

SHELLY CASHMAN SERIES®

DISCOVERING COMPUTERS 2000

CHAPTER 1 2 3 4 5 6 7 8 9 10 11 12 13 14 INDEX

AT THE MOVIES   www.scsite.com/dc2000/ch2/movies.htm

WELCOME to VIDEO CLIPS from CNN

WEB INSTRUCTIONS: *To display this page from the Web, launch your browser and enter the URL,* www.scsite.com/dc2000/ch2/movies.htm. *Click a picture to view a video. After watching the video, close the video window and then complete the exercise by answering the questions about the video. To view the videos, RealPlayer must be installed on your computer (download by clicking* here*).*

1 Internet Spam

Business advertisements take many forms. One form of advertisement and Internet communication that has been difficult for the Federal Trade Commission to regulate and Congress to legislate against is spam. What is spam? Have you ever received spam? Why would a company prefer e-mail advertisements to hard copy? If one form of advertisement is regulated, should all forms be regulated? What is the difference between unsolicited e-mail and junk mail? How might a U.S. Constitutional amendment protect the right to spam? What recourse do you have against spam?

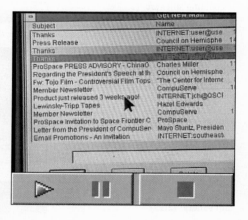

2 History Software

Have any of your history classes used software such as shown in the video clip? Do you think seeing film of speeches makes the person and event you are studying more real? How much interactivity do you think is necessary in software that teaches a subject? Would you rather just view the software or do you want to interact with it? How can you use software such as described in the video to research subject matter and prepare a report? What would be the best way to use the software shown in the video for your history assignments? In what ways could you use integrated application software suites, such as Microsoft Office or Corel PerfectSuite, with history software to enhance your reports? How would you reference the multimedia CD in a footnote or endnote?

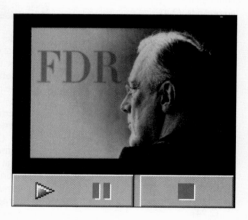

3 WebTV

What is WebTV? Is it expensive? How can users interact online by using WebTV? Is it compatible with Windows 98? What is the relationship between the Net Channel and WebTV? Explain how WebTV expands Microsoft's presence into the consumer electronics arena? Would you want to use WebTV to access the Internet?

CHAPTER 1 **2** 3 4 5 6 7 8 9 10 11 12 13 14 INDEX

CHECKPOINT   www.scsite.com/dc2000/ch2/check.htm

WEB INSTRUCTIONS: *To display this page from the Web, launch your browser and enter the URL, www.scsite.com/dc2000/ch2/check.htm. Click the links for current and additional information. To experience the animation and interactivity, Shockwave and the Flash Player must be installed on your computer (download by clicking here).*

Label the Figure

Instructions: *Identify the indicated elements in the Windows 98 graphical user interface.*

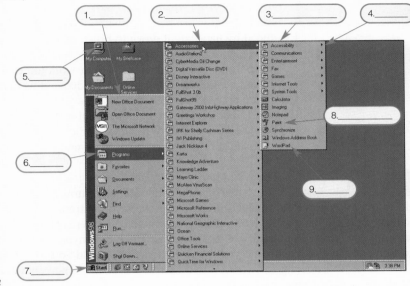

Matching

Instructions: *Match each application software feature from the column on the left with the best description from the column on the right.*

_____ 1. wordwrap

_____ 2. what-if analysis

_____ 3. validation

_____ 4. clip gallery

_____ 5. query

a. Database feature that compares data to a set of defined rules or values to determine if it is acceptable.

b. Presentation graphics feature consisting of images, pictures, and clips that can be incorporated into slides.

c. Word processing feature used to locate all occurrences of a particular character, word, or phrase.

d. Spreadsheet feature that displays data relationships in a graphical, rather than numerical, form.

e. Word processing feature that allows typing continually without pressing the ENTER key at the end of each line.

f. Database feature that is a specific set of instructions for retrieving data.

g. Spreadsheet feature in which certain values are altered to reveal the effects of those changes.

Short Answer

Instructions: *Write a brief answer to each of the following questions.*

1. How are creating, editing, and formatting a word processing document different? _____ What is the Clipboard and during which activity is it usually used? _____

2. What are the major advantages of a software suite? _____ How is a software suite different from integrated software? _____

3. Why do professional designers and graphic artists use DTP software instead of word processing packages? _____ What is a color library? _____

4. What is an Internet e-mail address? _____ What two parts of an e-mail address are separated by the at (@) sign? _____

5. What is online Help? _____ How do FAQs, wizards, and tutorials help software users? _____

SHELLY
CASHMAN
SERIES

DISCOVERING
COMPUTERS
2000

Student Exercises
WEB INFO
IN BRIEF
KEY TERMS
AT THE MOVIES
CHECKPOINT
AT ISSUE
CYBERCLASS
HANDS ON
NET STUFF
Special Features
TIMELINE 2000
GUIDE TO WWW SITES
MAKING A CHIP
BUYER'S GUIDE 2000
CAREERS 2000
TRENDS 2000
CHAT
INTERACTIVE LABS
NEWS
HOME

CHAPTER 1 2 3 4 5 6 7 8 9 10 11 12 13 14 INDEX

AT ISSUE
www.scsite.com/dc2000/ch2/issue.htm

WEB INSTRUCTIONS: *To display this page from the Web, launch your browser and enter the URL,* www.scsite.com/dc2000/ch2/issue.htm. *Click the links for current and additional information.*

ONE

Today, many commercial artists, creators of cartoons, book covers, and billboards use paint software. Paint programs authentically mimic art produced by hand, right down to brush strokes and surface textures. Artists can import graphic files and effortlessly change a work in progress. Some complain that computerization has made their work too easy. Knowing illustrations readily can be altered, clients are more demanding and less forgiving. Even worse, digital art has been denounced as having a bland quality that reflects little effort, feeling, or imagination. What is the future of paint software? Will it ever be widely accepted? Why or why not? How might paint software change commercial art? Will it ever be used by noncommercial artists? Why or why not?

TWO

Trained individuals have used polygraphs, or lie detectors, for years. Now, an application called Truster turns a PC into a polygraph. When a subject speaks into a microphone, a Truster algorithm measures vocal stress and reports relative veracity (Truth, Inaccurate, Slightly Inaccurate, Not Sure, False) on the computer screen. Sales have been brisk, much to some people's dismay. Polygraph use legally is restricted, but anyone can use Truster, even an instructor trying to find out if the dog really ate your homework. When would you be comfortable, and uncomfortable, with the use of lie-detecting software? Why? Truster claims an 85 percent accuracy rate. As accuracy rates improve, will you be more or less accepting of lie-detecting software? Why?

THREE

Industry experts claim more than 80 percent of entertainment and educational software is purchased by males. As computer literacy becomes increasingly important to career advancement, this figure indicates an added obstacle for females entering the workplace. Analysts insist much of the disparity in computer use is a result of the nature of entertainment and educational software. Men like the shoot-'em-up, win-lose character of most entertainment software. Women, on the other hand, prefer exploratory, less competitive software. Unless software adjusts, analysts predict female interest in using computers for entertainment and education will continue to wane. Are the analysts right? Do males and females favor different types of software? If so, should software developers adapt their products? Why or why not? Is it important to modify educational/entertainment software to meet the interests of different groups? Why?

FOUR

Software developed for elementary school children, kindergartners, and even preschoolers has won the praise of educators and child psychologists. Yet, controversy has erupted about "how young is too young" over Knowledge Adventure's® JumpStart Baby™ program, which is aimed at children nine- to twenty-four-months old. According to developers, JumpStart Baby™ makes even young children comfortable with computers. The software is tailored to tots and, supporters insist, certainly is more beneficial than an equal amount of time spent watching television. Knowledge Adventure® advocates that this software is designed as "lap-ware," meaning it is intended to be used by baby and parent together, which can serve as a springboard to stimulating activities rich in communication and social interaction during the critical developmental years. Critics feel, however, that digital blocks are no substitute for the real thing. Children need to experience the real world, not a cyber representation. When should children be introduced to computers? Why? How can parents ensure that a child's computer experience is worthwhile?

FIVE

Educational software has been developed for a wide range of subjects, including science, mathematics, grammar, history, foreign languages, even instrumental music. Educational software allows flexible scheduling, shows infinite patience, lets students learn at their own pace, and is available at reasonable cost. Unlike human instructors, however, educational software usually cannot recognize singular problems, presents material in a limited number of ways, provides limited feedback, and fails to address individual goals. Considering the strengths and weaknesses of educational software, for what subjects is it most suited? Why? For what subjects is it least appropriate? Why? If you could learn to play the guitar from either educational software or a human instructor, which would you choose? Why?

CYBERCLASS   www.scsite.com/dc2000/ch2/class.htm

WEB INSTRUCTIONS: *To display this page from the Web, launch your browser and enter the URL, www.scsite.com/dc2000/ch2/class.htm. To start Level I CyberClass, click a Level I link on this page or enter the URL, www.cyber-class.com. Click the Student button, click* Discovering Computers 2000 *in the list of titles, and then click the Enter a site button. To start Level II or III CyberClass (available only to those purchasers of a CyberClass floppy disk), place your CyberClass floppy disk in drive A, click Start on the taskbar, click Run on the Start menu, type* a:connect *in the Open text box, click the OK button, click the Enter CyberClass button, and then follow the instructions.*

I II III LEVEL **1. Flash Cards** Click Flash Cards on the Main Menu of the CyberClass web page. Click the plus sign before the Chapter 2 title. Click any subject you wish and answer all the cards in that section. If you have less than 80% correct, continue to answer cards in other sections until you have more than 80% correct. All users: Answer as many more flash cards as you desire. Close the Electronic Flash Card window and the Flash Cards window by clicking the Close button in each window.

I II III LEVEL **2. Practice Test** Click Testing on the Main Menu of the CyberClass web page. Click the Select a book box arrow and then click Discovering Computers 2000. Click the Select a Chapter test to take box arrow and then click the Chapter 2 title in the list. Click the Take Test button. If necessary, maximize the window. Take the practice test and then click the Submit Test button. Click the Display Study Guide button. Review the Study Guide. Scroll down and click the Return To CyberClass button. Click the Yes button to close the Study Guide window. If your score was less than 90%, click the Take another Test button to take another practice test. Continue taking tests until your score is greater than 90%. Then, click the Done button.

I II III LEVEL **3. Web Guide** Click Web Guide on the Main Menu of the CyberClass web page. When the Guide to World Wide Web Sites page displays, click Science. Go to the Exploratorium and explore. When you are finished, close the window and then prepare a brief report on what you found and why you would or would not return to the Exploratorium.

I II III LEVEL **4. Company Briefs** Click Company Briefs on the Main Menu of the CyberClass web page. Click a corporation name to display a case study. Read the case study. Write a brief report on how computers are used in this company.

II III LEVEL **5. CyberChallenge** Click CyberChallenge on the Main Menu of the CyberClass web page. Click the Select a book box arrow and then click Discovering Computers 2000. Click the Select a board to play box arrow and then click Chapter 2 in the list. Click the Play CyberChallenge button. Maximize the CyberChallenge window. Play CyberChallenge until you have answered all the 40 point and 50 point questions correctly. Close the CyberChallenge window.

II III LEVEL **6. Text Chat** Click Text Chat on the Main Menu of the CyberClass web page. If you have not created a chat account, follow the instructions on the screen to do so. If your instructor has assigned office hours for chat, ask any questions you wish. If not, see if anyone else is in the chat room and determine if you can agree on a use of chat for the classroom.

II III LEVEL **7. Send Messages and View Messages** Click Send Messages on the Main Menu of the CyberClass web page. Send a message to yourself by clicking the box beside your name in the Members section of the screen (a check mark will display in the box), entering a subject and the message itself, and then clicking the Send Message button. After sending the message, click View Messages on the Main Menu of the CyberClass web page and ensure the message was sent properly.

HANDS ON

www.scsite.com/dc2000/ch2/hands.htm

Student Exercises
WEB INFO
IN BRIEF
KEY TERMS
AT THE MOVIES
CHECKPOINT
AT ISSUE
CYBERCLASS
HANDS ON
NET STUFF
Special Features
TIMELINE 2000
GUIDE TO WWW SITES
MAKING A CHIP
BUYER'S GUIDE 2000
CAREERS 2000
TRENDS 2000
CHAT
INTERACTIVE LABS
NEWS
HOME

WEB INSTRUCTIONS: *To display this page from the Web, launch your browser and enter the URL,*
www.scsite.com/dc2000/ch2/hands.htm. Click the links for current and additional information.

One — Working with Application Programs

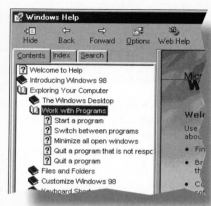

This exercise uses Windows 98 procedures.
Windows is a *multitasking operating system,* meaning you can work
on two or more applications that reside in memory at the same time.
To find out how to work with multiple application programs, click
the Start button on the taskbar, and then click Help on the Start
menu. Click the Contents tab. Click the Exploring Your Computer
book. Click the Work with Programs book. Click an appropriate
topic to answer each of the following questions:

- How do you start a program?
- How do you switch between programs?
- How do you quit a program that is not responding?
- How do you quit a program?

Close the Windows Help window.

Two — Creating a Word Processing Document

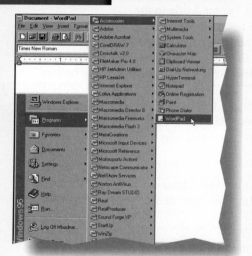

WordPad is a simple word processor included with the Windows operating system.
To create a document with WordPad, click the Start button on the taskbar, point to
Programs on the Start menu, point to Accessories on the Programs submenu, and
then click WordPad on the Accessories submenu. If necessary, when the WordPad
window displays, click its Maximize button. Click View on the menu bar. If a
check mark does not display before Toolbar, click it. Type a complete answer to
one of the AT ISSUE questions posed in this chapter or in Chapter 1. Your answer
should be at least two paragraphs long. Press the TAB key to indent the first line of
each paragraph and the ENTER key to begin a new paragraph. To correct errors,
press the BACKSPACE key to erase to the left of the insertion point and press the
DELETE key to erase to the right. To insert text, move the I-beam mouse pointer to
where the text should be inserted, click, and then begin typing. At the end of your
document, press the ENTER key twice and then type your name. When your document is complete, save it by inserting a floppy disk into drive A, clicking the Save
button on the toolbar, typing a:\h2-2 in the File name text box in the Save As
dialog box, and then clicking the Save button. Click the Print button on the toolbar
to print your document. Close WordPad.

Three — Using WordPad s Help

This exercise uses Windows 98 procedures. Open WordPad as described in HANDS ON 2 above.
Click Help on WordPad s menu bar and then click Help Topics. When the Help Topics, WordPad Help window displays, click
the Index tab. Type saving documents in the text box and then press the ENTER key. Click To save changes to a document in
the Topics Found window and then click the Display button. How can you save changes to a document? How can you save an
existing document with a new name? Close the Help window and WordPad.

Four — Productivity Software Products

What productivity software packages are on your computer? Click the Start button on the taskbar and
point to Programs on the Start menu. Scan the Programs submenu (if necessary, point to the arrow at the top or bottom of the
submenu to move the submenu up or down) for the names of popular productivity packages. Write down the package name
and the type of software application (see the chart on page 2.7 for help). When you are finished, click an empty area of the
desktop.

NET STUFF   www.scsite.com/dc2000/ch2/net.htm

WEB INSTRUCTIONS: *To display this page from the Web, launch your browser and enter the URL, www.scsite.com/dc2000/ch2/net.htm. To use the Word Processing lab or the Spreadsheet lab from the Web, Shockwave and Flash Player must be installed on your computer (download by clicking here).*

WORD PROCESSING LAB

1. Shelly Cashman Series Word Processing Lab

Follow the instructions in NET STUFF 1 on page 1.46 to start and use the Word Processing lab. If you are running from the Web, enter the URL, www.scsite.com/sclabs/menu.htm; or display this NET STUFF page (see instructions at the top of this page) and then click the WORD PROCESSING LAB button.

SPREADSHEET LAB

2. Shelly Cashman Series Spreadsheet Lab

Follow the instructions in NET STUFF 1 on page 1.46 to start and use the Working with Spreadsheets lab. If you are running from the Web, enter the URL, www.scsite.com/sclabs/menu.htm; or display the NET STUFF page (see instructions at the top of this page) and then click the SPREADSHEET LAB button.

SET UP E-MAIL

3. Setting Up an E-Mail Account

The fastest growing software application may be electronic mail (e-mail). One free e-mail service reports 30 million current subscribers with an additional 80,000 joining every day. To set up a free e-mail account, click the SET UP E-MAIL button. Follow the procedures to establish an e-mail account. When you are finished, send yourself an e-mail.

IN THE NEWS

4. In the News

It is a computer user's nightmare – a button is clicked accidentally or a key is pressed unintentionally and an important message, document, or presentation is deleted. Happily, new software called Save Butt can restore a sound night's sleep. Save Butt continuously copies open files to the hard drive. Not only are files kept safe, but you always can return to earlier versions of a project. Click the IN THE NEWS button and read a news article about a new software program. Who is introducing the program? What is the program called? What does it do? Who will benefit from using this software? Why? Where can the software be obtained? Would you be interested in this software? Why or why not?

vebutt.com/Reviews/Save_Reviews.cfm

PGSoft in the News
Press Releases • Product Reviews

Save Butt

Newsweek

December 14, 1998
"You know the sickening feeling you get in your stomach when you hit the wrong button and accidentally delete something important? Well, PGSoft can help avert that sinking sensation with its

WEB CHAT

5. Web Chat

A noted university psychology professor is advocating an Intelligent Essay Assessor, a software program that grades written essays. To establish a foundation, the program is given examples of good and bad essays that have been manually graded, and then is supplied with selections from experts. With this background, the Intelligent Essay Assessor understands student essays by comparing word usage to patterns in the samples. An essay that relates the same knowledge as that in the admirable examples receives a high score. In what subject areas, or at what levels, could an Intelligent Essay Assessor be used effectively? Why? What might be some drawbacks of the software? How could these drawbacks be addressed? Would you be willing to have your work evaluated by a software program? Why or why not? Click the WEB CHAT button to enter a Web Chat discussion related to this topic.

gUiDE tO wOrLD wIDe wEB sITeS

The World Wide Web is an exciting and highly dynamic medium. Every day, new Web sites are added, existing ones are changed, and still others cease to exist. Because of this, you may find that a URL listed here has changed or no longer is valid. In order to offer the most up-to-date information available, the *Discovering Computers 2000* Web site is continually checked and updated.

WEB INSTRUCTIONS: *To gain World Wide Web access to the most current version of the sites included in this special feature, launch your browser and enter the URL, www.scsite.com/dc2000/ch2/websites.htm.*

Categories

Art	History
Business and Finance	Humor
Careers and Employment	Internet
Computers and Computing	Museums
Education	News Sources
Entertainment	Reference
Environment	Science
Government and Politics	Shopping
Health and Medicine	Sports
	Travel
	Unclassified
	Weather

THE ANDY WARHOL MUSEUM

MUSEUM TOUR

The Underground Cafe

The Underground Cafe at the Andy Warhol Museum, serves light meals - soups, salads, sandwiches, and pastries. Also available are espresso and cappuccino, mineral water and soft drinks, including Coca-Cola in the original glass bottles. It is located in the Underground at the Museum.

The Underground Cafe is open to the public without an admission fee during museum hours. Please call 412.237.8300 for more information.

abn All Business Network

Welcome to the All Business Network - the destination for business on the Web!

Checkout This Great Online Music Catalog

Visit: The Complete Business Resource   GO!

plus Keyword Search, Headline News, The Job Bank, Online Databases, Business Services, Online Basics, Business Park

see why SMALL BUSINESS NEWS chose ABN as one of the Top 5 business sites!

JobOptions

Search Employers Post Resumes Job Alert Career Tools

Job Search

Post Your Resume
Our fast, easy-to-use resume builder gives you professional results that look great online, via email, and on the printed page.

Job Alert
Just sign up, and we'll search our jobs database and email you new openings that match your specifications.

YAHOO! FINANCE   Home - Yahoo! - Help -

Wed Oct 14 10:45am ET - U.S. Markets close in 5 hours 15 minutes.

Dow	7955.39 +17.25 (+0.22%)	Nasdaq	1523.62 +14.17 (+0.94%)	S&P 500	1000.16 +5.36
NYSE Volume	191,485,000	Nasdaq Volume	184,412,000	30-Yr Bond	5.043%

Microsoft **HomeAdvisor**

CollegeNET

About CollegeNET College Search CollegeBOT Crawler Scholarships Financial Aid Apply

the **computer museum**

HISTORY GALLERIES RESOURCES INFO DESK STORE

Learn about computers and have fun at the same time!

PLAY INTERACTIVE EXHIBITS
COMPUTER HISTORY RESOURCES
DOWNLOAD EDUCATIONAL MATERIALS

The Virtual FishTank!

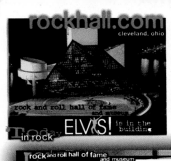

CATEGORY/SITE NAME	LOCATION	COMMENT
Art		
World Wide Arts Resources	wwar.com	Links to many art sites
Fine Art Forum	www.msstate.edu/Fineart_Online/home.html	Art and technology news
Leonardo da Vinci	sunsite.unc.edu/wm/paint/auth/vinci	Works of the famous Italian artist and thinker
The Andy Warhol Museum	www.clpgh.org/warhol	Famous American pop artist
The WebMuseum	mistral.culture.fr/louvre/louvrea.htm	Web version of Louvre Museum, Paris
World Art Treasures	sgwww.epfl.ch/BERGER	100,000 slides organized by civilization
Business and Finance		
FinanCenter, Inc.	www.financenter.com	Personal finance information
FINWEB All Business Network	www.all-biz.com	Links to Web business information
PC Quote	www.pcquote.com	Free delayed stock quotes
Yahoo! Finance	quote.yahoo.com	Free delayed stock quotes
Stock Research Group	www.stockgroup.com	Investment information
The Wall Street Journal	interactive.wsj.com	Financial news page
Careers and Employment		
CareerMagazine	www.careermag.com	Career articles and information
CareerMosaic®	www.careermosaic.com	Jobs from around the world
E-Span Job Options	www.joboptions.com	Searchable job database
CareerPath	www.careerpath.com	Job listings from U.S. newspapers
Computers and Computing		
Computer companies	Insert name or initials of most computer companies between www. and .com to find their Web site. Examples: www.ibm.com, www.microsoft.com, www.dell.com.	
MIT Media Lab	www.media.mit.edu	Information on computer trends
The Computer Museum	www.net.org	Exhibits and history of computing
Virtual Computer Library	www.utexas.edu/computer/vcl	Information on computers and computing
The Virtual Museum of Computing (VMoC)	www.comlab.ox.ac.uk/archive/other/ museums/computing.html	History of computing and online computer based exhibits
Education		
CollegeNET	www.collegenet.com	Searchable database of more than 2,000 colleges and universities
EdLinks	webpages.marshall.edu/~jmullens/ edlinks.html	Links to many educational sites
The Open University	www.open.ac.uk	Independent study courses from U.K.
Entertainment		
Classics World	www.bmgclassics.com/classics/index.html	Classical music information
Internet Underground Music Archive	www.iuma.com	Underground Music Database
Mr. Showbiz	www.mrshowbiz.com	Information on latest films
Music Boulevard	www.musicblvd.com	Search for and buy all types of music
Playbill On-Line	www.playbill.com	Theater news
Rock & Roll Hall of Fame	www.rockhall.com	Cleveland museum site

For an updated list: www.scsite.com/dc2000/ch2/websites.htm

CATEGORY/SITE NAME	LOCATION	COMMENT
Environment		
EnviroLink Network	www.envirolink.org	Environmental information
Greenpeace	www.greenpeace.org	Environmental activism
U.S. Environmental Protection Agency (EPA)	www.epa.gov	U.S. government environmental news
Government and Politics		
Canada Info	www.clo.com/~canadainfo/canada.html	List of Canadian Web sites
CIA	www.odci.gov/cia	Political and economic information on countries
FedWorld	www.fedworld.gov	Links to U.S. government sites
The Library of Congress	www.loc.gov	Variety of U.S. government information
The White House	www.whitehouse.gov	Take tour and learn about occupants
United Nations	www.un.org	Latest UN projects and information
U.S. Census Bureau	www.census.gov	Population and other statistics
Health and Medicine		
Centers for Disease Control and Prevention (CDC)	www.cdc.gov	How to prevent and control disease
CODI	codi.buffalo.edu	Resource for disability products and services
The Interactive Patient	medicus.marshall.edu/medicus.htm	Simulates visit to doctor
Women's Medical Health Page	www.cbull.com/health.htm	Articles and links to other sites

For an updated list: www.scsite.com/dc2000/ch2/websites.htm

CATEGORY/SITE NAME	LOCATION	COMMENT
History		
American Memory	rs6.loc.gov/amhome.html	American history
Historical Text Archive	www.msstate.edu/Archives/History/ USA/usa.html	U.S. documents, photos, and database
World History Archives	www.hartford-hwp.com/archives/index.html	Links to history sites
Virtual Library History	history.cc.ukans.edu/history/	Organized links to history sites
Humor		
Calvin & Hobbes Gallery	www.calvinandhobbes.com	Comic strip gallery
Comedy Central Online	www.comcentral.com	From comedy TV network
Late Show Top 10 Archive	marketing.cbs.com/lateshow/topten	David Letterman Top 10 lists
The Dilbert Zone	www.unitedmedia.com/comics/dilbert	Humorous insights about working
Internet		
Beginners Central Internet	northernwebs.com/bc	Beginners guide to the Internet
Internet Glossary	www.matisse.net/files/glossary.html	Definitions of Internet terms
WWW Frequently Asked Questions	www.boutell.com/faq/oldfaq/index.html	Common Web questions and answers

For an updated list: www.scsite.com/dc2000/ch2/websites.htm

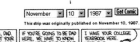

CATEGORY/SITE NAME	LOCATION	COMMENT
Museums		
The Smithsonian	www.si.edu	Information and links to Smithsonian museums
University of California Museum of Paleontology	www.ucmp.berkeley.edu	Great information on dinosaurs and other exhibits
U.S. Holocaust Memorial Museum	www.ushmm.org	Dedicated to World War II victims
News Sources		
C/NET	www.cnet.com	Technology news
CNN Interactive	www.cnn.com	CNN all-news network
Pathfinder	www.pathfinder.com	Excerpts from Time-Warner magazines
The Electronic Newsstand	www.enews.com	Articles from worldwide publications
USA TODAY	www.usatoday.com	Latest U.S. and international news
Wired News	www.wired.com	*Wired* magazine online and HotWired Network
Reference		
Bartlett's Quotations	www.columbia.edu/acis/bartleby/bartlett	Organized, searchable database of famous quotes
Dictionary Library	math-www.uni-paderborn.de/ HTML/Dictionaries.html	Links to many types of dictionaries
Internet Public Library	www.ipl.org	Literature and reference works
The New York Public Library	www.nypl.org	Extensive reference and research material
Science		
American Institute of Physics	www.aip.org	Physics research information
Exploratorium	www.exploratorium.edu	Interactive science exhibits
Internet Chemistry Index	www.chemie.de/	List of chemistry information sites
The NASA Homepage	www.nasa.gov	Information on U.S. space program
The Nine Planets	seds.lpl.arizona.edu/nineplanets/ nineplanets/	Tour the solar system

For an updated list: www.scsite.com/dc2000/ch2/websites.htm

CATEGORY/SITE NAME	LOCATION	COMMENT
Shopping		
Amazon.com	www.amazon.com	Books and gifts
BizWeb	www.bizweb.com	Search for products from more than 1,000 companies
CommerceNet	www.commerce.net	Index of products and services
Consumer World	www.consumerworld.org	Consumer information
Internet Bookshop	www.bookshop.co.uk	780,000 titles on more than 2,000 subjects
Internet Shopping Network	www.internet.net	Specialty stores, hot deals, computer products
The Internet Mall™	www.internet-mall.com	Comprehensive list of Web businesses
Sports		
ESPNET SportsZone	ESPN.SportsZone.com	Latest sports news
NBA Basketball	www.nba.com	Information and links to team sites
NFL Football	www.nfl.com	Information and links to team sites
Sports Illustrated	www.CNNSI.com	Leading sports magazine
Travel		
InfoHub WWW Travel Guide	www.infohub.com	Worldwide travel information
Excite City.Net	www.city.net	Guide to world cities
Lonely Planet Travel Guides	www.lonelyplanet.com	Budget travel guides and stories
Microsoft Expedia	expedia.msn.com	Complete travel resource
Travelocity℠	www.travelocity.com	Online travel agency
TravelWeb℠	www.travelweb.com	Places to stay
Unclassified		
Cool Site of the Day	cool.infi.net	Different site each day
Cupid's Network™	www.cupidnet.com	Links to dating resources
Pizza Hut	www.pizzahut.com	Order pizza online (limited areas)
Weather		
INTELLiCAST Guides	www.intellicast.com	International weather and skiing information
The Weather Channel	www.weather.com	National and local forecasts

For an updated list: www.scsite.com/dc2000/ch2/websites.htm

CHAPTER 3

THE COMPONENTS IN THE SYSTEM UNIT

OBJECTIVES

After completing this chapter, you will be able to:

▶ Identify the components in the system unit and explain their functions

▶ Explain how the CPU uses the four steps of a machine cycle to process data

▶ Compare and contrast various microprocessors on the market today

▶ Define a bit and describe how a series of bits is used to represent data

▶ Differentiate between the various types of memory

▶ Describe the types of expansion slots and expansion cards in the system unit

▶ Explain the difference between a serial and a parallel port

▶ Describe how buses contribute to a computer's processing speed

At some point during your professional career or personal endeavors, you probably will be involved in the decision to purchase a new computer or upgrade an existing computer. Thus, it is important that you understand the purpose of the components of a computer. As discussed in Chapter 1, a computer includes devices used for input, processing, output, storage, and communications. Many of these components are housed together in the system unit.

Chapter 3 presents the components in the system unit, describes how memory stores data, instructions, and information, and discusses the sequence of operations that occur when a computer executes an instruction. The chapter also includes a comparison of various microprocessors on the market today.

THE SYSTEM UNIT

The **system unit** is a box-like case that houses the electronic components of the computer that are used to process data. The system unit is made of metal or plastic and is designed to protect the electronic components from damage. On a desktop personal computer, the electronic components and most storage devices reside inside the system unit. Other devices, such as a keyboard, mouse, monitor, and printer, normally are located outside the system unit. A laptop computer houses almost all of its electronic components in the system unit (Figure 3-1).

At some point, you might find it necessary to open the system unit on a personal computer and replace or install a new component. For this reason, it is important that you have some familiarity with the inside of the system unit.

Figure 3-2 identifies some of the components inside a system unit, including the processor, memory module, several expansion cards, ports, and connectors. The processor, short for central processing unit, is the device that interprets and carries out the basic instructions that operate a computer. A memory module is a package that houses the memory that temporarily holds data and instructions while they are being processed by the CPU.

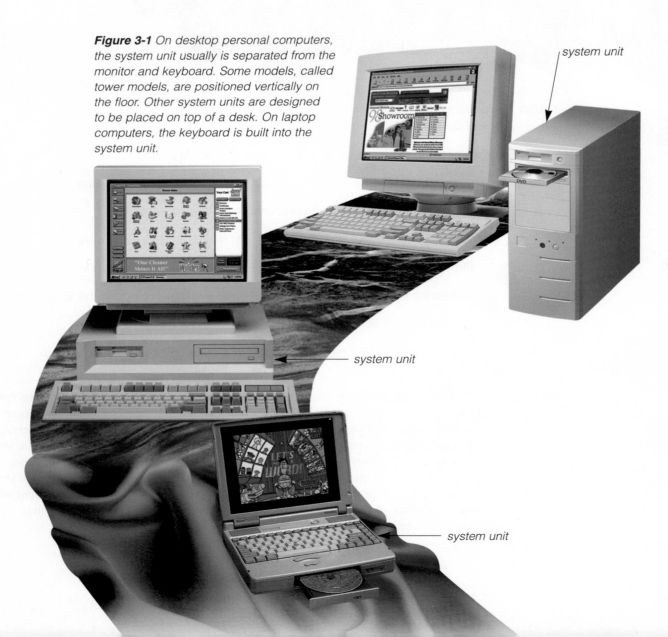

Figure 3-1 *On desktop personal computers, the system unit usually is separated from the monitor and keyboard. Some models, called tower models, are positioned vertically on the floor. Other system units are designed to be placed on top of a desk. On laptop computers, the keyboard is built into the system unit.*

system unit

system unit

system unit

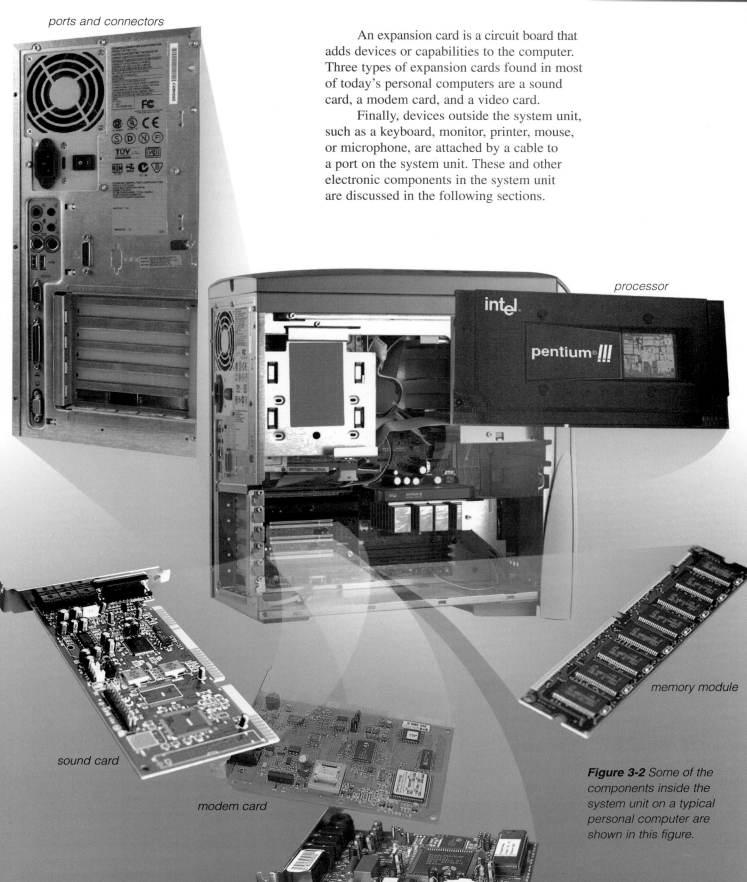

ports and connectors

An expansion card is a circuit board that adds devices or capabilities to the computer. Three types of expansion cards found in most of today's personal computers are a sound card, a modem card, and a video card.

Finally, devices outside the system unit, such as a keyboard, monitor, printer, mouse, or microphone, are attached by a cable to a port on the system unit. These and other electronic components in the system unit are discussed in the following sections.

processor

sound card

modem card

video card

memory module

Figure 3-2 Some of the components inside the system unit on a typical personal computer are shown in this figure.

The Motherboard

Many of the electronic components in the system unit reside on a circuit board called the **motherboard** or **system board**. Figure 3-3 shows a photograph of a personal computer motherboard and identifies some of its components, including several different types of chips.

CHIPS A **chip** is a small piece of semi-conducting material, usually no bigger than one-half-inch square, on which one or more integrated circuits are etched (Figure 3-4). An **integrated circuit (IC)** is a microscopic pathway capable of carrying electrical current. Each integrated circuit can contain millions of elements such as **transistors**, which act as electronic switches, or gates, that open or close the circuit for electronic signals. The motherboard in the system unit contains many different types of chips. Of these, one of the more important is the central processing unit (CPU).

clock chip

connectors for keyboard, mouse, monitor, and printer

PCI expansion slots

ISA expansion slots

memory slots

memory module (RAM chips)

heat sink

CPU chip

Figure 3-3 The motherboard in a personal computer contains many chips and other electronic components.

single edge contact (SEC) cartridge

pin grid array (PGA) package

dual inline package (DIP)

Figure 3-4 Chips are packaged so they can be connected to a circuit board. DIP and PGA packages contain thin metal feet, called pins, which attach the package to the circuit board. A dual inline package (DIP) consists of two parallel rows of downward-pointing pins. A pin grid array (PGA) package holds a larger number of pins because the pins are mounted on the bottom surface of the package. A single edge contact (SEC) cartridge, does not use pins; instead the cartridge connects to the motherboard on one of its edges.

CENTRAL PROCESSING UNIT

The **central processing unit (CPU)** interprets and carries out the basic instructions that operate a computer. The CPU, also referred to as the **processor**, significantly impacts overall computing power and manages most of a computer's operations. That is, most of the devices connected to the computer communicate with the CPU in order to carry out a task (Figure 3-5). The CPU contains the control unit and the arithmetic/logic unit. These two components work together to perform the processing operations.

On larger computers, such as mainframes and supercomputers, the various functions performed by the CPU are spread across many separate chips and sometimes multiple circuit boards. On a personal computer, the CPU usually is contained on a single chip and sometimes is called a **microprocessor** (Figure 3-6). In addition to the control unit and the arithmetic/logic unit, a microprocessor usually contains the registers and system clock. Each of these microprocessor components is discussed in the following sections.

WEB INFO
WEB INFO
For more information on microprocessors, visit the Discovering Computers 2000 Chapter 3 WEB INFO page (www.scsite.com/dc2000/ch3/webinfo.htm) and click Microprocessors.

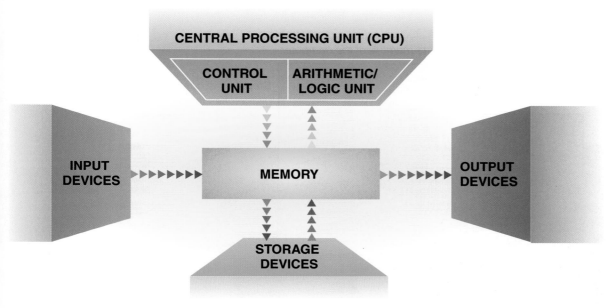

Figure 3-5 *Most of the devices connected to the computer communicate with the CPU in order to carry out a task. The arrows in this figure represent the flow of data, instructions, and information.*

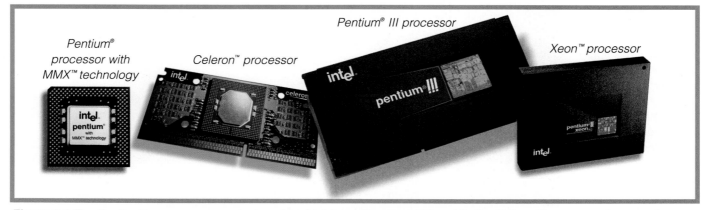

Figure 3-6 *The Pentium® processors are designed for higher-performance PCs, while the Celeron™ processor is geared toward the basic PCs that cost less than $1,000. The Xeon™ processor is geared toward servers and workstations.*

The Control Unit

As you know, a program or set of instructions must be stored in memory for a computer to process data. The CPU uses its control unit to execute these instructions. The **control unit**, one component of the CPU, directs and coordinates most of the operations in the computer. The control unit has a role much like a traffic cop: it interprets each instruction issued by a program and then initiates the appropriate action to carry out the instruction. For every instruction, the control unit repeats a set of four basic operations: (1) fetching an instruction, (2) decoding the instruction, (3) executing the instruction,

and, if necessary, (4) storing the result. Together, these four operations comprise the **machine cycle** or **instruction cycle** (Figure 3-7). **Fetching** is the process of obtaining a program instruction or data item from memory. **Decoding** is the process of translating the instruction into commands the computer understands. **Executing** is the process of carrying out the commands. **Storing** is the process of writing the result to memory. The time it takes to fetch is called **instruction time**, or **I-time**. The time it takes to decode and execute is called **execution time** or **E-time**. If you add together the I-time and E-time, you have the total time required for a machine cycle.

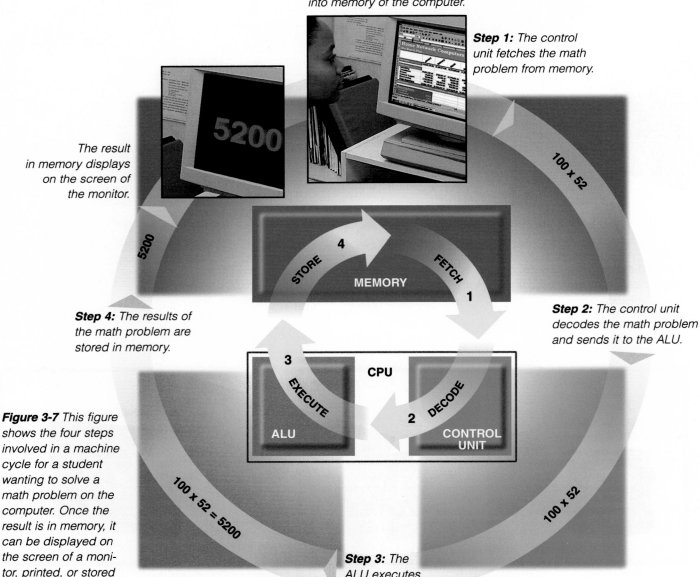

A student enters a math problem into memory of the computer.

Step 1: The control unit fetches the math problem from memory.

The result in memory displays on the screen of the monitor.

Step 2: The control unit decodes the math problem and sends it to the ALU.

Step 4: The results of the math problem are stored in memory.

Step 3: The ALU executes the math problem.

Figure 3-7 This figure shows the four steps involved in a machine cycle for a student wanting to solve a math problem on the computer. Once the result is in memory, it can be displayed on the screen of a monitor, printed, or stored on a disk.

Some computer professionals measure a computer's speed according to the number of instructions it can process in one second. Sometimes, this speed is measured in **MIPS**, which stands for **m**illion **i**nstructions **p**er **s**econd. Current personal computers, for example, can process more than 300 MIPS. Because different instructions require different amounts of processing time, however, no real standard for measuring MIPS exists. In addition, MIPS refers only to the CPU speed, whereas applications generally are limited by other factors such as input and output speed.

The Arithmetic/Logic Unit

The **arithmetic/logic unit (ALU)**, another component of the CPU, performs the execution part of a machine cycle as shown in Figure 3-7. Specifically, the ALU performs the arithmetic, comparison, and logical operations. **Arithmetic operations** include addition, subtraction, multiplication, and division. **Comparison operations** involve comparing one data item to another to determine if the first item is greater than, equal to, or less than the other item. Depending on the result of the comparison, different actions may occur. For example, to determine if an employee should receive overtime pay, the total hours the employee worked during the week have to be compared to straight-time hours allowed (40 hours, for instance). If the total hours worked is greater than 40, then an overtime wage is calculated; if total hours worked is

not greater than 40, no overtime wage is calculated. **Logical operations** work with conditions and logical operators such as AND, OR, and NOT. For example, if you wanted to search a job database for part-time work in the admissions office, you would search for any jobs classified as part-time *AND* listed under admissions.

Pipelining

In some computers, the CPU processes only a single instruction at a time. That is, the CPU waits until an instruction completes all four stages of the machine cycle (fetch, decode, execute, and store) before beginning work on the next instruction. With **pipelining**, the CPU begins executing a second instruction before the first instruction is completed. Pipelining results in faster processing, because the CPU does not have to wait for one instruction to complete the machine cycle before fetching the next. For example, by the time the first instruction is in the last stage of the machine cycle, three other instructions could have been fetched and started through the machine cycle (Figure 3-8).

Although formerly used only in high-performance processors, pipelining now is common in processors used in today's personal computers. For instance, most newer processor chips can pipeline up to four instructions. Superscalar CPUs have two or more pipelines that can process instructions simultaneously.

MACHINE CYCLE (without pipelining):

MACHINE CYCLE (with pipelining):

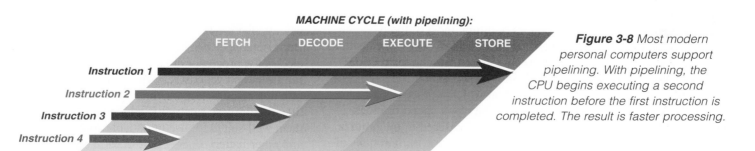

Figure 3-8 *Most modern personal computers support pipelining. With pipelining, the CPU begins executing a second instruction before the first instruction is completed. The result is faster processing.*

COMMON PREFIXES AND THEIR MEANINGS

Prefixes for Small Amounts	Meaning	Decimal Notation
MILLI	One thousandth of	.001
MICRO	One millionth of	.000001
NANO	One billionth of	.000000001
PICO	One trillionth of	.000000000001

Prefixes for Large Amounts	Meaning	Decimal Notation
KILO	One thousand	1,000
MEGA	One million	1,000,000
GIGA	One billion	1,000,000,000
TERA	One trillion	1,000,000,000,000

Figure 3-9 *This table outlines common prefixes and their meanings.*

Registers

The CPU uses temporary storage locations, called **registers**, to hold data and instructions. A microprocessor contains many different types of registers, each with a specific function. These functions include storing the location from where an instruction was fetched, storing an instruction while it is being decoded, storing data while the ALU processes it, and storing the results of a calculation.

The System Clock

The control unit relies on a small chip called the **system clock** to synchronize, or control the timing of, all computer operations. Just as your heart beats at a regular rate to keep your body functioning, the system clock generates regular electronic pulses, or ticks, that set the operating pace of components in the system unit. Each tick is called a **clock cycle**. A CPU requires a fixed number of clock cycles to execute each instruction. The faster the clock, the more instructions the CPU can execute per second. In addition, most of today's processors are **superscalar**, which means that they can execute more than one instruction per clock cycle.

The speed at which a processor executes instructions is called **clock speed** or **clock rate**. Clock speed is measured in **megahertz (MHz)**, which equates to one million ticks of

the system clock. In computer terminology, prefixes are used to describe items such as speed and storage capabilities. The table in Figure 3-9 outlines some common prefixes and their meanings. Thus, a computer that operates at 300 MHz has three hundred million clock cycles, or ticks, in one second.

The strength of a CPU frequently is determined by how fast it processes data. One of the major factors that affect this is the system clock. A higher clock speed means the CPU can process more instructions per second than the same CPU with a lower clock speed. For example, a 400 MHz CPU is faster than the same CPU operating at 200 MHz. The speed of the system clock affects only the CPU; it has no effect on peripherals such as a printer or disk drive.

The speed of the system clock varies among processors. Due to a technological breakthrough by IBM, many processors today operate at speeds in excess of 400 MHz. For nearly 30 years, aluminum was used to create the electronic circuitry on a single chip of silicon crystal. In 1997, IBM developed a process that uses copper instead of aluminum. Because copper is a better conductor of electricity, processor chips made using copper run faster and yet cost less. Another advantage of chips manufactured using copper is that they require less electricity, which makes them well-suited for use in portable computers and other battery-operated devices.

WEB INFO
WEB INFO

For more information on clock speed, visit the Discovering Computers 2000 Chapter 3 WEB INFO page (www.scsite.com/dc2000/ch3/webinfo.htm) and click Clock Speed.

Microprocessor Comparison

A microprocessor often is identified by its model name or model number. Figure 3-10 summarizes the historical development of the microprocessor and documents the increases in clock speed and number of transistors in chips since 1982.

Intel is the leading manufacturer of processors. With their earlier microprocessors, Intel used a model number to identify the various chips. After learning that CPU numbers could not be trademarked and protected from use by competitors, Intel decided to identify their microprocessors with names, not numbers – thus emerged their series of processors known as **Pentium® processors**. A second brand of Intel processor called the **Celeron**™ is designed for less expensive PCs. A third brand, called the **Xeon**™ processor, is geared toward workstations and servers.

Other companies such as Cyrix and AMD currently make **Intel-compatible microprocessors**. These microprocessors have the same internal design or architecture as Intel processors and perform the same functions, but often are less expensive. Intel and Intel-compatible processors are used in PCs.

An alternative to the Intel-style micro-processor is the **Motorola microprocessor**, which is found in Apple Macintosh and Power Macintosh systems. The processor used in Apple's PowerPC introduced a new architecture that increased the speed of the processor.

The **Alpha microprocessor**, which was developed by Digital Equipment Corporation, is used primarily in workstations and high-end servers. Current models of the Alpha chip run at clock speeds from 300 to 600 MHz.

Determining which processor to obtain when you purchase a computer depends on the type of computer you buy and how you plan to use the computer. If you purchase a PC (IBM-compatible), you will have the choice of an Intel processor or an Intel-compatible processor. Apple Macintosh and Power Macintosh users will want to choose a PowerPC processor.

Your intended use also will determine the clock speed of the processor you choose. The selection of the speed of the processor is an important consideration. A home user surfing the Web, for example, will need a less powerful processor than an artist working with graphics or applications requiring multimedia capabilities such as full-motion video.

COMPARISON OF WIDELY USED MICROPROCESSORS

NAME	DATE INTRODUCED	MANUFACTURER	CLOCK SPEED (MHz)	NUMBER OF TRANSISTORS
Pentium® III Xeon™	1999	Intel	500 and higher	7.5 million
Pentium® III	1999	Intel	400-500	7.5 million
Pentium® II Xeon™	1998	Intel	400	7.5 million
Celeron™	1998	Intel	266-400	7.5 million
AMD-K6	1998	AMD	300	8.8 million
Pentium® II	1997	Intel	233-450	7.5 million
Pentium® with MMX™ technology	1997	Intel	166-233	4.5 million
Pentium® Pro	1995	Intel	150-200	5.5 million
Pentium®	1993	Intel	75-200	3.3 million
80486DX	1989	Intel	25-100	1.2 million
80386DX	1985	Intel	16-33	275,000
80286	1982	Intel	6-12	134,000
PowerPC	1994	Motorola	50-333	Up to 50 million
68040	1989	Motorola	25-40	1.2 million
68030	1987	Motorola	16-50	270,000
68020	1984	Motorola	16-33	190,000
Alpha	1993	Digital	150-600	Up to 100 million

Figure 3-10 A comparison of some of the more widely used microprocessors. The greater the number of transistors, the more complex and powerful the chip.

Users of multimedia applications should obtain an Intel processor equipped with **MMX™ technology**, in which a set of instructions are built into the processor so it can manipulate and process multimedia data more efficiently. The Pentium® II processor includes MMX™ technology. Figure 3-11 describes guidelines for selecting an Intel processor. Remember, the higher the clock speed, the faster the processor – but also the more expensive the computer.

Processor Installation and Upgrades

A processor chip is inserted into an opening, or socket, on the motherboard. Most of today's computers are equipped with a **zero-insertion force (ZIF) socket**, which has a small lever or screw designed to facilitate the installation and removal of processor chips.

Instead of buying an entirely new computer, some processors can be upgraded to increase their performance. Processor upgrades take one of three forms: chip for chip, piggyback, or daughterboard. With a **chip for chip upgrade**, the existing processor chip is replaced with a new one. Because a

ZIF socket requires no force to remove and install a chip, users easily can upgrade the processor on computers equipped with this type of socket. Some motherboards also have a second ZIF socket, which is designed to hold an upgrade chip. In this case, the existing processor chip remains on the motherboard, and the upgrade chip is installed into the second ZIF socket. With a **piggyback upgrade**, the new processor chip is stacked on top of the old one. With a **daughterboard upgrade**, the new processor chip is located on a daughterboard. A **daughterboard** is a small circuit board that plugs into the motherboard, often to add additional capabilities to the motherboard.

Heat Sinks and Heat Pipes

Newer processor chips generate a lot of heat, which could cause the chip to burn up. Often, the computer's main fan generates enough airflow to cool the processor. Sometimes, however, a heat sink is required – especially when upgrading to a more powerful processor. A **heat sink** is a small ceramic or metal component with fins on its surface that is designed to absorb and ventilate heat produced by electrical components. Some

GUIDELINES FOR SELECTING AN INTEL PROCESSOR

Figure 3-11

Determining which processor to obtain when you purchase a computer depends on your computer usage. Today, most computers running Windows and Windows applications use some type of Intel processor.

INTEL PROCESSOR	CLOCK SPEED	USE
Xeon™	400 MHz and up	Power users with workstations; servers on a network
Pentium®	400 to 500 MHz	Users that work with graphics, full-motion video, encyclopedias, drawing, animation, photo-editing, art, games, or other applications requiring multimedia capabilities
	300 to 350 MHz	Businesses running financial, accounting, or intensive spreadsheet programs; users creating multimedia presentations; users that frequently surf the Web; home users into intense gaming
	266 MHz	Small businesses or home users that regularly work with databases, spreadsheets, or other number intensive packages designed for business use
	233 MHz	Home users surfing the Web and using basic software such as a word processing, spreadsheet, and finance
Celeron™	266 to 400 MHz	New home and business users with basic computing needs looking for a low-cost PC

heat sinks are packaged as part of the processor chip, while others must be installed on top of the chip. Because a heat sink consumes a lot of room, a smaller device called a **heat pipe** is used to cool laptop computers.

Coprocessors

Another way to increase the performance of a computer is through the use of a **coprocessor**, which is a special processor chip or circuit board designed to assist the processor in performing specific tasks. Users running engineering, scientific, or graphics applications, for instance, will notice a dramatic increase in speed with a **floating-point coprocessor**, provided the application is designed to take advantage of the coprocessor. Floating-point coprocessors also are called math or numeric coprocessors. Most of today's computers are equipped with a floating-point coprocessor upon purchase; for others, the coprocessor chip or card is installed later.

Parallel Processing

Some computers use more than one processor to speed processing times. Known as **parallel processing**, this method uses multiple processors simultaneously to execute a program (Figure 3-12). That is, parallel processing divides up a problem so that multiple processors work on their assigned portion of the problem at the same time. As you might expect, parallel processors require special software designed to recognize how to divide up the problem and then bring the results back together again. Supercomputers use parallel processing for applications such as weather forecasting.

DATA REPRESENTATION

To fully understand the way a computer processes data, it is important to understand how data is represented in a computer. People communicate using words that are combined into sentences in different ways each time we speak. Human speech is **analog**, meaning that it uses continuous signals to represent data and information. Most computers, by contrast, are **digital**, meaning that they understand only two discrete states: on and off. This is because

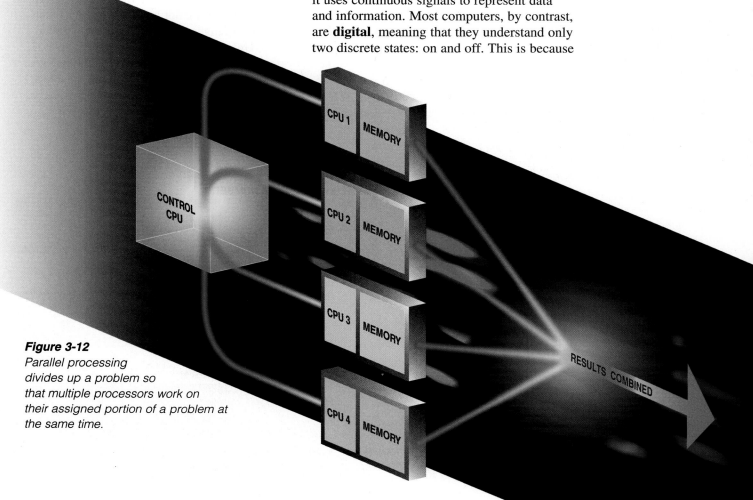

Figure 3-12
Parallel processing divides up a problem so that multiple processors work on their assigned portion of a problem at the same time.

computers are electronic devices powered by electricity, which has only two states: (1) on or (2) off.

These two states are represented easily by using two digits; 0 is used to represent the electronic state of off (absence of an electronic charge) and 1 is used to represent the electronic state of on (presence of an electronic charge) (Figure 3-13).

Figure 3-13 *A computer circuit represents the binary digits 0 or 1 electronically by the presence or absence of an electronic charge.*

BINARY DIGIT (BIT)	ELECTRONIC CHARGE	ELECTRONIC STATE
1		ON
0		OFF

When people count, they use the digits 0 through 9, which are digits in the decimal system. Because a computer understands only two states, it uses a number system that has just two unique digits, 0 and 1. This numbering system is referred to as the **binary** system.

Each on or off digital value is called a **bit** (short for **bi**nary dig**it**) and represents the smallest unit of data the computer can handle. By itself, a bit is not very informative. When eight bits are grouped together as a unit, they

are called a **byte**. A byte is informative because it provides enough different combination of 0s and 1s to represent 256 individual characters including numbers, uppercase and lowercase letters of the alphabet, punctuation marks, and other characters such as the letters of the Greek alphabet.

The combinations of 0s and 1s used to represent characters are defined by patterns called a coding scheme. Using one type of coding scheme, the number 1 is represented as 00110001, the number 2 as 00110010, and the capital letter M as 01001101 (Figure 3-14). Two popular coding schemes are ASCII and EBCDIC (Figure 3-15). The **American Standard Code for Information Interchange**, called **ASCII** (pronounced *ASK-ee*), is the most widely used coding system to represent data. ASCII is used on many personal computers and minicomputers. The **Extended Binary Coded Decimal Interchange Code**, or **EBCDIC** (pronounced *EB-see-dic*) is used primarily on mainframe computers.

The ASCII and EBCDIC codes are sufficient for English and Western European languages but are not large enough for Asian and other languages that use different alphabets. **Unicode** is a coding scheme capable of representing all the world's current languages. The ASCII, EBCDIC, and Unicode schemes, along with the parity bit and number systems, are discussed in the appendix of this book.

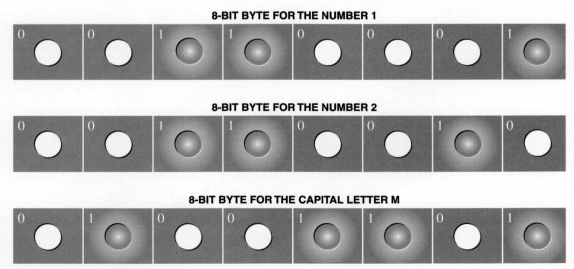

Figure 3-14 *Eight bits grouped together as a unit are called a byte. A byte is used to represent a single character in the computer and represents one storage location.*

ASCII	SYMBOL	EBCDIC
00110000	0	11110000
00110001	1	11110001
00110010	2	11110010
00110011	3	11110011
00110100	4	11110100
00110101	5	11110101
00110110	6	11110110
00110111	7	11110111
00111000	8	11111000
00111001	9	11111001
01000001	A	11000001
01000010	B	11000010
01000011	C	11000011
01000100	D	11000100
01000101	E	11000101
01000110	F	11000110
01000111	G	11000111
01001000	H	11001000
01001001	I	11001001
01001010	J	11010001
01001011	K	11010010
01001100	L	11010011
01001101	M	11010100
01001110	N	11010101
01001111	O	11010110
01010000	P	11010111
01010001	Q	11011000
01010010	R	11011001
01010011	S	11100010
01010100	T	11100011
01010101	U	11100100
01010110	V	11100101
01010111	W	11100110
01011000	X	11100111
01011001	Y	11101000
01011010	Z	11101001
00100001	!	01011010
00100010	"	01111111
00100011	#	01111011
00100100	$	01011011
00100101	%	01101100
00100110	&	01010000
00101000	(	01001101
00101001	)	01011101
00101010	*	01011100
00101011	+	01001110

Figure 3-15 *Two popular coding schemes are ASCII and EBCDIC.*

Coding schemes such as ASCII make it possible for humans to interact with a digital computer that recognizes only bits. When you press a key on a keyboard, the electronic signal is converted into a binary form the computer understands and is stored in memory. That is, every character is converted to its corresponding byte. The computer then processes that data in terms of bytes, which actually is a series of on/off electrical states. When processing is finished, the bytes are converted back into numbers, letters of the alphabet, or special characters to be displayed on a screen or be printed (Figure 3-16). All of these conversions take place so quickly that you do not realize they are occurring.

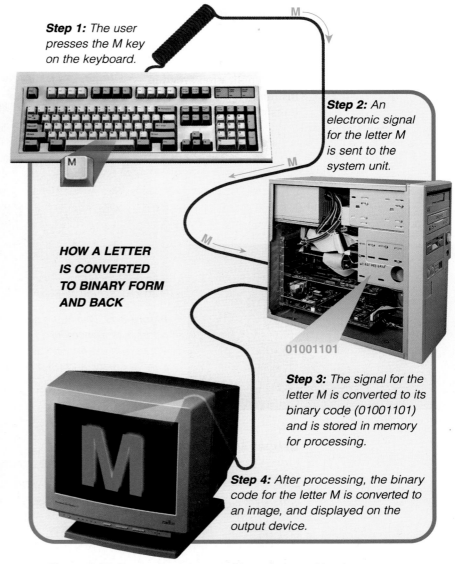

Step 1: *The user presses the M key on the keyboard.*

Step 2: *An electronic signal for the letter M is sent to the system unit.*

HOW A LETTER IS CONVERTED TO BINARY FORM AND BACK

01001101

Step 3: *The signal for the letter M is converted to its binary code (01001101) and is stored in memory for processing.*

Step 4: *After processing, the binary code for the letter M is converted to an image, and displayed on the output device.*

Figure 3-16 *Converting a letter to binary form and back*

MEMORY

While performing a processing operation, a processor needs a place to temporarily store instructions to be executed and the data to be used with those instructions. A computer's **memory** in the system unit is used to store data, instructions, and information. The memory chips on the circuit boards in the system unit perform this function. Memory stores three basic items: (1) the operating system and other system software that control the usage of the computer equipment; (2) application programs designed to carry out a specific task such as word processing; and (3) the data being processed by the application programs. This role of memory to store both data and programs is known as the **stored program concept**.

Recall that a character is stored in the computer as a group of 0s and 1s, called a byte. Thus, a byte is the basic storage unit in memory. When application program instructions and data are transferred into memory

from storage devices, they are stored as bytes, each of which is placed in a precise location in memory, called an **address**. This address is simply a unique number identifying the location of the byte in memory. The illustration in Figure 3-17 shows how seats in a stadium are similar to addresses in memory: (1) a seat holds one person at a time and an address in memory holds a single byte, (2) both a seat and an address can be empty, and (3) a seat has a unique identifying number and so does a memory address. Thus, to access data or instructions in memory, the computer references the addresses that contain bytes of data.

The size of memory is measured by the number of bytes available for use (Figure 3-18). A **kilobyte** of memory, abbreviated **KB** or **K**, is equal to exactly 1,024 bytes

seat #A1   seat #A2   seat #A3   seat #A4   seat #A5   seat #A6

Figure 3-17 This figure shows how seats in a stadium are similar to addresses in memory: (1) a seat holds one person at a time and an address in memory holds a single byte, (2) both a seat and an address can be empty, and (3) a seat has a unique identifying number and so does an address.

MEMORY AND STORAGE SIZES

Term	Abbreviation	Approximate Memory Size	Exact Memory Amount	Approximate Number of Pages of Text
Kilobyte	KB or K	1 thousand bytes	1,024 bytes	50
Megabyte	MB	1 million bytes	1,048,576 bytes	50,000
Gigabyte	GB	1 billion bytes	1,073,741,824 bytes	50,000,000
Terabyte	TB	1 trillion bytes	1,099,511,627,776 bytes	50,000,000,000

Figure 3-18 This table outlines terms used to define storage size.

(see Figure 3-18). To make storage definitions easier to identify, computer users often round a kilobyte down to 1,000 bytes. For example, if a memory chip can store 100 KB, it is said to hold 100,000 bytes (characters). A **megabyte**, abbreviated **MB**, is equal to approximately one million bytes.

The system unit contains two types of memory: volatile and nonvolatile. The contents of **volatile memory** are lost (erased) when the computer power is turned off. The contents of **nonvolatile memory**, on the other hand, are not lost when power is removed from the computer. RAM is an example of volatile memory. ROM, flash memory, and CMOS all are examples of nonvolatile memory. The following sections discuss each of these types of memory.

RAM

The memory chips in the system unit are called **RAM (random access memory)**. When the computer is powered on, certain operating system files (such as the files that determine how your Windows desktop displays) are loaded from a storage device such as a hard disk into RAM. These files remain in RAM as long as the computer is running. As additional programs and data are requested, they also are read from storage into RAM. The processor acts upon the data while it is in RAM. During this time, the contents of RAM may change as the data is processed (Figure 3-19). Multiple programs can be loaded into RAM simultaneously, provided you have enough RAM to accommodate all the programs. The program with which you are working currently displays on the screen.

WEB INFO

For more information on RAM, visit the Discovering Computers 2000 Chapter 3 WEB INFO page (**www.scsite.com/ dc2000/ch3/webinfo.htm**) and click RAM.

Figure 3-19 How application programs transfer in and out of RAM.

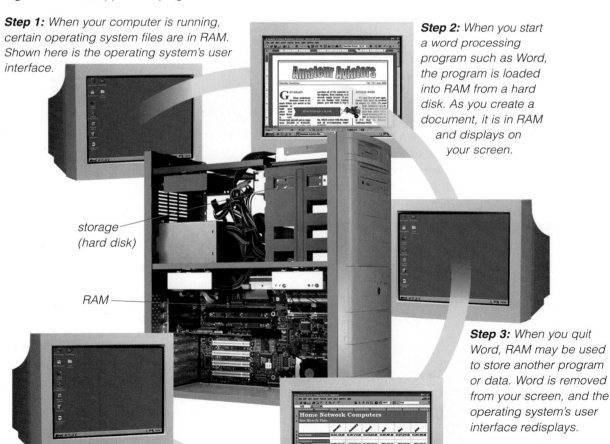

Step 1: When your computer is running, certain operating system files are in RAM. Shown here is the operating system's user interface.

Step 2: When you start a word processing program such as Word, the program is loaded into RAM from a hard disk. As you create a document, it is in RAM and displays on your screen.

storage (hard disk)

RAM

Step 3: When you quit Word, RAM may be used to store another program or data. Word is removed from your screen, and the operating system's user interface redisplays.

Step 5: When you quit Excel, RAM may be used to store another program or data. Excel is removed from your screen and the operating system's user interface redisplays.

Step 4: When you start a spreadsheet program such as Excel, the program is loaded into RAM from a hard disk. As you create a spreadsheet, it is in RAM and displays on your screen.

RAM is volatile, which means items stored in RAM are lost when the power to the computer is turned off. For this reason, any items needed for future use must be **saved**, or copied from RAM to a storage device such as a hard disk, before the power to the computer is turned off.

Two basic types of RAM exist: dynamic RAM and static RAM. When discussing RAM, users normally are referring to **dynamic RAM**, also called **DRAM** (pronounced DEE-ram), a type of memory that must be re-energized constantly or it loses its contents. A newer type of DRAM, called **Synchronous DRAM (SDRAM)** is much faster than DRAM because it is synchronized to the system clock. Most computers today use SDRAM.

Static RAM, also called **SRAM** (pronounced ESS-ram), is faster and more reliable than any form of DRAM. The term static refers to the fact that it does not have to be re-energized as often as DRAM. SRAM, however, is used for special purposes because it is much more expensive than DRAM.

RAM CHIPS Random access memory chips often are smaller in size than processor chips. RAM chips usually are packaged on a small circuit board that is inserted into the motherboard (Figure 3-20). One such circuit board is called a **single inline memory module (SIMM)** because it has RAM chips on only one side. Another type of circuit board is called a **dual inline memory module (DIMM)** because it has RAM chips on both

sides. The RAM chips used in SIMMs and DIMMs are DRAM chips.

CONFIGURING RAM The amount of RAM a computer requires often depends on the types of applications to be used on the computer. Remember that a computer only can manipulate data that is in memory. RAM is similar to the workspace you have on the top of your desk. Just as a desktop needs a certain amount of space to hold papers, pens, your computer, and so on, a computer needs a certain amount of memory to be able to store an applicaton program and files. The more RAM a computer has, the more programs and files it can work on at once.

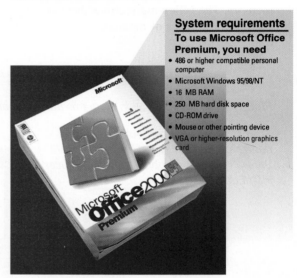

System requirements
To use Microsoft Office Premium, you need
- 486 or higher compatible personal computer
- Microsoft Windows 95/98/NT
- 16 MB RAM
- 250 MB hard disk space
- CD-ROM drive
- Mouse or other pointing device
- VGA or higher-resolution graphics card

Figure 3-21 *The minimum system requirements for Microsoft Office Premium are printed on the side of the box.*

A software package usually indicates the minimum amount of RAM it requires (Figure 3-21). If you want the application to perform optimally, typically you need more than the minimum specifications on the software package. For example, the optimum memory requirement for users running Microsoft Office Premium is 64 MB of RAM. In general, home users running Windows and using standard application software such as word processing should have at least 32 MB of RAM. Most business computers should be equipped with a minimum of 64 MB of RAM, so users can run accounting, financial, or spreadsheet programs, and programs requiring multimedia capabilities.

dual inline memory module

memory chip

Figure 3-20 *This photograph shows a dual inline memory module (DIMM).*

Users composing multimedia presentations or using graphics-intensive applications may want even more RAM. The table in Figure 3-22a provides guidelines for the amount of RAM you need on your computer.

The necessary amount of RAM varies according to the type of work you do and the type of software applications you are using. Remember, however, that the amount of RAM on your computer determines how many programs and how much data a computer can handle at one time and thus affects overall performance. As shown in Figure 3-22b, advertisements for computers normally contain the type of processor, the speed of the processor measured in MHz, and the amount of RAM installed.

Cache

Most of today's computers improve their processing times by using **cache** (pronounced cash). **Memory cache**, also called a cache store or RAM cache, helps speed the processes of the computer by storing frequently used instructions and data.

The rationale is that the processor is likely to request these items over and over again. When the processor needs an instruction or data, it first searches cache.

Most modern computers have two types, or layers, of cache: Level 1 and Level 2. **Level 1 (L1) cache,** also called **primary cache** or **internal cache**, is built directly into the processor chip. L1 cache usually has a very small capacity, ranging from 8 KB to 64 KB. For example, Pentium®, Pentium® Pro, and Pentium® II processors all have 16 KB of L1 cache.

Level 2 (L2) cache, or **external cache**, is not part of the processor chip; instead L2 cache consists of high-speed SRAM chips. L2 cache is slightly slower than L1 cache, but has a larger capacity. When discussing cache, most users are referring to L2 cache, which ranges in size from 64 KB to 2 MB.

As noted, cache speeds processing time by storing frequently used instructions and data. When the processor needs an instruction or data, it searches memory in this order: L1 cache, then L2 cache, then RAM – with a greater delay in processing for each level of memory it must search. If the instruction or data is not found in memory, then a slower speed storage device such as a hard disk or CD-ROM must be searched.

WEB INFO
WEB INFO
For more information on cache, visit the Discovering Computers 2000 Chapter 3 WEB INFO page (**www.scsite.com/ dc2000/ch3/webinfo.htm**) and click Cache.

Figure 3-22a
(RAM guidelines)

RAM (in MB)	32 MB (minimum)	64 MB (minimum)	128 to 256 MB
Use	Home and business users running Windows and using standard application software such as word processing	Users running advanced accounting, financial, or spreadsheet programs; users requiring basic multimedia capabilities such as sounds, photographs, and video; users running two or more programs simultaneously	Users running sophisticated CAD software, 3-D design software, or other graphics-intensive applications

Figure 3-22b
(Computers for sale)

Intel© Processor	366MHz Celeron™ Processor featuring MMX™ technology	433MHz Celeron™ Processor featuring MMX™ technology	400MHz Pentium© II Processor featuring MMX™ technology	450MHz Pentium© III Processor	500MHz Pentium© III Processor	500MHz Pentium© III Processor
Memory	32MB SDRAM Memory	64MB SDRAM Memory	96MB SDRAM Memory	128MB SDRAM Memory	128MB SDRAM Memory	256MB SDRAM Memory

Figure 3-22 Determining how much RAM you need depends on the applications you intend to run on your computer. Today, most computers running Windows and Windows applications include at least 32 MB of RAM. Advertisements for computers normally contain the type of processor, the speed of the processor measured in MHz, as well as the amount of RAM installed.

CONFIGURING CACHE A computer system with L2 cache usually performs at speeds that are 10 to 40 percent faster than those without any cache. To realize the largest increase in performance, the system should have from 256 K to 512 K of L2 cache (above that, the increases in performance are not significant). As shown in the advertisement in Figure 3-23, most current systems are equipped with 512 K of L2 cache.

Figure 3-23 *As shown in these advertisements, most current systems are equipped with 512 K of L2 cache.*

GP7-500

- Intel Pentium III Processor 500MHz with 512K Cache
- 128MB SDRAM
- VX900 19" Monitor (18" viewable)
- 16MB nVidia™ AGP Graphics
- 18GB 7200 RPM Ultra ATA Hard Drive
- MS Windows 98
- MS Office

L2 cache

9100XL

- 14.1" XGA TFT Color Display
- Intel Pentium II Processor 366MHz with 512K Cache
- 128MB SDRAM (expandable to 384MB)
- 4MB SGRAM 3D Graphics Accelerator
- Removable Combo DVD-ROM & 3.5" Diskette Drive
- 10GB Ultra ATA Hard Drive
- Two (2) Lithium Ion Batteries & AC Pack
- PC Card Modem w/56K Technology
- MS Office

ROM

Read-only memory (ROM) is the name given to memory chips storing data that only can be read. That is, the data stored in ROM chips cannot be modified – hence, the name read only. While RAM is volatile, ROM is nonvolatile; its contents are not lost when power to the computer is turned off. ROM chips thus contain data, instructions, or information that is recorded permanently. For example, ROM contains the sequence of instructions the computer follows to load the operating system and other files when you first turn the computer on.

The data, instructions, or information stored on ROM chips often are recorded when the chip is manufactured. ROM chips that contain permanently written data, instructions, or information are called **firmware**.

Another type of ROM chip, called a **programmable read-only memory (PROM)** chip, is a blank ROM chip on which you can permanently place items. The instructions used to program a PROM chip are called **microcode**. Once the microcode is programmed into the PROM chip, it functions like a regular ROM chip and cannot be erased or changed.

FLASH MEMORY Another type of nonvolatile memory is called **flash memory** or **flash ROM**. Unlike a PROM chip that can be programmed only once, flash memory can be erased electronically and reprogrammed. Flash memory is used to store programs on personal computers, as well as cellular telephones, printers, digital cameras, pagers, and personal digital assistants (Figure 3-24). Flash memory is available in sizes ranging from 1 to 40 MB.

Figure 3-24 *Flash ROM chips are used in personal computers, cellular telephones, digital cameras, pagers, and personal digital assistants.*

CMOS

Another type of memory chip in the system unit is complementary metal-oxide semiconductor memory. **Complementary metal-oxide semiconductor** memory, abbreviated **CMOS** (pronounced SEE-moss), is used to store configuration information about the computer, such as the type of disk drives, keyboard, and monitor; the current date and time; and other startup information needed when the computer is turned on. CMOS chips use battery power to retain information even when the power to the computer is turned off. Battery-backed CMOS memory thus keeps the calendar, date, and time current even when the computer is off. Unlike ROM, information stored in CMOS memory can be changed, such as when you change from standard time to daylight savings time.

Memory Access Times

The speed at which the processor can access data from memory directly affects how fast the computer processes data. This speed often is defined as **access time**. Access time is measured in fractions of a second (Figure 3-25). For memory, access times are measured in terms of a **nanosecond** (abbreviated **ns**), which is one billionth of a second. A nanosecond is extremely fast (Figure 3-26). In fact, electricity travels about one foot in a nanosecond.

The access time (speed) of memory contributes to the overall performance of the computer. DRAM chips normally have access times ranging from 50 to 70 ns, while SRAM chips commonly range in speed from 7 to 20 ns. ROM's access times range from 55 to 250 ns. For comparison purposes, accessing data on a fast hard disk takes between 8 and 15

ACCESS TIMES

TERM	ABBREVIATION	SPEED
Millisecond	ms	One-thousandth of a second
Microsecond	µs	One-millionth of a second
Nanosecond	ns	One-billionth of a second
Picosecond	psec	One-trillionth of a second

Figure 3-25 *Access times are measured in fractions of a second. This table outlines terms used to define access times.*

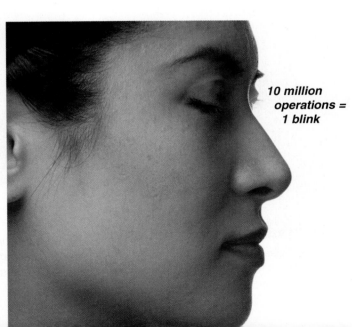

Figure 3-26 *It takes about one-tenth of a second to blink your eye, which is the equivalent of 100 million nanoseconds. A computer can perform some operations in as little as 10 nanoseconds. Thus, in the time it takes to blink your eye, a computer can perform some operations 10 million times.*

10 million operations = 1 blink

milliseconds. A **millisecond**, abbreviated **ms**, is one thousandth of a second. This means that accessing data in memory with a 70 ns access time is over 200,000 times faster than accessing data on a hard disk with a 15 ms access time.

While access times of memory greatly affect overall computer performance, manufacturers and retailers usually list a computer's memory in terms of its size, not its access time. Thus, an advertisement might describe a computer as having 512 K of L2 cache or 16 MB of SDRAM expandable to 256 MB.

Memory capacity can be expanded in a number of ways, such as installing additional memory in an expansion slot.

EXPANSION SLOTS AND EXPANSION CARDS

WEB INFO
WEB INFO

For more information on expansion cards, visit the Discovering Computers 2000 Chapter 3 WEB INFO page (**www.scsite.com/dc2000/ch3/webinfo.htm**) and click Expansion Cards.

An **expansion slot** is an opening, or socket, where a circuit board can be inserted into the motherboard. These circuit boards add new devices or capabilities to the computer such as more memory, higher-quality sound devices, a modem, or graphics capabilities (Figure 3-27). Many terms are used to refer to this type of circuit board:

expansion card, expansion board, adapter card, interface card, card, add-in, and add-on. Sometimes a device or feature is built into the expansion card; other times a cable is used to connect the expansion card to a device such as a scanner outside the system unit. Figure 3-28 shows an expansion card being plugged into an expansion slot on a personal computer motherboard.

Three types of expansion cards found in most of today's computers are a video card, a sound card, and an internal modem. A **video card**, also called a **video adapter** or **graphics card**, converts computer output into a video signal that is sent through a cable to the monitor, which displays an image on the screen. A **sound card** is used to enhance the sound-generating capabilities of a personal computer by allowing sound to be input through a microphone and output through speakers. An **internal modem** is a communications device that enables computers to communicate via telephone lines or other means.

In the past, installing an expansion card required setting switches and other elements on the motherboard. Many of today's computers support **Plug and Play**, which refers to the computer's capability to automatically configure expansion cards and other devices as they are installed. Having Plug and Play support means a user can plug in a device, turn on the computer, and then use, or play, the device without having to configure the system manually.

TYPES OF EXPANSION CARDS

Expansion Card	Function
Accelerator	To increase the speed of the CPU
Controller	To connect disk drives; being phased out because newer motherboards support these connections
Game	To connect a joystick
I/O	To connect input and output devices such as a printer or mouse; being phased out because newer motherboards support these connections
Interface	To connect other peripherals such as mouse devices, CD-ROMs, and scanners
Memory	To add more memory to the computer
Modem	To connect to other computers through telephone lines
Network	To connect to other computers and peripherals via a network
PC/TV	To connect to a television
Sound	To connect speakers or a microphone
Video	To connect a monitor
Video Capture	To connect a video camera

Figure 3-27 *This table lists some of the types of expansion cards and their functions.*

Figure 3-28 *This expansion card is being inserted into an expansion slot on the motherboard of a personal computer.*

PC Cards

Laptop and other portable computers have a special type of expansion slot used for installing PC Cards. A **PC Card** is a thin credit card-sized device that is used to add memory, disk drives, sound, and fax/modem capabilities to a laptop computer (Figure 3-29).

All PC Cards conform to standards developed by the **Personal Computer Memory Card International Association** (these cards originally were called **PCMCIA cards**), which help ensure that PC Cards can be interchanged between laptop computers. PC Cards thus are designed with the same length and width so they fit in a standard PC Card slot.

The height or thickness of PC Cards varies among three types, which are named Type I, Type II, and Type III. The thinnest **Type I cards** are used to add memory capabilities to the computer. **Type II cards** contain communications devices such as modems. The thickest **Type III cards** are used to house devices such as hard disks.

A PC Card slot usually is located on the side of a laptop computer. Unlike other expansion cards that require you to open the system unit and install the card onto the motherboard, a PC Card can be changed as needed without having to open the system unit or restart the computer. For example, if you need to send a fax, you can just insert the fax/modem card in the PC Card slot while the computer is running. The operating system automatically recognizes the new card and allows you to send the fax. The ability to add and remove devices while a computer is running is called **hot plugging** or **hot**

Figure 3-29 This picture shows a cellular telephone plugged into a modem card that is being inserted into a PC Card slot on a laptop computer.

WEB INFO

For more information on PC Cards, visit the Discovering Computers 2000 Chapter 3 WEB INFO page (**www.scsite.com/dc2000/ch3/webinfo.htm**) and click PC Cards.

swapping. Because of their small size and versatility, PC Cards also are used with consumer electronics products such as cable TV, automobiles, and digital cameras.

PORTS

External devices such as a keyboard, monitor, printer, mouse, and microphone, often are attached by a cable to the system unit. The interface, or point of attachment, to the system unit is called a **port**. Most of the time, ports are located on the back of the system unit (Figure 3-30), but they also can be placed on the front.

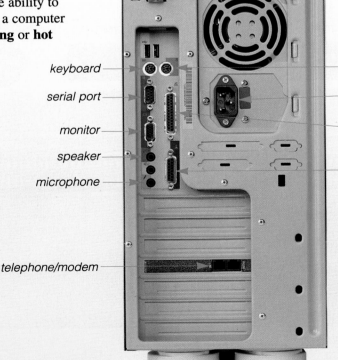

keyboard — — mouse
serial port — — power
monitor — — printer (parallel port)
speaker —
microphone — — joystick

telephone/modem —

Figure 3-30 A port is an interface that allows you to connect a peripheral device such as a printer, mouse, or keyboard to the computer. Usually, ports are on the back of the system unit and often are labeled.

Ports have different types of connectors. A **connector** is used to join a cable to a device (Figure 3-31). One end of a cable is attached to the connector on the system unit and the other end of the cable is attached to the peripheral device.

Most connectors are available in one of two genders: male or female. **Male connectors** have one or more exposed pins, like the end of an electrical cord you plug into the wall. **Female connectors** have matching holes to accept the pins on a male connector, like an electrical wall outlet.

Figure 3-32 shows the different types of connectors on a system unit. Some of these connectors are equipped with the computer when you buy it. Other connectors are added by inserting expansion cards into the computer. That is, the expansion card has a port, which enables you to attach a device to the expansion card. Understanding the differences among connector types is important, because the cables you purchase to connect peripheral devices to your computer often are identified by their types. For example, types of printer ports include a 25-pin female, 36-pin female, 36-pin Centronics female, and USB.

Sometimes a new peripheral device cannot be attached to the computer because the connector on the system unit is the same gender as the connector on the cable. Using a **gender changer**, which is a device used to join two connectors that are either both female or both male, can solve this problem.

Most computers are equipped with two types of ports: serial and parallel. The next section discusses each of these ports.

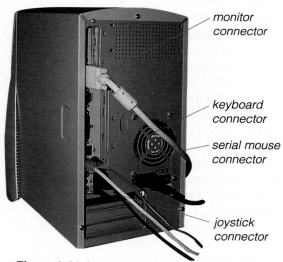

Figure 3-31 *A connector is used to attach an external device to the system unit.*

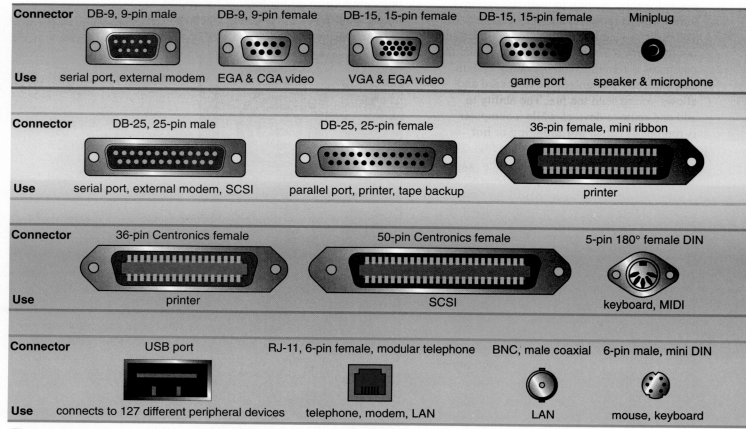

Figure 3-32 *Examples of different types of connectors on a system unit.*

Serial Ports

A **serial port** is one type of interface used to connect a device to the system unit. Because a serial port transmits only one bit of data at a time, it usually is used to connect devices that do not require fast data transmission rates, such as a mouse, keyboard, or modem (Figure 3-33). A modem, which connects the system unit to a telephone line, uses a serial port because the telephone line expects the data in a serial form. Serial ports conform to either the RS-232 or RS-422 standard, which specifies the number of pins used on the port's connector. Two common connectors for serial ports are a male 25-pin connector or a male 9-pin connector.

Parallel Ports

Unlike a serial port, a **parallel port** is an interface used to connect devices that are capable of transferring more than one bit at a time. Parallel ports originally were developed as an alternative to the slower speed serial ports.

Many printers connect to the system unit using a parallel port with a 25-pin female connector. This parallel port can transfer eight bits of data (one byte) simultaneously through eight separate lines in a single cable (Figure 3-34). A parallel port sometimes is called a Centronics interface, after the company that first defined the standard for communication between the system unit and a printer. Two newer types of parallel ports, the EPP (Enhanced Parallel Port) and the ECP (Extended Capabilities Port), use the same connectors as the Centronics port, but are more than ten times faster.

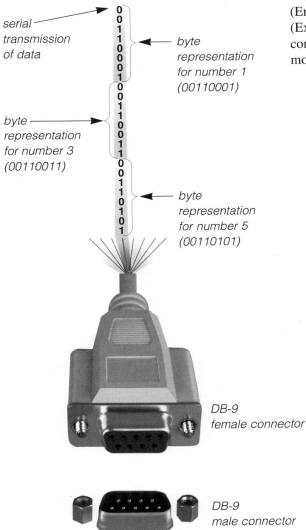

Figure 3-33 A serial port transmits data one bit at a time. One wire is used to send data; another is used to receive data; and the remaining wires are used for other communications operations.

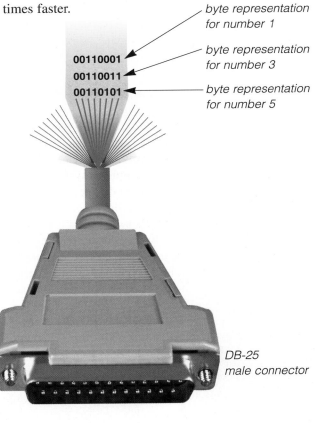

Figure 3-34 A parallel port is capable of transmitting more than one bit at a time. The port shown in this figure has eight wires that transmit data; the remaining wires are used for other communications operations.

Special-Purpose Ports

Five special-purpose ports used on many of today's computers are MIDI, SCSI, USB, 1394, and IrDA ports. Each of these ports is discussed in the following sections.

MIDI PORT A special type of serial port, called a **musical instrument digital interface,** or **MIDI** (pronounced MID-dee) **port,** is designed to connect the system unit to a musical instrument, such as an electronic keyboard. The electronic music industry has adopted MIDI as a standard to define how sounds are represented electronically by devices such as sound cards and synthesizers. A **synthesizer,** which can be a peripheral or a chip, creates sound from digital instructions. A system unit with a MIDI port has the capability of recording sounds that have been created by a synthesizer and then processing the sounds (the data) to create new sounds. Just about every sound card supports the MIDI standard, so sounds created using one computer can be played and manipulated by another.

SCSI PORT A special high-speed parallel port used to attach peripheral devices such as disk drives and printers is called a **SCSI port.** A SCSI port can transmit up to 32 bits at a time. Pronounced scuzzy, SCSI stands for **small computer system interface.** A total of seven SCSI devices can be daisy chained together, which means the first SCSI device connects to the computer, the second SCSI device connects to the first SCSI device, and so on. Some new computers are equipped with a SCSI port, while others have a slot that supports a SCSI expansion card.

UNIVERSAL SERIAL BUS PORT A **universal serial bus (USB) port** can connect up to 127 different peripheral devices with a single connector (Figure 3-35). Using this port, devices are daisy chained together outside the system unit.

A USB port also connects to newer peripherals such as digital cameras and joysticks. Having a standard port and connector greatly simplifies the process of attaching devices to a personal computer. The USB also supports hot plugging and Plug and Play, which means you can install peripherals while the computer is running.

1394 PORT Similarly to the USB port, the **1394 port** can connect multiple types of devices such as hard disks, printers, digital cameras, CD-ROM drives, and DVD-ROM drives to a single connector. The 1394 port also supports Plug and Play. Ports such as the USB and 1394 are expected someday to replace serial and parallel ports completely.

IrDA PORT Some peripheral devices do not use any cables; instead, they transmit data via infrared light waves. For these wireless devices to transmit signals to a computer, both the computer and the device must have an **IrDA port.** These ports must conform to standards developed by the **IrDA (Infrared Data Association).** Operating similar to a television remote control, the IrDA port on the computer and the IrDA port on the peripheral device must be aligned so that nothing obstructs the path of the infrared light wave. Devices that use IrDA ports include the keyboard, mouse, and printer.

BUSES

As previously explained, a computer processes and stores data as a series of electronic bits. These bits are transferred internally within the circuitry of the computer along electrical channels. Each channel, called a **bus,** allows the various devices inside and attached to the system unit to communicate with each other. Just as vehicles travel on a highway to move from one destination to another, bits travel on a bus (Figure 3-36).

WEB INFO
WEB INFO

For more information on buses, visit the Discovering Computers 2000 Chapter 3 WEB INFO page (www.scsite.com/dc2000/ch3/webinfo.htm) and click Bus.

Figure 3-35 *The universal serial bus (USB) port can connect up to 127 peripheral devices with a single connector.*

USB ports

Buses are used to transfer bits from input devices to memory, from memory to the CPU, from the CPU to memory, and from memory to output or storage devices. All buses consist of two parts: a data bus and an address bus. The data bus transfers actual data and the address bus transfers information about where the data should go in memory.

A bus is measured by its size. The size of a bus, called the **bus width**, determines the number of bits that can be transmitted at one time. For example, a 32-bit bus can transmit 32 bits (four bytes) at a time. On a 64-bit bus, bits are transmitted from one location to another 64 bits (eight bytes) at a time. The larger the number of bits handled by the bus, the faster the computer transfers data.

Using the highway analogy again, assume that one lane on a highway can carry one bit. A 32-bit bus, then, is like a 32-lane highway; and a 64-bit bus is like an 64-lane highway.

If a number in memory occupies eight bytes, or 64 bits, it must be transmitted in two separate steps when using a 32-bit bus: once for the first 32 bits and once for the second 32 bits. Using a 64-bit bus, however, the number can to be transmitted in a single step, transferring all 64 bits at once. The wider the bus, the fewer number of transfer steps required and the faster the transfer of data. Figure 3-37 summarizes some of the microprocessors currently in use and their bus widths.

In conjunction with the bus width, many computer professionals discuss a computer's word size. **Word size** is the number of bits

COMPARISON OF BUS WIDTHS

Name	Bus Width
Pentium® III Xeon™	100
Pentium® III	100
Pentium® II Xeon™	100
Pentium® II	64 or 100
Pentium® with MMX™ technology	64
Pentium® Pro	64
Pentium®	64
80486DX	32
80386DX	32
80286	16
PowerPC	64
68040	32
68030	32
68020	32
Alpha	64

Figure 3-37 *A comparison of bus widths on some of the more widely used microprocessors.*

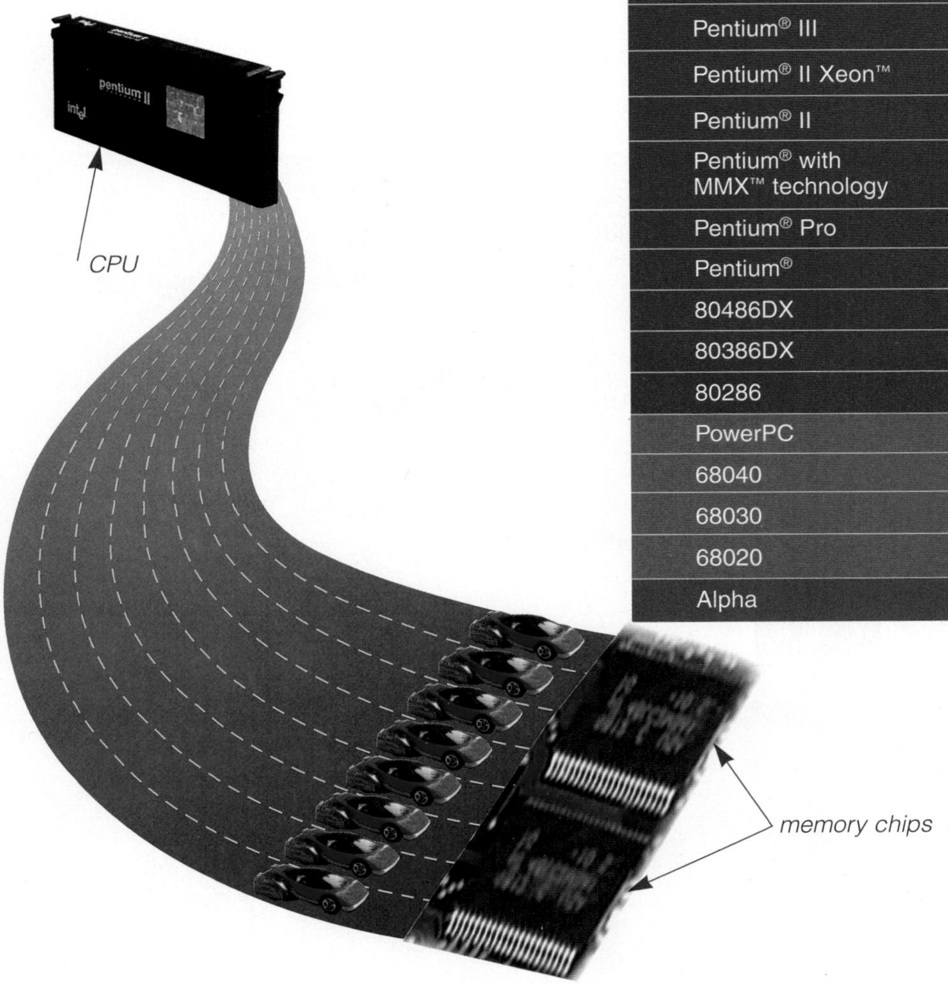

CPU

memory chips

Figure 3-36 *Just as vehicles travel on a highway to move from one destination to another, bits travel on a bus. Buses are used to transfer bits from input devices to memory, from memory to the CPU, from the CPU to memory, and from memory to output or storage devices.*

the CPU can process at a given time. That is, a 64-bit processor can manipulate 64 bits at a time. Computers with a larger word size can process more data in the same amount of time than computers with a smaller word size. In most computers, the word size is the same as the bus width.

Every bus also has a clock speed. Just like the processor, the clock speed for a bus is measured in megahertz. Recall that one megahertz (MHz) is equal to one million ticks per second. The higher the bus clock speed, the faster the transmission of data, which results in applications running faster.

Two basic types of buses are found in a computer: a system bus and an expansion bus. A **system bus** connects the CPU to main memory. An **expansion bus** allows the CPU to communicate with peripheral devices. When computer professionals use the term bus by itself, they usually are referring to the system bus.

Expansion Bus

Recall that a device outside the system unit is connected to a port on an expansion card, and an expansion card is inserted into an expansion slot. This expansion slot connects to the expansion bus, which allows the CPU to communicate with the peripheral device attached to the expansion card. Data transmitted to memory or the CPU travels from the expansion bus via the expansion bus and the system bus. The types of expansion buses on a motherboard determine the types of expansion cards you can add (Figure 3-38). For this reason, you should understand the following types of expansion buses: ISA bus, PCI bus, AGP bus, USB, 1394 bus, and PC Card bus.

• The most common and slowest expansion bus is the **ISA (Industry Standard Architecture) bus**. A mouse, modem card, sound card, and low-speed network card are examples of devices that connect to the ISA bus directly or through an ISA bus expansion slot.

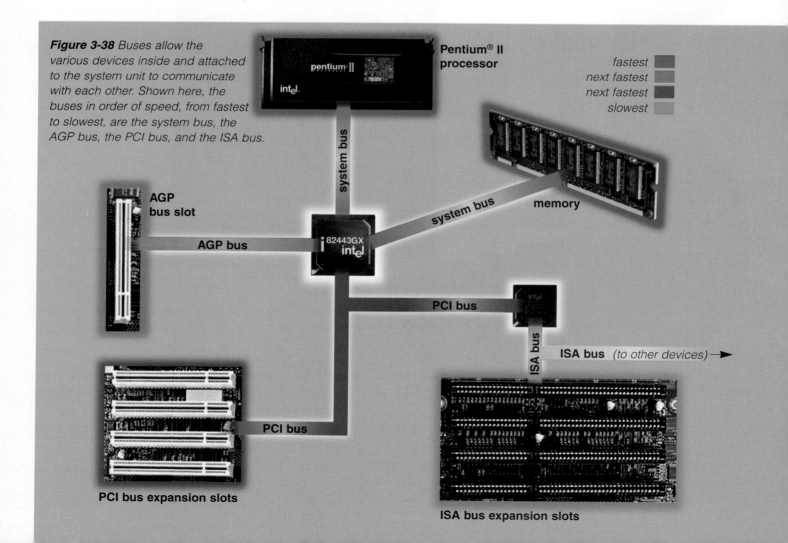

Figure 3-38 *Buses allow the various devices inside and attached to the system unit to communicate with each other. Shown here, the buses in order of speed, from fastest to slowest, are the system bus, the AGP bus, the PCI bus, and the ISA bus.*

- A **local bus** is a high-speed expansion bus used to connect higher speed devices such as hard disks. The first standard local bus was the **VESA local bus**, which was used primarily for video cards. The current local bus standard, however, is the **PCI (Peripheral Component Interconnect) bus** because it is more versatile than the VESA local bus. Types of cards inserted into a PCI bus expansion slot include video cards, SCSI cards, and high-speed network cards. The PCI bus transfers data about four times faster than the ISA bus. Most current personal computers have a PCI bus as well as an ISA bus.

- The **Accelerated Graphics Port (AGP)** is actually a bus designed by Intel to improve the speed with which 3-D graphics and video are transmitted. When an AGP video card is inserted in an AGP bus slot, the AGP bus provides a faster, dedicated interface between the video card and memory. Newer processors, such as the Pentium® II and Xeon™, support AGP technology.

- The **universal serial bus (USB)** and **1394 bus** are buses that eliminate the need to install expansion cards into expansion slots. In a computer equipped with a USB, for example, USB devices are connected to each other outside the system unit and then a single cable attaches to the USB port. The USB port then connects to the USB, which connects to the PCI bus on the motherboard. The 1394 bus works in a similar fashion. With these buses, you need not be concerned with running out of expansion slots.

- The expansion bus for a PC Card is the **PC Card bus**. With a PC Card inserted into a PC Card slot, data travels on the PC Card bus to the PCI bus.

BAYS

After you purchase a computer, you may want to install an additional device such as a disk drive to add storage capabilities to the system unit. A **bay** is an open area inside the system unit used to install additional equipment. Note that a bay is different from a slot, which is used for the installation of expansion cards. Because bays most often are used for disk drives, these spaces commonly are called **drive bays**.

Two types of drive bays exist: internal and external. An **external drive bay** or **exposed drive bay** allows access to the drive from outside the system unit. Floppy disk drives, CD-ROM drives, DVD-ROM drives, Zip® drives, and tape drives are examples of devices installed in external drive bays (Figure 3-39). An **internal drive bay** or **hidden drive bay** is concealed entirely within the system unit. Hard disk drives are installed in internal bays.

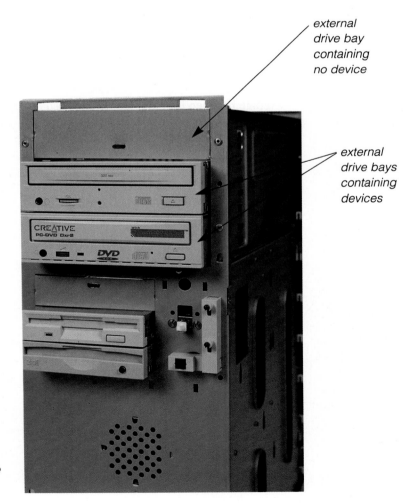

external drive bay containing no device

external drive bays containing devices

Figure 3-39 Bays, also called drive bays, usually are located beside or on top of one another. Each bay is about 6 inches wide and 1.75 inches high.

POWER SUPPLY

Many personal computers are plugged into standard wall outlets, which supply an alternating current (AC) of 115 to 120 volts. This type of power is unsuitable for use with a computer, which requires a direct current (DC) ranging from 5 to 12 volts. The **power supply** is the component in the system unit that converts the wall outlet AC power into DC power.

Some external peripheral devices such as an external modem or tape drive have an **AC adapter**, which is an external power supply. One end of the AC adapter plugs into the wall outlet and the other end attaches to the peripheral device. The AC adapter converts the AC power into DC power that the device requires.

LAPTOP COMPUTERS

As businesses expand to serve customers across the country and around the world, more and more people need to use a computer while traveling to and from a main office to conduct business. As noted in Chapter 1, users with such mobile computing needs – known as mobile users – often have a laptop computer (Figure 3-40). Weighing on average between four and ten pounds, usually these computers can run either using batteries or using a standard power supply.

Like their desktop counterparts, laptop computers have a system unit that contains electronic components used to process data (Figure 3-41). The difference is that many other devices also are built into the system unit. In addition to the motherboard, processor, memory, sound card, PC Card slot, and drive bay, the system unit also houses devices such as the keyboard, pointing device, and speakers. A laptop computer usually is more expensive than a desktop computer with the same capabilities.

Figure 3-41 Laptop computers have a system unit that contains electronic components used to process data.

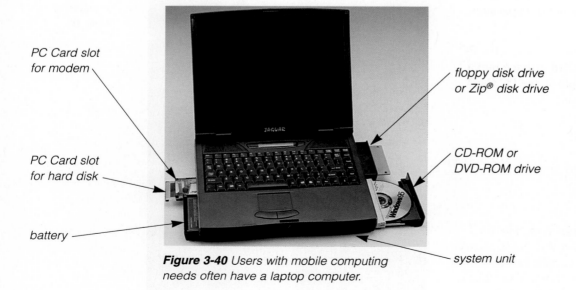

PC Card slot for modem

PC Card slot for hard disk

battery

floppy disk drive or Zip® disk drive

CD-ROM or DVD-ROM drive

system unit

Figure 3-40 Users with mobile computing needs often have a laptop computer.

The typical laptop computer often is equipped with serial, parallel, mouse, USB, video, IrDA, and docking station ports (Figure 3-42). Recall that a docking station is a device into which you place a laptop. The docking station contains connections to peripherals such as a keyboard, monitor, printer, and other devices. Some laptops also have a **port replicator**, which is a device that allows you to connect many peripheral devices (such as a printer, modem, and mouse) into it; the port replicator then is connected to the laptop computer.

PUTTING IT ALL TOGETHER

When you purchase a computer, you should have an understanding of the components in the system unit. Many factors inside the system unit influence the speed and power of a computer. The type of computer configuration you require depends on your intended use. The table in Figure 3-43 lists the suggested processor, clock speed, and RAM requirements based on the needs of various types of computer users.

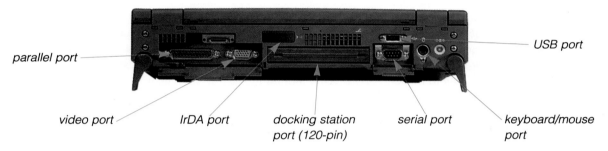

Figure 3-42 *A laptop computer often is equipped with serial, parallel, mouse, USB, video, IrDA, and docking station ports.*

SUGGESTED CONFIGURATIONS BY USER

USER	PROCESSOR AND CLOCK SPEED	RAM
Home User	Pentium® II or III – 400 MHz or higher; or Celeron™ – 400 MHz	32 MB
SMALL BUSINESS USER	Pentium® II or III – 400 MHz or higher	64 MB
MOBILE USER	Pentium® II – 350 MHz	64 MB
LARGE BUSINESS USER	Pentium® II or III – 450 MHz or higher	64 MB
POWER USER	Pentium® II or III Xeon™ – 500 MHz or higher	128 MB

Figure 3-43 *This table recommends suggested processor, clock speed, and RAM configurations.*

TECHNOLOGY TRAILBLAZERS

ANDY GROVE AND GORDON MOORE

The name Intel has become synonymous with microprocessors. From its inception, Gordon Moore and Andy Grove have been synonymous with Intel.

Gordon Moore's life-long interest in technology was kindled at an early age by a neighbor's chemistry set. Even then, he displayed the passion for practical outcomes that has typified his career. "With the chemistry set," he says, "I had to get a good explosion at the end or I wasn't happy." Yet, Moore was hardly a *science geek*. In high school, he devoted more time to athletics than to homework, lettering in four different sports. Moore was the first member of his family to attend college, graduating from the California Institute of Technology with a Ph.D. in chemistry and physics.

Moore worked with Bill Shockley, inventor of the transistor, at Shockley Semiconductor. There, he met Robert Noyce, and eventually the two left to join Fairchild Semiconductor. At Fairchild in 1965, Moore made a startling prediction. The power of silicon chips, he claimed, would *double* every eighteen months. This bold forecast, now known as Moore's Law, would prove amazingly accurate. Convinced of the future of silicon chips, and frustrated by the company's response to their work, in 1968 Moore and Noyce quit Fairchild to start Intel. "We saw a new way of storing information for computers," Moore notes. "A product area where... the existing semiconductor companies were not active."

Moore and Noyce were Intel's inspiration, but Andy Grove was the key to Intel's execution. Born in Budapest, Hungary, Grove survived the reigns of Hitler and Stalin, escaping to the United States in 1957. He completed his undergraduate degree in three years, while learning English and working as a waiter. After earning a Ph.D. in chemical engineering from the University of California at Berkeley, Grove worked as Moore's assistant at Fairchild. He was one of the first people recruited by Intel, where he was put in charge of production. According to Grove, by modern standards Intel's early assembly lines "looked like Willy Wonka's chocolate factory, with hoses and wires and contraptions chugging along." Grove fueled production with his firm, demanding style, emphasizing turnout over mere motion. "Stressing output is the key to productivity, while looking to increase activity can result in just the opposite." Grove adopted a team-based approach, encouraging managers and employees to meet one-on-one to impart data and foster a feeling of a shared effort. "People in the trenches," he points out, "are usually in touch with impending changes early."

Grove insists that recognizing and responding to changes is a crucial element in business success. In his book, *Only the Paranoid Survive*, Grove writes of "strategic inflection points" – changes that alter the fundamentals of a business. These changes can lead to opportunity or disaster. In the 1980s, a strategic inflection point occurred in the computer industry when a production glut resulted in an overabundance of memory chips. In response, Intel concentrated its efforts on microprocessors. Sales soared $789 million in 1981 to more than $3 billion in 1990. What momentous change will reshape today's businesses? Grove believes that "the mother of all strategic inflection points" is the Internet.

Both Moore and Grove share a key characteristic: the willingness to make a commitment even when results are unknown. This forward-looking approach is a hallmark of Intel's corporate philosophy. Grove writes, "The best thing is to make the right decision. Making a wrong decision is okay, too. The worst thing to do is hedge. To hedge is to fail." Moore concurs, noting that although they involve some risk, decisions should not be feared. After all, Moore says, "If everything you try works, then you are not trying hard enough."

Andrew S. Grove

Gordon E. Moore

COMPANY ON THE CUTTING EDGE

COMPANY ON THE CUTTING EDGE

INTEL

On an August day in 1968, Robert Noyce was mowing his lawn when Gordon Moore, a coworker at Fairchild Semiconductor, stopped by to talk. The two shared gripes, frustrated by the company's apparent disinterest in their work. Colleagues, who some called "Fairchildren," had left to form new companies. In a moment of inspiration, the pair decided to start their own company and manufacture a new product – semiconductors to replace the magnetic cores that comprised computer memory. Noyce typed a one-page business plan, an investment banker raised $2.5 million, the partners each put up $250,000, and a company called Moore Noyce emerged. The name, unfortunately, sounded a lot like "More Noise" – hardly suitable for an electronics firm – so they incorporated as NM Electronics. Later, after purchasing rights from a motel chain, a new name was adopted – Intel (for integrated electronics). From such humble beginnings came a company that today has more than $25 billion in sales.

Even if semiconductors could be used for memory storage, critics maintained it would cost much more to manufacture semiconductors than magnetic cores. Undismayed, Noyce and Moore, together with Andy Grove, another Fairchild expatriate, struggled to reduce production costs while packing more transistors on a chip. Moore had predicted that the power of silicon chips would continue to grow. If he was right, eventually memory chips would be less expensive and more popular than magnetic cores. As Intel perfected increasingly more powerful memory chips, sales climbed steadily.

Intel's most revolutionary product, however, was developed in answer to a customer request. A calculator manufacturer asked Intel to produce twelve custom chips. Instead of twelve separate chips, Ted Hoff, an Intel engineer, suggested designing a single chip that could function as twelve. The entire central processing unit would be placed on one, general-purpose programmable chip, saving money and time. This chip, introduced in 1971, was the first microprocessor. Dubbed the Intel 4004, the chip measured only 1/8 inch by 1/6 inch but had 2,300 transistors, could perform 60,000 operations per second, and packed as much power as ENIAC, the room-sized, vacuum-tube computer. The 4004 was one of the more important inventions in the history of technology.

Manufacturing and design rights were purchased from the calculator maker, and Intel began promoting its general-purpose programmable chip in the engineering community. Ever more powerful chips drove earnings to more than $660 million in the late 1970s. When IBM chose the Intel 8088 chip for its new personal computer in 1980, Intel chips became the standard for all IBM-compatible personal computers. Yet, competition was fierce as other chip manufacturers developed and marketed less-expensive clones. To meet the challenge, Intel introduced increasingly capable microprocessors, including the 386 and 486, the first chip to speed computations with a math coprocessor.

Intel's climb was not without missteps. The most jarring stumble occurred in 1994 when a design flaw was discovered in Intel's new Pentium® chip. For the average user, the defect resulted in a mistake only once in every 27,000 years, so Intel ignored the error. Faced with an unanticipated public outcry, however, the company reconsidered and offered replacement chips, at a cost of almost $500 million. An increased awareness of public perceptions caused Intel to launch an extensive new advertising campaign, immortalizing the slogan, "Intel Inside." By 1997, Intel controlled ninety percent of the microprocessor market.

Today, Intel employs more than 60,000 workers at sites around the world. The company supports a number of charities and encourages employees to aid schools and nonprofit organizations by volunteering via "Intel Involved." Through these efforts, Intel hopes to demonstrate its commitment not only to the development of new products, but also to the communities that use them.

SHELLY
CASHMAN
SERIES®
DISCOVERING
COMPUTERS
2000

CHAPTER 1 2 **3** 4 5 6 7 8 9 10 11 12 13 14 INDEX

IN BRIEF **www.scsite.com/dc2000/ch3/brief.htm**

WEB INSTRUCTIONS: *To display this page from the Web, launch your browser and enter the URL, www.scsite.com/dc2000/ch3/brief.htm. Click the links for current and additional information. To listen to an audio version of this IN BRIEF, click the Audio button to the right of the title, IN BRIEF, at the top of the page. To play the audio, RealPlayer must be installed on your computer (download by clicking here).*

 ## 1. What Are the Components of the System Unit?

The **system unit** is a box-like case housing the electronic components of a computer that are used to process data. System unit components include the processor, memory module, expansion cards, and ports and connectors. Many components reside on a circuit board called the **motherboard** or **system board**. The motherboard contains different types of **chips**, or small pieces of semiconducting material on which one or more **integrated circuits** (**IC**) are etched. One of the more important chips is the central processing unit.

 ## 2. How Does the CPU Process Data?

The **central processing unit** (**CPU**), sometimes referred to as the **processor**, interprets and carries out the basic instructions that operate a computer. The **control unit**, one component of the CPU, directs and coordinates most of the operations in the computer. For every instruction, the control unit repeats a set of four basic operations called the **machine cycle**: (1) **fetching** the instruction or data item from memory, (2) **decoding** the instruction into commands the computer understands, (3) **executing** the commands, and, if necessary, (4) **storing**, or writing, the result to memory. The arithmetic/logic unit, another component of the CPU, performs the execution part of the machine cycle.

 ## 3. How Do Pipelining and the System Clock Affect Processing Speed?

With **pipelining**, the CPU begins executing a second instruction before the first instruction is completed. Pipelining results in faster processing because the CPU does not have to wait for one instruction to complete the machine cycle. The **system clock** is a small chip that the control unit relies on to synchronize computer operations. The faster the clock, the more instructions the CPU can execute per second. The speed at which a processor executes instructions is called **clock speed**. Clock speed is measured in **megahertz** (**MHz**), which equates to one million ticks of the system clock.

 ## 4. What Are Some Microprocessors Available Today?

A personal computer's CPU usually is contained on a single chip called a **microprocessor**. Early Intel microprocessors were identified with numbers, but a more recent series is known as **Pentium®** **processors**. Intel processors with **MMX™ technology** have a built-in set of instructions that can be used to manipulate and process multimedia data more efficiently. **Intel-compatible microprocessors** have the same internal design as Intel processors and perform the same functions, but are made by other companies and often are less expensive. The **Motorola microprocessor** is an alternative to the Intel-style microprocessor and is found in Apple Macintosh and Power Macintosh systems. The **Alpha microprocessor**, from Digital Equipment Corporation, is used primarily in workstations and high-end servers.

IN BRIEF

 www.scsite.com/dc2000/ch3/brief.htm

 ## 5. How Do Series of Bits Represent Data?

Most computers are **digital**, meaning they understand only two discrete states: on and off. These states are represented using two digits, 0 (off) and 1 (on). Each on or off value is called a **bit** (short for **bi**nary dig**it**), which is the smallest unit of data a computer can handle. Eight bits grouped together as a unit are called a **byte**. A byte can represent 256 individual characters including numbers, letters of the alphabet, punctuation marks, and other characters. Combinations of 0s and 1s used to represent data are defined by patterns called coding schemes. Popular coding schemes are ASCII, **EBCDIC**, and **Unicode**.

 ## 6. What Are Different Types of Memory?

In the system unit, a computer's **memory** stores data, instructions, and information. The number of bytes it can store measures memory size – a **kilobyte** (**KB**) is approximately one thousand bytes, and a **megabyte** (**MB**) is approximately one million bytes. **RAM** (**random access memory**) is a memory chip that the processor can read from and write to. RAM is **volatile memory**, meaning that its contents are lost when the computer's power is turned off. **ROM** (**read-only memory**) is a memory chip that only can be read and used; that is, it cannot be modified. ROM is **nonvolatile memory**, meaning that its contents are not lost when the computer's power is turned off. **Flash memory**, or **flash ROM**, is nonvolatile memory that can be erased electronically and reprogrammed. **CMOS** memory is nonvolatile memory used to store configuration information about the computer.

 ## 7. What Are Expansion Slots and Expansion Boards?

An **expansion slot** is an opening, or socket, where a circuit board can be inserted into the motherboard. These circuit boards, sometimes referred to as **expansion boards** or **expansion cards**, add new devices or capabilities to the computer, such as a modem or more memory. **Plug and Play** refers to a computer's capability to automatically configure expansion boards and other devices as they are installed.

 ## 8. How Is a Serial Port Different from a Parallel Port?

A cable often attaches external devices to the system unit. The interface, or point of attachment, to the system unit is called a **port**. Ports have different types of **connectors** used to join a cable to a device. A **serial port** is an interface that transmits only one bit of data at a time. Serial ports usually are used to connect devices that do not require fast data transmission rates, such as a mouse, keyboard, or modem. A **parallel port** is an interface used to connect devices that are capable of transferring more than one bit at a time. Many printers connect to the system unit using a parallel port.

 ## 9. How Do Buses Contribute to a Computer's Processing Speed?

Bits are transferred internally within the circuitry of the computer along electrical channels. Each channel, called a **bus**, allows various devices inside and attached to the system unit to communicate with each other. The **bus width**, or size of the bus, determines the number of bits that can be transferred at one time. The larger the bus width, the faster the computer transfers data.

KEY TERMS www.scsite.com/dc2000/ch3/terms.htm

WEB INSTRUCTIONS: *To display this page from the Web, launch your browser and enter the URL, www.scsite.com/dc2000/ch3/terms.htm. Scroll through the list of terms. Click a term to display its definition and a picture. Click KEY TERMS on the left to redisplay the KEY TERMS page. Click the TO WEB button for current and additional information about the term from the Web. To see animations, Shockwave and Flash Player must be installed on your computer (download by clicking here).*

Student Exercises
WEB INFO
IN BRIEF
KEY TERMS
AT THE MOVIES
CHECKPOINT
AT ISSUE
CYBERCLASS
HANDS ON
NET STUFF
Special Features
TIMELINE 2000
GUIDE TO WWW SITES
MAKING A CHIP
BUYER'S GUIDE 2000
CAREERS 2000
TRENDS 2000
CHAT
INTERACTIVE LABS
NEWS
HOME

1394 bus (3.27)
1394 port (3.24)
AC adapter (3.28)
Accelerated Graphics Port (AGP) (3.27)
access time (3.19)
adapter card (3.20)
add-in (3.20)
add-on (3.20)
address (3.14)
Alpha microprocessor (3.9)
American Standard Code for Information Interchange (ASCII) (3.12)
analog (3.11)
arithmetic operations (3.7)
arithmetic/logic unit (ALU) (3.7)
bay (3.27)
binary (3.12)
bit (3.12)
bus (3.24)
bus width (3.25)
byte (3.12)
cache (3.17)
card (3.20)
Celeron (3.9)
central processing unit (CPU) (3.5)
chip (3.4)
chip for chip upgrade (3.10)
clock cycle (3.8)
clock rate (3.8)
clock speed (3.8)
comparison operations (3.7)
complimentary metal-oxide semiconductor (CMOS) (3.19)
connector (3.22)
control unit (3.6)
coprocessor (3.11)
daughterboard (3.10)
daughterboard upgrade (3.10)
decoding (3.6)
digital (3.11)
drive bays (3.27)
dual inline memory module (DIMM) (3.16)
dynamic RAM (DRAM) (3.16)
E-time (3.6)
executing (3.6)
execution time (3.6)
expansion board (3.20)
expansion bus (3.26)
expansion card (3.20)
expansion slot (3.20)
exposed drive bay (3.27)
Extended Binary Coded Decimal Interchange Code (EBCDIC) (3.12)
external cache (3.17)
external drive bay (3.27)
female connectors (3.22)
fetching (3.6)
firmware (3.18)
flash memory (3.18)

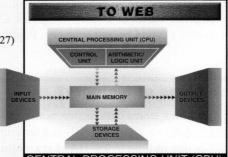

CENTRAL PROCESSING UNIT (CPU): Interprets and carries out the basic instructions that operate a computer. The CPU contains the control unit and the arithmetic/logic unit that work together to perform the processing operations. Also called processor, and on the personal computer it is called a microprocessor because it usually is contained on a single chip. (3.5)

flash ROM (3.18)
floating-point coprocessor (3.11)
gender changer (3.22)
graphics card (3.20)
heat pipe (3.11)
heat sink (3.10)
hidden drive bay (3.27)
hot plugging (3.21)
hot swapping (3.21)
Industry Standard Architecture bus (ISA) (3.26)
Infrared Data Association (IrDA) (3.24)
instruction cycle (3.6)
instruction time (3.6)
integrated circuit (IC) (3.4)
interface card (3.20)
internal cache (3.17)
internal drive bay (3.27)
internal modem (3.20)
IrDA port (3.24)
I-time (3.6)
kilobyte (KB or K) (3.14)
Level 1 (L1) cache (3.17)
Level 2 (L2) cache (3.17)
local bus (3.27)
logical operations (3.7)
machine cycle (3.6)
male connectors (3.22)
megabyte (MB) (3.15)
megahertz (MHz) (3.8)
memory (3.14)
memory cache (3.17)
microcode (3.18)
microprocessor (3.5)

millisecond (ms) (3.20)
MIPS (3.7)
MMX technology (3.10)
motherboard (3.4)
Motorola microprocessor (3.9)
musical instrument digital interface (MIDI) port (3.24)
nanosecond (ns) (3.19)
nonvolatile memory (3.15)
parallel port (3.23)
parallel processing (3.11)
PC Card (3.21)
PC Card bus (3.27)
PCMCIA cards (3.21)
Pentiumfi processors (3.9)
Peripheral Component Interconnect (PCI) bus (3.27)
piggyback upgrade (3.10)
pipelining (3.7)
Plug and Play (3.20)
port (3.21)
port replicator (3.29)
power supply (3.28)
primary cache (3.17)
processor (3.5)
programmable read-only memory (PROM) (3.18)
random access memory (RAM) (3.15)
read-only memory (ROM) (3.18)
registers (3.8)
saved (3.16)
serial port (3.23)
single inline memory module (SIMM) (3.16)
small computer system interface (SCSI) port (3.24)
sound card (3.20)
static RAM (SRAM) (3.16)
storing (3.6)
Superscaler (3.8)
synchronous DRAM (SDRAM) (3.16)
synthesizer (3.24)
system board (3.4)
system bus (3.26)
system clock (3.8)
system unit (3.2)
transistors (3.4)
Type I cards (3.21)
Type II cards (3.21)
Type III cards (3.21)
Unicode (3.12)
universal serial bus (USB) (3.27)
universal serial bus (USB) port (3.24)
VESA local bus (3.27)
video adapter (3.20)
video card (3.20)
volatile memory (3.15)
word size (3.25)
Xeon processor (3.9)
zero-insertion force (ZIF) socket (3.10)

AT THE MOVIES   www.scsite.com/dc2000/ch3/movies.htm

SHELLY
CASHMAN
SERIES®
DISCOVERING
COMPUTERS
2000

WELCOME to VIDEO CLIPS from CNN

WEB INSTRUCTIONS: *To display this page from the Web, launch your browser and enter the URL, www.scsite.com/dc2000/ch3/movies.htm. Click a picture to view a video. After watching the video, close the video window and then complete the exercise by answering the questions about the video. To view the videos, RealPlayer must be installed on your computer (download by clicking here).*

1 Grove Profile

Intel is the leading manufacturer of microprocessors, including the Pentium, Celeron, and Xeon processors. Intel grew to its present size with more than 60,000 employees as a result of the outstanding leadership of Andrew Grove. Based on the personal information you learned about Mr. Grove, describe how his early life struggles, his strong work ethic, and his vision of capitalizing on business trends have been the foundation for Intel's worldwide microprocessor empire. How might Andrew Grove's forward-growth visions for Intel continue to drive the company toward even greater success in the future?

2 IBM

IBM is keeping pace with the phenomenal rate of change in the computer technology industry by manufacturing microchips in a more desirable way than in the past. They have developed a breakthrough in semiconductor production that promises to affect IBM's business favorably. Confidence in the new process has been reflected by an increase in the value of the company's stock. Explain the new technology IBM has developed. How does it differ from the way chips have been made in the past? What are the benefits of the new technology to consumers and businesses?

3 Clone Buster

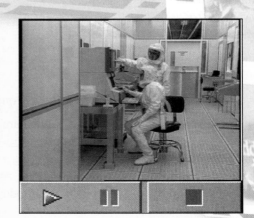

Although some felt the name, Pentium, would never take hold, the name has withstood the test of time. Why did Intel decide to move away from using numbers to name its chips? Why did Intel choose the name Pentium? Would you have chosen this name? If not, why?

SHELLY
CASHMAN
SERIES

DISCOVERING
COMPUTERS
2000

Student Exercises
WEB INFO
IN BRIEF
KEY TERMS
AT THE MOVIES
CHECKPOINT
AT ISSUE
CYBERCLASS
HANDS ON
NET STUFF
Special Features
TIMELINE 2000
GUIDE TO WWW SITES
MAKING A CHIP
BUYER'S GUIDE 2000
CAREERS 2000
TRENDS 2000
CHAT
INTERACTIVE LABS
NEWS
HOME

CHAPTER 1 2 **3** 4 5 6 7 8 9 10 11 12 13 14 **INDEX**

CHECKPOINT www.scsite.com/dc2000/ch3/check.htm

WEB INSTRUCTIONS: *To display this page from the Web, launch your browser and enter the URL, www.scsite.com/dc2000/ch3/check.htm. Click the links for current and additional information. To experience the animation and interactivity, Shockwave and Flash Player must be installed on your computer (download by clicking here).*

Label the Figure

Instructions: *Identify these components of the motherboard.*

1._____
2._____
3._____
4._____
5._____
6._____
7._____
8._____

Matching

Instructions: *Match each term from the column on the left with the best description from the column on the right.*

_____ 1. DRAM (dynamic RAM)

_____ 2. SRAM (static RAM)

_____ 3. SIMM (single inline memory module)

_____ 4. DIMM (dual inline memory module)

_____ 5. RAM cache (or memory cache)

a. Circuit board with RAM chips on only one side.

b. Type of memory that must be re-energized constantly or it loses its contents.

c. Nonvolatile memory that can be read and used but not modified.

d. Speeds processing time by storing frequently used instructions and data.

e. Circuit board with RAM chips on both sides.

f. Blank, nonvolatile memory chip on which items can be permanently placed.

g. More expensive type of memory that can be re-energized less often; used for special purposes.

Short Answer

Instructions: *Write a brief answer to each of the following questions.*

1. What is the purpose of the CPU? _____ What are registers? _____
2. How is instruction time, or I-time, different from execution time, or E-time? _____ In what unit is a computer's speed measured? _____
3. How are arithmetic operations, comparison operations, and logical operations different? _____
4. What are five special-purpose ports used in many of today's computers? _____ For what purpose is each port used? _____
5. How is a system bus different from an expansion bus? _____ How is an internal drive bay different from an external drive bay? _____

AT ISSUE   www.scsite.com/dc2000/ch3/issue.htm

WEB INSTRUCTIONS: *To display this page from the Web, launch your browser and enter the URL,* www.scsite.com/dc2000/ch3/issue.htm. *Click the links for current and additional information.*

From 1989 to 1998, the maximum clock speed of Intel's microprocessors increased 350 percent. New micron production processes and copper-based circuits continue the acceleration. Faster and less expensive microprocessors are anticipated, with clock speeds of 700 MHz or even 1 GHz (1,000 MHz). In the midst of this progress, whispers of planned obsolescence are heard among some naysayers. Faster processor speed and new software that demands it, they argue, will make a PC bought today obsolete in two years. Besides, they continue, is the increased speed really necessary? What do you think? Is greater processor speed a benefit for manufacturers and consumers alike, or a boon for builders and a burden for buyers? Why?

At a recent auto show, Citroen unveiled the first car equipped with Intel's Connected Car PC technology. The car PC lets drivers access e-mail (which is read by a text-to-speech converter), receive weather and traffic data, and obtain navigation information. Passengers can use the PC to watch movies on DVD. Developing and producing car PCs is expensive. Because of their special environment, they must be more durable and offer a simpler interface than desktop PCs. Many automakers wonder if car PCs offer buyers enough to justify their cost. Would you be interested in a car PC? Why or why not? How much would you be willing to add to the price of a new car for the convenience of a car PC?

THREE *Several terms that name system unit components or their functions also have* meanings in other contexts. For example, in the system unit a bay is an open area used to install additional equipment; in geography, a bay is an open area of water, partially surrounded by land, that is used to anchor ships. Comparing these meanings can help clarify, and make memorable, a term's definition. Make a list of terms from this chapter that have meanings in other contexts. Next to each term, write its meaning in relation to the system unit, its meaning in another context, and the ways in which the meanings are, or are not, similar. List as many terms as possible, including compound words (such as motherboard) that have parts (mother and board) with alternate meanings.

FOUR *Gordon Moore, cofounder of Intel, fears that* society is becoming a two-class society, "those who are wired and those who are not." A recent Commerce Department report echoes Moore's concerns. The report asserts that age, income, and education all are factors in computer use. Do those who "are wired" have an advantage over those who "are not wired?" In what way? If you do not have a computer and cannot access the Internet, can you still compete for good grades in school? What can be done to make computing available to everyone? Do the computers in public and school libraries solve the problem? Why or why not? If this situation continues, what will be the effects on society as a whole?

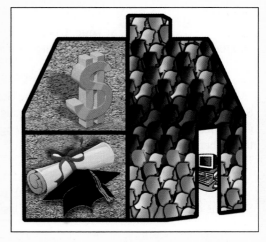

FIVE *In 1994, a design flaw in Intel's Pentium* microprocessor chip caused a rounding error once in nine billion division operations. For most users, this would result in a mistake only once in every 27,000 years, so Intel initially ignored the problem. After an unexpected public outcry, however, eventually Intel supplied replacements to anyone who wanted one at a cost of almost $500 million. Did people overreact? Did the demand for perfection divert funds that could have been better spent elsewhere? (Intel's costs were equivalent to half a year's research and development budget.) How much perfection do consumers have a right to expect?

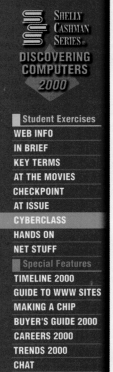

CHAPTER   1   2   3   4   5   6   7   8   9   10   11   12   13   14   INDEX

CYBERCLASS   www.scsite.com/dc2000/ch3/class.htm

WEB INSTRUCTIONS: *To display this page from the Web, launch your browser and enter the URL, www.scsite.com/dc2000/ch3/class.htm. To start Level I CyberClass, click a Level I link on this page or enter the URL, www.cyber-class.com. Click the Student button, click Discovering Computers 2000 in the list of titles, and then click the Enter a site button. To start Level II or III CyberClass (available only to those purchasers of a CyberClass floppy disk), place your CyberClass floppy disk in drive A, click Start on the taskbar, click Run on the Start menu, type* a:connect *in the Open text box, click the OK button, click the Enter CyberClass button, and then follow the instructions.*

I   II   III   LEVEL   **1. Flash Cards**   Click Flash Cards on the Main Menu of the CyberClass web page. Click the plus sign before the Chapter 3 title. Click CPU and Microprocessor and answer all the cards in that section. Choose other sections and continue until you have answered 20 questions. Record your percentage correct and hand in your score to your instructor. All users: Answer as many more Flash Cards as you desire. Close the Electronic Flash Card window and the Flash Cards window by clicking the Close button in the upper-right corner of each window.

I   II   III   LEVEL   **2. Practice Test**   Click Testing on the Main Menu of the CyberClass web page. Click the Select a book box arrow and then click Discovering Computers 2000. Click the Select a test to take box arrow and then click the Chapter 3 title in the list. Click the Take Test button. If necessary, maximize the window. Take the practice test and then click the Submit Test button. Click the Display Study  Guide button. Review the Study Guide and then print the Study Guide by clicking the Print button on the toolbar or by clicking File/Print on the menu bar. Scroll down and click the Return To CyberClass button. Click the Yes button to close the Study Guide window. Then, click the Done button. Hand in your printed Study Guide.

I   II   III   LEVEL   **3. Web Guide**   Click Web Guide on the Main Menu of the CyberClass web page. When the Guide to World Wide Web Sites page displays, click Humor. Examine the sites under humor until you find a joke or comic strip related to computers. Based on what you have learned so far in this course, is the joke or comic strip accurate or inaccurate? Do you think humor helps or hurts an understanding of computers? When you are finished, close the window. Hand in a brief synopsis of your answers to your instructor.

I   II   III   LEVEL   **4. Company Briefs**   Click Company Briefs on the Main Menu of the CyberClass web page. Click a corporation name to display a case study. Read the case study. Write a brief report on why computers are vital to the company you selected.

II   III   LEVEL   **5. CyberChallenge**   Click CyberChallenge on the Main Menu of the CyberClass web page. Click the Select a book box arrow and then click Discovering Computers 2000. Click the Select a board to play box arrow and then click Chapter 3 in the list. Click the Play CyberChallenge button. Maximize the CyberChallenge window. Play CyberChallenge until you have answered all the 10, 20, and 30 point questions correctly. Close the CyberChallenge window.

II   III   LEVEL   **6. Assignments and Syllabus**   Click Assignments on the Main Menu of the CyberClass web page. Ensure you are aware of all assignments and when they are due. Click Syllabus on the Main Menu of the CyberClass web page. Verify you are up to date on all activities for the class.

II   III   LEVEL   **7. Send Messages**   Visit a Web site you located through a magazine, newspaper, radio, or television. Send a message to your classmates (or selected classmates) indicating if you liked the Web site or not and the reasons why.

HANDS ON

www.scsite.com/dc2000/ch3/hands.htm

WEB INSTRUCTIONS: *To display this page from the Web, launch your browser and enter the URL,* www.scsite.com/dc2000/ch3/hands.htm. *Click the links for current and additional information.*

One — Installing New Hardware

This exercise uses Windows 98 procedures. Plug and Play technology is a key feature of the Windows operating system. Plug and Play technology allows users to install new devices without having to reconfigure the system manually. To find out how to install a new device with Plug and Play technology, click the Start button on the taskbar, and then click Help on the Start menu. Click the Contents tab. Click the Managing Hardware and Software book and then click the Installing New Hardware and Software book. Click Install a Plug and Play device. What are the three steps in installing a Plug and Play device? When would Windows not detect a Plug and Play device? How is a device that is not Plug and Play installed?

Two — Setting the System Clock

Double-click the time on the taskbar. In the Date/Time Properties dialog box, click the question mark button on its title bar and then click the picture of the calendar. Read the information in the pop-up window and then click the pop-up window to close it. Repeat this process for other areas of the dialog box and then answer these questions:

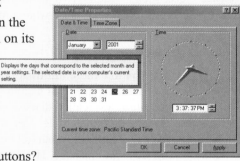

- ▲ What is the purpose of the calendar?
- ▲ How do you change the time zone?
- ▲ What is the difference between the OK and the Apply buttons?

Close the Date/Time Properties dialog box.

Three — Using Calculator to Perform Number System Conversion

Instead of the decimal (base 10) number system that people use, computers use the binary (base 2) or hexadecimal (base 16) number systems. It is not necessary to understand these number systems to use a computer, but it is interesting to see how decimal numbers look when in binary or hexadecimal form. Click the Start button on the taskbar, point to Programs on the Start menu, point to Accessories on the Programs submenu, and then click Calculator on the Accessories submenu. Click View on the menu bar and then click Scientific to display the scientific calculator. Perform the following tasks:

- ▲ Click Dec to select decimal. Enter 35 by clicking the numeric buttons or using the numeric keypad. Click Bin to select binary. What number displays? Click Hex to select hexadecimal. What number displays? Click the C (Clear) button.
- ▲ Convert the following decimal numbers to binary and hexadecimal: 7, 256, and 3,421.
- ▲ What decimal number is equal to 10010 in the binary system? What decimal number is equal to 2DA9 in the hexadecimal system?

Close Calculator.

Four — Power Management

This exercise uses Windows 98 procedures. Environmental and financial considerations make it important to manage the amount of power a computer uses. Click the Start button on the taskbar, point to Settings on the Start menu, and then click Control Panel on the Settings submenu. Double-click the Power Management icon in the Control Panel dialog box. In the Power Management Properties dialog box, click the Power Schemes tab. What is a power scheme? What power scheme currently is being used on your computer? After how many minutes of inactivity is the monitor turned off? After how many minutes of inactivity are the hard disks turned off? Close the Power Management dialog box and the Control Panel dialog box. How can the Power Management dialog box be used to make a computer more energy efficient?

SHELLY
CASHMAN
SERIES®
DISCOVERING
COMPUTERS
2000

CHAPTER 1 2 **3** 4 5 6 7 8 9 10 11 12 13 14 **INDEX**

NET STUFF   www.scsite.com/dc2000/ch3/net.htm

WEB INSTRUCTIONS: *To display this page from the Web, launch your browser and enter the URL, www.scsite.com/dc2000/ch3/net.htm. To use the Motherboard lab from the Web, Shockwave and Flash Player must be installed on your computer (download by clicking here).*

MOTHERBOARD LAB

1. Shelly Cashman Series Motherboard Lab

Follow the appropriate instructions in NET STUFF 1 on page 1.46 to start and use the Understanding the Motherboard lab. If you are running from the Web, enter the URL, www.scsite.com/sclabs/menu.htm, or display the NET STUFF page (see instructions at the top of this page) and then click the MOTHERBOARD LAB button.

MICRO-PROCESSOR

2. How a Microprocessor Works

After reading about what a microprocessor does and the way it interacts with other system unit components, it still can be difficult to understand how a microprocessor performs even a simple task such as adding two plus three. To find the answer, click the MICROPROCESSOR button and complete this exercise to learn what a microprocessor does to find the answer.

NEWSGROUPS

3. Newsgroups

Would you like more information about a special interest? Perhaps you would like to share opinions and advice with people who have the same interest. If so, you might be interested in newsgroups, also called discussion groups or forums. A newsgroup offers the opportunity to read articles on a specific subject, respond to the articles, and even post your own articles. Click the NEWSGROUPS button to find out more about newsgroups. What is lurking? What is Usenet? Click the Searching Newsgroups link at the bottom of the page. Read and print the Searching Newsgroups page. How can you locate a newsgroup on a particular topic?

IN THE NEWS

4. In the News

The ENIAC (Electronic Numerical Integrator and Computer) often is considered the first modern computer. Invented in 1946, the ENIAC weighed thirty tons and filled a thirty-by-fifty-foot room, yet its capabilities are dwarfed by current laptop computers. The ENIAC performed fewer than one thousand calculations per minute; today, PCs can process more than 300 million instructions per second. The rapid development of computing power and capabilities is astonishing, and that development is accelerating. Click the IN THE NEWS button and read a news article about the introduction of a new or improved computer component. What is the component? Who is introducing it? Will the component change the way people use computers? If so, how?

WEB CHAT

5. Web Chat

Winnie the Pooh may be less rumbley in the tumbley. Toy makers have put something in the stomach of stuffed versions of the bear – microprocessors. The stuffed Pooh chatters through twenty minutes of talk and song and can be programmed to use a child's name, discuss favorite foods and activities, and play games both at and away from a computer. Yet, some parents are not impressed with the bear's accomplishments. They maintain that a simple stuffed toy develops creativity through imaginary conversations and fanciful play, but the processor-enriched bear promotes little more than passive observation. Stuffed toys with microprocessors are available for about $100. Would you buy one for your child? Why or why not? Click the WEB CHAT button to enter a Web Chat discussion related to this topic.

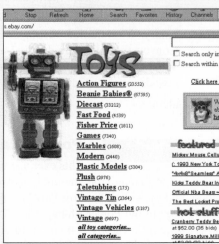

"The human tendency to regard little things as important has produced very many great things."

– G. C. Lichtenberg

WEB INSTRUCTIONS: *To gain World Wide Web access to additional and up-to-date information regarding this special feature, launch your browser and enter the URL shown at the top of this page.*

How Computer Chips Are Made

Computer chips are made by placing and removing thin layers of insulating, conducting, and semiconducting materials in hundreds of distinct steps. The chips are incredibly small — tinier than a human fingernail — and are becoming smaller. Intel recently released two chips using a 0.18-micron production process (a micron, or micrometer, is 0.000001 of a meter), instead of the 0.25-micron process used to produce Pentium and Pentium II processors. Smaller production processes make smaller chips and smaller circuitry possible. Because electricity travels faster over smaller circuits, these smaller chips are faster than ever. The smaller chips also are less expensive because manufacturers can create more chips from the same amount of raw materials.

Every computer chip consists of many layers of circuits and microscopic electronic components such as transistors, diodes, capacitors, and resistors. Connected together on a chip, these components are referred to as an **integrated circuit (IC)**. Most chips have at least four to six layers, but some have more than fifteen.

3.42

[FIGURE 1]▶

Computer chips, glass, artificial sweet-
eners, sandpaper, and even bathroom
cleansers all share at least one common
raw material: silicon. **Silicon**, which is the
second most common element on earth, is
found in sand, clay, bauxite, and quartz.
Although some companies use other materials to make chips (a German company, for
example, is experimenting with plastic), most
computer chips are made from silicon crystals
refined from quartz rocks. At 99.999999% pure,
the refined silicon is the purest material produced
commercially in large quantities.

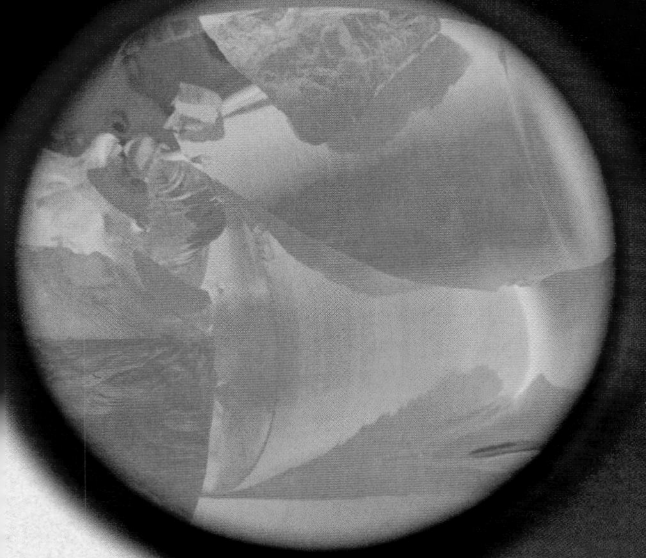

◀[FIGURE 2]

The first step in the manufacturing process involves melting the
silicon crystals. Next, a seed crystal is dipped into the melted
silicon and then slowly drawn out to form a cylindrical ingot that is
five to ten inches in diameter and several feet long. After being
smoothed, a diamond saw blade slices the silicon ingot into wafers
that are four to eight inches in diameter and 4/1000 of an inch
thick (about as thick as a credit card). The creation of these silicon
wafers is an essential phase in the chip manufacturing process and
usually takes from ten to thirty days. Each wafer forms the foundation for hundreds of chips.

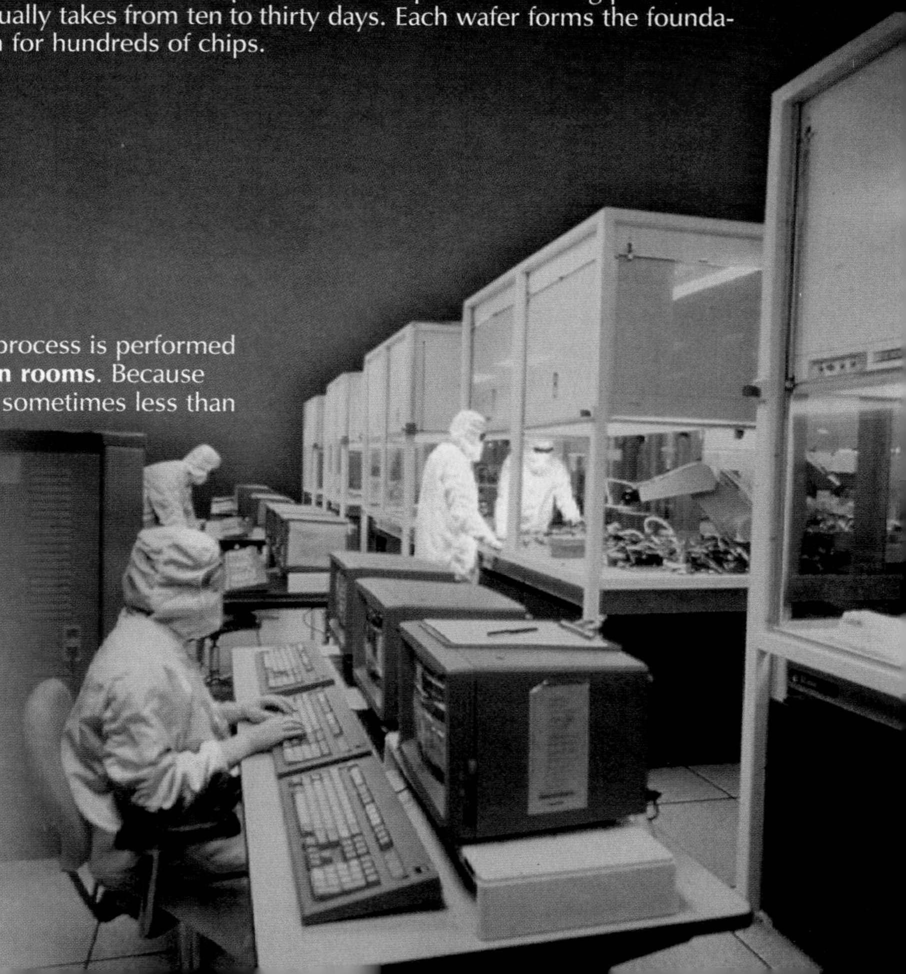

[FIGURE 3]▶

Much of the chip manufacturing process is performed
in special laboratories called **clean rooms**. Because
chip components are so small — sometimes less than
one-hundredth the diameter of a
human hair — even the smallest dust particle can ruin a
chip. Clean rooms are one
thousand times cleaner than a
hospital operating room, with
less than one particle per cubic
foot of air. People who work in
these facilities wear special protective clothing called **bunny
suits**. Before entering the manufacturing area, the workers use
an air shower to remove any
dust from their suits.

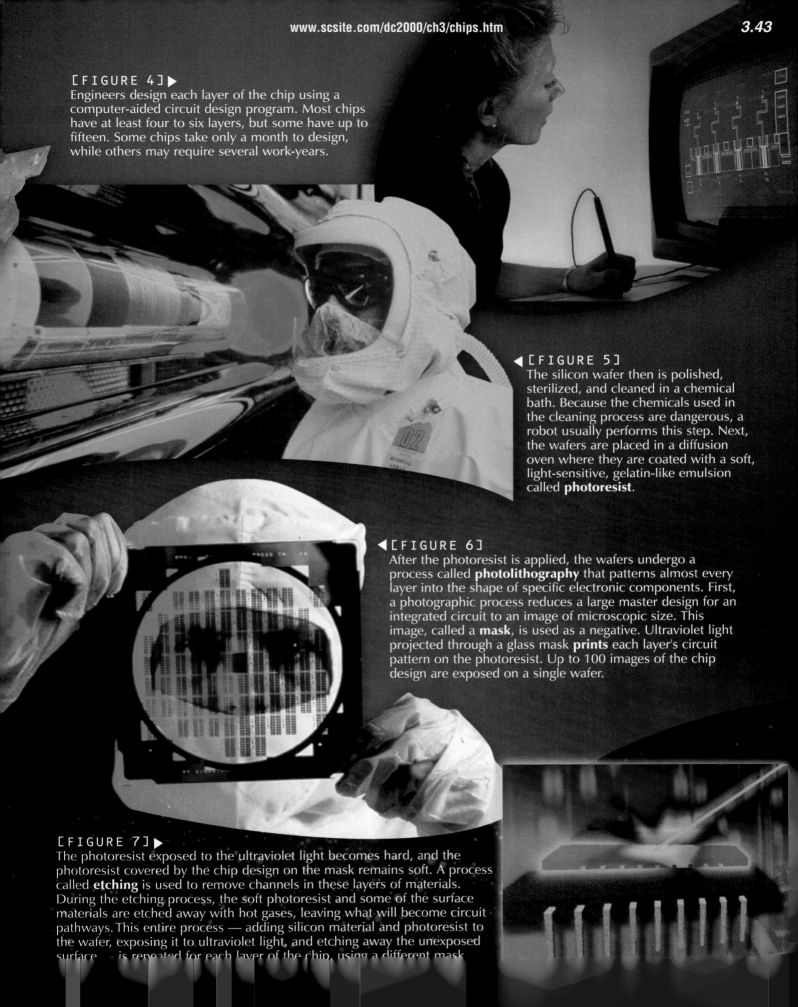

[FIGURE 4]▶
Engineers design each layer of the chip using a computer-aided circuit design program. Most chips have at least four to six layers, but some have up to fifteen. Some chips take only a month to design, while others may require several work-years.

◀[FIGURE 5]
The silicon wafer then is polished, sterilized, and cleaned in a chemical bath. Because the chemicals used in the cleaning process are dangerous, a robot usually performs this step. Next, the wafers are placed in a diffusion oven where they are coated with a soft, light-sensitive, gelatin-like emulsion called **photoresist**.

◀[FIGURE 6]
After the photoresist is applied, the wafers undergo a process called **photolithography** that patterns almost every layer into the shape of specific electronic components. First, a photographic process reduces a large master design for an integrated circuit to an image of microscopic size. This image, called a **mask**, is used as a negative. Ultraviolet light projected through a glass mask **prints** each layer's circuit pattern on the photoresist. Up to 100 images of the chip design are exposed on a single wafer.

[FIGURE 7]▶
The photoresist exposed to the ultraviolet light becomes hard, and the photoresist covered by the chip design on the mask remains soft. A process called **etching** is used to remove channels in these layers of materials. During the etching process, the soft photoresist and some of the surface materials are etched away with hot gases, leaving what will become circuit pathways. This entire process — adding silicon material and photoresist to the wafer, exposing it to ultraviolet light, and etching away the unexposed surface — is repeated for each layer of the chip, using a different mask

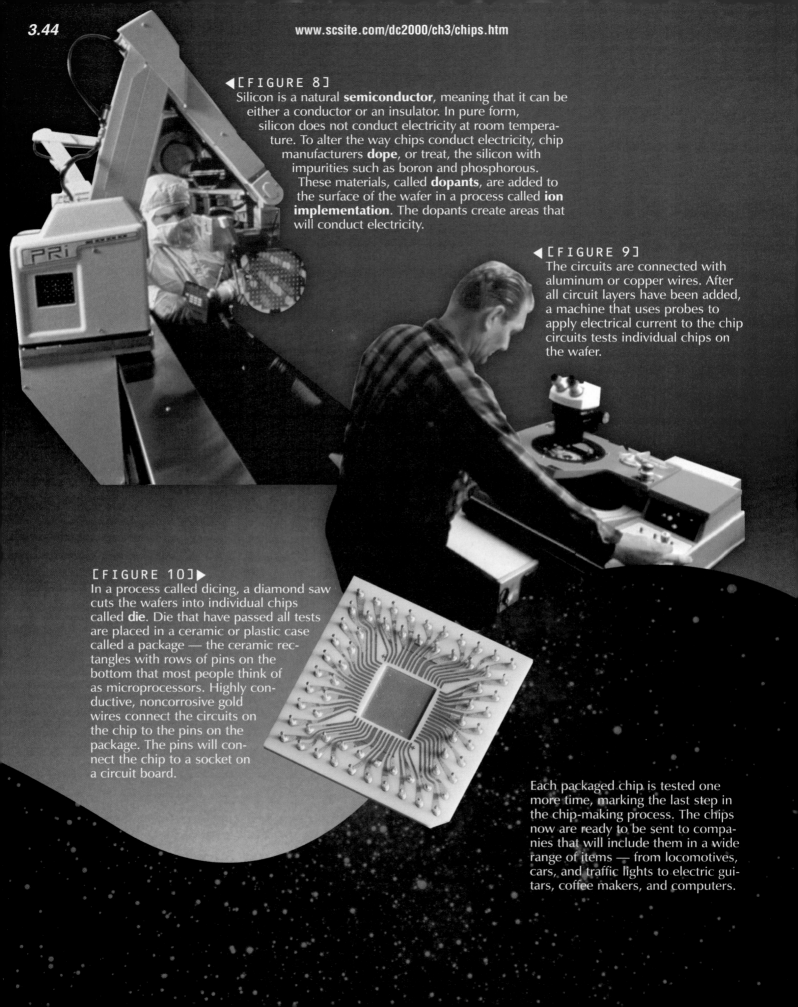

◀[FIGURE 8]

Silicon is a natural **semiconductor**, meaning that it can be either a conductor or an insulator. In pure form, silicon does not conduct electricity at room temperature. To alter the way chips conduct electricity, chip manufacturers **dope**, or treat, the silicon with impurities such as boron and phosphorous. These materials, called **dopants**, are added to the surface of the wafer in a process called **ion implementation**. The dopants create areas that will conduct electricity.

◀[FIGURE 9]

The circuits are connected with aluminum or copper wires. After all circuit layers have been added, a machine that uses probes to apply electrical current to the chip circuits tests individual chips on the wafer.

[FIGURE 10]▶

In a process called dicing, a diamond saw cuts the wafers into individual chips called **die**. Die that have passed all tests are placed in a ceramic or plastic case called a package — the ceramic rectangles with rows of pins on the bottom that most people think of as microprocessors. Highly conductive, noncorrosive gold wires connect the circuits on the chip to the pins on the package. The pins will connect the chip to a socket on a circuit board.

Each packaged chip is tested one more time, marking the last step in the chip-making process. The chips now are ready to be sent to companies that will include them in a wide range of items — from locomotives, cars, and traffic lights to electric guitars, coffee makers, and computers.

CHAPTER 4

INPUT

During the information processing cycle, a computer executes instructions and processes data (input) into information (output) and stores the information for future use. Input devices are used to enter instructions and data into the computer. This chapter describes the devices used for input and the various methods of entering input. Devices that can be used for both input and storage, such as disk drives, are covered in the discussion of storage in Chapter 6.

WHAT IS INPUT?

Input is any data or instructions you enter into the memory of a computer. Once input is in memory, the CPU can access it and process the input into output. Four types of input are data, programs, commands, and user responses (Figure 4-1):

- **Data** is a collection of unorganized facts that can include words, numbers, pictures, sounds, and videos. A computer manipulates and processes data into information, which is useful. Although technically speaking, a single item of data should be called a datum, the term data commonly is used and accepted as both the singular and plural form of the word.

- A **program** is a series of instructions that tells a computer how to perform the tasks necessary to process data into information. Programs are kept on storage media such as a floppy disk, hard disk, CD-ROM, or DVD-ROM. Programs respond to commands issued by a user.

- A **command** is an instruction given to a computer program. Commands can be issued by typing keywords or pressing special keys on the keyboard. A **keyword** is a specific word, phrase, or code that a program understands as an instruction. Some keyboards include keys that send a command to a program when you press them.

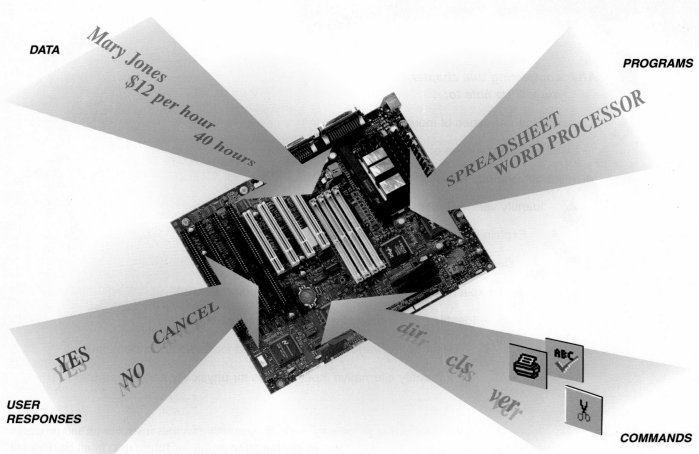

DATA

Mary Jones
$12 per hour
40 hours

PROGRAMS

SPREADSHEET
WORD PROCESSOR

USER
RESPONSES

YES   NO   CANCEL

dir
cls
ver

COMMANDS

Figure 4-1 Four types of input are data, programs, commands, and user responses.

Instead of requiring you to remember key words or special keys, many programs allow you to issue commands by selecting menu choices or graphical objects. For example, programs that are **menu-driven** provide menus as a means of entering commands. Today, most programs have a **graphical user interface** that use icons, buttons, and other graphical objects to issue commands. Of all of these methods, a graphical user interface is the most user-friendly way to issue commands.

- A **user response** is an instruction you issue to the computer by replying to a question posed by a computer program, such as *Do you want to save the changes you made?* Based on your response, the program performs certain actions. For example, if you answer, Yes, to this question, the program saves your changed file on a storage device.

WHAT ARE INPUT DEVICES?

An **input device** is any hardware component that allows you to enter data, programs, commands, and user responses into a computer. Input devices include the keyboard, pointing devices, scanners and reading devices, digital cameras, audio and video input devices, and input devices for physically challenged users. Each of these input devices is discussed in the following pages.

THE KEYBOARD

One of the primary input devices on a computer is the **keyboard** (Figure 4-2). You enter data into a computer by pressing the keys on the keyboard.

Desktop computer keyboards usually have from 101 to 105 keys, while keyboards for smaller computers such as laptops contain fewer keys. A computer keyboard includes keys that allow you to type letters of the alphabet, numbers, spaces, punctuation marks, and other symbols such as the dollar sign ($) and asterisk (*). A keyboard also contains special keys that allow you to enter data and

WEB INFO

For more information on keyboards, visit the Discovering Computers 2000 Chapter 4 WEB INFO page (**www.scsite.com/ dc2000/ch4/webinfo.htm**) and click Keyboard.

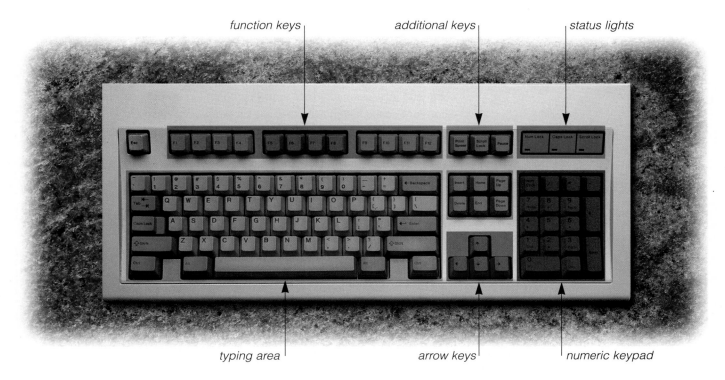

function keys   *additional keys*   *status lights*

typing area   *arrow keys*   *numeric keypad*

Figure 4-2 *A typical desktop computer keyboard. You can type using keys in the typing area and on the numeric keypad.*

instructions into the computer. The table in Figure 4-3 summarizes the purpose of special keys found on personal computer keyboards.

All computer keyboards have a typing area that includes the letters of the alphabet, numbers, punctuation marks, and other basic keys. Many desktop computer keyboards also have a numeric keypad located on the right side of the keyboard. A **numeric keypad** is a calculator-style arrangement of keys representing numbers, a decimal point, and some basic mathematical operators (see Figure 4-2 on the previous page). The numeric keypad is

designed to make it easier to enter numbers.

Across the top, most keyboards contain function keys, which are labeled with the letter F followed by a number (see Figure 4-2). **Function keys** are special keys programmed to issue commands and accomplish certain tasks. The command associated with a function key depends on the program you are using. For example, in many programs, pressing the function key F1 displays a Help window. When instructed to press a function key such as F1, do not press the letter F followed by the number 1; instead press the key labeled

PC KEYBOARD SUMMARY

Key Name	Key Purpose
ALT	Short for Alternate. When pressed in combination with another key(s), usually issues a command. Meaning varies depending on application.
Arrow keys	Moves the insertion point in the direction of the arrow. For example, the UP ARROW key moves the insertion point up one position.
BACKSPACE	Erases the character to the left of the insertion point.
Break	Often pressed in combination with another key to stop or suspend execution of a program.
CAPS LOCK	A toggle key that when activated, shifts alphabetic letters to uppercase. It does not affect keys with numbers, punctuation marks, or other symbols.
CTRL	Short for Control. When pressed in combination with another key(s), usually issues a command. Meaning of CONTROL key combinations varies depending on application.
DELETE	Erases the character to the right of the insertion point. Also used to erase selected objects. Sometimes abbreviated DEL.
END	Usually moves the insertion point to an ending position, such as the end of a line.
ENTER	Also called Return key. Used at end of a command to direct computer to process command. Also used to create a new paragraph in a word processing application.
ESC	Short for Escape. Often used to quit a program or operation.
Function keys	Labeled F1, F2, F3, and so on. Meaning of each function key varies depending on application.
HOME	Usually sends the insertion point to a beginning location, such as the top of a document or beginning of a line.
INSERT	Usually toggles between insert and overwrite modes.
NUM LOCK	Short for Numeric Lock. A toggle key that when activated, causes numeric keypad keys to function like a calculator. When deactivated, numeric keypad keys move insertion point.
PAGE DOWN	Causes the insertion point to move down a certain number of lines. Sometimes abbreviated PGDN.
PAGE UP	Causes the insertion point to move up a certain number of lines. Sometimes abbreviated PGUP.
Pause	Temporarily suspends a program or command.
PRINT SCREEN	Captures screen images.
SCROLL LOCK	Has no function in most current applications.
SHIFT	When pressed in combination with a letter key, causes the letter to be in uppercase.
TAB	Moves insertion point from place to place. Also used to insert tab characters into a word processing document.

Figure 4-3 Summary of keys found on personal computer keyboards.

F1. Function keys often are used in combination with other special keys (SHIFT, CTRL, ALT, and others) to issue commands. Many programs let you use a shortcut menu, a button, a menu, or a function key to obtain the same result (Figure 4-4).

Keyboards also contain keys that can be used to position the insertion point on the screen. The **insertion point** is a symbol that indicates where on the screen the next character you type will display. Depending on the program, the symbol may be a vertical bar, a rectangle, or an underline (Figure 4-5). **Arrow keys** allow you to move the insertion point left, right, up, or down. Most keyboards also contain keys such as HOME, END, PAGE UP, and PAGE DOWN, that you can press to move the insertion point to the beginning or end of a line, page, or document.

Most keyboards also include **toggle keys**, which can be switched between two different states. The NUM LOCK key, for example, is a toggle key. When you press it once, it locks the numeric keypad so you can use it to type numbers. When you press the NUM LOCK key again, the numeric keypad is unlocked so the same keys serve as arrow keys that move the insertion point. Many keyboards have status lights in the upper-right corner that light up to indicate that a toggle key is activated.

COMMAND SUMMARY

Command	Function Key(s)	Menu	Button
Close Word	ALT+F4	File|Exit	
Copy	SHIFT+F2	Edit|Copy	
Office Assistant	F1	Help|Microsoft Word Help	
Open	CTRL+F12	File|Open	
Print	CTRL+SHIFT +F12	File|Print	
Print Preview	CTRL+F2	File|Print Preview	
Save	SHIFT+F12	File|Save	
Spelling and Grammar	F7	Tools|Spelling and Grammar	

Figure 4-4 *Many programs allow you to use a button, a menu, or a function key to obtain the same result, as shown by these examples from Microsoft Word.*

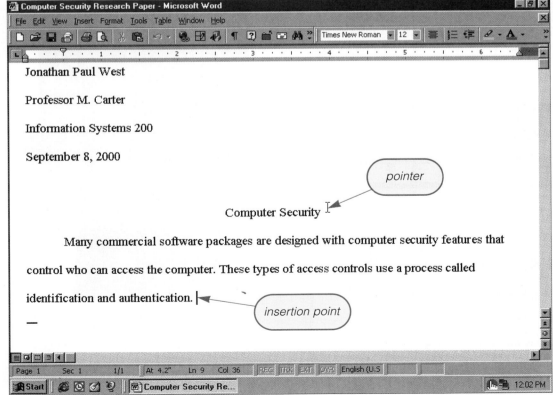

Figure 4-5 *In most Windows programs, such as Word, the insertion point is a blinking vertical bar. You can use the keyboard or the mouse to move the insertion point. The pointer, another symbol that displays on the screen, is controlled by using a mouse.*

Keyboard Types

A standard computer keyboard sometimes is called a **QWERTY keyboard** because of the layout of its typing area (Figure 4-6a). Pronounced KWER-tee, this keyboard layout is named after the first six leftmost letters on the top alphabetic line of the keyboard. Because of the way the keys are organized, a QWERTY keyboard might limit your typing speed.

A keyboard with an alternative layout was designed to improve typing speed. Called the **Dvorak keyboard** (pronounced de-VOR-zhak), this type of keyboard places the most frequently typed letters in the middle of the typing area (Figure 4-6b). Despite the more logical design of the Dvorak keyboard, the QWERTY keyboard is more widely used.

Most of today's desktop computer keyboards are **enhanced keyboards**, which means they have twelve function keys along the top, two CTRL keys, two ALT keys, and a set of arrow and additional keys between the typing area and the numeric keypad (see Figure 4-2 on page 4.3).

Although most keyboards attach to a serial port on the system unit via a cable, some keyboards – called **wireless keyboards** – transmit data via infrared light waves. For a wireless keyboard to transmit signals to a computer, both the computer and the wireless keyboard must have an IrDA port. These IrDA ports must be aligned so that nothing obstructs the path of the infrared light wave.

On laptops and many handheld computers, the keyboard is built into the top of the system unit (Figure 4-7). To fit in these smaller computers, the keyboards usually are smaller and have fewer keys. A typical laptop computer keyboard, for example, has only 85 keys, compared to the 105 keys on most desktop computer keyboards. To provide all of the functionality of a desktop computer keyboard, manufacturers design many of the keys to serve two or three different purposes.

Regardless of size, most keyboards have a rectangular shape with the keys aligned in rows. Users who spend a significant amount of time typing on these keyboards sometimes experience repetitive strain injuries of their wrists. For this reason, some manufacturers have redesigned their keyboards to minimize the chance of these types of workplace injuries (Figure 4-8). Keyboards such as these are called ergonomic keyboards. The goal of **ergonomics** is to incorporate comfort, efficiency, and safety into the design of items in the workplace.

Figure 4-7 On laptop and many handheld computers, the keyboard is built into the top of the system unit.

Figure 4-6
Comparison of the QWERTY and Dvorak keyboard layouts.

Figure 4-6a (QWERTY)

Figure 4-6b (Dvorak)

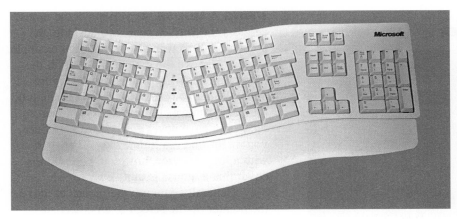

Figure 4-8 *The Microsoft Natural Keyboard is an ergonomic keyboard designed to minimize strain on your hands and wrists.*

POINTING DEVICES

A **pointing device** is an input device that allows you to control a pointer on the screen. In a graphical user interface, a **pointer** or **mouse pointer** is a small symbol on the display screen (see Figure 4-5 on page 4.5). A pointer often takes the shape of a block arrow (⌖), an I-beam (I), or a pointing hand (☝). Using a pointing device, you can position the pointer to move or select items on the screen. For example, you can use a pointing device to move the insertion point; select text, graphics, and other objects; and click buttons, icons, links, and menu commands.

Common pointing devices include the mouse, trackball, touchpad, pointing stick, joystick, touch screen, light pen, and graphics tablet. Each of these devices is discussed in the following sections.

Mouse

The mouse is the most widely used pointing device because it takes full advantage of a graphical user interface. Designed to fit comfortably under the palm of your hand, a **mouse** is an input device that is used to control the movement of the pointer on the screen and to make selections from the screen. The top of the mouse has one to four buttons; some also have a small wheel. The bottom of a mouse is flat and contains a multi-directional mechanism, usually a small ball, which senses movement of the mouse (Figure 4-9). The mouse often rests on a **mouse pad**, which usually is a rectangular rubber or foam pad that provides better traction for the mouse than the top of a desk. The mouse pad also protects the ball mechanism from a build up of dust and dirt, which could cause it to malfunction.

WEB INFO
WEB INFO

For more information on a mouse, visit the Discovering Computers 2000 Chapter 4 WEB INFO page (**www.scsite.com/ dc2000/ch4/webinfo.htm**) and click Mouse.

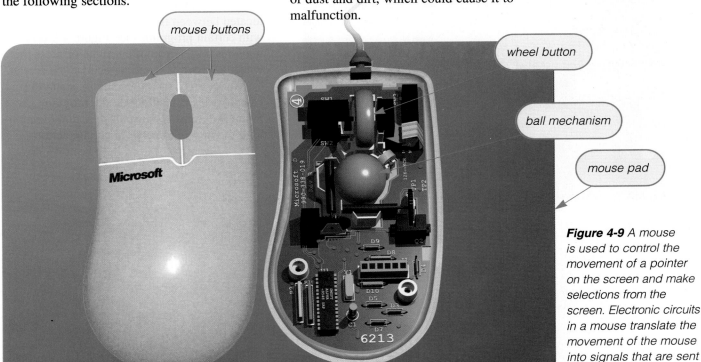

mouse buttons

wheel button

ball mechanism

mouse pad

Figure 4-9 *A mouse is used to control the movement of a pointer on the screen and make selections from the screen. Electronic circuits in a mouse translate the movement of the mouse into signals that are sent to the computer.*

Figure 4-10
MOVING THE MOUSE POINTER

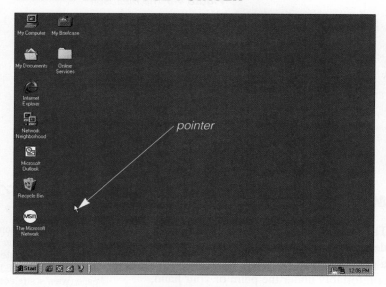

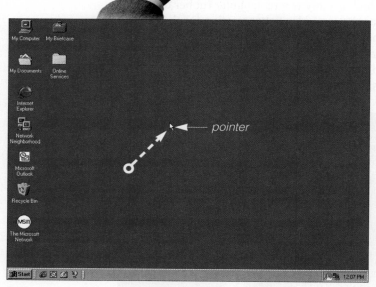

Step 1: Position the mouse on the lower-left edge of the mouse pad.

Step 2: Move the mouse diagonally toward the middle of the mouse pad to move the pointer on the screen.

USING A MOUSE As you move the mouse across a flat surface such as a desktop, the pointer on the screen also moves. For example, when you move the mouse to the right, the pointer moves right on the screen (Figure 4-10). When you move the mouse to the left, the pointer moves left on the screen, and so on. If you have never worked with a mouse, you might find it a little awkward at first; with a little practice, however, you will discover that a mouse is quite easy to use.

Generally, you use the mouse to move the pointer on the screen to an object such as a button, a menu, an icon, a link, or text and then press one of the mouse buttons to perform a certain action on that object. In Windows 98, for example, if you point to the Start button on the taskbar and then press, or **click**, the primary mouse button, the Start menu displays on the screen (Figure 4-11).

For a right-handed user, the primary mouse button typically is the left button, and the secondary mouse button typically is the right mouse button. The function of these buttons, however, can be reversed to accommodate left-handed people.

You can perform other operations using the mouse in addition to clicking. These operations include point, right-click, double-click, drag, and right-drag. The table in Figure 4-12 explains how to perform each of these mouse operations and the general function of each operation.

Some mouse devices also have a wheel located between two buttons that can be used with certain programs (see Figure 4-9 on the previous page). You often rotate or press the wheel to move text and objects on the screen. The function of the mouse buttons and the wheel varies depending on the program. Some programs also use keys in combination with the mouse to perform certain actions.

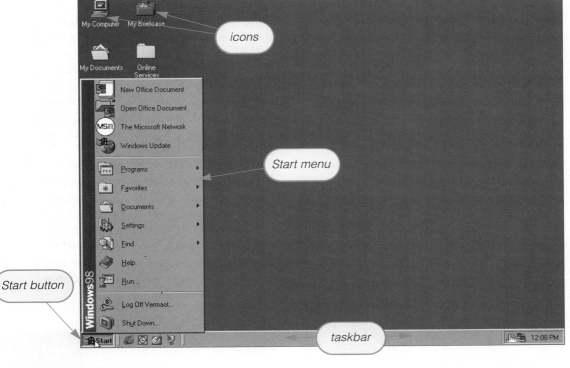

Figure 4-11 *In Windows 98, if you point to the Start button on the taskbar and then click the primary mouse button, the Start menu displays on the screen.*

MOUSE TYPES A mouse that has a rubber or metal ball on its underside is called a **mechanical mouse**. When the ball rolls in a certain direction, electronic circuits in the mouse translate the movement of the mouse into signals that are sent to the computer. Another type of mouse, called an **optical mouse**, has no moving mechanical parts inside; instead it uses devices that emit light to detect the mouse's movement. When using an optical mouse, you must use a special mouse pad that is capable of detecting motion. An optical mouse is more accurate than a mechanical mouse, but it also is more expensive.

MOUSE OPERATIONS

Operation	Mouse Action	Example
Point	Move the mouse across a flat surface until the pointer rests on the item of choice on the desktop.	Position the pointer on the screen.
Click	Press and release the primary mouse button, which usually is the left mouse button.	Select or deselect items on the screen or start a program or program feature.
Right-click	Press and release the secondary mouse button, which usually is the right mouse button.	Display a shortcut menu.
Double-click	Quickly press and release the primary mouse button twice without moving the mouse.	Start a program or program feature.
Drag	Point to an item, hold down the left mouse button, move the item to the desired location on the screen, and then release the left mouse button.	Move an object from one location to another or draw pictures.
Right-drag	Point to an item, hold down the right mouse button, move the item to the desired location on the screen, and then release the right mouse button.	Display a shortcut menu after moving an object from one location to another.
Rotate wheel	Roll the wheel forward or backward.	Scroll up or down a few lines.
Press wheel button	Press the wheel button while moving the mouse on the desktop.	Scroll continuously.

Figure 4-12 *The more common mouse operations.*

A mouse connects to your computer in one of two ways. Most connect using a cable that attaches to an RS-232C serial port, which usually is located on the back of the system unit. Some mouse devices are cordless, relying on battery power. Operating similarly to a television remote control, a **cordless mouse** uses infrared or radio waves to communicate with a receiver that usually is plugged into an IrDA port on the system unit (Figure 4-13). A cordless mouse frees up desk space and eliminates the clutter of a cord.

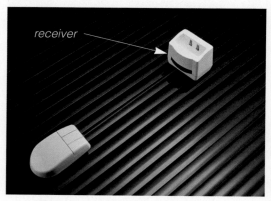

Figure 4-13 *This cordless mouse uses infrared remote transmission to communicate with the computer.*

Trackball

Some users opt for alternative pointing devices other than a mouse, such as a trackball. Whereas a mouse has a ball mechanism on the bottom, a **trackball** is a stationary pointing device with a ball mechanism on its top (Figure 4-14). The ball mechanism in a

larger trackball is about the size of a Ping-Pong ball; some laptop computers use small trackballs about the size of a marble (Figure 4-15).

To move the pointer using a trackball, you rotate the ball mechanism with your thumb, fingers, or the palm of your hand. Around the ball mechanism, usually a trackball also has one or more buttons that work just like mouse buttons.

Although it shares characteristics with a mouse, a trackball is not as accurate as a mouse. A trackball's ball mechanism also requires frequent cleaning because it picks up oils from your fingers and dust from the environment. If you have limited desk space, however, a trackball is a good alternative to a mouse because you do not have to move the entire device.

Figure 4-15 *Smaller trackballs are used with some laptop computers.*

trackball

WEB INFO
WEB INFO
For more information on trackballs, visit the Discovering Computers 2000 Chapter 4 WEB INFO page (**www.scsite.com/ dc2000/ch4/webinfo.htm**) and click Trackballs.

Figure 4-14 *A trackball is like an upside-down mouse. You rotate the ball mechanism with your thumb, fingers, or the palm of your hand to move the pointer.*

Touchpad

A **touchpad** or **trackpad** is a small, flat, rectangular pointing device that is sensitive to pressure and motion (Figure 4-16). To move the pointer using a touchpad, you slide your fingertip across the surface of the pad. Some touchpads have one or more buttons around the edge of the pad that work like mouse buttons; on others, you tap the pad's surface to simulate mouse operations such as clicking.

Although you can attach a stand-alone touchpad to any personal computer, touchpads are found more often on laptop computers.

Pointing Stick

A **pointing stick** is a pressure-sensitive pointing device shaped like a pencil eraser that was first developed by IBM for its laptop computers. Because of its small size, the pointing stick is positioned between keys on the keyboard (Figure 4-17). To move the

touchpad

Figure 4-16 *Laptop computers sometimes have a touchpad to control the movement of the pointer.*

pointer using a pointing stick, you push the pointing stick with your finger. The pointer on the screen moves in the direction that you push the pointing stick.

An advantage of using a pointing stick is that it does not require cleaning like a mouse or trackball. Whether you select a laptop that has a trackball, touchpad, or pointing stick is a matter of personal preference.

pointing stick

Figure 4-17 *Some laptop computers use a pointing stick to control the movement of the pointer.*

Joystick

Users running game software such as a driving or flight simulator may prefer to use a joystick as their pointing device. A **joystick** is a vertical lever mounted on a base (Figure 4-18). You move the lever in different directions to control the actions of a vehicle or player. The lever usually includes buttons called *triggers* that you can press to activate certain events. Some joysticks also have additional buttons that you can set to perform other actions.

Touch Screen

A monitor that has a touch-sensitive panel on the screen is called a **touch screen.** You interact with the computer by touching areas of the screen with your finger, which acts as an input device. Because they require a lot of arm movements, touch screens are not used to enter large amounts of data. Instead you touch words, pictures, numbers, or locations identified on the screen.

Touch screens often are used in kiosks located in stores, hotels, airports, and museums. Customers at Hallmark stores, for example, can use a kiosk to create personalized greeting cards (Figure 4-19).

Pen Input

Many input devices use an electronic pen instead of a keyboard or mouse for input. Some of these devices require you to point to onscreen objects with the pen; others allow you to input data using drawings, handwriting, and other symbols that are written with the pen on a surface.

LIGHT PEN A **light pen** is a handheld input device that contains a light source or can detect light. Some light pens require a specially designed monitor, while others work with a standard monitor (Figure 4-20). Instead of touching the screen with your finger to interact with the computer, you press the light pen against the surface of the screen or point the light pen at the screen and then press a button on the pen. Light pens are used in applications where desktop space is limited such as in the health-care field or when a wide variety of people use the application, such as electronic voting.

Figure 4-18 *A joystick is used with game software to control the actions of a vehicle or a player.*

Figure 4-19 *This kiosk allows you to create personalized Hallmark greeting cards.*

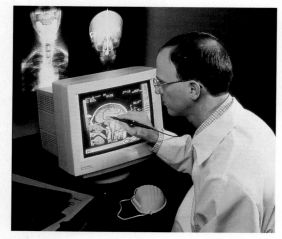

Figure 4-20 *To make selections with a light pen, you touch the pen against the surface of the screen or point the pen at the screen and then press a button on the pen.*

PEN COMPUTING Many handheld computers also allow you to input data using an electronic pen (Figure 4-21). The **pen** (also called a **stylus**) looks like a ballpoint pen but uses an electronic head instead of ink. Pen computers use **handwriting recognition software** that translates the letters and symbols used in handwriting into character data that the computer can use. Although most handwriting recognition software recognizes printed letters and can be trained to distinguish writing styles, pen-computing technology continues to be refined.

GRAPHICS TABLET A **graphics tablet**, also called a **digitizer** or **digitizing tablet**, consists of a flat, rectangular, electronic plastic board used to input drawings, sketches, or other graphical data (Figure 4-22). Each location on the graphics tablet corresponds to a specific location on the screen. When you draw on the tablet with either an electronic pen or a puck, the tablet detects and converts the movements into digital signals that are sent into the computer. A **puck** is a device that looks similar to a mouse, except that is has a window with cross hairs so the user can see through to the tablet. Users with precise pointing requirements such as mapmakers and architects use a puck.

Figure 4-21 Many handheld computers support handwriting input through a pen.

SCANNERS AND READING DEVICES

Some devices make the input process more efficient by eliminating the manual entry of data. Instead of a person entering data using a keyboard or pointing device, these devices capture data from a **source document**, which is the original form of the data. When using a keyboard or pointing device to enter data, the source document might be a timecard, order blank, invoice, or any other document that contains data to be processed.

Devices that capture data directly from source documents include optical scanners, optical character recognition devices, optical mark recognition devices, bar code scanners, and magnetic-ink character recognition readers. Examples of source documents used with these devices include advertisements, brochures, photographs, inventory tags, or checks. Each of these devices is discussed in the following pages.

Figure 4-22 Some graphics tablets use a pen as their input device. Architects and engineers, however, often use a puck with a graphics tablet to input drawings, sketches, or other graphical data.

Optical Scanner

An **optical scanner**, usually simply called a **scanner**, is a light-sensing input device that reads printed text and graphics and then translates the results into a form the computer can use (Figure 4-23). A scanner is similar to a copy machine except that it creates a file of the document instead of a paper copy. The file that contains the scanned object then can be stored on a disk, displayed on the screen, printed, faxed, sent via electronic mail, or included in another document. For example, you can scan a picture and then incorporate the picture into a brochure using a desktop publishing program.

When a document is scanned, the results are stored in rows and columns of dots called a **bitmap** (Figure 4-24). Each dot on a bitmap consists of one or more bits of data. The more bits used to represent a dot, the more colors and shades of gray that can be represented. For instance, one bit per dot is enough to represent simple one-color images, but for colors and shades of gray, each dot requires more than one bit of data.

Today's scanners range from 24 bit to 45 bit, with the latter being a higher quality, but more expensive.

Figure 4-23
HOW AN OPTICAL SCANNER WORKS

Step 1: The document to be scanned is placed face down on the glass window.

Step 2: A bright light moves underneath the scanned document.

Step 3: An image of the document is reflected into a series of mirrors.

Step 4: The light is converted to an analog electrical current by a chip called a charge-coupled device (CCD).

Step 5: The analog signal is converted to a digital signal by a device called an analog-to-digital converter (ADC).

Step 6: The digital information is sent to software in the computer to be used by illustration, or desktop publishing, or other software.

Step 7: The scanned image displays on the screen.

The density of the dots, known as the **resolution**, determines sharpness and clearness of the resulting image (Figure 4-25). Resolution typically is measured in **dots per inch (dpi)**, and is stated as the number of columns and rows of dots. For example, a 600 x 1200 (pronounced 600 by 1200) dpi scanner has 600 columns and 1200 rows of dots. If just one number is stated, such as 600 dpi, that number refers to both the number of rows and the number of columns. The more dots, the better the resolution, and the resulting image is of higher quality.

Some manufacturers refer to the actual scanned resolution as the *optical resolution*, differentiating it from *enhanced* or *interpolated resolution*. The enhanced resolution usually is higher because it uses a special formula to add dots between those generated by the optical resolution.

Most of today's affordable color desktop scanners for the home or small business user have an optical resolution ranging from 300 to 2000 dpi. Commercial scanners designed for power users range from 4000 to 6000 dpi. The table in Figure 4-26 summarizes the three basic types of scanners.

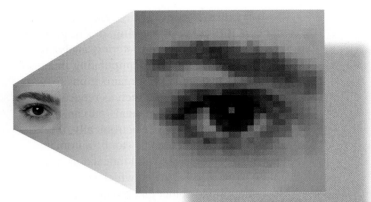

Figure 4-24 *Each dot on a bitmap consists of one or more bits of data. The more bits used to represent a dot, the more colors and shades of gray that can be represented. This is a bitmap for a woman's eye.*

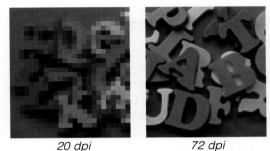

| 20 dpi | 72 dpi | 300 dpi |

Figure 4-25 *The higher the resolution or dots per inch (dpi), the sharper and clearer the resulting image. Today's scanners have a resolution of at least 300 dpi.*

TYPES OF SCANNERS

Scanner Photo	Method of Scanning/ Use	Scannable Items
Flatbed	• Similar to a copy machine. • Scanning mechanism passes under the item to be scanned, which is placed on a glass surface.	• Single-sheet documents • Bound material • Photographs • Slides (with an adapter)
Sheet-fed	• Item to be scanned is pulled into a stationary scanning mechanism. • Smaller and less expensive than a flatbed.	• Single-sheet documents • Photographs • Slides (with an adapter)
Drum	• Item to be scanned rotates around a stationary scanning mechanism. • Very large and expensive. • Used in publishing industry.	• Single-sheet documents • Photographs • Slides • Negatives

Figure 4-26 *This table lists the various types of scanners.*

Organizations use many types of scanners for **image processing**, or **imaging**, which consists of capturing, storing, analyzing, displaying, printing, and manipulating images (bitmaps). Image enables organizations to convert paper documents such as reports, memos, and procedure manuals into an electronic form. Once saved electronically, the routing of these documents can be automated. They also can be stored and indexed using an **image processing system**, which serves as an electronic filing cabinet that provides access to exact reproductions of the original documents. The government, for example, uses an image processing system to store property deeds and titles to provide quick access to the public, lawyers, and loan officers.

Optical Readers

An **optical reader** is a device that uses a light source to read characters, marks, and codes and then converts them into digital data that can be processed by a computer. The following sections discuss three types of optical readers: optical character recognition, optical mark recognition, and bar code.

OPTICAL CHARACTER RECOGNITION

Optical character recognition (OCR) is a technology that involves reading typewritten, computer-printed, or handwritten characters from ordinary documents and translating the images into a form that the computer can understand. Most **OCR devices** include a small optical scanner for reading characters and sophisticated software for analyzing what is read.

OCR devices range from large machines that can read thousands of documents per minute to handheld wands that read one document at a time. OCR devices are used to read characters printed using an OCR font. Although others exist, the standard OCR font is called OCR-A (Figure 4-27). During the scan of a document, an OCR device determines the shapes of characters by detecting patterns of light and dark. **Optical character recognition (OCR) software** then compares these shapes with predefined shapes stored in memory and converts the shapes into characters the computer can understand.

OCR software also is used with optical scanners such as flatbed and sheet-fed scanners. For example, suppose you need to modify a business report, but do not have the original word processing file. You could use a flatbed scanner to scan the document, but you still would not be able to edit the report. The scanner, which does not differentiate between text and graphics, will save the report as a bitmap image, which cannot be edited directly in a word processing program. To convert it into an editable text file that can be edited, you must have optical character recognition (OCR) software that works with the scanner. The resulting output can be stored in a variety of file formats, including those recognized by word processing software.

Current OCR software has a very high success rate and usually can identify more than 99 percent of scanned material. OCR software also will mark text it could not read, allowing you to make corrections easily.

Companies use OCR devices to increase the speed and accuracy of data entry. OCR is very useful when a significant amount of data must be entered into a computer and only the printed pages are available.

OCR also is used frequently for **turnaround documents**, which are documents designed to be returned (turned around) to the organization that created and sent them. For

WEB INFO
WEB INFO

For more information on OCR, visit the Discovering Computers 2000 Chapter 4 WEB INFO page (www.scsite.com/ dc2000/ch4/webinfo.htm) and click OCR.

ABCDEFGHIJKLMNOPQRSTUVWXYZ

1234567890-=■;',./

Figure 4-27 *A portion of the characters in the OCR-A font. Notice how characters such as the number 0 and the letter O are shaped differently so the reading device easily can distinguish between them.*

example, when you receive a gas bill, you tear off a portion of the bill and send it back to the gas company with your payment (Figure 4-28). The portion of the bill you return usually has your account number, payment amount, and other information printed in optical characters.

OPTICAL MARK RECOGNITION Optical **mark recognition (OMR)** devices read hand-drawn marks such as small circles or rectangles. A person places these marks on a form, such as a test, survey, or questionnaire answer sheet (Figure 4-29). The OMR device first reads a master document, such as an answer key sheet for a test, to record correct answers based on patterns of light; the remaining documents then are passed through the OMR device and their patterns of light are matched against the master document.

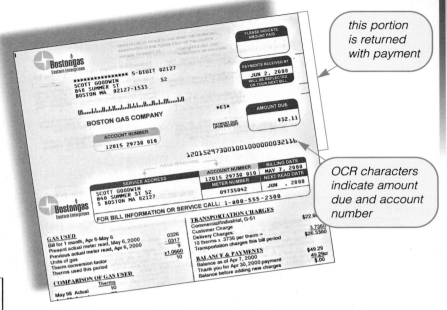

this portion is returned with payment

OCR characters indicate amount due and account number

Figure 4-28 *OCR is used frequently with turn-around documents. With this gas bill, you tear off the top portion and return it with your payment.*

Figure 4-29 *OMR devices commonly are used to scan test, survey, or questionnaire answer sheets.*

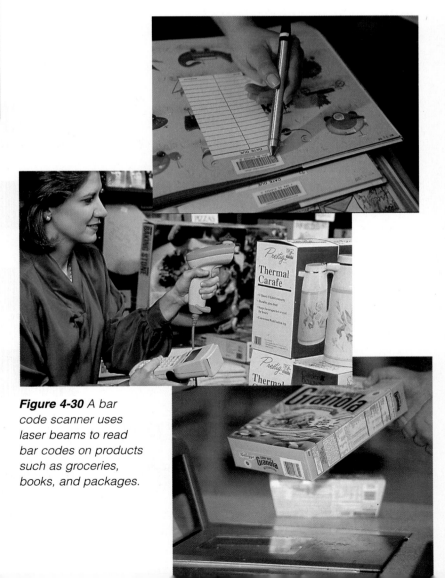

Figure 4-30 *A bar code scanner uses laser beams to read bar codes on products such as groceries, books, and packages.*

BAR CODE SCANNER A **bar code scanner** uses laser beams to read bar codes (Figure 4-30). A **bar code** is an identification code that consists of a set of vertical lines and spaces of different widths. The bar code, which represents some data that identifies the item, is printed on a product's package or on a label that is affixed to a product so it can be read by a bar code scanner. The bar code scanner uses light patterns from the bar code lines to identify the item.

Bar codes are used on a variety of products such as groceries, pharmacy supplies, vehicles, mail, and books. Each industry uses its own type of bar code. For example, the U.S. Postal Service uses a POSTNET bar code, while retail and grocery stores use the Universal Product Code, or UPC (Figure 4-31). The table in Figure 4-32 summarizes some of the more widely used types of bar codes.

10 OZ CHEERIOS UPC SYMBOL #

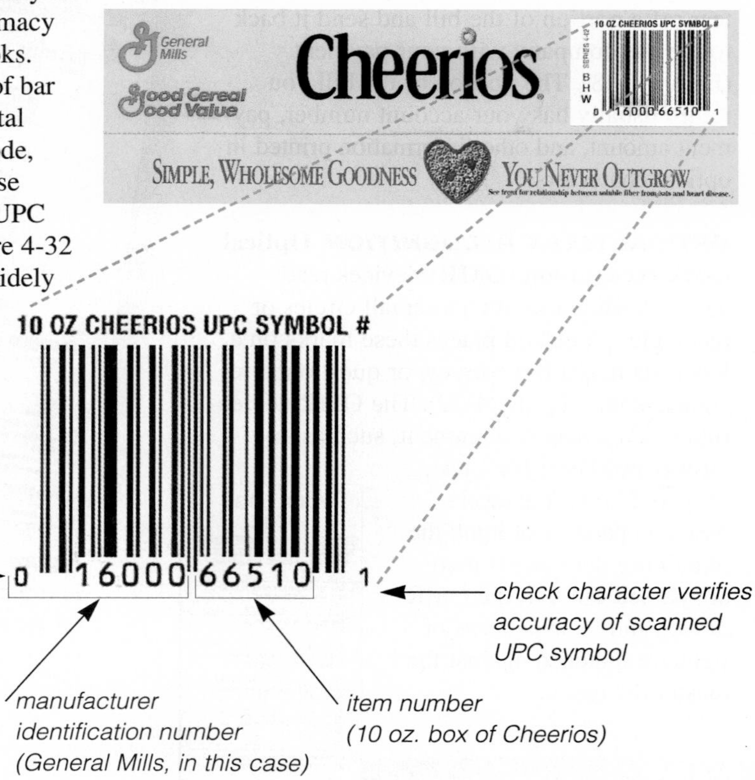

Figure 4-31 *This UPC identifies a box of General Mills Cheerios™.*

number system character identifies type of product

check character verifies accuracy of scanned UPC symbol

manufacturer identification number (General Mills, in this case)

item number (10 oz. box of Cheerios)

TYPES OF BAR CODES

Figure 4-32 *Some of the more widely used types of bar codes.*

Bar Code Name	Sample Bar Code	Primary Market
Codabar	Codabar — A 1 2 3 4 5 6 7 8 9 0 1 2 A	Libraries, blood banks, and air parcel carriers.
Code 39	C O D E 3 9	Nonretail applications such as manufacturing, military, and health applications requiring numbers and letters in the bar code.
EAN – European Article Numbering	EAN-13 — 1 234567 890128	Similar to UPC, except used in Europe. A variation of EAN is used for ISBNs on books.
Interleaved 2 of 5	Interleaved 2 of 5 — 1 2 3 4 5 6 7 8 9 0 1 2	Nonretail applications requiring only numbers in the bar code.
POSTNET – Postal Numeric Encoding Technique	(POSTNET bar code)	U.S. Postal Service to represent a postal code or delivery point code.
UPC – Universal Product Code	UPC-A with Supplemental — 0 12345 67890 s	Supermarkets, convenience, and specialty stores used to identify manufacturers and products.

Magnetic Ink Character Recognition Reader

A **magnetic-ink character recognition (MICR)** reader is used to read text printed with magnetized ink (Figure 4-33). MICR is used almost exclusively by the banking industry for check processing. Each check in your checkbook has precoded MICR characters on the lower-left edge; these characters represent the bank number, your account number, and the check number.

When a check is presented for payment, the bank uses an MICR inscriber to print the amount of the check in MICR characters in the lower-right corner (Figure 4-34). The check then is sorted or routed to the customer's bank, along with thousands of others. Each check is inserted into an MICR reader, which sends the check information – including the amount of the check – to a computer for processing. When you balance your checkbook, you should verify that the amount printed in the lower-right corner is the same as the amount written on the check; otherwise, your statement will not balance.

Figure 4-33 An MICR reader is used almost exclusively by the banking industry for check processing.

The banking industry has established an international standard not only for bank numbers, but also for the font of the MICR characters. This standardization makes it possible for you to write checks in another country.

Figure 4-34 The MICR characters preprinted on the check represent the bank number, your account number, and the check number. The amount of the check in the lower-right corner is added after you write the check.

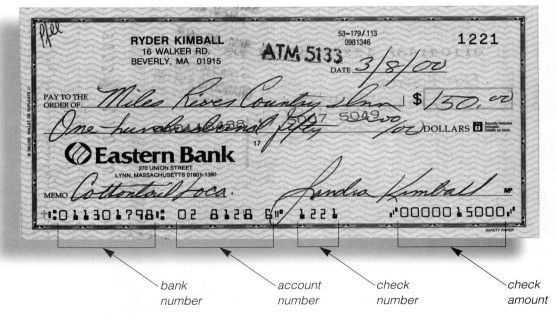

bank number

account number

check number

check amount

Data Collection Devices

Instead of reading or scanning data from a source document, **data collection devices** are designed and used to obtain data directly at the location where the transaction or event takes place. Data collection devices are used in factories, warehouses, or other locations where heat, humidity, and cleanliness are difficult to control. An example of this type of environment is a researcher who must be outside in the elements when collecting the data (points, lines, and area features) for a geographic information system (GIS). The data collection devices used to gather data for a GIS thus are rugged and durable, allowing researchers to create maps, analyze and interpret data for the maps, and capture images from the air or the ground (Figure 4-35).

DIGITAL CAMERAS

A **digital camera** allows you to take pictures and store the photographed images digitally instead of on traditional film (Figure 4-36). With some digital cameras, you **download**, or transfer a copy of, the stored pictures to your computer by connecting a cable between the digital camera and your computer and using special software included with the camera. With other digital cameras, the pictures are stored directly on a floppy disk or on a PC Card. You then copy the pictures to your computer by inserting the floppy disk into a disk drive or the PC Card into a PC Card slot. Once the pictures are on your computer, they can be edited with photo-editing software, printed, faxed, sent via electronic

Figure 4-36a (digital camera)

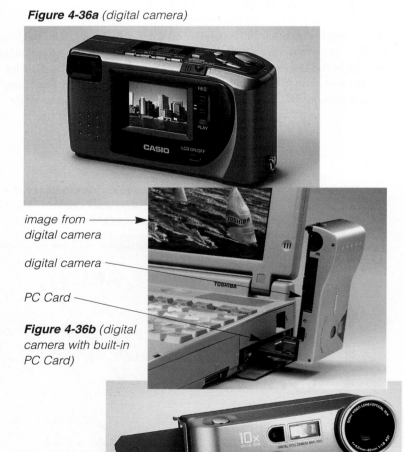

image from digital camera

digital camera

PC Card

Figure 4-36b (digital camera with built-in PC Card)

Figure 4-35 Civil engineers use GIS data collection device to locate sewers, roads, and public buildings.

Figure 4-36 A digital camera is used to take pictures and store the photographed images on the computer. Some digital cameras can save images directly onto a floppy disk or PC Card.

Figure 4-36c (digital camera with floppy disk)

mail, included in another document, or posted to a Web site for everyone to see (Figure 4-37).

The three basic types of digital cameras are studio cameras, field cameras, and point-and-shoot cameras. The most expensive and highest quality of the three, a **studio camera** is a stationary camera used for professional studio work. Often used by photojournalists, a **field camera** is a portable camera that has many lenses and other attachments; like the studio camera, a field camera can be quite expensive. A **point-and-shoot camera** is more affordable and lightweight and provides acceptable quality photographic images for the home or small business user. You can use a point-and-shoot camera to add pictures to personalized greeting cards, a computerized photo album, a family newsletter, certificates, awards, or your own Web site. The point-and-shoot camera also is ideal for mobile users such as real estate agents, insurance agents, and general contractors.

As with a scanner, the quality of a digital camera is measured by the number of bits it stores in a dot and the number of dots per inch, or resolution. The higher each number, the better quality, but the more expensive the camera. Most of today's point-and-shoot digital cameras are at least 24-bit with a resolution ranging from 640 x 480 to 1024 x 960. Other features of digital cameras are discussed in Chapter 13.

WEB INFO

For more information on digital cameras, visit the Discovering Computers 2000 Chapter 4 WEB INFO page (**www.scsite.com/dc2000/ ch4/webinfo.htm**) and click Digital Cameras.

Figure 4-37
HOW A DIGITAL CAMERA WORKS

Step 1: *Point to the image to photograph. Light passes into the lens of the camera.*

Step 2: *The image is focused on a chip called a charge-coupled device (CCD).*

Step 3: *The CCD generates an analog signal that represents the image.*

Step 4: *The analog signal is converted to a digital signal by an analog-to-digital converter (ADC).*

Step 5: *A digital signal processor (DSP) adjusts the quality of the image and stores the digital image on a PC Card, floppy disk, or other media in the camera.*

Step 6: *Images are transferred to a computer by plugging one end of the cable into a camera and the other end of the cable into a computer; or a PC Card or floppy disk is inserted into the computer and the images are copied to the hard disk.*

Step 7: *Using software supplied with the camera, the images are viewed on the screen.*

AUDIO AND VIDEO INPUT

Although characters (text and numbers) are still the primary form of input into a computer, the use of other types of input such as images, audio, and video is increasing. In the previous sections, you learned about a variety of ways to enter image data. The next sections discuss methods used to enter audio and video data into a computer. Other techniques for using images, audio, and video are discussed in Chapter 13.

Audio Input

Audio input is the process of entering (recording) music, speech, or sound effects. To record high quality sound, your personal computer must have a sound card. (Most new computers today come equipped with a sound card.) Sound is entered via a device such as a microphone, tape player, or audio CD player, each of which plugs into a port on the sound card. External MIDI devices such as an electric piano keyboard also can connect to the sound card for audio input (Figure 4-38).

Recall that, in addition to being a port, MIDI (musical instrument digital interface) is the electronic music industry's standard that defines how sounds are represented electronically by digital musical devices. Software programs that conform to the MIDI standard allow you to compose and edit music and other sounds. For example, you can change the speed, add notes, or rearrange the score to produce an entirely new sound.

With a microphone plugged into the microphone port on the sound card, you can record sound using the Windows Sound Recorder (Figure 4-39). Windows stores audio files as **waveforms**, which are called **WAV** files and have a .wav extension. Once you save the sound in a file, you can play it using the Sound Recorder, or edit it using music-editing software that conforms to the MIDI standard. You also can attach the audio file to an e-mail message or include it in a document such as a word processing report or presentation graphics slide show.

WAV files often are large – requiring more than 1 MB of storage space for a single minute of audio. For this reason, WAV files often are compressed so they take up less storage space.

Figure 4-39 *The waveform shown represents a portion of the word, Hello, as spoken into a microphone.*

Speech Recognition

Another use for a microphone is speech recognition. **Speech recognition**, also called **voice recognition**, is the computer's capability of distinguishing spoken words. Speech recognition programs do not understand speech; they only recognize a vocabulary of certain words. The vocabulary of speech recognition programs can range from two

Figure 4-38 *An electronic keyboard is an external MIDI device that can be used to play music, which can be stored in the computer.*

words (such as Yes and No) to more than sixty thousand words (Figure 4-40).

Speech recognition programs are either speaker dependent or speaker independent. With **speaker-dependent software**, the computer makes a profile of your voice, which means you have to train the computer to recognize your voice. To train the computer, you must speak each of the words in the vocabulary into the computer repeatedly. After *hearing* the spoken word repeatedly, the program develops and stores a digital pattern for the word. When you later speak a word, the program compares the spoken word to those stored. **Speaker-independent software** has a built-in set of word patterns, so you do not have to train a computer to recognize your voice.

Some speech recognition software requires **discrete speech**, which means you have to speak slowly and separate each word with a short pause. Higher-quality speech recognition software allows you to speak in a flowing conversational tone, called **continuous speech**. Several continuous-speech systems are available for personal computers, and advances in speech recognition continue to be made.

Speech recognition systems often are used in specialized applications in which a user's hands are occupied or disabled, or by users such as reporters and attorneys. Instead of typing or using a pointing device, the user speaks into a microphone to dictate words, issue commands, or perform other tasks. The table in Figure 4-41 summarizes three types of speech recognition applications and examples of their uses.

☑ **Continuous speech—increased productivity.** Speak to your computer without pausing between words. At speeds faster than that of an average typist, you can create documents more quickly than ever before. ViaVoice automatically spells each word correctly, so there's no need to spend time looking for spelling mistakes.

☑ **Dictate directly into Microsoft Word (version 6.0c, 7 & 97).** Save precious time by speaking directly into this popular word processing program. No need to cut and paste... dictate right into Word!

☑ **No initial training.** No initial enrollment is necessary (use ViaVoice out of the box). Just spend a few minutes with the Dictation Trainer to learn how to dictate, and you're off and running.

☑ **Adapts to the way you work.** As you use the system, it learns your vocabulary and usage patterns. The more you use the system, the more accurate it becomes. You can have any number of users and guests on a single system.

☑ **Shortcuts.** Use a key word to automatically trigger commonly used phrases, paragraphs, or pages. By simply dictating "T-letter" the entire text of a thank you letter can appear on your screen.

☑ **Accuracy.** Industry-leading technology. IBM's multi-patented breakthrough technology means you can spend less time correcting and more time creating.

☑ **Context recognition.** ViaVoice uses context to distinguish between similar sounding words and phrases (for example: there, their and they're; or whirled peas and world peace).

☑ **Text to speech.** Listen to your own documents or imported documents. In a rush? Let ViaVoice read aloud your e-mail as you prepare for that important meeting. Or, just give your tired eyes a rest.

☑ **Large vocabulary.** The base vocabulary of 22,000 words can be expanded to 64,000 words to accommodate your own personal preferences. ViaVoice also provides a 200,000 word back-up dictionary.

☑ **Expand your vocabulary.** Analyze text documents for new words with the option of adding them to your vocabulary. This is a quick and easy way to customize your vocabulary to the words used most often.

☑ **Ease of correction.** Many other programs insist that you correct errors as they occur. IBM ViaVoice allows you to complete your thoughts and make corrections at a convenient time or defer the corrections to a colleague. Simply click on a word to play back that word. This feature makes corrections a breeze and ensures your original intent and accuracy.

☑ **Includes noise-canceling headset microphone.** ViaVoice includes a top-of-the-line headset microphone.

Figure 4-40 *Speech recognition programs recognize a vocabulary of words. ViaVoice, for example, has a 22,000 word base vocabulary that can be expanded to 64,000 words.*

SPEECH RECOGNITION APPLICATIONS

Speech Recognition Application	Explanation	Example Uses
Command	Controls equipment	• Issue instructions to personal computer • Dial a cellular telephone • Route calls in an automated telephone system
Dictation/Data Entry	Types spoken words	• Office employees dictate letters • Doctors update hospital patient records • Reporters write stories • Lawyers develop briefs • Bankers transfer funds among bank accounts
Information Access	Enables access to products and services	• Access credit card account information • Access product information

Figure 4-41 *Summary of the three types of speech recognition applications and examples of their uses.*

Video Input

Video input or **video capture** is the process of entering a full-motion recording into a computer and storing the video on a hard disk or some other medium. To capture video, you plug a video camera, VCR, or other video device into a **video capture card**, which is an expansion card that converts the analog video signal into a digital signal that a computer can understand. (Most new computers are not equipped with a video capture card.) Once the video device is connected to the video capture card, you can begin recording. After you save the video on a hard disk, you can play it or edit it using video-editing software.

Just as with audio files, video files can require tremendous amounts of storage space. A three-minute segment, or clip, of high-quality video, for example, can take an entire gigabyte of storage (equal to approximately 50 million pages of text). To decrease the size of the files, video often is compressed. A popular video compression standard is defined by the **Moving Picture Experts Group (MPEG)**. DVD-ROMs use the MPEG standard to compress video data.

If you do not want to save an entire video clip on your computer, you can use a **video digitizer** to capture an individual frame from a video and then save the still picture in a file. To do this, you plug the recording device such as a video camera, VCR, or television into the video digitizer, which then usually connects to a parallel port on the system unit (Figure 4-42). As you watch the video using special software, you can stop it and capture any single frame. The resulting files are similar to those generated with a digital camera.

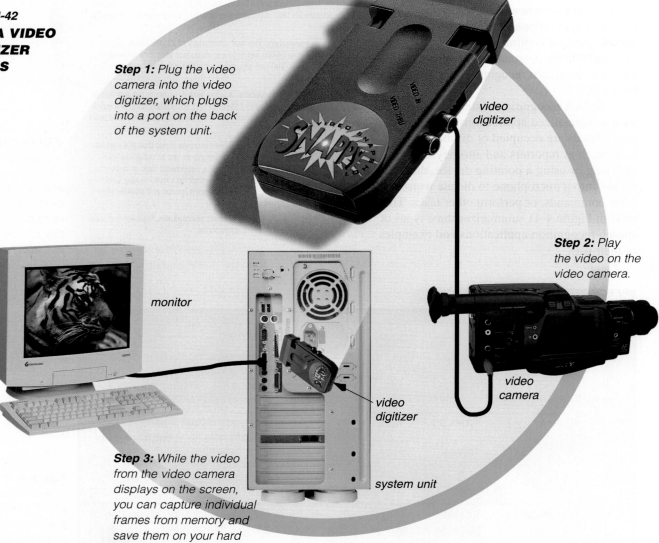

Figure 4-42
HOW A VIDEO DIGITIZER WORKS

Step 1: Plug the video camera into the video digitizer, which plugs into a port on the back of the system unit.

video digitizer

Step 2: Play the video on the video camera.

monitor

video digitizer

video camera

system unit

Step 3: While the video from the video camera displays on the screen, you can capture individual frames from memory and save them on your hard disk.

Videoconferencing

A **videoconference** is a meeting between two or more geographically separated individuals who use a network or the Internet to transmit audio and video data. To participate in a videoconference, you must have a microphone, speakers, and a video camera mounted on your computer (Figure 4-43). As you speak, members of the meeting hear your voice on their speakers. Any image in front of the video camera, such as a person's face, displays in a window on each participant's screen.

Another window on the screen that displays notes and drawings simultaneously on all the participants' screens, called a **whiteboard**, provides multiple users with an area on which they can write or draw. As the costs of videoconferencing hardware and software continue to decrease, more people and companies are taking advantage of this cost-effective way to conduct business meetings, corporate training, and educational classes.

WEB INFO
WEB INFO

For more information on videoconference, visit the Discovering Computers 2000 Chapter 4 WEB INFO page (**www.scsite.com/dc2000/ ch4/webinfo.htm**) and click Videoconference.

Figure 4-43 *As you speak, members of the videoconference hear your voice on their speakers. With the video camera facing you, an image of your face displays in a window on each participant's screen.*

INPUT DEVICES FOR PHYSICALLY CHALLENGED USERS

The growing presence of computers in everyone's lives has generated an awareness of the need to address computing requirements for those with physical limitations. Today, the **Americans with Disabilities Act (ADA)** requires that any company with 15 or more employees make reasonable attempts to accommodate the needs of physically challenged workers. Whether at work or at home, you may find it necessary to obtain input devices that address physical limitations. Besides speech recognition, which is ideal for blind or visually impaired users, several other input devices are available.

Users with limited hand mobility that wish to use a keyboard have several options. A **keyguard**, which is placed over the keyboard, allows you to rest your hand on the keyboard without accidentally pressing any keys; a keyguard also guides your finger or pointing device so you press only one key at a time (Figure 4-44).

Keyboards with larger keys also are available. Still another option is the screen-displayed keyboard, in which a graphic of a standard keyboard displays on the user's screen. Using a pointing device, the individual presses the keys on the screen-displayed keyboard.

Various pointing devices are available for users with motor disabilities. Small trackballs that can be controlled with a thumb or

Figure 4-44 *A keyguard allows you to rest your hand on the keyboard without accidentally pressing any keys and guides your finger or pointing device onto a key so you press only a single key at a time.*

one finger can be attached to a table, mounted to a wheelchair, or held in a user's hand. People with limited hand movement can use a **head-mounted pointer** to control the pointer or insertion point (Figure 4-45). To simulate the functions of a mouse button, you use a single-switch scanning display. The switch might be a pad you press with your hand, a foot pedal, a receptor that detects facial motions, or a pneumatic instrument controlled by puffs of air.

Figure 4-45 *A head-mounted pointer can be used to control the pointer on a screen-displayed keyboard, which is a graphical image of the standard keyboard.*

PUTTING IT ALL TOGETHER

When you purchase a computer, you should have an understanding of the input devices included with the computer, as well as those you may need that are not included. Many factors influence the type of input devices you may use: the type of input desired, the hardware and software in use, and the desired cost. The type of input devices you require depends on your intended use. Figure 4-46 outlines several suggested input devices for specific computer users.

SUGGESTED INPUT DEVICES BY USER

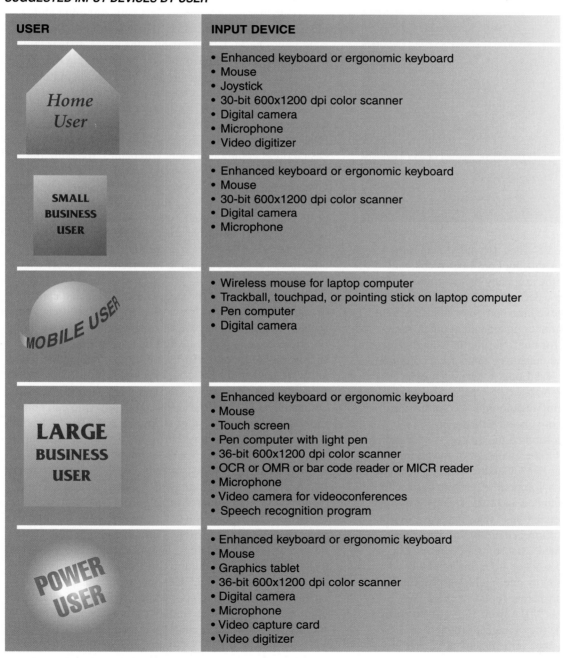

USER	INPUT DEVICE
Home User	• Enhanced keyboard or ergonomic keyboard • Mouse • Joystick • 30-bit 600x1200 dpi color scanner • Digital camera • Microphone • Video digitizer
SMALL BUSINESS USER	• Enhanced keyboard or ergonomic keyboard • Mouse • 30-bit 600x1200 dpi color scanner • Digital camera • Microphone
MOBILE USER	• Wireless mouse for laptop computer • Trackball, touchpad, or pointing stick on laptop computer • Pen computer • Digital camera
LARGE BUSINESS USER	• Enhanced keyboard or ergonomic keyboard • Mouse • Touch screen • Pen computer with light pen • 36-bit 600x1200 dpi color scanner • OCR or OMR or bar code reader or MICR reader • Microphone • Video camera for videoconferences • Speech recognition program
POWER USER	• Enhanced keyboard or ergonomic keyboard • Mouse • Graphics tablet • 36-bit 600x1200 dpi color scanner • Digital camera • Microphone • Video capture card • Video digitizer

Figure 4-46 *This table recommends suggested input devices.*

TECHNOLOGY TRAILBLAZER

LOU GERSTNER

In 1993, IBM faced a crisis. Beset by changing customer relationships, a shifting consumer focus, and increasing competition, the company had lost more than $8 billion. IBM's future – perhaps even its existence – was in doubt; some believed the computer industry giant should be broken into smaller, independent enterprises. In search of a solution, for the first time in its eighty-two year history IBM reached outside its ranks for a corporate leader. The man tapped was Louis V. Gerstner, chief executive officer at RJR Nabisco.

Why would an ailing technological colossus turn to a tobacco/food company executive for a cure? Surprisingly, Gerstner combined the qualities, education, and experience required to be chairman of the board and chief executive officer at IBM. Gerstner learned account-ability and discipline in a competitive private high school, where grades were announced and rules strictly enforced. (Years later, Gerstner detailed his views on education in *Reinventing Education: Entrepeneurship in America's Public Schools.*) He earned a bachelor's degree in engi-neering as a scholarship student at Dartmouth College. Colleagues remember him as intelligent, purposeful, and demanding. "He did not tolerate fools," a classmate recalls. After receiving an MBA from Harvard Business School, Gerstner became the youngest principal at McKinsey & Company, Inc., a management consulting firm. He moved on to become president of American

Express Company, where he showed the ability to invigorate an established business. At RJR Nabisco, his next stop, Gerstner demonstrated the willingness to make tough decisions in a variety of crises.

Gerstner did not announce a new corporate philoso-phy when he arrived at IBM. "The last thing IBM needs right now," he said, "is a vision." Instead, Gerstner took practical steps to stabilize the company: cutting the workforce, rebuilding the product line, and instituting cost reductions. He brought a no-nonsense approach to an organization where internal dissent was commonplace. Gerstner was an exacting boss: "I'm intense, competitive, focused, blunt, and tough, yes." Yet, he permitted the more casual dress common at other companies, rejecting the blue-suited conformity once demanded at *Big Blue*. Gerstner cast aside IBM's geographic divisions, reorganiz-ing along industry lines. He railed against the fanatic perfectionism that characterized IBM's labs. "You don't launch products here," Gerstner complained to technicians. "They escape." Gerstner speeded product development and, in 1996, IBM PCs using new technology were first to market.

Perhaps most surprising, Gerstner rejected calls to break up the company. Network computing, he believed, would "change the way we do business, the way we teach our children, communicate and interact as individuals." In a networked world, IBM's ability to combine hardware, software, and service was an important asset. "This technology stuff is hard," Gerstner said, "and if I'm a company, what I really want is somebody who can help me implement it." Gerstner set out to make IBM a leading source for the technology, hardware, software, installation, and maintenance of networked computing systems.

IBM still had to reestablish the customer confidence that once was taken for granted. An early adage claimed, *Nobody was ever fired for buying from IBM*, but in a changing marketplace the company no longer inspired that assurance. Technology alone was not enough. "We should be impressed by technology, but we shouldn't be distracted by it, or fooled into thinking that technology, unto itself, is the solution to anything," Gerstner maintained. Restoring customer faith required cooperation with each individual client. "We start with an understanding of what our cus-tomers need," Gerstner said, "and then we work together to fashion a solution." Gerstner seems on the way to fashioning his own solution at IBM. In June 1998, the once troubled company had total assets of $77.1 billion.

COMPANY ON THE CUTTING EDGE

IBM

What do meat and cheese slicers, commercial scales, industrial time recorders, tabulators, and punched cards have in common? These were some of the first products offered by IBM. It was more than thirty years before the company created its first computer. Despite the delayed start, today IBM, nicknamed Big Blue, is a leader in the computer industry with a reputation for innovative products.

In 1911, the Computing Scale Company of America, Herman Hollerith's Tabulating Machine Company, and the International Time Recording Company merged and incorporated to form the Computing – Tabulating – Recording Company (C-T-R). The company sold a variety of business-related gadgets, but Hollerith's tabulating machine presaged its future. The machine, which used punched cards to catalogue data, helped complete the 1890 census in record time and was an ancestor of the modern computer. Nine years after C-T-R was created, its name was changed to the International Business Machines Corporation (IBM).

IBM's first electronic computer, the Mark I, was completed in 1944. Designed to perform long computations automatically, the huge Mark I took about twelve seconds to divide – far slower than today's pocket calculators. In 1952, IBM produced its first vacuum tube computer. This IBM 701 executed 17,000 instructions per second and soon was employed for business applications. Five years later, IBM introduced the first computer disk storage system and FORTRAN, a scientific programming language. In 1959, IBM presented the IBM 7090, a mainframe that could perform 229,000 calculations per second.

In the 1960s and 1970s, IBM changed how computers were marketed and used. The System/360 was the first family of computers. Interchangeable software and peripherals allowed users to upgrade processors without having to replace the entire system. In 1969, IBM unbundled components (hardware, software, and services), and began to sell each separately – thus giving birth to the software and service industries. Three devices, now taken for granted, were invented at IBM in the 1970s: the supermarket price scanner, the automatic teller machine (ATM), and a new type of laser printer.

In 1981, the IBM Personal Computer (PC) revolutionized the computer industry. With 16 KB of RAM, a floppy disk drive, an optional color monitor, and prices starting at $1,565, more than 136,000 IBM PCs were sold in the first year and a half. For the first time, IBM had turned to outside companies for components – an Intel processor and a Microsoft operating system. As a result, a number of IBM PC-compatible clones with the same components were built by other companies. In 1992, IBM's new ThinkPad notebook computer combined two inventive input devices – a butterfly-like keyboard that expanded when the computer case was opened and a unique pointing device, called a TrackPoint, positioned between keys. The ThinkPad collected more than 300 awards for its creative design.

As purchasing decisions moved down the corporate ladder, customer relationships changed and many buyers turned to less-expensive IBM-compatible clones. With declining sales, some industry insiders advocated breaking up the company. New CEO Louis Gerstner, however, recognized that the rise of the Internet and network computing dovetailed with an IBM strength – the ability to provide integrated solutions. Building on this advantage, revenues climbed. Acquisitions such as Lotus Development Corporation in the mid 1990s increased IBM's market value by $50 billion.

In 1997, IBM had 369,465 employees with revenues of $78.5 billion and net earnings of more than $6 billion. The company also experienced a public relations coup when Deep Blue, an IBM supercomputer, defeated World Chess Champion Gary Kasparov in a six-game match, becoming the first computer to beat a reigning champion. The unprecedented success of Deep Blue is emblematic of Big Blue's determination to remain at the forefront of the computer revolution.

SHELLY
CASHMAN
SERIES®

**DISCOVERING
COMPUTERS
2000**

■ Student Exercises
WEB INFO
IN BRIEF
KEY TERMS
AT THE MOVIES
CHECKPOINT
AT ISSUE
CYBERCLASS
HANDS ON
NET STUFF
■ Special Features
TIMELINE 2000
GUIDE TO WWW SITES
MAKING A CHIP
BUYER'S GUIDE 2000
CAREERS 2000
TRENDS 2000
CHAT
INTERACTIVE LABS
NEWS
HOME

CHAPTER 1 2 3 [4] 5 6 7 8 9 10 11 12 13 14 INDEX

IN BRIEF **www.scsite.com/dc2000/ch4/brief.htm**

WEB INSTRUCTIONS: *To display this page from the Web, launch your browser and enter the URL, www.scsite.com/dc2000/ch4/brief.htm. Click the links for current and additional information. To listen to an audio version of this IN BRIEF, click the Audio button to the right of the title, IN BRIEF, at the top of the page. To play the audio, RealPlayer must be installed on your computer (download by clicking here).*

 1. What Are the Four Types of Input?

Input is any data or instructions entered into the memory of a computer. Four types of input are data, programs, commands, and user responses. **Data** is a collection of unorganized facts that can include words, numbers, pictures, sounds, and video. A **program** is a series of instructions that tell a computer how to process data into information. **Commands** are instructions given to a computer program. **User responses** are instructions a user issues to the computer by responding to questions posed by a computer program. Any component used to enter data, programs, commands, and user responses into a computer is an **input device**.

 2. What Are the Characteristics of a Keyboard?

The **keyboard** is a primary input device on a computer. All keyboards have a typing area used to type letters of the alphabet, numbers, punctuation marks, and other basic characters. A keyboard also may include a **numeric keypad** designed to make it easier to enter numbers, **function keys** programmed to issue commands and accomplish certain tasks, **arrow keys** used to move the **insertion point**, and **toggle keys** that can be switched between two different states.

 3. Describe the Various Types of Keyboards?

A standard computer keyboard sometimes is called a **QWERTY keyboard** because of the layout of its typing area. The **Dvorak keyboard** places the most frequently typed letters in the middle of the typing area. **Enhanced keyboards** have function keys, CTRL keys, ALT keys, and a set of arrow and additional keys. **Wireless keyboards** transmit data via infrared light waves. Laptop and handheld computer keyboards sometimes contain smaller and fewer keys.

 4. What Are Various Types of Pointing Devices?

Pointing devices control the movement of a pointer on the screen. A **mouse** is a pointing device that is moved across a flat surface, controls the movement of the pointer on the screen, and is used to make selections from the screen. A **trackball** is a stationary pointing device with a ball mechanism on its top. A **touchpad** is a flat, rectangular pointing device that is sensitive to pressure and motion. A **pointing-stick** is a pressure-sensitive pointing device shaped like a pencil eraser. Other pointing devices include a **joystick** (a vertical lever mounted on a base), a **touch screen** (a monitor with a touch-sensitive panel on the screen), a **light-pen** (a hand-held device that contains a light source or can detect light), and a **graphics tablet** (an electronic plastic board used to input graphical data).

 5. How Does a Mouse Work?

The bottom of a mouse is flat and contains a multidirectional mechanism, usually a small ball, which senses movement of the mouse. As the mouse is moved across a flat surface, electronic circuits in the mouse translate the movement into signals that are sent to the computer, and the pointer on the screen also moves.

 www.scsite.com/dc2000/ch4/brief.htm

SHELLY
CASHMAN
SERIES

**DISCOVERING
COMPUTERS
2000**

6. What Are Different Mouse Types?

A **mechanical mouse** has a rubber or metal ball on its underside. An <u>optical mouse</u> uses devices that emit light to detect the mouse's movement. A **cordless mouse** relies on battery power and uses infrared or radio waves to communicate with a receiver.

7. How Do Scanners and Other Reading Devices Work?

A **scanner** is a light-sensing input device that reads printed text and graphics and then translates the results into a form the computer can use. When a **source document** is scanned, a bright light moves across the document and an image is reflected into a series of mirrors. The light image is converted into an analog electrical current, which is converted into a digital signal that is sent to software in the computer. The scanned results are stored in rows and columns of dots, called a **bitmap**. An **optical reader** uses a light source to read characters, marks, and codes and converts them into digital data that can be processed by a computer. Three types of <u>optical readers</u> are **optical character recognition (OCR)**, **optical mark recognition (OMR)**, and **bar code scanners**.

8. Why Is a Digital Camera Used?

A <u>digital camera</u> is used to take pictures and store the photographed images digitally. The photographed image can be **downloaded**, or transferred, to a computer by a connecting cable; or it can be stored on a floppy disk or PC Card and copied to a computer through a disk drive or PC Card slot. Once on a computer, pictures can be edited with photo-editing software, printed, faxed, sent via electronic mail, included in another document, or posted to a Web site.

9. What Are Various Techniques Used for Audio and Video Input?

Audio input is the process of entering (recording) music, speech, or sound effects. Sound is entered via a microphone, tape player, audio CD player, or external <u>MIDI</u> (musical instrument digital interface) device such as an electric piano keyboard. Each plugs into a port on a computer's sound card. Audio files can be played, edited, attached to an e-mail message, or included in a document. **Video input** is the process of entering a full-motion recording into a computer and storing the video on a hard disk or some other medium. To capture video, a video camera is plugged into a video capture card, which is an expansion card that converts the analog video signal into a digital signal. A **video digitizer** can be used to capture an individual frame from a video and save the still picture in a file.

10. What Are Some Alternative Input Devices for Physically Challenged Users?

Speech recognition, or the computer's capability of distinguishing spoken words, is ideal for blind or visually impaired computer users. A **keyguard**, which is placed over the keyboard, allows people with limited hand mobility to rest their hands on the keyboard and guides a finger or pointing device so that only one key is pressed. Keyboards with larger keys and screen-displayed keyboards on which keys are pressed using a pointing device also can help. Pointing devices such as small track balls that can be controlled with a thumb or one finger and **head-mounted pointers** also are available for <u>users with motor disabilities</u>.

SHELLY CASHMAN SERIES®

DISCOVERING COMPUTERS 2000

■ Student Exercises
WEB INFO
IN BRIEF
KEY TERMS
AT THE MOVIES
CHECKPOINT
AT ISSUE
CYBERCLASS
HANDS ON
NET STUFF
■ Special Features
TIMELINE 2000
GUIDE TO WWW SITES
MAKING A CHIP
BUYER'S GUIDE 2000
CAREERS 2000
TRENDS 2000
CHAT
INTERACTIVE LABS
NEWS
HOME

CHAPTER 1 2 3 **4** 5 6 7 8 9 10 11 12 13 14 INDEX

KEY TERMS www.scsite.com/dc2000/ch4/terms.htm

WEB INSTRUCTIONS: *To display this page from the Web, launch your browser and enter the URL,* www.scsite.com/dc2000/ch4/terms.htm. *Scroll through the list of terms. Click a term to display its definition and a picture. Click KEY TERMS on the left to redisplay the KEY TERMS page. Click the TO WEB button for current and additional information about the term from the Web. To see animations, Shockwave and Flash Player must be installed on your computer (download by clicking* here*).*

Americans with Disabilities Act (ADA) (4.26)
arrow keys (4.5)
audio input (4.22)
bar code (4.17)
bar code scanner (4.17)
bitmap (4.14)
click (4.8)
command (4.2)
continuous speech (4.23)
cordless mouse (4.10)
data (4.2)
data collection devices (4.20)
digital camera (4.20)
digitizer (4.13)
digitizing tablet (4.13)
discrete speech (4.23)
dots per inch (dpi) (4.15)
download (4.20)
Dvorak keyboard (4.6)
enhanced keyboards (4.6)
ergonomics (4.6)
field camera (4.21)
function keys (4.4)
graphical user interface (4.3)
graphics tablet (4.13)
handwriting recognition software (4.13)
head-mounded pointer (4.26)
image processing (4.16)
image processing system (4.16)
imaging (4.16)
input (4.2)
input device (4.3)
insertion point (4.5)
joystick (4.12)
keyboard (4.3)
keyguard (4.26)

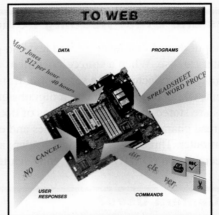

INPUT: Any data or instructions entered into the memory of a computer. Once in memory, the CPU can access it and process it into output. Four types of input are data, programs, commands, and user responses. (4.2)

keyword (4.2)
light pen (4.12)
magnetic-ink character recognition (MICR) (4.19)
mechanical mouse (4.9)
menu-driven (4.3)
mouse (4.7)
mouse pad (4.7)
mouse pointer (4.7)
Moving Picture Experts Group (MPEG) (4.24)
numeric keypad (4.4)
OCR devices (4.16)
optical character recognition (OCR) (4.16)
optical character recognition (OCR) software (4.16)
optical mark recognition (OMR) (4.17)

optical mouse (4.9)
optical reader (4.16)
optical scanner (4.14)
pen (4.13)
point-and-shoot camera (4.21)
pointer (4.7)
pointing device (4.7)
pointing stick (4.11)
program (4.2)
puck (4.13)
QWERTY keyboard (4.6)
resolution (4.15)
scanner (4.14)
source document (4.13)
speaker-dependent software (4.23)
speaker-independent software (4.23)
speech recognition (4.22)
studio camera (4.21)
stylus (4.13)
toggle keys (4.5)
touch screen (4.12)
touchpad (4.11)
trackball (4.10)
trackpad (4.11)
turnaround documents (4.16)
user response (4.3)
video capture card (4.24)
video digitizer (4.24)
video input (4.24)
videoconferencing (4.24)
voice recognition (4.22)
WAV (4.22)
waveforms (4.22)
whiteboard (4.25)
wireless keyboards (4.6)

CHAPTER 1 2 3 **4** 5 6 7 8 9 10 11 12 13 14 INDEX

AT THE MOVIES

www.scsite.com/dc2000/ch4/movies.htm

WELCOME to VIDEO CLIPS from CNN

WEB INSTRUCTIONS: *To display this page from the Web, launch your browser and enter the URL, www.scsite.com/dc2000/ch4/movies.htm. Click a picture to view a video. After watching the video, close the video window and then complete the exercise by answering the questions about the video. To view the videos, RealPlayer must be installed on your computer (download by clicking here).*

1 Walk Through Computer

What is the idea behind the oversized computer exhibit at the Computer Museum in Boston? How does a museum visitor interact with the computer? What input devices are included in this larger-than-life computer? Do you think that being inside a computer could help you understand how computers work? To learn more about the museum's latest exhibits, visit the Web site.

2 Joystick Review

Advances in joystick technology have created exciting new possibilities. Where would you expect to use a joystick? What two types of joysticks are described in the video? Describe the features of each. How do they differ from other input devices, such as a mouse? How are they the same? In relation to the joystick, what is meant by feedback technology? Which model of joystick would you purchase?

3 Faces in the Crowd

What are some applications of face-recognition technology? What types of input devices are used in a face-recognition system? In what segment of society are the privacy issues raised by use of these face-recognition systems? If you were recognized as someone else and detained, would you be upset? What can be done to make sure this technology is not abused? Who do you think is accountable for the responsible use of face-recognition technology – government or the private sector?

SHELLY CASHMAN SERIES®

DISCOVERING COMPUTERS 2000

Student Exercises
WEB INFO
IN BRIEF
KEY TERMS
AT THE MOVIES
CHECKPOINT
AT ISSUE
CYBERCLASS
HANDS ON
NET STUFF
Special Features
TIMELINE 2000
GUIDE TO WWW SITES
MAKING A CHIP
BUYER'S GUIDE 2000
CAREERS 2000
TRENDS 2000
CHAT
INTERACTIVE LABS
NEWS
HOME

SHELLY CASHMAN SERIES®

DISCOVERING COMPUTERS 2000

Student Exercises
WEB INFO
IN BRIEF
KEY TERMS
AT THE MOVIES
CHECKPOINT
AT ISSUE
CYBERCLASS
HANDS ON
NET STUFF
Special Features
TIMELINE 2000
GUIDE TO WWW SITES
MAKING A CHIP
BUYER'S GUIDE 2000
CAREERS 2000
TRENDS 2000
CHAT
INTERACTIVE LABS
NEWS
HOME

CHAPTER 1 2 3 4 5 6 7 8 9 10 11 12 13 14   INDEX

CHECKPOINT   www.scsite.com/dc2000/ch4/check.htm

WEB INSTRUCTIONS: *To display this page from the Web, launch your browser and enter the URL, www.scsite.com/dc2000/ch4/check.htm. Click the links for current and additional information. To experience the animation and interactivity, Shockwave and Flash Player must be installed on your computer (download by clicking here).*

Label the Figure

Instructions: *Identify these areas or keys on a typical desktop computer keyboard.*

1._____ 2._____ 3._____

4._____ 5._____ 6._____

Matching

Instructions: *Match each key name from the column on the left with the best description from the column on the right.*

_____ 1. ENTER

_____ 2. BACKSPACE

_____ 3. ESC

_____ 4. CTRL

_____ 5. NUM LOCK

a. Toggle key that causes numeric keypad keys to function like a calculator.
b. Erases the character to the right of the insertion point.
c. Used at the end of a command to direct the computer to process the command.
d. When pressed in combination with another key(s), usually issues a command.
e. Toggle key that shifts alphabetic letters to uppercase.
f. Often used to quit a program or operation.
g. Erases a character to the left of the insertion point.

Short Answer

Instructions: *Write a brief answer to each of the following questions.*

1. Why is resolution important when using a scanner? _____ How is resolution typically measured and stated? _____

2. How is optical character recognition different from optical mark recognition? _____

3. What is a bar code? _____ How are bar codes read? _____ On what products are they used? _____

4. How is speaker-dependent software different from speaker-independent software? _____ How is discrete speech recognition different from continuous speech recognition? _____

5. What is videoconferencing? _____ How does a whiteboard enhance videoconferencing? _____

AT ISSUE

www.scsite.com/dc2000/ch4/issue.htm

SCS SHELLY CASHMAN SERIES.
DISCOVERING COMPUTERS 2000

WEB INSTRUCTIONS: *To display this page from the Web, launch your browser and enter the URL, www.scsite.com/dc2000/ch4/issue.htm. Click the links for current and additional information.*

ONE *In addition to data, programs, commands, and user responses,* researchers are experimenting with a fifth type of input – human emotions. A development called affective computing uses input devices such as video cameras and skin sensors with software similar to speech recognition programs to allow a computer to read a user's emotions. For example, a furrowed brow and sweaty palms might indicate frustration. Emotional input could be invaluable in conjunction with <u>computer-aided instruction</u>, letting a computer know whether to speed up or slow down tutorials. Some people, however, see affective computing as an invasion of privacy. How do you feel? In what areas might affective computing be useful? Why? Would you be comfortable with a computer knowing how you feel? Why or why not?

TWO *Although input varies, in one way input devices do not; most are* encased in a bland, beige, plastic shell. A California company is changing that by offering keyboards and mouse units in oak, cherry, or maple. As a fitting adjunct, another company is selling <u>mouse pads</u> that replicate traditional Oriental or Persian carpets. Upgrading appearance is not cheap. A wooden keyboard costs more than $600, a wooden mouse more than $300, and the rodent rug almost $20. Yet, some people insist these devices provide a more attractive and, in the long run, more productive work setting. How much money would you spend to upgrade the appearance of your computer equipment? Why? Would this kind of upgrade increase productivity? Why or why not?

THREE *After one week of work at a fast-food restaurant, an Arizona teenager was thrilled to* receive a check for $16,834. Her dreams of a new car were dashed, however, when it was discovered that her hourly pay rate had been entered incorrectly in the restaurant's computer. Reliable output requires reliable input, a truism expressed by the acronym <u>GIGO</u> (Garbage In, Garbage Out). Data entered with some input devices is more likely to be accurate than data entered with others. What two input devices are more likely to produce accurate data? Why? What two input devices are more likely to produce inaccurate data? Why? What factors have the most effect on input accuracy?

FOUR *Experts agree that speech recognition capability* represents the future of software. Experts do not agree, however, that the future is now. The best <u>speech recognition</u> programs are ninety to ninety-five percent accurate. Yet, advocates admit that this assessment is based on expected speech and vocabulary. When confronted with unusual dialogue, accuracy drops; one speech recognition program translated the line, "I'll make him an offer he can't refuse" (from *The Godfather*) into "I held make them that off or he can refuse." Even a ninety percent accuracy rate means one out of ten words will be wrong. How accurate must speech recognition software be before it can be used effectively? When would speech recognition be an advantage? Might it ever be a disadvantage? Why?

FIVE *Getting ready to study for an exam can take longer than studying. By the time notes* written on scraps of paper, food wrappers, book covers, and so on have been collected and arranged, little study time may be left. Fortunately, a new device called CrossPad can assist less-than-organized scholars. The <u>portable digital notepad</u> allows students to jot notes with a digital pen (storing up to one hundred pages), download the notes to a PC, and then organize the information by date or keywords. How would a portable digital notepad change your study habits? If every student had a portable digital notepad, how might it change the way teachers teach? In what occupations could people benefit from a portable digital notepad? Why?

CHAPTER 1 2 3 [4] 5 6 7 8 9 10 11 12 13 14 INDEX

CYBERCLASS   www.scsite.com/dc2000/ch4/class.htm

WEB INSTRUCTIONS: *To display this page from the Web, launch your browser and enter the URL, www.scsite.com/dc2000/ch4/class.htm. To start Level I CyberClass, click a Level I link on this page or enter the URL, www.cyber-class.com. Click the Student button, click Discovering Computers 2000 in the list of titles, and then click the Enter a site button. To start Level II or III CyberClass (available only to those purchasers of a CyberClass floppy disk), place your CyberClass floppy disk in drive A, click Start on the taskbar, click Run on the Start menu, type* a:connect *in the Open text box, click the OK button, click the Enter CyberClass button, and then follow the instructions.*

ⓘ ⓘⓘ ⓘⓘⓘ LEVEL **1. Flash Cards**   Click Flash Cards on the Main Menu of the CyberClass web page. Click the plus sign before the Chapter 4 title and then click Pointing Devices. Complete all Pointing Devices questions. Then, choose a category and continue to answer flash cards until you have answered 20 questions. Record your percentage correct and hand in your score to your instructor. All users: Answer as many more flash cards as you desire. Close the Electronic Flash Card window and the Flash Cards window by clicking the Close button in the upper-right corner of each window.

ⓘ ⓘⓘ ⓘⓘⓘ LEVEL **2. Practice Test**   Click Testing on the Main Menu of the CyberClass web page. Click the Select a book box arrow and then click Discovering Computers 2000. Click the Select a test to take box arrow and then click the Chapter 4 title in the list. Click the Take Test button. If necessary, maximize the window. Take the practice test and then click the Submit Test button. If your percentage correct is less than 85%, click the Take another Test button and take another practice test. Record your test score(s) and hand them in to your instructor.

ⓘ ⓘⓘ ⓘⓘⓘ LEVEL **3. Web Guide**   Click Web Guide on the Main Menu of the CyberClass web page. When the Guide to World Wide Web Sites page displays, click News Sources. Then, click C/NET. Find a story about computers that interests you and write a brief synopsis of the story. Hand in the synopsis to your instructor.

ⓘ ⓘⓘ ⓘⓘⓘ LEVEL **4. Company Briefs**   Click Company Briefs on the Main Menu of the CyberClass web page. Click a corporation name to display a case study. Read the case study. Write a brief report on whether you would want to work for the company, based upon their use of computers.

ⓘⓘ ⓘⓘⓘ LEVEL **5. CyberChallenge**   Click CyberChallenge on the Main Menu of the CyberClass web page. Click the Select a book box arrow and then click Discovering Computers 2000. Click the Select a board to play box arrow and then click Chapter 4 in the list. Click the Play CyberChallenge button. Maximize the CyberChallenge window. Play CyberChallenge until you have answered correctly all questions for a given vertical column. Close the CyberChallenge window.

ⓘⓘ ⓘⓘⓘ LEVEL **6. Hot Links**   Determine a Web site on the World Wide Web that you think everyone in your class should visit. Click Hot Links on the Main Menu of the CyberClass web page. Click Add a Link within the Hot Links section. Enter the Link Name, the URL, and the Link Description. Click the Add Link button. Your link should display on the Hot Links screen.

ⓘⓘ ⓘⓘⓘ LEVEL **7. Send Messages**   Click Send Messages on the Main Menu of the CyberClass web page. Send a message to all members of your class to look at the Hot Links web site you entered in exercise 6 above by clicking the Send to all box in the Members section of the screen (a check mark will display in the box), entering a subject and the message itself, and then clicking the Send Message button.

HANDS ON

www.scsite.com/dc2000/ch4/hands.htm

WEB INSTRUCTIONS: *To display this page from the Web, launch your browser and enter the URL,*
www.scsite.com/dc2000/ch4/hands.htm. Click the links for current and additional information.

One   *About Your Computer*

Your computer probably has more than one input device. To learn a little bit about
the input devices on your computer, right-click the My Computer icon on the desktop. Click Properties on
the shortcut menu. When the System Properties dialog box displays, click the Device Manager tab. Click
View devices by type. Under Computer, a list of hardware device categories displays. What input devices
appear in the list? Click the plus sign next to each category. What specific input devices in each category are
connected to your computer? Click the Cancel button in the System Properties dialog box.

Two   *Customizing the Keyboard*

The Windows operating system provides several ways to customize the keyboard
for people with physical limitations. Some of these options are StickyKeys, FilterKeys, and ToggleKeys. To
find out more about each option, click the Start button, point to Settings on the Start menu, and then click
Control Panel on the Settings submenu. Double-click Accessibility Options in the Control Panel window.
Click the Keyboard tab in the Accessibility Properties dialog box. Click the question mark in the title bar,
click StickyKeys, read the information in the pop-up window, and then click the pop-up window to close it.
Repeat this process for FilterKeys and ToggleKeys. What is the purpose of each option? How might each
option benefit someone with a physical disability?

Three   *Using the Mouse and Keyboard to Interact with an Online Program*

See your instructor for the location of the Loan Payment Calculator program.
Click the Start button on the taskbar, and then click Run on the Start menu to
display the Run dialog box. In the Open text box, type the path and file name
of the program. For example, type `a:loancalc.exe` and then press the
ENTER key to display the Loan Payment Calculator window. Type `12500` in
the LOAN AMOUNT text box. Click the YEARS right scroll arrow or drag
the scroll box until YEARS equals 15. Click the APR right scroll arrow or
drag the scroll box until APR equals 8.5. Click the Calculate button. Write
down the monthly payment and sum of payments. Click the Clear button.
What are the monthly payment and sum of payments for each of these loan
amounts, years, and APRs: (1) 28000, 5, 7.25; (2) 98750, 30, 9; (3) 6000, 3,
8.75; (4) 62500, 15, 9.25. Close the Loan Payment Calculator.

Four   *MouseKeys*

A graphical user interface allows you to perform many tasks with just the point and click of a mouse.
Yet, what if you do not have, or cannot use, a mouse? The Windows operating system covers this possibility with an option
called MouseKeys. When the MouseKeys option is turned on, you can use numeric keypad keys to move the mouse pointer,
click, right-click, double-click, and drag. To find out how, click the Start button and click Help on the Start menu. Click the
Index tab. Type `MouseKeys` in the text box and click the Display button. To answer each of the following questions, click an
appropriate topic in the Topics Found dialog box, click the Display button, and read the Help information. To display a different topic, click the topic and then click the Display button.

- ♠ How do you turn on MouseKeys?
- ♠ How do you use MouseKeys to move the mouse pointer?
- ♠ How do you perform each of these operations using MouseKeys: click, right-click, double-click, drag?

Click the Close button to close the Windows Help dialog box.

SHELLY
CASHMAN
SERIES®
DISCOVERING
COMPUTERS
2000

■ **Student Exercises**
WEB INFO
IN BRIEF
KEY TERMS
AT THE MOVIES
CHECKPOINT
AT ISSUE
CYBERCLASS
HANDS ON
NET STUFF
■ **Special Features**
TIMELINE 2000
GUIDE TO WWW SITES
MAKING A CHIP
BUYER'S GUIDE 2000
CAREERS 2000
TRENDS 2000
CHAT
INTERACTIVE LABS
NEWS
HOME

NET STUFF

www.scsite.com/dc2000/ch4/net.htm

WEB INSTRUCTIONS: *To display this page from the Web, launch your browser and enter the URL, www.scsite.com/dc2000/ch4/net.htm. To use the Scanning Documents lab from the Web, Shockwave and Flash Player must be installed on your computer (download by clicking here).*

SCANNING
DOCUMENTS
LAB

1. Shelly Cashman Series Scanning Documents Lab

Follow the appropriate instructions in NET STUFF 1 on page 1.46 to start and use the Scanning Documents lab. If you are running from the Web, enter the URL, www.scsite.com/sclabs/menu.htm; or display the NET STUFF page (see instructions at the top of this page) and then click the SCANNING DOCUMENTS LAB button.

DIGITAL
CAMERAS

2. Digital Cameras

Digital cameras, which record photographs in the form of digital data, have fans and critics. Fans claim that digital cameras make it easy to store, organize, edit, and transmit photographs. Critics argue that digital cameras are difficult to use, produce poor-quality images, and cost too much money. Click the DIGITAL CAMERAS button and complete this exercise to learn more about digital cameras, see a live digital camera in action, and perhaps form your own opinion about their value.

SENDING
E-MAIL

3. Sending E-Mail

In Chapter 2, you set up an e-mail account. Now, you can use that account to send messages across the world, across the country, or across the room. To send an e-mail message, click the SENDING E-MAIL button to display your e-mail service. Log in to your e-mail service. When you are finished, send the message. Next, read any messages you have received. When you are finished, exit your e-mail service. Then, follow the procedure to compose a message. The subject of the message should be input devices. Enter the e-mail address of one of your classmates. In the message itself, type something your classmates should know about input devices.

IN THE NEWS

4. In the News

Input devices can enhance the productivity of users and increase the number of potential users. The U.S. Army recently discovered this by replacing the many buttons used to operate a tank's onboard computer with a joystick and just three buttons. To the Army's delight, tank-driver performance improved, and even individuals who scored poorly on Army intelligence tests handled the tanks effectively. Click the IN THE NEWS button and read a news article about a new or improved input device, an input device being used in a new way, or an input device being made more available. What is the device? Who is promoting it? How will it be used? Will the input device change the number, or effectiveness, of potential users? If so, why?

WEB CHAT

5. Web Chat

Although satisfactory for Western languages, the keyboard is inadequate for many Asian languages. While English uses 26 letters, even the simpler version of written Chinese used in mainland China has almost 7,000 characters. This presents a major roadblock to the introduction of computers in the world's largest country. Three solutions have been offered for the problem of Chinese input. The first, called pinyin, uses English letters to express the sound of Chinese words. Pinyin is difficult to learn and slow to use, however. The second remaps keyboard keys with strokes used to draw Chinese characters. As keys are pressed, software suggests a list of characters that incorporate those strokes. The program is easy to learn, but also is fairly slow. The third is speech recognition software. As users speak words into a microphone, the computer produces the Chinese characters. The software must be reprogrammed for regional dialects, requires a powerful computer, and is less than 100 percent accurate. What do you think is the best method to handle input in China? Why? Can you suggest a better approach? Click the WEB CHAT button to enter a Web Chat discussion related to this topic.

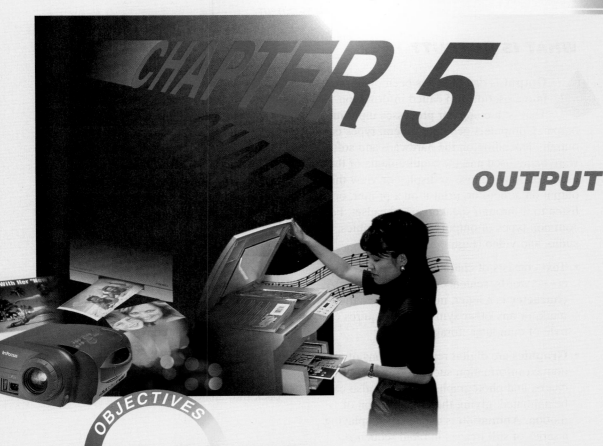

CHAPTER 5

OUTPUT

OBJECTIVES

*After completing this chapter,
you will be able to:*

Define the four types of output

Identify the different types of display devices

Describe factors that affect the quality of a monitor

Understand the purpose of a video card

Identify monitor ergonomic issues

Explain the differences among various types of printers

List various types of audio output devices

Identify the purpose of data projectors, fax machines, and multifunction devices

Explain how a terminal is both an input and output device

Identify output options for physically challenged users

Data is a collection of unorganized items that can include words, numbers, images, and sounds. Computers process and organize data into information, which has meaning and is useful. Output devices such as printers, monitors, and speakers are used to convey that information to a user. This chapter describes the various methods of output and several commonly used output devices.

WHAT IS OUTPUT?

Output is data that has been processed into a useful form called information. That is, a computer processes input into output. Computers generate several types of output, depending on the hardware and software being used and the requirements of the user. You may choose to display or view this output on a monitor, print it on a printer, or listen to it through speakers or a headset. Four common types of output are text, graphics, audio, and video (Figure 5-1).

- **Text** consists of characters that are used to create words, sentences, and paragraphs. A **character** is a letter, number, punctuation mark, or any other symbol that requires one byte of computer storage space.

- **Graphics** are digital representations of nontext information such as drawings, charts, and photographs. Graphics also can be animated, giving them the illusion of motion. **Animation** is created by displaying a series of still images in rapid sequence.

Many of today's software programs support graphics. For example, you can include a photograph in a word processing document or create a chart of data in a spreadsheet program.

Some software packages are designed specifically to create and edit graphics. Paint programs, for instance, allow you to create graphics that can be used in brochures, newsletters, and Web pages. **Image editing software** allows you to alter graphics by including enhancements such as blended colors, animation, and other special effects.

- **Audio** is music, speech, or any other sound. Recall that sound waves, such as the human voice or music, are analog. To store such sounds, a computer converts the sounds from a continuous analog signal into a digital format. Most output devices require that the computer convert the digital format back into analog signals.

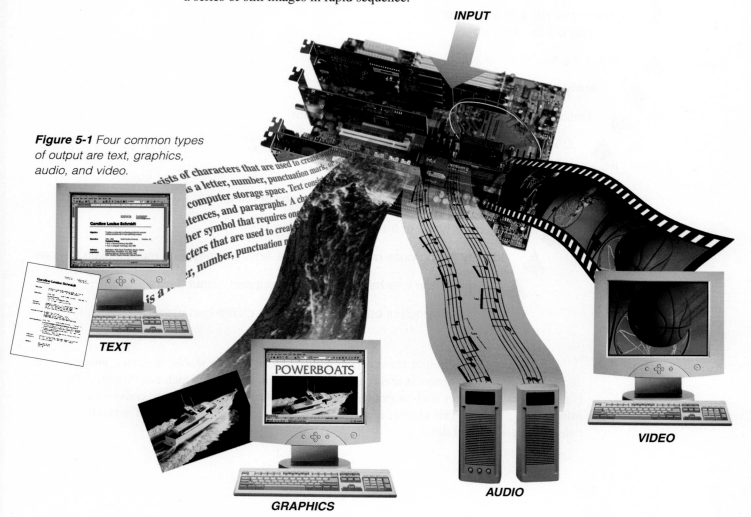

Figure 5-1 *Four common types of output are text, graphics, audio, and video.*

INPUT

TEXT

GRAPHICS

AUDIO

VIDEO

- **Video** consists of images that are played back at speeds that provide the appearance of full motion. Video often is captured with a video input device such as a video camera or VCR. Most video signals are analog; however, some video devices record the video images digitally.

A video capture card converts an analog video signal into a digital signal that a computer can understand. The digital signal then is stored on the computer's hard disk. Some output devices accept the digital signal, while others require that the computer convert the digital signals back into analog signals.

Figure 5-2 *A color monitor displays text, graphics, and video information in color.*

WHAT ARE OUTPUT DEVICES?

An **output device** is any computer component capable of conveying information to a user. Commonly used output devices include display devices, printers, speakers, headsets, data projectors, facsimile machines, and multifunction devices. Each of these output devices is discussed in the following pages.

DISPLAY DEVICES

A **display device** is an output device that visually conveys text, graphics, and video information. Information shown on a display device often is called **soft copy**, because the information exists electronically and is displayed for a temporary period of time.

Display devices include CRT monitors, flat-panel displays, and high-definition televisions.

CRT Monitors

A **CRT monitor**, or **monitor**, is a display device that consists of a screen housed in a plastic or metal case. A **color monitor** displays text, graphics, and video information in color (Figure 5-2). Color monitors are used widely with all types of computers because most of today's software is designed to display information in color.

Monitors that display only one color are considered monochrome. A **monochrome monitor** displays text, graphics, and video information in one color (usually white, amber, or green) on a black background.

Because monochrome monitors are less expensive than color monitors, some organizations use them for applications that do not require color or detailed graphics, such as order entry.

To enhance the quality of their graphics display, some monochrome monitors use **gray scaling**, which involves using many shades of gray from white to black to form the images.

Like a television set, the core of a CRT monitor is a large glass tube called a **cathode ray tube (CRT)** (Figure 5-3). The **screen**, which is the front of the tube, is coated with

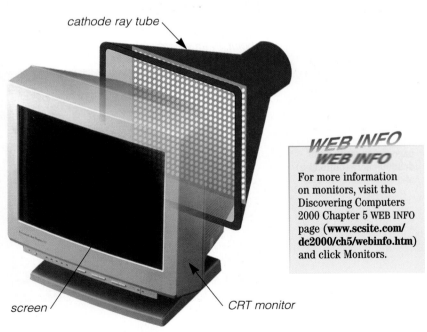

Figure 5-3 *The core of most desktop monitors is a cathode ray tube.*

WEB INFO

For more information on monitors, visit the Discovering Computers 2000 Chapter 5 WEB INFO page (**www.scsite.com/ dc2000/ch5/webinfo.htm**) and click Monitors.

tiny dots of phosphor material that glow when electrically charged. Inside the CRT, an electron beam moves back and forth across the back of the screen, causing the dots to glow, which produces an image on the screen.

Each dot, called a **pixel** (short for *pic*ture *el*ement), is a single point in an electronic image (Figure 5-4). Monitors consist of hundreds, thousands, or millions of pixels arranged in rows and columns that can be used to create images. The pixels are so close together that they appear connected.

CRT monitors are used with a variety of computers. The CRT monitors used with desktop computers are available in a number of sizes, with the more common being 15, 17, 19, and 21 inches. The size of a monitor is measured diagonally, from corner to corner.

Most monitors are referred to by their **viewable size**, which is the diagonal measurement of the cathode ray tube inside the

monitor and is larger than the actual viewing area provided by the monitor. A monitor listed as a 17-inch monitor, for example, may have a viewable size of only 15.7 inches. Manufacturers are required to list a monitor's viewable size in any advertisement.

Determining what size monitor to use depends on your intended use. A large monitor allows you to view more information on the screen at once, but usually is more expensive. If you work on the Web or use multiple applications at one time, however, you may want to invest in at least a 17-inch monitor. If you use your computer for intense graphing applications such as desktop publishing and engineering, you may want an even larger monitor.

Flat-Panel Displays

A **flat-panel display** is a lightweight, thin screen that consumes less power than a CRT monitor. Two common types of flat-panel displays are LCD and gas plasma.

LCD DISPLAYS LCD displays commonly are used in laptop computers, handheld computers, digital watches, and calculators because they are thinner and more lightweight than CRT monitors (Figure 5-5). While most LCD displays are color, some handheld computers use monochrome LCD displays to save battery power (Figure 5-6).

Figure 5-4 *A pixel is a single dot of color, or point, in an electronic image.*

WEB INFO

For more information on LCD displays, visit the Discovering Computers 2000 Chapter 5 WEB INFO page (www.scsite.com/dc2000/ch5/webinfo.htm) and click LCD Displays.

Figure 5-5 *Most laptop computers use an LCD display because it is lightweight and thin.*

Unlike a CRT monitor, an **LCD display** does not use a cathode ray tube (CRT) to create images on the screen; it instead uses a liquid crystal display (LCD). A **liquid crystal display (LCD)** has special molecules (called liquid crystals) deposited between two sheets of material. When an electric current passes through them, the molecules twist, causing some light waves to be blocked and allowing others to pass through, which then creates the desired images on the screen.

Like CRT monitors, the LCD displays used with laptop computers are available in a variety of sizes, with the more common being 12.1, 13.3, and 14.1 inches. LCD displays produce color using either passive matrix or active matrix technology. An **active-matrix display** uses a separate transistor for each color pixel and thus can display high-quality color that is viewable from all angles. Active-matrix displays sometimes are called **TFT displays**, named after the thin-film transistor (TFT) technology they use. Because they use many transistors, active-matrix displays require a lot of power.

A **passive-matrix display** uses fewer transistors and requires less power, but its color display often is not as bright as an active-matrix display. Images on a passive-matrix display can be viewed best when you work directly in front of the display. Passive-matrix displays are less expensive than active-matrix displays.

While LCD displays are used most often with laptops, stand-alone LCD monitors also can be used with desktop computers (Figure 5-7). (The term monitor typically is used for desktop display devices, while the term display is used for display devices on portable computers.) LCD monitors require less power and take up less desk space than traditional CRT monitors, making them ideal for users with space limitations. Some LCD monitors even can be mounted on the wall for increased space savings. Stand-alone LCD monitors, however, are more expensive than CRT monitors.

mounted on wall

on a desktop

Figure 5-7 *Desktop applications that have space and weight limitations sometimes use an LCD monitor.*

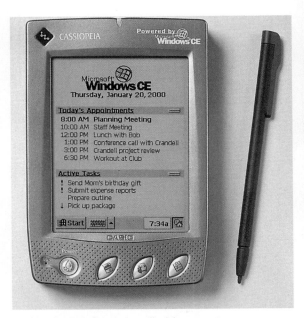

Figure 5-6 *Some handheld computers use monochrome displays to save battery power.*

GAS PLASMA MONITORS For even larger displays, some large business or power users prefer gas plasma monitors, which can measure more than 42 inches and hang directly on a wall (Figure 5-8). **Gas plasma monitors** use gas plasma technology, which substitutes a layer of gas for the liquid crystal material in an LCD monitor. When voltage is applied, the gas glows and produces the pixels that form an image. Gas plasma monitors offer larger screen sizes and higher display quality than LCD monitors but are much more expensive.

Monitor Quality

The quality of a monitor's display depends largely on its resolution, dot pitch, and refresh rate. The **resolution**, or sharpness and clarity, of a monitor is related directly to the number of pixels it can display. Resolution is expressed as two separate numbers: the number of columns of pixels and the number of rows of pixels a monitor can display.

Figure 5-8 *Large gas plasma displays can measure more than 42 inches and hang directly on a wall.*

A screen with a 640 x 480 (pronounced 640 by 480) resolution, for example, can display 640 columns and 480 rows of pixels (or a total of 307,200 pixels). Most modern monitors can display 800 x 600 and 1024 x 768 pixels; some high-end monitors can display 1280 x 1024, 1600 x 1200, or even 1800 x 1440 pixels.

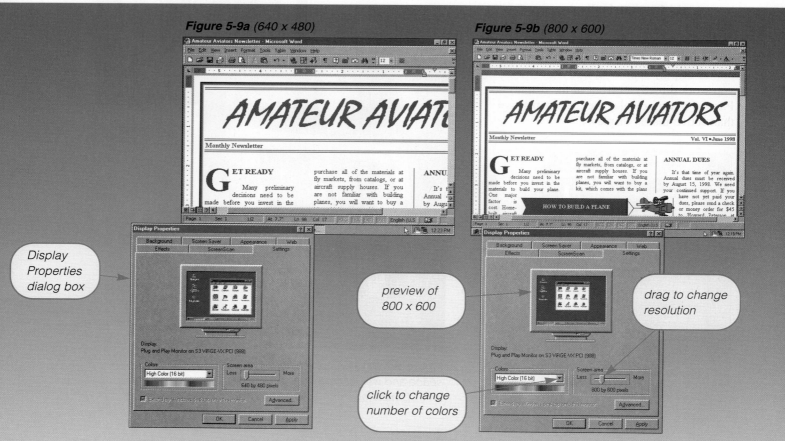

Figure 5-9 *The higher a screen's resolution, the smaller the images display on the screen. As the resolution increases from 640 x 480 (a) to 800 x 600 (b) to 1024 x 768 (c), the image on the screen becomes increasingly smaller.*

A monitor with a higher resolution displays a greater number of pixels, which provides a smoother image. A higher resolution, however, also causes images to display smaller on the screen. For this reason, you would not use a high resolution on a small monitor, such as a 14-inch monitor, because the small characters would be difficult to read. In Windows, you can change the resolution and other monitor characteristics using the Display Properties dialog box (Figure 5-9).

The ideal monitor resolution to use is a matter of preference. A higher resolution is desirable for graphics applications; a lower resolution usually is satisfactory for applications such as word processing.

Another factor that determines monitor quality is **dot pitch**, which is a measure of image clarity. The dot pitch is the vertical distance between each pixel on a monitor. The smaller the distance between the pixels,

Figure 5-10 *In this figure, the letter b on the right is easier to read because it has a smaller dot pitch.*

the sharper the displayed image. For example, as shown in Figure 5-10, text created with a smaller dot pitch is easier to read. To minimize eye fatigue, you should use a monitor with a dot pitch of .28 millimeters or smaller.

Recall that images are drawn on the screen as an electron beam moves back and forth across the back of the screen and causes pixels on the screen to glow. These pixels, however, glow for only a fraction of a second before beginning to fade. The monitor thus must redraw the picture many times per second so the image does not fade.

The speed that the monitor redraws images on the screen is called the **refresh rate**. Ideally, a monitor's refresh rate should be fast enough to maintain a constant, flicker-free image. A slower refresh rate causes the image to fade and then flicker as it is redrawn, which can cause headaches for users. Refresh rate is measured according to **hertz**, which is the number of times per second the screen is redrawn. Although most people can tolerate a refresh rate of 60 hertz, a high-quality monitor will provide a refresh rate of at least 75 hertz.

Some older monitors refresh images using a technique called interlacing. With **interlacing**, the electron beam draws only half the horizontal lines with each pass (for example, all odd-numbered lines on one pass and all even-numbered lines on the next pass). Because it happens so quickly, your brain perceives the two images as a single image. Interlacing originally was developed for monitors with slow refresh rates. Most of today's monitors are *noninterlaced*, and they provide a much better, flicker-free image than interlaced monitors.

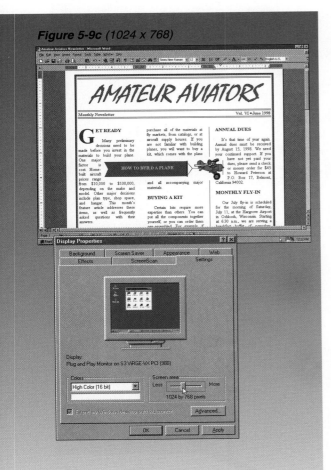

Figure 5-9c (1024 x 768)

Video Cards

To display color, a color monitor works in combination with a video card, which is included with today's personal computers. A **video card**, also called a **graphics card** or **video adapter**, converts digital output into an analog video signal that is sent through a cable to the monitor (Figure 5-11). The monitor separates the video signal into red, green, and blue signals. Electron guns then fire the three color signals to the front of the monitor. These three dots – one red, one green, and one blue – are combined to make up each single pixel.

The number of colors that a video card can display is determined by the number of bits it uses to store information about each pixel. For example, an 8-bit video card (also called 8-bit color) uses 8 bits to store information about each pixel and thus can display 256 different colors (computed as 2^8 or $2 \times 2 \times 2 \times 2 \times 2 \times 2 \times 2 \times 2$); a 24-bit video card uses 24 bits to store information about each pixel and can display 16.7 million colors (Figure 5-12). In Windows, you can change the number of displayed colors in the Display Properties dialog box (see Figure 5-9 on page 5.6).

Figure 5-11

HOW VIDEO TRAVELS FROM THE CPU TO YOUR MONITOR

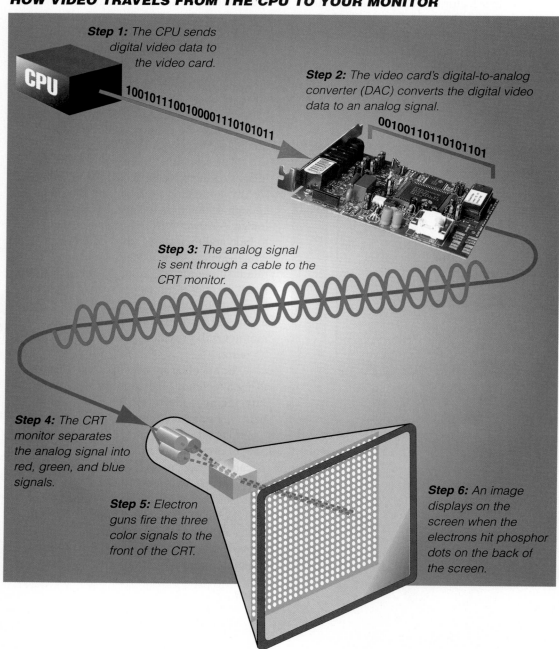

Step 1: The CPU sends digital video data to the video card.

CPU

100101110010000111010101011

Step 2: The video card's digital-to-analog converter (DAC) converts the digital video data to an analog signal.

0010011011010101101

Step 3: The analog signal is sent through a cable to the CRT monitor.

Step 4: The CRT monitor separates the analog signal into red, green, and blue signals.

Step 5: Electron guns fire the three color signals to the front of the CRT.

Step 6: An image displays on the screen when the electrons hit phosphor dots on the back of the screen.

Over the years, several video standards have been developed to define the resolution, number of colors, and other properties for various types of monitors. Today, just about every monitor supports the **super video graphics array (SVGA)** standard, which also supports resolutions and colors in the VGA standard. The table in Figure 5-13 outlines the suggested resolution and number of displayed colors in the MDA, VGA, XGA, and SVGA standards.

For a monitor to display images using the resolution and number of colors defined by a video standard, the monitor must support the video standard and the video card must be capable of communicating appropriate signals to the monitor. That is, the video card and the monitor must support the video standard to generate the desired resolution and number of colors.

Most video cards are equipped with memory, which is used to store information about each pixel. While some use dynamic RAM (DRAM), higher-quality video cards use **video RAM** or **VRAM** (pronounced *VEE*-ram) to improve the quality of graphics. As with other types of memory, VRAM is measured in megabytes.

VIDEO CARD DISPLAY DESIGNATIONS

Sample Display				
Number of Bits of Storage	4 bit	8 bit	16 bit (high color)	24 bit (true color)
Number of Possible Colors	16 (2^4)	256 (2^8)	65,536 (2^{16})	16.7 million (2^{24})

Figure 5-12 *The number of colors that can be displayed on a monitor is determined by the numbers of bits it uses to store information about each pixel. The greater the number of bits, the more colors. Most monitors today use at least 8-bit color.*

VIDEO STANDARDS

Standard	Suggested Resolution	Possible Simultaneous Colors
Monochrome Display Adapter (MDA)	720 x 350	1
Video Graphics Array (VGA)	640 x 480	16
	320 x 200	256
Extended Graphics Array (XGA)	1024 x 768	256
	640 x 480	65,536
Super Video Graphics Array (SVGA)	800 x 600	16 million
	1024 x 768	16 million
	1280 x 1024	16 million
	1600 x 1200	16 million

Figure 5-13 *The various video standards.*

Your video card must have enough memory to generate the resolution and number of colors you want to display. The table in Figure 5-14 outlines the amount of VRAM suggested for various screen resolutions and color displays. For example, if you wanted an 800 x 600 resolution with 16-bit color (65,536 colors), then your video card should have at least 1 MB of VRAM.

Monitor Ergonomics

Recall that the goal of ergonomics is to incorporate comfort, efficiency, and safety into the design of items in the workplace. Many monitors have features that help address ergonomic issues, such as the controls that allow you to adjust the brightness, contrast, positioning, height, and width of images. These controls usually are positioned on the front of the monitor for easy access. Newer monitors have digital controls that allow you to fine-tune the display in small increments (Figure 5-15).

Another advantage of digital controls is you quickly can return to the default settings. Many monitors have a tilt-and-swivel base, so you can adjust the angle of the screen to minimize neck strain and reduce glare from overhead lighting.

Because they use electricity, monitors produce a small amount of **electromagnetic radiation (EMR)**, which is a magnetic field that travels at the speed of light. Although no solid evidence exists to prove that EMR poses a health risk, an established set of standards, known as MPR II, define acceptable levels of EMR for a monitor. All high-quality monitors should comply with MPR II standards. To protect yourself even further, you should sit at arm's length from the monitor because electromagnetic radiation only travels a short distance. Also, electromagnetic radiation is greatest on the sides and back of the monitor.

VRAM REQUIREMENTS

Number of Colors	640 x 480	800 x 600	1024 x 768	1280 x 1024	1600 x 1200
16 (4 bit)	256 KB	256 KB	512 KB	1 MB	1 MB
256 (8 bit)	512 KB	512 KB	1 MB	2 MB	2 MB
65,536 (16 bit)	1 MB	1 MB	2 MB	4 MB	4 MB
16.7 million (24 bit)	1 MB	2 MB	4 MB	4 MB	6 MB

Figure 5-14 *The amount of video RAM required for various screen resolutions.*

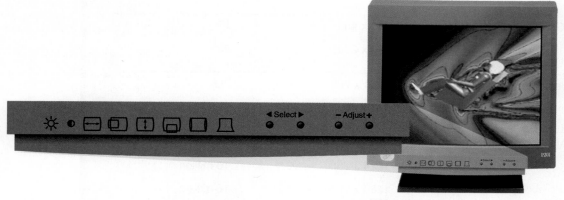

Figure 5-15 *Digital controls on many monitors allow a user to fine-tune the display in small increments.*

To help reduce the amount of electricity used by monitors and other computer components, the U.S. Department of Energy (DOE) and the U.S. Environmental Protection Agency (EPA) developed the **ENERGY STAR program**. This program encourages manufacturers to create energy-efficient devices that require little power when they are not in use. Monitors and devices that meet ENERGY STAR guidelines display an ENERGY STAR® label (Figure 5-16).

EPA POLLUTION PREVENTER

Figure 5-16 *Products with an ENERGY STAR® label are energy efficient as defined by the Environmental Protection Agency (EPA).*

High-Definition Television

High-definition television (HDTV) is a type of television set that works with digital broadcasting signals and supports a wider screen and higher resolution display than a standard television set. When you use a standard television set as a monitor for your computer, the output must be converted to an analog signal that can be displayed by the television set.

With HDTV, the broadcast signals are digitized when they are sent. Digital television signals provide two major advantages over analog signals. First, digital signals produce a higher-quality picture. Second, many programs can be broadcast on a single digital channel, whereas only one program can be broadcast on an analog channel. Because HDTV is capable of receiving text, graphics, audio, and video, you can use HDTV as a monitor while browsing the Internet. When the cost of HDTV becomes more reasonable, home users will begin to use it as their computer's display device.

PRINTERS

A **printer** is an output device that produces text and graphics on a physical medium such as paper or transparency film. Printed information is called **hard copy** because the information exists physically and is a more permanent form of output than that presented on a display device (soft copy).

Hard copy, also called a **printout**, can be printed in portrait or landscape orientation. A page with **portrait orientation** is taller than it is wide, with information printed across the shorter width of the paper; a page with **landscape orientation** is wider than it is tall, with information printed across the widest part of the paper (Figure 5-17). Letters, reports, and books typically are printed in portrait orientation; spreadsheets, slide shows, and graphics often are printed in landscape orientation.

WEB INFO
WEB INFO

For more information on HDTV, visit the Discovering Computers 2000 Chapter 5 WEB INFO page (www.scsite.com/dc2000/ch5/webinfo.htm) and click High-Definition Television.

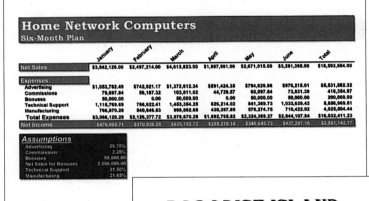

landscape orientation

portrait orientation

Figure 5-17 *Portrait orientation is taller than it is wide; landscape orientation is wider than it is tall.*

PRINTING REQUIREMENTS QUESTION SHEET

1. How fast must my printer print?

2. Do I need a color printer?

3. What is the cost per page for printing?

4. Do I need multiple copies?

5. Do I need to print graphics?

6. Do I need to print photographic-quality images?

7. What types of paper does the printer use?

8. What sizes of paper does the printer accept?

9. How much paper can the printer tray hold?

10. Will the printer work with my computer and software?

11. How much do supplies such as ink and paper cost?

12. Can the printer print on envelopes and transparencies?

13. What is my budget?

14. What will I be printing?

15. How much do I print now, and what will I be printing in a year or two?

Figure 5-18 *Questions to ask when purchasing a printer.*

Printing requirements vary greatly among users (Figure 5-18). Home computer users might print only a hundred pages or fewer a week. Small business computer users might print several hundred pages a day. Users of mainframe computers, such as large utility companies that send printed statements to hundreds of thousands of customers each month, require printers that are capable of printing thousands of pages per hour. These different needs have resulted in the development of printers with varying speeds, capabilities, and printing methods.

Generally, printers can be grouped into two categories: impact and nonimpact. Printers in each of these categories are discussed in the following sections.

Impact Printers

An **impact printer** forms characters and graphics on a piece of paper by striking a mechanism against an ink ribbon that physically contacts the paper. Because of the striking activity, impact printers generally are noisy.

Many impact printers do not provide letter quality print. **Letter quality (LQ)** output is a quality of print acceptable for business letters. Many impact printers produce **near letter quality (NLQ)** print, which is slightly less clear than letter quality. NLQ impact printers are used for jobs that require only near letter quality, such as printing mailing labels, envelopes, or invoices.

Impact printers also are ideal for printing multipart forms because they easily can print through many layers of paper. Finally, impact printers are used in many factories and at retail counters because they can withstand dusty environments, vibrations, and extreme temperatures.

Two commonly used types of impact printers are dot-matrix printers and line printers. Each of these printers is discussed in the following sections.

DOT-MATRIX PRINTERS A **dot-matrix printer** is an impact printer that produces printed images when tiny wire pins on a print head mechanism strike an inked ribbon (Figure 5-19). When the ribbon presses against the paper, it creates dots that form characters and graphics.

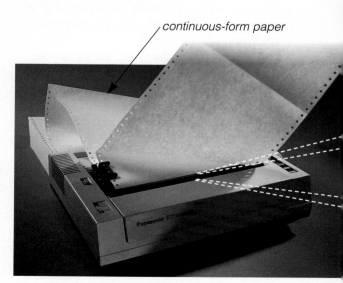

continuous-form paper

Figure 5-19 *A dot-matrix printer produces printed images when tiny pins strike an inked ribbon.*

Most dot-matrix printers use **continuous-form paper**, in which each sheet of paper is connected together. The pages generally have holes punched along two opposite sides so the paper can be fed through the printer. Perforations along the inside of the punched holes and at each fold allow the sheets to be separated into standard-sized sheets of paper, such as 8½ x 11 inches. One advantage of continuous-form paper is that it does not have to be changed very often because thousands of pages are connected together. Many dot-matrix printers also can be adjusted to print pages in either portrait or landscape orientation.

The print head mechanism on a dot-matrix printer can contain nine to twenty-four pins, depending on the manufacturer and the printer model. A higher number of pins means more dots are printed, which results in higher print quality.

The speed of a dot-matrix printer is measured by the number of **characters per second (cps)** it can print. The speed of dot-matrix printers ranges from 50 to 700 characters per second (cps), depending on the desired print quality.

LINE PRINTERS A **line printer** is a high-speed impact printer that prints an entire line at a time (Figure 5-20). The speed of a line printer is measured by the number of lines per minute (lpm) it can print. Capable of printing up to 3,000 lines per minute (lpm), these printers often are used with mainframes, minicomputers, or with a network in applications such as manufacturing, distribution, or shipping. Line printers typically use 11 x 17-inch

continuous-form paper, such as the greenbar paper used to print reports from mainframe computers.

Two popular types of line printers used for high-volume output are band and shuttle-matrix. A **band printer** prints fully-formed characters when hammers strike a horizontal, rotating band that contains shapes of numbers, letters of the alphabet, and other characters. A **shuttle-matrix printer** works more like a dot-matrix printer; the difference is the shuttle-matrix printer moves a series of print hammers back and forth horizontally at incredibly high speeds. Unlike a band printer, a shuttle-matrix printer can print characters in various fonts and font sizes.

Figure 5-20 *A line printer is a high-speed printer often connected to a mainframe, minicomputer, or network.*

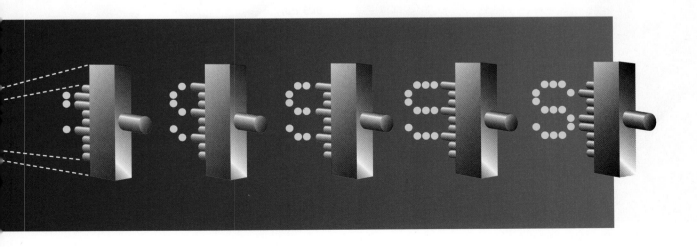

Nonimpact Printers

A **nonimpact printer** forms characters and graphics on a piece of paper without actually striking the paper. Some spray ink, while others use heat and pressure to create images. Because these printers do not strike the paper, they are much quieter than the previously discussed impact printers.

Three commonly used types of nonimpact printers are ink-jet printers, laser printers, and thermal printers. Each of these printers is discussed in the following sections.

INK-JET PRINTERS

An **ink-jet printer** is a type of nonimpact printer that forms characters and graphics by spraying tiny drops of liquid ink onto a piece of paper. Ink-jet printers usually use individual sheets of paper stored in a removable or stationary tray. These printers can produce letter-quality text and graphics in both black-and-white and color on various materials such as envelopes, labels, transparencies, or paper. Some ink-jet printers can print photo-quality images on any type of paper, while other ink-jet printers require a heavier weight premium paper for better-looking color documents. Many ink-jet printers are sold with software for creating greeting cards, banners, business cards, letterheads, and transparencies (Figure 5-21).

Because of their reasonable cost and letter-quality print, ink-jet printers have become the most popular type of color printer for use in the home. You can purchase an ink-jet printer of reasonable quality for a few hundred dollars.

One factor that determines the quality of an ink-jet printer is its resolution, or sharpness and clarity. Printer resolution is measured by the number of **dots per inch (dpi)** a printer can output. As shown in Figure 5-22, the higher the dpi, the better the print quality. With an ink-jet printer, a dot is a drop of ink. A higher dpi means the drops of ink are smaller, which provides a higher quality image. Most ink-jet printers have a dpi that ranges from 300 to 1,440 dpi. Typically, printers with a higher dpi are more expensive.

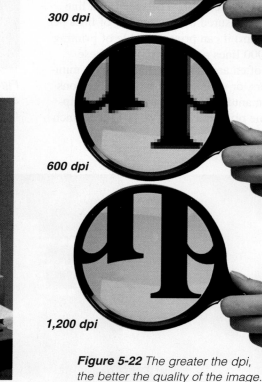

300 dpi

600 dpi

1,200 dpi

Figure 5-22 *The greater the dpi, the better the quality of the image.*

Figure 5-21 *Ink-jet printers are the most popular type of color printer for use in the home.*

The speed of an ink-jet printer is measured by the number of **pages per minute (ppm)** it can print. Most ink-jet printers print from one to eight pages per minute (ppm). Graphics and colors print at the slower rate.

The print head mechanism of an ink-jet printer contains ink-filled print cartridges, each with fifty to several hundred small ink holes, or nozzles. The steps in Figure 5-23 illustrate how a drop of ink appears on a page. Each nozzle in the print cartridge is similar to an individual pin on a dot-matrix printer. Just as any combination of dot-matrix pins can be activated, ink can be propelled by heat or pressure through any combination of the nozzles to form a character or image on the paper.

When the print cartridge runs out of ink, you simply replace the cartridge. Most ink-jet printers have at least two print cartridges: one containing black ink and the other(s) containing colors.

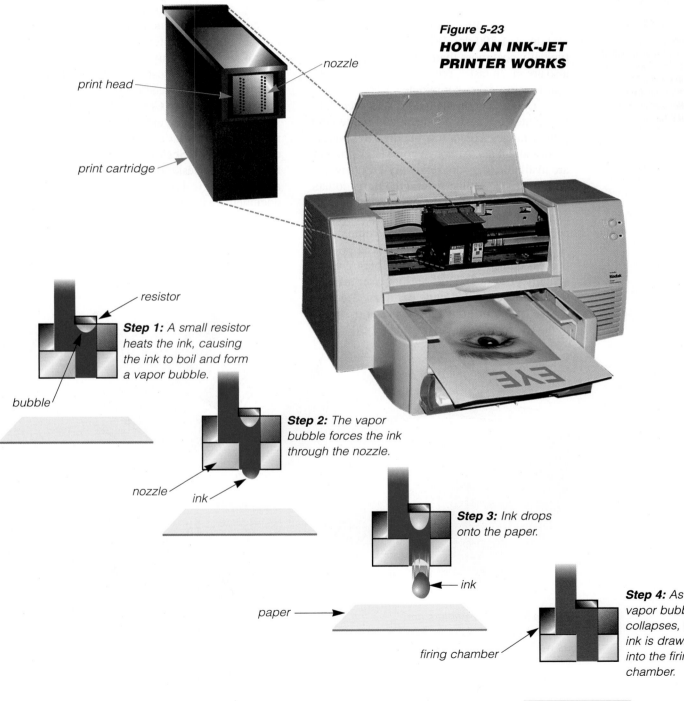

Figure 5-23
HOW AN INK-JET PRINTER WORKS

print head

nozzle

print cartridge

resistor

Step 1: A small resistor heats the ink, causing the ink to boil and form a vapor bubble.

bubble

Step 2: The vapor bubble forces the ink through the nozzle.

nozzle   ink

Step 3: Ink drops onto the paper.

ink

paper

firing chamber

Step 4: As the vapor bubble collapses, fresh ink is drawn into the firing chamber.

ink dot

LASER PRINTERS A **laser printer** is a high-speed, high-quality nonimpact printer (Figure 5-24). Laser printers for personal computers usually use individual sheets of paper stored in a removable tray that slides into the printer case. Some laser printers have trays that can accommodate different sizes of paper, while others require separate trays for letter- and legal-sized paper. Most laser printers have a manual feed slot where you can insert individual sheets and envelopes. You also can print transparencies on a laser printer.

Laser printers can print text and graphics in very high quality resolutions, ranging from 300 dpi to 1,200 dpi. While laser printers typically cost more than ink-jet printers, they also are much faster, printing text at speeds of four to thirty pages per minute.

Depending on the quality and speed of the printer, the cost of a black-and-white laser printer ranges from a few hundred to several thousand dollars. Although color laser printers are available, they are relatively expensive, with prices exceeding several thousand dollars. The higher the resolution and speed, the more expensive the printer. High-end fast laser printers are used with mainframe computers.

When printing a document, laser printers process and store the entire page before they actually print it. For this reason, laser printers sometimes are called **page printers**. Storing a page before printing requires laser printers to have a certain amount of memory.

WEB INFO
WEB INFO

For more information on laser printers, visit the Discovering Computers 2000 Chapter 5 WEB INFO page (**www.scsite.com/ dc2000/ch5/webinfo.htm**) and click Laser Printers.

Depending on the amount of graphics you intend to print, a laser printer can have up to 200 MB of memory. To print a full-page 600-dpi picture, for instance, you might need 8 MB of memory on the printer. If your printer does not have enough memory to print the picture, it either will print as much of the picture as its memory will allow or it will display an error message and not print any of the picture.

Laser printers use software that enables them to interpret a **page description language** (**PDL**). A PDL tells the printer how to layout the contents of a printed page. When you purchase a laser printer, it comes with at least one of two common page description languages: PCL or PostScript. Developed by Hewlett-Packard, a leading printer manufacturer, **PCL (Printer Control Language)** is a standard printer language designed to support the fonts and layout used in standard office documents. **PostScript** commonly is used in fields such as desktop publishing and graphic art because it is designed for complex documents with intense graphics and colors.

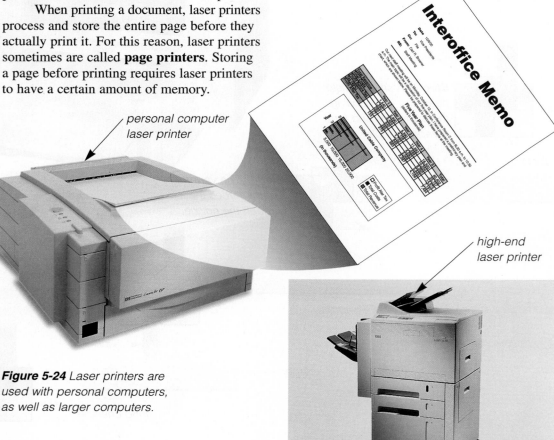

personal computer laser printer

high-end laser printer

Figure 5-24 *Laser printers are used with personal computers, as well as larger computers.*

Operating in a manner similar to a copy machine, a laser printer creates images using a laser beam and powdered ink, called **toner**, which is packaged in a cartridge. The laser beam produces an image on a special drum inside the printer. The light of the laser alters the electrical charge on the drum wherever it hits. When this occurs, the toner sticks to the drum and then is transferred to the paper through a combination of pressure and heat (Figure 5-25). When the toner runs out, you can replace the toner cartridge (Figure 5-26).

THERMAL PRINTERS A **thermal printer** generates images by pushing electrically heated pins against heat-sensitive paper. Standard thermal printers are inexpensive, but the print quality is low and the images tend to fade over time. Thermal printers are, however, ideal for use in small devices such as adding machines.

Figure 5-25
HOW A LASER PRINTER WORKS

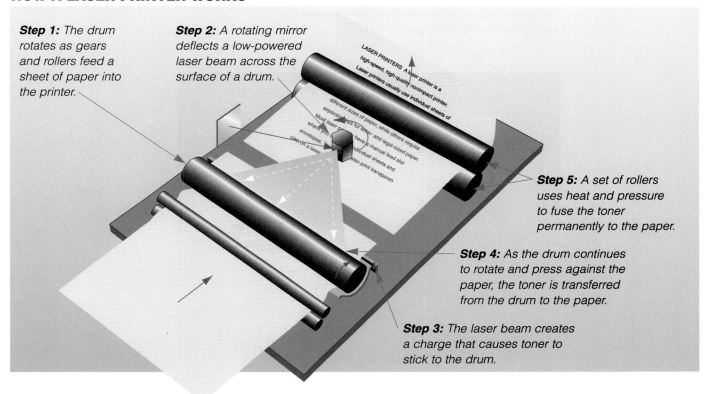

Step 1: *The drum rotates as gears and rollers feed a sheet of paper into the printer.*

Step 2: *A rotating mirror deflects a low-powered laser beam across the surface of a drum.*

Step 5: *A set of rollers uses heat and pressure to fuse the toner permanently to the paper.*

Step 4: *As the drum continues to rotate and press against the paper, the toner is transferred from the drum to the paper.*

Step 3: *The laser beam creates a charge that causes toner to stick to the drum.*

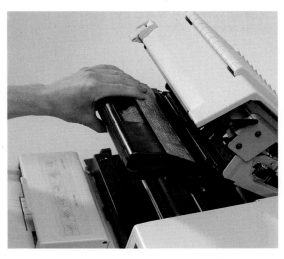

Figure 5-26 *Replacing the toner cartridge in a laser printer.*

Two special types of thermal printers have a much higher print quality. A **thermal wax-transfer printer**, also called a **thermal transfer printer**, generates rich, nonsmearing images by using heat to melt colored wax onto heat-sensitive paper. Thermal wax-transfer printers are more expensive than ink-jet printers, but less expensive than many color laser printers. A **dye-sublimation printer**, also called a **thermal dye transfer printer**, uses heat to transfer colored dye to specially coated paper. While among the more expensive types of printers, dye-sublimation printers can create images that are of photo-graphic quality. Some manufacturers offer a printer for a few thousand dollars that have both capabilities, that is, thermal wax-transfer and dye sublimation (Figure 5-27).

Portable Printers

A **portable printer** is a small, lightweight printer that allows a mobile user to print from a laptop or handheld computer while traveling (Figure 5-28). Barely wider than the paper on which they print, portable printers easily can fit in a briefcase alongside a laptop computer.

Some portable printers use ink-jet tech-nology, while others are thermal or thermal wax-transfer. Portable ink-jet printers provide better output quality than portable thermal printers, but usually are larger. Many of these printers connect to a parallel port; others have a built-in infrared port through which they communicate with the computer.

WEB INFO
WEB INFO

For more information on portable printers, visit the Discovering Computers 2000 Chapter 5 WEB INFO page (**www.scsite.com/dc2000/ch5/webinfo.htm**) and click Portable Printers.

Figure 5-27 *The printer shown in this figure by Fargo Electronics uses both thermal wax-transfer and dye-sublimation technology.*

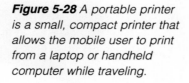

Figure 5-28 *A portable printer is a small, compact printer that allows the mobile user to print from a laptop or handheld computer while traveling.*

Plotters and Large-Format Printers

Plotters and large-format printers are sophisticated printers used to produce high-quality drawings such as blueprints, maps, circuit diagrams, and signs (Figure 5-29). Because blueprints, maps, and other such drawings can be quite large, these printers typically can handle paper with widths up to 60 inches. Some plotters and large-format printers use individual sheets of paper, while others take large rolls. These printers are used in specialized fields such as engineering, drafting, and graphic art and usually are very costly.

Two basic types of plotters are pen plotters and electrostatic plotters. A **pen plotter** uses one or more colored pens, light beams, or a scribing device to draw on paper or transparencies. Pen plotters differ from other printers in that they produce continuous lines, whereas most printers generate lines by printing a closely spaced series of dots.

An **electrostatic plotter** uses a row of charged wires (called styli) to draw an electrostatic pattern on specially coated paper and then fuses toner to the pattern. The printed image is composed of a series of very small dots, which provide high-quality output.

Operating like an ink-jet printer, but on a much larger scale, a **large-format printer** creates photo-realistic quality color prints. Used by graphic artists, these high performance printers are used for signs, posters, and other displays.

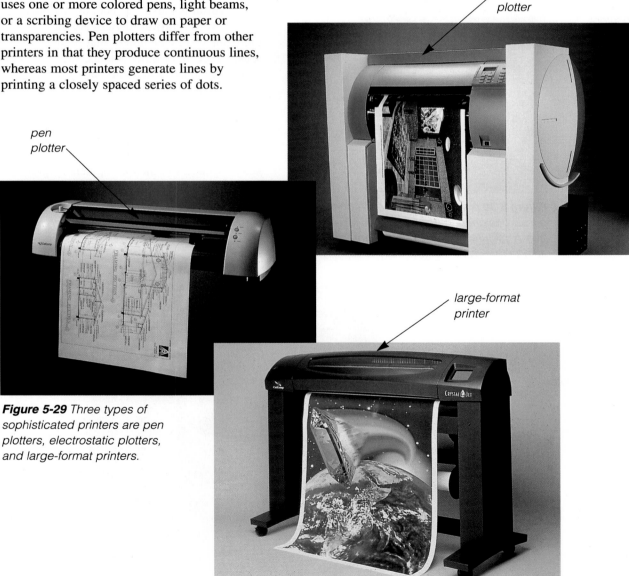

pen plotter

electrostatic plotter

large-format printer

Figure 5-29 *Three types of sophisticated printers are pen plotters, electrostatic plotters, and large-format printers.*

snapshot printer

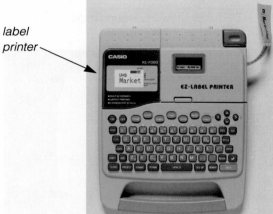

label printer

Figure 5-30 *A snapshot printer is a color printer designed to produce photo lab quality pictures. A label printer prints on an adhesive-type material used to identify a variety of items.*

Special-Purpose Printers

In addition to the printers just discussed, other printers have been developed for special purposes (Figure 5-30). A **snapshot printer** is a color printer designed to produce photo lab quality pictures from any image that has been scanned or taken with a digital camera. A **label printer** is a small printer that prints on an adhesive-type material that can be placed on a variety of items such as envelopes, disks, audiocassettes, photographs, and toys. Many label printers are used to print bar codes.

AUDIO OUTPUT

Audio is music, speech, or any other sound. **Audio output devices** are the components of a computer that produce music, speech, or other sounds, such as beeps. Two commonly used audio output devices are speakers and headsets.

Most personal computers have a small internal speaker that usually outputs only low-quality sound. For this reason, many personal computer users add higher-quality stereo speakers to their computers (Figure 5-31) or purchase PCs with larger speakers built into the sides of the monitor (see Figure 5-2 on page 5.3).

woofer

speakers

Figure 5-31 *Many personal computer users add high-quality stereo speakers and a woofer to their computers.*

To boost the low bass sounds, you can add a woofer (also called a subwoofer). The stereo speakers and woofer are connected to ports on the sound card. Most speakers have tone and volume controls so you can adjust these settings.

When using speakers, anyone within listening distance can hear the output. If you are in a computer laboratory or some other crowded environment, speakers might not be practical; instead, you can plug a headset into a port on the sound card (Figure 5-32). With the **headset**, only you can hear the sound from the computer.

Figure 5-32 *In a crowded environment where speakers are not practical, you can use a headset for audio output.*

OTHER OUTPUT DEVICES

Although monitors, printers, and speakers are the more widely used output devices, many other output devices are available for particular uses and applications. These include data projectors, facsimiles, and multifunction devices. Each of these devices is discussed in the following sections.

Data Projectors

A **data projector** takes the image that displays on a computer screen and projects it onto a screen so that an audience of people can see the image clearly (Figure 5-33). Data projectors can be large devices attached to a ceiling or wall in an auditorium, or they can be small portable devices. Two types of smaller, lower-cost units are LCD projectors and DLP projectors.

An **LCD projector**, which uses liquid crystal display technology, attaches directly to a computer and uses its own light source to display the information shown on the computer screen. Because LCD projectors tend to produce lower-quality images, some users prefer to use a DLP projector for sharper, brighter images.

A **digital light processing (DLP) projector** uses tiny mirrors to reflect light, producing crisp, bright, colorful images that remain in focus and can be seen clearly even in a well-lit room.

Figure 5-33 *An LCD data projector.*

Facsimile (Fax) Machine

A **facsimile (fax) machine** is a device that transmits and receives documents over telephone lines. The documents can contain text, drawings, or photographs, or can be handwritten. When sent or received via a fax machine, these documents are known as faxes. A stand-alone fax machine scans the original document, converts the image into digitized data, and transmits the digitized image (Figure 5-34). A fax machine at the receiving end reads the incoming data, converts the digitized data into an image, and prints or stores a copy of the original image.

Fax capability also can be added to your computer using a fax modem. A **fax modem** is a communications device that allows you to send (and sometimes receive) electronic documents as faxes (Figure 5-35). A fax modem transmits computer-prepared documents, such as a word processing letter, or documents that have been digitized with a scanner or digital camera. A fax modem is like a regular modem except that it is designed to transmit documents to a fax machine or to another fax modem.

When a computer (instead of a fax machine) receives a fax, you can view the document on the screen or print it using special fax software. The quality of the viewed or printed fax is less than that of a word processing document because the fax actually is a large image. If you have optical character recognition (OCR) software, you also can edit the document.

A fax modem can be an external peripheral that plugs into a port on the back of the system unit or an internal card that is inserted into an expansion slot on the motherboard. In addition, most fax modems function as regular modems.

Figure 5-34 A stand-alone fax machine.

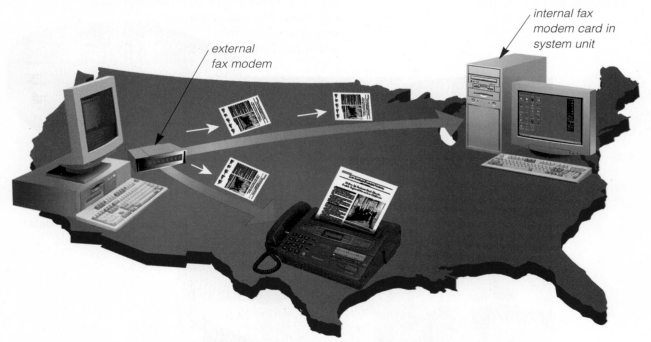

Figure 5-35 A fax modem allows you to send (and sometimes receive) electronic documents as faxes to a fax machine or another computer.

Multifunction Devices

A **multifunction device (MFD)** is a single piece of equipment that looks like a copy machine but provides the functionality of a printer, scanner, copy machine, and perhaps a fax machine (Figure 5-36). Sometimes called a multifunction peripheral, the features of multifunction devices vary widely. For example, some use color ink-jet printer technology, while others include a black-and-white laser printer.

Small offices and home offices use multifunction devices because they take up less space than having a separate printer, scanner, copy machine, and fax machine. Another advantage of an MFD is that it is significantly less expensive than if you purchased each device separately. The primary disadvantage of an MFD is that if the machine breaks down you lose all four functions. Given the advantages, however, increasingly more users are bringing multifunction devices into their offices and homes.

TERMINALS

A **terminal** is a device that performs both input and output because it consists of a monitor (output), a keyboard (input), and a video card. Terminals fall into three basic categories: dumb terminals, intelligent terminals, and special-purpose terminals.

A **dumb terminal** has no processing power, and thus, cannot function as an independent device (Figure 5-37). A dumb terminal is used to enter and transmit data to, or receive and display information from, a computer to which it is connected. Dumb terminals are connected to a **host computer** that performs the processing and then sends the output back to the dumb terminal. The host computer usually is a minicomputer, mainframe computer, or supercomputer.

In addition to a monitor and keyboard, an **intelligent terminal** also has memory and a processor that has the capability of performing some functions independent of the host computer. Intelligent terminals sometimes are called **programmable terminals** because they can be programmed by the software developer to perform basic tasks. In recent years, personal computers have replaced many intelligent terminals.

WEB INFO

For more information on MFDs, visit the Discovering Computers 2000 Chapter 5 WEB INFO page (**www.scsite.com/ dc2000/ch5/webinfo.htm**) and click Multifunction Devices.

Figure 5-36 *This OfficeJet by Hewlett-Packard is a color printer, scanner, and copy machine all in one device.*

Figure 5-37 *Dumb terminals have no processing power and usually are connected to larger computer systems.*

WEB INFO
WEB INFO

For more information
on POS terminals,
visit the Discovering
Computers 2000
Chapter 5 WEB INFO page
(www.scsite.com/dc2000/
ch5/webinfo.htm) and
click Point-of-Sale
Terminals.

WEB INFO
WEB INFO

For more information
on ATMs, visit the
Discovering Computers
2000 Chapter 5 WEB INFO
page (www.scsite.com/
dc2000/ch5/webinfo.htm)
and click Automatic
Teller Machines.

Other special-purpose terminals perform specific tasks and contain features uniquely designed for use in a particular industry (Figure 5-38). Two of these special-purpose terminals are point-of-sale terminals and automatic teller machines.

A **point-of-sale (POS) terminal** is used to record purchases at the point where the consumer purchases the product or service. The POS terminal used in a grocery store, for example, is a combination of an electronic cash register and bar code reader. When the bar code on the food product is scanned, the price of the item displays on the monitor, the name of the item and its price print on a receipt, and the item being sold is recorded so the inventory can be updated.

As indicated by this example, POS terminals serve as input to other computers to maintain sales records, update inventory, verify credit, and perform other activities associated with the sales transactions that are critical to running the business.

An **automatic teller machine (ATM)** is a self-service banking machine attached to a host computer through a telephone network. You insert a plastic bankcard with a magnetic strip into the ATM and enter your password, called a personal identification number (PIN), to access your bank account.

Some ATMs have touch screens, while others have special keyboards for input. Using an ATM, you can withdraw cash, deposit money, transfer funds, or inquire about an account balance.

OUTPUT DEVICES FOR PHYSICALLY CHALLENGED USERS

As discussed in Chapter 4, the growing presence of computers in everyone's lives has generated an awareness of the need to address computing requirements for those with physical limitations. For users with mobility, hearing, or vision disabilities, many different types of output devices are available. Hearing-impaired users, for example, can instruct programs to display words instead of sounds. With Windows, such users also can set options in the **Accessibility Properties dialog box** to instruct Windows to display visual signals in situations where normally it would make a sound (Figure 5-39).

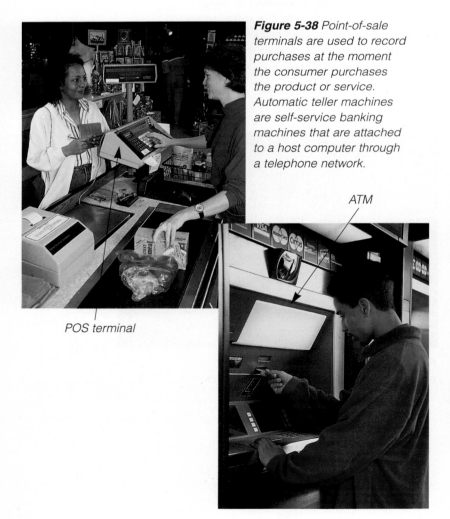

Figure 5-38 *Point-of-sale terminals are used to record purchases at the moment the consumer purchases the product or service. Automatic teller machines are self-service banking machines that are attached to a host computer through a telephone network.*

POS terminal

ATM

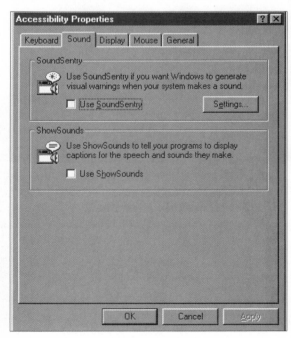

Figure 5-39 *Setting options in the Accessibility Properties dialog box makes Windows easier to use for physically challenged individuals.*

Figure 5-40 *A Braille printer.*

Visually impaired users can change Windows settings such as increasing the size or changing the color of the text to make the words easier to read. Instead of using a monitor, blind users can utilize speech output, where the computer *reads* the information that displays on the screen. Another alternative is a **Braille printer**, which outputs information in Braille onto paper (Figure 5-40).

PUTTING IT ALL TOGETHER

Many factors influence the type of output devices you should use: the type of output desired, the hardware and software in use, and the desired cost. Figure 5-41 outlines several suggested monitors, printers, and other output devices for various types of computer users.

SUGGESTED OUTPUT DEVICES BY USER

User	Monitor	Printer	Other
Home User	• 15- or 17-inch color CRT monitor	• Ink-jet color printer • Snapshot printer	• Speakers • Headset
SMALL BUSINESS USER	• 17- or 19-inch color CRT monitor • Monochrome or color LCD display for a handheld computer (PDA)	• Multifunction device; *or* • Ink-jet color printer; *or* • Laser printer, black and white • Label printer	• Fax machine • Speakers
MOBILE USER	• 14.1-inch color LCD display with a laptop computer • 17-inch color CRT monitor for a laptop docking station • Monochrome or color LCD display for a handheld computer (PDA)	• Portable printer • Ink-jet color printer; *or* • Laser printer, black and white, for in-office use	• Fax modem • Headset • LCD or DLP data projector
LARGE BUSINESS USER	• 17- or 19-inch color CRT monitor • 14.1-inch color LCD display for a laptop computer • Monochrome or color LCD display for a handheld computer (PDA)	• Laser printer, black and white • Line printer (for large reports from a mainframe) • Label printer	• Fax machine *or* fax modem • Speakers • LCD or DLP data projector • Dumb terminal
POWER USER	• 21-inch color monitor (for multimedia, desktop publishing, and engineering)	• Laser printer, black and white • Plotter • Snapshot printer • Dye-sublimation printer • Large format printer	• Fax machine *or* fax modem • Speakers • Headset

Figure 5-41 *This table recommends suggested output devices for various types of users.*

TECHNOLOGY TRAILBLAZERS

WILLIAM HEWLETT AND DAVID PACKARD

William Hewlett, David Packard

William Hewlett's children have formed a group called SPPW – the Society to Prove Papa Wrong. The group's objective is no small task. Hewlett's knowledge ranges from medicine, botany, and education to mountain climbing, fishing, and ranching. The subject that must be avoided most, however, is computer technology. Some sixty years ago William Hewlett, along with David Packard, co-founded Hewlett-Packard Company, the world's second largest manufacturer of computers and computer peripherals.

Hewlett and Packard met at Stanford University, where they both were students of Fred Terman, an inspirational teacher and author of a book on radio engineering, one of Packard's passions. Terman would become a mentor to both Hewlett and Packard. In the midst of the depression, Terman's electronics lab at Stanford was in the attic of a building badly in need of renovation. With no repair money, students scattered tar-paper-lined wooden baskets to catch water from a leaky roof. Yet, enthusiasm never waned; one winter, Hewlett stocked the baskets with goldfish to add a homey touch. Terman made up for a limited faculty by encouraging seminars in which students taught each other. To remedy Stanford's financial problems, Terman convinced the school to lease university lands to high-tech companies. He conducted tours of the labs and factories, pointing out that many were led by people with little conventional schooling. Just think, Terman mused, how successful someone with a formal engineering education

and a little business training could be. Terman's insights and advice colored decisions made by Hewlett and Packard and other entrepreneurs. Today, Terman often is called "The Intellectual Father of Silicon Valley," that region of California known for firms specializing in electronics and computer technology.

On a post-graduation camping trip in the Colorado mountains, Hewlett and Packard discovered similar attitudes and cemented a lasting friendship. Hewlett went on to MIT, while Packard accepted a job with General Electric. Eventually, both returned to Stanford to complete their graduate work. With Terman's encouragement, in 1938 they started their own electronics company, Hewlett-Packard Company, in Packard's garage. Terman checked on his ex-students' progress whenever he drove past. "If the car was in the driveway," he recalled, "business was good." The car often was in the driveway, for that first year started an astonishing run. "We made $1,536 in profits," Packard noted. "We would show a profit every year thereafter." To avoid competitors, the company created original products. "Never take a fortified position unless you have to," Hewlett said. "The world is a big place." Hewlett-Packard products were accepted enthusiastically by engineers and scientists. Sales representatives were hired, and World War II fired an explosion of government orders. From electronic components, the company expanded into medical equipment, chemical analysis, test and measurement instruments, and computer equipment, which today forms the bulk of the company's sales. Hewlett-Packard earned a reputation for innovation. Packard proudly stated, "HP continually strives to develop products that represent true advancements."

Innovative products were accompanied by an inventive managerial style. Perhaps reminiscent of Terman's student-led seminars, a recurring theme is the idea of sharing. Hewlett-Packard employees share setting and achieving goals, share professional development, share ownership (through stock purchases), and share in the company's highs and lows. In his book, *The HP Way*, Packard described the decentralized decision making, team orientation, and hands-on leadership that characterize working at Hewlett-Packard. A key principle is "management by walking around (MBWA)," which maintains that managers learn more in the plant than they do from behind a desk. *The HP Way* emphasizes seeking out, and hearing, what others have to say. Packard died in 1996, but listening remains a priority at Hewlett-Packard. As Hewlett points out, "I learned how to listen…What you learn is you have a great memory."

COMPANY ON THE CUTTING EDGE

COMPANY ON THE CUTTING EDGE

HEWLETT-PACKARD

In a one-car garage in 1938, two 26-year-old engineers started a business with a collection of simple tools (bench, vise, drill press, screwdriver, file, soldering iron, hacksaw, and some electrical supplies) and $538 in working capital. It was a humble beginning, but the business begun by William Hewlett and David Packard would become Hewlett-Packard (HP) Company, one of the largest companies in the computer industry, with 121,000 employees worldwide and revenues of more than $42.8 billion. Today, the Palo Alto garage is a California State Historical Landmark, a Silicon Valley milestone.

The Hewlett-Packard partnership was formed officially in 1939. A coin toss determined the company's name. The first product was an audio oscillator, which is an instrument that employed a light bulb to help test sound equipment. Walt Disney ordered eight oscillators to use in developing sound effects for the movie, *Fantasia*. In 1942, the company built its first Hewlett-Packard owned building — a 10,000-square-foot office/laboratory/factory. Business was good, but the founders designed the new facility so it easily could be converted into a grocery store if the electronics business failed.

Instead of failing, Hewlett-Packard grew. By 1962, the company had earned a place on *Fortune* magazine's list of the top 500 U.S. companies. During its first two decades, Hewlett-Packard introduced a variety of products, including microwave signal generators, high-speed frequency counters, and other instruments. Through a number of acquisitions, the company expanded into other fields. Today, Hewlett-Packard markets and services electronic components, test and measurement supplies, medical electronic equipment, chemical analysis instruments, and computer products.

Hewlett-Packard entered the computer field in 1966 with a computer designed as a controller for some of the company's test and measurement instruments. A flurry of computer-related products followed, including personal computers, electronic mail systems, printers, palmtop PCs, and handheld organizers. The company also achieved a number of *firsts*, such as the first desktop scientific calculators (presaging workstations) and the first scientific handheld calculators (making slide rules obsolete). By 1997, computer-related sales made up 82 percent of the company's revenues.

Hewlett-Packard's most successful product is the LaserJet printer. Interestingly, the company developed *two* new printers in the early 1980s: the HP Thinkjet ink-jet printer and the HP LaserJet laser printer. Some companies would have held back one of the competing printers for later release. Hewlett-Packard decided, however, that it would rather compete with itself than with another printer manufacturer. When the printers were introduced, Hewlett-Packard sales skyrocketed. By 1993, the company had sold 20 million printers, and it is estimated that 60 percent of printers sold bear the Hewlett-Packard logo.

Despite its well-earned reputation for innovation among industry insiders, Hewlett-Packard's image among home consumers is less inspiring. Recent company surveys found that if Hewlett-Packard was a person, it would be seen as a "trustworthy but boring computer geek wearing a turtleneck and sandals." Hewlett-Packard is working to change that picture, with a new marketing campaign, a new corporate slogan ("Expanding Possibilities"), and new services (such as automated printer-supply vending machines). The company hopes this fresh approach, coupled with the unique ability to combine measurement, computer, and communication technologies, will give Hewlett-Packard the recognition it deserves both inside and outside the computer industry.

IN BRIEF www.scsite.com/dc2000/ch5/brief.htm

WEB INSTRUCTIONS: *To display this page from the Web, launch your browser and enter the URL, www.scsite.com/dc2000/ch5/brief.htm. Click the links for current and additional information. To listen to an audio version of this IN BRIEF, click the Audio button to the right of the title, IN BRIEF, at the top of the page. To play the audio, RealPlayer must be installed on your computer (download by clicking here).*

1. What Are the Four Types of Output?

Output is data that has been processed into a useful form, called information. Four types of output are text, graphics, audio, and video. **Text** consists of **characters** that are used to create words, sentences, and paragraphs. **Graphics** are digital representations of nontext information such as drawings, charts, and photographs. **Audio** is music, speech, or any other sound. **Video** consists of images that provide the appearance of full motion.

2. What Are Different Types of Output Devices?

An **output device** is any computer component capable of conveying information to a user. A **display device** is an output device that visually conveys text, graphics, and video information. A **printer** is an output device that produces text and graphics on a physical medium such as paper or transparency film. An **audio output device** produces music, speech, or other sounds. Other output devices include **data projectors**, **facsimile (fax) machines**, and **multifunction devices**.

3. What Factors Affect the Quality of a Monitor?

A **monitor** is a display device that consists of a screen housed in a plastic or metal case. The **screen** is coated with tiny dots of phosphor material, called **pixels**, that glow when electrically charged. The quality of the resulting image depends on a monitor's resolution, dot pitch, and refresh rate. **Resolution**, or sharpness, is related to the number of pixels a monitor can display. Higher resolution means a greater number of pixels display, providing a smoother image. **Dot pitch**, a measure of image clarity, is the vertical distance between each pixel. The smaller the dot pitch, the clearer the displayed image. **Refresh rate** is the speed with which a monitor redraws images on the screen. Refresh rate should be fast enough to maintain a constant, flicker-free image.

4. Why Is a Video Card Used?

A **video card** converts digital output into an analog video signal that is sent through a cable to the monitor. The monitor separates the video signal into red, green, and blue signals. Electron guns fire the signals to the front of the monitor, and these three colored dots are combined to make up each single pixel. Several standards have been developed to define resolution, the number of colors, and other monitor properties. Today, most monitors and video cards support the **super video graphics array** (**SVGA**) standard.

5. What Are Monitor Ergonomic Issues?

Features that address monitor ergonomic issues include controls to adjust the brightness, contrast, positioning, height, and width of images. Many monitors have a tilt and swivel base so the angle of the screen can be altered to minimize neck strain and glare. Monitors produce a small amount of **electromagnetic radiation (EMR)**, which is a magnetic field that travels at the speed of light. High-quality monitors should comply with MPR II, which is a standard that defines acceptable levels of EMR for a monitor.

CHAPTER 1 2 3 4 **5** 6 7 8 9 10 11 12 13 14 INDEX

 IN BRIEF www.scsite.com/dc2000/ch5/brief.htm

 ## 6. How Are Various Types of Printers Different?

Printers can be grouped in two categories: impact and nonimpact. **Impact printers** form characters and graphics by striking a mechanism against an ink ribbon that physically contacts the paper. A **dot-matrix printer** is an impact printer that prints images when tiny wire pins on a print head mechanism strike an inked ribbon. A **line printer** is an impact printer that prints an entire line at one time. **Nonimpact printers** form characters and graphics without actually striking the paper. An **ink-jet printer** is a nonimpact printer that sprays drops of ink onto a piece of paper. A laser printer is a nonimpact printer that operates in a manner similar to a copy machine. A **thermal printer** is a nonimpact printer that generates images by pushing electrically heated pins against heat-sensitive paper.

 ## 7. What Are Various Types of Audio Output Devices?

Two commonly used audio output devices are speakers and headsets. Most personal computers have an internal speaker that outputs low-quality sound. Many users add high-quality stereo speakers or purchase PCs with larger speakers built into the sides of the monitor. A woofer can be added to boost low bass sounds. A **headset** plugged into a port on the sound card allows only the user to hear sound from the computer.

 ## 8. Why Are Data Projectors, Fax Machines, and Multifunction Devices Used?

A **data projector** takes the image on a computer screen and projects it onto a large screen so an audience of people can see the image. A **facsimile (fax) machine** transmits and receives documents over telephone lines. A **fax modem** is a communications device that sends (and sometimes receives) electronic documents as faxes. A multifunction device (MFD) is a single piece of equipment that looks like a copy machine but provides the functionality of a printer, scanner, copy machine, and sometimes a fax machine.

 ## 9. How Is a Terminal Both an Input and Output Device?

A **terminal** is a device that consists of a keyboard (input), a monitor (output), and a video card. A terminal is used to input and transmit data to, or receive and output information from, a **host computer**. Three basic categories of terminals are **dumb terminals**, **intelligent terminals**, and special-purpose terminals.

10. What Are Output Options for Physically Challenged Users?

Hearing-impaired users can instruct programs to display words instead of sounds. With Windows, the **Accessibility Properties dialog box** can be used to instruct Windows to display visual signals in situations where normally it would make a sound. Visually impaired users can change the size or color of text to make words easier to read. Blind users can utilize speech output, where the computer reads information that displays on the screen. A **Braille printer** outputs information in Braille onto paper.

CHAPTER 1 2 3 4 [5] 6 7 8 9 10 11 12 13 14 INDEX

KEY TERMS   www.scsite.com/dc2000/ch5/terms.htm

WEB INSTRUCTIONS: *To display this page from the Web, launch your browser and enter the URL, www.scsite.com/dc2000/ch5/terms.htm. Scroll through the list of terms. Click a term to display its definition and a picture. Click KEY TERMS on the left to redisplay the KEY TERMS page. Click the TO WEB button for current and additional information about the term from the Web. To see animations, Shockwave and Flash Player must be installed on your computer (download by clicking here).*

Accessibility Properties dialog box (5.24)
active-matrix display (5.5)
animation (5.2)
audio (5.2, 5.20)
audio output devices (5.20)
automatic teller machine (ATM) (5.24)
band printer (5.13)
Braille printer (5.25)
cathode ray tube (CRT) (5.3)
character (5.2)
characters per second (cps) (5.13)
color monitor (5.3)
continuous-form paper (5.13)
CRT monitor (5.3)
data projector (5.21)
digital light processing (DLP) projector (5.21)
display device (5.3)
dot pitch (5.7)
dot-matrix printer (5.12)
dots per inch (dpi) (5.14)
dumb terminal (5.23)
dye-sublimation printer (5.18)
electromagnetic radiation (EMR) (5.10)
electrostatic plotter (5.19)
ENERGY STAR program (5.11)
facsimile (fax) machine (5.22)
fax modem (5.22)
flat-panel display (5.4)
gas plasma monitors (5.6)
graphics (5.2)
graphics card (5.8)
gray scaling (5.3)
hard copy (5.11)
headset (5.21)
hertz (5.7)
high-definition television (HDTV) (5.11)
host computer (5.23)

TO WEB

300 dpi

600 dpi

1,200 dpi

DOTS PER INCH (DPI): Measure of printer resolution; the higher the dpi, the better the quality of the print image. (5.14)

image editing software (5.2)
impact printer (5.12)
ink-jet printer (5.14)
intelligent terminal (5.23)
interlacing (5.7)
label printer (5.20)
landscape orientation (5.11)
large-format printer (5.19)
laser printer (5.16)
LCD display (5.5)
LCD projector (5.21)
letter quality (LQ) (5.12)
line printer (5.13)
liquid crystal display (LCD) (5.5)
monitor (5.3)
monochrome monitor (5.3)
multifunction device (MFD) (5.23)
near letter quality (NLQ) (5.12)
nonimpact printer (5.14)

output (5.2)
output device (5.3)
page description language (PDL) (5.16)
page printers (5.16)
pages per minute (ppm) (5.15)
passive-matrix display (5.5)
PCL (Printer Control Language) (5.16)
pen plotter (5.19)
pixel (5.4)
point-of-sale (POS) terminal (5.24)
portable printer (5.18)
portrait orientation (5.11)
PostScript (5.16)
printer (5.11)
printout (5.11)
programmable terminals (5.23)
refresh rate (5.7)
resolution (5.6)
screen (5.3)
shuttle-matrix printer (5.13)
snapshot printer (5.20)
soft copy (5.3)
super video graphics array (SVGA) (5.9)
terminal (5.23)
text (5.2)
TFT displays (5.5)
thermal dye transfer printer (5.18)
thermal printer (5.17)
thermal transfer printer (5.18)
thermal wax-transfer printer (5.18)
toner (5.17)
video (5.3)
video adapter (5.8)
video card (5.8)
video RAM (5.9)
viewable size (5.4)
VRAM (5.9)

CHAPTER   1 2 3 4 5 6 7 8 9 10 11 12 13 14   INDEX

AT THE MOVIES   www.scsite.com/dc2000/ch5/movies.htm

WELCOME to VIDEO CLIPS from CNN

WEB INSTRUCTIONS: *To display this page from the Web, launch your browser and enter the URL, www.scsite.com/dc2000/ch5/movies.htm. Click a picture to view a video. After watching the video, close the video window and then complete the exercise by answering the questions about the video. To view the videos, RealPlayer must be installed on your computer (download by clicking here).*

1 IP Faxville Press

The use of the facsimile (fax) machine has changed many aspects of political life. Do you think the change is for the better? Why? Does the use of a fax give one candidate an advantage over another candidate? Is this good? What other activities have been altered by the use of fax machines? Describe what you see as problems with this instant communications device. Do you see any way of solving the problems or must we put up with whatever we are sent on a fax machine? Would you support "fax regulation?" Why?

2 Postage Computer

The United States Postal Service is the technology for testing e-stamps. What do you think of e-stamps? How are e-stamps placed on envelopes? Do you need a special printer to print the e-stamps? Can a person handwrite the address on an e-stamped envelope? What are the advantages and disadvantages of e-stamps? Will you use e-stamps? Why?

3 Biz Apple 20th

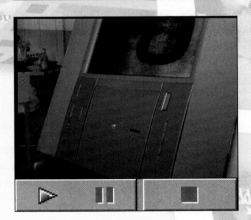

New versatile features of Apple laptop computers parallel trends in PC laptops. What are some of the new features offered on laptop models? What new types of input and output devices are used with laptops? Do you think laptops will look the same ten years from now? If not, how might laptops be different?

SHELLY
CASHMAN
SERIES
DISCOVERING
COMPUTERS
2000

Student Exercises
WEB INFO
IN BRIEF
KEY TERMS
AT THE MOVIES
CHECKPOINT
AT ISSUE
CYBERCLASS
HANDS ON
NET STUFF
Special Features
TIMELINE 2000
GUIDE TO WWW SITES
MAKING A CHIP
BUYER'S GUIDE 2000
CAREERS 2000
TRENDS 2000
CHAT
INTERACTIVE LABS
NEWS
HOME

CHAPTER 1 2 3 4 **5** 6 7 8 9 10 11 12 13 14 INDEX

CHECKPOINT   www.scsite.com/dc2000/ch5/check.htm

WEB INSTRUCTIONS: *To display this page from the Web, launch your browser and enter the URL, www.scsite.com/dc2000/ch5/check.htm. Click the links for current and additional information. To experience the animation and interactivity, Shockwave and Flash Player must be installed on your computer (download by clicking here).*

Label the Figure

Instructions: *Complete these steps to show how video travels from the CPU to the monitor.*

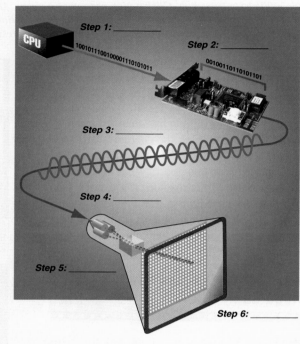

Matching

Instructions: *Match each term from the column on the left with the best description from the column on the right.*

_____ 1. LCD (liquid crystal display)

_____ 2. EMR (electromagnetic radiation)

_____ 3. NLQ (near letter quality)

_____ 4. PDL (page description language)

_____ 5. ATM (automatic teller machine)

a. Has special molecules deposited between two sheets of material.
b. Used by higher-quality video cards to improve the quality of graphics.
c. Print that is slightly less clear than letter quality but ideal for mailing labels and envelopes.
d. A magnetic field that travels at the speed of light.
e. A standard printer language designed to support the fonts and layouts used in standard documents.
f. Tells the printer how to layout the contents of a printed page.
g. A self-service banking machine attached to a host computer through a telephone network.

Short Answer

Instructions: *Write a brief answer to each of the following questions.*

1. How are color monitors, monochrome monitors, and monitors that use gray scaling different? _____ When are color monitors and monochrome monitors most widely used? _____

2. How is an active matrix display different from a passive matrix display? _____ What is a gas plasma monitor? _____

3. What is high-definition television (HDTV)? _____ What advantages does HDTV provide over analog signals? _____

4. How is hard copy different from soft copy? _____ How is portrait orientation different from landscape orientation? _____

5. How is a dumb terminal different from an intelligent terminal? _____ For what purpose is a point-of-sale terminal used? _____

AT ISSUE   www.scsite.com/dc2000/ch5/issue.htm

SHELLY
CASHMAN
SERIES®
**DISCOVERING
COMPUTERS
2000**

WEB INSTRUCTIONS: *To display this page from the Web, launch your browser and enter the URL,*
www.scsite.com/dc2000/ch5/issue.htm. Click the links for current and additional information.

Short of cash? Some college students found a solution to the
problem: they made some. With a scanner, personal computer, and color printer,
the students produced bogus bills and passed more than $1,000 in counterfeit
currency before they were caught. As printer quality improves, police have
arrested counterfeiters ranging from high school students to senior citizens, and
the problem is growing. Fake money usually can be spotted with a close inspec-
tion, but most people never look that closely. Once a counterfeit bill is accepted,
even as change, it is yours. Should printer manufacturers take some responsibility for this problem? Why or why not? What, if anything, could printer makers
do? Can you offer any other possible solutions?

Computer screens appear in unlikely places, but
perhaps no spot is more improbable than a cemetery. Never-
theless, a company called Leif Technologies is changing that by offering computerized
grave markers. The headstones have a 5-inch by 4-inch screen and a computer that
stores up to 85 pages of information about the deceased person. Visitors can access
records, stories, poems, and even photographs. Buyers think these modern memorials
will prove invaluable to future generations, but traditionalists feel the technological
tombstones are unseemly in such a solemn setting. Are computerized grave markers
appropriate? Why or why not? At a cost of $5,000, would you consider an interactive plaque? Why?

THREE *Many interior decorators feel CRT monitors are the most unattractive and inefficient*
component of the modern office. Perched on a desktop, these boxy devices add little to office allure
and subtract much from available workspace. Liquid crystal display (LCD) screens, however, soon may remedy this problem.
Modern LCDs provide resolution, screen sizes, and clarity equivalent to or better than the best CRTs and occupy much less
space. Designer LCDs also are available in a range of attractive colors and designs. Yet, high-quality LCDs can cost more than
$2,000, while a top-quality CRT monitor can be purchased for only $500. Is the extra expense worth it? When would you consider buying a designer LCD instead of a standard CRT monitor? Why?

FOUR *At one time, people predicted paperless offices in which all*
information was processed electronically, and hard copy was nonex-
istent. Instead, paper use has risen more than forty percent over the past thirty years, and the
largest increase is in the use of office paper. Experts explain this phenomenon by pointing out
that paper is less expensive and paper documents are easier to create than in the past. Every
office has computer printers, copying machines, and facsimile machines that reproduce documents at an ever-increasing rate. In addition, paper documents help sift the glut of electronic
information. Can, and should, people and organizations try to reduce paper use? Why or why
not? What can be done to make, if not a paperless office, at least a less-paper office?

FIVE *What are the most prevalent input devices and output devices for home computers?*
Not surprisingly, today's most popular input devices are the keyboard and the mouse, while the
most widespread output devices are the monitor and the printer. Yet, given advances in hardware and software, what does the
future hold? Will these two input devices and these two output devices still be the more commonly used 25 years from now?
Why or why not? What other input and output devices are personal computer users more likely to adopt? Why? How will the
use of these devices affect the way people work with computers?

SHELLY
CASHMAN
SERIES®
DISCOVERING
COMPUTERS
2000

Student Exercises
WEB INFO
IN BRIEF
KEY TERMS
AT THE MOVIES
CHECKPOINT
AT ISSUE
CYBERCLASS
HANDS ON
NET STUFF
Special Features
TIMELINE 2000
GUIDE TO WWW SITES
MAKING A CHIP
BUYER'S GUIDE 2000
CAREERS 2000
TRENDS 2000
CHAT
INTERACTIVE LABS
NEWS
HOME

CHAPTER 1 2 3 4 **5** 6 7 8 9 10 11 12 13 14 **INDEX**

CYBERCLASS www.scsite.com/dc2000/ch5/class.htm

WEB INSTRUCTIONS: *To display this page from the Web, launch your browser and enter the URL,* *www.scsite.com/dc2000/ch5/class.htm. To start Level I CyberClass, click a Level I link on this page or enter the URL, www.cyber-class.com. Click the Student button, click* Discovering Computers 2000 *in the list of titles, and then click the Enter a site button. To start Level II or III CyberClass (available only to those purchasers of a CyberClass floppy disk), place your CyberClass floppy disk in drive A, click Start on the taskbar, click Run on the Start menu, type* a:connect *in the Open text box, click the OK button, click the Enter CyberClass button, and then follow the instructions.*

I II III LEVEL **1. Flash Cards** Click Flash Cards on the Main Menu of the CyberClass web page. Click the plus sign before the Chapter 5 title and then click Output Devices. Complete all the Output Devices questions. Then, choose a category and continue to answer flash cards until you have answered 25 questions. Record your percentage correct and hand in your score to your instructor. All users: Answer as many more flash cards as you desire. Close the Electronic Flash Card window and the Flash Cards window by clicking the Close button in the upper-right corner of each window.

I II III LEVEL **2. Practice Test** Click Testing on the Main Menu of the CyberClass web page. Click the Select a book box arrow and then click Discovering Computers 2000. Click the Select a test to take box arrow and then click the Chapter 5 title in the list. Click the Take Test button. If necessary, maximize the window. Take the practice test and then click the Submit Test button. If your percentage correct is less than 85%, click the Take another Test button and take another practice test. Record your test score(s) and hand them in to your instructor.

I II III LEVEL **3. Web Guide** Click Web Guide on the Main Menu of the CyberClass web page. When the Guide to World Wide Web Sites page displays, click Computers and Computing. Then, click Virtual Computer Library. Find an article about computers that interests you and write a brief synopsis of the story. When you are finished, close the window. Hand in the synopsis to your instructor.

I II III LEVEL **4. Company Briefs** Click Company Briefs on the Main Menu of the CyberClass web page. Click a corporation name to display a case study. Read the case study. Write a brief report on whether you would want to work for the company, based upon their use of computers.

II III LEVEL **5. CyberChallenge** Click CyberChallenge on the Main Menu of the CyberClass web page. Click the Select a book box arrow and then click Discovering Computers 2000. Click the Select a board to play box arrow and then click Chapter 5 in the list. Click the Play CyberChallenge button. Maximize the CyberChallenge window. Play CyberChallenge until you have answered correctly all questions for a given vertical column. Close the CyberChallenge window.

II III LEVEL **6. Hot Links** Determine a Web site on the World Wide Web that pertains to Output you think that everyone in your class should visit. Click Hot Links on the Main Menu of the CyberClass web page. Click Add a Link within the Hot Links section. Enter the Link Name, the URL, and the Link Description. Click the Add Link button. Your link should display on the Hot Links screen.

II III LEVEL **7. Send Messages** Click Send Messages on the Main Menu of the CyberClass web page. Send a message to all members of your class to look at the Hot Links web site you entered in exercise 6 above by clicking the Send to all box in the Members section of the screen (a check mark will display in the box), entering a subject and the message itself, and then clicking the Send Message button.

CHAPTER   1   2   3   4   5   6   7   8   9   10   11   12   13   14   INDEX

HANDS ON   www.scsite.com/dc2000/ch5/hands.htm

WEB INSTRUCTIONS: *To display this page from the Web, launch your browser and enter the URL,* www.scsite.com/dc2000/ch5/hands.htm. *Click the links for current and additional information.*

One   *About Your Computer*

Your computer probably has more than one output device. To learn a little bit about the <u>output devices</u> on your computer, right-click the My Computer icon on the desktop. Click Properties on the shortcut menu. When the System Properties dialog box displays, click the Device Manager tab. Click View devices by type. Below Computer, a list of hardware device categories displays. What output devices display in the list? Click the plus sign next to each category. What specific output devices in each category are connected to your computer? Close the System Properties dialog box.

Two   *Accessibility Options*

The Windows operating system offers several <u>output options</u> for people with hearing or visual impairments. Three of these options are SoundSentry, ShowSounds, and High Contrast. To find out more about each option, click the Start button, point to Settings on the Start menu, and then click Control Panel on the Settings submenu. Double-click the Accessibility Options icon in the Control Panel window. Click the Sound tab in the Accessibility Properties dialog box. Click the question mark button on the title bar, click Use SoundSentry, read the information in the pop-up window, and then click the pop-up window to close it. Repeat this process for Use ShowSounds. Click the Display tab. Click the question mark button on the title bar and then click Use High Contrast. Read the information in the pop-up window, and then click the pop-up window to close it. What is the purpose of each option? Click the Cancel button. Click the Close button to close the Control Panel window.

Three   *Self-Portrait*

Windows includes a <u>drawing program</u> called Paint. The quality of graphics produced with this program depends on a variety of factors, including the quality of your printer, your understanding of the software, and (to some extent) your artistic talent. In this exercise, you will use Paint to create a self-portrait. To access Paint, click the Start button, point to Programs on the Start menu, point to Accessories on the Programs submenu, and then click Paint on the Accessories submenu. When the Paint windows displays, you will see the Paint toolbar on the left side of the window. Point to a toolbar button to see a tool's name; click a button to use that tool. Use the tools and colors available in Paint to draw a picture of yourself. If you make a mistake, you can click Undo on the Edit menu to undo your most recent action, you can erase part of your picture using the Eraser/Color Eraser tool, or you can clear the entire picture by clicking Clear Image on the Image menu. When your self-portrait is finished, print it by clicking Print on the File menu. Close Paint.

Four   *Microsoft Magnifier*

This exercise uses Windows 98 procedures. Microsoft Magnifier is a Windows <u>utility for the visually impaired</u>. To find out about the Microsoft Magnifier capabilities, click the Start button and then click Help on the Start menu. Click the Index tab. Type `magnifier` in the text box and then click the Display button. Click the Using Microsoft Magnifier topic and then click the Display button in the Windows Help window. Read the information and answer these questions:

▲ How does Microsoft Magnifier make the screen more readable for the visually impaired?
▲ What viewing options does Microsoft Magnifier have?
▲ What tracking options does Microsoft Magnifier have?

Click the Close button to close the Windows Help window.

SHELLY
CASHMAN
SERIES

DISCOVERING
COMPUTERS
2000

Student Exercises
WEB INFO
IN BRIEF
KEY TERMS
AT THE MOVIES
CHECKPOINT
AT ISSUE
CYBERCLASS
HANDS ON
NET STUFF
Special Features
TIMELINE 2000
GUIDE TO WWW SITES
MAKING A CHIP
BUYER'S GUIDE 2000
CAREERS 2000
TRENDS 2000
CHAT
INTERACTIVE LABS
NEWS
HOME

CHAPTER   1   2   3   4   5   6   7   8   9   10   11   12   13   14   INDEX

NET STUFF   www.scsite.com/dc2000/ch5/net.htm

WEB INSTRUCTIONS: *To display this page from the Web, launch your browser and enter the URL,* www.scsite.com/dc2000/ch5/net.htm. *To use the Setting Up to Print lab or the Configuring Your Display lab from the Web, Shockwave and Flash Player must be installed on your computer (download by clicking* here*).*

SETTING UP
TO PRINT LAB

1. Shelly Cashman Series Setting Up to Print Lab

Follow the appropriate instructions in NET STUFF 1 on page 1.46 to start and use the Setting Up to Print lab. If you are running from the Web, enter the URL, www.scsite.com/sclabs/menu.htm; or display the NET STUFF page (see instructions at the top of this page) and then click the SETTING UP TO PRINT LAB button.

CONFIGURING
YOUR DISPLAY
LAB

2. Shelly Cashman Series Configuring Your Display Lab

Follow the appropriate instructions in NET STUFF 1 on page 1.46 to start and use the Configuring Your Display lab. If you are running from the Web, enter the URL, www.scsite.com/sclabs/menu.htm; or display the NET STUFF page (see instructions at the top of this page) and then click the CONFIGURING YOUR DISPLAY LAB button.

NETIQUETTE

3. Newsgroup Etiquette

In Chapter 3, you learned about newsgroups. Before getting involved in a newsgroup, however, you should learn a little about newsgroup etiquette. Perfectly acceptable communication in e-mail messages to a friend may be highly inappropriate in postings to newsgroup readers. Click the NETIQUETTE button for an informative, amusing, common-sense guide to newsgroup etiquette. This site's Emily Post-like approach presents etiquette questions with unlikely answers. As you explore the guide, you will see that the actual answer to each question usually is the opposite of what the given answer suggests. Make a list of five etiquette questions presented. Using the satirical answer given and your own common sense, write a genuine reply to each question.

IN THE NEWS

4. In the News

Monitors continue to grow clearer and thinner. A newly introduced 50-inch gas plasma display presents near-photographic images and is less than four inches thick. At a cose of $25,000, the monitors probably will be seen first at stadiums, in airports, and as touch screens in stores. Yet, as prices fall, consumers surely will purchase the monitors for HDTV and crystal-clear Internet access. Click the IN THE NEWS button and then read a news article about a new or improved output device. What is the device? Who manufactures it? How is the output device better than, or different from, earlier devices? Who do you think is most likely to use the device? Why?

WEB CHAT

5. Web Chat

A photomosaic is a large image, often a portrait, made up of many small photographs. The result is a remarkable representation that is enchanting from a distance and stunning from up close. Photomosaics include an Abraham Lincoln composed of Civil War photographs, a Vincent Van Gogh comprised of nature scenes, and a Bill Gates consisting of various world currencies. Robert Silvers created the software to form photomosaics while a graduate student at MIT. The software digitizes a large image and then selects the smaller photographs from special collections or a huge database of stock pictures. The software then sorts the photographs based on color, tone, and discernible shapes. Finally, the small photographs are digitally arranged to create the large image. A photomosaic costs more than $75,000, but is it art? Silvers is not sure. He claims the entire process could be done by hand, although over a much longer period of time. Critics argue that photomosaics are little more than computer wizardry, but admirers insist photomosaics may express emotion, an essential characteristic of art, even better than conventional artwork. Would you consider a photomosaic a work of art? Why or why not? Click the WEB CHAT button to enter a Web Chat discussion concerning photomosaics.

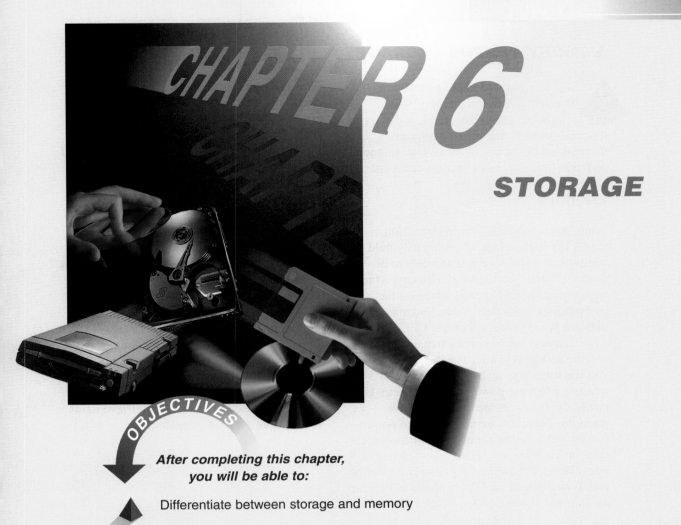

CHAPTER 6

STORAGE

OBJECTIVES

After completing this chapter,
you will be able to:

Differentiate between storage and memory

Identify various types of storage media and storage devices

Explain how data is stored on a floppy disk

Understand how to care for a floppy disk

Describe how a hard disk organizes data

List the advantages of using disks

Explain how data is stored on compact discs

Understand how to care for a compact disc

Differentiate between CD-ROMs and DVD-ROMs

Identify uses of tapes, PC Cards, smart cards, microfilm, and microfiche

Storage refers to the media on which data, instructions, and information are kept, as well as the devices that record and retrieve these items. This chapter explains various storage media and storage devices. Following completion of this chapter, you will have an understanding of all four operations in the information processing cycle: input, processing, output, and storage.

MEMORY VERSUS STORAGE

It is important to understand the difference between memory, which was discussed in Chapter 3, and storage, the focus of this chapter. To clarify the differences, the next section reviews memory and then discusses basic storage concepts.

Memory

While performing a processing operation, the CPU needs a place to temporarily hold instructions to be executed and data to be used with those instructions. Memory, which is composed of one or more chips on the motherboard, holds data and instructions while they are being processed by the CPU.

The two basic types of memory are volatile and nonvolatile. The contents of **volatile memory**, such as RAM, are lost (erased) when the power to the computer is turned off. The contents of **nonvolatile memory**, however, are not lost when power is removed from the computer. For example, once instructions have been recorded onto a nonvolatile ROM chip, they usually cannot be erased or changed, and the contents of the chip are not erased when power is turned off.

Storage

Storage, also called **secondary storage**, **auxiliary storage**, or **mass storage**, holds items such as data, instructions, and information for future use.

Think of storage as a filing cabinet used to hold file folders, and memory as the top of your desk. When you need to work with a file, you remove it from the filing cabinet (storage) and place it on your desk (memory). When you are finished with the file, you return it to the filing cabinet (storage).

Storage is nonvolatile, which means that items in storage are retained even when power is removed from the computer (Figure 6-1). A **storage medium** (media is the plural) is the physical material on which items are kept. One commonly used storage medium is a **disk**, which is a round, flat piece of plastic or metal with a magnetic coating on which items can be written. A **storage device** is the mechanism used to record and retrieve items to and from a storage medium.

AN ILLUSTRATION OF VOLATILITY

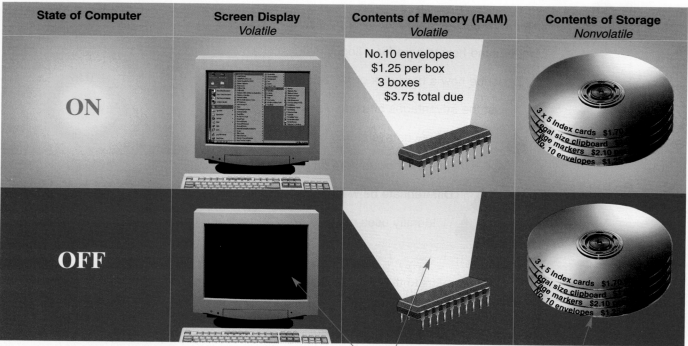

State of Computer	Screen Display *Volatile*	Contents of Memory (RAM) *Volatile*	Contents of Storage *Nonvolatile*
ON		No.10 envelopes $1.25 per box 3 boxes $3.75 total due	3 x 5 Index cards $1.70 Legal size clipboard $ Edge markers $2.10 No. 10 envelopes $1
OFF			3 x 5 Index cards $1.70 Legal size clipboard $ Edge markers $2.10 No. 10 envelopes $1

Figure 6-1 Both a screen display and RAM are volatile; that is, their contents are erased when power is removed from the computer. Storage, in contrast, is nonvolatile – its contents are retained when power is off.

screen display and contents of RAM (memory) erased when power is off

contents of storage retained when power is off

Storage devices can function as sources of input and output. For example, each time a storage device transfers data, instructions, and information from a storage medium into memory — a process called **reading** — it functions as an input source. When a storage device transfers these items from memory to a storage medium — a process called **writing** — it functions as an output source.

The speed of a storage device is defined by its **access time**, which is the minimum time it takes the device to locate a single item on a disk. Compared to memory, storage devices are slow. The access time of memory devices is measured in nanoseconds (billionths of a second), while the access time of storage devices is measured in milliseconds (thousandths of a second).

The size, or **capacity**, of a storage device, is measured by the number of bytes (characters) it can hold. Figure 6-2 lists the terms used to define the capacity of storage devices. For example, a typical floppy disk can store 1.44 MB of data (approximately 1,440,000 bytes) and a typical hard disk can store 8 GB of data (approximately 8,000,000,000 bytes).

Storage requirements among users vary greatly. Users of smaller computers, such as small business users, might need to store a relatively small amount of data. For example, a field sales representative might have a list of names, addresses, and telephone numbers of 50 customers, which he or she uses on a daily basis. Such a list might require no more than several thousand bytes of storage. Users of larger computers, such as banks, libraries, or insurance companies, process data for millions of customers and thus might need to store trillions of bytes worth of historical or financial records in their archives.

To meet the needs of a wide range of users, numerous types of storage media and storage devices exist. Figure 6-3 shows how different types of storage media and memory compare in terms of relative cost and speed. The storage media included in the pyramid are discussed in this chapter.

STORAGE TERMS

Storage Term	Abbreviation	Number of Bytes
Kilobyte	KB	1 thousand
Megabyte	MB	1 million
Gigabyte	GB	1 billion
Terabyte	TB	1 trillion

Figure 6-2 The capacity of a storage device is measured by the number of bytes it can hold.

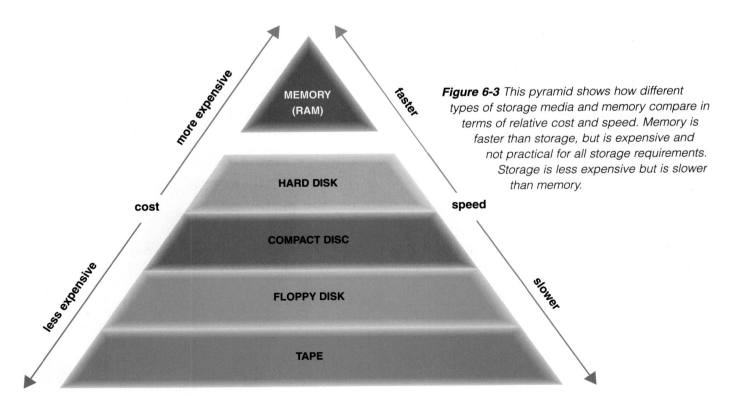

Figure 6-3 This pyramid shows how different types of storage media and memory compare in terms of relative cost and speed. Memory is faster than storage, but is expensive and not practical for all storage requirements. Storage is less expensive but is slower than memory.

FLOPPY DISKS

WEB INFO
WEB INFO

For more information on floppy disks, visit the Discovering Computers 2000 Chapter 6 WEB INFO page (www.scsite.com/dc2000/ch6/webinfo.htm) and click Floppy Disks.

A **floppy disk**, or **diskette**, is a portable, inexpensive storage medium that consists of a thin, circular, flexible plastic disk with a magnetic coating enclosed in a square-shaped plastic shell (Figure 6-4). In the early 1970s, IBM introduced the floppy disk as a new type of storage. Because these early 8-inch wide disks had flexible plastic covers, many users referred to them as floppies. The next generation of floppies looked much the same, but were only 5.25-inches wide.

Today, the most widely used floppy disk is 3.5-inches wide. The flexible cover of the earlier floppy disks has been replaced with a rigid plastic outer cover. Thus, although today's 3.5-inch disks are not at all floppy, the term floppy disk still is used.

As noted, a floppy disk is a portable storage medium. When discussing a storage medium, the term portable means you can remove the medium from one computer and carry it to another computer. For example, you can insert a floppy disk into and remove it from a floppy disk drive on many types of computers (Figure 6-5). A floppy disk drive is a device that can read from and write to a floppy disk.

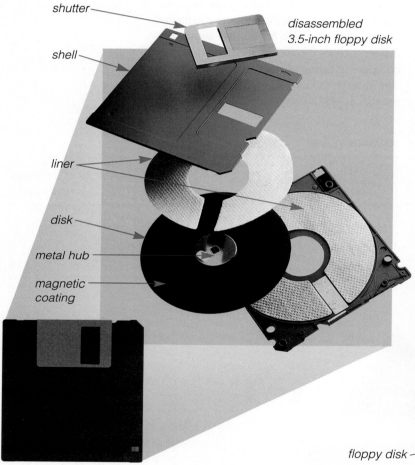

shutter

shell

liner

disk

metal hub

magnetic coating

disassembled 3.5-inch floppy disk

Figure 6-4 In a 3.5-inch floppy disk, the thin circular flexible disk is enclosed between two liners. A piece of metal called a shutter in the rigid plastic shell covers an opening to the recording surface.

Figure 6-5 Various types of floppy disk drives.

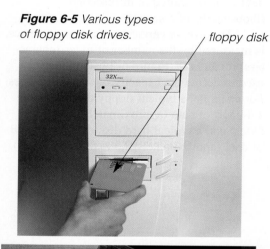

floppy disk

floppy disk

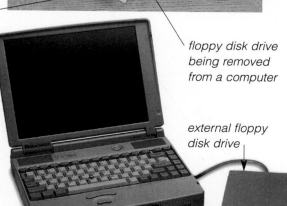

floppy disk drive being removed from a computer

external floppy disk drive

Characteristics of a Floppy Disk

A floppy disk is a type of a magnetic disk, which means it uses magnetic patterns to store items such as data, instructions, and information on the disk's surface. Most magnetic disks are **read/write** storage media; that is, you can access (read) data from and place (write) data on a magnetic disk any number of times, just as you can with an audiocassette tape.

A new, blank floppy disk has nothing stored on it. Before you can write on a new floppy disk, it must be formatted.

Formatting is the process of preparing a disk (floppy disk or hard disk) for reading and writing by organizing the disk into storage locations called tracks and sectors (Figure 6-6). A **track** is a narrow recording band that forms a full circle on the surface of the disk. The disk's storage locations then are divided into pie-shaped sections, which break the tracks into small arcs called sectors. A **sector** is capable of holding 512 bytes of data. A typical floppy disk stores data on both sides and has 80 tracks on each side of the recording surface with 18 sectors per track.

Sometimes, a sector is damaged or has a flaw and cannot store data. A sector that cannot be used due to a physical flaw on the disk is called a bad sector. When you format a disk, the operating system marks these bad sectors as unusable. If a sector that contains data is damaged, you may be able to use special software to recover the data.

For reading and writing purposes, sectors are grouped into clusters. A **cluster** consists of two to eight sectors (the number varies depending on the operating system). A cluster is the smallest unit of space used to store data. Even if a file consists of only a few bytes, an entire cluster is used for storage. Although each cluster holds data from only one file, one file can be stored in many clusters.

A disk's storage capacity is determined by the density of the disk. A higher density means that the disk has a larger storage capacity. Disk **density** is computed by

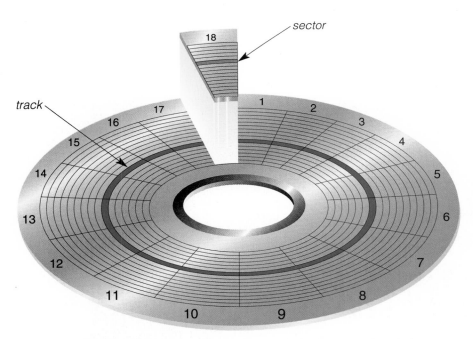

Figure 6-6 A track is a narrow recording band that forms a full circle on the surface of a disk. The disk's storage locations then are divided into pie-shaped sections, which break the tracks into small arcs called sectors. A sector can store 512 bytes of data.

multiplying together the number of sides on the disk, the number of tracks on the disk, the number of sectors per track, and the number of bytes in a sector. For example, for a typical 3.5-inch floppy disk, disk density is computed as follows: 2 (sides) x 80 (tracks) x 18 (sectors per track) x 512 (bytes per sector) = 1,474,560 bytes, or approximately 1.44 MB. The table in Figure 6-7 shows the number of sides, tracks, sectors per track, and bytes per sector for two densities of a 3.5-inch floppy disk. Most floppy disks used today are high density (storing 1.44 MB of data).

If you are using the Windows operating system, the formatting process also defines the **file allocation table (FAT)**, which is a table of information used to locate files on a disk. The FAT is like a library card catalog for your disk that contains a listing of all files, file types, and locations. If you format a disk that already contains data, instructions, or information, the formatting process erases the file location information and redefines the file allocation table for these items. The actual files on the disk, however, are not erased. For this reason, if you accidentally format a disk, you often can *unformat* it with special software.

To protect them from accidentally being erased, floppy disks have a write-protect notch. A **write-protect notch** is a small opening in the corner of the floppy disk with a tab that you slide to cover or expose the notch (Figure 6-8). The write-protect notch works much like the recording tab on a VHS tape: if the recording tab is removed, a VCR cannot record onto the VHS tape.

On a floppy disk, if the write-protect notch is exposed, or open, the drive cannot write on the floppy disk. If the write-protect notch is covered, or closed, the drive can write on the floppy disk. The write-protect notch only affects the floppy disk drive's capability of writing on the disk; a floppy disk drive can read from a floppy disk whether the write-protect notch is open or closed. Some floppy disks have a second opening on the opposite side of the disk that does not have the small tab; this opening identifies the disk as a high-density floppy disk.

TWO DENSITIES OF A 3.5-INCH FLOPPY DISK

	Double Density (DD)	High Density (HD)
Capacity	720 KB	1.44 MB
Number of sides	2	2
Number of tracks	80	80
Sectors per track	9	18
Bytes per sector	512	512
Sectors per disk	1,440	2,880

Figure 6-7 *The two densities of 3.5-inch floppy disks. Most of today's personal computers use high-density disks.*

notch open means you
cannot write on the disk

write-protected

not write-protected

notch closed means you
can write on the disk

Figure 6-8 *To protect data from being erased accidentally, floppy disks have a write-protect notch. By sliding a small tab, you can either cover or expose the notch.*

Floppy Disk Drives

As noted, a **floppy disk drive (FDD)** is a device that can read from and write on a floppy disk. Desktop personal computers usually have a floppy disk drive installed inside the system unit. Many laptop computers have removable floppy disk drives that can be replaced with other types of drives or devices, or they use an external floppy disk drive that plugs into the laptop (see Figure 6-5 on page 6.4).

If a computer has one floppy disk drive, the drive usually is designated *drive A*; if the computer has two floppy disk drives, the second one usually is designated *drive B*.

To read from or write on a floppy disk, a floppy disk drive must support that floppy disk's density. That is, to use a high-density floppy disk, you must have a high-density floppy disk drive. Floppy disk drives are **downward compatible**, which means they recognize and can use earlier media. Floppy disk drives are not **upward compatible**, however, which means they cannot recognize

Most floppy disks are preformatted by the disk's manufacturer. If you must format a floppy disk yourself, you do so by issuing a formatting command to the operating system (Figure 6-9). Because PC-compatible computers using the Windows operating system format floppy disks differently than Macintosh computers, a Macintosh computer cannot use a PC formatted floppy disk without special equipment or software. A disk drive such as the Apple Macintosh SuperDrive, however, can read from and write on both Macintosh and PC formatted floppy disks.

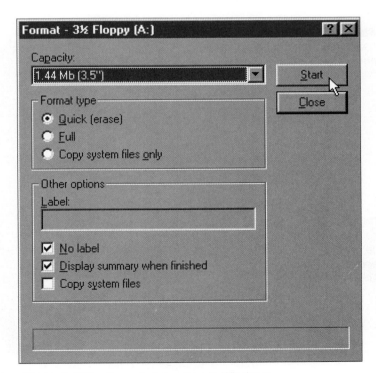

Figure 6-9 *The Format dialog box in Windows contains options to format a floppy disk.*

newer media. For example, a double-density floppy disk drive cannot read from or write on a high-density floppy disk.

On any 3.5-inch floppy disk, a piece of metal called the **shutter** covers an opening in the rigid plastic shell. When you insert a floppy disk into a floppy disk drive, the drive slides the shutter to the side to expose a portion of both sides of the floppy disk's recording surface.

The **read/write head** is the mechanism that actually reads items from or writes items on the floppy disk. Figure 6-10 illustrates the steps for reading and writing a floppy disk.

The average access time for current floppy disk drives to locate an item on the disk is 84 ms, or approximately $1/12$ of a second.

On the front of most floppy disk drives is a light emitting diode (LED) that lights up when the drive is accessing the floppy disk. You should not remove a floppy disk when the floppy disk drive is accessing the disk.

Sometimes, a floppy disk drive will malfunction when it is attempting to access a floppy disk and will display an error message on the computer's monitor screen. If the same error occurs with multiple floppy disks, the read/write heads in the floppy disk drive may have a buildup of dust or dirt. In this case, you can try cleaning the read/write heads using a floppy disk cleaning kit.

Figure 6-10
HOW A FLOPPY DISK DRIVE WORKS

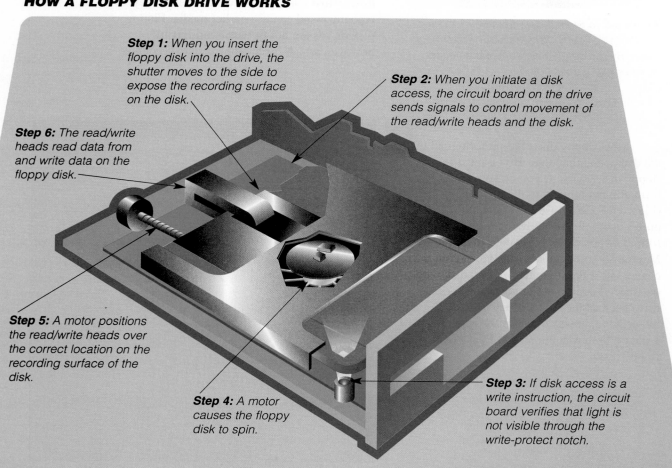

Step 1: *When you insert the floppy disk into the drive, the shutter moves to the side to expose the recording surface on the disk.*

Step 2: *When you initiate a disk access, the circuit board on the drive sends signals to control movement of the read/write heads and the disk.*

Step 6: *The read/write heads read data from and write data on the floppy disk.*

Step 5: *A motor positions the read/write heads over the correct location on the recording surface of the disk.*

Step 4: *A motor causes the floppy disk to spin.*

Step 3: *If disk access is a write instruction, the circuit board verifies that light is not visible through the write-protect notch.*

Care of Floppy Disks

With reasonable care, floppy disks can last at least seven years – providing an inexpensive and reliable form of storage. When handling a floppy disk, you should avoid exposing it to heat, cold, magnetic fields, and contaminants such as dust, smoke, or salt air. Exposure to any of these elements could damage or destroy the data, instructions, and information stored on the floppy disk. Figure 6-11 outlines some guidelines for the proper care of floppy disks.

High-Capacity Floppy Disks

Several manufacturers have high-capacity floppy disk drives that use disks with capacities of 100 MB and greater. With these high-capacity disks, you can store large files containing graphics, audio, or video; transport a large number of files from one computer to another; or make a backup of all of your important files. A **backup** is a duplicate of a file, program, or disk that can be used if the original is lost, damaged or destroyed.

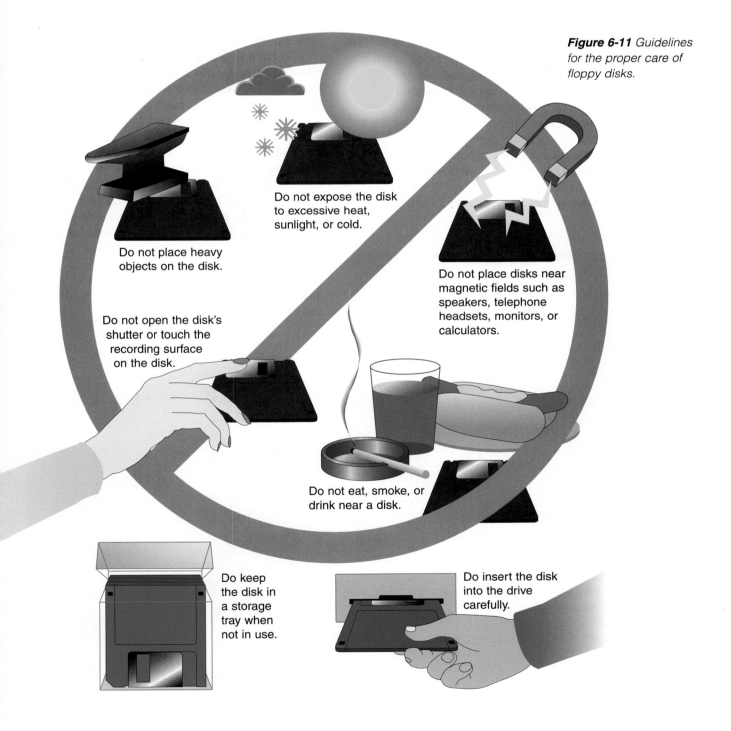

Figure 6-11 *Guidelines for the proper care of floppy disks.*

Do not place heavy objects on the disk.

Do not expose the disk to excessive heat, sunlight, or cold.

Do not open the disk's shutter or touch the recording surface on the disk.

Do not place disks near magnetic fields such as speakers, telephone headsets, monitors, or calculators.

Do not eat, smoke, or drink near a disk.

Do keep the disk in a storage tray when not in use.

Do insert the disk into the drive carefully.

A **SuperDisk™ drive** is a high-capacity disk drive developed by Imation that uses 120 MB SuperDisk™ floppy disks. Sony Electronics Inc. has developed **HiFD (High FD)**, a floppy disk drive technology that replaces existing floppy disk drives. The HiFD format uses 200 MB high-capacity floppy disks. Both the SuperDisk™ drive and the HiFD drive are downward compatible; that is, they can read from and write on standard 3.5-inch floppy disks as well as their own high-capacity disks.

Another type of disk drive is the Zip® drive. A **Zip® drive** is a special high-capacity disk drive developed by Iomega Corporation. Zip® drives use a 3.5-inch **Zip® disk**, which is slightly larger than and about twice as thick as a 3.5-inch floppy disk, and can store 100 MB of data — equivalent to about 70 high-density floppy disks. Today, many new computers are equipped with a built-in Zip® drive, so that using Zip® disks to store and transport large files is as easy as storing smaller files on a standard floppy disk. You also can add an external Zip® drive to a desktop or laptop computer (Figure 6-12).

WEB INFO
WEB INFO

For more information on a Zip® drive, visit the Discovering Computers 2000 Chapter 6 WEB INFO page (**www.scsite.com/dc2000/ch6/webinfo.htm**) and click Zip® Drives.

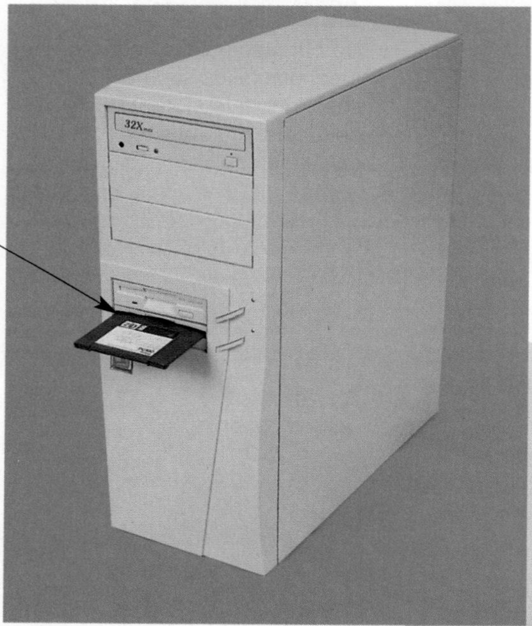

HARD DISKS

When personal computers were introduced, software programs and their related files required small amounts of storage and fit easily on floppy disks. As software became more complex and included graphical user interfaces and multimedia, file sizes and storage requirements increased. Today, hard disks — which provide far larger storage capacities and much faster access times than floppy disks — are the primary media for storing software programs and files. Current personal computer hard disks can store from 2 to 16 GB of data, instructions, and information.

A **hard disk** usually consists of several inflexible, circular disks, called platters, on which items are stored electronically. A **platter** in a hard disk is made of aluminum, glass, or ceramic and is coated with a material that allows items to be magnetically recorded on its surface. On hard disks, the platters, the read/write heads, and the mechanism for moving the heads across the surface of the disk are enclosed in an airtight, sealed case that protects the platters from contamination.

The hard disk in most desktop personal computers is housed inside the system unit. Such hard disks, which are not portable, are considered **fixed disks** (Figure 6-13). Hard disks also can be removable. Removable hard disks are discussed later in this chapter.

built-in Zip® drive

external Zip® drive

Figure 6-12 *Many new computers are equipped with a built-in Zip® drive. External Zip® drives sometimes are attached to desktop and laptop computers.*

Characteristics of a Hard Disk

Like a floppy disk, a hard disk is a type of magnetic disk that stores items using magnetic patterns. Hard disks also are read/write storage media; that is, you can both read from and write on a hard disk any number of times.

Hard disks undergo two formatting steps, and possibly a third process, called partitioning. The first format, called a **low-level format**, organizes both sides of each platter into tracks and sectors to define where items will be stored on the disk. Because a hard disk often has some bad sectors, the hard disk manufacturer usually performs the low-level format.

After low-level formatting is complete, the hard disk can be divided into separate areas called **partitions** by issuing a special operating system command. Each partition functions as if it were a separate hard disk drive. Partitioning often is performed to make hard disks more efficient (faster) or to allow you to install multiple operating systems on the same hard disk.

If a hard disk has only one partition, the hard disk usually is called, or designated, drive C. If the hard disk is divided into two partitions, the first partition is designated drive C and the second partition is designated drive D, and so on. Unless specifically requested by the consumer, most manufacturers define a single partition (drive C) on the hard disk.

After low-level formatting and partitioning, a **high-level format** command is issued through the operating system to define, among other items, the file allocation table (FAT) for each partition. Recall that the FAT is a table of information used to locate files on a disk. As with the low-level format, most hard disk manufacturers perform the high-level format for the consumer.

You can partition a hard disk yourself using special operating system commands. You then must issue a high-level format command for each partition.

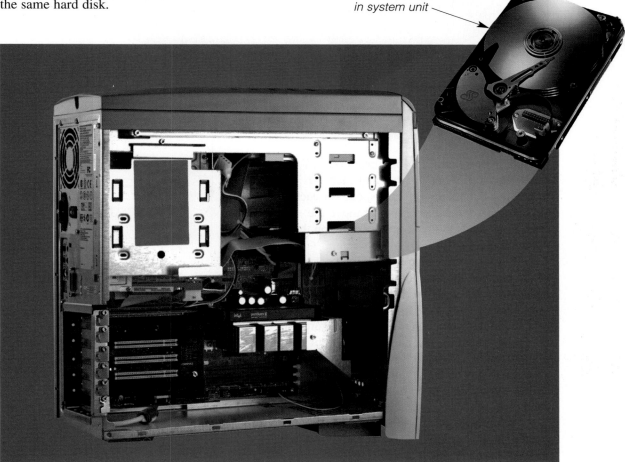

hard disk installed in system unit

Figure 6-13 *The hard disk in a desktop personal computer normally is housed permanently inside the system unit; that is, it is not portable.*

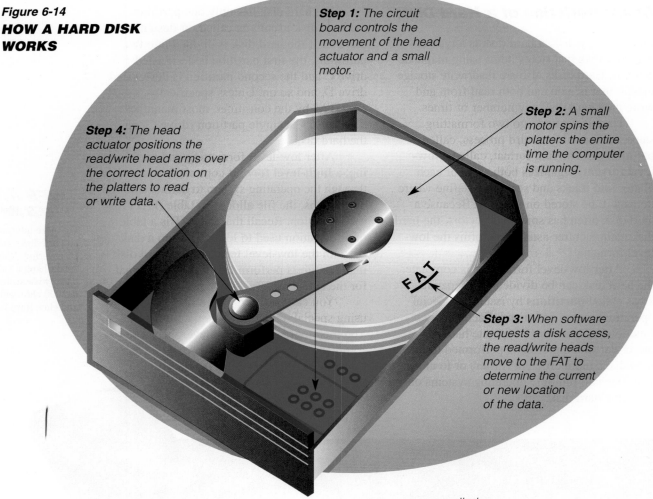

Figure 6-14

HOW A HARD DISK WORKS

Step 1: The circuit board controls the movement of the head actuator and a small motor.

Step 2: A small motor spins the platters the entire time the computer is running.

Step 4: The head actuator positions the read/write head arms over the correct location on the platters to read or write data.

Step 3: When software requests a disk access, the read/write heads move to the FAT to determine the current or new location of the data.

How a Hard Disk Works

Most hard disks have multiple platters stacked on top of one another and each platter has two read/write heads, one for each side. The hard disk has arms that move the read/write heads to the proper location on the platter (Figure 6-14).

Because of the stacked arrangement of the platters, the location of the read/write heads often is referred to by its cylinder instead of its track. A **cylinder** is the location of a single track through all platters (Figure 6-15). For example, if a hard disk has four platters (eight sides), each with 1,000 tracks, then it will have 1,000 cylinders with each cylinder consisting of eight tracks (two for each platter).

While your computer is running, the platters in the hard disk rotate at a high rate of speed, usually 3,600 to 7,200 revolutions per minute. The platters continue spinning until power is removed from the computer.

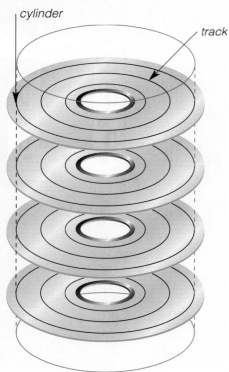

Figure 6-15 A cylinder is the location of a single track through all platters on a hard disk.

The spinning motion creates a cushion of air between the platter and its read/write head so the read/write head floats above the platter instead of making direct contact with the platter surface. The distance between the read/write head and the platter is approximately two millionths of an inch.

As shown in Figure 6-16, this close clearance leaves no room for any type of contamination. If contamination is introduced, the hard disk can have a head crash. A **head crash** occurs when a read/write head touches the surface of a platter, usually resulting in a loss of data or sometimes loss of the entire drive. Today's hard disks are built to withstand shocks and are sealed tightly to keep out contaminants, which means head crashes are less likely to occur.

Access time for today's hard disks ranges from eight to fifteen milliseconds. Access time for a hard disk is significantly faster than for a floppy disk for two reasons: (1) a hard disk spins much faster than a floppy disk and (2) a hard disk spins constantly, while a floppy disk starts spinning only when it receives a read or write command.

Some computers are able to improve the hard disk access time by using disk caching. **Disk cache** is a portion of memory that the CPU uses to store frequently accessed items (Figure 6-17). Disk cache works similarly to memory cache. When a program needs data, instructions, or information, the CPU checks

the disk cache. If the item is located in disk cache, the CPU uses that item and completes the process. If the CPU does not find the requested item in the disk cache, then the CPU must wait for the hard disk drive to locate and transfer the item from the disk to the CPU.

Some disk caching systems also attempt to predict what data, instructions, or information might be needed next and place them into cache before they are requested. Because disk caching significantly improves disk access times, almost all new disk drives work with some amount of disk cache.

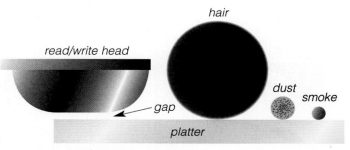

Figure 6-16 *Because the gap between a disk read/write head and the platter is so small, contaminants such as a smoke particle, dust particle, or human hair could render the drive unusable.*

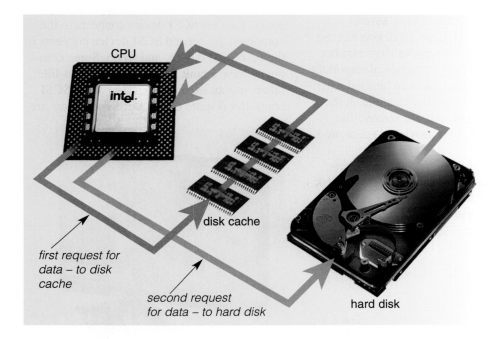

Figure 6-17 *When a program needs an item, the CPU checks the disk cache. If the item is located, the CPU uses it. If the CPU does not find the item in the disk cache, then the CPU must wait for the disk drive to locate and transfer the data from the disk.*

Removable Hard Disks

As noted, some hard disks are removable, which means they can be inserted and removed from a hard disk drive, much like a floppy disk. A **removable hard disk** or **disk cartridge** is a disk drive in which hard disks are enclosed in plastic or metal cases so they can be removed from the drive (Figure 6-18). A popular, reasonably priced, removable hard disk is the **Jaz**® **disk** by Iomega, which can store up to two gigabytes (GB) of data, instructions, and information.

Figure 6-18 *The Jaz® disk by Iomega is a removable hard disk with a capacity of up to 2 GB.*

Portable media, such as floppy disks and other removable disks, have several advantages over fixed disks. First, you can use a removable disk to transport a large number of files or to make backup copies of important files. Also, removable disks can be used when data security is an issue. For example, at the end of a work session, you can remove the hard disk and lock it up, leaving no data on the computer.

Networks, minicomputers, and mainframe computers often use disk packs. A **disk pack** is a collection of removable hard disks mounted in the same cabinet as the computer or enclosed in a large stand-alone cabinet.

Hard Disk Controllers

The flow of data, instructions, and information to and from a disk is managed by a special-purpose chip and its associated electronic circuits called the **disk controller**. Because a disk controller controls the transfer of items from the disk to the rest of the computer, it often is referred to as a type of interface.

A controller for a hard disk is called a **hard disk controller (HDC)**. On a personal computer, the hard disk controller either is built into the disk drive or is a separate expansion card that plugs into an expansion slot. Two types of hard disk controllers for personal computers are IDE and SCSI.

IDE The most widely used controllers, or interfaces, for hard disks are Integrated Drive Electronics (IDE) controllers. **Integrated Drive Electronics** (**IDE**) controllers support one or two hard disks with capacities up to 14 GB and can transfer data, instructions, and information to the disk at rates of up to 33 MB per second. IDE controllers also are referred to as **ATA**, short for the **AT Attachment**, that integrates the controller into the disk drive. Many versions of ATA exist, including ATA, ATA-4, Ultra ATA, Ultra DMA, and ATA/66.

SCSI **Small computer system interface**, or **SCSI**, (pronounced scuzzy) controllers can support multiple disk drives, as well as other peripherals such as scanners and printers. When using SCSI devices, you can daisy chain a total of seven devices together, which means the first SCSI device connects to the computer, the second SCSI device connects to the first SCSI device, and so on. Some computers have a built in SCSI controller, while others use an expansion card to add a SCSI controller (Figure 6-19). SCSI controllers are

Figure 6-19 *A SCSI expansion card.*

faster and have greater storage capacities than EIDE controllers, providing up to 100 MB per second transfer rates and supporting hard disks with storage capacities up to 25 GB. SCSI controllers, however, are more expensive than EIDE controllers. As with ATA, many versions of SCSI exist, including SCSI-3, Wide SCSI, Fast SCSI, and Ultra2 SCSI.

RAID

For networks and other applications that depend on reliable data access, it is crucial that the data is available when a user attempts to access it. For these applications, some manufacturers developed a type of hard disk system that connects several smaller disks into a single unit that acts like a single large hard disk. A group of two or more integrated hard disks is called a **RAID (redundant array of independent disks)**. Although quite expensive, RAID is more reliable than traditional disks and thus often is used with network and Internet servers (Figure 6-20).

Reliability is improved with RAID through the duplication of data, instructions, and information. This duplication is implemented in different ways, depending on the RAID storage design, or level, used. (These levels are not hierarchical; that is, higher levels are not necessarily better than lower levels.) The simplest RAID storage design is **level 1**, called **mirroring**, which has one backup disk

Figure 6-20 *A group of two or more integrated hard disks, called a RAID (redundant array of independent disks), often is used with network servers.*

WEB INFO

For more information on RAID, visit the Discovering Computers 2000 Chapter 6 WEB INFO page (**www.scsite.com/dc2000/ch6/webinfo.htm**) and click RAID.

for each disk (Figure 6-21a). A level 1 configuration enhances system reliability because, if a drive should fail, a duplicate of the requested item is available elsewhere within the array of disks.

Levels beyond level 1 use a technique called **striping**, which splits data, instructions, and information across multiple disks in the array (Figure 6-21b). Striping improves disk access times, but does not offer data duplication. For this reason, some RAID levels combine both mirroring and striping.

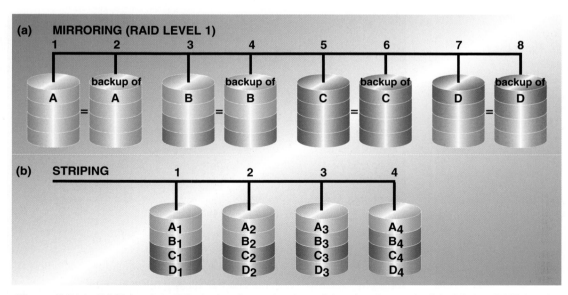

Figure 6-21 *In RAID level 1, called mirroring, a backup disk exists for each disk. Higher RAID levels use striping; that is, portions of each disk are placed on multiple disks.*

Maintaining Data Stored on a Hard Disk

Most manufacturers guarantee their hard disks to last somewhere between three and five years, although many last much longer with proper care. To prevent the loss of items stored on a hard disk, you should perform preventative maintenance such as defragmenting or scanning the disk for errors. As outlined in the table in Figure 6-22, operating systems such as Windows provide many maintenance and monitoring utilities. These and other utilities are discussed in more depth in Chapter 8.

COMPACT DISCS

In the past, when you purchased off-the-shelf software, you received one or more floppy disks that contained the files needed to install or run the software program. As software programs became more and more complex, the number of floppy disks required to store the programs increased, sometimes exceeding thirty disks. These more complex programs required a larger storage medium, which is why many of today's software programs are distributed on compact discs.

A **compact disc (CD)** is a flat, round, portable, metal storage medium that usually is 4.75 inches in diameter and less than one-twentieth of an inch thick (Figure 6-23). Compact disks store items such as data, instructions, and information by using

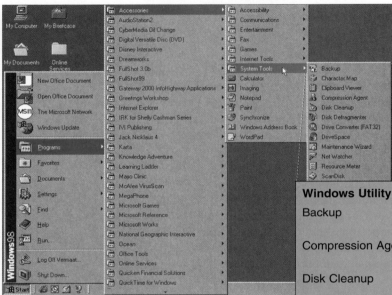

System Tools menu

Figure 6-22 *Windows provides many maintenance and monitoring utilities on the System Tools submenu. The table in this figure briefly describes each of these utilities.*

Windows Utility	Function
Backup	Creates a copy of files on a hard disk in case the original is damaged or destroyed.
Compression Agent	Recompresses files according to settings in DriveSpace (see below).
Disk Cleanup	Frees up space on a hard disk by listing files that can be deleted safely.
Disk Defragmenter	Reorganizes files and unused space on a hard disk so programs run faster.
Drive Converter (FAT 32)	Improves the FAT method of storing data, which frees up hard disk space and makes programs load faster.
DriveSpace	Compresses a hard disk or floppy disk to create free space on the disk.
Maintenance Wizard	Runs utilities that optimize your computer's performance.
Net Watcher	Monitors users and disk/file usage when computers are networked.
Resource Meter	Monitors system, user, and graphics resources being used by programs.
ScanDisk	Detects errors on a disk and then repairs the damaged areas.
Scheduled Tasks	Automatically runs a utility at a specified time.
System Monitor	Monitors disk access, the processor, memory, and network usage.

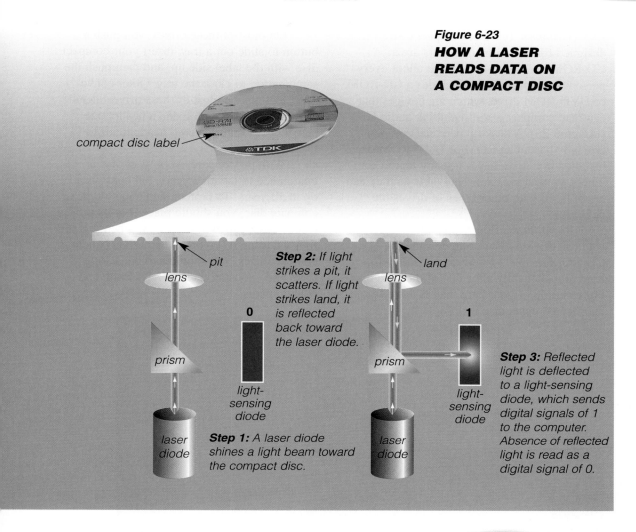

Figure 6-23

HOW A LASER READS DATA ON A COMPACT DISC

compact disc label

pit

lens

Step 2: If light strikes a pit, it scatters. If light strikes land, it is reflected back toward the laser diode.

land

lens

0

prism

light-sensing diode

1

prism

Step 3: Reflected light is deflected to a light-sensing diode, which sends digital signals of 1 to the computer. Absence of reflected light is read as a digital signal of 0.

light-sensing diode

laser diode

Step 1: A laser diode shines a light beam toward the compact disc.

laser diode

microscopic pits (indentations) and land (flat areas) that are in the middle layer of the disc. (Most manufacturers place a silk-screened label on the top layer of the disc so you can identify it.) A high-powered laser light creates the pits. A lower-powered laser light reads items from the compact disc by reflecting light through the bottom of the disc, which usually is either solid gold or silver in color. The reflected light is converted into a series of bits that the computer can process. Land causes light to reflect, which is read as binary digit 1. Pits absorb the light; this absence of light is read as binary digit 0.

A compact disc stores items in a single track that spirals from the center of the disc to the edge of the disc. As with a hard disk, this single track is divided into evenly sized sectors in which items are stored (Figure 6-24).

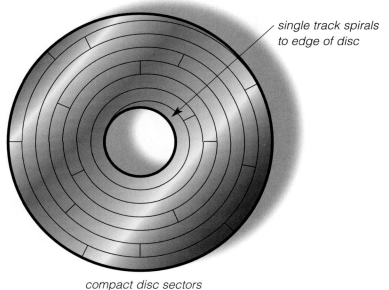

single track spirals to edge of disc

compact disc sectors

Figure 6-24 The data on a compact disc is stored in a single track that spirals from the center of the disc to the edge of the disc; this track is divided into evenly sized sectors.

Two basic types of compact discs designed for use with computers are a CD-ROM and DVD-ROM. Just about every personal computer today includes a CD-ROM or DVD-ROM drive, which are devices that can read compact discs, including audio CDs (Figure 6-25). A desktop personal computer typically has a CD-ROM or DVD-ROM drive installed in a drive bay; on many laptop computers, these drives are removable so they can be replaced with other types of drives or devices.

Recall that a floppy disk drive is designated as drive A. The drive designation of a CD-ROM or DVD-ROM drive usually follows alphabetically after that of the hard disk. For example, if your hard disk is drive C, then the compact disc is drive D.

On most of these drives, you push a button to slide out a tray, insert your compact disc with the label side up, and then push the same button to close the tray. Other convenient features on most of these drives include a volume control button and a headphone jack so you can use stereo headphones to listen to audio.

With proper care, a compact disc is guaranteed to last five years, but could last up to 50 years. To protect data on any type of compact disc, you should place it in its protective case, called a **jewel box**, when you are finished using it (Figure 6-26). When handling compact discs, you should avoid stacking them and exposing them to heat, cold, and contaminants.

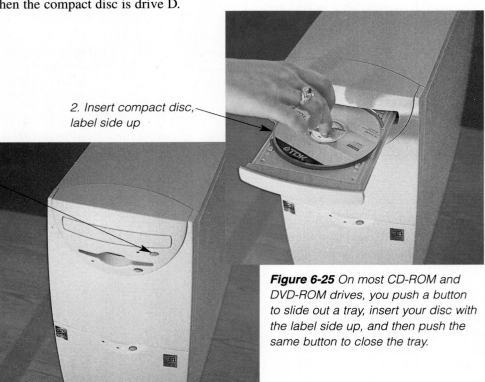

2. Insert compact disc, label side up

1. Push a button to slide out a tray

Figure 6-25 On most CD-ROM and DVD-ROM drives, you push a button to slide out a tray, insert your disc with the label side up, and then push the same button to close the tray.

Figure 6-26 To protect data on a compact disc, you should place it in a jewel box when you are finished using it.

Figure 6-27 outlines some guidelines for the proper care of compact discs. You can clean the bottom surface of a compact disc with a soft cloth and warm water or a specialized CD cleaning kit, but never clean the label side because this may destroy the data. You also can repair scratches on the bottom surface with a specialized CD repair kit.

Compact discs are available in a variety of formats. The following sections discuss two basic types used with personal computers: CD-ROMs and DVD-ROMs.

CD-ROMs

A **CD-ROM** (pronounced SEE-DEE-rom, which is an abbreviation for **compact disc read-only memory**) is a silver-colored compact disc that uses the same laser technology as audio CDs for recording music. Unlike an audio CD, a CD-ROM can contain text, graphics, and video, as well as sound. The contents of standard CD-ROMs are written, or **recorded**, by the manufacturer and only can be read and used. That is, they cannot be erased or modified — hence, the name read-only.

Figure 6-27 *Guidelines for the proper care of compact discs.*

Do not expose the disc to excessive heat or sunlight.

Do not touch the underside of the disc.

Do not eat, smoke, or drink near a disc.

Do not write on the label side of the disc.

Do not stack discs.

Do store the disc in a jewel box when not in use.

Do hold a disc by its edges.

For a computer to read items on a CD-ROM, you must place it into a **CD-ROM drive** or **CD-ROM player**. Because audio CDs and CD-ROMs use the same laser technology, you also can use your CD-ROM drive to listen to an audio CD while working on your computer.

A CD-ROM can hold nearly 700 MB of data, instructions, and information, or about 450 times that which can be stored on a high-density 3.5-inch floppy disk. Because CD-ROMs have such high storage capacities, they are used to store and distribute today's complex software (Figure 6-28). Some programs even require that the disc be in the drive each time you use the program.

Figure 6-28a (encyclopedia)

Figure 6-28b (word processing)

Figure 6-28c (flight simulator)

Figure 6-28 CD-ROMs are used to store and distribute multimedia and other complex software.

CD-ROM DRIVE SPEED The speed of a CD-ROM drive is extremely important when viewing animation or video such as those found in multimedia encyclopedias and games. A slower CD-ROM drive will result in choppy images or sound. A CD-ROM drive's speed is measured by its **data transfer rate**, which is the time it takes the drive to transmit data, instructions, and information from the CD-ROM to another device.

The original CD-ROM drive was a single-speed drive with a data transfer rate of 150 KB per second. All subsequent CD-ROM drives have been measured relative to this first CD-ROM drive and use an X to denote the original transfer rate of 150 KB per second. For example, a 16X CD-ROM drive has a data transfer rate of 2,400 (16 x 150) KB per second or 2.4 MB per second. Current CD-ROM drives have speeds ranging from 40X to 75X. The higher the number, the faster the CD-ROM drive, which results in smoother playback of images and sounds. Faster CD-ROM drives, however, are more expensive than slower drives.

CD-ROM VARIATIONS Three variations of the standard CD-ROM are the PhotoCD, the recordable CD, and the rewriteable CD. These CD-ROMs typically are **multisession**, which means additional data, instructions, and information can be written to the disc at a later time. (Most standard CD-ROMs are called **single-session** because all items must be written to the disc at the time it is manufactured.)

- Based on a file format developed by Eastman Kodak, a **PhotoCD** is a compact disc that only contains digital photographic images saved in the PhotoCD format. You can purchase PhotoCDs that already contain pictures or you can have your own pictures or negatives recorded on a PhotoCD so that you have digital versions of your photographs. The images on a PhotoCD can be printed, faxed, sent via electronic mail, included in another document, or posted to a Web site for everyone to see. Many film developers offer this service when you drop off film to be developed (Figure 6-29).

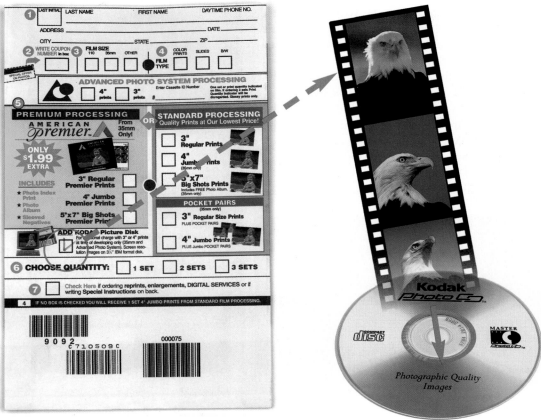

Figure 6-29 *Many film developers offer a PhotoCD service when you drop off film to be developed.*

WEB INFO
WEB INFO

For more information
on DVD-ROMs, visit the
Discovering Computers
2000 Chapter 6 WEB INFO
page (**www.scsite.com/
dc2000/ch6/webinfo.htm**)
and click DVD-ROMs.

- **CD-R (compact disc-recordable)** is a technology that allows you to write on a compact disc using your own computer. Whereas the disc's manufacturer records the data, instructions, and information on a standard CD-ROM, you record your own items onto a CD-R (compact disc-recordable). You can write on the disc in stages – writing on part of it one time and writing on another part at a later time. You can, however, write on each part only once. Once you have recorded the CD-R, you can read from it as many times as you wish. To differentiate them from silver-colored read-only compact discs, CD-R discs are gold-colored. In order to write on a CD-R, you must have CD-R software and a CD-R drive. A **CD-R drive** can read and write both audio CDs and standard CD-ROMs. While CD-R drives are somewhat more expensive than standard CD-ROM drives, their price continues to drop.

- A **CD-RW (compact disc-rewritable)** is an erasable disc that you can write on multiple times. CD-RW overcomes one of the disadvantages of CD-R disks — that you can write on them only once. With CD-RW, the disk acts like a floppy or hard disk, allowing you to write data, instructions, and information onto it multiple times. To write on a CD-RW disc, you must have CD-RW software and a CD-RW drive. The speed of these drives is quite slow, and they are not downward compatible with many standard CD-ROMs. For this reason, many believe that most users will wait for DVD technology to become less expensive, instead of purchasing CD-RW drives.

DVD-ROMs

Although CD-ROMs have huge storage capacities, even a CD-ROM is not large enough for many of today's complex programs. Some software, for example, is sold on five or more CD-ROMs. To meet these tremendous storage requirements, some software moved from CD-ROMs to the larger DVD-ROM format — a technology that can be used to store video items, such as motion pictures (Figure 6-30). A **DVD-ROM (digital video disc-ROM)** is an extremely high capacity compact disc capable of storing from 4.7 GB to 17 GB — more than enough to hold a telephone book containing every resident in the United States. Not only is the storage capacity of a DVD-ROM greater than a CD-ROM, a DVD-ROM's quality also far surpasses that of a CD-ROM. In order to read a DVD-ROM, you must have a **DVD-ROM drive** or DVD player. These drives can also read CD-ROMs.

DVD-ROM

DVD-ROM drive

DVD player

Figure 6-30 *A DVD-ROM is an extremely high capacity compact disc capable of storing 4.7 GB to 17 GB.*

At a glance, a DVD-ROM looks just like a CD-ROM. Although the size and shape are similar, a DVD-ROM stores data, instructions, and information in a slightly different manner and thus achieves a higher storage capacity. A DVD-ROM uses one of three storage techniques. The first technique involves making the disc more dense by packing the pits closer together. A second technique involves using two layers of pits. For this technique to work, the lower layer of pits is semitransparent so the laser can read through it to the upper layer. This technique doubles the capacity of the disc. Finally, some DVD-ROMs are double-sided, which means you must remove the DVD-ROM and turn it over to read the other side. The storage capacities of various types of DVD-ROMs are shown in the table in Figure 6-31.

DVD VARIATIONS DVDs are available in a variety of formats, one of which stores video such as digital movies and/or audio such as music. To view a movie that has been stored on a DVD, you insert the DVD into a DVD player that is connected to your television set, somewhat like the VCR you use to play VHS tapes. Movies on DVD have near-studio-quality video, which far surpasses VHS tapes. When music is stored on a DVD, it includes surround sound and has a much better quality than audio CDs.

As with compact discs, you can obtain recordable and rewritable versions of DVD. With a recordable DVD, you can write once on it and read (play) it many times. With a rewritable version of a DVD, you can erase and record on it multiple times. As the cost of DVD technologies becomes more reasonable, many industry professionals expect that DVD eventually will replace compact discs.

TAPES

One of the first storage media used with mainframe computers was **magnetic tape**, a magnetically coated ribbon of plastic capable of storing large amounts of data and information at a low cost. Tape storage requires **sequential access**, which refers to reading or writing data consecutively. Like a music tape, you must forward or rewind the tape to a specific point to access a specific piece of data.

DVD-ROM STORAGE CAPACITIES

Number of sides	1	1	2	2
Number of layers	1	2	1	2
Storage capacity	4.7 GB	8.5 GB	9.4 GB	17 GB

Figure 6-31 *Storage capacities of DVD-ROMs.*

For example, to access item W, you must pass sequentially through points A through V. Floppy disks, hard disks, and compact discs all use **direct access**, or **random access**, which means you can locate a particular data item or file immediately, without having to move consecutively through items stored in front of the desired data item or file. Because sequential access is much slower than direct access, tapes are no longer used as a primary method of storage. Instead, tapes are used most often for long-term storage and backup.

Similar to a tape recorder, a **tape drive** is used to read from and write data and information onto a tape. Although older computers used reel-to-reel tape drives, today's tape drives use tape cartridges. A **tape cartridge** is a small, rectangular, plastic housing for tape (Figure 6-32). Tape cartridges containing one-quarter-inch wide tape are slightly larger than audiocassette tapes and frequently are used for personal computer backup.

WEB INFO

For more information on tapes, visit the Discovering Computers 2000 Chapter 6 WEB INFO page (**www.scsite.com/ dc2000/ch6/webinfo.htm**) and click Tapes.

Figure 6-32 *Tape cartridges are an inexpensive, reliable form of storage often used for personal computer backup.*

Some personal computers have permanently mounted tape drives, while others have external units (Figure 6-33). On larger computers, tape cartridges are mounted in a separate cabinet (Figure 6-34).

Three common types of tape drives are QIC, DAT, and DLT, which is the fastest and most expensive of the three. The table in Figure 6-35 summarizes each of these tapes.

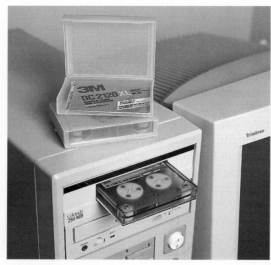

Figure 6-33 *Some personal computers have permanently mounted tape drives, while others have external units.*

PC CARDS

As discussed in Chapter 3, a **PC Card** is a thin, credit card-sized device that fits into a PC Card expansion slot on a personal computer. Different types and sizes of PC Cards are used to add storage, additional memory, communications, and sound capabilities to a computer. PC Cards most often are used with laptops and other portable computers (Figure 6-36). Some digital cameras also use PC Cards, sometimes called **picture cards** or **compact flash card**s, to store pictures, which are then transferred to a computer by inserting the card into the computer's PC Card slot.

Figure 6-34 *On larger computers, tape cartridges are mounted in a separate cabinet.*

POPULAR TYPES OF TAPES

Name	Abbreviation	Storage Capacity
Quarter-inch cartridge	QIC	40 MB to 5 GB
Digital audio tape	DAT	2 to 24 GB
Digital linear tape	DLT	20 to 40 GB

Figure 6-35 *Common types of tapes.*

Figure 6-36 *PC Cards normally are used with laptops and other portable computers.*

PC Cards are available in three types, which are designated Type I, Type II, and Type III. The thicker **Type III cards** are used to house hard disks and currently have storage capacities of more than 520 MB (Figure 6-37). The advantage of a PC Card hard disk is portability; that is, you easily can transport large amounts of data, instructions, and information from one machine to another. Type I and Type II cards are used to add memory or communications capabilities to a computer, are discussed in other chapters.

OTHER TYPES OF STORAGE

Although the majority of data, instructions, and information are stored on floppy disk, hard disk, compact disc, tape, and PC Cards, other more specialized means for storing these items also are used. These include smart cards and microfilm and microfiche. Each of these media is discussed in the following sections.

Smart Cards

A **smart card**, which is similar in size to a credit card or ATM card, stores data on a thin microprocessor embedded in the card (Figure 6-38). Two types of smart cards exist: intelligent and memory. An **intelligent smart card** contains a CPU and has input, process, output, and storage capabilities. In contrast, a **memory card** has only storage capabilities. When the smart card is inserted into a specialized card reader, the information on the smart card is read and, if necessary, updated.

WEB INFO

For more information on smart cards, visit the Discovering Computers 2000 Chapter 6 WEB INFO page (**www.scsite.com/dc2000/ch6/webinfo.htm**) and click Smart Cards.

Figure 6-37 *This Type III PC Card is a hard disk with 520 MB of storage space.*

front of card

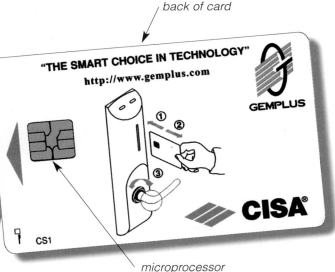

back of card

microprocessor

Figure 6-38 *Many hotels issue smart cards instead of keys to hotel guests. With the smart card, guests gain access to their rooms as well as hotel services such as cafeterias, swimming pools, lockers, and parking lots.*

WEB INFO
WEB INFO

For more information on e-money, visit the Discovering Computers 2000 Chapter 6 WEB INFO page (www.scsite.com/dc2000/ch6/webinfo.htm) and click E-money.

One popular use of smart cards is to store a prepaid dollar amount, as in a prepaid telephone calling card. You receive the card with a specific dollar amount stored in the microprocessor. Each time you use the card, the available amount of money is reduced. Using these cards provides convenience to the caller, eliminates the telephone company's need to collect coins from telephones, and reduces vandalism of pay telephones. Other uses of smart cards include storing patient records, vaccination data, and other health-care information; tracking information such as customer purchases or employee attendance; and storing a prepaid amount, such as electronic money.

Electronic money (e-money), also called **digital cash**, is a means of paying for goods and services over the Internet. A bank issues unique digital cash numbers that represent an amount of money. When you purchase digital cash, the amount of money is withdrawn from your bank account. One implementation of e-money places the digital cash on a smart card. To use the card, you swipe it through a card reader on your computer or one that is attached to your computer (Figure 6-39).

Microfilm and Microfiche

Microfilm and microfiche are used to store microscopic images of documents on roll or sheet film (Figure 6-40). **Microfilm** uses a 100- to 215-foot roll of film. **Microfiche** uses a small sheet of film, usually about four inches by six inches. The images are recorded onto the film using a device called a **computer output microfilm (COM) recorder**. The stored images are so small they can be read only with a microfilm or microfiche reader.

Figure 6-39 *To use a smart card to pay for products and services over the Internet, you swipe the card through a card reader connected to your computer.*

Figure 6-40 *Microfilm and microfiche are used to store microscopic images of documents on roll or sheet film.*

Applications of microfilm and microfiche are widespread. Libraries use these media to store back issues of newspapers, magazines, and genealogy records. Large organizations use microfilm and microfiche to archive inactive files. Banks, for example, use it to store transactions and cancelled checks, and the U.S. Army uses it to store personnel records. Using microfilm and microfiche provides a number of advantages: it greatly reduces the amount of paper firms must handle; it is inexpensive; and it has the longest life of any storage medium (Figure 6-41).

PUTTING IT ALL TOGETHER

Many factors influence the type of storage devices you should use: the amount of data, instructions, and information to be stored; the hardware and software in use; and the desired cost. The table in Figure 6-42 outlines several suggested storage devices for various types of computer users.

MEDIA LIFE EXPECTANCIES

Media Type	Guaranteed Life Expectancy	Potential Life Expectancy
Tape	2 to 5 years	20 years
Compact disc	5 years	50 years
Microfilm	100 years	200 years

Figure 6-41 *Microfilm is the medium with the longest life.*

SUGGESTED STORAGE DEVICES BY USER

USER	STORAGE DEVICE
Home User	• 3.5-inch high-density floppy disk drive • 100 MB Zip® drive • 8 GB hard disk • DVD-ROM drive or 24X CD-ROM drive
SMALL BUSINESS USER	• 3.5-inch high-density floppy disk drive • 16 GB hard disk • DVD-ROM drive or 40X CD-ROM drive • 2 GB Jaz® drive
MOBILE USER	• 3.5-inch high-density floppy disk drive • 8 GB hard disk • 520 MB PC Card hard disk • DVD-ROM drive or 24X CD-ROM drive
LARGE BUSINESS USER	• 3.5-inch high-density floppy disk drive • Tape drive • 16 GB hard disk • DVD-ROM drive or 40X CD-ROM drive • Smart card reader • Microfilm or microfiche • RAID
POWER USER	• 3.5-inch high-density floppy disk drive • 16 GB hard disk • DVD-ROM drive or 40X CD-ROM drive • 2 GB Jaz® drive

Figure 6-42 *This table recommends suggested storage devices.*

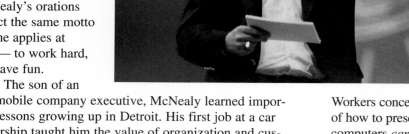

TECHNOLOGY TRAILBLAZER

SCOTT McNEALY

Scott McNealy — chairman of the board, president, and CEO of Sun Microsystems — is a sought-after speaker. His talks are laced with humor, insight, and controversy, causing listeners to rethink their opinions about the computer industry. In short, McNealy's orations reflect the same motto that he applies at Sun — to work hard, but have fun.

The son of an automobile company executive, McNealy learned important lessons growing up in Detroit. His first job at a car dealership taught him the value of organization and customer satisfaction. He also discovered that, in addition to superior technology, successful companies need vision and the knowledge of how to market their products. These lessons would be guiding principles for McNealy, who claims he would trade all he was taught in college for everything he learned working at the car dealership in the Motor City. A wealthy man today, McNealy still drives "good ol' Deeeeetroit iron."

Despite what he says, it is obvious that McNealy reaped the benefits of his schooling — earning a bachelor's degree at Harvard and an MBA at Stanford, with a concentration in manufacturing. After graduation, he worked in middle management at several companies. In 1982, former schoolmate Vinod Khosla asked McNealy to join him in forming a company to build engineering workstations in the network computer model. Together with Andreas Bechtolsheim and Bill Joy, Khosla and McNealy founded Sun Microsystems, Inc., a company that would work closely with the Stanford University Network (hence, the *SUN* in Sun Microsystems).

Company growth was rapid. The first Sun system, SUN 1, was built with inexpensive, readily available components and the UNIX operating system. In 1983, Sun and Computervision began to work together to develop and manufacture new workstation products.

Although McNealy had little technical expertise, he could envision and sell ideas and products. When appointed company president in 1984, McNealy championed his latest vision for Sun: "the network is the computer." According to McNealy, "[the personal computer] is a personal activity generator," McNealy says. "It was a brilliant stroke to call it a personal productivity tool." As an example, McNealy cites his own belief that productivity increased when presentation graphics software was banned at Sun. Workers concentrated on what they were producing instead of how to present it. He further states that, even if personal computers *can* improve individual productivity, networked workstations allow groups of people to work together, thus increasing overall productivity.

It is an idea that is working. By 1988, Sun became the fastest-growing computer company in history, reaching $1 billion in revenues just six years after its founding. By 1992, Sun was the world's second most profitable company. Today, Sun employs more than 17,000 people and has revenues of more than $8.5 billion.

One of Sun's key innovations is Java. Java combines two of Sun's founding principles: network computing and open systems that make software and information portable. Java is the first universal programming language designed to let developers write user-friendly applications that will run on any computer. "The problem with personal computers today," insists McNealy, "is that incompatible systems make it difficult to share information." According to McNealy, "Java is the way for everybody to share the technology they invent, to share the information they publish, and to provide an interactivity that has never been there before."

McNealy knows that not everyone accepts his, or Sun's, vision. "I want Sun to be controversial. If everyone believes in your strategy you have zero chance of profit." In the future, McNealy thinks network computers will replace the world of personal computers we know today. "I am a firm believer that my little boy is going to come to me some day and say, 'Daddy, you *really* had a computer in your home? Why?'"

COMPANY ON THE CUTTING EDGE

COMPANY ON THE CUTTING EDGE

SILICON GRAPHICS

The oldest and most celebrated event in international sailing is the series of races known as the America's Cup. Since 1851, when the sloop *America* brought home the first United States victory, U.S. ships have dominated the America's Cup. Now, a team from New Zealand has joined the short list of non-American winners using a new tool — networked computer workstations from Silicon Graphics, Inc.

Designing a winning racing yacht has been an exacting, expensive, and time-consuming process of trial and error. Team New Zealand, however, saved time and money by using Silicon Graphics's workstations and servers to test yacht designs under a range of conditions, do structural analysis simulations, and provide design corroboration before prototypes were built. "Our yachts are going faster than ever before because of this program," says the syndicate head for Team New Zealand. "New design ideas can be tested literally overnight and implemented as early as the next series of races."

Silicon Graphics, Inc. is a leading manufacturer of high-performance visual computing systems ranging from desktop workstations to servers and supercomputers. Dr. James Clark, an associate professor at Stanford University, and six graduate students founded the company in 1982. The firm was based on Clark's idea for a chip that would speed a computer's capability of displaying three-dimensional graphics. In 1983, Silicon Graphics shipped its first graphics terminals. The company released its first workstations one-year later and introduced its first RISC workstations in 1987.

In the 1990s, mergers resulted in two new Silicon Graphics subsidiaries, thus expanding the company's horizons. Alias|Wavefront became a leading innovator in graphics technology, creating software for markets including film, video games, interactive media, and industrial design. Cray Research, Inc. placed its focus on supercomputing technologies used for weather forecasts, molecular modeling, new car design, and hazardous waste site cleanup.

Silicon Graphics's first venture into the general consumer marketplace took place in 1993 — the result of an agreement with Nintendo to create the Nintendo 64™ video game system. The *Reality Immersion Technology* combined Silicon Graphics's digital media and computing technologies with MIPS microprocessor technology to power a highly realistic gaming experience. In 1998,

Silicon Graphics expanded its presence in the consumer marketplace through an alliance with Microsoft Corp. aimed at increasing graphics capabilities for a variety of customers.

Over the years, Silicon Graphics has pioneered four core technologies: graphics innovations for workstations, servers, and supercomputers; symmetric multiprocessing that optimizes the performance of applications; RISC CPUs based on the MIPS architecture; and digital media that integrates 3-D graphics, animation, and text with video, audio, and videoconferencing capabilities.

Today, Silicon Graphics is developing Internet and Web technologies. The company offers systems for Web server setup and Web page authoring packages designed for use with workstations. Silicon Graphics hopes to challenge Sun Microsystems's Solaris™ software (another proprietary version of UNIX) Internet servers for a larger portion of the Web server market.

With 10,300 employees worldwide and revenues of $3.1 billion for fiscal year 1998, Silicon Graphics is a major player in the computer industry. The company name may be less well known to the general public, but in recent years, its creations have become uncomfortably familiar to millions of movie-goers with its production of the life-like, computer-generated monsters in movies including *The Lost World* and *Godzilla*.

CHAPTER 1 2 3 4 5 **6** 7 8 9 10 11 12 13 14 **INDEX**

IN BRIEF www.scsite.com/dc2000/ch6/brief.htm

WEB INSTRUCTIONS: *To display this page from the Web, launch your browser and enter the URL,* *www.scsite.com/dc2000/ch6/brief.htm*. *Click the links for current and additional information. To listen to an audio version of this IN BRIEF, click the Audio button to the right of the title, IN BRIEF, at the top of the page. To play the audio, RealPlayer must be installed on your computer (download by clicking* here).

 ## 1. How Is Storage Different from Memory?

Memory, which is composed of one or more chips on the motherboard, holds data and instructions while they are being processed by the CPU. Storage holds items such as data, instructions, and information for future use.

 ## 2. What Are Storage Media and Storage Devices?

A **storage medium** (media is the plural) is the physical material on which items are kept. A **storage device** is the mechanism used to record and retrieve items to and from a storage medium. When a storage device transfers items from a storage medium into memory – a process called **reading** – it functions as an input device. When a storage device transfers items from memory to a storage medium – a process called **writing** – it functions as an output device.

 ## 3. How Is Data Stored on a Floppy Disk?

A **floppy disk** is a portable, inexpensive storage medium that consists of a thin, circular, flexible disk with a plastic coating enclosed in a square-shaped plastic shell. **Formatting** prepares a disk for reading and writing by organizing the disk into storage locations called **tracks** and **sectors**. When data is stored, a formatted floppy disk is inserted in a **floppy disk drive**, and the drive slides the shutter to the side to expose a portion of both sides of the floppy disk's recording surface. A circuit board on the drive sends signals to control the movement of the **read/write head**, the mechanism that reads items from or writes items on the floppy disk. The circuit board on the drive verifies that light is not visible through the disk's **write-protect notch**. A motor causes the floppy disk to spin and positions the read/write head over the correct position on the recording surface. The read/write head then writes data on the floppy disk.

 ## 4. How Do You Care for a Floppy Disk?

Floppy disks should not be exposed to excessive heat, sunlight, cold, magnetic fields, or contaminants such as dust, smoke, or salt air. Heavy objects should not be placed on a disk. The disk's shutter should not be opened and the recording surface should not be touched. Floppy disks should be inserted carefully into the disk drive and kept in a storage tray when not in use.

 ## 5. How Does a Hard Disk Organize Data?

A **hard disk** usually consists of several inflexible, circular disks called platters on which items are stored electronically. Hard disks undergo two formatting steps. A **low-level format** organizes both sides of each platter into tracks and sectors to define where items will be stored on the disk. After low-level formatting is complete, a hard disk can be divided into separate areas called **partitions**; each partition functions as if it were a separate hard disk drive. Partitioning makes the hard disk more efficient (faster). A **high-level format** defines, among other items, the **file allocation table (FAT)** for each partition, which is a table of information used to locate files on the disk.

 **IN BRIEF** www.scsite.com/dc2000/ch6/brief.htm

 ## 6. What Are the Advantages of Using Disks?

Disks are a nonvolatile, relatively inexpensive means for storing data. Floppy disks can be used to transport a large number of files or to make backup copies of important files. Removable disks can be used when security is an issue.

 ## 7. How Is Data Stored on Compact Discs?

A **compact disc (CD)** is a flat, round, portable metal storage medium that usually is 4.75 inches in diameter and less than one-twentieth of an inch thick. Compact discs store items in microscopic pits (indentations) and land (flat areas) that are under the printed label on the disc. A high-powered laser light creates the pits in a single track, divided into evenly spaced sectors, that spirals from the center of the disc to the edge of the disc. A low-powered laser reads items from the compact disc by reflecting light through the bottom of the disc surface. The reflected light is converted into a series of bits that the computer can process.

 ## 8. How Do You Care for a Compact Disc?

Compact discs should not be stacked or exposed to heat, cold, and contaminants. The label side should not be written on or the underside touched. A compact disc should be held by its edges and placed in its protective case, called a **jewel box**, when it is not being used. The bottom surface of the compact disc can be cleaned with a soft cloth and warm water or a specialized CD cleaning kit, but the label side should not be cleaned because this is where data is stored.

 ## 9. How Are CD-ROMs and DVD-ROMs Different?

A **CD-ROM** is a silver-colored compact disc that uses the same laser technology as audio CDs for recording music. A CD-ROM can hold nearly 700 MB of data, instructions, and information. A DVD-ROM is an extremely high capacity compact disc capable of storing from 4.7 GB (4,700 MB) to 17 GB (17,000 MB). Both the storage capacity and quality of a DVD-ROM surpass that of a CD-ROM. A DVD-ROM stores data in a different manner than a CD-ROM, making the disc more dense by packing pits closer together, using two layers of pits, or using both sides of the disc.

 ## 10. How Are Tapes, PC Cards, Smart Cards, Microfilm, and Microfiche Used?

Tape is a magnetically-coated ribbon of plastic capable of storing large amounts of data and information at a low cost. Tape storage requires **sequential access** which refers to reading or writing data consectively and is used for long-term storage and backup. A **PC Card** is a thin, credit card-sized device that fits into a PC Card expansion slot on a personal computer. PC Cards are used to add storage, memory, communications, and sound capabilities to laptops and other portable computers. A smart card stores data on a thin microprocessor embedded in the card similar in size to an ATM card. Smart cards are used to store prepaid dollar amounts such as electronic money, patient records in the health-care industry, and tracking information such as customer purchases. **Microfilm** and **microfiche** store microscopic images of documents on roll (microfilm) or sheet (microfiche) film. Libraries and large organizations use microfilm and microfiche to archive relatively inactive documents and files.

CHAPTER 1 2 3 4 5 6 7 8 9 10 11 12 13 14 INDEX

KEY TERMS

www.scsite.com/dc2000/ch6/terms.htm

WEB INSTRUCTIONS: *To display this page from the Web, launch your browser and enter the URL,* www.scsite.com/dc2000/ch6/terms.htm. *Scroll through the list of terms. Click a term to display its definition and a picture. Click KEY TERMS on the left to redisplay the KEY TERMS page. Click the TO WEB button for current and additional information about the term from the Web. To see animations, Shockwave and Flash Player must be installed on your computer (download by clicking* here).

access time (6.3)
AT Attachment (ATA) (6.14)
auxiliary storage (6.2)
backup (6.9)
capacity (6.3)
CD-R drive (6.22)
CD-ROM drive (6.20)
CD-ROM player (6.20)
cluster (6.5)
compact disc read-only
   memory (CD-ROM) (6.19)
compact disc-recordable
   (CD-R) (6.22)
compact disc-rewritable
   (CD-RW) (6.22)
compact disc (CD) (6.16)
compact flash cards (6.24)
computer output microfilm
   (COM) recorder (6.26)
cylinder (6.12)
data transfer rate (6.21)
density (6.5)
digital cash (6.26)
digital video disc-ROM
   (DVD-ROM) (6.22)
direct access (6.23)
disk (6.2)
disk cache (6.13)
disk cartridge (6.14)
disk controller (6.14)
disk pack (6.14)
diskette (6.4)
downward compatible (6.7)
DVD-ROM drive (6.22)
electronic money (e-money)
   (6.26)
file allocation table (FAT) (6.6)
fixed disks (6.10)
floppy disk (6.4)
floppy disk drive (FDD) (6.7)

TO WEB

TRACK: Narrow recording band that forms a full circle on the surface of a disk. The disk s storage locations are then divided into pie-shaped sections, which break the tracks into small arcs called sectors. A sector can store 512 bytes of data. (6.5)

formatting (6.5)
hard disk (6.10)
hard disk controller (HDC)
   (6.14)
head crash (6.13)
High FD (HiFD) (6.10)
high-level format (6.11)
Integrated Drive Electronics
   (IDE) (6.14)
intelligent smart card (6.25)
Jaz^fi disk (6.14)
jewel box (6.18)
level 1 (6.15)
low-level format (6.11)
magnetic tape (6.23)
mass storage (6.2)
memory card (6.25)
microfiche (6.26)
microfilm (6.26)
mirroring (6.15)

multisession (6.21)
nonvolatile memory (6.2)
partitions (6.11)
PC Card (6.24)
PhotoCD (6.21)
picture cards (6.24)
platter (6.10)
random access (6.23)
reading (6.3)
read/write (6.5)
read/write head (6.8)
recorded (6.19)
redundant array of independent
   disks (RAID) (6.15)
removable hard disk (6.14)
secondary storage (6.2)
sector (6.5)
sequential access (6.23)
shutter (6.8)
single-session (6.21)
small computer system interface
   (SCSI) (6.15)
smart card (6.25)
storage (6.2)
storage device (6.2)
storage medium (6.2)
striping (6.15)
SuperDisk drive (6.10)
tape (6.23)
tape cartridge (6.23)
tape drive (6.23)
track (6.5)
Type III cards (6.25)
upward compatible (6.7)
volatile memory (6.2)
write-protect notch (6.6)
writing (6.3)
Zip^fi disk (6.10)
Zip^fi drive (6.10)

AT THE MOVIES
www.scsite.com/dc2000/ch6/movies.htm

SHELLY
CASHMAN
SERIES®
DISCOVERING
COMPUTERS
2000

■ Student Exercises
WEB INFO
IN BRIEF
KEY TERMS
AT THE MOVIES
CHECKPOINT
AT ISSUE
CYBERCLASS
HANDS ON
NET STUFF
■ Special Features
TIMELINE 2000
GUIDE TO WWW SITES
MAKING A CHIP
BUYER'S GUIDE 2000
CAREERS 2000
TRENDS 2000
CHAT
INTERACTIVE LABS
NEWS
HOME

WELCOME to VIDEO CLIPS from CNN

WEB INSTRUCTIONS: *To display this page from the Web, launch your browser and enter the URL,* *www.scsite.com/dc2000/ch6/movies.htm. Click a picture to view a video. After watching the video, close the video window and then complete the exercise by answering the questions about the video. To view the videos, RealPlayer must be installed on your computer (download by clicking* here*).*

1   Biz IBM Storage

Based on what you learned in this video and in this chapter, will increased storage change the way you use a computer? Will it change the types of applications that can run on personal computers? What size storage do you think will be available in ten years? Why? How much has the cost of 1 MB of storage fallen since 1991? In the future, storage capacities will continue to increase. How much data will higher-density storage being developed by IBM allow you to store on 1 square inch of disk space? Why is greater storage capacity important? Does IBM intend to share this new technology with competitors?

2   SBT Online/NetFlix

Popularity is growing for sites like the NetFlix movie Web site where you can search for your favorite movie and then either rent or buy it in DVD-ROM format. What would it cost to rent a DVD movie online and how would you receive and return the movie? What are the advantages and disadvantages of an online DVD movie rental? What movie companies are strong players in the DVD movie market? Are you excited about renting DVD movies on-line? Why?

3   Internet Commerce

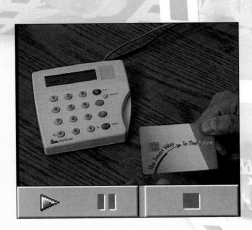

One practice soon to become commonplace is the use of bank-assigned smart cards. What is a smart card? How does it work? What kind of password-protection is used? What are the advantages of having a "personal ATM"? Are there disadvantages? Would you use a personal ATM rather than cash? Why? What are the most likely uses of your smart card. The least likely uses? Why?

Student Exercises
WEB INFO
IN BRIEF
KEY TERMS
AT THE MOVIES
CHECKPOINT
AT ISSUE
CYBERCLASS
HANDS ON
NET STUFF
Special Features
TIMELINE 2000
GUIDE TO WWW SITES
MAKING A CHIP
BUYER'S GUIDE 2000
CAREERS 2000
TRENDS 2000
CHAT
INTERACTIVE LABS
NEWS
HOME

CHAPTER 1 2 3 4 5 6 7 8 9 10 11 12 13 14 INDEX

CHECKPOINT www.scsite.com/dc2000/ch6/check.htm

WEB INSTRUCTIONS: *To display this page from the Web, launch your browser and enter the URL, www.scsite.com/dc2000/ch6/check.htm. Click the links for current and additional information. To experience the animation and interactivity, Shockwave and Flash Player must be installed on your computer (download by clicking here).*

Label the Figure

Instructions: *Identify each part of a 3.5-inch floppy disk.*

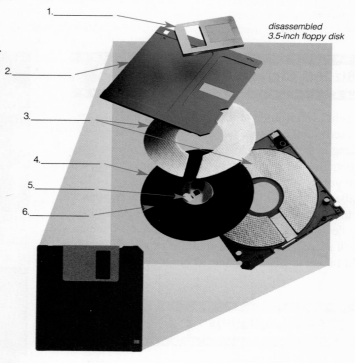

disassembled
3.5-inch floppy disk

Matching

Instructions: *Match each storage medium or storage device from the column on the left with the best description from the column on the right.*

_____ 1. SuperDisk drive

_____ 2. HiFD (High FD)

_____ 3. Zip^fi drive

_____ 4. Zip^fi disk

_____ 5. Jaz^fi disk

a. Floppy disk drive technology that replaces existing disk drives; uses 200 MB high-capacity floppy disks.

b. Silver-colored optical disk that uses the same laser technology as audio CDs.

c. Slightly larger than and about twice as thick as a 3.5-inch floppy disk and can store 100 MB of data.

d. High-capacity disk drive developed by Imation that uses 120 MB floppy disks.

e. Special high-capacity disk drive developed by Iomega Corporation that is built into many new computers.

f. Used to read a DVD-ROM, and is downward compatible with standard CD-ROMs.

g. Popular, reasonably priced, removable hard disk by Iomega, which can store up to 2 GB of data.

Short Answer

Instructions: *Write a brief answer to each of the following questions.*

1. What is access time? _____ Why is hard disk access time faster than floppy disk access time? _____
2. What is disk density? _____ What does it mean to say that floppy disk drives are downward compatible but not upward compatible? _____
3. What is a head crash? _____ How does a disk cache improve hard disk access time? _____
4. What is a disk controller? _____ How are EIDE controllers and SCSI controllers different? _____
5. How are multisession CD-ROMs different from single-session CD-ROMs? _____ What are three variations of the standard CD-ROM? _____

CHAPTER 1 2 3 4 5 6 7 8 9 10 11 12 13 14 INDEX

AT ISSUE www.scsite.com/dc2000/ch6/issue.htm

WEB INSTRUCTIONS: *To display this page from the Web, launch your browser and enter the URL,* www.scsite.com/dc2000/ch6/issue.htm. *Click the links for current and additional information.*

ONE *Up to 75 percent of today's data is "born digital" and has never* existed on paper. Although written documents can be read hundreds of years after they were created, rapid changes in computer technology can make digital records almost inaccessible in just one decade. Without the necessary hardware or software, information stored on once-popular 5¼-inch floppy disks can be impossible to access. Pennsylvania State University recently admitted that 2,986 student and school files could not be accessed due to lost or outdated software. Is the potential unavailability of digital data a problem? Why or why not? What can be done to keep today's digital information available in the future?

TWO *Apple Computer's iMac shocked* traditionalists. The new computer's translucent case and distinctive shape alone made it unlike conventional desktop computers, but perhaps its most controversial feature was the absence of a 3½-inch floppy disk drive. Steve Jobs, acting CEO of Apple Computer, claimed Apple was "leading the way" by abandoning an outmoded and superfluous technology. Is Jobs correct? Will larger hard drives, increased Internet access, and new

developments make 3½-inch floppy disks as antiquated as the 8-inch floppy disks used in the early 1980s? Why? Would you buy a computer without a 3½-floppy disk drive? Why or why not?

THREE **National Geographic** *recently released the* entire history of the magazine – 109 years worth of issues – on four DVDs. The DVDs also include the magazine's television specials. The discs are completely indexed, so users can find particular issues, special articles (or even specific advertisements), or articles on certain topics. The National Gallery in Washington, DC, the nation's premier art museum, also has stored its entire collection on optical disk. Is this the beginning of a trend? What other organizations or institutions would benefit from using optical disc technology to catalog their history or holdings? Why? What, if any, advantages are there by seeing an original work over viewing a representation on optical disc?

FOUR **Nothing lasts forever.** *This aphorism is true even in regards to computer storage.* NASA discovered almost 20 percent of the data collected during the Viking mission was lost on decaying magnetic tape. Veterans' files, census statistics, and toxic-waste records also have been lost on deteriorating storage media. One computer scientist admits, "Digital information lasts forever or five years – whichever comes first." A major problem with digital data is that, unlike the visible deterioration in a faded document, the extent of decay on a storage medium such as a CD-ROM may be invisible until it is too late. If you were the leader of an information-intensive organization, what medium would you choose to store your records? Why? What steps would you take to ensure the records were intact ten years from now? Twenty years from now?

FIVE *Today's sports cards are different from those you once traded, and not only are the* players new. Topps has introduced a series of plastic baseball cards, each of which has four seconds of game footage from Kodak. Eventually, Kodak hopes to add sound chips to the $10 cards. Donruss already offers CD-ROM trading cards. When the rectangular (yes, rectangular) $20 cards are inserted into a CD-ROM drive, they display a host of statistics, present personal information, and even show video highlights analyzing individual playing styles. Will the new sports cards eventually replace traditional trading cards? Why or why not? In light of what you have learned regarding computer storage, how else might sports cards be different in the future?

CHAPTER 1 2 3 4 5 6 7 8 9 10 11 12 13 14 INDEX

CYBERCLASS

www.scsite.com/dc2000/ch6/class.htm

WEB INSTRUCTIONS: *To display this page from the Web, launch your browser and enter the URL, www.scsite.com/dc2000/ch6/class.htm. To start Level I CyberClass, click a Level I link on this page or enter the URL, www.cyber-class.com. Click the Student button, click Discovering Computers 2000 in the list of titles, and then click the Enter a site button. To start Level II or III CyberClass (available only to those purchasers of a CyberClass floppy disk), place your CyberClass floppy disk in drive A, click Start on the taskbar, click Run on the Start menu, type* a:connect *in the Open text box, click the OK button, click the Enter CyberClass button, and then follow the instructions.*

I II III LEVEL **1. Flash Cards** Click Flash Cards on the Main Menu of the CyberClass web page. Click the plus sign before the Chapter 6 title and then click Magnetic Disk Storage. Complete all Magnetic Disk Storage questions. Then, choose a category and continue to answer flash cards until you have answered at least 15 questions. If you have not answered 80% correctly by the time you have answered 15 questions, continue until you have answered at least 15 questions correctly. All users: Answer as many more flash cards as you desire. Close the Electronic Flash Card window and the Flash Cards window by clicking the Close button in the upper-right corner of each window.

I II III LEVEL **2. Practice Test** Click Testing on the Main Menu of the CyberClass web page. Click the Select a book box arrow and then click Discovering Computers 2000. Click the Select a test to take box arrow and then click the Chapter 6 title in the list. Click the Take Test button. If necessary, maximize the window. Take the practice test and then click the Submit Test button. Hand in your score to your instructor.

I II III LEVEL **3. Web Guide** Click Web Guide on the Main Menu of the CyberClass web page. When the Guide to World Wide Web Sites page displays, click Reference and then click Internet Public Library. At the library site, visit the Reference Center and then click Computers and Internet. Find a subject of interest to you that explains an element of data storage. When you are finished, close the window. Write a brief synopsis of what you learned and hand it in to your instructor.

II III LEVEL **4. Company Briefs** Click Company Briefs on the Main Menu of the CyberClass web page. Click a corporation name to display a case study. Read the case study. Write a brief report describing the data storage needs for the company's computers.

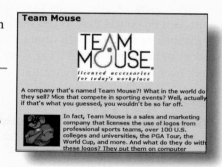

Team Mouse

TEAM MOUSE.
*licensed accessories
for today's workplace*

A company that's named Team Mouse?! What in the world do they sell? Mice that compete in sporting events? Well, actually if that's what you guessed, you wouldn't be so far off.

In fact, Team Mouse is a sales and marketing company that licenses the use of logos from professional sports teams, over 100 U.S. colleges and universities, the PGA Tour, the World Cup, and more. And what do they do with these logos? They put them on computer

I II III LEVEL **5. CyberChallenge** Click CyberChallenge on the Main Menu of the CyberClass web page. Click the Select a book box arrow and then click Discovering Computers 2000. Click the Select a board to play box arrow and then click Chapter 6 in the list. Click the Play CyberChallenge button. Maximize the CyberChallenge window. Play CyberChallenge until you have scored more than 500 points. Close the CyberChallenge window.

II III LEVEL **6. Student Bulletin Board** Click Student Bulletin Board on the Main Menu of the CyberClass web page. Read any bulletins that have been posted. Determine which message you find most interesting and write a brief report describing why. Hand in the report to your instructor. If no bulletins are posted, create a topic by clicking Add Topic. Then, place your own message on the bulletin board.

II III LEVEL **7. Text Chat** Arrange for your instructor to conduct office hours using CyberClass text chat. Then, at the appointed time, click Text Chat on the Main Menu of the CyberClass web page and ask any questions you may have about the course so far.

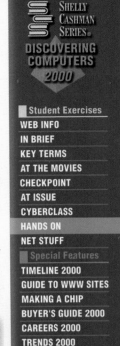

HANDS ON   www.scsite.com/dc2000/ch6/hands.htm

WEB INSTRUCTIONS: *To display this page from the Web, launch your browser and enter the URL,* www.scsite.com/dc2000/ch6/hands.htm. *Click the links for current and additional information.*

One   *Examining My Computer*

How many disk drives does your computer have? What letter is used for each? To find out more about the disk drives on your computer, right-click the My Computer icon in the upper-left corner on the desktop. Click Open on the shortcut menu. What is the drive letter for the floppy disk drive on your computer? What letter(s) are used for the hard disk drives on your computer? If you have a CD-ROM drive, what letter is used for it? Double-click the Hard disk (C:) drive icon in the My Computer window. The Hard disk (C:) window shows the file folders (yellow folder icons) stored on your hard disk. How many folders are on the hard disk? Click the Close button to close the Hard disk (C:) window.

Two   *Working with Files*

Insert the Discover Data Disk into drive A. If you do not have the Discover Data Disk, see the inside back cover of this book or your instructor. Double-click the My Computer icon on the desktop. When the My Computer window displays, right-click the 3½ Floppy (A:) icon. Click Open on the shortcut menu. Click View on the menu bar and then click Large Icons. Right-click the h2-2 icon. If h2-2 is not on the floppy disk, ask your instructor for a copy. Click Copy on the shortcut menu. Click Edit on the menu bar and then click Paste. How has the 3½ Floppy (A:) window changed? Right-click the new icon (Copy of h2-2) and then click Rename on the shortcut menu. Type h6-2 and then press the ENTER key. Right-click the h6-2 icon and then click Print on the shortcut menu. Close the 3½ Floppy (A:) window.

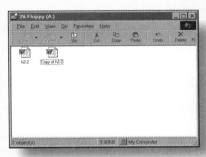

Three   *Learning About Your Hard Disk*

What are the characteristics of your hard disk? To find out, right-click the My Computer icon in the upper-left corner on the desktop. Click Open on the shortcut menu. Right-click the Hard disk (C:) icon in the My Computer window. Click Properties on the shortcut menu. If necessary, click the General tab and then answer the following questions:

- What Label is on the disk?
- What Type of disk is it?
- How much of the hard disk is Used space?
- How much of the hard disk is Free space?
- What is the total Capacity of the hard disk?

Close the Hard disk (C:) dialog box and the My Computer window.

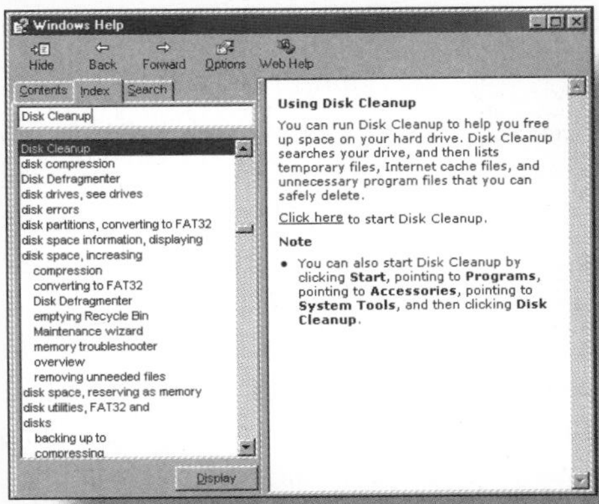

Four   *Disk Cleanup*

This exercise uses Windows 98 procedures. Just as people maintain they never can have too much money, computer users insist that you never can have too much hard disk space. Fortunately, Windows includes a utility program called Disk Cleanup that can increase available hard disk space. To find out more about Disk Cleanup, click the Start button and then click Help on the Start menu. Click the Index tab in the Windows Help window and then type Disk Cleanup in the Index sheet text box. Click the Display button. Click Using Disk Cleanup in the Topics Found dialog box and then click the Display button. How does Disk Cleanup help to free up space on the hard disk? How do you start Disk Cleanup using the Start button? Click the Close button to close the Windows Help window.

Right margin navigation:

■ **Student Exercises**
WEB INFO
IN BRIEF
KEY TERMS
AT THE MOVIES
CHECKPOINT
AT ISSUE
CYBERCLASS
HANDS ON
NET STUFF
■ Special Features
TIMELINE 2000
GUIDE TO WWW SITES
MAKING A CHIP
BUYER'S GUIDE 2000
CAREERS 2000
TRENDS 2000
CHAT
INTERACTIVE LABS
NEWS
HOME

SHELLY CASHMAN SERIES

DISCOVERING COMPUTERS 2000

Student Exercises
WEB INFO
IN BRIEF
KEY TERMS
AT THE MOVIES
CHECKPOINT
AT ISSUE
CYBERCLASS
HANDS ON
NET STUFF
Special Features
TIMELINE 2000
GUIDE TO WWW SITES
MAKING A CHIP
BUYER'S GUIDE 2000
CAREERS 2000
TRENDS 2000
CHAT
INTERACTIVE LABS
NEWS
HOME

CHAPTER 1 2 3 4 5 6 7 8 9 10 11 12 13 14 INDEX

NET STUFF   www.scsite.com/dc2000/ch6/net.htm

WEB INSTRUCTIONS: *To display this page from the Web, launch your browser and enter the URL,* www.scsite.com/dc2000/ch6/net.htm. *To use the Maintaining Your Hard Drive lab from the Web, Shockwave and Flash Player must be installed on your computer (download by clicking* here*).*

MAINTAINING YOUR HARD DRIVE LAB

1. Shelly Cashman Maintaining Your Hard Drive Lab

Follow the appropriate instructions in NET STUFF 1 on page 1.46 to start and use the Maintaining Your Hard Drive lab. If you are running from the Web, enter the URL, www.scsite.com/sclabs/menu.htm; or display the NET STUFF page (see instructions at the top of this page) and then click the MAINTAINING YOUR HARD DRIVE LAB button.

DVD

2. Digital Video Disk (DVD)

A DVD can hold almost twenty-five times more data than a CD. This translates into richer sound and images than ever seen or heard before. The quality of DVD storage is beginning to have a major impact on the market. Some expect the sales of DVD optical drives will soon pass the $4 billion mark. Click the DVD button and complete this exercise to learn more about DVDs.

PIM

3. Personal Information Management

Tired of forgetting birthdays, missing meetings, overlooking appointments, or neglecting to complete important tasks? If so, then personal information management software may be perfect for you. Click the PIM button to find out about a free, Internet-based calendar. How could this calendar help you organize your life? How might the calendar help you have more fun? After reading the information you may sign up to create your own Internet-based calendar.

IN THE NEWS

4. In the News

IBM recently unveiled a small disk drive, about the size of a quarter, that is capable of storing 340 megabytes of information, as much as 230 floppy disks. The drive will be used in devices such as digital cameras. What other storage devices are on the horizon? Click the IN THE NEWS button and read a news article about a new or improved storage device. What is the device? Who manufactures it? How is the storage device better than, or different from, earlier devices? How will the device be used? Why?

WEB CHAT

5. Web Chat

In McDonald's restaurants across Germany, you can get a Big Mac without handing over any cash. The sandwiches are not free, but customers at hundreds of McDonalds Deutschland, Inc., now can make their purchases by swiping a smart card through terminals at the restaurants' counters. With simple touch-screens that guide them through the process, customers also can use the terminals to add value to their smart cards by downloading money electronically from their bank accounts. Is McDonald's experiment a forerunner for the future? Smart cards offer greater security and provide more control (card-owners can restrict the type of purchases that can be made) than conventional currency. On the other hand, because transactions are recorded, smart cards eliminate anonymity in purchasing and may lead to invasion of privacy. What is the greatest advantage of smart cards? What is the greatest disadvantage? Do you think smart cards will someday replace money? Why or why not? Click the WEB CHAT button to enter a Web Chat discussion related to this topic.

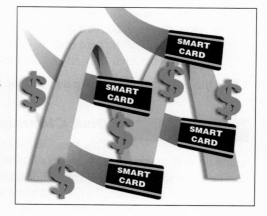

CHAPTER 7

THE INTERNET

OBJECTIVES

After completing this chapter, you will be able to:

Describe how the Internet works

Recognize how graphics, animation, audio, video, and virtual reality are used on the World Wide Web

Identify the tools required for Web publishing

Describe the uses of electronic commerce (e-commerce)

Explain how e-mail, FTP, Telnet, newsgroups, mailing lists, and chat rooms work

Identify the rules of netiquette

Understand security precautions for the Internet

Explain how network computers are used

Today, one of the major reasons business, home, and other users purchase computers is for Internet access. Many companies and organizations assume the public is familiar with the Internet. Web addresses appear on television, in radio broadcasts, in printed newspapers magazines, and other forms of advertising. Software companies use their Web sites as a place for you to download upgrades or enhancements to software products. The government publishes thousands of informational Web pages to provide individuals with material such as legislative updates, tax forms, and e-mail addresses for Congress members. To be successful today, you must have an understanding of the Internet. Without it, you are missing a tremendous resource for goods, services, and information. This chapter discusses the history and structure of the Internet and the various services available on the Internet.

THE INTERNET

You have learned that a **network** is a collection of computers and devices connected together via communications devices and media such as cables, telephone lines, modems, and satellites.

The world's largest network is the **Internet**, which is a worldwide collection of networks that links together millions of businesses, government offices, educational institutions, and individuals (Figure 7-1). Each of these networks provides resources that add to the abundance of goods, services, and information accessible via the Internet.

The many networks that comprise the Internet, also called the **Net**, are local, regional, national, and international. Although each network that constitutes the Internet is owned by a public or private organization, no single organization owns or controls the Internet. Each organization on the Internet is responsible only for maintaining its own network.

Today more than 100 million users around the world connect to the Internet for a variety of reasons. Some of the uses of the Internet are as follows:

- To access a wealth of information, news, research, and educational material

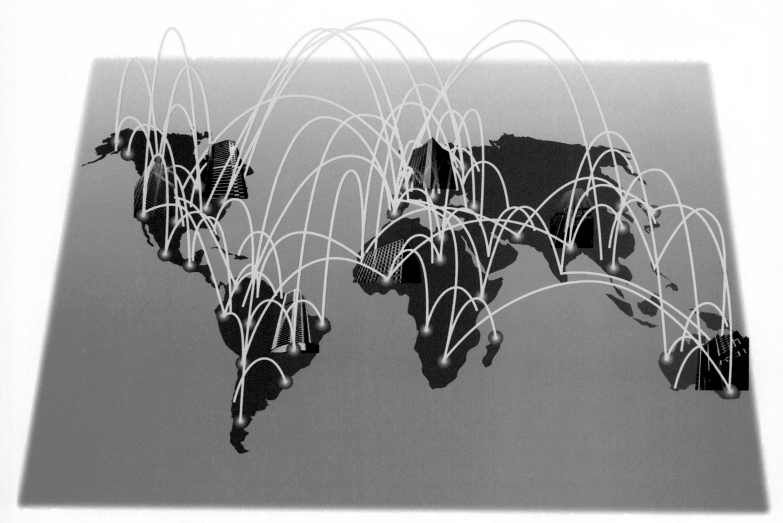

Figure 7-1 The world's largest network is the Internet, which is a worldwide collection of networks that link together millions of businesses, the government, educational institutions, and individuals.

- To conduct business or complete banking and investing transactions

- To access sources of entertainment and leisure such as online games, magazines, and vacation planning guides

- To shop for goods and services

- To meet and converse with people around the world in discussion groups or chat rooms

- To access other computers and exchange files

- To send messages to or receive messages from other connected users

Figure 7-2 shows Web pages that illustrate some of these uses.

To support these and other activities, the Internet provides a variety of services including the World Wide Web, electronic mail (e-mail), FTP, Telnet, newsgroups, mailing lists, and chat rooms. These services, along with a discussion of the history of the Internet and how the Internet works, are explained in the following pages.

Figure 7-2a (information)

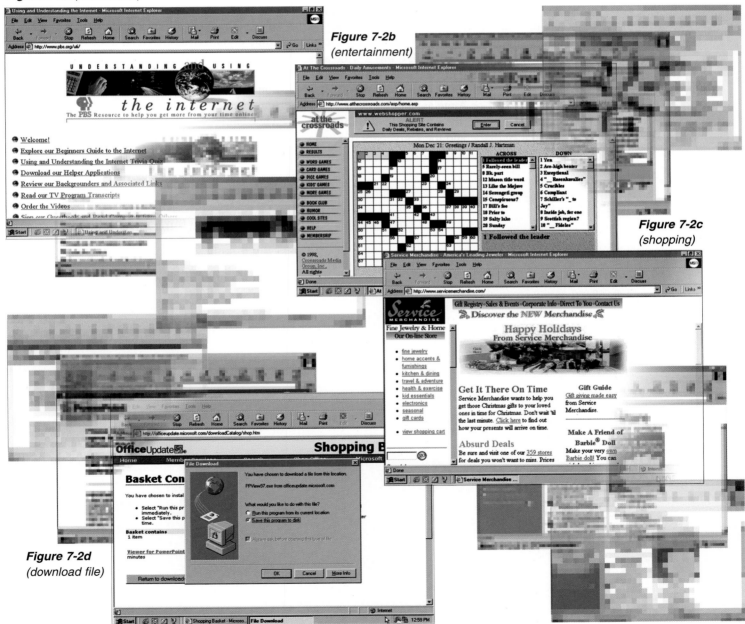

Figure 7-2b (entertainment)

Figure 7-2c (shopping)

Figure 7-2d (download file)

Figure 7-2 Today, more than 100 million users around the world connect to the Internet.

HISTORY OF THE INTERNET

Although the history of the Internet is relatively short, its growth has been explosive (Figure 7-3). The Internet has it roots in a networking project started by the Pentagon's **Advanced Research Projects Agency (ARPA)**, which is an agency of the U.S. Department of Defense. ARPA's goal was to build a network that (1) would allow scientists at different locations to share information and collaborate on military and scientific projects and (2) could function even if part of the network were disabled or destroyed by a disaster, such as a nuclear war. That network, called **ARPANET**, became functional in September 1969, effectively linking together scientific and academic researchers in the United States.

The original ARPANET was a wide area network consisting of four main computers, one each located at the University of California at Los Angeles, the Stanford Research Institute, the University of California at Santa Barbara, and the University of Utah.

Each of these four computers served as the network's host nodes. In a network, a **host node**, or **host**, is any computer directly connected to the network. A host often stores and transfers data and messages on high-speed communications lines and provides network connections for other computers. Hosts and communications lines are discussed in more depth in Chapter 9.

As researchers and others realized the great benefit of using ARPANET's electronic mail to share information and notes, ARPANET underwent phenomenal growth. By 1984, ARPANET had more than 1,000 individual computers linked as hosts. (Today, more than 35 million hosts are connected to the Internet.)

To take further advantage of the high-speed communications offered by ARPANET, some organizations decided to connect entire networks to ARPANET. In 1986, for example, the National Science Foundation (NSF) connected its huge network of five supercomputer centers, called **NSFnet**, to ARPANET. This configuration of complex networks and hosts became known as the Internet.

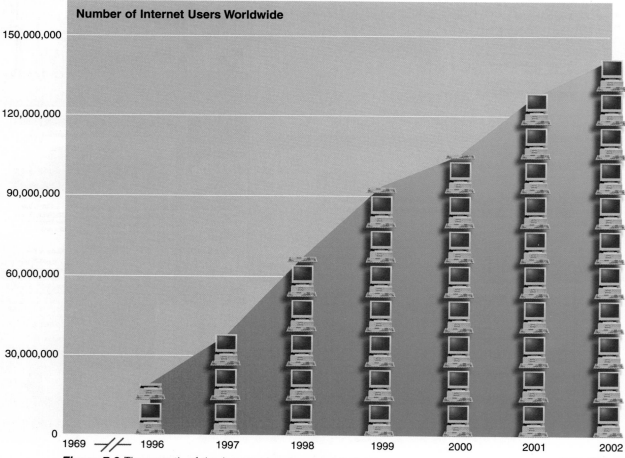

Figure 7-3 *The growth of the Internet has been explosive.*

source: eStats

Because of its advanced technology, NSFnet served as the major backbone network on the Internet until 1995. A **backbone** is a high-speed network that connects regional and local networks to the Internet; other computers then connect to these regional and local networks to access the Internet. A backbone thus handles the bulk of the communications activity, or **traffic**, on the Internet.

In 1995, NSFnet terminated its backbone network on the Internet to return its status to a research network. Since then, a variety of corporations, commercial firms, and other companies run backbone networks that provide access to the Internet.

These backbone networks, along with telephone companies, cable and satellite companies, and the government all contribute toward the internal structure of the Internet. Many donate resources, such as servers, communication lines, and technical specialists — making the Internet truly collaborative.

Even as it grows, the Internet remains a public, cooperative, and independent network. Although no single person, company, institution, or government agency controls or owns the Internet, several organizations contribute toward its success by advising, defining standards, and addressing other issues. The table in Figure 7-4 outlines the functions of some of these organizations.

WEB INFO

WEB INFO

For more information on the Internet backbone, visit the Discovering Computers 2000 Chapter 7 WEB INFO page (**www.scsite.com/dc2000/ ch7/webinfo.htm**) and click Internet Backbone.

INTERNET ADVISORY GROUPS AND ORGANIZATIONS

Organization	Abbreviation	Composition	Function
World Wide Web Consortium	W3C	Commercial and educational institutions	Oversees research and sets standards for many areas of the Web
Internet Society	ISOC	Individuals, corporations, nonprofit organizations, foundations, and government agencies	Concerned with use, maintenance, and development of Internet; oversees other boards and task forces; publishes Internet Society News; coordinates annual Internet conference called INET
Internet Architecture Board	IAB	Body of the ISOC	Defines the architecture of the Internet – including backbone and all attached networks; resolves standards' disputes
Internet Engineering Steering Group	IESG	Body of the ISOC	Responsible for Internet standards process; approves final Internet standards specifications
Internet Engineering Task Force	IETF	Body of the IESG	Studies technical problems and recommends solutions to the IAB and IESG
Internet Assigned Numbers Authority	IANA	Body of the IAB	Assigns and controls numeric designations on the Internet, such as IP addresses and protocols
Internet Network Information Center	InterNIC	National Science Foundation, AT&T, General Atomics, and Network Solutions, Inc.	Registers domain names and IP addresses; distributes information about the Internet
Internet Engineering and Planning Group	IEPG	Internet service providers	Coordinates technical efforts on the Internet; promotes usage of the Internet
Internet Research Task Force	IRTF	Volunteers	Makes recommendations about the Internet to the IAB

Figure 7-4 *The functions of the various organizations that define standards and make recommendations for Internet issues.*

HOW THE INTERNET WORKS

Data sent over the Internet travels via networks and communications lines owned and operated by many companies. Various ways to connect to these networks are presented in the following sections.

Internet Service Providers and Online Services

For more information on ISPs, visit the Discovering Computers 2000 Chapter 7 WEB INFO page (**www.scsite.com/ dc2000/ch7/webinfo.htm**) and click ISP.

An **Internet service provider (ISP)** is an organization that has a permanent Internet connection and provides temporary connections to individuals and companies for a fee. The most common ISP fee arrangement is a fixed amount, usually about $20 per month for an individual account. For this amount, many ISPs provide unlimited Internet access, while others specify a set number of access

hours per month, such as 100 hours. If you spend more time on the Internet than the allotted access hours, you are charged an additional amount, based on an hourly rate.

Two types of ISPs exist: local and national (Figure 7-5). A **local ISP** usually provides one or more local telephone numbers to provide access to the Internet. A **national ISP** is a larger business that provides local telephone numbers in most major cities and towns nation- wide; some also provide a toll-free telephone number. Because of their size, national ISPs offer more services and generally have a larger technical support staff than local ISPs. The most important consideration when selecting an ISP is to be sure that it provides a local telephone number for Internet access, called a **point of presence (POP)**; otherwise, you pay long-distance telephone bills for the time you are connected to the Internet.

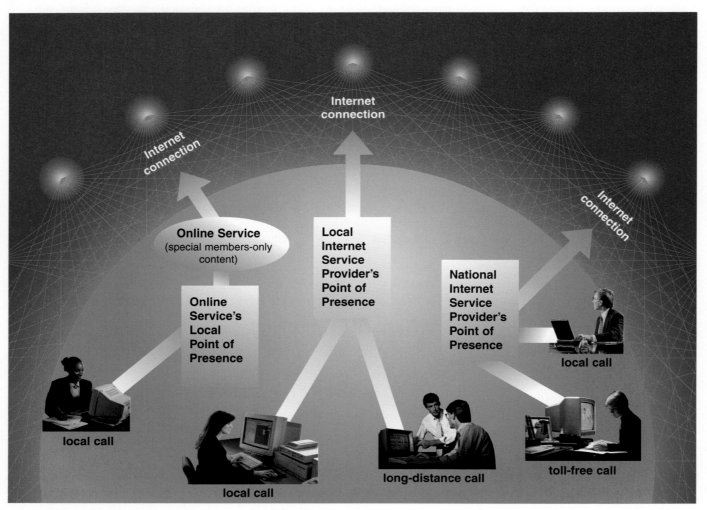

Figure 7-5 Common ways to access the Internet are through an online service or a local or national Internet service provider.

Like an ISP, an **online service** provides Internet access, but such online services also have members-only features that offer a variety of special content and services such as news; weather; legal information; financial data; hardware and software guides; games; and travel guides. For this reason, the fees for using an online service usually are slightly higher than fees for an ISP. Online services such as America Online and The Microsoft Network (MSN) usually have thousands of POPs all over the world and large customer and technical support staffs.

Connecting to the Internet

Many users connect to the Internet through a business or school network. In this instance, their computers usually are part of a local area network (LAN) that is connected to an ISP through a high-speed connection line leased from the local telephone company. Instead of connecting via a modem, a personal computer connects to the LAN using a network interface card (NIC), which is an expansion card that allows the computer to be networked.

When connecting from home or while traveling, individuals typically use dial-up access to connect to the Internet. With **dial-up access**, you might use your computer and a modem to dial into an ISP or online service over a regular telephone line. The computer at the receiving end, whether at an ISP or online service, also may use a modem. Dial-up access provides an easy way for mobile and home users to connect to the Internet to check e-mail, read the news, and access research material. Because dial-up access uses regular telephone lines, however, the speed of the connection is limited.

Newer technologies such as Integrated Services Digital Network (ISDN) and cable modems provide an alternative to dial-up access over regular telephone lines. ISDN provides users with faster-speed Internet connections. These technologies, along with modems, network interface cards, and other types of communications equipment and media are discussed in more detail in Chapter 9.

How Data Travels the Internet

Computers connected to the Internet work together to transfer data and information around the world using servers and clients. Recall that a **server** is a computer that manages the resources on a network and provides a centralized storage area for software programs and data. A **client** is a computer that can access the contents of the storage area on the server, including programs, data, and other resources. On the Internet, for example, your computer is a client that can access files and services on a variety of servers, which are called host computers.

When a client computer sends data over the Internet, the data is divided into small pieces, called **packets**. The data in a packet might be part of an e-mail message, a file, a document, or a request for a file. Each packet contains the data, as well as the recipient (destination), origin (sender), and sequence information used to reassemble the data at the destination. These packets are sent along the fastest available path to the recipient's computer via devices called **routers**. If the most direct path to the destination is overloaded or not operating, the routers send the packets along an alternate path.

If necessary, each packet can be sent over a different path to the destination. If the packets arrive out of sequence, the destination computer uses the sequence information contained in each packet to reassemble the original message, file, document, or request. This technique of breaking a message into individual packets, sending the packets along the best route available, and then reassembling the data is called **packet switching**.

For a technique such as packet switching to work, all of the devices on the network must follow certain standards, or protocols. A **communications protocol** specifies the rules that define how devices connect to each other and transmit data over a network. The protocol used to define packet switching on the Internet is a communications protocol known as **TCP/IP (transmission control protocol/Internet protocol)**.

WEB INFO
WEB INFO

For more information on online services, visit the Discovering Computers 2000 Chapter 7 WEB INFO page (**www.scsite.com/ dc2000/ch7/webinfo.htm**) and click Online Services.

The inner structure of the Internet works much like a transportation system. Just as highways connect major cities and carry the bulk of the automotive traffic across the country, several main communications lines carry the heaviest amount of traffic on the Internet. These communications lines are referred to collectively as the Internet **backbone**.

In the United States, the communications lines that make up the Internet backbone exchange data at several different locations. These locations, which function like a highway interchange, are one of two basic types: Network Access Points or Metropolitan Area Exchanges (Figure 7-6). Network Access Points (NAPs) and Metropolitan Area Exchanges (MAEs) are located in major cities and use high-speed equipment to transfer data packets from one network to another.

National ISPs, sometimes called **backbone providers**, use dedicated lines to connect directly to the Internet backbone at one or more NAPs or MAEs. Smaller regional networks and local ISPs, by contrast, lease lines from local telephone companies to connect to national ISPs. These smaller, slower-speed regional and local networks extend out from the backbone into regions and local communities. Figure 7-7 illustrates how these components of the Internet work together to transfer data over the Internet to and from your computer.

Internet Addresses

The Internet relies on an addressing system much like the postal service to send data to a computer at a specific destination. Each computer location on the Internet has a numeric address called an **IP (Internet protocol) address**. The IP address consists of four groups of numbers, each separated by a period. The number in each group is between 0 and 255. For example, the numbers, 198.112.168.223, are an IP address. In general, the first portion of each IP address identifies the network and the last portion identifies the specific computer.

Because these all-numeric IP addresses are difficult to remember and use, the Internet supports the use of a text name that represents one or more IP addresses. The text version of an IP address is called a **domain name**.

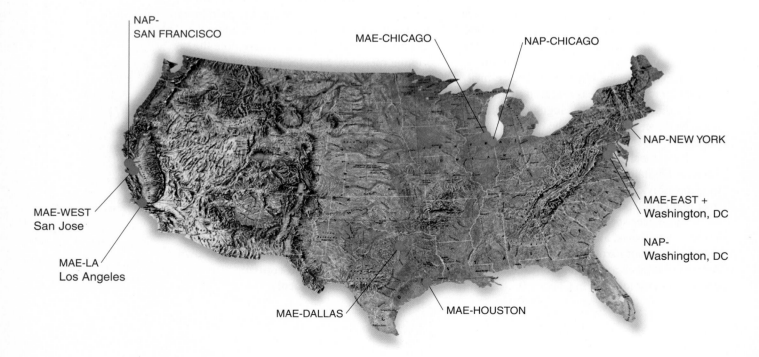

Figure 7-6 *The map shows where the MAEs and NAPs currently are located in the U.S.*

Figure 7-7

HOW DATA MIGHT TRAVEL THE INTERNET

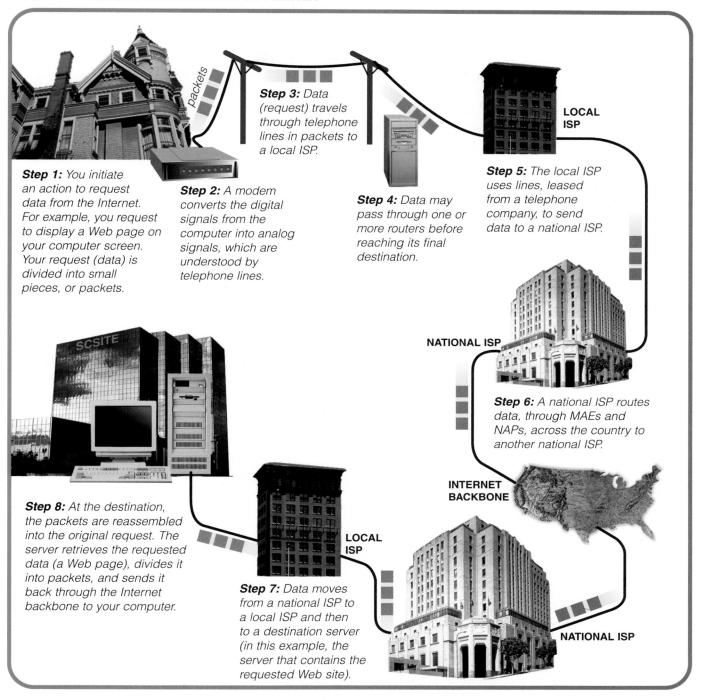

packets

Step 3: Data (request) travels through telephone lines in packets to a local ISP.

LOCAL ISP

Step 1: You initiate an action to request data from the Internet. For example, you request to display a Web page on your computer screen. Your request (data) is divided into small pieces, or packets.

Step 2: A modem converts the digital signals from the computer into analog signals, which are understood by telephone lines.

Step 4: Data may pass through one or more routers before reaching its final destination.

Step 5: The local ISP uses lines, leased from a telephone company, to send data to a national ISP.

NATIONAL ISP

Step 6: A national ISP routes data, through MAEs and NAPs, across the country to another national ISP.

INTERNET BACKBONE

Step 8: At the destination, the packets are reassembled into the original request. The server retrieves the requested data (a Web page), divides it into packets, and sends it back through the Internet backbone to your computer.

LOCAL ISP

Step 7: Data moves from a national ISP to a local ISP and then to a destination server (in this example, the server that contains the requested Web site).

NATIONAL ISP

Figure 7-8 shows an IP address and its associated domain name. Like an IP address, the components of a domain name are separated by periods.

Every domain name contains a **top-level domain (TLD)** abbreviation that identifies the type of organization that operates the site. In Figure 7-8, for example, the abbreviation, com, represents a top-level domain. For international Web sites, the domain name also includes a country code, which usually is

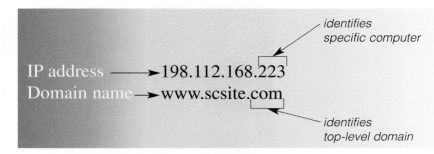

identifies specific computer

IP address ——→ 198.112.168.223
Domain name ——→ www.scsite.com

identifies top-level domain

Figure 7-8 *The IP address and domain name for the Shelly Cashman Series® Instructional Web site.*

TOP-LEVEL DOMAIN ABBREVIATIONS

Original Top-Level Domain Abbreviations	Type of Organization
com	Commercial organizations, businesses, and companies
edu	Educational institutions
gov	Government institution
mil	Military organizations
net	Network provider
org	Non-profit organizations

Newer Top-Level Domain Abbreviations	Type of Organization
arts	Arts and cultural-oriented entities
firm	Other businesses or firms
info	Information services
nom	Individuals or families
rec	Recreation/entertainment sources
store	Merchants, businesses offering goods to purchase
web	Parties emphasizing Web activities

Figure 7-9 With the explosive growth of the Internet over the last few years, the competition for domain names has increased. To address this problem, seven new top-level domain abbreviations have been created by the Internet Ad Hoc Committee (IAHC) to provide companies with additional possibilities for registering their names.

WEB INFO

For more information on the DNS, visit the Discovering Computers 2000 Chapter 7 WEB INFO page (**www.scsite.com/dc2000/ch7/webinfo.htm**) and click DNS.

placed at the end of a domain name — for countries outside the United States. Figure 7-9 lists the domain type abbreviations, and Figure 7-10 lists several country code abbreviations.

Domain names are registered in the **domain name system (DNS)** and are stored in Internet computers called **domain name system servers (DNS servers)**. Recall that the Internet is based on IP addresses. Every time you specify a domain name, a DNS server translates the domain name into its associated IP address, so that data can be routed to the correct computer.

Because the rapid growth of the Internet is expected to continue, an expanded IP addressing scheme is being implemented. The new address scheme will increase the number of addresses by a factor of four and will provide added security for data transfers.

Country Code Abbreviations	Country
au	Australia
ax	Antarctica
ca	Canada
de	Germany
dk	Denmark
fr	France
jp	Japan
nl	Netherlands
se	Sweden
th	Thailand
uk	United Kingdom
us	United States

Figure 7-10 A partial listing of country code abbreviations. The us code usually is omitted.

THE WORLD WIDE WEB

Although many people use the terms World Wide Web and Internet interchangeably, the World Wide Web is just one of the many services available on the Internet. The World Wide Web actually is a relatively new aspect of the Internet. While the Internet was developed in the late 1960s, the World Wide Web came into existence less than a decade ago — in the early 1990s. Since then, however, it has grown phenomenally to become the most widely used service on the Internet.

Recall that the **World Wide Web (WWW)**, or simply **Web**, consists of a worldwide collection of electronic documents that have built-in hyperlinks to other related documents. These hyperlinks, called **links**, allow users to navigate quickly from one document to another, regardless of whether the documents are located on the same computer or on different computers in different countries.

An electronic document on the Web is called a **Web page**; it can contain text, graphics, sound, and video, as well as links to other Web pages. A collection of related Web pages that you can access electronically is called a **Web site**. Most Web sites have a starting point, called a **home page**, which is similar to a book cover or table of contents for the site and provides information about the site's purpose and content.

Each Web page on a Web site has a unique address, called a **Uniform Resource Locator (URL)**. As shown in Figure 7-11, a URL consists of a protocol, a domain name, and sometimes the path to a specific Web page or location in a Web page. Most Web page URLs begin with **http**://, which stands for **hypertext transfer protocol**, the communications protocol used to transfer pages on the Web. You access and view Web pages using a software program called a **Web browser**, or **browser**. The more widely used Web browsers today are Microsoft Internet Explorer and Netscape Navigator.

The Web pages that comprise a Web site are stored on a server, called a Web server. A **Web server** is a computer that delivers (serves) requested Web pages. For example, when you enter the URL, http://www.sportsline.com/mlb/index.html in your browser, your browser sends a request to the server that stores the Web site of www.sportsline.com. The server then fetches the page named index.html and sends it to your browser.

Multiple Web sites can be stored on the same Web server. For example, many Internet service providers grant their subscribers storage space on a Web server for their personal or company Web sites.

A **Webmaster** is the individual responsible for developing Web pages and maintaining a Web site. Webmasters and other Web page developers create and format Web pages using hypertext markup language (HTML), which is a set of special codes that define the placement and format of text, graphics, video, and sound on a Web page. Because HTML can be difficult to learn and use, many user-friendly tools exist for Web publishing, which is the development and maintenance of Web pages. HTML and other Web publishing techniques are discussed later in this chapter.

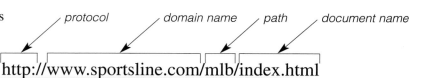

Figure 7-11 *Each Web page has a unique address, called a Uniform Resource Locator (URL).*

WEB INFO

For more information on plug-ins, visit the Discovering Computers 2000 Chapter 7 WEB INFO page (www.scsite.com/dc2000/ch7/webinfo.htm) and click Plug-ins.

Search Engines

No single organization controls additions, deletions, and changes to Web sites, which means no central menu or catalog of Web site content and addresses exists. Several companies, however, maintain organized directories of Web sites to help you find information on specific topics. The companies provide a software program, called a **search engine**, which helps you locate Web sites, Web pages, and Internet files (Figure 7-12). For additional information on search engines, see Chapter 2.

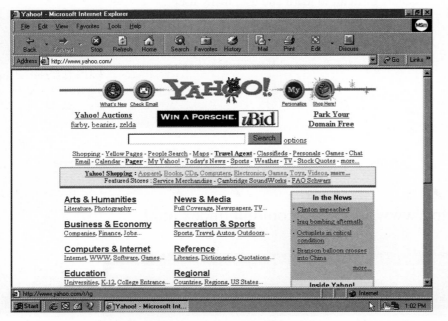

Figure 7-12 *Yahoo! is a popular search engine.*

Multimedia on the Web

Most Web pages include more than just formatted text and links. In fact, some of the more exciting Web developments involve multimedia. A Web page that incorporates color, sound, motion, and graphics with text has much more appeal than one with text on a gray background. Combining text, audio, video, animation, and sound brings a Web page to life; increases the types of information available on the Web; expands the Web's potential uses; and makes the Internet a more entertaining place to explore. Although multimedia Web pages often require more time to download because they contain large files such as video or audio clips, the pages usually are worth the wait.

Most browsers have the capability of displaying basic multimedia elements on a Web page. Sometimes, however, your browser might need an additional program, called a plug-in or helper application, which extends the capability of the browser. A **plug-in** runs multimedia elements within the browser window, while a **helper application** runs multimedia elements in a window separate from the browser. Plug-ins and helper applications can be downloaded, or copied, at no charge from many sites on the Web (Figure 7-13). In fact, Web pages that use multimedia elements often include links to Web sites that contain the required plug-in or helper. Some browsers include commonly used plug-ins, such as Shockwave, which is required for viewing many multimedia Web pages.

Some of the multimedia on the Web is developed in **Java**, which is a programming language specifically designed by Sun Microsystems for use on the Internet. Developers use Java to create small programs called **applets** that can be downloaded and run in a browser window. Applets can be used by just about any type of computer. Similar to an applet, an **ActiveX control** is a small program that can be downloaded and run in a browser, thus adding multimedia capabilities to Web pages. Although Microsoft initially developed ActiveX controls, programmers can develop ActiveX controls using Java as well as other programming languages. These programming languages are discussed in more detail in Chapter 12.

The following sections discuss how graphics, audio, animation, video, and virtual reality are used on the Web.

GRAPHICS **Graphics** were the first media used to enhance the text-based Internet. The introduction of graphical Web browsers allowed Web page developers to incorporate illustrations, logos, and other images into Web pages. Today, many Web pages use colorful graphical designs and images to convey messages (Figure 7-14).

POPULAR PLUG-IN/HELPER APPLICATIONS

Plug-In/Helper Application		Description	Web Site URL
Get Acrobat Reader Adobe	Acrobat Reader	View, navigate, and print Portable Document Format (PDF) files — documents formatted to look just as they look in print	www.adobe.com
macromedia SHOCKWAVE	Shockwave/Flash Player	Experience dynamic interactive multimedia, graphics, and streaming audio	www.macromedia.com
QuickTime logo	QuickTime	View animation, music, audio, video, and virtual reality panoramas and objects directly in a Web page	www.apple.com
FREE realplayer real G2	RealPlayer	Live and on-demand near-CD-quality audio and newscast-quality video; stream audio and video content for faster viewing	www.real.com
LIQUID AUDIO	Liquid MusicPlayer	Listen to and purchase CD-quality music tracks and audio CDs over the Internet; the first commercially viable and legally responsible system for this type of multimedia	www.liquidaudio.com
ichat logo	ichat	Access thousands of different chat rooms to chat with more than eight million ichat users	www.acuity.com
Cosmo Player /2.1 The Universal VRML 2.0 Client	Cosmo Player	View 3-D and other virtual reality applications written in Virtual Reality Modeling Language (VRML)	cosmosoftware.com

Figure 7-13 *Most of these popular plug-ins and helper applications can be downloaded free from the Web.*

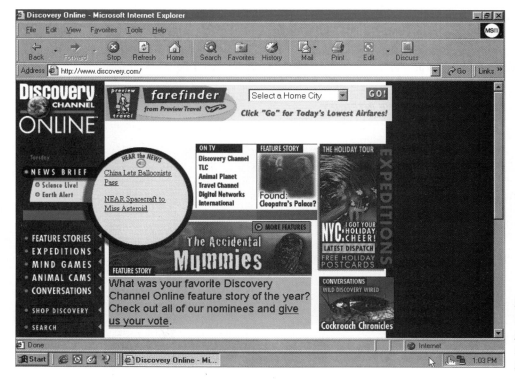

Figure 7-14 *Many Web pages use colorful graphic designs and images to convey their messages.*

Graphics files on the Web must be saved in a certain format. The two more common file formats for graphical images on the Web are JPEG and GIF. A **JPEG** (pronounced JAY-peg) file, which stands for **Joint Photographic Experts Group**, is a graphical image saved using compression techniques to reduce the file size for faster downloading from the Web. When you create a JPEG image, you can specify the image quality to reach a balance between image quality and file size. The JPEG format often is used for scanned photographs, artwork, and other images that include smooth color variations.

A graphical image saved as a **GIF** (pronounced jiff or giff) file, which stands for **Graphics Interchange Format**, also is saved using compression techniques to reduce its file size for downloading. The GIF format works best for images with only a few distinct colors, such as line drawings, single-color borders, and simple cartoons. The technique used to compress GIF files (called LZW compression), however, is patented, which means companies that make products using the GIF format must obtain a license. (Most Web users or businesses that include GIFs in their Web pages are not required to obtain a license.)

A patent-free replacement for the GIF, the PNG format, has been developed and approved by the World Wide Web Consortium as an Internet graphics standard. The **PNG** (pronounced ping) format, which stands for **portable network graphics**, also is a compressed file format that supports multiple colors and resolutions. These and other graphics formats used on the Web are shown in the table in Figure 7-15.

The Web contains thousands of image files on countless subjects, many of which can be downloaded free and used for non-commercial purposes. Because graphics files can be time consuming to download, some Web sites use thumbnails on their pages. A **thumbnail** is a small version of a larger graphical image that you usually can click to display the full-sized image (Figure 7-16).

ANIMATION Animation is the appearance of motion that is created by displaying a series of still images in rapid sequence. Animated graphics can make Web pages more visually interesting or draw attention to important information or links. For example, text that is animated to scroll across the screen, called a **marquee** (pronounced mar-KEE), can serve as a ticker to display stock updates, news, sports scores, or weather (Figure 7-17). Animation often is used in Web-based games; some animations even contain links to a different page.

One popular type of animation, called an **animated GIF**, is created using computer animation and graphics software to combine several images into a single GIF file. You also can create applets or ActiveX controls that include animation, or you simply can download many already-developed animations from the Web.

GRAPHICS FORMATS USED ON THE INTERNET

Acronym	Name	File Extension
JPEG (pronounced JAY-peg)	Joint Photographic Experts Group	.jpg
GIF (pronounced jiff)	Graphics Interchange Format	.gif
PNG (pronounced ping)	Portable Network Graphics	.png
TIFF	Tagged Image File Format	.tif
PCX	PC Paintbrush	.pcx
BMP	Bitmap	.bmp

Figure 7-15 Graphics formats used on the Internet.

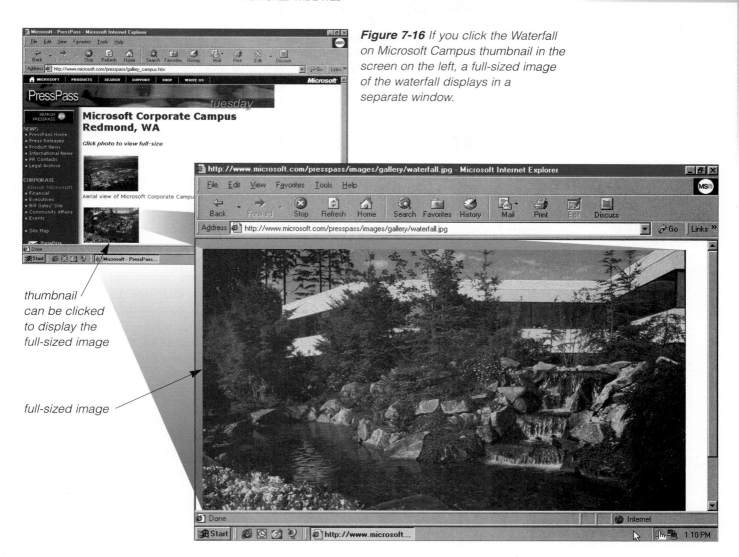

Figure 7-16 *If you click the Waterfall on Microsoft Campus thumbnail in the screen on the left, a full-sized image of the waterfall displays in a separate window.*

thumbnail can be clicked to display the full-sized image

full-sized image

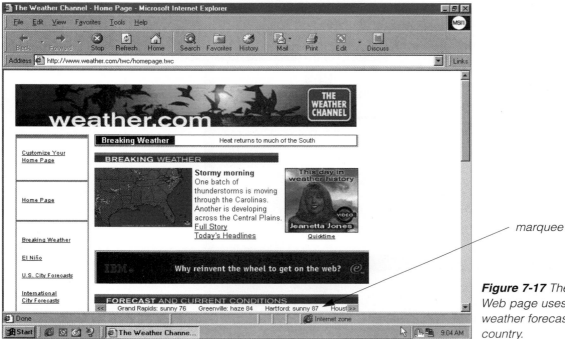

marquee

Figure 7-17 *The Weather Channel Web page uses a marquee to display weather forecasts in cities around the country.*

AUDIO Simple **Web audio applications** consist of individual sound files that must be downloaded completely before they can be played. As with graphics files, these sound files must be saved in a certain format. Two common formats used for audio files on the Internet are **WAV** and **AU**.

More advanced Web audio applications use streaming audio. **Streaming** is the process of transferring data in a continuous and even flow, which allows users to access and use a file before it has been transmitted completely. Streaming is important because most users do not have fast enough Internet connections to download a large multimedia file quickly. **Streaming audio**, enables you to listen to the sound (the data) as it downloads to your computer. Many radio and television stations use streaming audio to broadcast music, interviews, talk shows, sporting events, music videos, news, live concerts, and other segments (Figure 7-18). One

accepted standard for transmitting audio data on the Internet is **RealAudio**, which is supported by most current Web browsers.

Web-based audio can be used for **Internet telephone service**, also called **audioconferencing** and **Internet telephony**, which enables you to talk to other people over the Web. Internet telephony uses the Internet (instead of a public telephone network) to connect a calling party and one or more called parties. Internet telephony thus allows you to talk to friends or colleagues for just the cost of your Internet connection. As you speak into a computer microphone, **Internet telephone software** and your computer's sound card digitize and compress your conversation and then transmit the digitized audio over the Internet to the called parties. Software and equipment at the receiving end reverse the process so the receiving parties can hear what you have said, just as if you were on a telephone.

WEB INFO
WEB INFO

For more information on streaming media, visit the Discovering Computers 2000 Chapter 7 WEB INFO page (**www.scsite.com/ dc2000/ch7/webinfo.htm**) and click Streaming Media.

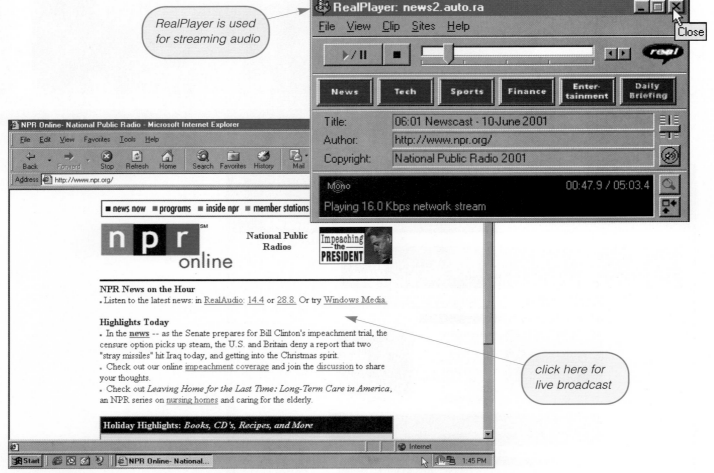

Figure 7-18 *Many radio and television stations use streaming audio. National Public Radio (NPR) transmits audio data in RealAudio, which is a component of RealPlayer.*

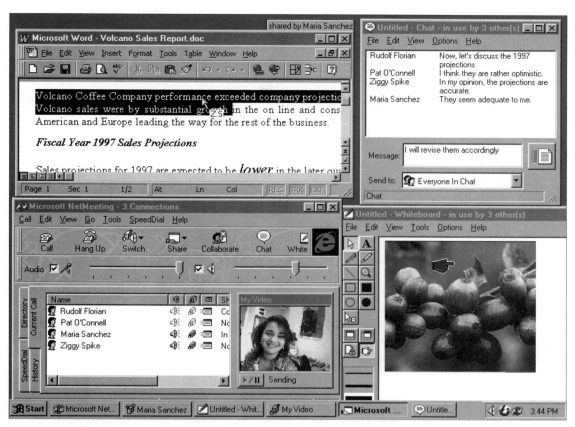

Figure 7-19 *NetMeeting, which is included with Internet Explorer, offers Internet telephony.*

Some of today's Web browsers include software such as CoolTalk and Microsoft NetMeeting, which supports Internet telephony (Figure 7-19). In addition to Internet telephony, these products typically offer additional services such as a whiteboard to display drawings, diagrams, and other graphics; chat tools to type text messages; and even videoconferencing so you can see images of the meeting participants.

VIDEO Like audio, simple **Web video applications** consist of individual video files, such as movie or television clips, that must be downloaded completely before they can be played on your computer. Because video files often are large and can take a long time to download, these video clips usually are quite short.

As with streaming audio, **streaming video** allows you to view longer or live video images as they are downloaded to your computer. A widely used standard for transmitting video data on the Internet is **RealVideo**. Like RealAudio, RealVideo is supported by most current Web browsers.

Streaming video also allows you to conduct Internet videoconferences, which work much like Internet telephony. As you are filmed by a video camera, videoconferencing software and your computer's video capture card digitize and compress the images and sounds. A popular video compression standard is defined by the **Motion Picture Experts Group** (**MPEG**). Files in the MPEG format typically have an .mpg extension.

This compressed data is divided into packets and sent over the Internet. Equipment and software at the receiving end assemble the packets, decompress the data, and present the image and sound as video. As with traditional videoconferencing, live Internet videoconferences can be choppy and blurry depending on the speed of the slowest communications link. As mentioned earlier, many products that support Internet telephony also have videoconferencing capabilities, thus allowing for face-to-face conversations over the Internet (see Figure 7-19).

VIRTUAL REALITY Virtual reality (VR) is the simulation of a real or imagined environment that appears as a three-dimensional (3-D) space. On the Web, VR involves the display of 3-D images that you can explore and manipulate interactively. Most Web-based VR applications are developed using **virtual reality modeling language**, or **VRML** (pronounced VER-mal), which is a language that defines how 3-D images display on the Web. Using VRML, a developer can create an entire 3-D site, called a **VR world**, that contains infinite space and depth. A VR world, for example, might show a room with furniture. You can walk through such a VR room by moving your pointing device forward, backward, or to the side. To view a VR world, you need a VRML browser or a VRML plug-in to a Web browser.

VR often is used for games, but it has many practical applications as well. Science educators can create VR models of molecules, organisms, and other structures for students to examine. Companies can use VR to showcase products or create advertisements (Figure 7-20). Architects can create VR models of buildings and rooms so they can show their clients how a completed construction project will look before it is built.

WEBCASTING

Until recently, when you wanted information from a Web site, you requested, or pulled, the information from the site by entering a URL in your browser or clicking a link. Some of today's browsers support **push technology**, in which Web-based content is downloaded automatically to your computer at regular intervals or whenever the site is updated. You can choose to have the entire site or just a portion of it, such as the

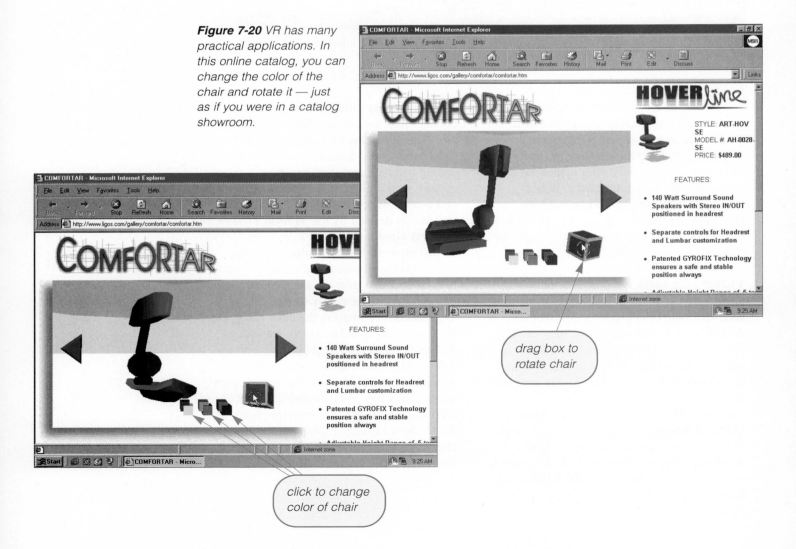

Figure 7-20 VR has many practical applications. In this online catalog, you can change the color of the chair and rotate it — just as if you were in a catalog showroom.

latest news, pushed to your computer (Figure 7-21). In Microsoft Internet Explorer, for example, push technology can be implemented through channels. A **channel** is a preselected Web site that automatically can send updated information. You can choose to view the information immediately or access it later. Push technology thus saves you time by delivering information at regular intervals, without your having to request it.

Another advantage to push technology is that once Web content has been pushed to your computer, you can view it whether you are online or **offline** — that is, when you are not connected to the Internet. With push technology, the contents of one or more Web sites are downloaded to your hard disk while you are online, thus making them available for browsing while you are offline. Offline browsing is ideal for mobile users because they do not always have access to the Internet.

The concept of using push and pull technologies to broadcast audio, video, and text information is called **webcasting**. With webcasting, you receive customized Web content that is updated regularly and automatically. The information you receive is based on the preferences you choose, such as selecting certain channels and setting times for updates.

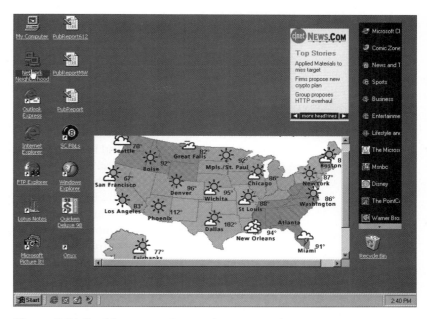

Figure 7-21 On this screen, the weather map and news headlines are pushed onto the desktop.

For more information on e-commerce, visit the Discovering Computers 2000 Chapter 7 WEB INFO page (**www.scsite.com/ dc2000/ch7/webinfo.htm**) and click E-commerce.

ELECTRONIC COMMERCE

When you conduct business activities online, you are participating in **electronic commerce**, also known as **e-commerce** (Figure 7-22). These activities include shopping, investing, and any other venture that uses either electronic money (e-money) or electronic data interchange. **Electronic data interchange (EDI)** is the transmission of business documents or data over communication lines. Many companies are using EDI on the Internet for buying, selling, or trading because it eliminates paperwork and increases response times.

One major advantage of e-commerce is that consumers can purchase directly from businesses, eliminating the middleman. For example, instead of visiting a computer retailer to purchase a computer, you now can order one designed to your specifications, right from the manufacturer's Web site. This practice enables businesses to provide goods and services at a lower cost.

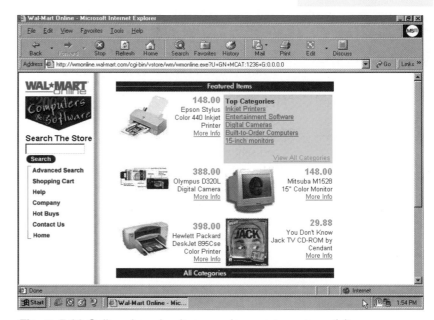

Figure 7-22 Online shopping is a popular e-commerce activity. Web sites, such as this one, allow you to purchase a range of products over the Internet.

Electronic money (e-money), also called **digital cash**, is a means of paying for goods and services over the Internet. With one method, you purchase digital certificates from a **certificate authority (CA)**, which is an authorized company or person that issues and verifies digital certificates. A **digital certificate** is an electronic credential that ensures a user is legitimate and the transfer of confidential materials is secure. Many banks, for example, allow you to purchase digital certificates that represent cash. Each digital cash certificate is assigned a unique number that represents an amount of money, just like the unique numbers on real currency.

Once you have the digital cash certificate, you can purchase goods or services over the Web. To do this, you transfer the digital cash certificate to the vendor, who then deposits the certificate number in a bank or transfers it to another vendor. Just like paper money, digital cash is reusable and anonymous; that is, the vendor has no information about the buyer. Because of this, many users prefer to pay with e-money instead of a credit card. Currently, no standard exists for e-money, and many companies offer various electronic payment schemes for use on the Internet.

A variation on e-money is **electronic credit** or an **electronic wallet**, which is a credit-card payment scheme for use on the Web. With electronic credit, a small program, called a **wallet**, stores your address and credit card information on your computer's hard disk. When you purchase something using electronic credit, you can choose from any of the credit cards in your wallet, and that information is transferred from your computer to the vendor's computer. Your credit card information is encrypted when it is stored on your computer and sent over communication lines. Encryption is the conversion of data into a form that cannot be easily understood by unauthorized people. Various encryption techniques are discussed in Chapter 14.

WEB INFO
WEB INFO

For more information on Web publishing, visit the Discovering Computers 2000 Chapter 7 WEB INFO page (**www.scsite.com/ dc2000/ch7/webinfo.htm**) and click Web Publishing.

WEB PUBLISHING

Before the advent of the Web, the means to share opinions and ideas with others easily and inexpensively was limited to classroom, work, or social environments. Generating an advertisement or publication that could reach a massive audience required a lot of expense. Today, businesses and individuals can convey information to millions of people by using Web pages. Individual Web pages are sometimes called **personal Web pages**.

As mentioned earlier in this chapter, Web pages are created and formatted using **hypertext markup language (HTML)**, which is a set of special codes used to format a file for use as a Web page. These codes, called **tags**, specify how the text and other elements display in a browser and where the links lead. Figure 7-23 shows the HTML document used to create the Web page shown in Figure 7-24. Your Web browser translates the document with HTML tags into a functional Web page.

The development and maintenance of Web pages, called **Web publishing**, is fairly easy as long as you have the proper tools.

- To incorporate pictures in your Web pages, you could use a digital camera to take digital photographs or a scanner to convert your existing photographs and other graphics into digital format. It also would be beneficial to have a collection of clip art and/or other images, which you can download from the Web or purchase on CD-ROM or DVD-ROM.

- With a sound card, you can add sounds to your Web pages. A microphone allows you to include your voice in a Web page.

- To incorporate videos, you could use a video capture card and a video camera. Or, you can purchase a video digitizer to capture still photographs from videos.

- If you are comfortable using HTML tags, you can create an HTML document using any text editor or standard word processing software. You must save the HTML document as an ASCII file with an **.htm** or **.html** extension, instead of as a formatted word processing document.

To develop a Web page, however, you do not have to be a computer programmer — or even learn more than basic HTML.

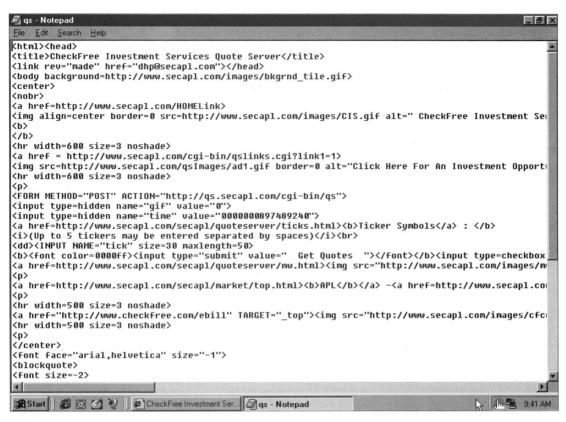

Figure 7-23 *This HTML document represents the top portion of the Web page shown in Figure 7-24. Web browser software interprets the HTML tags and displays the text, graphics, and links accordingly.*

Figure 7-24 *The Web page generated from the HTML shown in Figure 7-23.*

Instead, you can generate HTML tags with Web page authoring software — or just your word processing software. Many current word processing packages include Web page authoring features that help you to create basic Web pages that contain text and graphics (Figure 7-25).

To create more sophisticated Web pages that include video, sound, animation, and other special effects, you can use Web page authoring software such as Adobe PageMill or Microsoft FrontPage (Figure 7-26). Both new and experienced users can create fascinating Web sites with this software.

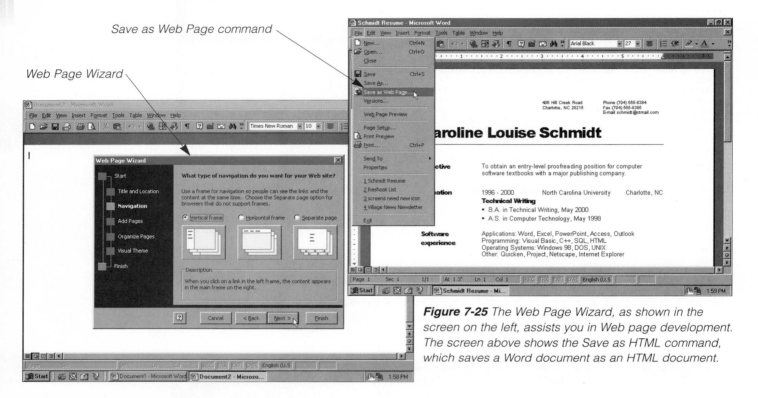

Save as Web Page command

Web Page Wizard

Figure 7-25 *The Web Page Wizard, as shown in the screen on the left, assists you in Web page development. The screen above shows the Save as HTML command, which saves a Word document as an HTML document.*

Figure 7-26a (Web page template)

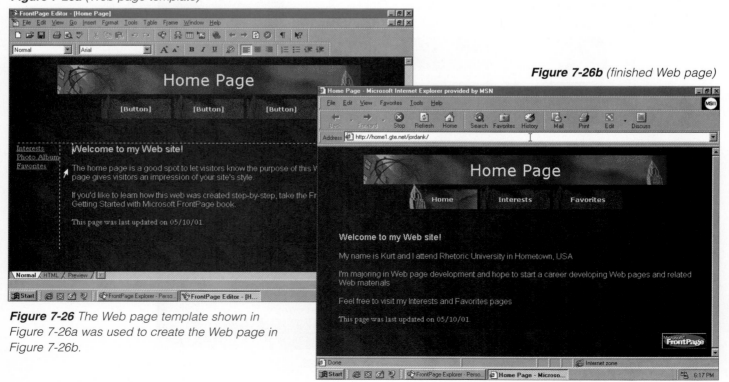

Figure 7-26b (finished Web page)

Figure 7-26 *The Web page template shown in Figure 7-26a was used to create the Web page in Figure 7-26b.*

Web page authoring software hides the complexity of HTML instructions used to format a Web page and allows a Web page developer to focus on Web page design and style. Many Web page authoring products provide templates and wizards, along with collections of design elements such as bullets, backgrounds, patterns, fonts, and graphics, to assist you with Web page development.

After your Web pages are created, you store them on a Web server. Many ISPs and online services provide their customers with a Web address and 1 to 10 MB of storage on a Web server without an additional charge. If your ISP does not include this service, companies called **Web hosting services** provide storage for your Web pages for a reasonable monthly fee. The fee charged by a Web hosting service varies based on factors such as the amount of storage your Web pages require, whether your pages use streaming or other multimedia, and whether the pages are personal or for business use.

Once you have created a Web page and located a Web server to store it, you need to **upload** the Web page, or copy it, from your computer to the Web server. A common procedure used to upload files is FTP, which is discussed later in this chapter.

To help others locate your Web site, you should register it with various search engines. Doing so ensures that your site will appear in the results returned for searches on keywords related to your site. Many search engines allow you to register your URL and keywords without cost.

Registering your site with the various search engines, however, can be an extremely time-consuming task. Instead, you can use a **submission service**, which is a Web-based business that usually offers free registration of your site with several search engines or a registration package in which you pay to register with hundreds of search engines (Figure 7-27).

In addition to supplying a title for your site, the URL, and a site description, the submission service probably will require you to identify several features of your site, such as whether the site is commercial or personal; a category and subcategory; and search keywords. For example, if your Web site business sells greeting cards, you could register under the Products and Services subcategory in the Business and Economy category, and specify keywords such as greeting cards, birthday cards, and anniversary cards.

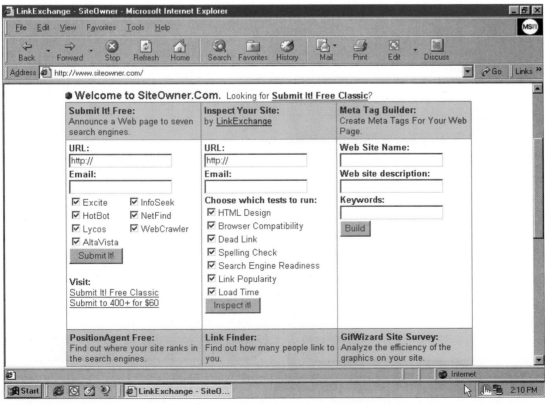

Figure 7-27 *Submit It! is a popular submission service that offers free registration to several search engines or a complete registration to hundreds of search engines for a fee.*

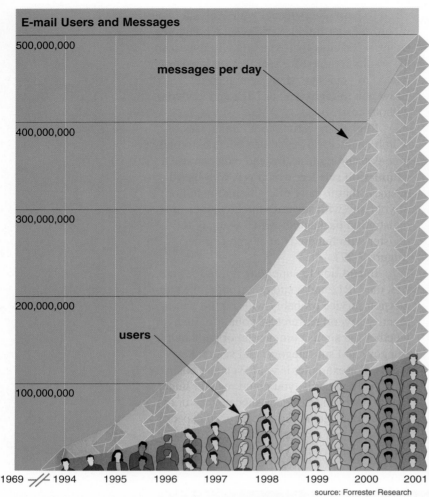

E-mail Users and Messages

500,000,000

messages per day

400,000,000

300,000,000

200,000,000

users

100,000,000

1969 —//— 1994   1995   1996   1997   1998   1999   2000   2001

source: Forrester Research

Figure 7-28 *The number of e-mail users and e-mail messages as indicated by this graph, has grown phenomenally in the past several years.*

OTHER INTERNET SERVICES

Although the World Wide Web is the most talked about service on the Internet, many other Internet services are used widely. These include e-mail, FTP, Telnet, newsgroups, mailing lists, and chat rooms. Each of these services is discussed in the following sections.

E-mail

E-mail (electronic mail) is the transmission of messages and files via a computer network. E-mail was one of the original services on the Internet, enabling scientists and researchers working on government-sponsored projects to communicate with colleagues at other locations. Today, e-mail quickly is becoming a primary communication method for both personal and business use (Figure 7-28).

Using an **e-mail program**, you can create, send, receive, forward, store, print, and delete messages (Figure 7-29). To receive messages, you need an **e-mail address**, which is a combination of a user name and a domain name that identifies a user (Figure 7-30). When you receive an e-mail message, the message is placed in your mailbox. A **mailbox** is a storage location usually residing on the computer that connects you to the Internet, such as the server operated by your Internet service provider (ISP). The server that contains the mailboxes often is called a **mail server**. Most ISPs and online services provide an Internet e-mail program and a mailbox on a mail server as a standard part of their Internet access services.

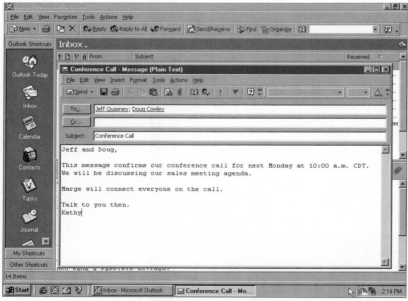

Figure 7-29 *Outlook is an e-mail program that allows you to create, send, receive, forward, store, print, and delete messages.*

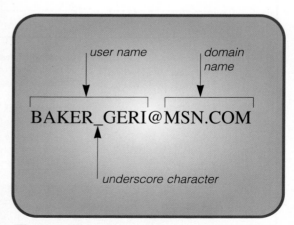

Figure 7-30 *An e-mail address is a combination of a user name and a domain name. The underscore character (_) often is used to separate sections of the user name.*

When you send a message, the message is transmitted according to a communications protocol called **SMTP (simple mail transfer protocol)**. The mail server uses SMTP to determine how to route the message through the Internet and then sends the message. When the message arrives at the recipient's mail server, the message is transferred to a POP or POP3 server. **POP (Post Office Protocol)** is a communications protocol used to retrieve e-mail from a mail server. The POP server holds the message until the recipient retrieves it with his or her e-mail software (Figure 7-31). The newest version of POP is **POP3**, or **Post Office Protocol 3**.

Most e-mail programs allow you to send messages that contain graphics, audio and video clips, and computer files, as attachments. These attachments must be converted, or encoded, to binary format so they can be sent over the Internet and then decoded when the recipient retrieves them. Most e-mail software includes **encoding schemes** that make it possible for attachments to arrive at the recipient's computer in the same format in which they left the sender's computer.

Figure 7-31

HOW AN E-MAIL MESSAGE TRAVELS FROM THE SENDER TO THE RECEIVER

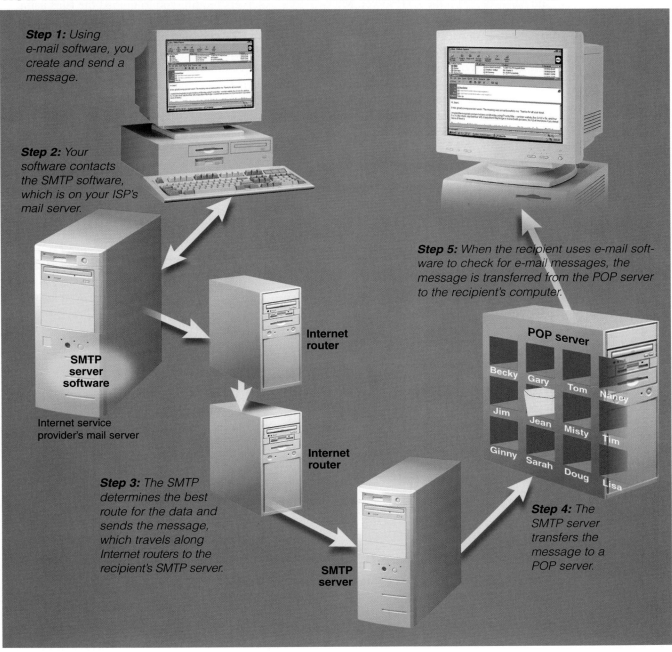

Step 1: Using e-mail software, you create and send a message.

Step 2: Your software contacts the SMTP software, which is on your ISP's mail server.

SMTP server software

Internet service provider's mail server

Internet router

Step 3: The SMTP determines the best route for the data and sends the message, which travels along Internet routers to the recipient's SMTP server.

Internet router

SMTP server

Step 5: When the recipient uses e-mail software to check for e-mail messages, the message is transferred from the POP server to the recipient's computer.

POP server

Becky Gary Tom Nancy
Jim Jean Misty Tim
Ginny Sarah Doug Lisa

Step 4: The SMTP server transfers the message to a POP server.

FTP

FTP (file transfer protocol) is an Internet standard that allows you to exchange files with other computers on the Internet. For example, if you click a link on a Web page that begins to download a file to your hard disk, you probably are using FTP (Figure 7-32).

An **FTP server** is a computer that allows users to upload and download files using FTP. An FTP server contains one or more FTP sites. An **FTP site** is a collection of files including text, graphics, audio, video, and program files that reside on an FTP server. Some FTP sites limit file transfers to individuals who have authorized accounts (user names and passwords) on the FTP server. Many FTP sites allow **anonymous FTP**, whereby anyone can transfer some, if not all, available files. Microsoft, for example, has an FTP site that uses anonymous FTP to allow customers to download software updates, manuals, and other files. Many program files on anonymous FTP sites are freeware or public domain software, while others are shareware.

To view or use a file on an FTP site, you first must download it to your computer. In most cases, you click the file name to begin the download procedure. Large files on FTP sites often are compressed to reduce storage space and download transfer time. Before you use a compressed file, you must expand it with a decompression program, such as WinZip. Such programs usually are available for download from the FTP site. Compression and decompression programs are discussed in more detail in Chapter 8.

In some cases, you may want to upload a file to an FTP site. For example, if you create personal Web pages, you will want to post them on a Web server. To do this, many Web servers require you to upload the files using FTP. To upload files from your computer to an FTP site, you use an **FTP program** (Figure 7-33). Many Internet service providers include an FTP program as part of their Internet access service; you also can download FTP programs from the Web.

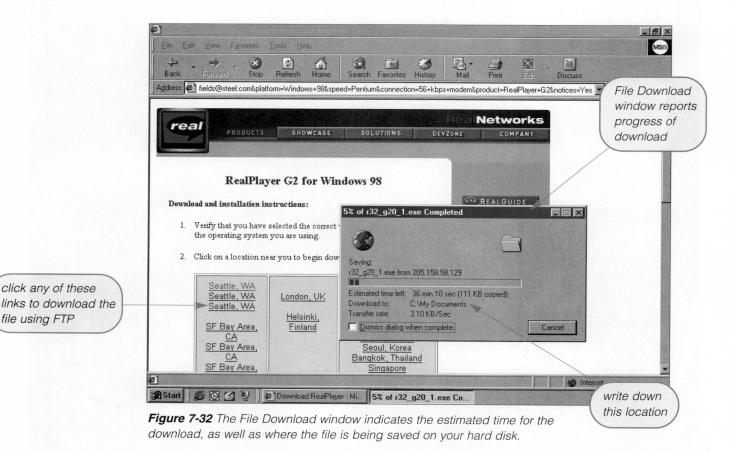

Figure 7-32 *The File Download window indicates the estimated time for the download, as well as where the file is being saved on your hard disk.*

Telnet

Telnet is a program or command that enables you to connect to a remote computer on the Internet. To make a Telnet connection to the remote computer, you enter a user name and password. Once connected, your computer acts like a terminal directly linked to the remote computer. Telnet access to many remote computers is free, while others are accessed for a fee. For convenience, some remote computers provide the Telnet program.

Some uses of Telnet include connecting to a remote computer to access databases, directories, and library catalogs. Online databases may contain research results, and directories containing lists of information such as people and organizations.

The widespread use of Internet service providers and Web browsers, however, has reduced the need to log in directly to remote computers using Telnet. Many libraries, for example, have converted their library databases to allow Web-based access.

Newsgroups

A **newsgroup** is an online area in which users conduct written discussions about a particular subject. To participate in a discussion, a user sends a message to the newsgroup, and other users in the newsgroup read and reply to the message. The entire collection of Internet newsgroups is called **Usenet**, which contains thousands of newsgroups on a multitude of topics. Some major topic areas include news, recreation, business, science, and computers.

A computer that stores and distributes newsgroup messages is called a **news server**. Many universities, corporations, ISPs, online services, and other large organizations have a news server. Some newsgroups require you to enter your user name and password to participate in the discussion. These types of newsgroups are used when the messages on the newsgroup are to be viewed only by authorized members, such as students taking a college course.

To participate in a newsgroup, you use a program called a **newsreader**, which is included with most browsers. The newsreader enables you to access a newsgroup to read a previously entered message, called an **article**. You also can add an article of your own, a process called **posting**. A newsreader also keeps track of which articles you have and have not read.

Newsgroup members frequently post articles as a reply to another article — either to answer a question or to comment on material

WEB INFO

For more information on newsgroups, visit the Discovering Computers 2000 Chapter 7 WEB INFO page (**www.scsite.com/ dc2000/ch7/webinfo.htm**) and click Newsgroups.

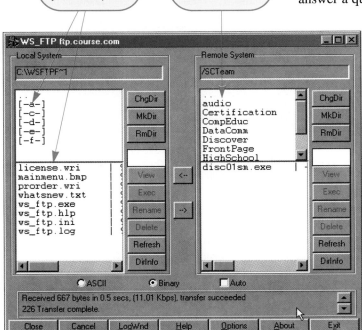

Figure 7-33 *You use an FTP program such as WS_FTP to upload a file to an FTP site.*

in the original article. These replies may cause the author of the original article, or others, to post additional articles related to the original article. The original article and all subsequent related replies are called a **thread** or **threaded discussion** (Figure 7-34). A thread can be short-lived or continue for some time, depending on the nature of the topic and the interest of the participants.

Using a newsreader, you can search for newsgroups discussing a particular subject, such as a type of musical instrument, brand of sports equipment, or employment opportunities. To help you determine what topics are discussed in a particular newsgroup, newsgroups are identified using a hierarchical naming system, with a major category divided into one or more subcategories. Each subcategory is separated by a period. Figure 7-35 lists major categories for newsgroups. If you like the discussion in a particular newsgroup, you can **subscribe** to it, which means its location is saved in your newsreader so you can access it easily in the future.

In some newsgroups, when you post an article, it is sent to a moderator instead of immediately displaying on the newsgroup. The **moderator** reviews the contents of the article and then posts it, if appropriate. Called a **moderated newsgroup**, the moderator decides if the article is relevant to the discussion. The moderator may choose to edit or discard inappropriate articles. For this reason, the content of a moderated newsgroup is considered more valuable.

Mailing Lists

A **mailing list** is group of e-mail names and addresses given a single name. When a message is sent to a mailing list, every person on the list receives a copy of the message in his or her mailbox. To add your e-mail name and address to a mailing list, you **subscribe** to it; to remove your name, you **unsubscribe** from the mailing list. Some mailing lists are called **LISTSERVs**, named after a popular mailing list software product.

Thousands of mailing lists exist on a variety of topics in areas of entertainment,

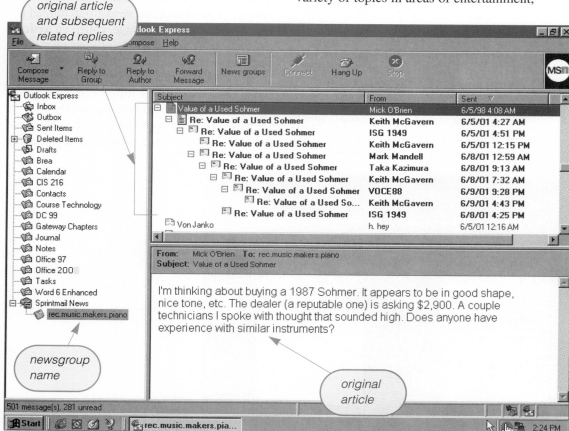

Figure 7-34 A newsgroup is an online area in which users conduct written discussions about a particular subject. Shown is a thread about the value of a used piano model.

business, computers, society, culture, health, recreation, and education. To locate a mailing list dealing with a particular topic, you can search for the keywords, mailing lists or LISTSERVs, using your Web browser.

Chat Rooms

A **chat** is a real-time typed conversation that takes place on a computer. **Real-time** means that you and the people with whom you are conversing must be online at the same time. When you enter a line of text on your computer screen, your words display on one or more participant's screens.

A **chat room** refers to the communications medium, or channel, that permits users to chat with each other. Anyone on the channel can participate in the conversation, which usually is specific to a particular topic. Each discussion is assigned a different channel.

To start a chat session, you connect to a chat server through a **chat client**, which is a program on your computer. Today's browsers usually include a chat client. If yours does not, you can download a chat client from the Web. Some chat clients are text-based, such as IRC (Internet relay chat) and ichat, while others, such as Microsoft Chat, support graphical and text-based chats.

Once you have installed a chat client, you then can create or join a conversation on the chat server to which you are attached. The channel name should indicate the topic of discussion. The person who creates a channel acts as the channel operator and has responsibility for monitoring the conversation and disconnecting anyone whom becomes disruptive. Operator status can be shared or transferred to someone else.

Several Web sites exist for the purpose of conducting chats. Some chat sites even allow participants to assume the role or appearance of a fictitious character.

Portals

A **portal** is a Web site designed to offer a variety of Internet services from a single, convenient location. Most portals offer the following free services: search engine; local, national, and worldwide news, sports, and weather; reference such as yellow pages and maps; shopping malls; e-mail; and chat rooms. Some portals also provide Internet access.

Popular portals include AltaVista, Excite, InfoSeek, Lycos, Microsoft Internet Start, Netscape Netcenter, Snap, and Yahoo! The goal of these portals is to be designated as your browser's starting Web page.

WEB INFO

For more information on portals, visit the Discovering Computers 2000 Chapter 7 WEB INFO page (**www.scsite.com/ dc2000/ch7/webinfo.htm**) and click Portals.

NEWSGROUP CATEGORIES

Category	Description	Examples
alt	Alternative	alt.family-names.hendricks alt.music.paul-simon
biz	Business	biz.jobs biz.marketplace.computers
comp	Computer	comp.graphics.animation comp.sys.handhelds
news	Newsgroups	news.announce.newsgroups news.groups.reviews
rec	Recreation	rec.autos.antique rec.travel.misc
soc	Social	soc.college.gradinfo soc.culture.spain
talk	Talk	talk.environment talk.politics.misc

Figure 7-35 *Major categories of newsgroups.*

NETIQUETTE

Netiquette, which is short for *Internet etiquette*, is the code of acceptable behaviors users should follow while on the Internet; that is, the conduct expected of individuals while online. Netiquette includes rules for all aspects of the Internet, including the World Wide Web, e-mail, FTP, Telnet, newsgroups, and chat rooms. Figure 7-36 outlines the rules of netiquette.

USING THE INTERNET: COOKIES AND SECURITY

While it is a vast and exciting resource, the Internet also is a public place, and as with all other public places, you should use common sense while there. The following sections explain guidelines for the use of cookies and security precautions for your consideration while using the Internet.

Netiquette

Golden Rule: *Treat others as you would like them to treat you.*

1. In e-mail, newsgroups, and chat rooms:
   • Keep messages brief, using proper grammar and spelling.
   • Be careful when using sarcasm and humor, as it might be misinterpreted.
   • Be polite. Avoid offensive language.
   • Avoid sending or posting **flames**, which are abusive or insulting messages. Do not participate in **flame wars**, which are exchanges of flames.
   • Avoid sending spam, which is the Internet's version of junk mail. **Spam** is an unsolicited e-mail message or newsgroup posting sent to many recipients or newsgroups at once.
   • Do not use all capital letters, which is the equivalent of SHOUTING!
   • Use **emoticons** to express emotion. Popular emoticons include

:)	Smile
:(	Frown
:I	Indifference
:\	Undecided
:o	Surprised

   • Use abbreviations and acronyms for phrases such as

BTW	by the way
FYI	for your information
FWIW	for what it's worth
IMHO	in my humble opinion
TTFN	ta ta for now
TYVM	thank you very much

   • Clearly identify a **spoiler**, which is a message that reveals a solution to a game or ending to a movie or program.

2. Read the **FAQ** (frequently asked questions), if one exists. Many newsgroups and Web sites have an FAQ.

3. Use your user name for personal purposes only.

4. Do not assume material is accurate or up to date. Be forgiving of other's mistakes.

5. Never read someone's private e-mail.

Figure 7-36 *The rules of netiquette.*

Cookies

Webcasting, e-commerce, and other Web applications often rely on cookies to track information about viewers, customers, and subscribers. A **cookie** is a small file that a Web server stores on your computer. Cookie files typically contain data about you, such as your user name or viewing preferences. Some Web sites send a cookie to your browser, which stores it on your computer's hard disk. The next time you visit the Web site, your browser retrieves the cookie from your hard disk and sends the data in the cookie to the Web site. Web sites use cookies for a variety of purposes.

• Web sites that allow for personalization often use cookies to track user preferences (Figure 7-37). On such sites, you may be asked to fill in a form requesting personal information, such as your name and site preferences. A news site, for example, might allow you to customize your viewing preferences to display business and sports news only. Your preferences are stored in a cookie on your hard disk.

• Online shopping sites generally use cookies to keep track of items in your shopping cart. This way, you can start an order during one Web session and finish it on another day in another session.

• Some Web sites use cookies to track how regularly you visit a site and the Web pages you visit while at the site.

• Web sites may use cookies to target advertisements. Your interests and browsing habits are stored in the cookie.

Although many believe that cookies allow other Web sites to read information on your computer, a Web site can read data only from its own cookie file; that is, it cannot access or view any other data on your hard disk — including another cookie file. Some Web sites do, however, sell or trade information stored in your cookie to advertisers — a practice many believe to be unethical. If

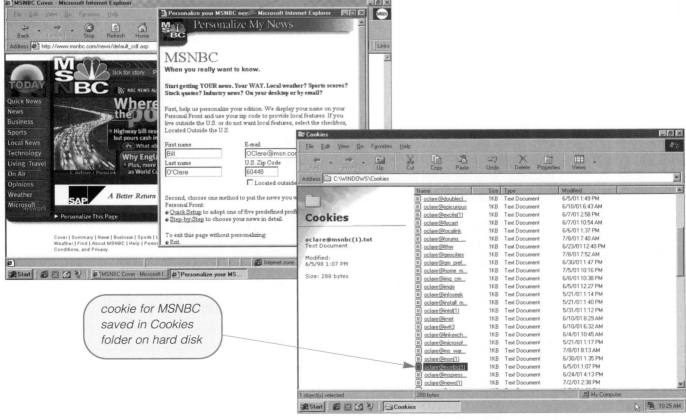

the personal information you enter in this form is stored in a cookie on your hard disk

cookie for MSNBC saved in Cookies folder on hard disk

Figure 7-37 *Some Web sites store user preferences in a cookie on your hard disk.*

you do not want your personal information being distributed, you should limit the amount of information you provide to a Web site. You can set your browser to accept cookies automatically, prompt you if you wish to accept a cookie, or disable cookie use altogether (Figure 7-38).

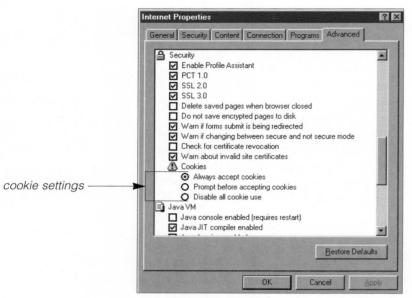

cookie settings

Figure 7-38 *Cookie settings are changed or viewed in the Windows Internet Properties dialog box.*

Internet Security

Even with netiquette guidelines, the Internet opens up the possibility for improper behaviors and content. For example, amidst the wealth of information and services on the Internet, some content may be inappropriate for certain people. Some Web sites, newsgroups, or chat rooms, for instance, contain content or discussions that are unsuitable for children. To assist parents with these types of issues, many browsers include software that can screen out unacceptable content. You also can purchase Internet **filtering software**, which allows parents, teachers, and others to block access to certain materials on the Internet.

Confidentiality is another important consideration on the Internet. For example, when shopping online, you should be sure that confidential or personal information such as your credit card number is encrypted during transmission. Reputable companies have secure servers that automatically encrypt this type of information while it is being transmitted.

One way to identify a secure Web page is to see if its URL begins with https://, instead of http:// (Figure 7-39). Many browsers today also include encryption software that allows you to encrypt e-mail messages or other documents. Attaching a digital signature to a document or message verifies your identity to the recipient, which is especially critical for e-commerce. Various types of encryption software and other security methods are discussed in Chapter 14.

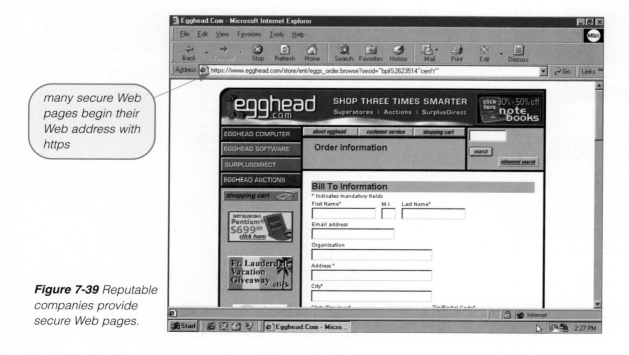

many secure Web pages begin their Web address with https

Figure 7-39 *Reputable companies provide secure Web pages.*

NETWORK COMPUTERS

For some applications, including many of the Internet services, a personal computer has more capability than the application requires. Jobs that primarily involve entering transactions or looking up information in a database — even viewing pages on the Web — do not require floppy disks, CD-ROMs, or large hard disks. These extra components contribute to both the cost and complexity of a personal computer; the more complex a computer is, the more expensive it is to maintain. As the costs of owning, operating, and maintaining a personal computer increase, many users are turning to network computers.

A **network computer (NC)**, sometimes called a **thin-client computer**, is a less expensive version of a personal computer designed specifically to connect to a network, especially the Internet. Most network computers cannot operate as a stand-alone computer; that is, they must be connected to a network to be functional. Network computers typically rely on the network for storage and, therefore, usually do not have a hard disk or CD-ROM drive (Figure 7-40).

A specific type of network computer used in business applications is the **network personal computer**, or **NetPC**, which was designed cooperatively by Microsoft and Intel. A NetPC primarily relies on the server for software and storage but does have a hard disk for storing some data and programs. A NetPC can run Java and other programs such as Microsoft Windows applications.

Low-cost network computers are well suited for use in the home, especially if a potential home user plans to purchase a computer only for Internet access. A network computer for the home, sometimes called a **set-top box**, is a device that incorporates Internet access into a television set. To keep the cost down, manufacturers have eliminated many standard computer features, such as any type of disk drive or monitor. Instead, your television set serves as the monitor. A set-top box is placed on top of your television set and allows you to access the Internet and navigate Web pages using a device that looks like a remote control (Figure 7-41). If you want to use the device to enter e-mail, you can use an optional wireless keyboard.

WEB INFO
WEB INFO

For more information on set-top boxes, visit the Discovering Computers 2000 Chapter 7 WEB INFO page (**www.scsite.com/dc2000/ch7/webinfo.htm**) and click Set-top Boxes.

Figure 7-40 *This thin-client computer is used in schools, businesses, medical facilities, and other applications designed specifically to connect to a network, especially the Internet.*

Figure 7-41 *A network computer that uses a television set as the display device is called a set-top box. With a system such as WebTV™, you can access the Internet and navigate Web pages using a device that looks like a remote control.*

TECHNOLOGY TRAILBLAZER

TIM BERNERS-LEE

Tim Berners-Lee is the creator of the World Wide Web, the innovation that revolutionized the way people use computers and obtain information. Millions access the Web every day, and many wonder why he did not commercialize his brainchild. Berners-Lee responds, "It's a strange question. By asking the question, people are suggesting that they respect people as a function of their net worth. That's worrying. It's not an assumption I was brought up with."

Tim Berners-Lee learned his values growing up in London, the child of mathematicians who met while working with the Ferranti Mark I, one of the first computers sold commercially. Berners-Lee had an early interest in both mathematics and electronics, playing with five-hole paper tape and making toy computers out of cardboard boxes. He attended Oxford University's Queen's College where, as a compromise between mathematics and electronics, he studied physics. While at Oxford, he also made his first working computer with a soldering iron, an M6800 processor, and an old television.

After graduating in 1976, Berners-Lee worked with transaction systems, message relays, bar code technology, typesetting software, multitasking operating systems, real-time control firmware, generic macro languages, and graphics and communications software. Looking back, his most significant work may have been a software program, called Enquire, that he wrote for his own use at CERN, the European Laboratory for Particle Physics based in Geneva, Switzerland. The program was inspired by the English edition of a book titled, *Enquire Within Upon Everything*. Enquire, which was intended as a resource you could use to learn about anything, foreshadowed the World Wide Web.

Computers always had stored information and worked with it mechanically, in tables and hierarchies. "One of the things computers have not done," Berners-Lee wrote, "is to be able to store random associations between disparate things, although this is something the brain has always done relatively well." Enquire not only stored text but also stored *random associations* in the form of hypertext links that pointed to related documents. Enquire's associations were limited, but in 1989, Berners-Lee suggested a universal system to let people everywhere share knowledge in a collection of hypertext documents. Associations would be sweeping and links could point to any document — primitive or polished, personal or public, everyday or exotic.

Early names for the project were rejected because Tim Berners-Lee was uncomfortable with their acronyms — Mine of Information (MOI) seemed self-centered ("moi" is "my" in French), and The Information Mine (TIM) was even worse. Finally, the World Wide Web (WWW) was chosen as both descriptive and memorable. The World Wide Web made its debut within CERN in December of 1990 and on the Internet at large in 1991. The Web's popularity exploded — each year from 1991 to 1994, the load on the first server was ten times greater than the year before.

As Web technology spread, initial specifications for URLs, HTML, and HTTP were refined. Questions remained, however, and in 1994 Berners-Lee became the director of the World Wide Web Consortium (W3C) based at the Massachusetts Institute of Technology (MIT). The Consortium consisted of, in 1999, more than 300 organizations — including Microsoft, IBM, Hewlett-Packard, and Lotus — that consider issues in the Web's evolution, hoping to realize its full potential and ensure its stability.

"We have to be careful," Berners-Lee warns, "because the sort of Web we end up with and the society we end up building on top of it will be determined by the decisions we make." Users shape the Web's future. The places people browse, the sites they setup, and the links they establish affect how the Web develops. "People have to be aware of this. We have the answers in our own hands."

COMPANY ON THE CUTTING EDGE

COMPANY ON THE CUTTING EDGE

YAHOO!

One of the more recognizable brands on the World Wide Web has one of the more unusual names: Yahoo! **Yahoo!** a leading global Internet media, is visited by millions of people worldwide every day. Supposedly, the name is an acronym for Yet Another Hierarchical Officious Oracle, but the co-founders claim they simply consider themselves yahoos (or tough guys). For millions of grateful users, however, the name is the cry of joy they utter when Yahoo! (www.yahoo.com) guides them to an elusive Web site. Whatever the origin, today Yahoo! is one of the more popular destinations.

Jerry Yang and David Filo, Ph.D. candidates in electrical engineering at Stanford University, started Yahoo! in 1994. Envisioned as a way of organizing their personal interests on the Internet, they began with collections of lists. As the lists became cumbersome, Yang and Filo transformed them into a tree-style database. Thousands of people soon were accessing the database, and software was developed to find, catalog, and edit material. Yang maintained the database on his student workstation, while Filo kept the search engine on his computer. The machines were dubbed *Akebono* and *Konishiki* in honor of two celebrated Hawaiian sumo wrestlers. Grappling with the Web went from a part-time pursuit to a full-time fixation, and Filo and Yang took a leave of absence from their doctoral work. In 1995, Marc Andreessen asked Yang and Filo to bring their operation to the large computers at Netscape Communications Corporation.

Yahoo!'s navigational guide and directory is a tailor-made database that runs on the UNIX platform and provides links to other Web sites. Links come from users who submit sites by clicking, Add URL, on the Yahoo! menu bar and from automated robots that seek out new sites. The database's renown stems from its simple indexing. Every site is hand placed in an appropriate category by human beings. A value in parentheses following a category name indicates the number of entries in that category, and an @ symbol at the end of a category means the heading appears in several different places in the Yahoo! hierarchy.

What differentiates the Yahoo! navigational guide from other online guides is that the directory is built by people. Every site is visited and evaluated by a Yahoo! staff member, or surfer. Site creators suggest the category under which a site belongs, but the Yahoo! surfers ultimately decide where each site is placed. To do this, staff members ride the surfboard of a typical user. While a book on building a chair, for example, may seem appropriate for the furniture category, most people surfing that category are interested in buying, not making, chairs. Therefore, Yahoo! surfers would place a site advertising the book in the how-to category. These decisions often are made in spontaneous staff meetings, which can take several days.

Yahoo! is the largest guide to the Web in terms of traffic and user reach. Services offered include Yahoo! Mail (http://mail.yahoo.com), Yahoo! Chat (http://chat.yahoo.com), and My Yahoo! (http://my.yahoo.com); and features such as What's New, What's Cool, and What's Popular. Yahoo! was incorporated in 1995 and became a publicly owned company in 1996. Today, Yahoo! employs more than 800 people. It costs nothing to use Yahoo! Revenue comes from advertising, including banner advertisements, sponsorships, promotion, keywords, and from electronic commerce, hosting, and licensing. People using this service may be asked for such information as their name, e-mail address, or other personal information that Yahoo! uses to target advertising at specific audiences based on their demographics, geographic location, interests, or other factors. Consolidated statistics also may be used to describe Yahoo! audiences to potential advertisers.

In 1998, Yahoo! recorded net revenues of more than $203 million. With traffic increased to 167 million page views per day in December 1998, Yahoo! corporate shareholders may have good reason to shout — well, you know.

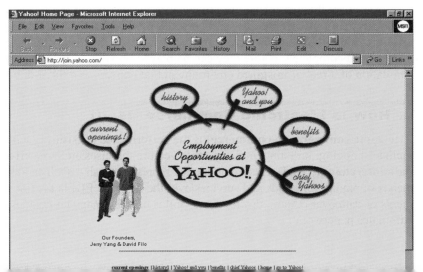

CHAPTER 1 2 3 4 5 6 **7** 8 9 10 11 12 13 14   INDEX

IN BRIEF www.scsite.com/dc2000/ch7/brief.htm

WEB INSTRUCTIONS: *To display this page from the Web, launch your browser and enter the URL,* www.scsite.com/dc2000/ch7/brief.htm. *Click the links for current and additional information. To listen to an audio version of this IN BRIEF, click the Audio button to the right of the title, IN BRIEF, at the top of the page. To play the audio, RealPlayer must be installed on your computer (download by clicking* here*).*

1. What Is the Internet?

The <u>Internet</u> is the world's largest network consisting of a worldwide collection of networks that links together millions of businesses, government offices, educational institutions, and individuals. Each of the networks provides an abundance of resources and uses. An **Internet service provider (ISP)** is an organization that has a permanent Internet connection and provides temporary connections to individuals and companies for a fee. An **online service** provides Internet access and offers a variety of special content and services. Individuals usually connect to the Internet using a modem and their personal computers. Other users connect to the Internet through a business or school network. With a network interface card (NIC), many people connect to a local area network (LAN) that is connected to an ISP.

2. How Does the Internet Work?

Data sent over the Internet travels via networks and communications lines. Computers connected to the Internet transfer data and information using **servers**, which are computers that manage network resources and provides centralized storage areas for software programs and data; and **clients**, which are computers that can access the contents of the storage areas on servers. When a <u>client computer</u> sends data over the Internet, the data is divided into small pieces called **packets**. The packets (containing data), move over communications lines (the main lines are referred to as the Internet **backbone**) through national ISPs and local ISPs to the destination server, where they are reassembled. Each computer on the Internet has a numeric address called an **IP** (**Internet protocol**) **address**, the text version of which is called a **domain name**.

3. What Is the World Wide Web and How Is Multimedia Used on the Web?

The **World Wide Web, WWW, or Web** consists of the worldwide collection of electronic documents, called **Web pages**, that have built-in **links** to other related Web pages. A collection of related Web pages is called a **Web site**, which can be viewed using a **Web browser** program. Web pages contain a variety of multimedia including graphics, animation, audio, video, and virtual reality. **Graphics** were the first media used to enhance the text-based Internet. **Animation** is the appearance of motion that is created by displaying a series of still images in rapid sequence. Simple **Web audio applications** and **Web video applications** consist of individual sound and video files that must be downloaded completely before they can be played on your computer. <u>**Virtual reality (VR)**</u> is the simulation of a real or imagined environment that appears as a three-dimensional (3-D) space.

4. How Is Electronic Commerce Used?

Electronic commerce (e-commerce) is the performance of business activities online. These activities include shopping, investing, and any other venture that uses either **electronic money** or **electronic data interchange (EDI)**. Electronic money represents cash – such as a **digital certificate** – and is a means of paying for goods and services over the Internet. <u>EDI</u> is the transmission of business documents or data over communication lines, and is used by many companies on the Internet because it eliminates paperwork and increases response times.

 **IN BRIEF**   www.scsite.com/dc2000/ch7/brief.htm

 ## 5. What Tools Are Required for Web Publishing?

Web publishing is the development and maintenance of Web pages. Web pages are created and formatted using **hypertext markup language** (**HTML**) which is a set of codes used to format a file for use as a Web page. Special codes, called **tags**, stipulate how elements display in the browser and where the links lead. Using tags, developers can create an HTML document with any text editor or word processor. Many word processing packages generate HTML tags and include authoring features that help users create basic Web pages. Web page authoring software such as Adobe PageMill or Microsoft FrontPage can be used to create more sophisticated Web pages. Other Web publishing tools include digital cameras, scanners, and clip art to incorporate pictures; sound cards and microphones to add sound; and video capture cards, video cameras, or video digitizers to incorporate videos.

 ## 6. How Do Internet Services Work?

Many services are available on the Internet. **E-mail** (**electronic mail**) is the transmission of messages and files via a computer network. An **e-mail program** is used to create and send messages to an **e-mail address**, a combination of a user name and a domain name that identifies a user. An **e-mail program**, can create, send, receive, forward, store, print, and delete messages. Messages are transmitted and received according to communications protocols. **FTP** (**file transfer protocol**) is an Internet standard that allows you to exchange files with other computers on the Internet. Telnet is a program or command that enables you to connect to a remote computer on the Internet. A **newsgroup** is an online area in which users conduct written discussions about a particular subject. A **mailing list** is a group of e-mail names and addresses given a single name. A **chat room** refers to the communications medium, or channel, that permits users to **chat** (type real-time conversations) with each other.

 ## 7. What Are the Rules of Netiquette?

Netiquette, short for Internet etiquette, is the code of acceptable behaviors when using the Internet. Rules for e-mail, newsgroups, and chat rooms include keeping messages short and polite; avoiding sarcasm, **flames** (abusive messages), **spam** (unsolicited junk mail); and reading the **FAQ** (frequently asked questions). Do not assume material is accurate or up to date, and never read private e-mail.

 ## 8. Why Are Security Precautions Necessary on the Internet?

The Internet is a public place. As with all public places, you should use common sense while there. Security precautions include understanding cookies, handling inappropriate behavior or content, and ensuring confidentiality. **Cookies** are small files containing data about you that a Web server stores on your computer. Your browser allows you to accept or disable cookie use. Internet **filtering software** can block access to certain material on the Internet, such as sites with content unsuitable for children. Using a browser that encrypts (codes) messages, or attaching a digital signal to a message are ways of insuring confidentiality when dealing with secure Web pages.

 ## 9. How Are Network Computers Used?

A **network computer** (**NC**) is a less expensive version of a personal computer designed specifically to connect to a network, especially the Internet. Network computers have fewer components and less software than personal computers and typically rely on a network for storage. A special type of network computer used in business applications is the **network personal computer**, or **NetPC**. Low-cost network computers are well-suited for use in the home, especially if a potential home user plans to purchase a computer primarily for Internet access.

SHELLY
CASHMAN
SERIES®

DISCOVERING
COMPUTERS
2000

CHAPTER 1 2 3 4 5 6 **7** 8 9 10 11 12 13 14 INDEX

KEY TERMS

www.scsite.com/dc2000/ch7/terms.htm

WEB INSTRUCTIONS: *To display this page from the Web, launch your browser and enter the URL, www.scsite.com/dc2000/ch7/terms.htm. Scroll through the list of terms. Click a term to display its definition and a picture. Click KEY TERMS on the left to redisplay the KEY TERMS page. Click the TO WEB button for current and additional information about the term from the Web. To see animations, Shockwave and Flash Player must be installed on your computer (download by clicking here).*

ActiveX control (7.12)
Advanced Research Projects Agency (ARPA) (7.4)
animated GIF (7.14)
animation (7.14)
anonymous FTP (7.26)
applets (7.12)
ARPANET (7.4)
article (7.27)
AU (7.16)
audioconferencing (7.16)
backbone (7.5, 7.8)
backbone providers (7.8)
browser (7.11)
certificate authority (CA) (7.20)
channel (7.19)
chat (7.29)
chat client (7.29)
chat room (7.29)
client (7.7)
communications protocol (7.7)
cookie (7.31)
dial-up access (7.7)
digital cash (7.20)
digital certificate (7.20)
domain name (7.8)
domain name system (DNS) (7.10)
domain name system servers (DNS servers) (7.10)
e-commerce (7.19)
electronic commerce (7.19)
electronic credit (7.20)
electronic data interchange (EDI) (7.19)
electronic mail (e-mail) (7.24)
electronic money (e-money) (7.20)
electronic wallet (7.20)
e-mail address (7.24)
e-mail program (7.24)
emoticons (7.30)
encoding schemes (7.25)
FAQ (7.30)
file transfer protocol (FTP) (7.26)
filtering software (7.32)
flame wars (7.30)
flames (7.30)
FTP program (7.26)
FTP server (7.26)
FTP site (7.26)
graphics (7.12)
Graphics Interchange Format (GIF) (7.14)
helper application (7.12)
home page (7.10)
host (7.4)
host node (7.4)
.htm (7.20)
.html (7.20)
hypertext markup language (HTML) (7.20)
hypertext transfer protocol (http:) (7.11)

ELECTRONIC COMMERCE (E-COMMERCE): Conducting business activities online, including shopping, investing, and any other venture that uses either electronic money (e-money) or electronic data interchange. Using online shopping allows users to purchase a range of products over the Internet. (7.19)

Internet (7.2)
Internet protocol (IP) address (7.8)
Internet service provider (ISP) (7.6)
Internet telephone service (7.16)
Internet telephone software (7.16)
Internet telephony (7.16)
Java (7.12)
Joint Photographic Experts Group (JPEG) (7.14)
links (7.10)
LISTSERVs (7.28)
local ISP (7.6)
mail server (7.24)
mailbox (7.24)
mailing list (7.28)
marquee (7.14)
moderated newsgroup (7.28)
moderator (7.28)
Motion Picture Experts Group (MPEG) (7.17)
national ISP (7.6)
Net (7.2)
netiquette (7.30)
NetPC (7.33)
network (7.2)
network computer (NC) (7.33)
network personal computer (NetPC) (7.33)
news server (7.27)
newsgroup (7.27)
newsreader (7.27)
NSFnet (7.4)
offline (7.19)
online service (7.7)

packet switching (7.7)
packets (7.7)
personal Web pages (7.20)
plug-in (7.12)
point of presence (POP) (7.6)
portable network graphics (PNG) (7.14)
portal (7.29)
Post Office Protocol (POP) (7.25)
Post Office Protocol 3 (POP3) (7.25)
posting (7.27)
push technology (7.18)
RealAudio (7.16)
real-time (7.29)
RealVideo (7.17)
routers (7.7)
search engine (7.12)
server (7.7)
set-top box (7.33)
simple mail transfer protocol (SMTP) (7.25)
spam (7.30)
spoiler (7.30)
streaming (7.16)
streaming audio (7.16)
streaming video (7.17)
submission service (7.23)
subscribe (7.28)
tags (7.20)
Telnet (7.27)
thin-client computer (7.33)
thread (7.28)
threaded discussion (7.28)
thumbnail (7.14)
top-level domain (TLD) (7.9)
traffic (7.5)
transmission control protocol/Internet protocol (TCP/IP) (7.7)
Uniform Resource Locator (URL) (7.11)
unsubscribe (7.28)
upload (7.23)
Usenet (7.27)
virtual reality (VR) (7.18)
virtual reality modeling language (VRML) (7.18)
VR world (7.18)
wallet (7.20)
WAV (7.16)
Web (7.10)
Web audio applications (7.16)
Web browser (7.11)
Web hosting services (7.23)
Web page (7.10)
Web publishing (7.20)
Web server (7.11)
Web site (7.10)
Web video applications (7.17)
webcasting (7.19)
Webmaster (7.11)
World Wide Web (WWW) (7.10)
Yahoo! (7.35)

AT THE MOVIES   www.scsite.com/dc2000/ch7/movies.htm

WELCOME to VIDEO CLIPS from

WEB INSTRUCTIONS: *To display this page from the Web, launch your browser and enter the URL, www.scsite.com/dc2000/ch7/movies.htm. Click a picture to view a video. After watching the video, close the video window and then complete the exercise by answering the questions about the video. To view the videos, RealPlayer must be installed on your computer (download by clicking here).*

1   New Internet

The U.S. government and businesses are partnering to make I-2, "The Next Generation Internet," happen. What is I-2? How fast will it be? What is meant by "World Wide Wait"? Who can use I-2 now? Who will be able to use it in the future? What are I-2's advantages? What is the expected growth in Internet traffic over the next few years? Is the World Wide Web too slow for you now? If I-2 is significantly faster, will your use of the Web change? How?

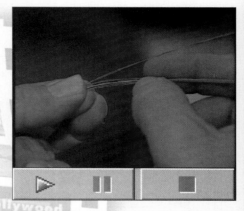

2   Yahoo! Millionaires

At the time two ingenious college students started Yahoo!, the success it now enjoys was inconceivable. Its founders became so wealthy that they now are million dollar benefactors of Stanford University. Who are the founders of Yahoo? How old are they? What services does Yahoo! offer? Have you ever used Yahoo!? What is the corporate culture like at Yahoo! Would you want to work at a firm like Yahoo!?

3   Chat Goes to Work

Chat is becoming a valuable business tool. Based on the video, what kinds of companies are using chat on their Web sites to support customers? Why do companies want to use chat in this manner? What are the advantages and disadvantages? Do you think using chat is more or less effective than using telephone and/or e-mail support? Would you prefer chat? If chat was the only support you received for a product, would you be more inclined, or less inclined to buy the product? Why? What other uses might chat have in a business environment?

SHELLY
CASHMAN
SERIES
DISCOVERING
COMPUTERS
2000

■ **Student Exercises**
WEB INFO
IN BRIEF
KEY TERMS
AT THE MOVIES
CHECKPOINT
AT ISSUE
CYBERCLASS
HANDS ON
NET STUFF
■ *Special Features*
TIMELINE 2000
GUIDE TO WWW SITES
MAKING A CHIP
BUYER'S GUIDE 2000
CAREERS 2000
TRENDS 2000
CHAT
INTERACTIVE LABS
NEWS
HOME

SHELLY
CASHMAN
SERIES®

DISCOVERING
COMPUTERS
2000

■ **Student Exercises**
WEB INFO
IN BRIEF
KEY TERMS
AT THE MOVIES
CHECKPOINT
AT ISSUE
CYBERCLASS
HANDS ON
NET STUFF
■ **Special Features**
TIMELINE 2000
GUIDE TO WWW SITES
MAKING A CHIP
BUYER'S GUIDE 2000
CAREERS 2000
TRENDS 2000
CHAT
INTERACTIVE LABS
NEWS
HOME

CHAPTER 1 2 3 4 5 6 **7** 8 9 10 11 12 13 14 **INDEX**

CHECKPOINT www.scsite.com/dc2000/ch7/check.htm

WEB INSTRUCTIONS: *To display this page from the Web, launch your browser and enter the URL,* www.scsite.com/dc2000/ch7/check.htm. *Click the links for current and additional information. To experience the animation and interactivity, Shockwave and Flash Player must be installed on your computer (download by clicking* here*).*

Label the Figure

Instructions: *Identify each part of the URL and e-mail address.*

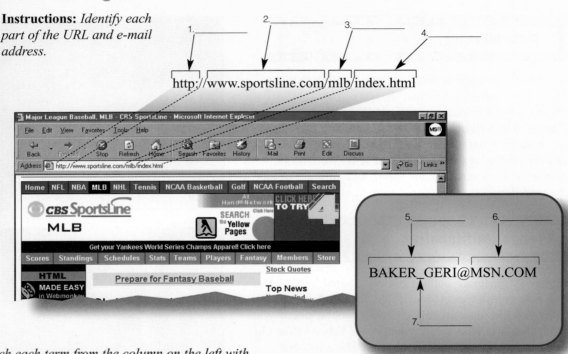

Matching

Instructions: *Match each term from the column on the left with the best description from the column on the right.*

_____ 1. TCP/IP

_____ 2. HTML

_____ 3. JPEG

_____ 4. VRML

_____ 5. SMTP

a. Set of special codes used to format a file for use as a Web page.

b. Popular standard used in compression of video and audio files.

c. Language that defines how 3-D images display on the Web.

d. Protocol used to define packet-switching on the Internet.

e. File format that uses compression techniques to reduce the size of graphical files.

f. Communications protocol used when e-mail messages are transmitted.

g. Communications protocol used to transfer pages on the Web.

Short Answer

Instructions : *Write a brief answer to each of the following questions.*

1. What is packet switching? _____ How do routers and communications protocols enable packet switching? _____

2. How are a Web page, Web site, and home page different? _____ What is a URL? _____

3. What is a search engine? _____ How is a plug-in different from a helper application? _____

4. What does it mean to subscribe to a newsgroup? _____ What is a thread? _____

5. Why do Web sites use cookies? _____ What cookie-related practice often is considered unethical? _____

AT ISSUE   www.scsite.com/dc2000/ch1/issue.htm

WEB INSTRUCTIONS: *To display this page from the Web, launch your browser and enter the URL,* www.scsite.com/dc2000/ch1/issue.htm. *Click the links for current and additional information.*

ONE   *A recent study of Pittsburgh families discovered a disturbing trend –* the more time subjects spent online, the more depressed and lonely they tended to be. The report concluded that one hour a week of Internet use led to an average increase of 1% on the depression scale and 0.04% on the loneliness scale. Researchers think time spent on the Internet may be deducted from contact with real people. Participants in a study reported a decline in interaction with family members and a reduction in numbers of friends. No matter how heartfelt, e-mail, chat rooms, and news-groups have an ephemeral quality compared to real human relationships. How does Internet communication affect mental health? Why? In terms of mental health, what do you think is the best way to use the Internet?

TWO   *A father sat down at a computer with his young child, typed what he* thought was the URL for a site of national interest, and was surprised to encounter pornographic material. "I should have paid closer attention to the (URL) suffix," he admitted. Stealth URLs – addresses similar to those of other Web pages – attract visitors and potential subscribers. Some Web pages adopt the URLs of popular Web sites, with minor changes in spelling or domain name. Critics claim this misleads consumers and weakens the value of the origi- nal name. Defendants counter that restrictions on URLs would violate rights to free speech. Do you think URLs should be regulated? Why or why not? How else can people deal with the problem of stealth URLs?

THREE   *Choosing a college once involved poring over catalogs,* mailing letters, completing applications, and anxiously awaiting letters of acceptance. Today, a college selection Web site allows students to answer a few questions, and the site presents links to appropriate schools. Click a link to tour the college's Web page and complete an online application. Though the process is great for students, some admissions offices have reservations. Colleges have little control over what schools are pro- moted, and cannot prevent chat-room slander by grumpy students. Online applications requires less commitment than paper forms, and admissions personnel see an increasing number of incomplete or fake online applications. What, if anything, do you think can be done to make Internet college selection a benefit for both candidates and colleges?

FOUR   *A recent study by America Online and Nielsen Media Research discovered* households connected to the Internet watch 15 percent less television than households without Internet access. The study confirmed the findings of a similar survey conducted two years ago. Before moving all commercials online, however, advertisers should consider that the study could not conclude Internet use *led* to watching less television. Other studies have found that Internet users tend to belong to more upscale demographic groups, people who generally watch less television. What impact, if any, do you think Internet use has on television viewership? If you were in charge of a com- pany's advertising, how would this study affect your decision on where to purchase promotional time? Why?

FIVE   *Almost 80 percent of America's public schools have Internet access. Although a* boon to students and teachers, Internet use could prove a headache for school administrators. Legally, a school's responsibility for Internet use is unclear. No one is sure of a school's liability if students access objection- able material, hack into other computers, or violate copyrights. So far, most schools have relied on filtering software and per- mission slips. Yet, filtering software can screen too much (students might be unable to research sextuplets), and permission slips have questionable legal value. Besides, neither teaches responsible Internet use. What can, and should, schools do to con- trol Internet use? Do you think schools should be required to take any steps? Why or why not? Where should responsibility for in-school Internet use ultimately lie? Why?

SHELLY CASHMAN SERIES®
DISCOVERING COMPUTERS 2000

Student Exercises
WEB INFO
IN BRIEF
KEY TERMS
AT THE MOVIES
CHECKPOINT
AT ISSUE
CYBERCLASS
HANDS ON
NET STUFF
Special Features
TIMELINE 2000
GUIDE TO WWW SITES
MAKING A CHIP
BUYER'S GUIDE 2000
CAREERS 2000
TRENDS 2000
CHAT
INTERACTIVE LABS
NEWS
HOME

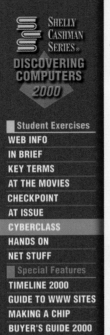

■ Student Exercises
WEB INFO
IN BRIEF
KEY TERMS
AT THE MOVIES
CHECKPOINT
AT ISSUE
CYBERCLASS
HANDS ON
NET STUFF
■ Special Features
TIMELINE 2000
GUIDE TO WWW SITES
MAKING A CHIP
BUYER'S GUIDE 2000
CAREERS 2000
TRENDS 2000
CHAT
INTERACTIVE LABS
NEWS
HOME

CHAPTER 1 2 3 4 5 6 **7** 8 9 10 11 12 13 14 INDEX

CYBERCLASS www.scsite.com/dc2000/ch7/class.htm

WEB INSTRUCTIONS: *To display this page from the Web, launch your browser and enter the URL,* *www.scsite.com/dc2000/ch7/class.htm*. *To start Level I CyberClass, click a Level I link on this page or enter the URL,* *www.cyber-class.com*. *Click the Student button, click* Discovering Computers 2000 *in the list of titles, and then click the Enter a site button. To start Level II or III CyberClass (available only to those purchasers of a CyberClass floppy disk), place your CyberClass floppy disk in drive A, click Start on the taskbar, click Run on the Start menu, type* a:connect *in the Open text box, click the OK button, click the Enter CyberClass button, and then follow the instructions.*

I II III LEVEL **1. Flash Cards** Click Flash Cards on the Main Menu of the CyberClass web page. Click the plus sign before the Chapter 7 title. Answer all the questions in any two subjects of your choosing. If you missed two consecutive questions, choose another subject and answer all the questions in that category. Continue this process until you can answer five flash cards without missing two consecutive questions. All users: Answer as many more flash cards as you desire. Close the Electronic Flash Card window and the Flash Cards window by clicking the Close button in the upper-right corner of each window.

I II III LEVEL **2. Practice Test** Click Testing on the Main Menu of the CyberClass web page. Click the Select a book box arrow and then click Discovering Computers 2000. Click the Select a test to take box arrow and then click the Chapter 7 title in the list. Click the Take Test button. If necessary, maximize the window. Take the practice test and then click the Submit Test button. If you missed more than three questions, click the Take another Test button. Continue to take tests until you miss no more than three questions.

I II III LEVEL **3. Web Guide** Click Web Guide on the Main Menu of the CyberClass web page. When the Guide to World Wide Web Sites page displays, click Internet. Visit one of the Internet sites and find some information about the Internet you did not already know. When you are finished, close the window. Write a brief report about what you learned.

I II III LEVEL **4. Company Briefs** Click Company Briefs on the Main Menu of the CyberClass web page. Click a corporation name to display a case study. Read the case study. Write a brief report indicating the use of the World Wide Web in this company.

II III LEVEL **5. CyberChallenge** Click CyberChallenge on the Main Menu of the CyberClass web page. Click the Select a book box arrow and then click Discovering Computers 2000. Click the Select a board to play box arrow and then click Chapter 7 in the list. Click the Play CyberChallenge button. Maximize the CyberChallenge window. Play CyberChallenge until you have answered correctly the 20, 30, 40, and 50 point questions diagonally left or right across the playing board.

II III LEVEL **6. Hot Links and Student Bulletin Board** Click Hot Links on the Main Menu of the CyberClass web page. Visit sites in Hot Links until you find one that uses state of the art Web technology. Then, click Student Bulletin Board, click Add Topic, type your name as the topic, click the Add Topic button, type a message subject and message body, and then click the Add Message button.

II III LEVEL **7. Text Chat** Read AT ISSUE exercise 5 on page 7.41. Then, click Text Chat on the Main Menu of the CyberClass web page and discuss with others in the chat room what responsibility schools should take for student use of the Internet.

CHAPTER 1 2 3 4 5 6 7 8 9 10 11 12 13 14 INDEX

HANDS ON   www.scsite.com/dc2000/ch7/hands.htm

WEB INSTRUCTIONS: *To display this page from the Web, launch your browser and enter the URL,* www.scsite.com/dc2000/ch7/hands.htm. *Click the links for current and additional information.*

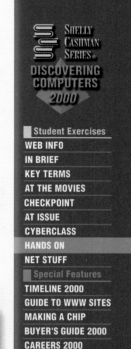

 ### Online Services

This exercise uses Windows 98 procedures. What online services are available on your computer? Right-click the Online Services icon on the desktop and then click Open on the shortcut menu. What online services have shortcut icons in the Online Services window? Right-click each shortcut and then click Properties on each shortcut menu. Click the General tab. When was each shortcut created? When was it modified? Close the dialog box and then click the Close button to close the Online Services window.

Two Understanding Internet Properties

Right-click an icon for a Web browser that displays on your desktop. Click Properties on the shortcut menu. When the Internet Properties dialog box displays, click the General tab. Click the question mark button on the title bar and then click one of the buttons. Read the information in the pop-up window and then click the pop-up window to close it. Repeat the process for other areas of the dialog box. Click the Cancel button.

Three Determining Dial-Up Networking Connections

This exercise uses Windows 98 procedures. Click the Start button on the taskbar. Point to Programs on the Start menu, point to Accessories on the Program submenu, point to Communications on the Accessories submenu, and then click Dial-Up Networking on the Accessories submenu. When the Dial-Up Networking window displays, right-click a connection displayed in the window and then click Connect on the shortcut menu. Write down the User name and the Phone number. Close the connect to dialog box and the Dial-Up Networking window.

 ### Using Help to Understand the Internet

This exercise uses Windows 98 procedures. Click the Start button on the taskbar and then click Help on the Start menu. Click the Contents tab. Click the Exploring the Internet book and then click the Explore the Internet topic. Click the Click here link to find out more about Internet Explorer. Answer the following questions:

- How can you update your favorite Web sites and view them at your leisure?
- How can you move around the Web faster and easier with the Explorer bar?
- How can you browse the Web safely?
- How can you view Web pages in other languages?

Close the Internet Explorer Help window and the Windows Help window.

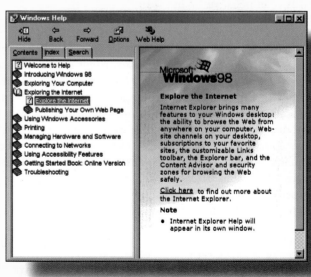

SHELLY
CASHMAN
SERIES®

DISCOVERING
COMPUTERS
2000

Student Exercises
WEB INFO
IN BRIEF
KEY TERMS
AT THE MOVIES
CHECKPOINT
AT ISSUE
CYBERCLASS
HANDS ON
NET STUFF
Special Features
TIMELINE 2000
GUIDE TO WWW SITES
MAKING A CHIP
BUYER'S GUIDE 2000
CAREERS 2000
TRENDS 2000
CHAT
INTERACTIVE LABS
NEWS
HOME

CHAPTER 1 2 3 4 5 6 **7** 8 9 10 11 12 13 14 INDEX

NET STUFF   www.scsite.com/dc2000/ch7/net.htm

WEB INSTRUCTIONS: *To display this page from the Web, launch your browser and enter the URL,* *www.scsite.com/dc2000/ch7/net.htm*. *To use the Connecting to the Internet lab or the World Wide Web lab from the Web, Shockwave and Flash Player must be installed on your computer (download by clicking* *here).*

CONNECTING
TO THE
INTERNET
LAB

1. Shelly Cashman Series Connecting to the Internet Lab

Follow the instructions in NET STUFF 1 on page 1.46 to start and use the Connecting to the Internet lab. If you are running from the Web, enter the URL www.scsite.com/sclabs/menu.htm; or display the NET STUFF page (see instructions at the top of this page) and then click the CONNECTING TO THE INTERNET LAB button.

WORLD WIDE
WEB LAB

2. Shelly Cashman Series World Wide Web Lab

Follow the instructions in NET STUFF 1 on page 1.46 to start and use the World Wide Web lab. If you are running from the Web, enter the URL, www.scsite.com/sclabs/menu.htm; or display the NET STUFF page (see instructions at the top of this page) and then click the WORLD WIDE WEB LAB button.

NEWSGROUP

3. Internet Newsgroups

One of the more popular topics for Internet news-groups is the Internet. Click the NEWSGROUP button for a list of newsgroups. Find one or more newsgroups that discuss something about the Internet. Read the newsgroup postings and briefly summarize the topic under discussion. If you like, post a reply to a message.

IN THE NEWS

4. In the News

In her book, *Caught in the Net*, Kimberly S. Young argues that the Internet can be addictive. Young's methodology and conclusions have been questioned by several critics, but Young remains resolute. She points out that at one time no one admitted the existence of alcoholism. Click the IN THE NEWS button and read a news article about the impact of Internet use on human behavior. What affect did the Internet have? Why? In your opinion, is the Internet's influence positive or negative? Why?

WEB CHAT

5. Web Chat

Some of the most unusual pages on the Web are remi-niscent of the movie, *The Truman Show*. With a digital camera, a desktop computer, some free software, and an arrangement with a server, people are setting up Web pages that display a room in their home twenty-four hours a day, seven days a week. Cyber-voyeurs can watch someone eat, sleep, read, watch television – in short, do anything that can be done in the room. Unlike characters in *The Truman Show*, however, people on these Web pages know they are being watched. Whether they are performance artists, homespun philosophers, or simple exhibition-ists, a growing number of people are opening their lives to anyone with Internet access. Would you be willing to put a room in your house on the Web? Why or why not? Would you be interested in accessing one of these Web pages? Why? Click the WEB CHAT button to enter a Web Chat discussion related to this topic.

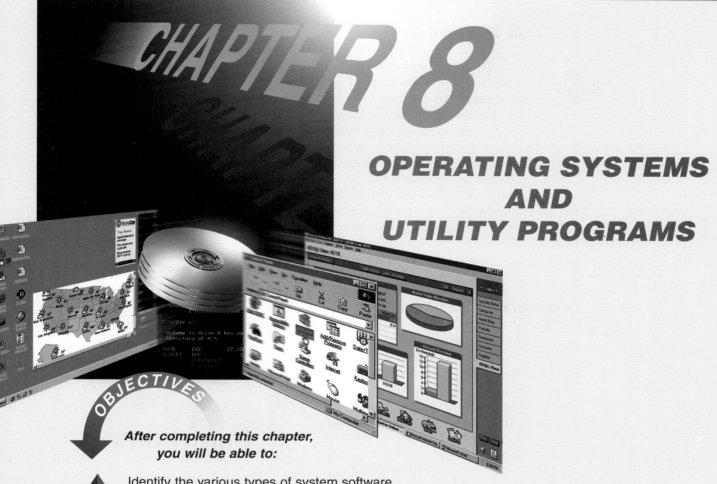

CHAPTER 8

OPERATING SYSTEMS AND UTILITY PROGRAMS

OBJECTIVES

After completing this chapter, you will be able to:

▸ Identify the various types of system software

▸ Differentiate between an operating system and utility program

▸ Describe the features of operating systems

▸ Describe the functions of an operating system

▸ Identify and briefly describe popular operating systems used today

▸ Explain the startup process for a personal computer

▸ Discuss the purpose of the following utilities: viewer, file compression, diagnostic, disk scanner, defragmenter, uninstaller, backup, antivirus, and screen saver

Like most computer users, you probably are familiar with application software, such as word processing, spreadsheet, e-mail, and a Web browser. To run any application software, also called an application, your computer also must be running another type of software -- an operating system. In addition to an operating system, modern computers also contain several utility programs. Together, operating systems and utility programs comprise a category of software called system software. This chapter discusses the operating system and its functions, as well as several utility programs used with today's personal computers.

SYSTEM SOFTWARE

System software consists of the programs that control the operations of the computer and its devices. Functions that system software performs include starting up the computer; opening, executing, and running applications; storing, retrieving, and copying files; formatting disks; reducing file sizes; and backing up the contents of a hard disk. As shown in Figure 8-1, system software serves as the interface between you (the user), your application software, and your computer's hardware. The two types of system software are operating systems and utility programs.

OPERATING SYSTEMS

An **operating system (OS)** is a set of programs containing instructions that coordinate all of the activities among computer hardware resources. For example, the operating system recognizes input from an input device such as the keyboard, mouse, or microphone; coordinates the display of output on the monitor; instructs a printer how and when to print information; and manages data, instructions, and information stored on disk. A computer cannot function without an operating system.

An operating system also contains instructions that allow you to run application software. Application software is written to run with particular operating systems. Thus, the operating system installed on your computer directly determines which application software you can and cannot run.

The operating system used on a computer sometimes is called the **software platform**. When you purchase application software, the package states the software platform (operating system) on which it runs.

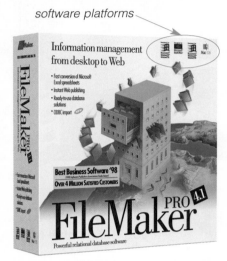

software platforms

Figure 8-2 *Some application software can run on multiple software platforms (operating systems) on which it runs.*

Figure 8-1 *System software serves as the interface between the user, application programs, and the computer's hardware.*

Applications that run identically on more than one operating system are referred to as **cross-platform**. FileMaker Pro, for example, runs on several operating systems, including several versions of Microsoft Windows and the Macintosh operating system (Figure 8-2).

An operating system usually is stored on the computer's hard disk. The core of an operating system, called the **kernel**, is responsible for managing memory, files, and devices; maintaining the computer's clock, which contains the current date and time; starting applications; and assigning the computer's resources, such as hardware devices, software programs, data, and information. Each time you turn on the computer, the kernel and other frequently used instructions in the operating system are copied from the hard disk (storage) to the computer's memory.

Any program or command that remains in memory while the computer is running is called **memory-resident**. This includes the operating system kernel and programs such as calendars and calculators that you access frequently or need to access quickly.

User Interfaces

A **user interface** is the part of the software with which you interact; it controls how data and instructions are entered and information is presented on the screen. Two types of user interfaces are command-line and graphical (Figure 8-3). Many operating systems use a combination of these types of user interfaces to define how you interact with your computer.

With a **command-line interface**, you type keywords or press special keys on the keyboard to enter data and instructions. Recall that a keyword is a special word, phrase, or code that a program understands as an instruction. Some keyboards also include keys that send a command to a program when you press them. When working with a command-line interface, the set of commands you use to interact with the computer is called the **command language**.

Figure 8-3a (command-line)

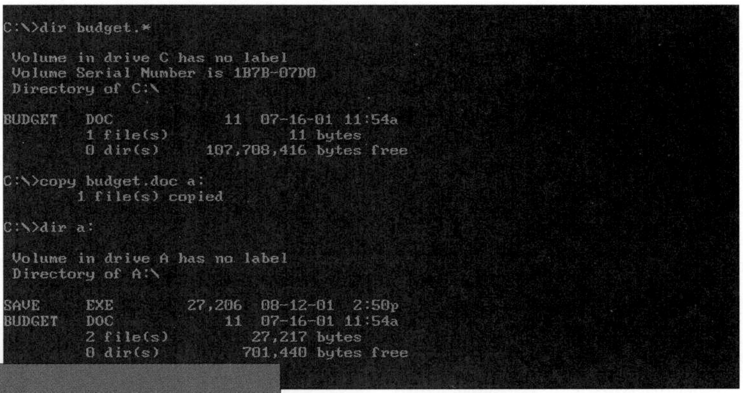

Figure 8-3b (graphical)

Figure 8-3 Examples of command-line and graphical user interfaces.

WEB INFO

For more information on graphical user interfaces, visit the Discovering Computers 2000 Chapter 8 WEB INFO page (**www.scsite.com/ dc2000/ch8/webinfo.htm**) and click Graphical User Interface.

As noted in Chapter 1, a **graphical user interface** allows you to use menus and visual images such as icons, buttons, and other graphical objects to issue commands.

Instead of requiring you to remember keywords or special keys, a **menu** displays a set of available commands or options from which you choose one or more. You can use a keyboard, mouse, or any other pointing device to select items on the menu. Because they do not require you to know a command language, menus typically are easier to learn and use than commands.

An **icon** is a small image that represents an item such as a program, an instruction, or a file.

Although any input device can be used with a graphical user interface, the mouse and other pointing devices are used more commonly. Of all the interfaces, a graphical user interface is the easiest to learn and work with, characteristics described as being **user-friendly**.

Today, many graphical user interfaces incorporate Web browser-like features, which increase their ease of use. In these browser-like graphical user interfaces, icons function like Web links, toolbar buttons look like those used in Web browsers, and Web pages can be delivered automatically to your computer (Figure 8-4).

Features of Operating Systems

Depending on its intended use, an operating system will support just one user running one program or thousands of users running multiple programs. These various capabilities of operating systems are described as single user, multiuser, multiprocessing, and/or multitasking. A single operating system may support one or all of these capabilities.

A **single user**, also called **single tasking**, operating system allows only one user to run one program at a time. Suppose, for example, you are typing a memorandum in a word processing program and decide to browse the Web for more information. If you are working with a single user operating system, you must quit the word processing program before you can run the Web browser. You then must close the Web browser before you restart the word processing program to finish the memorandum. Early operating systems were single user; however, most operating systems today are multitasking and multiuser.

Figure 8-4 This graphical user interface incorporates icons that function like Web links, and news and weather Web pages pushed onto the desktop.

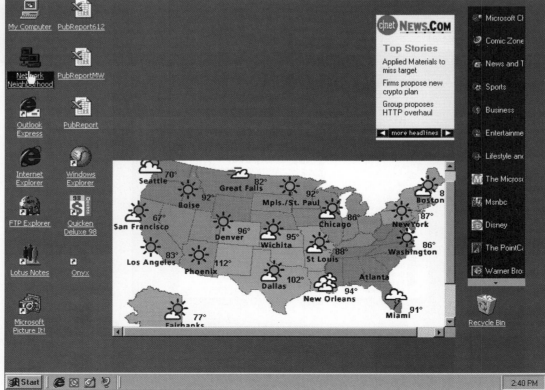

A **multitasking** operating system allows a single user to work on two or more applications that reside in memory at the same time. Using the example just cited, if you are working with a multitasking operating system, you do not have to quit the word processing program to run a Web browser; that is, both programs can run concurrently. When you are running multiple applications, the one that you currently are working with is in the **foreground**, and the others that are running but not being used are in the **background** (Figure 8-5).

A **multiuser** operating system enables two or more users to run a program simultaneously. Networks, minicomputers, mainframes, and supercomputers allow hundreds to thousands of users to be connected at the same time, and thus are multiuser.

A **multiprocessing** operating system can support two or more CPUs running programs at the same time. Multiprocessing works much like parallel processing, which was discussed in Chapter 3, and involves the coordinated processing of programs by more than one CPU. As with parallel processing, multiprocessing increases a computer's processing speed.

A computer with separate CPUs also can serve as a **fault-tolerant computer**; that is, one that continues to operate even if one of its components fails. Fault-tolerant computers are built with duplicate components such as CPUs, memory, and disk drives. If any one of these components fails, the computer switches to the duplicate component and continues to operate. Fault-tolerant computers are used for airline reservation systems, communications networks, bank teller machines, and other systems that are of critical importance and must be operational at all times.

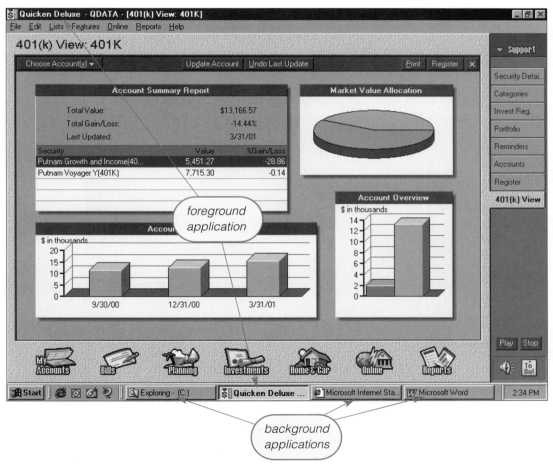

Figure 8-5 When running multiple applications, the one with which you currently are working is in the foreground; others that are running but not being used are in the background. In this screen, the buttons in the taskbar button area indicate that Quicken Deluxe is in the foreground and Windows Explorer, Microsoft Internet Explorer, and Microsoft Word are in the background.

Functions of an Operating System

An operating system performs a number of basic functions that enable you and the application software to interact with the computer: managing memory, spooling print jobs, configuring devices, monitoring system performance, administering security, and managing storage media and files. The following paragraphs describe these activities.

MEMORY MANAGEMENT The purpose of **memory management** is to optimize use of random access memory (RAM). Recall that RAM, often simply called memory, is one or more chips on the motherboard that temporarily hold items such as data and instructions while they are being processed

by the CPU. The operating system has the responsibility to allocate, or assign, these items to an area of memory while they are being processed; to monitor carefully the contents of these items in memory; and to clear these items from memory when they are no longer required by the CPU. For example, the operating system manages areas of memory or storage called buffers. A **buffer** is an area of memory or storage in which data and information is placed while waiting to be transferred to or from an input or output device. The contents of the buffers are managed by the operating system.

Some operating systems use virtual memory to optimize RAM. With **virtual memory** (**VM**), the operating system allocates a portion of a storage medium, usually the hard disk, to function as additional RAM (Figure 8-6). The area of the hard disk used for virtual memory is called a **swap file**

VIRTUAL MEMORY MANAGEMENT

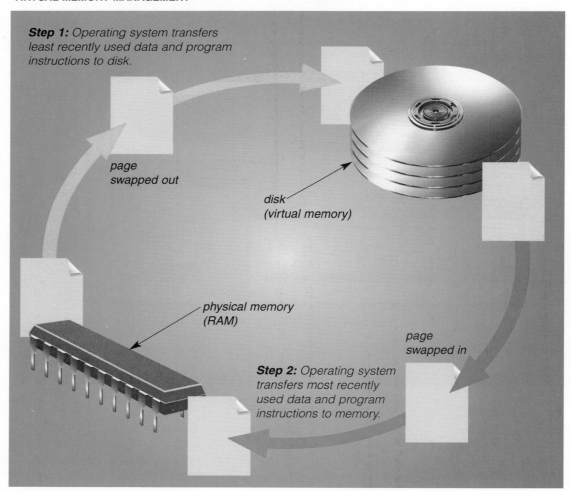

Step 1: Operating system transfers least recently used data and program instructions to disk.

page swapped out

disk (virtual memory)

physical memory (RAM)

page swapped in

Step 2: Operating system transfers most recently used data and program instructions to memory.

Figure 8-6 *With virtual memory (VM), the operating system allocates a portion of a storage medium, usually the hard disk, to function as additional RAM.*

because it is used to swap (exchange) data and program instructions between memory and storage. The amount of data and program instructions exchanged at a given time is called a **page**. Thus, the technique of swapping items between memory and storage often is called **paging**.

When an operating system spends much of its time paging, instead of executing application software, it is said to be **thrashing**. If application software, such as a Web browser, has stopped responding and the LED for your hard disk is blinking repeatedly, the operating system probably is thrashing. To stop the thrashing, you should quit the application that stopped responding. If thrashing occurs frequently, you may need to install more RAM in your computer.

SPOOLING PRINT JOBS When you instruct an application to print a document, such as a memorandum, newsletter, photograph, or e-mail message, the document you are printing is called a **print job**. Because the CPU sends print jobs to the printer at a rate much faster than the printer can print, operating systems typically use a technique called spooling to increase printer efficiency.

With **spooling**, the print jobs are placed in a buffer instead of being sent immediately to the printer. Recall that a buffer is an area of memory or storage that holds data and information waiting to be transferred from one device to another. In the case of print spooling, the buffer holds the information waiting to print while the printer prints from the buffer at its own printing rate. As soon as the print job is placed in the buffer, the CPU is available to process the next instruction, usually in less than a few seconds. Thus, once the print job is in the buffer, you can use your computer for other tasks.

Spooling allows you to send a second job to the printer without waiting for the first job to finish printing. Multiple print jobs are **queued**, or lined up, in the buffer. The program that manages and intercepts print jobs and places them in the queue is called the **print spooler** (Figure 8-7).

CONFIGURING DEVICES To communicate with each device in the computer, the operating system relies on device drivers. A **device driver** is a small program that accepts commands from another program and then converts these commands into commands that the device understands. Each device on a computer, such as the mouse, keyboard,

WEB INFO

For more information on device drivers, visit the Discovering Computers 2000 Chapter 8 WEB INFO page (**www.scsite.com/ dc2000/ch8/webinfo.htm**) and click Device Drivers.

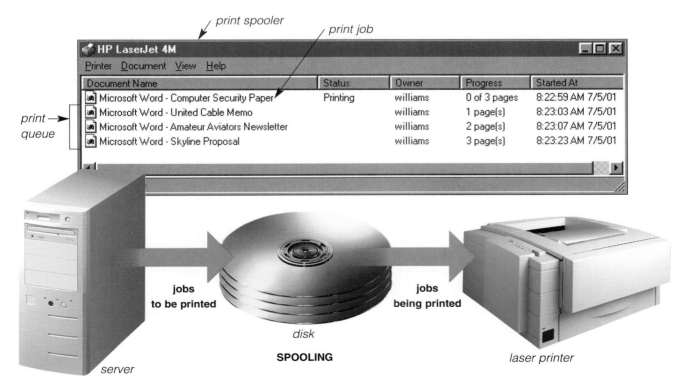

Figure 8-7 *Spooling increases both CPU and printer efficiency by writing print jobs to a disk before they are printed. In this figure, three jobs are in the queue and one is printing.*

monitor, and printer, has its own specialized set of commands and thus requires its own device driver, also called a **driver**. These devices will not function unless the correct device driver is installed on the computer. In Windows environments, most device drivers have a .drv extension.

If you add a new device to your computer, such as a printer or scanner, its driver must be installed before the device will be operational. Windows 98 provides a wizard to guide you through the installation steps (Figure 8-8). For many devices, your computer's operating system already may include the necessary device drivers. If it does not, you can install the drivers from the disk included with the device upon purchase. If, for some reason, you need a driver for your device and do not have the original disk, you can obtain the driver by contacting the vendor that sold you the device or contacting the manufacturer directly. Many manufacturers also post device drivers on their Web sites for anyone to download.

Figure 8-8

HOW TO INSTALL NEW HARDWARE IN WINDOWS 98

Step 1: Open the Control Panel window.

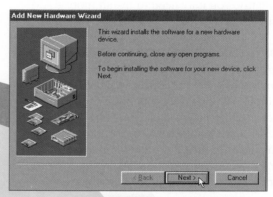

Step 2: Start the Add New Hardware Wizard by clicking the Add New Hardware icon. Follow the on-screen instructions.

Step 3: The Add New Hardware Wizard searches for Plug and Play devices on your system. If it finds any such devices, it installs them.

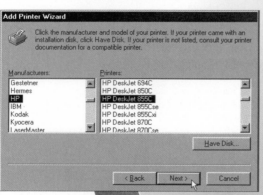

Step 5: You may be requested to insert the floppy disk, CD-ROM, or DVD-ROM that contains necessary driver files to complete the installation of the device.

Step 4: If the Add New Hardware Wizard cannot find any Plug and Play devices, you can select the type of device you want to install.

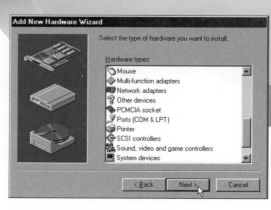

In the past, installing a new device often required setting switches and other elements on the motherboard. Installation of current devices is easier because most devices and operating systems support Plug and Play. As previously noted, **Plug and Play** is the computer's capability of recognizing any new device and assisting in the installation of the device by loading the necessary drivers automatically and checking for conflicts with other devices. Having Plug and Play support means a user can plug in a device, turn on the computer, and then use, or play, the device without having to configure the system manually.

When installing some components, occasionally you have to know which interrupt request the device should use for communications. An **interrupt request (IRQ)** is a communications line between a device and the CPU. Most computers have 15 IRQs (Figure 8-9). With Plug and Play, the operating system determines the best IRQ to use for these communications. If your operating system uses an IRQ that already is assigned to another device, an IRQ conflict will occur and the computer will not work properly. If an IRQ conflict occurs, you will have to obtain the correct IRQ for the device, which usually is specified in the installation directions that accompany the device.

MONITORING SYSTEM PERFORMANCE

Operating systems typically contain a **performance monitor**, which is a program that assesses and reports information about various system resources and devices (Figure 8-10). For example, you can monitor the CPU, disks, memory, and network usage, as well as the number of times a file is read or written. The information in these reports can help you identify problems with resources so you can attempt to resolve the problem. For example, if your computer is running extremely slow and you determine that the computer's memory is utilized to its maximum, then you might consider installing additional memory.

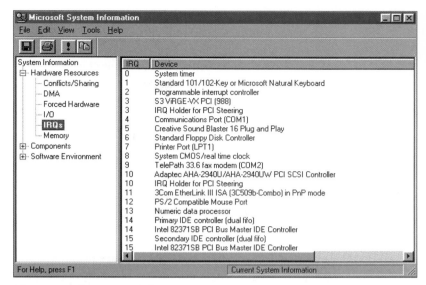

Figure 8-9 To display IRQs in Windows 98, click the Start button, point to Programs, point to Accessories, point to System Tools, and click System Information. When the Microsoft System Information window opens, click the Hardware Resources icon and then click IRQs.

WEB INFO

For more information on plug and play, visit the Discovering Computers 2000 Chapter 8 WEB INFO page (**www.scsite.com/dc2000/ch8/webinfo.htm**) and click Plug and Play.

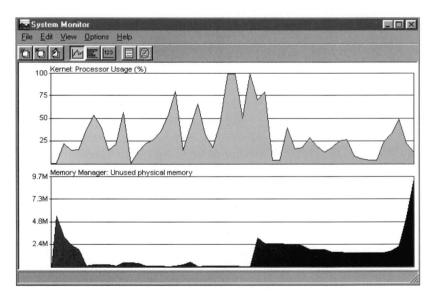

Figure 8-10 A performance monitor is a program that assesses and reports information about various system resources and devices. The System Monitor above is tracking the processor usage and the amount of unused physical memory.

ADMINISTERING SECURITY Most multiuser operating systems allow each user to **log on**, which is the process of entering a user name and a password into the computer (Figure 8-11). A **user name**, or **user ID**, is a unique combination of characters, such as letters of the alphabet or numbers, that identifies one specific user. Many users select a combination of their first and last names as their user name. A user named Rick Williams, for example, might choose, rwilliams, as his user name. A **password** is a combination of characters associated with your user name that allow you to access certain computer resources. To help prevent unauthorized users from accessing those computer resources, you should keep your password confidential. As you enter your password, most computers hide the actual password characters by displaying some other characters, such as asterisks (*). Guidelines for selecting good passwords are discussed in Chapter 14.

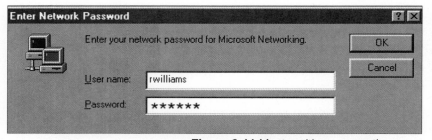

Figure 8-11 *Most multiuser operating systems allow each user to log on, which is the process of entering a user name and password into the computer.*

Before you can use a computer that requires a log on procedure, you must enter your user name and password correctly. As you enter these items, a computer compares your entries with a list of authorized user names and passwords. If your entries match the user name and password kept on file, you are granted access; otherwise, you are denied access. Both successful and unsuccessful log on attempts often are recorded in a file so the system administrator can review who is using or attempting to use the computer. System administrators also use these files to monitor computer usage.

Some operating systems also allow you to assign passwords to files so that only authorized users can open them.

MANAGING STORAGE MEDIA AND FILES
Operating systems also contain a type of program called a **file manager**, which performs functions related to storage and file management (Figure 8-12). Some of the storage and file management functions performed by a file manager are formatting and copying disks; displaying a list of files on a storage medium; checking the amount of used or free space on a storage medium; and copying, renaming, deleting, moving, and sorting files.

POPULAR OPERATING SYSTEMS

Many of the first operating systems were **device dependent**; that is, they were developed by manufacturers specifically for the computers in their product line. Software that is privately owned and limited to a specific vendor or computer model is called **proprietary software**. When manufacturers introduced a new computer or model, they often produced an improved and different proprietary operating system. Problems arose, however, when a user wanted to switch computer models or manufacturers. Because applications were designed to work with a specific operating system, the user's application software often would not work on the new computer.

Although some operating systems still are device dependent, the trend today is toward **device-independent** operating systems that will run on many manufacturers' computers. The advantage of device independent operating systems is that, even if you change computer models or vendors, you can retain existing application software and data files, which generally represent a sizable investment in time and money.

New versions of an operating system usually are downward compatible. A **downward-compatible** operating system is one that recognizes and works with application software that was written for an earlier version of the operating system. The application software, by contrast, is **upward compatible**; meaning it was written for an earlier version of the operating system, but runs under the new version.

The following sections discuss some of the more popular operating systems.

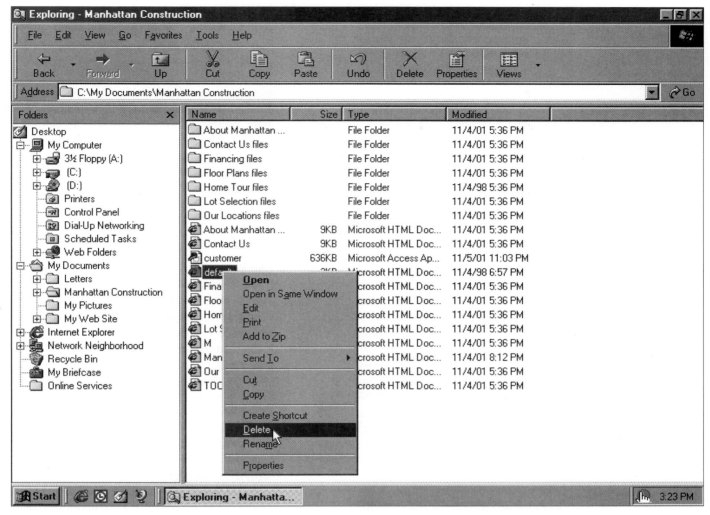

Figure 8-12 *Windows Explorer is a file manager. A file manager performs functions related to storage and file management.*

DOS

The term **DOS (Disk Operating System)** refers to several single user operating systems that were developed in the early 1980s for PCs. The two more widely used versions of DOS were PC-DOS and MS-DOS. Microsoft Corporation developed both PC-DOS and MS-DOS; the two operating systems were essentially the same. Microsoft developed PC-DOS (Personal Computer DOS) for IBM, and IBM installed and sold PC-DOS on its computers. At the same time, Microsoft marketed and sold MS-DOS (Microsoft DOS) to makers of IBM-compatible personal computers.

When first developed by Microsoft, DOS used a command-line interface. Later versions of DOS included both command-line and menu-driven user interfaces, as well as improved memory and disk management.

At its peak, DOS was a widely used operating system, with an estimated 70 million computers running it. Today, DOS no longer is widely used because it does not offer a graphical user interface and it cannot take full advantage of modern 32-bit microprocessors. Although it still has some users, many PC users prefer to use the graphical user interface of Windows platforms.

WEB INFO
WEB INFO

For more information on Windows, visit the Discovering Computers 2000 Chapter 8 WEB INFO page (**www.scsite.com/ dc2000/ch8/webinfo.htm**) and click Windows.

Windows 3.x

To meet the need for an operating system that had a graphical user interface, Microsoft developed **Windows**. **Windows 3.x** refers to three early versions of Microsoft Windows: Windows 3.0, Windows 3.1, and Windows 3.11. These Windows 3.x versions were not operating systems; instead they were operating environments. An **operating environment** is a graphical user interface that works in combination with an operating system to simplify its use.

Windows 3.x was designed to work as an operating environment for DOS. While DOS was the actual operating system, Windows 3.x provided a graphical user interface to simplify basic tasks such as formatting disks and copying files. Common features of an operating environment such as Windows 3.x include support for mouse usage, icons, and menus.

Introduced in 1990, **Windows 3.0** was the first graphical user interface for PCs. **Windows 3.1** was introduced in 1992 and provided a number of improvements to version 3.0. **Windows 3.11**, also called **Windows for Workgroups**, was a networking version of Windows 3.1. The Windows 3.x versions of Windows also supported multitasking, so you could have several applications running at the same time.

Windows 95

With **Windows 95**, also referred to as **Win95**, Microsoft developed a true multitasking operating system – not an operating environment like early versions of Windows. Windows 95 thus did not require DOS to run, although it included some DOS and Windows 3.x features to allow for downward compatibility.

One advantage of Windows 95 was its improved graphical user interface, which made working with files and programs easier than the earlier versions. In addition, most programs ran faster under Windows 95 because it was written to take advantage of 32-bit processors (versus 16-bit processors) and supported a more efficient form of multitasking. Windows 95 also included support for networking, Plug and Play technology, longer file names, and e-mail.

Windows 98

Microsoft developed an upgrade to the Windows 95 operating system, called Windows 98. The **Windows 98** operating system, also called **Win98**, was easier to use than Windows 95 and was more integrated with the Internet (Figure 8-13). For example, Windows 98 included **Microsoft Internet Explorer**, a popular Web browser. The Windows 98 file manager, called **Windows Explorer**, also had a Web browser look and feel. With Windows 98, you could have an Active Desktop™ interface, which allowed you to set up Windows so icons on the desktop and file names in Windows Explorer worked like Web links.

Windows 98 also provided faster system startup and shutdown, better file management, and support for new multimedia technologies such as DVD and WebTV. Windows 98 supported the Universal Serial Bus (USB) so you easily could add and remove devices on your computer. The table in Figure 8-14 lists features of Windows 98. Like Windows 95, Windows 98 could run 16- and 32-bit software, which means it could run software designed for DOS and earlier versions of Windows.

Windows 2000

Microsoft Windows 2000 is an upgrade to the Windows 98 and Windows NT operating systems. Microsoft **Windows NT**, also referred to as **NT**, was an operating system designed for client-server networks. Like Windows 98 and Windows NT, Windows 2000 is a complete multitasking operating system (not an operating environment) that has a graphical user interface. Two basic versions of Windows 2000 exist: **Windows 2000** for network servers and the **Windows 2000 Professional** for computers connected to the network. Windows 2000 includes all features of Windows 98, plus these additional features:

- Wizards to guide you through administrative activities such as adding user accounts
- Programs to monitor network traffic and applications
- Capability of working with multiple CPUs using multiprocessing
- Tools for Web site creation and management
- Features to support user and account system security

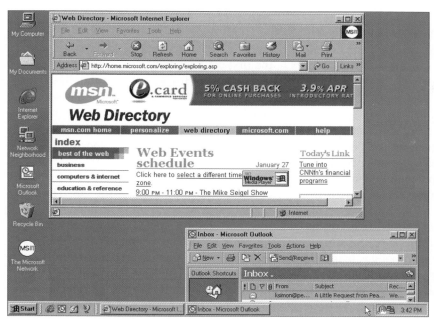

Figure 8-13 *Microsoft Windows 98 is easy to use, fast, and integrated with the Internet. This desktop view is called the Classic style; the desktop view shown in Figure 8-4 on page 8.4 is called the Web style.*

WINDOWS 98 FEATURES

Feature	Description
1. Active Desktop™	Allows you to set up Windows so icons on the desktop and file names in Windows Explorer work like Web links (single-click); create real-time windows that display television-style news or an animated ticker that provides stock updates, news, or other information; and display a window of channels on the desktop to which you can subscribe.
2. Taskbar/toolbars	Several new toolbars can be added to the taskbar by right-clicking the taskbar. These toolbars make it easier to use your computer.
3. Web browser look and feel in Web-style interface	Several Web browser tools have been added to the Web-style interface. For example, in Windows Explorer, your hard drive is viewed as an extension of the World Wide Web. Back and Forward buttons allow you easily to revisit folders you have selected previously. A Favorites menu allows you to view quickly your favorite folders. You also can view folder contents in Web-page format.
4. Increased speed	Faster startup and shutdown of Windows. Also, loads 32-bit applications faster.
5. Tune-Up Wizard	Makes your programs run faster, checks for hard disk problems, and frees up hard disk space.
6. Multiple display support	Makes it possible for you to use several monitors at the same time to increase the size of your desktop, run different programs on separate monitors, and run programs or play games with multiple views.
7. Universal Serial Bus Support	Add devices to your computer easily without having to restart.
8. Accessibility Settings Wizard	Accessibility options, such as StickyKeys, ShowSounds, and MouseKeys, are Wizards designed to help users with specific disabilities make full use of the computer.
9. Update Wizard	Reviews device drivers and system software on your computer, compares findings with a database on the Web, and then recommends and installs updates specific to your computer.
10. Registry Checker	A system maintenance program that finds and fixes registry problems.
11. FAT32	An improved version of the File Allocation Table (file system) that allows hard drives larger than two gigabytes to be formatted as a single drive.
12. New hardware support	Windows 98 supports a variety of new hardware devices, such as DVD, digital audio speakers, and recording devices. Improved Plug and Play capabilities make installing new hardware easier than early versions of Windows.

Figure 8-14 *Windows 98 offers a substantially improved operating system over its predecessors.*

WEB INFO
WEB INFO

For more information on
Mac OS, visit the
Discovering Computers
2000 Chapter 8 WEB INFO
page (**www.scsite.com/
dc2000/ch8/webinfo.htm**)
and click Mac OS.

Because it is more complex than pre-vious versions of Windows, Windows 2000 requires more disk space, memory, and faster processors.

Windows CE

Windows CE is a scaled-down Windows operating system designed for use on wireless communications devices and smaller computers such as handheld computers, in-vehicle devices, and network computers (Figure 8-15). Because it is designed for use on smaller computing devices, Windows CE requires lit-tle memory. On most of these devices, the Windows CE interface incorporates many ele-ments of the Windows graphical user inter-face. It also has multitasking, e-mail, and Internet capabilities.

Figure 8-15 *Windows CE is a scaled-down Windows operating system designed for use on wireless communications devices and smaller computers such as the Auto PC.*

Many applications, such as Microsoft Word and Microsoft Excel, have scaled-down versions that run under Windows CE.

Recently, Microsoft introduced the **Auto PC**, which is a device mounted onto a vehicle's dashboard that is powered by Windows CE. Using an automobile equipped with Auto PC, the driver can obtain informa-tion such as driving directions, traffic condi-tions, and weather; access e-mail; listen to the radio or a CD; and share information with a handheld computer. Because the Auto PC is directed through voice commands, it is ideal for the mobile user.

WEB INFO
WEB INFO

For more information on
OS/2, visit the Discovering
Computers 2000
Chapter 8 WEB INFO page
(**www.scsite.com/dc2000/
ch8/webinfo.htm**) and
click OS/2.

Mac OS

Apple's **Macintosh operating system** was the first commercially successful graphical user interface. It was released with Macintosh computers in 1984; since then, it has set the standard for operating system ease of use and has been the model for most of the new graphical user interfaces developed for non-Macintosh systems.

In recent years Apple changed the name of the operating system to **Mac OS**. The Mac OS is available only on computers manufactured by Apple. Figure 8-16 shows a screen of the latest version of Mac OS. This version includes the two more popular Web browsers: Netscape Navigator and Microsoft Internet Explorer. It also has the capability of opening, editing, and saving files created using the Windows and DOS platforms. Other features of the latest version of Mac OS include multitasking, built-in networking support, electronic mail, and enhanced multi-media capabilities.

OS/2

OS/2 (pronounced OH-ESS too) is IBM's multitasking graphical user interface operating system designed to work with 32-bit micro-processors (Figure 8-17). In addition to its capability of running programs written specifi-cally for OS/2, the operating system also can run programs written for DOS and most Windows 3.x programs. The latest version of OS/2, called **OS/2 Warp**, includes the following features:

- Enhanced graphical user interface

- Integrated business application software, including word processing, spreadsheet, database, fax, Internet access, and multi-media programs such as video editing software

- Speaker-independent speech recognition software for use in dictating data and commands

- Desktop objects that allow you to connect directly to Internet documents and services

- Integrated Java programming language that allows Java applications to run without a Web browser

- Support for multiple CPUs using multiprocessing

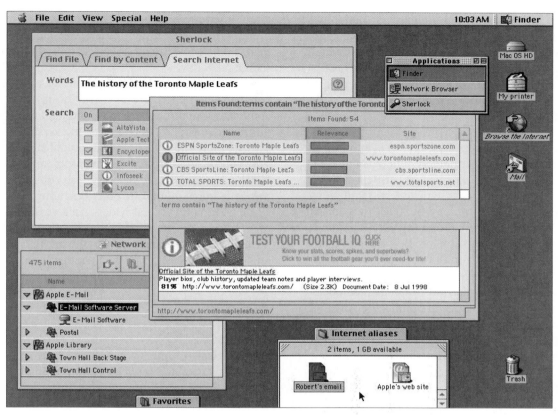

Figure 8-16 Mac OS is the operating system used with Apple Macintosh computers.

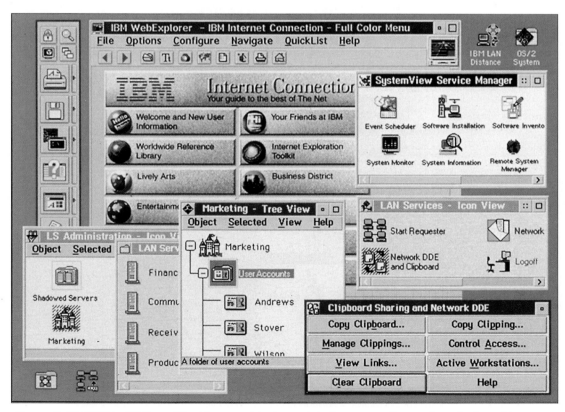

Figure 8-17 OS/2 is IBM's multitasking graphical user interface operating system designed to work with 32-bit microprocessors.

Because of IBM's long association with business computing and OS/2's strong networking support, OS/2 has been most widely used by businesses. As with Windows NT, a version of OS/2 exists for use on a server.

UNIX

WEB INFO
WEB INFO

For more information on UNIX, visit the Discovering Computers 2000 Chapter 8 WEB INFO page (**www.scsite.com/ dc2000/ch8/webinfo.htm**) and click UNIX.

UNIX (pronounced YOU-nix) is a multiuser, multitasking operating system developed in the early 1970s by scientists at Bell Laboratories. Because of federal regulations, Bell Labs (a subsidiary of AT&T) was prohibited from actively promoting UNIX in the commercial marketplace. Bell Labs instead licensed UNIX for a low fee to numerous colleges and universities where it obtained a wide following and was implemented on many different types of computers. After deregulation of the telephone companies in the 1980s, UNIX was licensed to many hardware and software companies.

Today, a version of UNIX is available for most computers of all sizes. UNIX is a powerful operating system, capable of handling a high volume of transactions in a multiuser environment and working with multiple CPUs using multiprocessing. UNIX thus is used most often on workstations and servers.

A weakness of UNIX is that it has a command-line interface, and many of its commands are difficult to remember and use. Some versions of UNIX, such as the version for the Apple Macintosh, offer a graphical user interface to help reduce this problem. UNIX also lacks some of the system administration features offered by other operating systems. Finally, several widely used versions of UNIX exist, each of which is slightly different. To move application software from one of these UNIX versions to another, you must rewrite some programs.

Linux

WEB INFO
WEB INFO

For more information on Linux, visit the Discovering Computers 2000 Chapter 8 WEB INFO page (**www.scsite.com/ dc2000/ch8/webinfo.htm**) and click Linux.

A popular, free, UNIX-like GUI operating system is called **Linux** (pronounced LINN-uks). Many software applications run on Linux. Red Hat Software, for example, sells products and services specifically developed for Linux (Figure 8-18).

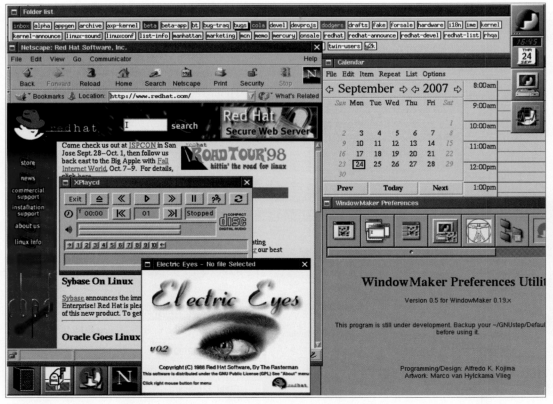

Figure 8-18 *Red Hat Software provides a version of Linux designed to run on many types of computers, including PCs.*

NetWare

Novell's **NetWare** is a widely used network operating system designed for client-server networks. NetWare has a server portion that resides on the network server and a client portion that resides on each client computer connected to the network. The server portion of NetWare allows you to share hardware devices attached to the server (such as a printer), as well as any files or application software stored on the server. The client portion of NetWare communicates with the server. Client computers also have a local operating system, such as Windows 98.

STARTING A COMPUTER

The process of starting or resetting a computer involves loading an operating system into memory – a process called **booting** the computer. When you turn on a computer after it has been powered off completely, you are performing a **cold boot**. A **warm boot**, by contrast, is the process of restarting, or resetting, a computer that already is on. When using Windows, you typically can perform a warm boot, also called a **warm start**, by pressing a combination of keyboard keys (CTRL+ALT+DEL), selecting options from a menu, or pressing a Reset button on your computer.

When you boot a computer, information displays on the screen (Figure 8-19). The actual information displayed varies depending on the make of the computer and the equipment installed. The boot process, however, is similar for large and small computers.

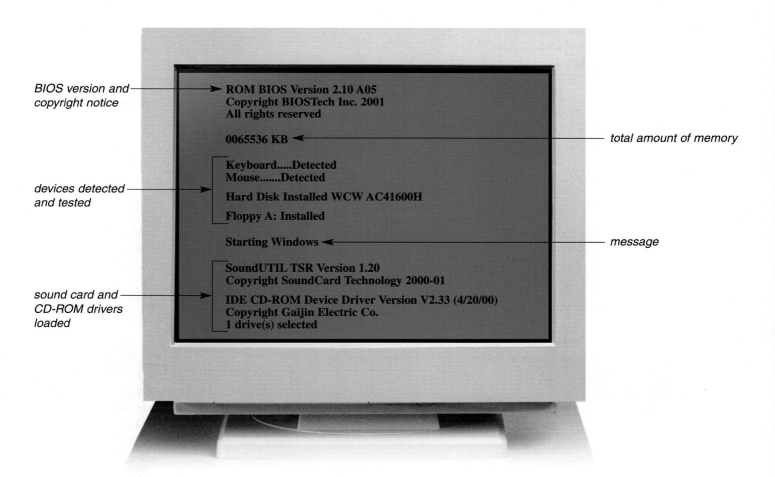

BIOS version and copyright notice

ROM BIOS Version 2.10 A05
Copyright BIOSTech Inc. 2001
All rights reserved

0065536 KB — *total amount of memory*

devices detected and tested

Keyboard.....Detected
Mouse.......Detected

Hard Disk Installed WCW AC41600H

Floppy A: Installed

Starting Windows — *message*

sound card and CD-ROM drivers loaded

SoundUTIL TSR Version 1.20
Copyright SoundCard Technology 2000-01

IDE CD-ROM Device Driver Version V2.33 (4/20/00)
Copyright Gaijin Electric Co.
1 drive(s) selected

Figure 8-19 *When you boot a computer, information displays on the screen. The actual information displayed varies depending on the make of the computer and the equipment installed.*

The following steps explain what occurs during a cold boot for a personal computer using the Windows operating system (Figure 8-20).

1. When you turn on your computer, the power supply sends an electrical signal to the motherboard and the other devices located in the system unit.

2. The surge of electricity causes the CPU chip to reset itself and look for the ROM chip(s) that contains the BIOS. The **BIOS** (pronounced BYE-oss), which stands for **basic input/output system**, is firmware that contains the computer's startup instructions. Recall that firmware consists of ROM chips that contain permanently written instructions and data.

Figure 8-20

HOW SEVERAL COMPONENTS ARE ACCESSED DURING THE BOOT PROCESS

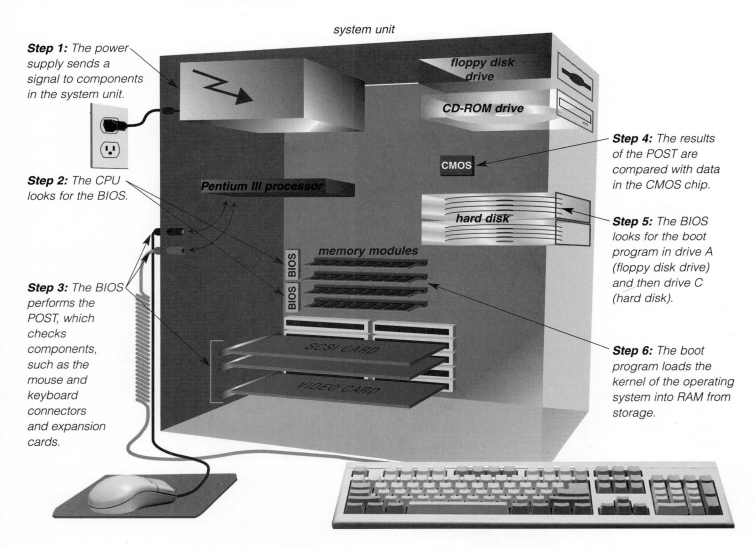

Step 1: The power supply sends a signal to components in the system unit.

Step 2: The CPU looks for the BIOS.

Step 3: The BIOS performs the POST, which checks components, such as the mouse and keyboard connectors and expansion cards.

system unit

floppy disk drive

CD-ROM drive

Pentium III processor

CMOS

hard disk

memory modules

BIOS BIOS

BIOS

SCSI CARD

VIDEO CARD

Step 4: The results of the POST are compared with data in the CMOS chip.

Step 5: The BIOS looks for the boot program in drive A (floppy disk drive) and then drive C (hard disk).

Step 6: The boot program loads the kernel of the operating system into RAM from storage.

Step 7: The operating system loads configuration information and displays the desktop on the screen.

3. The BIOS begins by executing a series of tests to make sure the computer hardware is connected properly and operating correctly. The tests, collectively called the **power-on self test** (**POST**), check the various system components such as the buses, system clock, expansion cards, RAM chips, keyboard, floppy disk drive(s), and hard disk. As the POST is performed, LEDs flicker on devices such as the disk drives and keyboard, several beeps sound, and messages display on the monitor's screen.

4. The results of the POST are compared with data in a CMOS chip on the motherboard. Recall that the CMOS chip stores configuration information about the computer, such as the amount of memory; type of disk drives, keyboard, and monitor; the current date and time; and other startup information needed when the computer is turned on. The CMOS chip is updated whenever new components are installed. If any problems are found, the computer may beep, display error messages, or cease operating — depending on the severity of the problem.

5. If the POST is completed successfully, the BIOS looks for the boot program that loads the operating system. Usually, it first looks in drive A (the designation for a floppy disk drive). If an operating system disk is not inserted into drive A, the BIOS looks in drive C, which is the designation usually given to the first hard disk. If neither drive A nor drive C contain the boot program, some computers look to the CD-ROM drive.

6. Once located, the boot program is loaded into memory and executed. The boot program then loads the kernel of the operating system into RAM. The operating system takes control of the computer.

7. The operating system loads system configuration information. In Windows, system configuration information is contained in several files called the **registry**. Windows constantly accesses the registry during the computer's operation for information such as installed hardware and software devices and individual user preferences for mouse speed, passwords, and other user-specific information.

For each hardware device identified in the registry, such as the sound card, a CD-ROM or DVD-ROM drive, or a scanner, the operating system loads a device driver. Recall that a device driver is a program that tells the operating system how to communicate with a device.

The remainder of the operating system is loaded into RAM and the desktop and icons display on the screen. The operating system executes programs in the StartUp folder, which contains a list of programs that open automatically when you boot your computer.

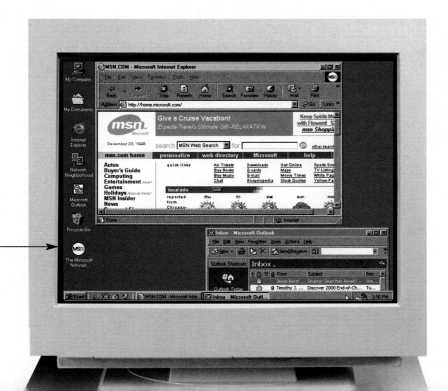

Boot Disk

Under normal circumstances, the drive from which your computer boots, called the **boot drive**, is drive C (the hard disk). If you cannot boot from the hard disk, for example if it is damaged or destroyed, you can boot from a boot disk. A **boot disk** is a floppy disk that contains certain operating system commands that will start the computer. For this reason, it is crucial you have a boot disk available — ready for use at any time.

When you install an operating system, one of the installation steps involves making a boot disk. You may not, however, have a boot disk because the operating system was pre-installed by the computer's manufacturer when you purchased the computer. If you do not have a boot disk, you should create one and keep it in a safe place. The steps in Figure 8-21 show how to create a boot disk in Windows 98.

Figure 8-21
HOW TO CREATE A BOOT DISK IN WINDOWS 98

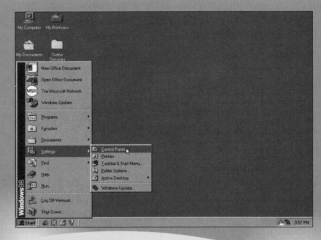

Step 1: Click the Start button on the taskbar, point to Settings on the Start menu, point to Control Panel on the Settings submenu.

Step 2: Click Control Panel on the Settings submenu to open the Control Panel window.

Step 4: Click the Startup Disk tab and then click the Create Disk button to create the boot disk. Follow the on-screen instructions.

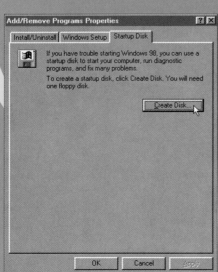

Step 3: Double-click the Add/Remove Programs icon in the Control Panel window to display the Add/Remove Programs Properties dialog box.

UTILITY PROGRAMS

A **utility program**, also called a **utility**, is a type of system software that performs a specific task, usually related to managing a computer, its devices, or its programs. Most operating systems include several utility programs. As shown in Figure 8-22, for example, Windows 98 provides access to many utility programs through the System Tools submenu. You also can buy stand-alone utilities that offer improvements over those supplied with the operating system.

Popular utility programs perform these functions: viewing files, compressing files, diagnosing problems, scanning disks, defragmenting disks, uninstalling software, backing up files and disks, checking for viruses, and displaying screen savers. Each of these utilities is briefly discussed in the following paragraphs.

- A **file viewer** is a utility that displays the contents of a file. An operating system's file manager often includes a file viewer. In Windows 98, for example, Windows Explorer has two viewers: one called **Quick View** to display the contents of text files and another called **Imaging Preview** for graphics files (Figure 8-23). The title bar of the file viewer window displays the name of the file being viewed.

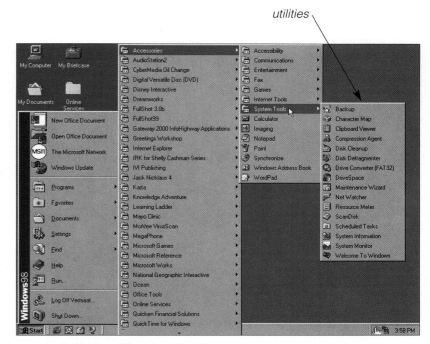

utilities

Figure 8-22 *Many Windows 98 utility programs are accessed on the System Tools submenu.*

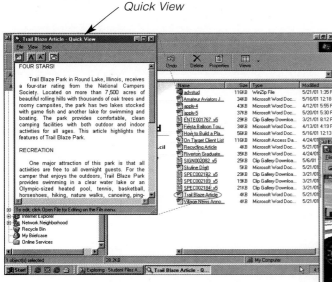

Quick View

Figure 8-23 *Windows Explorer has two viewers: Quick View that displays the contents of text files and Imaging Preview that displays graphics files.*

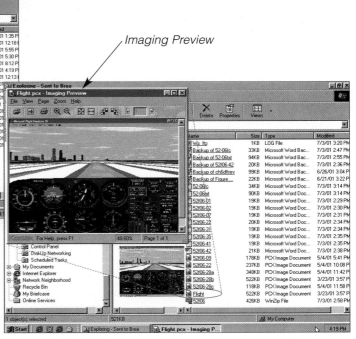

Imaging Preview

WEB INFO
WEB INFO

For more information on
file compression utilities,
visit the Discovering
Computers 2000
Chapter 8 WEB INFO page
(**www.scsite.com/dc2000/
ch8/webinfo.htm**) and
click File Compression
Utilities.

• A **file compression utility** reduces, or compresses, the size of a file. A compressed file takes up less storage space on a hard disk or floppy disk, which frees up room on the disk and improves system performance. Files available for download from the Internet often are compressed to reduce download time. Compressing files attached to e-mail messages also reduces the time needed for file transmission.

Because compressed files usually have a .zip extension, compressed files sometimes are called **zipped files**. When you receive a compressed file, you must **uncompress**, or **unzip**, the file — or restore it to its original form. Two popular stand-alone file compression utilities are PKZIP™ and WinZip®. WinZip® is shown in Figure 8-24.

• A **diagnostic utility** compiles technical information about your computer's hardware and certain system software programs and then prepares a report outlining any identified problems. For example, Windows 98 includes the diagnostic utility, Dr. Watson, which diagnoses problems as well as suggests courses of action (Figure 8-25).

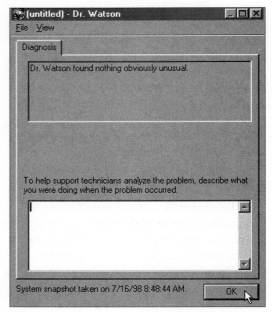

Figure 8-24 *WinZip® is a popular stand-alone file compression utility. This zipped file (ch1notes) contains 5 files for a total of 79 KB. Without being zipped, these files consume 478 KB. Thus, zipping the files reduced the amount of storage by 399 KB.*

Figure 8-25 *Dr. Watson is a diagnostic utility included with Windows 98.*

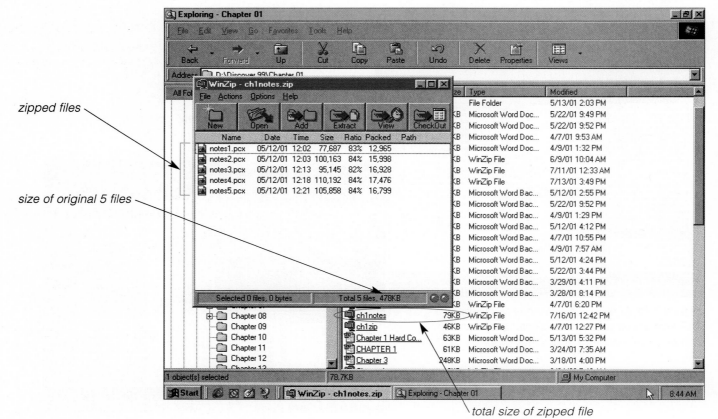

- A **disk scanner** is a utility that (1) detects and corrects both physical and logical problems on a hard disk or floppy disk and (2) searches for and removes unwanted files. A physical problem is one with the media, such as a scratch on the surface of the disk. A logical problem is one with the data, such as a corrupted file allocation table (FAT). Windows 98 includes two disk scanner utilities: **ScanDisk**, which detects and corrects problems, and **Disk Cleanup**, which searches for and removes unnecessary files such as temporary files (Figure 8-26).

- A **disk defragmenter** is a utility that reorganizes the files and unused space on a computer's hard disk so data can be accessed more quickly and programs can run faster. When a computer stores data on a disk, it places the data in the first available sector on the disk. Although the computer attempts to place data in sectors that are contiguous (next to each other), this is not always possible. When the contents of a file are scattered across two or more noncontiguous sectors, the file is **fragmented**. Fragmentation slows down disk access and thus the performance of the entire computer. The process of **defragmentation** — that is, reorganizing the disk so the files are stored in contiguous sectors — solves this problem (Figure 8-27). Windows 98 includes a disk defragmenter, called **Disk Defragmenter**.

Figure 8-26a (ScanDisk utility)

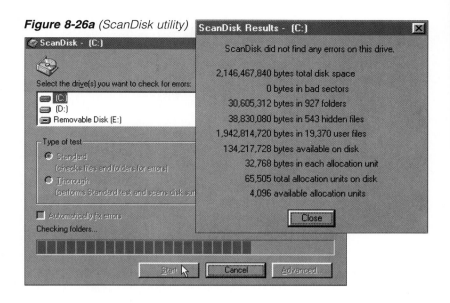

Figure 8-26b (Disk Cleanup utility)

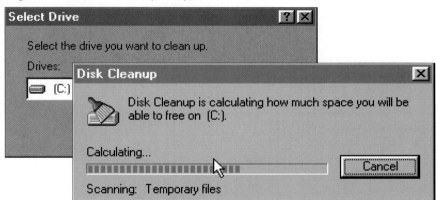

Figure 8-26 *ScanDisk detects and corrects problems on a disk, and Disk Cleanup searches for and removes unnecessary files.*

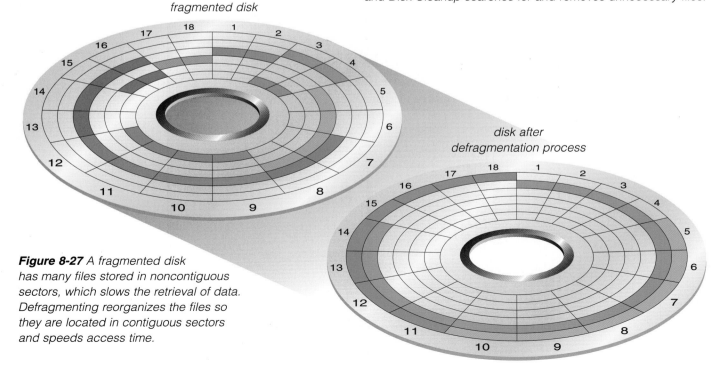

fragmented disk

disk after
defragmentation process

Figure 8-27 *A fragmented disk has many files stored in noncontiguous sectors, which slows the retrieval of data. Defragmenting reorganizes the files so they are located in contiguous sectors and speeds access time.*

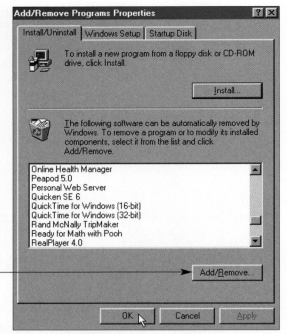

click
to uninstall
a program

Figure 8-28 *With Windows 98, you can uninstall programs by clicking the Add/Remove Programs icon in the Control Panel window.*

- An **uninstaller** is a utility that removes an application, as well as any associated entries in the system files (Figure 8-28). When you install an application, the operating system records the information that it uses to run the software in the system files. If you attempt to remove the application from your computer by deleting the files and folders associated with that program without running the uninstaller, the system file entries remain. Most operating systems include an uninstaller; you also can purchase a stand-alone program, such as CyberMedia's UnInstaller.

- A **backup utility** allows you to copy, or backup, selected files or your entire hard disk onto another disk or tape. During the backup process, the backup utility monitors progress and alerts you if additional disks or tapes are needed. Many backup programs will compress files during this process, so the backup files require less storage space than the original files.

  For this reason, backup files usually are not usable in their backed up form. In the event you need to use one of these files, a **restore program**, which is included with the backup utility, reverses the process and returns backed up files to their original form. You should back up files and disks regularly in the event your originals are lost, damaged, or destroyed. Windows 98 includes a backup utility, which also includes a restore program (Figure 8-29).

Figure 8-29 *A backup utility allows you to copy files or your entire hard disk to another disk or tape.*

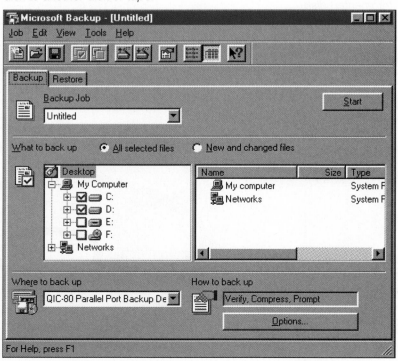

- An **antivirus** program is a utility that prevents, detects, and removes viruses from a computer's memory or storage devices. A **virus** is a program that copies itself into other programs and spreads through multiple computers. Viruses often are designed to damage a computer intentionally by destroying or corrupting its data. Antivirus programs and viruses are discussed in more depth in Chapter 14.

- A **screen saver** is a utility that causes the monitor's screen to display a moving image or blank screen if no keyboard or mouse activity occurs for a specified time period (Figure 8-30). When you press a key on the keyboard or move the mouse, the screen returns to the previously displayed image.

Screen savers originally were developed to prevent a problem called **ghosting**, in which images could be permanently etched on a monitor's screen. Although ghosting is not a problem with today's monitors, screen savers still are used for reasons of security, business, or entertainment. To secure a computer, for example, you can configure your screen saver so that you must enter a password to stop the screen saver and redisplay the previous image. Some screen savers use push technology so you receive updated and new information each time the screen saver displays.

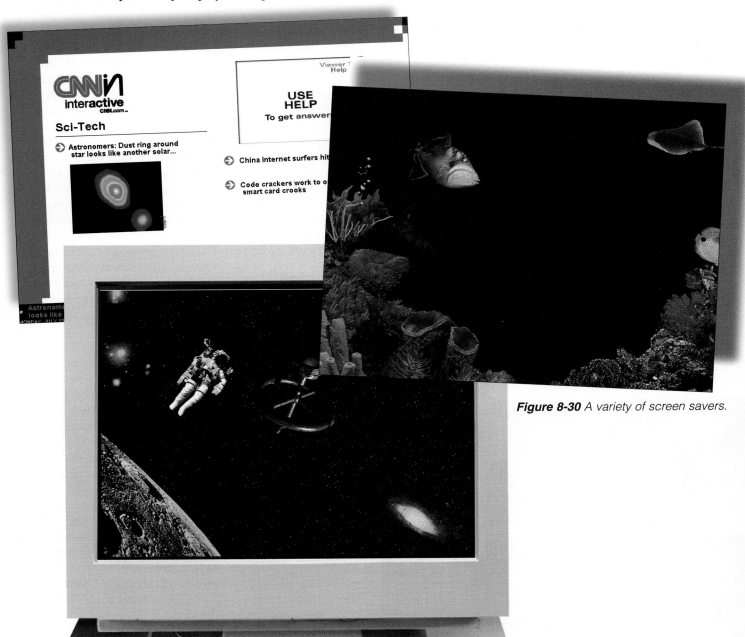

Figure 8-30 A variety of screen savers.

TECHNOLOGY TRAILBLAZERS

STEVE WOZNIAK AND STEVE JOBS

Before they were 35-years-old, Steve Wozniak and Steve Jobs built the first desktop personal computer, co-founded Apple Computer, marketed a revolutionary operating system, and became multimillionaires. Not bad.

Steve Wozniak always was interested in computers. Growing up, he devoted much of his time to designing and building sophisticated machines. "It was all self-done; I didn't ever take a course, didn't ever buy a book on how to do it. Just pieced it all together." Wozniak told his father, an engineer, that someday he would own a 4 KB computer. "Yeah, but they cost as much as a house!" his father exclaimed. "Well then," Wozniak replied, "I'll live in an apartment."

After dropping out of the University of California at Berkeley, Wozniak went to work at Hewlett-Packard where he met Steve Jobs, a summer employee. "Woz[niak] was the first person I met who knew more about electronics than I did," Jobs recalls. On his own time, Wozniak had built a *blue box* that, with a toy whistle from Cap'n Crunch cereal boxes, could be used to make free long-distance telephone calls. Jobs helped Wozniak sell the device.

In 1972, Jobs graduated from high school and attended Reed College for a semester. He took classes in philosophy, embraced the contemporary counterculture, and eventually journeyed to India in search of enlightenment. When he returned, he joined Wozniak's Homebrew Computer Club. The club's focus was on small computers that could empower individuals. "Never trust a computer you can't throw out a window," Wozniak said. Unfortunately,

Steve Wozniak & Steve Jobs

small computers were built from kits and programmed with a confusing array of switches. Wozniak envisioned a small computer "laid out like a typewriter with a video screen." The concept of an accessible computer would be a Wozniak benchmark.

When Wozniak designed a simple small computer, Jobs suggested they start a company and make the circuit boards. Even if the company failed, at least they could say they once *had* a company. The founders sold their most valuable possessions — Jobs's Volkswagen mini-bus and Wozniak's scientific calculator — for capital and built a prototype in Jobs's parent's garage. Marketed in 1976, the Apple I was an immediate success, earning Wozniak and Jobs almost $775,000 from sales. The Apple II, introduced the next year, earned much more. Wozniak and Jobs not only had a company, they had a very prosperous company.

As Apple grew, Jobs proved to be a demanding manager with an uncompromising drive for perfection. Yet, he also was a brilliant motivator, getting the best from the people around him. Employees joked about Jobs's "reality-distortion field" that allowed him to make seemingly unreasonable ideas appear reasonable. The Macintosh computer, announced in 1984, incorporated one of these ideas: a graphical user interface controlled by a mouse. To Jobs, just as the telegraph had been usurped by the easier-to-use telephone, interfaces requiring typed commands surely would be displaced by graphical user interfaces allowing people simply to point and click. Jobs was right, and the Macintosh was a hit.

Wozniak left Apple in 1985 to spend more time with his family, community projects, and work in computer education. He still serves as an adviser at Apple. Jobs also left in 1985. He would co-found NeXT Software and become Chairman and CEO of Pixar, the computer animation studio that developed the feature film, *Toy Story*. Both companies eventually were acquired by Apple.

In 1997, Jobs returned to a troubled Apple as interim CEO. A wealthy man with only one share of Apple stock, Jobs did not accept the post for financial reasons. Instead, he maintains that "the world would be a slightly better place with Apple Computer." In a short time, a quarterly profit of $45 million was announced. Perhaps the world *is* destined to be a "slightly better place."

COMPANIES ON THE CUTTING EDGE
COMPANIES ON THE CUTTING EDGE

APPLE VS. IBM COMPATIBLES – THE RIVALRY

The Montagues and the Capulets. The Yankees and the Red Sox. Coke and Pepsi. The list of famous feuds is lengthy, but few are more passionate than one that grips the computer industry: Apple computers and IBM compatibles.

Steve Jobs and Steve Wozniak founded Apple Computer in 1977. Jobs suggested the name Apple, but Wozniak says, "He doesn't always let on where ideas come from, or how they come into his head." The name may have reminded Jobs of time spent in an orchard, or of the Beatles's record label, or simply of his favorite fruit. Whatever the origin, Wozniak maintains that other names "all sounded boring compared to Apple." The company's logo is easier to explain — an apple with a bite (a play on byte) taken out of it.

Apple iMac

The company's first computer, the Apple I, had a video interface, built-in ROM, and a cost of $666. The Apple II followed with a similarly simple design, 4 KB of memory, and an interface that allowed it to work with a color television. The Apple II was the first mass-marketed personal computer. With Jobs's encouragement, independent programmers wrote about 16,000 applications for the Apple II. In three years, the Apple II earned almost $140,000,000. Several versions of the Apple II were marketed, and the machine became a school standard.

In 1981, IBM, which up to this time had ignored small computers, introduced the IBM PC. The IBM PC reflected two crucial decisions. First, Intel, an outside company, made the processor. Second, Microsoft created the operating system, DOS, but maintained the right to market DOS to other manufacturers. These decisions led to a whole family of IBM-compatible computers —machines with the same processor and operating system as IBM PCs — from companies such as Compaq, Dell, and Gateway. PC prices fell and IBM and IBM-compatible PCs soon dominated the market, particularly in the business world. The number of applications

written to work with DOS exploded. Because neither DOS nor its related applications were compatible with Apple computers, Apple's sales sagged.

Two new Apple efforts, the Apple III and the Lisa, failed. The Lisa's revolutionary graphical user interface, obtained from Xerox, made it easy to use, but the $10,000 price made it hard to buy. Apple's next computer, the Macintosh, also had a graphical user interface. The Macintosh had a larger processor and more memory than IBM PCs, but its greatest strengths were its flexibility, creative capabilities, and user-friendliness. Advertised as, *the computer for the rest of us*, the Macintosh was embraced enthusiastically, especially by customers in the humanities.

Microsoft responded by introducing Windows, a graphical face-lift for the DOS operating system. Apple sued unsuccessfully for copyright infringement, a move Wozniak feels was a mistake. "Had we gone to Microsoft and said, 'do anything the way we've already found is good, for 25 cents' the result might have been a commonality as beneficial to Apple as to Microsoft." Microsoft would improve on its initial Windows offering with *true* graphical operating systems, Windows 95 and Windows 98. *Wintel* (a word describing IBM compatibles that combine Windows operating systems and Intel processors) sales climbed while Apple's trade slumped and company morale tumbled. Nevertheless, Mac OS users remain extremely loyal. They insist their operating system is more stable, error-free, and user friendly than any version of Windows. Windows users counter that more applications are available for use with their operating system, and some insist even programs designed to work with both operating systems often work better with the Windows operating system.

Apple vs. IBM compatibles — the rivalry continues and may not end soon. Until it does, as the carnival barker says, "you pays your money and you takes your choice."

IBM PC

CHAPTER 1 2 3 4 5 6 7 8 9 10 11 12 13 14 INDEX

IN BRIEF www.scsite.com/dc2000/ch8/brief.htm

WEB INSTRUCTIONS: *To display this page from the Web, launch your browser and enter the URL, www.scsite.com/dc2000/ch8/brief.htm. Click the links for current and additional information. To listen to an audio version of this IN BRIEF, click the Audio button to the right of the title, IN BRIEF, at the top of the page. To play the audio, RealPlayer must be installed on your computer (download by clicking here).*

1. What Are Various Types of System Software?

System software consists of the programs that control the operations of the computer and its devices. System software performs a variety of functions, such as running applications and storing files, and serves as the interface between a user, the application software, and the computer's hardware. The two types of system software are operating systems and utility programs.

2. How Is an Operating System Different from a Utility Program?

An **operating system** (**OS**) is a set of programs containing instructions to coordinate all of the activities among computer hardware resources. The part of the software with which you interact is the user interface. Two types of user interfaces are command-line and graphical. With a **command-line interface**, you type keywords or press special keys on the keyboard to enter data and instructions. A **graphical user interface** (**GUI**) allows you to use **menus** and visual images such as **icons** and buttons to issue commands. A **utility program** is a type of system software that performs a specific task, usually related to managing a computer, its devices, or its programs. Most operating systems include several utility programs. Popular utility programs perform functions such as viewing files, compressing files, diagnosing problems, scanning disks, defragmenting disks, uninstalling software, backing up files and disks, checking for viruses, and displaying screen savers.

3. What Are the Features of Operating Systems?

Various capabilities of operating systems are described as single user, multiuser, multiprocessing, and multitasking. A **single user** operating system allows only one user to run one program at a time. A **multiuser** operating system enables two or more users to run a program simultaneously. A **multitasking** operating system allows a single user to work on two or more applications that reside in memory at the same time. A **multiprocessing** operating system can support two or more CPUs running programs at the same time.

4. What Are the Functions of an Operating System?

An operating system performs a number of basic functions that enable the user and the application software to interact with the computer. Operating systems manage memory, spool print jobs, configure devices, monitor system performance, administer security, and manage storage media and files. **Memory management** optimizes use of random access memory (RAM). **Spooling** increases efficiency by placing **print jobs** in a **buffer** until the printer is ready, freeing the CPU for other tasks. A **device driver** is a small program that configures devices by accepting commands and converting them into commands the device understands. **Plug and Play** is the computer's capability to recognize any new device and assist in the installation of the device. Having Plug and Play support means a user can plug in a device, turn on the computer, and then use, or play, the device without having to configure the system manually. A **performance monitor** assesses and reports information about various system resources and devices. Most multiuser operating systems administer security by allowing each user to **log on**, which is the process of entering a **user name** and **password**. A type of program called a **file manager** performs functions related to storage and file management.

 www.scsite.com/dc2000/ch8/brief.htm

5. What Are Popular Operating Systems Used Today?

DOS (Disk Operating System) refers to several single user, command-line and menu-driven operating systems developed in the early 1980s for PCs. **Windows 3.x** refers to three early **operating environments** that provided a graphical user interface to work in combination with DOS and simplify its use. **Windows 95** is a true multitasking operating system – not an operating environment – with an improved graphical interface. The **Windows 98** operating system is easier to use than Windows 95 and is more integrated with the Internet. **Windows 2000** is an upgrade to Windows 98 and **Windows NT**, an operating system designed for client-server networks. **Windows CE** is a scaled-down Windows operating system designed for use on wireless communications devices and smaller computers. The **Mac OS**, a descendant of the first commercially successful graphical user interface, is available only on Apple computers. **OS/2** is IBM's multitasking graphical user interface operating system designed to work with 32-bit processors. **UNIX** is a multiuser, multitasking, command-line operating system developed by scientists at Bell Laboratories. **Linux** is a popular, free, UNIX-like operating system. Novell's **NetWare** is a widely used operating system designed for client-server networks.

6. What Is the Startup Process for a Personal Computer?

Starting a computer involves loading an operating system into memory – a process called **booting**. When the computer is turned on, the power supply sends an electrical signal to devices located in the system unit. The CPU chip resets itself and looks for the ROM chip that contains the **BIOS (basic input/output system)**, which is firmware that holds the startup instructions. The BIOS executes the **power-on self test (POST)** to make sure hardware is connected properly and operating correctly. Results of the POST are compared with data in a CMOS chip on the motherboard. If the POST is completed successfully, the BIOS looks for the boot program that loads the operating system. Once located, the boot program is loaded into memory and executed. The boot program loads the **kernel** of the operating system into RAM. The operating system loads system configuration information from the **registry** for each hardware device. The remainder of the operating system is loaded into RAM, the desktop and icons display on the screen, and programs in the StartUp folder are executed.

7. Why Are Some Common Utility Programs Used?

A **file viewer** displays the contents of a file. A **file compression utility** reduces the size of a file. A **diagnostic utility** compiles technical information about a computer's hardware and certain system software programs and then prepares a report outlining any identified problems. A **disk scanner** detects and corrects problems on a disk and searches for and removes unwanted files. A **disk defragmenter** reorganizes files and unused space on a computer's hard disk so data can be accessed more quickly and programs can run faster. An **uninstaller** removes an application, as well as any associated entries in the system files. A **backup utility** copies or backups selected files or the entire hard drive onto another disk or tape. An **antivirus program** prevents, detects, and removes **viruses** (programs often designed to damage a computer) from a computer's memory or storage devices. A **screen saver** causes the monitor's screen to display a moving image on a blank screen if no keyboard or mouse activity occurs for a specific time period.

CHAPTER 1 2 3 4 5 6 7 **8** 9 10 11 12 13 14 INDEX

KEY TERMS   www.scsite.com/dc2000/ch8/terms.htm

WEB INSTRUCTIONS: *To display this page from the Web, launch your browser and enter the URL,* www.scsite.com/dc2000/ch8/terms.htm. *Scroll through the list of terms. Click a term to display its definition and a picture. Click KEY TERMS on the left to redisplay the KEY TERMS page. Click the TO WEB button for current and additional information about the term from the Web. To see animations, Shockwave and Flash Player must be installed on your computer (download by clicking* here).

antivirus (8.25)
Auto PC (8.14)
background (8.5)
backup utility (8.24)
basic input/output system
   (BIOS) (8.18)
boot disk (8.20)
boot drive (8.20)
booting (8.17)
buffer (8.6)
cold boot (8.17)
command language (8.3)
command-line interface (8.3)
cross-platform (8.3)
defragmentation (8.23)
device dependent (8.10)
device driver (8.7)
device-independent (8.10)
diagnostic utility (8.22)
Disk Cleanup (8.23)
disk defragmenter (8.23)
Disk Defragmenter (8.23)
Disk Operating System (DOS)
   (8.11)
disk scanner (8.23)
downward-compatible (8.10)
driver (8.8)
fault-tolerant computer (8.5)
file compression utility (8.22)
file manager (8.10)
file viewer (8.21)
foreground (8.5)
fragmented (8.23)
ghosting (8.25)
graphical user interface
   (GUI) (8.4)
icon (8.4)
Imaging Preview (8.21)
interrupt request (IRQ) (8.9)
kernel (8.3)
Linux (8.16)
log on (8.10)
Mac OS (8.14)

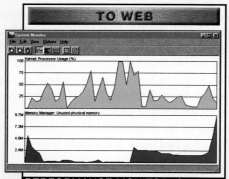

PERFORMANCE MONITOR: Operating system program that assesses and reports information about various system resources and devices. (8.9)

Macintosh operating system
   (8.14)
memory management (8.6)
memory-resident (8.3)
menu (8.4)
Microsoft Internet Explorer
   (8.12)
multiprocessing (8.5)
multitasking (8.5)
multiuser (8.5)
NetWare (8.17)
NT (8.12)
operating environment (8.12)
operating system (OS) (8.2)
OS/2 (8.14)
OS/2 Warp (8.14)
page (8.7)
paging (8.7)
password (8.10)
performance monitor (8.9)
Plug and Play (8.9)
power-on self test (POST) (8.19)
print job (8.7)
proprietary software (8.10)
queued (8.7)
Quick View (8.21)
registry (8.19)
restore program (8.24)

ScanDisk (8.23)
screen saver (8.25)
single tasking (8.4)
single user (8.4)
software platform (8.2)
spooling (8.7)
swap file (8.6)
system software (8.2)
thrashing (8.7)
uncompress (8.22)
uninstaller (8.24)
UNIX (8.16)
unzip (8.22)
upward-compatible (8.10)
user ID (8.10)
user interface (8.3)
user name (8.10)
user-friendly (8.4)
utility (8.21)
utility program (8.21)
virtual memory (VM) (8.6)
virus (8.25)
warm boot (8.17)
warm start (8.17)
Win95 (8.12)
Win98 (8.12)
Windows (8.12)
Windows 2000 (8.12)
Windows 2000 Professional
   (8.12)
Windows 3.0 (8.12)
Windows 3.1 (8.12)
Windows 3.11 (8.12)
Windows 3.x (8.12)
Windows 95 (8.12)
Windows 98 (8.12)
Windows CE (8.14)
Windows Explorer (8.12)
Windows for Workgroups (8.12)
Windows NT (8.12)
zipped files (8.22)

AT THE MOVIES

www.scsite.com/dc2000/ch8/movies.htm

WELCOME to VIDEO CLIPS from CNN

WEB INSTRUCTIONS: *To display this page from the Web, launch your browser and enter the URL, www.scsite.com/dc2000/ch8/movies.htm. Click a picture to view a video. After watching the video, close the video window and then complete the exercise by answering the questions about the video. To view the videos, RealPlayer must be installed on your computer (download by clicking here).*

■ Student Exercises
WEB INFO
IN BRIEF
KEY TERMS
AT THE MOVIES
CHECKPOINT
AT ISSUE
CYBERCLASS
HANDS ON
NET STUFF
■ Special Features
TIMELINE 2000
GUIDE TO WWW SITES
MAKING A CHIP
BUYER'S GUIDE 2000
CAREERS 2000
TRENDS 2000
CHAT
INTERACTIVE LABS
NEWS
HOME

1 Screen Savers

Today's office environment is filled with computer workstations. Because of the many interruptions that take employees away from their computers during the day, computer screens often remain open and idle for long periods. During this idle time, some pretty fascinating screen savers are popping up in the workplace. What is a screen saver? Why were screen savers initially created? Why are they used today? Do you have a screen saver on the computer you use? If you were an employer or instructor would you care whether your employees or students ran their own screen savers? Why or why not?

2 E-mail Virus

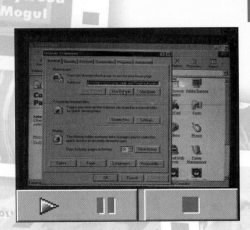

Think of a virus as a program designed intentionally to damage a computer by destroying or corrupting its data. Do you think companies should be held responsible for virus-infected software they sell when the software comes out of a box? Should the software company be held responsible for a virus that is planted by a hacker after the software is running on the computer? Should companies be required to notify customers of known viruses in their software? Could software companies alleviate the virus problem by including antivirus program software in their products that automatically checks for viruses?

3 Biz Hyper Speed Product

Because of the rapid change in online technology, early release of functional, but not perfect, browsers may take place. Advancement in Internet technology is the driving force behind these premature releases. Trying as hard as they can, software development firms nevertheless have difficulty detecting all bugs in new software. Yet, according to the video, consumers do benefit from the rapid release of new software. Do you agree or disagree? Is it acceptable for companies to release software with bugs? If you were a programmer, would you release a program with bugs?

SHELLY CASHMAN SERIES®
DISCOVERING COMPUTERS 2000

■ **Student Exercises**
WEB INFO
IN BRIEF
KEY TERMS
AT THE MOVIES
CHECKPOINT
AT ISSUE
CYBERCLASS
HANDS ON
NET STUFF
■ **Special Features**
TIMELINE 2000
GUIDE TO WWW SITES
MAKING A CHIP
BUYER'S GUIDE 2000
CAREERS 2000
TRENDS 2000
CHAT
INTERACTIVE LABS
NEWS
HOME

CHAPTER 1 2 3 4 5 6 7 **8** 9 10 11 12 13 14 **INDEX**

CHECKPOINT   www.scsite.com/dc2000/ch8/check.htm

WEB INSTRUCTIONS: *To display this page from the Web, launch your browser and enter the URL,* www.scsite.com/dc2000/ch8/check.htm. *Click the links for current and additional information. To experience the animation and interactivity, Shockwave and Flash Player must be installed on your computer (download by clicking* here*).*

Label the Figure

Instructions: *Identify the information displayed when you boot a computer.*

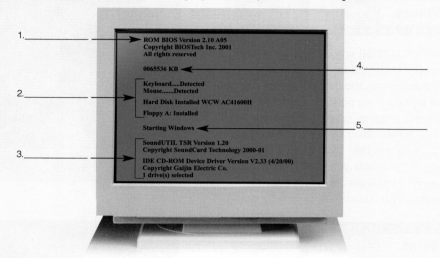

1.
2.
3.
4.
5.

ROM BIOS Version 2.10 A05
Copyright BIOSTech Inc. 2001
All rights reserved

0065536 KB

Keyboard.....Detected
Mouse.......Detected

Hard Disk Installed WCW AC41600H

Floppy A: Installed

Starting Windows

SoundUTIL TSR Version 1.20
Copyright SoundCard Technology 2000-01

IDE CD-ROM Device Driver Version V2.33 (4/20/00)
Copyright Gaijin Electric Co.
1 drive(s) selected

Matching

Instructions : *Match each popular operating system from the column on the left with the best description from the column on the right.*

_____ 1. DOS

_____ 2. Windows 98

_____ 3. Mac OS

_____ 4. OS/2

_____ 5. UNIX

    a. Single-user operating system with a command-line interface, developed in the early 1980s.
    b. Operating environment that works in combination with an operating system to simplify its use.
    c. Widely used network operating system designed for client-server networks.
    d. Powerful operating system capable of handling a high volume of transactions in a multi-user environment.
    e. IBM's multitasking graphical user interface operating system designed to work with 32-bit processors.
    f. Apple computer operating system that set the standard for ease of use.
    g. Internet integration allows for optional Web-page like user interface.

Short Answer

Instructions : *Write a brief answer to each of the following questions.*

1. How is a command-line interface different from a graphical user interface? _____ Why is a graphical user interface described as user-friendly? _____
2. What is a fault-tolerant computer? _____ For what type of systems are fault-tolerant computers used? _____
3. How does virtual memory (VM) optimize RAM? _____ What is a swap file? _____
4. How is a device-dependent operating system different from a device-independent operating system? _____ What is a downward-compatible operating system? _____
5. What is a boot disk? _____ Why is it important to have a boot disk available? _____

AT ISSUE   www.scsite.com/dc2000/ch8/issue.htm

SHELLY CASHMAN SERIES.
DISCOVERING COMPUTERS 2000

WEB INSTRUCTIONS: *To display this page from the Web, launch your browser and enter the URL,* www.scsite.com/dc2000/ch8/issue.htm. *Click the links for current and additional information.*

Developing icons for a graphical user interface is not an easy task. Although a good icon need not be a work of art, it must be a memorable symbol of the task it represents. According to Susan Kare, creator of the icons used with many popular GUIs, "The best icons are more like traffic signs than graphic illustrations." Choose *three* of the utilities described in this chapter and, using three sheets of graph paper, create an icon to represent each utility. Let each square on the graph paper stand for a pixel. Color the appropriate squares on the graph paper to create the image for each icon. On the back of the graph paper, explain why the icon is suitable for the utility you have chosen.

When Microsoft released Windows 98, it claimed the new operating system was *evolutionary*, not *revolutionary*. In other words, instead of being radically different, Windows 98 built on the model of its predecessor, Windows 95. Of the operating systems described in this chapter – DOS, Windows 3.x, Windows 95, Windows 98, Windows 2000, Windows CE, the Mac OS, OS/2, UNIX, Linux, and NetWare – which would you consider revolutionary? Why? Which would you call evolutionary? Why? Based on your experiences with each operating system, is a user better served using a revolutionary or evolutionary operating system? Why?

At a recent technical conference, a speaker from a noted software company told an audience of information-technology professionals that upgrading to a new operating system would be "seamless." The listeners responded with uncontrollable laughter. Adopting a new operating system seldom is easy. As a result, people often are reluctant to give up their old operating systems. Although critics claim Windows 95 and Windows 98 offer several advantages, Windows 3.1 remains popular. Why might people be reluctant to embrace new versions of an operating system? How could developers hasten the acceptance of a new operating system? If you generally were satisfied with your current operating system, would you upgrade? Why or why not?

New utility programs are being developed constantly to meet user needs. One new utility guards against computer theft by once a week making a silent call to a control center. If the call emanates from an appropriate number, the call is logged. If the computer has been reported stolen however, the center traces the call to locate the missing computer. What other needs could be addressed by a utility program? Identify three specific tasks (not described in this chapter) computer users would like to have performed that relate to managing or working with hardware, software, or files. Why would these tasks be important to a computer user? What would a utility program do to perform each task? If you were to market the utility program, what would you call it?

Futurists claim tomorrow's operating systems may be very different from those we use today. Innovations such as touch-screens, speech-recognition capabilities, automatic adaptability to individuals, and even recognition of user emotional states, have been suggested. Some innovators claim operating systems will be simpler, others think they will be more complex. What kind of operating system would you like to see? Write a description of the perfect operating system. Would it be a single-tasking, multitasking, or multiprocessing system? How would it handle such tasks as memory management, configuring devices, monitoring system performance, administering security, and managing storage media? What type of interface would it have? Of the operating systems with which you are familiar, which is most like, or most dislike, the perfect operating system? Why?

Student Exercises
WEB INFO
IN BRIEF
KEY TERMS
AT THE MOVIES
CHECKPOINT
AT ISSUE
CYBERCLASS
HANDS ON
NET STUFF
Special Features
TIMELINE 2000
GUIDE TO WWW SITES
MAKING A CHIP
BUYER'S GUIDE 2000
CAREERS 2000
TRENDS 2000
CHAT
INTERACTIVE LABS
NEWS
HOME

CHAPTER 1 2 3 4 5 6 7 8 9 10 11 12 13 14 INDEX

CYBERCLASS   www.scsite.com/dc2000/ch8/class.htm

WEB INSTRUCTIONS: *To display this page from the Web, launch your browser and enter the URL, www.scsite.com/dc2000/ch8/class.htm. To start Level I CyberClass, click a Level I link on this page or enter the URL, www.cyber-class.com. Click the Student button, click Discovering Computers 2000 in the list of titles, and then click the Enter a site button. To start Level II or III CyberClass (available only to those purchasers of a CyberClass floppy disk), place your CyberClass floppy disk in drive A, click Start on the taskbar, click Run on the Start menu, type* a:connect *in the Open text box, click the OK button, click the Enter CyberClass button, and then follow the instructions.*

I II III LEVEL   **1. Flash Cards**   Click Flash Cards on the Main Menu of the CyberClass web page. Click the plus sign before the Chapter 8 title. Select all the subjects under Chapter 8 and answer all the flash cards. Hand in the number right, the number wrong, and the percentage score to your instructor. All users: Close the Electronic Flash Card window and the Flash Cards window by clicking the Close button in the upper-right corner of each window.

I II III LEVEL   **2. Practice Test**   Click Testing on the Main Menu of the CyberClass web page. Click the Select a book box arrow and then click Discovering Computers 2000. Click the Select a test to take box arrow and then click the Chapter 8 title in the list. Click the Take Test button. If necessary, maximize the window. Take 4 practice tests by completing a test, clicking the Submit Test button, and then clicking the Take another Test button.

I II III LEVEL   **3. Web Guide**   Click Web Guide on the Main Menu of the CyberClass web page. When the Guide to World Wide Web Sites page displays, click Art. Visit one of the art sites. What are the advantages of viewing art on the Web? What are the disadvantages? When you are finished, close the window. Write a brief report indicating your responses to these questions.

I II III LEVEL   **4. Company Briefs**   Click Company Briefs on the Main Menu of the CyberClass web page. Click a corporation name to display a case study. Read the case study. Write a brief report indicating the variety of operating systems in use at the company. If the case study does not give information about operating systems, visit the Web site of the company and search to determine the use of operating systems.

II III LEVEL   **5. CyberChallenge**   Click CyberChallenge on the Main Menu of the CyberClass web page. Click the Select a book box arrow and then click Discovering Computers 2000. Click the Select a board to play box arrow and then click Chapter 8 in the list. Click the Play CyberChallenge button. Maximize the CyberChallenge window. Play CyberChallenge until you correctly answer all the 30, 40 and 50 point questions on the playing board. Close the CyberChallenge window.

II III LEVEL   **6. Assignments and Syllabus**   Click Assignments on the Main Menu of the CyberClass web page. Ensure you are aware of all assignments and when they are due. Click Syllabus on the Main Menu of the CyberClass web page. Verify you are up to date on all activities for the class.

II III LEVEL   **7. Text Chat and Send Messages**   Read How to Purchase, Install, and Maintain a Personal Computer, beginning on page 8.37. Then, click Text Chat on the Main Menu of the CyberClass web page and discuss with others in the chat room your most important criteria for purchasing a computer. If no one is in the chat room, click Send Messages on the Main Menu of the CyberClass web page and then send a message to two classmates explaining what you think is most important about buying a computer.

 **HANDS ON**   www.scsite.com/dc2000/ch8/hands.htm

WEB INSTRUCTIONS: *To display this page from the Web, launch your browser and enter the URL,* www.scsite.com/dc2000/ch8/hands.htm. *Click the links for current and additional information.*

■ Student Exercises
WEB INFO
IN BRIEF
KEY TERMS
AT THE MOVIES
CHECKPOINT
AT ISSUE
CYBERCLASS
HANDS ON
NET STUFF
■ Special Features
TIMELINE 2000
GUIDE TO WWW SITES
MAKING A CHIP
BUYER'S GUIDE 2000
CAREERS 2000
TRENDS 2000
CHAT
INTERACTIVE LABS
NEWS
HOME

One   ### About Windows

Double-click the My Computer icon on the desktop. When the My Computer window displays, click Help on the menu bar and then click About Windows 95 or About Windows 98. Answer the following questions:

- ▲ To whom is Windows licensed?
- ▲ How much physical memory is available to Windows?
- ▲ What percent of the system resources are free?

Click the OK button. Close the My Computer window.

Two   ### Using a Screen Saver

Right-click an empty area on the desktop and then click Properties on the shortcut menu. When the Display Properties dialog box displays, click the Screen Saver tab. Click the Screen Saver box arrow and then click Mystify Your Mind or any other selection. Click the Preview button to display the actual screen saver. Move the mouse to make the screen saver disappear. Answer the following questions:

- ▲ How many screen savers are available in your Screen Saver list?
- ▲ How many minutes does your system wait before activating a screen saver?

Click the Cancel button in the Display Properties dialog box.

Three   ### Changing Desktop Colors

Right-click an empty area on the desktop and then click Properties on the shortcut menu. When the Display Properties dialog box displays, click the Appearance tab. Perform the following tasks: (1) Click the question mark button on the title bar and then click the Scheme box. When the pop-up window displays, right-click it. Click Print Topic on the shortcut menu and then click the OK button in the Print dialog box. Click anywhere to remove the pop-up window. (2) Click the Scheme box arrow and then click Rose (large) to display the color scheme in Figure 8-31. Find a color scheme you like. Click the Cancel button.

Figure 8-31

Four   ### Customizing the Desktop for Multiple Users

This exercise uses Windows 98 procedures. If more than one person uses a computer, how can you customize the desktop for each user? Click the Start button on the taskbar and then click Help on the Start menu. Click the Contents tab. Click the Exploring Your Computer book. Click the The Windows Desktop book. Click the Customizing for Multiple Users book. Click an appropriate Help topic and read the Help information to answer each of the following questions:

- ▲ How can you display a list of users at startup?
- ▲ How can you add personalized settings for a new user?
- ▲ How can you change desktop settings for multiple users?

Click the Close button to close the Windows Help window.

SHELLY
CASHMAN
SERIES®

DISCOVERING
COMPUTERS
2000

CHAPTER 1 2 3 4 5 6 7 **8** 9 10 11 12 13 14   INDEX

NET STUFF   www.scsite.com/dc2000/ch8/net.htm

WEB INSTRUCTIONS: *To display this page from the Web, launch your browser and enter the URL,* www.scsite.com/dc2000/ch8/net.htm. *To use the Evaluating Operating Systems lab or the Working at Your Computer lab from the Web, Shockwave and Flash Player must be installed on your computer (download by clicking* here).

EVALUATING
OPERATING
SYSTEMS LAB

1. Shelly Cashman Series Evaluating Operating Systems Lab

Follow the instructions in NET STUFF 1 on page 1.46 to start and use the Evaluating Operating Systems lab. If you are running from the Web, enter the URL, www.scsite.com/sclabs/menu.htm; or display the NET STUFF page (see instructions at the top of this page) and then click the EVALUATING OPERATING SYSTEMS LAB button.

WORKING
AT YOUR
COMPUTER
LAB

2. Shelly Cashman Series Working at Your Computer Lab

Follow the instructions in NET STUFF 1 on page 1.46 to start and use the Working at Your Computer lab. If you are running from the Web, enter the URL, www.scsite.com/sclabs/menu.htm; or display the NET STUFF page (see instructions at the top of this page) and then click the WORKING AT YOUR COMPUTER LAB button.

PICTURES

3. A Picture's Worth a Thousand Words

Although she is not a programmer, Susan Kare's impact on the modern graphical user interface has been substantial. Kare is the person responsible for many of the icons used in modern graphical interfaces. According to *Forbes* magazine, "When it comes to giving personality to what otherwise might be cold and uncaring office machines, Kare is the queen of look and feel." Click the PICTURES button to learn more about Susan Kare and her approach to developing icons.

IN THE NEWS

4. In the News

When Windows 98 was launched in June, 1998, hundreds queued up at computer outlets. It is unclear, however, whether the anticipation was caused by the new operating system or by the promotions many dealers offered – one vendor gave system buyers the chance to also purchase a computer for $98. Click the IN THE NEWS button and read a news article about the impact, quality, or promotion of an operating system. What operating system was it? What was done to sell the operating system? Is the operating system recommended? Why or why not?

WEB CHAT

5. Web Chat

In 1998, a court began what some have called the trial of the century – U.S. vs. Microsoft. The Justice Department's antitrust suit alleged that the software giant took unjust advantage of its operating system dominance (Microsoft supplies almost 90 percent of world's operating systems). Specifically, by making its browser, Internet Explorer, an integral part of the Windows 98 operating system, the Justice Department claimed Microsoft engaged in unfair competition against rival browser suppliers, such as Netscape. Microsoft countered that its innovations are for the good of consumers. "Fortunately, this is a case where we've got customer benefit on our side," Bill Gates said. Should there be restrictions on what can, and cannot, be included with an operating system? Why? Should Microsoft be allowed to make any type of software (browser, speech recognition, word processing, spreadsheet, presentation graphics, etc.) part of its operating system, or would such an inclusion be unfair to other software developers? Click the WEB CHAT button to enter a Web Chat discussion related to this topic.

WEB INSTRUCTIONS: *To gain World Wide Web access to additional and up-to-date information regarding this special feature, launch your browser and enter the URL shown at the top of this page.*

The decision to buy a personal computer system is an important one – and finding and purchasing a personal computer system suited to your needs will require an investment of both time and money. In general, personal computer buyers fall into three categories: first-time buyers, replacement buyers, and upgrade buyers. A recent survey of North American consumers found that the

Buyer's Guide 2000
How to Purchase, Install, and Maintain a Personal Computer

largest of the three categories, first-time buyers, make up 40 percent of the PC market. Surprisingly, the survey also discovered that most first-time buyers have little computer experience. In fact, more than 70 percent of first-time home computer buyers do not even use a computer at work.

As with many buyers, you may have little computer experience and find yourself unsure of how to proceed. The following guidelines are presented to help you purchase, install, and maintain a computer system. These guidelines also apply to the purchase of a laptop computer. Purchasing a laptop also involves some additional considerations, which are addressed later in this special feature.

How to Purchase a Personal Computer

1. **Determine what application software products you will use on your computer.** Knowing what software applications you plan to use will help you decide on the type of computer to buy, as well as to define the memory, storage, and other requirements. Certain software products, for example, can run only on Macintosh computers, while others run only on a PC with the Windows operating system. Further, some software products require more memory and disk space than others, as well as additional input/output devices.

When you purchase a computer system, it may come bundled with several software products (although not all will). At the very least, you probably will want software for word processing and a browser to access the World Wide Web. If you need additional applications, such as a spreadsheet, database, or presentation graphics, consider purchasing a software suite that offers reduced pricing on several applications.

Before selecting a specific package, be sure the software contains the features necessary for the tasks you want to perform. Many Web sites and magazines, such as those listed in Figure 1, provide reviews of software products. These sites also frequently have articles that rate computer systems and software on cost, performance, and support.

Type of System	Web Site	URL
PC	PC Comparison	www.computers.com/scoreboard
	Computer Shopper	www.zdnet.com/computershopper/edit/howtobuy/C0000001
	PC World Magazine	www.pcworld.com
	Tech Web Buyer's Guides	www.techweb.com/infoseek/shopper/bguides.html
	Byte Magazine	www.byte.com
	PC Computing Magazine	www.zdnet.com/pccomp
	PC Magazine	www.zdnet.com/pcmag
	Ziff-Davis	www.zdnet.com/product
	Yahoo! Computers	computers.yahoo.com
	Family PC Magazine	www.zdnet.com/familypc/filters/fpc.hardware.html
	Compare.Net	compare.net
	Tips on Buying a PC	www.css.msu.edu/pc-guide.html
Macintosh	Byte Magazine	www.techweb.com/wire/apple/
	Ziff-Davis	www.zdnet.com/mac
	Macworld Magazine	www.macworld.com
	Apple	www.apple.com

For an updated list of hardware and software reviews and their Web sites, visit www.scsite.com/dc2000/ch8/buyers.htm.

Figure 1 Hardware and Software Reviews

2. **Before buying a computer system, do some research.** Talk to friends, coworkers, and instructors about prospective computer systems. What type of computer system did they buy? Why? Would they recommend their system and the company from which they bought it? You also should visit the Web sites or read reviews in the magazines listed in Figure 1. As you conduct your research, consider the following important criteria:

- Speed of the processor

- Size and types of memory (RAM) and storage (hard disk, floppy disk, CD-ROM, DVD-ROM, Zip® drive)

- Input/output devices included with the system (e.g., mouse, keyboard, monitor, printer, sound card, video card)

- Communications devices included with the system (modem, network interface card)

- Any software included with the system;

- Overall system cost

3. **Look for free software.** Many system vendors include free software with their systems. Some sellers even let you choose which software you want. Remember, however, that free software has value only if you would have purchased the software even if it had not come with the computer.

Figure 2 Some mail-order companies, such as Dell Computer, sell computers online.

4. **If you are buying a new computer system, you have several purchasing options: buying from your school bookstore, a local computer dealer, a local large retail store; or ordering by mail via telephone or the World Wide Web.** Each purchasing option has certain advantages. Many college bookstores, for example, sign exclusive pricing agreements with computer manufacturers and, thus, can offer student discounts. Local dealers and local large retail stores, however, more easily can provide hands-on support. Mail-order companies that sell computer systems by telephone or online via the Web (Figure 2) often provide the lowest prices but extend less personal service. Some major mail-order companies, however, have started to provide next-business-day, onsite services. A credit card usually is required to buy from a mail-order company. Figure 3 lists some of the more popular mail-order companies and their Web site addresses.

Type of System	Company	URL	Telephone Number 1
PC	Computer Shopper	www.computershopper.com	
	Compaq	www.compaq.com	1-800-888-0220
	CompUSA	www.compusa.com	1-800-266-7872
	Dell	www.dell.com	1-800-678-1626
	Gateway	www.gateway.com	1-800-846-4208
	IBM	www.ibm.com	1-800-426-7235
	Micron	www.micron.com	1-800-964-2766
	Packard Bell	www.packardbell.com	1-888-474-6772
	Quantex	www.quantex.com	1-800-346-6685
Macintosh	Apple Computer	store.apple.com	1-800-795-1000
	Club Mac	www.clubmac.com	1-800-258-2622
	MacBase	www.macbase.com	1-800-951-1230
	Mac Wholesale	www.macwholesale.com	1-800-531-4622
	Mac Exchange	www.macx.com	1-888-650-4488

For an updated list of new computer mail-order companies and their Web sites, visit www.scsite.com/dc2000/ch8/buyers.htm.

Figure 3 New computer mail-order companies

Figure 4
Used computer mail-order companies

Company	URL	Telephone Number
American Computer Exchange	www.amcoex.com	1-800-786-0717
Boston Computer Exchange	www.bocoex.com	1-617-625-7722
United Computer Exchange	www.uce.com	1-800-755-3033
Used Computer Exchange	www.usedcomputer exchange.com	1-888-256-0481

For an updated list, visit www.scsite.com/dc2000/ch8/buyers.htm

5. **If you are buying a used computer system, stick with name brands.** Although brand-name equipment can cost more, most brand-name systems have longer, more comprehensive warranties, are better supported, and have more authorized centers for repair services. As with new computer systems, you can purchase a used computer from local computer dealers, local large retail stores, or mail order via the telephone or the Web. Classified ads and used computer brokers offer additional outlets for purchasing used computer systems. Figure 4 lists several major used computer brokers and their Web site addresses.

How to Purchase a Personal Computer

6. **Use a worksheet to compare computer systems, services, and other considerations.** You can use a separate sheet of paper to take notes on each vendor's computer system and then summarize the information on a spreadsheet, such as the one shown in Figure 5. Most companies advertise a price for a base system that includes components housed in the system unit (processor, RAM, sound card, video card), disk drives (floppy disk, hard disk, CD-ROM, and DVD-ROM), a keyboard, mouse, monitor, printer, speakers, and modem. Be aware, however, that some advertisements list prices for systems with only some of these components. Monitors, printers, and modems, for example, often are not included in a base system price. Depending on how you plan to use the system, you may want to invest in additional or more powerful components. When you are comparing the prices of computer systems, make sure you are comparing identical or similar configurations.

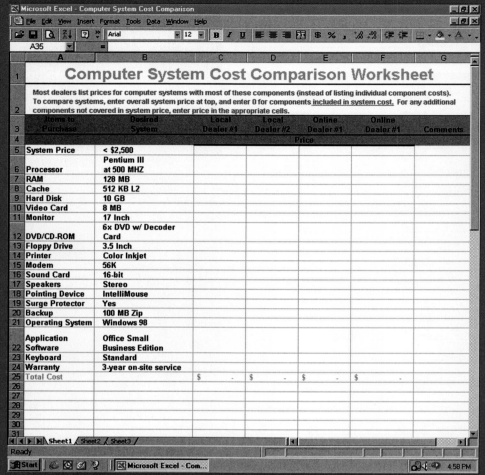

Figure 5 A spreadsheet is an effective tool for summarizing and comparing the prices and components of different computer vendors. A copy of the Computer System Cost Comparison workbook is on the Discover Data Disk. To obtain a copy of the Discover Data Disk, see the inside back cover of this book for instructions.

7. **Be aware of hidden costs.** Before purchasing, be sure to consider any additional costs associated with buying a computer, such as an additional telephone line, an uninterruptible power supply (UPS), computer furniture, floppy disks and paper, or computer training classes you may want to take. Depending on where you buy your computer, the seller may be willing to include some or all of these in the system purchase price.

8. Consider more than just price. The lowest cost system may not be the best buy. Consider such intangibles as the vendor's time in business, the vendor's regard for quality, and the vendor's reputation for support. If you need to upgrade your computer often, you may want to consider a leasing arrangement, in which you pay monthly lease fees but upgrade or add on to your computer system as your equipment needs change. If you are a replacement buyer, ask if the vendor will buy your old system; an increasing number of companies are taking trade-ins. No matter what type of buyer you are, insist on a 30-day, no questions-asked return policy on your computer system.

9. Select an Internet service provider (ISP) or online service. You can access the Internet in one of two ways: via an ISP or an online service. Both provide Internet access for a monthly fee that ranges from $5 to $20. Local ISPs offer Internet access through local telephone numbers to users in a limited geographic region. National ISPs provide access for users nationwide (including mobile users), through local and toll-free telephone numbers. Because of their size, national ISPs offer more services and generally have a larger technical support staff than local ISPs. Online services furnish Internet access as well as members-only features for users nationwide. Figure 6 lists several national ISPs and online services. Before you choose an Internet access provider, compare such features as the number of access hours, monthly fees, available services (e-mail, Web page hosting, chat), and reliability.

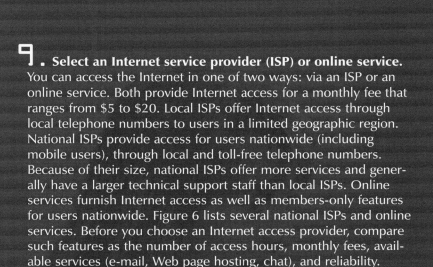

Figure 6 National ISPs and online services

Company	Service	URL	Telephone Number
America Online	ONLINE	www.americaonline.com	1-800-827-6364
AT&T Network Commerce Services	ISP	www.att.com/work-net	1-800-467-8467
CompuServe	ONLINE	www.compuserve.com/ gateway/default.asp	1-800-394-1481
Earthlink Network	ISP	www.earthlink.com	1-800-395-8425
GTE Internet	ISP	www.gte.net	1-888-GTE-SURF
IBM Internet Connection Services	ISP	www.ibm.net	1-800-455-5056
MCI	ISP	www.mciworldcom.com	1-800-1-888-0800
Microsoft Network	ONLINE	www.msn.com	1-800-386-5550
Prodigy/Prodigy Classic	ISP/ONLINE	www.prodigy.com	1-800-PRODIGY
UUNet Technologies	ISP	www.uu.net	1-800-4UUNET4

For information on local ISPs or to learn more on any ISPs and online services listed here, visit The List™ at thelist.internet.com. The List™ — the most comprehensive and accurate directory of ISPs and online services on the Web — compares dial-up services, access hours, and fees for over 5,000 access providers.

For an updated list of ISPs and online service providers, visit www.scsite.com/dc2000/ch8/buyers.htm.

10. Buy a system compatible with the ones you use elsewhere. If you use a personal computer at work or in some other capacity, make sure the computer you buy is compatible. For example, if you use a PC at work, you may not want to purchase a Macintosh for home use. Having a computer compatible with the ones at work or school will allow you to transfer files and spend time at home on work- or school-related projects.

How to Purchase a Personal Computer

11. **Consider purchasing an onsite service agreement.** If you use your computer system for business or are unable to be without your computer, consider purchasing an onsite service agreement through a local dealer or third-party company. Most onsite service agreements state that a technician will come to your home, work, or school within 24 hours. If your system includes onsite service only for the first year, think about extending the service for two or three years when you buy the computer.

13. **Avoid buying the smallest system available.** Computer technology changes rapidly, meaning a computer that seems powerful enough today may not serve your computing needs in a few years. In fact, studies show that many users regret they did not buy a more powerful system. Plan to buy a system that will last you for two to three years. You can help delay obsolescence by purchasing the fastest processor, most memory, and largest hard drive you can afford. If you must buy a smaller system, be sure you can upgrade it with additional memory and auxiliary devices as your system requirements grow. Figure 7 includes minimum recommendations for each category of user discussed in this book: Home User, Small Business User, Mobile User, Large Business User, and Power User. The Home User category is divided into two groups, Application Home User and Game Home User.

12. **Use a credit card to purchase your system.** Many credit cards now offer purchase protection and extended warranty benefits that cover you in case of loss of or damage to purchased goods. Paying by credit card also gives you time to install and use the system before you have to pay for it. Finally, if you are dissatisfied with the system and are unable to reach an agreement with the seller, paying by credit card gives you certain rights regarding withholding payment until the dispute is resolved. Check your credit card agreement for specific details.

BASE SYSTEM COMPONENTS

	Application Home User	Game Home User	Small Business User	Mobile User	Large Business User	Power User
HARDWARE						
Processor	Pentium III at 450 MHz	Pentium III at 500 MHz	Pentium III at 500 MHZ	Pentium II at 366 MHz	PentiumIII at 500 MHz	Pentium III Xeon at 500 MHz
RAM	96 MB	128 MB	128 MB	96 MB	192 MB	256 MB
Cache	512 KB L2	512 KB L2	512 KB L2	512 KB L2	512 KB L2	512 KB L2
Hard Drive	12.9 GB	12.9 GB	17.2 GB	10 GB	17.2 GB	16.8 GB
Video Graphics Card	8 MB	16 MB	8 MB	8 MB	8 MB	16 MB
Monitor	17"	19"	17"	15" active matrix	19"	21"
DVD/CD-ROM Drive	40X CD-ROM	5X DVD with Decoder Card	40X CD-ROM	24X CD-ROM	40X CD-ROM	5X DVD with Decoder Card
Floppy Drive	3.5"	3.5"	3.5"	3.5"	3.5"	3.5"
Printer	Color ink-jet	Color ink-jet	8 ppm laser	Portable ink-jet	24 ppm laser	8 ppm laser
Fax/modem	56 K	56 K	56 K	56 K	ISDN	ISDN
Sound Card	16-bit	16-bit	16-bit	Built-In	16-bit	16-bit
Speakers	Stereo	Full-Dolby surround	Stereo	Stereo	Stereo	Full-Dolby surround
Pointing Device	IntelliMouse	IntelliMouse and Joystick	IntelliMouse	Touchpad or Pointing Stick and IntelliMouse	IntelliMouse	IntelliMouse and Joystick
Keyboard	Yes	Yes	Yes	Built-In	Yes	Yes
Backup Disk/Tape Drive	100 MB Zip	1 GB Jaz	1 GB Jaz and Tape	100 MB Zip	2 GB Jaz and Tape	2 GB Jaz and Tape
SOFTWARE						
Operating System	Windows 98	Windows 98	Windows 98	Windows 98	Windows NT	Windows NT
Application Software Suite	Office Standard	Office Standard	Office Small Business Edition	Office Small Business Edition	Office Professional	Office Professional
Internet Access	Online Service or ISP	Online Service or ISP	LAN (ISDN)	ISP	LAN/WAN (T1/T3)	LAN
OTHER						
Surge Protector	Yes	Yes	Yes	Portable	Yes	Yes
Warranty	3-year on-site service	3-year on-site service	3-year on-site service	3-year on-site service	3-year on-site service	3-year on-site service
Other		Headset		Docking Station Carrying case		

Optional Components for all Categories
digital camera
multifunction device (MFD)
scanner
uninterruptable power supply
ergonomic keyboard
network interface card
TV/FM tuner
recordable CD-ROM
video camera
mouse pad/wrist rest

Figure 7 Base system components and optional components

How to Purchase a Laptop Computer

If you need computing capability when you travel, you may find a laptop computer to be an appropriate choice. The guidelines mentioned in the previous section also apply to the purchase of a laptop computer (Figure 8). The following are additional considerations unique to laptops.

Figure 8 Laptop computer

1. **Purchase a laptop with a sufficiently large active-matrix screen. Active-matrix screens** display high-quality color that is viewable from all angles. Less expensive, passive matrix screens sometimes are hard to see in low-light conditions and cannot be viewed from an angle. Laptop computers typically come with a 12.1-inch, 13.3-inch, or 14.1-inch display. For most users, a 13.3-inch display is satisfactory. If you intend to use your laptop as a desktop replacement, however, you may opt for a 14.1-inch display. If you travel a lot and portability is essential, consider that most of the lightest machines are equipped with a 12.1-inch display. Regardless of size, the resolution of the display should be at least 800 x 600 pixels.

2. **Experiment with different pointing devices and keyboards.** Laptop computer keyboards are far less standardized than those for desktop systems. Some laptops, for example, have wide wrist rests, while others have none. Laptops also use a range of pointing devices, including pointing sticks, touchpads, and trackballs. Before you purchase a laptop, try various types of keyboard and pointing devices to determine which is easiest for you to use. Regardless of the pointing device you select, you also may want to purchase a regular mouse unit to use when you are working at a desk or other large surface.

3. **Make sure the laptop you purchase has a CD-ROM or DVD-ROM drive.** Loading software, especially large software suites, is much faster if done from a CD-ROM or DVD-ROM. Today, most laptops come with either an internal or external CD-ROM drive; others have an internal and external unit that allows you to interchange the 3.5-inch floppy drive and the CD-ROM drive. An advantage of a separate CD-ROM drive is that you can leave it behind to save weight. Some users prefer a DVD-ROM drive to a CD-ROM drive. Although DVD-ROM drives are more expensive, they allow you to read CD-ROMs and to play movies using your laptop.

4. **If you plan to use your laptop both on the road and at home or in the office, consider a docking station.** A docking station usually includes a floppy disk drive, a CD-ROM or DVD-ROM drive, and a connector for a full-sized monitor. When you work both at home and in the office, a docking station is an attractive alternative to buying a full-sized system. A docking station essentially turns your laptop into a desktop, while eliminating the need to transfer files from one computer to another.

5. **If necessary, upgrade memory and disk storage at the time of purchase.** As with a desktop computer system, upgrading your laptop's memory and disk storage usually is less expensive at the time of initial purchase. Some disk storage systems are custom designed for laptop manufacturers, meaning an upgrade might not be available two or three years after you purchase your laptop.

6. **If you are going to use your laptop on an airplane, purchase a second battery.** Two batteries should provide enough power to last through most airplane flights. If you anticipate running your laptop on batteries frequently, choose a system that uses **lithium-ion batteries** (they last longer than nickel cadmium or nickel hydride batteries).

7. **Purchase a well-padded and well-designed carrying case.** An amply padded carrying case will protect your laptop from the bumps it will receive while traveling. A well-designed carrying case will have room for accessories such as spare floppy disks; an external floppy disk, CD-ROM, or DVD-ROM drive; a user manual; pens; and paperwork (Figure 9).

8. **If you travel overseas, obtain a set of electrical and telephone adapters.** Different countries use different outlets for electrical and telephone connections. Several manufacturers sell sets of adapters that will work in most countries (Figure 10).

Figure 10
Set of electrical and telephone adapters

9. **If you plan to connect your laptop to a video projector, make sure the laptop is compatible with the video projector.** Some laptops will not work with certain video projectors; others will not allow you to display an image on the laptop and projection device at the same time (Figure 11). Either of these factors can affect your presentation negatively.

Figure 11 Video projector

Figure 9 Well-designed carrying case

How to Install a Personal Computer

1. **Read the installation manuals before you start to install your equipment.** Many manufacturers include separate installation instructions with their equipment that contain important information. You can save a great deal of time and frustration if you make an effort to read the manuals.

2. **Do some research.** To locate additional instructions on installing your computer, review the computer magazines or Web sites listed in Figure 12 to search for articles on installing a computer system.

WEB SITE	URL
Getting Started/Installation	
Once You've Bought It	www.newsday.com/plugin/ c101main.htm
HelpTalk Online	www.helptalk.com
Ergonomics	
Ergonomic Computing	cobweb.creighton.edu/training/ergo.htm
Healthy Choices for Computer Users	www-ehs.ucsd.edu/vdttoc.htm
Video Display Health Guidelines	www.uhs.berkeley.edu/facstaff/ergonomics/ ergguide.html

For an updated list of reference materials, visit www.scsite.com/dc2000/ch8/buyers.htm.

Figure 12 Web references on setting up and using your computer

3. **Set up your computer in a well-designed work area, with adequate workspace around the computer.** **Ergonomics** is an applied science devoted to making the equipment and its surrounding work area safer and more efficient. Ergonomic studies have shown that using the correct type and configuration of chair, keyboard, monitor, and work surface will help you work comfortably and efficiently, and help protect your health. For your computer workspace, experts recommend an area of at least two feet by four feet. Figure 13 illustrates additional guidelines for setting up your work area.

4. **Install bookshelves.** Bookshelves above and/or to the side of your computer area are useful for keeping manuals and other reference materials handy.

5. **Have a telephone outlet and telephone near your workspace so you can connect your modem and/or place calls while using your computer.** To plug in your modem to dial up and access the World Wide Web, you will need a telephone outlet close to your computer. Having a telephone nearby also helps if you need to place business or technical support calls while you are working on your computer. Often, if you call a vendor about a hardware or software problem, the support person can talk you through a correction while you are on the telephone. To avoid data loss, however, do not place floppy disks on the telephone or near any other electrical or electronic equipment.

Figure 13 A well-designed work area should be flexible to allow adjustments to the height and build of different individuals. Good lighting and air quality also are important considerations.

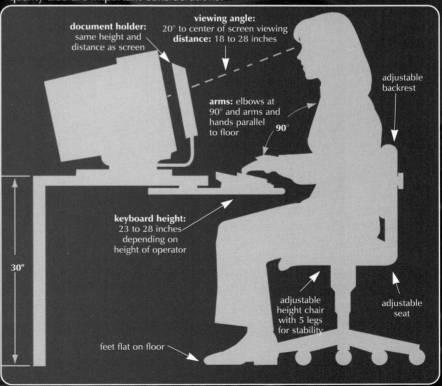

document holder: same height and distance as screen

viewing angle: 20° to center of screen **viewing distance:** 18 to 28 inches

arms: elbows at 90° and arms and hands parallel to floor

90°

adjustable backrest

adjustable seat

keyboard height: 23 to 28 inches depending on height of operator

adjustable height chair with 5 legs for stability

30"

feet flat on floor

6. While working at your computer, be aware of health issues. Working safely at your computer requires that you consider several health issues. To minimize neck and eye discomfort, for instance, obtain a document holder that keeps documents at the same height and distance as your computer screen. To provide adequate lighting that reduces eye strain, use non-glare light bulbs that illuminate your entire work area. Figure 14 lists additional computer user health guidelines.

Computer User Health Guidlines

1. Work in a well-designed work area. See Figure 13 on the previous page.

2. Alternate work activities to prevent physical and mental fatigue. If possible, change the order of your work to provide some variety.

3. Take frequent breaks. Every fifteen minutes, look away from the screen to give your eyes a break. At least once per hour, get out of your chair and move around. Every two hours, take at least a fifteen-minute break.

4. Incorporate hand, arm, and body stretching exercises into your breaks. At lunch, try to get outside and walk.

5. Make sure your computer monitor is designed to minimize electromagnetic radiation (EMR). If it is an older model, consider adding EMR reducing accessories.

6. Try to eliminate or minimize surrounding noise. Noisy environments contribute to stress and tension.

7. If you frequently use the telephone and the computer at the same time, consider using a telephone headset. Cradling the telephone between your head and shoulder can cause muscle strain.

8. Be aware of symptoms of repetitive strain injuries: soreness, pain, numbness, or weakness in neck, shoulders, arms, wrists, and hands. Do not ignore early signs; seek medical advice.

Figure 14 Following these health guidelines will help computer users maintain their health.

7. Obtain a computer tool set.
Computer tool sets include any screwdrivers and other tools you might need to work on your computer. Computer dealers, office supply stores, and mail-order companies sell these tool sets. To keep all the tools together, get a tool set that comes in a zippered carrying case.

8. Save all the paperwork that comes with your system. Keep the documents that come with your system in an accessible place, along with the paperwork from your other computer-related purchases. To keep different-sized documents together, consider putting them in a manila file folder, large envelope, or sealable plastic bag.

9. Record the serial numbers of all your equipment and software. Write the serial numbers of your equipment and software on the outside of the manuals packaged with these items. As noted in Figure 16 on the next page, you also should create a single, comprehensive list that contains the serial numbers of all your equipment and software.

10. Complete and send in your equipment and software registration cards. When you register your equipment and software, the vendor usually enters you in its user database. Being a registered user not only can save you time when you call with a support question, it also makes you eligible for special pricing on software upgrades.

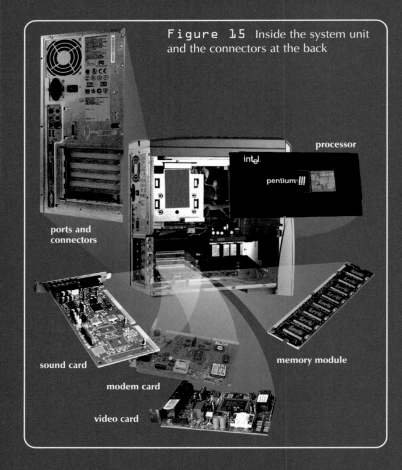

Figure 15 Inside the system unit and the connectors at the back

processor

intel

pentium·III

ports and connectors

sound card

modem card

video card

memory module

11. **Keep the shipping containers and packing materials for all your equipment.** Shipping containers and packing materials will come in handy if you have to return your equipment for servicing or must move it to another location.

12. **Identify device connectors.** At the back of your system, you will find a number of connectors for your printer, monitor, mouse, telephone line, and so forth (Figure 15). If the manufacturer has not identified them for you, use a marking pen to write the purpose of each connector on the back of the computer case.

13. **Install your system in an area where you can maintain the temperature and humidity.** You should keep the system in an area with a constant temperature between 60°F and 80°F. High temperatures and humidity can damage electronic components. Be careful when using space heaters, for example, as the hot, dry air they generate can cause disk problems.

14. **Keep your computer area clean.** Avoid eating and drinking around your computer. Also, avoid smoking. Cigarette smoke can cause damage to the floppy disk drives and floppy disk surfaces

15. **Check your home or renter's insurance policy.** Some renter's insurance policies have limits on the amount of computer equipment they cover. Other policies do not cover computer equipment at all if it is used for business. In this instance, you may want to obtain a separate insurance policy.

How to Maintain Your Personal Computer

1. **Start a notebook that includes information on your system.** Keep a notebook that provides a single source of information about your entire system, both hardware and software. Each time you make a change to your system, such as adding or removing hardware or software or altering system parameters, record the change in your notebook. Include the following items in your notebook.

- Vendor support numbers from your user manuals
- Serial numbers of all equipment and software
- User IDs, passwords, and nicknames for your ISP or online service, network access, Web sites, and so on
- Vendor and date of purchase for all software and equipment
- Trouble log that provides a chronological history of equipment or software problems
- Notes on any discussions with vendor support personnel

Figure 16 provides a suggested outline for the contents of your notebook.

PC OWNER'S NOTEBOOK OUTLINE

1. Vendors
Vendor
City/State
Product
Telephone #
URL

2. Internet and online services information
Service provider name
Logon telephone number
Alternate logon
   telephone number
Technical support
   telephone number
User ID
Password

3. Web site information
Web site name
URL
User ID
Password
Nickname

4. Serial numbers
Product
Manufacturer
Serial #

5. Purchase history
Date
Product
Manufacturer
Vendor
Cost

6. Software log
Date installed/uninstalled

7. Trouble log
Date
Time
Problem
Resolution

8. Support calls
Date
Time
Company
Contact
Problem
Comments

9. Vendor paperwork

Figure 16 To keep important information about your computer on hand and organized, use an outline such as this sample outline.

How to Maintain Your Personal Computer

2. Before you work inside your computer, turn off the power and disconnect the equipment from the power source. Working inside your computer with the power on can affect both you and the computer adversely. Thus, you should turn off the power and disconnect the equipment from the power source before you open a computer to work inside. In addition, before you touch anything inside the computer, you should touch an unpainted metal surface such as the power supply. Doing so will help discharge any static electricity that could damage internal components.

3. Keep the area surrounding your computer dirt and dust free. Reducing the dirt and dust around your computer will reduce the need to clean the inside of your system. If dust builds up inside the computer, remove it carefully with compressed air and a small vacuum. Do not touch the components with the vacuum.

4. Back up important files and data. Use the operating system or utility program to create an emergency or rescue disk to help you restart your computer if it crashes. You also regularly should copy important data files to disks, tape, or another computer.

5. Protect your system from computer viruses. A computer virus is a potentially damaging computer program designed to infect other software or files by attaching itself to the software or files with which it comes in contact. Virus programs are dangerous because often they destroy or corrupt data stored on the infected computer. You can protect your computer from viruses by installing an antivirus program.

6. Keep your system tuned. Most operating systems include several system tools that provide basic system maintenance functions. One important system tool is the disk defragmenter. Defragmenting your hard disk reorganizes files so they are in contiguous (adjacent) clusters, making disk operations faster. Some programs allow you to schedule system maintenance tasks for times when you are not using your computer. If necessary, leave your computer on at night so the system can run the required maintenance programs. If your operating system does not provide the system tools, you can purchase a stand-alone utility program to perform basic system maintenance functions.

7. Learn to use system diagnostic tools. Diagnostic tools help you identify and resolve system problems, thereby helping to reduce your need for technical assistance. Diagnostic tools help you test system components, monitor system resources such as memory and processing power, undo changes made to system files, and more. As with basic maintenance tools, most operating systems include system diagnostic tools; you also can purchase or download many stand-alone diagnostic tools.

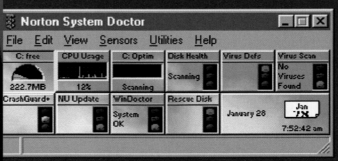

CHAPTER 9

COMMUNICATIONS AND NETWORKS

OBJECTIVES

**After completing this chapter,
you will be able to:**

Define the components required for successful communications

Describe uses of communications

Identify the various types of transmission media

Explain the purpose of communications software

Describe commonly used communications devices

Explain the difference between a local area network and a wide area network

Understand the various communications protocols

Identify uses of intranets and extranets

When computers first were produced, they were stand-alone devices. As computers became more widely used, hardware and software were designed so computers could exchange data, instructions, or information with other computers — a process called communications. Originally, only large computers had communications capabilities; today, even the smallest computers can communicate with other computers.

This chapter provides an overview of communications terminology and applications and explains various communications devices, media, and procedures as they relate to computers. It also discusses how you can join computers together into a network, allowing them to communicate and share resources such as hardware, software, data, and information.

COMMUNICATIONS

When referring to computers, **communications** describes a process in which one computer transfers data, instructions, and information to another computer(s). Figure 9-1 shows a basic model for this type of communications, sometimes called **data communications** or **telecommunications**. The model consists of the following:

- A sending device that initiates an instruction to transmit data, instructions, or information

- A communications device that converts the data, instructions, or information from the sending device into signals that can be carried by a communications channel

- A **communications channel**, or path, over which the signals are sent

- A communications device that receives the signals from the communications channel and converts them into a form understood by the receiving device

- A receiving device that accepts the data, instructions, or information

The most common type of sending and receiving device in this communications model is a computer. Other devices, such as fax machines and digital cameras, also can function as sending and/or receiving devices.

A communications device, such as a modem, typically sends and receives signals to and from a communications channel. For instance, a modem connected to a sending device such as a computer converts the computer's digital signals into analog signals. The analog signals then are sent over a standard telephone line (the communications channel). At the receiving end, another modem converts the analog signals back into digital signals that a receiving computer can understand.

A communications channel consists of one or more transmission media, including cables, telephone lines, and airwaves. Throughout this chapter, various types of transmission media are discussed.

The basic model of communications also includes communications software, which consists of programs that manage the transmission of data, instructions, and information between computers. Communications software is discussed later in the chapter.

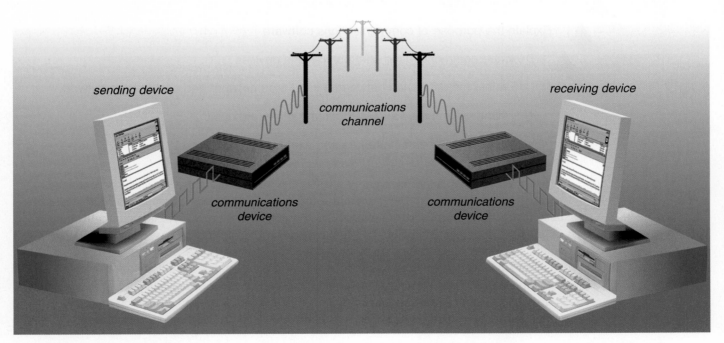

Figure 9-1 *In this basic model of communications, the sending device and receiving devices are personal computers, the communications devices are modems, and the communications channel consists of telephone lines.*

USES OF COMMUNICATIONS

Communications technologies have changed the way individuals interact, by allowing for instant and accurate information transfer, 24 hours a day. Today, uses of communications technology are all around you. In the course of a day, for example, you might use, or use information generated by, one or more of the following communications technologies: e-mail, voice mail, fax, telecommuting, videoconferencing, groupware, a global positioning system (GPS), a bulletin board system (BBS), the Internet, the World Wide Web, e-commerce, or telephony.

Previous chapters have presented many of these communications technologies, as they related to a particular topic. For instance, Chapter 2 presented e-mail and groupware as software applications; Chapter 4 introduced videoconferencing as a form of input; and Chapter 5 discussed fax machines as output devices. Chapter 7 explained communications technologies such as the Internet; the World Wide Web; and e-commerce and telephony, which are two popular Web-based activities. The following sections review these technologies and present new technologies as they specifically relate to communications.

E-mail

E-mail (**electronic mail**) is the exchange of text messages and computer files transmitted via a communications network such as a local area network or the Internet. Communications devices, such as modems, transfer the e-mail messages to and from computers or terminals on the same network or a separate network. To send and receive e-mail messages, you use e-mail software installed on your computer.

When another user sends you an e-mail message, the message is placed in your **mailbox**, which is a storage location on the computer that connects you to the local area network or the Internet. Using your e-mail software, you can retrieve, read, and reply to that message or delete it from your mailbox.

Voice Mail

Voice mail, which functions much like an answering machine, allows callers to leave a voice message for a called party. Unlike answering machines, however, a computer in the voice mail system converts an analog voice message into digital form. Once digitized, the message is stored in a **voice mailbox**, which is a storage location on a computer in the voice mail system. A voice mail system usually provides individual voice mailboxes for many users (for example, employees in a company or students and faculty at a college).

By accessing his or her voice mailbox, a called party can listen to messages; add comments to a message; and reply or forward a message to another voice mailbox in the voice mail system. Some voice mail systems allow you to send the same message to a specific group of individuals or everyone listed in the system's database. Colleges, for example, can use voice mail to notify every student of registration deadlines and weather-related school closings.

Fax

A **fax** (**facsimile**) **machine** is a device that sends and receives documents via telephone lines. Such a document, called a **fax**, can contain handwritten or typed text, illustrations, photographs, or other graphics. You can send or receive a fax using a stand-alone fax machine or a fax modem.

A **stand-alone fax machine** scans a printed document, digitizes the text and graphical images, and transmits the digitized data. A fax machine at the receiving end reads the incoming data, converts the digitized data back into text and graphical images, and prints or stores a copy of the original document.

A **fax modem** allows you to send and receive faxes using your computer. Because the fax modem must be connected to a computer, it can transmit only documents that already are digitized, such as a word processing letter or a digital photograph.

WEB INFO

For more information on telecommuting, visit the Discovering Computers 2000 Chapter 9 WEB INFO page (**www.scsite.com/dc2000/ch9/webinfo.htm**) and click Telecommuting.

Telecommuting

Telecommuting is a work arrangement in which employees work away from a company's standard workplace, but communicate with the office using some communications technology (Figure 9-2). A telecommuter often works at home and connects to the main office's network using a personal computer equipped with communications software and a communications device. Once connected, the employee can read and answer e-mail, access databases, and send and receive project-related information.

Telecommuting benefits both employers and employees. Because it provides flexibility, telecommuting increases employee productivity and job satisfaction in these ways.

1. It reduces the time used to commute to the office.

2. Travel during unsafe weather conditions is eliminated.

3. It provides a convenient, comfortable work environment for disabled employees or workers recovering from injuries or illnesses.

4. Employees are allowed to combine work and personal responsibilities, such as child care.

In addition, telecommuting positively impacts the environment by reducing the air pollution caused by vehicles driven to and from an office.

Videoconferencing

Videoconferencing involves using video and computer technology to conduct a meeting between participants at two or more geographically separate locations (Figure 9-3). Videoconferencing allows participants to collaborate as if they were in the same room. Popular uses of videoconferencing include technical support, distance learning, job recruiting interviews, and telecommuting.

Conducting a videoconference requires computers with microphones, speakers, video cameras, and communications devices and software. The communications devices and software digitize and compress the video and audio data and then transmit it over a communications channel, such as a standard telephone line.

Figure 9-2 *Telecommuting allows you to work from your home or some other location away from a main office.*

Figure 9-3 *Software, such as the Intel® Team Station™ System, allows individual users to participate in a videoconference.*

Groupware

Groupware is a software application that helps groups of people work together on projects and share information over a network. Groupware is a component of a broad concept called **workgroup computing**, which includes specific hardware and software that enables group members to communicate, manage projects, schedule meetings, and make group decisions. To assist with these activities, most groupware provides personal information manager (PIM) functions, such as an electronic appointment calendar, an address book, and a notepad.

Global Positioning System

A **global positioning system** (**GPS**) consists of one or more earth-based receivers that accept and analyze signals sent by satellites in order to determine the receiver's geographic location. A GPS receiver can be handheld or mounted on an object such as an automobile, boat, airplane, farm and construction equipment, or a computer. A GPS often is used to locate a person or object; ascertain the best route between two points; monitor the movement of a person or object; or create a map.

Today, GPSs help scientists, farmers, pilots, dispatchers, and rescue workers operate more productively and safely. A rescue worker, for example, might use a GPS to locate a motorist stranded in a blizzard; a surveyor might use a GPS to create design maps for construction projects (Figure 9-4).

GPSs also are used in travel and recreation activities. For example, many rental cars use GPSs to provide directions to a destination and some golf carts even include a GPS to show the layout of each hole and distances to the green.

Bulletin Board System

An electronic **bulletin board system** (**BBS**) is a computer that maintains a centralized collection of electronic messages. You access a BBS by using your computer to connect to the main BBS computer. Once you connect to the BBS, you can add or delete messages, read existing messages, or upload and download software. An individual called the **system operator**, or **sys op**, creates and updates the BBS.

Today, tens of thousands of BBSs exist. Many hardware and software vendors, for example, have BBSs to provide online product support. Others BBSs function as electronic meeting rooms for special-interest groups to share information about hobbies such as games, music, genealogy, and astronomy. Still other BBSs are strictly social, allowing users to meet friends and conduct conversations by posting messages to the bulletin board. Because you can use the Internet to access many of the same services, however, BBS usage is declining.

Figure 9-4 This GPS receiver used by land surveyors communicates with satellites to provide information on the user's location.

The Internet

The **Internet** is a worldwide collection of networks that links together millions of businesses, government offices, educational institutions, and individuals via modems, telephone lines, satellites, and other communications devices and media.

As discussed in Chapters 2 and 7, most users connect to the Internet through an Internet service provider (ISP) or an online service (Figure 9-5). After subscribing to an ISP or online service, you can use communications software and devices to connect to a computer operated by the ISP or online service. Once connected to your ISP or online service, you can access the Internet.

Although the Internet itself is based on communications technology, it offers a variety of services that also are based on this technology, some of which are presented in the following sections.

THE WEB Today, one of the more popular uses for communications is to access the World Wide Web. Recall that the **World Wide Web**, **WWW**, or **Web**, consists of a worldwide collection of electronic documents (Web pages) that have built-in links to other related documents. Connected users browse pages on the Web to access a wealth of information, news, research, and educational material, as well as sources of entertainment and leisure.

E-COMMERCE A growing use of the Web is **e-commerce** (**electronic commerce**), which includes activities such as shopping, banking, investing, and any other venture that uses either electronic money (e-money) or electronic data interchange. **Electronic money** (**e-money**) is a means of paying for goods and services over the Internet. **Electronic data interchange** (**EDI**) is the transmission of business documents or data over communications media. Many companies use EDI to transmit routine documents such as invoices, purchase orders, or shipping information.

TELEPHONY **Internet telephony** enables you to talk to other people over the Web. Internet telephony uses the Internet (instead of the public switched telephone network) to connect a calling party and one or more called parties. To place an Internet telephone call, you need Internet telephone software. As you speak into a computer microphone, **Internet telephone software** and your computer's sound card digitize and compress your conversation (the audio) and then transmit the digitized audio over the Internet to the called parties. Software and equipment at the receiving end reverse the process so the receiving parties can hear what you have said, just as if you were speaking on a telephone.

WEB INFO

For more information on telephony, visit the Discovering Computers 2000 Chapter 9 WEB INFO page (**www.scsite.com/dc2000/ch9/webinfo.htm**) and click Telephony.

Figure 9-5a (The Microsoft Network)

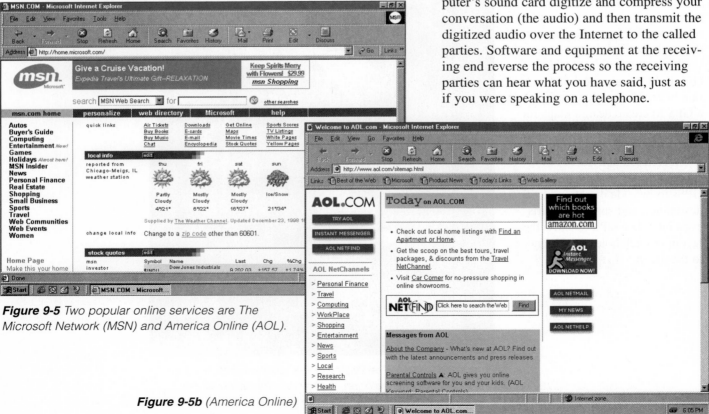

Figure 9-5 Two popular online services are The Microsoft Network (MSN) and America Online (AOL).

Figure 9-5b (America Online)

COMMUNICATIONS CHANNEL

An important aspect of communications is the **channel**, which is the communications path between two devices. A communications channel is composed of one or more transmission media. **Transmission media** consists of materials or techniques capable of carrying a signal.

Transmission media are one of two types: physical or wireless. **Physical transmission media** use wire, cable, and other tangible (touchable) materials to send communications signals; **wireless transmission media** send communications signals through the air or space using radio, microwave, and infrared signals.

PHYSICAL TRANSMISSION MEDIA

Physical transmission media used in communications include twisted-pair cable, coaxial cable, and fiber-optic cable. These cables typically are used within buildings or underground. The following sections discuss each of these types of cables.

Twisted-Pair Cable

One of the more commonly used transmission media for network cabling and telephone systems is twisted-pair cable. **Twisted-pair cable** consists of one or more twisted-pair wires bundled together (Figure 9-6). Each **twisted-pair wire** consists of two separate insulated copper wires that are twisted together. The wires are twisted together to reduce **noise**, which is an electrical disturbance that can degrade communications.

One type of twisted-pair cable, called **shielded twisted-pair** (**STP**) cable, has a metal wrapper around each twisted-pair wire, which further reduces noise. Cables that do not have this shielding are called **unshielded twisted-pair** (**UTP**). Inexpensive and easy-to-install, UTP cables commonly are used in telephone networks. Because STP cables are more insulated than UTP cables, STP cables are used in environments susceptible to noise, such as in a local area network. STP cables, however, are more expensive than UTP cables.

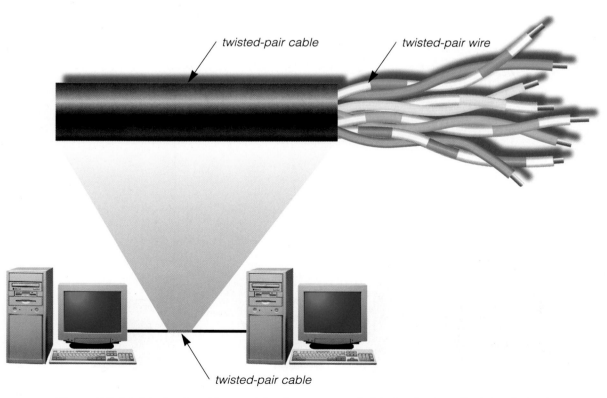

twisted-pair cable

twisted-pair wire

twisted-pair cable

Figure 9-6 *A twisted-pair cable consists of one or more twisted-pair wires. Each twisted-pair wire usually is color coded for identification. Twisted-pair cable often is used in telephone networks and local area networks.*

Coaxial Cable

A second type of physical transmission media is coaxial cable. **Coaxial cable**, often referred to as **coax** (pronounced CO-ax), consists of a single copper wire surrounded by three layers: (1) an insulating material, (2) a woven or braided metal, and (3) a plastic outer coating (Figure 9-7).

Cable television wiring often uses coaxial cable because it can be cabled over longer distances than twisted-pair cable. Coaxial cable also is insulated more heavily than twisted-pair cable, and thus is not as susceptible to noise. Most of today's computer networks, however, do not use coaxial cable because other transmission media such as fiber-optic cable transmit signals at faster rates.

Fiber-Optic Cable

Another type of physical transmission media is fiber-optic cable. The core of a **fiber-optic cable** consists of dozens or hundreds of thin strands of glass or plastic that use light to transmit signals. Each strand, called an **optical fiber**, is as thin as a human hair. Inside the fiber-optic cable, an insulating glass cladding and a protective coating surround each optical fiber (Figure 9-8).

Fiber-optic cables have several advantages over cables that use wire, such as twisted-pair and coaxial cables. These advantages include the following.

- Capability of carrying significantly more signals than wire cables

- Faster data transmission

- Less susceptible to noise (interference) from other devices such as a copy machines

- Better security for signals during transmission because they are less susceptible to noise

- Smaller size (much thinner and lighter weight)

Disadvantages of fiber-optic cable are that it costs more than twisted-pair or coaxial cable and can be difficult to install and modify. Despite these limitations, many local and long-distance telephone companies and cable TV operators are replacing existing telephone and coaxial cables with fiber-optic cables. Many companies also are using fiber-optic cables in high-traffic networks or as the main cable in a network.

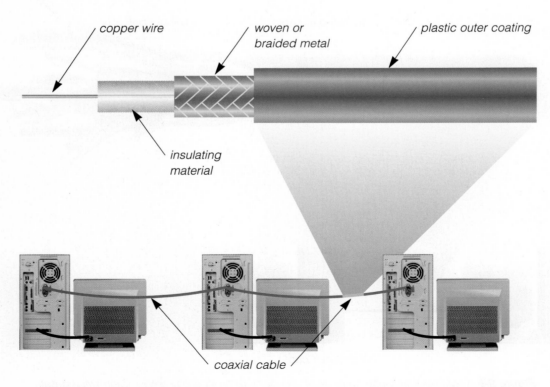

copper wire

woven or braided metal

plastic outer coating

insulating material

coaxial cable

Figure 9-7 *On a coaxial cable, data travels through the copper wire. This illustration shows computers networked together with coaxial cable.*

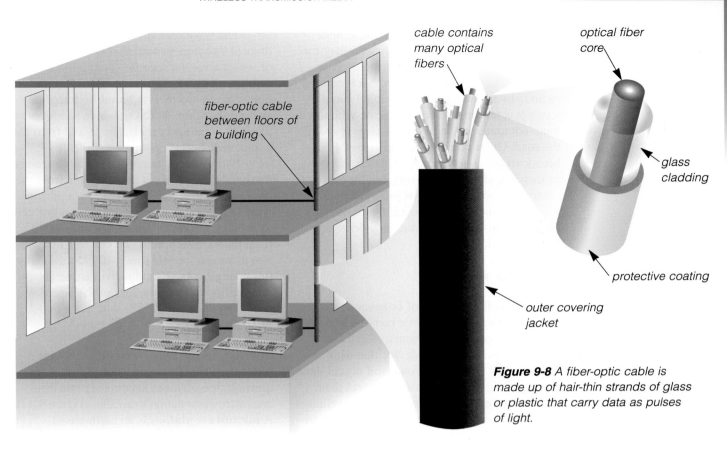

cable contains many optical fibers

optical fiber core

glass cladding

protective coating

outer covering jacket

Figure 9-8 *A fiber-optic cable is made up of hair-thin strands of glass or plastic that carry data as pulses of light.*

fiber-optic cable between floors of a building

WIRELESS TRANSMISSION MEDIA

Wireless transmission media used in communications include broadcast radio, cellular radio, microwaves, communications satellites, and infrared. Wireless transmission media are used when it is impractical or impossible to install cables. The following sections discuss several types of wireless transmission media.

Broadcast Radio

Broadcast radio is a wireless transmission medium that distributes radio signals through the air over long distances such as between cities, regions, and countries. For radio transmissions, you need a transmitter to send the broadcast radio signal and a receiver to accept it. To receive the broadcast radio signal, the receiver has an antenna that is located in the range of the signal. Some networks use a **transceiver**, which both sends and receives signals from wireless devices.

You use broadcast radio when listening to AM and FM radio stations, watching television stations, and talking on a citizens band (CB) radio. Each station uses a different

frequency, as assigned by the Federal Communications Commission (FCC). This allows you to select which station you wish to receive.

Some companies have their own broadcast radio networks to support mobile communications to their network (Figure 9-9).

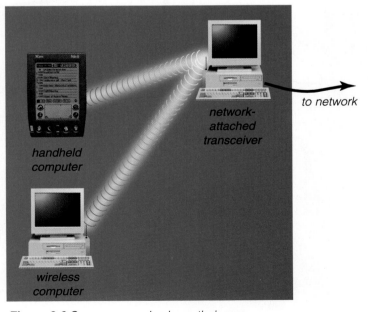

handheld computer

network-attached transceiver

to network

wireless computer

Figure 9-9 *Some companies have their own broadcast radio networks to support wireless communications.*

Wireless devices such as terminals, laptop computers, or PDAs have antenna so they can communicate with the network transceiver. For example, in a warehouse with a broadcast radio network, warehouse personnel can use a wireless terminal to communicate with the main computer while in the warehouse or on the road. Other common applications of broadcast radio networks include order processing, shipping, delivery, and inventory control. Although broadcast radio networks are slower and more susceptible to noise than physical transmission media, they do provide flexibility and portability.

Cellular Radio

Cellular radio is a form of broadcast radio that is used widely for mobile communications, specifically cellular telephones. A **cellular telephone** is a telephone device that uses radio signals to transmit voice and digital data messages. Some mobile users connect their laptop or other portable computer to a cellular telephone to access the Internet, e-mail, or an office network while traveling.

The broadcast area for cellular radio is divided into honeycombed-shaped **cells**, each of which covers a specific geographic area and has its own base station. The base stations communicate with a **mobile telephone switching office** (**MTSO**), which sends and receives voice and data traffic to and from the public switched telephone network.

Every cellular telephone has a transceiver that sends and receives radio signals from the base station in a particular cell. As a person with a cellular telephone travels from one cell to another, the radio signals are transferred from the base station in one cell to a base station in another cell (Figure 9-10). Occasionally, this change in base stations will cause an interruption or even the loss of the signal.

Microwaves

Microwaves are radio waves that provide a high-speed signal transmission. Microwave transmission involves sending signals from one microwave station to another (Figure 9-11). A **microwave station** is an earth-based reflective dish that contains the antenna, transceivers, and other equipment necessary for microwave communications.

Figure 9-10 *As a person with a cellular telephone drives from one cell to another, the radio signals are transferred from the base station in one cell to a base station in another cell.*

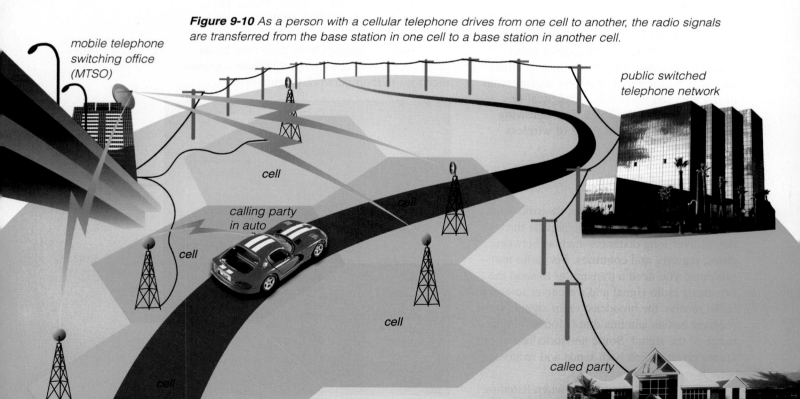

mobile telephone switching office (MTSO)

public switched telephone network

cell

calling party in auto

cell

cell

cell

cell

cell

called party

base station

Microwaves are limited to **line-of-sight transmission**, which means that microwaves must be transmitted in a straight line with no obstructions between microwave antennas. To avoid possible obstructions, such as buildings or mountains, microwave stations often are positioned on the tops of buildings, towers, or mountains.

Microwave transmission is used in environments where installing physical transmission media is difficult or impossible and where line-of-sight transmission is available. For example, microwave transmission is used in wide-open areas such as deserts or lakes; between buildings in a close geographic area; or to communicate with a satellite. Current users of microwave transmission include universities, hospitals, city governments, cable TV providers, and telephone companies.

Communications Satellite

A **communications satellite** is a space station that receives microwave signals from an earth-based station, amplifies (strengthens) the signals, and broadcasts the signals back over a wide area to any number of earth-based stations (Figure 9-12). These earth stations often are microwave stations, but other devices, such as handheld portable computers, also are used. A transmission from an earth station to a satellite is called an **uplink**; a transmission from a satellite to an earth station is called a **downlink**.

Communications satellites usually are placed about 22,300 miles above the earth's equator. Because these satellites orbit (revolve in a circular path) at the same rate as the earth, they are considered **geosynchronous satellites**. A geosynchronous satellite maintains its position over the same location of the earth's surface because the satellite moves at the same rate as the earth.

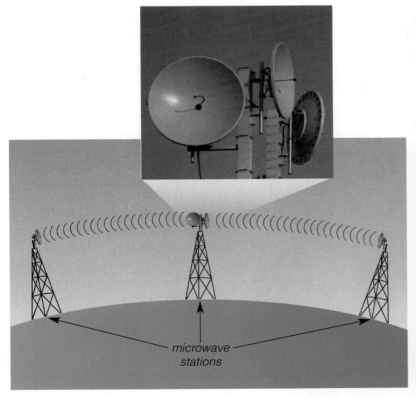

Figure 9-11 *A microwave station is a ground-based reflective dish that contains the antenna and other equipment necessary for microwave communications.*

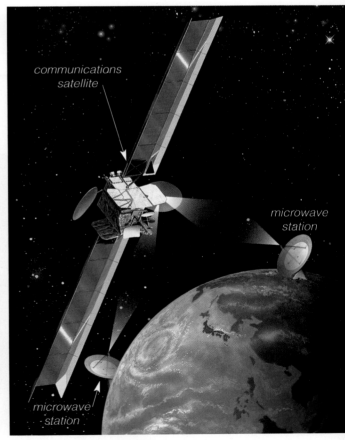

Figure 9-12 *Communications satellites are placed about 22,300 miles above the earth's equator.*

Communications satellites are used in applications such as air navigation, television and radio broadcasts, videoconferencing, paging, and global positioning systems. Businesses with operations in multiple locations often use private satellite systems to communicate information such as retail inventory management or credit verification. Such businesses often use a small communications satellite called a **VSAT** (**Very Small Aperture Terminal**) for applications that involve transmitting small amounts of data.

Infrared

Infrared (**IR**) is a wireless transmission media that sends signals using infrared light waves. Like microwaves, infrared transmission requires a line-of-sight transmission; that is, the sender and the receiver must be aligned so that nothing obstructs the path of the infrared light wave.

As discussed in Chapter 3, many computers and devices, such as mouse units, printers, docking stations, and digital cameras,

have an IrDA port that enables the transfer of data from one device to another using infrared light waves. A laptop computer or printer also can use IR transmission to communicate with other devices on a network. Figure 9-13 shows an infrared network access device that allows any IR-equipped device to communicate with the network.

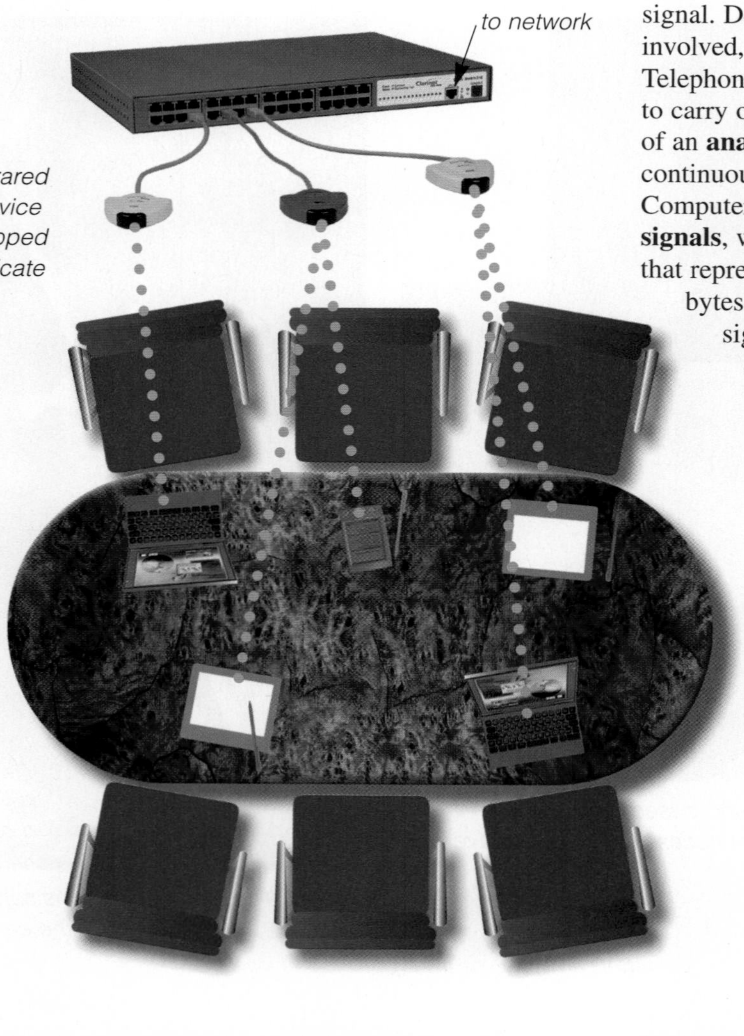

TRANSMISSION CHARACTERISTICS

Recall that communications involves the transmission of data, instructions, and information among computers. Any transmissions sent during these communications can be categorized by a number of characteristics including the signal type, transmission mode, transmission direction, and transmission rate. Each of these characteristics is discussed in the following sections.

Signal Type: Analog or Digital

As discussed, communications requires a signal. Depending on the devices and media involved, that signal is either analog or digital. Telephone equipment originally was designed to carry only voice transmission in the form of an **analog signal**, which consists of a continuous electrical wave (Figure 9-14). Computers, however, process data as **digital signals**, which are individual electrical pulses that represent the bits grouped together into bytes. For telephone lines to carry digital signals, a special piece of equipment called a modem converts between digital signals (0s and 1s) and analog signals. Modems are discussed in more detail later in this chapter.

to network

Figure 9-13 An infrared network access device allows any IR-equipped device to communicate with a network.

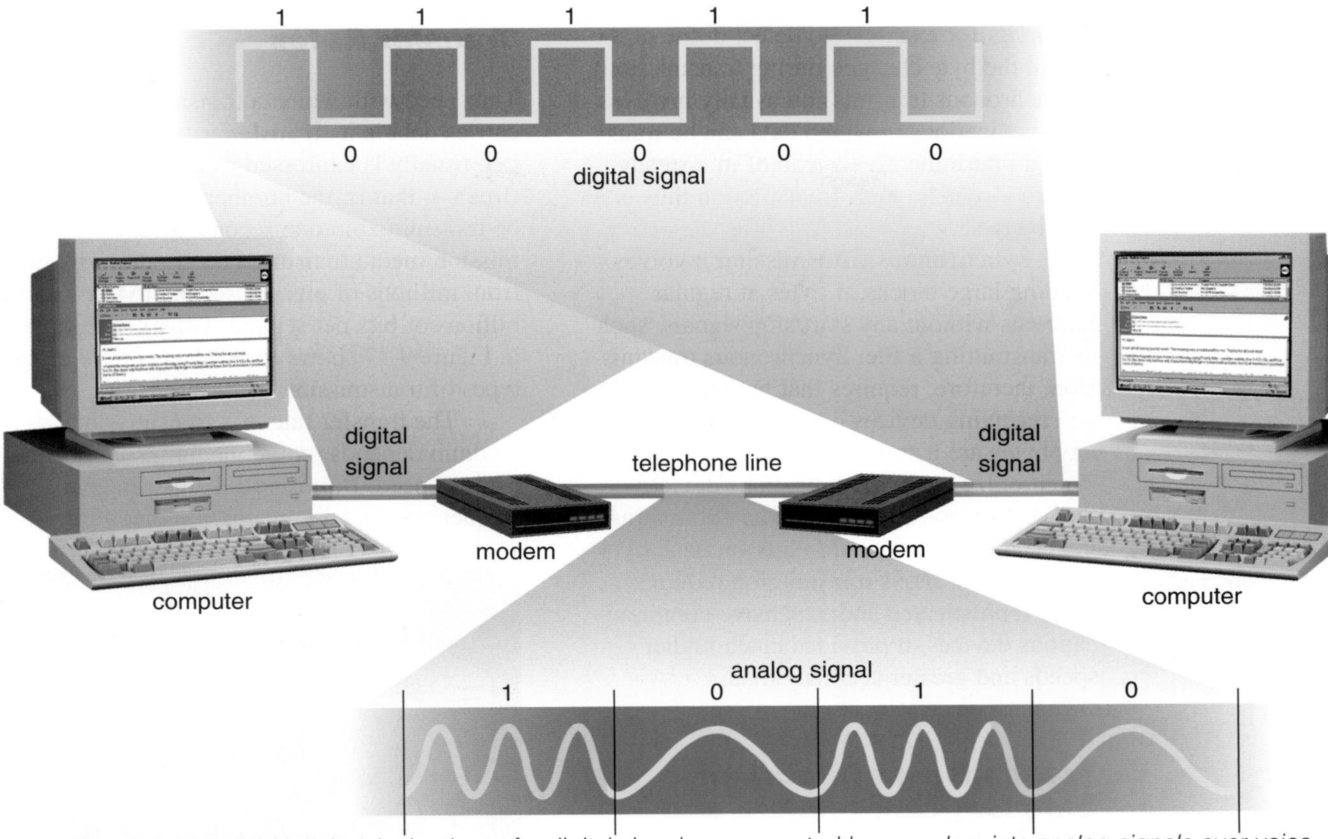

1 1 1 1 1

digital signal

0 0 0 0 0

digital signal **digital signal**

telephone line

modem **modem**

computer **computer**

analog signal

1 0 1 0

Figure 9-14 *Individual electrical pulses of a digital signal are converted by a modem into analog signals over voice telephone lines. At the receiving computer, another modem converts the analog signals back into digital signals that can be processed by the computer.*

Transmission Modes: Asynchronous and Synchronous

When two devices exchange data, the data flows between the devices as a continuous stream of bits. As the bits flow between the sending and receiving devices, these devices extract bytes (characters) from the bit stream. Two basic transmission techniques are used to separate the groups of bits: asynchronous transmission and synchronous transmission (Figure 9-15).

With **asynchronous transmission**, transmissions are not synchronized — that is, transmission does not occur at predetermined or regular intervals such as when you enter data. A sending device thus can transmit bytes at any time, and the receiving device must be ready to accept them as they arrive. To help the receiving device identify each byte, a *start bit* marks the beginning of the byte and a *stop bit* marks the end of the byte. An additional bit called a *parity bit* sometimes is included at the end of each byte to allow for error

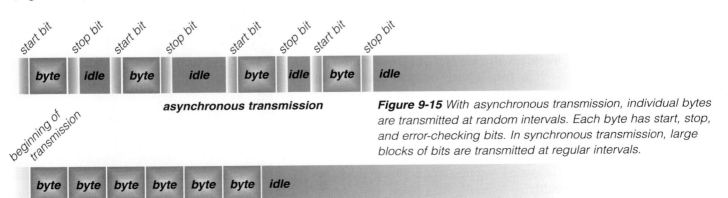

start bit stop bit start bit stop bit start bit stop bit start bit stop bit

byte **idle** **byte** **idle** **byte** **idle** **byte** **idle**

beginning of transmission

asynchronous transmission

Figure 9-15 *With asynchronous transmission, individual bytes are transmitted at random intervals. Each byte has start, stop, and error-checking bits. In synchronous transmission, large blocks of bits are transmitted at regular intervals.*

byte **byte** **byte** **byte** **byte** **byte** **idle**

synchronous transmission

checking (for example, to detect if one of the bits in the byte changed during transmission). Asynchronous transmission usually involves communications in which data can be transmitted intermittently instead of in a steady stream. Asynchronous transmission thus is relatively slow.

Synchronous transmission involves sending large blocks of bytes at regular intervals without any start/stop signals, such as transmitting a file. Synchronous transmission, therefore, requires that both the sending and receiving devices be synchronized before any bytes are transmitted. Timing signals synchronize the communications devices at the sending and receiving ends, eliminating the need for start and stop bits for each byte. While synchronous transmission requires more sophisticated and expensive communications devices, it provides much higher speeds and greater accuracy than asynchronous transmission.

Transmission Direction: Simplex, Half-Duplex, and Full-Duplex

The direction in which data flows along transmission media is classified in one of three types: simplex, half-duplex, or full-duplex (Figure 9-16).

In **simplex transmission**, data flows only in one direction — from the sending device to the receiving device. Simplex transmission is used only when the sending device does not require a response from the receiving device. Security systems and fire alarms that contain a sensor, for example, use simplex transmission.

In **half-duplex transmission**, data can flow in either direction — from sender to receiver and back — but only in one direction at a time. Citizens band (CB) radio, for example, uses half-duplex transmission; you can talk or listen, but you cannot do both at the same time. Many fax machines, credit card verification systems, and automatic teller machines also use half-duplex transmission.

In **full-duplex transmission**, data can flow in both directions at the same time. A regular telephone line, for example, supports full-duplex transmission, meaning both parties can talk at the same time. Full-duplex transmission is used for applications with intensive computing requirements or those with heavy traffic.

WEB INFO
WEB INFO

For more information on bandwidth, visit the Discovering Computers 2000 Chapter 9 WEB INFO page (**www.scsite.com/ dc2000/ch9/webinfo.htm**) and click Bandwidth.

Transfer Rates

The speed with which a transmission medium carries data is its **transfer rate**. Transfer rate usually is expressed as **bits per second (bps)** — that is, the number of bits that can be transmitted in one second. Today's transmission media transmit data at rates ranging from millions of bits per second (Mbps) to billions of bits per second (Gbps). The table in Figure 9-17 shows transfer rates for various types of transmission media.

The transfer rate of a transmission medium depends on the medium's bandwidth and its speed. **Bandwidth** is the range of frequencies that a transmission medium can

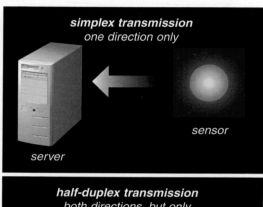

simplex transmission
one direction only

sensor

server

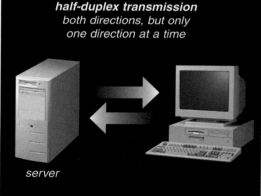

half-duplex transmission
both directions, but only one direction at a time

server

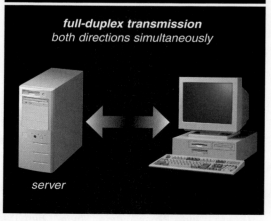

full-duplex transmission
both directions simultaneously

server

Figure 9-16 *Three types of data flow are simplex, half-duplex, and full-duplex.*

TRANSFER RATES FOR VARIOUS TYPES OF TRANSMISSION MEDIA

Channel	Transfer Rates
Twisted pair	1 to 128 Mbps
Coaxial cable	Up to 200 Mbps
Fiber-optic cable	100 Mbps to 2 Gbps
Broadcast radio	Up to 2 Mbps
Microwave radio	45 Mbps
Communications satellite	50 Mbps
Cellular radio	9,600 bps to 14.4 Kbps
Infrared	1 to 4 Mbps

Figure 9-17 *Today's transmission media transmit data in ranges of millions of bits per second and billions of bits per second.*

carry in a given period of time. The higher the bandwidth of a medium, the more frequencies it can transmit. Because data can be assigned to different frequencies, a larger bandwidth means more data can be transmitted at one time.

For analog signals, bandwidth is expressed in hertz (Hz), or cycles per second (cps). For digital signals, bandwidth is expressed in bits per second, or bps. Each year, transfer rates and bandwidth increase as communications companies develop new communications techniques and technologies.

THE TELEPHONE NETWORK

The **public switched telephone network (PSTN)** is the worldwide telephone system that handles regular voice telephone calls. Telephone service carried by the PSTN is sometimes called **plain old telephone service (POTS)**. While initially it was built to handle voice communications, the public switched telephone system also is an integral part of data communications.

The PSTN uses transmission media and switching offices that route the analog (voice) and digital (data) signals to their destinations. Today, the PSTN uses a variety of media. Fiber-optic cables, microwaves, and communications satellites, for example, typically are used for long-distance lines and networks with heavy traffic. The final link from the local telephone company to a home or office, however, often uses analog twisted-pair cable. Figure 9-18 shows how a telephone network might use various transmission media.

Data, instructions, and information can be sent over the PSTN using dial-up lines or dedicated lines. The following sections discuss each of these types of connections.

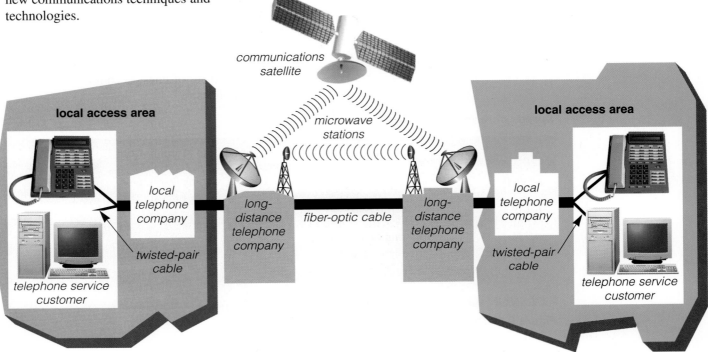

Figure 9-18 *When you send data via the telephone network, it may travel over a variety of transmission media.*

Dial-Up Lines

A **dial-up line** is a temporary connection that uses one or more analog telephone lines for communications. A dial-up connection is not permanent; each time a call is placed, the telephone company switching offices select the line to use to establish the connection. Using a dial-up line to transmit data is similar to using a telephone to make a call. A modem at the sending end dials the telephone number of the modem at the receiving end. When the modem at the receiving end answers the call, a connection is established and the data is transmitted. When the transmission is complete, the modem at either end terminates the call by hanging up, and the communications connection ends.

One advantage of a dial-up line is that it costs no more than making a regular telephone call. Another advantage is that computers at any two locations can establish a connection using modems and the PSTN. Mobile users, for example, often use dial-up lines to connect to the main office network so they can read e-mail messages, access the Internet, and upload files.

A disadvantage of dial-up lines is that you cannot control the quality of the connection because the telephone company's switching office randomly selects the line.

Dedicated Lines

A **dedicated line** is a connection that always is established between two communications devices (unlike a dial-up line where the connection is reestablished each time it is used). Because dedicated lines provide a constant connection, the quality and consistency of the connection is better than a dial-up line.

Businesses often use dedicated lines to connect geographically distant offices. Businesses can buy and maintain their own dedicated lines, or they can lease a dedicated line from a telephone or communications service company, in which case it is called a **leased line**. The cost of leased lines varies according to the distance between the two connected points and the speed at which the line transmits data. The charges for leased lines, however, usually are flat fees, meaning you pay a fixed monthly amount for 24-hour a day access.

Leased lines can be either analog or digital. As with dial-up lines, analog leased lines require modems at both the sending and receiving ends. Digital leased lines use any of the following transmission media: twisted-pair cable, coaxial cable, fiber-optic cable, microwaves, or infrared. Because they provide faster transmission rates than analog lines, digital leased lines increasingly connect home and business users to networks around the globe. Four popular types of digital leased lines are ISDN lines, digital subscriber lines, T-carrier lines, and asynchronous transfer mode. The table in Figure 9-19 lists the transfer rates and approximate monthly costs of these types of lines, as compared with dial-up lines.

Speeds of Various Telephone Connections

Type of Line	Transmission Rates	Approximate Monthly Cost
Dial-up	1.2 to 56 Kbps	Local or long-distance rates
ISDN	Up to 128 Kbps	$10 to $40
ADSL	16 Kbps to 8.45 Mbps	$60 to $110
T1	1.544 Mbps	$1,000 or more
T3	45 Mbps	$10,000 or more

Figure 9-19 *The speeds of various telephone connections.*

ISDN LINES For the small business and home user, an Integrated Services Digital Network (ISDN) line provides faster transmission rates than regular telephone lines. **Integrated Services Digital Network (ISDN)** is a set of standards for digital transmission of data over analog telephone lines. With ISDN, the same twisted-pair telephone line that could carry only one computer signal, now can carry three or more signals at once, through the same line, using a technique called multiplexing.

ISDN requires that both ends of the connection have an ISDN adapter installed instead of a modem. ISDN lines also require a special ISDN telephone for voice communications. Home and business users who choose ISDN adapters benefit from faster Web page downloads and clearer videoconferencing. Digital ISDN connections also produce voice conversations that are very clear.

Depending on the type of ISDN line, it can carry from three to twenty-four signals. The most affordable ISDN line, called a **Basic Rate Interface** (**BRI**), carries three signals and has transmission rates up to 128 Kbps. These ISDN lines typically cost $10 to $40 more than basic residential monthly telephone rates. An ISDN line that carries 24 signals, called a Primary Rate Interface (PRI), is comparable in speed to a T-1 line and is intended for large business use. Most ISPs support ISDN line connections, but they cost about $20 more per month than a standard dial-up connection.

DIGITAL SUBSCRIBER LINES Another digital line alternative for the small business or mobile user is a digital subscriber line (DSL). A **digital subscriber line** (**DSL**) uses sophisticated techniques to transmit a greater number of bytes on a standard twisted-pair cable. DSL provides slightly higher transfer rates than ISDN lines and thus is slightly more expensive, ranging from $60 to $110 per month. To connect to a digital subscriber line, a customer must have a DSL modem.

One of the more popular DSLs is an **asymmetric digital subscriber line** (**ADSL**), which is a type of DSL that supports faster transmission rates when receiving data (the downstream rate) than when sending data (the upstream rate). For example, ADSL downstream rates range from 1.54 Mbps to 8.45 Mbps and upstream rates range from 16 Kbps to 640 Kbps. Because most users download more information from the Internet than upload, an asymmetric digital subscriber line is ideal for Internet access. DSL is a fairly new technology, thus many ISPs do not yet offer it.

T-CARRIER LINES A **T-carrier line** is any of several types of digital lines that carry multiple signals over a single communications line. Whereas a standard analog telephone line carries only one signal, digital T-carrier lines use a technique called multiplexing so that multiple signals can share the telephone line. While T-carrier lines do provide high transmission rates, they also are expensive. For this reason, T-carrier lines are used by medium to large organizations that can afford this investment.

The most popular T-carrier line is the T-1 line. In the United States, a **T-1 line** can carry 24 separate signals at a transmission rate of 64 Kbps each — for a total transmission rate of 1.544 Mbps (24 * 64,000 + 8,000). (The remaining 8 Kbps manage the transmission.) Businesses often use T-1 lines to connect to the Internet; many Internet service providers (ISPs) also use T-1 lines to connect to the Internet backbone.

A **T-3 line** is equal to twenty-eight T-1 lines; that is, a T-3 line can carry 672 individual signals (28 * 24) at a transmission rate of 64 Kbps each — for a total transmission rate of 43 Mbps. T-3 lines are quite expensive. Main users of T-3 lines include large organizations, telephone companies, and Internet service providers connecting to the Internet backbone. The Internet backbone itself also uses T-3 lines.

ASYNCHRONOUS TRANSFER MODE **Asynchronous transfer mode** (**ATM**) is a service designed to carry voice, data, video, and multimedia at high speeds — currently up to 622 Mbps. ATM is used in telephone networks, on the Internet, and for other networks with large amounts of traffic. Some experts predict that ATM will become the Internet standard for data transmission.

WEB INFO

For more information on digital subscriber lines, visit the Discovering Computers 2000 Chapter 9 WEB INFO page(**www.scsite.com/ dc2000/ch9/webinfo.htm**) and click DSLs.

COMMUNICATIONS CHANNEL EXAMPLE

When you send data from your computer to another device, the signal carrying that data most likely travels over a variety of transmission media — especially when the transmission is sent over a long distance. Figure 9-20 illustrates a typical communications channel — much like the one that connects a computer to the World Wide Web — and shows the variety of transmission media used to complete the connection. Although many media and devices are involved, the entire communications process could take less than one second.

COMMUNICATIONS SOFTWARE

As mentioned at the beginning of this chapter, the basic communications model includes **communications software**, which consists of programs that manage the transmission of data, instructions, and information between computers. For two computers to communicate, they must have compatible communications software.

Some communications devices are pre-programmed to accomplish communications tasks. Other communications devices require a separate communications software program to ensure proper transmission of data.

WEB INFO
WEB INFO

For more information on communications software, visit the Discovering Computers 2000 Chapter 9 WEB INFO page (www.scsite.com/dc2000/ch9/webinfo.htm) and click Communications Software.

Figure 9-20

AN EXAMPLE OF A COMMUNICATIONS CHANNEL SENDING A REQUEST OVER THE INTERNET

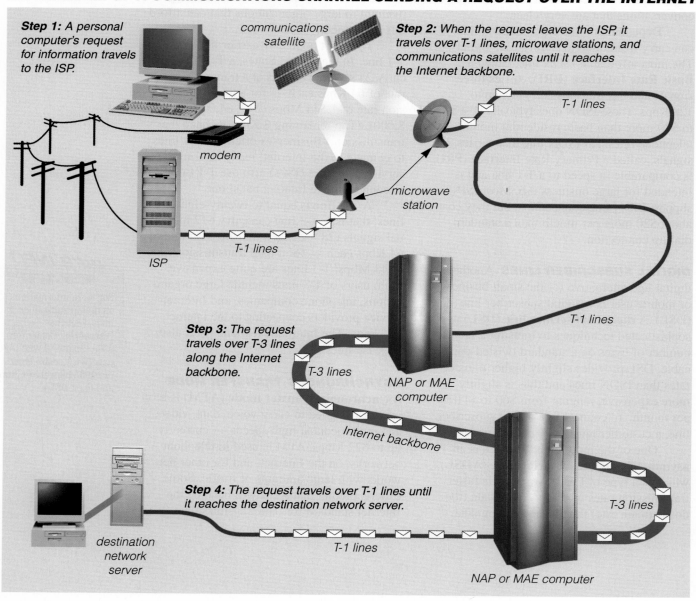

Step 1: A personal computer's request for information travels to the ISP.

communications satellite

Step 2: When the request leaves the ISP, it travels over T-1 lines, microwave stations, and communications satellites until it reaches the Internet backbone.

T-1 lines

modem

microwave station

T-1 lines

ISP

T-1 lines

Step 3: The request travels over T-3 lines along the Internet backbone.

T-3 lines

NAP or MAE computer

Internet backbone

Step 4: The request travels over T-1 lines until it reaches the destination network server.

T-3 lines

destination network server

T-1 lines

NAP or MAE computer

Communications software helps you establish a connection to another computer and manage the transmission of data between computers; it resides in the main memory of the sending and receiving computers while the connection is established.

To help you establish a connection to another computer, communications software uses wizards, dialog boxes, and other onscreen messages to prompt you for information and automate tasks where possible. Communications software usually includes one or more of the following features: dialing, file transfer, terminal emulation, and Internet access. Figure 9-21 shows dialog boxes and windows that illustrate each of these features.

The **dialing feature** of communications software allows you to store, review, select, and dial telephone numbers to connect to another computer.

Communications software that supports **file transfer** allows you to send one or more files from one computer to another. For file transfers to work, both the sending and receiving computers must have file transfer software or communications software with file transfer capabilities.

As discussed in Chapter 1, users often access a minicomputer or mainframe via a terminal, which is a device with a monitor and keyboard for input and output. The **terminal emulation feature** of communications software allows a personal computer to act as a specific type of terminal, so the personal computer user can connect to and access data and resources on a minicomputer or mainframe.

Figure 9-21a (dialing)

Figure 9-21b (file transfer)

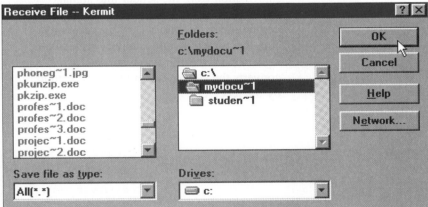

Figure 9-21c (terminal emulation)

Figure 9-21d (Internet access)

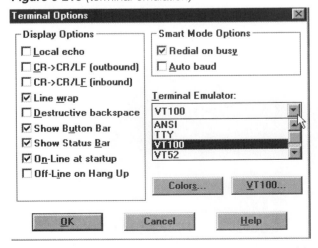

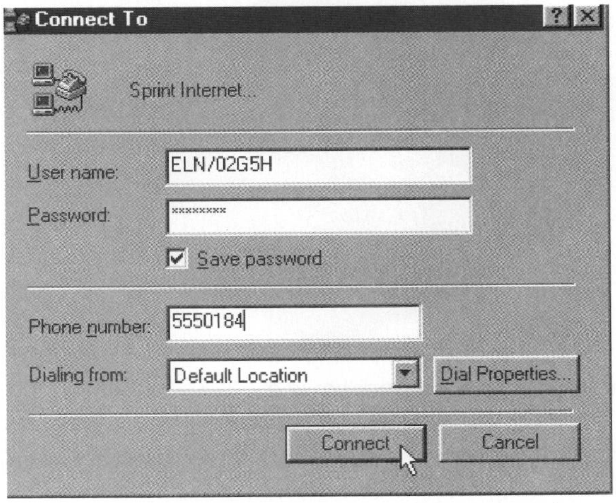

Figure 9-21 Communications software typically provides dialing, file transfer, terminal emulation, and Internet access features.

The **Internet access feature** allows you to use the computer to connect to the Internet to send e-mail, participate in chat rooms, visit World Wide Web sites, and so on.

When you purchase a modem, it usually includes a basic communications software package so you can connect to other computers, such as ones used for a bulletin board system. When you subscribe to an online service or Internet service provider, the provider typically sends you a separate communications software package, which you must use to connect to their computers so you can access the Internet, send e-mail, and use their other services.

COMMUNICATIONS DEVICES

A **communications device** is any type of hardware capable of transmitting data, instructions, and information between a sending device (sender) and a receiving device (receiver). At the sending end, a communications device converts the data, instructions, or information from the sender into signals understood by the transmission media on the communications channel. At the receiving end, the communications device receives the signals from the communications channel and converts the signals into a form understood by the receiver.

Recall that sending and receiving devices include a variety of types of hardware such as handheld computers, laptop computers, desktop computers, minicomputers, mainframes, digital cameras, and fax machines. The type of communications device used in a communications system depends on the type of sending and/or receiving devices, as well as the type of transmission media.

Some of the more common types of communications devices are modems, cable modems, multiplexers, and network interface cards. The following sections describe each one.

Modems

As previously discussed, a computer's digital signals must be converted to analog signals before they are transmitted over standard telephone lines. The communications device that performs this conversion is a **modem**. The word, modem, is derived from a combination of the words, **modulate**, to change into an analog signal and, **demodulate**, to convert an analog signal into a digital signal. Both the sending and receiving ends of a communications channel must have a modem for data transmission to occur.

A modem can be an external or an internal device (Figure 9-22). An **external modem** is a stand-alone (separate) device that attaches to a serial port on a computer with a cable and to a telephone outlet with a standard telephone cord. Because external modems are stand-alone devices, you easily can move the modem from one computer to another.

an external modem is connected to a terminal or computer and to a telephone outlet

Figure 9-22 *An external modem is a stand-alone device, whereas an internal modem is an expansion card.*

internal modem

An **internal modem** is an expansion card that you insert into an expansion slot on a computer's motherboard; the modem then attaches to a telephone outlet with a standard telephone cord. Devices other than computers use internal modems. A stand-alone fax machine, for example, has an internal modem that converts a scanned digitized image into an analog signal that can be sent to the recipient's fax machine. One key advantage of internal modems over external modems is that they do not require desk space.

Laptop and other portable computers can use a modem in the form of a PC Card that you insert into a PC Card slot on the computer. The PC Card modem attaches to a telephone outlet with a standard telephone cord. Mobile users without access to a telephone outlet also can use a special cable to attach the PC Card modem to a cellular telephone, thus enabling them to transmit data over a cellular telephone.

Most personal computer modems transmit data between 28.8 Kbps and 56 Kbps. The faster the transfer rate, the faster you can send and receive messages.

Many modems today are called **fax modems** because they can send computer-prepared documents as faxes and also receive faxes. When you purchase a fax modem, you also receive the software needed to send a fax.

Cable Modems

A **cable modem** is a modem that sends and receives data over the cable television (CATV) network, which consists largely of coaxial cable (Figure 9-23). With more than 100 million homes wired for cable television, cable modems provide an alternative to standard modems or ISDN for home users wanting fast Internet access. Cable modems currently can transmit data at speeds of 500 Kbps to 2 Mbps — much faster than either a standard modem or ISDN. Industry experts predict cable modems eventually will be able to transmit at 30 Mbps.

To access the Internet using a cable modem, you use a cable to connect the cable modem to your cable television outlet. As with standard modems, two types of cable modems exist: external and internal. An **external cable modem** is a stand-alone (separate) device that you connect with a cable to a port on your computer's network interface card, which is

an expansion card that allows hardware to be connected to a network. Using an external cable modem thus requires your computer to have a network interface card installed. An **internal cable modem** is an expansion card that you insert into an expansion slot on a computer or other device.

You also can add or integrate a cable modem with a set top box to provide faster viewing of multimedia Web sites. As described in Chapter 7, a **set-top box** is a low-cost network computer placed on top of your television set that allows you to access the Internet and navigate Web pages using a device that looks like a remote control.

To support the use of cable modems, CATV networks must upgrade from a one-way system to a two-way system. Currently, most CATV networks broadcast signals in just one direction — into subscribers' homes. On the Internet, however, communications must flow in both directions — from the cable TV operator to homes and vice versa. Although it is an expensive investment, some CATV operators in the United States already have upgraded their systems and offer Internet service for $30 to $70 per month. As more CATV operators upgrade, the public increasingly may switch from standard modems to cable modems to take advantage of the many resources available on the Internet and other networks.

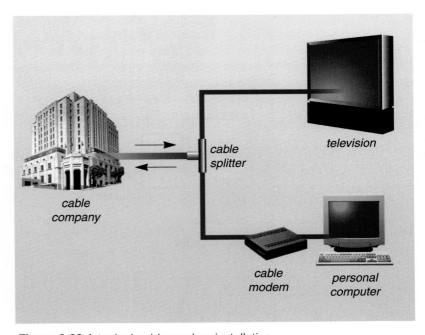

Figure 9-23 *A typical cable modem installation.*

Multiplexers

Recall that T-carrier and ISDN lines are two types of digital lines that carry more than one separate signal in a single telephone line. To combine multiple signals (analog or digital) for transmission over a single line or media, these lines use a technique called **multiplexing**.

A **multiplexer**, sometimes referred to as a **MUX**, is a device that combines two or more input signals from various devices into a single stream of data and then transmits it over a single transmission medium (Figure 9-24). By combining the separate data streams into one, a multiplexer increases the efficiency of communications and reduces the need for, and cost of, using separate transmission media.

As with modems, both the sending and the receiving devices need a multiplexer for data transmission to occur. The multiplexer at the sending end codes each character with an identifier before combining the data streams. It then compresses the data and sends it over the communications channel. The multiplexer at the receiving end takes the transmitted signal, uses the character identifiers to separate the combined data stream into its original parts, and sends the data to the appropriate device.

Network Interface Card

A **network interface card**, or **NIC** (pronounced nick), is an expansion card that you insert into an expansion slot of a personal computer or other device, such as a printer, enabling the device to connect to a network (Figure 9-25). Also called a **LAN adapter**, a network interface card coordinates the transmission and receipt of data, instructions, and information to and from the computer or device containing the NIC.

A NIC provides an attachment point to connect a specific type of transmission media, such as twisted-pair, coaxial, or fiber-optic cable or infrared light. A NIC for a desktop computer, for example, has a port where a cable connects. A NIC for laptop and other portable computers is in the form of a PC Card. Many of these NICs have more than one type of port, enabling different types of cables to attach to the card. The NIC for a wireless transmission, by contrast, typically has an antenna.

A network interface card also is designed to work with a particular type of protocol, such as Ethernet or token ring. These and other protocols are discussed later in this chapter.

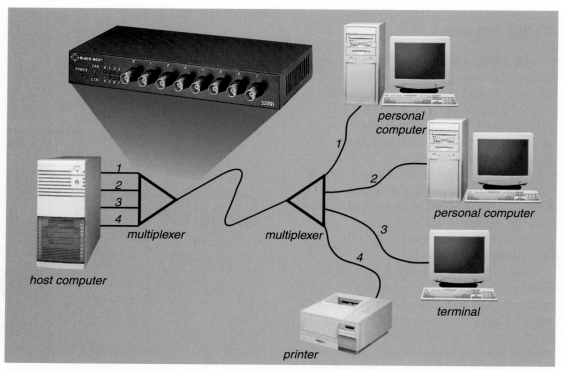

Figure 9-24 At the sending end, a multiplexer (MUX) combines separate data transmissions into a single data stream. At the receiving end, the MUX separates the single stream into its original parts.

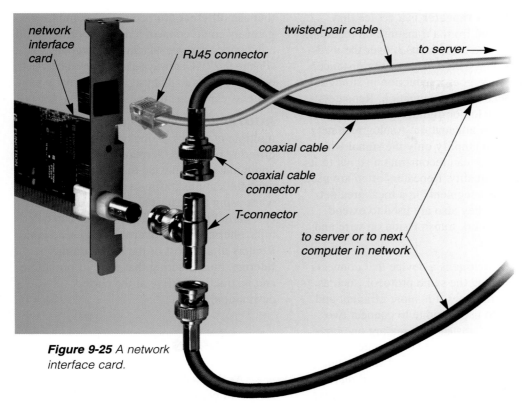

Figure 9-25 *A network interface card.*

Connecting Networks

Today, thousands of computer networks exist, ranging from small networks operated by home users to global networks operated by numerous telecommunications firms. To interconnect the many types of networks that exist, various types of communications devices are used, including hubs, repeaters, bridges, gateways, and routers.

HUB A **hub**, also called a **concentrator** or **multistation access unit** (**MAU**), is a device that provides a central point for cables in a network (Figure 9-26). Hubs usually contain ports for eight to twelve computers and other devices.

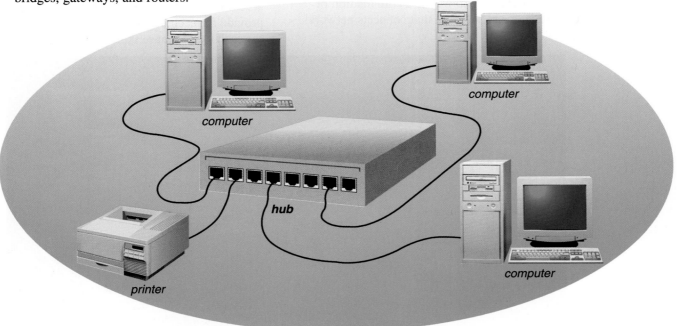

Figure 9-26 *A hub is a central point where all the cables in a network are joined together.*

REPEATER A **repeater** is a device that accepts a signal from a transmission medium, amplifies it, and retransmits it over the medium. As a signal travels over a long distance, the signal undergoes a reduction in strength, an occurrence called attenuation. Repeaters regenerate analog or digital signals that can be distorted by attenuation. Analog repeaters frequently can amplify only the signal while digital repeaters can reconstruct a signal to its near-original quality. Repeaters often are used to interconnect segments in a local area network (LAN); they also are used to extend wide area network transmission on wire and wireless media.

BRIDGE A **bridge** is a device that connects two LANs using the same protocol, such as Ethernet. Sometimes it is more efficient and economical to use a bridge to connect two separate LANs, instead of creating one large LAN that combines the two separate LANs. For example, if a company had similar but separate LANs in its accounting and marketing departments, the company could connect the networks with a bridge. In this example, using a bridge is more efficient than joining all the computers into a single LAN because the individual departments only access information in the other department occasionally.

To use a bridge, the transmission media used in the LANs does not have to be the same. One LAN could use coaxial cable, while the other might use twisted-pair cable.

GATEWAY A **gateway** is a combination of hardware and software that connects networks that use different protocols. For example, a gateway could connect a network of PCs with a network of Apple Macintosh computers (Figure 9-27). Gateways also are used between e-mail systems so that users on different e-mail systems can exchange messages.

ROUTER A **router** is a device that connects multiple networks — including those with differing protocols. A router is an intelligent communications device that sends (routes) communications traffic to the appropriate network using the fastest available path. In case of a partial network failure, routers can determine alternate paths over which to send data. Routers direct most of the traffic on the Internet, thus ensuring that data, information, and instructions arrive at the correct destination.

NETWORKS

As defined earlier, a **network** is a collection of computers and devices connected by communications channels that allows users to share data, information, hardware, and software with other users. Individuals and organizations connect computers in a network for a variety of reasons, including the ability to share hardware, data and information, and software; and to facilitate communications.

- **Hardware Sharing**. In a networked environment, each computer on a network can access and use hardware that is too costly to provide for each user or cannot be justified for each user because the equipment is used

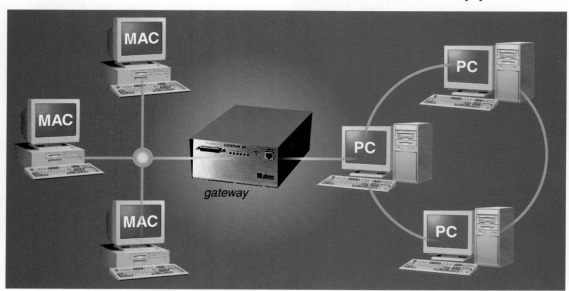

Figure 9-27 *A gateway connects networks that use differing protocols.*

infrequently. For example, suppose a number of personal computers on a network each require the use of a laser printer. If the personal computers and the laser printer are connected into a network, each personal computer user can access the laser printer over the network as he or she needs it.

- **Data and Information Sharing**. In a networked environment, any authorized user can use a computer on a network to access data and information stored on other computers in the network. A large company, for example, might store a database of customer information on a server's hard disk. Any authorized person, including a mobile user using a modem to connect to the network, can access this database. As shown by this example, sharing data and information resources (the customer database) and sharing hardware resources (the server's hard disk) often are combined. The capability of providing access to and storage of data and information on shared storage devices is an important feature of many networks.

- **Software Sharing**. With software sharing, frequently used software is stored on a server's hard disk so multiple users on the network can access the software. To support software sharing, most software vendors sell network versions of their software. When you purchase a network version of a software package, software vendors issue a legal agreement called a **site license**,

which allows many users to run the software package. The site license fee usually is based on the number of users or the number of computers attached to the network. Sharing software via a network usually costs less than buying individual copies of the software package for each computer. As with data and information sharing, software sharing also requires the capability of sharing hardware resources, such as space on the server's hard disk.

- **Facilitated Communications**. Using a network, people can communicate efficiently and easily via e-mail, telephony, and videoconferencing. E-mail messages usually are delivered almost instantaneously. With telephony and videoconferencing, users in geographically dispersed areas can conduct meetings — for only the cost of the required hardware, software, and network access time.

Networks exist in a range of sizes, from a small network connecting two computers to a global network such as the Internet, which connects millions of computers around the world. Networks also can connect computers of all sizes, from handheld computers to supercomputers. Two types of networks more widely used in business are local area networks and wide area networks.

Local Area Network (LAN)

A **local area network** (**LAN**) is a network that connects computers in a limited geographical area, such as a school computer laboratory, office, or group of buildings. A LAN consists of a communications channel, networked computers and devices, a network interface card, and a network operating system (Figure 9-28).

network interface card in each computer

Figure 9-28 A local area network consists of a network operating system, networked computers and other devices, a network interface card, and a communications channel that connects computers in a limited geographic area.

Network Operating System

A **network operating system**, or **NOS** (pronounced nauss), is the system software that organizes and coordinates the activities on a local area network. In most networks, a NOS is a set of programs separate from the operating system. The NOS either is installed on each computer in addition to the current operating system or installed on the network server to which each computer connects. When you start your computer, the operating system loads into the computer first, and then the NOS loads. While the network is active, the NOS takes over most of the functions of the operating system. Some operating systems, such as Windows NT, include networking capabilities that enable them to be considered a network operating system.

Some of the tasks performed by a NOS include the following.

- **Administration.** Includes adding, deleting, and organizing users and performing maintenance tasks such as backup.

- **File Management.** Locates and transfers files

- **Printer Management.** Involves prioritizing print jobs and reports sent to specific printers on the network.

- **Security.** Consists of monitoring and, when necessary, restricting access to network resources

Just as application software runs with certain operating systems, a NOS also works with certain operating systems. Additionally, a network operating system works with a certain type of LAN. Figure 9-29 outlines popular network operating systems, the operating systems with which they work, and the type of LAN for which they are designed.

Types of LANs

As indicated by the table in Figure 9-29, two popular types of LANs are peer-to-peer and client/server. The major difference between these types of LANs lies in how the data and information is stored.

PEER-TO-PEER NETWORK A **peer-to-peer network** is a simple, inexpensive network designed to connect less than ten computers together using twisted-pair cable or coaxial cable. Each computer on a peer-to-peer network can share the hardware (such as a printer), data, or information located on any other computer in the network (Figure 9-30). Each computer, or **peer**, stores files on its own storage devices. A network operating system and application software thus must be installed on each computer in the network. Only one computer on the network, however, needs to connect to peripherals, such as a printer, scanner, or fax modem; the other computers on the network share these hardware resources.

While peer-to-peer networks typically do not offer e-mail, telephony, or video-conferencing capabilities, these networks are ideal for very small businesses and home users. Some operating systems, such as Windows, include a peer-to-peer networking utility that allows you to set up a basic peer-to-peer network.

Popular Network Operating Systems

Network Operating System	Operating System Required	LAN type
Novell NetWare	DOS	Client/server
Artisoft LANtastic	DOS	Peer-to-peer
Microsoft Windows 95, Windows 98, and Windows for Workgroups	Windows	Peer-to-peer
Microsoft Windows NT	Windows NT	Client/server
Banyan Vines	UNIX	Client/server
Microsoft OS/2 LAN Manager	OS/2	Client/server

Figure 9-29 A listing of popular network operating systems. A network operating system is designed to work with a certain operating system, as well as a certain type of LAN.

network operating system
and application software
installed on each computer

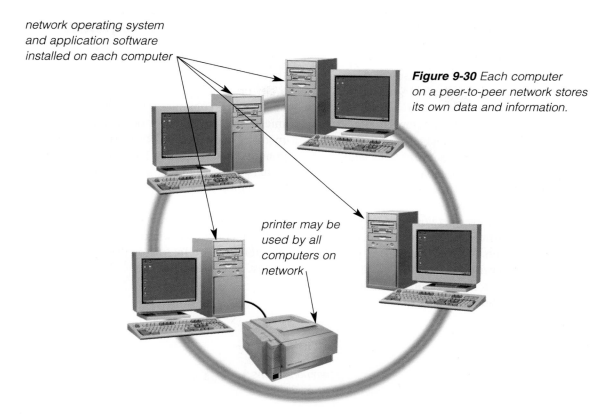

Figure 9-30 Each computer
on a peer-to-peer network stores
its own data and information.

printer may be
used by all
computers on
network

CLIENT/SERVER NETWORK A **client/ server network** is a network in which one or more computers are designated as a server(s) and the other computers on the network, called clients, can request services from the server, such as providing database access or queuing print jobs (Figure 9-31). A **server** controls access to the hardware and software on the network and provides a centralized storage area for programs, data, and information. The other computers on the network, called **clients**, rely on the servers for these resources, such as files, devices, processing power, and storage. A server, for example, might store a network version of a word processing program, so that every client can access the word processing program on the server.

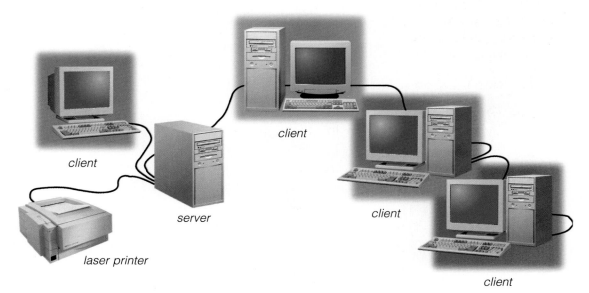

client

client

server

client

laser printer

client

client

Figure 9-31 On a client/server network, one or more computers are designated as a server, and the other computers on the network are called clients.

The major difference between the server and the client computers is that the server ordinarily is faster and has more storage space. Thus, the server generally performs most of the processing tasks. Some servers are dedicated to performing a specific task. For example, a **file server** stores and manages files; a **print server** manages printers and print jobs; a **database server** stores and provides access to a database; and a **thin server**, intended for the home user, provides access to the Internet.

A client/server network typically provides an efficient means to connect ten or more computers together. Because of the size of a client/server network, most client/server networks have a **network administrator**, who is the person in charge of operations

Wide Area Network (WAN)

A **wide area network** (**WAN**) is a network that covers a large geographical area (such as a city or country) using a communications channel that combines telephone lines, microwave, satellites, or other transmission media (Figure 9-32). Today, a WAN typically consists of two or more LANs connected by routers that ensure that data, instructions, and information are delivered to the correct destination. Computers often are connected to a wide area network via public networks such as the telephone system or by dedicated lines or satellites. The Internet is the world's largest wide area network.

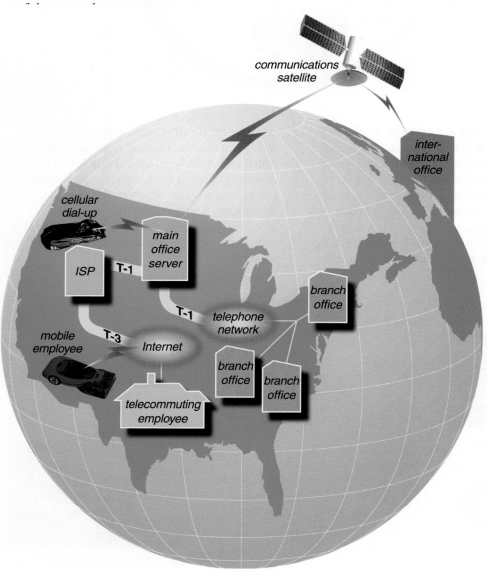

Figure 9-32 *An example of a WAN.*

Metropolitan Area Network (MAN)

A **metropolitan area network (MAN)** is a backbone network that connects local area networks in a metropolitan area such as a city or town and handles the bulk of communications activity, or traffic, across that region. MANs also frequently provide a shared connection to other networks using a link to a WAN.

A MAN typically includes one or more LANs but covers a smaller geographic area than a WAN. The state of Pennsylvania, for example, has a metropolitan area network that connects state agencies and individual users in the region around the state capital.

A MAN usually is managed by a consortium of users or by a single network provider who sells the service to the users. Local and state governments, for example, regulate some MANs. Telephone companies, cable television operators, and other organizations provide users with connections to the MAN via bridges and routers.

Network Topologies

The configuration, or physical arrangement, of the devices in a communications network is called the **network topology** or **network architecture**. Network architecture is similar to the architecture of a building. Like a blueprint, which shows the physical layout of the building, a drawing of a network architecture provides a pictorial representation of the physical layout of the network. Three commonly used network topologies are bus, ring, and star. Networks also can use combinations of these topologies.

BUS NETWORK A **bus network** consists of a single central cable, to which all computers and other devices connect (Figure 9-33). The **bus** is the physical cable that connects the computers and other devices. The bus in a bus network can transmit data, instructions, and information in both directions. Only one device, such as a computer, can transfer items at one time, however. When a sending device transmits data, a destination address is included with the transmission so that the data is routed to the appropriate receiving device.

The bus topology is used primarily for local area networks. Bus networks are flexible in that computers and other devices can be attached or detached from the network at any point without disturbing the rest of the network. Failure of one device also does not affect the rest of the bus network: the transmission simply bypasses the failed device. The greatest risk to a bus network is that the bus itself might become inoperable. If that happens, the network remains inoperative until the bus is back in working order.

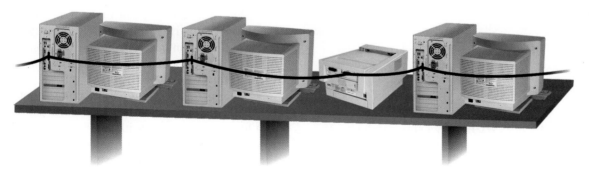

Figure 9-33 *Devices in a bus network share a single data path.*

RING NETWORK A **ring network** is designed so a cable forms a closed ring, or loop, with all computers and devices arranged along the ring (Figure 9-34). Data transmitted on a ring network travels from device to device around the entire ring, in one direction. When a computer sends data, the data travels to each computer on the ring until it reaches its destination.

If a device on a ring network fails, all devices before the failed device are unaffected, but those after the failed device cannot function.

The ring topology primarily is used for LANs, but also is used to connect a mainframe to a WAN. Personal computer LANs connected in a ring network normally use a token ring protocol, which is discussed in the next section.

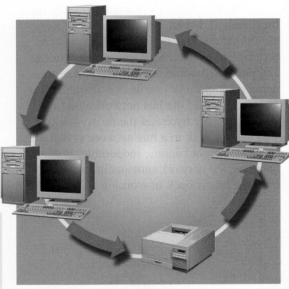

Figure 9-34 *In a ring network, all the devices are connected in a continuous loop.*

STAR NETWORK In a **star network**, all of the devices in the network connect to a central computer, thus forming a star (Figure 9-35). The central computer that provides a common connection point for devices in the network is called the **hub**. All data that transfers from one computer to another passes through the hub.

Because each device in a star network connects directly to the hub, if one device fails, only that device is affected. The other devices continue to operate normally. If the hub fails, however, the entire network is inoperable until the hub is repaired. Most large star networks, therefore, keep backup hubs available in case the primary hub fails.

Communications Protocols

A **protocol** is a set of rules and procedures for exchanging information among computers. Protocols define how the communications channel is established, how information is transmitted, and how errors are detected and corrected. Using the same protocols, different types and makes of computers can communicate with each other. Depending on the task, a single computer can use multiple protocols. For example, a computer might use one protocol to communicate with another computer on the LAN and a different protocol to communicate with a computer at an ISP.

Numerous protocols have been developed over the years, some of which are designed to work together. Ethernet and token ring are the two more widely used protocols for LANs. TCP/IP is one of the major protocols used on the Internet.

ETHERNET Developed at Xerox in 1976, Ethernet was approved as the first industry standard LAN protocol in 1983. **Ethernet** is a LAN protocol that allows personal computers to contend for access to the network. Today, Ethernet is the most popular LAN protocol because it is relatively inexpensive and easy to install and maintain. A network that uses the Ethernet protocol sometimes is called an **Ethernet network**.

Ethernet is based on a bus topology, but Ethernet networks can be wired in a star pattern by using a hub. As with any bus network, when a sending device transmits data over an Ethernet network, the data travels along the network until it arrives at the receiving device. If two computers on an Ethernet network attempt to send data at the same time, a collision occurs, and the computers must attempt to send their messages again.

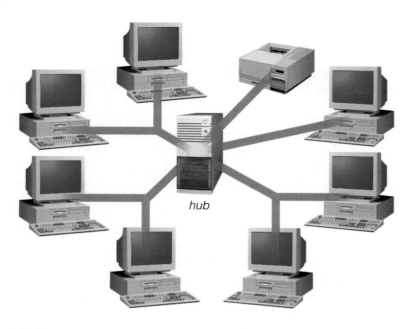

hub

Figure 9-35 *A star network contains a single, centralized host computer with which all the devices in the network communicate.*

To avoid collisions, Ethernet networks use an access method called **Carrier Sense Multiple Access/Collision Detection (CSMA/CD)**. CSMA/CD is an access-control technique that attempts to detect possible collisions. If a computer with data to transmit senses that data is already on the network, it waits a random amount of time before attempting to retransmit the data, thus helping to avoid collisions.

Ethernet networks use twisted-pair cable, coaxial cable, or fiber-optic cable as their transmission media. The maximum transmission rate on a standard Ethernet network is 10 Mbps, which is not very fast by today's standards. For small to medium networks, however, the Ethernet protocol works quite well. Another type of protocol, called **Fast Ethernet**, transmits at 100 Mbps. **Gigabit Ethernet** provides an even higher speed of transmission, 1,000 Mbps (1 gigabit or 1 billion bits per second).

TOKEN RING Token ring is the second more widely used protocol for LAN networks. A **token ring** protocol controls access to the network by requiring that a special signal, called a token, is shared or passed among network devices. Only the device with the token can transmit data over the network, ensuring that only one computer can transmit data at a time. If a device has nothing to transmit, the device passes the token to the next device. As with CSMA/CD, the token-passing scheme helps prevent the collision between two devices that want to send data at the same time.

Token ring is based on a ring topology (although it can use a star topology). Networks using a token ring protocol are called **token ring networks**. A token ring network can operate at speeds of 4 Mbps using unshielded twisted-pair cables or 16 Mbps using shielded twisted-pair cables. While the token-passing scheme used in a token ring network is more complex than an Ethernet network, access to the network is more equitable because each device has an equal chance to transmit.

WEB INFO
WEB INFO

For more information
on intranets, visit the
Discovering Computers
2000 Chapter 9 WEB INFO
page (**www.scsite.com/
dc2000/ch9/webinfo.htm**)
and click Intranets.

TCP/IP Short for **Transmission control protocol/Internet protocol, TCP/IP** is a set of protocols used to manage the transmission of data by breaking it up into packets. TCP/IP is widely used on the Internet. Recall from Chapter 7 that when a computer sends data over the Internet, the data is divided into small pieces, called **packets**. The TCP/IP protocol defines how to break the message into packets, provides routing information for message delivery, and reassembles the message at the receiving end. TCP/IP also establishes a connection between two computers so they can send messages back and forth for a period of time.

TCP/IP was developed in 1973 for use in the ARPANET. Since then, TCP/IP has developed into a protocol used by both WANs and LANs. In 1983, TCP/IP was adopted as the Internet standard; all hosts on the Internet are required to use TCP/IP.

Intranets

Recognizing the efficiency and power of the Web, many organizations have applied Web technologies to their own internal networks. Internal networks that use Internet and Web technologies are called **intranets** (intra means inside). An intranet, sometimes called an **enterprise network**, essentially is a small version of the Internet used within an organization: it uses TCP/IP protocols; supports multimedia Web pages coded in HTML, and is accessible via a browser. Users can post and update information on the intranet by creating and posting a Web page, using a method much like that used on the Internet. Other users can access the Web page using a standard Web browser, such as Microsoft Internet Explorer.

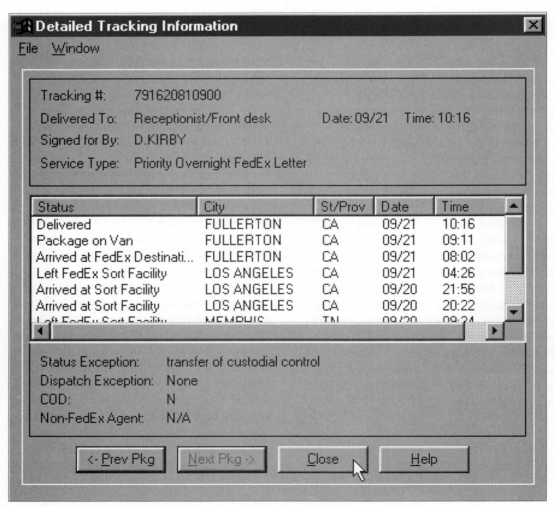

Figure 9-36 *Federal Express uses an extranet to allow customers to ship and track packages. As shown in this figure, customers can track the progress of shipped packages as the packages travel to their destination.*

Intranets generally make company information accessible to employees and facilitate working in groups. Simple intranet applications include Web pages that provide basic organizational information such as telephone directories, event calendars, procedure manuals, employee benefits information, e-mail, and job postings. More sophisticated uses of intranets include groupware applications such as project management, newsgroups, group scheduling, and video-conferencing.

Typically, an intranet includes a connection to the Internet through one or more gateways. Sometimes an organization allows others to access its intranet. Federal Express, for example, allows customers to access their intranet to print air bills, schedule pickups, and even track shipped packages as they travel to their destination (Figure 9-36). An intranet that extends to authorized users outside the company and facilitates communications among a company's customers or suppliers is called an **extranet**.

FIREWALLS As a public network, anyone with the proper connection can access the Internet. A private corporate intranet or extranet, by contrast, is restricted to specific authorized users, usually employees, suppliers, and customers. To prevent unauthorized access to data and information, an intranet or extranet often is protected by a firewall. A **firewall** is a general term that refers to both hardware and software used to restrict access to data and information on a network (Figure 9-37). Organizations use firewalls to deny network access to outsiders and to restrict employees' access to sensitive data such as payroll or personnel records.

Figure 9-37 *A firewall is hardware or software used to restrict access to data and information on a network.*

TECHNOLOGY TRAILBLAZER

ROBERT METCALFE

At 3Com Corporation in Santa Clara, California, a plaque honors Robert M. Metcalfe, the company's cofounder and inventor of the most widely used system for networking computers. The plaque includes a picture of Metcalfe and bears a motto attributed to him: "The only difference between being visionary and being stubborn is whether you're right." In the world of computer technology, Bob Metcalfe has proven to be visionary.

Metcalfe first evidenced an interest in electronics in fourth grade. With a last-minute book report due, he remembers grabbing a book from his father's bookshelf. The book turned out to be a college textbook on electrical engineering. Because the book was incomprehensible, Metcalfe wrote the type of generic report typical of most ten year olds: "I read this book and it had its high points and it had its low points, but on average it sort of averaged out." To guarantee a good grade, Metcalfe added that he planned to attend the Massachusetts Institute of Technology and major in engineering.

In high school, Metcalfe won several mathematics and science awards. "I learned an important lesson at graduation," Metcalfe says, "which is, the amount of money that I got from the science/technology award was much more than the amount of money [the winner of the humanities award] got!"

After graduation, Metcalfe headed to MIT, a move in line with his fourth grade prediction. Here, Metcalfe earned the dubious distinction of being among the first to fall victim to computer theft. As an MIT senior, Metcalfe taught a computer-programming course. One day he arrived at class to find a $30,000 computer borrowed from Digital Equipment Corporation (DEC) was missing. Fortunately, DEC accepted the loss, and even took pride in having created a computer small enough to be stolen! A few months later, less one computer but true to his book report, Metcalfe graduated from MIT with a degree in electrical engineering.

Metcalfe went on to earn a master's degree in applied mathematics and a Ph.D. in computer science from Harvard. His doctoral dissertation dealt with the Advanced Research Projects Agency Network (ARPANET), the first Internet network. While earning his Ph.D., Metcalfe worked at Xerox's Palo Alto Research Center (PARC), the birthplace of such innovations as the personal computer and graphical user interface. Here, Metcalfe set out to connect the building's many computers to what Metcalfe believes was the first laser printer. "It wasn't that anyone particularly doubted that you could do it," Metcalfe recalls. "They just didn't know why…you would want to." Together with D.R. Boggs, Metcalfe invented Ethernet, a local area network (LAN) protocol consisting of hardware and software that joins computers within a building. Ethernet one day would link more than fifty million computers worldwide, allowing even computers from different manufacturers to communicate.

In 1979, Metcalfe left Xerox to found 3Com Corporation, so named for three words — computer, communication, and compatibility. 3Com worked to make Ethernet the standard for computer communications. Metcalfe served in several posts, including CEO, president, and chairman of the board. For Metcalfe, however, "the most fun was being head of sales and marketing…when we went from approximately zero in sales to one million dollars a month in sales." In that position, Metcalfe discovered that inventors need more than creative talent. "My basic message to engineers is that you can invent Ethernet or whatever your version of that is, but you have to *sell* it." Metcalfe's ability to sell Ethernet has made 3Com a $5 billion company.

Metcalfe retired from 3Com in 1990. Today, Metcalfe is a technology pundit, writing articles voicing his observations, criticisms, and predictions for the computer industry. What does the future hold? For Metcalfe, all you need to do is look around. "Everything that's going to happen in twenty-five years, it's already happening somewhere…Whatever it is in twenty-five years, it's probably around if you were just aware of it."

COMPANY ON THE CUTTING EDGE

COMPANY ON THE CUTTING EDGE

NOVELL

Once, personal computers were stand-alone machines that independently processed data, produced information, and stored the results. Today, most computers are interconnected. Personal computers produce, store, and *communicate* information. Several companies played a part in this transformation, but none had a larger role than Novell, a leading provider of network software.

In 1981, Jack Davis and George Canova founded Novell Data Systems. Originally, Novell manufactured terminals for IBM mainframe computers. When Novell incorporated in 1983, the firm shifted its focus toward developing operating system software for local area networks (LANs). Novell's first operating system product, NetWare, provided an effective tool for maintaining shared files and furnishing access to network hardware. Throughout the 1980s, Novell dominated the LAN market.

The early 1990s, however, proved challenging for Novell. In 1993, CEO Ray Noorda expanded Novell's software interests, acquiring AT&T's UNIX operating system. The next year, Novell purchased WordPerfect, a word processing program, and Quattro Pro, a spreadsheet program, seemingly a challenge to Microsoft. Even as Novell moved into application software, however, Microsoft's Windows NT made quiet inroads into Novell's network operating system dominance. Novell's application software venture soon floundered, and its plan to integrate UNIX and NetWare into a *super* network operating system failed. Once a prominent player in the computer software game, Novell appeared destined for the sidelines.

In 1994, Robert Frankenberg became Novell's CEO. Frankenberg's goal was to return life to Novell by returning Novell to its strength — networking. Novell sold UNIX to Santa Cruz Operation (SCO) in 1995, and sold WordPerfect and Quattro Pro to Corel Corporation in 1996. Staff cuts of more than one thousand employees trimmed company fat, and Novell seemed rejuvenated. Then, a new wrinkle in network communications confronted the company — the Internet. The Internet's reliance on wide area networks (WANs), simple interfaces, and accessible services bypassed Novell's strengths. Novell's commanding 50 percent market share fell to just over 27 percent.

Frankenberg resigned in 1996, and Dr. Eric Schmidt took over as Novell CEO. Schmidt was a respected figure in the computer industry, but when confronted with Novell's problems he admitted, "I was in over my head." The unassuming CEO took the unusual step of asking other industry executives, such as Intel's Andy Grove, for advice. He also appealed to the best people at Novell for their views on what was right and wrong with the company. Although Schmidt would have to layoff almost 20 percent of Novell's staff, his openness earned the workers' confidence and respect.

Schmidt combined everything he learned from Novell employees with his own technical vision. Instead of confronting Microsoft, he focused Novell's efforts on areas in which Microsoft did not dominate. To address customer concerns regarding Novell's tendency to deliver products late, Schmidt cut the number of projects in development by 75 percent. The smaller workload allowed Novell to release the latest version of its network operating system, NetWare 5, ten days early — a feat that earned Novell near-universal praise. To expand their market, Novell made Novell Directory Services (NDS), a distributed database of network information that is a key part of NetWare 5, compatible with Windows NT and UNIX. Schmidt also concentrated on products adaptable to both corporate networks and the Internet, moving Novell to the center of electronic commerce. In 1998, Novell shipped NetWare 5, the first version of NetWare based entirely on Internet Protocol (IP) and other open standards. Its strong reception in the marketplace helped drive a turnaround year for Novell, with the company returning to profitability and profits increasing progressively in all four quarters.

Today, Novell is again a growing company with more than 4,500 employees in more than 30 countries. More than 80 percent of Fortune 500 companies use NetWare, and Novell's directory technology provides management and security for networks serving more than 40 million users. With annual sales of $1.1 billion in 1998 and more than $100 million in profit, Novell appears to have successfully adapted its networking business to an era dominated by the biggest network, the Internet.

CHAPTER 1 2 3 4 5 6 7 8 9 10 11 12 13 14 INDEX

IN BRIEF

 www.scsite.com/dc2000/ch9/brief.htm

WEB INSTRUCTIONS: *To display this page from the Web, launch your browser and enter the URL, www.scsite.com/dc2000/ch9/brief.htm. Click the links for current and additional information. To listen to an audio version of this IN BRIEF, click the Audio button to the right of the title, IN BRIEF, at the top of the page. To play the audio, RealPlayer must be installed on your computer (download by clicking here).*

1. What Components Are Required for Successful Communications?

When referring to computers, **communications** describes a process in which one computer transfers data, instructions, and information to another computer(s). Communications requires: a device that initiates the transfer (a sending device); a communications device (such as a modem) that converts the sent material into signals capable of being carried by a communications channel; a **communications channel** over which the signals are sent; a communications device that receives the signals and converts them into a form understood by the receiving device; and a device that accepts the sent material (a receiving device).

2. How Is Communications Used?

E-mail (electronic mail) is the exchange of text messages and computer files via a communications network. **Voice mail** functions much like an answering machine but converts an analog voice message into digital form. A **fax (facsimile)** machine sends and receives documents via telephone lines. **Telecommuting** allows employees to work away from the standard workplace and communicate using some communications technology. **Videoconferencing** involves using video and computer technology to conduct a meeting between participants at two or more geographically separate locations. **Groupware** is a software application that helps people work together and share information over a network. A **global positioning system (GPS)** consists of earth-based receivers that analyze satellite signals to determine the receiver's geographic location. An electronic **bulletin board system (BBS)** is a computer that maintains a centralized collection of electronic messages. The **Internet**, a worldwide collection of networks, offers the **World Wide Web** and such popular Web-based activities as **e-commerce** and **Internet telephony**.

3. What Are Various Types of Physical Transmission Media?

Transmission media consists of materials or techniques capable of carrying a signal. **Physical transmission media**, which use tangible (touchable) materials to send communications signals, include twisted-pair cable, coaxial cable, and fiber-optic cable. **Twisted-pair cable** consists of **twisted-pair wires** bundled together. **Coaxial cable** consists of a single copper wire surrounded by three layers (insulating material, braided metal and a plastic outer coating). **Fiber-optic cable** consists of dozens or hundreds of thin strands of glass or plastic that use light to transmit data.

4. What Are Various Types of Wireless Transmission Media?

Wireless transmission media, which send communications signals through air or space, include broadcast radio, cellular radio, microwaves, communications satellites, and infrared. **Broadcast radio** distributes radio signals through the air over long distances. **Cellular radio** is a form of broadcast radio used widely for mobile communications. **Microwaves** are radio waves that provide a high-speed signal transmission. A **communications satellite** is a space station that receives microwave signals from an earth-based station, amplifies the signals, and broadcasts the signals back over a wide area to any number of earth-based stations. **Infrared** sends signals using infrared light waves.

IN BRIEF www.scsite.com/dc2000/ch9/brief.htm

5. Why Is Communications Software Used?

<u>Communications software</u> manages the transmission of data, instructions, and information between computers. For two computers to communicate, they must have compatible communications software. Communications software usually includes a **dialing feature** (for storing, reviewing, selecting and dialing), a **file transfer** feature (for sending one or more files from one computer to another), a **terminal emulation feature** (allows a personal computer to act as a terminal), and an **Internet access feature** (for sending e-mail, participating in chat rooms, and visiting Web sites).

6. What Are Commonly Used Communications Devices?

A **communications device** is any type of hardware capable of transmitting data, instructions, and information between a sending device and a receiving device. A <u>modem</u> converts a computer's digital signals into analog signals (*mo*dulate) so they can be transmitted over standard telephone lines, and then reconverts the analog signals into digital signals (*dem*odulate) that a computer can understand. A **cable modem** is a modem that sends and receives data over the cable television (CATV) network, which consists largely of coaxial cable. A **multiplexer** combines input signals from telephone lines or communications devices into a single stream of data and then transmits it over a transmission medium. A **network interface card** is an expansion card inserted into an expansion slot of a PC or other device, enabling the device to connect to a network. Various devices are used to interconnect networks, including **hubs**, **repeaters**, **bridges**, **gateways**, and **routers**.

7. How Is a Local Area Network Different from a Wide Area Network?

A <u>local area network (LAN)</u> is a network that connects computers in a limited geographical area, such as a school computer laboratory, office, or group of buildings. Two popular types of LANs are **peer-to-peer networks** and **client/server networks**. A **wide area network (WAN)** is a network that covers a large geographical area (such as a city or country) using a communications channel that combines telephone lines, microwave, satellites, or other transmission media.

8. What Are Communications Protocols?

A **protocol** is a set of rules and procedures for exchanging information among computers. Using the same protocols, different types and makes of computers can communicate with each other. <u>Ethernet</u> is a LAN protocol that allows personal computers to contend for access to a network. A **token ring** protocol controls access to a network by requiring that a special signal called a token is shared or passed among network devices. **TCP/IP (Transmission control protocol/Internet protocol)** is a set of protocols used to manage data transmission by breaking it up into packets.

9. How Are Intranets and Extranets Used?

Intranets are internal networks that use Internet and Web technologies. <u>Intranets</u> make company information accessible to employees and facilitate working in groups. An **extranet** is an intranet that extends to authorized users outside the company. Extranets facilitate communications among a company's customers or suppliers. A **firewall** denies intranet and extranet access to outsiders.

Student Exercises
WEB INFO
IN BRIEF
KEY TERMS
AT THE MOVIES
CHECKPOINT
AT ISSUE
CYBERCLASS
HANDS ON
NET STUFF
Special Features
TIMELINE 2000
GUIDE TO WWW SITES
MAKING A CHIP
BUYER'S GUIDE 2000
CAREERS 2000
TRENDS 2000
CHAT
INTERACTIVE LABS
NEWS
HOME

KEY TERMS   www.scsite.com/dc2000/ch9/terms.htm

WEB INSTRUCTIONS: *To display this page from the Web, launch your browser and enter the URL,* www.scsite.com/dc2000/ch9/terms.htm. *Scroll through the list of terms. Click a term to display its definition and a picture. Click KEY TERMS on the left to redisplay the KEY TERMS page. Click the TO WEB button for current and additional information about the term from the Web. To see animations, Shockwave and Flash Player must be installed on your computer (download by clicking* here).

analog signal (9.12)
asymmetric digital subscriber line (ADSL) (9.17)
asynchronous transfer mode (ATM) (9.17)
asynchronous transmission (9.13)
bandwidth (9.14)
Basic Rate Interface (BRI) (9.17)
bits per second (bps) (9.14)
bridge (9.24)
broadcast radio (9.9)
bulletin board system (BBS) (9.5)
bus (9.29)
bus network (9.29)
cable modem (9.21)
Carrier Sense Multiple Access/Collision Detection (CSMA/CD) (9.31)
cells (9.10)
cellular radio (9.10)
cellular telephone (9.10)
channel (9.7)
client/server network (9.27)
clients (9.27)
coax (9.8)
coaxial cable (9.8)
communications (9.2)
communications channel (9.2)
communications device (9.20)
communications satellite (9.11)
communications software (9.18)
concentrator (9.23)
data communications (9.2)
database server (9.28)
dedicated line (9.16)
dialing feature (9.19)
dial-up line (9.16)
digital signals (9.12)
digital subscriber line (DSL) (9.17)
downlink (9.11)
electronic commerce (e-commerce) (9.6)
electronic data interchange (EDI) (9.6)
electronic mail (e-mail) (9.3)
electronic money (e-money) (9.6)
enterprise network (9.32)
Ethernet (9.30)
Ethernet network (9.30)
external cable modem (9.21)
external modem (9.20)
extranet (9.33)
facsimile machine (fax) (9.3)
Fast Ethernet (9.31)
fax modem (9.3)
fax modems (9.21)
fiber-optic cable (9.8)
file server (9.28)
file transfer (9.19)
firewall (9.33)
full-duplex transmission (9.14)
gateway (9.24)

TO WEB

TELECOMMUTING: Work arrangement in which employees work away from a company's standard workplace, such as a home, but communicate with the office using some communications technology. (9.4)

geosynchronous satellites (9.11)
Gigabit Ethernet (9.31)
global positioning system (GPS) (9.5)
groupware (9.5)
half-duplex transmission (9.14)
hub (9.23, 9.30)
infrared (IR) (9.12)
Integrated Services Digital Network (ISDN) (9.17)
internal cable modem (9.21)
internal modem (9.21)
Internet (9.6)
Internet access feature (9.20)
Internet telephone software (9.6)
Internet telephony (9.6)
intranets (9.32)
LAN adapter (9.22)
line-of-sight transmission (9.11)
leased line (9.16)
local area network (LAN) (9.25)
mailbox (9.3)
metropolitan area network (MAN) (9.29)
microwave station (9.10)
microwaves (9.10)
mobile telephone switching office (MTSO) (9.10)
modem (9.20)
multiplexer (9.22)
multiplexing (MUX) (9.22)
multistation access unit (MAU) (9.23)
network (9.24)
network administrator (9.28)

network architecture (9.29)
network interface card (NIC) (9.22)
network operating system (NOS) (9.26)
network topology (9.29)
noise (9.7)
optical fiber (9.8)
packets (9.32)
peer (9.26)
peer-to-peer network (9.26)
physical transmission media (9.7)
plain old telephone service (POTS) (9.15)
print server (9.28)
protocol (9.30)
public switched telephone network (PSTN) (9.15)
repeater (9.24)
ring network (9.30)
router (9.24)
server (9.27)
set-top box (9.21)
shielded twisted-pair (STP) (9.7)
simplex transmission (9.14)
site license (9.25)
stand-alone fax machine (9.3)
star network (9.30)
synchronous transmission (9.14)
system operator (sys op) (9.5)
T-1 line (9.17)
T-3 line (9.17)
T-carrier line (9.17)
telecommunications (9.2)
telecommuting (9.4)
terminal emulation feature (9.19)
thin server (9.28)
token ring (9.31)
token ring networks (9.31)
transfer rate (9.14)
transceiver (9.9)
Transmission control protocol/Internet protocol (TCP/IP) (9.32)
transmission media (9.7)
twisted-pair cable (9.7)
twisted-pair wire (9.7)
unshielded twisted-pair (UTP) (9.7)
uplink (9.11)
Very Small Aperture Terminal (VSAT) (9.12)
videoconferencing (9.4)
voice mail (9.3)
voice mailbox (9.3)
Web (9.6)
wide area network (WAN) (9.28)
wireless transmission media (9.7)
workgroup computing (9.5)
World Wide Web (9.6)
WWW (9.6)

CHAPTER 1 2 3 4 5 6 7 8 **9** 10 11 12 13 14 **INDEX**

SHELLY
CASHMAN
SERIES®

DISCOVERING
COMPUTERS
2000

AT THE MOVIES   www.scsite.com/dc2000/ch9/movies.htm

WELCOME to VIDEO CLIPS from CNN

WEB INSTRUCTIONS: *To display this page from the Web, launch your browser and enter the URL, www.scsite.com/dc2000/ch9/movies.htm. Click a picture to view a video. After watching the video, close the video window and then complete the exercise by answering the questions about the video. To view the videos, RealPlayer must be installed on your computer (download by clicking here).*

1 Internet Car

Specially built vehicles are able to connect to the Internet and make use of global positioning wherever they go. The communication technology in these vehicles does not come cheaply, however. What kinds of communications channels are used to connect the car to the Internet? List and describe some of the communications applications the car supports. What safety features does the car have? Would you ever purchase an Internet car? Why or why not? In your opinion, what are the pros and cons of having cars connected to the Internet?

2 Distance Learning

Important lessons are being taught and learned simultaneously each day to students at separate educational facilities. What type of communications equipment is used to connect the schools and how is it used? How does a distance-learning environment differ from a regular classroom? Would you want to be in classroom like this? In your opinion, what unique challenges might teachers and students face while working in a distance-learning environment?

3 Internet Speed (Cable Modems)

Internet Web pages no longer need to load at a snail's pace. Expeditious Internet commerce can take place through shared telephone lines on ASDL. What is ASDL? How does it work? How much faster is it than a standard modem using regular phone lines? How does a cable modem transmit data? Which is faster – ADSL or cable modem?

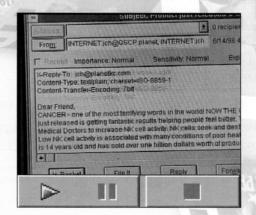

SHELLY CASHMAN SERIES®

DISCOVERING COMPUTERS 2000

CHAPTER   1 2 3 4 5 6 7 8 [9] 10 11 12 13 14   INDEX

CHECKPOINT   www.scsite.com/dc2000/ch9/check.htm

WEB INSTRUCTIONS: *To display this page from the Web, launch your browser and enter the URL, www.scsite.com/dc2000/ch9/check.htm. Click the links for current and additional information. To experience the animation and interactivity, Shockwave and Flash Player must be installed on your computer (download by clicking here).*

Label the Figure

Instructions: *Identify each element in this basic model for communications.*

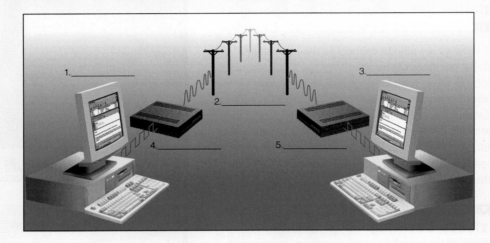

1. _____
2. _____
3. _____
4. _____
5. _____

Matching

Instructions: *Match each communications device from the column on the left with the best description from the column on the right.*

_____ 1. hub

_____ 2. repeater

_____ 3. bridge

_____ 4. gateway

_____ 5. router

a. Provides a central point for cables in a network.
b. Connects multiple networks – including those with different protocols.
c. Combines multiple input signals into a single stream of data and then transmits it.
d. Connects two LANs using the same protocol.
e. Accepts a signal from a transmission medium, amplifies it, and retransmits it over the medium.
f. Connects networks using different protocols.
g. Converts a computer's digital signals into a telephone's analog signals.

Short Answer

Instructions: *Write a brief answer to each of the following questions.*

1. What is noise? _____ Why are shielded twisted-pair (STP) cables used instead of unshielded twisted-pair (UTP) cables in environments susceptible to noise? _____

2. How are analog signals different from digital signals? _____ Why must both the sending and receiving ends of some communications channels have a modem for data transmission to occur? _____

3. What is a network operating system (NOS)? _____ What tasks does a network operating system perform? _____

4. How is a peer-to-peer network different from a client/server network? _____ What is the role of a network administrator? _____

5. What is network topology? _____ How are bus networks, ring networks, and star networks different? _____

AT ISSUE

www.scsite.com/dc2000/ch9/issue.htm

WEB INSTRUCTIONS: *To display this page from the Web, launch your browser and enter the URL,* www.scsite.com/dc2000/ch9/issue.htm. *Click the links for current and additional information.*

ONE *Some Florida law enforcement agencies have adopted an intranet to* help solve crime. The internal network lets various bureaus access crime reports, rap sheets, mug shots, fingerprints, and other crime-related data stored by different agencies. Investigators can collect information in minutes that once might have taken days to gather. In addition, sophisticated search algorithms can pinpoint connections that may not have been recognized by human detectives. The intranet cost $1.5 million to establish, and future intranets will cost $300,000. Despite the intranet's success, some complain the money would be better spent putting more officers on the street. Do you think the intranet is worth the cost? Why or why not? If it were your tax dollars, how would you prefer to have the money spent? Why?

TWO *A recent survey found that more than 12 million U.S. workers* telecommute. Telecommuting offers several advantages to employees – flexible work hours, no rush hour traffic, and casual dress codes – and employers claim telecommuters are 15 to 25 percent more productive than their office-bound brethren. Yet, some feel there also are disadvantages, including an inability to leave the job at the office, lack of personal contact, and an "out of sight, out of mind" attitude when it comes to promotion. How can the disadvantages of telecommuting be addressed? What type of personality do you think is needed to be a successful telecommuter? For what types of jobs would telecommuting be a viable alternative? Why? Given your personality and the career you plan to pursue, would you be a successful telecommuter? Why or why not?

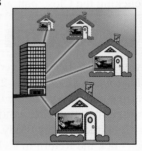

THREE *About a score of U.S. day-care centers offer parents a new form of communication –* a Web site with live video of center activities. Parents who log on can see their children learning the alphabet, playing a game, singing a song, or participating in other activities. Although developed partly in response to criticisms of staff at some centers, most day-care workers are comfortable with the new technology. Critics contend, however, that the systems foster mistrust; the still-primitive video can make an innocent pat on the cheek look like a slap. They also insist the systems' cost would be better spent hiring, training, or compensating staff. As a day-care center worker, how would you feel about Web site video? How would you feel as a parent? Would you be willing to pay a larger fee to have a real-time video of your child's day-care center available? Why or why not?

FOUR *Cardinal Richelieu, chief minister for Louis XIII, wrote, "If you give me six lines* written by the most honest man, I will find something in them to hang him." E-mail authors should heed Richelieu's warning. Tasteless postings and tactless messages have cost companies millions in damages and lost employees their jobs. People write things in e-mail that they would never put on paper. Yet, while paper eventually is destroyed, e-mail often survives. In minutes, it can be searched for a damning phrase. Why are people so unfettered in their e-mail communications? How should people ensure their e-mail communications are not used in an unintended fashion? If you were a senior company officer, what e-mail guidelines would you offer employees?

FIVE *Automobile leasing regulations are constantly changing. Unanticipated shifts in* lease policies can turn a done deal into no deal. To keep sales staff abreast of leasing regulations, Chrysler Corporation has tried an intranet with an online training program called LearnLinc. In electronic meetings, LearnLinc integrates multimedia, audioconferencing, application sharing, and Web-based courseware to convey the latest lease tips and techniques. Specific questions can be asked by clicking a link, and all trainees hear the answers. In addition, the intranet can be used to obtain up-to-date lease information. In what other areas do you think an intranet training program might be valuable? Why? What, if any, advantages do traditional training programs have over intranet training programs? Would you be comfortable taking part in a training program via an intranet? Why or why not?

SHELLY
CASHMAN
SERIES
DISCOVERING
COMPUTERS
2000

Student Exercises
WEB INFO
IN BRIEF
KEY TERMS
AT THE MOVIES
CHECKPOINT
AT ISSUE
CYBERCLASS
HANDS ON
NET STUFF
Special Features
TIMELINE 2000
GUIDE TO WWW SITES
MAKING A CHIP
BUYER'S GUIDE 2000
CAREERS 2000
TRENDS 2000
CHAT
INTERACTIVE LABS
NEWS
HOME

SHELLY
CASHMAN
SERIES®
DISCOVERING
COMPUTERS
2000

Student Exercises
WEB INFO
IN BRIEF
KEY TERMS
AT THE MOVIES
CHECKPOINT
AT ISSUE
CYBERCLASS
HANDS ON
NET STUFF
Special Features
TIMELINE 2000
GUIDE TO WWW SITES
MAKING A CHIP
BUYER'S GUIDE 2000
CAREERS 2000
TRENDS 2000
CHAT
INTERACTIVE LABS
NEWS
HOME

CHAPTER 1 2 3 4 5 6 7 8 **9** 10 11 12 13 14 **INDEX**

CYBERCLASS www.scsite.com/dc2000/ch9/class.htm

WEB INSTRUCTIONS: *To display this page from the Web, launch your browser and enter the URL,* www.scsite.com/dc2000/ch9/class.htm. *To start Level I CyberClass, click a Level I link on this page or enter the URL,* www.cyber-class.com. *Click the Student button, click Discovering Computers 2000 in the list of titles, and then click the Enter a site button. To start Level II or III CyberClass (available only to those purchasers of a CyberClass floppy disk), place your CyberClass floppy disk in drive A, click Start on the taskbar, click Run on the Start menu, type* a:connect *in the Open text box, click the OK button, click the Enter CyberClass button, and then follow the instructions.*

(I) (II) (III) LEVEL **1. Flash Cards** Click Flash Cards on the Main Menu of the CyberClass web page. Click the plus sign before the Chapter 9 title and then click Examples of How Communications Is Used. Answer flash cards until you correctly answer five in a row. Then, choose the subject, Transmission Media, and answer the flash cards until you correctly answer five in a row. Choose two more subjects and correctly answer five in a row for each subject. All users: Answer as many more flash cards as you desire. Close the Electronic Flash Card window and the Flash Cards window by clicking the Close button in the upper-right corner of each window.

(I) (II) (III) LEVEL **2. Practice Test** Click Testing on the Main Menu of the CyberClass web page. Click the Select a book box arrow and then click Discovering Computers 2000. Click the Select a test to take box arrow and then click the Chapter 9 title in the list. Click the Take Test button. If necessary, maximize the window. Take the practice test and then click the Submit Test button. Click the Display Study Guide button. Review the Study Guide. Scroll down and then click the Return to CyberClass button. If you missed two consecutive questions, click the Take another Test button. Continue to take tests until you do not miss consecutive questions in the test.

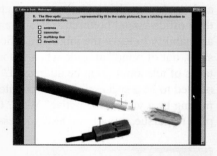

(I) (II) (III) LEVEL **3. Web Guide** Click Web Guide on the Main Menu of the CyberClass web page. When the Guide to World Wide Web Sites page displays, click Weather and then visit one of the weather sites. Determine the weather forecast for your area of the country during the next five days. Write a brief synopsis and hand it in to your instructor.

(I) (II) (III) LEVEL **4. Company Briefs** Click Company Briefs on the Main Menu of the CyberClass web page. Click a corporation name to display a case study. Read the case study. Write a brief report describing the use of computers and communications within the company.

(II) (III) LEVEL **5. CyberChallenge** Click CyberChallenge on the Main Menu of the CyberClass web page. Click the Select a book box arrow and then click Discovering Computers 2000. Click the Select a board to play box arrow and then click Chapter 9 in the list. Click the Play CyberChallenge button. Maximize the CyberChallenge window. Play CyberChallenge and answer only the 40 point questions until you get a score of 195 (using the time bonuses). Close the CyberChallenge window.

(II) (III) LEVEL **6. Assignments** Click Assignments on the Main Menu of the CyberClass web page. Ensure you are aware of all assignments and when they are due.

(II) (III) LEVEL **7. View Messages and Reply** Click View Messages on the Main Menu of the CyberClass web page. Review any messages that have been sent to you from classmates or from your instructor. Click Reply below the Subject line for any of the messages you feel need a reply and send a reply by entering a subject and the message itself. Then click the Send Message button.

CHAPTER 1 2 3 4 5 6 7 8 **9** 10 11 12 13 14 INDEX

HANDS ON   www.scsite.com/dc2000/ch9/hands.htm

SHELLY
CASHMAN
SERIES®

DISCOVERING
COMPUTERS
2000

WEB INSTRUCTIONS: *To display this page from the Web, launch your browser and enter the URL,* www.scsite.com/dc2000/ch9/hands.htm. *Click the links for current and additional information.*

One *Understanding Your Modem*

This exercise requires that you have a modem. Click the Start button on the taskbar, point to Settings on the Start menu, and then click Control Panel on the Settings submenu. Double-click the Modems icon in the Control Panel window. When the Modems Properties dialog box displays, click the General tab and then click the Properties button. Answer the following questions:

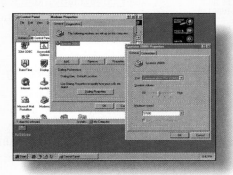

- ▲ What is the name of the modem?
- ▲ To which port is the modem connected?
- ▲ What is the maximum speed of the modem?

Click the Connection tab and then answer the following questions:

- ▲ What is the number of data bits?
- ▲ What is the parity?
- ▲ What is the number of stop bits?
- ▲ Which call preferences (if any) are set on your modem?

Close the dialog boxes and then click the close button to close the Control Panel window.

Two *Phone Dialer*

This exercise uses Windows 98 procedures. Click the Start button on the taskbar and then click Help on the Start menu. Click the Index tab. Type phone dialer in the text box and then click the Display button to learn about using Phone Dialer to dial from your computer. What is Phone Dialer? How do you start Phone Dialer after clicking the Start button? How can you obtain information about how to use Phone Dialer? Click the Close button to close the Windows Help window.

Three *Network Access*

Double-click the My Computer icon on the desktop. Dougle-click the Control Panel icon in the My Computer window. Click the Network icon in the Control Panel window. When the Network dialog box displays, click the Identification tab. What is the Computer name? What is the Workgroup? What, if any, is the Computer Description? Click the Access Control tab. How is Share-level access control different from User-level access control? Click the Close button to close each window.

Four *Using Help to Understand Networks*

This exercise uses Windows 98 procedures. Click the Start button on the taskbar and then click Help on the Start menu. Click the Contents tab. Click the Connecting to Networks book. Click the Connecting to a Network book. Click an appropriate Help topic to answer the following questions:

- ▲ How do you log on to a network?
- ▲ How do you connect to another computer on your network?
- ▲ How do you log off the network?

Click the Close button to close the Windows Help window.

NET STUFF www.scsite.com/dc2000/ch9/net.htm

WEB INSTRUCTIONS: *To display this page from the Web, launch your browser and enter the URL, www.scsite.com/dc2000/ch9/net.htm. To use the Exploring the Computers of the Future lab from the Web, Shockwave and Flash Player must be installed on your computer (download by clicking here).*

EXPLORING THE COMPUTERS OF THE FUTURE LAB

1. Shelly Cashman Series Exploring the Computers of the Future Lab

Follow the instructions in NET STUFF 1 on page 1.46 to start and use the Exploring the Computers of the Future lab. If you are running from the Web, enter the URL, www.scsite.com/sclabs/menu.htm; or display the NET STUFF page (see instructions at the top of this page) and then click the EXPLORING THE COMPUTERS OF THE FUTURE LAB button.

GPS

2. Global Positioning Systems

In 1998, a group of adventurers retraced Leif Ericson's voyage from Greenland to North America. The crew sailed a replica of a Viking boat, slept on the deck, ate dried foods, and used (for the most part) authentic navigational tools. The modern mariners did have, however, one instrument that was not available to Leif almost 1,000 years ago – a handheld global positioning system (GPS). Click the GPS button to learn more about global positioning systems.

ATTACHMENTS

3. Attachments

People often attach files to e-mail messages. To send an e-mail message with an attachment, click the ATTACHMENTS button to display your e-mail service. Enter your Login Name and Password. When the In-Box screen displays, click Compose. Type a classmate's e-mail address in the To: text box and type Attachments in the Subject: text box. Click the Attachments button. Insert your floppy disk in drive A. Type `a:\h2-2.doc` in the Attach File text box. This is the document you wrote to complete Chapter 2 Hands On Exercise 2. Click Attach to Message. Click Done. Click in the message box and then type a brief message about which At Issue question the attached document answers. When you are finished, click Send. Click the OK button on the Compose: sent Message Confirmation screen. Read newly arrived mail. When you have read all of your messages, click Log Out to exit the e-mail service.

IN THE NEWS

4. In the News

Theoretically, business travelers can access e-mail, fax documents, and transmit data from anywhere in the world. In practice, however, incompatible telephone standards and mismatched phone jacks can frustrate even experienced globetrotters. 3Com's Megahertz International PC Card addresses this problem. The modem and accompanying software allows travelers to use computer communications with more than 250 telephone systems simply by selecting the appropriate country from a menu and attaching a suitable adapter plug. Click the IN THE NEWS button and read a news article about a product that is changing computer communications. What is the product? What does it do? Who is more likely to use this product?

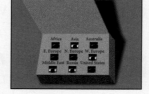

WEB CHAT

5. Web Chat

For years, junk mail has plagued postal customers. Junk e-mail, often called spam, has become an equivalent annoyance for computer users. America Online believes that almost 30 percent of the e-mail it transmits from the Internet is spam. Wading through spam to get to important messages is one of the more-stated complaints of America Online members. Not only is spam a continued nuisance, but an overflow of junk e-mail can slow network communications to a crawl. Several companies have created software to block spam, but no program is entirely effective. A movement to make spam illegal is gaining momentum, yet spammers maintain that any restrictions on e-mailings violate free enterprise. Do you think spam should be outlawed? Why or why not? If spam is made illegal, it must be specifically defined. How would you define spam? Click the WEB CHAT button to enter a Web Chat discussion related to this topic.

CHAPTER 10

DATABASES AND INFORMATION MANAGEMENT

*After completing this chapter,
you will be able to:*

Explain why data and information are important to an organization

Identify data maintenance techniques

Differentiate between file processing and databases

Discuss the advantages of using a database management system (DBMS)

Describe characteristics of relational and object-oriented databases

Explain how to use a query language

Discuss the responsibilities of the data and database administrators

Describe the various types of information systems

To provide maximum benefit to an individual or organization, data must be managed carefully, organized efficiently, and used effectively. Today, many users store data in databases — from the school's database of students, to the library card catalog, from your e-mail address book, to the vast, searchable databases behind search engines on the World Wide Web. Databases affect how individuals work, learn, and live. Therefore, understanding them is an important skill.

This chapter provides a review of data and information concepts and presents methods for maintaining high-quality data. The chapter then discusses the advantages of organizing data in a database, describes various types of databases, and examines the role of the data and database administrators in larger organizations. Finally, the chapter outlines the qualities of valuable information and presents various types of information systems.

DATA AND INFORMATION

Data is a collection of items such as words, numbers, images, and sounds that are not organized and have little meaning individually. Data is processed into information. **Information** is data that is organized, has meaning, and, therefore, is useful. A student grade report (information), for example, contains several data items, including student identification (ID) number, student first name, student last name, course names, course codes, credit hours, and course grades (Figure 10-1).

As discussed in Chapter 2, a **database** is a collection of data organized in a manner that allows access, retrieval, and use of that data. Database software, also called a database management system (DBMS), allows you to create a computerized database; add, change, and delete data; sort and retrieve data from the database; and create forms and reports using the data.

Most organizations realize that data is among their more valuable assets. Without data and information, an organization could not complete many business activities. Information accumulated on sales trends, competitors' products and services, production processes, and even employee skills, for example, allow a company to make decisions and develop, create, and distribute products and services. This information is a valuable resource that would be difficult, if not impossible, to replace. Because information cannot be generated without data, an organization must manage, maintain, and protect its data resources just as it would any other resource. Two critically important aspects of this include ensuring that data has integrity and is kept secure.

Data Integrity

For a computer to output accurate information, the data used to create the information must have integrity. **Data integrity** is the degree to which data is accurate. If your name is misspelled in a student database, for example, the data is inaccurate and is considered a violation of data integrity.

Although accurate data does not guarantee accurate information, it is impossible to produce accurate information from erroneous

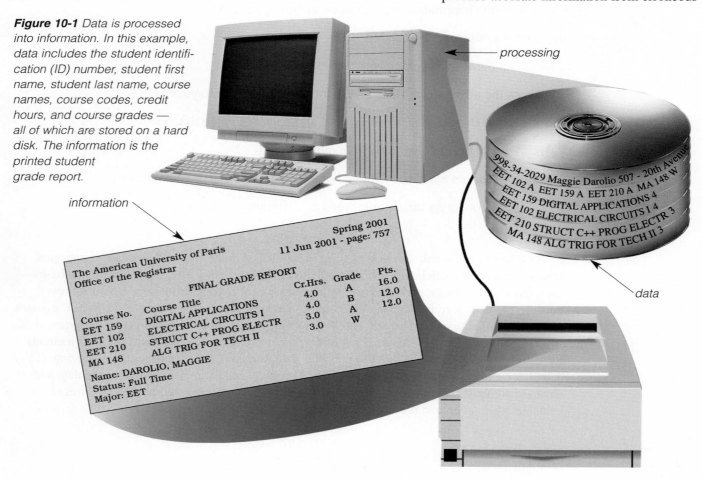

Figure 10-1 Data is processed into information. In this example, data includes the student identification (ID) number, student first name, student last name, course names, course codes, credit hours, and course grades — all of which are stored on a hard disk. The information is the printed student grade report.

processing

information

data

998-34-2029 Maggie Darolio 507 - 20th Avenue
EET 102 A EET 159 A EET 210 A MA 148 W
EET 159 DIGITAL APPLICATIONS 4
EET 102 ELECTRICAL CIRCUITS I 4
EET 210 STRUCT C++ PROG ELECTR 3
MA 148 ALG TRIG FOR TECH II 3

The American University of Paris
Office of the Registrar

Spring 2001
11 Jun 2001 - page: 757

FINAL GRADE REPORT

Course No.	Course Title	Cr.Hrs.	Grade	Pts.
EET 159	DIGITAL APPLICATIONS	4.0	A	16.0
EET 102	ELECTRICAL CIRCUITS I	4.0	B	12.0
EET 210	STRUCT C++ PROG ELECTR	3.0	A	12.0
MA 148	ALG TRIG FOR TECH II	3.0	W	

Name: DAROLIO, MAGGIE
Status: Full Time
Major: EET

data. This computing principle, often referred to as **garbage in, garbage out** (**GIGO**), means that, if you enter erroneous data into a computer (garbage in), the computer will produce inaccurate information (garbage out). Data integrity is critical because computers and individuals use information generated from data to make decisions and take actions. When you place an order with a mail-order company, for example, a sales representative enters the product number for each item you order. If he or she enters an incorrect product number, the warehouse likely will package and ship an item you did not intend to order.

Data Security

Data security involves protecting data so it is not misused or lost. Most schools, for example, have procedures that allow only authorized personnel to access confidential student data. The school also performs backup procedures to protect against the loss of data. As described

in Chapter 5, backup refers to making duplicate copies of data, files, programs, or disks, which can be used if the originals are lost, damaged, or destroyed. Making backup copies ensures that you can recover data in a timely manner and that processing can continue. Chapter 14 discusses these and other methods of data security in more detail.

THE HIERARCHY OF DATA

Data is organized in a hierarchy in which each higher level consists of one or more elements from the lower level preceding it. Depending on the application and the user, different terms describe the various levels of the hierarchy. Commonly used terms are character, field, record, file, and database. As shown in Figure 10-2, and a database contains files, a file contains records, and a record contains fields. Each field is defined by a variety of characteristics, one of which is the field size, or number of characters (bytes) it contains.

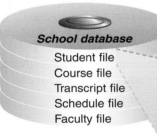

Figure 10-2 *A sample school database with five files: Student file, Course file, Transcript file, Schedule file, and Faculty file. The sample Student file contains eight records. Each record contains twelve fields. The State field can contain a maximum of two characters (bytes).*

School database

Student file
Course file
Transcript file
Schedule file
Faculty file

Student file

records

996-77-2775	Deborah	Peterson	305 - 14th Avenue	Highland	IN	4 . . .
997-23-1928	Brandon	Cloak	722 Bay Boulevard	Munster	IN	4 . . .
997-40-1827	Tim	Smith	908 W. Capital Way	Highland	IN	4 . . .
997-75-9282	Anne	Winters	722 Eastern Street	Mokena	IL	6 . . .
998-01-4987	Wesley	Peacock	4110 Wood Road	New Lenox	IL	6 . . .
998-20-9001	Matthew	Dunn	14 Garrett Drive	Hammond	IN	4 . . .
998-34-2029	Maggie	Darolio	507 - 20th Avenue	Hammond	IN	4 . . .
998-69-2286	Anita	Johnson	45 Francis Boulevard	Highland	IN	4 . . .

fields in each record

Student ID
First Name
Last Name
Address
City
State
Zip
Birthdate
Email Address
HS GPA
HS Graduation Date
Major

characteristics of State field

General	Lookup
Field Size	2
Format	
Input Mask	
Caption	State
Default Value	"IN"
Validation Rule	
Validation Text	
Required	Yes
Allow Zero Length	No
Indexed	No

characters in State field

Recall from Chapter 3 that a bit represents the smallest unit of data the computer can handle. Eight bits grouped together in a unit comprise a byte. Each byte represents an individual **character**, such as a number (8), letter (M), punctuation mark (!), or other symbol (@).

A **field** is a combination of one or more characters and is the smallest unit of data you can access. Typical fields in a database containing data about people include First Name, Last Name, Address, City, State, and Zip. A field often is defined by its data type and field length. As described in Chapter 2, the **data type** specifies the kind of data a field can contain. Common data types include:

- **Text**: letters, numbers, or special characters

- **Numeric**: numbers only

- **Currency**: dollar and cent amounts or numbers containing decimal values

- **Date**: month, day and year information

- **Memo**: longer text entries

- **Hyperlink**: Web address that links to a Web page

The **field length** is the maximum number of characters a field can contain. The State field, for example, stores text and can contain a total of two characters (for the state abbreviation); a Date field contains a date/time value and can store up to eight characters (for the format, mm/dd/yyyy).

A **record** is a group of related fields. A student record, for example, is a collection of fields about one student. The record might contain fields such as Student ID, First Name, Last Name, Address, City, State, Zip,

Birthdate, Email Address, HS (high school) GPA, HS Graduation Date, and Major.

A **key field**, or **primary key**, is a field that differentiates the records in a file. The data stored in a key field contains data that is unique to a specific record. A student record, for example, would use Student ID as a key field because it uniquely identifies each student.

A **data file**, also called a **file**, is a collection of related records stored on a disk such as a floppy disk, hard disk, or CD-ROM. A school's Student file, for example, would consist of thousands of individual student records. Each student record in the file would contain the same fields. Figure 10-3 illustrates a small sample Student file containing seven student records, each with twelve fields.

As defined in previous chapters, file also refers to word processing, spreadsheet, or other application files. These types of files, sometimes called **program files**, contain programs, instructions, or documents.

A database is a group of related data files. A school's database, for example, might have many individual files related to class scheduling and registration, such as a Student file, a Course file, and a Schedule file. The data files in a database are organized so that a particular database management system can access them.

MAINTAINING DATA

Data maintenance, sometimes called **file maintenance**, refers to the procedures used to keep data current. Data maintenance procedures include adding records to, changing records in, or deleting records from a file.

Figure 10-3 *A sample data file stored on a hard disk that contains seven records, each with twelve fields.*

Student ID	First Name	Last Name	Address	City	State	Zip	Birthdate
996-77-2775	Deborah	Peterson	305 - 14th Avenue	Highland	IN	46322-	10-17-1980
997-23-1928	Brandon	Cloak	722 Bay Boulevard	Munster	IN	46321-	01-15-1976
997-40-1827	Tim	Smith	908 W. Capital Way	Highland	IN	46322-	04-02-1979
997-75-9282	Anne	Winters	722 Eastern Street	Mokena	IL	60448-	05-12-1980
998-01-4987	Wesley	Peacock	4110 Wood Road	New Lenox	IL	60451-	11-27-1979
998-20-9001	Matthew	Dunn	14 Garrett Drive	Hammond	IN	46323-	12-06-1978
998-34-2029	Maggie	Darolio	507 - 20th Avenue	Hammond	IN	46323-	07-14-1977

records

fields

Adding Records

Records are added to a file when additional data is required to make it current. If a school admits a new student, for example, the admissions department would need to add a record containing the data for the new student to the school's Student file. The process required to add this record to the file includes the following steps:

1. An admissions counselor in the admissions department starts a Student Maintenance program that gives him or her access to the database. The admissions counselor then clicks the New Record button, which begins the process of adding a record to the Student file.

2. The admissions counselor assigns a Student ID to the new student. This number serves as the primary key for the student record.

3. The counselor enters data to fill in the fields in the student record. (For purposes of this example, the data entered is kept to a minimum.)

4. Once the admissions counselor verifies the data on the screen, he or she clicks the New Record button to add the new student record to the Student file. The program that manages the disk determines where to write the record on the disk. In some cases, the new record is written between existing records in the file. In other cases, such as illustrated in Figure 10-4, it writes the new record to the end of the file.

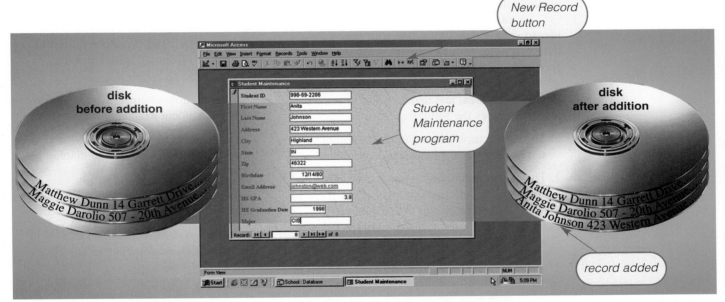

Figure 10-4 *Using the Student Maintenance program, an admissions counselor adds a new student record. After the admissions counselor confirms that the data is correct, the counselor clicks the New Record button to add the record to the file.*

Email Address	HS GPA	HS Grad	Major
deborah@west.com	3.9	1998	MGMT
bcloak@net.com	3.8	1994	CIS
timsmith@star.com	3.4	1997	MKTG
awinters@suburb.com	3.2	1998	ENGL
pea@suburb.com	3.6	1997	EDUC
dunnmatt@star.com	3.5	1996	CIS
darolio@star.com	3.5	1995	MGMT

Changing Records

Generally, you change a record in a file for two primary reasons: (1) to correct inaccurate data or (2) to update older data with newer data.

As an example of the first type of change, assume that an administrative assistant entered a new student's name as Anita Jonson, instead of Anita Johnson. When the student receives her schedule of classes, she notices the error, contacts the registration department, and requests that the department correct the spelling of her name.

To do this, an administrative assistant in the registration department retrieves the record and changes the last name field from Jonson to Johnson. The change thus corrects the inaccurate data and replaces it with accurate data.

A more common reason to change a record is to update older data with newer data. Suppose, for example, that Anita Johnson moves from 423 Western Avenue to 45 Francis Boulevard. The process required to change the address and update Anita Johnson's record includes the following steps:

1. The registration administrative assistant starts the Student Maintenance program.

2. The registration administrative assistant enters Anita Johnson's Student ID of 998-69-2286 to display Anita Johnson's record on the screen. If the assistant did not have the Student ID available, he or she

could enter the student's last name, which would retrieve all students with that same last name.

3. The program displays data about Anita Johnson. By reviewing this data on the screen, the assistant can confirm that the correct Student ID was entered.

4. The administrative assistant enters the new street address of 45 Francis Boulevard.

5. Once the administrative assistant verifies the data on the screen, she clicks the Save button to change the record in the Student file. The program changes the record on the disk (Figure 10-5).

Deleting Records

When a record no longer is needed, it is deleted from a file. In this example, a student named Brandon Cloak has requested a transfer to another school. The process required to delete a record from a file includes the following steps:

1. The registration administrative assistant starts the Student Maintenance program.

2. The assistant enters Brandon Cloak's Student ID of 997-23-1928 to display his record on the screen.

3. The program displays Brandon Cloak's name and personal data on the screen.

4. Once the assistant verifies that this is the record to be deleted, he or she clicks

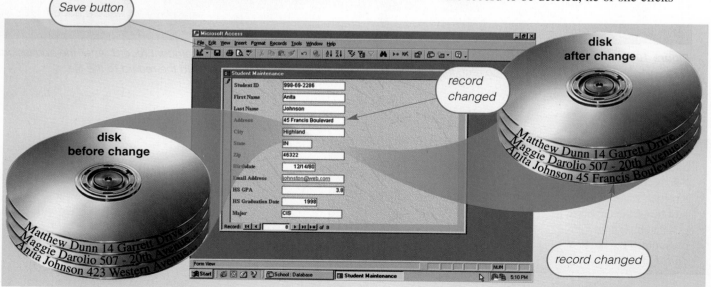

Figure 10-5 *The registration administrative assistant enters a Student ID to display the associated student record. The assistant reviews the record on the screen to confirm the correct Student ID has been entered and then changes the student's address. After the assistant verifies that the new address is correct, he or she clicks the Save button to change the student record on disk.*

the Delete Record button to delete the record from the Student file. The actual processing that occurs to delete a record from a file depends on the application. Sometimes, the record is removed from the file immediately. Other times, as in this example, the record is not removed from the file. Instead, the record is *flagged*, or marked, in some manner so the program will not process it again. In this case, an asterisk (*) is placed at the beginning of the record (Figure 10-6).

Although the record still physically is stored on the disk, it effectively is deleted because the program will not retrieve it for processing. Flagged records commonly are used in applications where inactive data must be maintained for some period of time. A bank, for example, might flag closed accounts and remove them after one year. Periodically, you should run a utility program that removes flagged records and reorganizes current records. Deleting unneeded records reduces the size of files and creates additional storage space.

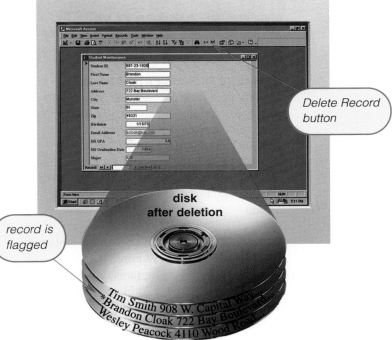

Figure 10-6 *The registration administrative assistant enters a Student ID to display the associated student record. After the assistant verifies that the correct student record displays, he or she clicks the Delete Record button to delete the record. The program flags the student record on disk by placing an asterisk in the first position of the record.*

Data Validation

As you learned in Chapter 2, **validation** is the process of comparing the data to a set of rules or values to determine if the data is accurate. Many programs perform a **validity check** that analyzes entered data to help ensure that the data is current and accurate. For instance, when an assistant adds or changes data in a record, the database management system performs a validity check to test the entered data.

A range check is an example of a validity check. For example, if you were entering high school grade point averages, you would expect values in the range of 0.0 to 4.0. A value of −10 or 85 clearly is outside of

the valid range. If the entered data does not pass a validity check, the computer usually displays an error message and asks you to re-enter the data. Validity checks, also called **validation rules**, minimize data entry errors and thus enhance the integrity of the data before the data is stored.

Various types of validity checks include alphabetic checks, numeric checks, completeness checks, range checks, consistency checks, and check digits. The table in Figure 10-7 illustrates several validity checks and shows valid data (data that passes these tests) and invalid data

WEB INFO
WEB INFO

For more information on validity checks, visit the Discovering Computers 2000 Chapter 10 WEB INFO page (**www.scsite.com/ dc2000/ch10/webinfo.htm**) and click Validity Checks.

Sample Valid and Invalid Data

Validity Check	Field Being Checked	Valid Data	Invalid Data
Alphabetic Check	City	Hammond	Hamm9nd
Numeric Check	HS GPA	4	R
Completeness Check	Last Name	Johnson	
Range Check	HS GPA	3.7	52
Consistency Check	Birthdate	07-12-1980	05-05-1979
	HS Graduation Date	06-03-1998	06-10-1975

Figure 10-7 *In this table of sample valid and invalid data, the first column lists commonly used validity checks. The second column lists the name of the field that contains data being tested. The third column shows valid data that passes the validity checks. The fourth column shows invalid data that fails the validity checks.*

(data that fails these tests) for each. The following paragraphs describe the purpose of these validity checks.

ALPHABETIC/NUMERIC CHECK An **alphabetic check** ensures that only alphabetic data is entered into an alphabetic field and a **numeric check** ensures that only numeric data is entered into a numeric field. For example, data in a City field should contain only alphabetic characters and data in a HS GPA (Grade Point Average) field should contain only numbers.

COMPLETENESS CHECK A **completeness check** verifies that all required data is present. In many application programs, you cannot leave the Last Name field blank. A completeness check on this field ensures data exists in it (Figure 10-8).

RANGE CHECK As just described, a **range check** determines whether a number is within a specified range. When data in the HS GPA field must be between 0.0 and 4.0, any number outside this range is invalid.

CONSISTENCY CHECK A **consistency check** tests the data entered in two or more fields to determine whether a known relationship between the fields is reasonable. For example, a High School Graduation Date cannot occur before a Birthdate.

CHECK DIGIT A **check digit** verifies the accuracy of a primary key. Bank account numbers, credit card numbers, and identification numbers often include a check digit. A check digit is a number(s) or character(s) that is appended to or inserted into a primary key value.

The value of a check digit is determined by applying a formula to the numbers in the primary key. A simple formula for computing a check digit would involve adding together the numbers in the primary key. For example, if the primary key is 4359, this check digit formula would add together these numbers $(4 + 3 + 5 + 9)$ for a sum of 21. The formula then would add together the numbers in the result $(2 + 1)$ to generate the check digit of 3. The primary key then would be 43593 (the primary key value, 4359, with the check digit, 3, appended).

When the data entry clerk enters the primary key, 43593, the program applies the formula to the first four digits of the primary key to test if its check digit is valid. If the computed check digit is the same as the entered check digit (3, in this case), the program assumes the entered primary key is valid. If the program computes any other number as the check digit, it displays an error message.

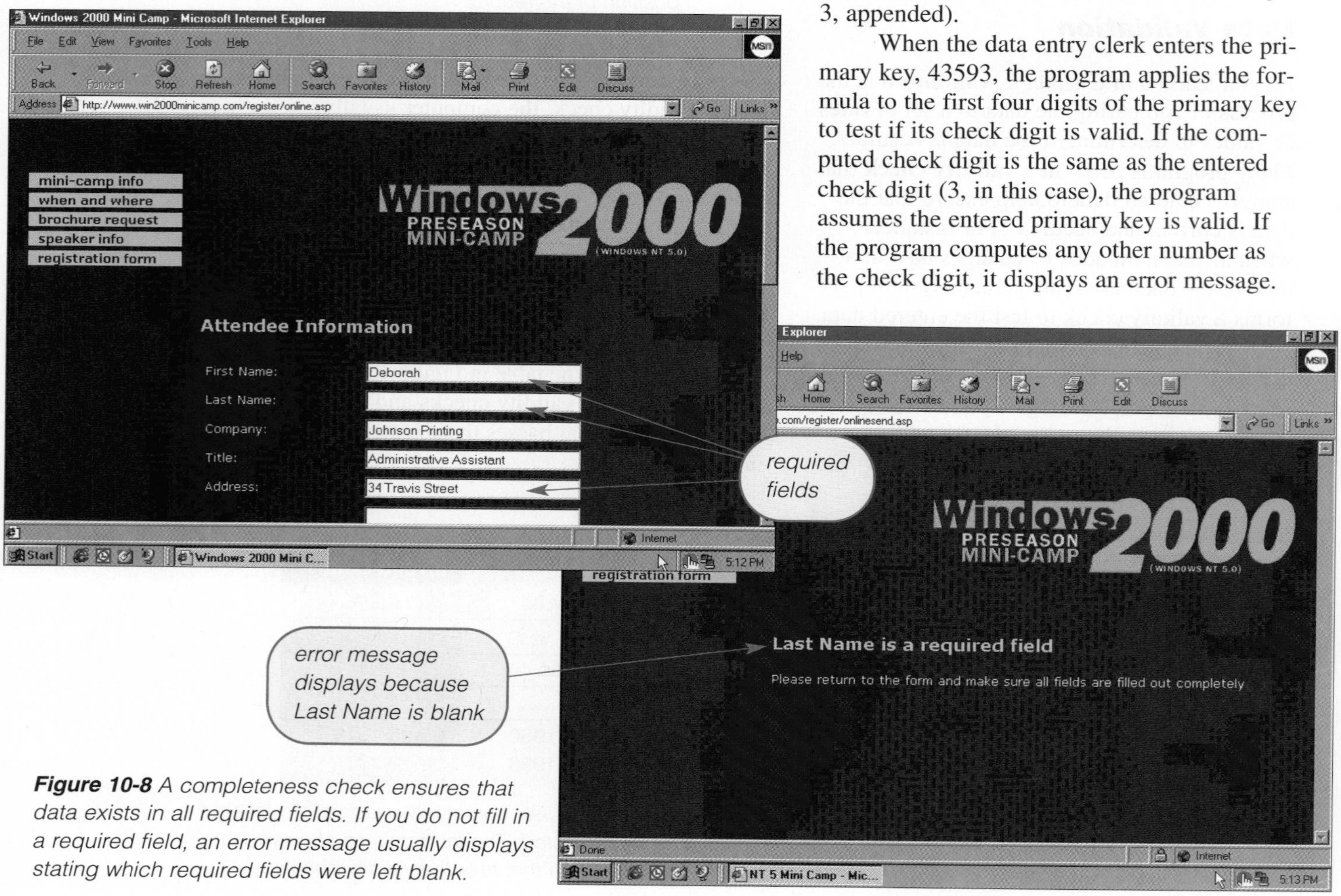

Figure 10-8 *A completeness check ensures that data exists in all required fields. If you do not fill in a required field, an error message usually displays stating which required fields were left blank.*

FILE PROCESSING VERSUS DATABASES

Almost all application programs use data that is stored in either files or databases. These two approaches to storing data are discussed in the following sections.

File Processing Systems

In the past, many organizations stored data in files on tape or disk and managed the data using file processing systems. In a typical **file processing system**, each department within an organization has its own set of files, designed specifically for their own applications, and the records in one file are not related to the records in any other file. Figure 10-9 illustrates an example of how a school might use a file processing system. The admissions department has its own files to admit a student into the school, and the registration department has its own set of files to register students for classes.

Although organizations have used file processing systems for many years, these systems do have major disadvantages. Two of these disadvantages are data redundancy and isolated data.

• **Data Redundancy**. Because each department has it own files in a file processing system, the files often must store the same (redundant) data. Both the admissions department files and the registration department files, for example, must store a student's name and address. Data redundancy wastes resources such as storage space and employee time. Storing the same data in more than one file requires increased storage capacity. When data is added or changed, data maintenance takes

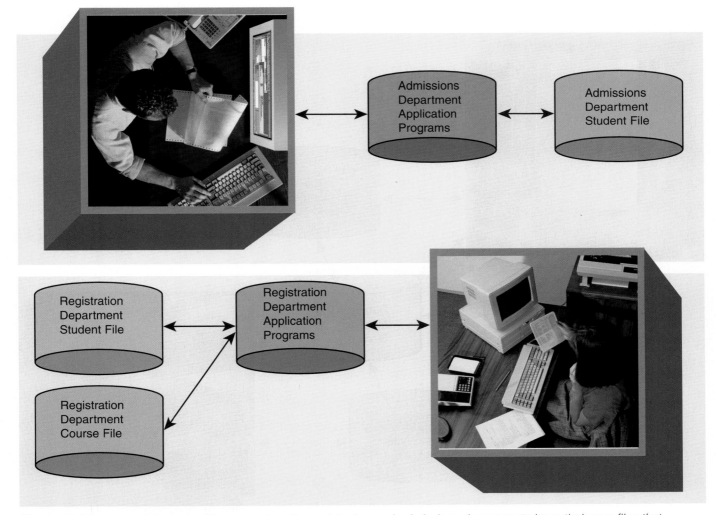

Figure 10-9 *In a school that uses file processing, the registration and admissions departments have their own files that are designed specifically for their applications.*

more time because employees must update more than one file. Data redundancy also compromises data integrity. If a student relocates, for example, the school must update the student's Address field in the admission and registration files, as well as any other department that contains the student's Address field throughout the school. If the field is not changed in all the files, then discrepancies among the files will exist.

- **Isolated Data**. When data is stored in multiple files in multiple departments, often it is difficult to access the data. For example, to generate a report listing the majors of a particular class of students, you would need to access and use data in both the admissions department files and the registration department files because the admissions files store the students' major and the registration files store the class rosters. Sharing data from multiple, separate files to generate such a list often is a complicated procedure and typically requires the expertise of an experienced computer programmer.

To overcome these and other problems associated with file processing systems, many companies use the database approach for managing data.

The Database Approach

As previously described, a database is a shared collection of data. With the **database approach**, many application programs in an organization could use the data in this single, shared database. A school's database, for example, would contain data about students and courses. As shown in Figure 10-10, departments within the school, such as admissions and registration, would share the data in this database.

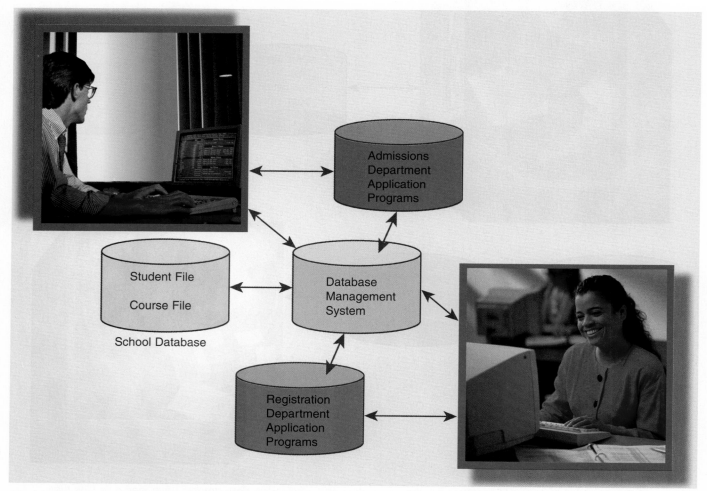

Figure 10-10 *In a school that uses a database, the registration and admissions departments access data in a single database through the database management system.*

Users access the data in the database using database software, which often is called a database management system (DBMS). As noted at the beginning of this chapter, a database management system (DBMS) is a software program designed to control access to the database and manage the data resources efficiently. While a user is working with the database, the DBMS resides in the memory of the computer. The next section presents the features of a DBMS in detail.

The database approach overcomes many of the limitations of file processing systems by reducing data redundancy and allowing for sharing of data. These and other advantages of the database approach are presented next.

- **Reduced Data Redundancy**. Using the database approach, all data is stored together, which greatly reduces data redundancy. A school database, for example, would store a student's name and address only once. When student data is entered or changed, one employee makes the change once. Figure 10-11 contrasts a database application to a file processing application with respect to data redundancy.

- **Improved Data Integrity**. Because most data is stored in only one location, the database approach increases the data's integrity by reducing the likelihood of introducing inconsistencies. When data in the database is changed, all applications have access to the same updated data.

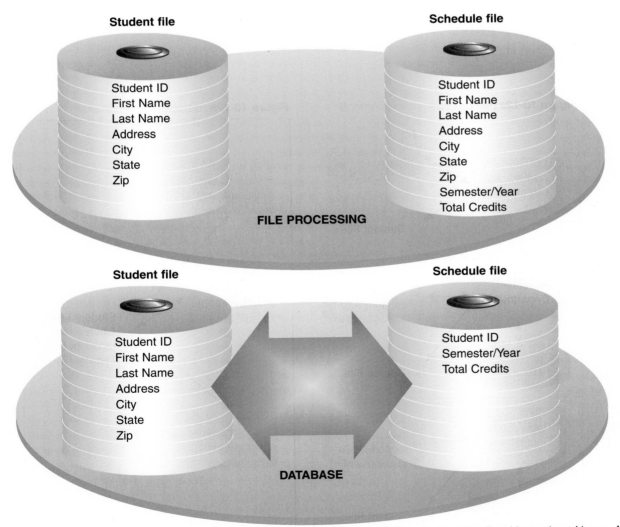

Figure 10-11 In this file processing environment, both files contain the Student ID, First Name, Last Name, Address, City, State, and Zip fields. In a database environment, only the Student file contains the First Name, Last Name, Address, City, State, and Zip fields. Other files, however, such as the Schedule file, contain the Student ID, which is used to retrieve the student's personal data when it is needed.

- **Shared Data**. Whereas each application in a file processing environment has its own set of files, the data in a database environment belongs to and is shared by the entire organization. Figure 10-12 compares how a database application stores data versus a file processing application. Organizations using databases typically set up controls to define who can access, add, change, and delete the data in a database.

- **Reduced Development Time**. A database organizes data more efficiently than a file processing system, thus it often is easier and faster to develop programs that use this data. Many database management systems also provide several tools to assist in program development, thus further reducing the development time. The next section discusses these and other DBMS features.

- **Easier Reporting**. The database approach allows nontechnical users to access and manipulate data. Although computer professionals typically develop larger databases and their associated programs, many computer users are developing smaller databases themselves, without professional assistance.

While it has many advantages, the database approach does have the disadvantages of cost and vulnerability. For one, the initial investment in the hardware and software required for a database usually is high. A large database also can be more complex than a file processing system and thus require trained individuals to develop these applications. These larger databases also require more memory, storage, and processing power than file processing systems.

Figure 10-12a *(file processing environment)*

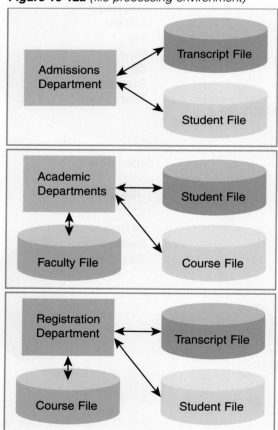

Figure 10-12b *(database environment)*

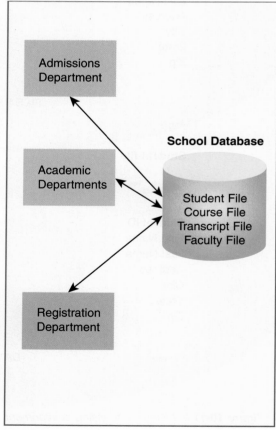

Figure 10-12 *The admissions department, registration department, and academic departments all have their own files in the file processing environment. In a database environment, these departments all share the same files.*

A second disadvantage of the database approach is its increased vulnerability. Because all data is stored in a single location and shared by application programs, many users depend on the data in the database. If the database is not operating properly or is damaged or destroyed, many users will not be able to perform their jobs. In some cases, certain application programs may cease to operate. To protect their valuable database resource, individuals and organizations should establish and follow security procedures. Chapter 14 discusses these and other security methods.

Despite these limitations, many business and home users work with databases because of their tremendous advantages.

DATABASE MANAGEMENT SYSTEMS

As previously discussed, a **database management system** (**DBMS**) is a software program or set of programs designed to control access to the database and manage the data resources efficiently. While a user is working with the database, the DBMS resides in the memory of the computer.

Database management systems are available for many sizes and types of computers (Figure 10-13). Whether designed for a mainframe or a personal computer, every database management system has a number of common features. These features include a data dictionary, and functions such as data maintenance and retrieval, data security, and backup and recovery. The following pages discuss these features of a DBMS.

WEB INFO
WEB INFO
For more information on database management systems, visit the Discovering Computers 2000 Chapter 10 WEB INFO page (**www.scsite.com/ dc2000/ch10/webinfo.htm**) and click DBMS.

Popular Database Management Systems

Database	Computer Type
Microsoft Pocket Access	Handheld personal computer
Microsoft Access	Personal computer, server
Corel Paradox	Personal computer, server
Lotus Approach	Personal computer, server
Microsoft Visual FoxPro	Personal computer, server
Oracle	Personal computer server, minicomputer, mainframe
DB2	Personal computer server, minicomputer, mainframe
Informix	Personal computer server, minicomputer, mainframe

Figure 10-13 *Some databases run on only a single type of computer, while others run on multiple types of computers.*

WEB INFO

For more information on the data dictionary, visit the Discovering Computers 2000 Chapter 10 WEB INFO page (www.scsite.com/dc2000/ch10/webinfo.htm) and click Data Dictionary.

Data Dictionary

A **data dictionary** stores data about each file in the database and each field within those files. For each file, a data dictionary stores data including the file name, description, and the file's relationship to other files. For each field, a data dictionary stores data including the field name, field size, description, type of data (e.g., text, numeric, or date/time), default value, validation rules, and the field's relationship to other fields. Figure 10-14 shows how a data dictionary might list data about the files and fields in a Student database.

A DBMS uses the data dictionary to perform validation checks and maintain the integrity of the data. When you enter data, the data dictionary verifies that the entered data matches the field's data type. The HS Graduation Date field, for example, must contain a number. A data dictionary also allows you to specify a default value for certain fields. A **default value** is a value that the DBMS automatically displays in a field. For example, if most students that attend a school live in Indiana, then the DBMS could display a default value of IN in the State field. Displaying a default value minimizes the possibility of errors, because commonly used data items are entered for you. Usually, you can override a default value if it does not apply for a certain record. For example, you can change the value, IN, to MI if you need to add a student that lives in Michigan.

Data Maintenance and Retrieval

A DBMS provides several facilities to enable users and programs to maintain data in and retrieve data from the database. As you have learned, data maintenance involves adding new records, changing data in existing

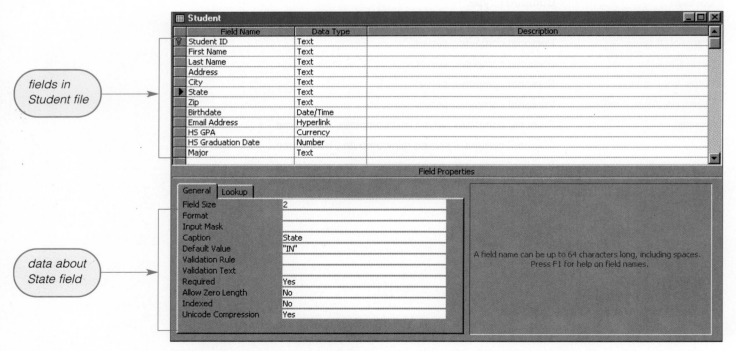

Figure 10-14 A sample data dictionary entry shows the fields in the Student file and the properties of the State field.

records, and removing unwanted records from the database. To retrieve data from a database, a process called a **query**, involves extracting specific data from the database and displaying, printing, or storing it. As described in Chapter 2, the capability of retrieving (selecting) database information based on an instruction, called **criteria**, specified by the user is one of the more powerful features of a database.

Often, a variety of users, from experienced professionals to nontechnical users, need to maintain and retrieve the data in a database. A DBMS thus provides several methods of accessing data, each of which requires varying levels of database expertise. Of these, query languages, forms, and report generators provide a user-friendly means to maintain and retrieve data from the database. Each of these methods is described in the following paragraphs.

A **query language** consists of simple, English-like statements that allow you to specify the data you want to display, print, or store. Although each query language has its own grammar and vocabulary, a person without a programming background usually can learn these languages in a short time. Although you can maintain data with a query language, most users utilize a query language only to retrieve data. To simplify the process, many DBMSs provide wizards to guide a user through the steps of building a query. Figure 10-15 shows a Simple Query Wizard and the query it generates.

Most database management systems also include a feature called query-by-example. Instead of learning the grammar and vocabulary associated with a query language, you can use a **query-by-example** (**QBE**) to

Figure 10-15a *(Simple Query Wizard)*

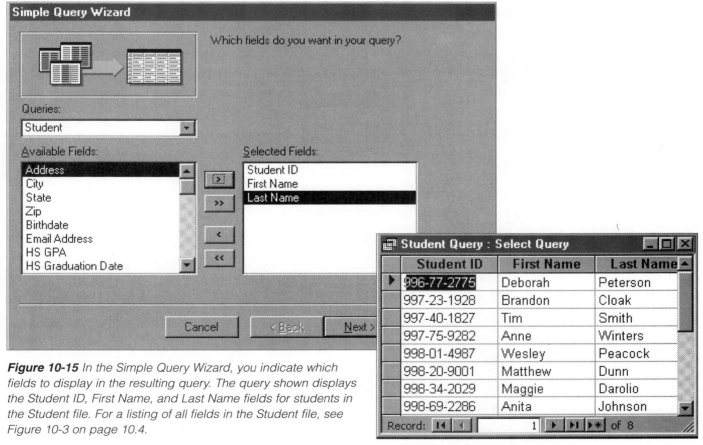

Figure 10-15 *In the Simple Query Wizard, you indicate which fields to display in the resulting query. The query shown displays the Student ID, First Name, and Last Name fields for students in the Student file. For a listing of all fields in the Student file, see Figure 10-3 on page 10.4.*

Figure 10-15b *(query results)*

extract data from the database. QBEs have a graphical user interface that assists you with retrieving data. Figure 10-16 shows a sample QBE screen for a query that searches for students that live in Illinois. Later in the chapter, specific query languages are presented in more depth.

A **form**, sometimes called a **data entry form**, is a window on the screen that provides areas for entering or changing data in a database. You use forms to retrieve (Figure 10-16) and maintain (Figure 10-17) the data in a database. Forms usually provide a means for validating data so as to reduce data entry

errors. When designing a form using a DBMS, you can make the form attractive and easy to use by incorporating color, shading, lines, and boxes; varying the fonts and font styles; and using other formatting features.

A **report generator**, also called a **report writer**, allows you to design or layout a report on the screen, extract data into the report layout, and then display or print the report (Figure 10-18). Unlike a form, a report generator is used only to retrieve data. Report generators usually allow you to format report page numbers and dates; report titles and column headings; subtotals and totals; and fonts, font sizes, color, and shading.

Figure 10-16a (QBE screen)

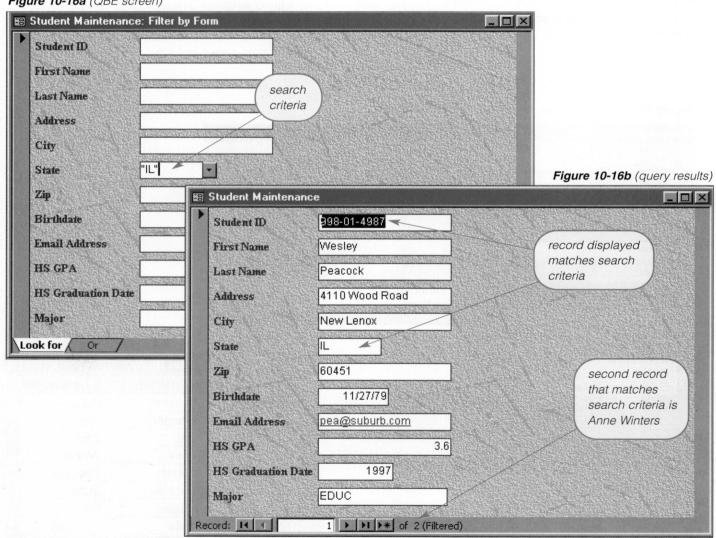

Figure 10-16b (query results)

Figure 10-16 *Microsoft Access has QBE capabilities. One of the more simple to use is Filter by Form, which uses a form to show available fields. Access retrieves records that match criteria you enter in the form fields. This example searches for records whose State is equal to IL and displays the first matching record.*

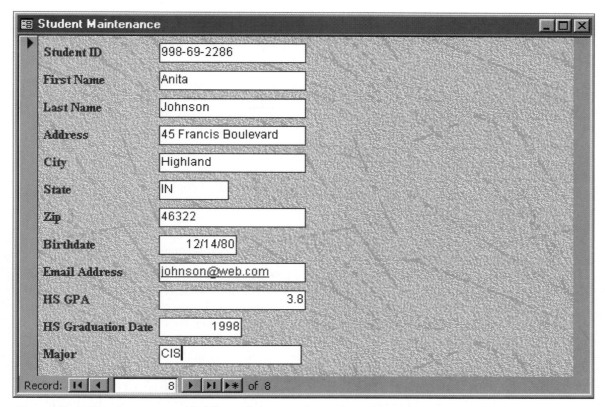

Figure 10-17 This form, created in Microsoft Access, is used to add or change student records in the Student file.

Figure 10-18 This report, created in Microsoft Access, displays student e-mail addresses by student major.

Student E-mail Addresses by Major

Major	Last Name	First Name	Student ID	Email Address
CIS				
	Cloak	Brandon	997-23-1928	bcloak@net.com
	Dunn	Matthew	998-20-9001	dunnmatt@star.com
	Johnson	Anita	998-69-2286	johnson@web.com
EDUC				
	Peacock	Wesley	998-01-4987	pea@suburb.com
ENGL				
	Winters	Anne	997-75-9282	awinters@suburb.com
MGMT				
	Darolio	Maggie	998-34-2029	darolio@star.com
	Peterson	Deborah	996-77-2775	deborah@west.com
MKTG				
	Smith	Tim	997-40-1827	timsmith@star.com

Data Security

To ensure that the data in a database is not misused, a DBMS provides mechanisms so that only authorized users can access data at permitted times. In addition, most database management systems allow you to specify different levels of access privileges for each field in the database. These **access privileges** define the activities allowed by a specific user or group of users.

Access privileges for data involve establishing who can enter new data, change existing data, delete unwanted data, and retrieve data. In the school database, for example, a faculty advisor might have **read-only privileges** for student transcripts; that is, the advisor could retrieve the transcript data, but cannot change it. The school's registrar, by contrast, would have **full-update privileges** to transcript data, meaning that the registrar can retrieve and change the data. Finally, a student would have no access privileges to the transcript data and can neither retrieve nor change the data. Chapter 14 covers access privileges and other security techniques in more depth.

Backup and Recovery

Occasionally, a database is damaged or destroyed because of hardware failure, a problem with the software, human error, or a catastrophe such as fire or flood. A DBMS provides a variety of techniques to restore the database to a usable form in case it is damaged or destroyed.

- On a regular basis, you should make a **backup**, or copy, of the entire database. Some DBMSs include backup utilities, while others rely on the backup utilities included with operating systems or those purchased separately.

- More sophisticated DBMSs maintain a **log**, or listing, of activities that have affected the database. If you change a student address, for example, the change appears in the log. In this situation, the DBMS places the following in the log: a copy of the student record prior to the change, called the **before image**; the actual change of address data; and a copy of the student record after the change, called the **after image** (Figure 10-19).

Figure 10-19a *(Before Image)*

Student ID	First Name	Last Name	Address	City	State	Zip	Birthdate
997-23-1928	Brandon	Cloak	722 Bay Boulevard	Munster	IN	46321-	01-15-1976

Email Address	HS GPA	HS Grad	Major Code
bcloak@net.com	3.8	1994	CIS

Figure 10-19b *(Change)*

Address
45 Green Street

Figure 10-19c *(After Image)*

Student ID	First Name	Last Name	Address	City	State	Zip	Birthdate
997-23-1928	Brandon	Cloak	45 Green Street	Munster	IN	46321-	01-15-1976

Email Address	HS GPA	HS Grad	Major
bcloak@net.com	3.8	1994	CIS

Figure 10-19 *If you make a change to a record, the DBMS often places three items in the log: the before image of the record; the actual change; and the after image of the record.*

- A DBMS that maintains a log often also provides a recovery utility that uses the logs to restore a database in the event it is damaged or destroyed. Depending on the type of failure, the recovery utility restores the database using rollback or rollforward techniques. In a **rollback**, also called **backward recovery**, the log is used to reverse or undo any changes made to the database during a certain period of time, such as an hour. Once the database is restored, you must re-enter the transactions entered during this period of time. In a **rollforward**, also called **forward recovery**, the log is used to re-enter changes automatically since the last database save or backup. Some database recovery utilities use a combination of both techniques.

RELATIONAL AND OBJECT-ORIENTED DATABASES

Every database and database management system is based on a particular data model. A **data model** consists of rules and standards that define how data is organized in a database. Five data models are hierarchical, network, relational, object oriented, and object relational.

In the past, databases often were organized according to the hierarchical or network data model. In a **hierarchical database**, data is organized in a series like a family tree or organization chart. As with a family tree, the hierarchical database has branches made up of parent and child records. Each *parent record* can have multiple child records. Each *child record*, however, can have only one parent. A **network database** is similar to a hierarchical database except that each child record can have more than one parent.

Because hierarchical and network databases offer only limited data access and lack flexibility, database developers prefer two other database models: relational and object oriented. A newer data model, the **object-relational data model**, combines features of the relational and object-oriented data models. The table in Figure 10-20 lists popular DBMSs based on these data models. The following sections discuss the features of relational and object-oriented data models and the databases based on them.

Relational Databases

Today, the most commonly used database, the relational database, is based on the relational data model. A **relational database** stores data in tables that consist of rows and columns. Each row has a primary key and each column has a unique name.

WEB INFO

For more information on relational databases, visit the Discovering Computers 2000 Chapter 10 WEB INFO page (**www.scsite.com/ dc2000/ch10/webinfo.htm**) and click Relational Databases.

Data Models and Associated DBMSs

Data Model	Popular DBMSs
Relational	Microsoft Access Corel Paradox Lotus Approach Microsoft Visual FoxPro Informix Oracle DB2
Object-oriented	GemStone Objectstore Versant Ontos
Object-relational	Illustra O2 UniSQL

Figure 10-20 *Two popular data models are relational and object oriented. Most DBMSs are based on one of these models.*

Data Terminology

File Processing Developer	Relational Database Developer	Relational Database User
File	Relation	Table
Record	Tuple	Row
Field	Attribute	Column

Figure 10-21 *In this data terminology table, the first column identifies the terms used by developers in a file processing environment. The second column presents the terms used by developers of a relational database. The third column indicates the terms to which the users of a relational database refer.*

A relational database uses terminology different from a file processing environment to represent data. A relational database developer, for example, refers to a file as a **relation**, a record as a **tuple**, and a field as an **attribute**.

A user of a relational database, however, refers to a file as a **table**, a record as a **row**, and a field as a **column** (Figure 10-21). This chapter uses the terms, table, row, and column, when discussing relational databases.

In addition to storing data, a relational database also stores any associations among the data, which are called **relationships**. With a relational database, you can establish a relationship between tables at any time, provided the tables have a common column (field). You would relate the Student table and the Schedule table, for example, using the Student ID column. Figure 10-22 illustrates these relational database concepts. In a relational database, the only data redundancy exists in the common columns (fields) that establish relationships.

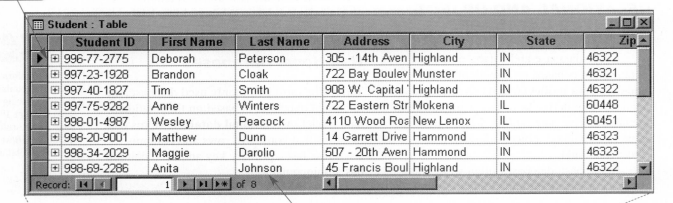

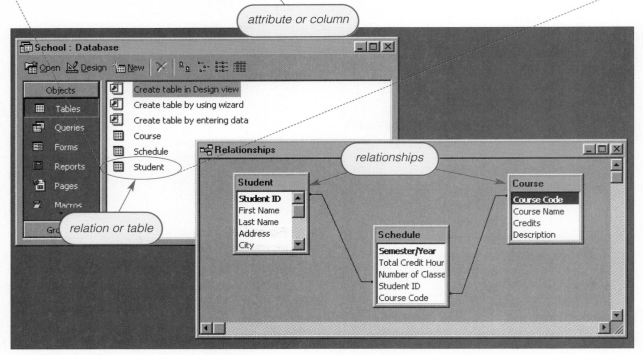

Figure 10-22 *The Student table is linked to the Schedule table through the Student ID column. The Schedule table is linked to the Course table through the Course Code column.*

RELATIONAL ALGEBRA Relational databases often use relational algebra to manipulate data. **Relational algebra** uses variables and operations to build a new relation. Three commonly used relational operations are projection, selection, and join operations.

To understand the function of the three operations, consider a query that uses these three operations to retrieve a list of students enrolled in ENGL 104 (Figure 10-23). First, the **projection operation** extracts columns (fields) from a relation, that is, a vertical subset of a table. In the example, the projection operation retrieves the Student ID, First Name, and Last Name columns from the Student table. The **selection operation** then retrieves certain rows (records) based on the criteria you specify, that is, a horizontal subset of a table. In the example, the selection operation retrieves all rows containing students in ENGL 104 in the Schedule table. The **join operation** then combines the data from the two queries based on a common column. In the example, the join operation uses the Student ID to combine the data retrieved from the Student and the Schedule tables.

STRUCTURED QUERY LANGUAGE
Relational databases use a query language called **Structured Query Language (SQL)** to manipulate and retrieve data. SQL includes keywords and rules used to implement relational algebra operations. The SQL statement in Figure 10-24, for example, would execute a query that retrieves students enrolled in ENGL 104. This SQL statement would generate the relation shown in Figure 10-23c.

WEB INFO
WEB INFO
For more information on SQL, visit the Discovering Computers 2000 Chapter 10 WEB INFO page (**www.scsite.com/ dc2000/ch10/webinfo.htm**) and click SQL.

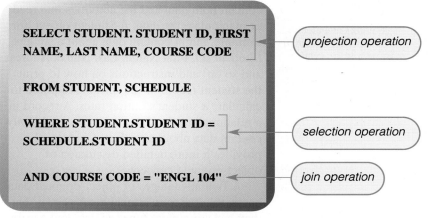

Figure 10-24 *This SQL statement would generate the results shown in Figure 10-23c.*

Query: Display students in ENGL 104

Figure 10-23a *(Student table)*

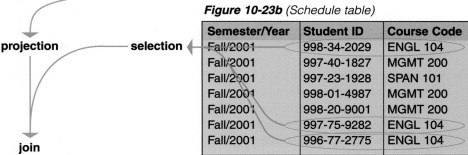

Student ID	First Name	Last Name	Address	City	State	Zip	
998-34-2029	Maggie	Darolio	507 - 20th Avenue	Hammond	IN	46323-	. . .
997-40-1827	Tim	Smith	908 W. Capital Way	Highland	IN	46322-	. . .
997-23-1928	Brandon	Cloak	722 Bay Boulevard	Munster	IN	46321-	. . .
998-01-4987	Wesley	Peacock	4110 Wood Road	New Lenox	IL	60451-	. . .
998-20-9001	Matthew	Dunn	14 Garrett Drive	Hammond	IN	46323-	. . .
997-75-9282	Anne	Winters	722 Eastern Street	Mokena	IL	60448-	. . .
996-77-2775	Deborah	Peterson	305 - 14th Avenue	Highland	IN	46322-	. . .

projection   **selection**

Figure 10-23b *(Schedule table)*

Semester/Year	Student ID	Course Code
Fall/2001	998-34-2029	ENGL 104
Fall/2001	997-40-1827	MGMT 200
Fall/2001	997-23-1928	SPAN 101
Fall/2001	998-01-4987	MGMT 200
Fall/2001	998-20-9001	MGMT 200
Fall/2001	997-75-9282	ENGL 104
Fall/2001	996-77-2775	ENGL 104

join

Figure 10-23c *(query results)*

Student ID	First Name	Last Name	Course Code
998-34-2029	Maggie	Darolio	ENGL 104
997-75-9282	Anne	Winters	ENGL 104
996-77-2775	Deborah	Peterson	ENGL 104

Figure 10-23 *The selection, projection, and join operations are used to produce a response to the query.*

Most relational database products for minicomputers and mainframes support Structured Query Language (SQL). Many personal computer database system vendors also have developed or modified existing packages to support SQL.

Object-Oriented Databases

An **object-oriented database** is based on an object-oriented data model and, thus, maintains objects. An **object** is an item that can contain both data and the activities that read or manipulate the data. A Student object, for example, might contain data about a student (Student ID, First Name, Last Name, Address, and so on) and instructions on how to print the student record or the formula required to calculate a student's tuition rates. A record in a relational database, by contrast, would *only* contain data about a student. Chapter 12 provides a more detailed discussion of object-oriented concepts.

Two advantages of object-oriented databases, relative to relational databases, is that they can store more types of data and access this data faster. With an object-oriented database, you can store unstructured data such as photographs, video clips, audio clips, and documents more efficiently than in a relational database. Further, if you run a query to extract data from an object-oriented database, the object-oriented database often returns results more quickly than the same query of a relational database. Examples of applications appropriate for an object-oriented database include the following:

- A **multimedia database** that stores images, audio clips, and/or video clips. A geographic information system (GIS) database, for example, stores maps; a voice mail system stores audio messages; and a television broadcast database stores audio and video clips.

- A **groupware database** that stores documents such as schedules, calendars, manuals, memos, and reports. Users can perform queries to search the document contents. One query, for example, might search the schedules for available meeting times.

- A **computer-aided design (CAD) database** that stores data about engineering, architectural, and scientific designs. This data in the database includes a list of components of the item being designed, the relationship among the components, and archived versions of the design drafts.

- A **hypertext database** contains text links to other documents, and a **hypermedia database** also contains graphics, video, and sound. A variety of hypertext and hypermedia databases are accessible via the Web. You can search one of these databases for items such as documents, graphics, audio and video clips, and links to Web pages (Figure 10-25).

Some companies also are developing **object-relational databases** to take advantage of features of both the relational and object-oriented data models.

OBJECT QUERY LANGUAGE Object-oriented and object-relational databases often use a query language called **object query language (OQL)** to manipulate and retrieve data. OQL is similar to SQL in that it uses many of the same rules, grammar, and vocabulary. Because OQL is a relatively new standard query language, however, not all object databases support it.

Figure 10-26 illustrates a sample OQL statement. When you enter search criteria or click a link, the DBMS generates the associated OQL statement that accesses that data from the database. In this case, the database is one on the Web.

DATABASE ADMINISTRATION

Keeping an organization's data centralized in a database requires a great deal of cooperation and coordination on the part of the database users. In file processing systems, if you wanted to track or store data, typically you would just create another file, often duplicating data already stored by someone else, in another file. In a database environment, if you want to track or store data, first you check to see if some or all of the data already is in the database or, if not, how you can add the data to the database. The role of coordinating the use of the database belongs to the data and database administrators.

WEB INFO
WEB INFO

For more information on object-oriented databases, visit the Discovering Computers 2000 Chapter 10 WEB INFO page (**www.scsite.com/dc2000/ch10/webinfo.htm**) and click Object-Oriented Databases.

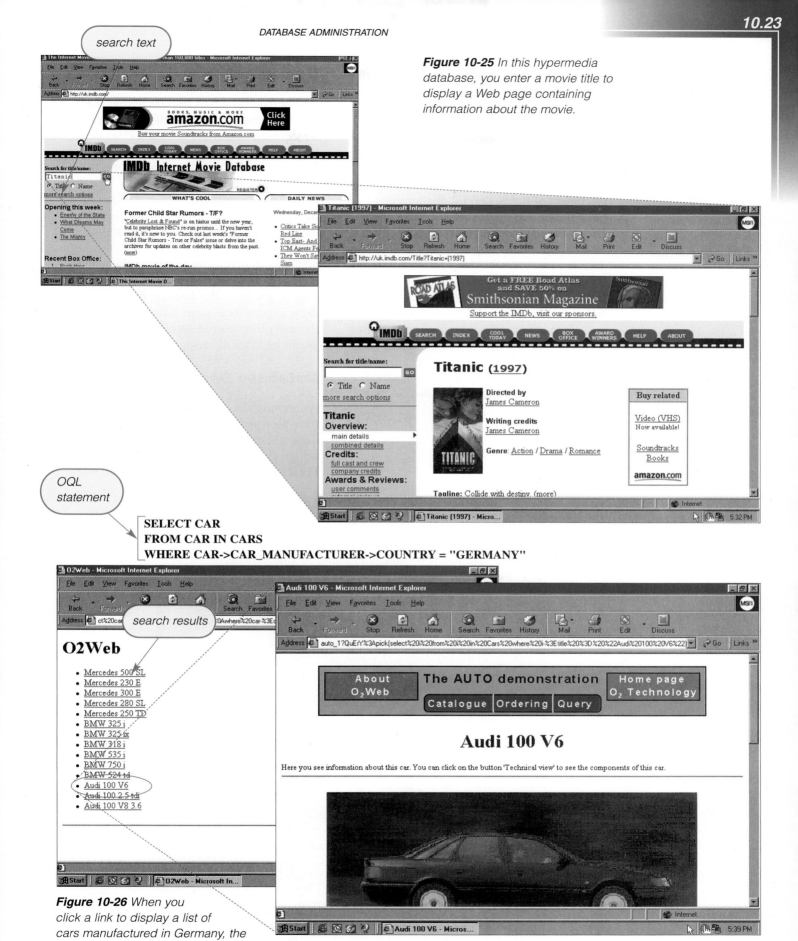

search text

Figure 10-25 In this hypermedia database, you enter a movie title to display a Web page containing information about the movie.

OQL statement

```
SELECT CAR
FROM CAR IN CARS
WHERE CAR->CAR_MANUFACTURER->COUNTRY = "GERMANY"
```

search results

Figure 10-26 When you click a link to display a list of cars manufactured in Germany, the DBMS executes the OQL statement. From the list of cars, you can display the picture and other information about a model you select by clicking the desired link.

Role of the Data and Database Administrators

The data and database administrators are responsible for managing and coordinating all database activities. The **data administrator (DA)** is responsible for designing the database; that is, the DA determines the proper placement of fields, defines relationships among data, and outlines users' access privileges. The **database administrator (DBA)** is responsible for creating and maintaining the data dictionary, establishing and monitoring security of the database, monitoring the performance of the database, and implementing and testing backup and recovery procedures.

In small organizations, one person often serves as both the data administrator and the database administrator. In larger organizations, the responsibilities of the data and database administrators are split among two or more persons.

Role of the User

One of the user's first responsibilities is to familiarize himself or herself with the data in the existing database. First-time database users often are amazed at the wealth of information available to help them perform their jobs more effectively.

Another responsibility of the user is to take an active role in specifying additions to the database. The maintenance of an organization's database is an ongoing task that organizations should measure constantly against their overall goals. Users thus should participate in designing the database that will help them achieve those goals. Chapter 11 discusses the role of the user in system development, which includes the design of the database.

Database Design Guidelines

A carefully designed database makes it easier for a user to query the database, modify the data, and create reports. Certain database design guidelines, including those shown in Figure 10-27, apply to databases of all sizes.

WEB INFO
WEB INFO
For more information on data and database administrators, visit the Discovering Computers 2000 Chapter 10 WEB INFO page (**www.scsite.com/dc2000/ch10/webinfo.htm**) and click DAs and DBAs.

Figure 10-27 *Guidelines for developing a database.*

Database Design Guidelines

1. Determine the purpose of the database.

2. Design the tables.

   • Design the tables on paper first.

   • Each table should contain data about one subject. The Student table, for example, contains data about students.

3. Design the fields for each table.

   • Be sure every field has a unique primary key.

   • Use separate fields for logically distinct items. For example, a name should be stored in six fields: Salutation (Mr., Mrs., Dr., etc.), First Name, Middle Name, Last Name, Suffix (Jr., Sr., etc.), and Nickname.

   • Do not create fields for information that can be derived from entries in other fields. For example, do not include a field for Age. Instead, store the birthdate and compute the age.

   • Allow enough space for each field.

   • Set default values for frequently entered data.

4. Determine the relationships among the tables.

QUALITIES OF VALUABLE INFORMATION

As with data, information should have certain characteristics to make it valuable. The characteristics of **valuable information** include being accurate, verifiable, timely, organized, meaningful, useful, and cost effective.

- **Accurate information** is correct information. Inaccurate information often is worse than no information, because **inaccurate information** can lead to incorrect decisions. Students, for example, assume that their transcripts correctly list their grades. If your transcript incorrectly reports low grades in your major courses, a potential employer might deny you an interview.

- **Verifiable** means that you can confirm information. For example, before relying on the cumulative grade point average (GPA) on your transcript, a potential employer might want to check that the GPA is calculated correctly. The potential employer can verify the accuracy of the accumulated GPA by calculating it from the individual semester GPA values.

- **Timely information** has an age suited to its use. Your transcript, for example, has value for a potential employer only if the employer receives it in time to make a hiring decision. Although most information loses its value with time, some information, such as information on trends, gains value as time passes and more information is obtained. Your transcript, for example, gains value as you complete more coursework because it reflects your work ethic and dedication over a time period.

- **Organized information** is arranged to suit the needs and requirements of the user. An advisor, for example, might want a schedule of classes organized by course codes, while a student would prefer a schedule organized by the day and time the courses meet.

- **Meaningful information** is relevant to the person who receives it. Because certain information is meaningful only to specific individuals or groups, you should eliminate unnecessary information and always consider the audience when you are accumulating or reporting information. A graduating student, for instance, probably does not need information on next year's plan for first-year student housing.

- **Cost-effective information** costs less to produce than the value of the resulting information. Most organizations periodically review the information they produce in reports to determine if the reports provide valuable information. Based on that review, the companies can determine whether to continue, scale back, or even eliminate these reports.

Sometimes the value of information is difficult to determine. If an organization cannot determine the value of information, it might choose to generate the information only as people require it, instead of on a regular basis. Another alternative is to make the information available online, thus allowing users to access and print it as they need it.

How Managers Use Information

All employees in an organization need information to perform their jobs effectively; the primary users of information, however, are managers. In an organization, **managers** are responsible for coordinating the use of resources such as people, money, materials, and information so the organization can operate efficiently and prosper. Managers work toward these goals by performing the four management activities of planning, organizing, leading, and controlling.

- **Planning** involves establishing goals and objectives and establishing the strategies or tactics needed to meet these goals and objectives.

- **Organizing** includes identifying and bringing together the resources necessary to achieve the plans of an organization. Organizing also involves establishing the management structure of an organization, such as the departments and reporting relationships.

- **Leading**, sometimes referred to as directing, involves instructing and authorizing others to perform the necessary work.

- **Controlling** involves measuring performance and, if necessary, taking corrective action.

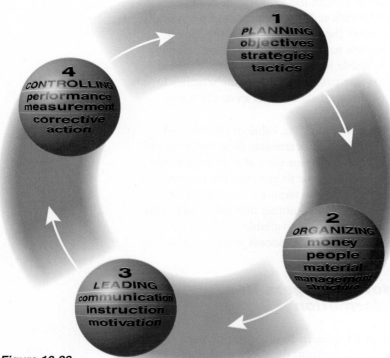

Figure 10-28

The four management activities of planning, organizing, leading, and controlling usually are performed in sequence that form a cycle.

Figure 10-28 shows how these four management activities usually are performed in a sequence that forms a recurring cycle. During the controlling activity, managers measure actual performance against a previously established plan. As a result of this measurement, they may revise the plan, which can result in additional organizational and leadership activities. Performance then is measured against the revised plan, and the cycle repeats itself. The four tasks are related and a change in one task usually affects one or more of the other tasks.

Levels of Users

The types of information required by a user often depends on the user's classification in the organization. Users typically are classified into four levels: executive management, middle management, operational management, and nonmanagement employees (Figure 10-29).

EXECUTIVE MANAGEMENT Executive **management**, also referred to as senior management or top management, includes the highest management positions in an organization. Executive management is concerned with the long-range direction of the organization. Senior managers primarily are responsible

Sample Job Titles

chief executive officer
chief Information officer
president
vice president

personnel manager
director of public relations
purchasing manager

office manager
shop floor foreman
supervisor

accountant
engineer
secretary
order entry clerk

EXECUTIVE MANAGEMENT
(strategic decisions)

MIDDLE MANAGEMENT
(tactical decisions)

OPERATIONAL MANAGEMENT
(operational decisions)

NONMANAGEMENT EMPLOYEES
(on-the-job decisions)

Figure 10-29 *The information requirements of a user often depend on the user's level in the organization. This pyramid illustrates the levels of users, sample job titles of each level of user, and the types of decisions these users make.*

for **strategic decisions** that deal with the overall goals and objectives of an organization. Executive management supervises middle management personnel.

MIDDLE MANAGEMENT

Middle management is responsible for implementing the strategic decisions of executive management. To do this, middle managers make **tactical decisions**, also called **short-range decisions**, that implement specific programs and plans necessary to accomplish the stated objectives. Middle management supervises operational management.

OPERATIONAL MANAGEMENT

Operational management supervises the production, clerical, and other nonmanagement employees of an organization. In performing their duties, operational managers make **operational decisions** that deal with day-to-day activities within the organization. The operational decisions should be consistent with and support the tactical decisions made by middle management.

NONMANAGEMENT EMPLOYEES

Nonmanagement employees, who include production, clerical, and staff personnel, also need frequent information to perform their jobs. Today, these employees have more information available to them than in the past. This is part of a trend toward giving lower-level, nonmanagement employees the information they need to make decisions previously made by managers.

TYPES OF INFORMATION SYSTEMS

An **information system** is a collection of hardware, software, data, people, and procedures that are designed to generate information that supports the day-to-day, short range, and long-range activities of users in an organization (Figure 10-30). Information systems generally are classified into five categories: office information systems, transaction processing systems, management information systems, decision support systems, and expert systems. The following sections present each of these information systems.

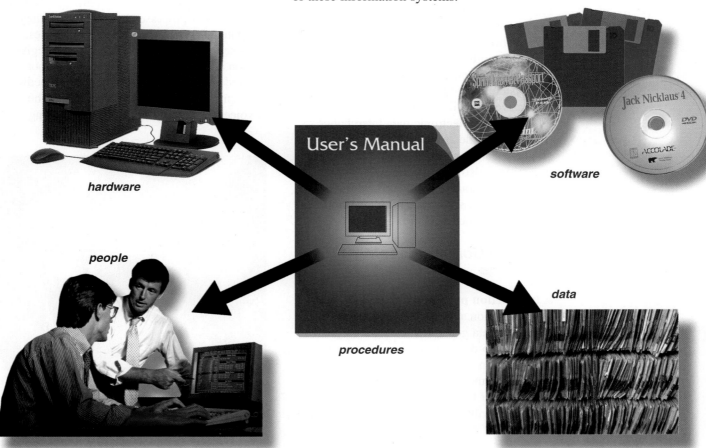

Figure 10-30 *An information system typically contains five components: hardware, software, data, people, and procedures.*

WEB INFO
WEB INFO

For more information on an office information system, visit the Discovering Computers 2000 Chapter 10 WEB INFO page (**www.scsite.com/dc2000/ch10/webinfo.htm**) and click OIS.

Office Information Systems

An **office information system**, or **OIS** (pronounced *oh-eye-ess*), is an information system that uses hardware, software, and networks to enhance work flow and facilitate communications among employees. With an office information system, also described as **office automation**, employees perform tasks electronically using computers and other electronic devices, instead of manually. With an office information system, for example, a registration department might post the class schedule on the Internet and e-mail students when the schedule is updated. In a manual system, the registration department would photocopy the schedule and mail it to each student's house.

An office information system supports a range of business office activities such as creating and distributing graphics and/or documents, sending messages, scheduling, and accounting. All levels of users from executive management to nonmanagement employees utilize and benefit from the features of an OIS.

The software an office information system uses to support these activities include word processing, spreadsheets, databases, presentation graphics, e-mail, Web browsers, Web page authoring, personal information management, and groupware. Office information systems use communications technology such as voice mail, facsimile (fax), videoconferencing, and electronic data interchange (EDI) for the electronic exchange of text, graphics, audio, and video. An office information system also uses a variety of hardware, including computers equipped with modems, video cameras, speakers, and microphones; scanners; and fax machines.

Transaction Processing Systems

A **transaction processing system (TPS)** is an information system that captures and processes data generated during an organization's day-to-day transactions (Figure 10-31). A transaction is a business activity such as a deposit, payment, order, or reservation. Clerical staff typically perform the activities associated with transaction processing, which include the following:

WEB INFO
WEB INFO

For more information on a transaction processing system, visit the Discovering Computers 2000 Chapter 10 WEB INFO page (**www.scsite.com/dc2000/ch10/webinfo.htm**) and click TPS.

1. Recording a business activity such as a student's registration, a customer's order, an employee's timecard, or a client's payment

2. Confirming an action or triggering a response, such as printing a student's schedule, sending a thank-you note to a customer, generating an employee's paycheck, or issuing a receipt to a client

3. Maintaining data, which involves adding new data, changing existing data, or removing unwanted data

Transaction processing systems were among the first computerized systems developed to process business data — a function originally called **data processing**. Usually, the TPS computerized an existing manual system to allow for faster processing, reduced clerical costs, and improved customer service.

The first transaction processing systems usually used batch processing. With **batch processing**, transaction data is collected over a period of time and all transactions are processed later, as a group. As computers became more powerful, system developers built online transaction processing systems. With **online transaction processing (OLTP)**, the computer processes transactions as they are entered. When you register for classes, your school probably uses OLTP. The registration administrative assistant enters your desired schedule and the computer immediately prints your statement of classes. The invoices, however, often are printed using

Figure 10-31 *Transaction processing systems process the day-to-day activities of an organization.*

batch processing, meaning all student invoices are printed and mailed at a later date.

Today, most transaction processing systems use online transaction processing. Some routine processing tasks such as calculating paychecks or printing invoices, however, are performed more efficiently on a batch basis. For these activities, many organizations still use batch processing techniques.

Management Information Systems

While computers were ideal for routine transaction processing, managers soon realized that the computers' capability of performing rapid calculations and data comparisons could produce meaningful information for management. Management information systems thus evolved out of transaction processing systems. A **management information system**, or **MIS** (pronounced *em-eye-ess*), is an information

system that generates accurate, timely, and organized information so managers and other users can make decisions, solve problems, supervise activities, and track progress. Because it generates reports on a regular basis, a management information system sometimes is called a **management reporting system** (**MRS**).

Management information systems often are integrated with transaction processing systems. To process a sales order, for example, the transaction processing system records the sale, updates the customer's account balance, and makes a deduction from inventory. Using this information, the related management information system can produce reports that recap daily sales activities; summarize weekly and monthly sales activities; list customers with past due account balances; graph slow or fast selling products; and highlight inventory items that need reordering. A management information system focuses on generating information that management and other users need to perform their jobs.

An MIS generates three basic types of information: detailed, summary, and exception (Figure 10-32). **Detailed information** typically confirms transaction processing

Figure 10-32a (detailed report)

DETAILED ORDER REPORT for January 17, 2001			
Customer	Part Number	Part Description	Quantity
Arbogast Construction	87143	ink-jet printer	5
Carlton Paper Products	89620	laser printer	2
Baker Produce	98083	label printer	1
Milton Service	93042	17-inch monitor	3

Figure 10-32 Three basic types of information generated in an MIS.

Figure 10-32b (summary report)

one summary line for each part →

INVENTORY SUMMARY REPORT as of January 17, 2001 by Part Number			
Part Number	Part Description	Total Quantity on Hand	Warehouse Location
87143	ink-jet printer	972	A
89620	laser printer	509	A
98083	label printer	178	A
93042	17-inch monitor	837	C

Figure 10-32c (exception report)

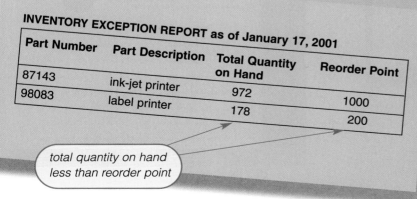

INVENTORY EXCEPTION REPORT as of January 17, 2001			
Part Number	Part Description	Total Quantity on Hand	Reorder Point
87143	ink-jet printer	972	1000
98083	label printer	178	200

total quantity on hand less than reorder point

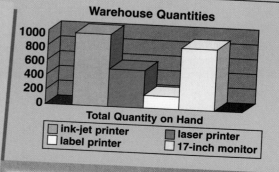

Warehouse Quantities

Total Quantity on Hand

- ink-jet printer
- label printer
- laser printer
- 17-inch monitor

activities. A Detailed Order Report is an example of a **detail report**. **Summary information** consolidates data into a format that an individual can review quickly and easily. To help synopsize information, a summary report typically contains totals, tables, or graphs. An Inventory Summary Report is an example of a **summary report**.

Exception information filters data to report information that is outside of a normal condition. These conditions, called the **exception criteria**, define the range of what is considered normal activity or status. An example of an **exception report** is an Inventory Exception Report that notifies the purchasing department of items it needs to reorder. Exception reports help managers save time because they do not have to search through a detailed report for exceptions. Instead, an exception report brings exceptions to the manager's attention in an easily identifiable form. Exception reports thus help them focus on situations that require immediate decisions or actions.

Decision Support Systems

Transaction processing and management information systems provide information on a regular basis. Frequently, however, users need information not provided in these reports to help them make decisions. A sales manager, for example, might need to determine how high to set yearly sales quotas based on increased sales and lowered product costs. Decision support systems help provide information to support such decisions.

A **decision support system** (**DSS**) is an information system designed to help users reach a decision when a decision-making situation arises. A variety of DSSs exist to help with a range of decisions. Figure 10-33, for

WEB INFO
WEB INFO

For more information on a decision support system, visit the Discovering Computers 2000 Chapter 10 WEB INFO page (www.scsite.com/dc2000/ch10/webinfo.htm) and click DSS.

Figure 10-33
A SAMPLE DSS FOR GOODYEAR CUSTOMERS

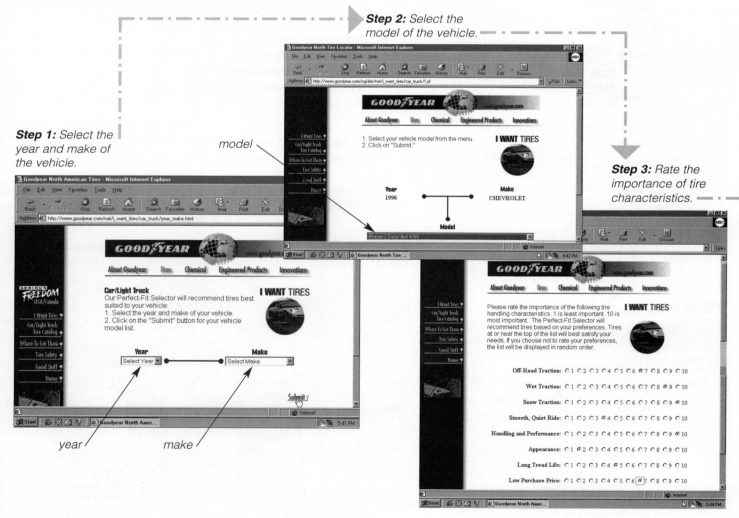

Step 1: Select the year and make of the vehicle.

Step 2: Select the model of the vehicle.

Step 3: Rate the importance of tire characteristics.

example, shows a DSS that helps users select a Goodyear tire that best suits their needs.

A decision support system uses data from internal and/or external sources. **Internal sources** of data might include sales, manufacturing, inventory, or financial data from an organization's database. Data from **external sources** could include interest rates, population trends, costs of new housing construction, or raw material pricing. Users of a DSS, often managers, can manipulate the data used in the DSS to help with decisions.

Some decision support systems include query languages, statistical analysis capabilities, spreadsheets, and graphics that help you extract data and evaluate the results. Some decision support systems also include capabilities that allow you to create a model of the factors affecting a decision. A simple model for determining the best product price, for example, would include factors for the expected sales volume at each price level. With the model, you can ask what-if questions by changing one or more of the factors and viewing the projected results. Many people use application software packages to perform DSS functions. Using spreadsheet software, for example, you can complete simple modeling tasks or what-if scenarios.

A special type of DSS, called an **executive information system** (**EIS**), is designed to support the information needs of executive management. Information in an EIS is presented in charts and tables that show trends, ratios, and other managerial statistics (Figure 10-34). Because executives usually focus on strategic issues, EISs rely on external data

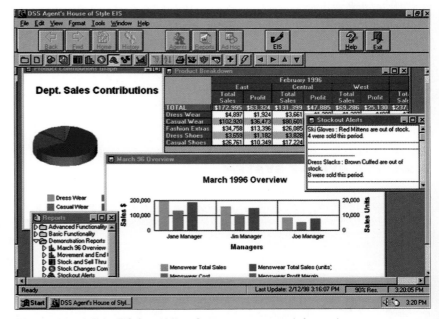

Figure 10-34 *This EIS from MicroStrategy presents information to executive management in the form of tables and charts.*

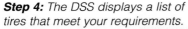

Step 4: *The DSS displays a list of tires that meet your requirements.*

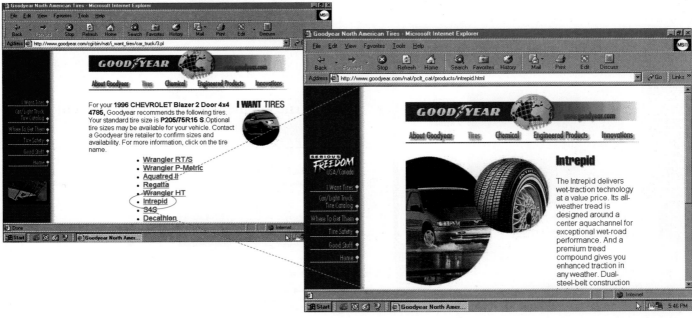

WEB INFO

For more information
on data warehouses,
visit the Discovering
Computers 2000
Chapter 10 WEB INFO
page (**www.scsite.com/
dc2000/ch10/webinfo.htm**)
and click Data Warehouses.

sources, such as the Dow Jones News/Retrieval service or the Internet. These external data sources can provide current information on interest rates, commodity prices, and other leading economic indicators.

To store all the necessary decision-making data, DSSs or EISs often use extremely large databases, called data warehouses. A **data warehouse** stores and manages the data required to analyze historical and current business circumstances.

Expert Systems

An **expert system** is an information system that captures and stores the knowledge of human experts and then imitates human reasoning and decision-making processes for those who have less expertise (Figure 10-35). Expert systems are composed of two main components: a knowledge base and inference rules. A **knowledge base** is the combined subject knowledge and experiences of the human experts. The **inference rules** are a set of logical judgments applied to the knowledge base each time a user describes a situation to the expert system (Figure 10-36).

Although expert systems can help decision-making at any level in an organization, nonmanagement employees are the primary users, who utilize them to help with job-related decisions. Expert systems also successfully have resolved such diverse

Figure 10-35
A SAMPLE EXPERT SYSTEM

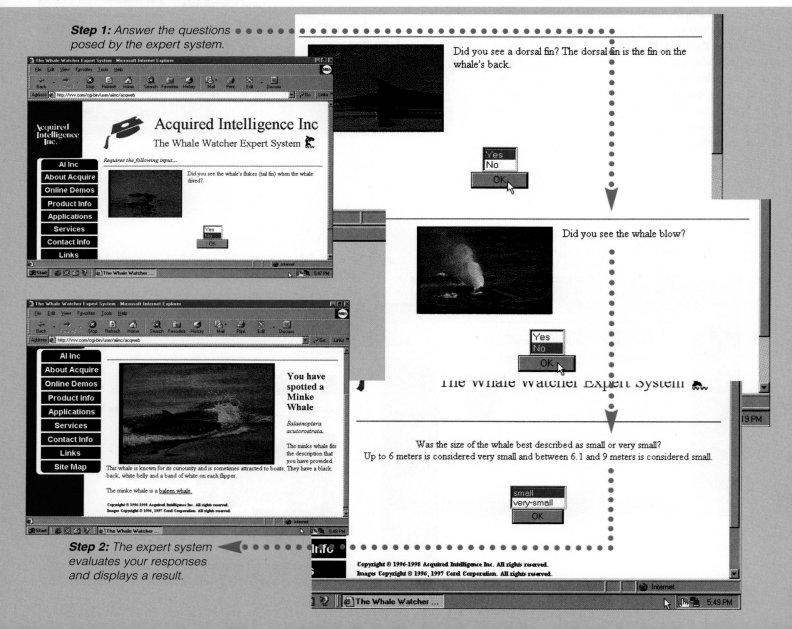

Step 1: Answer the questions posed by the expert system.

Step 2: The expert system evaluates your responses and displays a result.

problems as diagnosing illnesses, searching for oil, and making soup.

Expert systems are one part of an exciting branch of computer science called artificial intelligence. **Artificial intelligence (AI)** is the application of human intelligence to computers. AI technology can sense your actions and, based on logical assumptions and prior experience, will take the appropriate action to complete the task. AI has a variety of capabilities, including speech recognition, logical reasoning, and creative responses.

Experts predict that AI eventually will be incorporated into most computer systems and many individual software applications. Many word processing programs, for example, already include speech recognition.

Integrated Information Systems

With today's sophisticated hardware, software, and communications technologies, it often is difficult to classify a system as belonging uniquely to one of the five information system types discussed. Much of today's application software, for instance, supports transaction processing and generates management information. Other applications provide transaction processing, management information, and decision support. Although expert systems still operate primarily as separate systems, organizations increasingly are consolidating their information needs into a single, integrated information system.

WEB INFO
WEB INFO

For more information on an expert system, visit the Discovering Computers 2000 Chapter 10 WEB INFO page (**www.scsite.com/dc2000/ch10/webinfo.htm**) and click Expert System.

Figure 10-36 *The inference rules for the sample expert system shown in Figure 10-35.*

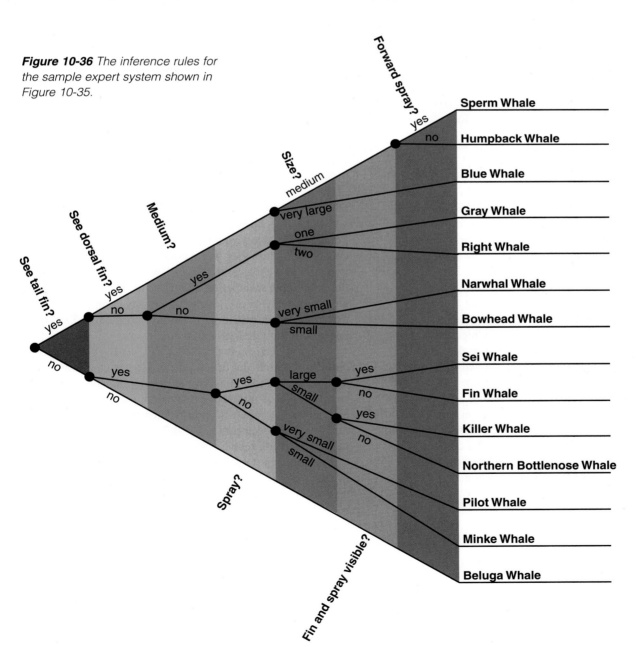

TECHNOLOGY TRAILBLAZER

LARRY ELLISON

Larry Ellison is the most flamboyant figure in Silicon Valley. Recently ranked the fifth wealthiest man in the world, Ellison does nothing in a half-hearted manner. His flashy lifestyle features designer clothes, expensive cars, celebrity friends, and a $40-million mansion that replicates a Japanese palace. Ellison's toys include a jet fighter and a 78-foot racing yacht, and his leisure activities are hardly tame — he has broken bones both surfing and bicycle racing. Yet, despite his larger-than-life presence, Ellison's greatest impact has been as founder and CEO of Oracle Corporation, the world's dominant software database company.

Ellison says he was raised in a lower middle-class neighborhood on the south side of Chicago. Notwithstanding his humble beginnings, Ellison downplays any rags-to-riches story. "The gap between rich and poor was not nearly so great as it is today," Ellison recalls, "and certainly the opportunity gap was very different than it is today." He had an early interest in science and mathematics but little enthusiasm for school. Ellison preferred constructing solutions to memorizing facts. "I was a lousy student," he says, "but a good builder." Colleagues maintain that Ellison still is at his best when faced with difficult technical problems.

Ellison attended the University of Chicago but did not graduate. Although he had no formal background in computer science, Ellison left school, moved to California, and obtained a job as a computer programmer. "I just picked up a book and started programming." At about this time, he also visited the city of Kyoto. Ellison is fascinated with Japanese culture and insists it influences his approach to business and to life. He believes Oracle's corporate philosophy reflects the same combination of confidence and humility evidenced in Japanese thinking.

After returning from Japan and working in some unsuccessful companies doomed by poor management, Ellison decided to start his own company. "I thought, I don't need leadership to [bankrupt a company]. I can run a company out of business all by myself… Next time, if the company was going to go down, I was going to be out front." In 1976, Ellison learned about relational database theory. Relational databases were powerful and easy-to-use, but industry experts believed they were too slow to be commercially feasible. Accepting the challenge, Ellison set out to develop a commercially viable relational database. With three cofounders, Ellison started Oracle Corporation in 1977.

"There is really nothing riskier than not taking risks," Ellison says. "When you think you have this really great idea and everyone else thinks you're nuts, there's one of two possibilities: you have a really great idea, [or] the other possibility is you're nuts." Ellison recognized that advances in technology had made relational databases practical. For two years, Oracle's cofounders worked as consultants while they wrote code. When the Oracle relational database was released, Ellison spent five weeks on the road doing installation and training. The product was an immediate success, changing the way companies stored and managed information. From four consultants Oracle has grown to more than 4,000 employees.

Today, Ellison is Oracle's CEO, yet his passion remains research and development. He has committed his time, insight, and enthusiasm to developing and promoting such projects as interactive television, parallel processing, and network computers. Industry insiders claim he also maintains an eccentric feud with Bill Gates and Microsoft, to which Ellison replies, "Eccentric? Me? Eccentric? Silly. Certainly, I want Oracle to be the largest software company in the world. If I didn't, they should get rid of me. That's my job. It's more fun being first than second." Ellison has been described as being everything from a "charming rogue" to "a bit of P.T. Barnum," but there is one thing he has never been called — boring.

COMPANY ON THE CUTTING EDGE

COMPANY ON THE CUTTING EDGE

ORACLE CORPORATION

In 1977, Larry Ellison and three colleagues founded Oracle Corporation on a wish and a prayer. Their wish was that they would find financial backing for the fledgling company. They did not. Their prayer was that they could successfully develop and market a new type of database.

They did. Two decades later, Oracle is the world's second largest software company and the foremost supplier of information management software.

Databases are crucial to a prosperous business. Well-maintained databases help a company track production, sales, costs, and profits. Early business databases were hierarchical — fast but functionally limited. In 1976, IBM research published a paper detailing the merits of relational databases and SQL, a language for accessing the databases. Relational databases offered an improved way to organize and connect data. Yet, conventional wisdom insisted they were too slow to be practical commercially. Oracle's cofounders, however, believed relational databases could be made commercially viable. "Because conventional wisdom was in error," Ellison recalls, "this gave us a tremendous advantage: we were the only ones trying to do it."

Silicon Valley investors were unenthusiastic about new software companies with untried ideas. Fortunately, writing software is not a capital-intensive business. Each Oracle cofounder scraped up $2,000 to start the company. While they wrote database code, the Oracle quartet ran a successful consultant business. Much to their banker's dismay, after two years and with $200,000 in their account, the foursome quit consulting to concentrate on product development. The timing was almost perfect; the account lasted just until the release of the Oracle relational database in 1979.

Oracle's first customer was Wright-Patterson Air Force Base. "Who but the Federal Government would buy database technology from four guys in California?" Ellison asks. As it turns out, the Federal Government made a wise decision. Oracle's relational database software set a new standard for business databases, changing the way companies stored and managed information. For the first time separate data tables, such as factory production records and sales orders, could be connected by a common field, such as a product number. Companies could construct data relationships that might have taken months to develop with a hierarchical database, if they could be developed at all.

As one of the first companies to produce network computing databases and products, Oracle seized a dominant place in the database market. According to a recent survey, Oracle receives forty percent of the almost $9 billion spent worldwide on purchasing and maintaining relational databases. Oracle8, the company's flagship product, is a network computing database that manages large amounts of information reliably, securely, and economically. Oracle develops and markets Oracle® database servers for data management, tools for creating network applications, and packaged application software for business operations. In 1996, Oracle introduced Network Computing Architecture™, which allows applications to be developed on various platforms and used across both corporate networks and on the Web. Oracle also has worked on projects such as network computers, video-on-demand, and massively parallel computing. In addition, Oracle offers consulting, support, and educational services.

Oracle's typical customer is a large, Fortune 500 company with a substantial investment in databases and related software. Because a complete Oracle system, including hardware, can cost $125 million, some suggest that the well of potential Oracle customers may be running dry. Large corporations are unlikely to buy more databases, and smaller companies might settle for less powerful, and less expensive, solutions. Yet, with 36,000 employees worldwide, earnings of more than $955 million, revenues up twenty-six percent over the past year, and a variety of innovative products and ideas, Oracle's leadership remains optimistic. For Ellison, Oracle's goal remains clear: "We want to make it easy for anyone in a company to access information."

CHAPTER 1 2 3 4 5 6 7 8 9 **10** 11 12 13 14 INDEX

 www.scsite.com/dc2000/ch10/brief.htm

WEB INSTRUCTIONS: *To display this page from the Web, launch your browser and enter the URL,* www.scsite.com/dc2000/ch10/brief.htm. *Click the links for current and additional information. To listen to an audio version of this IN BRIEF, click the Audio button to the right of the title, IN BRIEF, at the top of the page. To play the audio, RealPlayer must be installed on your computer (download by clicking* here*).*

1. How Is Data Different from Information?

Data is a collection of items such as words, numbers, images, and sounds that are not organized and have little meaning individually. Data is processed into information. **Information** is data that is organized, has meaning, and, therefore, is useful. A database is a collection of data organized in a manner that allows access, retrieval, and use of that data.

2. Why Are Data and Information Important to an Organization?

Organizations need data and information to complete many business activities. Information allows a company to make decisions and develop, create, and distribute products and services. Because information is generated with data, an organization must manage, maintain, and protect its data resources.

3. What Is the Hierarchy of Data?

Data is organized in a hierarchy (ranking) in which each higher level is composed of elements from the level preceding it. Different terms describe the various levels. A byte represents a **character**, such as a number, a letter, a punctuation mark, or another symbol. A **field** is a combination of one or more characters and is the smallest unit of data that can be accessed. A record is a group of related fields. A **data file**, also called a **file**, is a collection of related records stored on a disk. A database is a group of related data files.

4. What Are Data Maintenance Techniques?

Data maintenance refers to procedures used to keep data current. Data maintenance includes adding records when additional data is needed to keep a file up to date, changing records to correct inaccurate data or update older data, deleting records when they no longer are needed, and validating data to determine its accuracy.

5. How Is File Processing Different from Databases?

In a file processing system, each department within an organization has its own set of files, designed specifically for their own applications, and the records in one file are not related to the records in another file. Disadvantages of file processing are **data redundancy** (duplication of data) and **isolated data** (data that is difficult to access). A database is a single, shared collection of data that can be used by many application programs in an organization. The **database approach** reduces data redundancy and development time, improves data integrity, facilitates data sharing, and makes reporting easier.

6. What Are the Advantages of Using a Database Management System (DBMS)?

A database management system (DBMS) is a software program designed to control access to the database and manage data resources efficiently. As well as the advantages of the database approach, database management systems include a **data dictionary** that stores data about each file, and provides functions such as data maintenance and retrieval, data security, and **backup** and recovery.

 www.scsite.com/dc2000/ch10/brief.htm

7. What Are the Characteristics of Relational and Object-Oriented Databases?

A **relational database** is based on the relational data model and stores data in tables that consist of rows and columns. A file is referred to as a **relation** or **table**, a record as a **tuple** or **row**, and a field as an **attribute** or **column**. A relational database also stores associations among data, which are called **relationships**. An **object-oriented database** is based on an object-oriented data model and thus, maintains objects. An **object** is an item that can contain both data and the activities that read or manipulate the data. Object-oriented databases can store more types of data and access that data faster than relational databases.

8. How Is a Query Language Used?

A **query language** consists of simple, English-like statements used to specify the data you want. Structured Query Language (SQL) is used to manipulate and retrieve data in relational databases. SQL includes keywords and rules used to implement **relational algebra** operations. **Object query language** (OQL) is a query language often used to manipulate and retrieve data in object-oriented and object-relational databases. OQL uses many of the same rules, grammar, and vocabulary as SQL.

9. What Are the Responsibilities of Data and Database Administrators?

A **data administrator** (**DA**) designs a database; that is, the DA determines the proper placement of fields, defines data relationships, and outlines access privileges. The **database administrator (DBA)** is responsible for creating and maintaining the data dictionary, establishing and monitoring database security, monitoring database performance, and implementing and testing backup and recovery procedures.

10. What Are the Qualities of Valuable Information?

Valuable information is **accurate** (correct), **verifiable** (capable of being confirmed), **timely** (of an age suited to its use), **organized** (arranged to meet user requirements), **meaningful** (relevant to the person who receives it), and **cost-effective** (less expensive to produce than its ultimate value).

11. What Are Different Types of Information Systems?

An **information system** is a collection of hardware, software, data, people, and procedures designed to generate information that supports the activities of users in an organization. An **office information system** (**OIS**) uses hardware, software, and networks to enhance work flow and facilitate communications among employees. A **transaction processing system** (**TPS**) is an information system that captures and processes data generated during an organization's day-to-day transactions. A management information system (MIS) generates accurate, timely and organized information so managers can make decisions, solve problems, supervise activities, and track progress. A **decision support system** (**DSS**) is an information system designed to help users when a decision-making situation arises. An **expert system** is an information system that captures the knowledge of human experts and then imitates human reasoning and decision-making processes for those who have less expertise.

SHELLY
CASHMAN
SERIES®

**DISCOVERING
COMPUTERS
2000**

CHAPTER 1 2 3 4 5 6 7 8 9 **10** 11 12 13 14 INDEX

KEY TERMS

www.scsite.com/dc2000/ch10/terms.htm

WEB INSTRUCTIONS: *To display this page from the Web, launch your browser and enter the URL, www.scsite.com/dc2000/ch10/terms.htm. Scroll through the list of terms. Click a term to display its definition and a picture. Click KEY TERMS on the left to redisplay the KEY TERMS page. Click the TO WEB button for current and additional information about the term from the Web. To see animations, Shockwave and Flash Player must be installed on your computer (download by clicking here).*

access privileges (10.18)
accurate information (10.25)
after image (10.18)
alphabetic check (10.8)
artificial intelligence (AI) (10.33)
attribute (10.20)
backup (10.18)
backward recovery (10.19)
batch processing (10.28)
before image (10.18)
character (10.4)
check digit (10.8)
column (10.20)
completeness check (10.8)
computer-aided design (CAD) database (10.22)
consistency check (10.8)
controlling (10.26)
cost-effective information (10.25)
criteria (10.15)
data (10.2)
data administrator (DA) (10.24)
data dictionary (10.14)
data entry form (10.16)
data file (10.4)
data integrity (10.2)
data maintenance (10.4)
data model (10.19)
data processing (10.28)
data security (10.3)
data type (10.4)
data warehouse (10.32)
database (10.2)
database administrator (DBA) (10.24)
database approach (10.10)
database management system (DBMS) (10.13)
decision support system (DSS) (10.30)
default value (10.14)
detail report (10.30)
detailed information (10.29)
exception criteria (10.30)
exception information (10.30)
executive information system (EIS) (10.31)
executive management (10.26)
expert system (10.32)
external sources (10.31)
field (10.4)
field length (10.4)
file (10.4)
file maintenance (10.4)

TO WEB

TRANSACTION PROCESSING SYSTEM (TPS): Information system that captures and processes data generated during an organization's day-to-day transactions. A transaction is a business activity such as a deposit, payment, order, or reservation, and typically is performed by clerical staff. (10.28)

file processing system (10.9)
form (10.16)
forward recovery (10.19)
full-update privileges (10.18)
garbage in, garbage out (GIGO) (10.3)
groupware database (10.22)
hierarchical database (10.19)
hypermedia database (10.22)
hypertext database (10.22)
inaccurate information (10.25)
inference rules (10.32)
information (10.2)
information system (10.27)
internal sources (10.31)
join operation (10.21)
key field (10.4)
knowledge base (10.32)
leading (10.26)
management information system (MIS) (10.29)
management reporting system (MRS) (10.29)
managers (10.25)
meaningful information (10.25)
middle management (10.27)
multimedia database (10.22)
network database (10.19)
nonmanagement employees (10.27)
numeric check (10.8)

object (10.22)
object query language (OQL) (10.22)
object-oriented database (10.22)
object-relational data model (10.19)
object-relational databases (10.22)
office automation (10.28)
office information system (OIS) (10.28)
online transaction processing (OLTP) (10.28)
operational decisions (10.27)
operational management (10.27)
organized information (10.25)
organizing (10.25)
planning (10.25)
primary key (10.4)
program files (10.4)
projection operation (10.21)
query (10.15)
query language (10.15)
query-by-example (QBE) (10.15)
range check (10.8)
read-only privileges (10.18)
record (10.4)
relation (10.20)
relational algebra (10.21)
relational database (10.19)
relationships (10.20)
report generator (10.16)
report writer (10.16)
rollback (10.19)
rollforward (10.19)
row (10.20)
selection operation (10.21)
short-range decisions (10.27)
strategic decisions (10.27)
Structured Query Language (SQL) (10.21)
summary information (10.30)
summary report (10.30)
table (10.20)
tactical decisions (10.27)
timely information (10.25)
transaction processing system (TPS) (10.28)
tuple (10.20)
validation (10.7)
validation rules (10.7)
validity check (10.7)
valuable information (10.25)
verifiable (10.25)

CHAPTER 1 2 3 4 5 6 7 8 9 **10** 11 12 13 14 **INDEX**

AT THE MOVIES   www.scsite.com/dc2000/ch10/movies.htm

WELCOME to VIDEO CLIPS from

WEB INSTRUCTIONS: *To display this page from the Web, launch your browser and enter the URL,* www.scsite.com/dc2000/ch10/movies.htm. *Click a picture to view a video. After watching the video, close the video window and then complete the exercise by answering the questions about the video. To view the videos, RealPlayer must be installed on your computer (download by clicking* here).

1   Biz Database Privacy

Using online information available on the World Wide Web, you can search a database of phone numbers, names, addresses, and even maps to find anyone you want. How do you feel about that? Do you think you should have a right to own your personal information? Or is it public information? Much of this information already is available in local government offices. How is it different if it's on the Internet? For further research on this topic, use a search engine to conduct a search for your own name on the Internet. How many times does your name appear on the Web? Are you listed in any online phone books or e-mail directories? Type `http://people.yahoo.com/` to see if you are listed in its database.

2   Illicit Term Papers

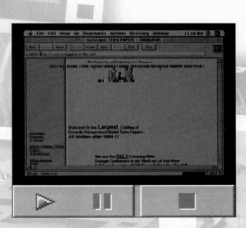

Some Web sites sell pre-written term papers for students to download, customize, and turn in as their own. Does the Internet facilitate cheating? In late 1997, Boston University sued eight online-term-paper vendors for distributing and selling term papers and contributing to cheating. They also listed "Purchased term papers and turned in as own work" as an example of academic misconduct. Should it be against the law for a business to sell term papers over the Net? Why or why not?

3   Internet Security

When visiting a Web site, you often are asked to complete information about yourself in a registration form. But without your even knowing it, you might be providing even more information. Should a company be required to tell you if it is collecting your personal information and storing it in a database? What kind of data and information can someone operating a Web site learn from your computer? What precautionary steps can you take to keep companies from recording your personal data and information?

SHELLY
CASHMAN
SERIES

DISCOVERING
COMPUTERS
2000

Student Exercises
WEB INFO
IN BRIEF
KEY TERMS
AT THE MOVIES
CHECKPOINT
AT ISSUE
CYBERCLASS
HANDS ON
NET STUFF
Special Features
TIMELINE 2000
GUIDE TO WWW SITES
MAKING A CHIP
BUYER'S GUIDE 2000
CAREERS 2000
TRENDS 2000
CHAT
INTERACTIVE LABS
NEWS
HOME

SHELLY
CASHMAN
SERIES®
DISCOVERING
COMPUTERS
2000

Student Exercises
WEB INFO
IN BRIEF
KEY TERMS
AT THE MOVIES
CHECKPOINT
AT ISSUE
CYBERCLASS
HANDS ON
NET STUFF
Special Features
TIMELINE 2000
GUIDE TO WWW SITES
MAKING A CHIP
BUYER'S GUIDE 2000
CAREERS 2000
TRENDS 2000
CHAT
INTERACTIVE LABS
NEWS
HOME

CHAPTER 1 2 3 4 5 6 7 8 9 10 11 12 13 14 INDEX

CHECKPOINT   www.scsite.com/dc2000/ch10/check.htm

WEB INSTRUCTIONS: *To display this page from the Web, launch your browser and enter the URL,* www.scsite.com/dc2000/ch10/check.htm. *Click the links for current and additional information. To experience the animation and interactivity, Shockwave and Flash Player must be installed on your computer (download by clicking* here).

Label the Figure

Instructions: *Identify each component of a relational database.*

1._____

2._____

3._____

4._____

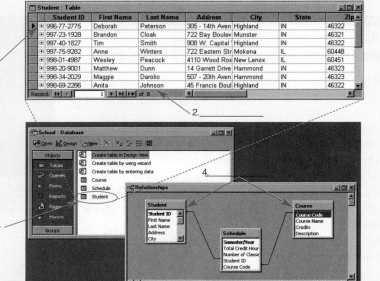

Matching

Instructions: *Match each validity check from the column on the left with the best description from the column on the right.*

_____ 1. alphabetic/numeric check

_____ 2. completeness check

_____ 3. range check

_____ 4. consistency check

_____ 5. check digit

a. Tests data to ascertain whether it was entered consistently by a qualified user.
b. Determines whether a number is within specified limits.
c. Verifies the accuracy of a primary key.
d. Ensures that letters are entered into alphabetic fields and numbers are entered into numeric fields.
e. Tests data to determine whether a known relationship between the fields is reasonable.
f. Verifies that all required data is present.
g. Ensures that each alphabetic field and each numeric field contain an appropriate number of characters.

Short Answer

Instructions: *Write a brief answer to each of the following questions.*

1. Why are data integrity and data security important? _____ What is GIGO? _____
2. What are access privileges? _____ How are read-only privileges different from full-update privileges? _____
3. How is a hierarchical database different from a network database? _____ Why do database developers prefer relational and object-oriented data models? _____
4. What is relational algebra? _____ How are the projection operator, selection operator, and join operator different? _____
5. What do the four management activities involve? _____ How are the information requirements of executive management, middle management, operational management, and nonmanagement employees different? _____

AT ISSUE   www.scsite.com/dc2000/ch10/issue.htm

WEB INSTRUCTIONS: *To display this page from the Web, launch your browser and enter the URL, www.scsite.com/dc2000/ch10/issue.htm. Click the links for current and additional information.*

In California, police officers employ a controversial database. Based on Megan's Law – the statute named for a seven-year-old girl who was violated and killed by a convicted child molester – the database lists the names and ZIP codes of 64,000 registered offenders. Touted as a valuable tool in crime prevention, people outside of law enforcement also may be using the database; one paroled offender's car was firebombed only days after his name was listed. Some fear the database will spur more vigilantism. Do you think a database of paroled or released criminal offenders should be compiled? Why or why not? Should such a database include accused, but not convicted, offenders? Why or why not? Where such a database is developed, who should have access to it? Why?

SoundScan revolutionized the recording industry. SoundScan is a database, put together using point-of-sale data, that shows what music is selling, where it is selling, and the stores in which it is selling. By purchasing the database, record producers can decide on artists to contract, and merchants can determine the music to market. SoundScan is attempting to make a similar impact on the publishing industry with BookScan, but not everyone is enthusiastic. Many fear that if publishers and vendors become too enamored with sales figures, titles that slowly gain recognition over time may never be given a chance. New authors could be ignored, no matter how good their work. Overall, will a book-sales database have a positive or negative effect on publishers? Retailers? Authors? Readers? Why? How could potential disadvantages be addressed?

Because it is a comprehensive collection of data, database security is an important consideration. Most database management systems can specify various access privileges. Individuals may be granted no access privileges, read-only privileges (data can be read but not changed), limited access privileges (only certain data can be read and/or changed), or full-update privileges (all data can be read and changed). When a database is created, access policies are determined. Consider a student file. In addition to a name, address, and grades, this file may contain information on ethnicity, gender, finances, family, health, activities, discipline, and so on. Using this file as an example, list the access privileges each of the following should be granted: the student, other students, faculty, administrators, potential employers, and other outside groups. Explain your answers.

In Feist v. Rural Telephone, the United States Supreme Court removed much of the protection that corporate databases previously enjoyed. The court decision held that, despite the effort involved in compiling a database, database creators did not deserve copyright protection, the legal right of creators to the exclusive distribution of their work, in the same manner as a book. That is, corporate databases can be copied, distributed, or displayed without the creator's permission. Why did the court decide as it did? In terms of copyright protection, how is a book different from a database? Was the Supreme Court's decision the right one? Why or why not? What effect, if any, will the decision have on database administrators? Why?

For many students, the cost to go to college is even more depressing than the quality of some dining hall food. A free Web service can ease the money crunch by helping students find scholarships that match their qualifications, plans, and chosen schools. When a student registers, the service queries a database of more than 180,000 records in search of suitable scholarships and then returns the results. Ironically, those least likely to benefit from the scholarship search may be those who need it most. Because students from less affluent backgrounds usually have less computer experience, they may be unaware of, or unable to access, the scholarship search service. How can the Web service be made more universally available? Who do you think should assume the leading role in extending access to the service? Why?

CHAPTER 1 2 3 4 5 6 7 8 9 **10** 11 12 13 14 INDEX

CYBERCLASS   www.scsite.com/dc2000/ch10/class.htm

WEB INSTRUCTIONS: *To display this page from the Web, launch your browser and enter the URL,* www.scsite.com/dc2000/ch10/class.htm. *To start Level I CyberClass, click a Level I link on this page or enter the URL,* www.cyber-class.com. *Click the Student button, click* Discovering Computers 2000 *in the list of titles, and then click the Enter a site button. To start Level II or III CyberClass (available only to those purchasers of a CyberClass floppy disk), place your CyberClass floppy disk in drive A, click Start on the taskbar, click Run on the Start menu, type* a:connect *in the Open text box, click the OK button, click the Enter CyberClass button, and then follow the instructions.*

I II III LEVEL   **1. Flash Cards**   Click Flash Cards on the Main Menu of the CyberClass web page. Click the plus sign before the Chapter 10 title and then select the subject of your choice. Answer 4 flash cards. If you missed any of the questions, select another subject and answer 4 more flash cards. Continue until you answer 4 questions in a row without missing one. All users: Answer as many more flash cards as you desire. Close the Electronic Flash Card window and the Flash Cards window by clicking the Close button in the upper-right corner.

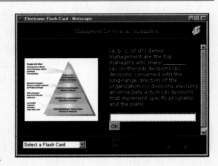

I II III LEVEL   **2. Practice Test**   Click Testing on the Main Menu of the CyberClass web page. Click the Select a book box arrow and then click Discovering Computers 2000. Click the Select a test to take box arrow and then click the Chapter 10 title in the list. Click the Take Test button. If necessary, maximize the window. Take a practice test by completing a test and clicking the Submit Test button. If you are happy with your score, hand in the results to your instructor. If you think you can do better, take another test by clicking the Take another Test button. When you are satisfied with your test score, hand in the results to your instructor.

I II III LEVEL   **3. Web Guide**   Click Web Guide on the Main Menu of the CyberClass web page. When the Guide to World Wide Web Sites page displays, click Business and Finance. Visit several of the sites. Do you find any advantage of visiting these sites over reading magazines or the newspaper? If you were investing, does the Web offer more timely information than printed materials? When you are finished, close the window. Which is your favorite site? Why? Write a brief report explaining your answers to these questions.

I II III LEVEL   **4. Company Briefs**   Click Company Briefs on the Main Menu of the CyberClass web page. Click a corporation name to display a case study. Read the case study. Write a brief report explaining the data security issues this company faces.

II III LEVEL   **5. CyberChallenge**   Click CyberChallenge on the Main Menu of the CyberClass web page. Click the Select a book box arrow and then click Discovering Computers 2000. Click the Select a board to play box arrow and then click Chapter 10 in the list. Click the Play CyberChallenge button. Maximize the CyberChallenge window. Play CyberChallenge until you answer 16 or more of the questions. Close the CyberChallenge window.

II III LEVEL   **6. Hot Links**   Click Hot Links on the Main Menu of the CyberClass web page. Review three different sites referenced in Hot Links. Write a brief report explaining why you like one site better than the others.

II III LEVEL   **7. Student Bulletin Board**   Read At Issue exercise 1 on page 10.41. Click Student Bulletin Board on the Main Menu of the CyberClass web page, click Add Topic, type your name as the topic, click the Add Topic button, type a message of 50 words or less explaining whether you think a database of paroled or released criminal offenders should be distributed to local law enforcers, and then click the Add Message button.

HANDS ON

www.scsite.com/dc2000/ch10/hands.htm

WEB INSTRUCTIONS: *To display this page from the Web, launch your browser and enter the URL, www.scsite.com/dc2000/ch10/hands.htm. Click the links for current and additional information.*

One — Managing Files and Folders

This exercise uses Windows 98 procedures. Click the Start button on the taskbar and then click Help on the Start menu. Click the Contents tab. Click the Exploring Your Computer book. Click the Files and Folders book. Click the Managing Files book. Click an appropriate Help topic to answer the following questions:

▲ How do you create a <u>folder</u>?
▲ How do you move a file or folder?
▲ How do you delete a file or folder?

Click the Close button to close the Windows Help window.

Two — Working with Folders

Right-click the My Computer <u>icon</u> on the desktop. Click Explore on the shortcut menu to open Windows Explorer. Maximize the Exploring - My Computer window. Click View on the menu bar and then click Large Icons. Insert the Discover Data Disk into drive A. If you do not have the Discover Data Disk, see the inside back cover of this book or see your instructor. If necessary, drag the vertical scroll box to the top of the scroll bar in the All Folders area. Click the 3½ Floppy (A:) icon in the All Folders area to display the contents of drive A. Click File on the menu bar, point to New, and then click Folder on the submenu. When the new folder displays, type Hands On and then press the ENTER key. Click View on the menu bar, point to Arrange Icons, and then click by Name. Click the plus sign next to the 3½ Floppy (A:) icon in the All Folders area to display the Hands On folder in the All Folders area. Click the Hands On folder in the All Folders area to display its contents. What is in the Hands On folder? Click the Close button to close the Exploring window.

Three — Working with Files in Folders

To complete this exercise, you first must complete Hands On 2 in Chapter 2 on page 2.54. Complete Hands On 2 above before proceeding with this lab. Open Windows Explorer as explained in Hands On 2. Maximize the Exploring window. Insert your <u>floppy disk</u> into drive A. Click the 3½ Floppy (A:) icon in the All Folders area to display the contents of drive A. Click the plus sign next to the 3½ Floppy (A:) icon in the All Folders area to display the Hands On folder in the All Folders area. To move the file you created in Chapter 2 (h2-2) into the Hands On folder, follow the procedure suggested in Help (see Hands On 1 above) or perform the following steps:

▲ Click the h2-2 icon to select the file.
▲ Right-drag the h2-2 icon to the Hands On folder.
▲ When the Hands On folder is highlighted, release the right mouse button.
▲ Click Move Here on the shortcut menu.

To delete file h6-2 (the copy of file h2-2 that you created in Chapter 6), follow the procedure suggested in Help (see Hands On 1 above) or perform the following steps:

▲ Right-click the h6-2 icon.
▲ Click Delete on the shortcut menu.
▲ Click Yes in the Confirm File Delete dialog box.

Click the Hands On folder in the All Folders area. What is in the Hands On folder? Click the 3½ Floppy (A:) icon in the All Folders area. What displays in the window? Click the Close button to close the Exploring window.

Student Exercises
WEB INFO
IN BRIEF
KEY TERMS
AT THE MOVIES
CHECKPOINT
AT ISSUE
CYBERCLASS
HANDS ON
NET STUFF
Special Features
TIMELINE 2000
GUIDE TO WWW SITES
MAKING A CHIP
BUYER'S GUIDE 2000
CAREERS 2000
TRENDS 2000
CHAT
INTERACTIVE LABS
NEWS
HOME

CHAPTER 1 2 3 4 5 6 7 8 9 **10** 11 12 13 14 INDEX

NET STUFF   www.scsite.com/dc2000/ch10/net.htm

WEB INSTRUCTIONS: *To display this page from the Web, launch your browser and enter the URL, www.scsite.com/dc2000/ch10/net.htm. To use the Designing a Database lab from the Web, Shockwave and Flash Player must be installed on your computer (download by clicking here).*

DESIGNING A
DATABASE LAB

1. Shelly Cashman Series Designing a Database Lab

Follow the instructions in NET STUFF1 on page 1.46 to start and use the Designing a Database lab. If you are running from the Web, enter the URL, www.scsite.com/sclabs/menu.htm; or display the NET STUFF page (see instructions at the top of this page) and then click the DESIGNING A DATABASE LAB button.

SHOPPING

2. Shopping Online

Online shopping is an increasingly prevalent Internet activity. Buying on the Web is especially popular among people with lots of money. During a recent holiday season, a survey found that almost 75 percent of upper-income families made at least one purchase online. Web sites that offer products for sale must provide database search capability as well as online order entry. Click the SHOPPING button and complete this exercise to learn more about database query and order entry in a large online music store.

NEWSGROUP
FAQs

3. Newsgroup FAQs

Just as redundant data takes up storage space and employee time, redundant questions, or frequently asked questions (FAQs), test the patience of newsgroup veterans. To spare experienced newsgroup participants from having to deal repeatedly with the same questions, most newsgroups compile a list of frequently asked questions. Click the NEWSGROUP FAQs button for a listing of newsgroups with FAQs. Click a newsgroup folder link in which you are interested. Continue clicking folder links until you see a file link called faq.html. Click the faq.html link to see the newsgroup's FAQs. Read the frequently asked questions. What question (or answer) is most surprising to you? Why?

IN THE NEWS

4. In the News

To spare harried dispatchers, police officers used to request suspect information only when it was urgent. Now, IBM's eNetwork Law Enforcement Express lets officers directly access real-time databases of stolen cars, mug shots, and warrants. With a few taps on a laptop keyboard, police officers can find out if a suspect stopped for speeding is wanted for any more serious infractions. Click the IN THE NEWS button and read a news article about a database that is being used in a new way. Who is using the database? How is it being used? How will the database benefit the user?

WEB CHAT

5. Web Chat

Most corporations have personnel databases containing data on an employee's position, salary, employment history, attendance, and job performance. Employee databases also may include a picture, personal information (health, family, interests, and so on), and the opinions of supervisors ("Has problems with authority.") Because these databases are a key factor in determining promotion, some people feel that private or unsubstantiated information has no place in personnel files. Appearance or personal history, they argue, should not affect a promotion decision, and a supervisor's opinion is, after all, only an opinion. Is this criticism of personnel databases justified? Why or why not? What kind of information legitimately can be included in a personnel database? What kind of information do you think should not be included? Why? Click the WEB CHAT button to enter a Web Chat discussion related to this topic.

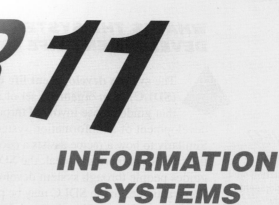

CHAPTER 11

INFORMATION SYSTEMS DEVELOPMENT

After completing this chapter,
you will be able to:

Explain the phases in the system development life cycle

Identify the guidelines for system development

Discuss the importance of project management, feasibility assessment, data and information gathering techniques, and documentation

Describe how structured tools such as entity-relationship diagrams and data flow diagrams are used in analysis and design

Differentiate between packaged software and custom software

Identify program development as part of the system development life cycle

Discuss techniques used to convert to a new system and support an information system

A system is a set of components that interact to achieve a common goal. The components of an information system include hardware, software, data, people, and procedures. The goal of an information system is to provide users with high-quality information so they can make effective decisions. The kinds and types of information that users need often change over time.

When information requirements change, the information system must meet the new requirements. In some cases, the current information system is modified; in other cases, an entirely new information system is developed. As a computer user, you someday may participate in the modification of an existing system or the development of a new system. Information system development consists of phases, referred to collectively as the system development life cycle.

This chapter discusses and illustrates the activities in each phase of this process by using a case study about Manhattan Construction. The case study addresses a request from customers asking that Manhattan Construction post construction progress information on the Web.

WHAT IS THE SYSTEM DEVELOPMENT LIFE CYCLE?

The **system development life cycle (SDLC)** is an organized set of activities that guides those involved through the development of an information system. Similarly to how a recipe assists a cook through the steps in preparing a meal, the SDLC guides people through system development. Some activities in the SDLC may be performed at the same time, while other activities are performed sequentially. Depending on the type and complexity of the information system being developed, the duration of the specific activities varies from one system to the next; in some cases, an activity may be skipped entirely. The many activities of the SDLC are grouped into five larger categories called **phases**.

WEB INFO
WEB INFO

For more information on the system development life cycle, visit the Discovering Computers 2000 Chapter 11 WEB INFO page (**www.scsite.com/dc2000/ch11/webinfo.htm**) and click SDLC.

Phases in the SDLC

The system development life cycle can be grouped into the following five major phases:

1. Planning

2. Analysis

3. Design

4. Implementation

5. Support

As illustrated in Figure 11-1, the phases in the SDLC form a loop; that is, information system development is an ongoing process for an organization. Notice that a loop forms because the support phase points to the planning phase. This connection occurs when the information system requires changing, which may happen for a variety of reasons such as a

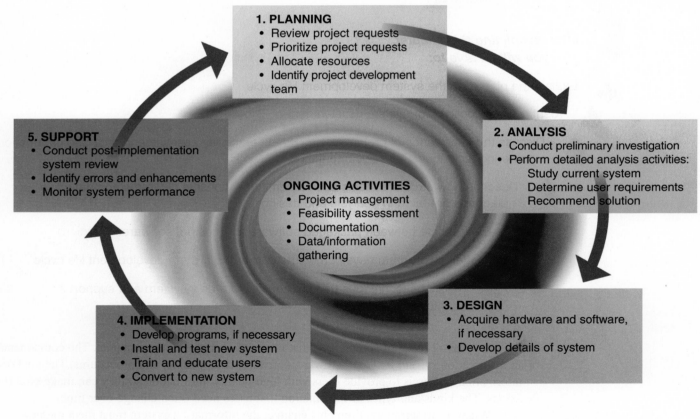

1. PLANNING
- Review project requests
- Prioritize project requests
- Allocate resources
- Identify project development team

5. SUPPORT
- Conduct post-implementation system review
- Identify errors and enhancements
- Monitor system performance

ONGOING ACTIVITIES
- Project management
- Feasibility assessment
- Documentation
- Data/information gathering

2. ANALYSIS
- Conduct preliminary investigation
- Perform detailed analysis activities:
  Study current system
  Determine user requirements
  Recommend solution

4. IMPLEMENTATION
- Develop programs, if necessary
- Install and test new system
- Train and educate users
- Convert to new system

3. DESIGN
- Acquire hardware and software, if necessary
- Develop details of system

Figure 11-1 *The system development life cycle consists of five phases that form a loop. Several ongoing activities also take place throughout the entire system development life cycle.*

report generates an incorrect total, information requirements of users change, a new version of software is released, or hardware becomes obsolete. Thus, the planning phase for a new or modified system begins and the system development life cycle starts again.

Before continuing with an explanation of each phase in the SDLC, the next section presents general guidelines for system development. Then, participants of the various phases of the life cycle are identified. Also addressed are the ongoing activities that take place throughout the entire system development life cycle, specifically project management, feasibility assessment, documentation, and data and information gathering.

Guidelines for System Development

The development of an information system should follow three general guidelines: (1) use a phased approach, (2) involve the users, and (3) develop standards.

First, the system development life cycle should be grouped into phases, each of which contains activities or tasks. Using a phased approach involves defining the phases of the SDLC and determining what activities and tasks will occur in each phase. Many SDLCs contain the five major phases outlined in Figure 11-1, while others have more or fewer phases. Regardless, all life cycles perform the same activities and tasks. For example, some SDLCs place the activity called Develop Programs, which is in the Implementation phase (see Figure 11-1) in an entirely separate phase named Construction or Development. Other differences among SDLCs are the terminology used, the order of activities, and the level of detail within each phase.

Second, system developers must involve users throughout the entire system development process. **Users** include anyone for whom the system is being built. Customers, data entry clerks, accountants, sales managers,

and owners are all examples of users. System developers must remember that they ultimately deliver the system to the user. If the system is to be successful, the user must contribute in all stages of development.

Third, standards for the development of the information system should be defined and written. **Standards** are sets of rules and procedures that an organization expects employees to accept and follow. Having standards helps multiple people working on the same development project produce consistent results. For example, one developer might refer to a part number in a database as a Part ID, while another calls it a part identification number, and still others call it a part number, part no., part #, part code, and so on. A system created in this way would be so confusing that it could never function correctly! If a standard is defined and agreed upon, then everyone involved uses one term, such as part number.

Who Participates in the System Development Life Cycle?

Any person who will be affected by the proposed information system should participate in its development. Participants can be categorized as users and information systems personnel, which includes systems analysts and programmers. A **systems analyst** is responsible for designing and developing an information system. A **programmer** uses a programming language to write the instructions necessary to direct the computer to process data into information. The next chapter discusses programming languages.

Systems analysts are the liaison between the users and the programmers; that is, they convert user requests into technical specifications. Throughout the entire life cycle, systems analysts prepare many reports, drawings, and diagrams. They also meet with users, management, other analysts, data and database administrators, network administrators, programmers, vendors, and the steering committee to discuss various aspects of the system development project (Figure 11-2). The **steering committee** is a decision-making body of an organization. Not only must systems analysts be familiar with business operations and computer programming techniques, they also must have excellent communication and interpersonal skills.

For each system development project, the organization usually establishes a **project team** to work on the project from beginning to end. The project team consists of both users and information systems personnel, usually including a systems analyst. One member of the team, designated as the **project leader**, manages and controls the budget and schedule of the project.

Project Management

Project management is the process of planning, scheduling, and then controlling the activities during the system development life cycle. The goal of project management is to deliver an acceptable system to the user in an agreed-upon time frame, while maintaining costs.

To plan and schedule a project effectively, the project leader must identify the following components of the project:

- The **scope**; that is, the goal, objectives, and expectations of the project
- Activities to be completed
- Time estimates for each activity
- Cost estimates for each activity
- The order in which activities must occur
- Activities that may be performed concurrently

Once identified, the project leader usually records these items in a **project plan**. A popular tool used to plan and schedule the time relationships among project activities is

Figure 11-2 A systems analyst meets with a variety of people during a system development project.

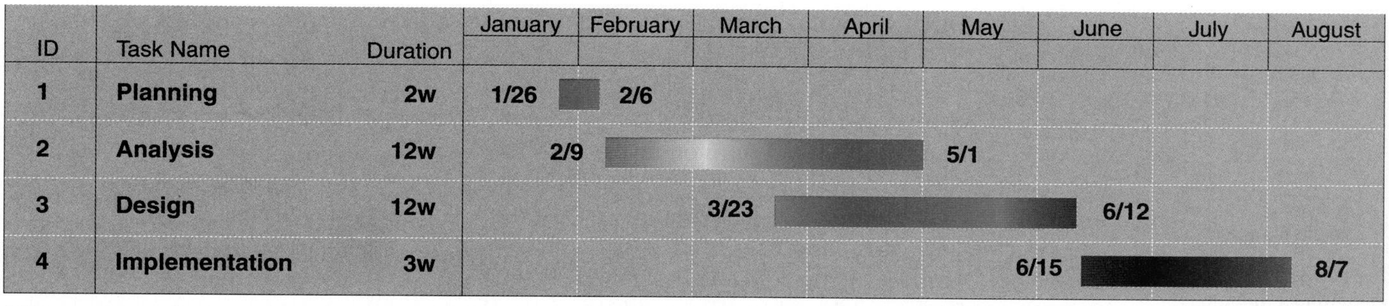

ID	Task Name	Duration	January	February	March	April	May	June	July	August
1	Planning	2w	1/26 ▮ 2/6							
2	Analysis	12w		2/9 ▬▬▬▬▬▬ 5/1						
3	Design	12w			3/23 ▬▬▬▬▬ 6/12					
4	Implementation	3w						6/15 ▬▬▬▬ 8/7		

Figure 11-3 *A Gantt chart is an effective way of showing the time relationships of a project's activities.*

called a Gantt chart (Figure 11-3). A **Gantt chart**, developed by Henry L. Gantt, is a bar chart that uses horizontal bars to represent project phases or activities. The left side, or vertical axis, displays the list of activities to be completed; and a horizontal axis across the top or bottom of the chart depicts time.

Time estimates assigned to activities should be realistic; otherwise, the success of a project is in jeopardy from the beginning. If project members do not believe the schedule is reasonable, they may not participate to the full extent of their abilities, which could lead to missed deadlines and delivery dates.

Once a project begins, the project leader monitors and controls the project. Some activities will take less time than originally planned and others will take longer. It is possible the project leader may realize that due to excessive time devoted to a particular activity, the original expected completion date of a project will not be met. In these cases, the scheduled completion date may be extended or the scope of the system development may be reduced, which results in a less comprehensive system being delivered at the originally scheduled completion date. In either case, the project leader revises the first project plan and presents the new plan to users for approval.

One aspect of managing projects is making sure each deliverable is transmitted on time and according to plan. A **deliverable** is any tangible item, such as a chart, diagram, report, or program file. **Project management software**, such as Microsoft Project, enables project leaders to plan, schedule, and control system development projects effectively and efficiently.

Feasibility Assessment

Feasibility is a measure of how suitable the development of a system will be to the organization. A project determined feasible at one point might become infeasible at a later point in the life cycle. Thus, systems analysts reassess feasibility frequently during the SDLC.

Systems analysts use four criteria to test feasibility of a project: operational feasibility, schedule feasibility, technical feasibility, and economic feasibility. **Operational feasibility** measures how well the proposed information system will work in the organization. In other words, operational feasibility addresses these questions, Will the users like the new system? Will they use it? Will it meet their requirements? Will it cause any changes to their work environment?

Schedule feasibility measures whether the established deadlines for the project are reasonable. If a deadline is not reasonable, a new schedule might be developed. If a deadline is mandatory and cannot be extended, then the scope of the project might be reduced so the mandatory deadline can be met.

Technical feasibility measures whether the organization has or can obtain the hardware, software, networks, and people needed to deliver and then support the proposed information system. For most system projects, the technology exists; the challenge is obtaining funds to pay for such resources, which is addressed in economic feasibility.

WEB INFO
WEB INFO

For more information on project management software, visit the Discovering Computers 2000 Chapter 11 WEB INFO page (**www.scsite.com/ dc2000/ch11/webinfo.htm**) and click Project Management Software.

WEB INFO
WEB INFO

For more information on a project dictionary, visit the Discovering Computers 2000 Chapter 11 WEB INFO page (**www.scsite.com/ dc2000/ch11/webinfo.htm**) and click Project Dictionary.

Economic feasibility, also called **cost/benefit feasibility**, measures whether the lifetime benefits of the proposed information system will exceed its lifetime costs. Many financial techniques, such as return on investment and payback analysis, are used to perform this cost/benefit analysis. Often, the systems analyst is unfamiliar with these financial techniques so he or she requests the assistance of a financial analyst (Figure 11-4) to assess economic feasibility.

Documentation

During the entire system development life cycle, project team members produce much documentation. **Documentation** is the compilation and summarization of data and information; it includes reports, diagrams, programs, or any other deliverable generated during the SDLC. The entire collection of documentation for a single project is stored in a **project notebook**. The project notebook might be a simple one, such as a large three-ring binder, or it may be more sophisticated, such as an automated project notebook that can be created and stored using a computerized analysis and design software package. An automated project notebook often is called a **project dictionary** or **repository**.

Well-written, thorough documentation makes it easier for everyone involved to understand all aspects of the life cycle, from economic decisions to system features to security considerations. Documentation should be an ongoing part of the system development life cycle. Too often, documentation is put off because project team members consider it an unimportant or unproductive part of system development. In these cases, documentation is pushed to the end of the life cycle or not done at all. Without complete and accurate documentation, users and information systems personnel may not know how to use, operate, or support the system. Having quality documentation also makes it easier to modify the system to meet changing information requirements.

Figure 11-4 *Often, the systems analyst requests the expertise of a financial analyst to determine if the proposed system is economically feasible.*

Data and Information Gathering Techniques

Throughout the SDLC, the project team gathers data and information. System developers need accurate and timely data and information for many reasons, such as to keep a project on schedule, to assess feasibility, and to ensure that the system is meeting requirements. Analysts and other system developers use several techniques during the system development life cycle to gather data and information: reviewing system documentation, observing, sending questionnaires, interviewing, conducting JAD sessions, and researching.

- **Reviewing Current System Documentation.** By reviewing documentation such as a company's organization chart, memos, and meeting minutes, you can learn the history of a project and aspects of the business such as its operations, weaknesses, and strengths.

- **Observing.** Observing an employee or machine can help you understand exactly how a system functions or a task is performed.

- **Sending Questionnaires.** To obtain data and information from a large number of people, you could send a questionnaire.

- **Interviewing.** The interview is the most important data and information gathering technique because it enables you to clarify responses and probe for feedback from users face to face. An interview can be unstructured or structured. An **unstructured interview** relies on the interviewee (the user) to direct the conversation based on a general subject. In a **structured interview**, the interviewer (the systems analyst) directs the conversation by following a specific set of topics and asking predefined questions. Structured interviews tend to be more successful for the systems analyst.

- **Conducting JAD Sessions.** As an alternative to the one-on-one interview, some companies use joint-application design sessions. A **joint-application design (JAD) session** is a lengthy, structured, group work session where all involved in the SDLC, including users and information systems personnel, discuss an aspect of the project (Figure 11-5). The goal of a JAD session is to obtain group agreement on an issue, such as problems associated with an existing system or information requirements of a new system.

WEB INFO

For more information on a JAD session, visit the Discovering Computers 2000 Chapter 11 WEB INFO page (**www.scsite.com/ dc2000/ch11/webinfo.htm**) and click JAD Session.

Figure 11-5 *During a JAD session, the systems analyst is the moderator, or leader, of the discussion. Another member, called the scribe, records facts and action items assigned during the discussion.*

- **Researching.** Computer magazines, trade journals, reference books, and the World Wide Web are excellent sources of information (Figure 11-6). These resources can provide you with information such as the latest hardware, software, and networking products; details of how others dealt with similar problems; and explanations of new processes and procedures.

WHAT INITIATES THE SYSTEM DEVELOPMENT LIFE CYCLE?

A user may request a new or modified information system for a variety of reasons, some external and some internal. An external reason would be that management or some other governing body mandates that you make a change to a system. For example, a nation-wide bank might require all offices to use the same e-mail software. Competition is another external reason for systems development. For example, once one bank offers Internet access

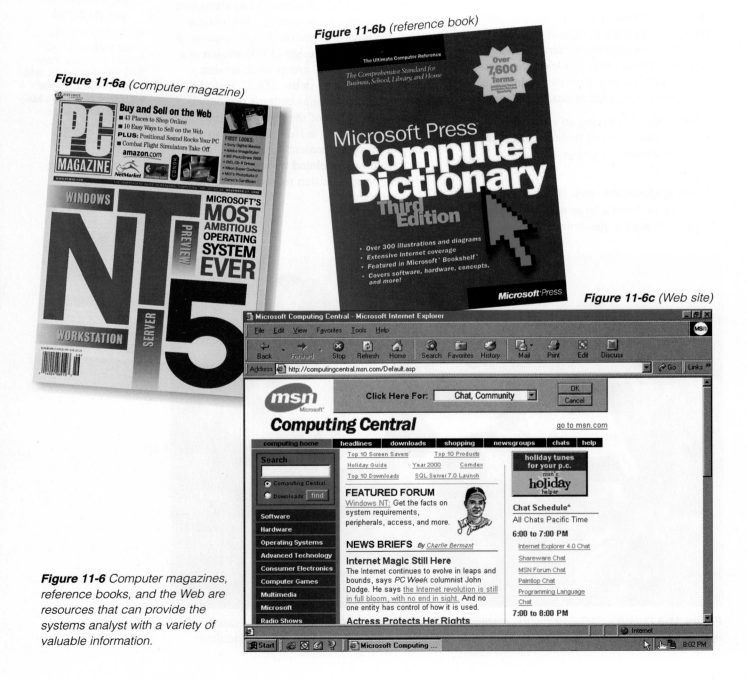

Figure 11-6b (reference book)

Figure 11-6a (computer magazine)

Figure 11-6c (Web site)

Figure 11-6 Computer magazines, reference books, and the Web are resources that can provide the systems analyst with a variety of valuable information.

to account information, others will have to follow suit, or run the risk of losing customers.

One internal reason for changing an information system is to improve or enhance it. For example, if a school wants to provide students with the ability to register for classes via the telephone, the school would have to modify the existing registration system to include this enhancement. The most obvious internal reason for changing an information system is to correct a problem. For example, the stock-on-hand listed on a report may not match the actual stock-on-hand in the warehouse.

The initial request for a new or modified information system may be communicated verbally or written as a memo or e-mail message but eventually should be written on a standard form. This form, called a **request for system services** or **project request**, becomes the first item of documentation in the project notebook (Figure 11-7). It is important that this request be completed so that all requests are organized in a similar format for the first phase of the system development life cycle: planning.

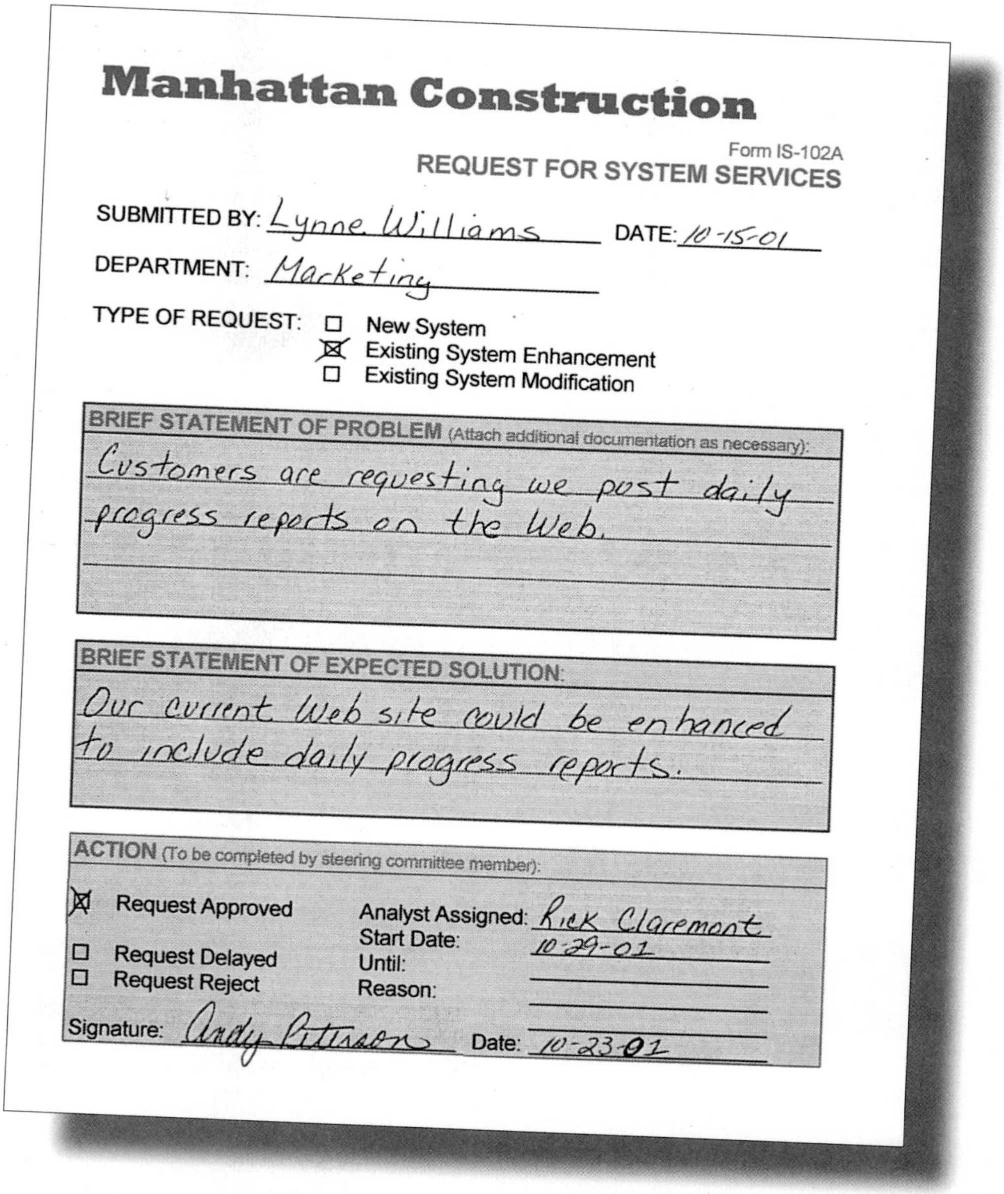

Manhattan Construction

Form IS-102A

REQUEST FOR SYSTEM SERVICES

SUBMITTED BY: _Lynne Williams_   DATE: _10-15-01_

DEPARTMENT: _Marketing_

TYPE OF REQUEST: ☐ New System
 ☒ Existing System Enhancement
 ☐ Existing System Modification

BRIEF STATEMENT OF PROBLEM (Attach additional documentation as necessary):

Customers are requesting we post daily progress reports on the Web.

BRIEF STATEMENT OF EXPECTED SOLUTION:

Our current Web site could be enhanced to include daily progress reports.

ACTION (To be completed by steering committee member):

☒ Request Approved   Analyst Assigned: _Rick Claremont_
 Start Date: _10-29-01_
☐ Request Delayed   Until:
☐ Request Reject   Reason:

Signature: _Andy Peterson_   Date: _10-23-01_

Figure 11-7 The system development life cycle usually is initiated by a project request. Requests often are documented on a form such as this Request for System Services to provide a written record of the request.

Manhattan Construction — A Case Study

To help you understand real-world applications of the system development life cycle, this chapter presents an ongoing case study following the discussion of each life cycle phase. To help you easily identify the case study in this chapter, it is shaded in the color yellow. Although the case is based on a fictitious construction company, it is designed to be as realistic as possible. The following paragraphs present a background on Manhattan Construction.

Since its inception in 1972, Manhattan Construction has earned a reputation for building high-quality, affordable homes for middle-income families. Named the 1998 Residential Builder of the Year, Manhattan Construction not only builds your dream house, but also has staff available to assist in lot selection, floor plan design, and financing. Headquartered in Chicago, Manhattan Construction is a national company with offices across the country.

Manhattan Construction prides itself on completing home construction projects within budget and on schedule. George Manhattan, president of Manhattan Construction, claims that much of the company's success is due to its impeccable record keeping. Today, practically all company operations are computerized including job bidding, cost tracking, inventory control, sales, accounts receivable, accounts payable, and payroll.

Manhattan Construction keeps its computer hardware, software, and networking capabilities up to date so it can continue to provide the best possible service to its customers. To maintain its competitive edge, Manhattan Construction has a home page on the Internet (Figure 11-8). Using this Web site, potential customers can tour completed homes and view floor plans for a variety of Manhattan Construction projects.

In last month's billing statements, Lynne Williams, vice president of marketing, included a customer satisfaction survey. After tabulating the results, Lynne was pleased to

Figure 11-8 To help you understand real-world applications of the SDLC, this chapter presents a case study about Manhattan Construction. To maintain its competitive edge, Manhattan Construction has a home page on the Internet. Many systems analysts assist companies with developing home pages, such as this, on the World Wide Web.

learn that customers are extremely satisfied with the quality of work and services provided by Manhattan Construction. The one suggestion that was mentioned several times, however, came from customers with access to the Web. For example, one customer wrote, "We are thrilled with the progress of our new home construction. It's so amazing to see our dream turn into a reality. We do appreciate receiving the monthly progress reports, but we would like more frequent updates. We wondered if you could post daily progress reports on the Web. These reports could notify us as to the physical construction progress of our home and also the financial status of the construction, which would be extremely helpful for the bank."

After Lynne discusses this suggestion with other vice presidents, she decides that posting daily progress reports on the Web not only would make Manhattan Construction customers happier, but also it could save Manhattan Construction a great deal of time and money. For example, the billing department cannot generate statements until the progress reports are complete. If the billing department mailed statements in a more timely fashion, the construction company would receive bank payouts more quickly.

Daily Web progress reporting, thus, could benefit many areas of the construction company. A key consideration, however, with progress reports posted on the Web is security; that is, ensuring that only authorized people can access this information on the Web. To begin the project investigation, Lynne fills out a Request for System Services form (Figure 11-7 on page 11.9) and submits it to Andy Peterson, chair of Manhattan Construction's steering committee.

PLANNING PHASE

The **planning phase** for a project begins when the steering committee receives a project request. As mentioned earlier, the steering committee is a decision-making body for an organization, usually consisting of five to nine people and including a mix of vice presidents, managers, users, and information systems personnel.

During the planning phase, four major activities are performed: (1) review the project requests, (2) prioritize the project requests, (3) allocate resources such as money, people, and equipment to approved projects, and (4) identify a project development team for each approved project.

Any project requests that management or some other governing body mandates receive the highest priority and are given immediate attention. The steering committee evaluates the remaining project requests based on their value to the organization. The steering committee rejects some projects and approves others. Of the approved projects, it is possible that only a few will begin their system development life cycle immediately. Others will have to wait for additional funds or resources to become available.

Planning at Manhattan Construction

After receiving the completed project request (Figure 11-7 on page 11.9), Andy Peterson distributes it to all members of the steering committee so they are prepared to discuss it at their next meeting. The steering committee members of Manhattan Construction are as follows: Andy Peterson, controller and chair of the steering committee; Kim Rivers, vice president of sales; Bill Henrickson, senior general contractor; Anita Davis, construction engineer; Rick Claremont, senior systems analyst; and Sarah Eastman, vice president of information systems. Andy also invites Lynne Williams to the next steering committee meeting to answer any additional questions because she originated the project request.

During the meeting, the committee decides that the project request identifies an enhancement to the system, instead of a problem. They feel that the nature of the enhancement (to post daily progress reports on the Web) could lead to considerable savings for the construction company, as well as provide better service for the customers. The committee discusses security features that must be included to ensure that only customers and authorized management can access these progress reports and, further, that each customer has access to only his or her construction project.

The request is approved. Andy indicates that the construction company has adequate funds in its budget to begin the project immediately. Thus, a system development project team is assembled and Rick Claremont, senior systems analyst, is assigned as the project leader for the Web Reporting Project. Rick and his team immediately begin the next phase: analysis.

ANALYSIS PHASE

The **analysis phase** consists of two major tasks: (1) conducting a preliminary investigation and (2) performing detailed analysis. Detailed analysis contains three activities: (1) study how the current system works; (2) determine the user's wants, needs, and requirements; and (3) recommend a solution.

The Preliminary Investigation

The purpose of the **preliminary investigation**, sometimes called the **feasibility study**, is to determine whether or not the problem or enhancement identified in a project request is worth pursuing. Should the company continue committing resources to this project? To answer this question, the systems analyst performs a very general investigation and then compiles his or her findings in a report also called a **feasibility study** or **feasibility report** (Figure 11-9).

Manhattan Construction
MEMORANDUM

To: **Steering Committee**
From: **Rick Claremont**
           Project Leader
Date: **November 7, 2001**
Subject: **Feasibility Report of Web Reporting Project**

Below is the feasibility report in response to the request for Web progress reports. Your approval is necessary before the next phase of the project will begin.

Introduction

The purpose of this feasibility report is to determine whether it is beneficial for Manhattan Construction to continue studying the Web Reporting Project. Customers have indicated a desire to have daily progress reports of home construction posted on the Web, instead of receiving a printed monthly progress report. This project would affect personnel involved with the current progress reports: construction crew, general contractor, office manager, administrative assistants, and the webmaster.

Existing System

Background

Manhattan Construction has tried to remain current with its computer hardware and software capabilities so it could continue to provide the best possible service to its customers. To maintain its competitive edge, a customer satisfaction survey was sent in recent monthly statements. An analysis of the results indicated that customers were, for the most part, extremely satisfied with Manhattan Construction's products and services – with one exception. Customers preferred having daily Web access to their construction progress reports. With the current procedure, customers receive a monthly progress report, which is mailed to a billing address.

Problems

The following problems have been identified with Manhattan Construction's current information system:

■ Customers are beginning to complain about the time period between progress reports

■ Some progress reports contain errors due to the administrative assistant not being able to read the general contractor's handwritten notes

■ Employees sometimes are duplicating effort by sending multiple statements to the same address – because some customers are contractors with multiple jobs

■ Resources are wasted including employee time, equipment usage, and supplies

Figure 11-9 *A feasibility report presents the results of the preliminary investigation. To be effective, the report must be prepared professionally and be well organized. This feasibility report was prepared using a professional report template provided with a popular word processing package.*

The most important aspect of the preliminary investigation is to define accurately the problem or enhancement. The perceived problem or enhancement identified in the project request may or may not be the actual problem. For example, suppose a project request indicates that the customers of a construction company complain it takes too long for the billing department to send statements. An investigation might reveal that the billing department has to request customers' construction information from other departments in the company, and the responses from the other departments can take days or weeks.

The preliminary investigation determines the real problem is that the customers' information is not easily accessible or readily available to the administrative assistants in the billing department.

The preliminary investigation begins with an interview of the user who submitted the project request. In the case of the construction company, the vice president of marketing submitted the request on behalf of the customers. Depending on the nature of the request, other users may be interviewed as well. For example, a request might involve data or a process affecting more than one

---

FEASIBILITY REPORT
Page 2

Benefits of a New System

The following benefits could be realized if a new consolidated statement system were developed:

- Customers would be more satisfied

- Bank payouts would be received sooner because billing statements could be prepared earlier

- Supplies expenses would be reduced by 20%

- Through a more efficient use of employees' time, the construction company could realize a 10% reduction in temporary clerks

- Printers would last 40% longer, due to a much lower usage rate

Feasibility of a New System

Operational

A new system will decrease the amount of equipment usage and paperwork. Employees will have time to complete meaningful job duties, alleviating the need to hire some temporary clerks. Progress reports will be available on the Web daily for access by both employees and customers. Customers will be more satisfied with the construction company's services.

Technical

Manhattan Construction will need to acquire a database server to handle the increased volume of data in its database. It also must either acquire the progress reporting software or write the programs in-house.

Economic

A detailed summary of the costs and benefits, including all assumptions, is attached. Depending on whether packaged software can be acquired or whether the programs need to be developed by our own staff, the potential costs of the proposed solution could range from $15,000 to $30,000. The estimated savings in supplies and postage alone will exceed $20,000.

If you have any questions on the attached detailed cost/benefit summary or require further information, please contact me.

Recommendation

Based on the findings presented in this report, we recommend to continue studying the Web Reporting Project.

department. In the construction company scenario just described, the systems analyst would interview the senior general contractor, the controller to determine job costing, and possibly one or two customers. During the preliminary investigation, the development team also may use other data gathering techniques, such as reviewing documentation. The time spent on the preliminary investigation is quite short when compared to the remainder of the project, usually just a few days.

Upon completion of the preliminary investigation, the systems analyst writes the feasibility report that presents his or her findings and a recommendation to the steering committee. The feasibility report contains these major sections: introduction, existing system, benefits of a new system, feasibility of a new system, and the recommendation.

The introduction identifies the purpose of the report, states the problem or enhancement, and defines the scope of the project. The existing system section outlines the background of the request and the problems and limitations of the current system. The benefits section addresses the benefits that could be realized from the proposed solution. The feasibility section assesses operational, schedule, technical, and economic feasibility of a new or modified information system. The recommendation section addresses whether or not to continue with further study of the problem or enhancement.

In some cases, as a result of the preliminary investigation, the company decides to end the project based on cost; in other words, the project is deemed infeasible so it is abandoned. If, however, the recommendation is to continue and the steering committee approves this recommendation, then detailed analysis begins.

Analysis: Preliminary Investigation at Manhattan Construction

Rick Claremont, senior systems analyst assigned to this project, meets with Lynne Williams to discuss her project request. During the interview, Rick reviews the questionnaires sent to customers and confirms that several of Manhattan Construction's customers requested daily progress reports posted on the Web.

Rick interviews Terry Hanson, vice president of construction, to obtain a general understanding of how the progress reports currently are communicated to customers. When asked for his perspective on posting daily progress reports on the Web, Terry thinks it is a great idea. Rick's final interview is with Andy Peterson, controller, to obtain some general cost and benefit figures for the feasibility study.

After preparing the feasibility study (Figure 11-9 on pages 11.12 and 11.13), Rick submits it to the steering committee for review and approval. Rick's recommendation is to continue into the detailed analysis phase for this project. The steering committee agrees. Rick and his team begin detailed analysis.

Detailed Analysis

Detailed analysis involves three major activities: (1) study the existing system in depth so you thoroughly understand the current operations, uncover all possible problems and enhancements, and determine the causes and effects of these problems or enhancements; (2) determine the users' requirements for the proposed system, which includes their wants and needs; and (3) present alternative solutions to the problem or enhancement and then recommend a proposed solution. Detailed analysis sometimes is called **logical design** because you develop the proposed solution without regard to any specific hardware or software, and no attempt is made to identify which procedures should be automated and which should be manual.

During detailed analysis, all of the data and information gathering techniques are used: reviewing system documentation, observing, sending questionnaires, interviewing, conducting JAD sessions, and researching. While obtaining data and information, the systems analyst uses a questioning approach with a problem-solving attitude. Often, systems analysts find that users do not perform certain tasks because the tasks are not efficient or effective or because they have never been performed.

An important benefit from studying the existing system and determining user requirements is that these activities build valuable relationships among the systems analyst and users. The systems analyst has much more credibility with users if he or she understands how the users currently perform their job responsibilities and respects their concerns. This point may seem obvious, but many systems are created or modified without these activities, or even worse, without any user participation.

Structured Analysis and Design Tools

The systems analyst collects vast amounts of data and information as he or she studies the current system and identifies user requirements. One of the difficulties in analyzing any system is documenting the findings in a way that can be understood by users, programmers, and other systems analysts. **Structured analysis and design** addresses this problem by using graphics to present the findings. Structured analysis and design uses tools such as entity-relationship diagrams, data flow diagrams, and the project dictionary to document specifications of an information system in the project notebook.

ENTITY-RELATIONSHIP DIAGRAMS One of the more difficult tasks in the analysis phase is to organize and document all of the data and information that an organization needs. For example, a construction company might need to store data about vendors, items, orders, customers, statements, and jobs. Each object about which data is stored, is called an **entity**. An **entity-relationship diagram (ERD)** is a tool that represents graphically the associations between entities in the project (Figure 11-10).

WEB INFO

For more information on an entity-relationship diagram, visit the Discovering Computers 2000 Chapter 11 WEB INFO page (**www.scsite.com/dc2000/ch11/webinfo.htm**) and click ERD.

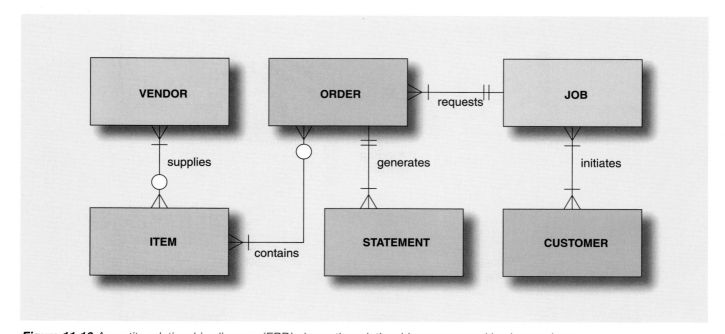

Figure 11-10 *An entity-relationship diagram (ERD) shows the relationships among entities in a project.*

On the ERD, entity names usually are described with a noun and written in all capital letters. Relationships describe the association between two entities. The relationship between the CUSTOMER and JOB entities in Figure 11-10 on page 11.15 is read as follows: a CUSTOMER initiates one or more JOBs, and a JOB is initiated by one or more CUSTOMERs.

Because they are visual, ERDs particularly are useful for reviewing the existing or proposed entities with the user. Once users approve the ERD, all data items associated with an entity are identified. For example, an entity called CUSTOMER might have these data items: Customer Number, First Name, Middle Name, Last Name, Address, City, State, Zip Code, Telephone Number, and Balance Due.

DATA FLOW DIAGRAMS A time-consuming task of analysis is to organize and document the flow of data within an organization. A **data flow diagram** (**DFD**) is a tool that represents graphically the *flow of data* in a system. The key components of a DFD are the data flows, the processes, the data stores, and the sources (Figure 11-11). A **data flow**, represented by a line with an arrow, shows the input or output of data or information into or out from a process. A **process**, which transforms an input data flow into an output data flow, is drawn as a rounded rectangle. A **data store**, shown as a rectangle, represents a holding place for data and information, such as a filing cabinet, a checkbook register, or an electronic file or database in a computer. A **source**, or **agent**, is drawn as a square and identifies an entity outside the scope of the system that sends data into the system or receives information from the system.

Because these also are visual, DFDs are useful for reviewing the existing or proposed system with the user. Systems analysts prepare DFDs on a level-by-level basis. The top level DFD, called a **context diagram**, identifies only the major process; that is, the system being studied. Lower-level DFDs add detail and definition to the higher levels, similarly to *zooming* in on a computer screen. For example, in Figure 11-11, the Web Reporting System process might be split into three subprocesses: gathering and organizing construction data, entering progress data into a database, and updating the Web page to reflect the new database contents.

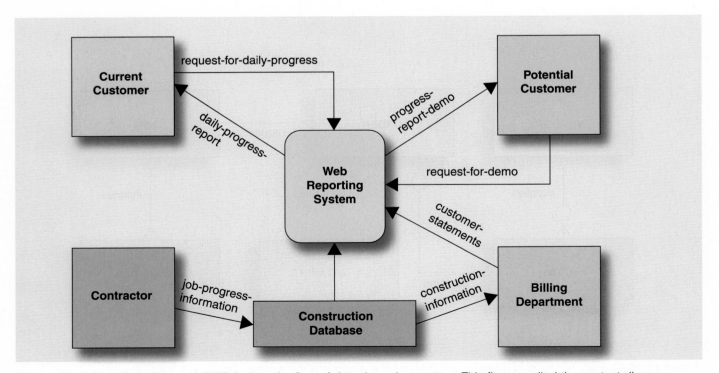

Figure 11-11 *Data flow diagrams (DFDs) show the flow of data through a system. This figure, called the context diagram, includes only one process — the Web Reporting System being studied. The construction database is a data store. Data sources both send and receive data to and from the system.*

PROJECT DICTIONARY The **project dictionary**, also called the **repository**, contains all the documentation and deliverables associated with a project. The project dictionary helps those involved keep track of the huge amount of details in every system. It begins with the project request and includes diagrams such as the ERD and DFDs. Another section of the project dictionary describes every item on these diagrams; that is, each process, data store, data flow, and source on every DFD, and every entity on the ERD and corresponding data items have an entry in the project dictionary. Because some systems can be represented with 25 or more DFDs and have hundreds of data items, the number of entries added to the dictionary at this point can be enormous. Thus, this particular activity requires a tremendous amount of time.

Several different techniques exist to describe the entries from the DFDs and ERDs in the project dictionary. Some of these include structured English, decision tables and decision trees, and the data dictionary.

STRUCTURED ENGLISH Each process on every DFD must have an entry in the project dictionary. One technique that systems analysts use to write these process specifications is called **structured English**, which is a style of writing that describes the steps in a process. Figure 11-12 shows an example of structured English describing the process of generating customer invoices, which are created from the contents of the Web progress reports.

For each customer, perform the following steps:

    Report the customer information.

    For each transaction, perform the following steps:

        Report the transaction.

        Compute the extended price as quantity ordered multiplied by price.

    Sum extended prices.

    If customer is tax-exempt then:

        Report 0 as tax due

    Otherwise (customer is not tax-exempt) then:

        Compute tax due as 6.5% of summed extended prices.

    Compute gross amount due.

    Compute discount.

    Compute net amout due.

    Print invoice.

Figure 11-12 *Structured English is a technique used to describe a process in the project dictionary. This structured English example describes the process for creating a customer invoice at Manhattan Construction.*

DECISION TABLES AND DECISION TREES Two techniques used to document processes that consist of many conditions or rules are decision tables and decision trees. A **decision table** is a tabular representation of actions to be taken given various conditions, and a **decision tree** is a graphical representation. Figures 11-13 and 11-14 show a decision table and decision tree for the process of computing customer discounts on invoices.

		RULES							
		1	2	3	4	5	6	7	8
CONDITIONS	Customer Type (Residential or Contractor)	R	C	R	C	R	C	R	C
	Gross Amount Due > $5,000?	Y	Y	N	N	Y	Y	N	N
	Coupon?	Y	Y	Y	Y	N	N	N	N
ACTIONS	No Discount							X	
	5% Discount			X		X			X
	10% Discount	X			X		X		
	15% Discount		X						

Figure 11-13 *This decision table describes the policy for computing a customer's discount at Manhattan Construction. For example, a residential customer with a gross amount due of $2,550 who has a coupon would receive a 5% discount on this order.*

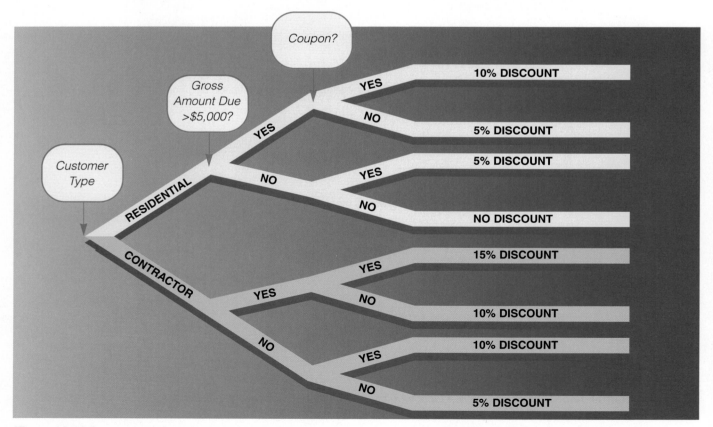

Figure 11-14 *Some systems analysts prefer the decision trees instead of decision tables because decision trees are graphical. The decision tree in this figure represents the same conditions shown in the decision table in Figure 11-13.*

DATA DICTIONARY Each data item has an entry in the **data dictionary** section (Figure 11-15) of the project dictionary. Recall from Chapter 10 that the data dictionary stores the data item's name and description, as well as details about the characteristics of each data item such as its length, type (e.g., text, numeric, and date), default value, and validation rules. The systems analyst creates the data dictionary in detailed analysis and refers to and updates it in all subsequent phases of the system development life cycle.

The Build-or-Buy Decision

After the systems analyst studies the current system and determines all user requirements, he or she communicates alternative solutions for the project to the steering committee as a verbal presentation or in a formal report. Often called the **system proposal**, its goal is to assess the feasibility of each alternative solution and then recommend the most feasible solution for the development project. Thus, the systems analyst reassesses feasibility at this point in the SDLC, especially economic feasibility. If the steering committee approves the recommended solution or one of the alternate solutions, the project enters the design phase.

When the steering committee discusses the system proposal and decides which alternative to implement, it often is facing a **build-or-buy decision**. That is, the organization is deciding whether to buy packaged software from an outside source or build its own custom software.

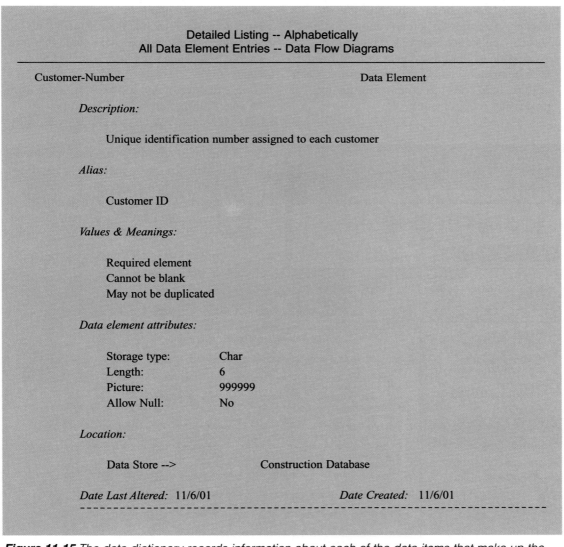

Detailed Listing -- Alphabetically
All Data Element Entries -- Data Flow Diagrams

Customer-Number   Data Element

Description:

 Unique identification number assigned to each customer

Alias:

 Customer ID

Values & Meanings:

 Required element
 Cannot be blank
 May not be duplicated

Data element attributes:

 Storage type: Char
 Length: 6
 Picture: 999999
 Allow Null: No

Location:

 Data Store -->   Construction Database

Date Last Altered: 11/6/01   *Date Created:* 11/6/01

Figure 11-15 *The data dictionary records information about each of the data items that make up the data flows and entities in the system. This is a dictionary entry for the Customer-Number data element.*

PACKAGED SOFTWARE Packaged software, sometimes called **commercial off-the-shelf software**, is already developed software available for purchase. This prewritten software is available for computers of all sizes. Chapter 2 presented numerous application packages available for personal computers, such as word processing, spreadsheet, database, desktop publishing, paint/image editing, Web page authoring, personal finance, legal, tax preparation, educational/reference, e-mail, and Web browser software.

Vendors offer two types of packaged software: horizontal and vertical. Software applications such as those presented in Chapter 2 that can be used by many different types of organizations are called **horizontal application software**. If an organization has a unique way of accomplishing activities, however, then it also may require **vertical application software**, which is software specifically designed for that business or industry. Examples of organizations that use vertical application software include real estate offices, libraries, dental offices, insurance companies, and construction firms. Each of these industries has unique information processing requirements.

Horizontal application software packages tend to be widely available because they can be used by a greater number of organizations; thus, they usually are less expensive than vertical application software packages. You can search the Internet for names and vendors of vertical and horizontal packages simply by entering your requirement as the search criteria (Figure 11-16). Other sources for names and vendors include computer magazines and **trade publications**, which are magazines written for specific businesses or industries. Companies and individuals who have written software for these industries often advertise in trade publications.

CUSTOM SOFTWARE Application software developed by the user or at the user's request is called **custom software**. With so many software application packages available commercially, why would an organization choose to build its own application software? The most common reason is the organization's software requirements are so unique that it is unable to locate a package that meets all its needs. In this case, the organization can choose to develop the software in-house using its own information systems personnel or have an outside source develop it specifically for them.

The main advantage of custom software is that it matches the organization's requirements exactly. The main disadvantages are that usually it is more expensive than packaged software and takes longer to design and implement.

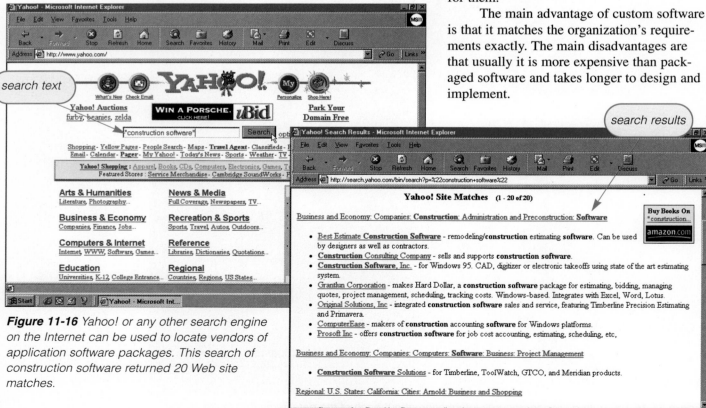

Figure 11-16 *Yahoo! or any other search engine on the Internet can be used to locate vendors of application software packages. This search of construction software returned 20 Web site matches.*

Detailed Analysis at Manhattan Construction

Rick and his team begin performing the activities in the detailed analysis phase of the Web Reporting Project. As part of the study and requirements activities, they use several of the data and information gathering techniques available to them: interviewing several people throughout the construction company, interviewing customers, observing the preparation and distribution of the monthly progress reports, and reviewing the questionnaires. They prepare many documents to record their findings including an entity-relationship diagram (see Figure 11-10 on page 11.15), a data flow diagram (see Figure 11-11 on page 11.16), a process specification using structured English (see Figure 11-12 on page 11.17), a process specification using a decision table (see Figure 11-13 on page 11.18), and a data dictionary entry for the customer number data item (see Figure 11-15 on page 11.19).

After two months of studying the existing system and obtaining user requirements, Rick discusses his findings with his supervisor, Sarah Eastman. Rick recommends that the customer progress be stored in a database and then posted to the Web daily from the database. Based on Rick's findings, Sarah writes a system proposal for the steering committee to review. The report assesses the feasibility of build-versus-buy scenarios; that is, should Manhattan Construction buy a construction progress reporting package or should they build a custom application?

Sarah recommends the project team attempt to find a suitable package that will meet their requirements and integrate with their current relational database. Sarah also recommends Manhattan Construction invest in a database server. The steering committee agrees with Sarah's request, but adds that if a package of this nature does not exist, then a custom construction progress reporting application will be built. Rick and his team begin the design phase of the project.

DESIGN PHASE

The **design phase** consists of two major activities: (1) if necessary, acquire hardware and software and (2) develop all of the details of the information system to be implemented.

The systems analyst often performs these two activities concurrently instead of sequentially.

Acquiring Necessary Hardware and Software

Once the steering committee approves a solution, you begin the tasks to acquire essential hardware and software to meet the requirements of the approved solution. It is possible that this activity is skipped if no new hardware or software is required. If it is required, the selection of appropriate products is crucial for the success of the information system. The activity consists of four major tasks: (1) identify technical specifications, (2) solicit vendor proposals, (3) test and evaluate vendor proposals, and (4) make a decision.

Identifying Technical Specifications

The first step in acquiring necessary hardware and software is to identify all the hardware, software, and networking requirements with respect to functionality, features, and performance. To obtain this criteria, the systems analyst researches using a variety of techniques such as talking with other analysts, visiting vendors' stores, and surfing the Web. Many trade journals, newspapers, and magazines now are online on the Web, allowing the analyst to locate information more quickly and easily than in the past (Figure 11-17).

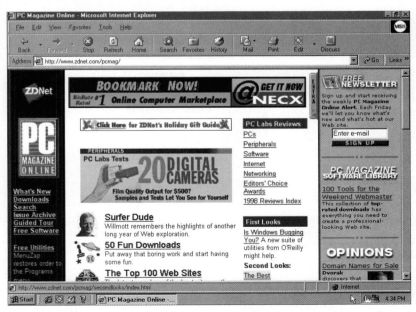

Figure 11-17 *The systems analyst can save time by researching on the Internet. Many magazines, such as PC Magazine Online shown in this figure, are on the Web.*

WEB INFO

For more information on a value-added reseller, visit the Discovering Computers 2000 Chapter 11 WEB INFO page (www.scsite.com/dc2000/ch11/webinfo.htm) and click VAR.

Once the technical requirements have been defined, the systems analyst summarizes these requirements in either a request for quotation or a request for proposal to send to prospective vendors. A **request for quotation** (**RFQ**) is used when you know which product(s) you want. With an RFQ, the vendor quotes a price for the specified product(s). A **request for proposal** (**RFP**) is used when you want the vendor to select the product(s) that meets your requirements and then quote the price(s). Just as the depth of an information system varies, so does the length of an RFQ or RFP; some can be as short as a couple of pages, with others consisting of more than one hundred pages. Some companies prefer to use a **request for information** (**RFI**), which is a less formal method using a standard form to request information about a product or service.

Soliciting Vendor Proposals

With either an RFQ or RFP in hand, you send it to potential hardware, software, and/or networking vendors. Many vendors post their product catalogs on the Internet so you have up-to-date and easy access to products, prices, technical specifications, and ordering information (Figure 11-18). If you are unable to locate a vendor on the Internet, you could visit local computer stores or contact computer manufacturers.

Another source for hardware, software, and networking products is a **value-added reseller** (**VAR**), which is a company that purchases products from manufacturers and then resells these products to the public — offering additional services with the product. Examples of additional services include user support, equipment maintenance, training, installation, and warranties. A **warranty** is a guarantee that a product will function properly for a specified time period. Some VARs offer one product or service, while others provide complete systems (Figure 11-19). The advantage of a full-scale VAR is that you deal with only one company for an entire system.

Another means of identifying software suppliers is to hire a computer **consultant**. Many consultants specialize in assisting organizations of all sizes with the task of identifying and installing software packages. Although consultant's fees may be high, it may be worth the expert advice. For a reliable consultant reference, contact a professional organization in your industry or a local university.

Testing and Evaluating Vendor Proposals

After you send RFQs and RFPs to potential vendors, you will receive completed quotations and proposals. A difficult task is to evaluate the proposals and then select the best one. A popular technique is to establish a scoring system that you can use to rate each proposal. You should be as objective as possible while rating each proposal.

During this task, you will use many information-gathering techniques. You should obtain user references from the software vendors, talk to current users of the software for their opinions, and ask the vendor for a demonstration of the product(s) specified. You may, however, prefer to test the software yourself. In this case, the vendor could supply you with a demonstration copy of the software to test on your equipment or set up a hardware and software configuration at its site so you can be sure it will meet the organization's needs. Some vendors allow you to download a demonstration copy directly from their Web sites (Figure 11-20).

If you are concerned about whether the software can handle a certain volume of transactions efficiently, you may want to conduct a benchmark test. A **benchmark test**

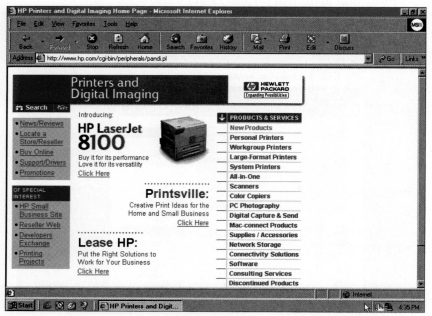

Figure 11-18 *Many hardware and software vendors are posting their products and services catalogs on the Web. This figure shows available products and services for Hewlett Packard's printers and digital imaging devices.*

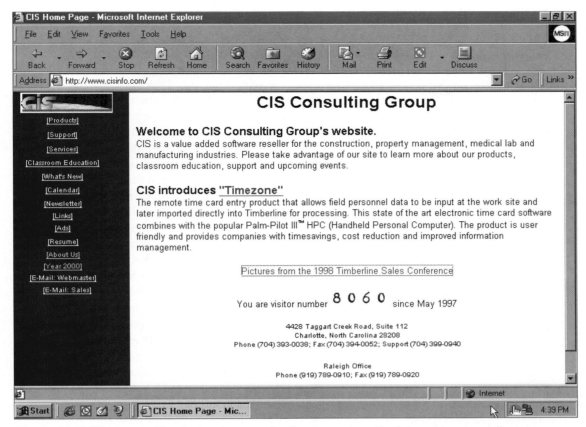

Figure 11-19 *When searching for hardware and software vendors, the Internet is an excellent resource. Many VARs advertise on the Internet. This figure shows the home page for Construction Information Services (CIS), a provider of computer systems for construction and other companies.*

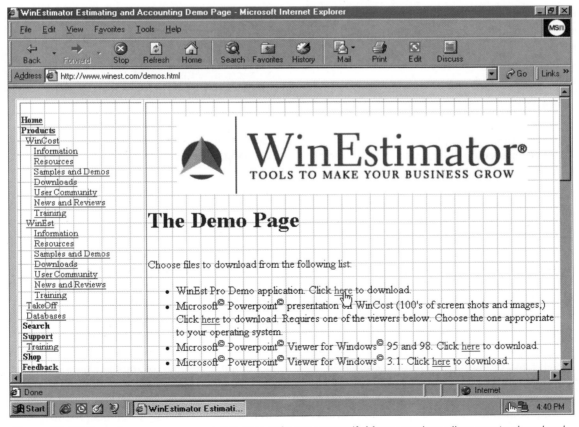

Figure 11-20 *Sometimes, you may want to test software yourself. Many vendors allow you to download a demonstration copy directly from their Web sites.*

measures the performance of hardware or software. For example, a benchmark test could measure the time it takes a payroll package to print 50 paychecks. Comparing the time it takes various accounting packages to print the same 50 paychecks is one way of measuring the package's relative performance. Many computer magazines conduct benchmark tests while evaluating hardware and software and then publish these results for consumers to review (Figure 11-21).

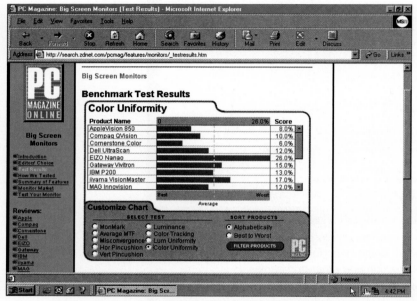

Figure 11-21 *Many publications, both online and hard copy, regularly evaluate software and hardware. This benchmark test from PC Magazine Online compares the color quality of a variety of big screen monitors.*

Making a Decision

Having rated the proposals, the systems analyst presents a recommendation to the steering committee. The recommendation could be to award a contract to a vendor or to not make any purchases at this time. When you purchase hardware, you usually own it; however, when you purchase software, you do not. With software, you purchase an **end-user license agreement**, which is the right to use the software under certain terms and conditions (Figure 11-22). Most license agreements state that the software may not be used on more than one computer or by more than one user. Other license restrictions include copying the software, modifying it, or translating it to another language. These restrictions protect the rights of software developers, who do not want someone else to benefit unfairly from their work.

Design: Hardware and Software Acquisition at Manhattan Construction

Based on the direction of the steering committee, Rick and his team compile a requirements list from the information obtained during analysis. They prepare an RFP and submit it to fifteen vendors: nine through the Internet and six local computer stores. Fourteen vendors send a response within the three-week deadline set by Manhattan Construction.

Of the fourteen replies, Manhattan Construction selects two to evaluate. They eliminate the other twelve because these vendors did not offer adequate warranties for the database server. The project team asks for demonstration copies of the software from the remaining two vendors. In addition, they contact three current users of each package for their opinions. After evaluating these two software packages, the team is disappointed because both require substantial modifications to meet Manhattan Construction's job costing and estimating procedures.

Rick summarizes his team's findings in a report to the steering committee. Manhattan Construction now faces a build decision. That is, should they develop the construction progress reporting application themselves or have an outside party develop it? After discussing the alternatives, the steering committee authorizes the information systems department to begin development of custom application for the Web Reporting Project. As a courtesy and to maintain good working relationships, Rick sends a letter to all fourteen vendors informing them of Manhattan Construction's decision.

Detailed Design

Once the data and process requirements have been identified, the next step is to develop detailed design specifications for the components in the proposed solution. Whereas detailed analysis sometimes is referred to as logical design, detailed design sometimes is called **physical design** because it specifies hardware and software for automated procedures. The activities to be performed include developing designs for the databases, inputs, outputs, and programs. Depending on whether packaged software is being purchased or custom software is being developed, the length

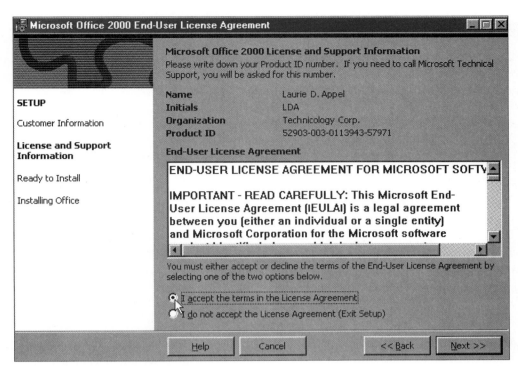

Figure 11-22 *When you install software, you must accept the terms of the end-user license agreement.*

and complexity of each of these activities may vary. For example, many of these steps would be skipped entirely with most purchased software packages.

DATABASE DESIGN Data is the central resource in an information system. Thus, it is crucial that the content of the data dictionary be current, consistent, and correct. During database design, the systems analyst builds upon the data dictionary developed during the analysis phase so it represents accurately the data requirements of the organization. The systems analyst works closely with the data and database administrators to identify those data elements that currently exist within the organization and those that must be developed.

With relational database systems, the structure of each table in the system must be defined, as well as relationships among the tables. Table structure definitions include details of columns within the rows. Another issue that the systems analyst addresses is user access privileges; that is, the analyst must define which data elements each user can access, when they can access the data elements, what actions they can perform on the data elements, and under what circumstances they can access the elements, called the constraints (Figure 11-23). Users with similar items, actions, or constraints would be grouped into a class, which then would be implemented for the security of the database. The systems analyst also must consider the volume of database activity. For example, large, frequently accessed tables may be organized in a manner so that inquiries are processed in an acceptable time frame.

USER NAME	ITEM	ACTION	CONSTRAINT
Mary Edwards	Customer Name	Inquiry, Add, Modify	None
Harry Travis	Customer Name	Inquiry	None
Harry Travis	Customer Name	Add, Modify	Not Allowed
Grace Owens	Laborer Hourly Wage	Inquiry	Hourly Wage < $35
Grace Owens	Laborer Hourly Wage	Add, Modify	Not Allowed
Vince Dexter	Laborer Hourly Wage	Inquiry, Add	None
Vince Dexter	Laborer Hourly Wage	Modify	Hourly Wage < $70

Figure 11-23 *Data security is an important issue that the systems analyst must address. This figure shows one method of data security.*

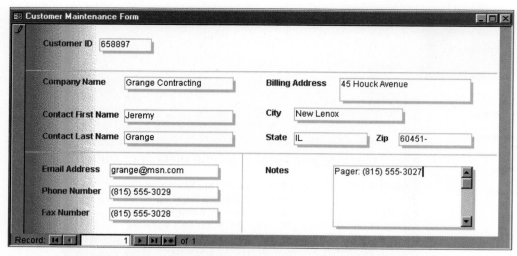

Figure 11-24 *Users must give their approval on all inputs and outputs. This input screen is a mockup (containing actual data) for the user to review.*

INPUT AND OUTPUT DESIGN Because users ultimately will be working with the inputs and outputs, it is crucial to involve users during input and output design. During this activity, the systems analyst carefully designs every menu, screen, and report specified in the requirements. Usually, the outputs are designed first because they help define the requirements for the inputs.

The systems analyst develops two types of designs for each input and output: a mockup and a layout chart. A **mockup** is a sample of the input or output that contains actual data

(Figure 11-24). Mockups are shown to users for their approval. Once the mockup is approved, the systems analyst develops a **layout chart** for the programmer. Layout charts are more technical and contain programming-like notations for the data items (Figure 11-25). Other issues that must be addressed during input and output design include the types of media to use (paper, video, audio); formats (graphical or narrative); and data entry validation techniques, which include making sure the inputted data is correct (for example, a pay rate cannot be less than 0).

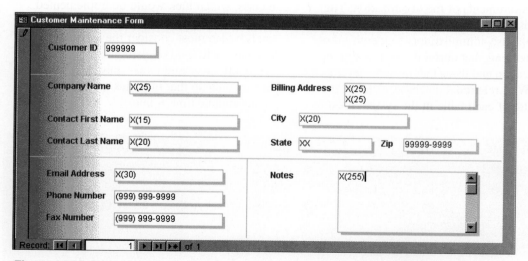

Figure 11-25 *Once users approve a mockup, the layout chart (with technical specifications) is given to the programmer. This layout chart is for the mockup in Figure 11-24.*

PROGRAM DESIGN During program design, the systems analyst identifies the processing requirements, or the **logic**, for each program in the system. To accomplish this, the analyst uses top-down and structured programming techniques, which are discussed in the next chapter.

Once the processing requirements are developed, the systems analyst prepares the **program specification package**, which communicates program requirements clearly to the programmer. The program specification package contains the relationship among each program in a process, as well as the input, output, processing, and database specifications.

Relationships among programs in a process sometimes are documented with systems flowcharts (Figure 11-26). A **systems flowchart** shows a major process, which may require one or more programs; the timing of the process; the outputs generated (including their distribution and media); database tables required; and the types of input devices that will provide data to the system. A systems flowchart is very different from a data flow diagram. A DFD shows the flow of data through the system; whereas, a system flowchart shows methods and procedures.

Prototyping

Many systems analysts today use a prototyping approach to perform detailed design activities. A **prototype** is a working model of the proposed system. That is, the analyst actually builds a functional form of the solution during design. The main advantage of a prototype is that users can work with the system before it is completed — to make sure it meets their needs.

The Customer Maintenance Screen shown in Figure 11-24 is a prototype created in Microsoft Access. Once users approve a prototype, the solution is implemented more quickly than without a prototype. In many cases, prototyped systems do not require a programmer for implementation; the analyst can convert the working model to the actual solution. That is, these systems are developed rapidly. Thus, the process of developing applications with prototypes is a component of **rapid application development** (**RAD**) which is discussed in the next chapter.

Some organizations use prototyping during design, while others begin earlier during analysis or even planning. Beginning a prototype in the planning phase or the analysis

WEB INFO
WEB INFO
For more information on a prototype, visit the Discovering Computers 2000 Chapter 11 WEB INFO page (**www.scsite.com/ dc2000/ch11/webinfo.htm**) and click Prototype.

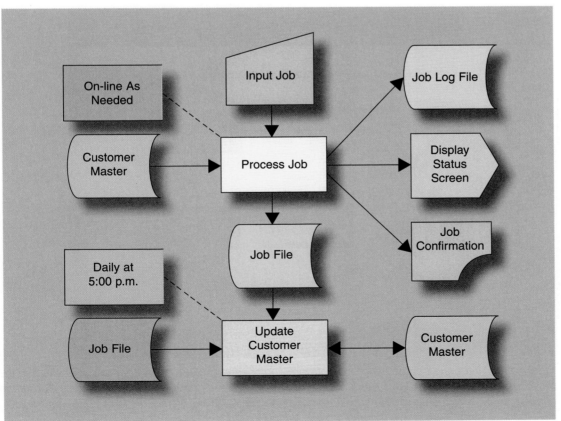

Figure 11-26 This system flowchart describes the process of a transaction being entered, such as a customer initiating a job. This chart contains five symbols with these meanings: rectangle with a slanted top - data entry; rectangle - program; rectangle with curved edges - file; rectangle with cut corner - hard copy; rectangle with no right side - comment. Comments are connected to the chart with dotted lines because they represent timing, not data flow.

phase might lead to problems. When the project development team sees a working model so early in the life cycle, they tend to skip critical analysis and design steps and overlook key features in the proposed solution.

A common pitfall of a prototype is that it is documented inadequately, or worse, not documented at all. Prototyping can be an effective tool if the development team and the users discipline themselves to follow all activities within the life cycle. Prototyping should not eliminate or replace activities — just improve the quality of these activities.

CASE Tools

Many systems analysts use computer software to assist in the system development life cycle. **Computer-aided software engineering** (**CASE**) products are computer-based tools designed to support one or more activities of the SDLC. This technology is intended to increase the efficiency and productivity of the project development team.

Some CASE tools exist separately; that is, one software package is a dictionary while another enables you to generate drawings. The most effective tools, however, are those developed as an integrated product,

sometimes called I-CASE or a CASE workbench (Figure 11-27).

I-CASE products include the following capabilities.

- Project repository facility that stores diagrams, specifications, descriptions, programs, and any other deliverable generated during the life cycle activities

- Graphics facility that enables the drawing of diagrams, such as DFDs and ERDs

- Prototyping facility used to create models of the proposed system

- Quality assurance facility to analyze deliverables, such as graphs and the data dictionary for accuracy

- Code generators that create actual computer programs from design specifications

- Housekeeping facility that establishes user accounts and provides backup and recovery functions

CASE tools support a variety of system development life cycles. Depending on the one your organization adopts and follows, you can customize the tools so all deliverables, such as DFDs and ERDs, are standardized.

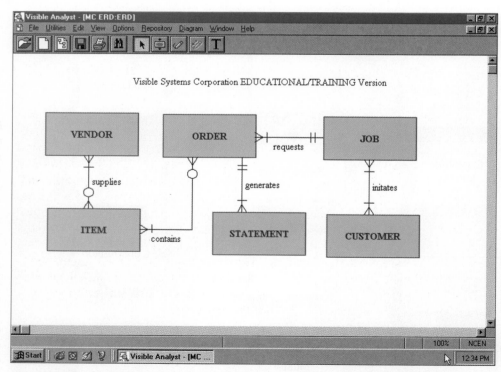

Figure 11-27 *Integrated computer-aided software engineering (I-CASE) packages assist analysts in the development of an information system. Visible Analyst Workbench (VAW) by Visible Systems Corporation enables analysts to create structured diagrams, as well as build the project dictionary. Figures 11-10, 11-11, 11-15, and 11-26 all were created using VAW.*

Quality Review Techniques

Before you submit the detailed design specifications to the programming team, the specifications should be reviewed by users, the senior systems analyst, and members of the project team. One popular review technique is a **structured walkthrough**, which is a step-by-step review of any deliverable. Deliverables that may be walked through include reports, diagrams, mockups, layout charts, and dictionary entries. The purpose of a walkthrough is to identify errors in the deliverable being reviewed. If any errors are identified, the information systems personnel must correct them. Structured walkthroughs are used throughout the entire SDLC to review a variety of deliverables.

As at the end of other phases in the life cycle, the systems analyst once again performs a feasibility assessment to determine if it still is beneficial to implement the proposed solution. It does not happen often, but some projects are terminated at this point because they become infeasible. Although you may feel that much time and money has been wasted, it is less costly in the long run to terminate the project than to implement an inadequate or incorrect solution. If the steering committee decides the project still is feasible, the project enters the implementation phase.

Detailed Design at Manhattan Construction

As approved by the steering committee, Rick and his team begin designing the Web reporting system. After studying existing progress reports and interviewing more users and customers, the team is able to design modifications to the construction company's database, Web site, and the associated programs. They prepare several documents including a mockup (see Figure 11-24 on page 11.26), a layout chart (see Figure 11-25 on page 11.26), and a systems flowchart (see Figure 11-26 on page 11.27).

After completing the detailed design, Rick meets with several users and the information systems personnel to walkthrough the deliverables. They locate two errors, which he corrects prior to presenting the design specifications to the steering committee. The committee agrees with the design solution and consents to implement it.

IMPLEMENTATION PHASE

Once the design is completed, the project enters the **implementation phase**. The purpose of implementation is to construct, or build, the new or enhanced system and then deliver it to the users. Four major activities are performed in this phase: (1) if necessary, develop programs; (2) install and test the new system; (3) train and educate users; and (4) convert to the new system. The following sections discuss each of these activities.

Develop Programs

If the project development team decides to write custom software, instead of purchasing packaged software, then the programmers will develop programs from the program specification package created during analysis. Just as the system development life cycle follows an organized set of activities, so does program development. The **program development life cycle (PDLC)** follows these six steps: (1) analyze the problem, (2) design the programs, (3) code the programs, (4) test the programs, (5) formalize the solution, and (6) maintain the programs. Chapter 12 explains the program development life cycle in depth. The important concept to understand now is that the PDLC is a part of the implementation phase, which is part of the SDLC.

Install and Test the New System

If new hardware was acquired, the hardware must be installed and tested at this point. Both packaged software and custom software programs have to be installed on the hardware. It is extremely important that the hardware and software be tested thoroughly. Just as you test individual programs, you also should test that all the programs work together in the system. It is better to find errors now so you can correct them before putting the system into production; that is, delivering it to the users.

Three types of tests are performed to test the new system:

- **Systems test**: verifies that all programs in an application work together properly

- **Integration test**: verifies that an application works with other applications

- **Acceptance test**: performed by end-users, checks that the new system works with actual data

Train and Educate Users

For a system to be effective, users must be trained properly on its functionality. They must be trained on how to use both the hardware and the software. **Training** involves showing users exactly how they will use the new system. This type of training could include one-on-one sessions or classroom-style lectures (Figure 11-28). Whichever technique is used, it should include hands-on sessions using realistic sample data. Well-designed user manuals also should be provided to users for reference.

Figure 11-28
Organizations must ensure that users are trained properly on the new system. One training method is classroom-style lectures.

Education is the process of learning new principles or theories that helps users understand the system. For example, many companies use **total quality management (TQM)** to maintain quality in a system. In this case, employees need to be educated on the concepts and practices of TQM.

Convert to the New System

The final activity in implementation is to change from the old system to the new system. This conversion can take place using one or more of the following conversion strategies: direct, parallel, phased, or pilot (Figure 11-29).

With **direct conversion**, the user stops using the old system and begins using the new system on a certain date. The advantage of this strategy is it requires no transition costs and is a quick implementation technique, which explains why some analysts call it an **abrupt cut-over**. The disadvantage is it is extremely risky and can disrupt operations seriously if the new system does not work correctly the first time.

Parallel conversion consists of running the old system alongside the new system for a specified time period. Results from both systems are compared, and if they agree, the old system either is terminated abruptly or is phased out. The advantage of this strategy is that any problems with the new system can be solved before the old system is terminated. The disadvantage is that it is costly to operate two systems simultaneously.

Phased conversion, sometimes called **location conversion**, is used with larger systems that are split into individual sites. Each site is converted separately at different times using either a direct or parallel conversion. An example of a phased conversion could be for an accounting system, with the accounts receivable, accounts payable, general ledger, and payroll sites all being converted in separate phases.

With a **pilot conversion**, only one location in the organization uses the new system — so it can be tested. Once the pilot site approves the new system, other sites convert using one of the aforementioned conversion strategies.

At the beginning of the conversion, existing data must be made ready for the new system. Converting existing manual and computer-based files so they can be used by a new system is called **data conversion**.

Implementation at Manhattan Construction

Upon receiving the program specification package, an implementation team of Mary Krammer, a programmer; Julie Regal, the company Webmaster; and Mark Hatley, a database designer; work together to develop the Web reporting system. Rick works closely with the team to answer questions about the design and to check the progress of their work. When the implementation team completes its work, the custom application is given to Rick for testing.

Rick arranges several training classes for the employees of Manhattan Construction on how to use the Web Progress Reporting

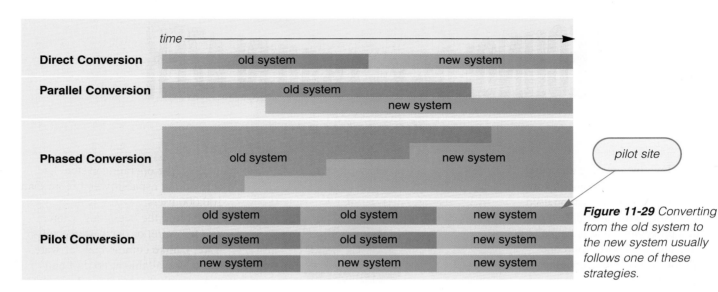

Figure 11-29 *Converting from the old system to the new system usually follows one of these strategies.*

application. He prepares a detailed user guide for each employee that has access to the system. Rick wants to be sure that everyone is prepared thoroughly for the new Web pages once they are posted. Rick also sends a letter to all customers informing when this new service will be available and how to use it.

SUPPORT PHASE

The purpose of the **support phase** is to provide ongoing assistance for an information system and its users after it is implemented. The support phase consists of four major activities: (1) conduct a post-implementation system review, (2) identify errors, (3) identify enhancements, and (4) monitor system performance.

One of the first activities performed in the support phase is the **post-implementation system review**, which is a meeting with users to determine if the information system is performing according to their expectations. If it is not, you must determine what must be done to satisfy the users — which means you begin planning all over again. Thus, the loop forms in the system development life cycle.

Sometimes, users identify errors in the system; that is, it does not produce correct results. These errors are caused from problems with design (logic) or programming (syntax). Often these errors are minor. For example, the total of a column might be incorrect on a customer statement. Other times, however, the error requires more serious investigation by the systems analyst before a correction can

be determined — back to the planning phase.

In some cases, users would like the system to do more; that is, they have additional requirements. **System enhancement** involves modifying or expanding an existing application system — back to the planning phase.

Performance monitoring is another activity that the systems analyst performs during the support phase. The purpose is to determine if the system is inefficient at any point and if the inefficiency is causing a problem. For example, is the time it takes to print a customer statement reasonable? If not, the analyst must investigate solutions to make the information system's response times more acceptable — back to the planning phase.

Support at Manhattan Construction

During the post-implementation system review, Rick learns that the customers of Manhattan Construction are extremely satisfied with the new Daily Progress Report on their Web site. Management is very happy because the project has saved the construction company a huge amount of money.

Six months after the new Web reporting system has been in operation, Lynne Williams sends another customer satisfaction survey to determine if the customers have any other wants or needs of Manhattan Construction. When Karen tabulates the survey results, she is delighted to learn that not a single customer who responded is dissatisfied! Karen passes the good news on to the steering committee.

TECHNOLOGY TRAILBLAZER

LINUS TORVALDS

Imagine creating an operating system that compares favorably with Windows, can be used effectively with older 386/486 Intel processors, and is backed by a technical support group one-million strong. Now, imagine giving that operating system away. Unimaginable? Well, that is what happened when Linus Torvalds created the Linux operating system.

In 1991, Linus Torvalds was a computer-science student at the University of Helsinki in Finland. Frustrated with the limitations of DOS, the most popular personal computer operating system at the time, Torvalds decided to create his own operating system. This might seem a daunting task, but the optimistic young programmer was confident. "I knew I was the best programmer in the world," Torvalds recalls. "Every twenty-one-year-old programmer knows that. How hard can it be? It's just an operating system." Torvalds announced his project in an Internet newsgroup: "Hello everybody… I'm doing a (free) operating system (just a hobby, won't be big and professional like gnu) for 386(486) AT clones… I'd like any feedback on things people like/dislike in Minix [a small, UNIX-like operating system for personal computers], as my OS resembles it somewhat… I'll get something practical within a few months, and I'd like to know what features most people would want. Any suggestions are welcome, but I won't promise I'll implement them. :-)."

Torvalds soon posted the first version of the operating system. Ten people downloaded the program, and five sent back bug fixes, improvements, and enhancements. Torvalds incorporated the changes and, despite fears that it would sound egocentric, adopted a suggested name, Linux (rhymes with cynics). As he continued to post new versions, the process was repeated and the number of users, and revisers, grew. Torvalds's ability to identify positive changes and make contributors feel appreciated made the system increasingly popular. When Linux 1.0 was released

in 1994, the operating system had networking capability and more than 100,000 users.

From the beginning, Linux was freeware, or open-source software. Unlike commercial software, Linux is available at no cost and comes with the source code — the commands written by the programmer. Other programmers can see the developer's design and fix, or customize, the program. Advocates claim this continual evaluation and revision of freeware by thousands of users, as opposed to the limited checks performed on commercial software by a small coterie of testers, is freeware's real strength. Torvalds eventually copyrighted Linux under a GPL license, allowing versions to be sold as long as the source code, and any alterations, remain public. Today, Linux (with a cute penguin as its unofficial symbol) is sold by companies such as Red Hat Software and Caldera.

Linux use is increasing at more than 40 percent a year. Corporations tend to be leery of freeware — companies like to have someone specific to call, and blame, if something goes wrong. Nevertheless, due to the operating system's reliability, flexibility, and affordability corporate use of Linux is up 30 percent. Linux was employed by the company that created the illusions in the movie, Titanic, and had more than seven million users by 1998. Because of Linux's popularity among college student-programmers (tomorrow's software designers), experts predict that its use will continue to grow. To become truly accepted, however, many feel that Linux still needs bona fide technical support, more compatible application programs, and a standardized graphical user interface.

Today, Linus Torvalds works for a chip design company, lives in a modest house, and drives a rental car look-alike. A celebrity among programmers, Torvalds still works with Linux and has no regrets about making the operating system available at no cost. "A big part of personal satisfaction is having your work recognized by your peers," Torvald points out. "That's fundamental in any human psyche."

COMPANY ON THE CUTTING EDGE
COMPANY ON THE CUTTING EDGE

SAP

In September 1998, a crowd of 15,000 people strong gathered in Los Angeles. Was it a presidential appearance? No. UFOs were not sighted, nor were any celebrities. It was SAPPHIRE '98, a user conference for customers of SAP, the German software giant.

SAP is short for Systeme, Anwendungen, und Produkte in der Datenverarbeitung. The acronym for its English translation works just as well: Systems, Applications, and Products in data processing. The company was founded in 1972 by five IBM system engineers in Walldorf, Germany, who believed that the time was ripe for a fully integrated software product that could be used for all facets of a company's operations. An IBM client had, in fact, asked for precisely such a product. Amazingly, IBM did not believe the concept to be feasible at that time. Convinced the opposite was true, the five formed their own company. Today, SAP is the world's largest enterprise software company.

From its inception, SAP thought globally. Although they were working at night on borrowed computers, the engineers developed all their software to run on a multi-national/multilingual level. By 1979, they began developing the R/2 Enterprise System for mainframes, a powerful database that enabled companies to organize all their data into a single database, then choose only those program modules they wanted. The freestanding modules, in turn, could be customized to fit each customer's needs.

Word soon spread overseas, and by the late 1980s, SAP had begun the expansion that elevated it to the lofty status it now enjoys. SAP International, a Swiss-based subsidiary, was created, followed by SAP America, based in Philadelphia. Fate lent a hand here, because it was in the 1992 that R/3 was released. Designed for client-server environments, it was touted as being less labor-intensive, quicker, and more integratable than R/2. Its release coincided neatly with the trend of corporate downsizing;

productivity had to be increased, and SAP was there, poised and waiting.

Inevitably, as with anything wildly successful, criticisms began. Some users claimed SAP products were too complex, difficult to install, and pricey. An average installation cost starts at around $1 million, the sky basically being the limit. Conventional wisdom holds that for every dollar spent on software, up to ten dollars will be spent on consulting and training fees. Needless to say, this makes for some lucrative jobs. SAP has responded by delivering TeamSAP, an online technical support service. Another option is SAP-Net, which allows users to send comments directly to SAP via the Internet. Explains Hasso Plattner, SAP CEO and co-founder, "Now you give people a kind of a vote… This feedback will help us measure the problem and either change the system or point at an easier way of doing things." Users are further assured they will receive an answer within a day or two at most.

Today, SAP employs more than 18,000 people in 50 countries and serves more than 18,000 installations. It is the vendor of choice for nine of the ten largest U.S. corporations, and fully one-third of the Fortune 500 companies. Said Jim Shepherd, of Advanced Marketing Research, a company that tracks the enterprise software industry, "here's a… company that grew 175% a year. Most companies have a heart attack if they grow at 15% a year, and SAP is more than doubling its work force every year. With no end in sight."

Besides future growth, what can be expected of SAP in the future? Just for starters, a new *geomarketing* application is in the works. Using maps and spatial data, it provides sales people with crucial information to help target customers in selected areas. The completed application will include graphics and animation, which should be interesting. According to Hasso Plattner, "I learned a lot from Stephen Spielberg and those guys. I think they are the future of business computing."

 IN BRIEF   **www.scsite.com/dc2000/ch11/brief.htm**

WEB INSTRUCTIONS: *To display this page from the Web, launch your browser and enter the URL,* *www.scsite.com/dc2000/ch11/brief.htm*. *Click the links for current and additional information. To listen to an audio version of this IN BRIEF, click the Audio button to the right of the title, IN BRIEF, at the top of the page. To play the audio, RealPlayer must be installed on your computer (download by clicking* here).

 1. What Are the Phases in the System Development Life Cycle?

The system development life cycle (SDLC) is an organized set of activities that guides those involved through the development of an information system. The many activities of the SDLC are grouped into five **phases**. The **planning phase** involves reviewing and prioritizing project requests; allocating resources; and identifying the project development team. The **analysis phase** consists of conducting a preliminary investigation and performing detailed analysis activities. The **design phase** calls for acquiring the necessary hardware and software and developing details of the system. The **implementation phase** includes developing programs; installing and testing the new system; training and educating users; and converting to the new system. The **support phase** entails conducting post-implementation system review; identifying errors and enhancements; and monitoring system performance.

 2. What Are Guidelines for System Development?

The development of an information system should follow three general guidelines. First, use a phased approach. Second, involve the **users**, who include anyone for whom the system is being built. Finally, develop **standards**, or sets of rules and procedures, that the organization expects employees to accept and follow.

▲ **3. Why Are Project Management, Feasibility Assessment, Data and Information Gathering Techniques, and Documentation Important?**

Project management is the process of planning, scheduling, and then controlling the activities during the SDLC. The goal is to deliver an acceptable system in an agreed-upon time frame, while maintaining costs. Feasibility is a measure of how suitable the development of a system will be to an organization. Analysts use four criteria to test feasibility: **operational feasibility**, **schedule feasibility**, **technical feasibility**, and **economic feasibility**. **Documentation** is the compilation and summarization of data and information. Well-written, thorough documentation makes it easier to understand all aspects of the life cycle. Data and information gathering techniques supply system developers with accurate and timely data in order to keep the project on schedule, assess feasibility, and ensure that the system is meeting requirements.

 4. How Are Structured Tools Such As Entity-Relationship Diagrams and Data Flow Diagrams Used in Analysis and Design?

Structured analysis and design uses graphics to present a systems analyst's findings in a way that can be understood by users, programmers, and other systems analysts. In structured analysis and design, an entity-relationship diagram (ERD) is a tool that graphically represents the associations between entities (vendors, orders, customers, jobs, and so on) in the project. A **data flow diagram (DFD)** is a tool that graphically represents the flow of data (input or output of data or information) in a system.

   www.scsite.com/dc2000/ch11/brief.htm

 5. Why Is the Project Dictionary Important?

The project dictionary, also called the **repository**, contains all the documentation and **deliverables** (tangible items) associated with a project. The project dictionary helps those involved to keep track of the huge number of details in every system. The project dictionary uses techniques such as **structured English** to describe process specifications, **decision tables** and **decision trees** to provide tabular and graphical representations of actions to be taken given various conditions, and a **data dictionary** to store details about the characteristics of each data item.

 6. How Is Packaged Software Different from Custom Software?

When a **steering committee** discusses the **system proposal** and determines which alternative to implement, it often faces a build-or-buy decision. That is, the committee must decide whether to buy packaged software or build its own custom software. **Packaged software** is already developed software available for purchase. **Custom software** is application software developed by the user or at the user's request. Custom software exactly matches an organization's requirements but usually is more expensive than packaged software and takes longer to design and implement.

 7. Why Is Program Development Part of the System Development Life Cycle?

If the project development team decides to write custom software, then programmers develop programs from the program specification package created during analysis. Program development is part of the implementation phase of the SDLC. The **program development life cycle** (**PDLC**) follows six steps: (1) analyze the problem, (2) design the programs, (3) code the programs, (4) test the programs, (5) formalize the solution, and (6) maintain the programs.

 8. What Techniques Are Used to Convert to a New System and Support an Information System?

Conversion to a new system can take place using one or more strategies. With **direct conversion**, the user stops using the old system and begins using the new system on a certain date. **Parallel conversion** consists of running the old system alongside the new system for a specified period of time. Phased conversion is used with larger systems that are split into individual sites, each of which converts separately at different times using either a direct or parallel conversion. With a **pilot conversion**, only one location in the organization uses the new system – so it can be tested. To support a new information system, the systems analyst performs a **post-implementation system review**, which is a meeting with users to determine if the information system is performing according to their specifications. The systems analyst also conducts **performance monitoring** to determine if the system is inefficient in any way and if the inefficiency is causing a problem.

Student Exercises
WEB INFO
IN BRIEF
KEY TERMS
AT THE MOVIES
CHECKPOINT
AT ISSUE
CYBERCLASS
HANDS ON
NET STUFF
Special Features
TIMELINE 2000
GUIDE TO WWW SITES
MAKING A CHIP
BUYER'S GUIDE 2000
CAREERS 2000
TRENDS 2000
CHAT
INTERACTIVE LABS
NEWS
HOME

KEY TERMS

www.scsite.com/dc2000/ch11/terms.htm

WEB INSTRUCTIONS: *To display this page from the Web, launch your browser and enter the URL,* *www.scsite.com/dc2000/ch11/terms.htm*. *Scroll through the list of terms. Click a term to display its definition and a picture. Click KEY TERMS on the left to redisplay the KEY TERMS page. Click the TO WEB button for current and additional information about the term from the Web. To see animations, Shockwave and Flash Player must be installed on your computer (download by clicking* here).

abrupt cut-over (11.30)
agent (11.16)
analysis phase (11.12)
benchmark test (11.22)
build-or-buy decision (11.19)
commercial off-the-shelf
    software (11.20)
computer-aided software
    engineering (CASE) (11.28)
consultant (11.22)
context diagram (11.16)
cost/benefit feasibility (11.6)
custom software (11.20)
data conversion (11.30)
data dictionary (11.19)
data flow (11.16)
data flow diagram (DFD)
    (11.16)
data store (11.16)
decision table (11.18)
decision tree (11.18)
deliverable (11.5)
design phase (11.21)
detailed analysis (11.14)
direct conversion (11.30)
documentation (11.6)
economic feasibility (11.6)
education (11.30)
end-user license agreement
    (11.24)
entity (11.15)
entity-relationship diagram
    (ERD) (11.15)
feasibility (11.5)
feasibility report (11.12)
feasibility study (11.12)
Gantt chart (11.5)
horizontal application software
    (11.20)
implementation phase (11.29)
joint-application design (JAD)
    session (11.7)
layout chart (11.26)
location conversion (11.30)
logic (11.27)

JOINT-APPLICATION DESIGN (JAD) SESSION: A lengthy, structured, group work session where all involved in the SDLC, including users and information systems personnel, discuss an aspect of a project. (11.7)

logical design (11.14)
mockup (11.26)
operational feasibility (11.5)
packaged software (11.20)
parallel conversion (11.30)
performance monitoring (11.31)
phased conversion (11.30)
phases (11.2)
physical design (11.24)
pilot conversion (11.30)
planning phase (11.11)
post-implementation system
    review (11.31)
preliminary investigation (11.12)
process (11.16)
program development life cycle
    (PDLC) (11.29)
program specification package
    (11.27)
programmer (11.3)
project dictionary (11.6, 11.17)
project leader (11.4)
project management (11.4)
project management software
    (11.5)

project notebook (11.6)
project plan (11.4)
project request (11.9)
project team (11.4)
prototype (11.27)
rapid application development
    (RAD) (11.27)
repository (11.6, 11.17)
request for information (RFI)
    (11.22)
request for proposal (RFP)
    (11.22)
request for quotation (RFQ)
    (11.22)
request for system services
    (11.9)
schedule feasibility (11.5)
scope (11.4)
source (11.16)
standards (11.3)
steering committee (11.4)
structured analysis and design
    (11.15)
structured English (11.17)
structured interview (11.7)
structured walkthrough (11.29)
support phase (11.31)
system development life cycle
    (SDLC) (11.2)
system enhancement (11.31)
system proposal (11.19)
systems analyst (11.3)
systems flowchart (11.27)
technical feasibility (11.5)
total quality management (TQM)
    (11.30)
trade publications (11.20)
training (11.30)
unstructured interview (11.7)
users (11.3)
value-added reseller (VAR)
    (11.22)
vertical application software
    (11.20)
warranty (11.22)

AT THE MOVIES

www.scsite.com/dc2000/ch11/movies.htm

WELCOME to VIDEO CLIPS from CNN

WEB INSTRUCTIONS: *To display this page from the Web, launch your browser and enter the URL,* *www.scsite.com/dc2000/ch11/movies.htm. Click a picture to view a video. After watching the video, close the video window and then complete the exercise by answering the questions about the video. To view the videos, RealPlayer must be installed on your computer (download by clicking* here).

1 Parents Online

What is an Internet student information system (ISIS)? What information does it provide to a parent? What family and school changes have made such an information system more valuable? For a parent and for a student, what are the advantages and disadvantages of using such a system? If you were a student at a school that used an ISIS, how would you feel about the system?

2 Artificial Intelligence

With the assistance of artificial intelligence, a computer could very well be the next operations manager at your favorite car manufacturing facility. Obviously, car manufacturing is not the only process that will gain from AI. Where do you think AI could best be used? What other uses can you envision for artificial intelligence? Do you think computers might one day become too intelligent? What could be the implications if computers became managers for more and more industries? Is this good or bad? Why?

3 Net Profit

In your opinion, what would help make an Internet business successful? What have you learned in your use of the Web that would make you a successful Web entrepreneur? If you could start your own Internet business, what kind of company would you start? From what you have learned in the video, would you want to start your own Internet business? Why or why not?

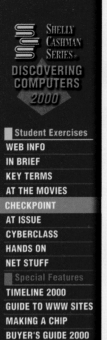

■ Student Exercises
WEB INFO
IN BRIEF
KEY TERMS
AT THE MOVIES
CHECKPOINT
AT ISSUE
CYBERCLASS
HANDS ON
NET STUFF
■ Special Features
TIMELINE 2000
GUIDE TO WWW SITES
MAKING A CHIP
BUYER'S GUIDE 2000
CAREERS 2000
TRENDS 2000
CHAT
INTERACTIVE LABS
NEWS
HOME

CHAPTER 1 2 3 4 5 6 7 8 9 10 11 12 13 14 INDEX

CHECKPOINT www.scsite.com/dc2000/ch11/check.htm

WEB INSTRUCTIONS: *To display this page from the Web, launch your browser and enter the URL, www.scsite.com/dc2000/ch11/check.htm. Click the links for current and additional information. To experience the animation and interactivity, Shockwave and Flash Player must be installed on your computer (download by clicking here).*

Label the Figure

Instructions: *Identify the phases in the system development life cycle.*

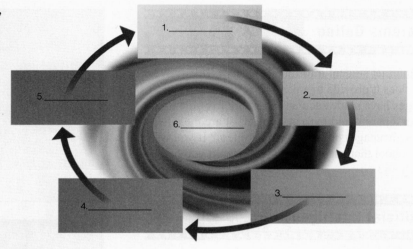

Matching

Instructions: *Match each term from the column on the left with the best description from the column on the right.*

_____ 1. feasibility

_____ 2. operational feasibility

_____ 3. schedule feasibility

_____ 4. technical feasibility

_____ 5. economic feasibility

a. A measure of how different the proposed system is from the needs of the organization.

b. Measures how well the proposed system combines with the emotional and financial needs of company employees.

c. Measures whether the lifetime benefits of the proposed information system will exceed its lifetime costs.

d. Measures whether the organization has or can obtain the hardware, software, networks, and people needed to deliver and support the proposed information system.

e. Measures whether the established deadlines for the project are reasonable.

f. A measure of how suitable the development of a system will be to the organization.

g. Measures how well the proposed information system will work in the organization.

Short Answer

Instructions: *Write a brief answer to each of the following questions.*

1. What is project management? _____ To plan and schedule a project effectively, what components of the project must the project leader identify? _____

2. How is an unstructured interview different from a structured interview? _____ What is a JAD session? _____

3. How is horizontal application software different from vertical application software? _____ What are trade publications? _____

4. How are a request for quotation (RFQ), request for proposal (RFP), and request for information (RFI) different? _____ What is a benchmark test? _____

5. What are computer-aided software engineering (CASE) products? _____ What capabilities do I-CASE products include? _____

AT ISSUE   www.scsite.com/dc2000/ch11/issue.htm

WEB INSTRUCTIONS: *To display this page from the Web, launch your browser and enter the URL,* *www.scsite.com/dc2000/ch11/issue.htm*. *Click the links for current and additional information.*

ONE *From 1950 to 1970, productivity – output per hour of work –* increased almost 3 percent annually. Since that time, however, despite an expanding use of computer information systems, annual increases in productivity have been substantially less. During the first half of the 1990's, growth was under 1 percent. Economists are baffled. Some argue that information systems make the most positive impact where productivity is hard to measure, such as in finance and health care. Others suspect that advancing technology causes workers to spend more time learning new systems than the workers using systems to be more productive. Still others claim workers spend too much time on non-productive computer activities, such as surfing the Net or playing games. Which, if any, of these explanations do you think is correct? Why? What other reasons might there be? How can companies ensure that information systems will make their workers more productive?

TWO *Decision support systems – information systems that help managers* make a determination by summarizing or comparing data – are playing an increasingly important role in business management. Airlines such as United, Delta, and American are using decision support systems to sum up flight histories, aircraft wear, and employee records to optimize seat availability, reduce traffic congestion, anticipate equipment damage, and improve worker performance. By helping managers project trends, the airline decision support systems have increased efficiency, lowered costs, reduced ticket prices, and shortened customer lines. In what other industries do you think decision support systems could be used effectively? Why? Where would decision support systems probably have little impact? Why?

THREE *Most information systems professionals are happy with their work, but a recent* study suggests that the level of satisfaction may be declining. Of the information systems professionals surveyed, 37 percent report their job satisfaction has decreased, and 61 percent feel they are not working to their full potential. The professionals cite a number of reasons for this trend, including uncertain corporate climates, misunderstanding of the role of information systems, lack of power, and limited access to new technologies. In short, many information systems professionals feel senior management fails to understand, and appreciate, the contributions information systems make to an organization. Do you think the discontent of some information systems professionals is a legitimate concern? Why or why not? What can companies do to reduce the disaffection of information systems professionals?

FOUR *Eighteen months after a $5 million information system was placed in full operation,* workers for a New York county were grumbling that the system was plagued with errors. The head of the county's Civil Service Employees Association reported complaints from almost every department. The cost of remedying the flawed system was prohibitive, and county legislators were incensed. During system development, problems are easier and less expensive to fix at some phases in the system development life cycle than at others. When would it be simplest and least costly to identify and solve problems? Why? At what phase would it be more expensive? Why? If you were the project leader, how would your beliefs color the way you manage each phase of the SDLC?

FIVE *Imagine you are head of the information systems department for a small* manufacturing firm. Several department managers have complained that the current information system is outdated and no longer meets their needs. You have organized a committee to investigate the problem. Martha, a department manager, believes that because Colonial Computing supplied the software for the current system, a representative from that vendor should have a featured part in the system development process. George, another manager, disagrees. He maintains that if a new system is necessary, the firm should turn to vendors other than the one who provided software for the current, inadequate system. What do you think are the strengths and weaknesses of the suggestions made by each department manager? As head of the committee, how would you resolve the conflict?

SHELLY
CASHMAN
SERIES®

DISCOVERING
COMPUTERS
2000

Student Exercises
WEB INFO
IN BRIEF
KEY TERMS
AT THE MOVIES
CHECKPOINT
AT ISSUE
CYBERCLASS
HANDS ON
NET STUFF
Special Features
TIMELINE 2000
GUIDE TO WWW SITES
MAKING A CHIP
BUYER'S GUIDE 2000
CAREERS 2000
TRENDS 2000
CHAT
INTERACTIVE LABS
NEWS
HOME

CHAPTER 1 2 3 4 5 6 7 8 9 10 **11** 12 13 14 **INDEX**

CYBERCLASS   www.scsite.com/dc2000/ch11/class.htm

WEB INSTRUCTIONS: *To display this page from the Web, launch your browser and enter the URL, www.scsite.com/dc2000/ch11/class.htm. To start Level I CyberClass, click a Level I link on this page or enter the URL, www.cyber-class.com. Click the Student button, click Discovering Computers 2000 in the list of titles, and then click the Enter a site button. To start Level II or III CyberClass (available only to those purchasers of a CyberClass floppy disk), place your CyberClass floppy disk in drive A, click Start on the taskbar, click Run on the Start menu, type* a:connect *in the Open text box, click the OK button, click the Enter CyberClass button, and then follow the instructions.*

I II III LEVEL **1. Flash Cards**   Click Flash Cards on the Main Menu of the CyberClass web page. Click the plus sign before the Chapter 11 title. Click What Is the System Development Life Cycle and answer all the cards in that section. If you have less than 80% correct, continue to answer cards in other sections until you have more than 80% correct. All users: Answer as many more flash cards as you desire. Close the Electronic Flash Card window and the Flash Cards window by clicking the Close button in the upper-right corner of each window.

I II III LEVEL **2. Practice Test**   Click Testing on the Main Menu of the CyberClass web page. Click the Select a book box arrow and then click Discovering Computers 2000. Click the Select a test to take box arrow and then click the Chapter 11 title in the list. Click the Take Test button. If necessary, maximize the window. Take the practice test and then click the Submit Test button. Click the Display Study Guide button. Review the Study Guide. Scroll down and click the Return to CyberClass button. If you missed two consecutive questions, click the Take another Test button. Continue to take tests until you do not miss consecutive questions in the test.

I II III LEVEL **3. Web Guide**   Click Web Guide on the Main Menu of the CyberClass web page. When the Guide to World Wide Web Sites page displays, click Sports. Visit several of the sites. Do you think sports news is delivered better on the Web than in a newspaper or magazine? What about sports scores that are changed while a game is in progress? Write a brief report explaining and defending your position.

II III LEVEL **4. Company Briefs**   Click Company Briefs on the Main Menu of the CyberClass web page. Click a corporation name to display a case study. Read the case study. Write a report on the training issues the company faces based upon their computer use.

SnapOn

Snap-on Diagnostics

Even if you're one of those talented people who can change your car's oil and tune its engine, there will probably come a time when you have to take your car to a mechanic or automotive technician. Where do you go? Who can you trust? How can you get the work done for the best price? How can you be an intelligent consumer?

One company that has helped consumers answer these questions is Snap-on . This vibrant 77 year old company is the leading supplier of automotive diagnostics and repair products in the world, and in 1996 earned 1.5 billion dollars in revenue. Snap-on is dedicated to finding solutions to every auto shop and repair problem, from diagnostic engine analysis equipment to the simplest

I II III LEVEL **5. CyberChallenge**   Click CyberChallenge on the Main Menu of the CyberClass web page. Click the Select a book box arrow and then click Discovering Computers 2000. Click the Select a board to play box arrow and then click Chapter 11 in the list. Click the Play CyberChallenge button. Maximize the CyberChallenge window. Play CyberChallenge until you have answered correctly all questions for a given vertical column. Close the CyberChallenge window.

II III LEVEL **6. Assignments and Syllabus**   Click Assignments on the Main Menu of the CyberClass web page. Ensure you are aware of all assignments and when they are due. Click Syllabus on the Main Menu of the CyberClass web page. Verify you are up to date on all activities for the class.

II III LEVEL **7. Hot Links**   Click Hot Links on the Main Menu of the CyberClass web page. Click two links that you find in the Hot Links section of the Web page and review the sites where these links take you. Write a brief report indicating which site you liked better and why.

HANDS ON   www.scsite.com/dc2000/ch11/hands.htm

WEB INSTRUCTIONS: *To display this page from the Web, launch your browser and enter the URL,* *www.scsite.com/dc2000/ch11/hands.htm. Click the links for current and additional information.*

One   *Traffic Sign Tutorial*

Insert the Discover Data Disk into drive A. If you do not have the Discover Data Disk, see the inside back cover of this book or see your instructor. Click the Start button on the taskbar and then click Run on the Start menu. In the Open text box, type a:traffic.exe and then press the ENTER key to display the Traffic Sign Tutorial window. This program was written in Visual Basic. Drag the signs to their correct containers. Click Options on the menu bar and then click Clear to reset the tutorial. Click Options on the menu bar and then click Show. Click Options on the menu bar and then click Clear. Click Options on the menu bar and then click Quiz. Answer the quiz questions.

Two   *Dr. Watson*

This exercise uses Windows 98 procedures. Dr. Watson is a <u>Windows diagnostic</u> <u>tool</u> used to identify faults in a system. To find out more about Dr. Watson, click the Start button on the taskbar and then click Help on the Start menu. Click the Index tab. Type Dr. Watson in the text box and then click the Display button. Click an appropriate Help topic in the Topics Found dialog box, click the Display button, and answer the following questions:

- ▲ How is Dr. Watson used to diagnose system faults?
- ▲ How can you open Dr. Watson from the Start menu?
- ▲ How do you use Dr. Watson to create a system snapshot?

Click the Close button to close the Windows Help window.

Three   *Creating a Drawing*

Click the Start button on the taskbar, point to Programs on the Start menu, point to Accessories on the Programs submenu, and then click Paint on the Accessories submenu. Maximize the <u>Paint</u> window. If necessary, drag the lower-right corner of the white rectangle to the right to increase its size. Change the background color to orange by right-clicking the color orange in the color box at the bottom of the Paint window, clicking the Fill With Color tool (row 2, column 2) in the toolbox on the left edge of the window, and right-clicking the white

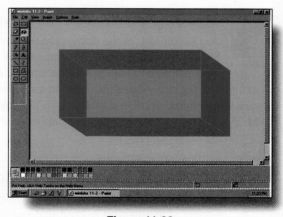

Figure 11-30

rectangle. Change the foreground color to red by clicking the color red in the color box. Use the Rectangle tool (row 7, column 1) and the Line tool (row 6, column 1) in the toolbox to draw the box (Figure 11-30). Use the Fill With Color tool (row 2, column 2) in the toolbox and color box to color the box. If you make a mistake, click Edit on the menu bar and then click Undo to erase your last draw. Click File on the menu bar and then click Save. With a floppy disk in drive A type a:h11-3 in the File name text box. Click the Save button. Click File on the menu bar and then click Print. Click the OK button. Close Paint.

Four   *Capturing Screen Images*

Click the Start button on the taskbar, point to Programs on the Start menu, and point to Accessories on the Programs submenu. Press the PRINT SCREEN key on your keyboard. Click WordPad on the Accessories submenu. In <u>WordPad</u>, type Below is a Windows Screen Shot: and press the ENTER key twice. Click Edit on the menu bar and then click Paste. Use the scroll bar to scroll the document. Click the Print button on the toolbar to print the file. Close WordPad. Do not save the file.

SHELLY CASHMAN SERIES®

DISCOVERING COMPUTERS 2000

Student Exercises
WEB INFO
IN BRIEF
KEY TERMS
AT THE MOVIES
CHECKPOINT
AT ISSUE
CYBERCLASS
HANDS ON
NET STUFF
Special Features
TIMELINE 2000
GUIDE TO WWW SITES
MAKING A CHIP
BUYER'S GUIDE 2000
CAREERS 2000
TRENDS 2000
CHAT
INTERACTIVE LABS
NEWS
HOME

CHAPTER   1   2   3   4   5   6   7   8   9   10   **11**   12   13   14   **INDEX**

NET STUFF   www.scsite.com/dc2000/ch11/net.htm

WEB INSTRUCTIONS: *To display this page from the Web, launch your browser and enter the URL,* *www.scsite.com/dc2000/ch11/net.htm.*

CUSTOMIZING YOUR E-MAIL

1. Customizing Your E-Mail Program

Many e-mail programs can be customized to block messages from certain senders, direct mail to particular folders, or add a signature to outgoing messages. To customize your e-mail program, click the CUSTOMIZING YOUR E-MAIL button to display your e-mail service. Enter your Login Name and Password. When the In-Box screen displays, click Options. On the Options sheet, click the Filters link in the Mail Handling column. Follow the directions on the Options: Filters sheet to block senders of mail you do not want to receive and direct incoming messages to specific folders. Click the OK button. On the Options sheet, click the Signature link in the Additional Options column. Follow the directions on the Options: Signature sheet to create a signature that will be added to outgoing messages. Click the OK button. Read any new mail. When you have read all of your messages, click Log Out to exit.

SDLC

2. System Development Life Cycle (SDLC)

People deal with problems in a variety of ways. Education alone does not guarantee success at problem solving. An anthropologist studying workers in Silicon Valley tells the story of an engineer who kept a list of dilemmas he faced and possible answers. When the list got too long, the engineer's solution simply was to combine the problems into a shorter list. The core of the SDLC is based on a standard, more effective approach to problem solving. To learn about different approaches, click the SDLC button and complete this exercise.

CASE

3. Computer-Aided Software Engineering (CASE)

A difficult task in the design phase is to systematize all of the information needed by an organization and to document the flow of data within the organization. One estimate indicates that the amount of material amassed in this phase is greater than the quantity of information an average person in the seventeenth century would come upon in a lifetime. To learn more about one of the many CASE products available for managing information and tracking data, click the CASE button and complete this exercise.

Consistency
Completeness
Conformation to Standards

IN THE NEWS

4. In the News

When teams from around the world gathered in France for the World Cup soccer championship, more than 60 groups of researchers met at a Paris café for another event – the annual Robot Football World Cup. The contest pits squads of automatons in modified soccer games designed to refine robotics, advance artificial intelligence, and offer some fun. Click the IN THE NEWS button and read a news article about an innovative development or use of a computer information system. Who developed or used the system? In what way is the development or use of the system original?

WEB CHAT

5. Web Chat

When the Denver Broncos won the Super Bowl, every player and coach received a ring as a symbol of victory in football's ultimate contest. A more unexpected recipient of the coveted ring was the head of the team's information systems department. Computerized information systems (IS) are used throughout the season to evaluate players, develop game plans, and even handle travel accommodations. Nevertheless, some wonder if the technological wizards earned the same symbolic award as the playing-field warriors. The importance of information systems in any organization's success or failure is a hotly disputed issue. When sales slip or profits plunge, IS professionals often complain if staff or bonuses are cut, especially if the downturn is attributed to corporate mistakes. Should IS professionals be rewarded or penalized based on the overall performance of an organization? Why? How closely should an organization's success or failure be tied to evaluation of information systems? Why? Click the WEB CHAT button to enter a Web Chat discussion related to this topic.

CHAPTER 12

PROGRAM DEVELOPMENT AND PROGRAMMING LANGUAGES

OBJECTIVES

After completing this chapter, you will be able to:

Explain the six steps in the program development life cycle

Describe top-down program design

Explain structured program design and the three basic control structures

Explain the differences among the categories of programming languages

Describe the object-oriented approach to program development

Identify programming languages commonly used today

Identify the uses of application generators, macros, and RAD tools

Describe various Web page development tools, including HTML, DHTML, and XML

As you learned in Chapter 11, the system development life cycle consists of five phases, one of which is implementation. If, during the analysis phase, the development team recommends building custom software (instead of purchasing packaged software), then a major part of the implementation phase involves writing and testing computer programs.

Although you may never write a computer program yourself, you may request information that requires a program to be written or modified. Thus, you will benefit from an understanding of how programmers develop the programs that meet those information requirements. Program development consists of six steps, which collectively are referred to as the program development life cycle. This chapter discusses each step in the program development life cycle and presents the tools used to make this process efficient. This chapter also explains various programming languages and program development tools used to write and develop computer programs.

WHAT IS A COMPUTER PROGRAM?

A **computer program** is a set of instructions that directs a computer to perform the tasks necessary to process data into information. A computer programmer might write these instructions using a **programming language**, which are sets of words, symbols, and codes used to create instructions a computer can process and execute. The steps that a programmer uses to build a computer program collectively are called the program development life cycle.

THE PROGRAM DEVELOPMENT LIFE CYCLE

The **program development life cycle (PDLC)** is a set of steps that programmers use to build computer programs. Whereas much of the system development life cycle guides systems analysts through the development of an information system, the program development life cycle guides computer programmers through the development of a program. The program development life cycle consists of six steps (Figure 12-1).

1. Analyze Problem

2. Design Programs

3. Code Programs

4. Test Programs

5. Formalize Solution

6. Maintain Programs

As illustrated in Figure 12-1, the steps in the PDLC form a loop; that is, program development is an ongoing process within the system development life cycle. The Maintain Programs step connects to the Analyze Problem step to complete the loop. Each time a user, programmer, or analyst identifies errors in or improvements to a program and requests program modifications, the Analyze Problem step begins again, and the program development life cycle starts over.

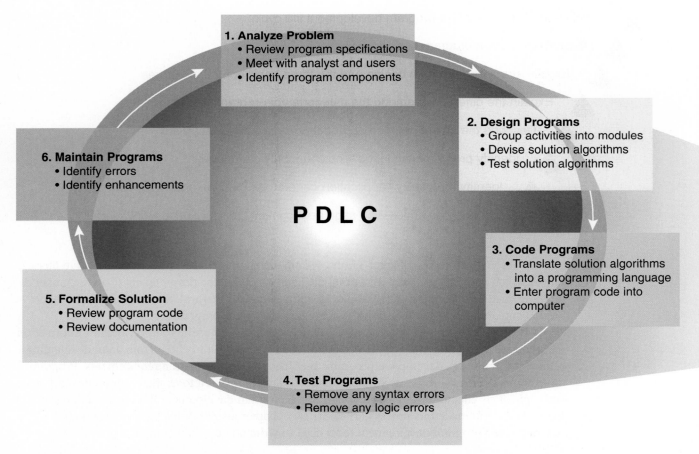

Figure 12-1 *The program development life cycle consists of six steps that form a loop.*

What Initiates the Program Development Life Cycle?

Requests for a new or modified program usually are made at the end of the analysis phase of the system development life cycle (SDLC). Recall from Chapter 11 that the SDLC consists of five major phases: planning, analysis, design, implementation, and support. At the end of the analysis phase, the company often faces a build-or-buy decision; that is, management must determine whether to buy packaged software or build custom software specifically designed to meet its needs.

If the company decides to build custom software, it then must decide whether to develop the software in-house using its own information systems personnel or have an outside source develop it specifically for the company. If the company opts for in-house development, the design phase of the SDLC focuses on creating a detailed set of system and program requirements for the programmer(s). These detailed design specifications, called the **program specification package**, include the relationship among programs in a system, as well as the input, output, processing, and data requirements of each program.

Preparing the program specification package is the last activity in the design phase of the SDLC. Once the programmer receives the program specification package, the implementation phase begins, with the programmer analyzing the problem to be solved. The program development life cycle thus begins at the start of the implementation phase. The steps of the PDLC are completed within the implementation phase of the system development life cycle (Figure 12-2).

The scope of the program specification package largely determines the number of programmers working on the program development. If the specifications have a large scope, a group of programmers, called the **programming team**, usually develops the programs. If the specifications are fairly simple, a single programmer might complete all of the development tasks. Whether a single programmer or a programming team, all of the programmers involved must interact with members of the system development project team (including the systems analyst and the users) throughout the program development life cycle.

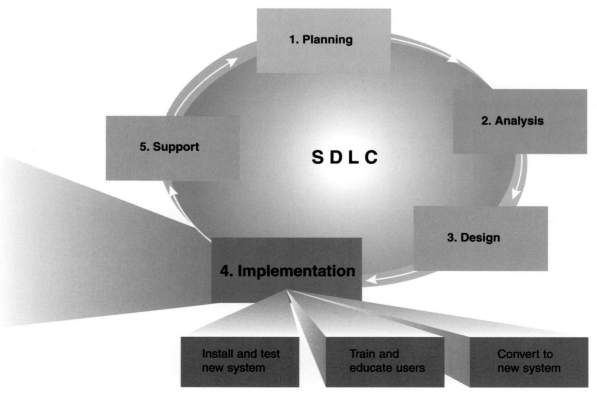

Figure 12-2 *The program development life cycle is part of the implementation phase of the system development life cycle.*

By following the steps in the PDLC, programmers can create programs that are correct (produce accurate information) and maintainable (easy to modify). Involving the project team further helps programmers build programs that meet user requirements. The following sections address each of the steps in the program development life cycle.

STEP 1 – ANALYZE PROBLEM

The first step in the program development life cycle is to analyze the problem the program(s) should solve so you can begin to develop an appropriate solution. In most cases, the solution requires more than one program. This analysis step consists of three major tasks: (1) reviewing the program specifications package, (2) meeting with the systems analyst and users, and (3) identifying each program's input, output, and processing components.

First, you review the program specifications package, which contains relationships among programs in the system, as well as the input, output, processing, and data requirements for each program. Within the program specifications package, these requirements are presented as a variety of deliverables such as charts, diagrams, reports, and files. For example, you use screen and report layout charts to document input and output requirements. System flowcharts, structured English, decision tables, and decision trees document program design (processing) requirements. The data dictionary identifies the data requirements. Thoroughly reviewing these deliverables helps the programmer understand the nature and requirements of each program.

In addition to reviewing the deliverables, the programmer should meet with the systems analyst and the users to understand the purpose of the program from the users' perspective. Recall from Chapter 11 that a guideline of system development is to involve users throughout the entire system development process.

If, after reviewing the program specifications package and meeting with the systems analyst and users, the programmer recommends a change to some aspect of the design specifications, he or she discusses the change with the systems analyst and the users. If everyone agrees with the change, the programmer can modify the design specifications. A programmer never should make any change without both the systems analyst's and users' approval.

Once design specifications are established, the programmer defines the input, processing, and output (IPO) requirements for each program. To help collect and better define these requirements, many programmers use an IPO chart (Figure 12-3). An **IPO chart**, also called a **defining diagram**, identifies the inputs to a program, the outputs the program will generate, and the processing steps required to transform the inputs into the outputs. As with the program specifications package, you should review the contents of the IPO chart with the systems analyst and the users to ensure you completely understand *what* the program is to accomplish; that is, the program requirements. Once the problem analysis is complete, the programmer begins designing programs to solve the problem.

INPUT	PROCESSING	OUTPUT
Unit price	Read unit price, quantity purchased, discount code	Net amount due
Quantity purchased	Calculate gross amount due	
Discount code	If discount applies, calculate discount amount	
	Calculate net amount due	
	Print net amount due	

Figure 12-3 *An IPO (Input Process Output) chart is a tool that assists the programmer in analyzing a program.*

STEP 2 – DESIGN PROGRAMS

Designing the programs involves three tasks: (1) grouping each program's activities into modules, (2) devising a solution algorithm for each module, and (3) testing the solution algorithms. The first task is called top-down design, which continues to focus on *what* the program should do (the requirements). The last two tasks, which are part of a process called structured design, determine *how* to build the programs based on the requirements.

Top-Down Design

Top-down design breaks down the original set of program specifications into smaller, more manageable sections, each of which is easier to solve than the original one. With top-down design, the programmer uses a telescopic approach to view a program, that is, beginning with the big picture and then zooming in on the details.

The first step in top-down design is to identify the major function of a program, sometimes called the main routine. Next, you decompose (break down) the main routine into smaller sections, which often are called

subroutines because they are subordinate to the main routine. Then, you analyze each subroutine to determine if it can be decomposed further. You continue decomposing subroutines until each one performs a single function. A section of a program dedicated to performing a single function is called a **module**. Each subroutine is a module; the main routine often is called the main module.

Programmers use a **hierarchy chart**, also called a **structure chart** or **top-down chart**, to represent these program modules graphically (Figure 12-4). The hierarchy chart represents each module with a rectangle labeled with the module name. The main module is located at the top of the chart. All other modules are placed below the main module, connected by lines that indicate their relationships. In Figure 12-4, for example, the initialization, process, and wrap-up modules are subordinate to the main module.

Programs developed using the top-down approach benefit from the simplicity of their design — they usually are reliable and easy to read and maintain. For these reasons, many computer professionals and programmers recommend the top-down approach to program design.

WEB INFO
WEB INFO

For more information on top-down design, visit the Discovering Computers 2000 Chapter 12 WEB INFO page (**www.scsite.com/ dc2000/ch12/webinfo.htm**) and click Top-Down Design.

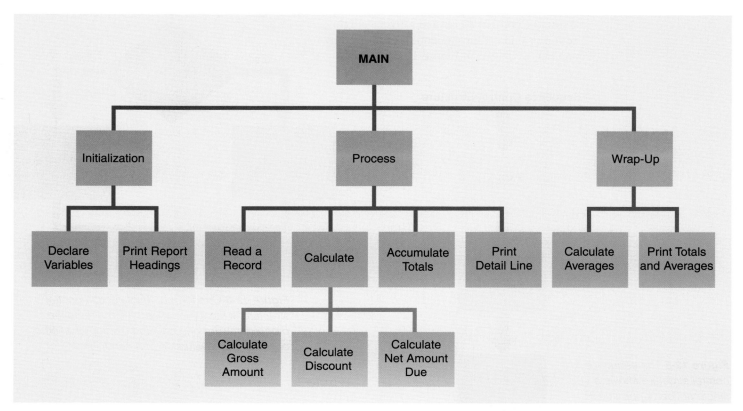

Figure 12-4 *The hierarchy chart is a tool the programmer uses during top-down design. On the hierarchy chart, the program modules are drawn as rectangles. All modules are subordinate to the main module.*

Structured Design

Once the programmer has identified the modules for a program (the *what*), the next step is to identify the logical order of the tasks required to accomplish the function described in each module (the *how*). A graphical or written description of the step-by-step procedures for a module is called the **solution algorithm** or **program logic**. Determining the logic for a program usually is a programmer's most challenging task, one that requires an understanding of structured design concepts, as well as creativity. Thus, defining the solution algorithm is both an art and a skill.

Structured design is an approach in which all program logic is constructed from a combination of three control structures. A **control structure**, or **construct**, is a design that controls the logical order in which program instructions are executed so that actions take place. Actions can be inputs, processes, and outputs, such as reading a record, calculating averages and totals, or printing totals. Each module in a program typically contains more than one control structure. Structured design uses three basic control structures: sequence, selection, and repetition.

SEQUENCE CONTROL STRUCTURE A **sequence control structure** shows a single action or one action sequentially followed by another, as shown in Figure 12-5.

WEB INFO

For more information on structured design, visit the Discovering Computers 2000 Chapter 12 WEB INFO page (**www.scsite.com/ dc2000/ch12/webinfo.htm**) and click Structured Design.

SELECTION CONTROL STRUCTURE A **selection control structure** tells the program which action to take, based on a certain condition. When the condition is evaluated, its result is either true or false. A condition is represented by a diamond symbol. The if-then-else control structure and the case control structure are two common types of selection control structures.

When the condition in an **if-then-else control structure** is evaluated, it yields one of two possibilities: true or false (Figure 12-6). If the result of the condition is true, then one action is performed; if it is false, a different (or possibly no) action is performed. For example, the selection control structure can determine if an employee should receive overtime pay. In this case, a possible condition might be the following: Is Hours Worked greater than 40? If the response is yes (true), then the action would calculate straight-time pay and overtime pay. If the response is no (false), then the action would calculate only straight-time pay.

Sequence Control Structure

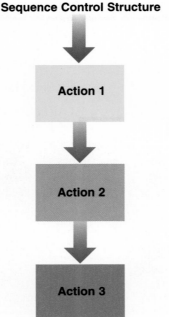

Figure 12-5 *The sequence control structure shows a single action or one action followed by another.*

Selection Control Structure

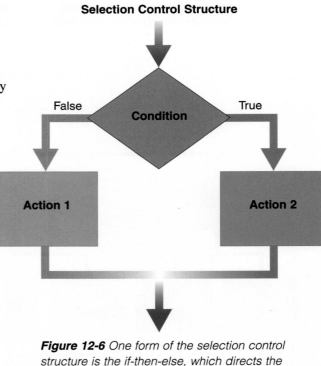

Figure 12-6 *One form of the selection control structure is the if-then-else, which directs the program toward one course of action or another based on the evaluation of a condition.*

The **case control structure** is a variation of the if-then-else control structure that is used when a condition can yield one of three or more possibilities (Figure 12-7). The size of a soft drink, for example, might be one of four possibilities: small, medium, large, or extra large. A case control structure would determine the price based on the size purchased.

REPETITION CONTROL STRUCTURE

The **repetition control structure**, also called the **iteration control structure**, is used when one or more actions are to be performed repeatedly as long as a certain condition is met. Each iteration sometimes is called a loop. Two forms of the repetition control structure are the do-while and do-until.

The **do-while control structure** repeats one or more times as long as a condition is true (Figure 12-8). The do-while control structure tests a condition at the *beginning* of the loop and, if the result of the condition is true, the action(s) inside the loop is executed. Then, the program loops back and tests the condition again. If the result of the condition is still true, the action(s) inside the loop is executed again. This looping process continues until the condition being tested becomes false. At that time, the program stops looping and moves to another set of actions in the algorithm.

The do-while control structure frequently is used to process all records in a file. A payroll program using a do-while control structure, for example, loops once for each employee and stops looping when it processes the last employee's paycheck.

The **do-until control structure** is similar to the do-while but has two major differences: where it tests the condition and when it stops looping. First, the do-until control structure tests the condition at the *end* of the loop (Figure 12-9). The action(s) in a do-until control structure thus always will execute at least once. A do-while control structure, by contrast, might not execute at all — if the condition is false the first time it is tested. Second, unlike a do-while control structure that continues to loop *while* the condition is true, a do-until control structure continues looping *until* the condition is true — and then stops.

Do-While Control Structure

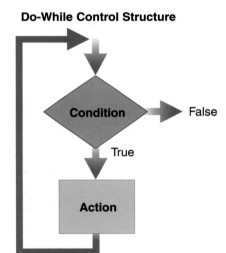

Figure 12-8 One form of the repetition control structure is the do-while, which tests the condition at the beginning of the loop.

Do-Until Control Structure

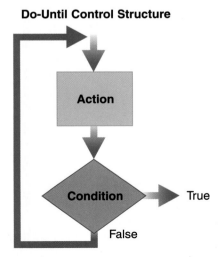

Figure 12-9 Another form of the repetition control structure is the do-until, which tests the condition at the end of the loop.

Case Control Structure

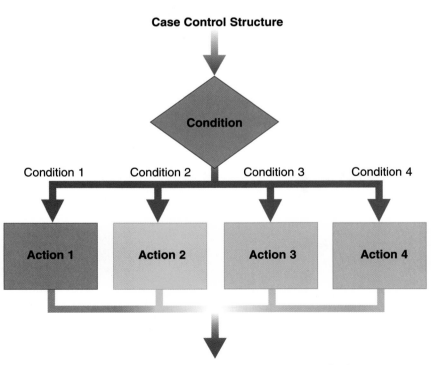

Figure 12-7 Another form of the selection control structure is the case, which allows for more than two alternatives when the condition is evaluated.

Proper Program Design

Programs designed using top-down and structured techniques are simple, yet effective. These programs also are reliable and easy to use and maintain. When using top-down and structured techniques, a programmer must take care to ensure that each program adheres to proper program design rules. A **proper program** is constructed in such a way that the program, each of its modules, and each of its control structures has the following characteristics.

1. No dead code

2. No infinite loops

3. One entry point

4. One exit point

    Dead code is any code, or program instruction, that a program never executes. Sometimes, while a programmer is writing a program, he or she will write a section of code in the program, and then decide not to use the code, but will leave the code in the program anyway. This unused code, called dead code, serves no purpose and should not exist.

    An **infinite loop** is a set of instructions that repeats indefinitely, or forever. Properly designed business programs should not contain infinite loops.

    An **entry point** is the location where a program, a module, or a control structure begins; an **exit point** is where it ends. Figure 12-10 shows the entry and exit points of a module with two control structures: an if-then-else control structure within a do-while control structure. The entry point of the do-while control structure is just prior to the first condition; the exit point occurs when the result of this condition is false. The entry point of the if-then-else control structure occurs just prior to the second condition; the exit point occurs just after one of the two actions is executed.

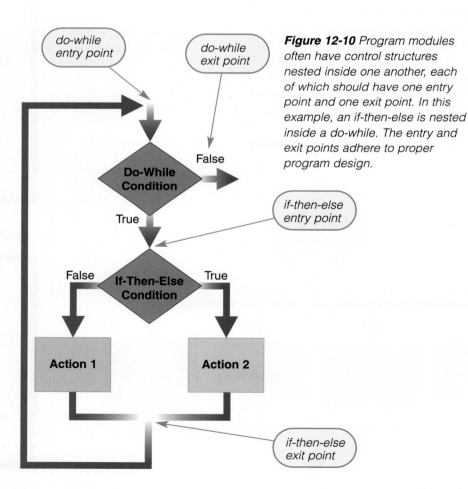

Figure 12-10 Program modules often have control structures nested inside one another, each of which should have one entry point and one exit point. In this example, an if-then-else is nested inside a do-while. The entry and exit points adhere to proper program design.

A properly designed program, module, or control structure has only one entry point and one exit point. Prior to the introduction of this concept, many programs were designed with multiple entry and exit points, which meant that frequently they jumped from one section of code to another. Such poorly designed programs often were called *spaghetti code*, because if you drew a line connecting all of the jumps together, the resulting line would look like cooked spaghetti! If you restrict program logic to the three basic control structures, however, your algorithms naturally will follow the single entry and single exit point rule.

Design Tools

To help develop a solution algorithm, programmers use **design tools**. Three commonly used design tools are program flowcharts, Nassi-Schneiderman charts, and pseudocode.

PROGRAM FLOWCHART A **program flowchart**, or simply **flowchart**, graphically shows the logic in a solution algorithm. The American National Standards Institute (ANSI) published a set of standards for program flowcharts in the early 1960s. These standards, still used today, specify symbols that represent various operations in a program's logic (Figure 12-11).

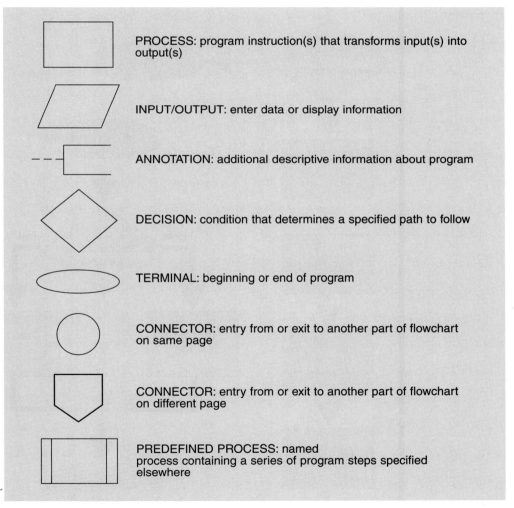

PROCESS: program instruction(s) that transforms input(s) into output(s)

INPUT/OUTPUT: enter data or display information

ANNOTATION: additional descriptive information about program

DECISION: condition that determines a specified path to follow

TERMINAL: beginning or end of program

CONNECTOR: entry from or exit to another part of flowchart on same page

CONNECTOR: entry from or exit to another part of flowchart on different page

PREDEFINED PROCESS: named process containing a series of program steps specified elsewhere

Figure 12-11 *Standard symbols used to create program flowcharts.*

WEB INFO
WEB INFO

For more information
on flowcharting software,
visit the Discovering
Computers 2000
Chapter 12 WEB INFO
page (**www.scsite.com/
dc2000/ch12/webinfo.htm**)
and click Flowcharting
Software.

Most symbols on a program flowchart are connected by solid lines that show the direction of the program. Dotted lines are used to connect **comment symbols**, also called **annotation symbols**, which explain or clarify logic in the algorithm. Figure 12-12 shows the program flowchart for three modules of the program shown in the hierarchy chart in Figure 12-4 on page 12.5.

In the past, programmers used a template to trace the symbols for a flowchart on paper. Today, programmers use commercial **flowcharting software** to develop flowcharts, which makes these flowcharts easy to modify and update (Figure 12-13). Today's flowcharts also use structured design constructs, which early program flowcharts did not use.

NASSI-SCHNEIDERMAN CHART A **Nassi-Schneiderman (N-S) chart** also graphically shows the logic in a solution algorithm. Because Nassi-Schneiderman charts are designed to represent each of the three basic control structures, they sometimes are called **structured flowcharts**. Unlike program flowcharts, an N-S chart does not use lines to

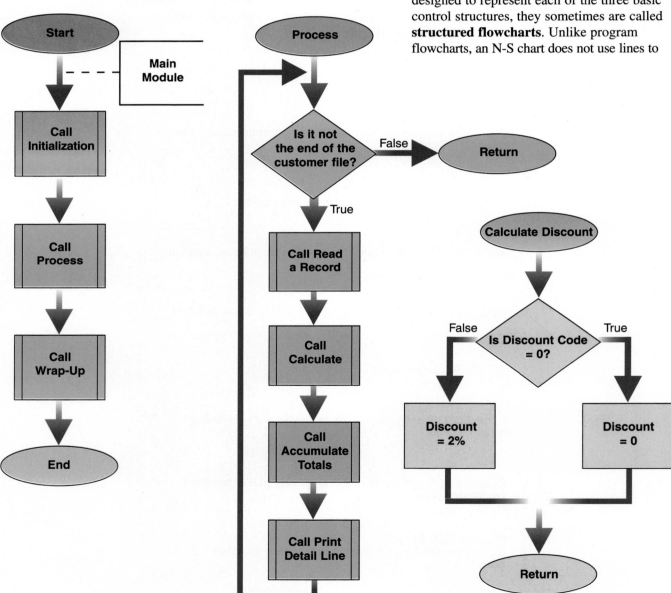

Figure 12-12 *A program flowchart is drawn for each module on the hierarchy chart. Three modules are shown in this figure: main, process, and calculate discount from Figure 12-4. Notice the main module is terminated with the word, End; whereas, the subordinate modules end with the word, Return, because they return to a higher-level module.*

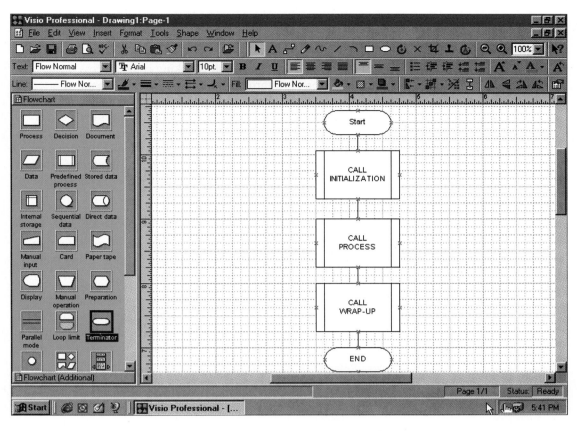

Figure 12-13 Visio is a popular flowcharting software package.

show direction. Instead, N-S charts use a series of rectangular boxes, one below the next, with the flow always moving from top to bottom. In Figure 12-14, the same three program modules shown in Figure 12-12 are illustrated in the form of an N-S chart.

PSEUDOCODE Some programmers prefer to explain the logic of a solution algorithm with a more English-like technique (instead of a graphical flowcharting technique). **Pseudocode** uses an abbreviated form of English to outline program logic. You identify the three basic control structures by their **indentation**: the beginning and end of the module start at the left margin, and the

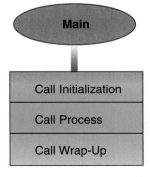

Figure 12-14 An N-S chart is an alternative method of showing program logic. This figure shows the same three modules (main, process, and calculate discount) as illustrated in Figure 12-12 with program flowcharts.

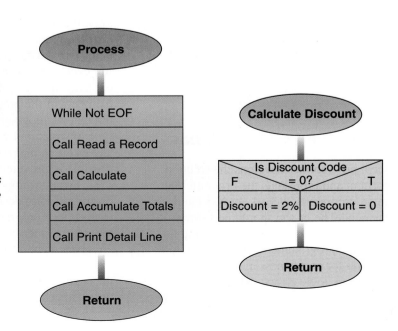

actions within the module are indented. The actions within a control structure in a module also are indented so you clearly can identify the beginning and end of the control structure. Figure 12-15 shows the pseudocode for the same three program modules represented in Figures 12-12 on page 12.10 and 12-14 on page 12.11.

```
MAIN MODULE:

        CALL Initialization
        CALL Process
        CALL Wrap-Up

END

PROCESS MODULE:

        DO WHILE Not EOF
                CALL Read a Record
                CALL Calculate
                CALL Accumulate Totals
                CALL Print Detail Line
        ENDDO

RETURN

CALCULATE DISCOUNT MODULE:

        IF Discount Code = 0 THEN
                Discount = 0
        ELSE
                Discount = .02
        ENDIF

RETURN
```

Figure 12-15 *Pseudocode is yet another alternative method of showing program logic. This figure shows the same three modules (main, process, and calculate discount) as illustrated in Figure 12-12 with program flowcharts and Figure 12-14 with N-S charts.*

Quality Review Techniques

Once a programmer develops the solution algorithm and represents the program logic using a program flowchart, an N-S chart, or pseudocode, he or she should perform a **quality review** of the program. During this review, the programmer checks the solution algorithm for correctness and attempts to uncover any logic errors. A **logic error** is a flaw in the design that generates inaccurate results. Desk checking and structured walk-throughs are two techniques used to check a solution algorithm.

Desk checking is the process of stepping through the logic of the algorithm with test data. **Test data** is sample data that simulates data the program might process when it is implemented. The programmer that developed the solution algorithm usually performs the desk check, but another programmer also can perform the desk check. Desk checking involves five steps.

1. Developing sets of test data (inputs)

2. Determining the expected result (output) for each set of data, without using the solution algorithm

3. Stepping through the solution algorithm using one set of test data and writing down the actual result obtained (output) using the solution algorithm

4. Comparing the expected result from Step 2 to the actual result from Step 3

5. Repeating Steps 3 and 4 for each set of test data

If the expected result and actual result do not match for each set of the data, the program has a logic error. If this occurs, you must review the logic of the solution algorithm to determine the source of the error and then correct it.

A more formal technique for checking the solution algorithm is a structured walk-through. As discussed in Chapter 11, a systems analyst commonly uses a **structured walk-through** to review deliverables during the system development life cycle. A programmer also can request a walkthrough of a solution algorithm during the program development life cycle. In this case, the programmer explains the logic of the algorithm while members of the programming team step through the program logic. The purpose of this type of structured walkthrough is to identify any errors in the program logic and check for possible improvements in program design.

Errors or improvements discovered during program design usually are corrected easily. Once program design is complete and the programmer begins coding, however, errors are more difficult to fix. Early detection of errors and program design improvements thus reduces the overall program development time and cost.

STEP 3 – CODE PROGRAMS

Coding a program involves two steps: (1) translating the solution algorithm into a programming language and (2) entering the programming language code into the computer. As previously mentioned, many different programming languages exist. Each of these has a particular **syntax**, or set of grammar and rules, that specifies how to write the instructions in a solution algorithm. An instruction to add three numbers, for example, is written differently in each programming language, according to its syntax. Fortunately, many of the commonly used programming languages follow a set of code standards developed by the American National Standards Institute (ANSI). Following these code standards ensures that the final program will run on many different types of computers, as well as many different operating systems.

As you enter a program into the computer, you should take time to document the program code thoroughly. In addition to any external program documentation such as flowcharts or N-S charts, a program also has its own documentation, called **comments** or **remarks**. A program should include both global and internal comments (Figure 12-16). For best results, position global comments at the top of the program to identify the program, its author, and the date written and to explain the program's purpose. Write internal comments throughout the body of the program to explain the purpose of the code statements within the program. Programs that are documented thoroughly are much easier to maintain.

STEP 4 – TEST PROGRAMS

Once a programmer codes the solution algorithm, the next step is to test the program. Thorough testing is very important, because once the program is put into use, many users will rely on the program and its output to support daily activities and decisions. The goal of **program testing** thus is to ensure that the program runs correctly and is error free. Errors uncovered during this step usually are one of two types: (1) syntax errors or (2) logic errors.

A **syntax error** occurs when the code violates the syntax, or grammar, of the programming language. Misspelling a command, leaving out required punctuation, or typing command words out of order all will cause syntax errors. Syntax errors often are discovered the first time the computer executes the program code. When a syntax error is located, a message either displays on the screen immediately or is written to a log file. Either way, the programmer must review and correct all syntax errors.

The procedure for testing for logic errors at this step is much like the desk checking techniques used in the Design Programs step. First, you develop test data. Unlike the Design Programs step, in which the programmer develops the test data, the systems analyst usually develops the test data in the Test Programs step to ensure that the test data is unbiased. The test data should include both valid (correct) and invalid (incorrect) input data. When valid test data is input, the program should output the correct

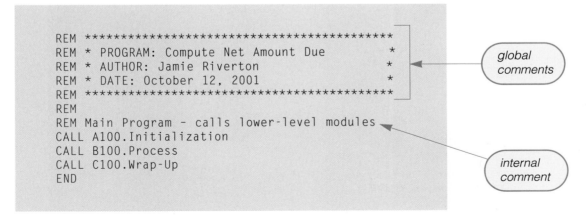

Figure 12-16 *Thorough documentation leads to maintainable programs. A program should contain global comments (at the top of the program) and internal comments (throughout the body of the program). In this QuickBASIC program, comments are identified by the letters, REM, which are an abbreviation for REMARK.*

result. If the expected result and actual result do not match, the program has a logic error. In this case, you must review the logic of the program code to determine the source of the logic error and then correct it.

Another purpose of using test data is to try to *crash* the system; that is, try to make it fail. For example, if the pay rate for employees cannot exceed $55 per hour, then the test data should use some valid pay rates, such as $25 and $10.50, as well as some invalid ones, such as $-32.00 and $72.50. When you input an invalid pay rate, the program should display an error message and allow you to re-enter the pay rate. If, however, the program accepts an invalid pay rate, it contains a logic error.

The process of locating and correcting syntax and logic errors in a program is called **debugging**. The errors themselves are referred to as **bugs**; thus, removing the errors is debugging. A popular story is that the term, bug, originated when the failure of one of the first computers was traced to an actual bug, a moth, that was lodged in the computer's electronic components (Figure 12-17). Most programming languages include a debug utility. A **debug utility**, or **debugger**, allows you to identify syntax errors and to find logic errors by examining program values (such as the result of a calculation) while the program runs in slow motion.

A bug found in many computers was the **Millenium Bug**, also called the **Year 2000 Bug** or **Y2k Bug**, which has the potential to cause serious financial losses. With this bug, on January 1, 2000 dates were read by non-Y2k compliant computers as 01/01/00, a year that is indistinguishable from 1900 or 3000, which caused some computer hardware and software to operate according to the wrong date.

If a program has been well designed during the Design Programs step, then testing should not require much time. If the programmer did not test the solution algorithm thoroughly during design, however, many logic errors may exist and testing can take longer. As a general rule, the more time and effort a programmer spends in analyzing and designing the solution algorithm, the less time he or she will spend debugging the program.

STEP 5 – FORMALIZE SOLUTION

In formalizing the solution, the programmer performs two activities: (1) reviewing the program code and (2) reviewing all the documentation.

First, you review the program for any dead code and remove it. Then, you should run the program one final time to verify it

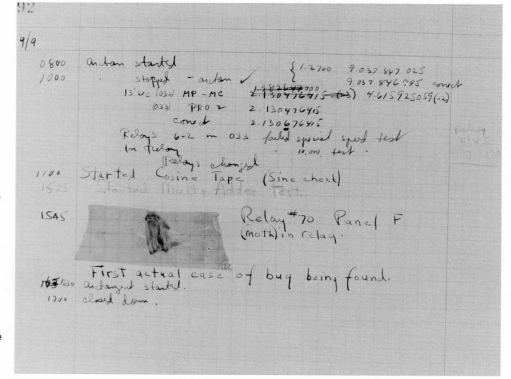

Figure 12-17 In 1945, the cause of the temporary failure of the world's first electro-mechanical computer, the Mark 1, was traced to a dead moth (shown taped to the log book) caught in the electrical components. Some say this event is the origin of the term, bug, meaning computer error.

After reviewing the program code, the programmer gives the program and all of the documentation to the systems analyst. The documentation includes the following: a hierarchy chart; a solution algorithm in the form of a program flowchart, an N-S chart, or pseudocode; test data; and program code listings containing global and internal comments. You should review each of these documents for completeness and accuracy.

Documentation becomes especially valuable if the program requires changes at a later date. One year later, for example, a new programmer might have to update the programs. Proper documentation substantially reduces the amount of time the new programmer spends learning about the programs so he or she can make changes effectively and efficiently.

STEP 6 – MAINTAIN PROGRAMS

Maintaining programs involves two activities: (1) correcting errors and (2) adding enhancements. Once programs are **implemented**, or placed into production, users interact with the programs to process real, or *live*, transactions. During the course of their use, programs may require maintenance. One type of maintenance occurs when users find syntax or logic errors. If the solution algorithm and program code were tested thoroughly in the previous steps, the number of errors found during production should be very small.

A more common type of maintenance occurs when a user would like the programs to have different features or functionality. **Program enhancement** involves modifying or expanding the existing programs.

When a user identifies an error or enhancement, he or she typically notifies the systems analyst, who in turn contacts and meets with a programmer. Sometimes, the systems analyst meets with the programmer who wrote the original program; if that programmer is unavailable, the systems analyst will meet with a different programmer. During the initial meeting, the systems analyst and the programmer begin analyzing the problem or enhancement, which is Step 1 in the program development life cycle. The program development life cycle thus completes its loop and begins again.

PROGRAMMING LANGUAGES AND PROGRAM DEVELOPMENT TOOLS

A computer programmer can select from a variety of programming languages or program development tools to create solutions to information system requirements. A **programming language** is a set of words, symbols, and codes that enables a programmer to communicate a solution algorithm to the computer. Just as humans understand a variety of spoken languages (English, Spanish, French, and so on), computers recognize a variety of programming languages.

A **program development tool** consists of user-friendly software products designed to assist in the creation of information system solutions. These program development tools automatically create the programming language instructions necessary to communicate with the computer. With program development tools, a developer typically does not need to learn a programming language.

The following sections discuss programming languages and program development tools.

CATEGORIES OF PROGRAMMING LANGUAGES

Several hundred programming languages exist, each with its own language rules, or syntax. Some languages were developed for specific computers; others were developed for specific uses, such as scientific or business applications. As previously noted, the American National Standards Institute (ANSI) has standardized some of these languages. Programs written in an ANSI-standard language thus can run on many different types of computers, as well as many different operating systems.

Programming languages are classified into five major categories: machine languages, assembly languages, third-generation languages, fourth-generation languages, and natural languages. Machine and assembly languages are referred to as low-level languages; third-generation, fourth-generation, and natural languages are called high-level languages. A **low-level language** is written to run on one particular computer. A **high-level language** can run on many different types of computers.

Machine Languages

The only language that the computer directly understands is **machine language**, which also is called a first-generation language (Figure 12-18). Machine language instructions use a series of binary digits (1s and 0s) that correspond to the on and off electrical states of a computer.

Machine language programs run only on the computer for which they were developed; that is, they are **machine-dependent**. One disadvantage of machine language programs then is that they are not portable to other computers. Second, as you might imagine, coding in the 1s and 0s of machine language can be tedious and time-consuming.

Assembly Languages

Because machine language programs were so difficult to write, a second generation of programming languages, called assembly languages, evolved. With an **assembly language**, instructions are written using abbreviations and codes (Figure 12-19). As with machine languages, assembly languages often are difficult to learn and are machine-dependent.

Assembly languages do have several advantages over machine languages. Instead of using a series of bits, the programmer uses meaningful abbreviations for program instructions, called **symbolic instruction codes**, or **mnemonics**. With an assembly language, a programmer writes codes such as A for

```
                                          00090
000090   50E0   30B2                      010B4
000094   1B44
000096   1B77
000098   1B55
00009A   F273   30D6   2C81   010D8        00C83
0000A0   4F50   30D6                       010D8
0000A4   F275   30D6   2C7B   010D8        00C7D
0000AA   4F70   30D6                       010D8
0000AE   5070   304A                       0104C
0000B2   1C47
0000B4   5050   304E                       01050
0000B8   58E0   30B2                       010B4
0000BC   07FE
                                          000BE
0000BE   50E0   30B6                       010B8
0000C2   95F1   2C85          00C87
0000C6   4770   20D2          000D4
0000CA   1B55
0000CC   5A50   35A6                       015A8
0000D0   47F0   2100          00102
0000D4   95F2   2C85          00C87
0000D8   4770   20E4          000E6
0000DC   1B55
0000DE   5A50   35AA                       015AC
0000E2   47F0   2100          00102
000102   1B77
000104   5870   304E                       01050
000108   1C47
00010A   4E50   30D6                       010D8
00010E   F075   30D6   003E   010D8        0003E
000114   4F50   30D6                       010D8
000118   5050   3052                       01054
00011C   58E0   30B6                       010B8
000120   07FE
                                          00122
000122   50E0   30BA                       010BC
000126   1B55
000128   5A50   304E                       01050
00012C   5B50   3052                       01054
000130   5050   305A                       0105C
000134   58E0   30BA                       010BC
000138   07FE
```

Figure 12-18 *The machine language version (printed in hexadecimal) of these three modules in the program designed earlier in Figure 12-4 on page 12.5: calculate gross amount, calculate discount, and calculate net amount due.*

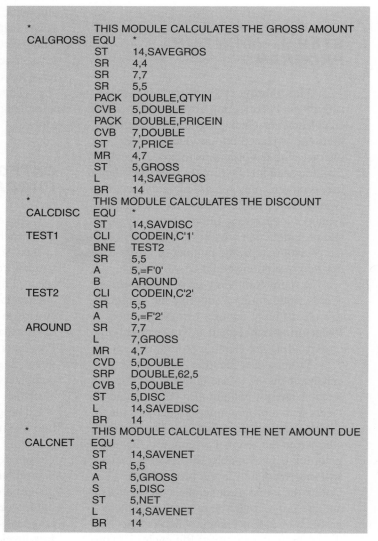

```
*                    THIS MODULE CALCULATES THE GROSS AMOUNT
CALGROSS   EQU    *
           ST     14,SAVEGROS
           SR     4,4
           SR     7,7
           SR     5,5
           PACK   DOUBLE,QTYIN
           CVB    5,DOUBLE
           PACK   DOUBLE,PRICEIN
           CVB    7,DOUBLE
           ST     7,PRICE
           MR     4,7
           ST     5,GROSS
           L      14,SAVEGROS
           BR     14
*                    THIS MODULE CALCULATES THE DISCOUNT
CALCDISC   EQU    *
           ST     14,SAVDISC
TEST1      CLI    CODEIN,C'1'
           BNE    TEST2
           SR     5,5
           A      5,=F'0'
           B      AROUND
TEST2      CLI    CODEIN,C'2'
           SR     5,5
           A      5,=F'2'
AROUND     SR     7,7
           L      7,GROSS
           MR     4,7
           CVD    5,DOUBLE
           SRP    DOUBLE,62,5
           CVB    5,DOUBLE
           ST     5,DISC
           L      14,SAVEDISC
           BR     14
*                    THIS MODULE CALCULATES THE NET AMOUNT DUE
CALCNET    EQU    *
           ST     14,SAVENET
           SR     5,5
           A      5,GROSS
           S      5,DISC
           ST     5,NET
           L      14,SAVENET
           BR     14
```

Figure 12-19 *The assembly language version of the machine language shown in Figure 12-18.*

addition, C for compare, L for load, and M for multiply. Another advantage of assembly languages is that the programmer can refer to storage locations with **symbolic addresses**. For example, instead of using the actual numeric storage address of a unit price, a programmer can use the symbolic name PRICE.

One disadvantage of an assembly language program is that it must be translated into machine language before the computer can understand it. The program containing the assembly language code is called the **source program**. The computer cannot understand or execute this source program until it is translated. A program called an **assembler** converts the assembly language source program into machine language that the computer can understand.

One assembly language instruction usually translates into one machine language instruction. In some cases, however, the assembly language includes **macros**, which generate more than one machine language instruction for a single assembly language instruction. Macros save the programmer time during program development, because one assembly language instruction can trigger several actions.

Third-Generation Languages

The disadvantages of low-level machine and assembly languages led to the development of high-level languages in the late 1950s and 1960s. Unlike low-level languages, high-level languages make it easy for programmers to develop and maintain programs. In addition to being easy for programmers to learn and use, high-level languages are **machine-independent**, meaning they run on many different types of computers. Three categories of high-level languages exist: third-generation languages, fourth-generation languages, and natural languages.

A **third-generation language (3GL)** instruction is written as a series of English-like words. For example, a programmer writes ADD for addition or PRINT to print. Many third-generation languages also use arithmetic operators such as * for multiplication and + for addition. These English-like words and arithmetic notations simplify the program development process for the programmer.

Third-generation languages require that the program instructions tell the computer *what* to accomplish and *how* to do it; thus, 3GLs often are called **procedural languages**. With most 3GLs, these procedures are developed using both the top-down approach (modules) and structured constructs (sequence, selection, and repetition) within each module.

As in an assembly language program, the 3GL code is called the source program, which must be translated to machine language before the computer can understand it. This translation process often is very complex, because one 3GL source program instruction translates into many machine language instructions. For third-generation languages, the translation is performed using one of two types of programs: a compiler or an interpreter.

A **compiler** converts the entire source program into machine language at one time. The machine language version that results from compiling the 3GL is called the **object code** or **object program**. The object code is stored on disk for execution at a later time.

While it is compiling the source program into object code, the compiler checks the source program's syntax and verifies that the program properly defines the data it will use in calculations or comparisons. The compiler then produces a program listing, which contains the source code and a list of any syntax errors. This listing helps the programmer make necessary changes to the source code and debug the program. Figure 12-20 illustrates the compilation process.

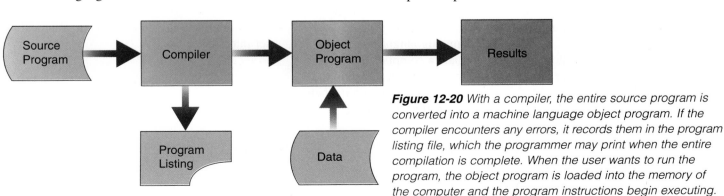

Figure 12-20 With a compiler, the entire source program is converted into a machine language object program. If the compiler encounters any errors, it records them in the program listing file, which the programmer may print when the entire compilation is complete. When the user wants to run the program, the object program is loaded into the memory of the computer and the program instructions begin executing.

While a compiler translates an entire program at once, an **interpreter** translates one program code statement at a time. That is, an interpreter reads a code statement, converts it to one or more machine language instructions, and then executes the machine language instructions, all before moving to the next code statement in the program. Each time you run the source program, it is interpreted into machine language, statement by statement, and then executed. No object program is produced. Figure 12-21 illustrates the interpretation process.

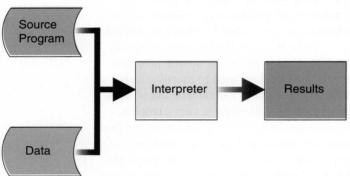

Figure 12-21 *With an interpreter, one line of the source program at a time is converted into machine language and then immediately executed by the computer. If the interpreter encounters an error while converting a line of code, an error message immediately displays on the screen and the interpretation stops.*

One advantage of an interpreter is that it immediately displays feedback when it finds a syntax error. The programmer can correct any errors, that is, debug the code, before the interpreter evaluates the next line. The disadvantage is that interpreted programs do not run as fast as compiled programs because the program must be translated to machine language each time it is executed.

Many programming languages include both an interpreter and a compiler. The programmer can use the interpreter to debug the program, and then compile the program when it is ready to be delivered to the users.

Fourth-Generation Languages

Like a 3GL, a **fourth-generation language** (**4GL**) uses English-like statements. A 4GL, however, is a **nonprocedural language**, which means the programmer only specifies *what* the program should accomplish without explaining *how*. Consequently, coding programs in a 4GL requires much less time and effort on the part of the programmer. In fact, 4GLs are so easy to use that users with very little programming background can develop programs using a fourth-generation language.

Many 4GLs work in combination with a database and its project dictionary. These powerful languages allow database administrators to define the database and its structure, help programmers maintain the data in the database, and allow users to query the database. Chapter 10 discussed SQL (Structured Query Language), which is a popular ANSI-standard 4GL used with relational database management systems (Figure 12-22). Recall that SQL is a **query language** enabling users and programmers to retrieve data from database tables. One query, for example, might request a list of all customers receiving a discount.

Some database management systems provide a report writer. As discussed in Chapter 10, a **report writer** or **report generator** is software that enables a developer to design or lay out a report on the screen; extract data into the report layout; and then display or print the report. Behind the scenes, these report writers build a 4GL query that enables you to access the data. The advantage of a report writer is that you can retrieve data without having to learn a query language. Another advantage is you easily can include page numbers and dates; report titles and column headings; subtotals and totals; numeric formatting (such as dollars and cents); and other formatting features such as fonts, font sizes, color, and shading. Report writers usually are menu-driven and have a graphical user interface.

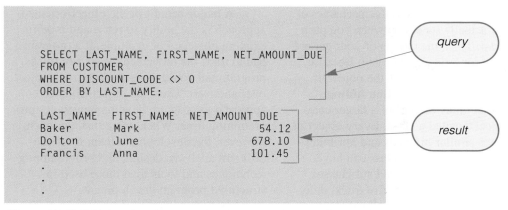

Figure 12-22 *SQL is a fourth-generation language that can be used to query database tables. This query produces an alphabetical list of those customers who receive a discount; that is, their discount code is not equal to zero.*

Natural Languages

Whereas a fourth-generation language program must follow a specific set of rules and syntax, a natural language program does not. A **natural language**, sometimes called a fifth-generation language, is a type of query language that allows the user to enter requests that resemble human speech. For example, an SQL query to obtain a list of GPAs that exceed 3.5 might be written as SELECT LAST_NAME, FIRST_NAME FROM STUDENT WHERE GPA > 3.5. A natural language version of that same query might be written or spoken as TELL ME THE NAMES OF STUDENTS WITH GPA OVER 3.5.

Natural languages often are associated with expert systems and artificial intelligence. These systems are popular in the medical field, but are not widely used in business applications.

OBJECT-ORIENTED PROGRAM DEVELOPMENT

As discussed earlier in this chapter, the introduction of structured program design and its three basic constructs largely solved the problem of spaghetti code. Structured program design, however, does not provide a way to keep the data and the program (or procedure) together. Each program, therefore, has to define how it will use the data for that particular program. This can result in redundant programming code that must change every time the structure of the data is changed, such as when a new field is added to a table in a database.

A newer approach to developing software, called the object-oriented approach, eliminates this problem. With the **object-oriented** approach, the programmer can package the data and the program (or procedure) into a single unit called an **object**. As you learned in Chapter 10, an **object** is an item that can contain both data and the procedures that read or manipulate the data. A Student object, for example, might contain data about a student (Student ID, First Name, Last Name, Address, and so on) and instructions on how to print the student record or the formula required to calculate a student's tuition rates.

The procedures in the object are called **methods**, or **operations**, which contain activities that read or manipulate the data. The data elements are called **attributes**, or **variables**.

The concept of packaging methods and attributes into a single object is called **encapsulation**; that is, the details of the object are encapsulated, or *hidden*, from the user. The user knows the method that can be requested of the object but does not know the specifics of how the method is performed. For example, while you know how to accelerate your car, you might not know the mechanics of how the car actually speeds up when you push the gas pedal. Thus, the details of your car are encapsulated, or hidden, from you. Because encapsulation hides details of the object, it sometimes is called **information hiding**.

An object may be part of a larger category of objects, called a **class**. Every object in a class shares similar methods and attributes as the original object. Each class can have one or more lower levels called **subclasses** (Figure 12-23). For example, fire truck, delivery truck, and dump truck are all subclasses of the higher-level class, truck. The higher-level class is called a **superclass**. Each subclass inherits the methods and attributes of the objects in its superclass. For example, all trucks have clearance lights (which would be an attribute in the truck object), but only fire trucks have fire hoses. This concept of lower levels inheriting methods and attributes of higher levels is called **inheritance**.

A specific occurrence of an object or object class is called an **object instance**. For example, Engine 12 sitting in the fire station in your town is an instance of the fire truck object.

To make an object do something, you send it a message. A **message** tells the object what to do; that is, it indicates the name of the method to be used. For example, turn right might be a method of the truck object.

A major benefit of the object-oriented approach is the ability to reuse and modify existing objects. For example, if a program had to track the movement of six fire trucks, a programmer could reuse the fire truck object over and over. Thus, the object-oriented approach to program development saves programming time. When using this approach, however, the development team must use different analysis, design, and programming techniques and tools than those used in structured program development.

Object-Oriented Programming

If the object-oriented approach to program development is used, then the programming language used to implement the design model is an **object-oriented programming (OOP) language**.

One feature of an OOP language is that it is event-driven. **Event** is simply the OOP term for *message*. An event-driven program checks for and responds to a set of messages or events. An event could be pressing a key on the keyboard, clicking the mouse, or typing a value into a text box. Some programming languages are event-driven; others are complete object-oriented languages. The next section covers specific examples of these and other programming languages in more detail.

WEB INFO
WEB INFO

For more information on object-oriented programming languages, visit the Discovering Computers 2000 Chapter 12 WEB INFO page (**www.scsite.com/ dc2000/ch12/webinfo.htm**) and click OOP languages.

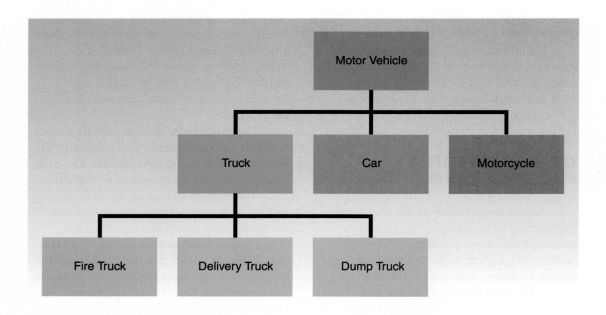

Figure 12-23 *A generalization hierarchy is an object-oriented analysis tool that shows the relationship among classes of an object. In this figure, truck has three subclasses. A subclass inherits (or acquires) the attributes and methods of its higher class.*

POPULAR PROGRAMMING LANGUAGES

Although hundreds of programming languages exist, only a few are used widely enough today for the industry to recognize them as standards. Most of these are high-level languages that work on a variety of computers. This section discusses the commonly used programming languages, their origins, and their primary purpose.

To illustrate the similarities and differences among these languages, the program code for each language is shown. The code solves the same basic problem shown in the machine language program in Figure 12-18 on page 12.16 and in the assembly language program in Figure 12-19 on page 12.16. Using the same problem in each — computing the net amount due from a customer — allows you to compare programming languages. To compute the net amount due, you multiply the quantity purchased by the unit price to obtain the gross amount. Then, you compute the discount as follows: customers with a code of 0 receive no discount; all others receive a 2% discount. Finally, you subtract the discount from the gross amount to determine the net amount due from the customer.

BASIC

John Kemeny and Thomas Kurtz developed a programming language called **B**eginner's **A**ll-purpose **S**ymbolic **I**nstruction **C**ode, or **BASIC**, in the mid-1960s at Dartmouth College. Kemeny and Kurtz designed BASIC for use as a simple, interactive problem-solving language (Figure 12-24). Because it is so easy to learn and use, BASIC originally was intended as, and often is still, the language used in the introductory programming course for students. Today, BASIC is used on both personal computers and minicomputers to develop some business applications. Many versions of BASIC exist, including QBasic, QuickBASIC, and MS-BASIC.

WEB INFO
WEB INFO
For more information on BASIC, visit the Discovering Computers 2000 Chapter 12 WEB INFO page (**www.scsite.com/ dc2000/ch12/webinfo.htm**) and click BASIC.

```
REM COMPUTE GROSS AMOUNT
Gross.Amount = Unit.Price * Quantity.Purchased

REM COMPUTE NET AMOUNT DUE
IF Discount.Code = 0 THEN
    Net.Amount.Due = Gross.Amount
ELSE
    Discount.Amount = .02 * Gross.Amount
    Net.Amount.Due = Gross.Amount - Discount.Amount
END IF

REM PRINT NET AMOUNT DUE
PRINT USING "The net amount due is $##,###.##"; Net.Amount.Due
```

Figure 12-24 An excerpt from a BASIC program. The code shows the computations for gross amount, discount amount, and net amount due; the decision to evaluate the discount value; and the output of the net amount due.

Visual Basic

WEB INFO
WEB INFO

For more information on Visual Basic, visit the Discovering Computers 2000 Chapter 12 WEB INFO page (**www.scsite.com/dc2000/ch12/webinfo.htm**) and click Visual Basic.

Developed by Microsoft Corporation in the early 1990s, **Visual Basic** is a Windows-based application designed to assist programmers in developing other event-driven Windows-based applications. The first step in building a Visual Basic application is to design the graphical user interface using Visual Basic objects (Steps 1 and 2 in Figure 12-25). Visual Basic objects, or *controls*, include items such as command buttons, text boxes, and labels.

Next, you write any code needed to define program events (Step 3 in Figure 12-25). An event in Visual Basic can be the result of an action initiated by a user. For example, when a user clicks an object in a Visual Basic application, the application executes the Click event. You define Visual Basic events using code statements written in Visual Basic's own programming language, which is very similar to BASIC and easy to learn and use. Once you have completed these steps, you can generate the final application (Step 4 in Figure 12-25).

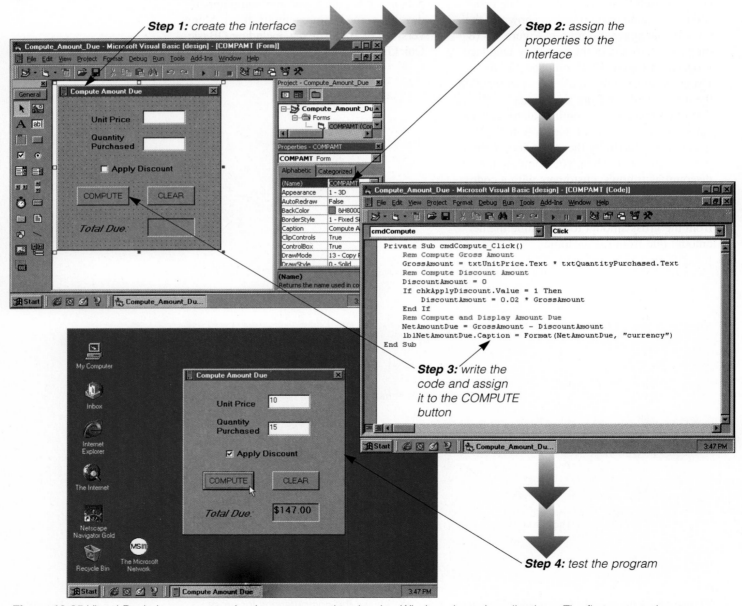

Figure 12-25 *Visual Basic is a programming language used to develop Windows-based applications. The first screen shows how the programmer designs the user interface. The user enters data in the Unit Price and Quantity Purchased text boxes. If appropriate, the user selects the Apply Discount check box, and finally, clicks the COMPUTE button to display the Total Due. The second screen shows the program code associated with the COMPUTE button. The code shows the computations for gross amount, discount amount, and net amount due; the decision to evaluate the discount value; and the output of the net amount due. The third screen shows the finished application with values entered and the resulting Total Due displaying.*

Because it is so easy to use, novice programmers can create professional Windows-based applications using Visual Basic.

COBOL

COBOL (**CO**mmon **B**usiness-**O**riented **L**anguage) developed out of a joint effort between the U.S. government, businesses, and major universities in the early 1960s. Naval officer Grace Hopper, a pioneer in computer programming, was a prime developer of the COBOL language.

COBOL is one of the more widely used procedural programming languages for business applications. Although COBOL programs often are lengthy, their English-like statements make them easy to read, write, and maintain (Figure 12-26). While COBOL is especially useful for processing transactions on mainframes, computers of all sizes run COBOL programs. The most popular personal computer COBOL program is Micro Focus Personal COBOL, which supports both procedural and object-oriented programming.

C

The **C** programming language, developed in the early 1970s by Dennis Ritchie at Bell Laboratories, originally was designed as a language to write system software. Today, C is used to develop a wide variety of software, including operating systems and application software such as word processing and spreadsheet programs. While C is a powerful programming language that requires professional programming skills, its expanded use allows it to be categorized as a general-purpose language that is effective for both business and scientific applications (Figure 12-27 on the next page). C runs on practically any type of computer with any operating system, but most often is used with the UNIX operating system. In fact, most of the UNIX operating system is written in C.

C++

Developed in the 1980s by Bjarne Sroustrup at Bell Laboratories, **C++** (pronounced *SEE-plus-plus*) is an object-oriented programming language. An extension of the C programming

```
*   COMPUTE GROSS AMOUNT
    MULTIPLY UNIT-PRICE BY QUANTITY-PURCHASED
        GIVING GROSS-AMOUNT.

*   COMPUTE NET AMOUNT DUE
    IF DISCOUNT-CODE = 0
        MOVE GROSS-AMOUNT TO NET-AMOUNT-DUE
    ELSE
        MULTIPLY .02 BY GROSS-AMOUNT
            GIVING DISCOUNT-AMOUNT
        SUBTRACT DISCOUNT-AMOUNT FROM GROSS-AMOUNT
            GIVING NET-AMOUNT-DUE.

*   PRINT NET AMOUNT DUE
    MOVE NET-AMOUNT-DUE TO NET-AMOUNT-DUE-OUT.
    WRITE REPORT-LINE-OUT FROM DETAIL-LINE
        AFTER ADVANCING 2 LINES.
```

Figure 12-26 An excerpt from a COBOL program. The code shows the computations for gross amount, discount amount, and net amount due; the decision to evaluate the discount value; and the output of the net amount due. Notice how much wordier this program is compared with the BASIC program in Figure 12-24 on page 12.21. It is, however, much more readable than the BASIC program.

language shown in Figure 12-27, C++ includes all the elements of the C language plus has additional features for working with objects, classes, events, and other object-oriented concepts. Programmers commonly use C++ to develop application software, such as word processing and spreadsheet programs, as well as database and Internet applications. Although C++ is an outgrowth of the C programming language, you do not need C programming experience to be a successful C++ programmer.

FORTRAN

FORTRAN, which stands for **for**mula **tran**slation, was one of the first high-level programming languages. Developed in the late 1950s by a team of IBM programmers led by John Backus, FORTRAN was intended for scientific applications (Figure 12-28). Because FORTRAN is designed to handle complex mathematical and logical expressions, scientists, engineers, and mathematicians use it most.

```
/* Compute Gross Amount                                          */
gross = price * qty_purch;

/* Compute Net Amount Due                                        */
if (disc_code == 0)
    net = gross;
else
    {
    disc_amt = .02 * gross;
    net = gross - disc_amt;
    }

/* Print Net Amount Due                                          */
printf("The net amount due is %d\n", net);
```

Figure 12-27 *An excerpt from a C program. The code shows the computations for gross amount, discount amount, and net amount due; the decision to evaluate the discount value; and the output of the net amount due.*

```
C       COMPUTE GROSS AMOUNT
        GROSS = PRICE * QTY

C       COMPUTE NET AMOUNT DUE
        IF (CODE .EQ. 0) THEN
            NET = GROSS
        ELSE
            DISC = .02 * GROSS
            NET = GROSS - DISC
        ENDIF

C       PRINT NET AMOUNT DUE
        WRITE(CRTOUT,*) 'THE NET AMOUNT DUE IS $', NET
```

Figure 12-28 *An excerpt from a FORTRAN program. The code shows the computations for gross amount, discount amount, and net amount due; the decision to evaluate the discount value; and the output of the net amount due.*

Pascal

In the late 1960s, a Swiss scientist named Niklaus Wirth created the **Pascal** programming language for the purpose of teaching structured programming concepts to students (Figure 12-29). He named the programming language in honor of the seventeenth-century French mathematician Blaise Pascal, who developed one of the earliest calculating machines. Today, Pascal typically is used on personal computers and minicomputers to develop scientific applications. Turbo Pascal is an object-oriented version of Pascal.

Ada

In the late 1970s, the U.S. Department of Defense developed the **Ada** programming language, which derived from the Pascal programming language. For years, the U.S. Department of Defense required that programmers use Ada for all U.S. government military software development. The Department of Defense named the programming language after Augusta Ada Lovelace Byron, the Countess of Lovelace, who is thought to be the first female computer programmer. Ada originally was designed to meet the needs of embedded computer systems, which are computer systems that act as a control mechanism inside other computers. Programmers, however, also use the Ada language for business applications (Figure 12-30).

```
(* COMPUTE GROSS AMOUNT *)
GROSSAMOUNT := UNITPRICE * QUANTITYPURCHASED

(* COMPUTE NET AMOUNT DUE *)
IF DISCOUNTCODE = 0 THEN
    NETAMOUNTDUE := GROSSAMOUNT
ELSE
    BEGIN
        DISCOUNTAMOUNT := 02 * GROSSAMOUNT;
        NETAMOUNTDUE := GROSSAMOUNT - DISCOUNTAMOUNT
    END
END IF

(* PRINT NET AMOUNT DUE *)
WRITELN ('THE NET AMOUNT DUE IS $', NETAMOUNTDUE:7:2)
```

Figure 12-29 An excerpt from a Pascal program. The code shows the computations for gross amount, discount amount, and net amount due; the decision to evaluate the discount value; and the output of the net amount due.

```
-- COMPUTE GROSS AMOUNT
GROSS_AMOUNT := UNIT_PRICE * QUANTITY_PURCHASED;

-- COMPUTE NET AMOUNT DUE
if DISCOUNT_CODE = 0 then
    NET_AMOUNT_DUE := GROSS_AMOUNT;
else
    DISCOUNT_AMOUNT := 02 * GROSS_AMOUNT;
    NET_AMOUNT_DUE := GROSS_AMOUNT - DISCOUNT_AMOUNT;
end if;

-- PRINT NET AMOUNT DUE
PUT ("THE NET AMOUNT DUE IS $");
PUT (NET_AMOUNT_DUE,7,2);
```

Figure 12-30 An excerpt from an Ada program. The code shows the computations for gross amount, discount amount, and net amount due; the decision to evaluate the discount value; and the output of the net amount due.

RPG

In the early 1960s, IBM introduced **RPG**, which stands for **R**eport **P**rogram **G**enerator, to assist businesses in generating reports (Figure 12-31). Today, businesses also use RPG for complex computations and file updating. Because RPG is a nonprocedural language, many advocates of RPG (and other report generators) claim it paved the way for 4GLs. Although a version with limited functionality is available for the personal computer, RPG primarily is used for application development on IBM midrange computers, such as the AS/400.

Other Programming Languages

In addition to the commonly used programming languages just discussed, a number of other languages sometimes are used. Figure 12-32 lists some of these languages and their primary applications.

Figure 12-31 An excerpt from an RPG program. The code shows the computations for gross amount, discount amount, and net amount due; the decision to evaluate the discount value; and the output of the net amount due.

```
C* COMPUTE GROSS AMOUNT
C            PRICE     MULT QTY          GROSS    72
C*
C* COMPUTE NET AMOUNT DUE
C            CODE      IFEQ 0
C                      Z-ADDNET          GROSS    72
                       ELSE
C            GROSS     MULT .02          DISC     52
C            GROSS     SUB  DISC         NET      72
C                      ENDIF
C
C* PRINT NET AMOUNT DUE
C                      EXCPTDETAIL
C*
O* OUTPUT SPECIFICATIONS
OQPRINT E 2           DETAIL
O                                  23 'THE NET AMOUNT DUE IS $'
O                          NET    J 34
```

ALGOL	ALGOrithmic Language, the first structured procedural language
APL	A Programming Language, a scientific language designed to manipulate tables of numbers
FORTH	Similar to C, used for device control applications
HYPERTALK	An object-oriented programming language developed by Apple to manipulate cards that can contain text, graphics, and sound
LISP	LISt Processing, a language used for artificial intelligence applications
LOGO	An educational tool used to teach programming and problem-solving to children
MODULA-2	A successor to Pascal used for developing systems software
PILOT	Programmed Inquiry Learning Or Teaching, used to write computer-aided instruction programs
PL/I	Programming Language One, a business and scientific language that combines many features of FORTRAN and COBOL
PROLOG	PROgramming LOGic, used for development of expert systems
SMALLTALK	Object-oriented programming language

Figure 12-32 Other programming languages.

PROGRAM DEVELOPMENT TOOLS

Program development tools are user-friendly software products designed to help both program developers and nontechnical users create solutions to information system requirements. The emergence of this alternative to programming languages has improved system development time for computer professionals and empowered nontechnical users. Program development tools **empower** nontechnical users by giving these users the ability to write simple programs and satisfy information processing requests on their own. This allows programmers and other system developers to focus development efforts on larger information systems projects, while empowered users create their own small applications or simple programs within applications.

Examples of program development tools include query languages and report writers, which were discussed earlier in this chapter and Chapter 10. In addition to query languages and report writers, other software development tools include application generators, macros, and RAD tools.

Application Generators

An **application generator**, sometimes called a **program generator**, is a program that allows you to build an application without writing the extensive code required by a third generation programming language. For this reason, programmers using an application generator can be more productive in a shorter time frame. In fact, many users unfamiliar with programming concepts can build applications with an application generator. Thus, application generators empower users by providing them with the ability to create applications on their own.

When using an application generator, the developer (a programmer or user) works with menu-driven tools that have graphical user interfaces. Some application generators create source code; others simply create object code. Although application generators are available as stand-alone programs, most often, they are bundled with or part of a database management system. An application generator typically includes a report writer, form, and menu generator.

As discussed earlier, a report writer is a software tool that enables a developer to design and format a report on the screen, extract data into the report layout, and then display or print the report. Recall from Chapter 10 that a form is a window on the screen that provides areas for entering or changing data in a database. With both a report writer and a form, the developer types titles and headings directly on the screen and then describes the data elements to be used, usually by clicking the location where the desired data element should display or print. The data elements are defined in the data dictionary; thus, the format specifications such as length, type, and validation, already are defined. When the developer uses a defined data element, the report writer or form accesses the data dictionary for the format specifications of the data element. Figure 12-33 shows a sample form design and the resulting form it generates.

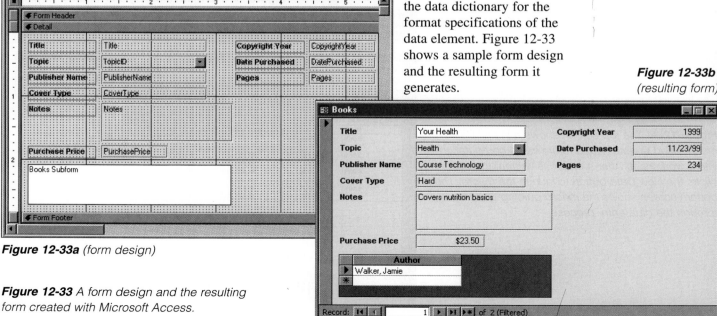

Figure 12-33a (form design)

Figure 12-33 A form design and the resulting form created with Microsoft Access.

Figure 12-33b
(resulting form)

A **menu generator** allows the developer to create a menu, or list of choices, for the application options. For example, if you create three reports and two forms for an application, your menu would contain at least six options: one for each report, one for each form, and one to exit, or quit, the application.

Macros

Empowered users also can create simple programs within applications by writing macros. A **macro** is a series of statements that instructs an application how to complete a task. Macros are used to automate routine, repetitive, or difficult tasks in an application such as word processing, spreadsheet, or database programs. You usually create a macro in one of two ways: (1) record the macro or (2) write the macro.

If you want to automate a routine or repetitive task such as formatting or editing, you would record a macro. A **macro recorder** is similar to a movie camera, in that it records all actions you perform until you turn it off.

To record a macro, you begin the macro recorder in the application and then record a series of actions, such as clicks of the mouse or keystrokes. Once the macro is recorded, you can run it any time you want to perform that same set of actions. For example, you could record the actions required to format a number as a subscript, and then run the Format Number As Subscript macro repeatedly to change a selected number in a document to a subscript.

If you are familiar with programming techniques, you can write your own macros instead of recording them. Many applications use Visual Basic or a similar language as their macro programming language. Macros written in Visual Basic code use the three basic structured programming constructs (sequence, selection, and iteration) within modules as well as objects, classes, and other object-oriented concepts. The objects in a Visual Basic macro, however, apply only to the specific application for which the macro was developed. For example, in a spreadsheet, an object might be a cell, a range of cells, a chart, or the worksheet.

The macro in Figure 12-34a shows an Excel macro used to automate the data entry process to determine the future value of an investment. Figure 12-34b shows the dialog box generated from the macro that prompts the user to enter the amount of money being invested each month.

Figure 12-34a (Visual Basic macro)

Figure 12-34b (macro dialog box in Excel window)

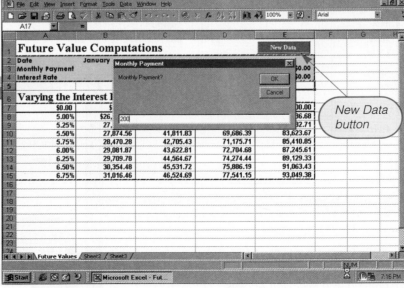

Figure 12-34 The top screen shows a Visual Basic macro used to automate a future value computation into a worksheet. After a macro is written, the user clicks the New Data button to launch the macro. The bottom screen shows the macro guiding the user through the data entry process.

RAD Tools: Visual Basic, Delphi, and PowerBuilder

Rapid application development (**RAD**) is the process of developing software throughout the system development process, instead of waiting until the implementation phase. A common approach used in RAD is prototyping. As you learned in Chapter 11, a **prototype** is a working model of the proposed system. With a prototype, it only requires a minimum amount of work to convert the prototype into an implemented solution; thus, programmers can develop the application rapidly.

Rapid application development uses RAD tools, which allow you to develop easy-to-maintain, component-based applications. A component is simply another term for object. Thus, a RAD tool typically includes an object-oriented programming language. Three popular RAD tools are Visual Basic, Delphi, and PowerBuilder.

VISUAL BASIC Recall that Microsoft's Visual Basic is a Windows-based application designed to assist programmers in developing other event-driven Windows-based applications. Visual Basic was one of the first programming environments to provide a visual programming environment that allowed developers to drag-and-drop objects to build programs. The ease of use of Visual Basic's event-driven programming makes it a popular RAD tool.

DELPHI Delphi is another popular RAD tool. This powerful tool offers a drag-and-drop visual programming environment. Whereas Visual Basic uses only an event-driven language, Delphi provides full object-oriented capabilities. Because it has more functionality and features than Visual Basic, Delphi is slightly more complicated to learn and use.

POWERBUILDER Another RAD tool, called **PowerBuilder**, uses a proprietary language to help with rapid application development (Figure 12-35). This language, called PowerScript, is similar to BASIC and C. Although PowerBuilder is not completely object-oriented like Delphi, it can be used to create powerful applications. Because of its extended functionality, PowerBuilder can be difficult to learn.

WEB PAGE PROGRAM DEVELOPMENT

Recall that the collection of linked documents accessible on the Internet is known as the World Wide Web, or simply, the Web. Each document on the Web, called a Web page, is a linked document that can contain text, graphics, video, and sound. The designers of Web pages, called **Web page authors**, may use a variety of techniques to develop Web pages. The following sections discuss these techniques.

WEB INFO

For more information on rapid application development, visit the Discovering Computers 2000 Chapter 12 WEB INFO page (www.scsite.com/dc2000/ch12/webinfo.htm) and click RAD.

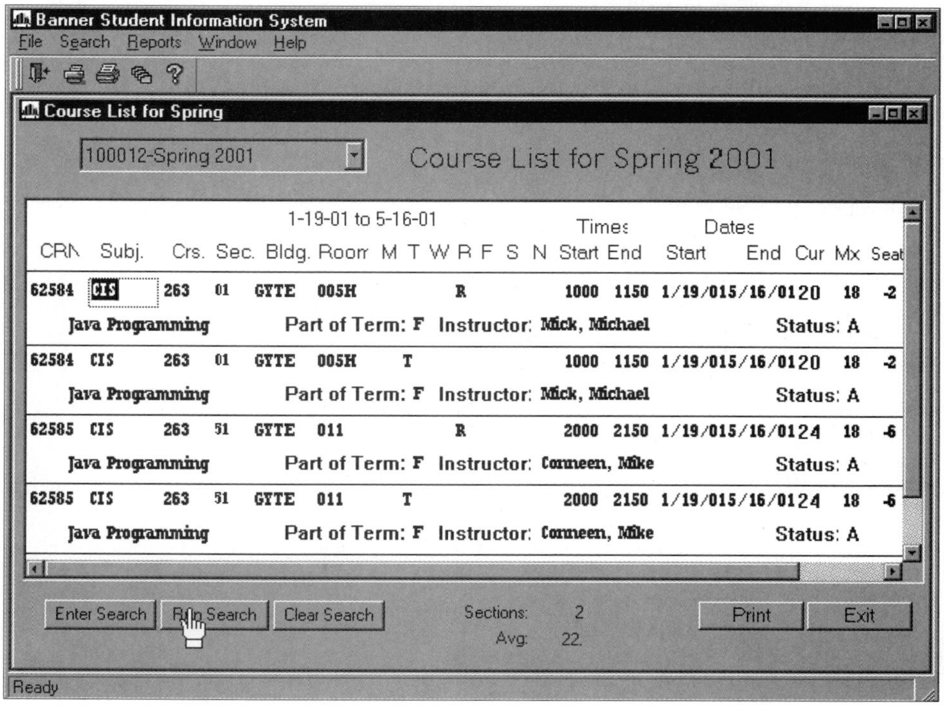

Figure 12-35 A PowerBuilder application.

HTML

Hypertext markup language (**HTML**) is a special formatting language used to create Web pages. You view a Web page written with HTML in a Web browser, such as Microsoft Internet Explorer or Netscape Navigator.

Although not actually a programming language, HTML is a language that has specific syntax rules for defining the placement and format of text, graphics, video, and sound on a Web page. HTML uses **tags**, or **markups**, which are codes that specify links to other documents, as well as how the Web page displays. A Web page, thus, is a file that contains both text and HTML tags. HTML tags *mark* the text page to define how it displays when viewed as a Web page on the World Wide Web. Examples of tags are <B> to bold text, <P> to indicate a new paragraph, and <HR> to display a horizontal rule across the page. Figure 12-36 shows part of the HTML code used to create the Web page shown in Figure 12-37.

```
<HTML>
<HEAD>
<TITLE>Course Technology Products -- Detail
</TITLE>
<META NAME="description" CONTENT="0-7895-4693-0: This is the Course Technology prod-
uct catalog detail page for the JavaScript Introductory Concepts and Techniques. Part of the
highly successful Shelly Cashman Series, this Introductory text leads the user through a clear,
step-by-step, screen-by-screen approach to learning the basics of JavaScript.">
<META NAME="keywords" CONTENT="education, textbooks, computer, learning, buy a book,
purchase, sell, Shelly/Cashman, JavaScript Introductory Concepts and Techniques, Internet,
Programming">
<META NAME="Title" CONTENT="Course Technology Catalog: JavaScript Introductory
Concepts and Techniques">
</HEAD>
<BODY LEFTMARGIN=10 TOPMARGIN=10 VLINK="#0000FF" LINK="#0000FF"
ALINK="#FFFFFF" background="/images/backgrounds/products_bg2.gif">
<A NAME="top"> </A>
<TABLE BORDER=0 CELLPADDING=0 CELLSPACING=0 WIDTH="575">
<MAP NAME="topnav">
<AREA SHAPE="RECT" COORDS="1, 1, 85, 24" HREF="/about/">
<AREA SHAPE="RECT" COORDS="86, 1, 575, 24" HREF="/home.cfm">
</MAP>
<TR BGCOLOR="#000000">
<TD WIDTH="100%" BGCOLOR="#000000" COLSPAN=2><IMG
SRC="/images/top_course_575.gif" ALT="Course Technology" BORDER=0 USEMAP="#top-
nav"></A></TD>
</TR>
</TABLE>
<TABLE BORDER=0 CELLPADDING=0 CELLSPACING=0 WIDTH="550">
<TR ALIGN=LEFT VALIGN=TOP>
<TD WIDTH=90 ROWSPAN=3>
<A HREF="/products/scseries/">
<IMG SRC="/images/logos/sc_logo.gif" BORDER=0 WIDTH="89" ></A>
</TD>
<MAP NAME="mininav">
<AREA SHAPE="RECT" COORDS="1, 1, 102, 14" HREF="/products/">
<AREA SHAPE="RECT" COORDS="103, 1, 220, 14" HREF="/downloads/">
<AREA SHAPE="RECT" COORDS="221, 1, 319, 14" HREF="/contacts/">
<AREA SHAPE="RECT" COORDS="320, 1, 450, 14" HREF="/news/">
</MAP>
<TD WIDTH=450 COLSPAN=2>
<IMG SRC="/images/nav/mini_text_450.GIF" WIDTH=450 HEIGHT=14 BORDER=0 ALT=""
USEMAP="#mininav">
<IMG SRC="/images/tdot.gif" WIDTH=450 HEIGHT=15 BORDER=0 ALT="">
</TD>
</TR>
<TR>
```

Figure 12-36 Hypertext markup language (HTML) is used to create Web pages. Illustrated is part of the HTML code used to generate a portion of the Web page shown in Figure 12-37.

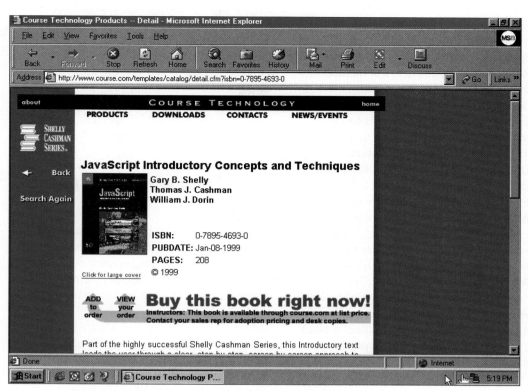

Figure 12-37 Web page created from part of the HTML code illustrated in Figure 12-36.

You can write HTML code using any text editor or standard word processing software package. You must save the code, however, as an ASCII file with an .htm or .html extension, instead of as a formatted word processing document. You also can use an HTML editor to create a Web page. Two basic types of HTML editors exist: stand-alone and add-on. A **stand-alone HTML editor** is a complete editing software package in itself; that is, it does not require any other program to create the Web page. An **add-on HTML editor** is an editing software tool that requires an existing software package, such as word processing software. One advantage of an add-on HTML editor is that the functionality of the existing software and the add-on tool usually are quite similar, so you can learn to use the editing tool very quickly.

Recall from Chapter 7 that you do not need to learn HTML to develop a basic Web page. Instead, you can generate HTML tags using specially designed Web page authoring software, or just your word processing software. Many current word processing packages include Web page authoring features that help you create basic Web pages that contain text and graphics. To create more sophisticated Web pages that include video, sound, animation, and other special effects, Web page authors can use Web page authoring software such as Adobe PageMill or Microsoft FrontPage.

To fine-tune the formatting of your Web pages, however, you should learn HTML.

Scripts, Applets, and Servlets

HTML tells your browser how to display text and images, set up lists and option buttons, and establish hyperlinks on a Web page. You can bring these Web pages to life by adding dynamic content and interactive elements, such as scrolling messages, animated graphics, forms, pop-up windows, and interactive quizzes. To do this, you develop small programs in the form of scripts, applets, or servlets.

Scripts, applets, and servlets are short programs that are executed inside of another program — unlike regular programs, which are executed by the operating system. In the case of Web pages, your Web browser executes these short programs. Recall that, when your computer is connected to the Web, it is the client computer. A **script** is an interpreted program that runs on the client; that is, it runs on your computer, as opposed to running on a Web server. An **applet** also usually runs on the client, but it is *compiled*, which means it usually runs faster than a script. Because scripts and applets run on the client, they shift the computational work from the Web server to your computer. A **servlet** is an applet that runs on the server.

A major reason for using scripts, applets, and servlets is to add multimedia capabilities to your Web pages. Examples of such scripts, applets, and servlets include animated graphics, scrolling messages, calendars, and advertisements. Another reason to use scripts, applets, and servlets is to send information from your computer to a Web server. The **common gateway interface (CGI)** is the communications protocol that defines how a Web server passes a user's request to a program and receives and sends data back to the user. Cookies, shopping carts, games, counters, image maps, and processing forms, for example, are types of scripts, applets, and servlets that allow you to transfer information to and from a Web server.

A **counter** tracks the number of visitors to a Web site. An **image map** is a graphic that points to a URL. Image maps are used in place of, or in addition to, plain text hyperlinks. When you click a certain part of the graphic, your Web browser sends the coordinates of the clicked location to the Web server, which in turn locates the corresponding URL and sends the Web page to your computer.

A **processing form** collects data from visitors to a Web site, who fill in blank fields and then click a Submit or Send button (Figure 12-38). When you click the Submit or Send button on the processing form, the script or applet is executed. It transmits your data to the server, processes it, and then, if appropriate, sends information back to your Web browser via the server.

Java, JavaScript, and Perl

You can download scripts, applets, and servlets from the Web; you can purchase them; or you can write them yourself. The more common scripting languages are C, C++, JavaScript, and Perl. Applets and servlets commonly are written using Java.

JAVA Developed by Sun Microsystems, **Java** is a compiled object-oriented programming language used to write stand-alone applications, as well as applets and servlets. The Java language is very similar to C++. Because of its simplicity, robustness, and portability, many programmers believe that Java will be the programming language of the future.

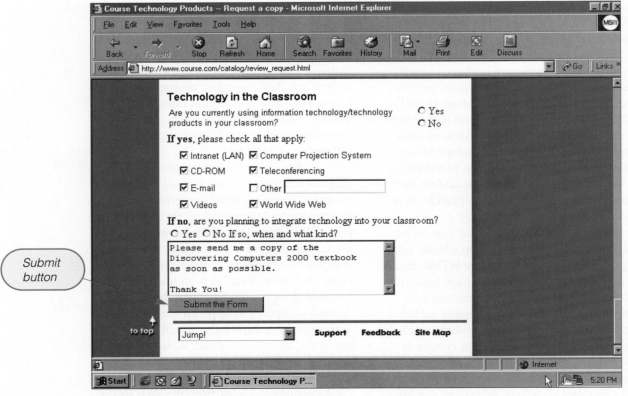

Figure 12-38 *One popular use of a script is to create a processing form. Instructors use this processing form to request review copies of textbooks.*

JAVASCRIPT **JavaScript** is an interpreted scripting language that allows you to add functionality to your Web pages by inserting JavaScript code within an HTML document. Whereas HTML tells your browser how to display text and images; set up lists and option buttons; and establish hyperlinks, JavaScript brings your Web page to life by adding dynamic content and interactive elements such as scrolling messages and data input forms. Although it shares many of the features of the full Java language, JavaScript is a simpler language (Figure 12-39).

JavaScript is the result of a joint venture between Sun Microsystems and Netscape Communications Corporation. Netscape originally began developing a scripting language called LiveScript, while Sun was trying to simplify its Java programming language. Today, JavaScript is endorsed by a number of software companies and is an open language that anyone can use without purchasing a license. JavaScript thus allows you to improve the appearance of your Web pages without spending a large amount of money or learning a high-level programming language.

PERL **Perl**, which stands for **P**ractical **E**xtraction and **R**eporting **L**anguage, originally was developed by Larry Wall as a procedural language similar to C. The latest release of PERL however, is an interpreted scripting language, especially designed for processing text. Because of its strong text processing capabilities, Perl has become a popular language for writing scripts.

WEB INFO

For more information on JavaScript, visit the Discovering Computers 2000 Chapter 12 WEB INFO page (www.scsite.com/dc2000/ch12/webinfo.htm) and click JavaScript.

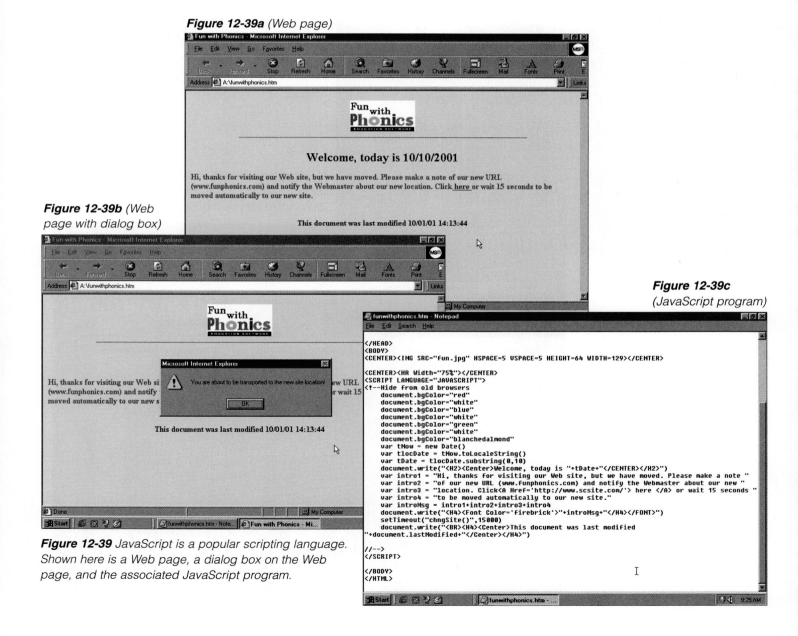

Figure 12-39a *(Web page)*

Figure 12-39b *(Web page with dialog box)*

Figure 12-39c *(JavaScript program)*

Figure 12-39 *JavaScript is a popular scripting language. Shown here is a Web page, a dialog box on the Web page, and the associated JavaScript program.*

Dynamic HTML

WEB INFO
WEB INFO

For more information on dynamic HTML, visit the Discovering Computers 2000 Chapter 12 WEB INFO page (www.scsite.com/dc2000/ch12/webinfo.htm) and click DHTML.

Dynamic HTML (DHTML) is a newer type of HTML that allows you to include more graphical interest and interactivity in a Web page, without the Web page having to access the Web server. That is, Web pages using DHTML update and change themselves on the client computer, which results in much faster display than those Web pages created with basic HTML. Figure 12-40 shows an example of a Web page containing DHTML; it displays and hides blocks of text as you point to various menus on the Web page.

In addition to basic HTML, dynamic HTML also includes the document object model, style sheets, and scripting languages such as JavaScript. The **document object model (DOM)** defines every item on a Web page, such as graphics and headlines, as an object. With DHTML, you can assign properties, such as color or size, to these objects. A **style sheet** contains the formats for how a particular object should display in the browser. For example, a style sheet might specify items such as colors, fonts, and font sizes. Once the objects are defined and formatted, a scripting language manipulates the objects, such as moving them, displaying them, or hiding them in response to mouse movements or clicks.

To use DHTML, you must be sure your browser supports it. The World Wide Web Consortium is developing standards so future browsers use the same DHTML.

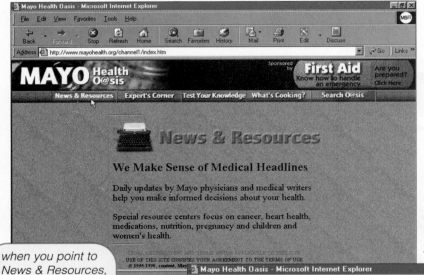

Figure 12-40 *The Mayo Health Oasis Web page uses DHTML to display and hide blocks of text as you point to various menus on the page.*

when you point to News & Resources, this object displays

when you point to What's Cooking?, this object displays

XML

The World Wide Web Consortium also is developing a specification for **eXtensible Markup Language** (**XML**), which some industry experts predict will replace HTML as a Web development tool. XML is more versatile than HTML. It allows Web page developers to create customized tags, as well as using predefined tags. With XML, you can define a link that points to multiple Web sites instead of a single site.

XML separates the Web page content from its format, allowing your browser to display Web page contents in a form appropriate for your display device. For example, the same XML page could be displayed on a handheld computer, a laptop computer, and a desktop computer. A Web page written with HTML probably would require multiple versions to run on each of these types of computers.

MULTIMEDIA PROGRAM DEVELOPMENT

Specialized software, called **multimedia authoring software**, is required to display text, graphics, animation, audio, and video into an electronic interactive presentation. Once created, these interactive multimedia presentations can be used to facilitate learning and elicit direct student participation. Multimedia presentations usually are stored and delivered via a CD-ROM or DVD-ROM over a local area network or via the Internet.

A variety of multimedia authoring software products are available, such as Asymetrix Toolbook, Macromedia Authorware, and Macromedia Director. These products, along with other multimedia program development issues, are discussed in more depth in Chapter 13.

SELECTING A PROGRAMMING LANGUAGE OR PROGRAM DEVELOPMENT TOOL

Although each programming language and program development tool has its own unique characteristics, it often is difficult to select one for a program development task. When making that decision, you should consider the following factors.

1. **Standards of the organization**. Many organizations have standards that require programmers to use a particular language or development tool for all applications.

2. **Interface with other programs**. If a program is to work with other programs, you should write it in the same language or with the same development tool as the other programs or a language or development tool compatible with the other programs.

3. **Suitability of the language to the application**. Most languages and development tools are designed to work with particular applications, such as business applications or scientific applications.

4. **Portability to other systems**. If an application is to run on multiple types of computers (hardware platforms) and operating systems (software platforms), you should select a language or development tool common to these platforms.

WEB INFO

For more information on eXtensible Markup Language, visit the Discovering Computers 2000 Chapter 12 WEB INFO page (**www.scsite.com/ dc2000/ch12/webinfo.htm**) and click XML.

TECHNOLOGY TRAILBLAZER

GRACE HOPPER

In the summer of 1945, a moth flew into the Mark II computer at Harvard University and caused a relay to fail. The engineers removed the moth and informed their boss that they were *debugging* the computer. A cultural catchword thus was born. The moth, scotch-taped into the logbook, is preserved for posterity at the Naval Museum in Virginia. Grace Hopper taped it there, and made, along with history, the notation, "first actual case of bug being found." It was to be one of many firsts she would experience in her long and eventful life.

The woman who would come to be known as, *Amazing Grace* or *Grandma COBOL* was born Grace Brewster Murray in New York City on December 9, 1906. Her parents taught her early on that anything was possible with training and education. Grace took their teaching very seriously and embarked on a career that would span several decades. In 1924, she entered Vassar College and pursued a degree in mathematics and physics, mainly because no engineering courses were offered to women. By 1934, she had acquired a bachelor's degree in mathematics and physics from Vassar, as well as a master's degree and a doctorate in mathematics, both from Yale.

When America entered World War II, Grace took it as a personal challenge and tried to enlist in the Navy. First denied because of her age (too old), then her weight (too light), she managed to obtain waivers, place first in her class at Midshipman's School, and be assigned to the Bureau of Ordnance Computation Project at Harvard University. Ironically, she had never considered a career in computer work because, as she puts it, "there were no computers to go into. In the 1940s, you could have all the computer people in the country in one small room."

During her stint at Harvard, she worked on several incarnations of early computers, helped develop parallel processors, and wrote countless lines of code. In 1949,

Grace accepted a position at Eckert-Mauchly Computer Corporation (later Sperry-Rand Corp.) where she began pushing for standardization of programming languages, an idea most companies, including IBM, found ludicrous. Grace, who would later become famous for her quote, "it's easier to ask forgiveness than it is to get permission," remained determined, further insisting that if computers could be *taught* English, more people could use them. To this end, she developed COBOL (COmmon Business Oriented Language). Its English-like commands made it possible for non-scientific people to understand it, and countless businesses and the U.S. government eventually adopted it.

She briefly retired from the Navy in 1966, but was called back to standardize COBOL. Originally slated as a six-month assignment, it stretched into twenty more years of naval service. In 1984, she was inducted into the Engineering and Science Hall of Fame, keeping company with George Washington Carver, Thomas Edison, and Jonas Salk. She finally retired in 1986 at the age of 79. The Navy retirement ceremony was barely over when she accepted a job as senior consultant for Digital Equipment Corporation. For the remainder of her long life, she gave hundreds of talks each year, in which she urged people to not be bound by convention and fear of change.

One goal Grace did not achieve was her desire to ring in the millennium and attend the New Year's Eve party to end all parties. Sadly, on New Year's Day 1992, she died in her sleep at age 85.

Prior to her death, in 1985, ground was broken for the Grace Murray Hopper Service Center for the Navy Regional Data Automation Center in San Diego. Fittingly, the cake at the facility's dedication ceremony was inscribed with one of Grace's favorite maxims, "A ship in port is safe, but that is not what ships are built for."

COMPANY ON THE CUTTING EDGE

COMPANY ON THE CUTTING EDGE

COMPAQ COMPUTER CORPORATION

In the summer of 1981, three men wanted to start a business. Each had approximately $1,000 to invest. After tossing about ideas, including one in which they would manage a Mexican restaurant, the three decided to build portable personal computers. They called their new company Compaq Computer Corporation. Because their company is now the second largest computer company in the world with yearly revenues exceeding $25 billion, one can only guess how happy they are for having nixed the restaurant idea.

It all started with three senior managers from Texas Instruments: Joseph R. Canion, James M. Harris, and William H. Murto. Once they decided on the name and the business, they approached Ben Rosen, president of Sevin-Rosen Partners, a Houston-based high-technology venture capital firm. Rosen agreed to invest $2.5 million. It was a risk well-taken; in less than three years, his original investment would be valued at $30 million.

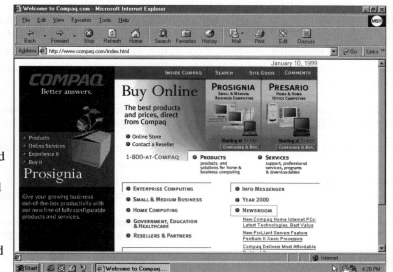

Compaq started with just twenty employees, seasoned professionals culled from Texas Instruments and IBM. In 1982, the same year Compaq formally was founded, IBM began marketing its first personal computer. Compaq burst on the scene, offering IBM *clones*, look-alike computers that performed like IBMs, but were less costly. Success was instantaneous. In its first full year of operation, Compaq generated $111.2 million in sales, the most successful first year sales ever recorded for a U.S. company. Four years later, another first: Compaq became the first company to achieve Fortune 500 status in less than four years. It is now the world's largest personal computer vendor, having successfully ousted IBM from the number-one spot. It employs more than 10,000 people, sells its products in 100 different countries, and was named the *Forbes* 1997 Company of the Year.

Compaq might have entered the personal computer market on IBM's heels, but IBM has been struggling to keep up since then. From the beginning, quick turnaround time has been a key ingredient to Compaq's success. While most computer-industry products have a development cycle of about twelve to eighteen months, Compaq delivers in about six to nine months. This has enabled Compaq to earn the admiration and loyalty of both vendors and users everywhere.

Compaq was ahead of IBM in the European game, too. As early as 1984, Compaq was selling to European markets, long before most other U.S. makers. By 1989, it had become the second largest supplier of business personal computers to Europe, tallying up $1.3 billion in international sales the first year alone. Because Europe's computer market is growing about one-third faster than that of the U.S., Compaq stands to profit even more handsomely. Today, sales outside the U.S. and Canada account for about half of all Compaq sales.

A few short years ago, the large mainframe market was dominated by IBM, Hewlett-Packard, and Digital Equipment Corporation (DEC). With the advent of servers, however, many older mini-computer and mainframe companies, IBM among them, are watching their former clients opt for Compaq systems. In fact, Walt Disney has chosen Compaq to power its new DisneyQuest operations, as has the New York-based International Securities Exchange (ISE). Already, 106 of 112 exchanges worldwide use Compaq systems for some or all of their operations, including NASDAQ.

One criticism of Compaq has been directed at its support force. In early 1998, its sales and support people numbered less than 8,000. Compaq addressed the problem, in part, by acquiring DEC. Although it reportedly cost Compaq $9.6 billion, it gained DEC's 25,000 field engineers and support staff. At the time of acquisition, about 45 percent of DEC's revenues came from its services division. Compaq is, once again, ideally positioned to benefit.

Compaq also countered the criticisms with the introduction of products like SalesPAQ, an incentive program for indirect sellers, and CarePAQ, a service and support package. And just think, it could have been offering TacoPAQs.

Student Exercises
WEB INFO
IN BRIEF
KEY TERMS
AT THE MOVIES
CHECKPOINT
AT ISSUE
CYBERCLASS
HANDS ON
NET STUFF
Special Features
TIMELINE 2000
GUIDE TO WWW SITES
MAKING A CHIP
BUYER'S GUIDE 2000
CAREERS 2000
TRENDS 2000
CHAT
INTERACTIVE LABS
NEWS
HOME

CHAPTER 1 2 3 4 5 6 7 8 9 10 11 12 13 14 INDEX

IN BRIEF   www.scsite.com/dc2000/ch12/brief.htm

WEB INSTRUCTIONS: *To display this page from the Web, launch your browser and enter the URL,*
www.scsite.com/dc2000/ch12/brief.htm. Click the links for current and additional information. To listen to
an audio version of this IN BRIEF, click the Audio button to the right of the title, IN BRIEF, at the top of
the page. To play the audio, RealPlayer must be installed on your computer (download by clicking here).

 ### 1. What Are the Six Steps in the Program Development Life Cycle?

The program development life cycle (PDLC) is a set of steps that programmers use to build a **computer program**, which is the set of instructions that directs the computer to perform the steps necessary to process data into information. Step 1, analyze problem, consists of reviewing program specifications; meeting with the analyst and users; and identifying program input, output, and processing components. Step 2, design programs, involves grouping activities into modules, devising **solution algorithms**, and testing the algorithms. Step 3, code programs, entails translating the solution algorithm into a programming language and entering programming language code into the computer. Step 4, test programs, consists of correcting **syntax errors** or **logic errors**. Step 5, formalize solution, includes reviewing program code and documentation. Step 6, maintain programs, involves correcting errors and adding enhancements.

 ### 2. What Is Top-Down Program Design?

Top-down design breaks the original set of program specifications into smaller, more manageable sections. A section of program dedicated to performing a single function is called a **module**. Programmers use a **hierarchy chart** to represent program modules graphically. Programs developed using the top-down approach usually are reliable and easy to read and maintain.

 ### 3. What Are Structured Program Design and Control Structures?

Structured design is an approach in which all program logic is constructed from a combination of three **control structures**, or designs that direct the order in which program instructions are executed. A **sequence control structure** shows a single action or one action sequentially followed by another. A **selection control structure** tells the program which action to take based on a certain condition. A **repetition control structure** is used when one or more actions are to be performed repeatedly as long as a certain condition is met.

 ### 4. How Are the Categories of Programming Languages Different?

A programming language is a set of words, symbols, and codes that enables a programmer to communicate a solution algorithm to the computer. **Machine language** uses a series of binary digits that correspond to the on and off electrical states of a computer. **Assembly language** instructions are written using abbreviations and codes. **Third-generation language (3GL)** instructions, which use a series of English-like words, are **procedural languages** because the computer must be told what to accomplish and how to do it. A **fourth-generation language (4GL)**, which also uses English-like statements, is a **nonprocedural language** because a programmer only specifies what the program should accomplish without explaining how. A **natural language** is a type of query language that allows the user to enter requests resembling human speech. Machine and assembly languages are **low-level languages** written to run on one particular computer. Third-generation, fourth-generation, and natural languages are **high-level languages** that can run on many different types of computers.

 www.scsite.com/dc2000/ch12/brief.htm

■ Student Exercises
WEB INFO
IN BRIEF
KEY TERMS
AT THE MOVIES
CHECKPOINT
AT ISSUE
CYBERCLASS
HANDS ON
NET STUFF
  Special Features
TIMELINE 2000
GUIDE TO WWW SITES
MAKING A CHIP
BUYER'S GUIDE 2000
CAREERS 2000
TRENDS 2000
CHAT
INTERACTIVE LABS
NEWS
HOME

5. What Is the Object-Oriented Approach to Program Development?

With the **object-oriented** approach, a programmer can package the data and the procedure into a single unit called an **object**. The data elements in the object are called **attributes**, and the procedures are called **methods**. An object-oriented programming (OOP) language is used to implement the object-oriented approach to program development.

6. What Programming Languages Are Commonly Used Today?

BASIC is a simple, interactive problem-solving language often used in the introductory programming course. **Visual Basic** is a programming language used to develop Windows-based applications. **COBOL** is a widely used procedural programming language widely used for business applications. The **C** programming language is used to develop a variety of software, including operating systems and application programs. C++ is an object-oriented extension of the C programming language. **FORTRAN** was one of the first high-level programming languages used for scientific applications. **Pascal** is a programming language created to teach structured programming concepts. **Ada** was originally designed for embedded computer systems. **RPG** is a nonprocedural language used for application development on IBM midrange computers.

7. Why Are Application Generators, Macros, and RAD Tools Used?

Program development tools such as application generators, macros, and RAD tools are user-friendly software products designed to create solutions to information systems requirements. An **application generator** is a program used to build an application without writing extensive code. A **macro** is a series of statements that instructs an application how to complete a routine, repetitive, or difficult task. Rapid application development (RAD) tools – such as Visual Basic, **Delphi**, and **Power-Builder** – are used to develop software throughout the system development process instead of waiting until the implementation phase.

8. What Are the HTML, DHTML, and XML Web Page Development Tools?

Hypertext markup language (HTML) is a special formatting language used to create Web pages. It uses specific syntax rules for defining the placement and format of text, graphics, video, and sound on a Web page. **Dynamic HTML (DHTML)** is a newer version of HTML used to include more graphical interest and interactivity, without having to access the Web server. A specification for **eXtensible Markup Language (XML)** allows Web page developers to create customized **tags** (codes that specify links to other documents and how the Web page displays), as well as the use of predefined tags. XML allows you to define a link that points to multiple Web sites.

9. What Are Scripts, Applets, and Servlets?

Scripts, applets, and servlets are short programs that are executed inside of another program. They are used to add multimedia capabilities to Web pages. A **script** is an interpreted program that runs on the client computer. An **applet** also usually runs on the client, but it is compiled, which means generally it runs faster than a script. A **servlet** is an applet that runs on the server. The more common scripting languages are C, C++, **JavaScript**, and **Perl**. Applets and servlets commonly are written using Java.

CHAPTER 1 2 3 4 5 6 7 8 9 10 11 **12** 13 14 INDEX

KEY TERMS   www.scsite.com/dc2000/ch12/terms.htm

WEB INSTRUCTIONS: *To display this page from the Web, launch your browser and enter the URL,* *www.scsite.com/dc2000/ch12/terms.htm. Scroll through the list of terms. Click a term to display its definition and a picture. Click KEY TERMS on the left to redisplay the KEY TERMS page. Click the TO WEB button for current and additional information about the term from the Web. To see animations, Shockwave and Flash Player must be installed on your computer (download by clicking here).*

Ada (12.25)
add-on HTML editor (12.31)
annotation symbols (12.10)
applet (12.31)
application generator (12.27)
assembler (12.17)
assembly language (12.16)
attributes (12.19)
BASIC (12.21)
bugs (12.14)
C (12.23)
C++ (12.23)
case control structure (12.7)
class (12.20)
COBOL (12.23)
coding (12.13)
comment symbols (12.10)
comments (12.13)
common gateway interface (CGI) (12.32)
compiler (12.17)
computer program (12.2)
construct (12.6)
control structure (12.6)
counter (12.32)
dead code (12.8)
debug utility (12.14)
debugger (12.14)
debugging (12.14)
defining diagram (12.4)
Delphi (12.29)
design tools (12.9)
desk checking (12.12)
document object model (DOM) (12.34)
do-until control structure (12.7)
do-while control structure (12.7)
Dynamic HTML (DHTML) (12.34)
empower (12.27)
encapsulation (12.19)
entry point (12.8)
event (12.20)
exit point (12.8)
eXtensible Markup Language (XML) (12.35)
flowchart (12.9)
flowcharting software (12.10)
FORTRAN (12.24)
fourth-generation language (4GL) (12.18)
hierarchy chart (12.5)
high-level language (12.15)
hypertext markup language (HTML) (12.30)
if-then-else control structure (12.6)
IPO chart (12.4)
image map (12.32)
implemented (12.15)
indentation (12.11)

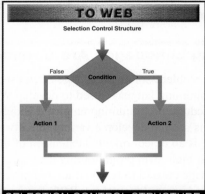

TO WEB

Selection Control Structure

False   Condition   True

Action 1   Action 2

SELECTION CONTROL STRUCTURE:
Used in structured design, a control structure that tells the program which action to take, based on a certain condition. When the condition is evaluated, its result is either true or false. Two types of selection control structures are the if-the-else control structure and the case control structure. (12.6)

infinite loop (12.8)
information hiding (12.20)
inheritance (12.20)
interpreter (12.18)
IPO chart (12.4)
iteration control structure (12.7)
Java (12.32)
JavaScript (12.33)
logic error (12.12)
low-level language (12.15)
machine language (12.16)
machine-dependent (12.16)
machine-independent (12.17)
macro (12.17, 12.28)
macro recorder (12.28)
maintaining (12.15)
markups (12.30)
menu generator (12.28)
message (12.20)
methods (12.19)
Millenium Bug (12.14)
mnemonics (12.16)
module (12.5)
multimedia authoring software (12.35)
Nassi-Schneiderman (N-S) chart (12.10)
natural language (12.19)
nonprocedural language (12.18)
object (12.19)
object code (12.17)
object instance (12.20)
object program (12.17)

object-oriented (12.19)
object-oriented programming (OOP) language (12.20)
operations (12.19)
Pascal (12.25)
Perl (12.33)
PowerBuilder (12.29)
procedural languages (12.17)
processing form (12.32)
program development life cycle (PDLC) (12.2)
program development tool (12.15, 12.27)
program enhancement (12.15)
program flowchart (12.9)
program generator (12.27)
program logic (12.6)
program specification package (12.3)
program testing (12.13)
programming language (12.2, 12.15)
programming team (12.3)
proper program (12.8)
prototype (12.29)
pseudocode (12.11)
quality review (12.12)
query language (12.18)
rapid application development (RAD) (12.29)
remarks (12.13)
repetition control structure (12.7)
report generator (12.18)
report writer (12.18)
RPG (12.26)
script (12.31)
selection control structure (12.6)
sequence control structure (12.6)
servlet (12.31)
solution algorithm (12.6)
source program (12.17)
stand-alone HTML editor (12.31)
structure chart (12.5)
structured design (12.6)
structured flowcharts (12.10)
structured walkthrough (12.12)
style sheet (12.34)
subclasses (12.20)
superclass (12.20)
symbolic addresses (12.17)
symbolic instruction codes (12.16)
syntax (12.13)
syntax error (12.13)
tags (12.30)
test data (12.12)
third-generation language (3GL) (12.17)
top-down chart (12.5)
top-down design (12.5)
variables (12.19)
Year 2000 Bug (Y2K Bug) (12.14)
Visual Basic (12.22)
Web page authors (12.29)

CHAPTER 1 2 3 4 5 6 7 8 9 10 11 **12** 13 14 **INDEX**

AT THE MOVIES

www.scsite.com/dc2000/ch12/movies.htm

WELCOME to VIDEO CLIPS from CNN

WEB INSTRUCTIONS: *To display this page from the Web, launch your browser and enter the URL, www.scsite.com/dc2000/ch12/movies.htm. Click a picture to view a video. After watching the video, close the video window and then complete the exercise by answering the questions about the video. To view the videos, RealPlayer must be installed on your computer (download by clicking here).*

SHELLY CASHMAN SERIES

DISCOVERING COMPUTERS 2000

Student Exercises
WEB INFO
IN BRIEF
KEY TERMS
AT THE MOVIES
CHECKPOINT
AT ISSUE
CYBERCLASS
HANDS ON
NET STUFF
Special Features
TIMELINE 2000
GUIDE TO WWW SITES
MAKING A CHIP
BUYER'S GUIDE 2000
CAREERS 2000
TRENDS 2000
CHAT
INTERACTIVE LABS
NEWS
HOME

1 Software Big Bucks

Growth in the U.S. software industry sector is faster than in any other major sector. How many people will work in the software industry by 2005? What is the average salary of a software producer? Why do you think software developers can command higher salaries than other professionals? The video suggests that firms are willing to pay software developers more to recoup their investment in training. Can you think of any other reasons why the professionals would expect higher-than-average salaries? Describe what you think will be employment opportunities in the programming field ten years from now.

2 Year 2000 Bug

The U.S. Securities and Exchange Commission has been so deeply concerned over the Year 2000 situation that it has required technology-based companies to report on their efforts to control the problem. What is the Year 2000 Bug? What could happen? What systems will it affect? What will it cost to re-program computers to ensure they will not stop functioning correctly at that time? Have you or anyone you know been affected by Y2K? How could this problem happen in the first place? What other widespread programming problems can you envision? How can these problems be corrected?

3 Electronic Libraries

Does your school library use computers? Have you ever used a library computer to do research on the Web? What are the advantages and disadvantages of this shift to electronic data? Do you think that traditional libraries will only exist to house publicly accessible computers and a collection of texts required for verifying digitized versions? Do you think print-based books will ever disappear? Why or why not?

Student Exercises
WEB INFO
IN BRIEF
KEY TERMS
AT THE MOVIES
CHECKPOINT
AT ISSUE
CYBERCLASS
HANDS ON
NET STUFF
Special Features
TIMELINE 2000
GUIDE TO WWW SITES
MAKING A CHIP
BUYER'S GUIDE 2000
CAREERS 2000
TRENDS 2000
CHAT
INTERACTIVE LABS
NEWS
HOME

CHAPTER 1 2 3 4 5 6 7 8 9 10 11 12 13 14 INDEX

CHECKPOINT   www.scsite.com/dc2000/ch12/check.htm

WEB INSTRUCTIONS: *To display this page from the Web, launch your browser and enter the URL, www.scsite.com/dc2000/ch12/check.htm. Click the links for current and additional information. To experience the animation and interactivity, Shockwave and Flash Player must be installed on your computer (download by clicking here).*

Label the Figure

Instructions: *Identify the steps in the program development life cycle (PDLC).*

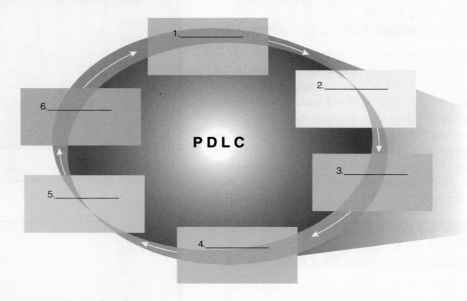

Matching

Instructions: *Match each programming aid from the column on the left with the best description from the column on the right.*

_____ 1. IPO chart

_____ 2. hierarchy chart

_____ 3. program flowchart

_____ 4. Nassi-Schneiderman (N-S) chart

_____ 5. pseudocode

a. Graphically reviews the deliverables during the system development life cycle.

b. Used to identify syntax and logic errors by examining values while the program runs in slow motion.

c. Represents each module in a program with a rectangle labeled with the module name.

d. Uses an abbreviated form of English to outline program logic.

e. Graphically shows the logic in a solution algorithm, but does not use lines to show direction.

f. Identifies program inputs, the program outputs, and the processing steps required.

g. Graphically shows the logic in a program according to standards published by ANSI.

Short Answer

Instructions: *Write a brief answer to each of the following questions.*

1. How is the if-then-else control structure different from the case control structure? _____ How is the do-while control structure different from the do-until control structure? _____

2. What is proper program design? _____ What are dead code, infinite loops, entry points, and exit points? _____

3. How is a logic error different from a syntax error? _____ What is desk checking? _____

4. How is a compiler different from an interpreter? _____ What is an advantage of an interpreter? _____

5. What factors should be considered when selecting a programming language? _____

AT ISSUE www.scsite.com/dc2000/ch12/issue.htm

WEB INSTRUCTIONS: *To display this page from the Web, launch your browser and enter the URL, www.scsite.com/dc2000/ch12/issue.htm. Click the links for current and additional information.*

The U.S. Department of Commerce predicts that more than a million new technology workers will be needed over the next five years. Typical programmers earn up to $90,000, with substantial signing bonuses and annual pay hikes. Yet, applicant supply is not keeping up with corporate demand. To ease the shortage, companies are tempting high-school students with attractive training programs that lead to lucrative jobs. The market for programmers has fluctuated wildly, and today's need is no guarantee of tomorrow's employment. Will students who begin technological training right out of high school have a background general enough for other pursuits if their interest fades or the market withers? Do you think companies should be allowed to sign high-school students? Why or why not? What can be done to address long-term concerns?

Linux is a fast-growing, innovative new operating system. One of the things that makes Linux different from other operating systems is that Linux can be downloaded from the Web at no cost, and its source code, along with any changes, must remain public. Since its introduction in 1991, Linux has been altered, adapted, and improved by hundreds of programmers. While Linux is an open-source program, program code often is a zealously guarded secret. At a large software developer firm, an employee claims that operating system programmers have little opportunity to contribute to application programs because they have no access to the application program source code. Why are many commercial software developers reluctant to share program code? What are the advantages of making program code public? What are the disadvantages?

"100% Pure Java" may soon be as familiar on software packages as it is on coffee shop menus. Java has been called the programming language of the future. A simple language, Java utilizes an object-oriented approach, module orientation, and an easy-to-use GUI. In addition, Java offers a cross-platform capability that allows it to be used in any computing environment. Some software companies, however, are releasing nonstandard Java applications. This contaminated Java, which incorporates certain proprietary elements, runs only on specific computers. A number of vendors want standard Java applications to be awarded a "100% Pure Java" logo. Do you think this is a good idea? Why or why not? Who would test, and confirm, the purity of Java applications? Who might oppose this certification? Why?

The consequences of bugs in computer programs can be staggering. One mistake in the code controlling a Canadian nuclear facility caused more than 3,000 gallons of radioactive water to be spilled. A bug in AT&T's long-distance switching software cost the company $60 million. Despite sophisticated debugging utilities, experts estimate that one in every 5,000 lines of code contains an error. Given that many programs contain hundreds of thousands, even millions, of code lines, is it possible to remove all the bugs from a program? Why or why not? What can be done to reduce the number of software bugs? If software bugs are inevitable, or at least to be expected, what steps can people relying on computer programs take to deal with the bugs?

Computer programmers have an unenviable image. They frequently are pictured as boring technocrats lucky enough to be in the right place at the right time; socially awkward introverts with thick glasses and plastic pocket protectors (a perception implied in the title of Robert X. Cringely's book, *Accidental Empires: How the Boys of Silicon Valley Make Their Millions, Battle Foreign Competition, and Still Can't Get a Date*). In reality, programmers are like other highly talented white-collar workers. Successful programmers have described their jobs as a combination of engineer, inventor, entrepreneur, and artist. What does this mean? What other occupations, if any, demand similar abilities? Is computer programming a science, a skill, a craft, or an art? Why? Would you make a good computer programmer? Why or why not?

Student Exercises
WEB INFO
IN BRIEF
KEY TERMS
AT THE MOVIES
CHECKPOINT
AT ISSUE
CYBERCLASS
HANDS ON
NET STUFF
Special Features
TIMELINE 2000
GUIDE TO WWW SITES
MAKING A CHIP
BUYER'S GUIDE 2000
CAREERS 2000
TRENDS 2000
CHAT
INTERACTIVE LABS
NEWS
HOME

CHAPTER 1 2 3 4 5 6 7 8 9 10 11 `12` 13 14 INDEX

CYBERCLASS   www.scsite.com/dc2000/ch12/class.htm

WEB INSTRUCTIONS: *To display this page from the Web, launch your browser and enter the URL,* www.scsite.com/dc2000/ch12/class.htm. *To start Level I CyberClass, click a Level I link on this page or enter the URL,* www.cyber-class.com. *Click the Student button, click Discovering Computers 2000 in the list of titles, and then click the Enter a site button. To start Level II or III CyberClass (available only to those purchasers of a CyberClass floppy disk), place your CyberClass floppy disk in drive A, click Start on the taskbar, click Run on the Start menu, type* a:connect *in the Open text box, click the OK button, click the Enter CyberClass button, and then follow the instructions.*

I II III LEVEL **1. Flash Cards** Click Flash Cards on the Main Menu of the CyberClass web page. Click the plus sign before the Chapter 12 title and then click Popular Programming Languages. Answer all flash cards in this subject. If you missed two consecutive questions, choose another subject and answer all the flash cards for the subject. Continue until you answer all flash cards in a subject without missing two consecutive questions. All users: Answer as many more flash cards as you desire. Close the Electronic Flash Card window and the Flash Cards window by clicking the Close button in the upper-right corner of each window.

I II III LEVEL **2. Practice Test** Click Testing on the Main Menu of the CyberClass web page. Click the Select a book box arrow and then click Discovering Computers 2000. Click the Select a test to take box arrow and then click the Chapter 12 title in the list. Click the Take Test button. If necessary, maximize the window. Take the practice test and then click the Submit Test button. If your score was less than 80%, click the Take another Test button. Continue taking tests until your score is greater than 80%. Then click the Done button.

I II III LEVEL **3. Web Guide** Click Web Guide on the Main Menu of the CyberClass web page. When the Guide to World Wide Web Sites page displays, click Museums and then click The Smithsonian. At the Smithsonian Institute, explore for information about computers. Write a brief report about the role programming languages have played in the development of computers.

I II III LEVEL **4. Company Briefs** Click Company Briefs on the Main Menu of the CyberClass web page. Click a corporation name to display a case study. Read the case study. Visit the company's Web site to find the programming languages the company uses.

II III LEVEL **5. CyberChallenge** Click CyberChallenge on the Main Menu of the CyberClass web page. Click the Select a book box arrow and then click Discovering Computers 2000. Click the Select a board to play box arrow and then click Chapter 12 in the list. Click the Play CyberChallenge button. Maximize the CyberChallenge window. Play CyberChallenge until you have answered all the 30, 40, and 50 point questions for a board. Close the CyberChallenge window.

II III LEVEL **6. Hot Links and Student Bulletin Board** Click Hot Links on the Main Menu of the CyberClass web page. Visit sites in Hot Links until you find one that uses sound or video. Then click Student Bulletin Board, click Add Topic, type your name as the topic, click the Add Topic button, type a message subject and message body that tells your fellow students about this site, and then click the Add Message button.

II III LEVEL **7. Text Chat** Arrange for your instructor to conduct office hours using CyberClass text chat. Then at the appointed time, click Text Chat on the Main Menu of the CyberClass web page and ask any questions you may have about programming languages and the design of computer programs.

HANDS ON   www.scsite.com/dc2000/ch12/hands.htm

WEB INSTRUCTIONS: *To display this page from the Web, launch your browser and enter the URL,* www.scsite.com/dc2000/ch12/hands.htm. *Click the links for current and additional information.*

One   Searching for Executable Files

In Windows, application files have an .exe extension, meaning that they are executable. To find the executable program files on your computer, click the Start button on the taskbar, point to Find on the Start menu, and then click Files or Folders on the Find submenu. In the Find: All Files window, click the Name & Location tab, click View on the menu bar, and then click Details. Type *.exe in the Named text box. Type c:\ in the Look in text box. Select Include subfolders. Click the Find Now button. Sort the files alphabetically by name by clicking the Name column heading. Scroll through the list of files and find the file name, Notepad. In what folder is Notepad located? How large is the file? Close the Find window.

Two   Movie Box Office Simulation

Insert the Discover Data Disk into drive A. If you do not have the Discover Data Disk, see the inside back cover of this book or your instructor. Click the Start button on the taskbar and then click Run on the Start menu. In the Open text box, type a:movie.exe and then press the ENTER key. This program was written in Visual Basic. The first customer wishes to purchase three tickets to a matinee performance of *The Abyss*. Notice the amount due and then click the Enter button. Enter the following transactions and write down the amount due for each transaction: (1) *The Client*, no matinee, 3 tickets; (2) *Forrest Gump*, matinee, 1 ticket; (3) *Beverly Hills Cop*, matinee, 2 tickets.

Three   Adjusting Keyboard Speed

Windows allows users to adjust the keyboard to their own specifications. To customize the keyboard, click the Start button on the taskbar, point to Settings on the Start menu, and then click Control Panel on the Settings submenu. Double-click the keyboard icon in the Control Panel window. When the Keyboard Properties dialog box displays, click the Speed tab (Figure 12-41). Use the question mark button on the title bar to answer the following questions: What is repeat delay? What is repeat rate? Click the Cancel button. Close the Control Panel window.

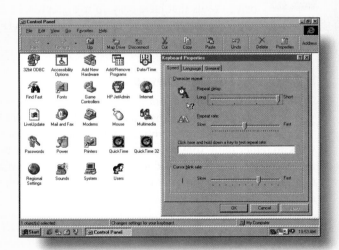

Figure 12-41

Four   Loan Payment Calculator

Insert the Discover Data Disk into drive A. If you do not have the Discover Data Disk, see the inside back cover of this book or your instructor. Click the Start button on the taskbar, and then click Run on the Start menu to display the Run dialog box. In the Open text box, type a:loancalc.exe and then press the ENTER key to display the Loan Payment Calculator window. This program was written in Visual Basic. Type 12500 in the LOAN AMOUNT text box. Click the YEARS right scroll arrow or drag the scroll box until YEARS equals 15. Click the APR right scroll arrow or drag the scroll box until APR equals 8.5. Click the Calculate button. Write down the monthly payment and sum of payments. Click the Clear button. What are the monthly payment and sum of payments for each of these loan amounts, years, and APRs? (1) 28000, 5, 7.25; (2) 98750, 30, 9; (3) 6000, 3, 8.75; and (4) 62500, 15, 9.25. Close Loan Payment Calculator.

SHELLY
CASHMAN
SERIES
DISCOVERING
COMPUTERS
2000

CHAPTER 1 2 3 4 5 6 7 8 9 10 11 **12** 13 14 INDEX

NET STUFF   www.scsite.com/dc2000/ch12/net.htm

WEB INSTRUCTIONS: *To display this page from the Web, launch your browser and enter the URL, www.scsite.com/dc2000/ch12/net.htm. To use the Choosing a Programming Language lab from the Web, Shockwave and Flash Player must be installed on your computer (download by clicking here).*

CHOOSING A PROGRAMMING LANGUAGE LAB

1. Shelly Cashman Series Choosing a Programming Language Lab

Follow the instructions in NET STUFF 1 on page 1.46 to start and use the Choosing a Programming Language lab. If you are running from the Web, enter the URL, www.scsite.com/sclabs/menu.htm; or display the NET STUFF page (see instructions at the top of this page) and then click the CHOOSING A PROGRAMMING LANGUAGE LAB button.

IMAGE MAPS

2. Image Maps

One common use of a script is to create an image map – a Web page picture that points to a URL and is used in place of, or in addition to, plain text hyperlinks (Figure 12-42). When you click a part of the picture, the Web browser locates the corresponding URL and sends the Web page to your computer. To work with image maps on Web pages, complete this exercise.

Figure 12-42

APPLICATION GENERATORS

3. Application Generators

When using an application generator, a developer works with menu-driven tools that have easy-to-use graphical interfaces. To use an application generator to produce Web pages (Figure 12-43), complete this exercise.

IN THE NEWS

4. In the News

Programming is not just for programmers anymore. Yaroze is a Japanese expression meaning, let us work together. Net Yaroze is a new project that lets anyone with a computer and some programming experience work together with Sony to create their own games for Sony's Playstation. Increasingly, entertainment and productivity applications are offering tools, such as macros, that allow users to program their own innovations. Click the IN THE NEWS button and read a news article about programming. Who is doing the programming? How is the programming different?

Figure 12-43

WEB CHAT

5. Web Chat

America is a litigious society. Almost half the world's lawyers practice law in the United States, and computer software is an increasingly fertile field for litigation. Some cases deal with antitrust issues, but a substantial number are concerned with errors in software programs. For example, estimates place the cost of settling lawsuits arising over the Y2K Bug – the software glitch that, because only the last two digits were used to specify a year, causes computers to interpret the year 2000 as the year 1900 – at nearly $600 billion. Together with other suspected software slips, the new millenium may see a flurry of computer-related lawsuits. When an individual, or group of individuals, suffers from a software flaw, who should be responsible? The organization using the software? The software developer? The programmer? Why? How will enthusiastic prosecution of cases related to software flaws affect software development? What, if anything, can be done to mitigate any negative impact? Click the WEB CHAT button to enter a Web Chat discussion related to this topic.

CAREERS 2000
Planning, Prerequisites, Potential

WEB INSTRUCTIONS: *To gain World Wide Web access to additional and up-to-date information regarding this special feature, launch your browser and enter the URL shown at the top of this page.*

In today's technology-rich world, a great demand for computer and information systems professionals exists and continues to grow. In fact, the U.S. Commerce Department's Office of Technology Policy recently reported that by the year 2006, American businesses and schools will require more than 1.3 million new systems analysts, computer scientists, engineers, and programmers. Today, however, fewer than 3 percent of college freshmen are majoring in a computer-related field. When you consider these two facts together, it is clear the demand for computer and information systems professionals could become a shortage quickly. For individuals worldwide, this means that incredible opportunities increase daily.

The computer and information systems (also called information technology or IT) industry offers many rewarding careers, which can require a unique combination of hands-on skills, creative problem solving, and an understanding of business needs. This special feature on Computer Careers discusses the positions available, preparing for a job, and planning for career development in the computer and information systems industry.

Positions in the Computer Industry

With annual sales of nearly $400 billion, the computer industry is one of the larger worldwide industries. Approximately one-half of this $400 billion total is related to equipment sales; the other half comes from software and service sales.

Job opportunities in the industry are found primarily in four areas:

- companies that manufacture computer-related equipment (hardware)
- companies that develop software
- companies that hire information systems professionals to work with these products
- companies and organizations that provide computer-related training and education

As in any major industry, the computer industry includes many service companies that support each of these four areas. Examples of such companies include firms that sell computer supplies or provide consultation on analysis, design, programming, and networking projects. You can find information on specific positions in each of these industries via typical job-searching methods, as well as on career-oriented sites on the World Wide Web (Figure 1).

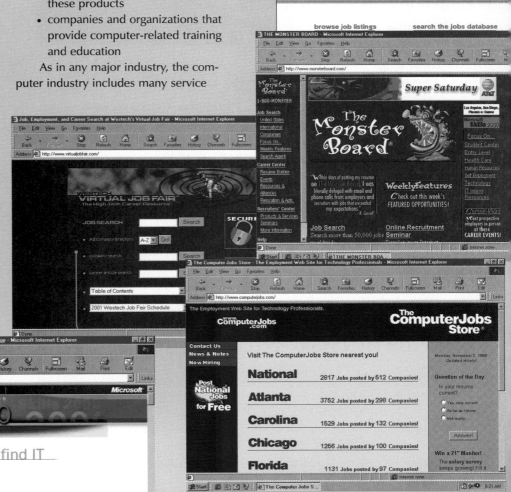

Figure 1

Information on computer-related jobs is available on many sites on the World Wide Web.

The Computer Equipment Industry

The computer equipment, or hardware, industry, consists of manufacturers and distributors of computer systems and computer-related equipment such as disk and tape drives, monitors, printers, and communications equipment (Figure 2).

Figure 2
A computer system is assembled carefully.

Computer equipment manufacturers include such companies as Apple, Compaq, Cisco, Dell, Gateway2000, Hewlett-Packard, IBM, Intel, Sun Microsystems, and 3Com. Many of these firms are huge organizations with thousands of employees worldwide. IBM, for example, is one of the largest computer companies with over 200,000 employees and annual sales of more than $80 billion.

The computer equipment industry also is well known for the many start-up companies that appear each year. These new companies take advantage of rapid changes in equipment technology, such as wireless communications, networking, multimedia, and fiber optics, to create new products and new job opportunities. Often these companies offer stock options to induce college graduates to join their firm instead of the larger, more established companies. Many young graduates have become millionaires overnight by taking a chance with a start-up company.

In addition to the companies that make end user equipment, thousands of companies build components that most users never see. These companies manufacture chips, motherboards, power supplies, peripherals, and the hundreds of other parts that go inside your computer.

Some of the more popular job titles that involve the design and manufacture of computer equipment are described in Figure 3. In larger companies there are several levels to each job title, including management positions.

Many companies list their job openings, internship opportunities, and career opportunities on their Web site. The upper left columns in Figure 4 list the Web site addresses of some of the major computer equipment companies. If you are serious about interviewing with a company, you often can obtain a wealth of information about the firm and its employment opportunities by visiting the company's Web site. Some companies even allow you to submit your resume online.

The Computer Software Industry

The computer software industry is composed of companies that develop, manufacture, and support a wide range of software products, such as operating systems and other systems software; productivity software; network software; software development tools; and Internet software and technologies. Some software companies specialize in a particular type of software product such as business productivity software, utility programs, or multimedia and graphic design tools. Other software companies, especially larger firms, produce and sell multiple software products.

The software industry is a huge one, with annual sales exceeding $200 billion. Leading software companies include Apple, Adobe Systems, Computer Associates, IBM, Intuit, Macromedia, Microsoft, Novell, Oracle, SAP, and Symantec. The largest software company, Microsoft, has more than 300 products and technologies, 20,500 employees, and annual sales of more than $11 billion.

Career opportunities in the software

COMPUTER EQUIPMENT INDUSTRY JOB TITLES

Job Title	Function	Minimum Education	Median Salary Range (in thousands of $)
Computer engineer	Design, build, test, and evaluate computer chips, circuit boards, computer systems, and peripheral devices	B.S. in Electrical or Computer Engineering	62.9
Software engineer	Develop system software such as operating systems, utilities, and software drivers	B.S. in Computer Science	64.4
Technical writer	Produce technical publications including manuals and product documentation	B.S. in Engineering, Science, or a related technology; good writing skills	39.5

(Source: U.S. Bureau of Labor Statistics and Source EDP, 1998 Salary Survey)

Figure 3
The more popular job titles involving the design and manufacture of computer equipment

industry involve designing and programming all kinds of software products, including application software for business, productivity software, educational programs, entertainment software, and systems software. Figure 5 describes some of the more popular job titles used for positions related to the development of software.

The upper right columns in Figure 4 list the Web site addresses of some of the major software companies. As with the computer equipment companies, you may wish to visit a software company's Web site to obtain information on specific job openings and career opportunities.

Information Systems Professionals

In many companies, the information systems department (IS) includes information systems professionals — the people who set up and manage the computer equipment and software to ensure that it produces information for the end user. In addition to other positions, information systems professionals include programmers and systems analysts that companies hire to work in an information systems department. The section beginning on page 12.50 discusses these and other positions available within most information systems departments.

WEB SITE ADDRESSES FOR MAJOR COMPANIES

Hardware

Company	URL
Apple Computer, Inc.	www.apple.com
Ascend Communications, Inc.	www.ascend.com
Cisco Systems, Inc.	www.cisco.com
Compaq	www.compaq.com
Dell Computer Corporation	www.dell.com
Gateway2000 Inc.	www.gateway.com
Hewlett-Packard Company	www.hp.com
IBM Corporation	www.empl.ibm.com
Intel Corporation	www.intel.com
Lucent Technologies	www.lucent.com
Sun Microsystems, Inc.	www.sun.com
3Com Corporation	www.3com.com

Software

Company	URL
Apple Computer, Inc.	www.apple.com
Adobe Systems Incorporated	www.adobe.com
Computer Associates International, Inc.	www.cai.com
IBM Corporation	www.ibm.com
Intuit Inc.	www.intuit.com
Macromedia® Inc.	www.macromedia.com
Microsoft Corporation	www.microsoft.com/jobs
Network Associates, Inc.	www.nai.com/about
Novell, Inc.	www.novell.com
Oracle Corporation	www.oracle.com
Sybase, Inc.	www.sybase.com
Symantec Corporation	www.symantec.com/us.index.html

Noncomputer Related

Company	URL
AT&T	www.att.com/att
The Boeing Company	www.boeing.com
Caterpillar Inc.	www.cat.com
Chevron Corporation	www.chevron.com
Disney	www.disney.go.com
General Motors Corporation	www.gm.com/about/index.html
McDonald's Corporation	www.mcdonalds.com
Merck & Co., Inc.	www.merck.com
Merrill Lynch & Co., Inc.	www.ml.com
Pfizer	www.pfizer.com
Procter & Gamble	www.pg.com
Union Carbide	www.unioncarbide.com
Wal-Mart Stores, Inc.	www.wal-mart.com

Internet

Company	URL
Amazon.com, Inc.	www.amazon.com
America Online, Inc.	www.aol.com
broadcast.com	www.broadcast.com/about
EarthLink Network, Inc.	www.earthlink.com
eBay Inc.	www.ebay.com/aboutebay98
VCash International	www.e-trade.com
Excite Inc.	www.excite.com
Lycos, Inc.	www.lycos.com/lycosinc/lycosjobs.html
Microsoft Corporation	www.microsoft.com
Netscape	www.netscape.com
RealNetworks, Inc.	www.real.com/company/index.html
Yahoo! Inc.	www.yahoo.com/docs/hr

Figure 4

This table lists the Web site addresses for the major hardware, software, noncomputer-related, and Internet companies. When you visit a site, you may have to click a link, such as About or Company Information, to obtain a list of employment opportunities and other career-related information. For an updated list, visit www.scsite.com/dc2000/ch12/careers.htm.

COMPUTER SOFTWARE INDUSTRY JOB TITLES

Job Title	Function	Minimum Education	Median Salary Range (in thousands of $)
Programmer/software engineer	Design, write, and test computer programs	B.S. in Computer Science or Computer Technology	55.7
Software analyst	Analyze software requirements, design software solutions, and oversee the software development process	B.S. in Computer Science	61.2
Technical writer	Produce technical publications including manuals, online Help, and product documentation	B.S. in Computer Science, Computer Technology, or a related technology with good writing skills	39.5

(Source: U.S. Bureau of Labor Statistics and Source EDP, 1998 Salary Survey)

Figure 5

Some popular job titles for software development positions

Information Systems Career Opportunities

Without computers, few companies could operate in today's economy. For some, computers help ensure smooth communication between corporate offices. Other firms use computers to order raw materials automatically, control manufacturing, and ship finished goods. In many cases, the only time a human being is involved in the process is in designing and writing the programs that tell the computer what to do each step of the way. This dependency on computers has created thousands of new high-tech jobs, even in noncomputer-related companies. For many firms, the use of technology separates them from their competitors and is a distinction they highlight on their Web sites (lower left columns in Figure 4 on the previous page).

Because of rapid changes in technology, many current jobs did not even exist just a few years ago. For example, the World Wide Web, which began in 1993, has spawned thousands of Internet Content/Commerce/Provider companies (lower right columns in Figure 4 on the previous page) that demand Web designers and network specialists to create and maintain their Web sites.

The following sections describe some current career opportunities in an information systems department.

Working in an Information Systems Department

The people in an information systems department work together as a team to meet the information demands of their organization. Several job positions have been discussed previously, including database administrators (Chapter 10), systems analysts (Chapter 11), and programmers (Chapter 12). In addition to these jobs, many other positions exist. Generally, these positions fall into four main groups:

1. Operations
2. System development
3. Technical services
4. End user computing

The table in Figure 6 shows some of the nonmanagement positions in each group in the typical information system department. The operations group is responsible for operating the centralized computer equipment and administering the network including both data and voice communications. The system development group is responsible for analyzing, designing, developing, and implementing new information systems and maintaining and improving existing systems. The technical services group is responsible for evaluating and integrating new technologies, administering the organization's data resources, and supporting the centralized computer operating system or servers. The end user computing group is responsible for assisting end users in working with existing systems and in using productivity software and query languages to obtain the information necessary to perform their jobs.

An information systems department provides career opportunities for people with a variety of skills and talents. Other information industry jobs are found in the areas of education and training, sales, service and repair, and consulting.

NONMANAGEMENT INFORMATION SYSTEMS JOB TITLES

Group	Job Title	Function	Minimum Education	Median Salary Range (in thousands of $)
Operations	Computer operator	Performs equipment-related activities such as monitoring performance, running jobs, backup, and restore	High School diploma	34.5
	Communications specialist	Evaluates, installs, and monitors data and/or voice communications equipment and software and is responsible for connections to the Internet and other wide area networks	B.S. in Information Systems or Electrical Engineering Technology	59.3
	Network (LAN) engineer	Installs and maintains local area networks	B.S. in Information Systems or Electrical Engineering Technology	58
System development	Systems analyst	Works closely with users to analyze their requirements and design an information system solution	B.S. in Management Information Systems	62.4
	Application programmer	Converts the system design into the appropriate computer language, such as C, Java, and COBOL	A.A.S. in Information Systems	47.4
	Webmaster	Maintains an organization's Web site; creates or helps users create Web pages	A.A.S. in Information Systems	42.5
	Technical writer	Works with the analyst, programmer, and user to create system documentation and user manuals	B.S. in Information Systems	39.5
Technical services	Database analyst	Assists systems analysts and programmers in developing or modifying applications that use the company's database	B.S. in Computer Science or Information Systems	59.6
	System programmer	Installs and maintains operating system software and provides technical support to the programmers' staff	B.S. in Computer Science or Information Systems	60.2
	Quality assurance specialist	Reviews programs and documentation to ensure they meet the organization's standards	B.S. in Information Systems	55
End user computing	PC support specialist	Installs and supports personal computer equipment and software	A.A.S. in Information Systems	39.8
	Help desk analyst	Provides user/customer telephone support for hardware, software, or telecommunications systems	A.A.S. in Information Systems	44.2

(Source: U.S. Bureau of Labor Statistics and Source EDP, 1998 Salary Survey)

Figure 6

This table shows some of the nonmanagement positions in each of the four main groups in a typical information systems department.

Education and Training

The increased sophistication and complexity of today's computer products has opened extensive opportunities in computer-related education and training (Figure 7). Schools, colleges, universities, and private companies all need qualified instructors. The high demand for instructors, in fact, has led to a shortage of qualified instructors at the university level as educators increasingly are lured into private industry by the promise of higher pay. This shortage probably will not end in the near future because the supply of educators with Ph.D. degrees (the degree usually required to teach at the university level) is not keeping pace with the demand.

Sales

Sales representatives must have a general understanding of computers and a specific knowledge of the product they are selling. Strong interpersonal, or people, skills are important, including listening ability and strong oral and written communication skills. Companies usually pay sales representatives based on the

Figure 7
A high demand exists in schools and industry for qualified instructors who can teach information processing subjects.

amount of product they sell; top sales representatives often are among an organization's more highly compensated employees.

Some sales representatives work directly for hardware and software manufacturers (top half of Figure 4 on page 12.49). Others work for resellers, including retailers that sell personal computer products such as Comp USA, Best Buy, and Office Max (Figure 8).

Service and Repair

Being a service and repair technician is a challenging job for individuals who like to troubleshoot and solve problems and have a strong background in electronics (Figure 9). In the early days of computers, technicians often made repairs at the site of the computer equipment. Today, however, technicians first will replace a malfunctioning component, such as a hard disk, and then take the faulty part back for repair at his or her office or at a special repair facility. Many computer equipment manufacturers include special diagnostic software with their computer equipment that helps service technicians identify any problems. Some computer systems even use a modem to telephone a computer automatically at a service technician's office to leave a message that a malfunction has been detected.

Consulting

After building experience in one or more computer and IS-related areas, an individual might decide to become a consultant, someone who draws upon his or her experiences to give advice to others. Consultants not only must have strong technical skills in their area of expertise, but also must have the people skills necessary to communicate their suggestions effectively to their clients. Qualified consultants are in high demand for tasks such as computer system selection, system design, communications network design and installation, and Web development.

Figure 9
Computer service and repair requires a knowledge of electronics.

Figure 8
Computer retailers need sales people who understand personal computers and have good people skills.

Preparing for a Career in the Computer Industry

To prepare for a career in the computer industry, you first must decide on the area in which you are interested and then obtain education in that field. According to the U.S. Bureau of Labor Statistics, the fastest growing computer career positions through the year 2006 will be computer engineer, systems analyst, computer repair technician, and programmer (Figure 10). The Web sites listed under the Getting Started category in Figure 11 will guide you through the prerequisites and opportunities in each field. The Microsoft Skills 2000 Web site is especially helpful. You also can obtain career information by visiting the Web sites listed under the Professional Organizations and Job Opportunities categories in Figure 11.

Choosing the Right Course of Study

Three broad disciplines in higher education produce the majority of entry-level employees in the computer industry: computer information systems, computer science (also referred to as software engineering), and computer engineering. The characteristics of each program are summarized in Figure 12 and discussed in the following paragraphs.

Computer information systems (CIS) programs emphasize the practical aspects of computing. After two years of study, students often receive an Applied Associate in Science degree (A.A.S.) with an emphasis in application programming. In four-year programs, students work toward and receive a Bachelor's of Science degree (B.S.) with an emphasis in systems programming, systems analysis and design, or networking. In many cases, local community colleges offer the A.A.S. degree. Students then transfer to a four-year college or university to complete their B.S. degree. If you are attending a community college, ask your advisor if the school has an articulation agreement with a nearby college or university. An articulation agreement ensures that, if you transfer to a college or university, you will receive credit for most of the courses you took at the community college level. In general, a computer information systems program does not require its majors to have a strong mathematics and science background, but it does help.

Computer science (CS), also called software engineering (SE), programs stress the theoretical side of programming. A computer science curriculum typically emphasizes systems programming, rather than applications programming. In general, CS programming courses are more rigorous than CIS programming courses. Students thus are required to take several mathematics and science courses before enrolling in the majority of computer science courses.

Computer engineering (CE) programs teach students how to design and develop the electronic components found in computers and peripheral devices. Students usually are required to take mathematics, physics, and basic engineering courses before taking the more serious computer engineering design and development courses.

As in most other industries, an individual with a more advanced degree in a specific field has a better chance of success. Thus, to round out their education, instead of continuing down a narrow path with a second degree in the computer area, many graduates with a computer degree change direction and obtain a Masters in Business Administration (M.B.A.) degree.

Attending a Trade School

An alternative to enrolling in a college or

PROJECTED GROWTH 1996 - 2006

	1996	2006	Change	% Change
Computer engineers	235,000	491,000	256,000	109
Systems analysts	520,000	1,055,000	535,000	103
Computer repair technicians	42,000	66,000	24,000	52
Programmers	568,000	738,000	170,000	30

(Source: U.S. Bureau of Labor Statistics and Source EDP, 1998 Salary Survey)

Figure 10
Projected growth rates for computer-related careers

WEB SITE TITLE	URL
Getting Started	
Computer Programmers	stats.bls.gov/oco/ocos110.htm
Careers in Computing	www.tcm.org/html/resources/cmp-careers/cnc-topdrawer.html
Making College Count	www.makingcollegecount.com/home.html
Microsoft Skills 2000	www.microsoft.com/skills2000/findit/resource.htm
Scholarships	www.fastweb.com
Bureau of Labor Statistics	stats.bls.gov/blshome.htm
Professional Organizations	
Association for Information Systems	www.aisnet.org
Association of Computing Machinery	www.acm.org
Association of Information Technology Professionals (formally DPMA)	www.aitp.org
Institute of Electrical and Electronics Engineers	www.ieee.org
The World's Computer Society	www.computer.org
Job Opportunities	
The ComputerJobs Store®	www.computerjobs.com
e-span's JobOptions™	www.espan.com
softwarejobs.com	www.softwarejobs.com
monster.com	www.monsterboard.com
Westech Virtual Job Fair™	www.virtualjobfair.com
Computer Industry Training	
Microsoft Training & Certification Programs	www.microsoft.com/train_cert/train
Novell: Education: Authorized Training Options	education.novell.com/general/trainopt.htm
Certification	
Institute for Certification of Computer Professionals	www.iccp.org
Computing Technology Industry Association (CompTIA)	www.comptia.org/
Microsoft Training & Certification Programs	www.microsoft.com/train_cert
Novell Professional Certifications	education.novell.com/certinfo
Cisco Connection Online	www.cisco.com
Sun Educational Services	suned.sun.com/
Adobe Certified Training Programs	partners.adobe.com/supportservice/training/main.html
Publications and Web News Sites	
Computerworld	www.computerworld.com
InfoWorld	www.infoworld.com
Datamation	www.datamation.com
internet.com	www.internet.com
PC Week Online	www.zdnet.com/pcweek

Figure 11
These Web sites help in career preparation in the computer industry. For an updated list, visit www.scsite.com/dc2000/ch12/careers.htm.

DISCIPLINE DIFFERENCES

Computer Information Systems	Computer Science/Software Engineering	Computer Engineering
Practical and application-oriented	Theoretical oriented	Design oriented
Business and management oriented	Mathematics and science oriented	Mathematics and science oriented
Understanding how to design and implement information systems	Understanding the fundamental nature of software	Understanding the fundamental nature of hardware
Degrees include A.A.S., B.S., M.S., Ph.D.	Degrees include B.S., M.S., Ph.D.	Degrees include B.S., M.S., Ph.D.

Figure 12
The major differences among the computer science/software engineering, computer engineering, and computer information systems disciplines

Attending a Trade School

An alternative to enrolling in a college or university is to attend a trade school. Trade schools offer programs primarily in the areas of programming and maintenance. One advantage of attending a trade school is time: students often can complete trade school programs in a shorter time than college and university programs, because they generally are not required to take science or humanities courses. As with any post-secondary school, when deciding on a trade school you should compare curricula, laboratory facilities, instructors, and the types of jobs the school's graduates have obtained. While not having a college degree may limit a person's opportunities for securing a top position, it will prevent neither entry into nor preclude success in the computer industry.

Planning for Career Development

The computer- and information systems-related industry is one of the more fluid parts of today's marketplace. Someone who is an expert today can be a has-been tomorrow. As a computer professional, you must find methods to keep up to date on industry trends and technologies, to develop new skills, and to increase recognition among your peers within your company. Three primary ways to achieve these objectives are through professional organizations, certification, and professional growth and continuing education activities. Numerous computer publications also can help an individual keep up with changes in the computer industry.

Professional Organizations

Computer professionals with common interests and a desire to extend their proficiency have formed computer-related professional organizations to share their knowledge. Two professional organizations that have been influential in the industry are the Association for Computing Machinery (ACM) and the Association of Information Technology Professionals (AITP). The Association for Computing Machinery (ACM) is a scientific and educational organization dedicated to advancing information technology. The ACM is composed of professionals and students working and interested in computer science and computer science education. A large number of college and university computer educators are members of the ACM. The Association of Information Technology Professionals, formerly called the Data Processing Management Association (DPMA), is a professional association of programmers, systems analysts, and information processing managers. Both ACM and AITP offer the following features and benefits:

- Chapters throughout the United States, for both professionals and students
- Monthly meetings
- Workshops, seminars, and conventions
- Publications, including magazines, journals, and books that help computing professionals negotiate industry and career challenges
- Special Interest Groups (SIGs), that bring together members with shared interests, needs, knowledge and experience
- Programs to help with continuing education needs

Attending professional meetings provides an excellent opportunity for students to learn about the information processing industry and to meet and talk with professionals in the field. Figure 11 presents a list of professional organizations and their URLs.

In addition to these and other professional organizations, user groups exist for a wide range of computers, operating systems, application software, and more. A user group is a collection of people with common computer equipment or software interests that meets regularly to share information. Most metropolitan areas have one or more local computer societies that convene monthly to discuss mutual interests about personal computers. Figure 13 shows a list of major user group organizations and their URLs. For anyone employed or simply interested in the computer industry, these groups can be an effective and rewarding way to learn and continue career development.

USER GROUP ORGANIZATIONS

Organization	URL
Association of Personal Computer User Groups (APCUG)	www.apcug.org
Computer User Groups Alliance (CUGA)	cuga.xopen.org
Microsoft Mindshare User Group Program	www.microsoft.com/mindshare
User Group Relations	www.ugr.com

Figure 13
The Web sites for the major user group organizations

Figure 14
COMDEX, held each year in Las Vegas, Nevada, is one of the larger computer product trade shows in the world. More than 2,000 vendors display their newest products and services to more than 250,000 attendees.

Certification

Certification is a way for employers to ensure a level of competency, skills, or quality in a particular area. Many vendors such as Microsoft and Novell offer technical certification programs for their software products. These vendors use examinations to determine if a person is qualified for certification. Some of the benefits of certification include:

- A certificate is proof of professional achievement, a level of competence commonly accepted and valued by the industry.
- A certificate enhances job opportunities. Many employers give preference in hiring applicants with certification. They view this as proof that a new hire knows the procedures and technologies required.
- A certificate offers opportunity for advancement. Certification can be a plus when an employer awards job advancements and promotions.

The Institute for Certification of Computing Professionals (ICCP) administers one of the more widely recognized professional certification programs in the computer industry. Several professional organizations, including the ACM and AITP, sponsor and support the Institute. You also can become certified through professional organizations. The ICCP confers a certificate titled Certified

Computing Professional (CCP) to those who have at least four years of experience or two years of experience and a college degree. To qualify, individuals must pass a core examination plus exams in two specialty areas, or exams in one specialty area and two programming languages. Those with less computing experience can take a certification exam to become an Associate Computing Professional (ACP). The ACP designation is ideal for a recent college graduate who wishes to gain professional credentials substantiating his or her level of computing knowledge. To qualify, an individual must pass a core examination plus an exam on one programming language.

A recent trend in certification is for vendor-specific certification. Microsoft, for example, has certification programs for end users (Microsoft Office User Specialist) and professionals (Microsoft Certified Professional); while Novell certification proves your knowledge of computer networking and your ability to support Novell networking products. Cisco Career Certifications provide proof of skills in the disciplines of network design or network support. For more information on certification, visit the Web sites listed in the Certification category in Figure 11 on page 12.52.

Professional Growth and Continuing Education

Staying aware of new products and services in the computer industry can be a challenging task because tech-nology changes so rapidly. One way to stay informed about the industry is to participate in professional growth and continuing education activities. This broad category includes events such as workshops, seminars, conferences, conventions, and trade shows. These events provide both general and specific information on equipment, software, services, and issues affecting the industry. Workshops and seminars usually last one or two days, while conferences,

conventions, and trade shows can run for a week. One of the larger trade shows in the United States, COMDEX, brings together more than 2,000 vendors and 250,000 attendees (Figure 14).

Many companies also offer training on their products in the form of books, video-based training, computer-based training (CBT), Web-based training (WBT), and instructor-led training in a classroom.

Computer Publications

Another way to stay informed about what is going on in the computer industry is to read regularly one or more computer industry publications (Figure 15). Hundreds of publications are available from which to choose. Some magazines, such as PC Week, Computerworld, and InfoWorld, are like newspapers and cover a wide range of issues. Other periodicals are oriented toward a particular topic such as communications, personal computers, or a specific equipment manufacturer. You can find many of the more popular publications in public or school libraries; most of them also have Web sites you can visit for news on the latest developments in the computer industry. For exact Web site addresses, review the Publications and Web News Sites category in Figure 11 on page 12.52.

Figure 15
Numerous computer industry publications are available.

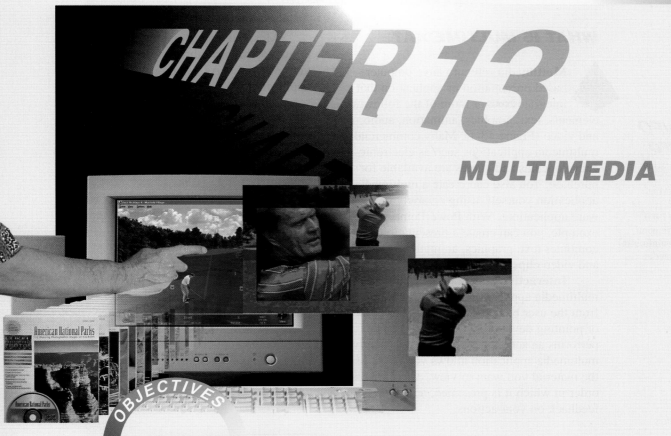

CHAPTER 13
MULTIMEDIA

OBJECTIVES

***After completing this chapter,
you will be able to:***

Define multimedia

Describe types of media used in multimedia applications

List and describe the various uses of multimedia applications

Identify types of multimedia hardware

Explain how to develop a multimedia application

Identify features of several multimedia authoring software packages

Today, multimedia plays an increasingly important role in business, industry, entertainment, and education. Multimedia involves the use of computers to present text, graphics, animation, audio, video, and other media elements in an integrated way into one application. Unlike television, which combines and presents these media elements in a predefined order, most multimedia applications are interactive, allowing the user to participate directly with the application. Interactivity makes multimedia well suited for applications such as video games, flight simulators, virtual reality, electronic magazines, and educational and training tutorials. Multimedia authoring software allows you to combine media elements and build interactive multimedia applications.

This chapter introduces you to many basic multimedia concepts and describes various media components used in multimedia applications. Then, you will learn about various types and uses of multimedia applications. Next, the chapter covers the various hardware components needed to create and view multimedia applications. Finally, you learn how to develop a multimedia application and about the authoring software packages you use to build a multimedia application.

WHAT IS MULTIMEDIA?

Multimedia refers to any computer-based presentation or application that integrates one or more of the following elements: text, graphics, animation, audio, and video (Figure 13-1). Many commercial multimedia applications such as electronic encyclopedias and games are available for purchase. You also can create a multimedia application yourself, using a variety of software applications. With PowerPoint, for example, you can create a presentation that combines text, graphics, animation, and audio and video clips.

Interactive multimedia describes a multimedia application that accepts input from the user by means of a keyboard, voice, or pointing device such as a mouse and performs an action in response. An interactive multimedia application allows you to choose the material you want to view, define the order in which it is presented, and obtain feedback on your actions.

Most interactive multimedia applications allow you to move through the materials at your own pace. As you progress through the application or complete certain tasks, you receive feedback in the form of a sound, score, or other response. The multimedia application shown in Figure 13-1, for example, allows you to select from numerous geographical locations to learn about cities and countries around the world.

The ability for users to interact with a multimedia application is one of its more unique and important features — a feature that has the potential to change dramatically the way individuals gather information and learn. Interactive multimedia allows users to define their own learning paths, investigate topics in depth, and get immediate feedback from drill-and-practice or exploration activities. Multimedia applications also tend to engage and challenge users, thus encouraging them to think creatively and independently.

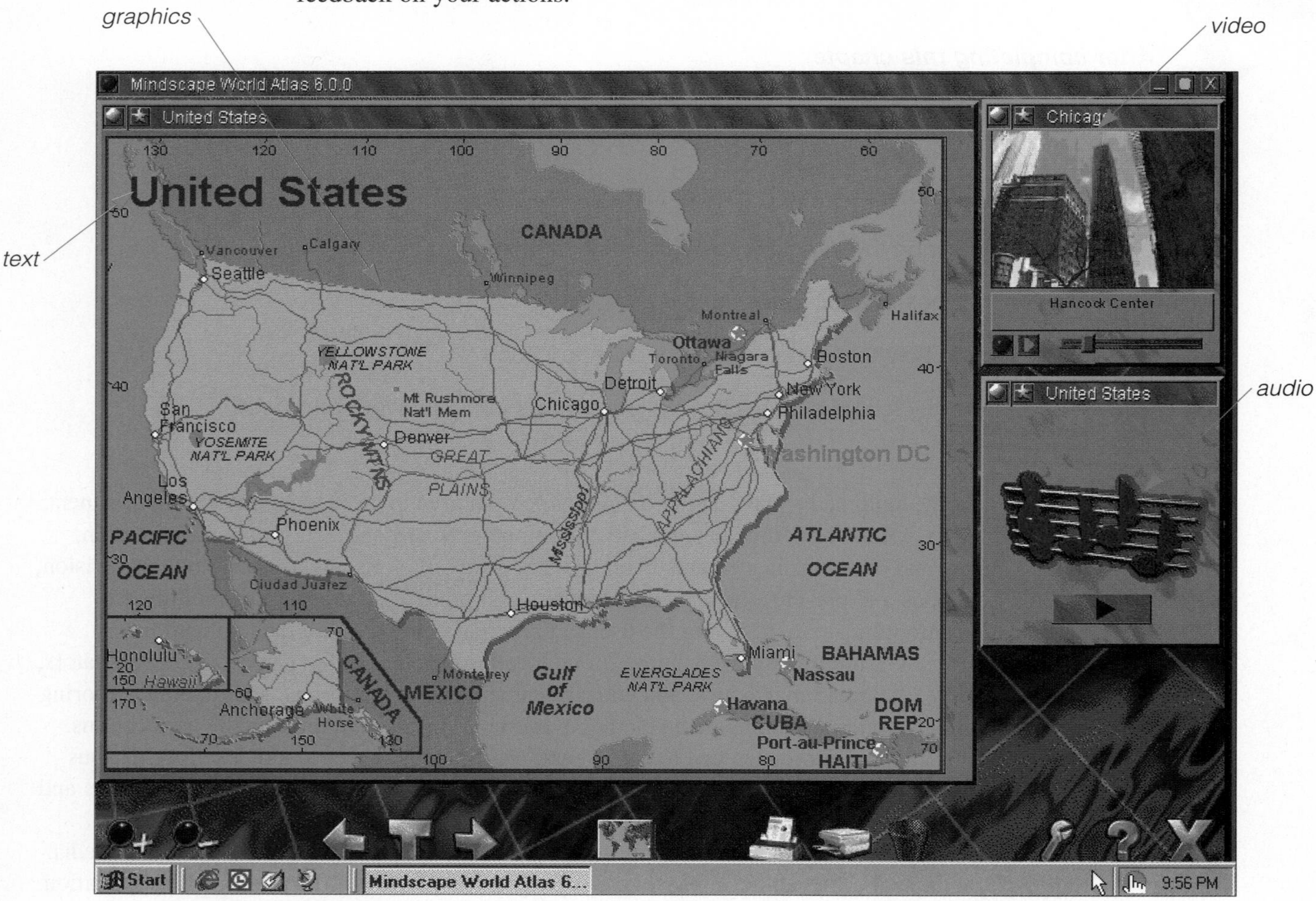

WEB INFO
WEB INFO

For more information on multimedia, visit the Discovering Computers 2000 Chapter 13 WEB INFO page (**www.scsite.com/dc2000/ch13/webinfo.htm**) and click Multimedia.

Figure 13-1 This World Atlas multimedia application consists of text, graphics, audio, and video. The window on the left contains a map of the United States. The upper-right window shows a video about Chicago, and the lower-right window plays the Star Spangled Banner — the national anthem of the United States.

Interactive multimedia applications often use a variety of media elements to present information in various ways. The following sections provide an introduction to the different media elements contained in multimedia applications.

Text

Text, characters that are used to create words, sentences, and paragraphs, is a fundamental element used in many multimedia applications. Multimedia applications not only use ordinary text to convey basic information, they also use a variety of textual effects to emphasize and clarify information. A different font size, color, or style, for example, often is used to emphasize certain words or phrases; and various colors help emphasize different blocks of text on a screen (Figure 13-2). Many multimedia applications also use text-based menus that allow you to select and display information on a certain topic.

Graphics

Recall from Chapter 5 that a **graphic** is a digital representation of nontext information, such as a drawing, chart, or photograph. A graphic, also called a graphical image or still graphical image, contains no movement or animation.

Graphics play an important role in multimedia because people are visually oriented more than ever. Television, movies, and highly visual magazines, for example, are a key source of information for many. In multimedia applications, graphics serve several functions.

- Graphics can illustrate certain concepts more vividly than text. A picture of Saturn, for example, clearly depicts the planet's rings in a way that text cannot.

- Graphics play an important role in the learning process: many individuals, called *visual learners*, comprehend concepts faster and retain a higher percentage of material if they *see* the information presented graphically.

Figure 13-2 This PowerPoint slide uses a variety of font sizes, styles, and color.

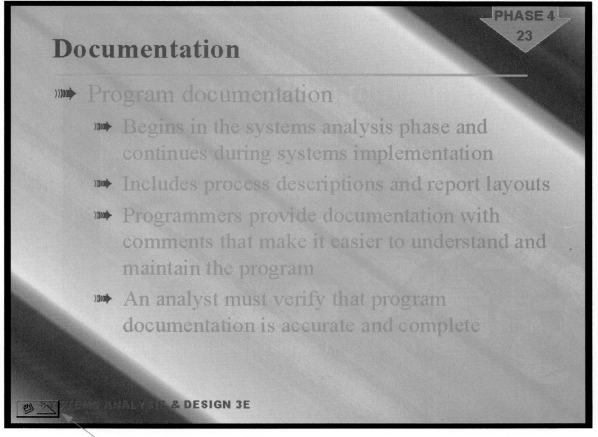

click to advance to next slide

- Graphics serve as navigation elements in many software packages. Multimedia applications often use graphics as buttons that link to more information. The popularity of the graphical user interfaces used on PCs and Macintosh computers and graphical Web browsers also demonstrates the importance of graphics when using computers.

You can obtain graphical images for a multimedia application in several ways. Many presentation graphics and multimedia authoring packages provide their own collection of basic clip art. As discussed in Chapter 2, you also can buy a clip art/image gallery, which is a collection of previously created clip art and photographs grouped by themes, or you can create your own graphical images using paint/image editing software.

If you want to use photographs in a multimedia application, you can use a color scanner to digitize them, take the photographs with a digital camera, or even buy them in a photograph collection on a CD-ROM or DVD-ROM. Some stock photograph agencies even let you purchase and download photographs from the Web.

Many presentation graphics and multimedia authoring packages also include simple drawing, paint, and image editing tools that allow you to create and modify graphics. Figure 13-3 shows a PowerPoint slide that contains clip art and a scanned photograph.

Animation

Displaying a series of still graphics creates an **animation**, which is a graphic that has the illusion of motion (Figure 13-4). Animations range in scope from a basic graphic with simple motion (for example, a blinking icon) to a detailed image with complex movements (such as a simulation of how an avalanche starts). As with graphics, animations can convey information more vividly than text alone. An animation showing the up-and-down movement of pistons and engine valves, for example, provides a better illustration of the workings of an internal combustion engine than a written explanation.

photograph

clip art

Figure 13-3 *Many multimedia applications use clip art and photographs.*

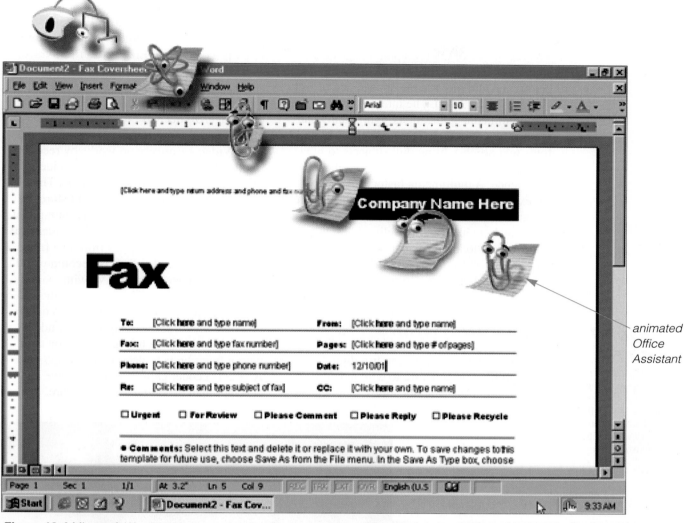

Figure 13-4 *Microsoft Word 2000 uses animation to represent the Office Assistant, which assists you in developing documents.*

You can create your own detailed and highly dynamic animations using a graphics animation software package. Commercial graphics animation software packages allow programmers to create animations that can be used by most popular multimedia authoring software packages. You also can obtain previously created animations from a CD-ROM or on the Web.

Audio

Audio is music, speech, or any other sound. To store these sounds, a computer converts the analog sound waves into a digital format. As with animation, audio allows you to provide information in a manner not otherwise conveyed in the computer environment. For example, the vibration of a human heartbeat or the melodies of a symphony are concepts difficult to convey without the use of sound. Using audio in a multimedia application to supplement text and graphics enhances understanding. An actor's narration added to the text of a Shakespearean play, for example, reinforces a student's grasp of the passage.

You can obtain audio for multimedia applications in several ways. One method is to capture the sounds using a microphone, CD-ROM, DVD-ROM, radio, or any other audio input device that is plugged into a port on a sound card. Recall from Chapter 4 that you also can play and store music from a synthesizer, keyboard, or other musical device that is connected to a sound card via a MIDI port. As with graphics and animations, you can purchase audio clips on a CD-ROM or DVD-ROM or download them from the Web.

Video

Video consists of photographic images that are played back at speeds of 15 to 30 frames per second and provide the appearance of full motion (Figure 13-5). The integration of video into multimedia applications significantly can impact the user's experience. Videos can reinforce text articles, bring dull subjects to life, and show items that users could not otherwise experience. A multimedia history CD-ROM, for example, might allow you to read the text of one of Martin Luther King's speeches and then watch a video of him delivering that same speech to an excited crowd.

To use video in a multimedia application, you first must capture, digitize, and edit the video segments using special video production hardware and software. As described in Chapter 4, video often is captured digitally with a video input device such as a video camera or VCR. You also can use digital video production software to edit and add video to multimedia applications.

Due to the size of video files, incorporating video into a multimedia application often is a challenge. Like audio files, video files require tremendous amounts of storage space: a three-minute segment, or clip, of high-quality video can take an entire gigabyte of storage. To decrease the size of the files, video often is compressed.

Video compression works by recognizing that only a small portion of the video image changes from frame to frame. Thus, a video compression program might store the first reference frame and then, assuming that the following frames will be almost identical to it, store only the changes from one frame to the next. The video then is decompressed before it is viewed. Prior to viewing, video compression software decompresses the video segment. Instead of using software to decompress the video, some computers include a **video decoder**, which is an expansion card whose function is to decompress video data. A video decoder card is more effective and efficient than decompression software.

WEB INFO

For more information on video decoders, visit the Discovering Computers 2000 Chapter 13 WEB INFO page (**www.scsite.com/dc2000/ch13/webinfo.htm**) and click Video Decoders.

Figure 13-5 *This Jack Nicklaus 4 instructional DVD-ROM features videos of the golf legend.*

The **Moving Pictures Experts Group** has defined a popular standard for video compression and decompression, called **MPEG** (pronounced *em-peg*). MPEG compression methods can reduce the size of video files up to 95 percent, while retaining near-television quality. Video compression and other improvements in video technology have allowed video to play a more important role in multimedia applications. Technologies such as streaming video also have made video a viable part of multimedia on the Web.

Links

With many multimedia applications, you navigate through the content by clicking links with a pointing device such as a mouse.

Recall from Chapter 2 that Web pages use hyperlinks, or links, to allow users to navigate quickly from one document to another. In a multimedia application, a **link** serves a similar function, allowing users to access information quickly and navigate from one topic to another in a nonlinear fashion. For example, when using a multimedia encyclopedia, you can click the keyword, cheetahs, to read about the animals, display a map of their habitat, or watch a video of them living in the wild. In a multimedia application, any clickable object — text, graphics, animation, and even videos — can function as a link. Figure 13-6 shows a multimedia application that uses text and graphics as links to access additional sources of information.

WEB INFO
WEB INFO

For more information on the Moving Pictures Experts Group, visit the Discovering Computers 2000 Chapter 13 WEB INFO page (**www.scsite.com/ dc2000/ch13/webinfo.htm**) and click MPEG.

Step 1: *Click Look Up (graphical link).*

Figure 13-6 *How to use links to navigate through the Swinging Safari CD-ROM by National Geographic.*

Step 2: *Click World Encyclopedia (graphical link).*

graphical links

Step 4: *Read about cheetas and then click Exit (graphical link).*

Cheetahs Growing Up In the Wild   Contents

All is quiet on a grassy plain in East Africa. Suddenly there's movement in tall grass just behind some tangled bushes. A young spotted cat appears and dashes around a tree trunk. Another chases it. They tumble on the ground and wrestle. Returning to their hiding place, the two jump on four other young cats.

What are these playful creatures? They're cheetahs, shy and speedy wild cats of the African plains. At birth, cheetahs are about the size of grown guinea pigs. Born with their eyes still closed, the cubs are helpless. Yet after only two months, young cheetahs

graphical link

Step 3: *Click Cheetas: Growing Up In the Wild (text link).*

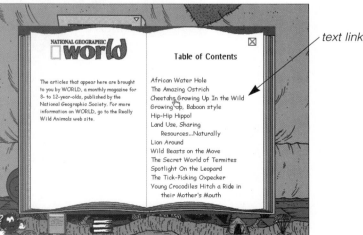

text link

NATIONAL GEOGRAPHIC
world

The articles that appear here are brought to you by WORLD, a monthly magazine for 8- to 12-year-olds, published by the National Geographic Society. For more information on WORLD, go to the Really Wild Animals web site.

Table of Contents

African Water Hole
The Amazing Ostrich
Cheetahs Growing Up In the Wild
Growing Up, Baboon style
Hip-Hip Hippo!
Land Use, Sharing
    Resources...Naturally
Lion Around
Wild Beasts on the Move
The Secret World of Termites
Spotlight On the Leopard
The Tick-Picking Oxpecker
Young Crocodiles Hitch a Ride in
    their Mother's Mouth

MULTIMEDIA APPLICATIONS

A **multimedia application** involves the use of multimedia technology for business, education, and entertainment. Businesses use multimedia, for example, in interactive advertisements and for job- and skill-training applications. Teachers use multimedia applications to deliver classroom presentations that enhance student learning. Students, in turn, use multimedia applications to learn by reading, seeing, hearing, and interacting with the subject content. A huge variety of computer games and other types of entertainment also use multimedia.

Another important application of multimedia is to create **simulations**, which are computer-based models of real-life situations. Multimedia simulations often replace costly and sometimes hazardous demonstrations and training in areas such as chemistry, biology, medicine, and aviation.

The following sections provide a more detailed look at the various types of multimedia applications, such as business presentations, computer- and Web-based training and education, electronic books and references, how-to guides, and magazines. The sections also address the use of multimedia for entertainment, virtual reality, and kiosks, as well as its importance on the World Wide Web.

Business Presentations

Many businesses and industries use multimedia to create marketing presentations that advertise and sell products. Multimedia authoring software, for instance, has made producing television commercials with unique media effects easier and less expensive. Sales representatives also use multimedia in marketing presentations created using presentation graphics software (Figure 13-7). To deliver these presentations to a large audience, users can connect their computer to a video projector that displays the presentation on a full screen.

WEB INFO

For more information on simulations, visit the Discovering Computers 2000 Chapter 13 WEB INFO page(**www.scsite.com/dc2000/ch13/webinfo.htm**) and click Simulations.

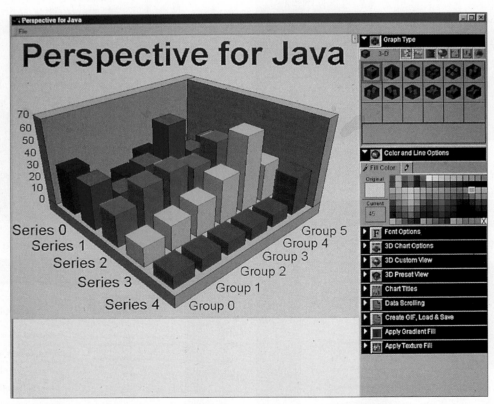

Figure 13-7 *Business users incorporate multimedia into their presentations for customers and employees.*

Computer-Based Training

Computer-based training (**CBT**) is a type of education in which students learn by using and completing exercises with instructional software (Figure 13-8). Also called **computer-aided instruction** (**CAI**), computer-based training is popular in business, industry, and schools to teach new skills or enhance the existing skills of employees, teachers, or students. Athletes, for example, use multimedia computer-based training programs to practice baseball, football, soccer, tennis, and golf skills, while airlines use multimedia CBT simulations to train employees for emergency situations. Schools are using CBT to train teachers in various disciplines and to teach students math, language, and software skills. Interactive CBT software called **courseware** usually is available on CD-ROM or DVD-ROM or shared over a network.

Computer-based training allows for flexible, on-the-spot training. Businesses, for example, can set up corporate training labs, so employees can update their skills without leaving the workplace. Installing CBT software on an employee's computer or on the company network provides even more flexibility — allowing employees to update their job skills right at their desks, at home, or while traveling.

Computer-based training provides a unique learning experience because learners receive instant feedback in the form of positive response for correct answers or actions, additional information on incorrect answers, and immediate scoring and results. Testing and self-diagnostic features allow instructors to verify that a learner has mastered curriculum objectives and identify those who need additional instruction or practice. CBT is especially effective for teaching software skills if the CBT is integrated with the software application, because it allows students to practice using the software as they learn.

WEB INFO
WEB INFO
For more information on computer-based training, visit the Discovering Computers 2000 Chapter 13 WEB INFO page (**www.scsite.com/dc2000/ch13/webinfo.htm**) and click CBT.

Figure 13-8 Boeing uses flight CBT to train new pilots and maintenance personnel. Clicking the right-pointing arrow displays the next screen in the CBT.

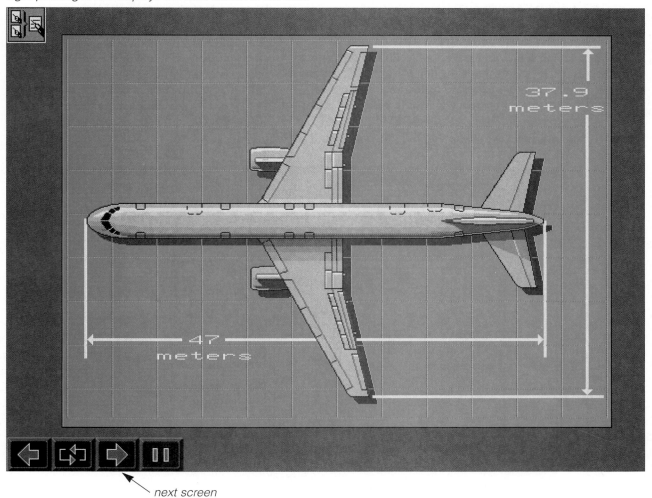

next screen

Some of the many other advantages of CBT over traditional training include:

- **Self-paced study**. Students can progress at their own pace, skipping strong areas to focus on areas of weakness.

- **Unique content**. The multimedia content appeals to many types of learners and can help make difficult concepts simple. Various media elements used to present the same information provide reinforcement.

- **Unique instructional experience**. Simulations allow students to learn skills in hazardous, emergency, or other real-world situations.

- **Reduced training time**. Self-paced instruction encourages students to take the most efficient path to content mastery.

- **One-on-one interaction**. Trainers can spend more time with trainees, because computers handle test delivery and grading.

- **Reduced training costs**. Decreasing training time and eliminating travel reduces costs.

For these reasons, schools also use CBT programs. These programs make the learning process more interesting, allow students to perform experiments in a risk-free environment, and provide instant feedback and testing. CBT also appeals to various learning styles and provides a new type of learning experience. A student using a CBT study guide, for example, could listen to a speaker reciting French vocabulary to help with the pronunciation of difficult words. You can buy many CBT programs such as these on CD-ROM or DVD-ROM from a local retailer or merchant on the Web (Figure 13-9).

Web-Based Training (WBT) and Distance Learning

Web-based training (**WBT**) is an approach to computer-based training (CBT) that employs the technologies of the Internet and the World Wide Web. As with CBT, Web-based training typically consists of self-directed, self-paced instruction on a topic. Because it is delivered via the Web, however, WBT has the advantage of being able to offer up-to-date content on any type of computer platform.

Over the past few years, the number of organizations using Web-based training has exploded. Today, many major corporations in the United States provide employees with some type of Web-based training to teach new skills or upgrade their current skills.

Web-based training, computer-based training, and other materials often are combined as materials for distance learning courses. **Distance learning**, also called **distance education**, is the delivery of education at one location while the learning takes place at other locations. Some national and international corporations also save millions of dollars by using distance learning to train employees — thus eliminating the costs of airfare, hotels, and meals for centralized training sessions.

WEB INFO

For more information on Web-based training, visit the Discovering Computers 2000 Chapter 13 WEB INFO page (www.scsite.com/dc2000/ch13/webinfo.htm) and click WBT.

WEB INFO
WEB INFO

For more information on distance learning, visit the Discovering Computers 2000 Chapter 13 WEB INFO page (www.scsite.com/dc2000/ch13/webinfo.htm) and click Distance Learning.

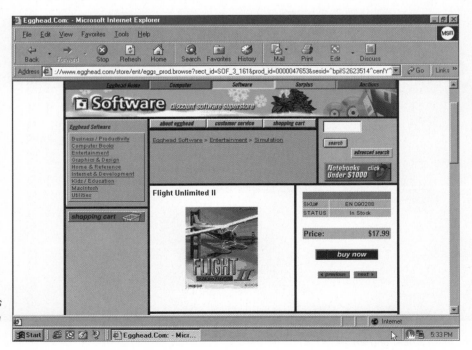

Figure 13-9 You can purchase CBTs, such as this flight simulator, from retailers on the Web.

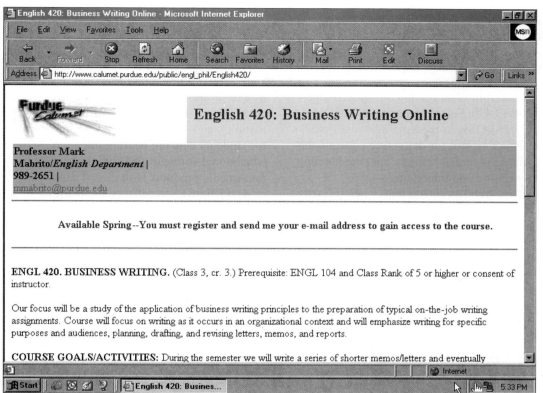

Many colleges and universities offer numerous distance learning courses, usually in the form of Web-based or Web-enhanced courses (Figure 13-10). Web-based courses offer many advantages for students who live far from a college campus or work full time, allowing them to attend class from home or at any time that fits their schedules. A number of colleges and universities now offer master's degree programs in which every required course is taught over the Web.

Web-based training also is available for individuals at home or at work. Today, anyone with access to the Web can take advantage of hundreds of multimedia tutorials offered online. Such tutorials cover a wide range of topics, from how to change a flat tire to creating presentations in PowerPoint. Many of these Web sites are free (Figure 13-11); others ask you to register and pay a fee to take the complete Web-based course.

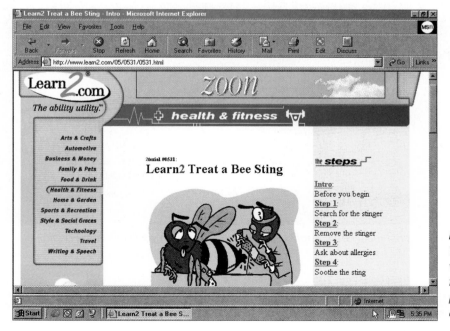

Figure 13-11 *This Learn2 Web site offers steps for a variety of activities ranging from cooking to first aid to personal care to making crafts.*

Classroom and Special Education

Multimedia applications also are used for the classroom education and training of students in grades from kindergarten through college (Figure 13-12). From interactive CD-ROMs and DVD-ROMs to presentations, multimedia is an effective tool for delivering educational material to potential learners, making learning more exciting and interesting.

Research has shown that, when properly evaluated and integrated into teaching at the point of instruction, multimedia applications are a highly effective teaching tool. When using a multimedia application, students become actively involved in the learning process instead of passive recipients of information. Interactive multimedia applications engage students by asking them to define their own paths through an application, which often lead them to explore many related topics.

Multimedia applications also are well suited for both physically impaired and learning disabled students. Students who are visually impaired, for example, benefit from the audio capabilities of multimedia applications, as well as the use of graphics and larger font sizes. Visual materials, such as graphics, animation, and video also make learning easier for students who are hearing impaired. Many educational software companies also offer multimedia products with closed captioning or sign language to enhance the learning experience for hearing-impaired students. The ability of individuals to work at their own pace is a major benefit for the learning disabled. Being able to practice and review at their pace aids people with learning disabilities, by alleviating the pressure to keep up with peers.

Figure 13-12 *An educational multimedia application designed to teach young learners basic reading skills.*

Electronic Books

One type of **electronic book** is a digital text that uses links to give the user access to information. These electronic books have many of the elements of a regular book, including *pages* of text and graphics. You generally turn pages of this type of electronic book by clicking icons. A table of contents, glossary, and index also are available at the click of a button. To display a definition or a graphic, play a sound or a video sequence, or connect to a Web site, you simply click a link (often a bold or underlined word).

A newer type of electronic book, called an **e-book**, uses a small book-sized computer that can hold up to 4,000 pages, or about 10 books' worth of text and small graphics. By clicking a button, users can move forward or backward, they can add notes, and highlight text stored in the e-book. A photograph of an e-book is on page 14.51 of the Trends 2000 special feature that follows Chapter 14.

Electronic Reference

An **electronic reference** text is a digital version of a reference book, which uses text, graphics, sound, animation, and video to explain a topic or provide additional information. The multimedia encyclopedia, Microsoft Encarta, for example, includes the complete text of a multivolume encyclopedia. In addition to text-based information, Microsoft Encarta includes thousands of photographs, animations, audio and video clips, and detailed illustrations (Figure 13-13). This array of multimedia information is accessible via menus and links.

WEB INFO

For more information on e-books, visit the Discovering Computers 2000 Chapter 13 WEB INFO page (**www.scsite.com/ dc2000/ch13/webinfo.htm**) and click E-Books.

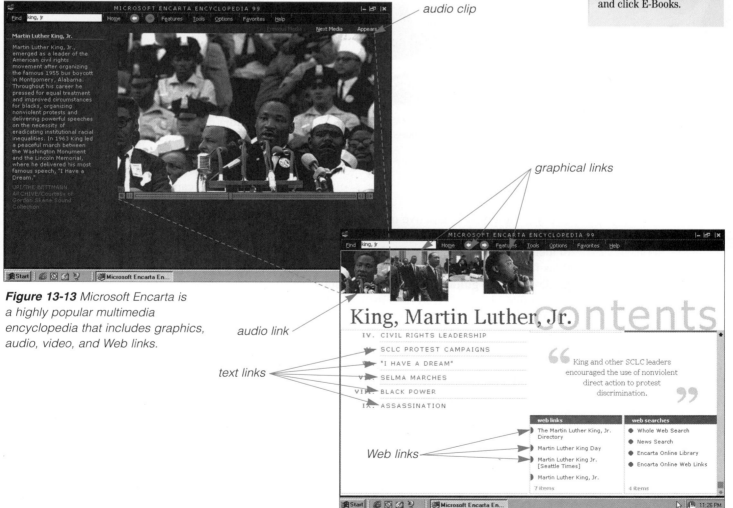

audio clip

graphical links

audio link

text links

Web links

Figure 13-13 *Microsoft Encarta is a highly popular multimedia encyclopedia that includes graphics, audio, video, and Web links.*

Health and medicine are two areas in which multimedia reference texts play an important role. Instead of using volumes of books, health professionals and students rely on reference CD-ROMs and DVD-ROMs for information, illustrations, animations, and photographs on hundreds of health and first aid topics (Figure 13-14).

How-to guides can help you with activities such as buying a home or a car; designing a garden; planning a vacation; and repairing your home, car, or computer. The tree selector how-to guide shown in Figure 13-15 details how to select trees best suited for an area. Multimedia how-to-guides are available on CD-ROM, DVD-ROM, and the Web.

Newspapers and Magazines

A **multimedia newspaper** is a digital version of a newspaper distributed on CD-ROM, DVD-ROM, or via the World Wide Web. A **multimedia magazine** is a digital version of a magazine, also distributed on CD-ROM, DVD-ROM, or via the World Wide Web. Today, many print-based magazines and newspapers have companion Web sites that provide multimedia versions of some or all of the magazine's printed content. An **electronic magazine** or **e-zine** is a multimedia magazine created specifically for distribution via the Web.

Multimedia newspapers and magazines usually include the sections and articles found in their print-based versions, including departments, editorials, and more (Figure 13-16). Unlike printed publications, however, multimedia magazines and newspapers use many types of media to convey information. Audio and video clips, for example, can showcase recent album or movie releases, and animations can depict weather patterns or election results. Multimedia magazines and newspapers usually are distributed on CD-ROM, DVD-ROM, or via the World Wide Web.

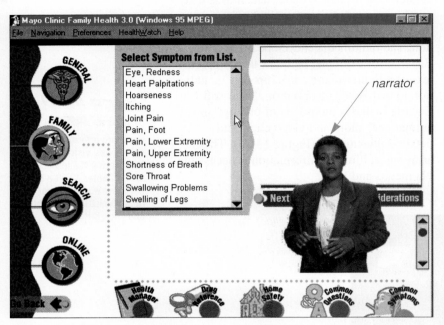

narrator

Figure 13-14 *The Mayo Clinic Family Health CD-ROM provides a narrator to guide you through the steps in addressing family health issues.*

How-To Guides

Today, a variety of interactive multimedia applications are available to help individuals in their daily lives. These multimedia applications fall into the broad category of how-to guides. **How-to guides** are multimedia applications that include step-by-step instructions and interactive demonstrations to teach you practical new skills. Much like the computer-based training applications used by businesses, how-to guides allow you to train, acquire new skills, and try out your skills in a risk-free environment. The skills you learn with a how-to guide, however, usually apply to enhancing talents outside of your job.

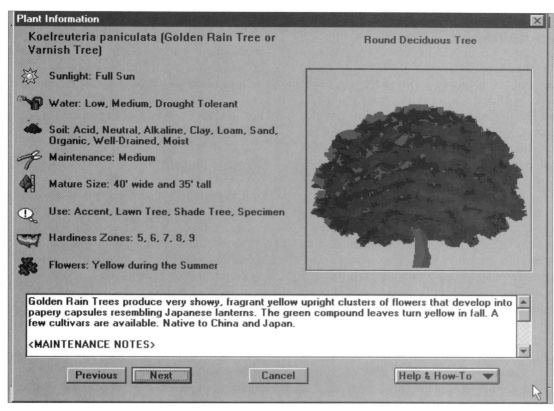

Figure 13-15 *Using this tree selector, you can choose trees best suited for any climate and soil.*

Figure 13-16a *(The New York Times on the Web)*

Figure 13-16b *(BusinessWeek ONLINE)*

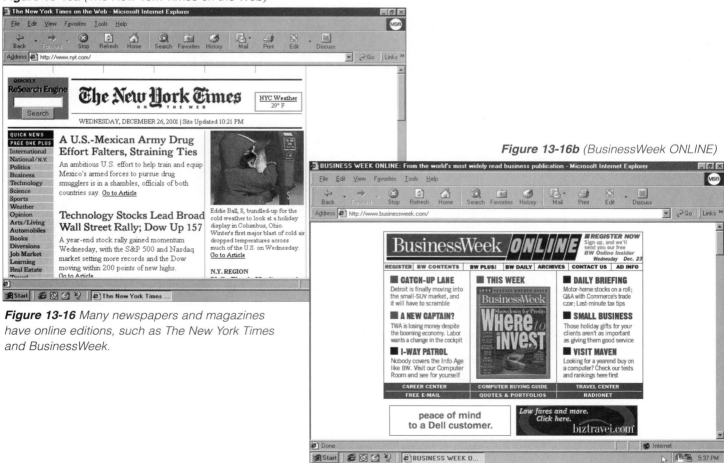

Figure 13-16 *Many newspapers and magazines have online editions, such as The New York Times and BusinessWeek.*

Entertainment and Edutainment

As described, multimedia combines the media elements of television *and* interactivity, thus making it ideal for entertainment. Multimedia computer games, for example, use a combination of graphics, audio, and video to create a realistic and entertaining game situation. Often the game simulates a real or fictitious world, in which you play the role of a character and have direct control of what happens in the game. The music industry also sells interactive multimedia applications on CD-ROM and DVD-ROM. Some interactive music CD-ROMs, for example, allow you to play musical instruments along with your favorite musician, read about the musician's life and interests, and even create your own version of popular songs. Like interactive games, these applications give you a character role and put you in control of the application.

Other multimedia applications are used for **edutainment**, which is an experience meant to be both educational and entertaining (Figure 13-17). Many edutainment CD-ROMs

and DVD-ROMs, such as the *Reader Rabbit* and *Carmen Sandiego* series, are designed specifically to teach children in a fun and appealing way. Others, such as *Baseball's Greatest Hits, The Way Things Work,* and standardized test preparation CD-ROMs and DVD-ROMs provide content for individuals of all ages.

Virtual Reality

Virtual reality (**VR**) is the use of a computer to create an artificial environment that appears and feels like a real environment and allows you to explore a space and manipulate the environment (Figure 13-18). In its simplest form, a virtual reality application displays a view that appears to be a three-dimensional view of a place or object, such as a landscape, building, molecule, or red blood cell, which users can explore. Architects are using this type of software to show clients how a building will look after a construction or remodeling project.

WEB INFO

For more information on virtual reality, visit the Discovering Computers 2000 Chapter 13 WEB INFO page (**www.scsite.com/ dc2000/ch13/webinfo.htm**) and click Virtual Reality.

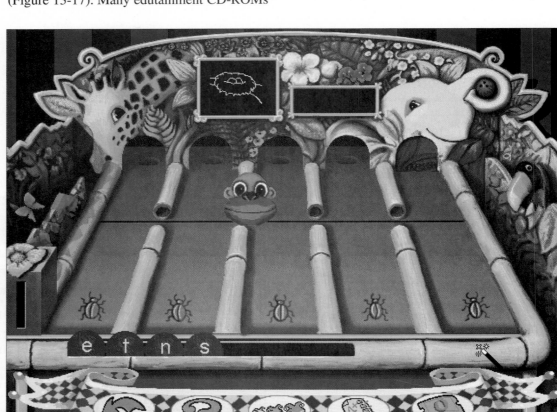

Figure 13-17 *Many edutainment applications use multimedia elements to entertain children while they learn. In this example, the child places the letters in the correct slot to spell the word that represents the picture shown (nest, in this case), before the bugs reach the finish line.*

Figure 13-18 *Virtual Glider by Intel takes the rider on a hang-gliding trip through the Grand Canyon.*

In more advanced forms, VR software requires you to wear specialized headgear, body suits, and gloves to enhance the experience of the artificial environment (Figure 13-19). The headgear displays the artificial environment in front of both of your eyes. The body suit and the gloves sense your motion and direction, allowing you to move through and pick up and hold items displayed in the virtual environment. Experts predict that eventually the body suits will provide tactile feedback so you can experience the touch and feel of the virtual world.

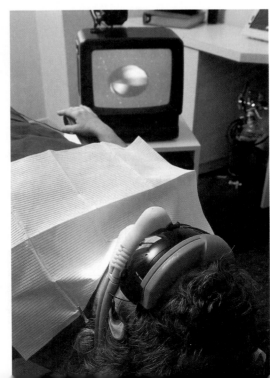

Figure 13-19 *In this dentist office, patients wear virtual reality headsets to relax them during their visit with the dentist.*

Your first encounter with VR likely will be a virtual reality game such as a flight simulator. In these games, special visors allow you to see the computer-generated environment. As you walk around the game's electronic landscape, sensors in the surrounding game machine record your movements and change your view of the landscape accordingly. You also might use a Web-based VR application developed using virtual reality modeling language (VRML). Web sites use virtual reality to allow you to take tours of a city, view hotel accommodations, or interact with local attractions. The United States Senate Web site, for example, provides a virtual tour of the U.S. Capitol building.

Companies are beginning to use VR for more practical, commercial applications, as well. Automobile dealers, for example, have created virtual showrooms in which customers can view the exterior and interior of available vehicles (Figure 13-20). Airplane manufacturers are using virtual prototypes to test new models and shorten product design time. Telecommunications firms and others even are using personal computer-based VR applications for employee training. As computing power and the use of the Web increase, practical applications of VR will continue to emerge in education, business, and entertainment.

Figure 13-20a (front view)

Figure 13-20b (side view)

Figure 13-20c (rear view)

Figure 13-20 At the Microsoft CarPoint site on the Web, you can view and rotate the interior of a featured car, such as the Saturn SL shown here.

Kiosks

A **kiosk** is a computerized information or reference center that allows you to select various options to browse through or find specific information. A typical kiosk is a self-service structure equipped with computer hardware and software. Kiosks often use touch screen monitors or keyboards for input devices and contain all of the data and information needed for the application stored directly on the computer (Figure 13-21).

Kiosks often provide information in public places where visitors or customers have common questions. Locations such as shopping centers, airports, museums, and libraries, for example, use kiosks to provide information on available services, product and exhibit locations, maps, and other information. Kiosks also are used for marketing. A kiosk might contain an interactive multimedia application that allows you to try options and explore scenarios related to a product or service. For example, you might be able to try different color combinations or take short quizzes to determine which product suits you best. The interactive multimedia involves customers with the product, thus increasing the likelihood of purchase.

The World Wide Web

Multimedia applications also play an important role on the **World Wide Web**, which is the part of the Internet that supports multimedia. In fact, much of the information on the Web today relies on multimedia. Using multimedia brings a Web page to life; increases the types of information available on the Web; expands the Web's potential uses; and makes the Internet a more entertaining place to explore. As described in Chapter 2, the Web uses many types of media to deliver information and enhance a user's Web experience (Figure 13-22). Graphics and animations reinforce text-based content and provide updated information. Online radio stations, movie rental sites, and games use audio and video clips to provide movie and music clips or deliver the latest news.

Figure 13-21 *Many camera shops now have kiosks that allow you to copy, enlarge, reduce, or crop photographs.*

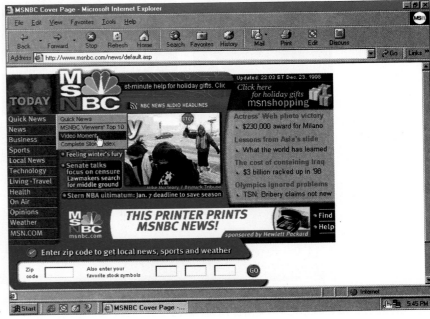

Figure 13-22 *MSNBC is one of the many sites on the Web that incorporate multimedia features.*

Many of the multimedia applications previously described, including computer- and Web-based training, e-zines, games, and virtual reality, are deliverable via the Web. New multimedia authoring software packages include tools for creating and delivering multimedia applications via the World Wide Web. Some of these authoring software packages allow you to create applications in the Windows environment and then convert them to HTML and Java for use on the Web.

MULTIMEDIA HARDWARE

Hardware selection is an important process in both the development and delivery of multimedia products. Previous chapters have presented many of these hardware components, including sound cards and video cards (Chapter 3); data projectors, digital cameras, and scanners (Chapter 4); monitors and HDTV (Chapter 5); and CD-ROMs, DVD-ROMs, and PhotoCDs (Chapter 6). The following section briefly reviews these and presents additional hardware needed to develop and display a multimedia presentation or application.

Multimedia Personal Computer

A **multimedia personal computer** (**MPC**) is a computer that uses specific hardware and software components to input, process, and output the various types of media (Figure 13-23). In the early to mid 1990s, multimedia personal computers met standards defined by the Multimedia PC Marketing Council. Today's personal computers meet standards defined by the Multimedia PC Working Group, which superseded the Marketing Council. These standards define the minimum hardware and software specifications for running multimedia software. The current highest level of standard is known as PC 97. To be considered a **PC 97** computer, it must include a 120 MHz Pentium processor with 16 MB of RAM and a USB port. In general, any multimedia personal computer purchased in the past two years has the capability of running most CD-ROM, DVD-ROM, and Web-based multimedia applications. For authoring multimedia applications, you should consider a computer with a 450 MHz Pentium® III processor and 128 MB RAM. For more information on the **Pentium® III processor** and RAM, see Chapter 3.

Figure 13-23 *Most multimedia personal computers are equipped with devices such as a microphone, a CD-ROM or DVD-ROM drive, speakers, and a high-resolution monitor.*

In addition to these required components, many other devices and components are used in multimedia computers. Along with the audio and video components, multimedia computers often use a number of input and output devices such as overhead projection systems, scanners, digital cameras, PhotoCDs, and laser disks.

SOUND CARD A **sound card** is an expansion card that provides both audio input and output (Figure 13-24). The typical sound card has three primary components: an audio digitizer, a wavetable synthesizer, and a mixer. The **audio digitizer** is a pair of analog-to-digital and digital-to-analog converters. The **wavetable synthesizer** has the capability of producing sounds. The **mixer** combines these two signals along with mixing audio from a CD-ROM or DVD-ROM.

The sound card can be used to record almost any audio signal. The sound card has two jacks for input and one for output. The microphone plugs into one jack, while the other jack accepts input from a radio, stereo, tape player, external CD player, or any other audio source. The remaining jack connects devices such as speakers, headphones, or a stereo sound system that are used for the final playback of the sound.

CD-ROM AND DVD-ROM DRIVES A **compact disc** is an optical storage medium that can hold a tremendous amount of data. Two basic types of compact discs designed for use with computers are a CD-ROM and a DVD-ROM. The large storage capacity of these devices makes them excellent media for storing and distributing multimedia applications that contain many large graphics, audio, and video files.

Today, most computer systems include a CD-ROM or DVD-ROM drive as standard equipment. A DVD-ROM drive is backward compatible; that is, it can read both CD-ROMs and DVD-ROMs. When you are buying a multimedia personal computer, the most important consideration for these drives is speed. The faster the transfer rate of the drive, the better quality the video playback will be. Drives with slower transfer rates tend to output poorer quality video, in which the audio and video is choppy.

Most CD-ROM and DVD-ROM drives sold today are internal; that is, they are installed inside the system unit of the personal computer. Most of these drives also have a headphone plug on the front of the drive and connectors that allow the CD-ROM or DVD-ROM to be connected directly to the sound card. By connecting the CD-ROM or DVD-ROM to the sound card and then connecting the sound card to a stereo system or speakers, you can obtain high-quality audio output.

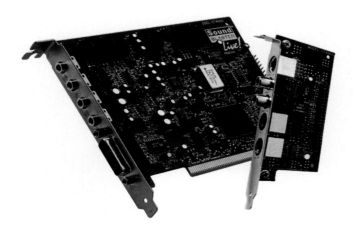

Figure 13-24 A sound card, such as the Creative Labs, Inc. SoundBlaster Live! sound cards shown here, provides both audio input and output.

SPEAKERS Small stereo **speakers**, such as those shown in Figure 13-23 on page 13.20, provide an easy and inexpensive way to play audio on a multimedia personal computer. For presentations, you might want to invest in amplified speakers or even a stereo system, which can be connected directly to the sound card.

DISPLAY DEVICE The **display device** is an important part of a multimedia personal computer. When choosing a display for your multimedia personal computer, you must evaluate both the monitor and the video card. The video card generates the output required to display text and graphics on a monitor. To display multimedia applications effectively, your system should have at least an SVGA monitor and video card that can display a resolution of 800 x 600.

Televisions and Data Projectors

Delivering a multimedia presentation to an audience often requires a data projector or projection system so the audience can see and hear the presentation clearly. For presentations to individuals or small groups, a large SVGA monitor often is appropriate. For larger group presentations, you might want to use a large-screen television set or HDTV (Figure 13-25). Connecting the multimedia computer to a standard television set requires an **NTSC converter**, which converts the digital signal to an analog signal that can be displayed on the television set. NTSC stands for **National Television System Committee**, which is the organization that sets the standards for most video and broadcast television equipment. Because HDTV is a type of television set that works with digital broadcasting signals, HDTV does not require the NTSC converter.

Figure 13-25 *HDTV is a newer technology for presenting to a large group.*

For presenting to even larger groups, you can use a **data projector**, which is connected directly to a computer with a cable and uses its own light source to display a multimedia application or presentation onto a screen. Recall that two types of data projectors are LCD projectors and DLP projectors. An **LCD projector** attaches directly to a computer and uses its own light source to display the information shown on the computer screen. A **digital light processing (DLP) projector**, by contrast, uses tiny mirrors to reflect light, producing crisp, bright, colorful images that remain in focus and can be seen clearly even in a well-lit room. Most LCD projectors require an NTSC converter, while DLP projectors can display SVGA output directly from the computer (Figure 13-26). Both LCD and DLP projectors usually have audio capabilities, as well.

Figure 13-26 A DLP projector, such as this Proxima Ultralight DS1, is ideal for the mobile user because it is lighweight (11 pounds) and portable.

Video Capture Card

A **video capture card** is an expansion card that enables you to connect a video camera or VCR to a computer and manipulate the video input. **Video capture software** used with the card compresses the video data so the video files are small enough to be stored on a hard disk. Many manufacturers of video capture cards use Intel's proprietary **digital video interleave**, or **DVI**, compression technology for their video compression. As with MPEG compression, DVI compression is capable of reducing the size of the file while maintaining the image quality. Unlike early versions of MPEG, DVI creates video files that can be replayed using only software; no other adapters or hardware are needed. Early versions of MPEG required additional hardware, but today several software-only MPEG technologies exist.

Scanners, Digital Cameras, and PhotoCDs

Multimedia developers can add color images and photographs to multimedia applications using color scanners, digital cameras, and photo CDs. A **color scanner** converts images into a digitized format for use in multimedia applications (Figure 13-27). More expensive scanners can produce images at a resolution as high as 2,000 dpi (dots per inch) in 16.7 million colors. Less-expensive scanners can produce decent-quality graphical images at a resolution of 600 dpi and 256 colors. The basic software included with scanners allows scanned images to be saved in many different

Figure 13-27 A color scanner converts images into digitized format for use in multimedia applications.

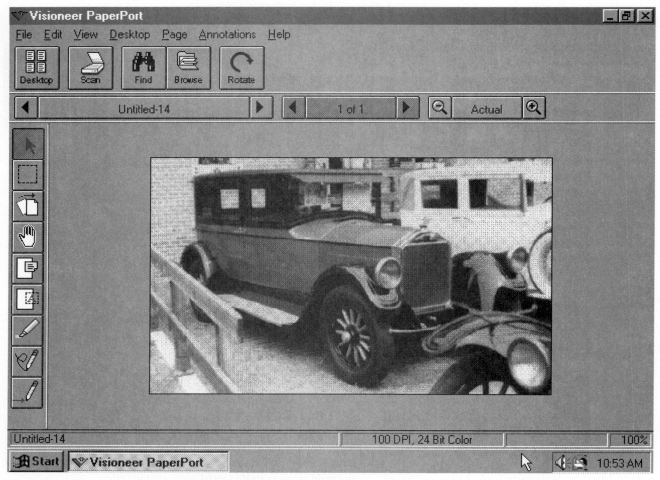

Figure 13-28 *The basic software included with scanners allows scanned images to be saved in many different file formats.*

file formats (Figure 13-28). If a wider variety of image editing possibilities are needed, more sophisticated software packages are available. Many times, the quality of a photograph can be improved using this software.

Another easy and effective way to obtain color photographs for a multimedia application is by using a digital camera (Figure 13-29). **Digital cameras** work similarly to regular cameras, except they use a small reusable disk, PC Card, or internal memory to store digital photographs. These photographs then are input into a computer using the appropriate hardware and software. You can incorporate these stored images into a multimedia application.

Figure 13-29 *An easy and effective way to obtain digitized color photographs is by using a digital camera. Once the photographs are input into a computer, you can incorporate them into a multimedia application.*

A relatively new way of obtaining and storing digital images is the PhotoCD (Figure 13-30). A **PhotoCD** uses a write-once compact disc to store photographic images that can be integrated into multimedia applications. You can purchase PhotoCDs that already contain pictures or you can have your own pictures or negatives recorded on a PhotoCD. Photographs stored on a PhotoCD can be read by practically any computer with a CD-ROM or DVD-ROM drive. You also can view them on a television set using a PhotoCD player.

Figure 13-30 *PhotoCDs are write-once compact discs that can store about 100 photographic images.*

Laser Disks and Laser Disk Players

Laser disks and **laser disk players** are part of a read-only video disk system based on the same optical disk technology used for compact discs. Laser disks and laser disk players provide high-quality display of audio and video. As the costs of DVD players continue to drop, however, experts predict that eventually they will replace laser disk players.

DEVELOPING MULTIMEDIA APPLICATIONS

As with all program development, developing multimedia applications follows a standard process with several phases. While some of the terminology is different, the basic activities completed within each phase closely follow those of the program development life cycle presented in Chapter 12. Figure 13-31 lists some basic guidelines that apply to the various phases of the multimedia application development process. The next sections focus on a few of these phases — analysis, design, and production — as well as introducing you to several popular multimedia authoring software packages.

FACTOR	ACTIVITY
Know you audience	Include a self-assessment test to gauge learner needs.
Give the user control	Provide a means for the user to navigate his or her own course.
Use icons with clear meanings	Use left and right arrows for sequential pages, a stop sign for exit, and so on.
Immerse the user	Recreate the tasks users have to perform.
Require interaction	Ask questions and provide feedback.
Review concepts	Use self-building exercises.
Engage the user	Make the program attractive and appealing to the eye and ear.
Test the program	Test on the target platform with a target audience.

Figure 13-31 *Multimedia development guidelines.*

Analysis

Careful planning during the **analysis** phase leads to success in a multimedia project. The first step is to involve all of the individuals in determining the objectives and requirements for the application and specifying the essential elements needed for the actual production. For larger projects with specific learning objectives, analysis particularly is important. For example, if you are building a multimedia training program, you must determine basic content needs, testing and scoring features, number of users it should support, and so on. Larger projects, such as commercial CD-ROM and DVD-ROM products, usually involve a project team, including a producer, an art director, an interface designer, a content designer, and the programmer. For smaller multimedia projects, the developer can play a variety of roles, which may include content developer, interface designer, and programmer.

Design

Once basic requirements have been determined, the **design** phase begins. Careful planning is critical during the design phase of a multimedia project. Throughout design, an important tool for the project team is a flowchart, or map, which includes all of the various media elements in the application and serves as a blueprint to which the project team or individual developer can refer. Another important tool used during the design phase of a multimedia project is the project script. The **project script** provides more detailed information to supplement the flowchart and provides a written record of how the various media elements will be used in the production.

Another important part of designing an effective multimedia application is the process of screen design. The colors and layout used for individual screens greatly influence the overall effect of the finished product. Simple screens with consistent backgrounds and a few bright colors, for example, usually are clearer and less distracting to a reader. Other basic screen design principles are shown in Figure 13-32.

Production

Multimedia **production** is the actual process of creating the various media elements used in the multimedia application and putting them together using a multimedia authoring software program. Original graphics and animations are created by artists using the various computerized paint/illustration software packages, and photographs are obtained by scanning images or using a digital camera or PhotoCD. Digital video and audio clips are recorded using recording devices and a video capture or sound card. When all of the media elements have been obtained, authoring begins. During authoring, the programmer or developer uses a multimedia authoring software package to combine these elements together. Finally, the developer tests the program to verify it performs the way it was designed.

DESIGN ELEMENT	EXPLANATION
Alignment	Use left-alignment to provide a more natural reading flow.
Balance	Avoid centering objects on the page. Place a graphic off to one side and text on the other.
Brevity	Use short, concise phrases.
Color	Keep the number of colors to a minimum, and use light text on a dark, consistent background.
Emphasis	Emphasize key concepts by using media elements such as video, audio, and graphics.
Font size	Use a font size big enough for your audience to read.
Formatting	Use appropriate formatting, such as bold formatting of keywords, to ensure your message is clear.
Navigation	Place navigation buttons at the bottom of the screen.
Number of ideas	Present only a few ideas per page.

Figure 13-32 *Effective screen design principles.*

Multimedia Authoring Software

The development of an interactive multimedia application involves the use of multimedia authoring software. **Multimedia authoring software** allows you to combine text, graphics, animation, audio, and video into an application. Authoring programs also allow you to design the screen on which the material is presented to create interactivity; that is, to create places in the program that respond to user input. Once various media elements are added to the program, you use the multimedia authoring software to assign relationships and actions to elements. The programs also help you create a structure that lets the user navigate through the material presented.

One of the more important activities of the production phase of multimedia development is the selection of the multimedia authoring software package. The following are important factors to consider when selecting a multimedia authoring software package.

- Quality of application developed
- Ease of use and documentation
- Responsiveness of vendor's service and technical support
- Compatibility with other applications
- Ease of programming
- Functionality
- System requirements for both user and developer

Most of today's popular authoring packages share similar features and are capable of creating similar applications. The major differences exist in the ease of use for development. This section will provide a closer look at three popular multimedia authoring packages: Toolbook, Authorware, and Director.

TOOLBOOK **ToolBook**, from Asymetrix Corporation, is one of the more widely used multimedia authoring software packages. ToolBook uses a graphical user interface and an object-oriented approach so you can design your applications using basic objects such as buttons, fields, graphics, backgrounds, and pages. Figure 13-33 shows a sample application developed in ToolBook.

WEB INFO

For more information on multimedia authoring software, visit the Discovering Computers 2000 Chapter 13 WEB INFO page (**www.scsite.com/ dc2000/ch13/webinfo.htm**) and click Multimedia Authoring Software.

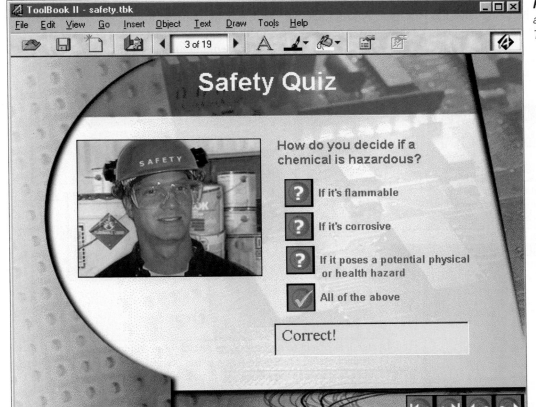

Figure 13-33 *A sample application developed in ToolBook.*

ToolBook uses a familiar **book metaphor** to help you build a multimedia application. The program or application that you build is called a book, and each screen is called a page. You begin building an application by creating a series of pages. Next, you add objects such as text fields, buttons, and graphics to each page.

Objects eliminate much of the programming involved in developing multimedia applications. Using objects, you easily can define navigation and add media components such as animation, audio, video, and clip art. Objects also assist in adding questions, feedback, and scoring capabilities to multimedia applications (Figure 13-34).

ToolBook has a catalog that contains objects that are prescripted, or contain properties that give them a certain behavior. If the catalog does not contain an object you need, you can write your own scripts to define objects and their behaviors. ToolBook also provides basic layout templates for items such as tests, glossaries, and Internet applications.

In ToolBook, you can convert your multimedia application into HTML and Java so it can be distributed over the Internet. Many businesses and colleges use ToolBook to create content for distance learning courses, in which students and employees at remote locations take training courses and other classes via the World Wide Web.

AUTHORWARE Authorware, from Macromedia, is another multimedia authoring software package that provides the tools developers need to build interactive multimedia training and educational programs.

Authorware uses a **flowchart metaphor** to help you build a multimedia application. You drag icons from a fixed set of icons into a flow line, which graphically represents the flow, or sequence, of action in the application. Each icon in the flow line represents a specific programming task; the flow line can be expanded to include more icons or content without programming.

Authorware offers a powerful authoring environment for the development of interactive multimedia magazines, catalogs, reference titles for CD-ROMs and DVD-ROMs, and applications for kiosks. Authorware also offers tools for bundling the content, student tracking, and course management components of a Web-based training or other distance learning course. Authorware applications distributed over the Web can be viewed using the Shockwave plug-in.

DIRECTOR Director, also from Macromedia, is a popular multimedia authoring program with powerful features that allow you to create highly interactive multimedia applications. Figure 13-35 shows a multimedia application created in Director.

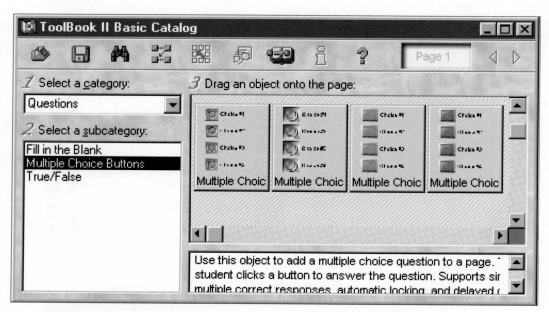

Figure 13-34 *A sample ToolBook screen.*

Director uses a **theater**, or **movie production**, **metaphor** to help you build a multimedia application. Three integrated windows — Cast, Score, and Paint — are used to create and sequence text and other media elements. The **Cast window** serves as a database of various media, such as text, graphics, animations, audio, and video. The **Score window**, which is the heart of Director, lets you create and edit animations, synchronize the various media elements such as audio and video, and precisely control transitions, colors, and the speed or tempo of the application. The **Paint window** contains a complete drawing and painting program for creating and editing graphics and adding animation effects (Figure 13-36). Director's programming language, **Lingo**, also can be used to add interactivity to a multimedia application.

Director's powerful features make it well suited for developing electronic presentations, CD-ROMs or DVD-ROMs for education and entertainment, simulations, and more. As with Authorware, applications developed in Director can be viewed on the Web using the Shockwave browser plug-in.

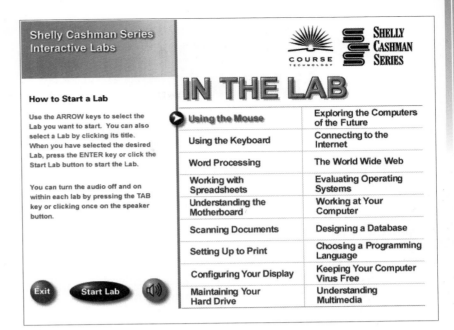

Figure 13-35 *A sample Director application.*

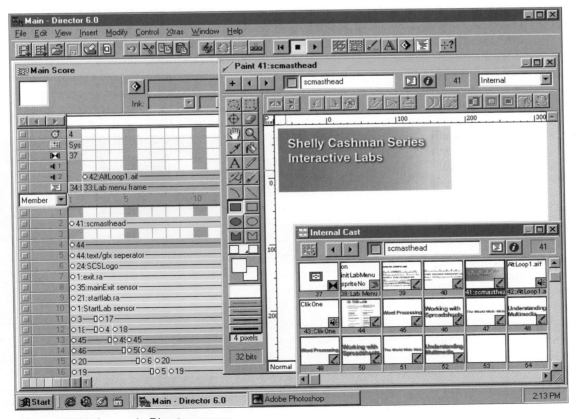

Figure 13-36 *A sample Director screen.*

TECHNOLOGY TRAILBLAZER

MICHAEL DELL

He dropped out of school and stored his products in a bathtub. He's the youngest person ever to head a Fortune 500 corporation, and his company's online sales are in the millions each day. He's been called many names: an upstart, a maverick, a whiz kid, and a boy wonder.

Michael Dell was born in 1965 in Houston, Texas, the second of three sons. While his parents wanted him to become a doctor, Dell's business acumen manifested itself early in life. At age eight, he sent away for an information packet on high school equivalency diplomas, not wanting to squander his adolescence on scholarly pursuits. This, as it turns out, was an omen of sorts, or at least a sign of his predilection for business.

When Dell was 12, he traded stamps through a mail order catalog and earned $2,000. By high school, he had progressed from the mail order business to a paper route. He was no ordinary paperboy, however. He visited the local marriage bureau to obtain names and addresses of newlyweds in order to target subscribers better. His efforts paid off handsomely. When his net profits reached $18,000 — and that is a *lot* of newspapers — he paid cash for a BMW.

By 1983, he was graduated from high school and enrolled at the University of Texas at Austin, majoring in biology. This is where fate, serendipity, karma — call it what you will — stepped in. Dell's fascination with computers led him to the conclusion that the demand for personal computers was not being met in a cost-efficient manner. He firmly believed — then, as now — that retail stores were going about things all wrong. The sales forces were not knowledgeable about the products, and the prices were marked up too high. Getting rid of the middleman is hardly a new concept, but applying the adage to personal computers was.

From his dorm room, he began building and selling personal computers via telephone orders. Placing advertisements in computer periodicals and buying surplus stock at cost from retail outlets, he began his business. Most orders were (and still are) from seasoned users who recognized quality merchandise at discount prices. He used some of his early profits to incorporate his business as Dell Computer Corporation, selling products under the PCs Limited trademark until mid-1987 and formally changing the company name to Dell Computer Corporation in 1987.

First year sales were $6 million, which made the young company one of the fastest growing businesses in the country. By 1993, sales soared to $2 billion. Even with the unbelievable growth, all was not perfect. The rapid growth had caused internal communications problems in the company, and a disastrous plan for laptop computers helped cause stocks to plummet that year. As Dell put it, "Hypergrowth can tax a company." Dell rallied by hiring talent in the form of computer industry executives and engineers, discontinuing retail sales, overhauling the laptop idea, and refocusing entirely on direct sales.

Today, Dell Computer Corporation is the world's second largest personal computer maker, growing at nearly four times the industry rate. More than 23,000 employees in 33 countries worldwide oversee the product line, which includes desktops, laptops, servers, and workstations.

A huge factor in Dell's success has always been his foresight. That foresight, coupled with his nearly uncanny ability to sense market trends, was exhibited in 1996, when Dell opened an Internet store. Online sales are about $10 million per day. Online sales, combined with other sale methods, total about $16.8 billion per year. Dell, a true believer in e-commerce (electronic business transactions via the Internet), said, "(The Internet) … is the ultimate catalyst for our industry. Essentially, a stand-alone computer was a good thing, a networked computer was a great thing, and the Internet is nirvana."

COMPANY ON THE CUTTING EDGE

COMPANY ON THE CUTTING EDGE

MACROMEDIA, INC.

If you have not visited the Web lately, prepare to be shocked. If you have surfed the Web recently, undoubtedly you already have been shocked, in the technological sense if not in the spiritual, that is. Oh, and certainly you have been flashed, too. If you have played music, viewed animation, or looked at charts and drawings, you have witnessed Macromedia's Shockwave and/or Flash.

Macromedia, Inc. is almost single-handedly responsible for the richly designed Web pages proliferating the Internet. Based in San Francisco, it is a relatively young company, having been founded formally in 1992. It has since grown to employ 550 people worldwide, with 80 distributors vending its products.

Macromedia's Web page claims its mission is, To bring life to the Web. In that, it certainly has succeeded. Its products are multimedia authoring tools, which are used to incorporate graphics, sound, text, and video into documents, presentations, and Web pages. Although it markets several products, the three principal products responsible for its success are Director, Authorware, and FreeHand.

Macromedia's Director allows users to create multimedia for Web pages, CD-ROMs, and DVD-ROMs. Because it contains the Lingo programming language, Director is capable of producing richly detailed, highly creative multimedia presentations. Authorware, billed as a Web learning tool, is used for creating interactive learning applications usually contained on CD-ROMs. FreeHand, a design tool for print and Internet graphics, was recently standardized by Knight Ridder/Tribune (KRT), which is a company that provides both printed and interactive news features to news organizations all over the world.

In addition to the three major products, Macromedia produces Shockwave, the world's most popular player for entertainment on the Web. If you view graphics created with either Flash or Director (both Macromedia products), you need Shockwave to play it back. Shockwave's success has been phenomenal. It is downloaded from

Macromedia's Web site (www.macromedia.com) approximately nine million times each month. This equates to about 300,000 daily downloads. In view of the astounding demand, several companies recently announced that they would ship Shockwave as part of their product package, including Windows 98, America Online, Netscape Navigator and Communicator, Internet Explorer, and Macintosh OS8. These announcements cemented Shockwave's place as the Web standard.

Another popular Macromedia application is Flash. Like Director, it is a design tool that allows users to create animation and graphics on the Web. Flash, however, is not programmable, and this results in a trade-off. It has several advantages, the chief one being that because the files generated are simpler and smaller, it is faster. Another advantage is that even the amateur can achieve remarkable results with no programming necessary. On the down side, the sophistication afforded by being programmable is missing.

No matter. In April 1998, Macromedia announced that the Flash file format would be available as an open Internet standard, a move that was embraced by the likes of IBM, Sun Microsystems, and Web TV.

Macromedia's success and popularity are due in large part to its appeal to a broad range of users, from educational institutions to large companies and just about every sized business in between. Additionally, its products are developed for both Windows and Macintosh platforms, with revenues generated fairly equally (56 percent Windows and 44 percent Macintosh).

But success in this industry also requires looking ahead to the future by identifying trends and responding to them. A recent source of pride for Macromedia was receiving *PC Computing* magazine's MVP (Most Valuable Product) award, as well as *PC Magazine's* Technical Excellence Award in Software, both in November 1998.

All the accolades and awards add up to one fact: Macromedia products rule the Web. And there's nothing "shocking" about that.

CHAPTER 1 2 3 4 5 6 7 8 9 10 11 12 13 14 INDEX

IN BRIEF www.scsite.com/dc2000/ch13/brief.htm

WEB INSTRUCTIONS: *To display this page from the Web, launch your browser and enter the URL,* *www.scsite.com/dc2000/ch13/brief.htm*. *Click the links for current and additional information. To listen to an audio version of this IN BRIEF, click the Audio button to the right of the title, IN BRIEF, at the top of the page. To play the audio, RealPlayer must be installed on your computer (download by clicking* here).

 1. What Is Multimedia?

Multimedia refers to any computer-based presentation or application that integrates one or more of the following elements: text, graphics, animation, audio, and video. A multimedia application that accepts input from the user by means of a keyboard, voice, or pointing device such as a mouse, is described as **interactive multimedia**.

 2. What Types of Media Are Used in Multimedia Applications?

Multimedia applications can use text, graphics, animation, audio, video, and links. **Text**, characters that are used to create words, sentences, and paragraphs, is a fundamental element used in many multimedia applications. **Graphics** are digital representations of nontext information such as a drawing, chart, or photographs which play an important comprehension role in the learning process. Animation, which is produced by displaying a series of still graphics, is a graphic that has the illusion of motion. **Audio** is music, speech, or any other sound that the computer converts from analog sound/waves into a digital format. **Video** consists of photographic images that are played back at speeds of 15 to 30 frames per second and provide the appearance of full motion. A **video compression** program works by recognizing only a small portion of the video changes from frame to frame. **Links** in a multimedia application allow users to access information quickly and navigate from one topic to another in a nonlinear manner.

 3. How Are Multimedia Applications Used?

Multimedia applications involve the use of multimedia technology for business, education, and entertainment. In business, multimedia applications are used for job- and skill-training and to create marketing presentations. In education, multimedia applications are used in computer-based training, Web-based training, and distance learning. Computer-based training (CBT) is a type of education in which students learn by using and completing exercises with instructional software, and receive instant feedback (also called **computer-aided instruction (CAI)**). **Web-based training (WBT)** is an approach to CBT that employs the techniques of the Internet and the World Wide Web. Web-based training typically consists of self-directed, self-paced instruction on a topic. **Distance learning**, also called **distance education**, is the delivery of education from one location while the learning takes place at other locations. Multimedia applications such as **electronic books**, **electronic references**, **how-to guides**, **multimedia newspapers**, and **multimedia magazines** also can be valuable educational tools. Because multimedia combines the media elements of television and interactivity, it is ideal for entertainment. Multimedia applications are used for **edutainment**, an experience meant to be both entertaining and educational. Multimedia applications also are used in **simulations** (computer-based models of real-life situations), **virtual reality** (computer-based environments that appear and feel like real environments and allow a space to be explored and manipulated), **kiosks** (computerized information or reference centers), and the **World Wide Web** (part of the Internet that supports and relies on multimedia).

IN BRIEF   www.scsite.com/dc2000/ch13/brief.htm

SHELLY
CASHMAN
SERIES®
**DISCOVERING
COMPUTERS
2000**

Student Exercises
WEB INFO
IN BRIEF
KEY TERMS
AT THE MOVIES
CHECKPOINT
AT ISSUE
CYBERCLASS
HANDS ON
NET STUFF
Special Features
TIMELINE 2000
GUIDE TO WWW SITES
MAKING A CHIP
BUYER'S GUIDE 2000
CAREERS 2000
TRENDS 2000
CHAT
INTERACTIVE LABS
NEWS
HOME

 4. What Are Different Types of Multimedia Hardware?

A **multimedia personal computer** (**MPC**) is a computer that uses specific hardware and software components to input, process, and output various types of media. Hardware components include **sound cards** (for audio input and output), **compact disk** (**CD-ROM**) drives and DVD-ROM drives (hold large amounts of data), **speakers** (play audio), and **display devices** (important for optimum viewing of multimedia). Connecting a multimedia computer to a standard television set requires an **NTSC converter**, which converts the digital signal to an analog signal that can be displayed on the television set. A **video capture card** is an expansion card that enables a video camera or VCR to be connected to a computer and the video input to be manipulated. **Color scanners** convert digital images into a digitized format for use in multimedia applications. **Digital cameras** use a small reusable disk, PC card, or internal memory to store digital photographs. A **photo CD** uses write-once compact disks to store photographic images that can be integrated into multimedia applications. **Laser disks** and **laser disk players** are part of a read-only video disk system based on the same optical disk technology used for compact disks.

5. How Is a Multimedia Application Developed?

Developing multimedia applications follows a standard process with several phases. The **analysis** phase determines the objectives and requirements for the application and specifies the essential elements needed for the actual production. Larger projects usually involve a project team, including a producer, art director, interface designer, content designer, and programmer. The **design** phase requires careful planning to determine a project blueprint and screen design. Throughout design, the project team employs a flowchart, which includes the various media elements in the application, and a **project script**, which provides a more detailed written record of how the media elements will be used. The **production** phase is the actual process of creating the various media elements used in the multimedia application and putting them together using a multimedia authoring program. Finally, the developer tests the program to verify that it performs the way it was designed.

 6. What Are Features of Multimedia Authoring Software Packages?

Multimedia authoring software allows text, graphics, animation, audio, and video to be combined into an application. Three popular multimedia authoring packages are ToolBook, Authorware, and Director. **ToolBook** uses a familiar **book metaphor** to help build a multimedia application. ToolBook employs a graphical user interface and an object-oriented approach. **Authorware**, from Macromedia, uses a **flowchart metaphor** to create a multimedia application. Developers drag icons into a flow line that graphically represents the sequence of action in the application. **Director** uses a **theater** or **movie production metaphor** to help build a multimedia application. Three integrated windows – the **Cast window**, the **Score window**, and the **Paint window** – are used to create and sequence text and other media elements.

CHAPTER 1 2 3 4 5 6 7 8 9 10 11 12 13 14 INDEX

KEY TERMS
www.scsite.com/dc2000/ch13/terms.htm

WEB INSTRUCTIONS: *To display this page from the Web, launch your browser and enter the URL, www.scsite.com/dc2000/ch13/terms.htm. Scroll through the list of terms. Click a term to display its definition and a picture. Click KEY TERMS on the left to redisplay the KEY TERMS page. Click the TO WEB button for current and additional information about the term from the Web. To see animations, Shockwave and Flash Player must be installed on your computer (download by clicking here).*

analysis (13.26)
animation (13.4)
audio (13.5)
audio digitizer (13.21)
Authorware (13.28)
book metaphor (13.28)
Cast window (13.29)
color scanner (13.23)
compact disk (13.21)
computer-aided instruction (CAI) (13.9)
computer-based training (CBT) (13.9)
courseware (13.9)
data projector (13.23)
design (13.26)
digital cameras (13.24)
digital light processing (DLP) projector (13.23)
digital video interleave (DVI) (13.23)
Director (13.28)
display device (13.22)
distance education (13.10)
distance learning (13.10)
edutainment (13.16)
electronic book (13.13)
electronic magazine (13.14)
electronic reference (13.13)
e-book (13.13)
e-zine (13.14)
flowchart metaphor (13.28)
graphic (13.3)
how-to guides (13.14)
interactive multimedia (13.2)

VIRTUAL REALITY (VR): The use of a computer to create an artificial environment that appears and feels like a real environment and allows the user to explore a space and manipulate the environment. Advanced forms of VR require the user to wear specialized headgear, body suits, and gloves to enhance the experience of the artificial environment. (13.17)

kiosk (13.19)
laser disk players (13.25)
laser disks (13.25)
LCD projector (13.23)
Lingo (13.29)
link (13.7)
mixer (13.21)
movie production metaphor (13.29)
Moving Pictures Experts Group (MPEG) (13.7)

multimedia (13.2)
multimedia application (13.8)
multimedia authoring software (13.27)
multimedia magazine (13.14)
multimedia newspaper (13.14)
multimedia personal computer (MPC) (13.20)
National Television System Committee (NTSC) (13.22)
NTSC converter (13.22)
Paint window (13.29)
PC 97 (13.20)
Pentium® III processor (13.20)
PhotoCD (13.25)
production (13.26)
project script (13.26)
Score window (13.29)
simulations (13.8)
sound card (13.21)
speakers (13.22)
text (13.3)
theater metaphor (13.29)
ToolBook (13.27)
video (13.6)
video capture card (13.23)
video capture software (13.23)
video compression (13.6)
video decoder (13.6)
virtual reality (VR) (13.16)
wavetable synthesizer (13.21)
Web-based training (WBT) (13.10)
World Wide Web (13.19)

CHAPTER 1 2 3 4 5 6 7 8 9 10 11 12 **13** 14 INDEX

AT THE MOVIES
www.scsite.com/dc2000/ch13/movies.htm

WELCOME to VIDEO CLIPS from

WEB INSTRUCTIONS: *To display this page from the Web, launch your browser and enter the URL,* www.scsite.com/dc2000/ch13/movies.htm*. Click a picture to view a video. After watching the video, close the video window and then complete the exercise by answering the questions about the video. To view the videos, RealPlayer must be installed on your computer (download by clicking* here*).*

1 Knowledge Adventure

Educational enrichment and creative discovery are primary buzzwords in the edutainment software industry. Describe edutainment software. What are some types of edutainment software being created by software companies today? What end users and age groups are targeted markets for edutainment software? Do you use any edutainment software in your learning environment? If so, what is it?

2 SBT Tech Guide Animation

Multimedia applications often use a variety of media elements to present information in a variety of ways. What kinds of media are used on the Web site to bring jazz to life? What types of multimedia Web technologies are used? Of the media and Web technologies used, which do you think is the most effective? What other media could you add to the site to make it more interesting and informative?

3 Internet Traffic School

Web-based training (WBT) is one approach to computer-based training (CBT) that employs the technologies of the Internet and the World Wide Web. What are the advantages of using WBT for an "Internet traffic school" for the city? What are the advantages of Web-based traffic school for students? Are there any disadvantages? What ethical concerns does an online traffic school create? If you had to attend traffic school, would you prefer to take an online traffic school or the traditional classroom-based traffic school?

SHELLY
CASHMAN
SERIES®
**DISCOVERING
COMPUTERS
2000**

CHAPTER   1   2   3   4   5   6   7   8   9   10   11   12   13   14   INDEX

CHECKPOINT   www.scsite.com/dc2000/ch13/check.htm

WEB INSTRUCTIONS: *To display this page from the Web, launch your browser and enter the URL, www.scsite.com/dc2000/ch13/check.htm. Click the links for current and additional information. To experience the animation and interactivity, Shockwave and Flash Player must be installed on your computer (download by clicking here).*

Label the Figure

Instructions: *Identify the indicated elements of a multimedia application.*

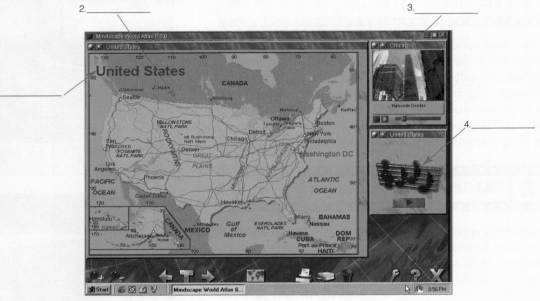

Matching

Instructions: *Match each multimedia hardware component from the column on the left with the best description from the column on the right.*

_____ 1. sound card

_____ 2. compact disc

_____ 3. speakers

_____ 4. display device

_____ 5. video capture card

a. Optical storage medium that can hold a tremendous amount of data.

b. An expansion card used to connect a video camera or VCR to a computer and manipulate the video image.

c. Converts images into a digitized format for use in multimedia applications.

d. An important part of a multimedia personal computer that should be evaluated in terms of both the monitor and the video card.

e. Work similarly to regular cameras, except they use a small reusable disk, PC card, or internal memory to store digital photographs.

f. An expansion card that provides both audio input and output.

g. Provide an easy and inexpensive way to play audio on a multimedia personal computer.

Short Answer

Instructions: *Write a brief answer to each of the following questions.*

1. What functions can graphics serve in multimedia applications? _____
2. What advantages does computer-based training (CBT) have over traditional training? _____
3. How is an electronic book different from an e-book? _____ What is a how-to guide? _____
4. What are two types of data projectors? _____ How are they different? _____
5. What factors should be considered when selecting a multimedia authoring package? _____

AT ISSUE   www.scsite.com/dc2000/ch13/issue.htm

WEB INSTRUCTIONS: *To display this page from the Web, launch your browser and enter the URL,* www.scsite.com/dc2000/ch13/issue.htm. *Click the links for current and additional information.*

ONE

Thanks to multimedia, even the most nervous driver education teachers finally may be able to relax. A recently released multimedia application, which comes complete with a steering wheel, simulates a driving experience for student motorists. After passing a written test, learners get behind the wheel and take to the virtual road, navigating streets, encountering traffic, dealing with ambulances and school buses, and even parallel parking. The software teaches rules of the road for every state and can be customized for specific locales. What advantages does a multimedia software application have over traditional driver education? What are the disadvantages? What approach would be more likely to produce a safe driver – a multimedia training program or an actual driving experience? Why?

TWO

For those who like the idea of a pet but dislike such realities as fleas or messes on the carpet, a virtual pet may be the answer. Originally simple digital facsimiles that attached to a key chain, virtual pets have evolved into sensitive companions that "live" in a personal computer. The detailed, three-dimensional images can represent a dog or cat, or a less conventional creature such as a fish-bird combination. Interactive multimedia allows virtual pets to sense both movement and sound. Sit in front of the computer and the virtual pet runs to greet you. Feed, play, or talk to the pet and depending on the species it might purr, sing songs, or do tricks. Who would more likely benefit from virtual pets? Why? Do you think virtual pets teach children the same sense of responsibility as some feel children learn from real pets? Why or why not?

THREE

Thirty high schools have been awarded a five-year grant to develop classes where students would participate via the Internet. These "netclasses" deal with subjects not ordinarily offered in high schools, from stellar astronomy to Russian studies to comparative Eastern and Western thought. Students read books but they use e-mail to do homework, take tests, join in discussions, and collaborate on multimedia projects. Distance learning participants applaud the opportunity to pursue unusual topics, communicate with experts, and work with classmates from different backgrounds. Some students, however, miss the personal contact that characterizes a conventional class. What subjects would be more appropriate for distance learning? What subjects would be least appropriate? Why? What type of student would be happiest in a distance learning class? Why? Would you be interested in distance learning? Why or why not?

FOUR

Couch potatoes take heart. A new multimedia game lets virtual mountain-bike racers leap hills, speed down inclines, and jump water holes, all without leaving the living room. The game's display shows one of nine different tracks, and the attached handlebars and brake lever can be used to corner sharply, downshift gradually, or stop quickly when the terrain becomes too rough. If you wipe out you will know it; the handlebars vibrate. Despite their apparent reality, critics claim multimedia sports applications miss the real value in a sports experience. Do you think multimedia sports applications ignore the real value of sports? Why or why not? When are multimedia sports applications appropriate? Could these applications be a legitimate part of a physical education course? Why or why not?

FIVE

One of the more popular how-to-guides is the "Complete Do-It-Yourself Guide" from Reader's digest. This CD-ROM offers a wide range of household projects. Step-by-step instructions are provided for hundreds of home-repair tasks from caulking windows to splicing wires. A feature called The Estimator approximates the cost of a project. Who would be most likely to use the Reader's Digest guide? Why? What advantages does a multimedia how-to-guide offer over traditional how-to-guide books? What are the disadvantages? In what other areas might multimedia how-to-guides be used? Why?

CHAPTER 1 2 3 4 5 6 7 8 9 10 11 12 **13** 14 INDEX

CYBERCLASS

www.scsite.com/dc2000/ch13/class.htm

WEB INSTRUCTIONS: *To display this page from the Web, launch your browser and enter the URL,* www.scsite.com/dc2000/ch13/class.htm. *To start Level I CyberClass, click a Level I link on this page or enter the URL,* www.cyber-class.com. *Click the Student button, click Discovering Computers 2000 in the list of titles, and then click the Enter a site button. To start Level II or III CyberClass (available only to those purchasers of a CyberClass floppy disk), place your CyberClass floppy disk in drive A, click Start on the taskbar, click Run on the Start menu, type* a:connect *in the Open text box, click the OK button, click the Enter CyberClass button, and then follow the instructions.*

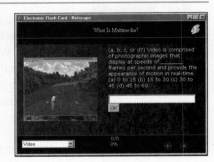

I II III LEVEL **1. Flash Cards** Click Flash Cards on the Main Menu of the CyberClass web page. Click the plus sign before the Chapter 13 title. Select all the subjects under the Chapter 13 title and answer all the flash cards. Hand in the number right, the number wrong, and the percentage score to your instructor. All users: Close the Electronic Flash Card window and the Flash Cards window by clicking the Close button in the upper-right corner of each window.

I II III LEVEL **2. Practice Test** Click Testing on the Main Menu of the CyberClass web page. Click the Select a book box arrow and then click Discovering Computers 2000. Click the Select a test to take box arrow and then click the Chapter 13 title in the list. Click the Take Test button. If necessary, maximize the window. Take the practice test and then click the Submit Test button. If you miss more than one question, take another test by clicking the Take another Test button. Continue to take tests until you miss no more than one question.

I II III LEVEL **3. Web Guide** Click Web Guide on the Main Menu of the CyberClass web page. When the Guide to World Wide Web Sites page displays, click Careers and Employment. Visit one or more of the Careers and Employment sites to look for jobs in the computer and information technology industry. Write a brief report listing available jobs, approximate salaries, and the number of positions open for these jobs.

II III LEVEL **4. Company Briefs** Click Company Briefs on the Main Menu of the CyberClass web page. Click a corporation name to display a case study. Read the case study. Visit the company's Web site to see how the company uses multimedia on its site.

I II III LEVEL **5. CyberChallenge** Click CyberChallenge on the Main Menu of the CyberClass web page. Click the Select a book box arrow and then click Discovering Computers 2000. Click the Select a board to play box arrow and then click Chapter 13 in the list. Click the Play CyberChallenge button. Maximize the CyberChallenge window. Play CyberChallenge as many times as you want to see if you can place you and your school in the CyberChallenge list of top scores. Close the CyberChallenge window.

II III LEVEL **6. Assignments and Syllabus** Click Assignments on the Main Menu of the CyberClass web page. Ensure you are aware of all assignments and when they are due. Click Syllabus on the Main Menu of the CyberClass web page. Verify you are up to date on all activities for the class.

II III LEVEL **7. Hot Links** Click Hot Links on the Main Menu of the CyberClass web page. Click Add a Link. Click New Link Topic. Type your name and the word, Multimedia, in the Link Topic Name box. Click the Create Link Topic button. Type the link name in the Link Name box, the URL in the URL (Internet address) box, and the link description in the Link Description box to revisit a multimedia Web site you think is outstanding. Click the Add Link button.

HANDS ON

www.scsite.com/dc2000/ch13/hands.htm

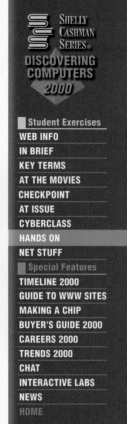

SHELLY CASHMAN SERIES®

DISCOVERING COMPUTERS 2000

■ **Student Exercises**
WEB INFO
IN BRIEF
KEY TERMS
AT THE MOVIES
CHECKPOINT
AT ISSUE
CYBERCLASS
HANDS ON
NET STUFF
■ **Special Features**
TIMELINE 2000
GUIDE TO WWW SITES
MAKING A CHIP
BUYER'S GUIDE 2000
CAREERS 2000
TRENDS 2000
CHAT
INTERACTIVE LABS
NEWS
HOME

WEB INSTRUCTIONS: *To display this page from the Web, launch your browser and enter the URL, www.scsite.com/dc2000/ch13/hands.htm. Click the links for current and additional information.*

 ### Playing Audio Compact Disks

This exercise uses Windows 98 procedures. Click the Start button on the taskbar, point to Programs on the Start menu, and point to Accessories on the Programs submenu. Point to Entertainment on the Accessories submenu, and then click CD Player on the Entertainment submenu. When the CD Player window displays (Figure 13-37), click Help on the menu bar and then click Help Topics. Answer these questions:

♠ How do you play a CD?
♠ How do you stop a CD?
♠ How do you eject a CD from the drive?

Figure 13-37

Close the CD Player Help window. If your system has a <u>CD-ROM drive</u> and a sound card, insert a CD into the CD-ROM drive and then play it. Close the CD Player window.

Understanding Multimedia Properties

Click the Start button on the taskbar, point to Settings on the Start menu, and then click Control Panel. Double-click the Multimedia icon in the Control Panel window. When the Multimedia Properties dialog box displays, click the Audio tab and then answer the following questions:

♠ What is the Playback preferred device?
♠ Will the volume control display on the taskbar of your computer?

Click the Advanced or Devices tab. For each <u>multimedia device</u> listed, if a plus sign (+) displays in the box to its left, click the plus sign to change it to a minus sign (–). For each device driver listed, write down the name(s) of the hardware device(s) installed on your system. Close the Multimedia Properties dialog box and Control Panel.

Using Help to Understand the Media Player

This exercise uses Windows 98 procedures. Click the Start button on the taskbar and then click Help on the Start menu. Click the Index tab, type `multimedia files` in the text box, and then click the Display button. In the Topics Found dialog box, double-click Using Media Player. Read and print the information. Click the Click here link in the Windows Help window to start Media Player. When the Media Player window displays, click Help on its menu bar and then click Help Topics. If necessary, click Playing Audio, Video, and Animation Files to open the book. Read and print each of these subtopics: Play an audio CD, Rewind a multimedia file, and Fast-forward a multimedia file. Close any open Help windows. Click File on the Media Player menu bar and then click Open. When the Open dialog box displays, be sure the Media folder is open in the Look in box and then double-click Beethoven's 5th Symphony. Play the <u>multimedia file</u>. Close the Media Player. Close the Windows Help window.

System Sounds

Double-click the My Computer icon on the Desktop. Double-click the Control Panel icon in the My Computer window. Double-click the Sounds icon in the Control Panel window. In the Sounds Properties dialog box, some of the items in the Events area have an associated sound. To hear the sound for an event, click the event in the Events area and then click the right arrow button in the Preview area. What events have the same <u>sound</u>? Do any events listed have no sound? Close the Sounds Properties dialog box and close each window.

SHELLY CASHMAN SERIES®

DISCOVERING COMPUTERS 2000

Student Exercises
WEB INFO
IN BRIEF
KEY TERMS
AT THE MOVIES
CHECKPOINT
AT ISSUE
CYBERCLASS
HANDS ON
NET STUFF
Special Features
TIMELINE 2000
GUIDE TO WWW SITES
MAKING A CHIP
BUYER'S GUIDE 2000
CAREERS 2000
TRENDS 2000
CHAT
INTERACTIVE LABS
NEWS
HOME

CHAPTER 1 2 3 4 5 6 7 8 9 10 11 12 **13** 14 INDEX

NET STUFF www.scsite.com/dc2000/ch13/net.htm

WEB INSTRUCTIONS: *To display this page from the Web, launch your browser and enter the URL, www.scsite.com/dc2000/ch13/net.htm. To use the Understanding Multimedia lab from the Web, Shockwave and Flash Player must be installed on your computer (download by clicking here).*

UNDER-STANDING MULTIMEDIA LAB

1. Shelly Cashman Series Understanding Multimedia Lab

Follow the instructions in NET STUFF 1 on page 1.46 to start and use the Understanding Multimedia lab. If you are running from the Web, enter the URL, www.scsite.com/sclabs/menu.htm; or display the NET STUFF page (see instructions at the top of this page) and then click the UNDERSTANDING MULTIMEDIA LAB button.

DIGITAL CAMERAS

2. Digital Cameras

The Elph Jr. APS is a pocket wonder manufactured by Canon. The tiny digital camera is smaller than four inches and weighs less than five ounces, but offers autoflash, autofocus, and autoexposure. Digital cameras work much like regular cameras except they use a small reusable disk or internal memory to store digital photographs. To learn more about digital cameras, complete this exercise.

ANIAMATION AND GRAPHICS

3. Animation and Graphics

Animation and graphics add interest to any multimedia application. Recent multimedia games have used detailed animation and graphics to add verisimilitude to Louis XIV's Versailles, provide integrity to the shah's Istanbul, and offer substance to Scottish golf courses. Graphics and animation also are used to reinforce Web page content. Complete this exercise to visit a Web page with hundreds of free animations and graphics you can download on your Web pages.

IN THE NEWS

4. In the News

Lara Croft may be the world's most famous non-person. Made up of 540 polygons, the adventurous archaeologist star of Core Design's multimedia game Tomb Raider has appeared on the cover of over forty magazines, receives voluminous e-mail, and dominates more than one hundred Web sites. With Lara's help, more than three million copies of Tomb Raider have been sold worldwide and Core Design turned a loss of almost three million dollars into a profit of more than fourteen million dollars. Click the IN THE NEWS button and read a news article about another company involved in multimedia applications. What company is it? What applications have they developed? Do you think the applications will be successful? Why or why not?

WEB CHAT

5. Web Chat

Most people remember dissecting a frog in high school biology class – the odor of formaldehyde, the nervous laughter, the unsuspecting classmate who finds a webbed foot in her lunch bag. For many students, conventional dissections are being replaced by multimedia applications. Students use computers to view color graphics of a frog's anatomy, videos of biological systems, and interactive quizzes that cheer ("ribbet") correct answers. Although these multimedia programs are supported by animal-rights activists and squeamish students, many biology teachers believe there is no substitute for genuine traditional dissection. Can multimedia applications replace hands-on experience? Why or why not? Who do you think should make the choice between multimedia programs and traditional dissection? Why? On what basis should the choice be made? Click the WEB CHAT button to enter a Web Chat discussion related to this topic.

CHAPTER 14

SECURITY, PRIVACY, AND ETHICS

OBJECTIVES

After completing this chapter, you will be able to:

▶ Identify the various types of security risks that can threaten computers

▶ Describe ways to safeguard a computer

▶ Describe how a computer virus works and the steps individuals can take to prevent viruses

▶ Explain why computer backup is important and how it is accomplished

▶ Discuss the steps in a disaster recovery plan

▶ Examine the issues relating to information privacy

▶ Discuss ethical issues with respect to the information age

▶ Identify and explain Internet-related security and privacy issues

Every day, home and business users depend on computers to perform a variety of significant tasks, such as tracking finances, recording transactions, creating documents and reports, and sending e-mail. Because people increasingly rely on computers to create, store, and manage critical information, it is important to ensure that computers and the data they store are accessible and available when needed and protected from loss, damage, and misuse. Businesses, for example, must take precautions to ensure that information such as credit records, employee and customer data, and product information are secured from loss and kept confidential.

This chapter identifies some potential risks to computers and software and the safeguards that schools, businesses, and individuals can implement to minimize these risks. The chapter also discusses information privacy, including current laws designed to keep certain data confidential. Then, the chapter presents concerns about the ethical use of computers and which activities are right, wrong, or even criminal. Finally, the chapter covers security and privacy issues that relate to the Internet.

COMPUTER SECURITY: RISKS AND SAFEGUARDS

Any event or action that could cause a loss of or damage to computer hardware, software, data, information, or processing capability is considered a **computer security risk**. Breaches to computer security may be intentional or unintentional. An intentional breach of computer security often involves a deliberate act that is against the law. Any illegal act involving a computer generally is referred to as a **computer crime**.

The following sections describe some of the more common computer security risks and protective measures, or **safeguards**, you can take to minimize or prevent their consequences. This section concludes with a discussion of how to develop an overall computer security plan.

WEB INFO
WEB INFO

For more information on computer viruses, visit the Discovering Computers 2000 Chapter 14 WEB INFO page (**www.scsite.com/ dc2000/ch14/webinfo.htm**) and click Computer Virus.

Computer Viruses

A **computer virus** is a potentially damaging computer program designed to affect, or *infect*, your computer negatively by altering the way it works without your knowledge or permission. More specifically, a computer virus is a segment of program code that implants itself in a computer file and spreads systematically from one file to another. Viruses can spread to your computer if an infected floppy disk is in the disk drive when you boot the computer, if you run an infected program, or if you open an infected data file in a program. Figure 14-1 shows how a virus can spread from one computer to another.

Computer viruses, however, do not generate by chance. Creators, or programmers, of computer virus programs write them for a specific purpose — usually to cause a certain

A COMPUTER VIRUS: WHAT IT IS AND HOW IT SPREADS

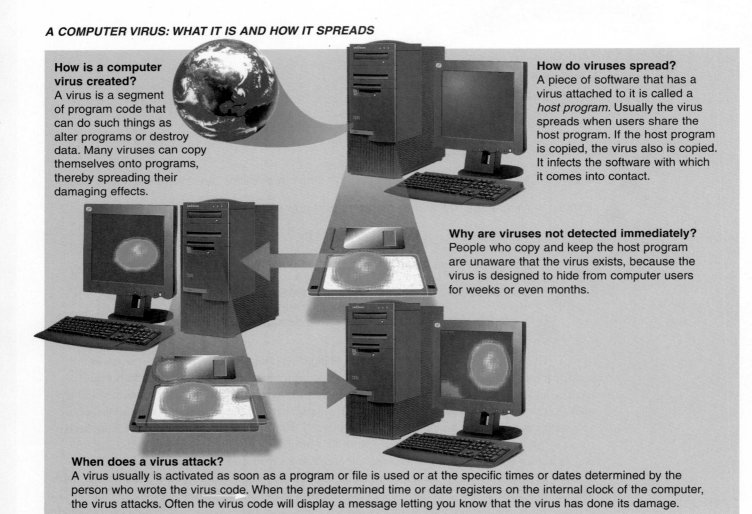

How is a computer virus created?
A virus is a segment of program code that can do such things as alter programs or destroy data. Many viruses can copy themselves onto programs, thereby spreading their damaging effects.

How do viruses spread?
A piece of software that has a virus attached to it is called a *host program.* Usually the virus spreads when users share the host program. If the host program is copied, the virus also is copied. It infects the software with which it comes into contact.

Why are viruses not detected immediately?
People who copy and keep the host program are unaware that the virus exists, because the virus is designed to hide from computer users for weeks or even months.

When does a virus attack?
A virus usually is activated as soon as a program or file is used or at the specific times or dates determined by the person who wrote the virus code. When the predetermined time or date registers on the internal clock of the computer, the virus attacks. Often the virus code will display a message letting you know that the virus has done its damage.

Figure 14-1 *This figure shows how a virus can spread from one computer to another.*

type of symptom or damage. Some viruses are harmless pranks that simply freeze a computer temporarily or display sounds or messages. When the Music Bug virus is triggered, for example, it instructs the computer to play a few chords of music. Other viruses, by contrast, are designed to destroy or corrupt data stored on the infected computer. Thus, the symptom or damage caused by a virus can be harmless or cause significant damage, as planned by the creator.

Viruses have become a serious problem in recent years. Currently, more than 13,000 known virus programs exist and an estimated six new virus programs are discovered each day (Figure 14-2). The increased use of networks, the Internet, and e-mail has accelerated the spread of computer viruses, by allowing individuals to share files — and any related viruses — more easily than ever.

Although numerous variations are known, four main types of viruses exist: boot sector viruses, file viruses, Trojan horse viruses, and macro viruses. A **boot sector virus** replaces the boot program used to start a computer with a modified, infected version of the boot program. When the computer runs the infected boot program, the computer loads the virus into its memory. Once the virus is in memory, it spreads to any disk inserted into the computer. A **file virus** attaches itself to or replaces program files; the virus then spreads to any file that accesses the infected program. A **Trojan horse virus** (named after the Greek myth) is a virus that hides within or is designed to look like a legitimate program. A **macro virus** uses the macro language of an application, such as word processing or spreadsheet, to hide virus code. When you open a document with an infected macro, the

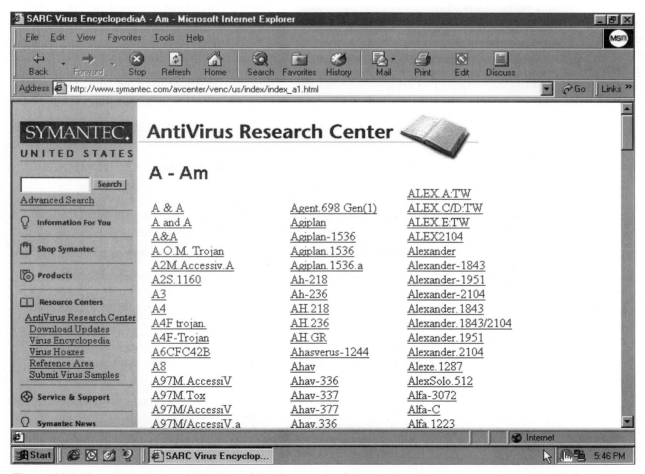

Figure 14-2 Many Web sites maintain lists of the thousands of viruses in existence, so you can obtain information of a specific virus if your computer is infected. The Symantec AntiVirus Research Center Web page, for example, organizes the virus names alphabetically.

macro virus loads into memory. Certain actions, such as opening the document, activate the virus (Figure 14-3). The creators of macro viruses often hide them in templates so they will infect any document created using the template.

Depending on the virus, certain actions can trigger the virus. Many viruses activate as soon as a computer accesses or runs an infected file or program. Other viruses, called logic bombs or time bombs, activate based on specific criteria. A **logic bomb** is a computer virus that activates when it detects a certain condition. One disgruntled worker, for example, planted a logic bomb that began destroying files when his name appeared on a list of terminated employees. A **time bomb** is a type of logic bomb that activates on a particular date. A well-known time bomb is the Michelangelo virus, which destroys data on your hard disk on March 6, Michelangelo's birthday.

WEB INFO

For more information on antivirus programs, visit the Discovering Computers 2000 Chapter 14 WEB INFO page (**www.scsite.com/dc2000/ch14/webinfo.htm**) and click Antivirus Programs.

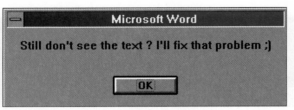

Picture from http://www.DataFellows.com/

Figure 14-3 *One Word macro virus displays the dialog box shown here when the user opens a document on the 6th or the 8th of the month.*

Another type of malicious program is a worm. Although often it is called a virus, a worm, unlike a virus, does not attach itself to another program. Instead, a **worm** program copies itself repeatedly in memory or on a disk drive until no memory or disk space remains. When no memory or disk space remains, the computer stops working. Some worm programs even copy themselves to other computers on a network.

Virus Detection and Removal

No completely effective methods exist to ensure that a computer or network is safe from computer viruses. You can, however, take precautions to protect your home and work computers from virus infections. Figure 14-4 summarizes these precautions, which are discussed in the following paragraphs.

An **antivirus program** protects a computer against viruses by identifying and removing any computer viruses found in memory, on storage media, or on incoming memory, on storage media, or on incoming files (Figure 14-5a). Most antivirus programs also protect against malicious ActiveX code and Java applets that might be included in files you download from the Web. An antivirus program scans for programs that attempt to

TIPS FOR PREVENTING VIRUS INFECTIONS

1. Install an antivirus program on all of your computers. Obtain updates to the antivirus signature files. The cost of antivirus software is much less than the cost of rebuilding damaged files. As a result, most businesses and large organizations have adopted this policy.
2. Write-protect your rescue disk by sliding the write-protect tab into the write-protect position.
3. Never start your computer with a floppy disk in drive A. All floppy disks contain a boot sector. During the startup process, the computer attempts to execute the boot sector on a disk in drive A. Even if the attempt is unsucessful, any virus on the floppy disk's boot sector can infect the computer's hard disk.
4. Before using any floppy disk, use the antivirus scan program to check the disk for viruses. This holds true even for shrink-wrapped software from major developers. Even commercial software has been infected and distributed to unsuspecting users.
5. Check all downloaded programs for viruses. Viruses often are placed in seemingly innocent programs so that they will affect a large number of users.
6. Back up your files regularly. Scan the backup program prior to backing up disks and files to ensure the backup program is virus free.

Figure 14-4 *With the growing number of new viruses, no single antivirus program can prevent all computer viruses. Thus, it is crucial you take steps to protect your computer. To protect your computer from virus infection, experts recommend the precautions listed here.*

modify the boot program, the operating system, and other programs that normally are read from but not modified.

Antivirus programs also identify a virus by looking for specific patterns of known virus code, called a **virus signature**, which they compare to a virus signature file. You should update your antivirus program's virus signature files frequently so it includes the virus signatures for newly discovered viruses and can protect against viruses written after the antivirus program was released (Figure 14-5b). Typically, you download updates to virus signature files from the vendor's Web site.

Even with an updated virus signature file, however, antivirus programs can have difficulty detecting some viruses. One such virus is a **polymorphic virus**, which modifies its program code each time it attaches itself to another program or file. Because its code never looks the same, an antivirus program cannot detect a polymorphic virus by its virus signature.

Another technique that antivirus programs use to detect viruses is to inoculate existing program files. To **inoculate** a program file, the antivirus program records information such as the file size and file creation date in a separate inoculation file. The antivirus program then can use this information to detect if a computer virus tampers with the inoculated program file. Some sophisticated viruses, however, take steps to avoid detection. Such a virus, called a **stealth virus**, can infect a program file, but still report the size and creation date of the original, uninfected program.

Once an antivirus program identifies an infected file, it can remove the virus or quarantine the infected file. When you **quarantine a file**, the antivirus program places the infected file in a separate area of your computer until you can remove the virus, thus insuring that other files will not become infected.

Figure 14-5a (virus scanner)

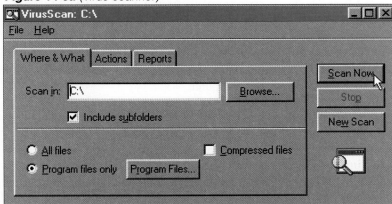

Figure 14-5b
(updated signature file)

Figure 14-5 Antivirus programs check disk drives and memory for computer viruses. Many antivirus programs allow you to update signature files automatically from the Web without cost.

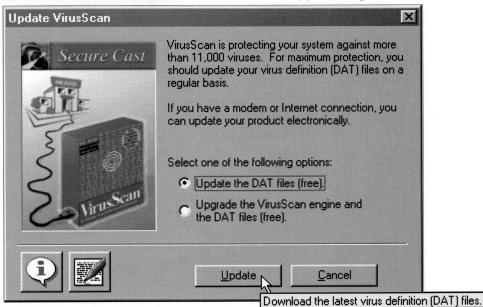

In addition to detecting and inoculating against viruses, most antivirus programs also have utilities to remove or repair infected programs and files. If the virus has infected the boot program, however, the antivirus program first will require you to restart the computer with a floppy disk called a rescue disk. The **rescue disk**, or **emergency disk**, is a disk that contains an uninfected copy of key operating system commands and startup information that enables the computer to restart correctly. Once you have restarted the computer using a rescue disk, you can run repair and removal programs to remove infected files and repair damaged files. If the program cannot repair the damaged files, you may have to replace, or *restore*, them with uninfected backup copies of the files. Later sections in the chapter review backup and restore procedures in detail.

Unauthorized Access and Use

Unauthorized access is the use of a computer or network without permission. An individual who tries to access a computer or network illegally is called a **cracker** or a hacker. The term **hacker**, although originally a complimentary word for a computer enthusiast, now has a derogatory connotation — referring to people who try to break into a computer often with the intent of stealing or corrupting its data. Crackers and hackers typically break into computers by connecting to them via a modem and logging in as a legitimate user. Some intruders do no damage; they merely access data, information, or programs on the computer before logging off. Other intruders leave some evidence of their presence either by leaving a message or deliberately altering data.

Unauthorized use is the use of a computer or its data for unapproved or possibly illegal activities. Unauthorized use can range from an employee using a company computer to send personal e-mail or track his or her child's soccer league scores to someone gaining access to a bank computer and performing an unauthorized transfer.

One way to prevent unauthorized access and unauthorized use of computers is to implement access controls. An **access control** is a security measure that defines who can access a computer, when they can access it,

and what actions they can take while accessing the computer. Many commercial software packages implement access controls using a two-phase process called identification and authentication. **Identification** verifies that you are a valid user; **authentication** verifies that you are who you claim to be. Four methods of identification and authentication exist: user identification and passwords, possessed objects, biometric devices, and a callback system.

USER IDENTIFICATION AND PASSWORDS With a **user identification** (user ID) and **password**, you are required to enter a word or series of characters that matches an entry in an authorization file stored on the computer or a network server. As discussed in Chapter 8, most multiuser operating systems require that you correctly enter a user ID and a password before you can access the data, information, and programs stored on a computer or network. When you enter your user ID and a password, the operating system checks to see if the user ID and password match entries stored in an authorization file. If the entries match, the operating system grants access to the computer or network. If they do not match, the operating system will deny your access to the computer.

You often are asked to select your own password by choosing a word or series of characters that will be easy to remember. If your password is too obvious, however, such as your initials or birthday, others can guess it easily. Longer passwords also provide greater security: each character added to a password significantly increases the number of possible combinations and the length of time it might take for someone to guess the password (Figure 14-6).

When choosing a password, be guided by the following criteria:

- Make the password at least eight characters (if supported by the software)

- Join two words together

- Mix initials and dates together

- Add one or more numbers at the beginning, middle, or end of a word

- Add letters to or subtract letters from an existing word

- Choose words from other languages

WEB INFO

For more information on crackers and hackers, visit the Discovering Computers 2000 Chapter 14 WEB INFO page (www.scsite.com/ dc2000/ch14/webinfo.htm) and click Crackers and Hackers.

- Choose family names far back in your family tree

- Choose names of obscure places in other countries

Generally, the more creative you are when selecting a password, the more difficult it is for someone to figure out. Even long and creative passwords, however, do not provide complete protection against unauthorized access. Some additional precautions to take include:

- Do not post passwords near your computer

- If possible, use a password that is easy for you to remember so you do not have to write it down

- Use a password that you can type quickly, without having to look at the keyboard

- Do not share your passwords with other users

Following these guidelines can help ensure that unauthorized users will not use your password to access data, programs, or sensitive information stored on your computer or network.

Many software programs have certain guidelines you must follow when you create your password. Many, for example, require passwords to have a minimum length of six characters and use a mixture of numbers and letters. Suppose a software package requires a password with a length between six and ten characters, two of which must be numeric. Following these guidelines, the password JEAN5 is invalid (it is too short), but JEAN0512 is valid. This password also is easy for the user to remember — JEAN is the user's daughter's name and May 12 is Jean's birthday (05/12) — but not so simple that it will be guessed easily.

To provide authentication further, users sometimes are asked to enter one of several possible items of personal information that they choose randomly from information on file. Such items can include a spouse's first name, a birthdate or place of birth, or a mother's maiden name. As with a password, if the user's response does not match the information on file, access is denied.

POSSESSED OBJECTS A **possessed object** is any item that you must carry to gain access to a computer or computer facility. Examples of possessed objects are badges, cards, and keys. Possessed objects often are used in combination with personal identification numbers. A **personal identification number (PIN)** is a numeric password, either assigned by an organization or selected by you. Like the PIN you must enter when using an automatic teller machine (ATM) card, a PIN used with a possessed object provides an additional level of security.

WEB INFO
WEB INFO

For more information on personal identification numbers, visit the Discovering Computers 2000 Chapter 14 WEB INFO page (**www.scsite.com/ dc2000/ch14/webinfo.htm**) and click PINs.

PASSWORD PROTECTION

NUMBER OF CHARACTERS	POSSIBLE COMBINATIONS	AVERAGE TIME TO DISCOVER	
		HUMAN	COMPUTER
1	36	3 minutes	.000018 second
2	1,300	2 hours	.00065 second
3	47,000	3 days	.02 second
4	1,700,000	3 months	1 second
5	60,000,000	10 years	30 seconds
10	3,700,000,000,000,000	580 million years	59 years

- *Possible characters include the letters A-Z and numbers 0-9*
- *Human discovery assumes one try every 10 seconds*
- *Computer discovery assumes one million tries per second*
- *Average time assumes password would be discovered in approximately half the time it would take to try all possible combinations*

Figure 14-6 *This table shows the effect of increasing the length of a password made up of letters and numbers. The longer the password, the more effort required to discover it. Long passwords, however, are more difficult for users to remember.*

WEB INFO
WEB INFO

For more information on biometric devices, visit the Discovering Computers 2000 Chapter 14 WEB INFO page (www.scsite.com/dc2000/ch14/webinfo.htm) and click Biometric Devices.

BIOMETRIC DEVICES A **biometric device** authenticates a person requesting access by verifying personal characteristics such as fingerprints, hand size, signature and typing patterns, and retinal (eye) and voice patterns. A biometric device translates a personal characteristic into a digital code that is compared to a digital code stored in the computer. If the digital code in the computer does not match the personal characteristics code, access is denied.

Many types of biometric devices currently are in use to provide security. **Fingerprint** or **thumbprint scanners**, for example, are used to verify fingerprints. Biometric devices also can measure the shape, size, and other characteristics of a person's hand using **hand geometry systems** (Figure 14-7). **Biometric pens** measure the pressure exerted and the motion used to write signatures, while **keystroke analysis devices** measure typing patterns and rhythms. **Retinal scanners** (Figure 14-8) even can read patterns in the tiny blood vessels in the back of the eye, which are as unique as a fingerprint. Finally, biometric devices can verify a person's voice by digitizing spoken words and comparing them against previously recorded digital patterns.

Biometric devices are gaining popularity as a security precaution because they are a virtually foolproof method of identification and authentication. Unlike user IDs and passwords or possessed objects that people can lose, copy, duplicate, or steal, personal characteristics are unique and cannot be forgotten or misplaced. Biometric devices do have some disadvantages, however. If you cut your finger, for example, a fingerprint scanner might reject you; if you are nervous, a voice, signature, or typing pattern might not match the one on file. Biometric devices also can be more expensive, especially the initial investment in equipment, than other identification and authentication techniques and thus primarily are used by government security organizations, the military, and financial institutions that deal with highly sensitive data.

Figure 14-8 *A retinal scanner identifies a user by reading the tiny blood vessel patterns in the back of the eye.*

CALLBACK SYSTEM A callback system is an access control method sometimes used to authenticate remote users. With a **callback system**, you can connect to a computer only after the computer calls you back at a previously established telephone number. To initiate the callback system, you call the computer and enter a user ID and password. If these entries are valid, the computer instructs you to hang up and then calls you back at the previously established number. A callback system thus provides an additional layer of security: even if a person steals or guesses a user ID and password, that person also must be at the authorized telephone number to access the computer.

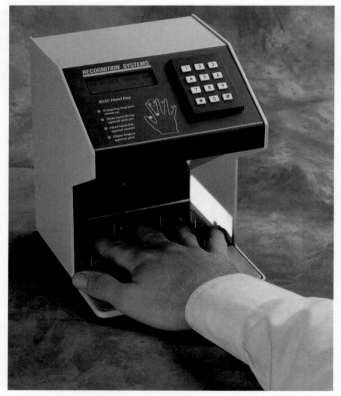

Figure 14-7 *A user's identity can be verified by his or her hand with a hand geometry system.*

Callback systems work best for users who regularly work at the same remote location, such as from home or a branch office. Mobile users that need to access a computer from different locations and telephone numbers can use a callback system, but they have to change the callback number stored by the callback system each time they move to a different location.

The authentication technique an organization uses should correspond to the degree of risk associated with the unauthorized access. In addition, an organization regularly should review users' authorization levels to determine if they still are appropriate.

No matter what type of identification and authentication techniques an organization uses, the computer should record both successful and unsuccessful access attempts in a file called an **audit trail** or **log**. Organizations should investigate unsuccessful access attempts immediately to ensure they were not attempted security breaks; they also should review successful access for irregularities, such as use of the computer after normal working hours or from remote computers.

In addition, organizations should have written policies regarding the use of computers by employees for personal reasons. Some organizations prohibit such use entirely, while others allow personal use on the employee's own time. Most organizations have informal policies, which are determined on a case-by-case basis. Whatever the policy, an organization should document the policy and explain it to employees.

Hardware Theft

Hardware theft and vandalism present a difficult security challenge. In the case of desktop and larger computers in a home or office, hardware theft generally is not a problem. To help minimize theft of computers and associated equipment, however, organizations can implement a variety of security precautions. Physical access controls, such as locked doors and windows, usually are adequate to protect the equipment, although many businesses, schools, and some homeowners install alarm systems to provide additional security. School computer labs and other areas with a large number of semi-frequent users often install additional physical security devices such as cables that lock the equipment to a desk, cabinet, or floor (Figure 14-9).

With portable equipment such as laptop computers or personal digital assistants (PDAs), hardware theft poses a more serious risk. Increasingly, businesses and schools are providing laptop computers to employees and students, in addition to loaning them out for short periods. Users of laptop computers must take special care to protect their equipment. High-end notebook computers, some of which cost more than $5,000, are particularly at risk; their size and weight make them easy to steal, and their value makes them tempting targets for thieves.

Common sense and a constant awareness of the risk are the best preventive measures against theft of laptop computers and other portable equipment. You should never, for example, leave a laptop computer unattended in a public place such as an airport or a restaurant or out in the open such as on the seat of a car. You also may want to use a physical device such as a cable to lock a portable computer temporarily to a desk or table. As a precaution in case of theft, you also should back up the files stored on your laptop computer regularly.

In addition to hardware theft, another area of concern for businesses and schools is

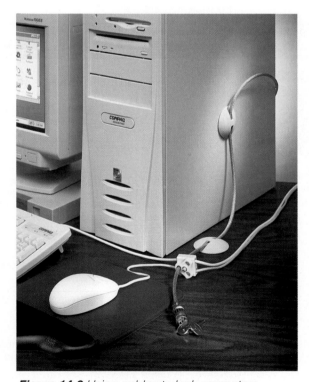

Figure 14-9 Using cables to lock computers can help prevent the theft of desktop and portable computer equipment.

vandalism. **Computer vandalism** takes many forms, from someone cutting a computer cable or deleting important files, to individuals breaking in a business or school computer lab and randomly smashing computers. Most organizations have written policies and procedures for dealing with the various types of vandalism.

Software Theft

WEB INFO
WEB INFO

For more information on an end-user license agreement, visit the Discovering Computers 2000 Chapter 14 WEB INFO page (**www.scsite.com/ dc2000/ch14/webinfo.htm**) and click EULA.

As with hardware theft and vandalism, **software theft** can take many forms — from someone physically stealing a DVD-ROM, CD-ROM, or floppy disk to intentional piracy of software. **Software piracy**, which is the unauthorized and illegal duplication of copyrighted software, is by far the most common form of software theft.

When you purchase software, you actually do not *own* the software; instead, you have purchased the right to use the software, as outlined in the software license. A **software license** is an agreement that provides specific conditions for use of the software,

which users must accept before using the software. The terms of a software license usually are displayed when you install the software, or, in the case of software downloaded via the Web, on a page at the manufacturer's site (Figure 14-10). Use of the software constitutes acceptance of the terms on the user's part.

The most common type of license included with software packages purchased by individual users is a **single-user license**, also called an **end-user license agreement (EULA)**. A single-user license agreement typically includes numerous conditions, including the following:

- Users can install the software on only *one* computer

- Users cannot install the software on a network, such a school computer lab network

- Users can make *one* copy for backup purposes

- Users cannot give copies to friends and colleagues

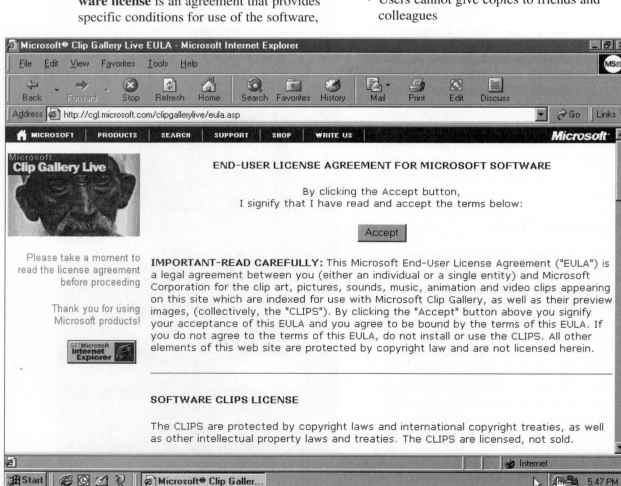

Figure 14-10 *When you download software from a Web site, typically you must accept the manufacturer's end-user license agreement online.*

Unless otherwise specified by a software license, you do not have the right to copy, loan, rent, or in any way distribute the software. Doing so not only is a violation of copyright law, it also is a federal crime. Despite this, experts estimate that, for every authorized copy of software in use, at least one unauthorized copy exists. One study reported that software piracy resulted in worldwide losses of more than $12 billion per year.

Software piracy continues for several reasons. In some countries, legal protection for software does not exist; while in others, laws rarely are enforced. In addition, many buyers believe they have the right to copy the software for which they have paid hundreds, even thousands of dollars. Finally, particularly in the case of floppy disks, software piracy is a simple crime to commit.

Software piracy, however, is a serious offense. For one, it introduces a number of risks into the software market: it increases the chance of viruses; reduces your ability to receive technical support; and significantly drives up the price of software for all users. Further, software companies take illegal copying seriously. In some cases, offenders have been prosecuted to the fullest extent of the law with penalties including fines up to $250,000 and five years in jail. To promote a better understanding of piracy problems and, if necessary, to take legal action, a number of major U.S. software companies formed the **Business Software Alliance (BSA)**. BSA operates a Web site (Figure 14-11) and antipiracy hotlines in the United States and more than 55 other countries.

Many organizations and businesses also have strict written policies governing the installation and use of software and enforce their rules by periodically checking computers to ensure that all software is licensed properly. If you are not completely familiar with your school or employer's policies governing installation of software, you should always

WEB INFO
WEB INFO

For more information on the Business Software Alliance, visit the Discovering Computers 2000 Chapter 14 WEB INFO page (**www.scsite.com/ dc2000/ch14/webinfo.htm**) and click BSA.

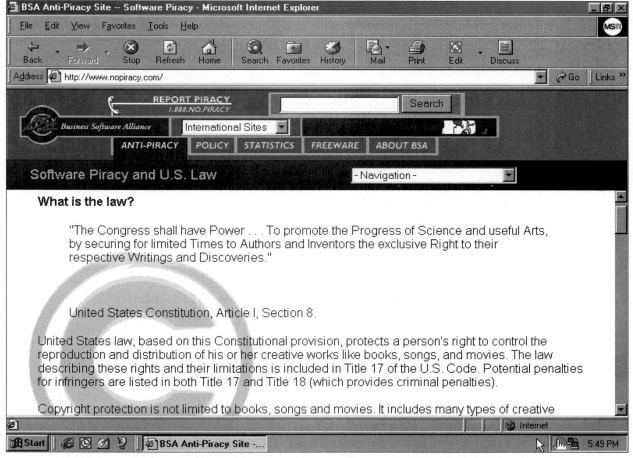

Figure 14-11 *The Business Software Alliance (BSA) Web site provides the latest information about software piracy. BSA fights against software piracy by conducting educational programs and operating antipiracy hotlines in the United States and more than 55 other countries.*

check with the information systems department or your school's technology coordinator.

To reduce software costs for organizations with large numbers of users, software vendors often offer special discount pricing or site licensing. With discount pricing, the more copies of a program an organization purchases, the greater the discount. Purchasing a software **site license** gives the buyer the right to install the software on multiple computers at a single site. Site license fees usually cost significantly less than purchasing individual copies of software for each computer.

Many software packages also have network versions, for which an organization also can purchase a network site license. A **network site license** allows network users to share a single copy of the software, which resides on the network server. Software companies typically price network software site licenses based on a fixed fee for an unlimited number of users, a maximum number of users, or on a per-user basis.

Information Theft

As discussed in Chapter 10, information is a valuable asset to an organization, and thus, if stolen, can cause as much damage as (if not more than) the theft of hardware or software. **Information theft** typically occurs for a variety of reasons — from organizations stealing or buying stolen information to learn about a competitor to individuals stealing credit card and telephone charge card numbers to make purchases. Information theft often is linked to other types of computer crime. An individual, for example, might first gain unauthorized access to a computer and then steal credit card numbers stored in a firm's accounting department.

WEB INFO

For more information on encryption, visit the Discovering Computers 2000 Chapter 14 WEB INFO page (**www.scsite.com/ dc2000/ch14/webinfo.htm**) and click Encryption.

Most organizations prevent information theft by implementing the user identification and authentication controls discussed earlier in this chapter. These controls, however, work best to prevent the theft of information that resides on computers located on an organization's premises. Information transmitted over networks offers a higher degree of risk because it can be intercepted during transmission. Portable computers that contain sensitive company information generally do not have the same level of access controls and, therefore, also carry a higher risk of information theft.

ENCRYPTION One way to protect sensitive data is to encrypt it. **Encryption** is the process of converting readable data into unreadable characters to prevent unauthorized access. Once data is encrypted, you can send it in e-mail messages or store it, just as with any other data. To read the data, the recipient must **decrypt**, or decipher, it into a readable form.

In the encryption process, the unencrypted, readable data is called **plaintext**, and the encrypted data is called **ciphertext**. To encrypt the data; that is, to convert the plaintext into ciphertext, the originator of the data applies a formula that uses a code, called an **encryption key**. The recipient of the data then uses an encryption key to decrypt it. Many data encryption methods exist. Figure 14-12 shows examples of some simple encryption methods. An encryption key often will use more than one of these methods, such as a combination of transposition and substitution. While most organizations use available software packages for encryption, some develop their own encryption programs.

The two basic types of encryption are private key and public key. With **private key encryption**, both the originator and recipient use the same encryption key to encrypt and decrypt the data. The most popular private key encryption system is the **data encryption standard** (**DES**), which is widely used by the U.S. government.

Public key encryption uses two encryption keys: a public key known to everyone and a private key known by only the sender or the receiver (Figure 14-13). For example, if the originator uses a public key to

SIMPLE ENCRYPTION METHODS

NAME	METHOD	PLAINTEXT	CIPHERTEXT	EXPLANATION
Transposition	Switch the order of characters	MICROPHONE	IMRCPOOHEN	Adjacent characters swapped
Substitution	Replace characters with others	SPEAKERS	ADVNQVXA	Each letter replaced with another
Expansion	Insert characters between existing characters	MODEM	MAOADAEAMA	Letter A inserted after each character
Compaction	Remove characters and store elsewhere	SOFTWARE	SOTWRE	Every third letter removed (F and A)

Figure 14-12 *This table shows four methods of encryption, which is the process of translating plaintext into ciphertext. Most encryption programs use a combination of these four methods.*

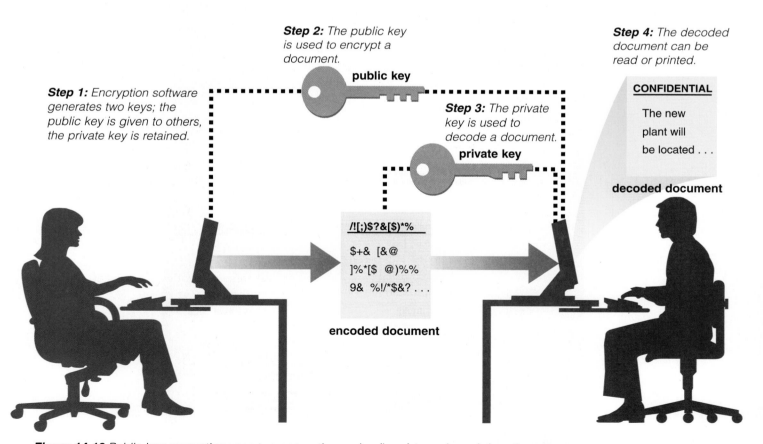

Step 2: *The public key is used to encrypt a document.*

public key

Step 4: *The decoded document can be read or printed.*

Step 1: *Encryption software generates two keys; the public key is given to others, the private key is retained.*

Step 3: *The private key is used to decode a document.*

private key

CONFIDENTIAL

The new plant will be located . . .

decoded document

/![;)$?&[$)*%

$+& [&@
]%*[$ @)%%
9& %!/*$&? . . .

encoded document

Figure 14-13 *Public key encryption uses two encryption codes (keys) to code and decode messages.*

encrypt data, then the recipient uses a private key to decipher the data. **RSA**, named from its inventors, Rivest, Shamir, and Adleman, is a powerful public key encryption technology used to encrypt data transmitted over the Internet. RSA technology is built into many software and public key encryption programs, including Pretty Good Privacy (PGP) and newer versions of Netscape Navigator and Microsoft Internet Explorer (Figure 14-14).

Since 1993, the U.S. government has proposed several ideas for developing a standard for voice and data encryption that would enable government agencies, such as the National Security Agency (NSA) and the Federal Bureau of Investigation (FBI), to monitor private communications. An early government proposal called for the use of an encryption formula implemented in a tamper-resistant microprocessor called the **Clipper chip**. Widespread opposition to this hardware

approach caused the idea to be abandoned. In its place, the government proposed a key escrow plan, similar to the public key encryption method. The government's **key escrow** plan proposed using independent escrow organizations that would have custody of private keys that could decode encrypted messages. If necessary, authorized government agencies could obtain the necessary key. This plan also has been opposed and has not yet been implemented.

System Failure

Theft is not the only cause of hardware, software, data, or information loss. Any of these also can occur during a **system failure**, which is the prolonged malfunction of a computer. System failures can be attributed to a variety of reasons which include aging hardware; natural disasters such as fires, floods, or storms; and events such as electrical power problems.

Figure 14-14 The upper window shows an e-mail message. The lower window shows the encrypted e-mail message.

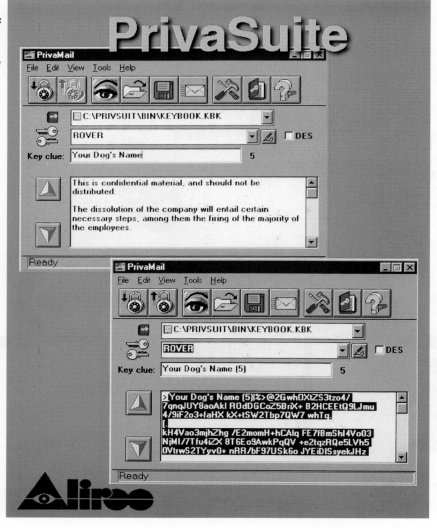

One of the more common causes of system failures is an electrical power variation. Electrical power variations can cause loss of data or loss of equipment. If the computer equipment is connected to a network, multiple systems can be damaged with a single power disturbance. Electrical disturbances include noise, undervoltages, and overvoltages.

Noise is any unwanted signal, usually varying quickly, that is mixed with the normal voltage entering the computer. Noise is caused by external devices such as fluorescent lighting, radios, and televisions, as well as from components within the computer itself. While noise generally is not a risk to hardware, software, or data, computer power supplies do filter out noise.

An **undervoltage** occurs when the electrical supply drops. In North America, electricity normally flows from the wall plug at approximately 120 volts. Any significant drop below 120 volts is considered an undervoltage. A **brownout** is a prolonged undervoltage; a **blackout** is a complete power failure. Undervoltages can cause data loss but generally do not cause equipment damage.

An **overvoltage**, or **power surge**, occurs when the incoming electrical power increases significantly above the normal 120 volts. A momentary overvoltage, called a **spike**, occurs when the power increase lasts for less than one millisecond (one thousandth of a second). Spikes are caused by uncontrollable disturbances such as lightning bolts or turning on a piece of equipment that is on the same electrical circuit. Overvoltages can cause immediate and permanent damage to hardware.

To protect against overvoltages and undervoltages, surge protectors are used. A **surge protector**, also called a **surge suppressor**, uses special electrical components to smooth out minor noise, provide a stable current flow, and keep an overvoltage from reaching the computer and other electronic equipment (Figure 14-15). Resembling a power strip, the computer and other devices plug into the surge protector, which plugs into the power source. The surge protector absorbs small overvoltages — generally without damage to the computer and equipment. Large overvoltages, such as those caused by a lightning strike, often causes the surge protector to fail in order to protect the computer and other equipment.

Surge protectors are not 100 percent effective. Large power surges can bypass the protector and repeated small overvoltages can weaken a surge protector permanently. Some experts recommend replacing surge protectors every two to three years. Typically, the amount of protection offered by a surge protector is proportional directly to its cost; that is, the more expensive, the more protection. The surge protector you purchase should indicate it meets the safety specification for surge suppression products as defined by the **Underwriters Laboratories** (**UL**) **1449 standard**, allowing no more than 500 maximum volts passing through the line. The surge protector also should have a Joule rating of at least 200. A **Joule** is the amount of energy a surge protection device can absorb before it can be damaged. The higher the Joule rating, the better the protection.

If your computer connects to a network or the Internet, you should be sure to have protection for your modem, telephone lines, and network lines. Many surge protectors include plug-ins for telephone lines and other cables. You also can purchase separate devices to protect these lines.

WEB INFO

For more information on a surge protector, visit the Discovering Computers 2000 Chapter 14 WEB INFO page (**www.scsite.com/ dc2000/ch14/webinfo.htm**) and click Surge Protector.

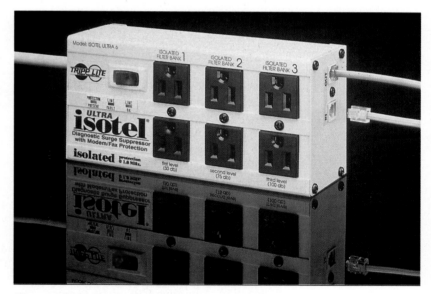

Figure 14-15 *Circuits inside a surge protector safeguard against overvoltages and undervoltages.*

WEB INFO
WEB INFO

For more information on
an uninterruptable power
supply, visit the
Discovering Computers
2000 Chapter 14 WEB INFO
page (**www.scsite.com/
dc2000/ch14/webinfo.htm**)
and click UPS.

For additional electrical protection, many users connect an uninterruptable power supply to the computer. An **uninterruptable power supply** (**UPS**), which connects between your computer and a power source, is a device that contains surge protection circuits and one or more batteries that can provide power during a temporary or permanent loss of power (Figure 14-16). Two types of UPSs

Figure 14-16 *If power fails, an uninterruptable power supply (UPS) uses batteries to provide electricity for a limited amount of time.*

are standby and online. A **standby UPS**, sometimes called an **offline UPS**, switches to battery power when a problem occurs in the power line. The amount of time a standby UPS allows you to continue working depends on the electrical requirements of the computer and the size of the batteries in the UPS. A UPS for a personal computer should provide from ten to thirty minutes of use in the case of a total power loss. This should be enough time to save current work and shut down the computer properly. An **online UPS** always runs off the battery, thus providing continuous protection. An online UPS, thus, is much more expensive than a standby UPS.

Backup Procedures

To prevent against data loss caused by a system failure, computer users should have backup procedures. A **backup** is a duplicate of a file, program, or disk that can be used if the original is lost, damaged, or destroyed. Thus, to back up a file means to make a copy, or duplicate, of it. In the case of a system failure or the discovery of corrupted files, you **restore** the files by copying the backed up files to their original location on the computer.

Backup copies normally are kept in fireproof safes or vaults, or offsite in a building separate from the computer site. Companies often use offsite storage so that a single disaster, such as a fire, does not destroy both the original and the backup copy of the data.

An organization or individual can perform three types of backup: full, differential, or incremental. A **full backup** duplicates all of the files in the computer. Because it involves copying all program and data files, a full backup provides the best protection against data loss. A full backup can take a long time, however; organizations thus often use full backups in combination with differential and incremental backups. A **differential backup** duplicates only the files that have changed since the last full backup. An **incremental backup** duplicates only the files that have changed since the last full or incremental backup.

The main difference between a differential backup and an incremental backup is the number of backup files and the time required for backup. With a differential backup, you always have two backups: the full backup and the differential backup of all changes since the last full backup. With incremental backups, you have the full backup copy and one or more incremental backup copies. The first incremental backup contains copies of files that have changed since the last full backup. Subsequent incremental backups contain copies of files that have changed since the previous incremental backup. For files that contain many changes and comprise a large portion of the total data, incremental backup usually is fastest. If files contain only a few changes, differential backups may be appropriate.

VARIOUS BACKUP METHODS

TYPE OF BACKUP	ADVANTAGES	DISADVANTAGES
Full	Fastest recovery method. All files are saved.	Longest backup time.
Differential	Fast backup method. Requires minimal space to back up.	Recovery is time consuming because need last full backup plus the differential backup.
Incremental	Fastest backup method. Requires minimal space to back up. Only most recent changes saved.	Recovery is most time consuming because need last full backup and all incremental backups since last full backup.

Figure 14-17 The advantages and disadvantages of various backup methods.

Figure 14-17 outlines the advantages and disadvantages of each type of backup.

Backup procedures specify a regular plan of copying and storing important data and program files. Generally, an organization develops backup procedures in which a full backup is performed at regular intervals, such as at the end of each week and at the end of the month. Between full backups, differential or incremental backups are performed. Figure 14-18 shows a sample approach for backing up a system for one month. This combination of full and incremental backups provides an efficient way of protecting data. Whatever backup procedures an organization adopts, they should be clearly stated, documented in writing, and followed consistently.

February 2001

Monday	Tuesday	Wednesday	Thursday	Friday	Sat/Sun
29 DAILY INCREMENTAL	30 DAILY INCREMENTAL	31 END OF MONTH FULL BACKUP	1 DAILY INCREMENTAL	2 WEEKLY FULL BACKUP	3/4
5 DAILY INCREMENTAL	6 DAILY INCREMENTAL	7 DAILY INCREMENTAL	8 DAILY INCREMENTAL	9 WEEKLY FULL BACKUP	10/11
12 DAILY INCREMENTAL	13 DAILY INCREMENTAL	14 DAILY INCREMENTAL	15 DAILY INCREMENTAL	16 WEEKLY FULL BACKUP	17/18
19 DAILY INCREMENTAL	20 DAILY INCREMENTAL	21 DAILY INCREMENTAL	22 DAILY INCREMENTAL	23 WEEKLY FULL BACKUP	24/25
26 DAILY INCREMENTAL	27 DAILY INCREMENTAL	28 END OF MONTH FULL BACKUP	1 DAILY INCREMENTAL	2 WEEKLY FULL BACKUP	3/4

Figure 14-18 This calendar shows a backup strategy for a month. The backup media used for Monday, Tuesday, Wednesday, and Thursday would be the same each week. The backup media used for the Friday backups would be used again the following month. A new medium would be used each month for the end-of-month backup. End-of-month backups usually are kept for at least one year.

Sometimes, a **three-generation backup policy** is used in which important individual files are backed up separately. The oldest copy of the file is called the **grandparent**. The second oldest copy of the file is called the **parent**. The most recent copy of the file is called the **child**.

Backup and restore programs are available from many sources including most developers of antivirus programs and utility software. Backup and restore programs also are included with most operating systems and with backup devices such as tape or cartridge disk drives.

Disaster Recovery Plan

Because the prolonged loss of computing capability can seriously damage an organization's ability to function, a disaster recovery plan should be developed. A **disaster recovery plan** is a written plan describing the steps an organization would take to restore computer operations in the event of a disaster. A disaster recovery plan contains four major components: the emergency plan, the backup plan, the recovery plan, and the test plan.

THE EMERGENCY PLAN An **emergency plan** specifies the steps to be taken immediately after a disaster strikes. The emergency plan usually is organized by type of disaster, such as fire, flood, or earthquake. Depending on the nature and extent of the disaster, some emergency procedures will differ. All emergency plans, however, should contain the following information:

1. Names and telephone numbers of people and organizations to be notified (e.g., management, fire department, police department)

2. Procedures to be followed with the computer equipment (e.g., equipment shutdown, power shutoff, file removal)

3. Employee evacuation procedures

4. Return procedures; that is, who can re-enter the facility and what actions they are to perform

THE BACKUP PLAN Once the procedures in the emergency plan have been executed, the next step is to follow the backup plan. The **backup plan** specifies how an organization will use backup files and equipment to resume information processing. Because an organization's normal location may be destroyed or unusable, the backup plan should specify the location of an alternate computer facility. The backup plan identifies these items:

1. The location of backup data, supplies, and equipment

2. The personnel responsible for gathering backup resources and transporting them to the alternate computer facility

3. A schedule indicating the order and approximate time each application should be up and running

For a backup plan to be successful, it is crucial that all critical resources are backed up; that is, hardware, software, data, facilities, supplies, and documentation. Because personnel could be injured in a disaster, it also is crucial that additional people, including possibly non-employees, are trained in the backup and recovery procedures.

The location of the alternate computer facility also is important. It should be close enough to be convenient, yet not too close that a single disaster, such as an earthquake, could destroy both the main and alternate computer facilities. The alternate computer facility might already have the necessary hardware, software, and communications equipment installed. To save on costs of maintaining this type of facility, the alternate computer facility might be an empty facility that can accommodate the necessary computer resources. Another alternative is to enter into a **reciprocal backup relationship** with another firm; that is, in case of disaster, one firm provides space and sometimes equipment to the other.

THE RECOVERY PLAN The **recovery plan** specifies the actions to be taken to restore full information processing operations. As with the emergency plan, the recovery plan differs for each type of disaster. To prepare for disaster recovery, planning committees should be established, with each one responsible for different forms of recovery. For example, one committee could be in charge of hardware replacement, while another could be responsible for software replacement.

THE TEST PLAN To provide assurance that the disaster plan is complete, it should be tested. A disaster recovery **test plan** contains information for simulating different levels of disasters and recording an organization's ability to recover. In a simulation, all personnel would be required to follow the steps outlined in the disaster recovery plan. Any needed recovery actions that are not specified in the plan should be added. Although simulations can be scheduled, the best test of the plan is to simulate a disaster without advance notice.

Developing a Computer Security Plan

The individual risks and safeguards previously mentioned and the disaster recovery plan all should be incorporated into an overall computer security plan. A **computer security plan** summarizes in writing all of the safeguards that are in place to protect an organization's information assets. A computer security plan should do the following:

1. Identify all information assets of an organization including hardware, software, documentation, procedures, people, data, facilities, and supplies.

2. Identify all security risks that may cause an information asset loss. Risks should be ranked from most likely to occur to least likely to occur. An estimated value should be placed on each risk including the value of lost business. For example, what is the estimated loss if customers cannot place orders for one hour, one day, or one week?

3. For each risk, identify the safeguards that exist to detect, prevent, and recover from a loss.

The computer security plan should be updated annually or more frequently for major changes in information assets, such as the addition of a new computer or the implementation of a new application. In developing the plan, you should keep in mind that some degree of risk is unavoidable. The more secure a system is, the more difficult it is for everyone to use. The goal of a computer security plan is to match an appropriate level of safeguards against the identified risks. Fortunately, most organizations will never experience a major information system disaster. Because many organizations and individuals rely heavily on computers, however, disaster recovery must be planned.

Companies and individuals who need help with computer security plans can contact the **International Computer Security Association** (**ICSA**) via the telephone or on the Web for assistance (Figure 14-19).

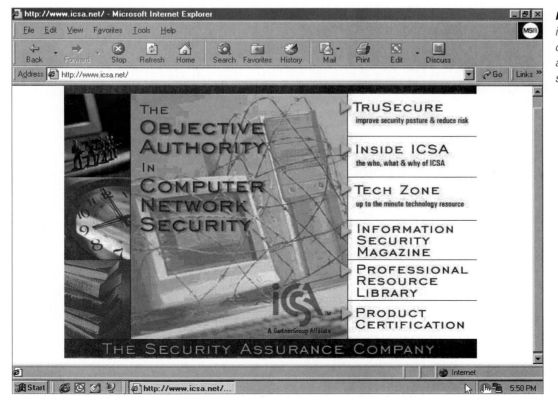

Figure 14-19 The ICSA is available for companies or individuals that need assistance with computer security plans.

INFORMATION PRIVACY

Information privacy refers to the right of individuals and organizations to deny or restrict the collection and use of information about them. In the past, information privacy was easier to maintain because information tended to be kept in separate locations: individual stores had their own credit files, government agencies had separate records, doctors had separate files, and so on. It is now, however, technically and economically feasible to store large amounts of related data about individuals in one database. Computers also can be used to monitor employee activities. As a result, many have concerns about how the unauthorized collection and use of data and monitoring affects their privacy.

Unauthorized Collection and Use of Information

Many individuals are surprised to learn that information provided for magazine subscriptions, product warranty registration cards, contest entry forms, and other documents often is sold to national marketing organizations. By combining this acquired data with other information obtained from public sources such as driver's license and vehicle registration information, national marketing organizations can create an electronic profile of an individual. This electronic profile then is sold to organizations that want to send information on their products, services, or causes to a specific group of individuals, such as all sports car owners over 40 years of age living in the southeastern United States. Direct marketing supporters say that using information in this way lowers overall selling costs, which, in turn, lowers product prices. Critics contend that the combined information in electronic profiles can reveal more about individuals than anyone has a right to know; they claim that, at a minimum, individuals should be informed that the information they furnish may be provided to others and have the right to deny such use. Figure 14-20 lists some techniques you can use to keep personal data private.

HOW TO SAFEGUARD PERSONAL INFORMATION

1. Fill in only necessary information on rebate, warranty, and registration forms.

2. Do not have your telephone number or social security number preprinted on personal checks.

3. Have an unlisted or unpublished telephone number.

4. If Caller ID is available in your area, find out how to block your number from displaying on the receiver's system.

5. Do not write your telephone number on charge or credit receipts.

6. Ask merchants to not write credit card numbers, telephone numbers, social security numbers, and drivers license numbers on the back of your personal checks.

7. Purchase goods with cash, rather than credit or checks.

8. Avoid shopping clubs and buyers' cards.

9. If a merchant asks personal questions, find out why before releasing the information.

10. Ask, in writing, to be removed from mailing lists.

11. Obtain your credit report once a year and correct any errors.

12. Request a free copy of your medical record once a year from the Medical Information Bureau.

Figure 14-20 Techniques to keep personal data private.

The concern about privacy has led to federal and state laws regarding the storage and disclosure of personal data (Figure 14-21). Common points in some of these laws include the following:

1. Information collected and stored about individuals should be limited to what is necessary to carry out the function of the business or government agency collecting the data.

2. Once collected, provisions should be made to restrict access to the data to those employees within the organization who need access to it to perform their job duties.

3. Personal information should be released outside the organization collecting the data only when the person has agreed to its disclosure.

4. When information is collected about an individual, the individual should know that the data is being collected and have the opportunity to determine the accuracy of the data.

DATE	LAW	PURPOSE
1997	No Electronic Theft (NET) Act	Closed a narrow loophole in the law that allowed people to give away copyrighted material (such as software) on the Internet without legal repercussions.
1996	National Information Infrastructure Protection Act	Penalizes theft of information across state lines, threats against networks, and computer system trespassing.
1994	Computer Abuse Amendments Act	Amends 1984 act to outlaw transmission of harmful computer code such as viruses.
1992	Cable Act	Extends privacy of Cable Communications Policy Act of 1984 to include cellular and other wireless services.
1991	Telephone Consumer Protection Act	Restricts activities of telemarketers.
1988	Computer Matching and Privacy Protection Act	Regulates the use of government data to determine the eligibility of individuals for federal benefits.
1988	Video Privacy Protection Act	Forbids retailers from releasing or selling video-rental records without customer consent or a court order.
1986	Electronic Communications Privacy Act (ECPA)	Provides the same right of privacy protection for the postal delivery service and telephone companies to the new forms of electronic communications, such as voice mail, e-mail, and cellular telephones.
1984	Cable Communications Policy Act	Regulates disclosure of cable TV subscriber records.
1984	Computer Fraud and Abuse Act	Outlaws unauthorized access of federal government computers.
1978	Right to Financial Privacy Act	Strictly outlines procedures federal agencies must follow when looking at customer records in banks.
1974	Privacy Act	Forbids federal agencies from allowing information to be used for a reason other than for which it was collected.
1974	Family Educational Rights and Privacy Act	Gives students and parents access to school records and limits disclosure of records to unauthorized parties.
1970	Fair Credit Reporting Act	Prohibits credit reporting agencies from releasing credit information to unauthorized people and allows consumers to review their credit records.

Figure 14-21 Summary of the major U.S. government laws concerning privacy.

Several federal laws deal specifically with computers. The 1986 **Electronic Communications Privacy Act (ECPA)** provides the same protection that covers mail and telephone communications to electronic communications such as voice mail. The 1988 **Computer Matching and Privacy Protection Act** regulates the use of government data to determine the eligibility of individuals for federal benefits. The 1984 and 1994 **Computer Fraud and Abuse Acts** outlaw unauthorized access to federal government computers and the transmission of harmful computer code such as viruses.

One law with an apparent legal loophole is in the 1970 **Fair Credit Reporting Act.** Although the act limits the rights of others viewing a credit report to those with a legitimate business need, a legitimate business need is not defined. The result is that just about anyone can say they have a legitimate business need and gain access to someone's credit report. Credit reports contain much more than just balance and payment information on mortgages and credit cards. The largest credit bureaus maintain information on family income, number of dependents, employment history, bank balances, driving records, lawsuits, and Social Security numbers. In total, these credit bureaus have more than 400 million records on more than 160 million people. Some credit bureaus sell combinations of the data they have stored in their databases to direct marketing organizations. Because of continuing complaints about credit report errors and the invasion of privacy, the U.S. Congress is considering a major revision of the Fair Credit Reporting Act.

Employee Monitoring

Employee monitoring involves the use of computers to observe, record, and review an individual's use of a computer, including communications such as e-mail, keyboard activity (used to measure productivity), and Internet sites visited. It is legal, for example, for an employer to use a software program that scans your computer to determine the content on the hard disk.

A frequently discussed issue is whether or not an employer has the right to read employee e-mail messages. Actual policies vary widely with some organizations declaring that e-mail messages will be reviewed regularly and others stating that e-mail is considered private. Most organizations, estimated in one study to be approximately 75 percent, do not have formal e-mail policies, which, in effect, means that e-mail can be read without employee notification. One survey discovered that more than 30 percent of companies search and/or read employee files, voice mail, e-mail, and other networking communications.

At present, no laws exist relating to e-mail. The 1986 **Electronic Communications Privacy Act** does not cover communications within an organization. Because many believe that such internal communications should be private, several lawsuits have been filed against employers. In response to the issue of workplace privacy, the U.S. Congress proposed the **Privacy for Consumers and Workers Act**, which states that employers must notify employees if they are monitoring electronic communications. Supporters of the legislation hope that it also will restrict the types and amount of monitoring that employers can conduct legally.

ETHICS AND THE INFORMATION AGE

As with any powerful technology, computers can be used for both good and bad actions. The standards that determine whether an action is good or bad are called ethics. **Computer ethics** are the moral guidelines that govern the use of computers and information systems (Figure 14-22). Five areas of computer ethics discussed frequently are unauthorized use of computer systems, software theft (piracy), information privacy, information accuracy, and codes of ethical conduct. Unauthorized use, software piracy, and information privacy were discussed earlier in this chapter. The following section deals with the accuracy of computer information and codes of conduct.

Information Accuracy

Organizations have been concerned constantly about the accuracy of computer input. Inaccurate input can result in erroneous information and incorrect decisions based on that information. **Information accuracy** today is even more of an issue because many users access information maintained by other organizations, such as on the Internet. Sometimes, the organization providing access to the information did not create the information. An example is the airline flight schedules available from several online service providers. The question that arises is, who is responsible for the accuracy of the information? Does the responsibility rest solely with the original creator of the information or does the service that passes along the information also have some responsibility to verify its accuracy? Legally, these questions have not been resolved.

	ETHICAL	UNETHICAL
1. A company requires employees wear badges that track their whereabouts while at work.	☐	☐
2. A supervisor reads an employee's e-mail.	☐	☐
3. An employee uses his computer at work to send e-mail to a friend.	☐	☐
4. An employee sends an e-mail message to several co-workers and blind copies his supervisor.	☐	☐
5. An employee forwards an e-mail message to a third party without permission from the sender of the message.	☐	☐
6. An employee uses her computer at work to complete a homework assignment for school.	☐	☐
7. The vice president of your Student Government Association (SGA) downloads a photograph from the Web and uses it in a flier recruiting SGA members.	☐	☐
8. A student copies text from the Web and uses it in a research paper for his English Composition class.	☐	☐
9. An employee sends political campaign material to individuals on her employer's mailing list.	☐	☐
10. As an employee in the registration office, you have access to student grades. You look up grades for your friends so they do not have to wait for delivery of grade reports from the postal service.	☐	☐
11. An employee makes a copy of software and installs it on her computer at home. No one uses her computer at home while she is at work, and she uses her computer at home only to finish projects from work.	☐	☐
12. An employee that has been laid off installs a computer virus on his employer's computer.	☐	☐

Figure 14-22 Indicate whether you think the situation described is ethical or unethical. Discuss your answers with your instructor and other students.

In addition to concerns about the accuracy of computer input, some people have raised questions about the ethics of using computers to alter output, primarily graphic output such as retouched photographs. Using graphics equipment and software, photographs can be digitized and edited to add, change, or remove images (Figure 14-23). One group that is opposed to any manipulation of an image is the National Press Photographers Association. It believes that allowing even the slightest alteration eventually could lead to deliberately misleading photographs. Others believe that digital photograph retouching is acceptable as long as the significant content or meaning of the photograph is not changed. Digital retouching is another area where legal precedents have not yet been established.

Codes of Conduct

Recognizing that individuals and organizations need specific standards for the ethical use of computers and information systems, a number of computer-related organizations have established **codes of conduct**, which are written guidelines that help determine whether a specific computer action is ethical or unethical (Figure 14-24). Many businesses have adopted similar codes of conduct and made them known to their employees.

One of the problems with ethical issues in business is that some people believe that ethical decisions are the responsibility of management, not employees. This often is true in service departments, such as information systems or accounting, whose organizational function can be interpreted as providing information or services requested by management. Establishing codes of conduct that apply to an entire organization can help all employees, including management, make ethical decisions by providing a standard against which they can measure their actions.

Figure 14-23 *A digitally altered photograph shows sports star Michael Jordan (born 1963) meeting famous scientist Albert Einstein (who died in 1955).*

CODE OF CONDUCT

1. **Computers may not be used to harm other people.**

2. **Employees may not interfere with other's computer work.**

3. **Employees may not meddle in other's computer files.**

4. **Computers may not be used to steal.**

5. **Computers may not be used to bear false witness.**

6. **Employees may not copy or use software illegally.**

7. **Employees may not use other's computer resources without authorization.**

8. **Employees may not use other's output.**

9. **Employees shall consider the social impact of programs and systems they design.**

10. **Employees should always use computers in a way that demonstrates consideration and respect for fellow humans.**

Figure 14-24 *A sample code of conduct that an employer may distribute to employees.*

INTERNET SECURITY AND PRIVACY ISSUES

Information transmitted over networks has a higher degree of security risk than information kept on the organization's premises. Many security issues related to the Internet were addressed in this and previous chapters. For example, Chapter 7 presented cookies, which often raise concerns about information privacy.

In addition to identification and authentication techniques presented earlier in this chapter, intranets can use firewalls to prevent unauthorized access to data and information. On a vast network such as the Internet with no central administrator, the risk is even greater; every computer along the route your data takes can look at what is being sent or received. Fortunately, most Web browsers and many Web sites use techniques to keep data secure and private.

Internet Encryption

To provide secure data transmission, many Web browsers use encryption. Newer versions of Netscape Navigator and Microsoft Internet Explorer, for example, use RSA, which recall is a very popular public key encryption technology. Most browsers offer at least a 40-bit encryption but also provide for a higher level of protection at 128-bit encryption for applications requiring more security, such as credit card or other financial transactions with banks, brokerage firms, or online retailers. Two popular uses of encryption on the Internet include Secure Sockets Layer and digital signatures.

SECURE SOCKETS LAYER One of the more popular Internet encryption methods is **Secure Sockets Layer (SSL)**, which provides two-way encryption along the entire route data travels to and from your computer. SSL uses a private key to encrypt data. Web pages that use SSL typically begin with the https protocol, instead of the http protocol (Figure 14-25). Web servers that use SSL sometimes are called **secure servers**.

DIGITAL SIGNATURES A **digital signature**, also called a **digital ID**, is an encrypted code that a person, Web site, or company attaches to an electronic message. Digital signatures often are used to ensure that an impostor is not participating in an Internet transaction. Digital signatures use a public key to encrypt the signature; some also encrypt the message.

A digital signature is a type of digital certificate; another type is e-money or digital cash, which was discussed in Chapter 7. A **certificate** or **digital certificate** is a notice that guarantees a user or a Web site is legitimate. A **certificate authority (CA)** is an authorized company or person that issues and verifies digital certificates. Thus, to obtain a digital signature or digital cash, you apply for the digital certificate from a certificate authority (Figure 14-26). Your digital certificate typically contains your name, your public key and its expiration date, the issuing CA's name and signature, and the serial number of the certificate.

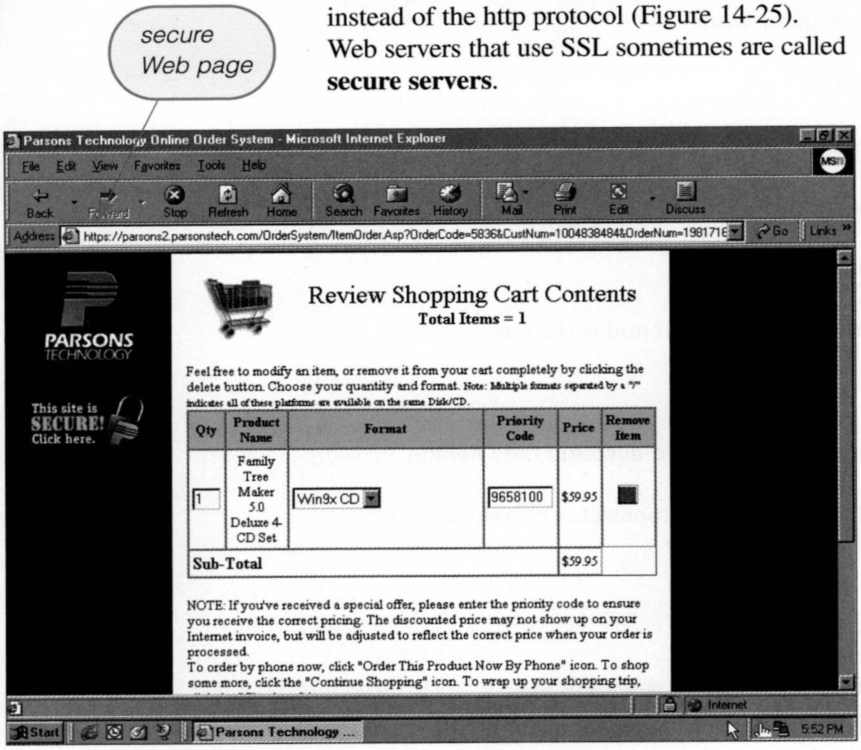

secure
Web page

Figure 14-25 *Secure Web pages often begin with the https protocol instead of the http protocol.*

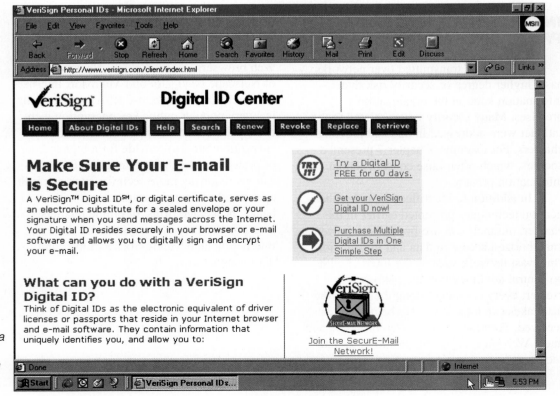

Figure 14-26 *VeriSign is a certificate authority that issues and verifies digital cerificates.*

Objectionable Materials on the Internet

The most discussed ethical issue concerning the Internet is the availability of objectionable material, such as racist literature and obscene pictures. Some believe that such materials should be banned, while others believe that the materials should be restricted and unavailable to minors. Opponents argue that banning any materials violates constitutional guarantees of free speech. Responding to pressure for restrictions, in February 1996, President Clinton signed the **Communications Decency Act**, which made it a criminal offense to distribute indecent or patently offensive material online. The law was appealed immediately and, in June 1996, it was declared unconstitutional.

One approach to restricting access to certain material is a rating system similar to those used for videos (Figure 14-27). If content at the Web site goes beyond the rating limitations set in the Web browser software, you are not allowed access to the site. Concerned parents can set the rating limitations and prevent them from being changed by using a password.

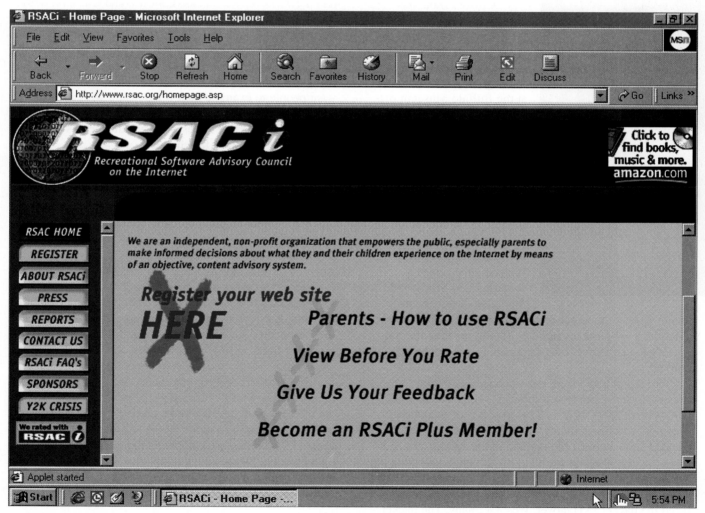

Figure 14-27 *Many Web browsers use the ratings of the Recreational Software Advisory Council on the Internet (RSACi), which allows you to specify a rating level for material unsuitable for minors.*

TECHNOLOGY TRAILBLAZER

CLIFFORD STOLL

cuckoo's egg — an egg laid in the nest of another bird
snake oil — colloquialism for a worthless medicine
sold as a cure-all

Technology Trailblazers have invented computer hardware, developed computer software, changed the way individuals and organizations use computers, and led prominent companies in the computer industry. Clifford Stoll, however, does not create computer technology. Instead, Stoll provokes people to *think* about how they use computer technology.

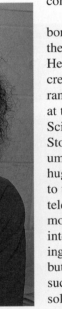

Clifford Stoll was born in Buffalo, New York, the son of a hotel bartender. He was an intelligent, creative boy with a wide-ranging curiosity. A curator at the Buffalo Museum of Science recalls a preteen Stoll appearing at the museum's doorstep, lugging a huge press camera, asking to use the astronomy lab's telescope to photograph the moon. Stoll nurtured his interest in astronomy working summers at the museum, but found time to master such singular topics as soldering and Morse code. Stoll also developed a unique style — a mentor recalls that when Stoll house-sat, he let the lawn grow all summer, finally mowing the message, Welcome Home, into the turf before the owners returned.

Stoll graduated from the University at Buffalo as an astrophysicist and took a job as systems manager at the Lawrence Berkley Lab. There, a 75-cent accounting discrepancy (a few minutes worth of computer time) revealed an unauthorized presence in the system. Instead of simply expelling the intruder, Stoll spent a year tracking the elusive hacker. Following the trail through computer networks and agencies worldwide, in 1989, Stoll finally traced the hacker to Hanover, West Germany. The hacker turned out to be part of a spy ring selling computer secrets to the Soviet Union's KGB for money and drugs.

Stoll's adventure made him a national figure. In *The Cuckoo's Egg: Tracking a Spy Through the Maze of Computer Espionage*, Stoll recounted the first true tale of computer spying. The book was a best-seller that espionage author Tom Clancy called, "a spy story for the 90s." Soon recognized as an authority on computer security, Stoll gave talks before such prestigious groups as NSA, the CIA, and the U.S. Senate.

Yet, as he lectured, Stoll started to ask questions about the way people use computers and networks. Does the Internet really bring people together? Can computers and networks replace books, libraries, and teachers? Why do networks promise so much more than they deliver? In 1995, Stoll wrote *Silicon Snake Oil: Second Thoughts on the Information Highway*, a book he calls a "perplexed meditation." Stoll maintains the book is not an anti-computer tirade ("I like them a lot"). He does, however, want people to examine their relationship with computer technology. "This idea that you must be online in order to have a rich life, I feel at best it's unchallenged. At worst it's a simple and gross falsehood."

Computers and the Internet deliver a great deal of data (perhaps too much) and some information. Yet, Stoll insists that a huge gap exists between information and wisdom, which is gained through experience and judgment. "Life in the real world is far more interesting, far more important, far richer, than anything you'll ever find on a computer screen." No matter how realistic, a virtual-reality game on cave exploring is far different from the actual experience of exploring a cave. "Wisdom comes from knowing how to deal with people and deal with information and deal with the environment around us. That takes time. You can't download it in an evening."

For Stoll, what is most important is how individuals use computers. "So what if you've got a fast computer… So what? Is there any content there? Are you doing something creative with it?" He insists he is not an authority, but Clifford Stoll has inspired both enthusiastic agreement and hearty rejection. Above all, he has made people think about the way they use computers today and their impact on tomorrow. "Makes me wonder what history we're leaving behind. Footprints across an artificial reality are as evanescent as data on the Ethernet."

COMPANY ON THE CUTTING EDGE
COMPANY ON THE CUTTING EDGE

NETWORK ASSOCIATES, INC.

You feel it first in the pit of your stomach, a sinking, queasy sensation. Next, your heart begins racing, your palms begin sweating, and your hands start shaking. The symptoms snowball, and you cannot do much to alleviate your suffering once you have been exposed. Few feelings compare to the ones experienced by those exposed to a virus — a computer virus, that is.

Viruses come in a wide array of types, but they all destroy data; hence, the symptoms described above. With Internet usage at an all-time high, increasingly more people than ever before are likely to pick up a computer virus. Fortunately, industry has addressed the need for added security and detection, with one company holding the lion's share of antidotes. Network Associates, Inc., head-quartered in Santa Clara, California, is the number one provider of antivirus and network security software.

Network Associates, Inc. was created by the 1997 merger of McAfee Associates and Network General. Although Network Associates caters mainly to corporate networks, several recent acquisitions have enabled it to broaden its offering of products and support, namely Dr. Solomon's Group (the number one antivirus company in Europe), CyberMedia, Pretty Good Privacy, and others. These acquisitions have added to Network Associates' ability to provide solutions to a wider range of users. A current estimate is that Network Associates' products reside on more than 60 million desktops around the world. With more than 2,500 employees and 1997 revenues of $727 million, Network Associates continues to grow impressively. By late 1998, Network Associates had displaced its main competitor, Symantec, as the antivirus market leader. A recent Dataquest report that analyzed the antivirus market said, "The clear leader in the antivirus market is Network Associates."

Its growth is due partly to shrewd acquisitions as well as market forces. Analysts predict that the market will continue to consolidate (e.g., more antivirus companies will merge) and few new companies will emerge. Another reason for growth is good, old-fashioned value. One of Network Associates' more popular products is Total Virus Defense (TVD), which provides antivirus defenses at several points: the desktop, the file server, the groupware server, and the Internet gateway.

The McAfee Software division of Network Associates concentrates on desktop products, and it has won several awards and accolades in recent years. The company recently ousted Symantec from the number two spot in utility software publishing (Microsoft is number one), and garnered awards from *PC Guide* and *Windows Magazine*, as well as two of *PC Computing's* Most Valuable Product (MVP) Awards.

A McAfee Software product that contributes greatly to the division's success is the recently released McAfee Office, which combines ten award-winning utilities in one product. In the past, users needed to install several different utility programs to ensure that their personal computers were not only protected from viruses and destructive code, but that the machines were optimized and in good working order. Naturally, because several products were involved, features overlapped. "McAfee Office is the first and only product in the marketplace to offer ten utilities in one complete solution," explains Peter Stewart, General Manager of McAfee Software. McAfee Office, he continues, "is a much greater value than our nearest competitor. Almost half of the products in McAfee Office have been on the Top-10 Retail Best Seller's list in the last year."

If any further proof was needed to place Network Associates at the top of the antivirus heap, consider this: all entry points within the U.S. Department of Defense (DOD) are guarded by Network Associates TVD. The DOD has the world's largest private network, with more than three million nodes, including the Army, Air Force, Navy, Marines, all DOD employee home computers, and all DOD-owned computers. In short, Network Associates' products not only are protecting countless users from malice every day, they also are defending the entire U.S. armed forces. And that in itself ought to make you feel better.

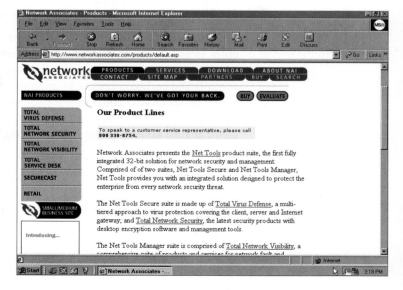

IN BRIEF   www.scsite.com/dc2000/ch14/brief.htm

WEB INSTRUCTIONS: *To display this page from the Web, launch your browser and enter the URL, www.scsite.com/dc2000/ch14/brief.htm. Click the links for current and additional information. To listen to an audio version of this IN BRIEF, click the Audio button to the right of the title, IN BRIEF, at the top of the page. To play the audio, RealPlayer must be installed on your computer (download by clicking here).*

1. What Are the Various Types of Security Risks that Can Threaten Computers?

A **computer security risk** is any event or action that could cause a loss of or damage to computer hardware, software data, information, or processing capability. Computer security risks include computer viruses, unauthorized access and use, hardware theft, software theft, information theft, and system failure. **Safeguards** are protective measures that can be taken to minimize or prevent the consequences of computer security risks. A **computer virus** is a potentially damaging computer program designed to affect or infect a computer negatively by altering the way it works. **Unauthorized access** is the use of a computer or network without permission; **unauthorized use** is the use of a computer or its data for unapproved or possibly illegal activities. An individual who tries to access a computer or network illegally is called a **cracker** or a **hacker**. **Hardware theft**, **software theft**, and **information theft** present difficult security challenges. The most common form of software theft is **software piracy**, which is the unauthorized and illegal duplication of copyrighted software. A **system failure** is the prolonged malfunction of a computer.

2. How Does a Computer Virus Work and What Steps Can Individuals Take to Prevent Viruses?

A virus spreads when users share the host program to which the virus is attached. A virus can replace the boot program with an infected version (**boot sector virus**), attach itself to a file (**file virus**), hide within a legitimate program (**Trojan horse virus**), or use an application's macro language to hide virus code (**macro virus**). The virus is activated when a certain action takes place (**a logic bomb**) or at a specific time (**a time bomb**). Viruses can be prevented by installing an antivirus program, write-protecting a **rescue disk** or **emergency disk**, never starting a computer with a disk in drive A, scanning floppy disks for viruses, checking downloaded programs, and regularly backing up files.

3. How Can a Computer Be Safeguarded?

An **antivirus program** protects a computer against viruses by identifying and removing any computer viruses found in memory. **Access controls** prevent unauthorized access and use by defining who can access a computer, when they can access it, and what actions they can take. Physical access controls and common sense can minimize hardware theft. A **software license** addresses software piracy by specifying conditions for software use. Encryption reduces information theft by converting readable data into unreadable characters. **Surge protectors** and **uninterruptable power supplies** guard against system failure by controlling power irregularities.

IN BRIEF www.scsite.com/dc2000/ch14/brief.htm

 SHELLY CASHMAN SERIES®
DISCOVERING COMPUTERS 2000

■ Student Exercises
WEB INFO
IN BRIEF
KEY TERMS
AT THE MOVIES
CHECKPOINT
AT ISSUE
CYBERCLASS
HANDS ON
NET STUFF
■ Special Features
TIMELINE 2000
GUIDE TO WWW SITES
MAKING A CHIP
BUYER'S GUIDE 2000
CAREERS 2000
TRENDS 2000
CHAT
INTERACTIVE LABS
NEWS
HOME

 ### 4. Why Is Computer Backup Important and How Is It Accomplished?

A **backup** is a duplicate of a file, program, or disk that can be used if the original is lost, damaged, or destroyed. In case of system failure or the discovery of corrupted files, the backup can be used to **restore** the files by copying the backed up files to their original location. <u>Backup procedures</u> specify a regular plan of copying and storing important data and program files. Organizations can accomplish a backup using one of, or combinations of, three methods: a **full backup**, which duplicates all files; a **differential backup**, which duplicates only files changed since the last full backup; or an **incremental backup**, which duplicates only files changed since the last full or incremental backup.

 ### 5. What Are the Components of a Disaster Recovery Plan?

A <u>disaster recovery plan</u> is a written plan describing the steps an organization would take to restore computer operations in the event of a disaster. A disaster recovery plan has four major components. An **emergency plan** specifies the steps to be taken immediately after a disaster strikes. A **backup plan** details how an organization will use backup files and equipment to resume information processing. A **recovery plan** stipulates the actions to be taken to restore full information processing operations. A **test plan** contains information for simulating different levels of disasters and recording an organization's ability to recover.

 ### 6. What Are Issues Relating to Information Privacy?

<u>Information privacy</u> refers to the right of individuals and organizations to deny or restrict the collection and use of information about them. Information privacy issues include unauthorized collection and use of information and employee monitoring. Unauthorized collection and use of information involves the compilation of data about an individual from a variety of sources. The data is combined to create an electronic profile that, without an individual's permission, may be sold to other organizations. **Employee monitoring** involves the use of computers to observe, record, and review an individual's use of a computer, including communications, keyboard activity, and Internet sites visited.

 ### 7. What Are Ethical Issues with Respect to the Information Age?

Computer ethics are the moral guidelines that govern the use of computers and information systems. Unauthorized use of computer systems, software theft, and information privacy are frequently discussed ethical issues. Other important <u>ethical issues</u> are the responsibility for **information accuracy** and **codes of conduct** that help determine whether a specific computer action is ethical or unethical.

8. What Are Internet-Related Security and Privacy Issues?

Information transmitted over networks has a higher degree of security risk than information kept on an organization's premises. On a vast network such as the Internet, the risk is even greater. To provide <u>secure data transmission</u>, many Web browsers use Internet encryption methods such as **Secure Socket Layers** and **digital signatures**. The most discussed ethical issue concerning the Internet is the availability of objectionable material.

Shelly
Cashman
Series.

DISCOVERING
COMPUTERS
2000

KEY TERMS   www.scsite.com/dc2000/ch14/terms.htm

WEB INSTRUCTIONS: *To display this page from the Web, launch your browser and enter the URL, www.scsite.com/dc2000/ch14/terms.htm. Scroll through the list of terms. Click a term to display its definition and a picture. Click KEY TERMS on the left to redisplay the KEY TERMS page. Click the TO WEB button for current and additional information about the term from the Web. To see animations, Shockwave and Flash Player must be installed on your computer (download by clicking here).*

access control (14.6)
antivirus program (14.4)
audit trail (14.9)
authentication (14.6)
backup (14.16)
backup plan (14.18)
backup procedures (14.17)
biometric device (14.8)
biometric pens (14.8)
blackout (14.15)
boot sector virus (14.3)
brownout (14.15)
Business Software Alliance (BSA) (14.11)
callback system (14.8)
certificate (14.26)
certificate authority (CA) (14.26)
child (14.18)
ciphertext (14.12)
Clipper chip (14.14)
codes of conduct (14.24)
Communications Decency Act (14.27)
computer crime (14.2)
computer ethics (14.23)
Computer Fraud and Abuse Acts (14.22)
Computer Matching and Privacy Protection Act (14.22)
computer security plan (14.19)
computer security risk (14.2)
computer vandalism (14.10)
computer virus (14.2)
cracker (14.6)
data encryption standard (DES) (14.12)
decrypt (14.12)
differential backup (14.16)
digital certificate (14.26)
digital ID (14.26)
digital signature (14.26)
disaster recovery plan (14.18)
Electronic Communications Privacy Act (ECPA) (14.22)
emergency disk (14.6)
emergency plan (14.18)
employee monitoring (14.22)
encryption (14.12)
encryption key (14.12)
end-user license agreement (EULA) (14.10)

TO WEB

HAND GEOMETRY SYSTEM: Biometric device that provides security by measuring the shape, size, and other characteristics of a person's hand. The measurements are used to verify a user's identity. (14.8)

Fair Credit Reporting Act (14.22)
file virus (14.3)
fingerprint scanners (14.8)
full backup (14.16)
grandparent (14.18)
hacker (14.6)
hand geometry systems (14.8)
hardware theft (14.9)
identification (14.6)
incremental backup (14.16)
information accuracy (14.23)
information privacy (14.20)
information theft (14.12)
inoculate (14.5)
International Computer Security Association (ICSA) (14.19)
Joule (14.15)
key escrow (14.14)
keystroke analysis devices (14.8)
log (14.9)
logic bomb (14.4)
macro virus (14.3)
network site license (14.12)
noise (14.15)
offline UPS (14.16)
online UPS (14.16)
overvoltage (14.15)

parent (14.18)
password (14.6)
personal identification number (PIN) (14.7)
plaintext (14.12)
polymorphic virus (14.5)
possessed object (14.7)
power surge (14.15)
Privacy for Consumers and Workers Act (14.22)
private key encryption (14.12)
public key encryption (14.12)
quarantine a file (14.5)
reciprocal backup relationship (14.18)
recovery plan (14.18)
rescue disk (14.6)
restore (14.16)
retinal scanners (14.8)
RSA (14.14)
safeguards (14.2)
secure servers (14.26)
Secure Sockets Layer (SSL) (14.26)
single-user license (14.10)
software license (14.10)
software piracy (14.10)
software theft (14.10)
spike (14.15)
standby UPS (14.16)
stealth virus (14.5)
surge protector (14.15)
surge suppressor (14.15)
system failure (14.14)
test plan (14.19)
three-generation backup policy (14.18)
thumbprint scanners (14.8)
time bomb (14.4)
Trojan horse virus (14.3)
unauthorized access (14.6)
unauthorized use (14.6)
undervoltage (14.15)
Underwriters Laboratories (UL) 1449 standard (14.15)
uninterruptable power supply (UPS) (14.16)
user identification (14.6)
virus signature (14.5)
worm (14.4)

CHAPTER 1 2 3 4 5 6 7 8 9 10 11 12 13 **14** INDEX

AT THE MOVIES www.scsite.com/dc2000/ch14/movies.htm

WELCOME to VIDEO CLIPS from CNN

WEB INSTRUCTIONS: *To display this page from the Web, launch your browser and enter the URL, www.scsite.com/dc2000/ch14/movies.htm. Click a picture to view a video. After watching the video, close the video window and then complete the exercise by answering the questions about the video. To view the videos, RealPlayer must be installed on your computer (download by clicking here).*

1 Code Crackers

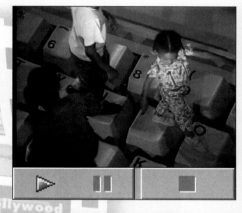

Governments and businesses rely on the security of encryption for their more confidential documents. But even the most complicated encryption code can be broken. Because privacy code can be broken, the U.S. government has placed restrictions on encryption code technology that is exported. Do you agree with these government restrictions? Should governments and companies be allowed to restrict encryption? What is DES (data encryption standards)?

2 Internet Copyright

Intellectual property protection is a world-wide concern. Some countries frequently violate copyrights on intellectual material. What is a copyright? How have Web carriers increased the likelihood of copyright infringement on content? The U.S. government is considering new laws to help curb copyright infringement. What might the positive and negative effects of these laws be? For example, how might they affect schools? ISPs? Other online content providers?

3 Biz Software Snoop

Employee monitoring involves the use of computers to observe, record, and review an individual's use of a computer, including game playing, e-mail, keyboard activity, and Internet sites visited. Is employee monitoring ethical? How much money do firms lose each year due to workers playing games or doing personal tasks during work hours? Some suggest that this is not a new problem—workers always have spent some time at work being unproductive. Do you think computers have made the situation better or worse? If you knew your firm used employee monitoring, how might it alter your behavior?

CHAPTER 1 2 3 4 5 6 7 8 9 10 11 12 13 14 INDEX

CHECKPOINT www.scsite.com/dc2000/ch14/check.htm

WEB INSTRUCTIONS: *To display this page from the Web, launch your browser and enter the URL, www.scsite.com/dc2000/ch14/check.htm. Click the links for current and additional information. To experience the animation and interactivity, Shockwave and Flash Player must be installed on your computer (download by clicking here).*

Label the Figure

Instructions: *Identify the three types of backup.*

VARIOUS BACKUP METHODS

TYPE OF BACKUP	ADVANTAGES	DISADVANTAGES
1. _____	Fastest recovery method. All files are saved.	Longest backup time.
2. _____	Fast backup method. Requires minimal space to back up.	Recovery is time consuming because need last full backup plus the differential backup.
3. _____	Fastest backup method. Requires minimal space to back up. Only most recent changes saved.	Recovery is most time consuming because need last full backup and all incremental backups since last full backup.

Matching

Instructions: *Match each method of identification and authentication from the column on the left with the best description from the column on the right.*

_____ 1. user ID and password

_____ 2. possessed object

_____ 3. personal identification number (PIN)

_____ 4. biometric device

_____ 5. callback system

a. Authenticates by verifying a physical characteristic such as fingerprints or retinal pattern.

b. Word or series of characters that must match an authentication file stored on a computer.

c. Encrypted code that a person, Web site, or company attaches to an electronic message.

d. Connects to a computer only after the computer calls back at a previously established number.

e. Numeric password, either assigned by an organization or selected by the user.

f. Item that must be carried to gain access to a computer or computer facility.

g. Uses special electrical components to smooth out minor noise and provide a stable flow.

Short Answer

Instructions: *Write a brief answer to each of the following questions.*

1. In terms of computer viruses, how is a logic bomb different from a time bomb? _____ What is a worm? _____

2. What is a virus signature? _____ Why is a polymorphic virus difficult to detect? _____

3. What conditions typically are included in a single-user license agreement? _____ What is the Business Software Alliance (BSA)? _____

4. How is private key encryption different from public key encryption? _____ What is the government's key escrow plan? _____

5. What are some common points shared by federal and state laws regarding the storage and disclosure of personal data? _____

AT ISSUE

www.scsite.com/dc2000/ch14/issue.htm

WEB INSTRUCTIONS: *To display this page from the Web, launch your browser and enter the URL,* www.scsite.com/dc2000/ch14/issue.htm. *Click the links for current and additional information.*

SHELLY
CASHMAN
SERIES®
DISCOVERING
COMPUTERS
2000

■ Student Exercises
WEB INFO
IN BRIEF
KEY TERMS
AT THE MOVIES
CHECKPOINT
AT ISSUE
CYBERCLASS
HANDS ON
NET STUFF
■ Special Features
TIMELINE 2000
GUIDE TO WWW SITES
MAKING A CHIP
BUYER'S GUIDE 2000
CAREERS 2000
TRENDS 2000
CHAT
INTERACTIVE LABS
NEWS
HOME

ONE *In a recent survey, more than 60 percent of organizations* questioned admitted to security breaches within the past year. Invasions were committed by curiosity seekers, pranksters, criminals, and even terrorists. The transgressors accessed and erased confidential records, caused airport computers to malfunction, and even paralyzed hospital information systems. In response to computer crime, a new breed of detective has emerged. The Computer Security Institute consists of more than 5,000 cyber-sleuths whose clues are hard drives instead of footprints. Fighting computer crime is a challenging task. Because computer crime is a relatively new phenomenon, computer detectives lack the proven crime-fighting techniques that have been used for centuries to solve other crimes. What skills and abilities must a cyber-sleuth possess? Why? Would you be a good computer security expert? Why or why not?

TWO *Employers can use a number of products to monitor their* employees' use of the Internet. These products report an employee's access of non-business related Web sites. Advocates insist that these products conserve network resources, make workers more productive, and discourage downloading of objectionable material. Opponents maintain, however, that determining business-related sites often is a matter of opinion. In addition, the time spent at home on work-related issues more than balances any office non-business Internet use. Companies have devised a range of Internet policies, from strict limitations on personal use to reliance on employee's discretion. Should there be limitations on an employee's access to the Internet? Why or why not? What might be the disadvantages of allowing unlimited access? What might be the advantages?

THREE *A popular Web site lets people construct personal Web pages for free and is proud* of its communal atmosphere. The Federal Trade Commission (FTC), however, had reservations about the Web site's policies. The FTC found that the Web site was selling personal information collected from registration forms without the permission of members. The Web site agreed to change its policies and was not prosecuted, but critics insist this is not enough. How sternly should companies be punished for selling information without permission? What, if any, limitations should be placed on the type of information that can be sold? Why?

FOUR *Computers and computer peripherals can be expensive. Because computer literacy* is an essential element in modern education, some school systems are accepting a degree of commercialism in return for the hardware. ZapMe!, a computer service group, has agreed to supply computers to a number of schools in return for a small advertisement placed in the corner of the screen. ZapMe! contends they are supplying essential resources at no greater cost than that of a simple advertisement students could see on the Web anyway, but critics insist the company is using a public forum to promote their products. What conditions should schools accept, and not accept, in return for computer equipment? Why? If you were a school administrator, would you accept ZapMe!'s demands? Why or why not?

FIVE *Information accuracy is a concern of all legitimate journalists. In Web journalism,* however, information accuracy is an even greater worry. Web journalism consists of news-related Web sites posted by organizations such as the Wall Street Journal, or by individuals such as cyberspace's Matt Drudge. Unlike its print and broadcast brethren, Web journalism knows no press time. As a result, the push is to distribute stories as soon as possible, sometimes before double-checking sources. Individual Web journalists often do not have the resources to check sources. If you were responsible for a news-related Web site, how would you balance information accuracy with the pressure to publish first? As a viewer, would you have the same faith in Web journalism that you have in print or broadcast journalism? Why or why not?

SHELLY
CASHMAN
SERIES®

DISCOVERING
COMPUTERS
2000

CHAPTER 1 2 3 4 5 6 7 8 9 10 11 12 13 **14** INDEX

CYBERCLASS   www.scsite.com/dc2000/ch14/class.htm

WEB INSTRUCTIONS: *To display this page from the Web, launch your browser and enter the URL,* www.scsite.com/dc2000/ch14/class.htm. *To start Level I CyberClass, click a Level I link on this page or enter the URL,* www.cyber-class.com. *Click the Student button, click* Discovering Computers 2000 *in the list of titles, and then click the Enter a site button. To start Level II or III CyberClass (available only to those purchasers of a CyberClass floppy disk), place your CyberClass floppy disk in drive A, click Start on the taskbar, click Run on the Start menu, type* a:connect *in the Open text box, click the OK button, click the Enter CyberClass button, and then follow the instructions.*

I II III LEVEL   **1. Flash Cards**   Click Flash Cards on the Main Menu of the CyberClass web page. Click the plus sign before the Chapter 14 title and then click Computer Security: Risks and Safeguards. Complete all questions in this category. Then, choose another category and continue to answer flash cards until you have answered at least 15 questions. If you have not answered 80% correctly by the time you have answered 15 questions, continue until you have answered at least 15 questions correctly. All users: Answer as many more flash cards as you desire. Close the Electronic Flash Card window and the Flash Cards window by clicking the Close button in the upper-right corner.

I II III LEVEL   **2. Practice Test**   Click Testing on the Main Menu of the CyberClass web page. Click the Select a book box arrow and then click Discovering Computers 2000. Click the Select a test to take box arrow and then click the Chapter 14 title in the list. Click the Take Test button. If necessary, maximize the window. Take the practice test and then click the Submit Test button. Click the Display Study Guide button. Review the Study Guide and then print the Study Guide by clicking the Print button on the toolbar or by clicking File/Print on the menu bar. Scroll down and click the Return To CyberClass button. Click the Yes button to close the Study Guide window. Then, click the Done button. Turn in your printed Study Guide to your instructor.

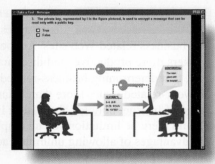

I II III LEVEL   **3. Web Guide**   Click Web Guide on the Main Menu of the CyberClass web page. When the Guide to World Wide Web Sites page displays, click Travel. Visit one or more of the travel sites and then write a brief report explaining how the World Wide Web can help a traveler plan and take a trip.

I II III LEVEL   **4. Company Briefs**   Click Company Briefs on the Main Menu of the CyberClass web page. Click a corporation name to display a case study. Read the case study. Visit the company's Web site to find material about the backup procedures the company uses for its data. Write a brief report describing your findings.

II III LEVEL   **5. CyberChallenge**   Click CyberChallenge on the Main Menu of the CyberClass web page. Click the Select a book box arrow and then click Discovering Computers 2000. Click the Select a board to play box arrow and then click Chapter 14 in the list. Click the Play CyberChallenge button. Maximize the CyberChallenge window. Play CyberChallenge until you have accumulated a total of 1,000 points. Close the CyberChallenge window.

II III LEVEL   **6. Assignments**   Click Assignments on the Main Menu of the CyberClass web page. Ensure you are aware of all assignments and when they are due.

II III LEVEL   **7. Hot Links**   Click Hot Links on the Main Menu of the CyberClass web page. Visit sites in Hot Links until you find one that you think presents objectionable content. Write a report describing what you found and what you would do to correct the situation.

HANDS ON   www.scsite.com/dc2000/ch14/hands.htm

WEB INSTRUCTIONS: *To display this page from the Web, launch your browser and enter the URL, www.scsite.com/dc2000/ch14/hands.htm. Click the links for current and additional information.*

One   *Understanding Backup*

This exercise uses Windows 98 procedures. Click the Start button on the taskbar, point to Programs on the Start menu, and then point to Accessories on the Programs submenu. Point to System Tools on the Accessories submenu, and then click Backup on the System Tools submenu. If a Welcome screen displays, click the OK button. Click the Close button in the Microsoft Back Up dialog box. When the Microsoft Backup - [Untitled] window displays, maximize it and then click the Backup tab. Click Help on the menu bar and then click Help Topics. Click Back Up, and then click Backing Up Everything On Your Computer. How can you backup your system? Close the Backup Help window. Close the Microsoft Backup - [Untitled] window.

Two   *License Agreements*

This exercise uses Windows 98 procedures. Click the Start button on the taskbar. Click Help on the Start menu. Click the Contents tab. Click the Introducing Windows 98 book. Click the Register Your Software book. Click the License Agreement questions and answers topic. Click an appropriate link to answer each of the following questions:

- ♠ Where do you find your End User License Agreement?
- ♠ Is it legal to sell software you have bought and used?
- ♠ Can you make a second copy of operating system software for a home or portable computer?
- ♠ Can you transfer or give away old versions of products when you buy an upgrade?

Click the Close button to close the Windows Help window.

Three   *Scanning a Disk*

ScanDisk is a Windows utility that checks a disk for physical and logical errors. To run ScanDisk, click the Start button on the taskbar, point to Programs on the Start menu, and point to Accessories on the Programs submenu. Point to System Tools on the Accessories submenu, and then click ScanDisk on the System Tools submenu. Click the Advanced button in the ScanDisk window. When the ScanDisk Advanced Options dialog box displays, click Always in the Display summary area and then click the OK button. Insert your floppy disk into drive A. Click 3½ Floppy (A:) in the Select the driver(s) you want to check for errors area. Click Thorough in the Type of test area. Click the Start button in the ScanDisk dialog box. What errors, if any, are detected? In bytes, what is the total disk space? How many folders are on the floppy disk? How many user files are on the floppy disk? Close the ScanDisk Results dialog box and the ScanDisk - 3½ Floppy (A:) window.

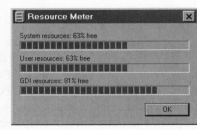

Four   *Checking System Resources*

Resource Meter monitors the system resources your programs are using. To run Resource Meter, click the Start button on the taskbar, point to Programs on the Start menu, and then point to Accessories on the Programs submenu. Point to System Tools on the Accessories submenu, and then click Resource Meter on the System Tools submenu. If a Resource Meter dialog box displays, read the information given and then click the OK button. Double-click the Resource Meter icon that displays to the left of the time on the taskbar. What percentage of system resources is free? What percentage of user resources is free? Click the OK button. Right-click the Resource Meter icon on the taskbar and then click Exit on the shortcut menu.

SHELLY
CASHMAN
SERIES®

DISCOVERING
COMPUTERS
2000

■ **Student Exercises**
WEB INFO
IN BRIEF
KEY TERMS
AT THE MOVIES
CHECKPOINT
AT ISSUE
CYBERCLASS
HANDS ON
NET STUFF
■ **Special Features**
TIMELINE 2000
GUIDE TO WWW SITES
MAKING A CHIP
BUYER'S GUIDE 2000
CAREERS 2000
TRENDS 2000
CHAT
INTERACTIVE LABS
NEWS
HOME

CHAPTER   1   2   3   4   5   6   7   8   9   10   11   12   13   14   INDEX

NET STUFF   www.scsite.com/dc2000/ch14/net.htm

WEB INSTRUCTIONS: *To display this page from the Web, launch your browser and enter the URL,* *www.scsite.com/dc2000/ch14/net.htm. To use the Keeping Your Computer Virus Free lab from the Web, Shockwave and Flash Player must be installed on your computer (download by clicking here).*

KEEPING YOUR
COMPUTER
VIRUS FREE
LAB

1. Shelly Cashman Series Keeping Your Computer Virus Free Lab

Follow the instructions in NET STUFF 1 on page 1.46 to start and use the Keeping Your Computer Virus Free lab. If you are running from the Web, enter the URL www.scsite.com/sclabs/menu.htm; or display the NET STUFF page (see instructions at the top of this page) and then click the KEEPING YOUR COMPUTER VIRUS FREE LAB button.

SOFTWARE
PIRACY

2. Software Piracy

Hong Kong once was the pirated software capital of the world. The availability of stolen software manufactured in China and smuggled over the border led to the use of pirated software by almost 65 percent of Hong Kong firms. To date, the impact of China's takeover of Hong Kong on the pirated software market is unknown. The Business Software Alliance (BSA) Web site provides the latest information about software piracy. To learn more, complete this exercise.

COMPUTER
CRIME

3. Computer Crime

The Federal Bureau of Investigation is taking computer crime seriously. The FBI has computer crime units in seven cities, and a team of 125 agents is responsible for coordinating investigations around the country. Part of their job is to anticipate, and prevent, the most catastrophic crimes computer crackers could commit. Many computer crimes fall under the jurisdiction of the FBI. Complete this exercise to learn more about the computer crimes the FBI investigates.

IN THE NEWS

4. In the News

Soon after Windows 98 was released, users reported attacks by a date-triggered virus that prevented their computers from booting up or kept them from accessing their hard drives. The virus spread slowly, however, and several companies quickly posted antivirus updates to combat the infection. Click the IN THE NEWS button and read a news story about a security, ethics, or privacy issue related to computers. What is the issue? Who does it affect? How do you think the issue can, or should, be resolved?

WEB CHAT

5. Web Chat

More than 85 percent of the United States' Pentagon's communications are sent over commercial telephone lines. At least a dozen countries have information-warfare programs, and the Pentagon admits that intrusions into their system are detected only 10 percent of the time. Pentagon security experts claim the best response to unauthorized access is to attach a virus to the intruder that will disable the attacker's system. Some point out, however, that trespassers often disguise their encroachment by utilizing systems in friendly countries. In addition, computer counterassaults constitute acts of war, which require congressional approval. Should security experts be limited in the steps they can take to protect classified data? Why or why not? What measures, other than attaching a counterattack virus, might be effective deterrents? Why? Click the WEB CHAT button to enter a Web Chat discussion related to this topic.

TRENDS 2000
A Look to the Future

WEB INSTRUCTIONS: *To gain World Wide Web access to additional and up-to-date information regarding this special feature, launch your browser and enter the URL shown at the top of this page.*

Advances in computing no longer impact only computer scientists, engineers, and information technologists. Today, computer advances impact all individuals, families, organizations, and schools. As you have learned throughout this book, computers already are an essential part of people's daily lives; they quickly are becoming a mainstay, as much as the automobile, television, and telephone. In the future, computers could take on many new roles and become an even more pervasive and critical part of homes, schools, and businesses. This special feature looks at several computer technology trends that will influence the direction of the computer field and then looks at the impact those technologies will have on information systems in business and personal computing.

Figure 1
In the future, computers could take on many new roles — providing vast information resources, fast communications, and powerful support for activities in homes, schools, and businesses.

TRENDS IN COMPUTER TECHNOLOGY

Over the next several years, the greatest advances in computer technology will come in areas such as ubiquitous computing, user interfaces, intelligent agents, human computer integration, virtual reality, the use of megaservers, the Internet and the Web, communications, and digital convergence.

Ubiquitous Computing

Computers are not yet everywhere, but as they get smaller, faster, and less expensive, they are being utilized in everything from toothbrushes and curling irons to cars and spaceships. Ralph Merkle, a research scientist at Xerox's Palo Alto Research Center, envisions a "not-so-distant future, maybe by 2020, definitely by 2050, [in which] we will have devices with the computational power of . . . roughly a billion Pentium computers." Having access to such enormous computational power will change the emphasis of computing from processing data to generating information to managing knowledge. Further, every device known to man, including the human body, will use some type of computer to help it function more efficiently and effectively.

Figure 2
A fingerprint reader captures the curves and indentations of a fingerprint.

Figure 3
Companies have prototype interfaces that resemble the human head to make voice recognition more realistic.

User Interface

Today, most computers use a graphical user interface (GUI), which developers have dubbed the **WIMP** (windows, icons, menus, and pointer) interface. To use the WIMP interface, you must learn a new mode of communication that includes pointing, clicking, dragging, and so on. Next-generation operating systems will be more natural and human-centric, meaning they will allow you to interface with a computer using many of the methods you now use to communicate with humans. Such methods will include natural language, hand gestures, facial expressions, and of course, spoken words.

The ability to understand a **natural language** means that a computer will be capable of translating your spoken statements intro computer instructions and responding in a similar fashion. Computers also will use video cameras to record and identify individuals through facial expressions and fingerprint recognition (Figure 2). In the near future, computers will support continuous-speech voice recognition and use artificial intelligence to determine the meaning of your spoken words.

In an even more advanced use of voice recognition, computers will recognize your voice commands and respond in a computer-generated voice through an on-screen presence that resembles a person, animal, or other object (Figure 3). IBM and Apple, for example, have developed prototype interfaces that resemble the human head. When using this interface, you turn off the computer by telling the character to go to sleep. The character closes its eyes and droops its head as the computer begins to shut down.

Increasingly, computers also will use biometric devices such as those discussed in Chapter 14. Rather than using a user ID and password, a **biometric device** authenticates your identity by using facial recognition, voice recognition, retinal (eye) recognition, or hand size and fingerprints (Figure 4).

Intelligent Agents

For more than 40 years, artificial intelligence (AI) experts promoted the advantages of **smart software**; that is, software with built-in intelligence. In recent years, as this concept has become reality, the term, **intelligent agent,** has evolved to describe any software program that independently asks questions, pays attention to work patterns, and carries out tasks on behalf of a user (Figure 5). Some intelligent agents are embedded and work within a single program. Other intelligent agents, sometimes called **network agents**, perform tasks on remote computers before bringing the results back to the user.

Intelligent agents already are a part of several productivity software packages. Some e-mail software, for example, includes intelligent agents that allow individuals and businesses to filter incoming messages and request immediate notification of messages about specific subjects or from specific individuals. The Intellisense™ technology built into Microsoft Office 2000 also is based on an intelligent agent. As you work, the intelligent agent understands the tasks you are trying to complete. The intelligent agent will correct text as you enter it, organize and update your menus and toolbars to display the frequently used commands and buttons, and suggest more efficient ways to complete tasks. A network agent generally is more sophisticated than an intelligent agent embedded in a single program because it performs its work on multiple remote computers with different platforms. Individuals often use network agents to search the Internet or other networks for information. Based on the user's instructions, the agent will search for, interpret, and synthesize the information on a particular subject. You could direct a network agent, for example, to research all references to Civil War battles in the state of Virginia; the agent then would return the results in the format you specify.

Some network agents require specific instructions, while others accept general instructions such as, "book a flight from New York to Boston on the morning of June 20." The intelligent agent then would choose an airline and a specific flight. Some network agents even can learn a user's interests, develop a user profile, and then search the entire Internet to find relevant documents.

Device	Description
Fingerprint Reader	Like an old-fashioned police ink blotter, it captures the curves and indentations of a fingerprint.
Iris Scanner	Analyzes the vein patterns of an eye, which are unique to every person.
Voice Recognition Scanner	Records your voice and then matches the intonations with the original recording.
Facial Recognition	Scans your face. The geometric shape of every face is different and cannot be altered by plastic surgery or makeup.

Figure 4
For many applications, biometric security devices will replace user IDs and passwords.

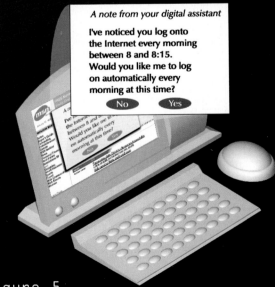

A note from your digital assistant

I've noticed you log onto the Internet every morning between 8 and 8:15. Would you like me to log on automatically every morning at this time?

No   Yes

Figure 5
Intelligent agents are software programs that can ask questions independently, pay attention to a user's work patterns, and carry out tasks on behalf of a user.

Human Computer Integration

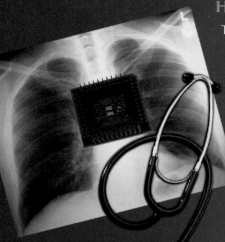

Today, microprocessors not only are used in computers, but also in the appliances you use everyday. Some believe the microprocessor eventually will become an integral part of the most complex device known — the human body (Figure 6).

Computers already are used inside the human body. Cochlear implants, for example, help some deaf people hear by stimulating the ear and the nerves that send information to the brain. The next step in human computer integration will involve implanting chips in the body to help it perform basic functions. A microprocessor, for example, could help regulate the release of hormones in the same way that a microprocessor regulates the fuel mixture in modern autos.

Canadian futurist Frank Ogden has conceived an even more futuristic use of embedded microprocessors, called CyberSight. With **CyberSight**, a microprocessor interfaces with a person's optic nerve to allow him or her to see information transmitted over a wireless link. The CyberSight system, for example, could transmit the floor plans of a building to a firefighter; the plans then would display in the vision of the firefighter, so that he or she can determine the best way to enter a burning building.

A further phase of human computer integration could involve making various disciplines such as mathematics, literature, and foreign languages available on microprocessors. If you wanted to learn Dutch, you could purchase a chip from a local retail store, much as you purchase a CD. Once you upload the chip to your brain through an implanted port, immediately you will know Dutch — without ever taking a class. While this may seem far-fetched, recent advances suggest it is possible. IBM, for example, already has prototyped a crude computer the size of an atom, called a **quantum computer**.

Figure 6
Eventually the microprocessor will become an integral part of the most complex device known — the human body.

Virtual Reality

Virtual reality (VR) is the use of computers to simulate a real or imagined environment that appears as a three-dimensional (3-D) space. VR allows you to explore and manipulate controls to experience the 3-D space fully (Figure 7). While most discussions of virtual reality focus on the thrilling aspects of virtual reality games, virtual reality has numerous practical applications. Virtual reality already is used in the areas of training, medicine, and manufacturing. Many companies use virtual reality simulations to train operators of expensive and complicated equipment such as airplanes and ships. In recent years, developers also have created VR simulations for less expensive, simpler equipment such as trucks and construction machinery. Medical schools also use VR for training — most often, to simulate surgery. Eventually, medical schools plan to use virtual patients to train medical personnel on all aspects of health care, from initial consultation to surgery, to post-operative rehabilitation. In manufacturing, companies are using VR to improve design, production, and maintenance activities. Eventually, computer-based virtual reality training will accompany all equipment repair manuals.

The use of virtual reality for entertainment also promises advancements. One futurist recently suggested that VR someday will allow moviegoers to pretend they are one of the movie characters. In such an environment, the virtual reality technology would link the moviegoer's sensory system (see, smell, hear, taste, and touch) to the character's sensory system.

Figure 7
Matsushita Electric Industrial Co., Ltd. has developed VR software that enables you to experience home remodeling changes before they are made. Using a head-mounted display and a data glove, you can walk through the remodeled room, open cabinets, and place items on shelves. You navigate the room by pointing a finger in the direction you want to travel.

Use of Megaservers

Today, an increasing number of information technologists advocate a return to a centralized computing environment, in which large megaservers store data, information, and programs, and less powerful client devices connect to the megaservers to access these items. The use of megaservers to store vast quantities of data, information, and programs is referred to as **information in the cloud** (Figure 8).

Already, online services such as America Online and The Microsoft Network operate numerous servers. Users connect to these servers to access the Internet, e-mail, online content, and other services. The next logical step is for firms to operate megaservers that give users access to additional personalized services and software — possibly even storing an individual's programs and personal files, such as a calendar, contact list, notes, and documents. Such an environment would catalyze the widespread use of inexpensive network computers (NCs). Subscribing home users, for example, could use an NC with a regular television set as a monitor to connect to a megaserver and access their files and programs. Mobile users could use wireless technology to access the megaservers using a pager, cellular telephone, or personal digital assistant (PDA).

You've got mail!

Dentist appointment at 3:30 PM

Your stock portfolio is worth $1,076,054.53

Your checking balance is $1,098.15

Meeting at 10:00 AM Lunch at noon with Jack

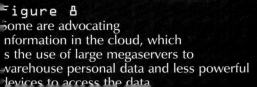

Figure 8
Some are advocating information in the cloud, which is the use of large megaservers to warehouse personal data and less powerful devices to access the data.

The Internet and the Web

Over the next decade, the Internet and the Web promise many exciting developments. Already, the Internet is the fastest growing segment of the computer industry and is a major reason why consumers are buying personal computers at a record pace. Today, more than one quarter of U.S. homes have access to the Internet. At present, individuals primarily use the Internet to access information and communicate using e-mail. In the future, individuals increasingly will rely on two other Internet-based communication applications — telephony and videoconferencing. As you learned in Chapter 7, Internet telephony uses the Internet (instead of a telephone network) to connect a calling party and one or more called parties. Currently, you can use Internet telephony to talk to someone anywhere in the world for just the cost of your Internet connection. Internet telephony often is used in combination with videoconferencing so you can see the person or persons with whom you are speaking. Videoconferencing involves the use of a digital camera device to transmit live video over the Internet or other networks.

Another future development will be the continued integration of television, networks, and computers. For now, the relatively inexpensive WebTV allows you to send e-mail and surf the Web using your television set. In the future, you will use WebTV in an interactive fashion to view your favorite movie, television show, concert, sporting event, or shopping guide.

E-commerce is another aspect of the Web that is gaining tremendous interest. Each year, individual and business consumers purchase more goods and services online. More than $7 billion of business was done over the Web in 1998 — and this number is expected to increase to more than $300 billion in the next few years. Figure 9 lists a number of popular Web sites, from which you can purchase books, automobiles, and more. Over the next few years, more e-commerce applications — and the technologies used to support them — will be developed. Many of these technologies will be focused on improving the security of and expediting credit card transactions.

Company	URL	Description
amazon.com	www.amazon.com	Sells books, music, and videos
BarclaySquare	www.barclaysquare.com	E-superstore located in England
e-buy®	www.ebuy.com	E-superstore
Egghead.com	www.egghead.com	Computer products/discount software superstore
E*TRADE	www.etrade.com	Online trading and portfolio management
Macy's	www.macys.com	Sells general merchandise and gift registry
Microsoft CarPoint	carpoint.msn.com	New and used car buying service
my-world	www.my-world.com	E-superstore located in Germany
NetGrocer	www.netgrocer.com	Internet SuperCenter — all products
Open Market	www.openmarket.com	Internet commerce software
Peapod	www.peapod.com	Order groceries online
theglobe.com	www.theglobe.com	E-superstore
United Buyers Advantage	www.ubuy.com	Auctions goods and services at a discount made available through suppliers
WebMarket	www.webmarket.com	Lists the best places on the Web to buy books, electronics, clothing, and more

For an updated list, visit the Discovering Computers 2000 Web site at www.scsite.com/dc2000/ch14/trends.htm

Figure 9
Major e-commerce Web sites

Communications

Over the next three to five years, home and business users can expect much faster access to the Internet as cable and telephone companies begin to provide broader bandwidth. As discussed in Chapter 9, **bandwidth** is a measure of the amount of data a communications channel can transmit over a given period of time. The key to speeding up Internet access is to increase the bandwidth of the communications channel between the user and the access provider. For most users, this part of the communications channel, which is called *the last mile*, often involves using a modem to dial up and connect to a server over slow analog telephone lines. Several cable

IRIDIUM® SYSTEM OVERVIEW

Figure 10
The Motorola IRIDIUM system will allow people to place telephone calls or send and receive digital information literally from anywhere on earth.

and telephone companies are working to increase the bandwidth of the last mile by using fiber optics, broadband cable (TV cable), and fast Digital Subscriber Lines (DSL). Higher-bandwidth communications channels will eliminate the use of dial-up modem connections and greatly increase Internet access speeds.

One of the more ambitious programs is Motorola's IRIDIUM system, which involves wireless communications using 66 low-earth orbit (LEO) satellites. Once implemented, the IRIDIUM system will allow individuals to make telephone calls or send and receive digital information from anywhere on earth (Figure 10). Smart wireless telephones that combine traditional telephone with e-mail, Web browsers, and personal management applications will make it easier for mobile users to stay in touch.

As soon as communications speeds improve, bandwidth-hungry Internet applications, such as virtual reality, distance education, downloadable audio and video libraries, and others, will gain more widespread acceptance.

Digital Convergence

More than 500 years ago, Johannes Gutenberg developed a printing press that made the written word accessible to the general public and revolutionized the way people shared information. Today, digital convergence drives the information revolution of the twenty-first century and helps shape the society of the future. **Digital convergence** describes the merging of technologies and products from the communications, entertainment, publishing, and computer industries. This merging, or convergence, is made possible by widespread use of digital data, information, and programs that can be processed, stored, and distributed over networks such as a corporate intranet or the Internet.

Digital convergence helps to advance many new applications, including networked virtual reality applications for training and collaboration, downloadable audio and video libraries, and remote scientific modeling. As noted by Judith Estrin, senior vice president and chief technology officer of Cisco Systems, "Everything eventually will be just a packet: data, video, and voice. This will be driven by new levels of bandwidth availability, especially 'last mile' technologies such as cable and fast Digital Subscriber Line . . . and competition among different service providers."

As digital convergence continues, the boundaries between communications, entertainment, publishing, and computer industries will dissolve, thus opening doors to vast information resources.

THE FUTURE OF INFORMATION SYSTEMS IN BUSINESS

Although millions of homes now include one or more computers, businesses by far are the largest users of computers. Around the world, businesses install and use millions of computers of all types — mainframes, personal computers, and more — for applications such as inventory control, billing, and accounting. These computers often are part of a large information system that includes data, people, procedures, hardware, and software.

Existing business information systems will undergo profound changes as a result of the computer trends just described. As computers become increasingly ubiquitous and technologies converge, businesses will rely on computers for communication — and users at all levels will need to be computer literate. Intelligent agents will help users sift through the vast amounts of data and information made available by the increased use of digital data and information and the expansion of the Internet. As shown in Figure 11, these and other trends will affect the information systems of tomorrow.

a

HARDWARE

- Use of smaller, faster, more efficient, more capacious, and less costly computers will continue.
- Use of Digital Subscriber Lines for communications and access to the Internet will increase, especially for e-commerce.
- Companies will adopt enterprise computing via megaservers so employees and business associates can access data or collaborate from any location.
- Wireless communications, laptops, and personal digital assistants will increase in popularity and use.
- Digital cameras for video conferencing and flat panel displays will become commonplace.
- Voice recognition capabilities will make inroads towards replacing the keyboard as the primary input device.
- Biometric devices will replace user IDs and passwords.

b

SOFTWARE

- Natural languages will enable users to communicate with the computer in a more conversational manner.
- Object orientation will combine processes and methods with data.
- Computer-aided software engineering (CASE) and rapid application development (RAD) will shorten the system development time frame.
- Increased use of expert systems will help users make decisions.
- Virtual reality will be common for training and recreation.
- User interfaces will allow for human-like communications.
- Applications software will create Web pages as easily as printed documents.

c

d

PROCEDURES

- Procedures will be stored electronically.
- Virtual reality will play a major role in training and education.
- Intelligent agents will simplify procedures.

PEOPLE

- Most people will be computer literate, with a basic understanding of how computers work and how to use them in their jobs.
- Individuals will be given increased responsibility for design, operation, and maintenance of information processing systems.
- Users increasingly will rely on computers to manage the continuing proliferation of information.
- Computers will be the primary mode of communication.
- Interface with users will increase.
- Telecommuting (working from home) will become the norm.

e

DATA

- Centralized data warehousing will outstrip storing data on local servers.
- Servers will use push technology to download data and preferences to users when they log on.
- Nearly all data will be input at the point where it is created.
- Compound documents will combine text, numbers, and non-text data such as voice, image, and full motion video.
- Debit and credit cards will become the major method of payment for goods purchased, especially on the Web.
- Improved search techniques will be established to allow users quicker access to data.
- Emphasis will change from how to capture and process data to how to use the available data and create information more effectively.

Figure 11
The major trends pertaining to the elements of an information system.

The Automated Office

The **automated office**, sometimes referred to as the **electronic office**, makes use of electronic devices such as computers, facsimile machines, copier machines, computerized telephone systems, scanners, and printers. Increasingly, computers connect to these devices via a network (Figure 12). In this networked environment, users can share hardware, software, data, and information as they work with automated office applications such as word processing, desktop publishing, e-mail, and voice mail.

The Digital Factory

As with the automated office, the goal of the **digital factory** is to increase productivity through the use of networked, computer-controlled equipment. A digital factory is any factory or manufacturing environment in which computers are used to help design products, run production machinery, or support other manufacturing operations. Technologies used in the digital factory include computer-aided design, computer-aided engineering, and computer-aided manufacturing. Once thought of as stand-alone technologies, companies now are linking them together to computerize the entire manufacturing process — a concept called computer-integrated manufacturing. As computers become more powerful, companies will become more dependent on these technologies, each of which is discussed in the following sections.

Computer-Aided Design (CAD)

Computer-aided design (CAD) uses a computer and special graphics software to aid in product design (Figure 13). In addition to the software, CAD systems require a high-resolution monitor; a mouse, light pen, or digitizing tablet for drawing; and a special printer or plotter for printing design specifications. Using CAD technology, designers can develop designs electronically. Using CAD offers several advantages over traditional laborious manual drafting methods. CAD, for example, allows a designer to modify a design more easily than before, as well as dynamically change the size of some or all of the product and view the design from different angles. Some CAD software even allows you to share

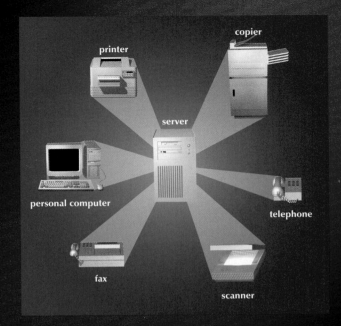

Figure 12
The trend is to network office devices together into an intranet so the office applications can share hardware and information.

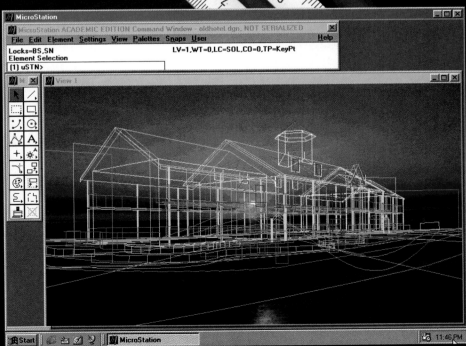

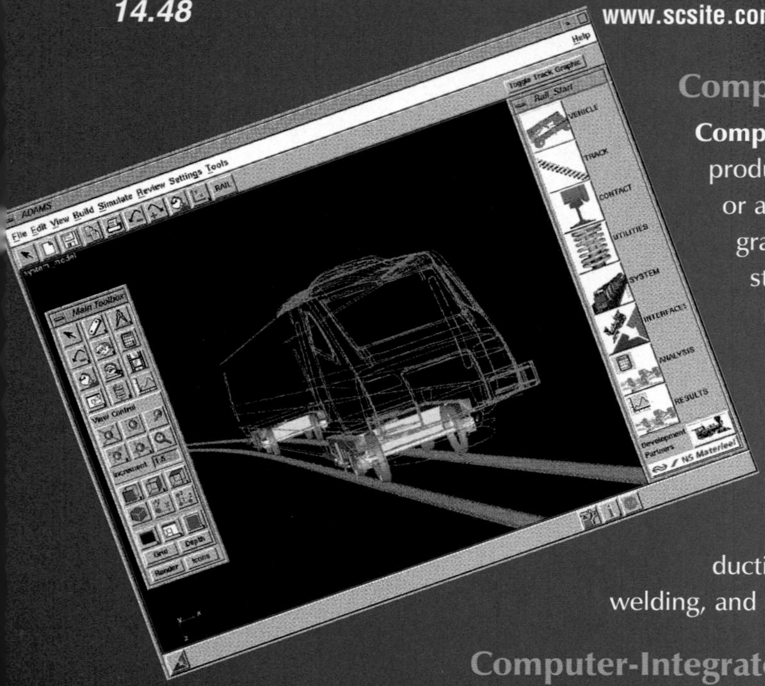

Computer-Aided Engineering (CAE)

Computer-aided engineering (CAE) is the use of computers to test product designs. Using CAE, engineers can test the design of a car or a bridge before it is built (Figure 14). These sophisticated programs simulate the effects of wind, temperature, weight, and stress on product shapes and materials. CAE also allows engineers to create a computer prototype for use in testing under a variety of conditions, including special conditions such as hurricanes and earthquakes.

Computer-Aided Manufacturing (CAM)

Computer-aided manufacturing (CAM) is the use of computers to control production equipment. CAM production equipment includes software-controlled drilling, lathe, welding, and milling machines.

Computer-Integrated Manufacturing (CIM)

Computer-integrated manufacturing (CIM) is the use of computers to integrate the many different operations of the manufacturing process, using such technologies as CAD, CAE, and CAM. Using CIM, a factory links individual production processes so that production is balanced, efficient, driven by customer demand, and results in high-quality products. In a CIM factory, most manufacturing processes — from design to machining to assembly to testing and packaging — are automated and linked. Under ideal CIM conditions, a product will move through the entire production process under computer control. Because CIM is so complex, smaller companies may never fully implement it. Many larger manufacturers, however, are planning to incorporate CIM into their new digital factories so they can reap the benefits of efficient demand-driven production.

Figure 14
Computer-aided engineering (CAE) allows the engineer to test a product design before the product is built.

The Virtual Corporation

Many management theorists believe that future companies will function as virtual corporations. A **virtual corporation** is a temporary network of companies that join together to provide goods and services. Virtual corporations form quickly and stay together only as long as the opportunity remains profitable.

In a virtual corporation, each partner contributes the essential skills, goods, services, and assets that differentiate it from other organizations — items known as core competencies. **Core competencies** are those characteristics a firm must develop and maintain in order to excel in current and future business activities. In a virtual corporation, for example, a company with a strong research focus might conceive the initial product idea, but another company would be responsible for product design, another for manufacturing, and a third for sales (Figure 15). As partners form a virtual corporation and include additional businesses, the virtual corporation's information system must also expand so each partnering company is part of the same network. The virtual corporation thus will have to develop an **interenterprise information system**, in which organizations share access to each other's data, information, hardware, software, and other resources.

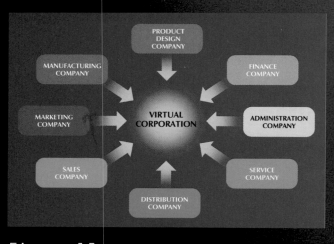

Figure 15
A virtual corporation is made up of several companies that have expertise in specific areas and work together as long as the corporation is profitable.

THE FUTURE OF PERSONAL COMPUTING

Just as the use of computers in businesses has changed the workplace, the use of computers in homes is changing family life. Already, consumers have purchased millions of personal computers for home use, and approximately 15 million homes in the United States have multiple PCs. The use of personal computers in the home is expected to increase dramatically over the next several years as the cost of computers continues to drop and more Internet applications become available.

Over the next ten years, computers will continue to decrease in price, but will be almost 100 times more powerful. Experts anticipate that in 2008, for example, the standard home personal computer will have a 4 GHz CPU, 8 GB of RAM, and a hard drive that provides almost a terabyte worth of storage.

Today and in the future, people will use home computers for a variety of applications. These applications usually fall into five general categories: (1) control of home systems, (2) personal services, (3) telecommuting, (4) education, and (5) entertainment.

Control of Home Systems

Over the next decade, computers will play an important role in the control of home systems such as security, temperature, televisions, stereos, lighting, smart appliances, and landscape sprinkler systems. To control such systems, personal computers usually are linked to special devices such as alarms for security; thermostats for temperature control; and timing devices for smart appliances, lighting, and sprinkler systems. If the computer has communications capabilities, a homeowner who is away can use a telephone or another computer to call home and change the operation of one of the control systems. Smart appliances can relieve you of the more time-consuming chores. For example, your refrigerator or cupboard may one day be linked through a home control system to the grocery store and order groceries without your intervention. Some busy people already order their groceries over the internet using Peapod (see Figure 9 on page 14.44) and have them delivered.

Currently, most installed home control systems consist of separate systems to control each set of devices. In the future, these homes will have integrated home control systems. Many new homes, for example, are being wired with cables to allow homeowners to install a network with a server. The server used in the home network, called a home server, can connect multiple PCs and smart appliances. Home servers will allow homeowners to network appliances, lighting systems, and other home products and control them using a consistent set of commands. The home server also can connect to Internet service providers via a computerized access device (Figure 16). Although not yet widely implemented, these changes will result in what many refer to as the intelligent home or smart house, in which computers automate lighting, heating and cooling, audio/video, art, and even pet care. Smart home products are expected to be a $4 billion a year business by the year 2001.

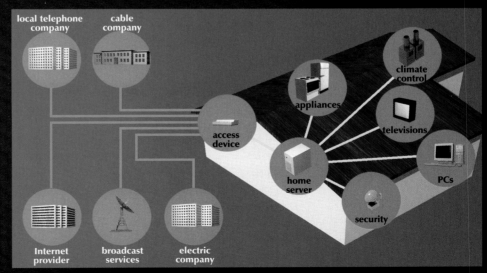

Figure 16
An integrated home network connects PCs, security, furnace and air conditioning, televisions, stereos, lights, sprinkler systems, and smart appliances to a home server. The home server is connected to service providers outside the home through a computerized access device.

Personal Services

Home computers also can help individuals manage their comm
and other aspects of home life. In many ways, running a home
small business. The productivity tools used by businesses, such
spreadsheets, databases, and Web browsers, also are valuable i
ware can help you create documents, file and organize data, ma
dar, send e-mail, and buy products over and gather information

Personal computer software also is available to help you pla
finances. Personal finance and home accounting software suppo
ing checkbooks, making household budgets, preparing tax retur
investments. Stock brokerage firms, such as E*TRADE, also allo
stocks online and track your investments (Figure 17). Eventually
perform all financial services from your home using a computer

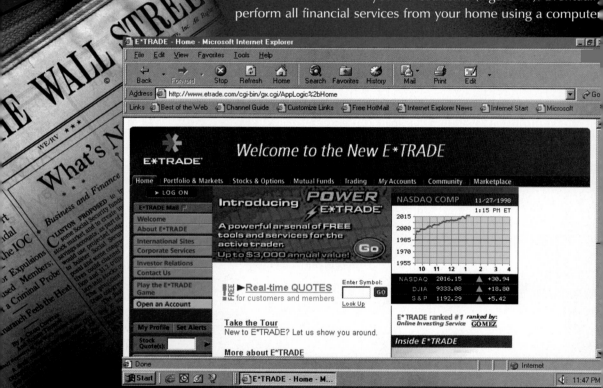

Figure 17
You can buy and sell stocks online for a considerable discount without using a stoc

Telecommuting

In the future, more individuals also will work from home. As dis
telecommuting is a work arrangement in which employees wor
standard workplace but communicate with the office using com
tions technology. Studies have shown that telecommuting increa
retention and recruiting, conserves energy, reduces air pollution
estate costs. According to one survey, nearly 15 million people
least two times a week. The number of telecommuters increases
year and is expected to include as many as 30 million workers h

Education

The use of personal computers in educational settings is another rapidly growing area. The Internet and the World Wide Web, however, promise to have the greatest impact on education in the future.

Ten years from now, for example, college no longer may be at a specific place or a specific time. Instead, education will be available where you need it, at almost any time. University professors may develop entire courses using video lectures with coordinated demonstrations on virtual blackboards — all distributed to students over the Internet. Students can view the professor's latest lecture whenever they have time, from home or workplace computers. Not only does this free students from rigid class schedules, it allows them to rewind and review difficult points or fast-forward past obvious ones. Students even can have live discussions with their classmates in a chat room or exchange e-mail with their instructor and other students.

Such courses are ideal for workers seeking advanced training but lacking the time to pursue on-campus studies or for undergraduates living far from campus. Already, many schools are offering online courses that count toward degrees — the first efforts at extending educational opportunities beyond the campus grounds.

As a result of these courses, the traditional campus could undergo a major change. Instead of attending classrooms for an academic year, students may make single annual visits to campuses to establish personal contacts with professors and classmates. Critics, however, argue that while the Internet can help with continuing education and professional retraining initiatives, a fully Internet-based education cannot capture the full value of the educational experience.

The Internet clearly will have a major impact on one familiar school structure: the library. Over the next decade, many libraries will begin to convert hard copy documents into digital form. Eventually, this could develop into an online universal library to which all schools have access. While looking for a book in this online universal library, you could search a network of individual online libraries to find the book, view any checkout terms or fees, and then view or download it from the site. Traditional libraries, however, still will exist, if only to house publicly accessible computers and a collection of texts required to verify digitized versions.

One recent breakthrough in digital books is the **electronic book**, or **e-book**. Several companies have introduced small book-sized computers (Figure 18) that can hold up to 4,000 pages, or about 10 books' worth of text. By pressing a button, you can move forward or backward through the text. You also can add notes or highlight text using a small pen input device. Although the tablet-sized displays will not have the clear resolution of ink on a page for years to come, Microsoft recently has developed a technology called **ClearType** that will enhance significantly the appearance of the font on a screen.

Figure 18
An electronic book (e-book) can hold up to 4,000 pages, or the equivalent of 10 books' worth of text, and it weighs less than 22 ounces.

Entertainment

For the younger members of the family, playing games using entertainment software always has had a large appeal. Many adults, however, are surprised to find that entertainment software also can provide them with hours of enjoyment. Popular types of **entertainment software** include arcade games, board games, simulations, and interactive adventure programs. The arcade-type games available for computers are similar to video games; computer board games provide computerized versions of traditional board games, such as chess, backgammon, and Trivial Pursuit. Simulations include games such as baseball and football and a variety of flight simulators that give you the experience of controlling and navigating different types of aircraft.

Entertainment software also includes a wide variety of interactive adventure games, which range from rescuing a princess from a castle's dungeon to solving a murder mystery. You can play many of these games in groups using a network or on the World Wide Web, or you can play with just the computer as your opponent. Entertainment software usually allows players to adjust the level of play to match their abilities; that is, beginner through advanced. With entertainment software, the computer becomes a fun, skillful, and challenging game partner.

In addition to playing games, some personal computer users use their home computers to support their personal hobbies and interests. Today, a variety of entertainment software allows hobbyists to create family photo albums; edit home videos; design quilt and stained glass patterns; organize stamp, doll, and photography collections; and write, transpose, play, and print musical scores.

CODING SCHEMES AND NUMBER SYSTEMS

CODING SCHEMES

As discussed in Chapter 3, a computer uses a coding scheme to represent characters. This section presents the ASCII, EBCDIC, and Unicode coding schemes and discusses parity.

ASCII and EBCDIC

Two widely used codes that represent characters in a computer are the ASCII and EBCDIC codes. **The American Standard Code for Information Interchange**, called ASCII (pronounced ASK-ee), is the most widely used coding system to represent data. Many personal computers and minicomputers use ASCII. The **Extended Binary Coded Decimal Interchange Code**, or **EBCDIC** (pronounced EB-see-dic) is used primarily on mainframe computers. Figure A-1 summarizes these codes. Notice how the combination of bits (0s and 1s) is unique for each character.

When the ASCII or EBCDIC code is used, each character that is represented is stored in one byte of memory. Other binary formats exist, however, that the computer sometimes uses to represent numeric data. For example, a computer may store, or pack, two numeric characters in one byte of memory. The computer uses these binary formats to increase storage and processing efficiency.

Unicode

The 256 characters and symbols that are represented by ASCII and EBCDIC codes are sufficient for English and western European languages but are not large enough for Asian and other languages that use different alphabets. Further compounding the problem is that many of these languages used symbols, called **ideograms**, to represent multiple words and ideas. One solution to this situation is Unicode. **Unicode** is a 16-bit code that has the capacity of representing more than 65,000 characters and symbols. Unicode represents

ASCII	SYMBOL	EBCDIC
00110000	0	11110000
00110001	1	11110001
00110010	2	11110010
00110011	3	11110011
00110100	4	11110100
00110101	5	11110101
00110110	6	11110110
00110111	7	11110111
00111000	8	11111000
00111001	9	11111001
01000001	A	11000001
01000010	B	11000010
01000011	C	11000011
01000100	D	11000100
01000101	E	11000101
01000110	F	11000110
01000111	G	11000111
01001000	H	11001000
01001001	I	11001001
01001010	J	11010001
01001011	K	11010010
01001100	L	11010011
01001101	M	11010100
01001110	N	11010101
01001111	O	11010110
01010000	P	11010111
01010001	Q	11011000
01010010	R	11011001
01010011	S	11100010
01010100	T	11100011
01010101	U	11100100
01010110	V	11100101
01010111	W	11100110
01011000	X	11100111
01011001	Y	11101000
01011010	Z	11101001
00100001	!	01011010
00100010	"	01111111
00100011	#	01111011
00100100	$	01011011
00100101	%	01101100
00100110	&	01010000
00101000	(	01001101
00101001	)	01011101
00101010	*	01011100
00101011	+	01001110

Figure A-1

all the world's current languages using more than 34,000 characters and symbols (Figure A-2). In Unicode, 30,000 codes are reserved for future use, such as ancient languages, and 6,000 codes are reserved for private use. Existing ASCII coded data is fully compatible with Unicode because the first 256 codes are the same. Unicode currently is implemented in several operating systems, including Windows NT and OS/2, and major system developers have announced plans eventually to implement Unicode.

	041	042	043	044	045	046	047
0	А	Р	а	р		Ѡ	Ѱ
1	Б	С	б	с	ё	ѡ	ѱ
2	В	Т	в	т	ђ	Ѣ	Ѳ
3	Г	У	г	у	ѓ	ѣ	ѳ
4	Д	Ф	д	ф	є	Ѥ	Ѵ
5	Е	Х	е	х	ѕ	ѥ	ѵ
6	Ж	Ц	ж	ц	і	Ѧ	Ѷ
7	З	Ч	з	ч	ї	ѧ	ѷ
8	И	Ш	и	ш	ј	Ѩ	Ѹ
9	Й	Щ	й	щ	љ	ѩ	ѹ
A	К	Ъ	к	ъ	њ	Ѫ	Ѻ
B	Л	Ы	л	ы	ћ	ѫ	ѻ
C	М	Ь	м	ь	ќ	Ѭ	Ѽ
D	Н	Э	н	э		ѭ	ѽ
E	О	Ю	о	ю	ў	Ѯ	Ѿ
F	П	Я	п	я	џ	ѯ	ѿ

Figure A-2

Parity

Regardless of whether ASCII, EBCDIC, or other binary methods are used to represent characters in memory, it is important that the characters be stored accurately. For each byte of memory, most computers have at least one extra bit, called a **parity bit**, that is used by the computer for error checking. A parity bit can detect if one of the bits in a byte has been changed inadvertently. While such errors are extremely rare (most computers never have a parity error during their lifetime), they can occur because of voltage fluctuations, static electricity, or a memory failure.

Computers are either odd- or even-parity machines. In computers with odd parity, the total number of on bits in the byte (including the parity bit) must be an odd number. In computers with even parity, the total number of on bits must be an even number (Figure A-3). The computer checks parity each time it uses a memory location. When the computer moves data from one location to another in memory, it compares the parity bits of both the sending and receiving locations to see if they are the same. If the system detects a difference or if the wrong number of bits is on (e.g., an odd number in a system with even parity), an error message displays. Many computers use multiple parity bits that enable them to detect and correct a single-bit error and detect multiple-bit errors.

NUMBER SYSTEMS

This section describes the number systems that are used with computers. Whereas thorough knowledge of this subject is required for technical computer personnel, a general understanding of number systems and how they relate to computers is all most users need.

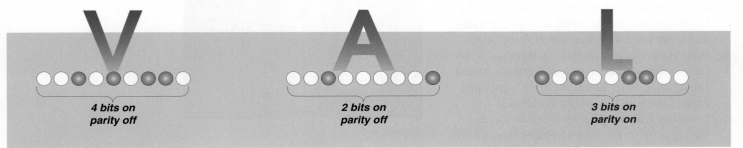

Figure A-3

As you have learned, the binary (base 2) number system is used to represent the electronic status of the bits in memory. It also is used for other purposes such as addressing the memory locations. Another number system that commonly is used with computers is **hexadecimal** (base 16). The computer uses the hexadecimal system to communicate with a programmer when a problem with a program exists, because it would be difficult for the programmer to understand the 0s and 1s of binary code. Figure A-4 shows how the decimal values 0 through 15 are represented in binary and hexadecimal.

The mathematical principles that apply to the binary and hexadecimal number systems are the same as those that apply to the decimal number system. To help you better understand these principles, this section starts with the familiar decimal system, then progresses to the binary and hexadecimal number systems.

DECIMAL	BINARY	HEXADECIMAL
0	0000	0
1	0001	1
2	0010	2
3	0011	3
4	0100	4
5	0101	5
6	0110	6
7	0111	7
8	1000	8
9	1001	9
10	1010	A
11	1011	B
12	1100	C
13	1101	D
14	1110	E
15	1111	F

Figure A-4

The Decimal Number System

The decimal number system is a base 10 number system (deci means ten). The base of a number system indicates how many symbols are used in it. The decimal number system uses 10 symbols: 0 through 9. Each of the symbols in the number system has a value associated with it. For example, 3 represents a quantity of three and 5 represents a quantity of five.

The decimal number system also is a positional number system. This means that in a number such as 143, each position in the number has a value associated with it. When you look at the decimal number 143, the 3 is in the ones, or units, position and represents three ones or (3 x 1); the 4 is in the tens position and represents four tens or (4 x 10); and the 1 is in the hundreds position and represents one hundred or (1 x 100). The number 143 is the sum of the values in each position of the number (100 + 40 + 3 = 143). The chart in Figure A-5 shows how you can calculate the positional values (hundreds, tens, and units) for a number system. Starting on the right and working to the left, the base of the number system, in this case 10, is raised to consecutive powers (10^0, 10^1, 10^2). These calculations are a mathematical way of determining the place values in a number system.

When you use number systems other than decimal, the same principles apply. The base of the number system indicates the number of symbols that are used, and each position in a number system has a value associated with it. By raising the base of the number system to consecutive powers beginning with zero, you can calculate the positional value.

power of 10	10^2	10^1	10^0	1	4	3	=	
				(1×10^2) +	(4×10^1) +	(3×10^0)	=	
positional value	100	10	1	(1×100) +	(4×10) +	(3×1)	=	
number	1	4	3	100 +	40 +	3	=	143

Figure A-5

The Binary Number System

As previously discussed, binary is a base 2 number system (bi means two), and the symbols it uses are 0 and 1. Just as each position in a decimal number has a place value associated with it, so does each position in a binary number. In binary, the place values, moving from right to left, are successive powers of two (2^0, 2^1, 2^2, 2^3) or (1, 2, 4, 8). To construct a binary number, you place ones in the positions where the corresponding values add up to the quantity you want to represent; you place zeros in the other positions. For example, in a four-digit binary number, the binary place values are (from right to left) 1, 2, 4, and 8. The binary number 1001 has ones in the positions for the values 1 and 8 and zeros in the positions for 2 and 4. Therefore, the quantity represented by binary 1001 is 9 (8 + 0 + 0 + 1) (Figure A-6).

The Hexadecimal Number System

The hexadecimal number system uses 16 symbols to represent values (hex means six, deci means ten). These include the symbols 0 through 9 and A through F (Figure A-4 on page A.3). The mathematical principles previously discussed also apply to hexadecimal (Figure A-7).

The primary reason why the hexadecimal number system is used with computers is because it can represent binary values in a more compact and readable form and because the conversion between the binary and the hexadecimal number systems is very efficient.

An eight-digit binary number (a byte) can be represented by a two-digit hexadecimal number. For example, in the ASCII code, the character M is represented as 01001101. This value can be represented in hexadecimal as 4D. One way to convert this binary number (4D) to a hexadecimal number is to divide the binary number (from right to left) into groups of four digits; calculate the value of each group; and then change any two-digit values (10 through 15) into the symbols A through F that are used in hexadecimal (Figure A-8).

Figure A-6

power of 2	2^3	2^2	2^1	2^0	1	0	0	1	=
positional value	8	4	2	1	$(1 \times 2^3) + (0 \times 2^2) + (0 \times 2^1) + (1 \times 2^0) =$				
					$(1 \times 8) + (0 \times 4) + (0 \times 2) + (1 \times 1) =$				
binary	1	0	0	1	8 + 0 + 0 + 1 = 9				

Figure A-7

power of 16	16^1	16^0	A	5	=
positional value	16	1	$(10 \times 16^1) + (5 \times 16^0) =$		
			$(10 \times 16) + (5 \times 1) =$		
hexadecimal	A	5	160 + 5 = 165		

Figure A-8

positional value	8421	8421
binary	0100	1101
decimal	4	13
hexadecimal	4	D

PHOTO CREDITS

Chapter 1: *Figure 1 Chapter opener* Bob Daemmrich/Stock Boston; *Figure 1-1a* Anthony Wood/Stock Boston; *Figure 1-1b* Andy Sacks/Tony Stone Images; *Figure 1-1c* Mark Richards/PhotoEdit; *Figure 1-1d* David Young-Wolff/PhotoEdit; *Figure 1-1e* Charles Gupton/Tony Stone Images; *Figure 1-2* Scott Goodwin Photography; *Figure 1-4a* '1999 PhotoDisc, Inc.; *Figure 1-4b* Courtesy of Intel Corporation; *Figure 1-4c* Courtesy of Intel Corporation; *Figure 1-4d* Courtesy of Intel Corporation; *Figure 1-4e* Phil A. Harrington/Peter Arnold, Inc.; *Figure 1-5* Scott Goodwin Photography; *Figure 1-6a* Courtesy of Seagate Technology; *Figure 1-6b* Courtesy of Iomega Corporation; *Figure 1-7* Courtesy of Toshiba America Information Systems, Inc.; *Figure 1-12* Scott Goodwin Photography; *Figure 1-17* PhotoEssentials, Inc.; *Figure 1-19* Courtesy of International Business Machines; *Figure 1-20* Terry Heferman/Courtesy of Apple Computer, Inc.; *Figure 1-21a* Courtesy of Hewlett Packard Company; *Figure 1-21b* Courtesy of International Business Machines; *Figure 1-22* Courtesy of Dell Computer Corporation; *Figure 1-24* Courtesy of Philips Consumer Electronics Company; *Figure 1-25* Courtesy of International Business Machines; *Figure 1-26* Courtesy of Hewlett Packard Company; *Figure 1-27* Bob Daemmrich/Tony Stone Images; *Figure 1-28* Courtesy of Hewlett Packard Company; *Figure 1-29* Courtesy of International Business Machines; *Figure 1-30* Courtesy of Randy Montoya/Sandia National Laboratories; *Figure 1-33* Courtesy of R-F Link, Inc.; *Figure 1-35* Churchill & Klehr/The Liaison Agency; *Figure 1-40a* Frank Wing/The Liaison Agency; *Figure 1-40b* Courtesy of Toshiba America Information Systems, Inc.; *Figure 1-40c* Michael Newman/PhotoEdit; *Figure 1-40d* Jim Vecchione/The Liaison Agency; *Figure 1-40e* Ed Lallo/Tony Stone Images; *Figure 1-41* Courtesy of Toshiba America Information Systems, Inc.; *Figure 1-42* Courtesy of Toshiba American Information Systems, Inc.; *Figure 1-43a* Bob Schatz/The Liaison Agency; *Figure 1-44b* Courtesy of Texas Instruments; *Figure 1-46* Courtesy of Kiosk Information Systems, Inc.; *Figure 1-47a* Spencer Grant/PhotoEdit; *Figure 1-47b* Kevin Horan/Tony Stone Images; *Figure 1-47c* Richard Pasley/Stock Boston; *Figure 1-48* Courtesy of Environmental Systems Research Institute, Inc. Copyright 1996. All rights reserved; *Figure 1-49* Courtesy of Microsoft Corporation; *Figure 1-50* Courtesy of Microsoft Corporation; **Timeline:** *1937* Courtesy of Iowa State University; *1937* Courtesy of Iowa State University; *1937* Courtesy of Iowa State University; *1943* The Computer Museum; *1943* The Computer Museum; *1945* Courtesy of the Institute for Advanced Studies; *1946* Courtesy of the University of Pennsylvania Archives; *1947* Courtesy of International Business Machines; *1951* Courtesy of Unisys Corporation; *1952* Courtesy of the Hagley Museum and Library; *1953* Courtesy of M.I.T. Archives; *1957* Courtesy of International Business Machines; *1957* Courtesy of the Department of the Navy; *1958* Courtesy of M.I.T. Archives; *1958* Courtesy of International Business Machines; *1959* Courtesy of International Business Machines; *1960* Courtesy of The Hagley Museum and Library; *1961* Courtesy of International Business Machines; *1965* Courtesy of Dartmouth College News Services; *1965* Courtesy of Digital Equipment Corporation; *1968* Courtesy of International Business Machines; *1970* Courtesy of International Business Machines; *1971* Courtesy of Intel Corporation; *1971* The Computer Museum; *1975* Courtesy of InfoWorld; *1976* Courtesy of Apple Computer, Inc.; *1976* Courtesy of Apple Computer, Inc.; *1976* Courtesy of Apple Computer, Inc.; *1979* The Computer Museum; *1980* Courtesy of International Business Machines; *1980* Courtesy of Microsoft Corporation; *1981* Courtesy of International Business Machines; *1982* Courtesy of Hayes; *1983* Courtesy of Lotus Development Corporation; *1983* '1982, Time, Inc.; *1984* Courtesy of International Business Machines; *1984* Courtesy of Hewlett Packard Company Archives; *1984* Courtesy of Apple Computer Company; *1987* Courtesy of Compaq Computer Corporation; *1989* Copyright '1997 - 1998 W3C (MIT, INRIA, Keio), All Rights Reserved; *1989* Courtesy of Intel Corporation; *1992* Courtesy of Microsoft Corporation; *1993* Courtesy of Intel Corporation; *1993* Jim Clark/The Liaison Agency; *1993* Courtesy of Netscape Communications; *1994* Courtesy of Netscape Communications Corporation; *1995* Courtesy of Microsoft Corporation; *1995* Courtesy of Sun Microsystems, Inc.; *1996* Courtesy of Palm Computing, Inc. 3Com Corporation; *1996* Reuters/Rick T. Wilking/Archive Photos; *1996* Courtesy of Microsoft Corporation; *1996* Courtesy of Web TV Networks Inc.; *1996* Courtesy of Web TV Networks Inc.; *1997* Courtesy of Intel Corporation; *1997* I. Uimonen/Sygma; *1997* Courtesy of International Business Machines; *1997* Motion Picture and Television Archives; *1998* Courtesy of Microsoft Corporation; *1998* Courtesy of Dell Computer; *1998* 'C o rel Corporation; *1998* Courtesy of Apple Computer Company; *1998* '1999 PhotoDisc, Inc.; *1999* Courtesy of Microsoft Computer Corporation; **Chapter 2:** *Figure 2-22* Courtesy of Palm Computing, Inc., a 3COM Company; *Figure 2-23* Courtesy of Microsoft Corporation; *Figure 2-23* Courtesy of Lotus Development Company; *Figure 2-25* Courtesy of Intuit Corporation; *Figure 2-27* Courtesy of AutoDesk, Inc.; *Figure 2-28* Courtesy of Adobe Systems Incorporated; *Figure 2-30* Courtesy of Adobe Systems Incorporated; *Figure 2-31* Courtesy of Asymetrix Learning Systems, Inc.; *Figure 2-34* Courtesy of Nolo Press, Inc.; *Figure 2-35* Courtesy of Block Financial Group Corp., makers of Kiplinger TaxCut; *Figure 2-39* Courtesy of Broderbund Software; *Figure 2-54* Scott Goodwin Photography; *Figure 2-55* Jim Clark/The Liaison Agency; *Figure 2-56* Courtesy of America Online, Inc.; **Chapter 3:** *Figure 3-1* Courtesy of International Business Machines; *Figure 3-2b* Courtesy of Intel Corporation; *Figure 3-3* Scott Goodwin Photography; *Figure 3-4c* Phil A. Harrington/Peter Arnold, Inc.; *Figure 3-4b* Courtesy of Intel Corporation; *Figure 3-4b* '1999 PhotoDisc, Inc.; *Figure 3-4d* Courtesy of Intel Corporation; *Figure 3-6a* Courtesy of Intel Corporation; *Figure 3-6b* Courtesy of Intel Corporation; *Figure 3-6c* Courtesy of Intel Corporation; *Figure 3-6d* Courtesy of Intel Corporation; *Figure 3-7* David Young Wolff/Tony Stone Images; *Figure 3-17* AP/Wide World Photos; *Figure 3-20* Scott Goodwin Photography; *Figure 3-21* Courtesy of Microsoft Corporation; *Figure 3-24* Courtesy of Intel Corporation; *Figure 3-26* '1999 PhotoDisc, Inc.; *Figure 3-28* Scott Goodwin Photography; *Figure 3-30* Scott Goodwin Photography; *Figure 3-39* Scott Goodwin Photography; *Figure 3-40* Courtesy of PC Notebook; *Figure 3-41* Scott Goodwin Photography; *Figure 3-42* Courtesy of International Business Machines; *Figure 3-45a* Courtesy of Intel Corporation; *Figure 3-45b* Courtesy of Andrew S. Grove/Intel Corporation; *Figure 3-44* Courtesy of Intel Corporation; **Computer Chip Feature:** *Figure 1* '1999 PhotoDisc, Inc.; *Figure 2* '1999 PhotoDisc, Inc.; *Figure 3* '1999 PhotoDisc, Inc.; *Figure 4* Courtesy of International Business Machines; *Figure 5* Hank Morgan/Science Source/Photo Researchers, Inc.; *Figure 6* Courtesy of Intel Corporation; *Figure 7* Courtesy of International Business Machines; *Figure 8* Courtesy of International Business Machines; *Figure 9* Courtesy of International Business Machines; *Figure 10* Courtesy of International Business Machines; *Figure 11* Rosenfeld Images LTD/Science Photo Library/Photo Researchers, Inc; **Chapter 4:** *Figure 4-1* Scott Goodwin Photography; *Figure 4-7a* Courtesy of International Business Machines; *Figure 4-7b* Courtesy of Casio, Inc.; *Figure 4-8* Courtesy of Microsoft Corporation; *Figure 4-13* Courtesy of Truedox Technology Corporation; *Figure 4-14* David Young Wolf/PhotoEdit; *Figure 4-15a* Amy C. Etra/PhotoEdit; *Figure 4-15b* Courtesy of Logitech, Inc.; *Figure 4-16* Scott Goodwin Photography; *Figure 4-17* Courtesy of International Business Machines; *Figure 4-18* Courtesy of Gravis Gaming Devices/Kensington Technology Group; *Figure 4-19* Michael Newman/PhotoEdit; *Figure 4-20* Courtesy of MicroTouch Systems, Inc.; *Figure 4-21a* Richard Pasley/Stock Boston; *Figure 4-21b* '1999 PhotoDisc, Inc.; *Figure 4-22a* Michael Newman/PhotoEdit; *Figure 4-22b* Zigy Kaluzny/Tony Stone Images; *Figure 4-26a* Courtesy of Microtek Lab, Inc.; *Figure 4-26b* Courtesy of Visioneer, Inc.; *Figure 4-26c* Courtesy of Howtek, Inc.; *Figure 4-28* Scott Goodwin Photography; *Figure 4-29* BMS Data Handling, Inc.; *Figure 4-29b* Courtesy of Scantron Corporation; *Figure 4-30a* Cassey Cohen/PhotoEdit; *Figure 4-30b* Courtesy of Symbol Technologies, Inc.; *Figure 4-30c* Novastock/PhotoEdit; *Figure 4-32* Courtesy of PenStock ECR; *Figure 4-33* Courtesy of NCR; *Figure 4-35* Courtesy of Trimble Corporation; *Figure 4-36a* Courtesy of Casio, Inc.; *Figure 4-36b* Courtesy of Toshiba America Information Systems, Inc.; *Figure 4-36c* Courtesy of Sony Electronics, Inc.; *Figure 4-38* Brian Smith/Stock Boston; *Figure 4-40* Courtesy of International Business Machines; *Figure 4-42* Courtesy of Play, Inc.; *Figure 4-43* Courtesy of Intel Corporation; *Figure 4-44* Courtesy of Orcca Technologies, Inc.; *Figure 4-45* Courtesy of Prentke Romich Company; *Figure 4-47* The Liaison Agency; *Figure 4-48* Peter Aaron/Esto Photographics /Courtesy of International Business Machines; **Chapter 5:** *Figure 5-2* Courtesy of International Business Machines; *Figure 5-5* Courtesy of Gateway Computer Company; *Figure 5-6* Courtesy of Casio, Inc.; *Figure 5-7* Courtesy of NEC Technologies, Inc.; *Figure 5-8* Courtesy of Fujitsu; *Figure 5-19* Scott Goodwin Photography; *Figure 5-20* Courtesy of Genicom Corporation; *Figure 5-21* Courtesy of Hewlett Packard Company; *Figure 5-24a* Courtesy of Hewlett-Packard Company; *Figure 5-24b* Courtesy of International Business Machines; *Figure 5-26* Scott Goodwin Photography; *Figure 5-27* Courtesy of Fargo Electronics, Inc.; *Figure 5-28* Courtesy of Citizen America; *Figure 5-29a* Courtesy of CalComp Technology; *Figure 5-29b* Courtesy of CalComp Technology; *Figure 5-29c* Courtesy of CalComp Technology; *Figure 5-30a* Courtesy of Fargo Electronics,Inc; *Figure 5-30b* Courtesy of Casio, Inc.; *Figure 5-31* Courtesy of Dell Computer Corporation; *Figure 5-32* Courtesy of Telex Communications, Inc.; *Figure 5-33a* Courtesy of In Focus Systems, Inc.; *Figure 5-33b* InFocus LP735 data/video projector. Jerome Hart Photography/Courtesy of InFocus, Inc.; *Figure 5-34* Bob Daemmrich/The Image Works; *Figure 5-36* Courtesy of Hewlett Packard Company; *Figure 5-37* Michael Rosenfeld/Tony Stone Images; *Figure 5-38a* Bob Daemmrich/The Image Works; *Figure 5-38b* Myrleen Ferguson/PhotoEdit; *Figure 5-40* Courtesy of Index; *Figure 5-41* Courtesy of Hewlett-Packard Company; *Figure 5-42* Courtesy of Hewlett-Packard Company; **Chapter 6:** *Figure 6-5* Scott Goodwin Photography; *Figure 6-12b* Courtesy of Toshiba America Information Systems, Inc.; *Figure 6-12* Scott Goodwin Photography; *Figure 6-12b* Courtesy of Iomega Corporation; *Figure 6-13* Courtesy of Seagate Technology; *Figure 6-18* Scott Goodwin Photography; *Figure 6-19* Courtesy of Adaptec Inc.; *Figure 6-20* Courtesy of ac&nc Corporation; *Figure 6-30* Courtesy of Pioneer Electronics; *Figure 6-32* Courtesy of Imation Corporation, Data Storage Products; *Figure 6-33* Scott Goodwin Photography; *Figure 6-34* Courtesy of m4Data Inc.; *Figure 6-36* Courtesy of International Business Machines; *Figure 6-37* Courtesy of Kingston Technology Company; *Figure 6-38* Courtesy of Gemplus; *Figure 6-39* Courtesy of Tritheim Technologies; *Figure 6-40* Courtesy of Eastman Kodak Company; *Figure 6-42* Courtesy of Sun Microsystems, Inc.; *Figure 6-43* Courtesy of Silicon Graphics Corporation; **Chapter 7:** *Figure 7-1* PhotoEssentials, Inc.; *Figure 7-5a* Bob Schatz/The Liaison Agency; *Figure 7-5b* Churchill & Klehr/The Liaison Agency; *Figure 7-5c* '1999 PhotoDisc, Inc.; *Figure 7-5d* Andy Sacks/Tony Stone Images; *Figure 7-7* PhotoEssentials, Inc.; *Figure 7-19* Courtesy of Microsoft Corporation; *Figure 7-40* Courtesy of Wyse Technology, Inc.; *Figure 7-41* Courtesy of Philips Consumer Electronics Company; *Figure 7-41* Copyright '1997-1998 W3C (MIT, INRIA, Keio). All rights reserved; *Figure 7-43* Courtesy of Yahoo!; **Chapter 8:** *Figure 8.1* Churchill & Klehr/The Liaison Agency; *Figure 8.2* Courtesy of Filemaker Inc.; *Figure 8.15* Courtesy of Clarion; *Figure 8.16* Courtesy of Apple Computer, Inc.; *Figure 8.17* Courtesy of International Business Machines; *Figure 8.18* Courtesy of Red Hat Software, Inc.; *Figure 8.31a* Jeffrey Braverman; *Figure 8.31b* Courtesy of Apple Computer, Inc.; *Figure 8.32a* Terry Heferman/Courtesy of Apple Computer, Inc.; *Figure 8.32b* Courtesy of International Business Machines; **Buyer's Guide 2000:** *Pages 8.37-8.48* '1999 PhotoDisc, Inc.; *Figure 8* Courtesy of International Business Machines; *Figure 9* Courtesy of Toshiba America, Inc.; *Figure 10* Courtesy of Xircom Corporation; *Figure 11* Courtesy of In Focus Corporation; **Chapter 9:** *Figure: 9-2* Index Stock Photography; *Figure: 9-3* Courtesy of Intel Corporation; *Figure: 9-4* Courtesy of Magellan Corporation; *Figure: 9-10* PhotoEssentials, Inc.; *Figure: 9-11* (c) 1999 PhotoDisc, Inc.; *Figure: 9-12* Courtesy of Hughes Space and Communications Company; *Figure: 9-13* Courtesy of Clarinet Systems, Inc.; *Figure: 9-22* Courtesy of Diamond Multimedia Systems, Inc.; *Figure: 9-24* Courtesy of Black Box Corporation; *Figure: 9-27* Courtesy of JBM Electronics, Inc.; *Figure: 9-28* Courtesy of 3Com Corporation; *Figure: 9-31* Courtesy of Intel Corporation; *Figure: 9-38* Courtesy of IDG/Robert Metcalfe; *Figure: 9-39* Courtesy of Novell; **Chapter 10:** *Figure: 10-9* (c) 1999 PhotoDisc, Inc.; *Figure: 10-9b* (c) 1999 PhotoDisc, Inc.; *Figure: 10-10a* (c) 1999 PhotoDisc, Inc.; *Figure: 10-10b* (c) 1999 PhotoDisc, Inc.; *Figure: 10-30* (c) 1999 PhotoDisc, Inc.; *Figure: 10-30* (c) 1999 PhotoDisc, Inc.; *Figure: 10-31* Bruce Ayers/Tony Stone Images; *Figure: 10-34* Copyright 1998 Microstrategy Inc., all rights reserved; *Figure: 10-37* Courtesy of Oracle Corporation; *Figure: 10-38* Courtesy of Oracle Corporation; **Chapter 11:** *Figure: 11-4* Michael Krasowitz/FPG International; *Figure: 11-5* (c) Adamsmith/FPG International; *Figure: 11-6a* Scott Goodwin Photography; *Figure: 11--6b* Courtesy of Microsoft Press Computer Dictionary, 3rd edition, ISBN 1-57231-743-4, Microsoft Press, Copyright 1997 by Microsoft Corp.; *Figure: 11-28* Terry Vine/Tony Stone Images; *Figure: 11-30* Christopher Gardner; *Figure: 11-31* Courtesy of SAP Americas, Inc.; **Chapter 12:** *Figure: 12-17* Courtesy of Naval Surface Warefare Center, Dalhgren, Virginia; *Figure: 12-35* Courtesy of Sybase; *Figure: 12-41* Courtesy of the Hagley Museum and Library; *Figure: 12-42* Courtesy of Compaq Computer Corporation; **Careers 2000 Feature:** *Figure 2* Andy Sacks/ Tony Stone Images; *Figure 7* Bill Bachman/The Image Works; *Figure 8* Bill Losh/FPG International; *Figure 9* Steven Rubin/The Image Works; *Figure 5-15* Scott Goodwin Photography; **Chapter 13:** *Figure: 13-7* Courtesy of Three D Graphics, Inc.; *Figure: 13-8* Courtesy of Wicat Technologies; *Figure: 13-16* Reproduced by Special Permission from the December 15, 1998 edition of The New York Times on the Web, copyright 1998 by The New York Times; *Figure: 13-16* Reproduced from the December 15th, 1998 issue of Business Week Online by special permission, copyright ' 1998 by The McGraw-Hill Companies, Inc. ; *Figure: 13-18a* (c) 1999 PhotoDisc, Inc.; *Figure: 13-18b* Courtesy of Intel Corporation; *Figure: 13-19* Gary Wagner/Stock Boston; *Figure: 13-21* MIchael Newman/PhotoEdit; *Figure: 13-23* Courtesy of NEC; *Figure: 13-24* Courtesy of Creative Labs, Inc.; *Figure: 13-25* Courtesy of Samsung HDTV; *Figure: 13-26* Courtesy of Proxima Corporation.; *Figure: 13-27* Courtesy of Epson America, Inc.; *Figure: 13-29* Courtesy of Eastman Kodak; *Figure: 13-30* Courtesy of Corel Corporation; *Figure: 13-38* AP/Wide World Photos; *Figure: 13-38* Courtesy of Macromedia, Inc.; **Chapter 14:** *Figure: 14-3* Courtesy of Data Fellows. , http://www.DataFellows.com; *Figure: 14-7* Courtesy of Recognition Systems, Inc.; *Figure: 14-8* Courtesy of EyeDentify, Inc.; *Figure: 14-9* Courtesy of Kensington Technology Group; *Figure: 14-14* Courtesy of Aliroo Ltd.; *Figure: 14-15* Courtesy of Tripp Lite; Chicago, FL; *Figure: 14-16* Courtesy of American Power Conversion; *Figure: 14-23* (c) Cynthia Satloff; *Figure: 14-28* Mikki Ansin/ The Liaison Agency; *Figure: 14-29* Courtesy of Network Associates, Inc.; **Trends 2000 Feature:** *Figure 1* (c) 1999 PhotoDisc, Inc.; *Figure 2* Courtesy of Biometric Access Corporation; *Figure 7* Courtesy of Matsushita; *Figure 8* (c) 1999 PhotoDisc, Inc.; *Figure 11a* Courtesy of International Business Machines; *Figure 11c* (c) 1999 PhotoDisc, Inc.; *Figure 15* Courtesy of Mechanical Dynamics, Inc.; *Figure 16* (c) 1999 PhotoDisc, Inc.; *Figure 19* Courtesy of Nuvo Media, Inc.; *Figure 19* (c) 1999 PhotoDisc, Inc.